UNIVERSITY CASEBOOK SERIES®

INTERNATIONAL LAW

EVOLVING DOCTRINE AND PRACTICE

SECOND EDITION

JENS DAVID OHLIN
Interim Dean and Professor of Law
Cornell Law School

FOUNDATION
PRESS

University Casebook Series is a trademark registered in the U.S. Patent and Trademark Office.

© 2018 LEG, Inc. d/b/a West Academic
© 2021 LEG, Inc. d/b/a West Academic
    444 Cedar Street, Suite 700
    St. Paul, MN 55101
    1-877-888-1330

Printed in the United States of America

ISBN: 978-1-64708-417-2

PREFACE

Each chapter of *International Law: Evolving Doctrine and Practice* has a consistent structure, one that is somewhat unique compared with other international law casebooks. Each chapter opens with an introduction that explains the topic and its relevance and also provides a roadmap of the subsequent subsections in the chapter. Usually, though not always, the subsections correspond with a subtopic, doctrine, or doctrinal element that the student must master to understand the chapter's topic. Each chapter ends with a conclusion that serves not only to bring together the subtopics into a coherent framework, but also functions as a list of de facto learning objectives for the students. By reading and reviewing the points articulated in the Conclusion section, the student can easily identify gaps in their comprehension of the material and take the necessary corrective steps by doubling back and reconsidering the more difficult material or complex doctrines.

Along the way, I have included short Problem Cases, usually a page or less, that force the reader to apply the legal doctrine—with all of its subtlety and rough edges—to a particular fact pattern, often one from current affairs. These Problem Cases are designed to both spark classroom discussion and to communicate to the reader what is at stake with each topic explored in the casebook. However, I have deliberately separated the Problem Cases from the presentation of the other materials in the chapter and I also have deliberately kept the Problem Cases to a reasonable length. The goal here is to present options for further discussion for both the professor and the student, though in a thoroughly *modular* format that can be skipped over without any loss of coherence to the chapter's presentation of the legal material. In other words, any particular Problem Case could be the basis for an enriching classroom discussion or it could be ignored in the classroom and treated as extracurricular food for thought—as the professor so desires.

In that sense, the internal structure of the casebook chapters was designed with pedagogical ecumenism in mind. Teachers with a variety of competing pedagogical approaches can succeed and thrive with the materials assembled in a truly flexible format. Moreover, this ecumenism is mirrored in the content of *International Law: Evolving Doctrine and Practice*. The last two decades have witnessed an explosion in new approaches to analyzing and framing international law, and many teachers of the subject have their own preferences about which theory they find most valuable. However, I have found over the years that it is best to prevent these theoretical debates from hijacking a casebook. I do not mean to suggest that a casebook should ignore these theoretical debates. Far from it. Rather, what I am suggesting is that a casebook that takes a *stand* on one of these theoretical debates, and presents the material in the casebook in a particular way to demonstrate the truth of that approach, will inevitably end up being useful only for instructors who already endorse that particular framework or theoretical lens. Casebooks can, and should, have a greater degree of flexibility. This is a large-tent casebook for all comers excited to teach international law to a class of American law school students.

That being said, despite this flexibility and ecumenism, it would be an exaggeration to suggest that there is no editorial vision at work in this casebook. Any time an author emphasizes some issues over others, or selects some cases for inclusion while rejecting others, there are normative inspirations for these decisions. To the extent that this is true here, the materials presented are designed to highlight, as the subtitle of the casebook suggests, that the substantive norms of international law are dynamic rather than static, which is to say that the international law of today is neither yesterday's nor tomorrow's law. The student should be able to appreciate how we got here while also participating in the collective project of imagining where we go from here. Along the way, the student is given a toolbox of norms—which are often in tension with each other—to help select which vision of international law will produce the most just world order. By engaging in this process, your students have already, in a sense, joined the invisible college of international lawyers.

I have followed several conventions while editing the cases and other materials in this volume. First, internal citations within the cases are often omitted without indication. Second, omissions or deletions in the text are indicated by ellipses (. . .). In particular, ellipses at the end of a paragraph may indicate an omission within that paragraph or in successive paragraphs. Third, some cases and excerpted material used numbered paragraphs in the original; I have kept that numbering and not used ellipses to indicate deleted paragraphs since a gap in the numbered sequence adequately communicates the existence of deleted material.

Professors are encouraged to consult the casebook website, hosted by Foundation Press and West Academic, where they can find ancillary material to guide their teaching, including a detailed set of PowerPoint slides for classroom lectures—one deck for each chapter of the casebook—as well as draft syllabi for an introductory course on international law.

I encourage adopters to send feedback to me at jdo43@cornell.edu for future editions. I am eager to hear about your experiences using the casebook and I am more than willing to incorporate your suggestions for new material in the third edition. I am grateful for the suggestions that formed the basis for this second edition. This is a collective and ongoing enterprise.

JENS DAVID OHLIN
CORNELL LAW SCHOOL

Ithaca, New York
January 2021

ACKNOWLEDGMENTS

There are many individuals who helped me with the preparation of this casebook—too numerous to mention. I initially learned international law from several talented professors while studying for my JD at Columbia Law School, an institution with a rich history intertwined with the development of international legal institutions, including the United Nations. Those classroom experiences sparked an intellectual interest that will continue to burn throughout my entire career.

As for the content of the casebook, many friends and colleagues have guided me on matters of controversy in international law. There are too many to name here, but they know who they are. Over the course of the last two decades, most of them have evolved from young doctoral candidates to become the leading scholars of our generation. My understanding of international law would not be what it is today without those enriching conversations.

Ryan Pfeiffer, Staci Herr, Mac Soto, Jon Harkness, and Kevin Schroder guided me through the submission process at Foundation Press and I'm grateful for their advice. I am also grateful to Greg Olson and the editorial and production teams at Foundation Press and West Academic.

At Cornell Law School, Kevin Clermont gave me general advice about pedagogy and specific advice about casebook organization. Zachary Clopton read and commented on a few crucial chapters while they were in draft form. I am also grateful to Harold Koh and other members of the Foundation Press Editorial Board for invaluable advice and feedback on this project when it was in its initial stages.

My wife Nancy Ohlin unfailingly supported my work on this project, which would never have come to fruition without her encouragement.

Finally, I would like to thank the following copyright holders for granting permission to reproduce the following materials in this casebook:

1. Yale Law Journal, for Oona Hathaway & Scott J. Shapiro, *Outcasting: Enforcement in Domestic and International Law*, 121 Yale L.J. 252 (2011). Reprinted with permission.

2. American Journal of International Law, for Anthony D'Amato, *Groundwork for International Law*, 108 Am. J. Int'l L. 650 (2014). Reprinted with permission.

3. Oxford University Press, for Independent International Commission on Kosovo, *The Kosovo Report: Conflict * International Response * Lessons Learned* (2001). Reprinted with permission.

SUMMARY OF CONTENTS

TABLE OF CONTENTS

TABLE OF CASES

The principal cases are in bold type.

UNIVERSITY CASEBOOK SERIES®

INTERNATIONAL LAW

EVOLVING DOCTRINE
AND PRACTICE

SECOND EDITION

CHAPTER 1

INTRODUCTION TO INTERNATIONAL LEGAL REGULATION

Introduction

International law is many things. First and foremost, it is a body of law that regulates the behavior of states—and perhaps other entities as well. International law is therefore a "normative" system akin to domestic law insofar as it announces how its subjects should behave. Just as domestic law tells individuals, corporations, and government actors how to behave, so too international law tells its subjects—usually nation-states but not always—how to behave.

Dig a little deeper and international law looks little like domestic law. It is *sui generis*. First, its sources of law are different. While domestic lawyers make their arguments with statutes, federal and state regulations, and judicial precedent, international lawyers focus on treaties, customary law, and general principles of international law. Second, international law's normative architecture is different from domestic law because the problems it seeks to solve are quite different. Third, methods of enforcement in international law share some commonalities with domestic law but also many differences.

That being said, there are many similarities between domestic and international law. Doctrines in one appear in the other. Judicial decision-making is important in both fields. Many of the basic principles of international law gain that status because they are principles shared in a majority of domestic legal systems. International and domestic law are therefore deeply intertwined with each other.

The goal of this course is certainly to master the formal doctrines of international law. No education of international law would be complete without a basic understanding of the ways that international law regulates and constrains state behavior. But along the way, the student of international law must understand the process of international law—how it is conducted, with what type of arguments, in which venues, and how success and failure is defined.

Before turning to the key doctrines outlined in the chapters that follow, this chapter starts with *background* principles that structure the entire enterprise of international law. Section A focuses on the role that natural law played in the development of international law and asks what role, if any, natural law still plays in international legal discourse today. Section B deals with the background assumption that states are permitted to do anything unless international law specifically prohibits it. Finally, Section C takes an outsider's perspective and looks at international law as a particular system in the hopes of identifying the key characteristics of the system. The rest of the materials in the casebook will frequently circle back to these core themes. The full import of these background principles will become more apparent as you grapple with the rest of the doctrines—and doctrinal controversies—covered in this course.

A. FROM THE LAW OF NATURE TO THE LAW OF NATIONS

For centuries, the concept of international law was dominated by natural law. In philosophy, "natural law" means that the content of moral philosophy flows from universal characteristics of human nature, which can be ascertained by human beings through the faculty of reason. For example, one element of natural law entails that all human beings are entitled to individual rights, simply by virtue of certain morally relevant characteristics shared by all human beings. In the natural law era, philosophers built entire intellectual systems that explained the content of ethics and moral philosophy using this methodology. Because these systems were based on common characteristics of humanity, the philosophical rules were supposedly universal, in the sense that they applied to all human beings, regardless of where they lived. Practice did not always live up to this philosophical ideal.

In the 17th Century, the content of international law was articulated through the lens of natural law. For example, the Dutch jurist Hugo Grotius (1583–1645) articulated basic principles of the international legal system by looking to natural law. So, while Grotius articulated some rules and norms that flowed from sources of law that today's lawyer might recognize—for example, international agreements between nation-states—many of the principles of international law articulated by Grotius stemmed from first-order principles about the nature of humanity, the nature of societies, and the nature of the international community. These principles of international law were then gathered together in highly influential treatises that read like a mixture of law and philosophy. For example, Grotius' most famous work was *De Jure Belli ac Pacis* (*On the Law of War and Peace*), which explored the rules regarding both the initiation of war and its conduct. In keeping with the methodology in vogue at the time, the rules referred to the conduct of states in prior armed conflicts but also basic principles that flowed from natural law. International lawyers consulted these and other treatises as authoritative statements regarding the requirements of international law, and they played a large role in determining the direction of state behavior in international relations.

Grotius was one of the most influential of the natural law theorists but certainly not the only one. Influential jurists such as Christian Wolff (1679–1754), Alberico Gentili (1552–1608), and Francisco Suárez (1548–1617) also wrote treatises based on a similar methodology. Taken together, the natural law method generated a series of transcendental and universal norms that provided the foundation for international law.

Over time, the natural law era of international law waned. In its place came legal positivism—an articulation of international legal rules based on more specific sources of law, such as treaties, judicial decisions, and international custom (the behavior of states). These "sources" of international law are how international law is "made" today. Today, international lawyers generally make arguments about the content of international law by referring to these sources, rather than referring to transcendental arguments about the nature of humanity or the nature of the international system. The modern lawyer would be more likely to refer to these natural law arguments as "philosophy" rather than law. A core tenet of positivism—or at least some versions of it—is that legal norms should be divorced from moral norms. Put this way, one can see why the natural law approach was eventually rejected, since natural law involved explicit recourse to moral principles that were found in nature. Put another way, international lawyers once looked to nature to *find* the natural law, whereas in today's world, it is assumed that international law is *made* by human beings when they engage in law-making behavior such as negotiating and signing a treaty.

One question is whether the era of legal positivism has completely eradicated all traces of natural law from our system of international law. Are appeals to the nature of humanity completely irrelevant? Consider the following case from the U.S. Supreme Court. In 1825, a slave ship called "The Antelope" was captured off the coast of Florida (at the time a territory of Spain) and brought to port in the United States. The ship was carrying 280 slaves. Ostensibly, the Antelope was supposed to be transporting slaves from Africa to Cuba, but there was some suggestion that the Antelope was bringing the slaves to the United States. At the time, the importation of foreign slaves to the U.S. was prohibited by federal law. Moreover, northern states in the U.S. had long since abolished slavery by law, though it was still permitted in southern states.

The Supreme Court was tasked with deciding the fate of the slaves on the ship, which hinged in part on whether the ship was violating international law (the law of nations) when it was captured and whether it could be considered a prize of war. As you read the case, pay particular attention to how the court determined the content of international law.

Did the international slave trade violate the law of nations? What role did natural law play in the court's analysis?

The Antelope
Supreme Court of the United States
23 U.S. 66 (1825)

■ MR. CHIEF JUSTICE MARSHALL delivered the opinion of the Court, and, after stating the case, proceeded as follows:

In prosecuting this appeal, the United States assert no property in themselves. They appear in the character of guardians, or next friends, of these Africans, who are brought, without any act of their own, into the bosom of our country, insist on their right to freedom, and submit their claim to the laws of the land, and to the tribunals of the nation.

The Consuls of Spain and Portugal, respectively, demand these Africans as slaves, who have, in the regular course of legitimate commerce, been acquired as property by the subjects of their respective sovereigns, and claim their restitution under the laws of the United States.

In examining claims of this momentous importance; claims in which the sacred rights of liberty and of property come in conflict with each other; which have drawn from the bar a degree of talent and of eloquence, worthy of the questions that have been discussed; this Court must not yield to feelings which might seduce it from the path of duty, and must obey the mandate of the law.

That the course of opinion on the slave trade should be unsettled, ought to excite no surprise. The Christian and civilized nations of the world with whom we have most intercourse, have all been engaged in it. However abhorrent this traffic may be to a mind whose original feelings are not blunted by familiarity with the practice, it has been sanctioned in modern times by the laws of all nations who possess distant colonies, each of whom has engaged in it as a common commercial business which no other could rightfully interrupt. It has claimed all the sanction which could be derived from long usage, and general acquiescence. That trade could not be considered as contrary to the law of nations which was authorized and protected by the laws of all commercial nations; the right to carry on which was claimed by each, and allowed by each.

The course of unexamined opinion, which was founded on this inveterate usage, received its first check in America; and, as soon as these States acquired the right of self-government, the traffic was forbidden by most of them. In the beginning of this century, several humane and enlightened individuals of Great Britain devoted themselves to the cause of the Africans; and, by frequent appeals to the nation, in which the enormity of this commerce was unveiled, and exposed to the public eye, the general sentiment was at length roused against it, and the feelings of justice and humanity, regaining their long lost ascendency, prevailed so far in the British parliament as to obtain an act for its abolition. The utmost efforts of the British government, as well as of that of the United States, have since been assiduously employed in its suppression. It has been denounced by both in terms of great severity, and those concerned in it are subjected to the heaviest penalties which law can inflict. In addition to these measures operating on their own people, they have used all their influence to bring other nations into the same system, and to interdict this trade by the consent of all.

Public sentiment has, in both countries, kept pace with the measures of government; and the opinion is extensively, if not universally entertained, that this unnatural traffic ought to be suppressed. While its illegality is asserted by some governments, but not admitted by all; while the detestation in which it is held is growing daily, and even those nations who tolerate it in fact, almost disavow their own conduct, and rather connive at, than legalize, the acts of their subjects; it is not wonderful that public feeling should march somewhat in advance of strict law, and that opposite opinions should be entertained on the precise cases in which our own laws may control and limit the practice of others. Indeed, we ought not to be surprised, if, on this novel series of cases, even Courts of justice should, in some instances, have carried the principle of suppression farther than a more deliberate consideration of the subject would justify.

The *Amedie*, (1 *Action's Rep.* 240.) which was an American vessel employed in the African trade, was captured by a British cruiser, and condemned in the Vice Admiralty Court of Tortola. An appeal was prayed; and Sir William Grant, in delivering the opinion of the Court, said, that the trade being then declared unjust and unlawful by Great Britain

> a claimant could have no right, upon principles of universal law, to claim restitution in a prize Court, of human beings carried as his slaves. He must show some right that has been violated by the capture, some property of which he has been dispossessed, and to which he ought to be restored. In this case, the laws of the claimant's country allow of no right of property such as he claims. There can, therefore, be no right of restitution. The consequence is, that the judgment must be affirmed.

The *Fortuna* was condemned on the authority of the *Amedie*, and the same principle was again affirmed.

The *Diana* was a Swedish vessel, captured with a cargo of slaves, by a British cruiser, and condemned in the Court of Vice Admiralty at Sierra Leone. This sentence was reversed on appeal, and Sir William Scott, in pronouncing the sentence of reversal, said, "the condemnation also took place on a principle which this Court cannot in any manner recognise, inasmuch as the sentence affirms, 'that the slave trade, from motives of humanity, hath been abolished by most civilized nations, *and is not, at the present time, legally authorized by any.*' This appears to me to be an assertion by no means sustainable." The ship and cargo were restored, on the principle that the trade was allowed by the laws of Sweden.

The principle common to these cases is, that the legality of the capture of a vessel engaged in the slave trade, depends on the law of the country to which the vessel belongs. If that law gives its sanction to the trade, restitution will be decreed; if that law prohibits it, the vessel and cargo will be condemned as good prize.

This whole subject came on afterwards to be considered in the *Louis*. The opinion of Sir William Scott, in that case, demonstrates the attention he had bestowed upon it, and gives full assurance that it may be considered as settling the law in the British Courts of Admiralty as far as it goes.

The *Louis* was a French vessel, captured on a slaving voyage, before she had purchased any slaves, brought into Sierra Leone, and condemned by the Vice Admiralty Court at that place. On an appeal to the Court of Admiralty in England, the sentence was reversed.

In the very full and elaborate opinion given on this case, Sir William Scott, in explicit terms, lays down the broad principle, that the right of search is confined to a state of war. It is a right strictly belligerent in its character, which can never be exercised by a nation at peace, except against professed pirates, who are the enemies of the human race. The act of trading in slaves, however detestable, was not, he said, "the act of freebooters, enemies of the human race, renouncing every country, and ravaging every country, in its coasts and vessels, indiscriminately." It was not piracy.

He also said, that this trade could not be pronounced contrary to the law of nations.

> A Court, in the administration of law, cannot attribute criminality to an act where the law imputes none. It must look to the legal standard of morality; and, upon a question of this nature, that standard must be found in the law of nations, as fixed and evidenced by general, and ancient, and admitted practice, by treaties, and by the general tenor of the laws and ordinances, and the formal transactions of civilized states; and, looking to those authorities, he found a difficulty in maintaining that the transaction was legally criminal.

The right of visitation and search being strictly a belligerent right, and the slave trade being neither piratical, nor contrary to the law of nations, the principle is asserted and maintained with great strength of reasoning, that it cannot be exercised on the vessels of a foreign power, unless permitted by treaty. France had refused to assent to the insertion of such an article in her treaty with Great Britain, and, consequently, the right could not be exercised on the high seas by a British cruiser on a French vessel.

> "It is pressed as a difficulty," says the Judge, "what is to be done, if a French ship, laden with slaves, is brought in?" I answer, without hesitation, restore the possession which has been unlawfully devested; rescind the illegal act done by your own subject, and leave the foreigner to the justice of his own country.

This reasoning goes far in support of the proposition, that, in the British Courts of admiralty, the vessel even of a nation which had forbidden the slave trade, but had not conceded the right of search, must, if wrongfully brought in, be restored to the original owner. But the Judge goes farther, and shows, that no evidence existed to prove that France had, by law, forbidden that trade. Consequently, for this reason, as well as for that previously assigned, the sentence of condemnation was reversed, and restitution awarded.

In the United States, different opinions have been entertained in the different Circuits and Districts; and the subject is now, for the first time, before this Court.

The question, whether the slave trade is prohibited by the law of nations has been seriously propounded, and both the affirmative and negative of the proposition have been maintained with equal earnestness.

That it is contrary to the law of nature will scarcely be denied. That every man has a natural right to the fruits of his own labour, is generally admitted; and that no other person can rightfully deprive him of those fruits, and appropriate them against his will, seems to be the necessary result of this admission. But from the earliest times war has existed, and war confers rights in which all have acquiesced. Among the most enlightened nations of antiquity, one of these was, that the victor might enslave the vanquished. This, which was the usage of all, could not be pronounced repugnant to the law of nations, which is certainly to be tried by the test of neral usage. That which has received the assent of all, must be the law of all.

Slavery, then, has its origin in force; but as the world has agreed that it is a legitimate result of force, the state of things which is thus produced by general consent, cannot be pronounced unlawful.

Throughout Christendom, this harsh rule has been exploded, and war is no longer considered as giving a right to enslave captives. But this triumph of humanity has not been universal. The parties to the modern law of nations do not propagate their principles by force; and Africa has not yet adopted them. Throughout the whole extent of that immense continent, so far as we know its history, it is still the law of nations that prisoners are slaves. Can those who have themselves renounced this law, be permitted to participate in its effects by purchasing the beings who are its victims?

Whatever might be the answer of a moralist to this question, a jurist must search for its legal solution, in those principles of action which are sanctioned by the usages, the national acts, and the general assent, of that portion of the world of which he considers himself as a part, and to whose law the appeal is made. If we resort to this standard as the test of international law, the question, as has already been observed, is decided in favour of the legality of the trade. Both Europe and America embarked in it; and for nearly two centuries, it was carried on without opposition, and without censure. A jurist could not say, that a practice thus supported was illegal, and that those engaged in it might be punished, either personally, or by deprivation of property.

In this commerce, thus sanctioned by universal assent, every nation had an equal right to engage. How is this right to be lost? Each may renounce it for its own people; but can this renunciation affect others?

No principle of general law is more universally acknowledged, than the perfect equality of nations. Russia and Geneva have equal rights. It results from this equality, that no one can rightfully impose a rule on another. Each legislates for itself, but its legislation can operate on itself alone. A right, then, which is vested in all by the consent of all, can be devested only by consent; and this trade, in which all have participated, must remain lawful to those who cannot be induced to relinquish it. As no nation can prescribe a rule for others, none can make a law of nations; and this traffic remains lawful to those whose governments have not forbidden it.

If it is consistent with the law of nations, it cannot in itself be piracy. It can be made so only by statute; and the obligation of the statute cannot transcend the legislative power of the state which may enact it.

If it be neither repugnant to the law of nations, nor piracy, it is almost superfluous to say in this Court, that the right of bringing in for adjudication in time of peace, even where the vessel belongs to a nation which has prohibited the trade cannot exist. The Courts of no country execute the penal laws of another; and the course of the American government on the subject of visitation and search, would decide any case in which that right had been exercised by an American cruiser, on the vessel of a foreign nation, not violating our municipal laws, against the captors.

It follows, that a foreign vessel engaged in the African slave trade, captured on the high-seas in time of peace, by an American cruiser, and brought in for adjudication, would be restored. . .

We think, then, that all the Africans, now in possession of the Marshal for the District of Georgia, and under the control of the Circuit Court of the United States for that District, which were brought in with the Antelope, otherwise called the General Ramirez, except those which may be designated as the property of the Spanish claimants, ought to be delivered up to the United States, to be disposed of according to law. So much of the sentence of the Circuit Court as is contrary to this opinion, is to be reversed, and the residue affirmed.

DECREE. . . On consideration whereof, this Court is of opinion, that there is error in so much of the sentence and decree of the said Circuit Court, as directs the restitution to the Spanish claimant of the Africans in the proceedings mentioned, in the ratio which one hundred and sixty-six bears to the whole number of those which remained alive at the time of pronouncing the said decree; and also in so much thereof, as directs restitution to the Portuguese claimant; and that so much of the said decree ought to be reversed, and it is hereby reversed and annulled. And this Court, proceeding to give such decree as the said Circuit Court ought to have given, doth DIRECT and ORDER, that the restitution to be made to the Spanish claimant, shall be according to the ratio which ninety-three (instead of one hundred and sixty-six) bears to the whole number, comprehending as well those originally on board the Antelope, as those which were put on board that vessel by the Captain of the Arraganta. After making the apportionment according to this ratio, and deducting from the number the rateable loss which must fall on the slaves to which the Spanish claimants were originally entitled, the residue of the said ninety-three are to be delivered to the Spanish claimant, on the terms in the said decree mentioned; and all the remaining Africans are to be delivered to the United States, to be disposed of according to law; and the said decree of the said Circuit Court is, in all things not contrary to this decree, affirmed.

NOTES & QUESTIONS

1. *The Slave Trade and the Birth of Human Rights.* What conclusion did the court reach regarding the fate of the slave trade under international law? Ultimately, the Supreme Court concluded that although an abolitionist spirit had prompted Britain and the United States to ban the international slave trade, plenty of other states were either continuing with the slave trade (such as Spain and Portugal) or had recently engaged in it. For this reason, the Supreme Court concluded that the slave trade did not violate the law of nations. However, other courts of that era were more willing to free slaves rescued from captured ships. In her book *The Slave Trade and the Origins of*

International Human Rights Law (2012), Jenny S. Martinez notes that after Britain passed the Act for the Abolition of the Slave Trade in 1807, the British Navy began enforcing the act by seizing ships that were engaged in illegal slave trading. The ships and the slaves they transported were then taken before special "courts of mixed commission" to adjudicate their fate, which often resulted in the slaves being freed. These courts, located in foreign cities, were created pursuant to bilateral treaties between Britain and the host nation where the court was located. Martinez argues that these courts were the forerunners to modern international human rights law—an application of international legal norms enforced for the purpose of protecting individual human beings. For a debate over this historical conclusion, see Philip Alston, *Does the Past Matter? On the Origins of Human Rights*, 126 Harv. L. Rev. 2043 (2013).

2.   *Natural Law Versus Positivism.* What role did natural law play in the court's analysis in *The Antelope*? The Supreme Court conceded that slavery was abhorrent and violated natural law. Nonetheless, the Court concluded that the law of nations was not constituted by natural law. In many ways, *The Antelope* was decided during a transitional period when international law was pivoting away from its natural law origins and towards a more positivist conception. The word "positivism" in this context refers to *positive* sources of law, such as treaties, judicial decisions, or even customary international law, which is the general practice of states and their views on what international law requires of them. Which of these positive sources of law most influenced the court's decision in the *Antelope*?

3.   *The Fate of Natural Law Today.* What role does natural law play today? Most international lawyers would argue none at all. Legal arguments are almost always won and lost by referring to positive sources of law, such as treaties, custom, or decisions from international courts or tribunals. But this conclusion may be slightly hasty. Even fully positivist international lawyers sometimes argue that some legal norms—called jus cogens—are universally required and cannot be derogated from (such as the prohibition against genocide or torture). The role of jus cogens will be explored in greater depth in Chapter 2. However, for the moment, just consider whether jus cogens is a covert reference to natural law, i.e., a positivistic gloss on a phenomenon that prior generations of lawyers would have simply referred to as natural law. Has natural law prevailed, in some small way, in the small real estate of international law that is non-derogable (universally mandatory)? For a discussion of modern international law arguments that rely on natural law, see Evan J. Criddle, *Three Grotian Theories of Humanitarian Intervention*, 16 Theoretical Inquiries in Law 473 (2015).

B. THE *LOTUS* PRESUMPTION

In 1926, the SS Lotus collided with the SS Bozkurt in water not far from Greece. The Lotus was a French ship and the Bozkurt was a Turkish vessel. The result of the collision was the destruction of the Bozkurt and the deaths of the eight Turkish sailors on board. Turkey prosecuted one of the French sailors on the Lotus and held him responsible for the accident and the deaths. France objected to Turkey's exercise of jurisdiction and sued Turkey before the Permanent Court of Justice, a forerunner of today's International Court of Justice in The Hague.

On one level, the *Lotus* case is about a complex jurisdictional dispute arising on the high seas. But on another level, the *Lotus* case is about something far deeper: the background assumptions against which international law operates. Are states required to articulate a legal rule before acting? Or is state action presumptively valid unless a rule of international law prohibits it? Is the default rule in international law that everything is permitted unless specifically prohibited? Or is the default rule the opposite: everything is prohibited unless specifically permitted? As you read the case, look for the court's answer to this foundational question.

The SS Lotus
(France v. Turkey)

Permanent Court of Justice
Sept. 7, 1927

The Facts

13. According to the statements submitted to the Court by the Parties' Agents in their Cases and in their oral pleadings, the facts in which the affair originated are agreed to be as follows:

14. On August 2nd, 1926, just before midnight, a collision occurred between the French mail steamer Lotus, proceeding to Constantinople, and the Turkish collier Boz-Kourt, between five and six nautical miles to the north of Cape Sigri (Mitylene). The Boz-Kourt, which was cut in two, sank, and eight Turkish nationals who were on board perished. After having done everything possible to succour the shipwrecked persons, of whom ten were able to be saved, the Lotus continued on its course to Constantinople, where it arrived on August 3rd.

15. At the time of the collision, the officer of the watch on board the Lotus was Monsieur Demons, a French citizen, lieutenant in the merchant service and first officer of the ship, whilst the movements of the Boz-Kourt were directed by its captain, Hassan Bey, who was one of those saved from the wreck.

16. As early as August 3rd the Turkish police proceeded to hold an enquiry into the collision on board the Lotus; and on the following day, August 4th, the captain of the Lotus handed in his master's report at the French Consulate-General, transmitting a copy to the harbour master.

17. On August 5th, Lieutenant Demons was requested by the Turkish authorities to go ashore to give evidence. The examination, the length of which incidentally resulted in delaying the departure of the Lotus, led to the placing under arrest of Lieutenant Demons without previous notice being given to the French Consul-General—and Hassan Bey, amongst others. This arrest, which has been characterized by the Turkish Agent as arrest pending trial (arrestation preventive), was effected in order to ensure that the criminal prosecution instituted against the two officers, on a charge of manslaughter, by the Public Prosecutor of Stamboul, on the complaint of the families of the victims of the collision, should follow its normal course.

18. The case was first heard by the Criminal Court of Stamboul on August 28th. On that occasion, Lieutenant Demons submitted that the Turkish Courts had no jurisdiction; the Court, however, overruled his objection. When the proceedings were resumed on September 11th, Lieutenant Demons demanded his release on bail: this request was complied with on September 13th, the bail being fixed at 6,000 Turkish pounds.

19. On September 15th, the Criminal Court delivered its judgment, the terms of which have not been communicated to the Court by the Parties. It is, however, common ground, that it sentenced Lieutenant Demons to eighty days' imprisonment and a fine of twenty-two pounds, Hassan Bey being sentenced to a slightly more severe penalty.

20. It is also common ground between the Parties that the Public Prosecutor of the Turkish Republic entered an appeal against this decision, which had the effect of suspending its execution until a decision upon the appeal had been given; that such decision has not yet been given; but that the special agreement of October 12th, 1926, did not have the effect of suspending "the criminal proceedings. . . . now in progress in Turkey."

21. The action of the Turkish judicial authorities with regard to Lieutenant Demons at once gave rise to many diplomatic representations and other steps on the part of the French Government or its representatives in Turkey, either protesting against the arrest of Lieutenant Demons or demanding his release, or with a view to obtaining the transfer of the case from the Turkish Courts to the French Courts.

22. As a result of these representations, the Government of the Turkish Republic declared on September 2nd, 1926, that "it would have no objection to the reference of the conflict of jurisdiction to the Court at The Hague."

23. The French Government having, on the 6th of the same month, given "its full consent to the proposed solution," the two Governments appointed their plenipotentiaries with a view to the drawing up of the

special agreement to be submitted to the Court; this special agreement was signed at Geneva on October 12th, 1926, as stated above, and the ratifications were deposited on December 27th, 1926.

The Law

24. Before approaching the consideration of the principles of international law contrary to which Turkey is alleged to have acted thereby infringing the terms of Article 15 of the Convention of Lausanne of July 24th, 1923, respecting conditions of residence and business and, jurisdiction, it is necessary to define, in the light of the written and oral proceedings, the position resulting from the special agreement. For, the Court having obtained cognizance of the present case by notification of a special agreement concluded between the Parties in the case, it is rather to the terms of this agreement than to the submissions of the Parties that the Court must have recourse in establishing the precise points which it has to decide. In this respect the following observations should be made:

25. The collision which occurred on August 2nd, 1926, between the S. S. Lotus, flying the French flag, and the S. S. Boz-Kourt, flying the Turkish flag, took place on the high seas: the territorial jurisdiction of any State other than France and Turkey therefore does not enter into account.

26. The violation, if any, of the principles of international law would have consisted in the taking of criminal proceedings against Lieutenant Demons. It is not therefore a question relating to any particular step in these proceedings—such as his being put to trial, his arrest, his detention pending trial or the judgment given by the Criminal Court of Stamboul—but of the very fact of the Turkish Courts exercising criminal jurisdiction. That is why the arguments put forward by the Parties in both phases of the proceedings relate exclusively to the question whether Turkey has or has not, according to the principles of international law, jurisdiction to prosecute in this case.

27. The Parties agree that the Court has not to consider whether the prosecution was in conformity with Turkish law; it need not therefore consider whether, apart from the actual question of jurisdiction, the provisions of Turkish law cited by Turkish authorities were really applicable in this case, or whether the manner in which the proceedings against Lieutenant Demons were conducted might constitute a denial of justice, and accordingly, a violation of international law. The discussions have borne exclusively upon the question whether criminal jurisdiction does or does not exist in this case.

28. The prosecution was instituted because the loss of the Boz-Kourt involved the death of eight Turkish sailors and passengers. It is clear, in the first place, that this result of the collision constitutes a factor essential for the institution of the criminal proceedings in question;

secondly, it follows from the statements of the two Parties that no criminal intention has been imputed to either of the officers responsible for navigating the two vessels; it is therefore a case of prosecution for involuntary manslaughter. The French Government maintains that breaches of navigation regulations fall exclusively within the jurisdiction of the State under whose flag the vessel sails; but it does not argue that a collision between two vessels cannot also bring into operation the sanctions which apply to criminal law in cases of manslaughter. The precedents cited by it and relating to collision cases all assume the possibility of criminal proceedings with a view to the infliction of such sanctions, the dispute being confined to the question of jurisdiction concurrent or exclusive—which another State might claim in this respect. As has already been observed, the Court has not to consider the lawfulness of the prosecution under Turkish law; questions of criminal law relating to the justification of the prosecution and consequently to the existence of a nexus causalis between the actions of Lieutenant Demons and the loss of eight Turkish nationals are not relevant to the issue so far as the Court is concerned. Moreover, the exact conditions in which these persons perished do not appear from the documents submitted to the Court; nevertheless, there is no doubt that their death may be regarded as the direct outcome of the collision, and the French Government has not contended that this relation of cause and effect cannot exist.

29. Lieutenant Demons and the captain of the Turkish steamship were prosecuted jointly and simultaneously. In regard to the conception of "connexity" of offences (connexité), the Turkish Agent in the submissions of his Counter-Case has referred to the Turkish Code of criminal procedure for trial, the provisions of which are said to have been taken from the corresponding French Code. Now in French law, amongst other factors, coincidence of time and place may give rise to "connexity" (connexité). In this case, therefore, the Court interprets this conception as meaning that the proceedings against the captain of the Turkish vessel in regard to which the jurisdiction of the Turkish Courts is not disputed, and the proceedings against Lieutenant Demons, have been regarded by the Turkish authorities, from the point of view of the investigation of the case, as one and the same prosecution, since the collision of the two steamers constitutes a complex of acts the consideration of which should, from the standpoint of Turkish criminal law, be entrusted to the same court.

30. The prosecution was instituted in pursuance of Turkish legislation. The special agreement does not indicate what clause or clauses of that legislation apply. No document has been submitted to the Court indicating on what article of the Turkish Penal Code the prosecution was based; the French Government however declares that

the Criminal Court claimed jurisdiction under Article 6 of the Turkish Penal Code, and far from denying this statement, Turkey, in the submissions of her Counter-Case, contends that that article is in conformity with the principles of international law. It does not appear from the proceedings whether the prosecution was instituted solely on the basis of that article.

31. Article 6 of the Turkish Penal Code, Law No. 765 of March 1st, 1926 (Official Gazette No. 320 of March 13th, 1926), runs as follows:

> Any foreigner who, apart from the cases contemplated by Article 4, commits an offence abroad to the prejudice of Turkey or of a Turkish subject, for which offence Turkish law prescribes a penalty involving loss of freedom for a minimum period of not less than one year, shall be punished in accordance with the Turkish Penal Code provided that he is arrested in Turkey. The penalty shall however be reduced by one third and instead of the death penalty, twenty years of penal servitude shall be awarded.

> Nevertheless, in such cases, the prosecution will only be instituted at the request of the Minister of Justice or on the complaint of the injured Party.

> If the offence committed injures another foreigner, the guilty person shall be punished at the request of the Minister of Justice, in accordance with the provisions set out in the first paragraph of this article, provided however that:

> (1) the article in question is one for which Turkish law prescribes a penalty involving loss of freedom for a minimum period of three years;

> (2) there is no extradition treaty or that extradition has not been accepted either by the government of the locality where the guilty person has committed the offence or by the government of his own country.

32. Even if the Court must hold that the Turkish authorities had seen fit to base the prosecution of Lieutenant Demons upon the above-mentioned Article 6, the question submitted to the Court is not whether that article is compatible with the principles of international law; it is more general. The Court is asked to state whether or not the principles of international law prevent Turkey from instituting criminal proceedings against Lieutenant Demons under Turkish law. Neither the conformity of Article 6 in itself with the principles of international law nor the application of that article by the Turkish authorities constitutes the point at issue; it is the very fact of the institution of proceedings which is held by France to be contrary to those principles. Thus the French Government at once protested against his arrest, quite independently of the question as to what clause of her legislation was

[handwritten margin note: Not whether they can, but whether they can't]

relied upon by Turkey to justify it. The arguments put forward by the French Government in the course of the proceedings and based on the principles which, in its contention, should govern navigation on the high seas, show that it would dispute Turkey's jurisdiction to prosecute Lieutenant Demons, even if that prosecution were based on a clause of the Turkish Penal Code other than Article 6, assuming for instance that the offence in question should be regarded, by reason of its consequences, to have been actually committed on Turkish territory.

33. Having determined the position resulting from the terms of the special agreement, the Court must now ascertain which were the principles of international law that the prosecution of Lieutenant Demons could conceivably be said to contravene.

34. It is Article 15 of the Convention of Lausanne of July 24th, 1923, respecting conditions of residence and business and jurisdiction, which refers the contracting Parties to the principles of international law as regards the delimitation of their respective jurisdiction.

35. This clause is as follows: "Subject to the provisions of Article 16, all questions of jurisdiction shall, as between Turkey and the other contracting Powers, be decided in accordance with the principles of international law."

36. The French Government maintains that the meaning of the expression "principles of international law" in this article should be sought in the light of the evolution of the Convention. Thus it states that during the preparatory work, the Turkish Government, by means of an amendment to the relevant article of a draft for the Convention, sought to extend its jurisdiction to crimes committed in the territory of a third State, provided that, under Turkish law, such crimes were within the jurisdiction of Turkish Courts. This amendment, in regard to which the representatives of France and Italy made reservations, was definitely rejected by the British representative; and the question having been subsequently referred to the Drafting Committee, the latter confined itself in its version of the draft to a declaration to the effect that questions of jurisdiction should be decided in accordance with the principles of international law. The French Government deduces from these facts that the prosecution of Demons is contrary to the intention which guided the preparation of the Convention of Lausanne.

37. The Court must recall in this connection what it has said in some of its preceding judgments and opinions, namely, that there is no occasion to have regard to preparatory work if the text of a convention is sufficiently clear in itself. Now the Court considers that the words "principles of international law," as ordinarily used, can only mean international law as it is applied between all nations belonging to the community of States. This interpretation is borne out by the context of

the article itself which says that the principles of international law are to determine questions of jurisdiction—not only criminal but also civil—between the contracting Parties, subject only to the exception provided for in Article 16. Again, the preamble of the Convention says that the High Contracting Parties are desirous of effecting a settlement in accordance "with modern international law," and Article 28 of the Treaty of Peace of Lausanne, to which the Convention in question is annexed, decrees the complete abolition of the Capitulations "in every respect." In these circumstances it is impossible—except in pursuance of a definite stipulation—to construe the expression "principles of international law" otherwise than as meaning the principles which are in force between all independent nations and which therefore apply equally to all the contracting Parties.

38. Moreover, the records of the preparation of the Convention respecting conditions of residence and business and jurisdiction would not furnish anything calculated to overrule the construction indicated by the actual terms of Article 15. It is true that the representatives of France, Great Britain and Italy rejected the Turkish amendment already mentioned. But only the British delegate—and this conformably to British municipal law which maintains the territorial principle in regard to criminal jurisdiction—stated the reasons for his opposition to the Turkish amendment; the reasons for the French and Italian reservations and for the omission from the draft prepared by the Drafting Committee of any definition of the scope of the criminal jurisdiction in respect of foreigners, are unknown and might have been unconnected with the arguments now advanced by France.

39. It should be added to these observations that the original draft of the relevant article, which limited Turkish jurisdiction to crimes committed in Turkey itself, was also discarded by the Drafting Committee; this circumstance might with equal justification give the impression that the intention of the framers of the Convention was not to limit this jurisdiction in any way.

40. The two opposing proposals designed to determine definitely the area of application of Turkish criminal law having thus been discarded, the wording ultimately adopted by common consent for Article 15 can only refer to the principles of general international law relating to jurisdiction.

41. The Court, having to consider whether there are any rules of international law which may have been violated by the prosecution in pursuance of Turkish law of Lieutenant Demons, is confronted in the first place by a question of principle which, in the written and oral arguments of the two Parties, has proved to be a fundamental one. The French Government contends that the Turkish Courts, in order to have jurisdiction, should be able to point to some title to jurisdiction

recognized by international law in favour of Turkey. On the other hand, the Turkish Government takes the view that Article 15 allows Turkey jurisdiction whenever such jurisdiction does not come into conflict with a principle of international law.

42. The latter view seems to be in conformity with the special agreement itself, No. I of which asks the Court to say whether Turkey has acted contrary to the principles of international law and, if so, what principles. According to the special agreement, therefore, it is not a question of stating principles which would permit Turkey to take criminal proceedings, but of formulating the principles, if any, which might have been violated by such proceedings.

43. This way of stating the question is also dictated by the very nature and existing conditions of international law.

44. International law governs relations between independent States. The rules of law binding upon States therefore emanate from their own free will as expressed in conventions or by usages generally accepted as expressing principles of law and established in order to regulate the relations between these co-existing independent communities or with a view to the achievement of common aims. Restrictions upon the independence of States cannot therefore be presumed.

45. Now the first and foremost restriction imposed by international law upon a State is that—failing the existence of a permissive rule to the contrary—it may not exercise its power in any form in the territory of another State. In this sense jurisdiction is certainly territorial; it cannot be exercised by a State outside its territory except by virtue of a permissive rule derived from international custom or from a convention.

46. It does not, however, follow that international law prohibits a State from exercising jurisdiction in its own territory, in respect of any case which relates to acts which have taken place abroad, and in which it cannot rely on some permissive rule of international law. Such a view would only be tenable if international law contained a general prohibition to States to extend the application of their laws and the jurisdiction of their courts to persons, property and acts outside their territory, and if, as an exception to this general prohibition, it allowed States to do so in certain specific cases. But this is certainly not the case under international law as it stands at present. Far from laying down a general prohibition to the effect that States may not extend the application of their laws and the jurisdiction of their courts to persons, property and acts outside their territory, it leaves them in this respect a wide measure of discretion, which is only limited in certain cases by prohibitive rules; as regards other cases, every State remains free to adopt the principles which it regards as best and most suitable.

47. This discretion left to States by international law explains the great variety of rules which they have been able to adopt without objections or complaints on the part of other States; it is in order to remedy the difficulties resulting from such variety that efforts have been made for many years past, both in Europe and America, to prepare conventions the effect of which would be precisely to limit the discretion at present left to States in this respect by international law, thus making good the existing lacunæ in respect of jurisdiction or removing the conflicting jurisdictions arising from the diversity of the principles adopted by the various States.

In these circumstances all that can be required of a State is that it should not overstep the limits which international law places upon its jurisdiction; within these limits, its title to exercise jurisdiction rests in its sovereignty.

48. It follows from the foregoing that the contention of the French Government to the effect that Turkey must in each case be able to cite a rule of international law authorizing her to exercise jurisdiction, is opposed to the generally accepted international law to which Article 13 of the Convention of Lausanne refers. Having regard to the terms of Article 15 and to the construction which the Court has just placed upon it, this contention would apply in regard to civil as well as to criminal cases, and would be applicable on conditions of absolute reciprocity as between Turkey and the other contracting Parties; in practice, it would therefore in many cases result in paralysing the action of the courts, owing to the impossibility of citing a universally accepted rule on which to support the exercise of their jurisdiction. . .

NOTES & QUESTIONS

1. *Defending the Lotus Presumption.* The court concluded that Turkey was not required to articulate a rule justifying its assertion of jurisdiction. Rather, France was required to articulate a rule that prohibited Turkey's behavior. The basic assumption in *Lotus* is that states have a sovereign right to act in any way they wish unless a specific rule of international law prohibits that behavior. What type of presumption applies in normal domestic life? For example, what is the background presumption that applies in domestic criminal law or domestic tort law? Do these fields operate according to a *Lotus* presumption or according to a reverse-*Lotus* presumption?

2. *Modern Examples of the Lotus Presumption.* Once you look for them, examples of the *Lotus* presumption appear everywhere. Often, the presumption is not explicitly articulated. But in other situations, the presumption is explicitly cited. For example, the International Court of Justice (ICJ) issued an Advisory Opinion in 2010 addressing whether the territory of Kosovo (in Serbia) had a right to unilaterally declare

independence. The ICJ concluded that there was no rule of international law explicitly prohibiting Kosovo from making such a declaration. See *Accordance with International Law of the Unilateral Declaration of Independence in Respect of Kosovo*, 2010 I.C.J. 404. This was clearly an application of the *Lotus* presumption. Writing in dissent, Judge Bruno Simma criticized the application of the *Lotus* presumption to the question of Kosovo's unilateral declaration of independence:

> The underlying rationale of the Court's approach reflects an old, tired view of international law, which takes the adage, famously expressed in the *Lotus* Judgment, according to which restrictions on the independence of States cannot be presumed because of the consensual nature of the international legal order. As the Permanent Court did in that case, the Court has concluded in the present Opinion that, in relation to a specific act, it is not necessary to demonstrate a permissive rule so long as there is no prohibition. In this respect, in a contemporary international legal order which is strongly influenced by ideas of public law, the Court's reasoning on this point is obsolete. . .

> The Court's reading of the General Assembly's question and its reasoning, leaping as it does straight from the lack of a prohibition to permissibility, is a straightforward application of the so-called *Lotus* principle. By reverting to it, the Court answers the question in a manner redolent of nineteenth-century positivism, with its excessively deferential approach to State consent. Under this approach, everything which is not expressly prohibited carries with it the same colour of legality; it ignores the possible degrees of non-prohibition, ranging from "tolerated" to "permissible" to "desirable."

What did Simma mean when he referred to positivism? What is the connection between the *Lotus* presumption and positivism? Do you see the *Lotus* presumption at work in the *Antelope* decision discussed above? Did the Supreme Court assume that the slave trade was legal under the law of nations unless a litigant could point to a rule of international law forbidding it? Finally, does the *Lotus* presumption represent an "excessively deferential approach" to state interests, as Simma suggests?

C. INTERNATIONAL LAW AS A LEGAL SYSTEM

International law is more than a body of law. It is also a legal system, with a distinctive ecology populated by actors—international lawyers—who use international law in a different way than domestic lawyers. In the following excerpt, Professor Anthony D'Amato takes a step back and rather than acting as an international lawyer within the system, he looks at international law as a discipline from the perspective of a social scientist. What does he see?

Groundwork for International Law

Anthony D'Amato

108 Am. J. Int'l L. 650 (2014)

International law is a system; its environment is the field of international relations. Although the word *system* is often used generically, it has a formal meaning in "general systems theory," an interdisciplinary methodology that grew out of cybernetics research in the 1970s. Since then, general systems theory has proved to be a significant heuristic in hundreds of disparate research areas. In describing international law from the viewpoint of an autopoietic system (to be defined shortly), this article intends not just to reexamine the foundations of international law but also to help litigators and negotiators make their international-law arguments sounder and more persuasive.

A general system is an entity that is separated from its environment by a skin, a membrane, or even just a description of its boundaries. The elements inside the system interact with each other. An open system interacts with its environment; a closed system (for example, a bacteria culture inside a sealed test tube) interacts only with itself. International law is an open system because it gets its information from diplomacy, and its rules, in turn, affect diplomatic strategy. The rules themselves are interconnected, as shown by the fact that any rule may be used as a sanction in cases of noncompliance with international law. Adding to the interconnectedness of rules is the fact that the states that cite or violate them form a nonscalar communications network of radio, television, the Internet, cell phones (the most ubiquitous product in history, with an increasing impact on human rights), trade, and cross-boundary movement of persons. In brief, international rules, norms, principles, privileges, duties, and entitlements (even when translations of these terms can be fuzzy) form an identifiable and coherent set within the system.

Autopoietic systems were discovered in 1973 by Chilean biologists Humberto Maurana and Francisco Varela. Their theory defines living systems as self-producing units that maintain their essential form, perpetuating themselves according to their internal organization. Not only do we now know that a living animal can be described by the autopoietic system, but we have the contrary claim—enormously successful as a heuristic in scientific research—that entities with an autopoietic organization can parsimoniously be studied as if they were alive. The international legal system is a living system because it is made up of jurists and practitioners (the invisible college, to be described below), and because these persons have invested their careers in the hope and reasonable expectation that the system will perpetuate itself into the foreseeable future. The system therefore "wants" to persist through time; indeed, it has survived since the fall of the Roman Empire.

The internal coherence of the international legal system is evidenced by the fact that it can be viewed anthropomorphically. This coherence is sometimes hard to see from the phenomenological perspectives of one's home state. General systems theory provides a top-down vantage point that helps, first, in providing an efficient descriptive model of the international system incorporating minimalist empirical assumptions of state behavior; second, in providing explanatory theories of causation for its set of norms; and third, in predicting generally the system's acceptance or rejection of new putative norms of customary international law.

All living systems want to survive over time. As a general matter, the international legal system's best tools in the Darwinian struggle to survive are, first, adhering to a set of noncontradictory rules and principles of public international law; second, applying these principles to all states equally; and third, recognizing a bias in the rules themselves (and in their formation) in favor of peaceful resolution of disputes, thus raising the odds of the system's survival. The same factors work in reinforcing and replenishing the perceived value of the system, thus increasing the prestige of its practitioners and experts.

The systemic rules I will be analyzing are rules about rules—rules of the general system of international law, or more simply, metarules. They can be taken as constitutive of present international law— "constitutive" meaning both epistemological and ontological. Thus, each of the systemic propositions. . . of this article can be challenged by the reader as empirically unfounded, ontologically invalid, or both. This potential double challenge has acted as a strong constraint upon my formulation of the propositions in this article. I have tried to formulate them as simply as possible (following Occam's razor) and to likewise limit their number, taking into account the great diversity of international law. The general template will, I hope, survive any errors within it, thus making it useful to others if they choose to substitute or add new propositions.

What make the present project feasible are two nonsubjective factors. First is the coherence of the international legal system itself. Its rules are well honed and well tested. It resembles a biological system that has evolved over time. The system strives to preserve itself by providing a normative peace-tilting check upon contested issues of international relations and diplomacy. Mutant conflict-stimulating rules that led to warfare have been replaced—in the Darwinian struggle to survive over the centuries—by cooperation-enabling rules. The second factor is the nature of law itself. Law is inherently conservative; its rules of decision emphasize adhering to precedents from the past. A peaceful past is a presumptive guide to a peaceful future. Stability can be seen as a function of rule preservation. Thus, the struggle for survival of the international legal system through time is coterminous with maintaining the integrity of the majority of its rules, norms, and principles.

For transparency of exposition, the theory presented here is broken down into its components: axioms, propositions, and corollaries. Four axioms describe basic requirements of the international legal system. Eleven propositions illustrate the sorting process that the system imposes on all potential legal rules that strive to become part of the system. Twelve corollaries present examples of the propositions and, in a few cases, examine related theories. By applying its three components, one applies the theory itself; there is nothing left over.

Taken together, the axioms, propositions, and corollaries herein offer a structured, internally consistent explanation of why the present rules of international law, instead of other imaginable or counterfactual rules, have turned out to be the fittest in the international legal system's Darwinian struggle to survive. Of course, mutant rules may arise at any time to replace one or more of the existing rules. However, a testable consequence of the groundwork offered here is that the probability of a potential rule replacing a current rule is a function of the former's having a tighter fit into the axiomatic scheme. Thus, the proffered axiomatic scheme has "bite": it is a filter for testing, accepting, or rejecting new rules.

Four Foundational Axioms

AXIOM 1. The primary purpose of the international legal system is not to regulate international relations but to preserve itself.

The general-systems point of view focuses primarily upon the system and only secondarily upon the system's goal or purpose. James Crawford's book *International Law as an Open System* takes the latter viewpoint: international law's purpose is to regulate international relations. By contrast, the general-systems viewpoint here takes an essentialist position in claiming that the rules and processes of international law can be best explained if we start with the self-protective nature of all aggregative, interconnected entities known as general systems.

International law is not a stack of rules on a library shelf. It is a professional industry, made up of national officials, diplomats and statespersons, international practitioners and scholars, law professors and students, UN officials, judges of international courts and their clerks, professional arbitrators, judges and clerks of bilateral claims commissions, and advocate-members of NGOs, among others—all of whom were well described by the late Oscar Schachter as an invisible college of international lawyers dedicated to a common intellectual enterprise. Because of the time that these persons have devoted to studying and learning international law, they have invested significant human capital in the system's continued utility and preservation. To be sure, they will often disagree as to whether an alleged rule belongs to the set of accepted rules of international law (especially if it is their job to come out the way that their employers or their governments demand), but even then they have a personal stake in preserving and maintaining the system of international rules. Governments turn to them for advice as to the international legality of a given policy that the government plans to implement—at the very least in order to help predict the reactions of the legally informed international community. These advisers, both official and unofficial, infuse the international legal system with a dynamic sense of purpose and persistence. Thus, to the tens of thousands of persons making up the invisible college around the world, international rules can sometimes seem incorrect but never irrelevant.

The greatest threat to the viability of the international-law system is anarchy. With total anarchy, international law would perish and might be replaced, if peace is restored, by something entirely different (such as a world dictatorship). Thus, when any controversy arises among nations and the relevant rules are in dispute, the international legal system's bias for self-preservation will tilt toward the rule that offers the greater probability of a peaceful resolution of the controversy and will bend away from the rule that prolongs or escalates it. That is not to say that justice is irrelevant to conflict resolution. But justice does not function in the abstract; rather, it is perceived justice that counts. And most of the time the perceived justice is symbiotic with the resolution that augurs future peace. Arguably, a justly perceived decision, both in domestic and international law, promotes stability. After the temper of a losing side cools down, the just decision may gradually be accepted as the right decision.

> *AXIOM 2. The international legal system, as it strives to persist through time, tends to evolve norms that reduce friction and controversies among states and to foster systemic equilibrium by prescribing how controversies may be avoided, mitigated, or resolved.*

Indefinite persistence through time is the foremost objective of any biological or behavioral system. Since war is the most dangerous predator of the international legal system, we can expect that for its own preservation the system will have generated rules or norms over time that serve both to reduce the temptation to resort to war (*jus ad bellum*) and to ameliorate the destructiveness of war should it break out (*jus in bello*). Thus, the ancient rule of diplomatic immunity was obviously intended to reduce international misunderstandings before they escalated into an unwanted war but also to provide a mechanism for facilitating peace negotiations at any time during a war that began when diplomacy failed.

How many rules are in the set of international rules? General systems theory provides some help. Theoretically, if a system has only one or two rules, it can quickly disequilibrate. The violation of one rule might invite a retaliatory response consisting of the violation of the other rule, leaving no remaining rules to help stabilize the impending rush toward anarchy. The propensity of systems toward homeostasis—to maintain a tolerable level of equilibrium—appears to require a larger number of rules in order to reduce the likelihood the rules will not be disregarded and then violated either all at once or, over time, through a process of escalating retaliation. The international legal system may be characterized as having a "rugged fitness landscape," to use Stuart Kauffman's concept derived from evolutionary biology. If the landscape were conceptually characterized by two tall mountains (two rules) with flat valleys between them, the system would include little room for "play"; states would have no place of refuge. But if the system consisted of many mountains, hills, and valleys, then a state's violation of a given rule could be met by migrations and adjustments in the other landscape configurations. Another concept from Kauffman is that the evolutionary viability of the survival of the fittest on earth favors progressive occupation of environmental niches in a rugged fitness landscape. By analogy, the varied topological landscape of the international legal system provides enough variety to allow thousands of applications of rules (consider the earth's jagged coastlines and island formations) without upsetting the rules themselves. As rules of international law increase in density and coverage, and as the more fit among them survive, they seek out niches for their own safety and stability. For example, in the Anglo-Norwegian *Fisheries* case, plaintiff Great Britain conceded in advance of litigation Norway's jurisdiction and control over numerous small-island configurations and drying rocks—which in our terminology were historical niches pragmatically belonging to Norway even though they were located beyond Norway's three-mile limit.

In addition, police rules (akin to antibodies in biological systems) will likely emerge to protect the substantive rules (humanitarian intervention might be an example). As a general matter, the more fine-meshed the web of protective rules is in peacetime, the farther away is the specter of war.

AXIOM 3. The general-systems viewpoint has practical payoffs.

A skeptical reader at this point might wonder whether the general-systems viewpoint is just an overblown metaphor. Of what use is it to a practitioner or scholar in the everyday world of litigating and practicing international law? The answer offered here is that when controversies arise among states, the international legal system immanently tilts in favor of the side whose position seems to auger greater peace and stability. The party having the advantage is the one who can argue that a legal resolution of the controversy in its favor will foster stabilization in international relations, whereas its opponent's position—irrespective of short-run considerations that might seem to justify it—will spawn further controversies over time. Such an argument finds its footing in general systems theory as set forth in the present essay. Axiom 2 contended that the international legal system "tends to evolve norms that reduce friction and controversies among states." It is just a short step to add that international courts and tribunals will tend to be more receptive to a party's arguments if the norms it cites and the principles it relies upon are those that are likely to increase international stability and reduce future friction and controversies. Litigators who are unaware of these dynamics may find themselves at an argumentative disadvantage—whether or not they use the jargon of general systems theory.

Prior to the Hague Conventions of 1899 and 1907, courts were not involved in questioning *jus in bellum*—the laws of war. Yet it was slowly realized, starting at the time of the Lieber Code of the American Civil War, expanded by the Hague Conventions of 1899 and 1907, and codified and restated in the Geneva Conventions of 1929 and 1949, that there was no need to kill prisoners of war or to kill unarmed civilians. Neither side would be militarily advantaged during a war if both sides regarded prisoners of war and civilians as *hors de combat*. However, this new practice—called "the humanitarian laws of war"—needs a theoretical explanation that coheres with the systemic bias in favor of future peace and stability.

To some students upon their first encounter with international law, the humanitarian laws of war seem proof of the "unreality" of the subject: after all, isn't war the ultimate all-out, winner-take-all, zero-sum activity? Rules of law, by definition, cannot restrain the conduct of warfare: norms do not stop bullets. To these students the very existence and specific development over the years of the laws of humanitarian warfare seem rooted in paradox. Either the paradox can be resolved by the simplistic conclusion that rules of law are pious norms ("positive morality" in John Austin's phrase), or else the paradox reveals the deep structure of the system: its tendency, above everything, to achieve homeostasis. The following brief argument is offered in support of the latter theory.

Is there a homeostatic reason for the international system to care enough about the degree of cruelty in the waging of war as to risk its norms in order to mitigate that cruelty? There is no doubt that its norms—and not just the norms concerning humanitarian warfare—

would be at risk: by putting the latter norms on the line, the international system takes the chance of their being ignored by military commanders on either side who want to win at all costs. The disobedience of the norms might then spread to all other norms of the international system, putting the entire legal structure at risk of collapse. Why would the international system take such a risk? Even more broadly, why should that system attempt to circumscribe military activity at all? Wouldn't unrestrained warfare bring war to a quicker termination?

Reducing cruelty per se is not the reason. The homeostatic, forward-looking reason for the international system to create humanitarian laws of warfare was suggested by Quincy Wright: "to prevent the war from providing the seeds for a new war." The international system has opted to protect its future equilibrium by outlawing certain defined kinds of cruel behavior during a period of disequilibrium. The norms against barbaric behavior (those for which legal prohibitions predated the war: bombing nonmilitary targets such as civilians, museums, churches, and synagogues; chemical warfare and the use of poisonous gas; shooting prisoners of war) remain robust even during total war. Violating those norms can lead to withdrawal of support during the war from neutrals or even allies, as well as to prosecution for war crimes after the war. In rare cases a new weapon can be so barbaric that a new prohibitory norm coalesces more or less immediately.

In domestic legal systems one can see something analogous to international law's favoring the side that argues that awarding it the judgment will reduce future conflicts. It is the famous "floodgates" argument: the defendant argues that allowing subject-matter jurisdiction in the present case will open the floodgates of future litigation on that issue. When a court is convinced by this argument, it will probably accept the defendant's motion to dismiss.

AXIOM 4. The actual practice of states constitutes, for the most part, practice that the system normatizes.

Louis Henkin has often been quoted for his observation: "Almost all nations observe almost all principles of international law and almost all of their obligations almost all of the time." But sometimes a minor rewording of a statement like Henkin's can yield a deeper truth: "Most nations cannot disobey most of the rules most of the time." If they did, then the rules could hardly be called rules. More rigorously, the reason that most states are law-abiding is a logical consequence of the proposition that the law that governs their behavior must in large part conform to that same behavior. In order for law violations to be punishable in any social organization, they must be relatively infrequent, minority phenomena. Hence, we may conclude that the rules of international law that survive over time are precisely those rules that describe majority behavior—whether or not we like that behavior. To be sure, the gap between law and behavior must be kept narrow lest the law itself precipitate a war.

Thus, in order to have an international "legal" system, majority behavior must be articulated and normatized. The system's principles for ensuring its own survival must then be internationalized. In short, it follows from the above variation of Henkin's observation that the system's articulation, selection, adoption, and normatization of its own principles is another way of describing the process of generating customary international law.

Custom includes events, incidents, and conflict resolutions. But as Quincy Wright cautioned, "events can hardly be described without a theory determining what is important and what should be looked for. Deduction and induction supplement one another." Since not all state practices amount to custom in the sense of customary international law, the system must also attempt to exclude the practices that lead to war. Those practices, if normatized, would give rise to dysfunctional rules of customary international law. For example, prior to the twentieth century, a king or a head of state could start an aggressive war against another state or states without violating any rule of international law. Yet the evidence indicates that there is even more state practice of abstaining from starting an aggressive war. An informal but intuitively correct compilation of available empirical evidence for the last seven centuries indicates that states have avoided war 97 percent of their lifetimes. Instead, they have sought to maximize their own welfare by engaging in peaceful activities such as international commerce, trade, and investment. States in the aggregate have desired an international system conducive to the maximization of their welfare, and hence over the centuries they have desired peace under law. The Ricardian doctrine of comparative advantage, which Ludwig von Mises pointed out is actually just an international extension of the economic principle of division of labor, allows individuals to increase their economic well-being and lifestyle when the interstate system allows free trade—a game that both sides win. In war, by contrast, there are always sunk costs—the total number of lives lost and the total worth of property destroyed on both sides. In a sense, war and free trade are jural opposites: on average, war is a lose-lose, and trade is a win-win, proposition.

The preceding example of many more states avoiding war than instigating it does not amount to a practice. Accordingly, it is hard to explain or contest international law's permissiveness in starting a war of aggression prior to the twentieth century. It took a series of multilateral treaties to outlaw recourse to war: the Hague Conventions of 1899 and 1907, the Covenant of the League of Nations, and the Kellogg-Briand Pact of 1928. A commitment by states not to resort to aggressive war is itself an anticipatory practice that is equivalent to custom.

In the short run, of course, some states find it to be politically or economically advantageous to take action in violation of a rule of international law. The system of rules, if sufficiently fine-meshed, can tolerate occasional and relatively isolated illegalities. However, every violation is a threat to the stability of the entire legal system, as we shall see below. Every violation that causes a rupture of the system must therefore be repaired by the system. Proportionate rules of sanction have evolved for the purpose of repair and deterrence.

Short-run deviations arise, for example, when a free-rider state wants the benefit of the treaties that it likes and the right to denounce all other treaties, or when a warrior state sees a "limited" war as serving its self-interest so long as other states refrain from intervening. But the system cannot afford to allow individual states to pick and choose from among the treaties it has ratified or to insulate a war from the intervention of third-party states. To reassemble the argument of Axiom 1, international law at any given time consists of rules that foster the persistence of the international system itself. Individual members of a system cannot tell the system what to do. It therefore devolves upon each state to calculate the cost of international-law compliance that constricts its freedom of action and to compare that cost to the overall benefit it derives from the existence of those rules. To be sure, the state's cost/benefit analysis cannot be reduced to an exact figure because, in a world of 193 states, other states at any time may *increase* the sanctions if those that are first applied do not deter the state in question. This conclusion reflects Henkin's aphorism—namely, that most states find it in their self-interest to obey most of the rules of international law most of the time. . . .

NOTES & QUESTIONS

1. *The Majority Always Wins.* Why does D'Amato argue that international law "normatizes" most state conduct? The basis for this conclusion is that states are the ones to *create* international law through the treaties they sign and through the customary law that is created by their own state conduct. So, is it any surprise that international law licenses most state conduct? Are there shades of this phenomenon in the *Antelope* case? The Supreme Court concluded that the slave trade is consistent with international law because most (or many) states engaged in it. Setting aside for the moment whether this conclusion was correct, the structure of the argument embodies D'Amato's point: international law is not likely to yield a legal rule that almost every state is violating. Does the *Lotus* presumption feed this dynamic? The Finnish legal scholar Martti Koskenniemi famously argued that international law is often caught between the extremes of utopia and apology. International law is utopian because it posits an ideal world with unrealistic norms or unrealistic levels of compliance. At the same time, international law often justifies or licenses existing behavior—for the very

reasons D'Amato articulates above—making international law an apologist for today's sorry state of affairs. See Martti Koskenniemi, *From Apology to Utopia: The Structure of International Legal Argument* (1989).

2.   *The Invisible College of International Lawyers.* D'Amato refers to the "invisible college" of international lawyers. What does he mean by this reference? More than forty years ago, Professor Schachter referred to the invisible college of international lawyers as a "professional community, though dispersed throughout the world and engaged in diverse occupations, [which] constitutes a kind of invisible college dedicated to a common intellectual enterprise." See Oscar Schachter, *The Invisible College of International Lawyers*, 72 Nw. U.L. Rev. 217 (1977). Simply put, although international lawyers often disagree with each other through an adversarial process, they are, in a deeper sense, cooperating with each other in a common enterprise—the enterprise of shaping something called international law. As you read through the materials for this course, consider the role played by this invisible college—a group you will one day join. Schachter asks whether the invisible college forms *la conscience juridique*—a judicial conscience for the international community that helps to define basic principles of "natural justice." According to Schachter, "Vague as that conception may seem, it has had a considerable influence in doctrine and in decisions as a basis for legal concepts of significant practical effect. Some examples that come to mind are reciprocity, good faith, abuse of rights, nonretroactivity, prescription, res judicata, proportionality and estoppel. . . . Whatever their justification, they have been applied by international lawyers in formulating general principles of law and in proposing standards for treaties and institutional arrangements." Is there a connection here with our prior discussion of natural law?

Conclusion & Summary

The rest of this course will focus on the substantive norms of international law. But as you learn and digest these norms, and understand how to apply them to concrete international controversies, do not forget that international law is a process, a practice, and a system. Recall the following points of process explored in this chapter:

1.   International law was once intertwined with, and inseparable from, natural law. However, the natural law-era of international law has long since ended, replaced by a positivist conception of law based on man-made sources of law such as treaties and custom. One might ask why the natural law conception of international law proved untenable. One might also ask whether natural law can be 100 percent eradicated from the discipline of international law and whether it survives in isolated cracks of the doctrine. This question should be central in your mind as you confront the material in each chapter. Would slavery be

OK if the positive sources of international law brought it back? How does one answer this question without reference to some conception of natural law?

2. It is generally presumed that states are entitled to act as they wish unless the action violates a rule of international law. This *Lotus* presumption is so central that many consider it the grounding principle of international law. One can think of the presumption as intimately tied to the concept of state sovereignty, i.e., that states have discretion over their internal affairs. Judge Simma of the ICJ referred to the *Lotus* presumption as being excessively deferential to state sovereignty. However, despite Simma's concerns, most international lawyers approach legal controversies with the assumption that a state is entitled to act as it wishes unless it violates a rule of international law. In other words, all is permitted unless it is prohibited. Throughout the rest of this casebook, look for examples where this binary opposition might not hold.

3. International law is a field of law that regulates the behavior of nation-states. But it is also a legal system with its own actors, processes, and norms of behavior. As a student of international law, you are already inside that system, adopting and participating in its collective project. However, it is useful, occasionally, to step back and take an outside perspective on the enterprise and question what role international lawyers are playing in the process. In every legal debate, the opposing viewpoints often share deeper principles that structure the conversation. It is helpful to identify and render explicit these deeper principles and to understand the role that lawyers—and other actors—play in the dissemination of these norms. The invisible college need not be invisible.

CHAPTER 2

CUSTOM AND OTHER SOURCES

Introduction

It is often said that the bulk of international legal norms stem not from treaty law but from custom—that strange process by which patterns of behavior among states ripen into legal obligations. Some of these customs will be codified in written instruments and become binding as a matter of treaty law, which is discussed in the next chapter. However, the majority of norms will never reach codification in a binding written instrument but will instead reside in the hinterland of legal sources known as customary international law.

Unlike domestic legal systems, where "unwritten" law is often considered anathema to a well-developed system of legal regulation, international law is much more comfortable with unwritten law in the form of custom. Generally speaking, states act in particular ways in their mutual interactions (state practice), and do so out of a sense of legal obligation (opinio juris). When they do so, the custom is a valid source of law. Often there will be a written record of the custom: a scholar will describe the custom or maybe even a document from a foreign diplomat might reference the practice. However, in those cases the written record is merely a description of the law rather than the law itself. The law is the custom itself in all its unwritten glory. Consequently, there is something magical about the radical bootstrapping of customary international law. States act in compliance with a rule and by doing so create the rule that gives rise to the legal obligation. It is unlike anything comparable in domestic law in its pure solipsism.

There is much to be said about why custom should be considered as a valid source of international law. One possibility is that it is based on the consent of the parties. After all, states engage in particular actions and in so doing participate in the process of constructing the norms of customary international law (since it is built from the raw materials of state practice). This "consent" picture is attractive because it dovetails with the underlying foundation for treaty law, which is clearly based on the principle that states voluntarily accept the legal obligations they will be subject to. One might therefore conclude that consent is the bedrock principle that underlies *all* of international law, regardless of the source.

On further reflection, however, there are cracks in that pristine picture. Although states participate in the formation of customary international law through their own practice, there is no requirement that state practice must be universal in the strict sense in order to form a rule. Of course, states that object to a rule of customary international law may exempt themselves from the rule by claiming "persistent objector status"—a rule that seems to be a doctrinal expression of the principle of consent. However, as we will learn below, there are strict requirements for successfully asserting persistent objector status, and it is rarely invoked. The most important limitation is that there are some legal norms—universal principles that are considered non-derogable—that are not subject to persistent objection and must be complied with regardless of whether the state consents to them or not. These legal norms are labelled jus cogens. As discussed below, international lawyers are generally in agreement that the category of jus cogens exists, but there is profound disagreement about which norms deserve that label. Moreover, there is great conceptual confusion over how legal norms obtain the status of jus cogens—the highest peak in the landscape of international law, where the state's consent to the norm is basically irrelevant because the norm is so imperative to the functioning of the global legal order. The most that can be said is that consent is a major building block of international law but may not constitute the entire foundation. There is some residual principle that grounds international law after the principle of consent is exhausted.

The following materials methodically introduce these key concepts and apply them in a series of concrete cases: state practice, opinio juris, persistent objection, jus cogens. The chapter ends with a consideration in the last section of other sources of international law that are not properly speaking classified as either treaty or custom, but which are identified in Article 38 of the Statute of the International Court of Justice as valid sources of international law. These include the somewhat nebulous "general principles" of international law, the decisions of international tribunals, and the teachings of "highly qualified publicists," i.e., the work of international legal scholars.

A. STATE PRACTICE

Customary law is built from the raw materials of state practice. Indeed, the process is somewhat akin to boot-strapping: a group of states act in a particular way, in their belief that the act is required by law, and in so doing the custom *becomes* law. How is this possible?

While the mysteries of customary law are deep and enduring, this source of law is also governed by concrete legal standards. International law distinguishes between "mere custom" and custom that has ripened into law. One of the key requirements is the nature of the underlying state practice. According to most observers who have studied the issue, the state practice must be constant and uniform, rather than isolated or sporadic. According to the International Law Commission, the following acts may constitute state practice:

1. Practice may take a wide range of forms. It includes both physical and verbal acts. It may, under certain circumstances, include inaction.

2. Forms of State practice include, but are not limited to: diplomatic acts and correspondence; conduct in connection with resolutions adopted by an international organization or at an intergovernmental conference; conduct in connection with treaties; executive conduct, including operational conduct "on the ground"; legislative and administrative acts; and decisions of national courts.

3. There is no predetermined hierarchy among the various forms of practice.

See ILC, Identification of Customary International Law, Draft Text, U.N. Doc. A/CN.4/L.872 (May 30, 2016). The ILC also has identified a requirement that state practice must be public, rather than secret, conduct. Also, the decisions or orders of international institutions or tribunals cannot be considered state practice because they are supranational institutions rather than organs of a particular state government.

The case below hinges on Article 6 of the Convention on the Continental Shelf Done at Geneva, on 29 April 1958, 499 U.N.T.S. 312–321:

1. Where the same continental shelf is adjacent to the territories of two or more States whose coasts are opposite each other, the boundary of the continental shelf appertaining to such States shall be determined by agreement between them. In the absence of agreement, and unless another boundary line is justified by special circumstances, the boundary is the median line, every point of which is equidistant from the nearest points of the baselines from which the breadth of the territorial sea of each State is measured.

2. Where the same continental shelf is adjacent to the territories of two adjacent States, the boundary of the continental shelf shall be determined by agreement between them. In the absence of agreement, and unless another boundary line is justified by special circumstances, the boundary shall be determined by application of the principle of equidistance from the nearest points of the baselines from which the breadth of the territorial sea of each State is measured.

As you read the following case, ask yourself whether the "equidistance" principle embodied in this provision is also binding on non-signatories as a matter of customary international law.

North Sea Continental Shelf
(Germany v. Denmark & Netherlands)

International Court of Justice
February 20, 1969

60. The conclusions so far reached leave open, and still to be considered, the question whether on some basis other than that of an a priori logical necessity, i.e., through positive law processes, the equidistance principle has come to be regarded as a rule of customary international law, so that it would be obligatory for the Federal Republic in that way, even though Article 6 of the Geneva Convention is not, as such, opposable to it. For this purpose it is necessary to examine the status of the principle as it stood when the Convention was drawn up, as it resulted from the effect of the Convention, and in the light of State practice subsequent to the Convention; but it should be clearly understood that in the pronouncements the Court makes on these matters it has in view solely the delimitation provisions (Article 6) of the Convention, not other parts of it, nor the Convention as such.

61. The first of these questions can conveniently be considered in the form suggested on behalf of Denmark and the Netherlands themselves in the course of the oral hearing, when it was stated that they had not in fact contended that the delimitation article (Article 6) of the Convention "embodied already received rules of customary law in the sense that the Convention was merely declaratory of existing rules." Their contention was, rather, that although prior to the Conference, continental shelf law was only in the formative stage, and State practice lacked uniformity, yet "the process of the definition and consolidation of the emerging customary law took place through the work of the International Law Commission, the reaction of governments to that work and the proceedings of the Geneva Conference"; and this emerging customary law became "crystallized in the adoption of the Continental Shelf Convention by the Conference."

62. Whatever validity this contention may have in respect of at least certain parts of the Convention, the Court cannot accept it as regards the delimitation provision (Article 6), the relevant parts of which were adopted almost unchanged from the draft of the International Law Commission that formed the basis of discussion at the Conference. The status of the rule in the Convention therefore depends mainly on the processes that led the Commission to propose it. These processes have already been reviewed in connection with the Danish-Netherlands contention of an a priori necessity for equidistance, and the Court

considers this review sufficient for present purposes also, in order to show that the principle of equidistance, as it now figures in Article 6 of the Convention, was proposed by the Commission with considerable hesitation, somewhat on an experimental basis, at most de lege ferenda, and not at all de lege lata or as an emerging rule of customary international law. This is clearly not the sort of foundation on which Article 6 of the Convention could be said to have reflected or crystallized such a rule.

63. The foregoing conclusion receives significant confirmation from the fact that Article 6 is one of those in respect of which, under the reservations article of the Convention (Article 12) reservations may be made by any State on signing, ratifying or acceding, for, speaking generally, it is a characteristic of purely conventional rules and obligations that, in regard to them, some faculty of making unilateral reservations may, within certain limits, be admitted—whereas this cannot be so in the case of general or customary law rules and obligations which, by their very nature, must have equal force for all members of the international community, and cannot therefore be the subject of any right of unilateral exclusion exercisable at will by any one of them in its own favour. Consequently, it is to be expected that when, for whatever reason, rules or obligations of this order are embodied, or are intended to be reflected in certain provisions of a convention, such provisions will figure amongst those in respect of which a right of unilateral reservation is not conferred, or is excluded. This expectation is, in principle, fulfilled by Article 12 of the Geneva Continental Shelf Convention, which permits reservations to be made to all the articles of the Convention "other than to Articles 1 to 3 inclusive"—these three Articles being the ones which, it is clear, were then regarded as reflecting, or as crystallizing, received or at least emergent rules of customary international law relative to the continental shelf, amongst them the question of the seaward extent of the shelf; the juridical character of the coastal State's entitlement; the nature of the rights exercisable; the kind of natural resources to which there relate; and the preservation intact of the legal status as high seas of the waters over the shelf, and the legal status of the superjacent air-space.

64. The normal inference would therefore be that any articles that do not figure among those excluded from the faculty of reservation under Article 12, were not regarded as declaratory of previously existing or emergent rules of law; and this is the inference the Court in fact draws in respect of Article 6 (delimitation), having regard also to the attitude of the International Law Commission to this provision, as already described in general terms. Naturally this would not of itself prevent this provision from eventually passing into the general corpus of customary international law by one of the processes considered in paragraphs 70–

81 below. But that is not here the issue. What is now under consideration is whether it originally figured in the Convention as such a rule.

65. It has however been suggested that the inference drawn at the beginning of the preceding paragraph is not necessarily warranted, seeing that there are certain other provisions of the Convention, also not excluded from the faculty of reservation, but which do undoubtedly in principle relate to matters that lie within the field of received customary law, such as the obligation not to impede the laying or maintenance of submarine cables or pipelines on the continental shelf seabed (Article 4), and the general obligation not unjustifiably to interfere with freedom of navigation, fishing, and so on (Article 5, paragraphs 1 and 6). These matters however, all relate to or are consequential upon principles or rules of general maritime law, very considerably ante-dating the Convention, and not directly connected with but only incidental to continental shelf rights as such. They were mentioned in the Convention, not in order to declare or confirm their existence, which was not necessary, but simply to ensure that they were not prejudiced by the exercise of continental shelf rights as provided for in the Convention. Another method of drafting might have clarified the point, but this cannot alter the fact that no reservation could release the reserving party from obligations of general maritime law existing outside and independently of the Convention, and especially obligations formalized in Article 2 of the contemporaneous Convention on the High Seas, expressed by its preamble to be declaratory of established principles of international law.

66. Article 6 (delimitation) appears to the Court to be in a different position. It does directly relate to continental shelf rights as such, rather than to matters incidental to these; and since it was not, as were Articles 1 to 3, excluded from the faculty of reservation, it is a legitimate inference that it was considered to have a different and less fundamental status and not, like those Articles, to reflect pre-existing or emergent customary law. It was however contended on behalf of Denmark and the Netherlands that the right of reservation given in respect of Article 6 was not intended to be an unfettered right, and that in particular it does not extend to effecting a total exclusion of the equidistance principle of delimitation, for, so it was claimed, delimitation on the basis of that principle is implicit in Articles 1 and 2 of the Convention, in respect of which no reservations are permitted. Hence the right of reservation under Article 6 could only be exercised in a manner consistent with the preservation of at least the basic principle of equidistance. In this connection it was pointed out that, of the no more than four reservations so far entered in respect of Article 6, one at least of which was somewhat far reaching, none has purported to effect such a total exclusion or denial.

67. The Court finds this argument unconvincing for a number of reasons. In the first place, Articles 1 and 2 of the Geneva Convention do not appear to have any direct connection with inter-State delimitation as such. Article 1 is concerned only with the outer, seaward, limit of the shelf generally, not with boundaries between the shelf areas of opposite or adjacent States. Article 2 is equally not concerned with such boundaries. The suggestion seems to be that the notion of equidistance is implicit in the reference in paragraph 2 of Article 2 to the rights of the coastal State over its continental shelf being "exclusive." So far as actual language is concerned this interpretation is clearly incorrect. The true sense of the passage is that in whatever areas of the continental shelf a coastal State has rights, those rights are exclusive rights, not exercisable by any other State. But this says nothing as to what in fact are the precise areas in respect of which each coastal State possesses these exclusive rights. This question, which can arise only as regards the fringes of a coastal State's shelf area is, as explained at the end of paragraph 20 above, exactly what falls to be settled through the process of delimitation, and this is the sphere of Article 6, not Article 2.

68. Secondly, it must be observed that no valid conclusions can be drawn from the fact that the faculty of entering reservations to Article 6 has been exercised only sparingly and within certain limits. This is the affair exclusively of those States which have not wished to exercise the faculty, or which have been content to do so only to a limited extent. Their action or inaction cannot affect the right of other States to enter reservations to whatever is the legitimate extent of the right.

69. In the light of these various considerations, the Court reaches the conclusion that the Geneva Convention did not embody or crystallize any pre-existing or emergent rule of customary law, according to which the delimitation of continental shelf areas between adjacent States must, unless the Parties otherwise agree, be carried out on an equidistance-special circumstances basis. A rule was of course embodied in Article 6 of the Convention, but as a purely conventional rule. Whether it has since acquired a broader basis remains to be seen: qua conventional rule however, as has already been concluded, it is not opposable to the Federal Republic.

70. The Court must now proceed to the last stage in the argument put forward on behalf of Denmark and the Netherlands. This is to the effect that even if there was at the date of the Geneva Convention no rule of customary international law in favour of the equidistance principle, and no such rule was crystallized in Article 6 of the Convention, nevertheless such a rule has come into being since the Convention, partly because of its own impact, partly on the basis of subsequent State practice, and that this rule, being now a rule of customary international law binding on all States, including therefore the Federal Republic,

should be declared applicable to the delimitation of the boundaries between the Parties' respective continental shelf areas in the North Sea.

71. In so far as this contention is based on the view that Article 6 of the Convention has had the influence, and has produced the effect, described, it clearly involves treating that Article as a norm-creating provision which has constituted the foundation of, or has generated a rule which, while only conventional or contractual in its origin, has since passed into the general corpus of international law, and is now accepted as such by the opinio juris, so as to have become binding even for countries which have never, and do not, become parties to the Convention. There is no doubt that this process is a perfectly possible one and does from time to time occur: it constitutes indeed one of the recognized methods by which new rules of customary international law may be formed. At the same time this result is not lightly to be regarded as having been attained.

72. It would in the first place be necessary that the provision concerned should, at all events potentially, be of a fundamentally norm-creating character such as could be regarded as forming the basis of a general rule of law. Considered in abstracto the equidistance principle might be said to fulfil this requirement. Yet in the particular form in which it is embodied in Article 6 of the Geneva Convention, and having regard to the relationship of that Article to other provisions of the Convention, this must be open to some doubt. In the first place, Article 6 is so framed as to put second the obligation to make use of the equidistance method, causing it to come after a primary obligation to effect delimitation by agreement. Such a primary obligation constitutes an unusual preface to what is claimed to be a potential general rule of law. Without attempting to enter into, still less pronounce upon any question of jus cogens, it is well understood that, in practice, rules of international law can, by agreement, be derogated from in particular cases, or as between particular parties, but this is not normally the subject of any express provision, as it is in Article 6 of the Geneva Convention. Secondly the part played by the notion of special circumstances relative to the principle of equidistance as embodied in Article 6, and the very considerable, still unresolved controversies as to the exact meaning and scope of this notion, must raise further doubts as to the potentially norm-creating character of the rule. Finally, the faculty of making reservations to Article 6, while it might not of itself prevent the equidistance principle being eventually received as general law, does add considerably to the difficulty of regarding this result as having been brought about (or being potentially possible) on the basis of the Convention: for so long as this faculty continues to exist, and is not the subject of any revision brought about in consequence of a request made under Article 13 of the Convention—of which there is at present no

official indication—it is the Convention itself which would, for the reasons already indicated, seem to deny to the provisions of Article 6 the same norm-creating character as, for instance, Articles 1 and 2 possess.

73. With respect to the other elements usually regarded as necessary before a conventional rule can be considered to have become a general rule of international law, it might be that, even without the passage of any considerable period of time, a very widespread and representative participation in the convention might suffice of itself, provided it included that of States whose interests were specially affected. In the present case however, the Court notes that, even if allowance is made for the existence of a number of States to whom participation in the Geneva Convention is not open, or which, by reason for instance of being land-locked States, would have no interest in becoming parties to it, the number of ratifications and accessions so far secured is, though respectable, hardly sufficient. That non-ratification may sometimes be due to factors other than active disapproval of the convention concerned can hardly constitute a basis on which positive acceptance of its principles can be implied: the reasons are speculative, but the facts remain.

74. As regards the time element, the Court notes that it is over ten years since the Convention was signed, but that it is even now less than five since it came into force in June 1964, and that when the present proceedings were brought it was less than three years, while less than one had elapsed at the time when the respective negotiations between the Federal Republic and the other two Parties for a complete delimitation broke down on the question of the application of the equidistance principle. Although the passage of only a short period of time is not necessarily, or of itself, a bar to the formation of a new rule of customary international law on the basis of what was originally a purely conventional rule, an indispensable requirement would be that within the period in question, short though it might be, State practice, including that of States whose interests are specially affected, should have been both extensive and virtually uniform in the sense of the provision invoked, and should moreover have occurred in such a way as to show a general recognition that a rule of law or legal obligation is involved.

75. The Court must now consider whether State practice in the matter of continental shelf delimitation has, subsequent to the Geneva Convention, been of such a kind as to satisfy this requirement. Leaving aside cases which, for various reasons, the Court does not consider to be reliable guides as precedents, such as delimitations effected between the present Parties themselves, or not relating to international boundaries, some fifteen cases have been cited in the course of the present proceedings, occurring mostly since the signature of the 1958 Geneva Convention, in which continental shelf boundaries have been delimited

according to the equidistance principle—in the majority of the cases by agreement, in a few others unilaterally—or else the delimitation was foreshadowed but has not yet been carried out. Amongst these fifteen are the four North Sea delimitations United Kingdom/Norway-Denmark-Netherlands, and Norway/Denmark already mentioned in paragraph 4 of this Judgment. But even if these various cases constituted more than a very small proportion of those potentially calling for delimitation in the world as a whole, the Court would not think it necessary to enumerate or evaluate them separately, since there are, a priori, several grounds which deprive them of weight as precedents in the present context.

76. To begin with, over half the States concerned, whether acting unilaterally or conjointly, were or shortly became parties to the Geneva Convention, and were therefore presumably, so far as they were concerned, acting actually or potentially in the application of the Convention. From their action no inference could legitimately be drawn as to the existence of a rule of customary international law in favour of the equidistance principle. As regards those States, on the other hand, which were not, and have not become parties to the Convention, the basis of their action can only be problematical and must remain entirely speculative. Clearly, they were not applying the Convention. But from that no inference could justifiably be drawn that they believed themselves to be applying a mandatory rule of customary international law. There is not a shred of evidence that they did and, as has been seen (paragraphs 22 and 23), there is no lack of other reasons for using the equidistance method, so that acting, or agreeing to act in a certain way, does not of itself demonstrate anything of a juridical nature.

77. The essential point in this connection—and it seems necessary to stress it—is that even if these instances of action by non-parties to the Convention were much more numerous than they in fact are, they would not, even in the aggregate, suffice in themselves to constitute the opinio juris; for, in order to achieve this result, two conditions must be fulfilled. Not only must the acts concerned amount to a settled practice, but they must also be such, or be carried out in such a way, as to be evidence of a belief that this practice is rendered obligatory by the existence of a rule of law requiring it. The need for such a belief, i.e., the existence of a subjective element, is implicit in the very notion of the opinio juris sive necessitatis. The States concerned must therefore feel that they are conforming to what amounts to a legal obligation. The frequency, or even habitual character of the acts is not in itself enough. There are many international acts, e.g., in the field of ceremonial and protocol, which are performed almost invariably, but which are motivated only by considerations of courtesy, convenience or tradition, and not by any sense of legal duty.

78. In this respect the Court follows the view adopted by the Permanent Court of International Justice in the *Lotus* case, as stated in the following passage, the principle of which is, by analogy, applicable almost word for word, mutatis mutandis, to the present case:

> Even if the rarity of the judicial decisions to be found. . . were sufficient to prove. . . the circumstance alleged. . ., it would merely show that States had often, in practice, abstained from instituting criminal proceedings, and not that they recognized themselves as being obliged to do so; for only if such abstention were based on their being conscious of having a duty to abstain would it be possible to speak of an international custom. The alleged fact does not allow one to infer that States have been conscious of having such a duty; on the other hand,. . . there are other circumstances calculated to show that the contrary is true.

Applying this dictum to the present case, the position is simply that in certain cases—not a great number—the States concerned agreed to draw or did draw the boundaries concerned according to the principle of equidistance. There is no evidence that they so acted because they felt legally compelled to draw them in this way by reason of a rule of customary law obliging them to do so—especially considering that they might have been motivated by other obvious factors.

79. Finally, it appears that in almost all of the cases cited, the delimitations concerned were median-line delimitations between opposite States, not lateral delimitations between adjacent States. For reasons which have already been given (paragraph 57) the Court regards the case of median-line delimitations between opposite States as different in various respects, and as being sufficiently distinct not to constitute a precedent for the delimitation of lateral boundaries. In only one situation discussed by the Parties does there appear to have been a geographical configuration which to some extent resembles the present one, in the sense that a number of States on the same coastline are grouped around a sharp curve or bend of it. No complete delimitation in this area has however yet been carried out. But the Court is not concerned to deny to this case, or any other of those cited, all evidential value in favour of the thesis of Denmark and the Netherlands. It simply considers that they are inconclusive, and insufficient to bear the weight sought to be put upon them as evidence of such a settled practice, manifested in such circumstances, as would justify the inference that delimitation according to the principle of equidistance amounts to a mandatory rule of customary international law, more particularly where lateral delimitations are concerned.

80. There are of course plenty of cases (and a considerable number were cited) of delimitations of waters, as opposed to seabed, being carried out on the basis of equidistance—mostly of internal waters (lakes, rivers,

etc.), and mostly median-line cases. The nearest analogy is that of adjacent territorial waters, but as already explained (paragraph 59) the Court does not consider this case to be analogous to that of the continental shelf.

81. The Court accordingly concludes that if the Geneva Convention was not in its origins or inception declaratory of a mandatory rule of customary international law enjoining the use of the equidistance principle for the delimitation of continental shelf areas between adjacent States, neither has its subsequent effect been constitutive of such a rule; and that State practice up-to-date has equally been insufficient for the purpose.

82. The immediately foregoing conclusion, coupled with that reached earlier (paragraph 56) to the effect that the equidistance principle could not be regarded as being a rule of law on any a priori basis of logical necessity deriving from the fundamental theory of the continental shelf, leads to the final conclusion on this part of the case that the use of the equidistance method is not obligatory for the delimitation of the areas concerned in the present proceedings. . .

NOTES & QUESTIONS

1. *Specially Affected States.* Does the practice of all states count equally when evaluating the existence of a putative norm of customary international law? In one sense yes, because all states are formally equal sovereigns as a matter of principle. But in another sense no, because some states are simply not impacted by a particular norm one way or the other. Recall what the ICJ said above in paragraph 74: "within the period in question, short though it might be, State practice, including that of States whose interests are specially affected, should have been both extensive and virtually uniform. . ." This is sometimes referred to as the doctrine of specially affected states. In *North Sea Continental Shelf*, which states are specially affected? Clearly the states with coastline along the shelf, but what of other states? What about states with a significant naval presence in the area? Which states are *not* specially affected? As the International Law Association described it:

> In the nature of things, who is "specially affected" will vary according to circumstances. There is no rule that major powers have to participate in a practice in order for it to become a rule of general customary law. Given the scope of their interests, both geographically and ratione materiae, they often will be "specially affected" by a practice; and to that extent and to that extent alone, their participation is necessary. However, it will not necessarily be only the major powers who are "specially affected." In the law of the sea, for instance, some of the States whose nationals are most heavily engaged in distant-water fishing would not normally be regarded as major powers; and the same is true of most of the

coastal States who have a special interest in offshore fisheries. These States have also played an important part in the evolution of customary rules in that domain.

See ILA, Statement of Principles Applicable to the Formation of General Customary International Law 26 (2000).

2. *Distinguishing a Violation from a Counter-Norm.* When a state engages in practice that runs counter to an established norm of customary international law, the state practice may be considered a violation of international law. However, another way of thinking of the practice is that the state is trying to create a new counter-norm. Indeed, both things may be true: the state may be breaking existing law in order to help create a new law. If other states join in the counter-practice, at some point these violations of customary law may become evidence of a new norm, thus transforming what would otherwise be a violation into an act of compliance. When is this legal line crossed? That depends on the context. In considering the breakdown of an old norm and the putative emergence of a counter-norm, the international lawyer must apply the regular standards for the existence of custom: a constant and uniform practice of states performed out of a sense of legal obligation (opinio juris). See Jonathan I. Charney, *The Power of the Executive Branch of the United States Government to Violate Customary International Law*, 80 Am. J. Int'l L. 913, 919 (1986) ("the United States must have the power to engage effectively in the customary lawmaking process; this process requires that, from time to time, the United States break that law"). Is it possible for state practice to be so split that the correct conclusion is that no customary rule exists?

B. OPINIO JURIS

Most commentators have concluded that state practice alone is not enough to establish a rule of customary international law. The practice must be accompanied by the correct "mental state," i.e., the practice must be performed from a sense of legal obligation, or *opinio juris*. This distinguishes "mere custom" from customary international *law*, which is custom that has ripened into law. However, not everyone is in agreement. For example, the ILA study on the formation of customary international law concluded that opinio juris is a sufficient but not strictly speaking *necessary* condition for the existence of a customary norm.

In practice, arguments about customary international law almost always rely on both state practice and *opinio juris*—an objective element combined with a subjective element. The following case is an example of that methodology. As you read the case, identify the possible motives that a state might have for engaging in a practice *other* than a sense of legal obligation. What examples does the court give?

Flores v. Southern Peru Copper Corp.

U.S. Court of Appeals for the Second Circuit
414 F.3d 233 (2003)

■ JOSÉ A. CABRANES, CIRCUIT JUDGE.

. . . Plaintiffs in this case are residents of Ilo, Peru, and the representatives of deceased Ilo residents. They brought personal injury claims under the ATCA against Southern Peru Copper Corporation ("SPCC"), a United States company, alleging that pollution from SPCC's copper mining, refining, and smelting operations in and around Ilo caused plaintiffs' or their decedents' severe lung disease. The ATCA states that "[t]he district courts shall have original jurisdiction of any civil action by an alien for a tort only, committed in violation of the law of nations or a treaty of the United States." Plaintiffs claimed that defendant's conduct violates the "law of nations"—commonly referred to as "international law" or, when limited to non-treaty law, as "customary international law." In particular, they asserted that defendant infringed upon their customary international law "right to life," "right to health," and right to "sustainable development." . . .

Definition of "Law of Nations" or "Customary International Law" for Purposes of the ATCA

The ATCA permits an alien to assert a cause of action in tort for violations of a treaty of the United States and for violations of "the law of nations," which, as used in this statute, refers to the body of law known as customary international law. The determination of what offenses violate customary international law, however, is no simple task. Customary international law is discerned from myriad decisions made in numerous and varied international and domestic arenas. Furthermore, the relevant evidence of customary international law is widely dispersed and generally unfamiliar to lawyers and judges. These difficulties are compounded by the fact that customary international law—as the term itself implies—is created by the general customs and practices of nations and therefore does not stem from any single, definitive, readily-identifiable source. All of these characteristics give the body of customary international law a "soft, indeterminate character," Louis Henkin, *International Law: Politics and Values* 29 (1995), that is subject to creative interpretation. Accordingly, in determining what offenses violate customary international law, courts must proceed with extraordinary care and restraint.

In short, customary international law is composed only of those rules that States universally abide by, or accede to, out of a sense of legal obligation and mutual concern.

First, in order for a principle to become part of customary international law, States must universally abide by it. *Filartiga,* 630 F.2d at 888 (holding that customary international law includes only "well-established, *universally recognized* norms of international law"); *see also Kadic,* 70 F.3d at 239; *id.* at 243 n. 8 (addressing whether a principle had "ripened into *universally accepted* norms of international law." Of course, States need not be universally successful in implementing the principle in order for a rule of customary international law to arise. If that were the case, there would be no need for customary international law. But the principle must be more than merely professed or aspirational.

Furthermore, a principle is only incorporated into customary international law if States accede to it out of a sense of legal obligation. *See, e.g., Chubb & Son, Inc. v. Asiana Airlines,* 214 F.3d 301, 307–08 (2d Cir. 2000) ("Customary international law results from a general and consistent practice of states followed by them *from a sense of legal obligation."* Practices adopted for moral or political reasons, but not out of a sense of legal obligation, do not give rise to rules of customary international law. *See Hain v. Gibson,* 287 F.3d 1224, 1243–44 (10th Cir. 2002) (noting that customary international law does not include those practices that States have adopted "for moral or political reasons (as opposed to any sense of legal obligation)"); *North Sea Continental Shelf,* 1969 I.C.J. 3, 44 ("[n]ot only must the acts concerned amount to a settled practice, but they must also be. . . carried out in such a way[ ] as to be evidence of a belief that this practice is rendered obligatory by the existence of a rule of law requiring it").

Finally, customary international law addresses only those "wrong[s]" that are "of *mutual,* and not merely *several,* concern" to States. Matters of "mutual" concern between States are those involving States' actions "performed. . . towards or with regard to the other," X Oxford English Dictionary 154 (2d ed. 1989)—matters that, as Judge Friendly aptly noted, concern the dealings of States "inter se," *Vencap,* 519 F.2d at 1015. Matters of "several" concern among States are matters in which States are separately and independently interested.

Even if certain conduct is universally proscribed by States in their domestic law, that fact is not necessarily significant or relevant for purposes of customary international law. As we explained in *Filartiga* and in *IIT v. Vencap, Ltd.*:

> [T]he mere fact that every nation's municipal [i.e., domestic] law may prohibit theft does not incorporate "the Eighth Commandment, 'Thou Shalt not steal'. . . [into] the law of nations." It is only where the nations of the world have demonstrated that *the wrong is of mutual, and not merely several, concern, by means of express international accords,* that a wrong generally recognized becomes an international law violation within the meaning of the statute.

Therefore, for example, murder of one private party by another, universally proscribed by the domestic law of all countries (subject to varying definitions), is not actionable under the ATCA as a violation of customary international law because the "nations of the world" have not demonstrated that this wrong is "of mutual, and not merely several, concern." By contrast, other offenses that may be purely intra-national in their execution, such as official torture, extrajudicial killings, and genocide, do violate customary international law because the "nations of the world" have demonstrated that such wrongs are of "mutual. . . concern," and capable of impairing international peace and security.

Sources and Evidence of Customary International Law

In determining whether a particular rule is a part of customary international law—i.e., whether States universally abide by, or accede to, that rule out of a sense of legal obligation and mutual concern—courts must look to concrete evidence of the customs and practices of States. As we have recently stated, "we look primarily to the formal lawmaking and official actions of States and only secondarily to the works of scholars as evidence of the established practice of States." *United States v. Yousef,* 327 F.3d 56, 103 (2d Cir. 2003).

In *United States v. Yousef,* we explained why the usage and practice of States—as opposed to judicial decisions or the works of scholars— constitute the primary sources of customary international law. In that case, we looked to the Statute of the International Court of Justice ("ICJ Statute")—to which the United States and all members of the United Nations are parties—as a guide for determining the proper sources of international law. Article 38 of the ICJ Statute provides in relevant part:

1.   The Court, whose function is to decide in accordance with international law such disputes as are submitted to it, shall apply:

a.   international conventions, whether general or particular, establishing rules expressly recognized by the contesting states;

b.   international custom, as evidence of a general practice accepted as law;

c.   the general principles of law recognized by civilized nations;

d.   subject to the provisions of Article 59, judicial decisions and the teachings of the most highly qualified publicists [*i.e.,* scholars or "jurists"] of the various nations, *as subsidiary means for the determination of rules of law.*

Article 38 embodies the understanding of States as to what sources offer competent proof of the content of customary international law. It establishes that the proper *primary* evidence consists only of those "conventions" (that is, treaties) that set forth "*rules* expressly recognized by the contesting states," "international custom" insofar as it provides "evidence of a general practice *accepted as law,*" and "the general principles of *law* recognized by civilized nations. It also establishes that acceptable *secondary* (or "subsidiary") sources summarizing customary international law include "judicial decisions," and the works of "the most highly qualified publicists," as that term would have been understood at the time of the Statute's drafting.

Notably absent from Article 38's enumeration of the sources of international law are conventions that set forth broad principles without setting forth specific rules—in the words of *Filartiga,* "clear and unambiguous" rules. Such a regime makes sense because, as a practical matter, it is impossible for courts to discern or apply in any rigorous, systematic, or legal manner international pronouncements that promote amorphous, general principles. Moreover, as noted above, customs or practices based on social and moral norms, rather than international legal obligation, are not appropriate sources of customary international law because they do not evidence any intention on the part of States, much less the community of States, to be legally bound.

Our recapitulation of the proper sources of international law is not novel. As one eminent authority has observed, "[t]he records or *evidence* of international law are the documents or acts proving the consent of States to its rules," and "[a]mong such records or *evidence,* treaties and *practice* play an essential part." Professor Parry's statement of the proper evidence of customary international law correctly emphasizes that the "acts" and "practice[s]" of States constitute the "essential" evidence of whether States follow a rule as a legal obligation. He also notes that recourse may be had to secondary sources such as "unilateral declarations, instructions to diplomatic agents, laws and ordinances, and *in a lesser degree,* to the writings of authoritative jurists," as evidence of the "acts" and "practice[s]" of States.

In sum, those clear and unambiguous rules by which States universally abide, or to which they accede, out of a sense of legal obligation and mutual concern, constitute the body of customary international law. But where the customs and practices of States demonstrate that they do not universally follow a particular practice out of a sense of legal obligation and mutual concern, that practice cannot give rise to a rule of customary international law. . .

NOTES & QUESTIONS

1. *The Paradox of Opinio Juris.* Some have noted that the requirement that state practice be accompanied by *opinio juris* generates a paradox, which is sometimes referred to as the "chronological paradox." If a state is engaging in a particular practice, the state can only be acting out of a sense of legal obligation if the custom is *already law*. However, how did the

custom become law in the first place? Presumably some state must have acted first and done so without opinio juris. But then other states that followed the norm would not have done so out of a sense of legal obligation. So, it is genuinely unclear how customary international law gets started and off the ground. Some international lawyers have concluded, on the basis of this paradox, that *opinio juris* is not, strictly speaking, an absolute requirement for customary law in all circumstances. For example, the ILA study on the formation of customary international law concluded that states "actively engaged in the creation of a new customary rule may well wish or accept that the practice in question will give rise to a legal rule, but it is logically impossible for them to have an *opinio juris* in the literal and traditional sense, that is, a belief that the practice is already legally permissible or obligatory." See ILA, Statement of Principles Applicable to the Formation of General Customary International Law 33 (2000). For more discussion, see Michael Byers, *Custom, Power, and the Power of Rules* 142–46 (1999); Jean d'Aspremont, *The Custom-Making Moment in Customary International Law*, in *The Theory and Philosophy of Customary International Law and Its Interpretation* (Merkouris et al. eds., 2021) ("Custom is always presupposed to have been made through actors' behaviours at some given point in the past and in a given place but neither the moment nor the place of such behaviours can be found or traced."). One possibility mentioned in the literature is that custom is formed when states erroneously believe that they are acting out of a sense of legal obligation at the time the act is performed—thus triggering the formation of the rule.

2.   *Obligation Versus Self-Interest.* In an influential article and book, Professors Eric Posner and Jack Goldsmith argued that states "do not comply with norms of [customary international law] because of a sense of moral or legal obligation; rather, their compliance and the norms themselves emerge from the states' pursuit of self-interested policies on the international stage." Jack L. Goldsmith & Eric A. Posner, *A Theory of Customary International Law*, 66 U. Chi. L. Rev. 1113 (1999). This theory was inspired by realism, which the authors noted "emphasizes that states act rationally to further their perceived national interest, and that the distribution of national power determines international behaviors. Realism is skeptical about international cooperation and international law." *Id.* at 1176. The authors concluded that customary international law "has real content, but it is much less robust than traditional scholars think, and it operates in a different fashion." Do you agree? One assumption of this argument is that acting out of a sense of legal obligation and acting from self-interest are mutually exclusive categories. Is it possible that states recognize that rational self-interest inspires them to comply, rather than reject, international law? In other words, might a refined "realism" suggest that states, even those acting out of self-interest, would select a general strategy of complying with international law rather than operating outside of it? For more discussion on this argument, see Jens David Ohlin, *Nash Equilibrium and International Law*, 96 Cornell L. Rev. 869 (2011) (discussing the strategy of constrained maximization).

C. Persistent Objectors

Treaty obligations are based on the concept of consent; states are free to voluntarily decide which obligations to accept through the negotiation and signing of a treaty. However, custom is different; a state may be subject to a rule of customary international law even if the state does not like the rule. In order to mitigate the harshness of this rule, scholars and practitioners of international law have recognized that states may exempt themselves from the application of a rule of customary international law by claiming "persistent objector status."

According to the International Law Association, which produced a report analyzing the formation of customary international law, the requirements for successfully asserting a persistent objector claim are quite stringent. As the report noted, there "is fairly widespread agreement that, even if there is a persistent objector rule in international law, it applies only when the customary rule is in the process of emerging. It does not, therefore, benefit States which came into existence only after the rule matured, or which became involved in the activity in question only at a later stage. Still less can it be invoked by those who existed at the time and were already engaged in the activity which is the subject of the rule, but failed to object at that stage. In other words, there is no 'subsequent objector' rule. The rule, if it exists, is available only those who object before the rule has fully emerged."

In addition to the limitation that the state must have objected to the rule as it was being formed, it is generally regarded that the persistent objector rule does not apply to any norm that has attained the status of jus cogens—a peremptory norm of international law. As you read the following case regarding the juvenile death penalty, ask yourself if there existed in 2002 a norm of customary international law prohibiting the juvenile death penalty. Furthermore, do you agree that the United States persistently objected to the emerging norm? If yes, should the U.S. be exempt from the norm?

Michael Domingues v. United States

Inter-American Commission on Human Rights
Case 12.285, Report No. 62/02 (2002)

1.   On May 1, 2000 the Inter-American Commission on Human Rights received a petition from Mr. William A. Courson of the Magnus Hirschfield Center for Human Rights against the United States of America. The Petition was presented on behalf of Mr. Michael Domingues, who is incarcerated on death row in the State of Nevada. . .

2.   The Petitioner states that Mr. Domingues had been convicted and sentenced to death in respect of two homicides that occurred in the state of Nevada in 1993. Mr. Domingues was 16 years old when the

crimes were committed. The Petitioner further states that on November 1, 1999 the Supreme Court of the United States declined to review a ruling by the Supreme Court of the State of Nevada permitting the execution of a person convicted of a crime committed while a juvenile. As of the date of this report, no date for Mr. Domingues' execution had been scheduled.

3.   The Petitioner alleges that Mr. Domingues has exhausted his domestic remedies and therefore that his petition is admissible. He also alleges that by sentencing Mr. Domingues to death for crimes committed while he was a juvenile, the State is in breach of Articles I (right to life), II (right to equality before law), VII (right to protection for mothers and children) and XXVI (right to due process of law) of the American Declaration of the Rights and Duties of Man ("the American Declaration"). . .

40. The Commission notes at the outset of its analysis that the Petitioner's arguments draw significantly upon the Commission's 1987 decision in the case of Roach and Pinkerton against the United States. That case concerned two juvenile offenders, James Terry Roach and Jay Pinkerton, who were sentenced to death in the states of, respectively, South Carolina and Texas, for crimes committed when they were seventeen years of age. Both petitioners were subsequently executed by those states. In determining the complaint brought before it on behalf of the Mr. Roach and Mr. Pinkerton, the Commission considered whether the United States had in sentencing the two prisoners to death and subsequently allowing their executions acted contrary to a recognized norm of jus cogens or customary international law. While the Commission determined the existence of a jus cogens norm prohibiting the execution of children, it found that uncertainty existed as to the applicable age of majority under international law. . .

41. The Commission ultimately concluded that there did not exist at that time a norm of jus cogens or other customary international law prohibiting the execution of persons under 18 years of age. . .

42. Accordingly, in determining the present complaint, the Commission must address whether the state of international law concerning the execution of individuals under the age of 18 has evolved since its decision in Roach and Pinkerton.

43. In addressing the claims raised by the Petitioner concerning the present status of rules governing the execution of minors under international law, it is first instructive to provide a brief overview of the categories of rules of international law pertinent to this analysis, namely customary international law and norms of jus cogens, as well as the principal means by which the contents of those rules are manifested.

44. In this connection, the Commission recalls that in interpreting and applying the Declaration, its provisions, including Articles I, VII and XXVI, should be considered in the context of the broader international and inter-American human rights systems, in the light of developments in the field of international human rights law since it was first composed. Due regard should in this respect be given to other relevant rules of international law applicable to member states against which complaints of violations of the Declaration are properly lodged as well as developments in the corpus juris gentium of international human rights law over time and in present-day conditions.

45. Developments in the corpus of international human rights law relevant to interpreting and applying the American Declaration may in turn be drawn from various sources of international law, including the provisions of other international and regional human rights instruments and customary international law, including those customary norms considered to form a part of jus cogens.

46. With respect to the rules of customary international law in particular, while these rules are of an inherently changeable nature and therefore cannot be the subject of a definitive or exhaustive enumeration, there nevertheless exists a broad consensus in respect of the component elements required to establish a norm of customary international law. These include:

a)   a concordant practice by a number of states with reference to a type of situation falling within the domain of international relations;

b)   a continuation or repetition of the practice over a considerable period of time;

c)   a conception that the practice is required by or consistent with prevailing international law;

d)   general acquiescence in the practice by other states.

48. Once established, a norm of international customary law binds all states with the exception of only those states that have persistently rejected the practice prior to its becoming law. While a certain practice does not require universal acceptance to become a norm of customary international law, a norm which has been accepted by the majority of States has no binding effect upon a State which has persistently rejected the practice upon which the norm is based.

49. Turning to the rules which govern the establishment of rules of jus cogens, this Commission has previously defined the concept of jus cogens as having been derived from ancient law concepts of a "superior order of legal norms, which the laws of man or nations may not contravene" and as the "rules which have been accepted, either expressly

by treaty or tacitly by custom, as being necessary to protect the public morality recognized by them." It has been said that the principal distinguishing feature of these norms is their "relative indelibility," in that they constitute rules of customary law which cannot be set aside by treaty or acquiescence but only by the formation of a subsequent customary rule of contrary effect. More particularly, as customary international law rests on the consent of nations, a state that persistently objects to a norm of customary international law is not bound by that norm. Norms of jus cogens, on the other hand, derive their status from fundamental values held by the international community, as violations of such preemptory norms are considered to shock the conscience of humankind and therefore bind the international community as a whole, irrespective of protest, recognition or acquiescence. Commonly cited examples of rules of customary law that have attained the status of jus cogens norms include genocide, slavery, forced disappearances and torture or other cruel, inhuman or degrading treatment or punishment. It has been suggested that a reliable starting point in identifying those international legal proscriptions that have achieved jus cogens status is the list of rights that international human rights treaties render non-derogable.

50. Therefore, while based on the same evidentiary sources as a norm of customary international law, the standard for determining a principle of jus cogens is more rigorous, requiring evidence of recognition of the indelibility of the norm by the international community as a whole. This can occur where there is acceptance and recognition by a large majority of states, even if over dissent by a small number of states.

51. Article I of the Declaration provides that "[e]very human being has the right to life, liberty and the security of his person."

52. The Commission notes that while Article I of the American Declaration does not explicitly refer to the issue of capital punishment, the Commission has in past decisions declined to interpret Article I of the Declaration as either prohibiting use of the death penalty per se, or conversely as exempting capital punishment from the Declaration's standards and protections altogether. Rather, in part by reference to the drafting history of the American Declaration as well as the terms of Article 4 of the American Convention on Human Rights, the Commission has found that Article I of the Declaration, while not precluding the death penalty altogether, prohibits its application when doing so would result in an arbitrary deprivation of life or would otherwise be rendered cruel, infamous or unusual punishment.

53. As noted above, the Petitioner argues that in the light of developments since 1986, a norm of customary international law now exists which prevents the execution of offenders aged 16 or 17 years old at the time of their crime. The Petitioner submits that this norm has

acquired the status of jus cogens. Consequently, the Petitioner asks that the Commission's decision in the case of Roach and Pinkerton be reviewed and extended, so as to find that Article I of the Declaration prohibits Mr. Domingues' execution as an offender who committed his crime when he was under 18 years of age.

54. In addressing this issue, the Commission must therefore evaluate whether the provisions of the American Declaration, when interpreted in the context of pertinent developments in customary international law and the norms of jus cogens, prohibit the execution of individuals who committed their crime when they were under the age of 18. In so doing, it is appropriate for the Commission to take into account evidence of relevant state practice as disclosed by various sources, including recitals in treaties and other international instruments, a pattern of treaties in the same form, the practice of the United Nations and other international governmental organizations, and the domestic legislation and judicial decisions of states.

55. Since 1987, several notable developments have occurred in relation to treaties that explicitly prohibit the execution of individuals who were under 18 years of age at the time of committing their offense. These developments include the coming into force of new international agreements as well as broadened ratifications of existing treaties.

56. Most significantly, on November 20, 1989 the U.N. General Assembly adopted the United Nations Convention on the Rights of the Child. Article 37(a) of the Convention provides that: "No child shall be subjected to torture or other cruel, inhuman or degrading treatment or punishment. Neither capital punishment nor life imprisonment without possibility of release shall be imposed for offences committed by persons below eighteen years of age."

57. The treaty subsequently entered into force on September 2, 1990, and as of September 2001 the Convention had 191 state parties with no explicit reservations taken to Article 37(a). The United States signed the Convention in February 1995, but has not yet ratified the Convention, joining Somalia as the only two states that are not parties to this treaty. In the Commission's view, the extent of ratification of this instrument alone constitutes compelling evidence of a broad consensus on the part of the international community repudiating the execution of offenders under 18 years of age.

58. The International Covenant on Civil and Political Rights (ICCPR) was adopted by the UN General Assembly in 1966 and entered into force in 1976. There are presently 64 signatories and 147 Parties to the ICCPR. Since 1986, sixty-four countries have acceded to or ratified the Covenant, including the United States in 1992. Article 6(5) of the ICCPR, like Article 37(a) of the Convention on the Rights of the Child,

provides that: "Sentence of death shall not be imposed for crimes committed by persons below eighteen years of age and shall not be carried out on pregnant women."

59. Of the states parties to this Convention, only the instruments of ratification of the U.S. and of accession by Thailand are presently accompanied by declarations or reservations in respect of Article 6(5). . .

61. For its part, the United States asserted the following reservation to Article 6(5) upon becoming a party to the ICCPR: "That the United States reserves the right, subject to its Constitutional constraints, to Impose capital punishment on any person (other than a pregnant woman) duly convicted under existing or future laws permitting the imposition of capital punishment, including such punishment for crimes committed by persons below eighteen years of age."

62. It is noteworthy that this reservation provoked condemnation within the international community and prompted eleven European States Parties to file objections declaring the reservation to be invalid, a majority on the basis that it was inconsistent with the aims and purposes of the ICCPR as provided by Article 19(c) of the Vienna Convention on the Law of Treaties. Moreover, in 1995 the U.N. Human Rights Committee declared this reservation to be contrary to the object and purpose of the ICCPR and recommended that the United States withdraw it.

63. Other international and regional human rights treaties that regulate the implementation of the death penalty have likewise witnessed an increase in states parties thereto since 1987. With regard to the inter-American human rights system in particular, Article 4 of the American Convention on Human Rights provides: "Capital punishment shall not be imposed upon persons who, at the time the crime was committed, were under 18 years of age."

64. There are presently 24 state parties to the American Convention. . . The Commission considers that this broad hemispheric adherence to the American Convention, including Article 4(5) thereof, constitutes compelling evidence of a regional norm repudiating the application of the death penalty to persons under 18 years of age even amongst those states such as Guatemala, Jamaica and Grenada that, like the United States, have retained the death penalty.

68. The foregoing analysis therefore indicates that since 1987, and consistent with events prior to that date, there has been concordant and widespread development and ratification of treaties by which nearly all of the world states have recognized, without reservation, a norm prohibiting the execution of individuals who were under 18 years of age at the time of committing their offense.

73. Also according to statistics compiled by Amnesty International, 115 states whose laws maintain the death penalty for some offences either have provisions in their laws which exclude the use of the death penalty against child offenders, or may be presumed to exclude such use by virtue of becoming parties to the International Covenant on Civil and Political Rights, the Convention on the Rights of the Child or the American Convention on Human Rights without entering a reservation to the relevant articles of these treaties. Since the beginning of 1994 at least 5 countries have changed their laws to eliminate the use of the death penalty against child offenders: Barbados, Pakistan, Yemen, Zimbabwe and China.

74. A small minority of states persist in executing juvenile offenders. Since 1990, 7 countries are known to have executed prisoners who were under 18 years old at the time of the crime—Congo (Democratic Republic), Iran, Nigeria, Pakistan, Saudi Arabia, U.S. and Yemen. A study of the worldwide executions of child offenders cite a total of 25 executions within that 10 year period. 14 of those executions were carried out by the United States of America, 6 were conducted in Iran and the remaining 5 nations carried out one execution each. Both Pakistan and Yemen are now reported to have abolished the death penalty for 16 and 17 year old offenders. In the year 2000, only 3 countries carried out any juvenile executions: the U.S., the Democratic Republic of Congo and Iran. In 1999 juvenile executions took place only in Iran and the U.S. In 1998, the U.S. was alone in its execution of 3 juvenile offenders. Yemen's sole execution took place in 1993, and Saudi Arabia's in 1992, with the consequence that since 1998, only three states, the U.S., Congo and Iran, have executed juvenile offenders sentenced to death.

75. As with adherence to regional treaties in the Western Hemisphere, it is pertinent to note that of the few states that have continued to execute juveniles, none but the United States are counted among the members of the inter-American system. In the Commission's view, this reinforces the existence of a particularly pervasive regional norm repudiating the application of the death penalty to persons under 18 years of age.

76. Domestic practice over the past 15 years therefore evidences a nearly unanimous and unqualified international trend toward prohibiting the execution of offenders under the age of 18 years. This trend crosses political and ideological lines and has nearly isolated the United States as the only country that continues to maintain the legality of the execution of 16 and 17 year old offenders, and then, as the following discussion indicates, only in certain state jurisdictions.

85. Moreover, the Commission is satisfied, based upon the information before it, that this rule has been recognized as being of a sufficiently indelible nature to now constitute a norm of jus cogens, a

development anticipated by the Commission in its Roach and Pinkerton decision. As noted above, nearly every nation state has rejected the imposition of capital punishment to individuals under the age of 18. They have done so through ratification of the ICCPR, U.N. Convention on the Rights of the Child, and the American Convention on Human Rights, treaties in which this proscription is recognized as non-derogable, as well as through corresponding amendments to their domestic laws. The acceptance of this norm crosses political and ideological boundaries and efforts to detract from this standard have been vigorously condemned by members of the international community as impermissible under contemporary human rights standards. Indeed, it may be said that the United States itself, rather than persistently objecting to the standard, has in several significant respects recognized the propriety of this norm by, for example, prescribing the age of 18 as the federal standard for the application of capital punishment and by ratifying the Fourth Geneva Convention without reservation to this standard. On this basis, the Commission considers that the United States is bound by a norm of jus cogens not to impose capital punishment on individuals who committed their crimes when they had not yet reached 18 years of age. As a jus cogens norm, this proscription binds the community of States, including the United States. The norm cannot be validly derogated from, whether by treaty or by the objection of a state, persistent or otherwise.

NOTES & QUESTIONS

1.   *Skepticism About Persistent Objector Status.* In this case, the inter-American Commission on Human Rights concluded that even if the U.S. had persistently objected from the norm prohibiting the juvenile death penalty, the objection is not capable of defeating a jus cogens norm. This argument implies that there is a class of non-jus cogens customary norms for which the persistent objector doctrine will clearly be relevant. However, not everyone agrees about the persistent objector doctrine. Some have called it an academic fiction that plays little role in actual international cases. One commentator noted: "There is, however, a rather puzzling anomaly. The support for the principle of the persistent objector in writing on the sources of international law is so broad and the legal consequences of being a persistent objector so decisive that one would expect to find a large number of instances in which states have claimed that status for themselves." See Ted L. Stein, *The Approach of the Different Drummer: The Principle of the Persistent Objector in International Law*, 26 Harv. Int'l. L. J. 457, 459 (1985). For more discussion, see Anthony D'Amato, *The Concept of Custom in International Law* (1973).

2.   *Two ICJ Precedents.* There are two major precedents where the ICJ appeared to rely on the notion of a persistent objector. The first is the *Fisheries Case*, in which the ICJ concluded, in a single hypothetical statement, that "[i]n these circumstances the Court deems it necessary to

point out that although the ten-mile rule has been adopted by certain States both in their national law and in their treaties and conventions, and although certain arbitral decisions have applied it as between these States, other States have adopted a different limit. Consequently, the ten-mile rule has not acquired the authority of a general rule of international law. In any event the ten-mile rule would appear to be inapplicable as against Norway inasmuch as she has always opposed any attempt to apply it to the Norwegian coast." *U.K. v. Norway,* 1951 I.C.J. 116, 131 (Dec. 18, 1951). The second case is the *Asylum Case,* in which the ICJ stated that "even if it could be supposed that such a custom existed between certain Latin-American States only, it could not be invoked against Peru which, far from having by its attitude adhered to it, has, on the contrary, repudiated it by refraining from ratifying the Montevideo Conventions of 1933 and 1939, which were the first to include a rule concerning the qualification of the offence in matters of diplomatic asylum." *Colombia v. Peru,* 1950 I.C.J. 266, 277–78 (Nov. 20, 1950). In both cases, the ICJ seemed to suggest that the existence of the rule of customary international law was deeply contested. Does the rule regarding persistent objectors exist outside of that context when the rule is well settled and clearly applicable?

3. *A Different Kind of Skepticism.* The basic understanding underlying the persistent objector rule is that states must object as the rule is crystallizing into law. Once a rule is fully formed, it becomes too late to exempt oneself from the rule's operation, because at that point the objection is not sufficiently persistent. This rule is even applied in cases where the state failed to object to the formation of the rule because the state did not yet exist at that time. Professors Bradley and Gulati have questioned this bedrock assumption and have asked why states cannot simply withdraw from international custom whenever they want. Why require states to persistently object when the rule is being formed rather than after the fact? After all, states *can* withdraw from a treaty obligation. As the authors note: "It is not obvious, however, why it should be easier to exit from treaties than from [custom], especially given the significant regulatory overlap that exists today between treaties and [custom]." Furthermore, "if the persistent objector doctrine is needed in order to ensure that CIL is consensual, why does that consent rationale not also require the allowance of opt-out through subsequent objection?" See Curtis A. Bradley & Mitu Gulati, *Withdrawing from International Custom,* 120 Yale L.J. 202, 205 (2010). Do you believe that the standard view should be revised?

D. JUS COGENS

Some norms of customary international law are so imperative that they are mandatory and bind all states without exception. Although there is much disagreement over the nature and content of jus cogens, the category is an indispensable tool for the modern international lawyer. In a sense, the term jus cogens is a trump card, because it defeats all manner of possible legal objections, including those pertaining to the persistent objector doctrine (discussed above), but also regarding other norms of customary or treaty law that might suggest a different outcome. If a rule is jus cogens, then a state must follow it. That being said, it is easier to assert jus cogens status than it is to actually defend it. Using the phrase jus cogens is not the end of the argument, it is the beginning. A lawyer must then demonstrate, through legal argumentation and evidence, that the asserted norm is in fact jus cogens and also demonstrate its content.

In the following case, the Democratic Republic of Congo (DRC) argued before the ICJ that the jus cogens prohibition on genocide also includes the ICJ's jurisdiction over disputes regarding genocide. Although Rwanda had signed the Genocide Convention, it had issued a reservation against the provision in the Convention granting the ICJ jurisdiction. The DRC viewed the ICJ jurisdictional provision as jus cogens and therefore not subject to reservation—it was part of the larger prohibition on genocide that had attained jus cogens status. As you read the case, ask yourself how the court treated this novel argument.

Armed Activities on the Territory of the Congo (DRC v. Rwanda)

International Court of Justice
2006 I.C.J. 6

64. The Court will begin by reaffirming that "the principles underlying the [Genocide] Convention are principles which are recognized by civilized nations as binding on States, even without any conventional obligation" and that a consequence of that conception is "the universal character both of the condemnation of genocide and of the co-operation required 'in order to liberate mankind from such an odious scourge' (Preamble to the Convention)." It follows that "the rights and obligations enshrined by the Convention are rights and obligations *erga omnes.*"

The Court observes, however, as it has already had occasion to emphasize, that "the *erga omnes* character of a norm and the rule of consent to jurisdiction are two different things," and that the mere fact that rights and obligations *erga omnes* may be at issue in a dispute would not give the Court jurisdiction to entertain that dispute.

The same applies to the relationship between peremptory norms of general international law (jus cogens) and the establishment of the Court's jurisdiction: the fact that a dispute relates to compliance with a norm having such a character, which is assuredly the case with regard to the prohibition of genocide, cannot of itself provide a basis for the jurisdiction of the Court to entertain that dispute. Under the Court's Statute that jurisdiction is always based on the consent of the parties.

65. As it recalled in its Order of 10 July 2002, the Court has jurisdiction in respect of States only to the extent that they have consented thereto. When a compromissory clause in a treaty provides for the Court's jurisdiction, that jurisdiction exists only in respect of the parties to the treaty who are bound by that clause and within the limits set out therein.

66. The Court notes, however, that it has already found that reservations are not prohibited under the Genocide Convention. This legal situation is not altered by the fact that the Statute of the International Criminal Court, in its Article 120, does not permit reservations to that Statute, including provisions relating to the jurisdiction of the International Criminal Court on the crime of genocide. Thus, in the view of the Court, a reservation under the Genocide Convention would be permissible to the extent that such reservation is not incompatible with the object and purpose of the Convention.

67. Rwanda's reservation to Article IX of the Genocide Convention bears on the jurisdiction of the Court, and does not affect substantive obligations relating to acts of genocide themselves under that Convention. In the circumstances of the present case, the Court cannot conclude that the reservation of Rwanda in question, which is meant to exclude a particular method of settling a dispute relating to the interpretation, application or fulfilment of the Convention, is to be regarded as being incompatible with the object and purpose of the Convention.

68. In fact, the Court has already had occasion in the past to give effect to such reservations to Article IX of the Convention. The Court further notes that, as a matter of the law of treaties, when Rwanda acceded to the Genocide Convention and made the reservation in question, the DRC made no objection to it.

69. In so far as the DRC contended further that Rwanda's reservation is in conflict with a peremptory norm of general international law, it suffices for the Court to note that no such norm presently exists requiring a State to consent to the jurisdiction of the Court in order to settle a dispute relating to the Genocide Convention. Rwanda's reservation cannot therefore, on such grounds, be regarded as lacking legal effect.

70. The Court concludes from the foregoing that, having regard to Rwanda's reservation to Article IX of the Genocide Convention, this Article cannot constitute the basis for the jurisdiction of the Court in the present case. . .

121. In its Counter-Memorial the DRC noted that Rwanda's Memorial invoked *inter alia* "the alleged irrelevance of the Congo's reference to the Vienna Convention on the Law of Treaties," and the DRC

referred the Court in this regard to the arguments which it had presented at the provisional measures phase. At the hearings, the DRC explained that Article 66 of the Vienna Convention on the Law of Treaties, to which Rwanda is a party, allows the Court to rule on any dispute concerning "the validity of a treaty which is contrary to a norm of jus cogens." In this regard the DRC argued that reservations to a treaty form an integral part thereof, and that they must accordingly "avoid either being in direct contradiction with a norm of jus cogens, or preventing the implementation of that norm." According to the DRC, Rwanda's reservation to Article IX of the Genocide Convention, as well as to "other similar provisions and compromissory clauses, seeks to prevent the . . . Court from fulfilling its noble mission of safeguarding peremptory norms, including the prohibition of genocide," and must therefore be regarded as "null and void."

122. In reply to Rwanda's reliance at the hearings on Article 4 of the Vienna Convention, which provides that the Convention applies only to treaties which are concluded by States after its entry into force with regard to such States, the DRC contended that "the supremacy and mandatory force of the norms referred to in this Convention (Articles 53 and 64) bind States irrespective of any temporal consideration or any treaty-based link"; according to the DRC, the rule can therefore "have retroactive effect in the overriding interest of humanity." In this connection, the DRC cited the Judgment of 27 June 1986 in the case concerning *Military and Paramilitary Activities in and against Nicaragua*, where the Court held that there was an obligation on the United States to respect the four Geneva Conventions "in all circumstances," since such an obligation "does not derive only from the Conventions themselves, but from the general principles of humanitarian law to which the Conventions merely give concrete expression." The DRC also invoked the "moral and humanitarian principles" to which the Court had referred in its Advisory Opinion on *Reservations to the Convention on the Prevention and Punishment of the Crime of Genocide*, and it asked the Court "to safeguard [those principles] by finding that it has jurisdiction."

123. For its part, Rwanda contended in its Memorial that the DRC's contention that the norms of jus cogens are capable of conferring jurisdiction on the Court is without foundation, since it ignores the principle, well established in the Court's jurisprudence, that jurisdiction is always dependent on the consent of the parties, even when the norm that a State is accused of violating is a jus cogens norm. Rwanda added that the same is true of the Court's jurisdiction to entertain a dispute concerning violation of a norm creating obligations *erga omnes*. It recalled that, in its *East Timor* Judgment, the Court held that "the *erga omnes* character of a norm and the rule of consent to jurisdiction are two

different things." Rwanda further contended that Article 66 of the Vienna Convention on the Law of Treaties did not provide for "any" dispute regarding contravention of a rule of jus cogens to be referred to the Court; it was concerned with "a very specific kind of dispute regarding one effect of norms of jus cogens." According to Rwanda, Article 66 "is part and parcel of the machinery for the settlement of disputes regarding the interpretation and application of the Vienna Convention" and confers jurisdiction on the Court "only in respect of disputes regarding the validity of a treaty which is said to contravene a rule of jus cogens," which is not at all the case in this instance. . .

SEPARATE OPINION OF JUDGE *AD HOC* DUGARD

1.   The Democratic Republic of the Congo (hereinafter the DRC) has failed to show that the Court has jurisdiction to hear the present Application, either in terms of the compromissory clauses of several treaties that it claims have been violated by Rwanda or in terms of a number of other bases for jurisdiction that it has advanced. In these circumstances I agree fully with the decision of the Court that it has no jurisdiction to entertain the Application filed by the DRC on 28 May 2002.

2.   There are, however, two issues on which I wish to add some comments of my own. First, as this is the first occasion on which the Court has expressly acknowledged the existence of peremptory norms (jus cogens), I wish to examine, albeit in a tentative manner, the role that jus cogens may play in international litigation and the limits that must be placed on its use, with special reference to the present Application. Secondly, I wish to comment on the subject of negotiations within the political organs of the United Nations for the purpose of satisfying the requirement in a compromissory clause for the exercise of jurisdiction that a dispute must be shown to be not capable of settlement by negotiation.

Jus Cogens in International Litigation

3.   The DRC has sought to invoke the jurisdiction of the Court on the basis of a number of arguments premised on the violation of peremptory norms (jus cogens) by Rwanda. These arguments, in essence, may be reduced to two. First, the allegation of the violation of a norm of jus cogens *per se* confers jurisdiction on the Court. Secondly, where a violation of a norm of jus cogens is alleged, the respondent State cannot raise a reservation to the Court's jurisdiction to defeat that jurisdiction. In such a case, jus cogens in effect trumps the reservation. Aware, no doubt, of the novelty and far-reaching implications of its argument, the DRC has urged the Court to act "boldly and creatively." The Court has responded boldly by acknowledging the existence of norms of jus cogens but it has, rightly, declined the DRC's invitation to go beyond this.

Instead it has, correctly in my judgment, rejected the DRC's submissions in holding that the fact that a dispute relates to compliance with a peremptory norm, such as genocide, cannot of itself provide a basis for the Court's jurisdiction; and that a reservation to the Court's jurisdiction cannot be held to be invalid on the ground that it violates a norm of jus cogens. In so finding the Court has emphasized that its jurisdiction is based on consent and that no peremptory norm requires States to consent to jurisdiction where the compliance with a peremptory norm is the issue before the Court.

4.   This is the first occasion on which the International Court of Justice has given its support to the notion of jus cogens. It is strange that the Court has taken so long to reach this point because it has shown no hesitation in recognizing the notion of obligation *erga omnes*, which together with jus cogens affirms the normative hierarchy of international law. Indeed, the Court itself initiated the notion of obligation *erga omnes* in 1970 in the *Barcelona Traction* case and has recently confirmed its adherence to the notion in its Advisory Opinion in the case concerning *Legal Consequences of the Construction of a Wall in the Occupied Palestinian Territory*. Until the present Judgment the Court carefully and deliberately avoided endorsing the notion of jus cogens despite the many opportunities it had to do so. In 1969 it refrained from pronouncing "on any question of jus cogens" (*North Sea Continental Shelf*); in 1986 it acknowledged that the International Law Commission had found the prohibition on the use of force to have the character of jus cogens, but declined to align itself with this position *(Military and Paramilitary Activities in and against Nicaragua)*; and in 2002 it failed to respond to an argument that the granting of immunity to a Foreign Minister for crimes against humanity violated a norm of jus cogens (*Arrest Warrant of 11 April 2000)*. Despite this, jus cogens has been invoked by individual judges in cases before the Court in separate and dissenting opinions going back to the 1960s. In 1960, in a dissenting opinion in the *Right of Passage* case, Judge *ad hoc* Fernandes referred to the "rules of *ius cogens*, over which no special practice can prevail." Then in 1966, in his dissenting opinion in the *South West Africa* cases, Judge Tanaka declared: "If we can introduce in the international field a category of law, namely jus cogens examined the International Law Commission, a kind of imperative law which constitutes the contrast to the *jus dispositivum*, capable of being changed by way of agreement between States, surely the law concerning the protection of human rights may be considered to belong to the jus cogens."

5.   The failure of the International Court to endorse or pronounce on the subject of jus cogens has not gone unnoticed. Its silence has been aggravated by the fact that both other international tribunals (*Al-Adsani* v. *United Kingdom*, European Court of Human Rights); *Prosecutor* v.

Furundzija, International Criminal Tribunal for the former Yugoslavia) and national courts have invoked the term jus cogens to portray higher norms of international law.

6.   The approval given to jus cogens by the Court in the present Judgment is to be welcomed. However, the Judgment stresses that the scope of jus cogens is not unlimited and that the concept is not to be used as an instrument to overthrow accepted doctrines of international law.

7.   The Court's endorsement of jus cogens raises the question of the future role of jus cogens and the legal consequences to be attached to a violation of jus cogens for, as Ian Brownlie states, "many problems of application remain" in respect of jus cogens.

8.   It is today accepted that a treaty will be void if at the time of its conclusion, it conflicts with "a peremptory norm of general international law" (Art. 53 of the Vienna Convention on the Law of Treaties of 1969); and that States must deny recognition to a situation created by the serious breach of a peremptory norm (Arts. 40 and 41 of the Draft Articles on the Responsibility of States for Internationally Wrongful Acts). Moreover, it has been suggested that a Security Council resolution will be void if it conflicts with a norm of jus cogens (see the separate opinion of Judge *ad hoc* Sir Elihu Lauterpacht in the case concerning the *Application of the Convention on the Prevention and Punishment of the Crime of Genocide (Bosnia and Herzegovina* v. *Yugoslavia (Serbia and Montenegro)*. Jus cogens does, however, have a less spectacular role to play in the judicial process and it is this role that becomes important now that the Court has finally recognized the existence of peremptory norms.

9.   In national law there is a wealth of literature on judicial lawmaking and the nature of the judicial process. International law, on the other hand, is characterized by a dearth of literature on this subject. Cf. Hersch Lauterpacht, *The Development of International Law by the International Court* (1958). This explains why little attention has been paid to the place of jus cogens in the judicial process despite the pivotal role that it could—and should—play.

10.   The judicial decision is essentially an exercise in choice. Where authorities are divided, or different general principles compete for priority, or different rules of interpretation lead to different conclusions, or State practices conflict, the judge is required to make a choice. In exercising this choice, the judge will be guided by principles (propositions that describe rights) and policies (propositions that describe goals) in order to arrive at a coherent conclusion that most effectively furthers the integrity of the international legal order.

Norms of jus cogens are a blend of principle and policy. On the one hand, they affirm the high principles of international law, which recognize the most important rights of the international order—such as the right to be free from aggression, genocide, torture and slavery and the right to self-determination; while, on the other hand, they give legal form to the most fundamental policies or goals of the international community—the prohibitions on aggression, genocide, torture and slavery and the advancement of self-determination. This explains why they enjoy a hierarchical superiority to other norms in the international legal order. The fact that norms of jus cogens advance both principle and policy means that they must inevitably play a dominant role in the process of judicial choice.

11. Several decisions of the International Court in which the Court might have invoked norms of jus cogens, but did not, illustrate the type of case in which norms of jus cogens might be employed. The Judgment of the Court in the *South West Africa* cases is an obvious example of such a case. There the Court was faced with a choice between the principle that a State must demonstrate a special, national, interest in the proceedings before the Court to enjoy legal standing and the "sacred trust of civilization" contained in the Mandate for South West Africa to promote to the utmost the well-being of the inhabitants of the territory. In preferring the former principle it chose not to accede to the higher norm; with serious consequences for the Court. In fairness, it must be added that this decision largely predated the recognition of norms of jus cogens although Judge Tanaka in his powerful dissenting opinion did refer to such norms.

Other cases in which norms of jus cogens might possibly have been invoked were *East Timor* and the *Arrest Warrant* case. In the former, the Court declined to apply its decision in the *Certain Phosphate Lands* case, and instead preferred the controversial precedent of the *Monetary Gold* case above the peremptory norm of self-determination, which was described as a norm of *erga omnes* rather than jus cogens by the Court. . . The Court has recently retreated from the *Monetary Gold* case and instead relied on the *Certain Phosphate Lands in Nauru* case in the case concerning *Armed Activities on the Territory of the Congo*. Although the Court did not indicate that its choice was influenced by the fact that norms of jus cogens were involved in this case, it may safely be assumed that the gravity of the issues raised influenced the Court's choice.

In the *Arrest Warrant* case the Court found that a Foreign Minister enjoyed immunity before a national court in respect of crimes against humanity on the basis of weak evidence of State practice rather than allowing the jus cogens character of the crime to prevail over the plea of immunity (see the dissenting opinions of Judge Al-Khasawneh and Judge *ad hoc* van den Wyngaert in the *Arrest Warrant* case, which advocate the choice of the jus cogens norm of the prohibition of crimes against humanity over the unsettled rule of immunity).

12. In the above cases the Court was faced with competing principles, State practice and precedents and preferred not to choose that solution which gave effect to a norm of jus cogens. The Court was not asked to invoke jus cogens to trump an established, accepted rule but instead to choose a principle of jus cogens or a precedent coinciding with a norm of jus cogens in preference to a principle, State practice or precedent that did not enjoy the status of jus cogens. It was simply asked to exercise its choice within the interstices of the law in a molecular rather than a molar fashion.

13. In the present case the Court is confronted with a very different situation. The Court is not asked, in the exercise of its legitimate judicial function, to exercise its choice between competing sources in a manner which gives effect to a norm of jus cogens. On the contrary, it is asked to overthrow an established principle—that the basis of the Court's jurisdiction is consent—which is founded in its Statute (Art. 36), endorsed by unqualified State practice and backed by *opinio juris*. It is, in effect, asked to invoke a peremptory norm to trump a norm of general international law accepted and recognized by the international community of States as a whole, and which has guided the Court for over 80 years. This is a bridge too far. The Court cannot be expected to accept the arguments raised by the DRC for by so doing it would not engage in molecular law-making, but molar law-making that goes beyond the legitimate judicial function. Only States can amend Article 36 of the Court's Statute.

14. For this reason the Court, in the present instance, has rightly held that although norms of jus cogens are to be recognized by the Court, and presumably to be invoked by the Court in future in the exercise of its judicial function, there are limits to be placed on the role of jus cogens. The request to overthrow the principle of consent as the basis for its jurisdiction goes beyond these limits. This, in effect, is what the Court has held. . .

NOTES & QUESTIONS

1. *The Origins of Jus Cogens.* Although the *existence* of jus cogens is rather uncontroversial, its origins are hotly contested, at least among scholars willing to discuss the esoteric issue. The "standard view," if there is one, is that jus cogens emerges from custom, i.e., a sub-class of customary norms that are considered so universal and imperative that they are obligatory and non-derogable. However, some have questioned this view and suggested that jus cogens might emerge from treaty based norms that are so universal that they apply even to non-signatories. In that case, does the jus cogens norm flow directly from treaty law or indirectly through the custom that emerges from a treaty that gains such widespread acceptance that it also embodies customary law as well? Another way of thinking about jus

cogens is that it represents the "positivization" of natural law. See Andrea Bianchi, *Human Rights and the Magic of Jus Cogens,* 19 Eur. J. Int'l L. 491, 492 (2008) (attributing the comment to René-Jean Dupuy). In other words, in prior eras, some possibilities would have been ruled "out of bounds" by international lawyers because they conflict with natural law. However, in today's era, natural law is largely disfavored as a legal category, but in its place international lawyers now refer to jus cogens as a way of expressing the notion that some possibilities, even if they were expressed in the positive law through treaty or custom, would be impermissible. Where do you think jus cogens comes from?

2.   *Jus Cogens or Erga Omnes.* What is the difference between a jus cogens norm and an *erga omnes* norm? In *DRC v. Rwanda* above, the ICJ refers to both without explicitly explaining the difference between them. As Bianchi, *supra* at 502, notes, "[w]hile the two notions may be complementary, they remain distinct, and to consider them as synonyms risks undermining the legal distinctiveness of each category." An *erga omnes* obligation is one that is owed to the entire world community, rather than owed reciprocally to a particular counter-party. A jus cogens violation is non-derogable and obligatory, regardless of the principle of consent. In practice, some human rights norms are both *erga omnes* and jus cogens at the same time, but it seems theoretically possible for there to be some *erga omnes* human rights obligations that are not yet obligatory in the sense of jus cogens. What are the legal obligations discussed in *DRC v. Rwanda*—jus cogens, *erga omnes,* or both?

3.   *Which Norms Are Jus Cogens?* Although every international lawyer agrees that there is a category of norms that are jus cogens, there is intense disagreement over which norms fit in that category. Indeed, making these arguments is precisely the job of international lawyers. On the minimalist view, jus cogens is limited mostly to axiomatic principles that are part and parcel of the architecture of international law, including, for example, the notion of *pacta sunt servanda,* a legal maxim that states that parties are bound by the elements of a treaty that they have signed. Without such a notion, all of treaty law would evaporate and therefore a state cannot exempt itself from the principle. However, a more modern view suggests that jus cogens includes more substantive norms as well. For example, the Restatement of Foreign Relations Law includes the following list as jus cogens: "A state violates international law if, as a matter of state policy, it practices, encourages, or condones (a) genocide, (b) slavery or slave trade, (c) the murder or causing the disappearance of individuals, (d) torture or other cruel, inhuman, or degrading treatment or punishment, (e) prolonged arbitrary detention, (f) systematic racial discrimination, or (g) a consistent pattern of gross violations of internationally recognized human rights." See Restatement (Third) of Foreign Relations Law § 702 (1987). Do you agree with this list?

E. OTHER SOURCES

Custom and treaties are not the only two sources of international law. Article 38 of the ICJ Statute also lists "the general principles of law recognized by civilized nations," as well as "judicial decisions, and the teachings of the most highly qualified publicists of the various nations, as subsidiary means for the determination of rules of law." This section will briefly discuss and analyze these three sources of law.

1. GENERAL PRINCIPLES

General principles of law are frequently invoked by international lawyers but poorly understood. There is no widely authoritative definition of what counts as a general principle, nor a universally accepted methodology for finding general principles. Unlike treaty interpretation, which is governed by the highly influential Vienna Convention on the Law of Treaties, general principles of law are invoked in particular legal arguments without an explicitly recognized methodology for their analysis.

With that being said, general principles as a category are undeniable and all international lawyers agree that they are a legitimate source. Where do they come from? One leading international lawyer, Oscar Schachter, developed a taxonomy in *International Law in Theory and Practice* 50–55 (1991), paraphrased here:

1. Principles of *domestic* law that are recognized by civilized nations. In other words, international law can take notice of abstract principles that are widely recognized and deployed by many nations in their domestic legal systems, and then "import" those principles into international law. The requirement that the principle be recognized by "civilized nations" suggests that the principle need not be universally shared among all legal systems—just those that are civilized. This qualifier allows the international lawyer a response to the objection that a particular state does not recognize the principle.

2. General principles that are part of the architecture of the international legal system as a distinct body of law. Examples of these principles include, for example, notions derived from the concept of sovereignty, including the idea that all states are formally equal before the law, and that all states must respect the territorial integrity of each other state.

3. Axiomatic principles that are elements of law. One might, for example, consider *pacta sunt servanda*—the idea that agreements must be kept—as a general principle of law.

Another example might be the idea of *lex specialis*, i.e., the idea that the more specific law shall prevail over the more general law.

4.   Principles that are considered universal because they are found in every human society. In a prior generation, these principles were labelled as natural law, but in today's more positivistic environment might be described with the language of human rights.

5.   Principles of justice that flow from the nature of human beings as rational animals.

See Neha Jain, *Judicial Lawmaking and General Principles of Law in International Criminal Law*, 57 Harv. J. Int'l L. 112, 117 (2016) (discussing the principles outlined above and concluding that "scholarship on the nature of the general principles presents an extremely chaotic picture" because general principles "are interpreted variously as principles common to all or most domestic legal systems, as general tenets underlying international legal rules, as inherent principles of natural law, and as principles deduced from legal logic").

One of the most common categories of general principles are those flowing from domestic legal systems, which are embodied in categories 1 and 3 above. The supposed rationale for this category is that if indeed international law is based on "consent"—states voluntarily accepting legal commitments—it is no problem for them to be bound by general principles of law that they already accept as part of their domestic legal systems. See Jain at 118; Jaye Ellis, *General Principles and Comparative Law*, 22 Eur. J. Int'l L. 949, 953–55 (2011).

One context where general principles of law come into play is international criminal law. International tribunals, such as the International Criminal Court (ICC) or the International Criminal Tribunal for the Former Yugoslavia (ICTY), prosecute individuals for war crimes, crimes against humanity, and genocide. The sources of law applied by those courts include treaty-based crimes and sometimes— more controversially—customary international law. (Customary international law might be used, for example, to clarify the scope of a legal norm, such as a war crime). However, these tribunals also sometimes refer to domestic legal norms, recognized in international law through the rubric of general principles.

For example, the ICTY adjudicated cases of rape as a war crime. Although the relevant treaty sources clearly establish that rape is a war crime, the definition of rape is not spelled out in the way that it would be in a domestic penal statute. In *Furundžija*, the ICTY looked to domestic legal precedents in multiple jurisdictions to establish the actus reus of the crime of rape. Taken individually, these precedents merely established that individual domestic penal systems define rape in a particular way. However, when taken together, and in combination with the general principle of respect for human dignity, the domestic precedents established that the definition of rape was a general principle of law, and therefore a legitimate source of law for an international court to apply. See *Prosecutor v. Furundžija*, Judgment, Case No. IT–95–17/1–T, para. 177 (Dec. 10, 1998).

A similar example is the case of Drazen Erdemović. The defendant pleaded guilty for an atrocity that involved the execution of innocent civilians but argued that his crime was excused by duress. The Trial Chamber was tasked with determining whether the defense of duress was applicable to a war crime and a crime against humanity that involved the murder of innocent civilians. To help answer this question, the court looked to domestic legal systems and their diverse approaches to the question of duress. The analysis was complicated by the fact that common law jurisdictions, following the precedent of *Dudley and Stephens*, generally do not permit the duress defense in murder cases, while in contrast civil law legal systems generally do not have a similar categorical exclusion. After finding him guilty, the ICTY repeated the same methodology to arrive at an appropriate sentence: "In order to review the scale of penalties applicable for crimes against humanity, the Trial Chamber will identify the features which characterise such crimes and the penalties associated with them under international law and national laws, which are expressions of general principles of law recognised by all nations." See *Prosecutor v. Erdemović,* Case No. IT–96–22–T (November 29, 1996).

2. JUDICIAL DECISIONS AND INTERNATIONAL SCHOLARSHIP

The second and third categories of sources listed in Article 38 involve judicial decisions from international tribunals and the teachings of highly qualified publicists. In both cases, these are considered subsidiary means of determining the law. To understand why they would be classified as "subsidiary," consider that international tribunals are generally viewed as applying the law rather than making it. In other words, an international tribunal is generally applying the same sources of law that we are learning about in this casebook: treaties, custom, and general principles. Therefore, a decision from an international tribunal can be cited as highly persuasive authority regarding the *content* of those legal obligations that flow from treaty, custom, or general principles. However, in that case, the international lawyer is citing the international decision for its derivative value. It is not strictly speaking a primary source of law itself but rather is a secondary form of law that embodies an authoritative gloss on the underlying sources. (Recall also that a decision from an international tribunal cannot be classified as customary international law because there is no state practice associated with an international tribunal.) Consequently, one might describe article 38 as representing a de facto hierarchy of sources under international law, with treaties and custom at the top, and the subsidiary modes at the bottom.

This leaves the teaching of highly qualified publicists. This colorful phrase refers to academic literature—the writings of international law scholars who articulate arguments about the content of legal norms. Yet again, these statements of the law are not primary sources but rather secondary sources that give us an authoritative gloss on the content of the primary sources. In practice, the citation of legal arguments by scholars is a crucial tool for international lawyers. The relative paucity of formal legal sources compared to domestic law (i.e., there are more domestic statutes than international treaties, for example) makes the citation of scholarly sources that much more important in international legal discourse.

In prior generations, the study of international law was a luxury for the scholarly few who published lengthy treatises summarizing the legal rules applicable to nations in their mutual conduct. A small number of treatises from a few "publicists" often dominated the conversation. Examples included Henry Wheaton's *Elements of International Law*, first published in 1836. Wheaton was a New York lawyer and politician who entered the foreign service as a diplomat. Today, the study of international law has been democratized, to an extent, with hundreds of academic journals available for professors around the world to publish their scholarly reflections. Some scholars even write for online blogs where complex legal questions are analyzed and debated. For almost every legal issue, there are dozens of academic articles or books discussing or analyzing the issue, making legal research both energizing and enervating. Schachter once referred to *The Invisible College of International Lawyers*, 72 Nw. U. L. Rev. 217 (1977–1978), his label for the tight-knit community of scholars that spans the globe. While scholars today often disagree intently on many angles of the law, this disagreement often takes place against a shared background of broad agreement on particular issues. Article 38 anticipates that international lawyers will cite these academic statements for their probative value of a scholarly consensus.

Conclusion & Summary

Custom is a "bread and butter" source of international law and no legal argument is complete without some reference to customary international law. Given its unwritten nature, though, it is a source of law unlike any found in domestic law. Consider carefully the following conclusions:

1. State practice must be constant and uniform. The practice and the associated custom may coalesce quickly or develop slowly over time. In determining how many states are required, international lawyers pay specific attention to states that are "specially affected" by the underlying issue. Some states may violate the rule and break the law, although once the number of states doing so grows large, it may suggest that the custom has changed.

2. Custom almost always requires the subjective element of *opinio juris*—acting from a sense of legal obligation. It may be difficult to determine the subjective element, though analysis of official government statements can clarify a state's reason for acting. Also, states may be motivated by a mixture of self-interest and legal obligation and the two may be intertwined; following the law might yield so many long-term benefits that the state thinks that engaging in the state practice advances its rational self-interest. The requirement of *opinio juris* may be dispensed with when a rule is first being formed as a way of solving the "chronological paradox."

3. States are not bound by a rule of customary international law if they "persistently objected" to a rule when it was being formed. A state exempting itself in this manner must consistently reaffirm its objection at relevant points in time. Once the state accepts the norm, it cannot withdraw from the obligation because its objection will no longer be persistent. Also, persistent objector status is unavailable for norms that rise to the level of jus cogens.

4. A jus cogens norm is non-derogable, meaning all states are required to abide by the rule, regardless of whether they consent to it or not. The category of jus cogens includes norms of customary international law that are so universally shared that they are considered obligatory. Some lawyers believe that a treaty provision also might rise to the level of jus cogens if the provision embodies virtually universal agreement. There is considerable disagreement about the source of jus cogens norms, nor is there widespread agreement over which norms qualify for that label. But the consequence of the label is clear: a treaty provision is invalid if it conflicts with jus cogens.

5. Custom and treaties do not exhaust the formal sources of international law. Article 38 of the ICJ Statute recognizes general principles of international law, which include, among other things, legal principles that are widely shared in the domestic legal systems of "civilized" nations. International lawyers can refer to these legal principles as a valid source of *international* law under the rubric of general principles.

6. The last two sources of international law are subsidiary: decisions of international tribunals and the teachings of highly qualified publicists, i.e., academics. Both are subsidiary sources of law because they may be consulted as indirect evidence of the content of international law, rather than direct sources of international law. They are secondary expressions of the law rather than the law itself. Nonetheless, they play a crucial role in the practice of international legal argumentation.

CHAPTER 3

TREATIES

Introduction

There are many reasons for states to formalize legal arrangements in the form of a written instrument. Sometimes treaties are drafted to codify legal obligations that are already part of customary international law. The benefit of codifying an existing legal obligation is to add clarity and precision to the content of the legal obligation and to remove ambiguity. Treaties can also provide a framework for enforcement or dispute resolution arising from the treaty.

In other situations, treaties create new legal obligations that the parties agree to through voluntary consent. When faced with a particularly acute international problem, a formal treaty between states establishes a set of legally binding rules between the parties.

Sometimes a rule created by treaty can later ripen into customary international law—and therefore become binding on states that are not parties to the treaty. In that situation, the regular standards for customary international law must be satisfied, including state practice and *opinio juris*. The existence of a treaty regime may encourage many states to coalesce around a particular practice, first among the treaty parties who are obligated, but then also among a wide audience of states that follow this lead. In this way, the treaty obligation may widen into a customary obligation.

Treaties are either bilateral or multilateral. Bilateral treaties between two states are negotiated to produce a tailored legal arrangement that both states consider beneficial. These agreements are typically negotiated and signed by an executive official with the capacity to represent the government and then often brought back "home" for ratification according to the requirements of domestic law. In the U.S., the ratification of treaties is handled by the federal government after the U.S. Senate gives its "advice and consent." During the time between signing but prior to domestic ratification, a state is only a "signatory" and not yet a "party" to the treaty, and therefore not yet subject to its obligations. However, a signatory does have a limited obligation not to engage in conduct that would defeat the object and purpose of the treaty.

Multilateral treaties are negotiated between a large number of states who wish to participate in a wide—perhaps even universal—legal framework. Examples include mutual defense treaties (such as NATO), economic arrangements such as the World Trade Organization, or human rights conventions such as the International Covenant on Civil and

Political Rights. In these situations, negotiations can be challenging, especially when states have competing ideas about how to structure the multilateral framework; it may be impossible to produce a document that all states can live with. In these situations, there are two options for the objecting state. Either it can refuse to sign the treaty and remain outside of the legal framework, or it can sign the treaty but attach a "Reservation" to the treaty that objects to, and exempts it from, isolated provisions within the treaty. As will be discussed in greater detail below, the permissibility of these reservations is evaluated by the rest of the state parties who may either accept or reject the reservations as legitimate or not. In practice, some states might object to the reservation while others might accept it, creating a messy patchwork of different obligations among participants in the multilateral regime.

Treaties are rarely eternal; they have a shelf life and outlive their usefulness at some point. Whether or how a state can leave a treaty is governed by the treaty itself, which may have terms explicitly articulating an exit process. In other situations, the treaty may be silent on the question, though treaty termination may be allowed if the parties implicitly assumed that unilateral termination would be allowed. Finally, a counter-party's material breach of the treaty may permit the other parties to terminate the treaty in response.

Under domestic law, the U.S. Constitution allocates the treaty-making power to both of the political branches of the federal government, and their relative authority has been debated, with little formal resolution by the Supreme Court, for centuries. For years, the typical process was treaty negotiation by the president or his representatives (in the State Department), followed by ratification after two-thirds of the Senate gives its "advice and consent," as dictated in the Constitution. However, this pattern is becoming less frequent, with alternative legal arrangements replacing full treaties, especially in situations where it would be impossible to secure a super-majority of senators to support ratification of the pact.

Sometimes the president might involve Congress in the process by getting congressional legislation, through simple majorities in both the House and the Senate. These agreements, though certainly "treaties" under international law, are referred to as "congressional-executive agreements" in American parlance. In extreme circumstances, particularly in the arena of national emergencies or military affairs, the president may sign a "sole executive agreement" with a foreign nation without any direct congressional involvement.

The following sections will meticulously guide you through these major conceptual building blocks, while demonstrating the practical and legal consequences for each. Section A will focus on how treaties are formed and interpreted when there is ambiguity in their terms. Section

B will detail the process of "reservations" in the context of multilateral conventions, with special reference to the Genocide Convention drafted after World War II, which was negotiated with the goal of receiving wide acceptance. Section C will analyze the federal treaty power, that is, whether there is any limit to what the federal government can make the subject of a treaty. Can the government use a treaty to do anything that it likes, or must the exercise of the treaty power comply with the structural restrictions of the Constitution, such as federalism or the Bill of Rights? Section D focuses on the distinction between self-executing and non-self-executing treaties—a classification that determines whether the treaty automatically becomes federal law or whether it requires further implementing legislation before becoming binding domestic law enforceable in federal court. Section E looks at when Presidents can conclude international agreements—such as sole executive agreements or congressional-executive agreements—without receiving the "advice and consent" from the Senate required under the Constitution for ratification of all treaties. Finally, Section F focuses on the unresolved question of the president's ability to unilaterally terminate a treaty that was ratified by the Senate.

As you read the following sections, remember that treaties are just one source of international law. In any legal situation, the relevant norms of international law will flow not just from treaties but also from custom, general principles of international law, and the decisions of international tribunals. Understanding the role of treaties in the international legal system—and the interplay with a domestic legal system—is just one piece of the larger architecture of international law.

A. TREATY FORMATION AND INTERPRETATION

The law governing treaty formation and interpretation was codified in the Vienna Convention on the Law of Treaties, which was signed in 1969 and entered into force in 1980. Although the United States is not a state party, the U.S. recognizes that the provisions of the Convention codify pre-existing customary law of treaty interpretation. Although the Vienna Convention is not the end of the analysis, its provisions are certainly the best starting point for any matter of law dealing with treaties. The following articles lay out the Convention's basic rules for how to interpret a treaty:

Vienna Convention on the Law of Treaties

1155 U.N.T.S. 331
May 23, 1969
Entered into force January 27, 1980

Article 31

General rule of interpretation

1.   A treaty shall be interpreted in good faith in accordance with the ordinary meaning to be given to the terms of the treaty in their context and in the light of its object and purpose.

2.   The context for the purpose of the interpretation of a treaty shall comprise, in addition to the text, including its preamble and annexes:

(a)   any agreement relating to the treaty which was made between all the parties in connexion with the conclusion of the treaty;

(b)   any instrument which was made by one or more parties in connexion with the conclusion of the treaty and accepted by the other parties as an instrument related to the treaty.

3.   There shall be taken into account, together with the context:

(a)   any subsequent agreement between the parties regarding the interpretation of the treaty or the application of its provisions;

(b)   any subsequent practice in the application of the treaty which establishes the agreement of the parties regarding its interpretation;

(c)   any relevant rules of international law applicable in the relations between the parties.

4.   A special meaning shall be given to a term if it is established that the parties so intended.

Article 32

Supplementary means of interpretation

Recourse may be had to supplementary means of interpretation, including the preparatory work of the treaty and the circumstances of its conclusion, in order to confirm the meaning resulting from the application of article 31, or to determine the meaning when the interpretation according to article 31:

(a)   leaves the meaning ambiguous or obscure; or

(b)   leads to a result which is manifestly absurd or unreasonable.

———————————

In the following case, the U.S. Supreme Court was tasked with interpreting the meaning of the phrase "chemical weapon." Although the term's most recent usage was in a federal statute, the statute was passed to implement international obligations under the Chemical Weapons Convention. As such, the Supreme Court had to determine what the phrase "chemical weapon" meant in both the federal statute and the international treaty. What canons of interpretation did the Supreme Court use? If you had to pick one sub-provision in articles 31 or 32 that best embodied the Supreme Court's methodology, which one would it be?

Bond v. United States
Supreme Court of the United States
572 U.S. 844 (2014)

■ CHIEF JUSTICE ROBERTS delivered the opinion of the Court.

The horrors of chemical warfare were vividly captured by John Singer Sargent in his 1919 painting Gassed. The nearly life-sized work depicts two lines of soldiers, blinded by mustard gas, clinging single file to orderlies guiding them to an improvised aid station. There they would receive little treatment and no relief; many suffered for weeks only to have the gas claim their lives. The soldiers were shown staggering through piles of comrades too seriously burned to even join the procession.

The painting reflects the devastation that Sargent witnessed in the aftermath of the Second Battle of Arras during World War I. That battle and others like it led to an overwhelming consensus in the international community that toxic chemicals should never again be used as weapons against human beings. Today that objective is reflected in the international Convention on Chemical Weapons, which has been ratified or acceded to by 190 countries. The United States, pursuant to the Federal Government's constitutionally enumerated power to make treaties, ratified the treaty in 1997. To fulfill the United States' obligations under the Convention, Congress enacted the Chemical Weapons Convention Implementation Act of 1998. The Act makes it a federal crime for a person to use or possess any chemical weapon, and it punishes violators with severe penalties. It is a statute that, like the Convention it implements, deals with crimes of deadly seriousness.

The question presented by this case is whether the Implementation Act also reaches a purely local crime: an amateur attempt by a jilted wife to injure her husband's lover, which ended up causing only a minor thumb burn readily treated by rinsing with water. Because our constitutional structure leaves local criminal activity primarily to the States, we have generally declined to read federal law as intruding on that responsibility, unless Congress has clearly indicated that the law should have such reach. The Chemical Weapons Convention Implementation Act contains no such clear indication, and we accordingly conclude that it does not cover the unremarkable local offense at issue here.

I

In 1997, the President of the United States, upon the advice and consent of the Senate, ratified the Convention on the Prohibition of the Development, Production, Stockpiling, and Use of Chemical Weapons and on Their Destruction. The nations that ratified the Convention (State Parties) had bold aspirations for it: "general and complete disarmament under strict and effective international control, including the prohibition and elimination of all types of weapons of mass destruction." This purpose traces its origin to World War I, when "[o]ver a million casualties, up to 100,000 of them fatal, are estimated to have been caused by chemicals. . ., a large part following the introduction of mustard gas in 1917." The atrocities of that war led the community of nations to adopt the 1925 Geneva Protocol, which prohibited the use of chemicals as a method of warfare.

Up to the 1990s, however, chemical weapons remained in use both in and out of wartime, with devastating consequences. Iraq's use of nerve agents and mustard gas during its war with Iran in the 1980s contributed to international support for a renewed, more effective chemical weapons ban. In 1994 and 1995, long-held fears of the use of chemical weapons by terrorists were realized when Japanese extremists carried out two attacks using sarin gas. The Convention was conceived as an effort to update the Geneva Protocol's protections and to expand the prohibition on chemical weapons beyond state actors in wartime. The Convention aimed to achieve that objective by prohibiting the development, stockpiling, or use of chemical weapons by any State Party or person within a State Party's jurisdiction. It also established an elaborate reporting process requiring State Parties to destroy chemical weapons under their control and submit to inspection and monitoring by an international organization based in The Hague, Netherlands.

The Convention provides:

(1) Each State Party to this Convention undertakes never under any circumstances:

(a) To develop, produce, otherwise acquire, stockpile or retain chemical weapons, or transfer, directly or indirectly, chemical weapons to anyone;

(b) To use chemical weapons;

(c) To engage in any military preparations to use chemical weapons;

(d) To assist, encourage or induce, in any way, anyone to engage in any activity prohibited to a State Party under this Convention.

"Chemical Weapons" are defined in relevant part as "[t]oxic chemicals and their precursors, except where intended for purposes not prohibited under this Convention, as long as the types and quantities are consistent with such purposes." "Toxic Chemical," in turn, is defined as "Any chemical which through its chemical action on life processes can cause death, temporary incapacitation or permanent harm to humans or animals. This includes all such chemicals, regardless of their origin or of their method of production, and regardless of whether they are produced in facilities, in munitions or elsewhere." "Purposes Not Prohibited Under this Convention" means "[i]ndustrial, agricultural, research, medical, pharmaceutical or other peaceful purposes," and other specific purposes not at issue here.

Although the Convention is a binding international agreement, it is "not self-executing." That is, the Convention creates obligations only for State Parties and "does not by itself give rise to domestically enforceable federal law" absent "implementing legislation passed by Congress." It instead provides that "[e]ach State Party shall, in accordance with its constitutional processes, adopt the necessary measures to implement its obligations under this Convention." "In particular," each State Party shall "[p]rohibit natural and legal persons anywhere... under its jurisdiction... from undertaking any activity prohibited to a State Party under this Convention, including enacting penal legislation with respect to such activity."

Congress gave the Convention domestic effect in 1998 when it passed the Chemical Weapons Convention Implementation Act. The Act closely tracks the text of the treaty: It forbids any person knowingly "to develop, produce, otherwise acquire, transfer directly or indirectly, receive, stockpile, retain, own, possess, or use, or threaten to use, any chemical weapon." It defines "chemical weapon" in relevant part as "[a] toxic chemical and its precursors, except where intended for a purpose not prohibited under this chapter as long as the type and quantity is consistent with such a purpose." "Toxic chemical," in turn, is defined in general as "any chemical which through its chemical action on life processes can cause death, temporary incapacitation or permanent harm to humans or animals. The term includes all such chemicals, regardless of their origin or of their method of production, and regardless of whether they are produced in facilities, in munitions or elsewhere." Finally, "purposes not prohibited by this chapter" is defined as "[a]ny peaceful purpose related to an industrial, agricultural, research, medical, or pharmaceutical activity or other activity," and other specific purposes. A person who violates section 229 may be subject to severe punishment:

imprisonment "for any term of years," or if a victim's death results, the death penalty or imprisonment "for life."

Petitioner Carol Anne Bond is a microbiologist from Lansdale, Pennsylvania. In 2006, Bond's closest friend, Myrlinda Haynes, announced that she was pregnant. When Bond discovered that her husband was the child's father, she sought revenge against Haynes. Bond stole a quantity of 10-chloro-10H-phenoxarsine (an arsenic-based compound) from her employer, a chemical manufacturer. She also ordered a vial of potassium dichromate (a chemical commonly used in printing photographs or cleaning laboratory equipment) on Amazon.com. Both chemicals are toxic to humans and, in high enough doses, potentially lethal. It is undisputed, however, that Bond did not intend to kill Haynes. She instead hoped that Haynes would touch the chemicals and develop an uncomfortable rash.

Between November 2006 and June 2007, Bond went to Haynes's home on at least 24 occasions and spread the chemicals on her car door, mailbox, and door knob. These attempted assaults were almost entirely unsuccessful. The chemicals that Bond used are easy to see, and Haynes was able to avoid them all but once. On that occasion, Haynes suffered a minor chemical burn on her thumb, which she treated by rinsing with water. Haynes repeatedly called the local police to report the suspicious substances, but they took no action. When Haynes found powder on her mailbox, she called the police again, who told her to call the post office. Haynes did so, and postal inspectors placed surveillance cameras around her home. The cameras caught Bond opening Haynes's mailbox, stealing an envelope, and stuffing potassium dichromate inside the muffler of Haynes's car.

Federal prosecutors naturally charged Bond with two counts of mail theft, in violation of 18 U.S.C. § 1708. More surprising, they also charged her with two counts of possessing and using a chemical weapon, in violation of section 229(a). . . The District Court sentenced Bond to six years in federal prison plus five years of supervised release, and ordered her to pay a $2,000 fine and $9,902.79 in restitution. . .

III

Section 229 exists to implement the Convention, so we begin with that international agreement. As explained, the Convention's drafters intended for it to be a comprehensive ban on chemical weapons. But even with its broadly worded definitions, we have doubts that a treaty about *chemical weapons* has anything to do with Bond's conduct. The Convention, a product of years of worldwide study, analysis, and multinational negotiation, arose in response to war crimes and acts of terrorism. There is no reason to think the sovereign nations that ratified the Convention were interested in anything like Bond's common law assault. . .

In the Government's view, the conclusion that Bond "knowingly" "use[d]" a "chemical weapon" in violation of section 229(a) is simple: The chemicals that Bond placed on Haynes's home and car are "toxic chemical[s]" as defined by the statute, and Bond's attempt to assault Haynes was not a "peaceful purpose." The problem with this interpretation is that it would "dramatically intrude[ ] upon traditional state criminal jurisdiction," and we avoid reading statutes to have such reach in the absence of a clear indication that they do. . .

In fact, a fair reading of section 229 suggests that it does not have as expansive a scope as might at first appear. To begin, as a matter of natural meaning, an educated user of English would not describe Bond's crime as involving a "chemical weapon." Saying that a person "used a chemical weapon" conveys a very different idea than saying the person "used a chemical in a way that caused some harm." The natural meaning of "chemical weapon" takes account of both the particular chemicals that the defendant used and the circumstances in which she used them.

When used in the manner here, the chemicals in this case are not of the sort that an ordinary person would associate with instruments of chemical warfare. The substances that Bond used bear little resemblance to the deadly toxins that are "of particular danger to the objectives of the Convention." More to the point, the use of something as a "weapon" typically connotes "[a]n instrument of offensive or defensive combat," Webster's Third New International Dictionary 2589 (2002), or "[a]n instrument of attack or defense in combat, as a gun, missile, or sword," American Heritage Dictionary 2022 (3d ed. 1992). But no speaker in natural parlance would describe Bond's feud-driven act of spreading irritating chemicals on Haynes's door knob and mailbox as "combat." Nor do the other circumstances of Bond's offense—an act of revenge born of romantic jealousy, meant to cause discomfort, that produced nothing more than a minor thumb burn—suggest that a chemical weapon was deployed in Norristown, Pennsylvania. Potassium dichromate and 10-chloro-10H-phenoxarsine might be chemical weapons if used, say, to poison a city's water supply. But Bond's crime is worlds apart from such hypotheticals, and covering it would give the statute a reach exceeding the ordinary meaning of the words Congress wrote.

In settling on a fair reading of a statute, it is not unusual to consider the ordinary meaning of a defined term, particularly when there is dissonance between that ordinary meaning and the reach of the definition. . . The Government would have us brush aside the ordinary meaning and adopt a reading of section 229 that would sweep in everything from the detergent under the kitchen sink to the stain remover in the laundry room. Yet no one would ordinarily describe those substances as "chemical weapons." The Government responds that because Bond used "specialized, highly toxic" (though legal) chemicals, "this case presents no occasion to address whether Congress intended [section 229] to apply to common household substances." That the statute *would* apply so broadly, however, is the inescapable conclusion of the Government's position: Any parent would be guilty of a serious federal offense—possession of a chemical weapon—when, exasperated by the children's repeated failure to clean the goldfish tank, he considers poisoning the fish with a few drops of vinegar. We are reluctant to ignore the ordinary meaning of "chemical weapon" when doing so would transform a statute passed to implement the international Convention on Chemical Weapons into one that also makes it a federal offense to poison goldfish. That would not be a "realistic assessment[ ] of congressional intent." . . .

In sum, the global need to prevent chemical warfare does not require the Federal Government to reach into the kitchen cupboard, or to treat a local assault with a chemical irritant as the deployment of a chemical weapon. There is no reason to suppose that Congress—in implementing the Convention on Chemical Weapons—thought otherwise. . .

NOTES & QUESTIONS

1. *Subsequent Practice of the Parties.* Article 31(3) of the Vienna Convention specifically allows for the consideration of the subsequent practice of the parties when interpreting a treaty provision. (Similarly, article 31(3) also refers to subsequent *agreements* between the parties. If the parties reach future agreements that are relevant to the underlying issues, these agreements may provide a window into the meaning of the earlier treaty.) In other words, one way of interpreting a treaty provision is to inquire how states have *acted* as they seek to fulfill their legal obligations under a treaty. This methodology raises several questions. Why look to the subsequent practice of the parties? Does it provide a window into what the parties intended when they drafted the agreement? Or does it suggest that parties may effectively *transform* the content of their legal obligations by changing their practice? If the latter, what recourse is available to state parties that object to these changes-via-practice? In 2014, the International Law Commission issued a report studying the methodology, which emphasized that the practice must be "in the application" of the treaty, which is not always easy to identify. See Second Report on Subsequent Agreements and Subsequent Practice in Relation to the Interpretation of Treaties, International Law Commission Sixty-sixth session Geneva, UN Doc. A/CN.4/671 (March 26, 2014).

The methodology can be used in many contexts. For example, Professor Jay Butler argued that "regime change triggers a legal obligation" on the part of states that use military force to "ensure that the successor regime, whose installation their military intervention and subsequent exercise of control over the territory facilitated, respects international human rights law." Butler's argument relied on an interpretation of the Fourth Geneva Convention based on the subsequent practice of states that used military force to depose a government. See Jay Butler, *Responsibility for Regime Change*, 114 Colum. L. Rev. 503, 507 (2014). For more discussion on the topic of subsequent practice, see generally *Treaties and Subsequent Practice* (Georg Nolte ed., 2013).

2.   *The Later-in-Time Rule.* What happens when two treaties conflict with each other? Or when a treaty conflicts with a statute? Federal courts that encounter this situation will often apply a "later-in-time" rule, on the assumption that the second obligation modified the first obligation. Since treaties and federal statutes are both considered federal law under the Supremacy Clause, it does not matter whether the first law was a treaty or statute—the second law should take precedence over the first. See *Medellín v. Texas*, 552 U.S. 491, 509 (2008) ("Indeed, a later-in-time federal statute supersedes inconsistent treaty provisions."). However, it should be noted that this is a rule for dealing with conflicting legal instruments, and not properly speaking a rule of interpretation. Consequently, if Congress passes a statute that conflicts with an earlier treaty obligation, federal courts will view the second law as authoritative as matter of U.S. law, but that does not alter the existence of the original obligation. As a matter of *international law*, then, the United States may be in breach of its obligations under the original treaty, depending on whether the original treaty allowed for unilateral termination or not, and under what circumstances.

3.   *Treaties with First Nations.* Many treaties were signed by European countries and First Nations, and this practice continued with the United States. So, for example, the Dutch signed the Kaswentah treaty in 1613 with the Haudenosaunee, which pledged non-interference between the nations. Under international law, First Nations have international legal personality and therefore have the right to negotiate and sign treaties. Article 37 of the UN Declaration on the Rights of Indigenous Peoples states that: "Indigenous peoples have the right to the recognition, observance and enforcement of treaties, agreements and other constructive arrangements concluded with States or their successors and to have States honour and respect such treaties, agreements and other constructive arrangements." Unfortunately, this obligation was not always upheld in practice, as the United States and other nations frequently negotiated and signed, but then broke, treaties with First Nations. For example, in *Cherokee Nation v. Georgia*, the Supreme Court ruled that it did not have jurisdiction to enforce a treaty between the Cherokee Nation and the State of Georgia because the Cherokee Nation was not a foreign state under the Constitution. Justice Marshall's majority opinion used language that was at once patronizing and offensive: "[T]hey are in a state of pupilage. Their relation to the United States resembles that of a ward to his guardian." 30 U.S. 1, 17 (1831). The Supreme Court changed course, ruling in 1832 that treaties with the Cherokee were enforceable: "The constitution, by declaring treaties already

made, as well as those to be made, to be the supreme law of the land, has adopted and sanctioned the previous treaties with the Indian nations, and, consequently, admits their rank among those powers who are capable of making treaties." *Worcester v. Georgia*, 31 U.S. 515, 519 (1832). The Supreme Court continues today to apply and enforce similar treaties, some of which were signed centuries ago. For example, in *Herrera v. Wyoming*, 139 S.Ct. 1686 (2019), the Supreme Court upheld and enforced an 1868 treaty signed between the Crow Tribe and the United States that granted hunting, fishing, and gathering rights on lands within Bighorn National Forest; the Court held that these rights did not expire when Wyoming was granted statehood. The use of treaties with First Nations to negotiate the purchase of land in exchange for other promises, which were then ignored or breached, was central to European colonization of North America—perhaps just as much as military conquest. For a discussion of international law and the role of treaties in the colonization of North America, see Saliha Belmessous (ed.), *Empire by Treaty: Negotiating European Expansion, 1600–1900* (2015).

B. RESERVATIONS TO TREATIES

What if a state disagrees with a proposed provision of a treaty? In a bilateral treaty, the state will simply negotiate to have the provision changed; without a satisfactory resolution of the issue, the state will not sign the treaty. However, things get much more complicated in a multilateral context when dozens of states are negotiating and drafting a treaty. One possibility is to simply require *every* state to accept the *entire* treaty. This rule would require that multilateral conventions be boiled down to the lowest common denominator. Instead, states are generally allowed to sign and ratify treaties but include a reservation exempting themselves from the application of a particular provision in the treaty.

As you read the following case from the International Court of Justice, identify the reasons that the ICJ identified in favor of allowing reservations. Also, are all reservations permissible? If not, what standard did the ICJ identify for when reservations would be accepted? Finally, who decides whether a treaty reservation is acceptable?

Reservations to the Convention on the Prevention and Punishment of the Crime of Genocide

International Court of Justice
1951 I.C.J. 15

. . .It is well established that in its treaty relations a State cannot be bound without its consent, and that consequently no reservation can be effective against any State without its agreement thereto. It is also a generally recognized principle that a multilateral convention is the result of an agreement freely concluded upon its clauses and that consequently none of the contracting parties is entitled to frustrate or impair, by means of unilateral decisions or particular agreements, the purpose and raison d'etre of the convention. To this principle was linked the notion of the integrity of the convention as adopted, a notion which in its traditional concept involved the proposition that no reservation was valid unless it was accepted by all the contracting parties without exception, as would have been the case if it had been stated during the negotiations.

This concept, which is directly inspired by the notion of contract, is of undisputed value as a principle. However, as regards the Genocide Convention, it is proper to refer to a variety of circumstances which would lead to a more flexible application of this principle. Among these circumstances may be noted the clearly universal character of the United Nations under whose auspices the Convention was concluded, and the very wide degree of participation envisaged by Article XI of the Convention. Extensive participation in conventions of this type has already given rise to greater flexibility in the international practice concerning multilateral conventions. More general resort to reservations, very great allowance made for tacit assent to reservations, the existence of practices which go so far as to admit that the author of reservations which have been rejected by certain contracting parties is nevertheless to be regarded as a party to the convention in relation to those contracting parties that have accepted the reservations-all these factors are manifestations of a new need for flexibility in the operation of multilateral conventions.

It must also be pointed out that although the Genocide Convention was finally approved unanimously, it is nevertheless the result of a series of majority votes. The majority principle, while facilitating the conclusion of multilateral conventions, may also make it necessary for certain States to make reservations. This observation is confirmed by the great number of reservations which have been made of recent years to multilateral conventions. In this state of international practice, it could certainly not be inferred from the absence of an article providing for reservations in a multilateral convention that the contracting States are prohibited from making certain reservations. Account should also be taken of the fact that the absence of such an article or even the decision not to insert such an article can be explained by the desire not to invite a multiplicity of reservations. The character of a multilateral convention, its purpose, provisions, mode of preparation and adoption, are factors which must be considered in determining, in the absence of any express provision on the subject, the possibility of making reservations, as well as their validity and effect.

Although it was decided during the preparatory work not to insert a special article on reservations, it is none the less true that the faculty for States to make reservations was contemplated at successive stages of the drafting of the Convention. . . Certain delegates clearly announced that their governments could only sign or ratify the Convention subject to certain reservations. . .

The Court recognizes that an understanding was reached within the General Assembly on the faculty to make reservations to the Genocide Convention and that it is permitted to conclude therefrom that States becoming parties to the Convention gave their assent thereto.

It must now determine what kind of reservations may be made and what kind of objections may be taken to them. The solution of these problems must be found in the special characteristics of the Genocide Convention. The origins and character of that Convention, the objects pursued by the General Assembly and the contracting parties, the relations which exist between the provisions of the Convention, inter se, and between those provisions and these objects, furnish elements of interpretation of the will of the General Assembly and the parties. The origins of the Convention show that it was the intention of the United Nations to condemn and punish genocide as "a crime under international law" involving a denial of the right of existence of entire human groups, a denial which shocks the conscience of mankind and results in great losses to humanity, and which is contrary to moral law and to the spirit and aims of the United Nations. The first consequence arising from this conception is that the principles underlying the Convention are principles which are recognized by civilized nations as binding on States, even without any conventional obligation. A second consequence is the universal character both of the condemnation of genocide and of the co-operation required "in order to liberate mankind from such an odious scourge" (Preamble to the Convention). The Genocide Convention was therefore intended by the General Assembly and by the contracting parties to be definitely universal in scope. It was in fact approved on December 9th, 1948, by a resolution which was unanimously adopted by fifty-six States.

The objects of such a convention must also be considered. The Convention was manifestly adopted for a purely humanitarian and civilizing purpose. It is indeed difficult to imagine a convention that might have this dual character to a greater degree, since its object on the one hand is to safeguard the very existence of certain human groups and on the other to confirm and endorse the most elementary principles of morality. In such a convention the contracting States do not have any interests of their own; they merely have, one and all, a common interest, namely, the accomplishment of those high purposes which are the raison d'etre of the convention. Consequently, in a convention of this type one cannot speak of individual advantages or disadvantages to States, or of the maintenance of a perfect contractual balance between rights and duties. The high ideals which inspired the Convention provide, by virtue of the common will of the parties, the foundation and measure of all its provisions.

The foregoing considerations, when applied to the question of reservations, and more particularly to the effects of objections to reservations, lead to the following conclusions. The object and purpose of the Genocide Convention imply that it was the intention of the General Assembly and of the States which adopted it that as many States as possible should participate. The complete exclusion from the Convention of one or more States would not only restrict the scope of its application, but would detract from the authority of the moral and humanitarian principles which are its basis. It is inconceivable that the contracting parties readily contemplated that an objection to a minor reservation should produce such a result. But even less could the contracting parties have intended to sacrifice the very object of the Convention in favour of a vain desire to secure as many participants as possible. The object and purpose of the Convention thus limit both the freedom of making reservations and that of objecting to them.

It follows that it is the compatibility of a reservation with the object and purpose of the Convention that must furnish the criterion for the attitude of a State in making the reservation on accession as well as for the appraisal by a State in objecting to the reservation. Such is the rule of conduct which must guide every State in the appraisal which it must make, individually and from its own standpoint, of the admissibility of any reservation. Any other view would lead either to the acceptance of reservations which frustrate the purposes which the General Assembly and the contracting parties had in mind, or to recognition that the parties to the Convention have the power of excluding from it the author of a reservation, even a minor one, which may be quite compatible with those purposes.

It has nevertheless been argued that any State entitled to become a party to the Genocide Convention may do so while making any reservation it chooses by virtue of its sovereignty. The Court cannot share this view. It is obvious that so extreme an application of the idea of State sovereignty could lead to a complete disregard of the object and purpose of the Convention.

On the other hand, it has been argued that there exists a rule of international law subjecting the effect of a reservation to the express or tacit assent of all the contracting parties. This theory rests essentially on a contractual conception of the absolute integrity of the convention as adopted. This view, however, cannot prevail if, having regard to the character of the convention, its purpose and its mode of adoption, it can be established that the parties intended to derogate from that rule by admitting the faculty to make reservations thereto. It does not appear, moreover, that the conception of the absolute integrity of a convention has been transformed into a rule of international law. The considerable part which tacit assent has always played in estimating the effect which is to be given to reservations scarcely permits one to state that such a rule exists, determining with sufficient precision the effect of objections made to reservations. In fact, the examples of objections made to reservations appear to be too rare in international practice to have given rise to such a rule. . .

It may, however, be asked whether the General Assembly of the United Nations, in approving the Genocide Convention, had in mind the practice according to which the Secretary-General, in exercising his functions as a depositary, did not regard a reservation as definitively accepted until it had been established that none of the other contracting States objected to it. If this were the case, it might be argued that the implied intention of the contracting parties was to make the effectiveness of any reservation to the Genocide Convention conditional on the assent of all the parties. The Court does not consider that this view corresponds to reality. It must be pointed out, first of all, that the existence of an administrative practice does not in itself constitute a decisive factor in ascertaining what views the contracting States to the Genocide Convention may have had concerning the rights and duties resulting therefrom. It must also be pointed out that there existed among the American States members both of the United Nations and of the Organization of American States, a different practice which goes so far as to permit a reserving State to become a party irrespective of the nature of the reservations or of the objections raised by other contracting States. The preparatory work of the Convention contains nothing to justify the statement that the contracting States implicitly had any definite practice in mind. . .

As has been pointed out above, each State which is a party to the Convention is entitled to appraise the validity of the reservation, and it exercises this right individually and from its own standpoint. As no State can be bound by a reservation to which it has not consented, it necessarily follows that each State objecting to it will or will not, on the basis of its individual appraisal within the limits of the criterion of the object and purpose stated above, consider the reserving State to be a party to the Convention. In the ordinary course of events, such a decision will only affect the relationship between the State making the reservation and the objecting State; on the other hand, as will be pointed out later, such a decision might aim at the complete exclusion from the Convention in a case where it was expressed by the adoption of a position on the jurisdictional plane.

The disadvantages which result from this possible divergence of views—which an article concerning the making of reservations could have obviated—are real; they are mitigated by the common duty of the contracting States to be guided in their judgment by the compatibility or incompatibility of the reservation with the object and purpose of the Convention. It must clearly be assumed that the contracting States are desirous of preserving intact at least what is essential to the object of the Convention; should this desire be absent, it is quite clear that the Convention itself would be impaired both in its principle and in its application. . .

Finally, it may be that a State, whilst not claiming that a reservation is incompatible with the object and purpose of the Convention, will nevertheless object to it, but that an understanding between that State and the reserving State will have the effect that the Convention will enter into force between them, except for the clauses affected by the reservation. . .

THE COURT IS OF OPINION, [i]n so far as concerns the Convention on the Prevention and Punishment of the Crime of Genocide, in the event of a State ratifying or acceding to the Convention subject to a reservation made either on ratification or on accession, or on signature followed by ratification, On Question I: by seven votes to five, that a State which has made and maintained a reservation which has been objected to by one or more of the parties to the Convention but not by others, can be regarded as being a party to the Convention if the reservation is compatible with the object and purpose of the Convention; otherwise, that State cannot be regarded as being a party to the Convention.

NOTES & QUESTIONS

1.   *Reservations Reconsidered.* Has the system of reservations worked out in practice as the ICJ envisioned? Recall that the ICJ suggested that the parties to the treaty itself would participate in a decentralized system of enforcing reservations, by determining which ones were consistent with the object and purpose of the treaty, and by extension, whether the reserving state should be considered a party to the agreement. In practice, do states scrutinize reservations issued by other parties and declare the state a non-party when their reservations run afoul of this standard? Consider the following statement from a dissenting opinion in the ICJ's decision *Armed Activities on the Territory of the Congo (DRC v. Rwanda)*, 2006 ICJ 126: "the Court in 1951 was clearly not unaware of the hazards inherent in its answers, in the sense that they would entail a veritable web of diverse reciprocal commitments within the framework of a multilateral convention." However, "the problems which the Court could already envisage in 1951 have turned out to be vastly greater than it could have foreseen. The Genocide Convention stood virtually alone in the sphere of human rights in 1951. Since then it has been added to by a plethora of reservations—often of a nature that give serious concern as to compatibility with the object and purpose of the treaty concerned. And the vast majority of states, who the Court in 1951 envisaged would scrutinize and object to such reservations, have failed to

engage in this task." With this information in mind, should the rule regarding treaty reservations be reversed?

2.   *CEDAW and Sharia.* Consider the Convention on the Elimination of All Forms of Discrimination against Women (CEDAW), which was finalized in 1979 and entered into force in 1981. Many human rights lawyers refer to CEDAW as an international bill of rights for women. For example, Article 15(2) declares that "States Parties shall accord to women, in civil matters, a legal capacity identical to that of men and the same opportunities to exercise that capacity. In particular, they shall give women equal rights to conclude contracts and to administer property and shall treat them equally in all stages of procedure in courts and tribunals." In signing the Convention, the United Arab Emirates included a reservation that stated that "The United Arab Emirates, considering this paragraph in conflict with the precepts of the sharia regarding legal capacity, testimony and the right to conclude contracts, makes a reservation to the said paragraph of the said article and does not consider itself bound by the provisions thereof." The UAE also issued reservations for several other provisions that were in conflict with Sharia law, as did several other nations. In response, the government of Denmark deposited the following statement: "The Government of Denmark considers that the reservations. . . referring to the contents of the sharia Law do not clearly specify the extent to which the United Arab Emirates feel committed to the object and purpose of the Convention. Consequently, the Government of Denmark considers the said reservations as being incompatible with the object and purpose of the Convention and accordingly inadmissible and without effect under international law."

3.   *Understandings and Declarations.* State parties also have the option of filing understandings and declarations, instead of reservations. In many cases the difference between a reservation and an understanding is rather formalistic. In theory, a reservation indicates that the state party accepts an interpretation of a particular norm but clarifies that it does not consider itself bound by the provision. In contrast, an understanding clarifies that the state understands the norm in a particular way, and its consent to the norm is conditional on that interpretation. For example, when the United States signed the International Covenant on Civil and Political Rights (ICCPR), it included the following understanding: "That the Constitution and laws of the United States guarantee all persons equal protection of the law and provide extensive protections against discrimination. The United States understands distinctions based upon race, colour, sex, language, religion, political or other opinion, national or social origin, property, birth or any other status—as those terms are used in article 2, paragraph 1 and article 26—to be permitted when such distinctions are, at minimum, rationally related to a legitimate governmental objective." In fact, the U.S. government uses declarations and understandings far more often than actual reservations. For a discussion, see Cindy Galway Buys, *Conditions in U.S. Treaty Practice: New Data and Insights on A Growing Phenomenon*, 14 Santa Clara J. Int'l L. 363, 379 (2016) ("The more frequent occurrence of

declarations may result, in part, from the multiple types of declarations that exist—everything from stand-alone legally binding documents to statements that seek to clarify the meaning of a particular treaty term. It may also be the result of States trying to fit international treaty obligations into their different legal systems and cultures.").

C. THE FEDERAL TREATY POWER

Is there any limit or restriction on what may be regulated by treaty? Specifically, could a state regulate conduct through a treaty that it could not regulate through a domestic statute? The question is particularly acute in the United States, whose constitutional structure grants the federal government limited powers and reserves all remaining legislative powers to the individual states. In the following case, the Supreme Court is tasked with deciding whether the federal government could sign a treaty regulating migratory birds if the regulation could not be established through a regular federal statute. In other words, can the federal government use the treaty power as an end-run around the constitutional constraints on federalism?

Missouri v. Holland

Supreme Court of the United States
252 U.S. 416 (1920)

■ MR. JUSTICE HOLMES delivered the opinion of the Court.

This is a bill in equity brought by the State of Missouri to prevent a game warden of the United States from attempting to enforce the Migratory Bird Treaty Act of July 3, 1918, and the regulations made by the Secretary of Agriculture in pursuance of the same. The ground of the bill is that the statute is an unconstitutional interference with the rights reserved to the States by the Tenth Amendment, and that the acts of the defendant done and threatened under that authority invade the sovereign right of the State and contravene its will manifested in statutes. The State also alleges a pecuniary interest, as owner of the wild birds within its borders and otherwise, admitted by the Government to be sufficient, but it is enough that the bill is a reasonable and proper means to assert the alleged quasi sovereign rights of a State. A motion to dismiss was sustained by the District Court on the ground that the Act of Congress is constitutional. The State appeals.

On December 8, 1916, a treaty between the United States and Great Britain was proclaimed by the President. It recited that many species of birds in their annual migrations traversed many parts of the United States and of Canada, that they were of great value as a source of food and in destroying insects injurious to vegetation, but were in danger of extermination through lack of adequate protection. It therefore provided

for specified closed seasons and protection in other forms, and agreed
that the two powers would take or propose to their lawmaking bodies the
necessary measures for carrying the treaty out. The above mentioned act
of July 3, 1918, entitled an act to give effect to the convention, prohibited
the killing, capturing or selling any of the migratory birds included in the
terms of the treaty except as permitted by regulations compatible with
those terms, to be made by the Secretary of Agriculture. Regulations
were proclaimed on July 31, and October 25, 1918. It is unnecessary to
go into any details, because, as we have said, the question raised is the
general one whether the treaty and statute are void as an interference
with the rights reserved to the States.

To answer this question it is not enough to refer to the Tenth
Amendment, reserving the powers not delegated to the United States,
because by Article 2, Section 2, the power to make treaties is delegated
expressly, and by Article 6 treaties made under the authority of the
United States, along with the Constitution and laws of the United States
made in pursuance thereof, are declared the supreme law of the land. If
the treaty is valid there can be no dispute about the validity of the statute
under Article 1, Section 8, as a necessary and proper means to execute
the powers of the Government. The language of the Constitution as to the
supremacy of treaties being general, the question before us is narrowed
to an inquiry into the ground upon which the present supposed exception
is placed.

It is said that a treaty cannot be valid if it infringes the Constitution,
that there are limits, therefore, to the treaty-making power, and that one
such limit is that what an act of Congress could not do unaided, in
derogation of the powers reserved to the States, a treaty cannot do. An
earlier act of Congress that attempted by itself and not in pursuance of a
treaty to regulate the killing of migratory birds within the States had
been held bad in the District Court. Those decisions were supported by
arguments that migratory birds were owned by the States in their
sovereign capacity for the benefit of their people, and that under cases
like *Geer v. Connecticut*, 161 U.S. 519, this control was one that Congress
had no power to displace. The same argument is supposed to apply now
with equal force.

Whether the two cases cited were decided rightly or not they cannot
be accepted as a test of the treaty power. Acts of Congress are the
supreme law of the land only when made in pursuance of the
Constitution, while treaties are declared to be so when made under the
authority of the United States. It is open to question whether the
authority of the United States means more than the formal acts
prescribed to make the convention. We do not mean to imply that there
are no qualifications to the treaty-making power; but they must be
ascertained in a different way. It is obvious that there may be matters of

the sharpest exigency for the national well being that an act of Congress could not deal with but that a treaty followed by such an act could, and it is not lightly to be assumed that, in matters requiring national action, "a power which must belong to and somewhere reside in every civilized government" is not to be found. *Andrews v. Andrews*, 188 U.S. 14, 33. What was said in that case with regard to the powers of the States applies with equal force to the powers of the nation in cases where the States individually are incompetent to act. We are not yet discussing the particular case before us but only are considering the validity of the test proposed. With regard to that we may add that when we are dealing with words that also are a constituent act, like the Constitution of the United States, we must realize that they have called into life a being the development of which could not have been foreseen completely by the most gifted of its begetters. It was enough for them to realize or to hope that they had created an organism; it has taken a century and has cost their successors much sweat and blood to prove that they created a nation. The case before us must be considered in the light of our whole experience and not merely in that of what was said a hundred years ago. The treaty in question does not contravene any prohibitory words to be found in the Constitution. The only question is whether it is forbidden by some invisible radiation from the general terms of the Tenth Amendment. We must consider what this country has become in deciding what that amendment has reserved.

The State as we have intimated founds its claim of exclusive authority upon an assertion of title to migratory birds, an assertion that is embodied in statute. No doubt it is true that as between a State and its inhabitants the State may regulate the killing and sale of such birds, but it does not follow that its authority is exclusive of paramount powers. To put the claim of the State upon title is to lean upon a slender reed. Wild birds are not in the possession of anyone; and possession is the beginning of ownership. The whole foundation of the State's rights is the presence within their jurisdiction of birds that yesterday had not arrived, tomorrow may be in another State and in a week a thousand miles away. If we are to be accurate we cannot put the case of the State upon higher ground than that the treaty deals with creatures that for the moment are within the state borders, that it must be carried out by officers of the United States within the same territory, and that but for the treaty the State would be free to regulate this subject itself.

As most of the laws of the United States are carried out within the States and as many of them deal with matters which in the silence of such laws the State might regulate, such general grounds are not enough to support Missouri's claim. Valid treaties of course "are as binding within the territorial limits of the States as they are elsewhere throughout the dominion of the United States." No doubt the great body of private relations usually fall within the control of the State, but a treaty may override its power. . .

Here a national interest of very nearly the first magnitude is involved. It can be protected only by national action in concert with that of another power. The subject matter is only transitorily within the State and has no permanent habitat therein. But for the treaty and the statute there soon might be no birds for any powers to deal with. We see nothing in the Constitution that compels the Government to sit by while a food supply is cut off and the protectors of our forests and our crops are destroyed. It is not sufficient to rely upon the States. The reliance is vain, and were it otherwise, the question is whether the United States is forbidden to act. We are of opinion that the treaty and statute must be upheld.

The next case, *Reid v. Covert*, presents a similar issue but in a unique context. The question is whether an international agreement can override the constitutional protections articulated in the Bill of Rights. As you read the case, ask yourself whether the reasoning from *Missouri v. Holland* applies with equal force to the defendants in this case. If the federal government can use the treaty power to regulate activity that it could not regulate through a federal statute, can the federal government also use a treaty to vitiate the constitutional right to a jury trial?

Reid v. Covert

Supreme Court of the United States
354 U.S. 1 (1957)

■ MR. JUSTICE BLACK announced the judgment of the Court and delivered an opinion, in which THE CHIEF JUSTICE, MR. JUSTICE DOUGLAS, and MR. JUSTICE BRENNAN join.

These cases raise basic constitutional issues of the utmost concern. They call into question the role of the military under our system of government. They involve the power of Congress to expose civilians to trial by military tribunals, under military regulations and procedures, for offenses against the United States thereby depriving them of trial in civilian courts, under civilian laws and procedures and with all the safeguards of the Bill of Rights. These cases are particularly significant because for the first time since the adoption of the Constitution wives of soldiers have been denied trial by jury in a court of law and forced to trial before courts-martial.

In No. 701 Mrs. Clarice Covert killed her husband, a sergeant in the United States Air Force, at an airbase in England. Mrs. Covert, who was not a member of the armed services, was residing on the base with her husband at the time. She was tried by a court-martial for murder under Article 118 of the Uniform Code of Military Justice (UCMJ). The trial was on charges preferred by Air Force personnel and the court-martial was composed of Air Force officers.

The court-martial asserted jurisdiction over Mrs. Covert under Article 2(11) of the UCMJ, which provides: "The following persons are subject to this code: (11) Subject to the provisions of any treaty or agreement to which the United States is or may be a party or to any accepted rule of international law, all persons serving with, employed by, or accompanying the armed forces without the continental limits of the United States. . ."

Counsel for Mrs. Covert contended that she was insane at the time she killed her husband, but the military tribunal found her guilty of murder and sentenced her to life imprisonment. . .

In No. 713 Mrs. Dorothy Smith killed her husband, an Army officer, at a post in Japan where she was living with him. She was tried for murder by a court-martial and despite considerable evidence that she was insane was found guilty and sentenced to life imprisonment. . .

The two cases were consolidated and argued last Term and a majority of the Court, with three Justices dissenting and one reserving opinion, held that military trial of Mrs. Smith and Mrs. Covert for their alleged offenses was constitutional. The majority held that the provisions of Article III and the Fifth and Sixth Amendments which require that crimes be tried by a jury after indictment by a grand jury did not protect an American citizen when he was tried by the American Government in foreign lands for offenses committed there and that Congress could provide for the trial of such offenses in any manner it saw fit so long as the procedures established were reasonable and consonant with due process. . .

Subsequently, the Court granted a petition for rehearing. Now, after further argument and consideration, we conclude that the previous decisions cannot be permitted to stand. . . We hold that Mrs. Smith and Mrs. Covert could not constitutionally be tried by military authorities.

I

At the beginning we reject the idea that when the United States acts against citizens abroad it can do so free of the Bill of Rights. The United States is entirely a creature of the Constitution. Its power and authority have no other source. It can only act in accordance with all the limitations imposed by the Constitution. When the Government reaches out to punish a citizen who is abroad, the shield which the Bill of Rights and other parts of the Constitution provide to protect his life and liberty should not be stripped away just because he happens to be in another land. This is not a novel concept. To the contrary, it is as old as government. It was recognized long before Paul successfully invoked his right as a Roman citizen to be tried in strict accordance with Roman law. . . The rights and liberties which citizens of our country enjoy are not protected by custom and tradition alone, they have been jealously preserved from the encroachments of Government by express provisions of our written Constitution.

Among those provisions, Art. III, s 2 and the Fifth and Sixth Amendments are directly relevant to these cases. . . The language of Art. III, s 2 manifests that constitutional protections for the individual were designed to restrict the United States Government when it acts outside of this country, as well as here at home. After declaring that all criminal trials must be by jury, the section states that when a crime is "not committed within any State, the Trial shall be at such Place or Places as the Congress may by Law have directed." If this language is permitted to have its obvious meaning, s 2 is applicable to criminal trials outside of the States as a group without regard to where the offense is committed or the trial held. From the very first Congress, federal statutes have implemented the provisions of s 2 by providing for trial of murder and other crimes committed outside the jurisdiction of any State "in the district where the offender is apprehended, or into which he may first be brought." The Fifth and Sixth Amendments, like Art. III, s 2, are also all inclusive with their sweeping references to "no person" and to "all criminal prosecutions."

This Court and other federal courts have held or asserted that various constitutional limitations apply to the Government when it acts outside the continental United States. While it has been suggested that only those constitutional rights which are "fundamental" protect Americans abroad, we can find no warrant, in logic or otherwise, for picking and choosing among the remarkable collection of "Thou shalt nots" which were explicitly fastened on all departments and agencies of the Federal Government by the Constitution and its Amendments. Moreover, in view of our heritage and the history of the adoption of the Constitution and the Bill of Rights, it seems peculiarly anomalous to say that trial before a civilian judge and by an independent jury picked from the common citizenry is not a fundamental right. . .

Trial by jury in a court of law and in accordance with traditional modes of procedure after an indictment by grand jury has served and remains one of our most vital barriers to governmental arbitrariness. These elemental procedural safeguards were embedded in our Constitution to secure their inviolateness and sanctity against the passing demands of expediency or convenience. . .

II

At the time of Mrs. Covert's alleged offense, an executive agreement was in effect between the United States and Great Britain which permitted United States' military courts to exercise exclusive jurisdiction over offenses committed in Great Britain by American servicemen or their dependents. For its part, the United States agreed that these military courts would be willing and able to try and to punish all offenses against the laws of Great Britain by such persons. In all material respects, the same situation existed in Japan when Mrs. Smith killed her husband. Even though a court-martial does not give an accused trial by jury and other Bill of Rights protections, the Government contends that article 2(11) of UCMJ, insofar as it provides for the military trial of dependents accompanying the armed forces in Great Britain and Japan, can be sustained as legislation which is necessary and proper to carry out the United States' obligations under the international agreements made with those countries. The obvious and decisive answer to this, of course, is that no agreement with a foreign nation can confer power on the Congress, or on any other branch of Government, which is free from the restraints of the Constitution.

Article VI, the Supremacy Clause of the Constitution, declares: "This Constitution, and the Laws of the United States which shall be made in Pursuance thereof; and all Treaties made, or which shall be made, under the Authority of the United States, shall be the supreme Law of the Land. . ." There is nothing in this language which intimates that treaties and laws enacted pursuant to them do not have to comply with the provisions of the Constitution. Nor is there anything in the debates which accompanied the drafting and ratification of the Constitution which even suggests such a result. These debates as well as the history that surrounds the adoption of the treaty provision in Article VI make it clear that the reason treaties were not limited to those made in "pursuance" of the Constitution was so that agreements made by the United States under the Articles of Confederation, including the important peace treaties which concluded the Revolutionary War, would remain in effect. It would be manifestly contrary to the objectives of those who created the Constitution, as well as those who were responsible for the Bill of Rights—let alone alien to our entire constitutional history and tradition—to construe Article VI as permitting the United States to exercise power under an international agreement without observing constitutional prohibitions. In effect, such construction would permit amendment of that document in a manner not sanctioned by Article V. The prohibitions of the Constitution were designed to apply to all branches of the National Government and they cannot be nullified by the Executive or by the Executive and the Senate combined.

There is nothing new or unique about what we say here. This Court has regularly and uniformly recognized the supremacy of the Constitution over a treaty. . .

This Court has also repeatedly taken the position that an Act of Congress, which must comply with the Constitution, is on a full parity with a treaty, and that when a statute which is subsequent in time is inconsistent with a treaty, the statute to the extent of conflict renders the treaty null. It would be completely anomalous to say that a treaty need not comply with the Constitution when such an agreement can be overridden by a statute that must conform to that instrument.

There is nothing in *Missouri v. Holland* which is contrary to the position taken here. There the Court carefully noted that the treaty involved was not inconsistent with any specific provision of the Constitution. The Court was concerned with the Tenth Amendment which reserves to the States or the people all power not delegated to the National Government. To the extent that the United States can validly make treaties, the people and the States have delegated their power to the National Government and the Tenth Amendment is no barrier.

In summary, we conclude that the Constitution in its entirety applied to the trials of Mrs. Smith and Mrs. Covert. Since their court-martial did not meet the requirements of Art. III, s 2, or the Fifth and Sixth Amendments we are compelled to determine if there is anything within the Constitution which authorizes the military trial of dependents accompanying the armed forces overseas.

III

Article I, s 8, cl. 14, empowers Congress "To make Rules for the Government and Regulation of the land and naval Forces." It has been held that this creates an exception to the normal method of trial in civilian courts as provided by the Constitution and permits Congress to authorize military trial of members of the armed services without all the safeguards given an accused by Article III and the Bill of Rights. But if the language of Clause 14 is given its natural meaning, the power granted does not extend to civilians—even though they may be dependents living with servicemen on a military base. The term "land and naval Forces" refers to persons who are members of the armed services and not to their civilian wives, children and other dependents. It seems inconceivable that Mrs. Covert or Mrs. Smith could have been tried by military authorities as members of the "land and naval Forces" had they been living on a military post in this country. Yet this constitutional term surely has the same meaning everywhere. The wives of servicemen are no more members of the "land and naval Forces" when living at a military post in England or Japan than when living at a base in this country or in Hawaii or Alaska. . .

We should not break faith with this nation's tradition of keeping military power subservient to civilian authority, a tradition which we believe is firmly embodied in the Constitution. The country has remained true to that faith for almost one hundred seventy years. Perhaps no group in the Nation has been truer than military men themselves. Unlike the soldiers of many other nations, they have been content to perform their military duties in defense of the Nation in every period of need and to perform those duties well without attempting to usurp power which is not theirs under our system of constitutional government. . .

Ours is a government of divided authority on the assumption that in division there is not only strength but freedom from tyranny. And under our Constitution courts of law alone are given power to try civilians for their offenses against the United States. . .

NOTES & QUESTIONS

1.   *Individual Rights.* Is *Missouri v. Holland* still good law after *Reid v. Covert*? What explains the different outcomes in the case? *Reid* involved an individual right, as opposed to the relative balance of power between Congress and the states. The Court in *Reid* notes that the power to conduct treaties was delegated by the states to the federal government. However, there is nothing in the Constitution that allows a federal treaty to abrogate the individual protections articulated in the Fifth and Sixth Amendments. Do you agree with this reasoning?

2.   *Limits on Missouri v. Holland?* After *Missouri v. Holland*, the Supreme Court did not have occasion to revisit its holding for many years, even though some legal commentators disapproved of its expansive interpretation of the federal treaty power. In 2014, the Supreme Court heard *Bond v. United States*, 572 U.S. 844, reprinted above, regarding the Chemical Weapons Convention and its companion federal implementing statute, 18 U.S.C. § 229(a)(1). At the time, many observers believed that the Supreme Court granted certiorari to revisit and limit, or even overrule, its original holding in *Missouri v. Holland*. Bond had argued unsuccessfully before the Court of Appeals that the statute was unconstitutional because it intruded "on the traditional state prerogative to punish assaults." *Bond*, 681 F.3d 149, 153 (3d Cir. 2012). However, the Supreme Court declined Bond's invitation to revisit or limit *Missouri*'s central holding and instead resolved the case in Bond's favor based on grounds of statutory and treaty interpretation. *Missouri* remains the law of the land.

D. SELF-EXECUTING VERSUS NON-SELF-EXECUTING TREATIES

In the United States, treaties are not necessarily enforceable in court as federal law. Federal courts generally distinguish between self-executing and non-self-executive treaties. The former are treaties ratified by the Senate with the expectation that they will become enforceable as federal law without any further domestic implementing legislation. In contrast, non-self-executing treaties are not enforceable in federal court absent domestic legislation. As you read the following case, ask yourself why the Supreme Court distinguishes treaties in this way.

Foster v. Neilson

Supreme Court of the United States
27 U.S. 253 (1829)

■ MR. CHIEF JUSTICE MARSHALL delivered the opinion of the Court.

This suit was brought by the plaintiffs in error in the court of the United States, for the eastern district of Louisiana, to recover a tract of land lying in that district, about thirty miles east of the Mississippi, and in the possession of the defendant. The plaintiffs claimed under a grant for 40,000 arpents of land, made by the Spanish governor, on the 2d of January 1804, to Jayme Joydra, and ratified by the king of Spain on the 29th of May 1804. The petition and order of survey are dated in September 1803, and the return of the survey itself was made on the 27th of October in the same year. The defendant excepted to the petition of the plaintiffs, alleging that it does not show a title on which they can recover; that the territory, within which the land claimed is situated, had been ceded, before the grant, to France, and by France to the United States; and that the grant is void, being made by persons who had no authority to make it. The court sustained the exception, and dismissed the petition. The cause is brought before this Court by a writ of error.

The case presents this very intricate, and at one time very interesting question: To whom did the country between the Iberville and the Perdido rightfully belong, when the title now asserted by the plaintiffs was acquired? . . .

In a controversy between two nations concerning national boundary, it is scarcely possible that the courts of either should refuse to abide by the measures adopted by its own government. There being no common tribunal to decide between them, each determines for itself on its own rights, and if they cannot adjust their differences peaceably, the right remains with the strongest. The judiciary is not that department of the government, to which the assertion of its interests against foreign powers is confided; and its duty commonly is to decide upon individual rights, according to those principles which the political departments of the nation have established. If the course of the nation has been a plain one, its courts would hesitate to pronounce it erroneous. . .

After these acts of sovereign power over the territory in dispute, asserting the American construction of the treaty by which the government claims it, to maintain the opposite construction in its own courts would certainly be an anomaly in the history and practice of nations. If those departments which are entrusted with the foreign intercourse of the nation, which assert and maintain its interests against foreign powers, have unequivocally asserted its rights of dominion over a country of which it is in possession, and which it claims under a treaty; if the legislature has acted on the construction thus asserted, it is not in its own courts that this construction is to be denied. A question like this respecting the boundaries of nations, is, as has been truly said, more a political than a legal question; and in its discussion, the courts of every country must respect the pronounced will of the legislature. . .

A treaty is in its nature a contract between two nations, not a legislative act. It does not generally effect, of itself, the object to be accomplished, especially so far as its operation is infra-territorial; but is carried into execution by the sovereign power of the respective parties to the instrument.

In the United States a different principle is established. Our constitution declares a treaty to be the law of the land. It is, consequently, to be regarded in courts of justice as equivalent to an act of the legislature, whenever it operates of itself without the aid of any legislative provision. But when the terms of the stipulation import a contract, when either of the parties engages to perform a particular act, the treaty addresses itself to the political, not the judicial department; and the legislature must execute the contract before it can become a rule for the Court. . .

Congress has reserved to itself the supervision of the titles reported by its commissioners, and has confirmed those which the commissioners have approved, but has passed no law, withdrawing grants generally for lands west of the Perdido from the operation of the 14th section of the act of 1804, or repealing that section.

We are of opinion then, that the court committed no error in dismissing the petition of the plaintiff, and that the judgment ought to be affirmed with costs.

NOTES & QUESTIONS

1. *The Supremacy Clause.* Is the concept of a non-self-executing treaty consistent with the Constitution's Supremacy Clause, which specifically declares that the "the Constitution, federal laws made pursuant to it, and treaties made under its authority, constitute the supreme law of the land." According to some scholars, a judicial declaration that a treaty is non-self-executing essentially removes the treaty from the orbit of federal law, in a way not contemplated by the drafters of the Supremacy Clause. Do you think the distinction between self-executing and non-self-executing treaties is consistent with the original meaning of the Constitution? For example, consider the views of Professor David Sloss: "The Framers included treaties

in the Supremacy Clause to help promote U.S. compliance with its treaty obligations. Whenever a court holds that a treaty is non-self-executing, that holding, if it matters at all, yields one of two results: (a) the court refuses to provide a remedy for an acknowledged treaty violation; or (b) the court refuses to decide whether the treaty has been violated. In the former case, the refusal to provide a remedy undermines the goal of treaty compliance by signaling relevant individuals and organizations that they can violate treaty norms without fear of domestic judicial sanctions." David Sloss, *Non-Self-Executing Treaties: Exposing A Constitutional Fallacy*, 36 U.C. Davis L. Rev. 1, 16–17 (2002). For a contrary view, see John C. Yoo, *Globalism and the Constitution: Treaties, Non-Self-Execution, and the Original Understanding*, 99 Colum. L. Rev. 1955, 1962 (1999) ("The Treaty Clause had created a democracy gap, as it were, because vesting the power partially in the Senate and excluding the House threatened to remove the people's most direct representatives from an important lawmaking function. Including the President in the treatymaking process and allowing treaties to be rendered non-self-executing—and, hence, in need of implementing legislation—ensured that the treaty power would retain majoritarian roots.").

2.   *The Role of Dualism.* One reason why federal courts deny that non-self-executive treaties can be enforced in federal court is because U.S. legal culture is strongly dualist. In other words, international law and American law are separate legal systems, and the former must be formally adopted into the latter for it to have legal effect in the court system. In contrast, other nations with a more monist outlook view international law and their domestic law as part of a single global legal system, with international law occupying a privileged place in that order. Accordingly, a country with a monist outlook on international law will be more likely to give all treaties automatic effect in their domestic courts. For a discussion, see David Sloss, *Domestic Application of Treaties*, in *The Oxford Guide to Treaties* (Duncan Hollis ed. 2012).

E. INTERNATIONAL AGREEMENTS WITHOUT SENATE RATIFICATION

The definition of the term "treaty" changes depending on whether you refer to international law or U.S. law. Under international law, a treaty is any binding written instrument between two or more states that creates legal obligations. However, a "treaty" under U.S. law is an international agreement that requires the advice and consent of the Senate. However, federal courts have long recognized that presidents have the power to create other international legal agreements without Senate ratification. These include congressional-executive agreements and sole-executive agreements. Are there any limits to this power? Can a president always sign one of these agreements instead of a full treaty? Is the choice of agreement up to the discretion of the President? The

Supreme Court answers that question—or rather *refuses* to answer that question—in the context of NAFTA in the following case.

Made in the USA Foundation v. United States
U.S. Court of Appeals for the Eleventh Circuit
242 F.3d 1300 (2001)

■ BETTY C. FLETCHER, CIRCUIT JUDGE:

This case presents complex issues of first impression in this circuit in the realm of constitutional interpretation—namely, whether certain kinds of international commercial agreements are "treaties," as that term is employed in Article II, Section 2 of the United States Constitution; and if so, whether the Treaty Clause represents the sole means of enacting such agreements into law. The appellants, comprised of national and local labor organizations as well as a nonprofit group that promotes the purchase of American-made products, urge that the North American Free Trade Agreement (commonly referred to as "NAFTA") be declared unconstitutionally void, as it was never approved by a two-thirds supermajority of the United States Senate pursuant to the constitutionally-mandated procedures governing treaty ratification. The Government, on the other hand, invokes the political question doctrine and also claims that this court lacks jurisdiction due to the appellants' lack of standing. In addition, the Government argues on the merits that NAFTA's enactment did not require Senate ratification as a "treaty." The parties' respective arguments thus require us to engage constitutional issues of unusual breadth, complexity and import. . .

We agree with the district court that the appellants have standing in this matter, and affirm the principle, as enunciated by the U.S. Supreme Court, that certain international agreements may well require Senate ratification as treaties through the constitutionally-mandated procedures of Art. II, § 2. *See, e.g., Holden v. Joy,* 84 U.S. 211, 242–43 (1872); *Missouri v. Holland,* 252 U.S. 416, 433 (1920). We nonetheless decline to reach the merits of this particular case, finding that with respect to international commercial agreements such as NAFTA, the question of just what constitutes a "treaty" requiring Senate ratification presents a nonjusticiable political question. Accordingly, we dismiss the appeal and remand with instructions to dismiss the action and vacate the decision of the district court.

I

The United States, Mexico and Canada entered negotiations in 1990 to create a "free trade zone" on the North American continent through the phased elimination or reduction of both tariff and non-tariff barriers to trade. Following extensive negotiations, the North American Free Trade Agreement was completed and signed by the leaders of the three countries on December 17, 1992. Through the passage of the NAFTA Implementation Act ("Implementation Act") on December 8, 1993, Congress approved NAFTA and provided for a series of domestic laws to effectuate and enforce NAFTA's provisions

Neither NAFTA nor the Implementation Act were subjected to the ratification procedures outlined in the Treaty Clause. Summoning primarily historical arguments, the appellants contend that this failure to go through the Art. II, § 2 procedures contravenes the original understanding of the Framers and therefore renders NAFTA and the Implementation Act unconstitutional. In support of their argument, the appellants marshal a considerable array of historical evidence. Relying heavily on the research of the late Arthur Bestor, a Professor of History at the University of Washington, the appellants claim that records from the Constitutional Convention evidence a careful and conscious decision on the part of the Framers to require a two-thirds Senate majority for approving treaties, with the deliberate intention of preventing national majorities from binding minority interests under the Supremacy Clause to international accords against their wishes. Furthermore, the appellants point to several early examples in our Nation's history (such as the Jay Treaty debate) when the United States entered into major commercial agreements with other countries, each of which was ratified as a treaty and approved by a two-thirds supermajority of the Senate.

Based on the near-contemporaneous writings of Emmerich de Vattel, the appellants contend that the key distinction in the minds of the Framers in determining whether a given agreement required ratification as a treaty turned on the relative importance of the accord; significant agreements were to be deemed treaties, while less important ones were to be considered compacts or executive agreements. Thus, according to the appellants, an accord such as NAFTA, with its wide-ranging scope and impact—including the harmonization of financial, commercial, labor, and environmental laws and regulations and the establishment of supranational adjudicatory bodies to settle disputes between the signatories—surely falls into the class of agreements which require ratification as a treaty. . .

Remarkably, although perhaps not altogether surprisingly, the United States Supreme Court has never in our nation's history seen fit to address the question of what exactly constitutes and distinguishes "treaties," as that term is used in Art. II, § 2, from "alliances," "confederations," "compacts," or "agreements," as those terms are employed in Art. I, § 10. Accordingly, the Court has never decided what sorts of international agreements, if any, might require Senate ratification pursuant to the procedures outlined in Art. II, § 2. . .

III

. . .According to the Government, because the text of the Constitution fails to define what is meant by a "treaty" or to dictate the proper procedure for approving international commercial agreements, and because the Constitution has clearly granted the political branches an enormous amount of authority in the areas of foreign affairs and commerce, the choice of what procedure to use for a given agreement is committed to the discretion and expertise of the Legislative and Executive Branches by virtue of the political question doctrine. We substantially agree with the Government's contentions that this case does not present the type of question that can be properly addressed by the judiciary, given our belief that Supreme Court precedent and historical practice confirm the wisdom of maintaining the practice of judicial nonintervention into such matters. . .

The political question doctrine emerges out of Article III's case or controversy requirement and has its roots in separation of powers concerns. *Baker v. Carr,* 369 U.S. 186, 210 (1962). In *Baker,* the Supreme Court enumerated six criteria that courts should consider in determining whether a case is nonjusticiable:

> Prominent on the surface of any case held to involve a political question is found (1) a textually demonstrable constitutional commitment of the issue to a coordinate political department; or (2) a lack of judicially discoverable and manageable standards for resolving it; or (3) the impossibility of deciding without an initial policy determination of a kind clearly for nonjudicial discretion; or (4) the impossibility of a court's undertaking independent resolution without expressing lack of the respect due coordinate branches of government; or (5) an unusual need for unquestioning adherence to a political decision already made; or (6) the potentiality of embarrassment from multifarious pronouncements by various departments on one question.

Significantly, any one of the above-listed characteristics may be sufficient to preclude judicial review.

In *Goldwater,* Justice Powell's concurrence suggested that the *Baker* analysis could be condensed into a three-question inquiry:

> (i)   Does the issue involve resolution of questions committed by the text of the Constitution to a coordinate branch of government?

> (ii) Would resolution of the question demand that a court move beyond areas of judicial expertise?

(iii) Do prudential considerations counsel against judicial intervention?

Inasmuch as it incorporates the *Baker* criteria without abridging them, we find Justice Powell's analytical framework to be useful and proceed to apply each of these inquiries to the present case.

A.   Constitutional Textual Commitment to Coordinate Branches

The term "treaties" appears four times in the text of the Constitution. The Treaty Clause states that the President "shall have Power, by and with the Advice and Consent of the Senate, to make Treaties, provided two-thirds of the Senators present concur." The Compacts Clause delineates the power of the states to deal with foreign powers, completely prohibiting the states from making "treaties" with foreign nations, but permitting states to enter into "agreements or compacts" with foreign powers with the consent of Congress. The Cases-and-Controversies Clause states, in pertinent part, that "the judicial power shall extend to all cases, in law and equity, arising under this Constitution, the laws of the United States, and treaties made . . . ." And finally, the Supremacy Clause states that "[t]his Constitution, and the laws of the United States which shall be made in pursuance thereof; and all treaties made, or which shall be made, under the authority of the United States, shall be the supreme law of the land." However, as noted earlier, the text of the Constitution does not (1) define the term "treaties"; (2) delineate the difference between treaties and other types of international agreements; (3) mandate that treaties are the exclusive means by which the federal government may make agreements with foreign powers; or (4) state that the Treaty Clause procedure is the only manner in which a treaty may be enacted.

The Constitution confers a vast amount of power upon the political branches of the federal government in the area of foreign policy—particularly foreign commerce. The breadth of the President's inherent powers in foreign affairs arises from his role as Chief Executive and as Commander in Chief. In addition to his power to "make Treaties" with the advice and consent of two-thirds of the Senators present, the President's authority in foreign affairs is further bolstered by his power to "appoint Ambassadors . . . and Consuls" and "to receive Ambassadors and other public Ministers." Meanwhile, Congress's enumerated powers in the realm of external affairs include its power "to declare war," "to raise and support armies," "to provide and maintain a navy," and the Senate's advice-and-consent role in the treaty-making process. Most significantly, the Constitution also confers on the entire Congress (and not just the Senate) authority "to regulate commerce with foreign nations"—an express textual commitment that is directly relevant to international commercial agreements such as NAFTA.

The Supreme Court has repeatedly recognized that the President is the nation's "guiding organ in the conduct of our foreign affairs," in whom the Constitution vests "vast powers in relation to the outside world." *Ludecke v. Watkins,* 335 U.S. 160, 173 (1948). With respect to NAFTA, it is especially important to note that the Supreme Court has long since recognized the power of the political branches to conclude international "agreements that do not constitute treaties in the constitutional sense." *Curtiss-Wright,* 299 U.S. at 318.

These cases interpreting the broad textual grants of authority to the President and Congress in the areas of foreign affairs leave only a narrowly circumscribed role for the Judiciary. As the Supreme Court stated in *Oetjen v. Central Leather,* 246 U.S. 297, 302 (1918), "The conduct of the foreign relations of our government is committed by the Constitution to the executive and legislative—'the political'— departments of the government, and the propriety of what may be done in the exercise of this political power is not subject to judicial inquiry or decision." Within this circuit, we have declared that "[m]atters relating to the conduct of foreign relations. . . are so exclusively entrusted to the political branches of government as to be largely immune from judicial inquiry or interference."

To be sure, the *Baker* Court deemed it "error to suppose that every case or controversy which touches foreign relations lies beyond judicial cognizance." Furthermore, the Court has recognized that "foreign commitments" cannot relieve the government of the obligation to "operate within the bounds laid down by the Constitution," and that "the prohibitions of the Constitution. . . cannot be nullified by the Executive or by the Executive and Senate combined." *Reid v. Covert,* 354 U.S. 1, 14, 17 (1957). We therefore have little doubt that courts have the authority— indeed, the duty—to invalidate international agreements which violate the express terms of the Constitution. Nonetheless, with respect to commercial agreements, we find that the Constitution's clear assignment of authority to the political branches of the Government over our nation's foreign affairs and commerce counsels against an intrusive role for this court in overseeing the actions of the President and Congress in this matter.

The appellants concede, as they must, that the Constitution affords the political branches substantial authority over foreign affairs and commerce. The appellants also concede that the Supreme Court has recognized the constitutional validity of the longstanding practice of enacting international agreements which do not amount to full-fledged treaties. Nonetheless, the appellants argue that what is at issue here is not the authority of a branch of government over a certain subject matter, but whether that branch "has chosen a constitutionally permissible means of implementing that power." This contention leads us to the second *Goldwater/Baker* inquiry: whether the resolution of this issue would require this court to move beyond recognized areas of judicial expertise.

B. *Judicial Expertise*

Under *Baker,* the second criterion by which we evaluate the justiciability of this case is whether or not there exist judicially manageable standards for determining when a given international commercial agreement must be approved pursuant to the Art. II, § 2 procedures. The Government contends that such a decision would require this court to consider areas beyond its judicial expertise. We agree.

As noted earlier, in *Goldwater v. Carter,* members of Congress challenged the President's unilateral termination of a mutual defense treaty with Taiwan (formerly known as the Republic of China). As in the present case, the crux of the challenge centered on the allegedly unconstitutional procedures used to abrogate the treaty, and not on the treaty's substantive provisions. A plurality of the Court determined that the case was nonjusticiable because the text of the Constitution failed to provide any guidance on the issue; joined by three other members of the Court, Justice Rehnquist noted that "while the Constitution is express as to the manner in which the Senate shall participate in the ratification of a treaty, it is silent as to the body's participation in the abrogation of a treaty." Justice Rehnquist thus concluded that "in light of the absence of any constitutional provision governing the termination of a treaty, and the fact that different termination procedures may be appropriate for different treaties. . . the instant case. . . must surely be controlled by political standards" rather than by judicial standards.

While the nature of the issue presented in *Goldwater* differs somewhat from the present case, we nonetheless find the disposition in *Goldwater* instructive, if not controlling, for our purposes, in that the Supreme Court declined to act because the constitutional provision at issue does not provide an identifiable textual limit on the authority granted by the Constitution. Indeed, just as the Treaty Clause fails to outline the Senate's role in the abrogation of treaties, we find that the Treaty Clause also fails to outline the circumstances, if any, under which its procedures must be adhered to when approving international commercial agreements.

Significantly, the appellants themselves fail to offer, either in their briefs or at argument, a workable definition of what constitutes a "treaty." Indeed, the appellants decline to supply any analytical framework whatsoever by which courts can distinguish international agreements which require Senate ratification from those that do not. Rather, the appellants offer up the nebulous argument that "major and significant" agreements require Art. II, § 2 ratification, without defining how courts should go about making such distinctions. According to the appellants, it is neither possible nor necessary to define the meaning of a "treaty" to decide this case, so long as we find that if any commercial agreement qualifies as a treaty requiring Senate ratification, NAFTA surely does. We disagree, given that under *Baker* and *Goldwater,* the ascertainment of judicially manageable standards is essential before we may rule that this court even has jurisdiction to reach the merits of the case. . .

IV

We therefore conclude that this case presents a nonjusticiable political question, thereby depriving the court of Article III jurisdiction in this matter. . . In dismissing this case as a political question, we do not mean to suggest that the terms of the Treaty Clause effectively allow the political branches to exercise unfettered discretion in determining whether to subject a particular international agreement to the rigors of that Clause's procedural requirements; to state as much would be tantamount to rendering the terms of Art. II, § 2, cl. 2 a dead letter. Indeed, as the Court stated in *Missouri v. Holland,* 252 U.S. 416, 433 (1920), "[i]t is obvious that there may be matters of the sharpest exigency for the national well being that an act of Congress could not deal with but that a treaty followed by such an act could." We only conclude that in the context of international commercial agreements such as NAFTA— given the added factor of Congress's constitutionally-enumerated power to regulate commerce with foreign nations, as well as the lack of judicially manageable standards to determine when an agreement is significant enough to qualify as a "treaty"—the issue of what kinds of agreements require Senate ratification pursuant to the Art. II, § 2 procedures presents a nonjusticiable political question.

In this second case, the Supreme Court evaluates the president's authority to sign a sole-executive agreement, the Algiers Accords, which terminated claims already filed in federal court. As you read the case, ask yourself why the Court was willing to resolve the question rather than dismiss it under the political question doctrine, as it did in *Made in the USA.*

Dames & Moore v. Regan
Supreme Court of the United States
453 U.S. 654 (1981)

■ JUSTICE REHNQUIST delivered the opinion of the Court.

The questions presented by this case touch fundamentally upon the matter in which our Republic is to be governed. Throughout the nearly two centuries of our Nation's existence under the Constitution, this subject has generated considerable debate. We have had the benefit of commentators such as John Jay, Alexander Hamilton, and James Madison writing in The Federalist Papers at the Nation's very inception, the benefit of astute foreign observers of our system such as Alexis deTocqueville and James Bryce writing during the first century of the Nation's existence, and the benefit of many other treatises as well as more than 400 volumes of reports of decisions of this Court. As these writings reveal it is doubtless both futile and perhaps dangerous to find any epigrammatical explanation of how this country has been governed. . .

Our decision today will not dramatically alter this situation, for the Framers "did not make the judiciary the overseer of our government." We are confined to a resolution of the dispute presented to us. That dispute involves various Executive Orders and regulations by which the President nullified attachments and liens on Iranian assets in the United States, directed that these assets be transferred to Iran, and suspended claims against Iran that may be presented to an International Claims Tribunal. This action was taken in an effort to comply with an Executive Agreement between the United States and Iran. We granted certiorari before judgment in this case, and set an expedited briefing and argument schedule, because lower courts had reached conflicting conclusions on the validity of the President's actions and, as the Solicitor General informed us, unless the Government acted by July 19, 1981, Iran could consider the United States to be in breach of the Executive Agreement. . .

Perhaps it is because it is so difficult to reconcile the foregoing definition of Art. III judicial power with the broad range of vitally important day-to-day questions regularly decided by Congress or the Executive, without either challenge or interference by the Judiciary, that the decisions of the Court in this area have been rare, episodic, and afford little precedential value for subsequent cases. The tensions present in any exercise of executive power under the tri-partite system of Federal Government established by the Constitution have been reflected in opinions by Members of this Court more than once. The Court stated in *United States v. Curtiss-Wright Export Corp.*, 299 U.S. 304, 319–320 (1936):

> [W]e are here dealing not alone with an authority vested in the President by an exertion of legislative power, but with such an authority plus the very delicate, plenary and exclusive power of the President as the sole organ of the federal government in the field of international relations—a power which does not require as a basis for its exercise an act of Congress, but which, of course, like every other governmental power, must be exercised in subordination to the applicable provisions of the Constitution.

And yet 16 years later, Justice Jackson in his concurring opinion in *Youngstown,* which both parties agree brings together as much combination of analysis and common sense as there is in this area, focused not on the "plenary and exclusive power of the President" but rather responded to a claim of virtually unlimited powers for the Executive by noting: "The example of such unlimited executive power that must have most impressed the forefathers was the prerogative exercised by George III, and the description of its evils in the Declaration of Independence leads me to doubt that they were creating their new Executive in his image."

As we now turn to the factual and legal issues in this case, we freely confess that we are obviously deciding only one more episode in the never-ending tension between the President exercising the executive authority in a world that presents each day some new challenge with which he must deal and the Constitution under which we all live and which no one disputes embodies some sort of system of checks and balances.

I

On November 4, 1979, the American Embassy in Tehran was seized and our diplomatic personnel were captured and held hostage. In response to that crisis, President Carter, acting pursuant to the International Emergency Economic Powers Act (IEEPA), declared a national emergency on November 14, 1979, and blocked the removal or transfer of "all property and interests in property of the Government of Iran, its instrumentalities and controlled entities and the Central Bank of Iran which are or become subject to the jurisdiction of the United States. . . ." . . . On November 26, 1979, the President granted a general license authorizing certain judicial proceedings against Iran but which did not allow the "entry of any judgment or of any decree or order of similar or analogous effect. . . ."

On December 19, 1979, petitioner Dames & Moore filed suit in the United States District Court for the Central District of California against the Government of Iran, the Atomic Energy Organization of Iran, and a number of Iranian banks. In its complaint, petitioner alleged that its wholly owned subsidiary, Dames & Moore International, was a party to a written contract with the Atomic Energy Organization, and that the subsidiary's entire interest in the contract had been assigned to petitioner. . . Petitioner contended, however, that it was owed $3,436,694.30 plus interest for services performed under the contract prior to the date of termination. The District Court issued orders of attachment directed against property of the defendants, and the property of certain Iranian banks was then attached to secure any judgment that might be entered against them.

On January 20, 1981, the Americans held hostage were released by Iran pursuant to an Agreement entered into the day before and embodied in two Declarations of the Democratic and Popular Republic of Algeria. The Agreement stated that "[i]t is the purpose of [the United States and Iran]... to terminate all litigation as between the Government of each party and the nationals of the other, and to bring about the settlement and termination of all such claims through binding arbitration." In furtherance of this goal, the Agreement called for the establishment of an Iran-United States Claims Tribunal which would arbitrate any claims not settled within six months. Awards of the Claims Tribunal are to be "final and binding" and "enforceable... in the courts of any nation in accordance with its laws." Under the Agreement, the United States is obligated

> to terminate all legal proceedings in United States courts involving claims of United States persons and institutions against Iran and its state enterprises, to nullify all attachments and judgments obtained therein, to prohibit all further litigation based on such claims, and to bring about the termination of such claims through binding arbitration.

In addition, the United States must "act to bring about the transfer" by July 19, 1981, of all Iranian assets held in this country by American banks. One billion dollars of these assets will be deposited in a security account in the Bank of England, to the account of the Algerian Central Bank, and used to satisfy awards rendered against Iran by the Claims Tribunal.

On January 19, 1981, President Carter issued a series of Executive Orders implementing the terms of the agreement...

On April 28, 1981, petitioner filed this action in the District Court for declaratory and injunctive relief against the United States and the Secretary of the Treasury, seeking to prevent enforcement of the Executive Orders and Treasury Department regulations implementing the Agreement with Iran. In its complaint, petitioner alleged that the actions of the President and the Secretary of the Treasury implementing the Agreement with Iran were beyond their statutory and constitutional powers and, in any event, were unconstitutional to the extent they adversely affect petitioner's final judgment against the Government of Iran and the Atomic Energy Organization, its execution of that judgment in the State of Washington, its prejudgment attachments, and its ability to continue to litigate against the Iranian banks...

II

The parties and the lower courts, confronted with the instant questions, have all agreed that much relevant analysis is contained in *Youngstown Sheet & Tube Co. v. Sawyer*, 343 U.S. 579 (1952). Justice

Black's opinion for the Court in that case, involving the validity of President Truman's effort to seize the country's steel mills in the wake of a nationwide strike, recognized that "[t]he President's power, if any, to issue the order must stem either from an act of Congress or from the Constitution itself." Justice Jackson's concurring opinion elaborated in a general way the consequences of different types of interaction between the two democratic branches in assessing Presidential authority to act in any given case. When the President acts pursuant to an express or implied authorization from Congress, he exercises not only his powers but also those delegated by Congress. In such a case the executive action "would be supported by the strongest of presumptions and the widest latitude of judicial interpretation, and the burden of persuasion would rest heavily upon any who might attack it." When the President acts in the absence of congressional authorization he may enter "a zone of twilight in which he and Congress may have concurrent authority, or in which its distribution is uncertain." In such a case the analysis becomes more complicated, and the validity of the President's action, at least so far as separation-of-powers principles are concerned, hinges on a consideration of all the circumstances which might shed light on the views of the Legislative Branch toward such action, including "congressional inertia, indifference or quiescence." Finally, when the President acts in contravention of the will of Congress, "his power is at its lowest ebb," and the Court can sustain his actions "only by disabling the Congress from acting upon the subject."

Although we have in the past found and do today find Justice Jackson's classification of executive actions into three general categories analytically useful, we should be mindful of Justice Holmes' admonition, quoted by Justice Frankfurter in *Youngstown*, that "[t]he great ordinances of the Constitution do not establish and divide fields of black and white." Justice Jackson himself recognized that his three categories represented "a somewhat over-simplified grouping," and it is doubtless the case that executive action in any particular instance falls, not neatly in one of three pigeonholes, but rather at some point along a spectrum running from explicit congressional authorization to explicit congressional prohibition. This is particularly true as respects cases such as the one before us, involving responses to international crises the nature of which Congress can hardly have been expected to anticipate in any detail.

III

In nullifying post-November 14, 1979, attachments and directing those persons holding blocked Iranian funds and securities to transfer them to the Federal Reserve Bank of New York for ultimate transfer to Iran, President Carter cited five sources of express or inherent power.

The Government, however, has principally relied on § 203 of the IEEPA. . . [which] provides in part:

> At the times and to the extent specified in section 1701 of this title, the President may, under such regulations as he may prescribe, by means of instructions, licenses, or otherwise—
>
> (A) investigate, regulate, or prohibit—
>
> (i) any transactions in foreign exchange,
>
> (ii) transfers of credit or payments between, by, through, or to any banking institution, to the extent that such transfers or payments involve any interest of any foreign country or a national thereof,
>
> (iii) the importing or exporting of currency or securities, and
>
> (B) investigate, regulate, direct and compel, nullify, void, prevent or prohibit, any acquisition, holding, withholding, use, transfer, withdrawal, transportation, importation or exportation of, or dealing in, or exercising any right, power, or privilege with respect to, or transactions involving, any property in which any foreign country or a national thereof has any interest;
>
> by any person, or with respect to any property, subject to the jurisdiction of the United States.

The Government contends that the acts of "nullifying" the attachments and ordering the "transfer" of the frozen assets are specifically authorized by the plain language of the above statute. . .

This Court has previously recognized that the congressional purpose in authorizing blocking orders is "to put control of foreign assets in the hands of the President. . . ." Such orders permit the President to maintain the foreign assets at his disposal for use in negotiating the resolution of a declared national emergency. The frozen assets serve as a "bargaining chip" to be used by the President when dealing with a hostile country. . .

IV

Although we have concluded that the IEEPA constitutes specific congressional authorization to the President to nullify the attachments and order the transfer of Iranian assets, there remains the question of the President's authority to suspend claims pending in American courts. Such claims have, of course, an existence apart from the attachments which accompanied them. In terminating these claims through Executive Order No. 12294 the President purported to act under authority of both the IEEPA and the so-called "Hostage Act."

We conclude that although the IEEPA authorized the nullification of the attachments, it cannot be read to authorize the suspension of the claims. The claims of American citizens against Iran are not in themselves transactions involving Iranian property or efforts to exercise any rights with respect to such property. An in personam lawsuit, although it might eventually be reduced to judgment and that judgment might be executed upon, is an effort to establish liability and fix damages and does not focus on any particular property within the jurisdiction. The terms of the IEEPA therefore do not authorize the President to suspend claims in American courts. . .

The Hostage Act, passed in 1868, provides:

> Whenever it is made known to the President that any citizen of the United States has been unjustly deprived of his liberty by or under the authority of any foreign government, it shall be the duty of the President forthwith to demand of that government the reasons of such imprisonment; and if it appears to be wrongful and in violation of the rights of American citizenship, the President shall forthwith demand the release of such citizen, and if the release so demanded is unreasonably delayed or refused, the President shall use such means, not amounting to acts of war, as he may think necessary and proper to obtain or effectuate the release; and all the facts and proceedings relative thereto shall as soon as practicable be communicated by the President to Congress.

We are reluctant to conclude that this provision constitutes specific authorization to the President to suspend claims in American courts. Although the broad language of the Hostage Act suggests it may cover this case, there are several difficulties with such a view. The legislative history indicates that the Act was passed in response to a situation unlike the recent Iranian crisis. Congress in 1868 was concerned with the activity of certain countries refusing to recognize the citizenship of naturalized Americans traveling abroad, and repatriating such citizens against their will. These countries were not interested in returning the citizens in exchange for any sort of ransom. This also explains the reference in the Act to imprisonment "in violation of the rights of American citizenship." Although the Iranian hostage-taking violated international law and common decency, the hostages were not seized out of any refusal to recognize their American citizenship—they were seized precisely because of their American citizenship. . .

Concluding that neither the IEEPA nor the Hostage Act constitutes specific authorization of the President's action suspending claims, however, is not to say that these statutory provisions are entirely irrelevant to the question of the validity of the President's action. We think both statutes highly relevant in the looser sense of indicating congressional acceptance of a broad scope for executive action in circumstances such as those presented in this case. As noted in Part III, the IEEPA delegates broad authority to the President to act in times of national emergency with respect to property of a foreign country. The Hostage Act similarly indicates congressional willingness that the President have broad discretion when responding to the hostile acts of foreign sovereigns. . .

Not infrequently in affairs between nations, outstanding claims by nationals of one country against the government of another country are "sources of friction" between the two sovereigns. To resolve these difficulties, nations have often entered into agreements settling the claims of their respective nationals. As one treatise writer puts it, international agreements settling claims by nationals of one state against the government of another "are established international practice reflecting traditional international theory." Consistent with that principle, the United States has repeatedly exercised its sovereign authority to settle the claims of its nationals against foreign countries. Though those settlements have sometimes been made by treaty, there has also been a longstanding practice of settling such claims by executive agreement without the advice and consent of the Senate. Under such agreements, the President has agreed to renounce or extinguish claims of United States nationals against foreign governments in return for lump-sum payments or the establishment of arbitration procedures. To be sure, many of these settlements were encouraged by the United States claimants themselves, since a claimant's only hope of obtaining any payment at all might lie in having his Government negotiate a diplomatic settlement on his behalf. But it is also undisputed that the "United States has sometimes disposed of the claims of its citizens without their consent, or even without consultation with them, usually without exclusive regard for their interests, as distinguished from those of the nation as a whole." It is clear that the practice of settling claims continues today. Since 1952, the President has entered into at least 10 binding settlements with foreign nations, including an $80 million settlement with the People's Republic of China.

Crucial to our decision today is the conclusion that Congress has implicitly approved the practice of claim settlement by executive agreement. This is best demonstrated by Congress' enactment of the International Claims Settlement Act of 1949. The Act had two purposes: (1) to allocate to United States nationals funds received in the course of an executive claims settlement with Yugoslavia, and (2) to provide a procedure whereby funds resulting from future settlements could be distributed. To achieve these ends Congress created the International Claims Commission, now the Foreign Claims Settlement Commission, and gave it jurisdiction to make final and binding decisions with respect to claims by United States nationals against settlement funds. By creating a procedure to implement future settlement agreements, Congress placed its stamp of approval on such agreements. Indeed, the legislative history of the Act observed that the United States was seeking settlements with countries other than Yugoslavia and that the bill contemplated settlements of a similar nature in the future. . .

In addition to congressional acquiescence in the President's power to settle claims, prior cases of this Court have also recognized that the President does have some measure of power to enter into executive agreements without obtaining the advice and consent of the Senate. In *United States v. Pink*, 315 U.S. 203 (1942), for example, the Court upheld the validity of the Litvinov Assignment, which was part of an Executive Agreement whereby the Soviet Union assigned to the United States amounts owed to it by American nationals so that outstanding claims of other American nationals could be paid. . .

In light of all of the foregoing—the inferences to be drawn from the character of the legislation Congress has enacted in the area, such as the IEEPA and the Hostage Act, and from the history of acquiescence in executive claims settlement—we conclude that the President was authorized to suspend pending claims pursuant to Executive Order No. 12294. As Justice Frankfurter pointed out in *Youngstown*, "a systematic, unbroken, executive practice, long pursued to the knowledge of the Congress and never before questioned. . . may be treated as a gloss on 'Executive Power' vested in the President by § 1 of Art. II." Past practice does not, by itself, create power, but "long-continued practice, known to and acquiesced in by Congress, would raise a presumption that the [action] had been [taken] in pursuance of its consent. . . ." Such practice is present here and such a presumption is also appropriate. In light of the fact that Congress may be considered to have consented to the President's action in suspending claims, we cannot say that action exceeded the President's powers.

Our conclusion is buttressed by the fact that the means chosen by the President to settle the claims of American nationals provided an alternative forum, the Claims Tribunal, which is capable of providing meaningful relief. The Solicitor General also suggests that the provision of the Claims Tribunal will actually enhance the opportunity for claimants to recover their claims, in that the Agreement removes a number of jurisdictional and procedural impediments faced by claimants in United States courts. Although being overly sanguine about the chances of United States claimants before the Claims Tribunal would require a degree of naiveté which should not be demanded even of judges, the Solicitor General's point cannot be discounted. Moreover, it is important to remember that we have already held that the President has the statutory authority to nullify attachments and to transfer the assets out of the country. The President's power to do so does not depend on his provision of a forum whereby claimants can recover on those claims. The fact that the President has provided such a forum here means that the claimants are receiving something in return for the suspension of their claims, namely, access to an international tribunal before which they may well recover something on their claims. Because there does appear to be a real "settlement" here, this case is more easily analogized to the more traditional claim settlement cases of the past.

Just as importantly, Congress has not disapproved of the action taken here. Though Congress has held hearings on the Iranian Agreement itself, Congress has not enacted legislation, or even passed a resolution, indicating its displeasure with the Agreement. Quite the contrary, the relevant Senate Committee has stated that the establishment of the Tribunal is "of vital importance to the United States." We are thus clearly not confronted with a situation in which Congress has in some way resisted the exercise of Presidential authority.

Finally, we re-emphasize the narrowness of our decision. We do not decide that the President possesses plenary power to settle claims, even as against foreign governmental entities... But where, as here, the settlement of claims has been determined to be a necessary incident to the resolution of a major foreign policy dispute between our country and another, and where, as here, we can conclude that Congress acquiesced in the President's action, we are not prepared to say that the President lacks the power to settle such claims...

NOTES & QUESTIONS

1. *The Interchangeability Thesis.* One school of thought holds that the president can do anything through a congressional executive agreement that he or she can do through a full treaty. Under this view, the choice is up to the discretion of the president, because congressional-executive agreements are fully "interchangeable" with treaties. For example, Professors Ackerman and Golove argue that the notion of interchangeability emerged in the New Deal era, which fundamentally transformed our constitutional system. See Bruce Ackerman & David Golove, *Is Nafta Constitutional?*, 108 Harv. L. Rev. 799, 808 (1995) ("The work of the New Deal scholars fed into a larger enterprise in constitutional reconstruction—one in which the American people reexamined their traditional isolationism amidst the sacrifices of the Second World War and resoundingly repudiated the Versailles precedent and the constitutional order that made it possible. It was only this decisive shift in public opinion that permitted the President and Congress to give constitutional substance to New Deal jurisprudence and introduce the congressional-executive agreement as a legitimate alternative to treaty-making."). The objection to this view is that it essentially writes the advice and consent provision of the Treaty Clause out of the Constitution. What do you think will happen in the future? Will presidents continue to sign treaties

or are we witnessing the slow death of treaties? For an argument that an end to treaties would not be all that bad, see Oona A. Hathaway, *Treaties' End: The Past, Present, and Future of International Lawmaking in the United States*, 117 Yale L.J. 1236, 1351 (2008).

2.   *Political (Non-Binding) Agreements*. Treaties may be experiencing a slow death in more ways than one. In addition to being replaced by congressional-executive and sole-executive agreements, they are also being replaced by non-binding "political" agreements that are not treaties at all in the international sense of that term. By design, these agreements do not impose any *legal* obligations on their signatories. Why sign such agreements when they do not impose legal obligations? In many situations, governments may be facing domestic political pressure that make a formal legal arrangement unpalatable. For example, in 2015 the United States negotiated and concluded a political agreement with Iran over its nuclear weapons program. The deal also was negotiated and signed by the major world powers who sit on the Security Council. The agreement laid out a common understanding regarding the termination of some nuclear activities and the transformation of other activities toward peaceful and civilian uses. Since the deal was not a legally binding instrument, there was no need for Senate advice and consent or even congressional agreement. Indeed, several members of the U.S. Senate vociferously objected to the deal and wrote a letter, ostensibly addressed to the Government of Iran, warning the Iranians that the deal was non-binding and could therefore be vitiated "by the stroke of a pen" by a future president. The Iranians ignored the warning and implemented the deal. The fact that the deal was non-binding was tempered by the fact that the deal called for the Security Council—whose permanent members all signed the agreement—to withdraw critical resolutions and sanctions once it could be verified that Iran had satisfied its political obligations under the deal. Could the Security Council use a similar structure for resolving thorny diplomatic disputes in the future?

PROBLEM CASE

In 2015, representatives from the world's major economies met in Paris to negotiate a framework for reducing gas emissions that are causing climate change. The agreement was drafted at the end of the year and signed in April of 2016. The question of its "bindingness" was the subject of great confusion when it was first announced, because Secretary of State John Kerry declared that it was non-binding while President Hollande of France insisted that it was a binding legal agreement. In fact, the agreement is legally binding in that it requires that states formally announce and submit their "nationally determined contributions" (NDCs) to reducing emissions. The agreement does not itself set those NDCs, which by definition are set by individual states after a non-binding international negotiation process.

The Obama Administration did not have enough support to submit the Paris Climate Deal to the Senate for ratification, nor did it have enough support to enact it as a congressional-executive agreement. Consequently, the deal was signed as a sole executive agreement. Do you agree with this decision? What are the costs and benefits of this approach?

The deal contemplates that each state will change emissions standards to meet the benchmarks laid out in the Paris Climate Deal. Without congressional involvement, how will this be possible? Moreover, future presidents may simply withdraw from the deal. Indeed, President Donald Trump made withdrawal from the Paris Climate Agreement a campaign issue during the 2016 election, insisting that the environmental regulations required by the deal would harm U.S. manufacturers and, by extension, manufacturing jobs in the Rust Belt states that Trump eventually carried in the electoral college. Trump carried through on his promise and in 2017 withdrew the United States from the accord, though President Biden reversed that decision and rejoined the Paris Agreement in 2021.

Would congressional involvement in the process have prevented this "seesaw" effect of joining, leaving, and rejoining the agreement? In the absence of domestic support for a full climate change *treaty*, should President Obama have refused to sign the agreement?

F. TREATY TERMINATION

As a matter of international law, the rules regarding treaty termination are relatively straightforward. According to the Vienna Convention, treaty termination is governed by the terms of the treaty itself. So, if a treaty explicitly calls for unilateral treaty termination, one party can terminate the treaty according to whatever standards the treaty articulates for unilateral withdrawal. In the absence of an explicit statement about treaty withdrawal, the default rule in article 56 is that a party may terminate a treaty if "(a) it is established that the parties intended to admit the possibility of denunciation or withdrawal; or (b) a right of denunciation or withdrawal may be implied by the nature of the treaty." Also, a state may terminate a treaty pursuant to article 60 if the other party engages in a "material breach" of its obligations under the treaty.

However, the issue of treaty termination under U.S. domestic law is fraught with unresolved legal questions. Can a president unilaterally terminate a treaty that was ratified by the Senate, even if the Senate would prefer to stay within the treaty regime? Can a president withdraw from a congressional-executive agreement even in the face of congressional objection? These questions were the subject of a lawsuit filed by Senator (and former presidential candidate) Barry Goldwater against President Jimmy Carter.

Goldwater v. Carter
Supreme Court of the United States
444 U.S. 996 (1979)

■ JUSTICE POWELL:

In this case, a few Members of Congress claim that the President's action in terminating the treaty with Taiwan has deprived them of their constitutional role with respect to a change in the supreme law of the land. Congress has taken no official action. In the present posture of this case, we do not know whether there ever will be an actual confrontation between the Legislative and Executive Branches. Although the Senate has considered a resolution declaring that Senate approval is necessary for the termination of any mutual defense treaty, no final vote has been taken on the resolution. Moreover, it is unclear whether the resolution would have retroactive effect. It cannot be said that either the Senate or the House has rejected the President's claim. If the Congress chooses not to confront the President, it is not our task to do so. I therefore concur in the dismissal of this case.

MR. JUSTICE REHNQUIST suggests, however, that the issue presented by this case is a nonjusticiable political question which can never be considered by this Court. I cannot agree. In my view, reliance upon the political-question doctrine is inconsistent with our precedents. As set forth in the seminal case of *Baker v. Carr* (1962), the doctrine incorporates three inquiries: (i) Does the issue involve resolution of questions committed by the text of the Constitution to a coordinate branch of Government? (ii) Would resolution of the question demand that a court move beyond areas of judicial expertise? (iii) Do prudential considerations counsel against judicial intervention? In my opinion the answer to each of these inquiries would require us to decide this case if it were ready for review.

First, the existence of "a textually demonstrable constitutional commitment of the issue to a coordinate political department," turns on an examination of the constitutional provisions governing the exercise of the power in question. No constitutional provision explicitly confers upon the President the power to terminate treaties. Further, Art. II, § 2, of the Constitution authorizes the President to make treaties with the advice and consent of the Senate. Article VI provides that treaties shall be a part of the supreme law of the land. These provisions add support to the view that the text of the Constitution does not unquestionably commit the power to terminate treaties to the President alone.

Second, there is no "lack of judicially discoverable and manageable standards for resolving" this case; nor is a decision impossible "without an initial policy determination of a kind clearly for nonjudicial discretion." We are asked to decide whether the President may terminate a treaty under the Constitution without congressional approval. Resolution of the question may not be easy, but it only requires us to apply normal principles of interpretation to the constitutional provisions at issue. The present case involves neither review of the President's activities as Commander in Chief nor impermissible interference in the field of foreign affairs. Such a case would arise if we were asked to decide, for example, whether a treaty required the President to order troops into a foreign country. But "it is error to suppose that every case or controversy which touches foreign relations lies beyond judicial cognizance." This case "touches" foreign relations, but the question presented to us concerns only the constitutional division of power between Congress and the President.

A simple hypothetical demonstrates the confusion that I find inherent in Mr. Justice REHNQUIST's opinion concurring in the judgment. Assume that the President signed a mutual defense treaty with a foreign country and announced that it would go into effect despite its rejection by the Senate. Under Mr. Justice REHNQUIST's analysis that situation would present a political question even though Art. II, § 2, clearly would resolve the dispute. Although the answer to the hypothetical case seems self-evident because it demands textual rather than interstitial analysis, the nature of the legal issue presented is no different from the issue presented in the case before us. In both cases, the Court would interpret the Constitution to decide whether congressional approval is necessary to give a Presidential decision on the validity of a treaty the force of law. Such an inquiry demands no special competence or information beyond the reach of the Judiciary.

Finally, the political-question doctrine rests in part on prudential concerns calling for mutual respect among the three branches of Government. Thus, the Judicial Branch should avoid "the potentiality of embarrassment [that would result] from multifarious pronouncements by various departments on one question." Similarly, the doctrine restrains judicial action where there is an "unusual need for unquestioning adherence to a political decision already made."

If this case were ripe for judicial review, none of these prudential considerations would be present. Interpretation of the Constitution does not imply lack of respect for a coordinate branch. If the President and the Congress had reached irreconcilable positions, final disposition of the question presented by this case would eliminate, rather than create, multiple constitutional interpretations. The specter of the Federal Government brought to a halt because of the mutual intransigence of the President and the Congress would require this Court to provide a resolution pursuant to our duty "to say what the law is."

In my view, the suggestion that this case presents a political question is incompatible with this Court's willingness on previous occasions to decide whether one branch of our Government has impinged upon the power of another. Under the criteria enunciated in *Baker v. Carr*, we have the responsibility to decide whether both the Executive and Legislative Branches have constitutional roles to play in termination of a treaty. If the Congress, by appropriate formal action, had challenged the President's authority to terminate the treaty with Taiwan, the resulting uncertainty could have serious consequences for our country. In that situation, it would be the duty of this Court to resolve the issue.

■ MR. JUSTICE REHNQUIST, with whom THE CHIEF JUSTICE, MR. JUSTICE STEWART, and MR. JUSTICE STEVENS join, concurring in the judgment.

I am of the view that the basic question presented by the petitioners in this case is "political" and therefore nonjusticiable because it involves the authority of the President in the conduct of our country's foreign relations and the extent to which the Senate or the Congress is authorized to negate the action of the President. . .

In light of the absence of any constitutional provision governing the termination of a treaty, and the fact that different termination procedures may be appropriate for different treaties, the instant case in my view also "must surely be controlled by political standards."

I think that the justifications for concluding that the question here is political in nature are even more compelling than in *Coleman* because it involves foreign relations—specifically a treaty commitment to use military force in the defense of a foreign government if attacked. In *United States v. Curtiss-Wright Corp.*, 299 U.S. 304 (1936), this Court said:

> Whether, if the Joint Resolution had related solely to internal affairs it would be open to the challenge that it constituted an unlawful delegation of legislative power to the Executive, we find it unnecessary to determine. The whole aim of the resolution is to affect a situation entirely external to the United States, and falling within the category of foreign affairs. . .

The present case differs in several important respects from *Youngstown Sheet & Tube Co. v. Sawyer*, 343 U.S. 579 (1952), cited by petitioners as authority both for reaching the merits of this dispute and for reversing the Court of Appeals. In *Youngstown*, private litigants brought a suit contesting the President's authority under his war powers to seize the Nation's steel industry, an action of profound and demonstrable domestic impact. Here, by contrast, we are asked to settle a dispute between coequal branches of our Government, each of which has resources available to protect and assert its interests, resources not available to private litigants outside the judicial forum. Moreover, as in *Curtiss-Wright,* the effect of this action, as far as we can tell, is "entirely external to the United States, and [falls] within the category of foreign affairs." Finally, as already noted, the situation presented here is closely akin to that presented in *Coleman,* where the Constitution spoke only to the procedure for ratification of an amendment, not to its rejection. . .

■ MR. JUSTICE BRENNAN, dissenting.

I respectfully dissent from the order directing the District Court to dismiss this case, and would affirm the judgment of the Court of Appeals insofar as it rests upon the President's well-established authority to recognize, and withdraw recognition from, foreign governments.

In stating that this case presents a nonjusticiable "political question," Mr. Justice REHNQUIST, in my view, profoundly misapprehends the political-question principle as it applies to matters of foreign relations. Properly understood, the political-question doctrine restrains courts from reviewing an exercise of foreign policy judgment by the coordinate political branch to which authority to make that judgment has been "constitutional[ly] commit[ted]." But the doctrine does not pertain when a court is faced with the *antecedent* question whether a particular branch has been constitutionally designated as the repository of political decisionmaking power. The issue of decisionmaking authority must be resolved as a matter of constitutional law, not political discretion; accordingly, it falls within the competence of the courts.

The constitutional question raised here is prudently answered in narrow terms. Abrogation of the defense treaty with Taiwan was a necessary incident to Executive recognition of the Peking Government, because the defense treaty was predicated upon the now-abandoned view that the Taiwan Government was the only legitimate political authority in China. Our cases firmly establish that the Constitution commits to the President alone the power to recognize, and withdraw recognition from, foreign regimes. That mandate being clear, our judicial inquiry into the treaty rupture can go no further. . . .

NOTES & QUESTIONS

1. *Re-Interpretation Versus Withdrawal.* One of President Ronald Reagan's signature policy initiatives was the Strategic Defense Initiative (SDI), also known as "Star Wars," which was announced in 1983. The goal of the SDI program was to create a system of space-based vehicles or satellites that could intercept and destroy intercontinental ballistic missiles carrying nuclear weapons from hostile nations such as the USSR. Unfortunately, Article V of the 1971 Anti-Ballistic Missile Treaty included the following restriction: "Each Party undertakes not to develop, test, or deploy ABM systems or components which are sea-based, air-based, space-based, or mobile land-based."

The Reagan Administration contended that continued research and development of SDI was consistent with the terms of the treaty. Administration officials pointed to, among other things, the following sentence contained in Agreed Statement D, an annex to the treaty: "In order to insure fulfillment of the obligation not to deploy ABM systems and their components except as provided in Article III of the Treaty, the Parties agree that in the event ABM systems based on other physical principles and including components capable of substituting for ABM interceptor missiles, ABM launchers, or ABM radars are created in the future, specific limitations on such systems and their components would be subject to discussion in accordance with Article XIII and agreement in accordance with Article XIV of the Treaty." According to the Reagan Administration, SDI was based on one such system and therefore did not fall under the prohibitory language of Article V.

Several members of the U.S. Senate disagreed sharply with this creative interpretation of the treaty. Moreover, the Senators complained that the President was attempting to *unilaterally* change—through reinterpretation—a treaty obligation ratified through advice and consent of the Senate. They objected that the power to reinterpret a treaty must be exercised jointly with the Senate. Consider the views of Professor Harold Koh in his testimony before Congress: "My. . . point is that the executive branch's current domination of the treaty process, with only limited participation by the other branches, hardly complies with the framers' original intent regarding treatymaking. This result has done a disservice to the long-term interests of the institutional presidency and the nation, even if it has appeared to serve President Reagan's short-term interests." Harold Hongju Koh et al, *The Treaty Power*, 43 U. Miami L. Rev. 101, 107 (1988).

The Supreme Court has never resolved this question, nor is it likely to do so, given the political question doctrine as it has been applied to the treaty power in *Goldwater v. Carter*. Do you think the Senate's original understanding of the treaty when it ratified a treaty should prevent the executive branch from subsequently issuing a divergent interpretation of a treaty provision? For more discussion of this issue, see David Gray Adler, *The Constitution and the Termination of Treaties* (1986).

2. *Withdrawing from the ABM.* In 2002, Congressman Dennis Kucinich sued President George W. Bush over the president's decision to terminate the 1972 Anti-Ballistic Missile (ABM) Treaty. In withdrawing from the treaty, Bush cited the following provision of the treaty: "Each Party shall, in exercising its national sovereignty, have the right to withdraw from this Treaty if it decides that extraordinary events related to the subject matter of this Treaty have jeopardized its supreme interests. It shall give notice of its decision to the other Party six months prior to withdrawal from the Treaty." The suit by Kucinich was dismissed on political question grounds in the same manner as *Goldwater v. Carter*. See *Kucinich v. Bush*, 236 F. Supp. 2d 1, 2 (D.D.C. 2002).

3. *Un-Signing a Treaty.* In the twilight of his second term in office, President Bill Clinton signed the Rome Statute, the treaty that created the International Criminal Court. The date was January 1, 2001, just days before George W. Bush would be inaugurated as the 43rd President of the United States. When he signed the treaty, Clinton noted that "The United States has a long history of commitment to the principle of accountability, from our involvement in the Nuremberg tribunals that brought Nazi war criminals to justice to our leadership in the effort to establish the International Criminal Tribunals for the Former Yugoslavia and Rwanda. Our action today sustains that tradition of moral leadership." President Bush held a starkly different view of the treaty. On May 6, 2002, the Bush Administration sent a letter to the U.N. Secretary General indicating that

the White House no longer intended to submit the treaty to the Senate for ratification and requesting that the Secretary General remove the name of the United States from its list of treaty signatories.

What effect did this "un-signing" have? To answer the question, first determine the effect of the original signature by President Clinton. According to the Vienna Convention (article 18), signatories that have not yet ratified a treaty are not subject to the obligations in the treaty, though they are subject to an affirmative obligation to "refrain from acts which would defeat the object and purpose of a treaty." By attempting to withdraw its signature, the Bush Administration sought to remove this positive obligation. International law scholars were divided on the question of whether a state could quash its positive obligations as a signatory by unilaterally declaring that it was "withdrawing" its signature—a process that is not explicitly discussed in the Vienna Convention. For a discussion of this controversy, see Edward T. Swaine, *Unsigning*, 55 Stan. L. Rev. 2061 (2003).

4.   *Rejoining Treaties.* Imagine the following scenario. A President signs a treaty and it is ratified after the Senate gives advice and consent. Then, some years later, a new President comes into office and decides to withdraw from the treaty, similar to the situation in *Goldwater v. Carter*. More years pass, and a third President is elected. If that third President *re-signs* the original treaty, does the President need to get Senate advice and consent again? Or is the original advice and consent still valid? This question, which has never been presented to a court, has practical consequences because the composition of the Senate, and the overall political landscape, might have changed in the intervening years. The Senate supermajority in support of the treaty that existed when the treaty was first ratified might no longer be available the next time around when the third President re-signs the treaty. Legal scholar Jean Galbraith argues that in this situation, a President would not need to return the treaty to the Senate but could instead rely on the earlier advice and consent. See Jean Galbraith, *Rejoining Treaties*, 106 Va. L. Rev. 73 (2020) (noting, inter alia, that "[a]s a textual matter, while the Senate often puts substantial conditions into its resolutions of advice and consent, it typically does not include language that renders them ineffective for purposes of rejoining").

Conclusion & Summary

The law of treaties involves a rich interplay between domestic and international law. The key principles that require mastery reside on the "life cycle" of international agreements: how they are formed, interpreted, applied in domestic courts, transformed into domestic legislation, and eventually terminated:

1.   International law points to domestic law to determine how international treaties are formed. Under the U.S. system, presidents negotiate and sign treaties which are then approved by the U.S. Senate through advice and consent.

However, the president can also sign other international agreements without Senate endorsement, and the Supreme Court has never determined whether there is any limit on the president's power to negotiate and sign these congressional-executive and sole-executive agreements.

2. Courts, both international and domestic, use a variety of interpretive canons to interpret treaty provisions. Generally speaking, treaty terms are given their ordinary meaning in accordance with the object and purpose of the treaty. In cases of ambiguity, courts may rely on a variety of other methodologies, including the consultation of the *travaux preparatoires* (legislative history), and any subsequent practice or agreements among the parties.

3. When signing a multilateral treaty, states may attach reservations, understandings, and declarations (RUDs) to the agreement that limit their obligations under particular provisions. The state parties may object to these reservations if they are so fundamental as to conflict with the object and purpose of the treaty. In making these objections, states have the option of declaring the treaty no longer in force between the objecting state and the reserving state.

4. The federal government may sign treaties to regulate conduct that could not otherwise be regulated through a federal statute pursuant to its enumerated powers, because the Constitution specifically allocated the treaty power to the federal government. However, the individual rights protected by the Bill of Rights continue to constrain the government when it signs international agreements.

5. Treaties can be divided into self-executing and non-self-executing agreements. The former are automatically enforceable in federal court while the latter only become directly enforceable as federal law once Congress passes implementing legislation. The categorization of a treaty as one or the other depends on the intention of the Senate when it ratified the treaty. Not all countries distinguish treaties in this way. In fact, some countries—especially ones with a monist posture—allow all treaties to be enforced in federal court.

6. Treaty termination is governed by the terms of the instrument, either express or implied. If a treaty is drafted in such a way as to require certain conditions prior to unilateral termination, then those conditions govern

withdrawal. Also, a party may withdraw from a treaty in response to a counter-party's material breach. On the domestic front, the Constitution says nothing explicitly about the relative authority of the political branches with regard to treaty termination, and the Supreme Court views the issue as a political question unsuitable for judicial regulation.

CHAPTER 4

STATES

Introduction

States are subjects and objects of international law. They are subjects in the sense that they create customary law through their state practice and treaty law through their bilateral and multilateral agreements. They are objects in the sense that international legal norms constrain and regulate the behavior of states. Although non-state actors, international and regional organizations, and individuals all increasingly participate in the international legal system, the "classical" view of international law is decidedly state-centric. States are an essential part of the universal grammar of international law.

One way of articulating this privileged position is to describe states as "legal persons" under international law. Just as all human beings are "persons" under domestic law, subject to both rights and responsibilities, so too states are "legal persons" under international law. Their "legal personality" is an expression of their formal legal equality under international law. Although states might differ in size, resources, power, and prestige, each is formally equal under international law and capable of participating in the international legal system on equal terms. This means that each state is capable of engaging in international relations, creating law through custom and treaty, and pursuing international dispute resolution through applicable channels.

So, determining what counts as a state is among the most crucial tasks for international law. States come into existence in a variety of ways. A state may dissolve into its component parts, each of which then becomes a state in its own right, with the parent state disappearing into an international abyss. Think here of Czechoslovakia dissolving into the Czech Republic and Slovakia. Or the reverse might happen. Two states might join together to create an entirely new entity. Or one state might absorb another.

The most common method by which a new state comes into existence is secession. In that case, a portion of a state, often a pre-existing political subunit such as a province or territory, breaks free from its parent state and declares independence as a new state with legal personality under international law. In some situations, a state's secession might be followed closely by its joining a different state—perhaps because the inhabitants of the breakaway territory have linguistic, cultural, or religious affinities with a different state. This process of disassociation and re-association is usually contentious, sometimes accomplished through referenda and peaceful negotiations. Or, the process might be accompanied by civil war, ethnic conflict, and even atrocities that violate international criminal law.

This chapter presents the relevant concepts and doctrines required for understanding states and their place in the international legal system. Section A focuses on the basic criteria for statehood: a permanent population, government, stable territory, and the capability of exercising international relations. In addition, according to something called the Constitutive View, a state must also be recognized as such by the international community before it may qualify for statehood. Section B focuses on the more normative criteria that some states apply before recognizing new states: a commitment to democracy and the rule of law, human rights, and the basic principles of the international legal order, especially the prohibition on the use of force.

Sections C and D focus on self-determination and secession, respectively. These are related but distinct concepts. Self-determination is a collective right that attaches to a "nation" or a "people," that is, a group of individuals with a shared heritage, perhaps through a common language, ethnic affiliation, religion, or culture. The content of the right protects a people's right to determine their own destiny through a particular political arrangement. For example, the concept of self-determination was crucial in the process of decolonization, as former colonies were granted self-rule and independence from their imperial rulers. In today's world, almost all colonies that wanted independence have received it, leaving self-determination as a legal concept on uncertain terrain. In concrete terms, the principle of self-determination might be satisfied by participation in a larger political union with other peoples. In other situations, however, self-determination might entail the creation of an independent state for that people. This latter possibility puts the principle of self-determination in tension—and perhaps direct conflict—with the principle of territorial sovereignty. All of these newly created states will be carved out of existing states that have a right under international law to control over their own territory.

These states might achieve their own independence through the process of secession, the focus of Section D. A negotiated solution with the parent state is relatively uncontroversial. Things get much more complicated when a territory unilaterally declares its independence over the objection of the parent state. In these cases, secession is the avenue through which a people's right of self-determination might be secured, followed by the creation of a new state that meets the criteria for statehood outlined in Section A. In these situations, the world community can either recognize the would-be state as a newly created independent state, complete with legal personhood under international law, or it could withhold recognition and declare the secession null and void. Some states might make these decisions based on principled criteria: rewarding states with recognition when they accomplish their independence through peaceful means and punishing states by withholding recognition when they seek independence through military force. In practice, though, plenty of states will simply base their decisions on far more pragmatic considerations, such as which entity has control over the territory and is capable of exercising the prerogatives of statehood. Or they may base their decision on geopolitical calculations—establishing alliances with key states and isolating enemies.

This brings us to the topic of Section E, the recognition of foreign governments. A change in government, or even a change in political structure, does not change the identity of a state. The state endures but usually under new leadership or with a new organization. Even in situations where a new government declares itself to be a "new" state, with a new name, other states may insist that the state assume the legal obligations of the prior state as a condition of receiving formal recognition. In some situations, however, states may simply forgo dispensing formal recognition and might instead opt for a form of de facto recognition, that is, opening diplomatic and legal relations with the new government without expressing an official position on its status.

Taken together, the following materials provide an introduction to the concept of statehood—a concept without which our modern system of international could not exist, or at the very least could not exist in its current form. Future chapters will explore entities larger than states (such as international organizations) or smaller than states (such as individual human beings and their rights protected by human rights law). Given that states are the building blocks of international law's DNA, their status as primary (but perhaps not exclusive) units of international law remains unquestioned.

A. CRITERIA FOR STATEHOOD

The criteria for statehood—population, territory, government, and international relations—are generally agreed on by most international lawyers. They are laid out in the so-called Montevideo Convention, which is listed below, a treaty signed in 1933 that codified the criteria, previously accepted as customary law, for the recognition of states under international law. However, the agreement regarding the basic criteria hides the bitter disagreements that follow over which entities should be recognized as states under international law. In other words, the controversy comes in the *application* of the criteria to specific cases, which is far more controversial.

Convention on Rights and Duties of States (Montevideo Convention)

December 26, 1933

Who, after having exhibited their Full Powers, which were found to be in good and due order, have agreed upon the following:

Article 1

The state as a person of international law should possess the following qualifications: a) a permanent population; b) a defined territory; c) government; and d) capacity to enter into relations with the other states.

Article 2

The federal state shall constitute a sole person in the eyes of international law.

Article 3

The political existence of the state is independent of recognition by the other states. Even before recognition the state has the right to defend its integrity and independence, to provide for its conservation and prosperity, and consequently to organize itself as it sees fit, to legislate upon its interests, administer its services, and to define the jurisdiction and competence of its courts.

The exercise of these rights has no other limitation than the exercise of the rights of other states according to international law.

Article 4

States are juridically equal, enjoy the same rights, and have equal capacity in their exercise. The rights of each one do not depend upon the power which it possesses to assure its exercise, but upon the simple fact of its existence as a person under international law.

Article 5

The fundamental rights of states are not susceptible of being affected in any manner whatsoever.

Article 6

The recognition of a state merely signifies that the state which recognizes it accepts the personality of the other with all the rights and duties determined by international law. Recognition is unconditional and irrevocable.

Article 7

The recognition of a state may be express or tacit. The latter results from any act which implies the intention of recognizing the new state.

Article 8

No state has the right to intervene in the internal or external affairs of another.

Article 9

The jurisdiction of states within the limits of national territory applies to all the inhabitants.

Nationals and foreigners are under the same protection of the law and the national authorities and the foreigners may not claim rights other or more extensive than those of the nationals.

Article 10

The primary interest of states is the conservation of peace. Differences of any nature which arise between them should be settled by recognized pacific methods.

Article 11

The contracting states definitely establish as the rule of their conduct the precise obligation not to recognize territorial acquisitions or special advantages which have been obtained by force whether this consists in the employment of arms, in threatening diplomatic representations, or in any other effective coercive measure. The territory of a state is inviolable and may not be the object of military occupation nor of other measures of force imposed by another state directly or indirectly or for any motive whatever even temporarily.

The process of *recognition*—states recognizing each other as sovereign entities—is central to the formation of states. Indeed, exercising the prerogatives of statehood is harder to do if other states refuse to recognize the would-be state as a co-equal sovereign. This has led some international lawyers to conclude that recognition of a state is an essential part of the requirements of statehood, such that a state that fulfills each of the other Montevideo conditions but is not recognized as such is not really a state at all. This is known as the *Constitutive View* because it entails that recognition constitutes one essential ingredient of statehood. The contrasting view is known as the *Declaratory View*, which is the idea that statehood exists independently of recognition, and that the process of recognition merely declares what is already true by virtue of the facts on the ground.

In the following case, a federal district court must decide if the Palestinian Authority has sovereign immunity—a doctrine that requires the court to decide if Palestine is a state, since in most situations only states enjoy sovereign immunity. Which criteria does the court use to determine statehood? Do you agree with the court's assessment of the status of Palestine?

Knox v. Palestine Liberation Organization

U.S. District Court for the Southern District of New York
306 F. Supp. 2d 424 (2004)

On the night of January 17, 2002, Ellis, an American citizen then 31 years old, was performing as a singer before approximately 180 relatives and guests celebrating the Bat Mitzvah of twelve-year-old Nina Kardoshova ("Nina") at the David's Palace banquet hall in Hadera, Israel. At approximately 10:45 p.m., random violence struck. While Nina, her family and guests were dancing, Hassuna, a named defendant in this case though now deceased, arrived at the banquet hall, burst through the door and, using a machine gun, opened fire into the crowd of celebrants. Six people were killed in the attack, including Ellis, and over 30 were wounded. And so, a moment of terror supplanted symbolism with reality; what began as an initiation ended in fatality. For Ellis and the other victims, a rite meant to commemorate an early passage into life was turned, instead, into a bloody ritual vainly exalting death.

Plaintiffs seek damages from Defendants, claiming that Hassana and the other individually named and unnamed defendants were employees, agents and/or co-conspirators of the PLO and PA and, as such, planned and carried out the attack acting in concert with or under instructions or inducements or with the assistance or material support and resources provided by the PLO the PA, Arafat and the other individual defendants.

The issues the parties' arguments and rebuttals present to the Court, however, far transcend the tragedy that ended Ellis's life and the compensation his heirs seek from Defendants. As framed in its larger dimensions, the dispute the parties portray implicates several other far-reaching questions. Is Palestine a state? Is the Israeli military occupation of Palestinian territories an illegal hostile act under international law, or a reality that bears on the validity of Palestine's claim to statehood? Are the PLO and PA constituted governmental entities of a state of Palestine entitled to sovereign immunity, or incubators and agents of international terrorism? Was the violent attack underlying this action carried out with the active knowledge, assistance or participation of Arafat and other high ranking PLO and PA officials? Are Defendants entitled to claim any form of state or governmental immunity to shield them from any further inquiry here into Plaintiffs' allegations? Does this Court possess authority to exercise jurisdiction over the subject matter or over any individual Defendants to permit discovery and further consideration of the merits of Plaintiffs' claims? . . .

A. STATEHOOD UNDER THE RESTATEMENT

1. Sovereign Immunity in General

The relevant civil remedies provision of the ATA provides that any United States national (or his heirs) may recover treble damages against those who cause him injury through acts of international terrorism. A 1992 amendment to the ATA bars any actions under that provision as against "a foreign state, an agency of a foreign state, or an officer or employee of a foreign state or an agency thereof acting within his or her official capacity or under color of legal authority." 18 U.S.C. § 2337. More broadly, the Foreign Sovereign Immunities Act, 28 U.S.C. § 1602, deprives federal courts of jurisdiction over any "foreign state" in any civil action, subject to exceptions not relevant here.

The PLO and PA assert that they are part of the "foreign state" of Palestine. Thus, they assert that the FSIA deprives this Court of jurisdiction to hear any aspect of this case and that § 2337 exempts them from the ATA cause of action in particular. . .

The Court must therefore determine whether there exists a "foreign state" of Palestine and, if so, whether the PLO and PA are essential elements of that state. Defendants need not demonstrate that either the PLO or PA would, by itself, satisfy the criteria for statehood. The Court concludes that PLO and PA are not entitled to sovereign immunity because there does not exist a state of Palestine which meets the legal criteria for statehood applicable to the Court's adjudication of the issue.

2. Brief Legal History of the PLO and PA

Although the Court will not endeavor to craft an impartial and comprehensive history of the struggle between the Palestinians and the Israelis over control of the territory historically known as Palestine, a brief mention of the events of legal significance to the motion now before the Court is instructive. At the end of World War I, the League of Nations placed Palestine (until then part of the Ottoman Empire) under British control, or "mandate," for the purpose of eventually establishing an independent state. From then and especially through and immediately following World War II, many Jews immigrated to the region, in spite of strong opposition from the local Arab inhabitants. Violence between Arabs and Jews prompted Great Britain to call for a special session of the United Nations General Assembly. In November 1947, the General Assembly adopted Resolution 181(II), which called for Palestine to be partitioned into a Jewish state and an Arab state, and contemplated that each state would gradually gain independence. See Future Government of Palestine, G.A. Res. 181(II), U.N. GAOR, Supp. No. 1, at 131, UN Doc. A/519 (1947). Resolution 181(II) engendered more violent conflict because leaders of the Palestinians rejected it, while Jewish leaders accepted it. When British forces pulled out of the region in May 1948,

Jewish leaders proclaimed the establishment of Israel, along the borders called for under Resolution 181(II), and full-blown war erupted between Israel and various neighboring Arab states. Israel prevailed and controlled much of the territory which had been allotted to the contemplated Arab state by Resolution 181(II), while Egypt and Jordan controlled the remaining portions—the Gaza Strip and the West Bank of the Jordan River (the "West Bank"), respectively. The war caused almost 750,000 Palestinians to become refugees.

Israel was admitted to the United Nations in 1949 and the situation in the region remained relatively without outbreak of major conflict until June 1967, when Israel, attacked by some of its Arab neighbors (Egypt, Jordan, and Syria), became involved in what became known as the Six-Day War. Israel again prevailed, and gained control of all of Palestine, including the West Bank, the Gaza Strip, and East Jerusalem—the areas which are now collectively called "Palestine," or the "occupied Palestinian territories." In November 1967, the United Nations Security Council adopted a resolution calling for "[w]ithdrawal of Israel armed forces from territories occupied in the recent conflict" and emphasized the need for "acknowledgment of the sovereignty, territorial integrity and political independence of every State in the area. . . ." S.C. Res. 242 (1967).

The PLO, which had formed in 1964, established a new charter in 1968 calling for the continued fight for Palestinian rights and independence. In 1974, the United Nations General Assembly recognized the PLO as "the principal party to the question of Palestine," and the PLO has since participated in the United Nations General Assembly as a permanent observer. See G.A. Res. 3210 and 3237 (1974). Neither the PLO nor Palestine has been admitted as a full member of the United Nations.

In 1988, the Palestinian National Council, the self-described Parliament in exile of the Palestinian people, issued a "Declaration of Independence" which purported to establish an independent state of Palestine, with Jerusalem as its capital. Within days, more than two dozen countries, including the Soviet Union and India, issued statements supporting the declaration or recognizing the new Palestinian state. The United States did not endorse the declaration, nor did it recognize a Palestinian state. Against this backdrop, a Second Circuit panel held in 1991 that the PLO was not a "foreign state" and therefore not entitled to sovereign immunity under the FSIA. See *Klinghoffer v. S.N.C. Achille Lauro*, 937 F.2d 44, 47–49 (2d Cir.1991). That panel held it "quite clear" that the PLO met *none* of the four legal prerequisites for statehood enunciated in the Restatement (Third). Nonetheless, Defendants contend that several fundamental international developments which occurred after *Klinghoffer* was decided produced agreements between the Palestinians and the Israelis and actual changes in Palestine that have materially altered the situation on the ground and cast doubt on the continuing validity of *Klinghoffer*.

Specifically, in September 1993, the PLO achieved a major milestone on the road towards a Palestinian state when, in a ceremony on the White House lawn, it agreed with the government of Israel to a Declaration of Principles on Interim Self-Government Arrangements (the "DOP"). The DOP "recognized [the] mutual legitimate and political rights" of the Palestinians and Israelis and sought to move the two sides towards a "just, lasting and comprehensive peace settlement. . . ." Declaration of Principles on Interim Self-Government Arrangements, Sept. 13, 1993, Preamble. In broad terms, the DOP established a five-year framework and timetable by which the two sides would negotiate the details for Israel to gradually transfer political and administrative authority in the West Bank and Gaza Strip to the Palestinians.

The DOP specified that, upon Israel's withdrawal of forces from the Gaza Strip and Jericho, the Palestinians would immediately establish a police force and would have immediate authority over "education and culture, health, social welfare, direct taxation, and tourism" in Palestine. The two sides agreed to begin negotiating an "Interim Agreement" which would, among other things, specify the structure of an interim Palestinian governmental authority and detail the transfer of powers from the Israeli government to that new Palestinian governmental authority. The DOP also called for the parties to begin "permanent status negotiations" to resolve the tougher questions of "Jerusalem, refugees, settlements, security arrangements, borders, relations and cooperation with other neighbors, and other issues of common interest."

In May 1994 one of many agreements augmenting the DOP established the interim governmental authority—the PA—with "all the legislative and executive powers and responsibilities" specified in that agreement. The DOP and such accompanying agreements are often collectively called the "Oslo Accords."

In September 1995, the parties completed the Interim Agreement. The Interim Agreement is far more comprehensive than the DOP and established in far greater detail the rights and obligations of the parties. It overhauled the structure of the PA and delineated its powers in much more detail. The Interim Agreement also provided for various security arrangements, including the redeployment of certain Israeli forces in the West Bank. As the constitutional document defining the PA and its official powers and functions, the Interim Agreement is crucial in answering the legal questions raised in this motion.

3. *Palestine's Claim to Statehood*

As an initial matter, neither the DOP, the Interim Agreement, nor any other of the Oslo Accords purports to create a state of Palestine. The

Interim Agreement explicitly states that the "status" of the occupied Palestinian territories "will be preserved during the interim period." A logical inference from these facts, and from the title of the Interim Agreement as "Interim," is that the Oslo Accords aim towards *eventual* statehood for Palestine (or some other permanent arrangement), not that the Oslo Accords have already created an independent state of Palestine. A close examination of the details of those agreements confirms this inference because, as the Court here stresses, the Oslo Accords consciously apportion political, administrative and diplomatic authority as between Israel and Palestine so as to make it clear that, under the relevant and well-established legal test, there does not exist, at present, an independent sovereign state of Palestine.

The Second Circuit has adopted the Restatement (Third)'s definition of "state" for purposes of the FSIA. Accordingly, for these purposes, "a state is an entity that has [1] a defined territory and a [2] permanent population, [3] under the control of its own government, and that [4] engages in, or has the capacity to engage in, formal relations with other such entities." Restatement (Third) § 201. The PLO and PA do not meet, nor are they part of any entity which meets, these criteria because, first, the PLO and PA do not sufficiently "control" Palestine and, second, they do not have sufficient capacity to engage in foreign relations.

Defendants argue that, at least since the United Nations called for a partition of British-mandated Palestine, Palestine has had a defined territory. While acknowledging that the borders have occasionally changed and that there is some dispute as to their exact contours, Defendants maintain that it is commonly recognized that Palestine today consists of the West Bank, Gaza Strip, and East Jerusalem. Moreover, Defendants remind the Court of what is an indisputable historical fact: that there has been a permanent population in Palestine for over two millennia.

Plaintiffs' briefing purports to challenge these first two requirements, but their arguments in this regard are, in essence, that neither the PLO nor PA has a defined territory *under its control,* nor a permanent population *under its control.* Accordingly, the Court moves directly to the third prong of the Restatement (Third) definition and addresses whether there is a government in Palestine in control of a defined territory and permanent population.

4.   *Control Over Territory and Population*

As evidence that the purported government of Palestine is in control of its population in the defined territory, Defendants assert that Palestinian government officials provide the complete services of a government, limited only to the extent that Israel forcibly imposes its occupation upon the Palestinians. Defendants emphasize that Israel's occupation—which Defendants contend is violent, oppressive, and illegal—cannot negate Palestine's claim to statehood. Defendants also direct the Court's attention to a law review article which concludes that "Palestine has a plausible claim to statehood. . . ." See John Quigley, *The Israel-PLO Interim Agreements: Are They Treaties?*, 30 Cornell Int'l L.J. 717 (1997). In that article, Professor Quigley argues that under the Interim Agreement, "the PLO came to administer both the Gaza Strip and the major towns of the West Bank," and thereby arguably satisfied the Restatement (Third)'s control requirement. Moreover, Professor Quigley asserts that "the control requirement has been relaxed in international practice where the putative state was seen to have a right to statehood and where there was not a competing entity seeking statehood in the same territory." He cites the examples of the Congo and Guinea-Bissau, which were admitted to the United Nations, even though their previous colonizers (Belgium and Portugal, respectively) had not yet fully ceded control to the new nations. On this point, the Court disagrees with the Defendants and Professor Quigley and is persuaded instead by the weight of judicial and scholarly authority pronouncing that, for statehood purposes, the PA and PLO do not meet the control requirement.

It is well-accepted under international law that, to meet the governmental control requirement, the entity "must be capable of acting independently of foreign governments." In other words, the entity must be "independent from direct orders from other State powers." The purported state must have "legal authority which is not in law dependent on any other earthly authority."

For example, a 1991 Second Circuit panel held that Palau, a group of approximately 200 islands in the Southwest Pacific, was not a foreign state within the meaning of the FSIA because the United States retained "ultimate authority over the governance of Palau." In this regard, following World War II, the United States entered into a Trusteeship Agreement with the United Nations Security Council regarding the governance of more than 2,100 islands (including Palau) formerly governed by Japanese mandate. Even though Palau "ha[d] been exercising sovereign powers pursuant to its Constitution adopted in January, 1981," the Second Circuit panel held that it was not entitled to sovereign immunity because, among other reasons, Palau was bound by pertinent United States laws, including executive orders of the Secretary of the Interior. The panel noted "that a political entity whose laws may be suspended by another cannot be said to be possessed of sovereignty of any kind, de facto or de jure."

An examination of the Interim Agreement confirms that the Oslo Accords have not created a Palestinian state because the Interim Agreement substantially circumscribes the PA's authority in many spheres of governance. The first words of Article I of the Interim Agreement make clear that the PA has limited jurisdiction: "Israel shall transfer powers and responsibilities as specified in this Agreement from the Israeli military government and its Civil Administration to the [PA] in accordance with this Agreement. *Israel shall continue to exercise powers and responsibilities not so transferred.*" In addition to Israel's Article I residual authority, the Interim Agreement is explicit that Israel, not the PA, has authority and jurisdiction regarding Israeli settlements, external security, and the Palestinian airspace. Moreover, the PA has virtually no jurisdiction over Israeli citizens, even when they are otherwise within the PA's territorial jurisdiction. Israel has authority to approve or reject visitors' permits to the West Bank and Gaza, and to approve or reject persons seeking permanent residence there. Under the Interim Agreement, a committee with an equal number of Israelis and Palestinians is in charge of "matters arising with regard to infrastructures, such as roads, water, and sewage systems, power lines and telecommunications infrastructure, which require coordination" between the parties.

In short, the PA's authority is subordinate to Israel's sovereign control, in many fundamental ways that conflict with and negate a claim of the existence of independent statehood for the Palestinian territory over which the PA exercises the limited governmental power specified in the Oslo Accords. . .

Defendants do not dispute any of these limitations on the PA's control, except to point out that they are the result of Israel's illegal and oppressive occupation. It is true that "belligerent occupation does not affect the continuity of the state." However, the predicate for this principle is that a sovereign entity satisfying all of the prerequisites for statehood existed prior to the occupation. In this case, Defendants have not argued that there was an independent state of Palestine immediately *before* Israel's allegedly illegal occupation. Under international law, a state will *maintain* its statehood during a belligerent occupation, but it would be anomalous indeed to hold that a state may *achieve* sufficient independence and statehood in the first instance while subject to and laboring under the hostile military occupation of a separate sovereign. In light of the preceding discussion, the Court concludes that neither the PLO nor PA possesses sufficient control over the disputed Palestinian territories to satisfy the "control" criterion of statehood.

5. *Capacity To Conduct Foreign Relations*

"An entity is not a state unless it has competence, within its own constitutional system, to conduct international relations with other states, as well as the political, technical, and financial capabilities to do so." Restatement (Third) § 201 cmt. e. The capacity of a state to engage in foreign relations with other sovereigns depends, in part, "on the entity concerned being separate for the purpose of [international] relations so that no other entity both carries out and accepts responsibility for them." Under the Interim Agreement, the PA is expressly prohibited from conducting foreign relations:

> In accordance with the DOP, the [PA] will not have powers and responsibilities in the sphere of foreign relations, which sphere includes the establishment abroad of embassies, consulates or other types of foreign missions and posts or permitting their establishment in the West Bank or the Gaza Strip, the appointment of or admission of diplomatic and consular staff, and the exercise of diplomatic functions.

Interim Agreement, art. IX. As Professor Watson explains, "The Interim Agreement starkly forbids the PA to engage in even the most fundamental aspect of foreign relations, [which] is obviously inconsistent with the suggestion that the PA now has the 'capacity to engage in foreign relations.'"

The Interim Agreement permits the PLO to negotiate and enter into international agreements regarding certain economic development plans, as well as certain cultural, scientific and educational agreements, "for the benefit of" the PA. However, the Interim Agreement explicitly declares that these limited activities "shall not be considered foreign relations." More importantly, the Interim Agreement provides no mechanism by which the PLO could actually implement any international commitments in the spheres of power delegated to the PA. Furthermore, neither the PLO nor the PA would be able to implement any international commitments in the spheres of authority which, as discussed above, remain with Israel, such as those relating to external threats, border control, and the movement of persons into the Palestinian territories. For this independent reason, Defendants have failed to carry their burden to demonstrate that the PLO or PA, even in combination, have sufficient capacity to conduct international relations to satisfy that criterion of statehood. . .

AFTERWORD

Much has changed since the SDNY released its decision in *Knox*. In 2006, elections and a subsequent military conflict between Hamas and Fatah brought the political party Hamas to power in Gaza, while the Palestinian Authority remains in control of the West Bank. The result is that the Palestinian territories are no longer governed by the same entity.

Also, since 2004 when *Knox* was decided, more states recognize Palestine as a state. In 2012, the UN General Assembly voted to grant Palestine Non-member observer status to the United Nations. Although the resolution did not admit Palestine to the United Nations as a full-fledged member—it was limited to observer status—the resolution was widely seen as a precursor to eventual recognition of statehood. The vote total for the resolution was 138 yes, 9 no, and 41 abstentions. Sweden announced in 2014 that it would formally recognize Palestine as a state, becoming the 135th state to do so. Although the United States and Canada do not, much of South America, Africa, and Asia recognize Palestine.

Most importantly, Israel removed most of its military forces from Gaza in 2005, though it retains some control over the Gaza coastline through a naval blockade. There is a dispute among international lawyers over whether Israel should still be described as an occupying power in Gaza. Israeli military forces continue to occupy parts of the West Bank.

In order to buttress its claim to statehood, the Palestinian Authority signed numerous international treaties and Conventions in 2015 and deposited their signatures with the United Nations Secretary General, who accepted the deposit. The conventions included the four Geneva Conventions originally drafted after World War II, and most controversially, the Rome Statute of the International Criminal Court. The latter was seen as a prelude to referring its situation to the ICC prosecutor for investigation of alleged crimes committed during an armed conflict with Israel. The move antagonized Israel which reacted strongly against the Palestinian attempt to use the international agreements as a way of bootstrapping its way into statehood.

In 2018, Palestine filed a suit against the United States at the ICJ alleging that President Trump's decision to move its Embassy from Tel Aviv to Jerusalem violated the Vienna Convention on Consular Relations. Palestine acceded to the Vienna Convention in 2014 and to the Optional Protocol to the Vienna Convention concerning the Compulsory Settlement of Disputes in 2018.

Why was the Palestinian Authority inclined to sign the treaties and file cases at the ICJ? As discussed above, the capacity to engage in international relations is one component of the criteria for statehood. In the final analysis, do you believe that Palestine is a state? Does it matter that a large number of states have recognized Palestine? Or is it the underlying facts that matter most?

NOTES & QUESTIONS

Continuity of Legal Obligations. When a new state is formed, there is often some ambiguity about the continuity of legal obligations from the prior state. A number of factors inform whether the new state will be subject to the prior legal obligations. The first factor is whether the new state is deemed a "successor" state or a genuinely new state. In the case of a successor state, legal obligations are more likely to be honored since the identity of the state is preserved through the transformation. If, on the other hand, the new state is considered to be an entirely new state, with a break in identity, it is less likely that other states will insist that prior legal obligations be honored. The second factor is whether states make the observance of prior legal obligations a condition of their recognition of the new state. In other words, a state might ask the newly formed state for assurances that it will honor certain legal obligations before issuing a statement formally recognizing the new state. One factor that constrains newly formed states is the logic of reciprocity. If a state wishes to receive the benefits of prior legal arrangements, it might have to accept legal obligations as well. For more discussion of these issues, see James R. Crawford, *The Creation of States in International Law* 34 (2006).

B. NORMATIVE CRITERIA FOR STATEHOOD

A state's decision whether to recognize another state depends on several factors—not just the factors listed in the Montevideo Convention. States occasionally filter their recognition decisions through their strategic objectives. Sometimes those strategic objectives are based on geopolitical concerns, which might favor recognizing states that will become allies and withholding recognition for states that will become enemies or, at the very least, geopolitical competitors.

In the early 1990s, the breakup of the former Yugoslavia, as well as the breakup of the Soviet Union, triggered a flurry of new would-be states seeking recognition from the world community. For the first time in years, established states were tasked with deciding whether they would recognize not just one but many states, and under what criteria.

In the statement below, the European Community articulates the standards it used for recognizing states. In addition to the classic Montevideo criteria, the European Community included several more normative criteria, i.e., expectations about how these states would be structured and governed—in accordance with the rule of law and respect for human rights—that were essential preconditions for recognition. As you read the following statement, ask yourself whether states should deploy their power of recognition in order to promote human rights or whether they should simply recognize states based on purely descriptive criteria, i.e., whether the state has control over its territory and population, regardless of whether they do so in a humane or liberal fashion. The implication of normative criteria for statehood is that states should withhold recognition from states governed by illiberal or repressive regimes. Is that an appropriate way of spreading democratic values?

European Community Declaration on Yugoslavia and on the Guidelines on the Recognition of New States
December 16, 1991
31 I.L.M. 1485

Declaration on Yugoslavia

The European Community and its member States discussed the situation in Yugoslavia in the light of their guidelines on the recognition of new states in Eastern Europe and in the Soviet Union. They adopted a common position with regard to the recognition of Yugoslav Republics. In this connection they concluded the following:

The Community and its member States agree to recognise the independence of all the Yugoslav Republics fulfilling all the conditions set out below. The implementation of this decision will take place on January 15, 1992.

They are therefore inviting all Yugoslav Republics to state by 23 December whether:

- they wish to be recognised as independent States;

- they accept the commitments contained in the above-mentioned guidelines;

- they accept the provisions laid down in the draft Convention—especially those in Chapter II on human rights and rights of national or ethnic groups—under consideration by the Conference on Yugoslavia;

- they continue to support the efforts of the Secretary General and the Security Council of the United Nations, and the continuation of the Conference on Yugoslavia.

The applications of those Republics which reply positively will be submitted through the Chair of the Conference to the Arbitration Commission for advice before the implementation date.

In the meantime, the Community and its member States request the UN Secretary General and the UN Security Council to continue their efforts to establish an effective cease-fire and promote a peaceful and negotiated outcome to the conflict. They continue to attach the greatest importance to the early deployment of a UN peace-keeping force referred to in UN Security Council Resolution 724.

The Community and its member States also require a Yugoslav Republic to commit itself, prior to recognition, to adopt constitutional and political guarantees ensuring that it has no territorial claims towards a neighbouring Community State and that it will conduct no hostile propaganda activities versus a neighbouring Community State, including the use of a denomination which implies territorial claims.

Declaration on the "Guidelines on the Recognition of New States in Eastern Europe and in the Soviet Union"

In compliance with the European Council's request, Ministers have assessed developments in Eastern Europe and in the Soviet Union with a view to elaborating an approach regarding relations with new states.

In this connection they have adopted the following guidelines on the formal recognition of new states in Eastern Europe and in the Soviet Union:

The community and its Member States confirm their attachment to the principles of the Helsinki Final Act and the Charter of Paris, in particular the principle of self-determination. They affirm their readiness to recognise, subject to the normal standards of international practice and the political realities in each case, those new states which, following the historic changes in the region, have constituted themselves on a democratic basis, have accepted the appropriate international obligations and have committed themselves in good faith to a peaceful process and to negotiations.

Therefore, they adopt a common position on the process of recognition of these new states, which requires:

- respect for the provisions of the Charter of the United Nations and the commitments subscribed to in the Final Act of Helsinki and in the Charter of Paris, especially with regard to the rule of law, democracy and human rights;

- guarantees for the rights of ethnic and national groups and minorities in accordance with the commitments subscribed to in the framework of the CSCE;

- respect for the inviolability of all frontiers which can only be changed by peaceful means and by common agreement;

- acceptance of all relevant commitments with regard to disarmament and nuclear non-proliferation as well as to security and regional stability;

- commitment to settle by agreement, including where appropriate by recourse to arbitration, all questions concerning state succession and regional disputes.

The Community and its Member States will not recognise entities which are the result of aggression. They would take account of the effects of recognition on neighbouring states.

The commitments to these principles opens the way to recognition by the Community and its Member States and to the establishment of diplomatic relations. It could be laid down in agreements.

NOTES & QUESTIONS

Constitutive Versus Declarative. Reconsider the distinction introduced at the very beginning of this section between the Declarative View and the Constitutive View of state recognition. One argument in favor of the constitutive view is that it grants recognition a real significance—the process *matters* for international law because without it, the state does not exist. Under the declarative view, the process of state recognition is superfluous, i.e., it does not change the outcome of the analysis. On the other hand, there is something suspicious about the Constitutive View. If a state meets the objective criteria for statehood—the facts on the ground, as it were—it seems strange that other states could deny it statehood simply by refusing to recognize it. Whether it exists as a state should be determined by objective criteria, not by the conferral of recognition that other states can withhold strategically. See James Crawford, *The Creation of States in International Law* (2d ed. 2006). As one commentator has put it: "Indeed, while constitutive theory may describe how recognition works in practice more accurately than declarative theory does, constitutive theory, by subjugating international law to political powers and political decisions, is both unsatisfying from a theoretical level and troubling from a moral perspective." See Gabriel Rossman, *Extremely Loud and Incredibly Close (but Still So Far): Assessing Liberland's Claim of Statehood*, 17 Chi. J. Int'l L. 306, 322 (2016). Do you agree with this assessment? For more discussion, see Mikulas Fabry, *Recognizing States: International Society & the Establishment of New States Since 1776* (2010).

C. THE RIGHT OF SELF-DETERMINATION

The right of self-determination is one of the most fundamental collective rights recognized by international law. It is codified in article 1 of the International Covenant on Civil and Political Rights (ICCPR), which states that "All peoples have the right of self-determination. By virtue of that right they freely determine their political status and freely pursue their economic, social and cultural development." Furthermore, article 1 of the UN Charter refers to "respect for the principle of equal rights and self-determination of peoples." The text of both instruments is clear that the right to self-determination is attributable to *peoples*— rather than states—and that peoples have a right to determine their own political destiny.

In many situations, though perhaps not all, the right of self-determination will entail statehood as a means of exercising the underlying right. This is where the rubber meets the road. While it is uncontested that there exists a general right of self-determination, it is the application of this right that is so contested. In concrete situations, international lawyers will debate whether the group in question constitutes "a people," and if the answer to that question is yes, then whether self-determination requires an independent state for that people. The following case is a classic example of that legal analysis. As you read the case, look for the key concepts that the Supreme Court of Canada uses to answer these questions.

In re Secession of Quebec
Supreme Court of Canada
2 S.C.R. 217 (1998)

This Reference requires us to consider momentous questions that go to the heart of our system of constitutional government. The observation we made more than a decade ago. . . . applies with equal force here: the present [case] "combines legal and constitutional questions of the utmost subtlety and complexity with political questions of great sensitivity." In our view, it is not possible to answer the questions that have been put to us without a consideration of a number of underlying principles. An exploration of the meaning and nature of these underlying principles is not merely of academic interest. On the contrary, such an exploration is of immense practical utility. Only once those underlying principles have been examined and delineated may a considered response to the questions we are required to answer emerge. . .

Question 2:   Does international law give the National Assembly, legislature or government of Quebec the right to effect the secession of Quebec from Canada unilaterally? In this regard, is there a right to self-determination under international law that would give the National Assembly, legislature or government of Quebec the right to effect the secession of Quebec from Canada unilaterally?

For reasons already discussed, the Court does not accept the contention that Question 2 raises a question of "pure" international law which this Court has no jurisdiction to address. Question 2 is posed in the context of a Reference to address the existence or non-existence of a right of unilateral secession by a province of Canada. The amicus curiae argues that this question ultimately falls to be determined under international law. In addressing this issue, the Court does not purport to act as an arbiter between sovereign states or more generally within the international community. The Court is engaged in rendering an advisory opinion on certain legal aspects of the continued existence of the Canadian federation. International law has been invoked as a consideration and it must therefore be addressed.

The argument before the Court on Question 2 has focused largely on determining whether, under international law, a positive legal right to unilateral secession exists. . . Arguments were also advanced to the effect that, regardless of the existence or non-existence of a positive right to unilateral secession, international law will in the end recognize effective political realities—including the emergence of a new state—as facts. [I]t should first be noted that the existence of a positive legal entitlement is quite different from a prediction that the law will respond after the fact to a then existing political reality. These two concepts examine different points in time. The questions posed to the Court address legal rights in advance of a unilateral act of purported secession. While we touch below on the practice governing the international recognition of emerging states, the Court is as wary of entertaining speculation about the possible future conduct of sovereign states on the international level as it was under Question 1 to speculate about the possible future course of political negotiations among the participants in the Canadian federation. In both cases, the Reference questions are directed only to the legal framework within which the political actors discharge their various mandates.

Secession at International Law

It is clear that international law does not specifically grant component parts of sovereign states the legal right to secede unilaterally from their "parent" state. This is acknowledged by the experts who provided their opinions on behalf of both the amicus curiae and the Attorney General of Canada. Given the lack of specific authorization for unilateral secession, proponents of the existence of such a right at international law are therefore left to attempt to found their argument (i) on the proposition that unilateral secession is not specifically prohibited and that what is not specifically prohibited is inferentially permitted; or (ii) on the implied duty of states to recognize the legitimacy of secession brought about by the exercise of the well-established international law right of "a people" to self-determination. The amicus curiae addressed the right of self-determination, but submitted that it was not applicable to the circumstances of Quebec within the Canadian federation, irrespective of the existence or non-existence of a referendum result in favour of secession. We agree on this point with the amicus curiae, for reasons that we will briefly develop.

A.   Absence of a Specific Prohibition

International law contains neither a right of unilateral secession nor the explicit denial of such a right, although such a denial is, to some extent, implicit in the exceptional circumstances required for secession to be permitted under the right of a people to self-determination, e.g., the right of secession that arises in the exceptional situation of an oppressed or colonial people, discussed below. As will be seen, international law places great importance on the territorial integrity of nation states and, by and large, leaves the creation of a new state to be determined by the domestic law of the existing state of which the seceding entity presently forms a part. Where, as here, unilateral secession would be incompatible with the domestic Constitution, international law is likely to accept that conclusion subject to the right of peoples to self-determination, a topic to which we now turn.

B.   The Right of a People to Self-determination

While international law generally regulates the conduct of nation states, it does, in some specific circumstances, also recognize the "rights" of entities other than nation states—such as the right of a people to self-determination.

The existence of the right of a people to self-determination is now so widely recognized in international conventions that the principle has acquired a status beyond "convention" and is considered a general principle of international law.

Article 1 of the Charter of the United Nations, states in part that one of the purposes of the United Nations (U.N.) is: "To develop friendly relations among nations based on respect for the principle of equal rights and self-determination of peoples, and to take other appropriate measures to strengthen universal peace. . ."

Article 55 of the U.N. Charter further states that the U.N. shall promote goals such as higher standards of living, full employment and human rights "[w]ith a view to the creation of conditions of stability and well-being which are necessary for peaceful and friendly relations among nations based on respect for the principle of equal rights and self-determination of peoples."

This basic principle of self-determination has been carried forward and addressed in so many U.N. conventions and resolutions that, as noted by Doehring, "The sheer number of resolutions concerning the right of self-determination makes their enumeration impossible."

For our purposes, reference to the following conventions and resolutions is sufficient. Article 1 of both the U.N.'s International Covenant on Civil and Political Rights, and its International Covenant on Economic, Social and Cultural Rights, states: "All peoples have the right of self-determination. By virtue of that right they freely determine their political status and freely pursue their economic, social and cultural development."

Similarly, the U.N. General Assembly's Declaration on Principles of International Law concerning Friendly Relations and Co-operation among States in accordance with the Charter of the United Nations, 24 October 1970, states: "By virtue of the principle of equal rights and self-determination of peoples enshrined in the Charter of the United Nations, all peoples have the right freely to determine, without external interference, their political status and to pursue their economic, social and cultural development, and every State has the duty to respect this right in accordance with the provisions of the Charter."

In 1993, the U.N. World Conference on Human Rights adopted the Vienna Declaration and Programme of Action, that reaffirmed Article 1 of the two above-mentioned covenants. The U.N. General Assembly's Declaration on the Occasion of the Fiftieth Anniversary of the United Nations (November 9, 1995), also emphasizes the right to self-determination by providing that the U.N.'s member states will: "Continue to reaffirm the right of self-determination of all peoples, taking into account the particular situation of peoples under colonial or other forms of alien domination or foreign occupation, and recognize the right of peoples to take legitimate action in accordance with the Charter of the United Nations to realize their inalienable right of self-determination. This shall not be construed as authorizing or encouraging any action that would dismember or impair, totally or in part, the territorial integrity or political unity of sovereign and independent States conducting themselves in compliance with the principle of equal rights and self-determination of peoples and thus possessed of a Government representing the whole people belonging to the territory without distinction of any kind. . ." [Emphasis added.]

The right to self-determination is also recognized in other international legal documents. For example, the Final Act of the Conference on Security and Co-operation in Europe (Helsinki Final Act) (1975) states: "The participating States will respect the equal rights of peoples and their right to self-determination, acting at all times in conformity with the purposes and principles of the Charter of the United Nations and with the relevant norms of international law, including those relating to territorial integrity of States. By virtue of the principle of equal rights and self-determination of peoples, all peoples always have the right, in full freedom, to determine, when and as they wish, their internal and external political status, without external interference, and to pursue as they wish their political, economic, social and cultural development."

As will be seen, international law expects that the right to self-determination will be exercised by peoples within the framework of existing sovereign states and consistently with the maintenance of the territorial integrity of those states. Where this is not possible, in the exceptional circumstances discussed below, a right of secession may arise.

International law grants the right to self-determination to "peoples." Accordingly, access to the right requires the threshold step of characterizing as a people the group seeking self-determination. However, as the right to self-determination has developed by virtue of a combination of international agreements and conventions, coupled with state practice, with little formal elaboration of the definition of "peoples," the result has been that the precise meaning of the term "people" remains somewhat uncertain.

It is clear that "a people" may include only a portion of the population of an existing state. The right to self-determination has developed largely as a human right, and is generally used in documents that simultaneously contain references to "nation" and "state." The juxtaposition of these terms is indicative that the reference to "people" does not necessarily mean the entirety of a state's population. To restrict the definition of the term to the population of existing states would render the granting of a right to self-determination largely duplicative, given the parallel emphasis within the majority of the source documents on the need to protect the territorial integrity of existing states, and would frustrate its remedial purpose.

While much of the Quebec population certainly shares many of the characteristics (such as a common language and culture) that would be considered in determining whether a specific group is a "people," as do other groups within Quebec and/or Canada, it is not necessary to explore this legal characterization to resolve Question 2 appropriately. Similarly, it is not necessary for the Court to determine whether, should a Quebec people exist within the definition of public international law, such a people encompasses the entirety of the provincial population or just a portion thereof. Nor is it necessary to examine the position of the aboriginal population within Quebec. As the following discussion of the scope of the right to self-determination will make clear, whatever be the correct application of the definition of people(s) in this context, their right of self-determination cannot in the present circumstances be said to ground a right to unilateral secession.

The recognized sources of international law establish that the right to self-determination of a people is normally fulfilled through internal self-determination—a people's pursuit of its political, economic, social and cultural development within the framework of an existing state. A right to external self-determination (which in this case potentially takes the form of the assertion of a right to unilateral secession) arises in only the most extreme of cases and, even then, under carefully defined circumstances. External self-determination can be defined as in the following statement from the Declaration on Friendly Relations as "[t]he establishment of a sovereign and independent State, the free association or integration with an independent State or the emergence into any other political status freely determined by a people constitute modes of implementing the right of self-determination by that people."

The international law principle of self-determination has evolved within a framework of respect for the territorial integrity of existing states. The various international documents that support the existence of a people's right to self-determination also contain parallel statements supportive of the conclusion that the exercise of such a right must be sufficiently limited to prevent threats to an existing state's territorial integrity or the stability of relations between sovereign states.

The Declaration on Friendly Relations, the Vienna Declaration and the Declaration on the Occasion of the Fiftieth Anniversary of the United Nations are specific. They state, immediately after affirming a people's right to determine political, economic, social and cultural issues, that such rights are not to "be construed as authorizing or encouraging any action that would dismember or impair, totally or in part, the territorial integrity or political unity of sovereign and independent States conducting themselves in compliance with the principle of equal rights and self-determination of peoples and thus possessed of a Government representing the whole people belonging to the territory without distinction. . ."

Similarly, while the concluding document of the Vienna Meeting in 1989 of the Conference on Security and Co-operation in Europe on the follow-up to the Helsinki Final Act again refers to peoples having the right to determine "their internal and external political status," that statement is immediately followed by express recognition that the participating states will at all times act, as stated in the Helsinki Final Act, "in conformity with the purposes and principles of the Charter of the United Nations and with the relevant norms of international law, including those relating to territorial integrity of States." Principle 5 of the concluding document states that the participating states (including Canada): ". . .confirm their commitment strictly and effectively to observe the principle of the territorial integrity of States. They will refrain from any violation of this principle and thus from any action aimed by direct or indirect means, in contravention of the purposes and principles of the Charter of the United Nations, other obligations under international law or the provisions of the [Helsinki] Final Act, at violating the territorial integrity, political independence or the unity of a State. No actions or situations in contravention of this principle will be recognized as legal by the participating States."

Accordingly, the reference in the Helsinki Final Act to a people determining its external political status is interpreted to mean the expression of a people's external political status through the government of the existing state, save in the exceptional circumstances discussed below. As noted by Cassese, given the history and textual structure of this document, its reference to external self-determination simply means that "no territorial or other change can be brought about by the central authorities of a State that is contrary to the will of the whole people of that State."

While the International Covenant on Economic, Social and Cultural Rights and the International Covenant on Civil and Political Rights do not specifically refer to the protection of territorial integrity, they both define the ambit of the right to self-determination in terms that are normally attainable within the framework of an existing state. There is no necessary incompatibility between the maintenance of the territorial integrity of existing states, including Canada, and the right of a "people" to achieve a full measure of self-determination. A state whose government represents the whole of the people or peoples resident within its territory, on a basis of equality and without discrimination, and respects the principles of self-determination in its own internal arrangements, is entitled to the protection under international law of its territorial integrity.

Accordingly, the general state of international law with respect to the right to self-determination is that the right operates within the overriding protection granted to the territorial integrity of "parent" states. However. . . there are certain defined contexts within which the right to the self-determination of peoples does allow that right to be exercised "externally," which, in the context of this Reference, would potentially mean secession: ". . .the right to external self-determination, which entails the possibility of choosing (or restoring) independence, has only been bestowed upon two classes of peoples (those under colonial rule or foreign occupation), based upon the assumption that both classes make up entities that are inherently distinct from the colonialist Power and the occupant Power and that their 'territorial integrity,' all but destroyed by the colonialist or occupying Power, should be fully restored. . ."

The right of colonial peoples to exercise their right to self-determination by breaking away from the "imperial" power is now undisputed, but is irrelevant to this Reference. . . The other clear case where a right to external self-determination accrues is where a people is subject to alien subjugation, domination or exploitation outside a colonial context. . .

A number of commentators have further asserted that the right to self-determination may ground a right to unilateral secession in a third circumstance. Although this third circumstance has been described in several ways, the underlying proposition is that, when a people is blocked from the meaningful exercise of its right to self-determination internally, it is entitled, as a last resort, to exercise it by secession. The Vienna Declaration requirement that governments represent "the whole people belonging to the territory without distinction of any kind" adds credence to the assertion that such a complete blockage may potentially give rise to a right of secession.

Clearly, such a circumstance parallels the other two recognized situations in that the ability of a people to exercise its right to self-determination internally is somehow being totally frustrated. While it remains unclear whether this third proposition actually reflects an established international law standard, it is unnecessary for present purposes to make that determination. Even assuming that the third circumstance is sufficient to create a right to unilateral secession under international law, the current Quebec context cannot be said to approach such a threshold. As stated by the amicus curiae: "The Quebec people is not the victim of attacks on its physical existence or integrity, or of a massive violation of its fundamental rights. The Quebec people is manifestly not, in the opinion of the amicus curiae, an oppressed people."

For close to 40 of the last 50 years, the Prime Minister of Canada has been a Quebecer. During this period, Quebecers have held from time to time all the most important positions in the federal Cabinet. During the 8 years prior to June 1997, the Prime Minister and the Leader of the Official Opposition in the House of Commons were both Quebecers. At present, the Prime Minister of Canada, the Right Honourable Chief Justice and two other members of the Court, the Chief of Staff of the Canadian Armed Forces and the Canadian ambassador to the United States, not to mention the Deputy Secretary-General of the United Nations, are all Quebecers. The international achievements of Quebecers in most fields of human endeavour are too numerous to list. Since the dynamism of the Quebec people has been directed toward the business sector, it has been clearly successful in Quebec, the rest of Canada and abroad.

The population of Quebec cannot plausibly be said to be denied access to government. Quebecers occupy prominent positions within the government of Canada. Residents of the province freely make political choices and pursue economic, social and cultural development within Quebec, across Canada, and throughout the world. The population of Quebec is equitably represented in legislative, executive and judicial institutions. In short, to reflect the phraseology of the international documents that address the right to self-determination of peoples, Canada is a "sovereign and independent state conducting itself in compliance with the principle of equal rights and self-determination of peoples and thus possessed of a government representing the whole people belonging to the territory without distinction."

The continuing failure to reach agreement on amendments to the Constitution, while a matter of concern, does not amount to a denial of self-determination. In the absence of amendments to the Canadian Constitution, we must look at the constitutional arrangements presently in effect, and we cannot conclude under current circumstances that those arrangements place Quebecers in a disadvantaged position within the scope of the international law rule.

In summary, the international law right to self-determination only generates, at best, a right to external self-determination in situations of former colonies; where a people is oppressed, as for example under foreign military occupation; or where a definable group is denied meaningful access to government to pursue their political, economic, social and cultural development. In all three situations, the people in question are entitled to a right to external self-determination because they have been denied the ability to exert internally their right to self-determination. Such exceptional circumstances are manifestly inapplicable to Quebec under existing conditions. Accordingly, neither the population of the province of Quebec, even if characterized in terms of "people" or "peoples," nor its representative institutions, the National Assembly, the legislature or government of Quebec, possess a right, under international law, to secede unilaterally from Canada.

We would not wish to leave this aspect of our answer to Question 2 without acknowledging the importance of the submissions made to us respecting the rights and concerns of aboriginal peoples in the event of a unilateral secession, as well as the appropriate means of defining the boundaries of a seceding Quebec with particular regard to the northern lands occupied largely by aboriginal peoples. However, the concern of aboriginal peoples is precipitated by the asserted right of Quebec to unilateral secession. In light of our finding that there is no such right applicable to the population of Quebec, either under the Constitution of Canada or at international law, but that on the contrary a clear democratic expression of support for secession would lead under the Constitution to negotiations in which aboriginal interests would be taken into account, it becomes unnecessary to explore further the concerns of the aboriginal peoples in this Reference. . .

AFTERWORD

Prior to the decision reprinted above, Quebec held a referendum on independence on October 30, 1995, with the no vote prevailing by a slim margin of 50.58% to 49.42%. (In a prior vote in 1980, the yes vote had received only 40%). The 1995 vote had a larger voter turnout. After the narrow defeat of the no-side in 1995, the Quebec Premier Jacques Parizeau remarked that the yes side lost because of money and the ethnic vote ("*l'argent puis des votes ethniques*"), a controversial comment that some political observers interpreted as anti-immigrant. The sovereigntist movement continued, although Quebec has not held another referendum on secession since 1995. It was against this backdrop that the Canadian Supreme Court decided to enter the fray and conclude that any secession would need to be accomplished through negotiation rather than unilateral declaration.

There is no question that under international law, a province or state can negotiate, consistent with its domestic legal process, a mutually agreeable separation from its parent state. There are several notable examples, including the dissolution of Czechoslovakia in 1993 into the Czech Republic and Slovakia. The separation was accomplished through an act of the country's Federal Assembly, though many Czechs and Slovaks opposed the separation.

The difficult question under international law pertains to unilateral claims of secession in the face of opposition from a parent state that enjoys territorial sovereignty under international law. In that situation, unilateral secession entails an infringement against the sovereignty of the existing state. For this reason, the international legal system views unilateral secession somewhat skeptically because of its potential to be a destabilizing force. The next section focuses on the consequences of a unilateral claim of secession by a sub-state entity in preciously those circumstances.

NOTES & QUESTIONS

1. *What Is a People?* The concept of self-determination is logically tied to the concept of a people. (Political scientists sometimes refer to "nations" and their pursuit of "nationalism," but international lawyers are more likely to refer to peoples.) The question is how to identify which collective groups count as peoples. Codified international law has remarkably little to say on the subject. See Antonio Cassese, *Self-Determination of Peoples: A Legal Reappraisal* 326 (1995) (noting lack of definition for what counts as a "people" under international law and noting that one should not expect international law to provide one). For answers, one must usually look beyond the law, to cognate disciplines in the social sciences, for an answer. The problem is that the criteria for statehood are relatively well-settled (see sections above), while the criteria for "people" are relatively contested.

2. *Decolonization and the Scope of Self-Determination.* Since the founding of the United Nations, there has been considerable dispute over the scope of the right of self-determination. Under one view, the right is limited

to the colonial context, so that the right of self-determination entails a right to be free from colonial rule but nothing in other contexts. See Frederic L. Kirgis, Jr., *The Degrees of Self-Determination in the United Nations Era*, 88 Am. J. Int'l L. 304, 304 (1994) (noting that "[f]or many years the majority of states in the UN General Assembly asserted that the expressed will of peoples to be free from colonial domination was the only face self-determination had"). On a broader view, decolonization was just one manifestation of the more general right of self-determination, which certainly applies in other situations as well. See, e.g., Declaration on Principles of International Law concerning Friendly Relations and Co-operation among States in accordance with the Charter of the United Nations, Annex to GA Res. 2625, UN Doc. A/8028, 9 I.L.M. 1292 (1970) ("The establishment of a sovereign and independent State, the free association or integration with an independent State or the emergence into any other political status freely determined by a people constitute modes of implementing the right of self-determination by that people."). Why would the broader view have difficulty gaining traction in international law? It is one thing for states to recognize that colonies have a right to independence, since most colonial powers have dismantled their colonies in favor of voluntary economic and political arrangements. It is quite another to concede that ethnic minorities located *within a state* have a right to self-determination and, by extension, the right to secede. In 2019, the ICJ signaled its support for the broader view, albeit in dicta, when it declared that "the right to self-determination, as a fundamental human right, has a broad scope of application." *Legal Consequences of the Separation of the Chagos Archipelago from Mauritius in 1965*, 2019 I.C.J. 95, 131.

3.   *The Doctrine of Uti Possidetis.* The concept of *uti possidetis* (derived from the maxim *uti possidetis, ita possideatis*) declares that colonial borders are to be respected even after a colony achieves independence. In other words, colonies should not take independence as an opportunity to reopen the question of the appropriate boundaries with their new neighbors. For an example, consider the ICJ's decision in *Burkino Faso v. Mali*, 1986 I.C.J. 554, 565 (Dec. 22), a territorial dispute between two former French colonies. There, the court observed:

> Since the two Parties have, as noted above, expressly requested the Chamber to resolve their dispute on the basis, in particular, of the "principle of the intangibility of frontiers inherited from colonization," the Chamber cannot disregard the principle of *uti possidetis juris*, the application of which gives rise to this respect for intangibility of frontiers. Although there is no need, for the purposes of the present case, to show that this is a firmly established principle of international law where decolonization is concerned, the Chamber nonetheless wishes to emphasize its general scope, in view of its exceptional importance for the African continent and for the two Parties. In this connection it should be noted that the principle of *uti possidetis* seems to have been first

invoked and applied in Spanish America, inasmuch as this was the continent which first witnessed the phenomenon of decolonization involving the formation of a number of sovereign States on territory formerly belonging to a single metropolitan State. Nevertheless the principle is not a special rule which pertains solely to one specific system of international law. It is a general principle, which is logically connected with the phenomenon of the obtaining of independence, wherever it occurs. Its obvious purpose is to prevent the independence and stability of new States being endangered by fratricidal struggles provoked by the challenging of frontiers following the withdrawal of the administering power.

To understand why the principle might have its detractors, consider for a moment that the boundaries between colonies might have been the product of administrative convenience at best, or outright injustice at worst. If the people of a colony did not participate in negotiating their own boundary, why should they be bound by that boundary when they achieve independence? Should the rule of *uti possidetis* apply outside of the decolonization context? For a discussion, see Steven R. Ratner, *Drawing A Better Line: Uti Possidetis and the Border of New States*, 90 Am. J. Int'l L. 590, 591 (1996) ("the extension of *uti possidetis* to modern breakups leads to genuine injustices and instability by leaving significant populations both unsatisfied with their status in new states and uncertain of political participation there").

4.   *Territorial Integrity and Self-Determination.* Although territorial integrity is usually associated with the concept of sovereignty, it also attaches to the collective right of self-determination. In 2019, the ICJ issued an Advisory Opinion regarding a longstanding dispute between the U.K. and Mauritius over the Chagos Peninsula, which is located in the middle of the Indian Ocean. For many years, the U.K. ruled Mauritius and the Chagos Peninsula as a single colony. Then, in 1965, the U.K. detached the islands of the Chagos Peninsula from Mauritius, and also detached several islands from the Seychelles, another U.K. colony. The detached islands were aggregated into a new colony called the "British Indian Ocean Territory." This all occurred during a period of sustained decolonization across the globe. The purpose of the detachment was to lease some of the islands of the newly created colony to the United States for the construction of U.S. military installations. In order to prepare the islands for the arrival of U.S. forces, the U.K. forcibly removed residents of the Chagos islands and also prevented them from returning. In 1968, Mauritius gained independence from Britain, but without the Chagos Peninsula. For decades, Mauritius claimed that the detachment was illegal and violated its self-determination. In a 2019 Advisory Opinion, the ICJ agreed, concluding that the Peninsula "was clearly an integral part of that non-self-governing territory" and that a 1965 agreement between Mauritius and the U.K. purporting to negotiate the detachment (while Mauritius was still a colony) "was not based on the free and genuine expression of the will of the people concerned." *Legal Consequences of the Separation of the Chagos Archipelago from Mauritius in*

1965, 2019 I.C.J. 95, 137. The ICJ ordered the U.K. to "complete" the decolonization of Mauritius by returning the Chagos Peninsula to Mauritius. At the time of the decision, the U.S. was still operating a military base there.

5. *External Versus Internal Self-Determination.* The Canadian Supreme Court's decision hinged largely on the distinction between external and internal self-determination. What exactly is the difference? What is the relationship between the two concepts? Presumably, a right of external self-determination is only triggered once internal self-determination is frustrated or impossible. Why did the Supreme Court conclude that Quebec's right of internal self-determination was already respected by the Canadian constitutional structure? For a discussion of the relationship between internal and external self-determination, see Russell A. Miller, *Self-Determination in International Law and the Demise of Democracy?*, 41 Colum. J. Transnat'l L. 601, 628 (2003); Karen Knop, *Diversity and Self-Determination in International Law* 18 (2002).

D. SECESSION

This section addresses a legal question that strictly speaking was not directly raised by the Quebec situation: What is the legal effect of a unilateral secession? In the Quebec case, the population rejected secession so Quebec never made such a declaration. But if a declaration *is* made, what is its legal effect? Does the sub-state entity automatically become a new state? Moreover, given the bedrock principle of state sovereignty, do unilateral declarations of secession, even when supported by the right of self-determination, violate international law?

In 2010, the International Court of Justice was asked to resolve these issues. The case came after a period of conflict in Kosovo, a province of Serbia with many ethnic Albanians and a minority population of ethnic Serbs. The ethnic Albanian population supported independence; a separatist force called the Kosovo Liberation Army (KLA) fought a civil war against the Serb Army to gain control over Kosovo. There were allegations of widespread atrocities and violations of the laws of war, many of which were subsequently investigated and prosecuted by the International Criminal Tribunal for the Former Yugoslavia (ICTY). The KLA alleged that the Serbs engaged in ethnic cleansing against ethnic Albanians; the KLA argued that independence was the only way to protect its population from Serbian violence.

NATO largely agreed with the KLA and intervened militarily against Serbia to pressure its officials to end its military involvement in Kosovo. The military campaign—mostly an air war—eventually succeeded, and soon UN peacekeeping troops patrolled Kosovo under the auspices of Security Council Resolution 1244 (creating the United Nations Interim Administration Mission in Kosovo). However, the resolution stopped short of explicitly recognizing Kosovo as an independent nation—something that Serbia (and Russia) certainly objected to.

In the following case, the ICJ was asked for its advisory opinion by Serbia on the legality of Kosovo's 2008 declaration of independence. As you read the case, ask yourself whether the court answered this question directly.

Accordance with International Law of the Unilateral Declaration of Independence in Respect of Kosovo

International Court of Justice
2010 I.C.J. 404

The Question Whether the Declaration of Independence is in Accordance with International Law

79. During the eighteenth, nineteenth and early twentieth centuries, there were numerous instances of declarations of independence, often strenuously opposed by the State from which independence was being declared. Sometimes a declaration resulted in the creation of a new State, at others it did not. In no case, however, does the practice of States as a whole suggest that the act of promulgating the declaration was regarded as contrary to international law. On the contrary, State practice during this period points clearly to the conclusion that international law contained no prohibition of declarations of independence. During the second half of the twentieth century, the international law of self-determination developed in such a way as to create a right to independence for the peoples of non-self-governing territories and peoples subject to alien subjugation, domination and exploitation. A great many new States have come into existence as a result of the exercise of this right. There were, however, also instances of declarations of independence outside this context. The practice of States in these latter cases does not point to the emergence in international law of a new rule prohibiting the making of a declaration of independence in such cases.

80. Several participants in the proceedings before the Court have contended that a prohibition of unilateral declarations of independence is implicit in the principle of territorial integrity. The Court recalls that the principle of territorial integrity is an important part of the international legal order and is enshrined in the Charter of the United Nations, in particular in Article 2, paragraph 4, which provides that: "AU Members shall refrain in their international relations from the threat or use of force against the territorial integrity or political independence of any State, or in any other manner inconsistent with the Purposes of the United Nations." . . .

81. Several participants have invoked resolutions of the Security Council condemning particular declarations of independence: see, inter alia, Security Council resolutions 216 (1965) and 217 (1965), concerning Southern Rhodesia; Security Council resolution 541 (1983), concerning northern Cyprus; and Security Council resolution 787 (1992), concerning the Republika Srpska. The Court notes, however, that in all of those instances the Security Council was making a determination as regards the concrete situation existing at the time that those declarations of independence were made; the illegality attached to the declarations of independence thus stemmed not from the unilateral character of these declarations as such, but from the fact that they were, or would have been, connected with the unlawful use of force or other egregious violations of norms of general international law, in particular those of a peremptory character (jus cogens). In the context of Kosovo, the Security Council has never taken this position. The exceptional character of the resolutions enumerated above appears to the Court to confirm that no general prohibition against unilateral declarations of independence may be inferred from the practice of the Security Council.

82. A number of participants in the present proceedings have claimed, although in almost every instance only as a secondary argument, that the population of Kosovo has the right to create an independent State either as a manifestation of a right to self-determination or pursuant to what they described as a right of "remedial secession" in the face of the situation in Kosovo. The Court has already noted (see paragraph 79 above) that one of the major developments of international law during the second half of the twentieth century has been the evolution of the right of self-determination. Whether, outside the context of non-self-governing territories and peoples subject to alien subjugation, domination and exploitation, the international law of self-determination confers upon part of the population of an existing State a right to separate from that State is, however, a subject on which radically different views were expressed by those taking part in the proceedings and expressing a position on the question. Similar differences existed regarding whether international law provides for a right of "remedial secession" and, if so, in what circumstances. There was also a sharp difference of views as to whether the circumstances which some participants maintained would give rise to a right of "remedial secession" were actually present in Kosovo.

83. The Court considers that it is not necessary to resolve these questions in the present case. The General Assembly has requested the Court's opinion only on whether or not the declaration of independence is in accordance with international law. Debates regarding the extent of the right of self-determination and the existence of any right of "remedial secession," however, concern the right to separate from a State. As the

Court has already noted (see paragraphs 49 to 56 above), and as almost all participants agreed, that issue is beyond the scope of the question posed by the General Assembly. To answer that question, the Court need only determine whether the declaration of independence violated either general international law or the lex specialis created by Security Council resolution 1244 (1999).

84. For the reasons already given, the Court considers that general international law contains no applicable prohibition of declarations of independence. Accordingly, it concludes that the declaration of independence of 17 February 2008 did not violate general international law. Having arrived at that conclusion, the Court now turns to the legal relevance of Security Council resolution 1244, adopted on 10 June 1999.

113. The question whether resolution 1244 (1999) prohibits the authors of the declaration of 17 February 2008 from declaring independence from the Republic of Serbia can only be answered through a careful reading of this resolution.

114. First, the Court observes that Security Council resolution 1244 (1999) was essentially designed to create an interim regime for Kosovo, with a view to channelling the long-term political process to establish its final status. The resolution did not contain any provision dealing with the final status of Kosovo or with the conditions for its achievement. In this regard the Court notes that contemporaneous practice of the Security Council shows that in situations where the Security Council has decided to establish restrictive conditions for the permanent status of a territory, those conditions are specified in the relevant resolution. . .

115. Secondly, turning to the question of the addressees of Security Council resolution 1244 (1999), it sets out a general framework for the "deployment in Kosovo, under United Nations auspices, of international civil and security presences." It is mostly concerned with creating obligations and authorizations for United Nations Member States as well as for organs of the United Nations such as the Secretary-General and his Special Representative. The only point at which resolution 1244 (1999) expressly mentions other actors relates to the Security Council's demand, on the one hand, "that the KLA and other armed Kosovo Albanian groups end immediately all offensive actions and comply with the requirements for demilitarization" and, on the other hand, for the "full co-operation by all concerned, including the international security presence, with the International Tribunal for the former Yugoslavia." There is no indication, in the text of Security Council resolution 1244 (1999), that the Security Council intended to impose, beyond that, a specific obligation to act or a prohibition from acting, addressed to such other actors. . .

118. Bearing this in mind, the Court cannot accept the argument that Security Council resolution 1244 (1999) contains a prohibition, binding on the authors of the declaration of independence, against declaring independence; nor can such a prohibition be derived from the language of the resolution understood in its context and considering its object and purpose. The language of Security Council resolution 1244 (1999) is at best ambiguous in this regard. The object and purpose of the resolution, as has been explained in detail, is the establishment of an interim administration for Kosovo, without making any definitive determination on final status issues. The text of the resolution explains that the "main responsibilities of the international civil presence will include . . . [o]rganizing and overseeing the development of provisional institutions for democratic and autonomous self-government pending a political settlement." The phrase "political settlement", often cited in the present proceedings, does not modify this conclusion. First, that reference is made within the context of enumerating the responsibilities of the international civil presence, i.e., the Special Representative of the Secretary-General in Kosovo and UNMIK, and not of other actors. Secondly, as the diverging views presented to the Court on this matter illustrate, the term "political settlement" is subject to various interpretations. The Court therefore concludes that this part of Security Council resolution 1244 (1999) cannot be construed to include a prohibition, addressed in particular to the authors of the declaration of 17 February 2008, against declaring independence.

119. The Court accordingly finds that Security Council resolution 1244 (1999) did not bar the authors of the declaration of 17 February 2008 from issuing a declaration of independence from the Republic of Serbia. Hence, the declaration of independence did not violate Security Council resolution 1244 (1999). . .

122. The Court has concluded above that the adoption of the declaration of independence of 17 February 2008 did not violate general international law, Security Council resolution 1244 (1999) or the Constitutional Framework. Consequently the adoption of that declaration did not violate any applicable rule of international law.

NOTES & QUESTIONS

1. *The "Question" Question.* Did the ICJ answer the question it was posed by the General Assembly? How did it interpret the question presented? The court focused on the narrow issue of whether the *declaration* of independence violated international law, without addressing the deeper, and far more pressing, question of whether that declaration was legally effective in transforming Kosovo into an independent state. The court stated in paragraph 56:

The Court is not required by the question it has been asked to take a position on whether international law conferred a positive entitlement on Kosovo unilaterally to declare its independence or, *a fortiori*, on whether international law generally confers an entitlement on entities situated within a State unilaterally to break away from it. Indeed, it is entirely possible for a particular act—such as a unilateral declaration of independence—not to be in violation of international law without necessarily constituting the exercise of a right conferred by it. The Court has been asked for an opinion on the first point, not the second.

Do you agree with the court in its parsing of the question presented to it? For more discussion of these issues, see Marko Milanović and Michael Wood (eds.), *The Law and Politics of the Kosovo Advisory Opinion* (2015).

2.   *Remedial Secession.* In some circumstances, secession can be viewed as a *remedy* for the denial of certain rights protected by international law. The right in question might simply be the collective right of self-determination. Or, in more extreme cases, a local population might be subjected to widespread and systemic human rights abuses or even violations of international criminal law such as crimes against humanity or genocide. The more extreme the human rights violations, the stronger the claim for remedial secession becomes—at least from the perspective of the world community. For more on the notion of remedial secession, see Thomas W. Simon, *Remedial Secession: What the Law Should Have Done, from Katanga to Kosovo*, 40 Ga. J. Int'l & Comp. L. 105, 110 (2011) (suggesting that a territory's secession should be recognized when its parent state has thwarted its internal self-determination or the group has "suffered or been threatened with harms that rise to the level of peremptory prohibitions"); John R. Ablan, *Signal and Affirm: How the United Nations Should Articulate the Right to Remedial Secession*, 45 Vand. J. Transnat'l L. 211, 237 (2012) (suggesting that the General Assembly adopt "a set of rules for determining where a state's sovereign right to territorial integrity ends and a peoples' right to remedial secession begins").

PROBLEM CASE

In February 2014, troops in unmarked vehicles (without identifying insignia) moved across Crimea and took up positions around key government locations. Crimea is a peninsula along the Black Sea. At the time, Crimea was part of Ukraine's sovereign territory. Although there was initial confusion about the identity of the troops, it soon became clear that the troops were part of the Russian armed services.

Russia's relationship with Ukraine had recently soured. Ukraine had been led by a pro-Russian president named Viktor Yanukovych. However, just days before the mysterious troops appeared in Crimea, Yanukovych was driven from power in Ukraine during a political uprising by Ukrainian nationalists who were upset by Yanukovych's pro-Russia policies. A violent confrontation resulted in Yanukovych fleeing the country and being replaced by a Ukrainian nationalist government that was not friendly with Russia. Russian President Vladimir Putin responded by deploying the covert military forces to Crimea.

Crimea's historical status is complex. Originally it was part of Russia and included a large number of Russian-speaking residents. When both Russia and Ukraine were part of the larger U.S.S.R. during the Cold War, Nikita Khrushchev transferred Crimea from Russia to Ukraine as a gift between the republics—a decision that had little significance at the time for Crimea's sovereignty because neither Russia nor Ukraine were independent political units. At the dissolution of the U.S.S.R. in 1991, Crimea was formally part of Ukraine, though it was governed locally with regional autonomy.

Ukraine had little military options for retaking Crimea, and ultimately capitulated in the face of Russia's de facto occupation of the territory. However, Ukraine's position is that Russia annexed the territory through military force in violation of international law. Under this view, secession may never be accomplished legally by outside military intervention in violation of the parent state's territorial sovereignty.

On March 16, 2014, a referendum was held and a majority of Crimean residents voted in favor of seceding from Ukraine. Although the referendum was not recognized by the government of Ukraine, the result of the referendum was not entirely surprising, given the large percentage of Russian-speaking residents in the territory. For this reason, Russia's legal position is that the Crimean people exercised its collective right to self-determination and decided to leave Ukraine and join Russia.

Should this case be described as a case of annexation, or secession, or both? More importantly, was the result justified by the principle of self-determination? Does it matter that Crimea's separation from Ukraine was accomplished, at least initially, by military force, and that Ukrainian forces only withdrew from Crimea because they felt ill-prepared to win a military confrontation with Russia?

Finally, why did the Russian troops who invaded Crimea remove their identifying insignia?

E. RECOGNITION OF FOREIGN GOVERNMENTS

International law poses few constraints on when a state can, or cannot, recognize a foreign government as the legitimate representative of a foreign state. However, the lack of any formal limit on the recognition power under international law does not mean that there is an absence of direction regarding how the power should be strategically deployed. In fact, lawyers, diplomats, and scholars have offered no shortage of theories on the subject. Here are the key possibilities:

1. *Tinoco Test.* This doctrine stipulates that international law should recognize a foreign government when it garners "effective control" over its state. The doctrine earned its names from an arbitration case called *Tinoco Concessions (Great Britain. v. Costa Rica),* 1 R.I.A.A. 369 (1923). The argument for the effective control test is that it makes sense to have diplomatic engagement with the entity that has actual control over the state and is in a position to act on its behalf. While the Tinoco Test has been criticized for its stark realism, the goal of the test is to decide about the existence of a government free from any value judgment about the government's conduct. Although such judgments are important in other matters, they have no place in recognition decisions per se.

2. *Tobar Doctrine.* In contrast, the Tobar Doctrine suggests that democratic legitimacy is the litmus test for determining the government of a state. Under this view, "governments" that come to power through "extra-constitutional" means are not legitimate governments at all and should therefore be denied recognition. In other words, the recognition of the putative government becomes an international referendum of sorts on the *manner* in which the government came to power. If the method was violent or involved a coup d'état, recognition of the government should be withheld. In contrast, if the method involved a free and fair election, recognition should be conferred.

3. *Estrada Doctrine.* The final option is, in a sense, a non-option. The Estrada Doctrine suggests that states should forego recognition as often as possible. Named for the Mexican official in 1930 who announced it, the Estrada Doctrine suggests that states should *not recognize any governments at all.* Under this view, recognition should be limited to *states*, because recognition of governments interferes with the internal politics of a foreign state. Whether a foreign government is "legitimate" involves sensitive matters of domestic politics that should remain outside the scope of formal recognition. For more discussion of this doctrine, see Phillip C. Jessup, Editorial Comment, *The Estrada Doctrine*, 25 Am. J. Int'l L. 719, 723 (1931).

Among these three doctrines, international practice has traditionally favored the Tinoco Test, with recognition decisions being made by wholly pragmatic considerations centered around de facto control. However, in some situations a state that is troubled by a government's conduct may consider that government the "de facto" seat of power but at the same time refuse to formally recognize that government as a "de jure" government. As one scholar has written: "A government could coherently recognize a regime's effective control over some territory—and therefore deal with that regime as its de facto government—but at the same time not extend the regime formal recognition—and therefore refuse to validate its de jure claim to legitimacy. This idea in part animates the debate over the spectrum between so-called de facto and de jure recognition." Robert D. Sloane, *The Changing Face of Recognition in International Law: A Case Study of Tibet*, 16 Emory Int'l L. Rev. 107, 125–26 (2002).

To get a sense of how recognition decisions are made in practice, consider the following exchange of letters between U.S. Secretary of State Hillary Clinton and the government of Somalia. As you read the letters, ask yourself which doctrine of recognition is best exemplified by the exchange.

Diplomatic Correspondence Between Somalia and the United States
January 17, 2013

Dear Mr. President:

On behalf of the Government of the United States of America, I congratulate the people of Somalia on their success in establishing a new Government of Somalia. The United States of America is pleased to recognize your government, upon confirmation of the following arrangements for the conduct of relations between the United States of America and Somalia.

First, recalling Somalia's existing legal obligations to the United States of America, including existing bilateral and multilateral treaty obligations and financial obligations to the United States of America, such as those that relate to the conduct of diplomatic and consular relations and those outlined under the Agreement effected by exchange of notes dated August 22, 1980, and the Agreement on Economic and Technical Cooperation, effected by exchange of notes dated June 14, October 12 and 13, 1981, I seek your commitment to work with the Government of the United States of America to fulfill these obligations. The United States of America is, of course, prepared to review any such treaties to determine whether they should be revised, terminated, or replaced to take into account developments in U.S.-Somalia relations.

Second, I seek your confirmation that the Government of Somalia will honor the United States of America's property rights in Somalia, including continued U.S. ownership of the entire 720,000 square meter site of the former U.S. embassy in Somalia. The United States of America is prepared to honor Somalia's property rights in the United States of America, including with regard to any properties or proceeds held by the United States of America.

Third, I seek your assurances that the Government of Somalia will respect human rights in accordance with international law and ensure democratic, just, and transparent governance in Somalia. This includes protecting rights enshrined in the International Covenant on Civil and Political Rights and meeting its other obligations under international human rights law. It also includes holding free and fair elections, protecting the rights necessary to permit civil society organizations to operate, taking necessary and appropriate steps to fight corruption, and enshrining the rule of law.

Fourth, I seek your confirmation that Somalia consents to the United States of America continuing to conduct its economic, technical, and security assistance programs throughout Somalia, including those in and with Somaliland and Puntland, on the understanding that future political and constitutional arrangements will clarify the respective responsibilities of the central government and regional administrative entities.

I look forward to receiving, by reply to this note, your concurrence with these arrangements and with the continued development of cordial and productive relations between the United States of America and Somalia.

Sincerely yours,

HILLARY RODHAM CLINTON

Dear Madam Secretary:

On behalf of the Government of Somalia, I thank the government and people of the United States of America for the recognition of our government. I am pleased to confirm the arrangements you have proposed for the conduct of relations between the United States of America and Somalia.

First, recalling Somalia's existing legal obligations to the United States of America, including existing bilateral and multilateral treaty obligations and financial obligations to the United States of America, such as those that relate to the conduct of diplomatic and consular relations and those outlined under the Agreement effected by exchange of notes dated August 22, 1980, and the Agreement on Economic and Technical Cooperation, effected by exchange of notes dated June 14, October 12 and 13, 1981, commit to work with the Government of the United States of America to fulfill these obligations. Somalia is also prepared to review any such treaties to determine whether they should be revised, terminated, or replaced to take into account developments in U.S.-Somalia relations.

Second, I confirm that the Government of Somalia will honor the United States of America's property rights in Somalia, including continued U.S. ownership of the entire 720,000 square meter site of the former U.S. embassy in Somalia. We appreciate that the United States of America is prepared to honor Somalia's property rights in the United States of America, including with regard to any properties or proceeds held by the United States of America.

Third, I assure you that the Government of Somalia will respect human rights in accordance with international law, as well as ensure democratic, just, and transparent governance in Somalia. This includes protecting rights enshrined in the International Covenant on Civil and Political Rights and meeting its other obligations under international human rights law. It also includes holding free and fair elections, protecting the rights necessary to permit civil society organizations to operate, taking necessary and appropriate steps to fight corruption, and enshrine the rule of law.

Fourth, I also confirm that Somalia consents to the United States of America continuing to conduct its economic, technical, and security assistance programs throughout Somalia, including those in and with Somaliland and Puntland, on the understanding that future political and constitutional arrangements will clarify the respective responsibilities of the central government and regional administrative entities.

We look forward to the continued development of cordial and productive relations between Somalia and the United States of America.

Sincerely,

HASSAN SHEIKH MOHAMUD

The recognition of Somalia was relatively uncontroversial. But sometimes the recognition of a foreign government can provoke political and diplomatic complications. In 2015, the Supreme Court heard a case from an American citizen born in Jerusalem who wanted "Israel" listed as his place of birth on his U.S. passport. The longstanding policy of the State Department called for official neutrality regarding the status of Jerusalem, while congress had passed a law directing that such passports, upon request, should include a reference to the State of Israel as the place of birth. In this conflict, which branch of government gets to control recognition decisions?

Zivotofsky v. Kerry
Supreme Court of the United States
576 U.S. 1 (2015)

■ JUSTICE KENNEDY delivered the opinion of the Court.

A delicate subject lies in the background of this case. That subject is Jerusalem. Questions touching upon the history of the ancient city and its present legal and international status are among the most difficult and complex in international affairs. In our constitutional system these matters are committed to the Legislature and the Executive, not the Judiciary. As a result, in this opinion the Court does no more, and must do no more, than note the existence of international debate and tensions respecting Jerusalem. Those matters are for Congress and the President to discuss and consider as they seek to shape the Nation's foreign policies.

The Court addresses two questions to resolve the interbranch dispute now before it. First, it must determine whether the President has the exclusive power to grant formal recognition to a foreign sovereign. Second, if he has that power, the Court must determine whether Congress can command the President and his Secretary of State to issue a formal statement that contradicts the earlier recognition. The statement in question here is a congressional mandate that allows a United States citizen born in Jerusalem to direct the President and Secretary of State, when issuing his passport, to state that his place of birth is "Israel."

I

Jerusalem's political standing has long been, and remains, one of the most sensitive issues in American foreign policy, and indeed it is one of the most delicate issues in current international affairs. In 1948, President Truman formally recognized Israel in a signed statement of "recognition." That statement did not recognize Israeli sovereignty over Jerusalem. Over the last 60 years, various actors have sought to assert full or partial sovereignty over the city, including Israel, Jordan, and the Palestinians. Yet, in contrast to a consistent policy of formal recognition of Israel, neither President Truman nor any later United States President has issued an official statement or declaration acknowledging any country's sovereignty over Jerusalem. Instead, the Executive Branch has maintained that "the status of Jerusalem. . . should be decided not unilaterally but in consultation with all concerned." . . .

The President's position on Jerusalem is reflected in State Department policy regarding passports and consular reports of birth abroad. Understanding that passports will be construed as reflections of American policy, the State Department's Foreign Affairs Manual instructs its employees, in general, to record the place of birth on a passport as the "country [having] present sovereignty over the actual area of birth." If a citizen objects to the country listed as sovereign by the State Department, he or she may list the city or town of birth rather than the country. The FAM, however, does not allow citizens to list a sovereign that conflicts with Executive Branch policy. Because the United States does not recognize any country as having sovereignty over Jerusalem, the FAM instructs employees to record the place of birth for citizens born there as "Jerusalem."

In 2002, Congress passed the Act at issue here, the Foreign Relations Authorization Act. Section 214 of the Act is titled "United States Policy with Respect to Jerusalem as the Capital of Israel." The subsection that lies at the heart of this case. . . seeks to override the FAM by allowing citizens born in Jerusalem to list their place of birth as "Israel." . . .

In 2002, petitioner Menachem Binyamin Zivotofsky was born to United States citizens living in Jerusalem. In December 2002, Zivotofsky's mother visited the American Embassy in Tel Aviv to request both a passport and a consular report of birth abroad for her son. She asked that his place of birth be listed as "Jerusalem, Israel." The Embassy clerks explained that, pursuant to State Department policy, the passport would list only "Jerusalem." Zivotofsky's parents objected and, as his guardians, brought suit on his behalf. . .

II

In considering claims of Presidential power this Court refers to Justice Jackson's familiar tripartite framework from *Youngstown Sheet & Tube Co. v. Sawyer,* 343 U.S. 579, 635–638 (1952) (concurring opinion). The framework divides exercises of Presidential power into three categories: First, when "the President acts pursuant to an express or implied authorization of Congress, his authority is at its maximum, for it includes all that he possesses in his own right plus all that Congress can delegate." Second, "in absence of either a congressional grant or denial of authority" there is a "zone of twilight in which he and Congress may have concurrent authority," and where "congressional inertia, indifference or quiescence may" invite the exercise of executive power. Finally, when "the President takes measures incompatible with the expressed or implied will of Congress. . . he can rely only upon his own constitutional powers minus any constitutional powers of Congress over the matter." To succeed in this third category, the President's asserted power must be both "exclusive" and "conclusive" on the issue.

In this case the Secretary contends that § 214(d) infringes on the President's exclusive recognition power by "requiring the President to contradict his recognition position regarding Jerusalem in official communications with foreign sovereigns." In so doing the Secretary acknowledges the President's power is "at its lowest ebb." Because the President's refusal to implement § 214(d) falls into Justice Jackson's third category, his claim must be "scrutinized with caution," and he may rely solely on powers the Constitution grants to him alone. . .

A

Recognition is a "formal acknowledgement" that a particular "entity possesses the qualifications for statehood" or "that a particular regime is the effective government of a state." It may also involve the determination of a state's territorial bounds. See 2 M. Whiteman, Digest of International Law § 1, p. 1 (1963) ("[S]tates may recognize or decline to recognize territory as belonging to, or under the sovereignty of, or having been acquired or lost by, other states"). Recognition is often effected by an express "written or oral declaration." It may also be implied—for example, by concluding a bilateral treaty or by sending or receiving diplomatic agents.

Legal consequences follow formal recognition. Recognized sovereigns may sue in United States courts, and may benefit from sovereign immunity when they are sued. The actions of a recognized sovereign committed within its own territory also receive deference in domestic courts under the act of state doctrine. Recognition at international law, furthermore, is a precondition of regular diplomatic relations. Recognition is thus "useful, even necessary," to the existence of a state.

Despite the importance of the recognition power in foreign relations, the Constitution does not use the term "recognition," either in Article II or elsewhere. The Secretary asserts that the President exercises the recognition power based on the Reception Clause, which directs that the President "shall receive Ambassadors and other public Ministers." Art. II, § 3. As Zivotofsky notes, the Reception Clause received little attention at the Constitutional Convention. In fact, during the ratification debates, Alexander Hamilton claimed that the power to receive ambassadors was "more a matter of dignity than of authority," a ministerial duty largely "without consequence."

At the time of the founding, however, prominent international scholars suggested that receiving an ambassador was tantamount to recognizing the sovereignty of the sending state. It is a logical and proper inference, then, that a Clause directing the President alone to receive ambassadors would be understood to acknowledge his power to recognize other nations.

This in fact occurred early in the Nation's history when President Washington recognized the French Revolutionary Government by receiving its ambassador. After this incident the import of the Reception Clause became clear—causing Hamilton to change his earlier view. He wrote that the Reception Clause "includes th[e power] of judging, in the case of a revolution of government in a foreign country, whether the new rulers are competent organs of the national will, and ought to be recognised, or not." As a result, the Reception Clause provides support, although not the sole authority, for the President's power to recognize other nations.

The inference that the President exercises the recognition power is further supported by his additional Article II powers. It is for the President, "by and with the Advice and Consent of the Senate," to "make Treaties, provided two thirds of the Senators present concur." In addition, "he shall nominate, and by and with the Advice and Consent of the Senate, shall appoint Ambassadors" as well as "other public Ministers and Consuls."

As a matter of constitutional structure, these additional powers give the President control over recognition decisions. At international law, recognition may be effected by different means, but each means is dependent upon Presidential power. In addition to receiving an ambassador, recognition may occur on "the conclusion of a bilateral treaty," or the "formal initiation of diplomatic relations," including the dispatch of an ambassador. The President has the sole power to negotiate treaties, and the Senate may not conclude or ratify a treaty without Presidential action. The President, too, nominates the Nation's ambassadors and dispatches other diplomatic agents. Congress may not send an ambassador without his involvement. Beyond that, the President himself has the power to open diplomatic channels simply by engaging in direct diplomacy with foreign heads of state and their ministers. The Constitution thus assigns the President means to effect recognition on his own initiative. Congress, by contrast, has no constitutional power that would enable it to initiate diplomatic relations with a foreign nation. Because these specific Clauses confer the recognition power on the President, the Court need not consider whether or to what extent the Vesting Clause, which provides that the "executive Power" shall be vested in the President, provides further support for the President's action here.

The text and structure of the Constitution grant the President the power to recognize foreign nations and governments. The question then becomes whether that power is exclusive. The various ways in which the President may unilaterally effect recognition—and the lack of any similar power vested in Congress—suggest that it is. So, too, do functional considerations. Put simply, the Nation must have a single policy regarding which governments are legitimate in the eyes of the United States and which are not. Foreign countries need to know, before entering into diplomatic relations or commerce with the United States, whether their ambassadors will be received; whether their officials will be immune from suit in federal court; and whether they may initiate lawsuits here to vindicate their rights. These assurances cannot be equivocal.

Recognition is a topic on which the Nation must "speak . . . with one voice." That voice must be the President's. Between the two political branches, only the Executive has the characteristic of unity at all times. And with unity comes the ability to exercise, to a greater degree, "[d]ecision, activity, secrecy, and dispatch." The President is capable, in ways Congress is not, of engaging in the delicate and often secret diplomatic contacts that may lead to a decision on recognition. He is also better positioned to take the decisive, unequivocal action necessary to recognize other states at international law. These qualities explain why the Framers listed the traditional avenues of recognition—receiving ambassadors, making treaties, and sending ambassadors—as among the President's Article II powers.

As described in more detail below, the President since the founding has exercised this unilateral power to recognize new states—and the Court has endorsed the practice. Texts and treatises on international law treat the President's word as the final word on recognition. See, e.g., Restatement (Third) of Foreign Relations Law § 204, at 89 ("Under the Constitution of the United States the President has exclusive authority to recognize or not to recognize a foreign state or government"); see also L. Henkin, Foreign Affairs and the U.S. Constitution 43 (2d ed. 1996) ("It is no longer questioned that the President does not merely perform the ceremony of receiving foreign ambassadors but also determines whether the United States should recognize or refuse to recognize a foreign government"). In light of this authority all six judges who considered this case in the Court of Appeals agreed that the President holds the exclusive recognition power.

It remains true, of course, that many decisions affecting foreign relations—including decisions that may determine the course of our relations with recognized countries—require congressional action. Congress may "regulate Commerce with foreign Nations," "establish an uniform Rule of Naturalization," "define and punish Piracies and Felonies committed on the high Seas, and Offences against the Law of Nations," "declare War," "grant Letters of Marque and Reprisal," and "make Rules for the Government and Regulation of the land and naval Forces." In addition, the President cannot make a treaty or appoint an ambassador without the approval of the Senate. The President, furthermore, could not build an American Embassy abroad without congressional appropriation of the necessary funds. Under basic separation-of-powers principles, it is for the Congress to enact the laws, including "all Laws which shall be necessary and proper for carrying into Execution" the powers of the Federal Government.

In foreign affairs, as in the domestic realm, the Constitution "enjoins upon its branches separateness but interdependence, autonomy but reciprocity." Although the President alone effects the formal act of recognition, Congress' powers, and its central role in making laws, give it substantial authority regarding many of the policy determinations that precede and follow the act of recognition itself. If Congress disagrees with the President's recognition policy, there may be consequences. Formal recognition may seem a hollow act if it is not accompanied by the dispatch of an ambassador, the easing of trade restrictions, and the conclusion of treaties. And those decisions require action by the Senate or the whole Congress.

In practice, then, the President's recognition determination is just one part of a political process that may require Congress to make laws. The President's exclusive recognition power encompasses the authority to acknowledge, in a formal sense, the legitimacy of other states and governments, including their territorial bounds. Albeit limited, the exclusive recognition power is essential to the conduct of Presidential duties. The formal act of recognition is an executive power that Congress may not qualify. If the President is to be effective in negotiations over a formal recognition determination, it must be evident to his counterparts abroad that he speaks for the Nation on that precise question.

A clear rule that the formal power to recognize a foreign government subsists in the President therefore serves a necessary purpose in diplomatic relations. All this, of course, underscores that Congress has an important role in other aspects of foreign policy, and the President may be bound by any number of laws Congress enacts. In this way ambition counters ambition, ensuring that the democratic will of the people is observed and respected in foreign affairs as in the domestic realm.

B

No single precedent resolves the question whether the President has exclusive recognition authority and, if so, how far that power extends. In part that is because, until today, the political branches have resolved their disputes over questions of recognition. The relevant cases, though providing important instruction, address the division of recognition power between the Federal Government and the States, or between the courts and the political branches—not between the President and Congress. As the parties acknowledge, some isolated statements in those cases lend support to the position that Congress has a role in the recognition process. In the end, however, a fair reading of the cases shows that the President's role in the recognition process is both central and exclusive.

During the administration of President Van Buren, in a case involving a dispute over the status of the Falkland Islands, the Court noted that "when the executive branch of the government" assumes "a fact in regard to the sovereignty of any island or country, it is conclusive on the judicial department." Once the President has made his determination, it "is enough to know, that in the exercise of his constitutional functions, he has decided the question. Having done this under the responsibilities which belong to him, it is obligatory on the people and government of the Union."

Later, during the 1930's and 1940's, the Court addressed issues surrounding President Roosevelt's decision to recognize the Soviet Government of Russia. In *United States v. Belmont,* 301 U.S. 324 (1937), and *Pink,* 315 U.S. 203, New York state courts declined to give full effect to the terms of executive agreements the President had concluded in negotiations over recognition of the Soviet regime. In particular the state courts, based on New York public policy, did not treat assets that had been seized by the Soviet Government as property of Russia and declined to turn those assets over to the United States. The Court stated that it "may not be doubted" that "recognition, establishment of diplomatic relations,. . . and agreements with respect thereto" are "within the competence of the President." In these matters, "the Executive ha[s] authority to speak as the sole organ of th[e] government." The Court added that the President's authority "is not limited to a determination of the government to be recognized. It includes the power to determine the policy which is to govern the question of recognition." Thus, New York state courts were required to respect the executive agreements.

It is true, of course, that *Belmont* and *Pink* are not direct holdings that the recognition power is exclusive. Those cases considered the validity of executive agreements, not the initial act of recognition. The President's determination in those cases did not contradict an Act of Congress. And the primary issue was whether the executive agreements could supersede state law. Still, the language in *Pink* and *Belmont,* which confirms the President's competence to determine questions of recognition, is strong support for the conclusion that it is for the President alone to determine which foreign governments are legitimate. . .

In a world that is ever more compressed and interdependent, it is essential the congressional role in foreign affairs be understood and respected. For it is Congress that makes laws, and in countless ways its laws will and should shape the Nation's course. The Executive is not free from the ordinary controls and checks of Congress merely because foreign affairs are at issue. It is not for the President alone to determine the whole content of the Nation's foreign policy.

That said, judicial precedent and historical practice teach that it is for the President alone to make the specific decision of what foreign power he will recognize as legitimate, both for the Nation as a whole and for the purpose of making his own position clear within the context of recognition in discussions and negotiations with foreign nations. Recognition is an act with immediate and powerful significance for international relations, so the President's position must be clear. Congress cannot require him to contradict his own statement regarding a determination of formal recognition. . .

C

. . .From the first Administration forward, the President has claimed unilateral authority to recognize foreign sovereigns. For the most part, Congress has acquiesced in the Executive's exercise of the recognition power. . .

President Carter recognized the People's Republic of China (PRC) as the government of China, and derecognized the Republic of China, located on Taiwan. As to the status of Taiwan, the President "acknowledge[d] the Chinese position" that "Taiwan is part of China," but he did not accept that claim. The President proposed a new law defining how the United States would conduct business with Taiwan. After extensive revisions, Congress passed, and the President signed, the Taiwan Relations Act. The Act (in a simplified summary) treated Taiwan as if it were a legally distinct entity from China—an entity with which the United States intended to maintain strong ties.

Throughout the legislative process, however, no one raised a serious question regarding the President's exclusive authority to recognize the PRC—or to decline to grant formal recognition to Taiwan. Rather, Congress accepted the President's recognition determination as a completed, lawful act; and it proceeded to outline the trade and policy provisions that, in its judgment, were appropriate in light of that decision.

This history confirms the Court's conclusion in the instant case that the power to recognize or decline to recognize a foreign state and its territorial bounds resides in the President alone. For the most part, Congress has respected the Executive's policies and positions as to formal recognition. At times, Congress itself has defended the President's constitutional prerogative. Over the last 100 years, there has been scarcely any debate over the President's power to recognize foreign states. In this respect the Legislature, in the narrow context of recognition, on balance has acknowledged the importance of speaking "with one voice." The weight of historical evidence indicates Congress has accepted that the power to recognize foreign states and governments and their territorial bounds is exclusive to the Presidency. . .

NOTES & QUESTIONS

1. *Is Zivotofsky About Government or State Recognition?* The legal issue in this case centers about a political dispute over the status of Jerusalem. The Supreme Court frames this as a question of recognition. But what kind of recognition is it? Is it state recognition or government recognition? The statements made by the court vacillate between the two, in one breath talking about governments and in the next talking about states. Does the court explain why the question of state or government recognition should extend to the issue of dispute boundaries and territories? Perhaps the dispute has nothing to do with recognition at all. After all, the State Department, while neutral about the status of Jerusalem, does not question the existence of the State of Israel or its legitimate government. In dissent, Justice Thomas noted that "no act of recognition is implicated here" and that "[r]ather than adopt a novel definition of the recognition power, the majority should have looked to other foreign affairs powers in the Constitution to resolve this dispute." 576 U.S. 1, 61. Do you agree?

2. *Continuity of Legal Obligations Redux.* What factors influence a state's decision to recognize—or not—a foreign government? Notice the demand from Secretary of State Hillary Clinton in her letter to Somalia for

assurances that the new government would accept certain legal obligations under international law, including multilateral human rights obligations and bilateral property obligations. What response did she receive and why?

F. CONSEQUENCES OF STATEHOOD

As noted above, statehood entails certain rights and responsibilities under international law. States enjoy legal sovereignty and with that sovereignty comes a package of entitlements including the capacity to engage in foreign relations. Sovereignty also implies a degree of independence, i.e., freedom from outside interference by other states. International lawyers often refer to this as the principle of non-intervention—a simple enough idea whose application is nonetheless deeply contested.

In the following section of the ICJ's *Nicaragua* decision, the Court concluded that the United States had violated the principle of non-intervention in its conduct against Nicaragua. The principle of non-intervention prohibits a state from interfering in the domaine reserve of another state—that zone of exclusive authority that a sovereign state is entitled to exercise on its own without interference from another state. In that sense, one can think of the principle of non-intervention as an outgrowth of Westphalian state sovereignty—the idea that what it means to be sovereign is to be free from outside interference from other states. Of course, this is an exaggeration, since in our globalized society, every sovereign state is subject every day of the week to some level of "interference" from other states, and most of them are considered lawful. Although it is not always clear which interventions are illegal under the principle of non-intervention, the ICJ in Nicaragua did conclude that the U.S. mining of the harbors around Nicaragua was illegal, in part because it had a coercive quality.

Case Concerning Military and Paramilitary Activities in and Against Nicaragua (Nicaragua v. United States)
International Court of Justice
1986 I.C.J. 14

202. The principle of non-intervention involves the right of every sovereign State to conduct its affairs without outside interference; though examples of trespass against this principle are not infrequent, the Court considers that it is part and parcel of customary international law. As the Court has observed: "Between independent States, respect for territorial sovereignty is an essential foundation of international relations," and international law requires political integrity also to be respected. Expressions of an opinio juris regarding the existence of the principle of non-intervention in customary international law are

numerous and not difficult to find. Of course, statements whereby States avow their recognition of the principles of international law set forth in the United Nations Charter cannot strictly be interpreted as applying to the principle of non-intervention by States in the internal and external affairs of other States, since this principle is not, as such, spelt out in the Charter. But it was never intended that the Charter should embody written confirmation of every essential principle of international law in force. The existence in the opinio juris of States of the principle of non-intervention is backed by established and substantial practice. It has moreover been presented as a corollary of the principle of the sovereign equality of States. A particular instance of this is General Assembly resolution 2625 (XXV), the Declaration on the Principles of International Law concerning Friendly Relations and Co-operation among States. In the *Corfu Channel* case, when a State claimed a right of intervention in order to secure evidence in the territory of another State for submission to an international tribunal (I.C.J. Reports 1949, p. 34), the Court observed that:

> the alleged right of intervention as the manifestation of a policy of force, such as has, in the past, given rise to most serious abuses and such as cannot, whatever be the present defects in international organization, find a place in international law. Intervention is perhaps still less admissible in the particular form it would take here; for, from the nature of things, it would be reserved for the most powerful States, and might easily lead to perverting the administration of international justice itself.

149 I.C.J. 35.

The principle has since been reflected in numerous declarations adopted by international organizations and conferences in which the United States and Nicaragua have participated, e.g., General Assembly resolution 2131 (XX), the Declaration on the Inadmissibility of Intervention in the Domestic Affairs of States and the Protection of their Independence and Sovereignty. It is true that the United States, while it voted in favour of General Assembly resolution 2131 (XX), also declared at the time of its adoption in the First Committee that it considered the declaration in that resolution to be "only a statement of political intention and not a formulation of law." However, the essentials of resolution 2131 (XX) are repeated in the Declaration approved by resolution 2625 (XXV), which set out principles which the General Assembly declared to be "basic principles" of international law, and on the adoption of which no analogous statement was made by the United States representative.

As regards inter-American relations, attention may be drawn to, for example, the United States reservation to the Montevideo Convention on Rights and Duties of States (26 December 1933), declaring the opposition of the United States Government to "interference with the freedom, the sovereignty or other internal affairs, or processes of the Governments of other nations"; or the ratification by the United States of the Additional Protocol relative to Non-Intervention (23 December 1936). . . .

205. Notwithstanding the multiplicity of declarations by States accepting the principle of non-intervention, there remain two questions: first, what is the exact content of the principle so accepted, and secondly, is the practice sufficiently in conformity with it for this to be a rule of customary international law? As regards the first problem—that of the content of the principle of non-intervention—the Court will define only those aspects of the principle which appear to be relevant to the resolution of the dispute. In this respect it notes that, in view of the generally accepted formulations, the principle forbids all States or groups of States to intervene directly or indirectly in internal or external affairs of other States. A prohibited intervention must accordingly be one bearing on matters in which each State is permitted, by the principle of State sovereignty, to decide freely. One of these is the choice of a political, economic, social and cultural system, and the formulation of foreign policy. Intervention is wrongful when it uses methods of coercion in regard to such choices, which must remain free ones. The element of coercion, which defines, and indeed forms the very essence of, prohibited intervention, is particularly obvious in the case of an intervention which uses force, either in the direct form of military action, or in the indirect form of support for subversive or terrorist armed activities within another State. As noted above, General Assembly resolution 2625 (XXV) equates assistance of this kind with the use of force by the assisting State when the acts committed in another State "involve a threat or use of force." These forms of action are therefore wrongful in the light of both the principle of non-use of force, and that of non-intervention. In view of the nature of Nicaragua's complaints against the United States, and those expressed by the United States in regard to Nicaragua's conduct towards El Salvador, it is primarily acts of intervention of this kind with which the Court is concerned in the present case.

206. However, before reaching a conclusion on the nature of prohibited intervention, the Court must be satisfied that State practice justifies it. There have been in recent years a number of instances of foreign intervention for the benefit of forces opposed to the government of another State. The Court is not here concerned with the process of decolonization; this question is not in issue in the present case. It has to consider whether there might be indications of a practice illustrative of belief in a kind of general right for States to intervene, directly or indirectly, with or without armed force, in support of an internal opposition in another State, whose cause appeared particularly worthy by reason of the political and moral values with which it was identified. For such a general right to come into existence would involve a

fundamental modification of the customary law principle of non-intervention.

207. In considering the instances of the conduct above described, the Court has to emphasize that, as was observed in the *North Sea Continental Shelf* cases, for a new customary rule to be formed, not only must the acts concerned "amount to a settled practice," but they must be accompanied by the opinio juris sive necessitatis. Either the States taking such action or other States in a position to react to it, must have behaved so that their conduct is "evidence of a belief that this practice is rendered obligatory by the existence of a rule of law requiring it. The need for such a belief, i.e., the existence of a subjective element, is implicit in the very notion of the opinio juris sive necessitatis." 1969 I.C.J. 44.

The Court has no jurisdiction to rule upon the conformity with international law of any conduct of States not parties to the present dispute, or of conduct of the Parties unconnected with the dispute; nor has it authority to ascribe to States legal views which they do not themselves advance. The significance for the Court of cases of State conduct prima facie inconsistent with the principle of non-intervention lies in the nature of the ground offered as justification. Reliance by a State on a novel right or an unprecedented exception to the principle might, if shared in principle by other States, tend towards a modification of customary international law. In fact however the Court finds that States have not justified their conduct by reference to a new right of intervention or a new exception to the principle of its prohibition. The United States authorities have on some occasions clearly stated their grounds for intervening in the affairs of a foreign State for reasons connected with, for example, the domestic policies of that country, its ideology, the level of its armaments, or the direction of its foreign policy. But these were statements of international policy, and not an assertion of rules of existing international law.

208. In particular, as regards the conduct towards Nicaragua which is the subject of the present case, the United States has not claimed that its intervention, which it justified in this way on the political level, was also justified on the legal level, alleging the exercise of a new right of intervention regarded by the United States as existing in such circumstances. As mentioned above, the United States has, on the legal plane, justified its intervention expressly and solely by reference to the "classic" rules involved, namely, collective self-defence against an armed attack. Nicaragua, for its part, has often expressed its solidarity and sympathy with the opposition in various States, especially in El Salvador. But Nicaragua too has not argued that this was a legal basis for an intervention, let alone an intervention involving the use of force.

209. The Court therefore finds that no such general right of intervention, in support of an opposition within another State, exists in

contemporary international law. The Court concludes that acts constituting a breach of the customary principle of non-intervention will also, if they directly or indirectly involve the use of force, constitute a breach of the principle of non-use of force in international relations.

NOTES & QUESTIONS

The Coercion Requirement. What is the relationship between the principle of non-intervention and the concept of coercion? In the excerpt above, the ICJ stated that coercion "forms the very essence of prohibited intervention." What exactly does this mean? The ICJ stated that some decisions are reserved to individual states which must be free from coercion in order to remain free choices. This includes, but is not limited to, "the choice of a political, economic, social and cultural system, and the formulation of foreign policy." Consequently, the ICJ concluded that U.S. activities were designed to coerce Nicaragua into changing its policy. This is what the ICJ meant when it stated that coercion was the sine qua non of prohibited interventions. In the modern era, scholars have debated whether coercion is always required for an intervention to be illegal, but nonetheless the coercion requirement has structured the analysis in most cases. For a discussion of the coercion requirement, see Mohamed S. Helal, *On Coercion in International Law*, 52 N.Y.U. J. Int'l L. & Pol. 1, 75 (2019) (arguing that "there is no conceptual reason or logical justification for excluding practices such as economic sanctions or cyber-interference from the understanding of coercion in international law").

PROBLEM CASE

In recent years, several foreign powers have interfered in U.S. elections. The most notable examples include Russia during the 2016 presidential and 2018 mid-term elections, but other foreign powers are also using election interference as a tool of statecraft, so the phenomenon is not limited to the United States. Typical examples of election interference include computer hacking and the operation of social media troll farms designed to promote distrust in democratic institutions or even to tilt the outcome of the election in favor of a preferred candidate. Doing so might augment the strategic objectives of the intervening state and disrupt democratic processes.

It is not difficult to see why states might resort to election interference. First, the conduct can occur covertly and therefore the state can seek to deflect responsibility for the behavior. Second, the conduct is relatively inexpensive, in the sense that the financial investment for creating a troll farm is relatively minor when compared to the cost of building and deploying military resources on a battlefield. In this sense, election interference allows weaker military states to gain an advantage in international relations. Third, the conduct is effective at promoting distrust in democratic institutions, thus destabilizing states that are usually powerful actors in the international arena.

Scholars and diplomats have argued over whether foreign election interference violates international law. Some lawyers have argued that it is lawful because there is nothing particularly coercive about election interference. Do you agree? Think carefully about the goals of election interference and try to identify a distinctively coercive aspect to it. If there is nothing especially coercive about it, does this suggest that election interference is lawful or conversely does it suggest that coercion is not always required for an intervention to be considered unlawful?

Conclusion & Summary

States, just like other entities, live and die. Their existence as actors on the international stage is governed by the following principles:

1. The definition of statehood is outlined by the criteria articulated in the Montevideo Convention as well as recognition by third parties, depending on whether one accepts the Constitutive View or not. Some states, especially those in Europe, insist that new states demonstrate their commitment to democratic values, human rights, and respect for international law.

2. International law grants every people the right of self-determination, which entails the right to determine their own destiny and political arrangements. Outside of the process of decolonization, the exact contours of self-determination are highly contested. Internal self-determination involves participation in a larger state—perhaps a confederation or some other political structure—in a way that allows sufficient access to democratic decision-making and cultural flourishing. In contrast, external self-determination involves the creation of a state for that people's self-government.

3. External self-determination might be achieved through the process of secession. Claims of secession are highly controversial. The ICJ has stated that unilateral declarations of secession are not per se prohibited under international law. However, just because a sub-national entity is not barred from declaring its independence does not necessarily mean that its independence will be deemed successful. Whether a sub-national entity is legally entitled to independent statehood is governed by the concept of external self-determination, which may or may not apply to the case in question.

4. States are not the only entities that can be recognized by third parties. Governments can also be recognized by third parties as the official government of a state. The three major approaches to formal recognition are the Tinoco Test, the Tobar Doctrine, and the Estrada Doctrine. A state might formally recognize a new government as the official representative of a state in exchange for certain promises about how that government will conduct itself. Or, a state might simply withhold formal recognition of a foreign government as the "de jure" government but still engage in diplomatic relations with it as a "de facto" government—

that is, refuse to take a potion on its legitimacy. In the United States, the power to recognize foreign governments (and states) resides with the president and the executive branch.

CHAPTER 5

INTERNATIONAL ORGANIZATIONS

Introduction

The United Nations is often synonymous with international law and many people falsely assume that all international institutions are somehow related to the UN. Of course, this is false. International institutions are fragmented and do not enjoy the same level of hierarchical organization found in a domestic political structure. To take just one example, the International Criminal Court (ICC) in the Hague, which adjudicates allegations of international crimes against individuals, is not an organ of the UN at all. It is an independent court created by a treaty that was signed and ratified by 124 states.

That being said, the UN is certainly the most important international institution in existence, and its actors are at the heart of resolving most international disputes. This chapter explains the basic structure of the UN, its key organizational components, and their respective authority.

The goal of creating a global institution for the resolution of international disputes goes back to World War I. At the conclusion of the "Great War," President Woodrow Wilson championed the creation of the League, which was created in 1920 as part of the global settlement—the Paris Peace Conference—that officially concluded the war. The League only attracted a few dozen members and never represented the majority of states in the world. The advent of the Second World War, and in particular the League's failure to adequately respond to German and Japanese aggression, spelled its demise.

In another sense, though, the League *was* a limited success. It created the template for the *idea* of an international organization. At the end of World War II, with Japan, Germany, Italy, and its allies defeated, the major powers resolved to create a new international institution, this time negotiated with lessons learned from the failure of the League. The results of those negotiations were the United Nations. In a sense, one can think of the UN as the League of Nations 2.0.

The basic structure of the United Nations was hammered out at a diplomatic meeting at a Washington, D.C. mansion called Dumbarton Oaks. Officially known as the "Washington Conversations on International Peace and Security Organization," the diplomatic conference is more commonly referred to simply as the Dumbarton Oaks conference. The meeting took place in 1944, before the end of the war, but when victory was on the horizon and the major powers were already conceiving of a new world order with one goal in mind: avoiding a repeat of the disaster of yet another world war.

In addition to the Americans, diplomats from China, Russia, and England participated in the Dumbarton Oaks conference. The result of the negotiations was the "United Nations"—an organization that would be devoted to the following goals:

1. To maintain international peace and security; and to that end to take effective collective measures for the prevention and removal of threats to the peace and the suppression of acts of aggression or other breaches of the peace, and to bring about by peaceful means adjustment or settlement of international disputes which may lead to a breach of the peace;

2. To develop friendly relations among nations and to take other appropriate measures to strengthen universal peace;

3. To achieve international cooperation in the solution of international economic, social and other humanitarian problems; and

4. To afford a center for harmonizing the actions of nations in the achievement of these common ends.

See Chapter I, Proposals for the Establishment of a General International Organization, Dumbarton Oaks, Washington, D.C. (October 7, 1944).

The details of the organization were laid out in a subsequent diplomatic conference in San Francisco. The Charter of the United Nations was signed on June 26, 1945. The organization included four principal organs: a legislative branch called the General Assembly, a Security Council tasked with primary responsibility for international peace and security with the five world powers serving as its permanent members, a judicial organ called the International Court of Justice, and an executive authority called the Secretariat, composed of a Secretary-General and his or her administrative staff. Although the Soviet Union and the United States were already suspicious of each other, as the two global superpowers remaining after the war, the organization served their interests because both the Soviet Union and the United States received a veto on the Security Council and thus had the ability to block any resolution pertaining to international peace and security. (China, France, and England also received veto power.) Without this privileged position, it is unclear whether the world's major powers would have joined forces to create the organization. For better or worse, the UN has been the primary clearinghouse for multilateral diplomacy since its creation in 1945, although certainly not the exclusive forum for such efforts. Other institutions, such as the World Trade Organization, are independent and not official organs of the UN.

This chapter is devoted to analyzing the authority of the various organs within the UN and their respective authority. Much of that authority is clearly spelled out in the details of the Charter. But at the margins there is considerable confusion or contestation. Are these co-equal branches, analogous to the federal branches of the U.S. government? Does the International Court of Justice enjoy supremacy because of its judicial function? Is the Security Council on top because of its ultimate responsibility to ensure international peace and security—the prime goal of the UN as envisioned at Dumbarton Oaks? What happens when the Security Council becomes deadlocked? Since 1945, these issues and more have been contested by international lawyers and diplomats working inside and outside the UN.

Section A focuses on the Security Council; Section B on the General Assembly; Section C on the International Court of Justice; and Section D on the Secretary-General. Finally, Section E focuses on the status of the United Nations under international law, i.e., its "legal personality" and its capacity to enter into official legal relations with states and other international organizations bearing legal personality.

A. THE SECURITY COUNCIL

The UN Charter assigns primary responsibility for the maintenance of international peace and security to the Security Council, which is currently composed of 15 member states. The so-called "permanent members" of the Security Council have the ability to veto any resolution that comes before it. These states include Russia, the United Kingdom, France, China, and the United States—the world powers at the end of World War II when the United Nations was created. The other 10 seats on the Security Council are rotating seats that are assigned by an election in the General Assembly. These "non-permanent members" serve on the Security Council for two-year terms.

1. THE AUTHORITY OF THE SECURITY COUNCIL UNDER THE UN CHARTER

The authority of the Security Council is outlined in the UN Charter provisions that are reprinted below. In one sense, the powers of the Security Council are relatively straightforward. The Council may "determine the existence of any threat to the peace, breach of the peace, or act of aggression" and in response order any non-military or military measures it finds necessary to repair the situation. The resulting resolutions are *binding* on all members of the United Nations. In another sense, though, the dividing line between the authority of the Security Council and the other organs of the United Nations is contested. Also, at the level of law-making authority, the most pertinent question is whether the Security Council's authority in the realm of international peace and security is fundamentally unbounded or whether the Security Council itself is constrained by some body of law. If it is so constrained, which institution or court—if any—has the power to review Security Council resolutions to test their legality?

The following materials present the key issues for the reader to resolve. First, consider this excerpt from the UN Charter on the powers of the Security Council.

Charter of the United Nations
June 26, 1945

Chapter V: The Security Council

Article 24

1.   In order to ensure prompt and effective action by the United Nations, its Members confer on the Security Council primary responsibility for the maintenance of international peace and security, and agree that in carrying out its duties under this responsibility the Security Council acts on their behalf.

2.   In discharging these duties the Security Council shall act in accordance with the Purposes and Principles of the United Nations. The specific powers granted to the Security Council for the discharge of these duties are laid down in Chapters VI, VII, VIII, and XII.

3.   The Security Council shall submit annual and, when necessary, special reports to the General Assembly for its consideration.

Article 25

The Members of the United Nations agree to accept and carry out the decisions of the Security Council in accordance with the present Charter.

Chapter VII: Action with Respect to Threats to the Peace,
Breaches of the Peace, and Acts of Aggression

Article 39

The Security Council shall determine the existence of any threat to the peace, breach of the peace, or act of aggression and shall make recommendations, or decide what measures shall be taken in accordance with Articles 41 and 42, to maintain or restore international peace and security.

Article 40

In order to prevent an aggravation of the situation, the Security Council may, before making the recommendations or deciding upon the measures provided for in Article 39, call upon the parties concerned to comply with such provisional measures as it deems necessary or desirable. Such provisional measures shall be without prejudice to the rights, claims, or position of the parties concerned. The Security Council shall duly take account of failure to comply with such provisional measures.

Article 41

The Security Council may decide what measures not involving the use of armed force are to be employed to give effect to its decisions, and it may call upon the Members of the United Nations to apply such measures. These may include complete or partial interruption of economic relations and of rail, sea, air, postal, telegraphic, radio, and other means of communication, and the severance of diplomatic relations.

Article 42

Should the Security Council consider that measures provided for in Article 41 would be inadequate or have proved to be inadequate, it may take such action by air, sea, or land forces as may be necessary to maintain or restore international peace and security. Such action may include demonstrations, blockade, and other operations by air, sea, or land forces of Members of the United Nations.

Article 43

All Members of the United Nations, in order to contribute to the maintenance of international peace and security, undertake to make available to the Security Council, on its call and in accordance with a special agreement or agreements, armed forces, assistance, and facilities, including rights of passage, necessary for the purpose of maintaining international peace and security.

Such agreement or agreements shall govern the numbers and types of forces, their degree of readiness and general location, and the nature of the facilities and assistance to be provided.

The agreement or agreements shall be negotiated as soon as possible on the initiative of the Security Council. They shall be concluded between the Security Council and Members or between the Security Council and groups of Members and shall be subject to ratification by the signatory states in accordance with their respective constitutional processes.

Article 44

When the Security Council has decided to use force it shall, before calling upon a Member not represented on it to provide armed forces in fulfilment of the obligations assumed under Article 43, invite that

Member, if the Member so desires, to participate in the decisions of the Security Council concerning the employment of contingents of that Member's armed forces.

Article 45

In order to enable the United Nations to take urgent military measures, Members shall hold immediately available national air-force contingents for combined international enforcement action. The strength and degree of readiness of these contingents and plans for their combined action shall be determined within the limits laid down in the special agreement or agreements referred to in Article 43, by the Security Council with the assistance of the Military Staff Committee.

Article 46

Plans for the application of armed force shall be made by the Security Council with the assistance of the Military Staff Committee.

Article 47

There shall be established a Military Staff Committee to advise and assist the Security Council on all questions relating to the Security Council's military requirements for the maintenance of international peace and security, the employment and command of forces placed at its disposal, the regulation of armaments, and possible disarmament.

The Military Staff Committee shall consist of the Chiefs of Staff of the permanent members of the Security Council or their representatives. Any Member of the United Nations not permanently represented on the Committee shall be invited by the Committee to be associated with it when the efficient discharge of the Committee's responsibilities requires the participation of that Member in its work.

The Military Staff Committee shall be responsible under the Security Council for the strategic direction of any armed forces placed at the disposal of the Security Council. Questions relating to the command of such forces shall be worked out subsequently.

The Military Staff Committee, with the authorization of the Security Council and after consultation with appropriate regional agencies, may establish regional sub-committees.

Article 48

The action required to carry out the decisions of the Security Council for the maintenance of international peace and security shall be taken by all the Members of the United Nations or by some of them, as the Security Council may determine.

Such decisions shall be carried out by the Members of the United Nations directly and through their action in the appropriate international agencies of which they are members.

Article 49

The Members of the United Nations shall join in affording mutual assistance in carrying out the measures decided upon by the Security Council.

Article 50

If preventive or enforcement measures against any state are taken by the Security Council, any other state, whether a Member of the United Nations or not, which finds itself confronted with special economic problems arising from the carrying out of those measures shall have the right to consult the Security Council with regard to a solution of those problems.

Article 51

Nothing in the present Charter shall impair the inherent right of individual or collective self-defence if an armed attack occurs against a Member of the United Nations, until the Security Council has taken measures necessary to maintain international peace and security. Measures taken by Members in the exercise of this right of self-defence shall be immediately reported to the Security Council and shall not in any way affect the authority and responsibility of the Security Council under the present Charter to take at any time such action as it deems necessary in order to maintain or restore international peace and security.

Chapter XVI: Miscellaneous Provisions

Article 103

In the event of a conflict between the obligations of the Members of the United Nations under the present Charter and their obligations under any other international agreement, their obligations under the present Charter shall prevail.

2. THE BINDING NATURE OF SECURITY COUNCIL RESOLUTIONS

Having reviewed the powers of the Security Council as outlined in the UN Charter, consider the following case arising from South Africa's occupation of Namibia, which it ruled under a system of racial apartheid. The backstory here is important and involves the precursor to the United Nations, the League of Nations, which came into existence briefly after World War I before atrophying in the 1930s on the eve of the Second World War. The League of Nations had approved of a South African "mandate" over Namibia. The point of the mandate system was that the territories were supposed to be governed for the benefit of the local population. When the United Nations was created after World War II, it eliminated the old mandate system and replaced it with a new "trustee" system. Although the trustee system, like the mandate system, allowed for imperial control over territories, there was one important and lasting difference. The mandate system contemplated perpetual imperial rule as long as it was benevolent and for the benefit of the local population. In contrast, the trustee system explicitly envisioned that the territories would be prepared for independence and eventual self-rule in the near future.

South Africa resisted the elimination of the Namibia mandate because it desired continual control over the territory. Both the General Assembly and the Security Council demanded South Africa's acquiescence. The following ICJ case outlines the relative authority of the General Assembly and the Security Council to demand compliance from South Africa. Which body has coercive authority over South Africa?

Legal Consequences for States of the Continued Presence of South Africa in Namibia (S.W. Africa) Notwithstanding Security Council Resolution 276

International Court of Justice
1971 I.C.J. 16

106. By resolution 2145 (XXI) the General Assembly terminated the Mandate. However, lacking the necessary powers to ensure the withdrawal of South Africa from the Territory, it enlisted the co-operation of the Security Council by calling the latter's attention to the resolution. . .

107. The Security Council responded to the call of the General Assembly. It "took note" of General Assembly resolution 2145 (XXI) in the preamble of its resolution 245 (1968); it took it "into account" in resolution 246 (1968); in resolutions 264 (1969) and 269 (1969) it adopted certain measures directed towards the implementation of General Assembly resolution 2145 (XXI) and, finally, in resolution 276 (1970), it reaffirmed resolution 264 (1969) and recalled resolution 269 (1969).

108. Resolution 276 (1970) of the Security Council, specifically mentioned in the text of the request, is the one essential for the purposes of the present advisory opinion. Before analysing it, however, it is necessary to refer briefly to resolutions 264 (1969) and 269 (1969), since these two resolutions have, together with resolution 276 (1970), a combined and a cumulative effect. Resolution 264 (1969), in paragraph 3 of its operative part, calls upon South Africa to withdraw its administration from Namibia immediately. Resolution 269 (1969), in view of South Africa's lack of compliance, after recalling the obligations of Members under Article 25 of the Charter, calls upon the Government of South Africa, in paragraph 5 of its operative part, "to withdraw its

administration from the territory immediately and in any case before 4 October 1969." The preamble of resolution 276 (1970) reaffirms General Assembly resolution 2145 (XXI) and espouses it, by referring to the decision, not merely of the General Assembly, but of the United Nations "that the Mandate of South-West Africa was terminated." In the operative part, after condemning the non-compliance by South Africa with General Assembly and Security Council resolutions pertaining to Namibia, the Security Council declares, in paragraph 2, that "the continued presence of the South African authorities in Namibia is illegal" and that consequently all acts taken by the Government of South Africa "on behalf of or concerning Namibia after the termination of the Mandate are illegal and invalid." In paragraph 5 the Security Council "Calls upon all States, particularly those which have economic and other interests in Namibia, to refrain from any dealings with the Government of South Africa which are inconsistent with operative paragraph 2 of this resolution."

109. It emerges from the communications bringing the matter to the Security Council's attention, from the discussions held and particularly from the text of the resolutions themselves, that the Security Council, when it adopted these resolutions, was acting in the exercise of what it deemed to be its primary responsibility, the maintenance of peace and security, which, under the Charter, embraces situations which might lead to a breach of the peace. In the preamble of resolution 264 (1969) the Security Council was "Mindful of the grave consequences of South Africa's continued occupation of Namibia" and in paragraph 4 of that resolution it declared 'that the actions of the Government of South Africa designed to destroy the national unity and territorial integrity of Namibia through the establishment of Bantustans are contrary to the provisions of the United Nations Charter." In operative paragraph 3 of resolution 269 (1969) the Security Council decided "that the continued occupation of the territory of Namibia by the South African authorities constitutes an aggressive encroachment on the authority of the United Nations. . ." In operative paragraph 3 of resolution 276 (1970) the Security Council declared further "that the defiant attitude of the Government of South Africa towards the Council's decisions undermines the authority of the United Nations."

110. As to the legal basis of the resolution, Article 24 of the Charter vests in the Security Council the necessary authority to take action such as that taken in the present case. The reference in paragraph 2 of this Article to specific powers of the Security Council under certain chapters of the Charter does not exclude the existence of general powers to discharge the responsibilities conferred in paragraph 1. Reference may be made in this respect to the Secretary-General's Statement, presented to the Security Council on 10 January 1947, to the effect that "the powers

of the Council under Article 24 are not restricted to the specific grants of authority contained in Chapters VI, VII, VIII and XII. . . the Members of the United Nations have conferred upon the Security Council powers commensurate with its responsibility for the maintenance of peace and security. The only limitations are the fundamental principles and purposes found in Chapter I of the Charter."

111. As to the effect to be attributed to the declaration contained in paragraph 2 of resolution 276 (1970), the Court considers that the qualification of a situation as illegal does not by itself put an end to it. It can only be the first, necessary step in an endeavour to bring the illegal situation to an end.

112. It would be an untenable interpretation to maintain that, once such a declaration had been made by the Security Council under Article 24 of the Charter, on behalf of all member States, those Members would be free to act in disregard of such illegality or even to recognize violations of law resulting from it. When confronted with such an internationally unlawful situation, Members of the United Nations would be expected to act in consequence of the declaration made on their behalf. The question therefore arises as to the effect of this decision of the Security Council for States Members of the United Nations in accordance with Article 25 of the Charter.

113. It has been contended that Article 25 of the Charter applies only to enforcement measures adopted under Chapter VII of the Charter. It is not possible to find in the Charter any support for this view. Article 25 is not confined to decisions in regard to enforcement action but applies to "the decisions of the Security Council" adopted in accordance with the Charter. Moreover, that Article is placed, not in Chapter VII, but immediately after Article 24 in that part of the Charter which deals with the functions and powers of the Security Council. If Article 25 had reference solely to decisions of the Security Council concerning enforcement action under Articles 41 and 42 of the Charter, that is to say, if it were only such decisions which had binding effect, then Article 25 would be superfluous, since this effect is secured by Articles 48 and 49 of the Charter.

114. It has also been contended that the relevant Security Council resolutions are couched in exhortatory rather than mandatory language and that, therefore, they do not purport to impose any legal duty on any State nor to affect legally any right of any State. The language of a resolution of the Security Council should be carefully analysed before a conclusion can be made as to its binding effect. In view of the nature of the powers under Article 25, the question whether they have been in fact exercised is to be determined in each case, having regard to the terms of the resolution to be interpreted, the discussions leading to it, the Charter provisions invoked and, in general, all circumstances that might assist

in determining the legal consequences of the resolution of the Security Council.

115. Applying these tests, the Court recalls that in the preamble of resolution 269 (1969), the Security Council was "Mindful of its responsibility to take necessary action to secure strict compliance with the obligations entered into by States Members of the United Nations under the provisions of Article 25 of the Charter of the United Nations." The Court has therefore reached the conclusion that the decisions made by the Security Council in paragraphs 2 and 5 of resolutions 276 (1970), as related to paragraph 3 of resolution 264 (1969) and paragraph 5 of resolution 269 (1969), were adopted in conformity with the purposes and principles of the Charter and in accordance with its Articles 24 and 25. The decisions are consequently binding on all States Members of the United Nations, which are thus under obligation to accept and carry them out.

116. In pronouncing upon the binding nature of the Security Council decisions in question, the Court would recall the following passage in its Advisory Opinion of 11 April 1949 on Reparation for Injuries Suffered in the Service of the United Nations:

> The Charter has not been content to make the Organization created by it merely a centre "for harmonizing the actions of nations in the attainment of these common ends." It has equipped that centre with organs, and has given it special tasks. It has defined the position of the Members in relation to the Organization by requiring them to give it every assistance in any action undertaken by it, and to accept and carry out the decisions of the Security Council.

Thus when the Security Council adopts a decision under Article 25 in accordance with the Charter, it is for member States to comply with that decision, including those members of the Security Council which voted against it and those Members of the United Nations who are not members of the Council. To hold otherwise would be to deprive this principal organ of its essential functions and powers under the Charter.

NOTES & QUESTIONS

1. *Reforming the Security Council.* The preceding materials make clear that the Security Council wields enormous legal authority. Among UN organs, it alone has the authority to issue binding resolutions—legal pronouncements that require other member states to undertake some measure or stop some behavior. Despite this great authority, the Security Council hardly embodies broad democratic representation. The Council is composed of 15 members, 10 of whom rotate through two-year terms following an election in the UN General Assembly. The other five (Russia, China, U.S., U.K., France) are permanent members, each of whom enjoys a

veto power over any resolution introduced in the Council. Consequently, the Council's authority is dominated by major global powers who enjoy the power to dictate terms to states with less power. For many critics of the Security Council, this structure simply replicates, in the international legal system, power imbalances on the global stage. The criticisms come from scholars who are part of "Third-World Approaches to International Law," a critical perspective that investigates the ways that the deep structure of international law is overly influenced by the interests of global powers and ignores the significance of states in the Third World. However, the call to reform the Security Council is no mere academic proposal; plenty of states and their diplomatic representatives have called for reform but the permanent members are unwilling to relinquish their authority. Indeed, reform of the Security Council would represent a sea change in the basic structure of the UN, which has remained relatively unchanged since its formation in 1945. Do you believe that the Security Council's unequal power structure requires reform? If the world's major powers—Russia, the United States, China—were not given special treatment on the Security Council, would they simply leave the United Nations? Could the Security Council fulfill its responsibility to protect international peace and security if the world's most powerful nations simply ignored it? Or do powerful nations already do that when international law conflicts with their self-interest?

2.   *Can the President Violate the UN Charter?* Under U.S. constitutional law, does the President have the authority to violate the UN Charter? Under one common view, the President needs the authority to ignore international law when doing so is in the national interest. This issue is especially germane in the context of the UN Charter's use-of-force framework, which generally prohibits military force unless taken in self-defense or authorized by the Security Council. But consider Article II of the Constitution, which obligates the President to "take care that the laws be faithfully executed." Recall that the Supremacy Clause explicitly includes treaties as the "supreme law of the land." By logical extension, does this entail that the President has a constitutional obligation to ensure that the United States complies with the UN Charter, which was enacted as a formal treaty of the United States? For an argument along these lines, see Brian Finucane, *Presidential War Powers, the Take Care Clause, and Article 2(4) of the U.N. Charter*, 105 Cornell L. Rev. 1809 (2020) (suggesting that only Congress, not the President, may decide to ignore the UN Charter by authorizing military force contrary to its requirements).

3.   SECURITY COUNCIL RESOLUTIONS VERSUS TREATIES

The next case arises from the bombing of Pan Am Flight 103 on December 21, 1988. The flight took off from Frankfurt, Germany and was over the town of Lockerbie, Scotland, when it exploded in midair, killing 259 individuals. A joint international investigation focused on two Libyan nationals as the suspected bombers, and arrest warrants for the two men were issued in 1991.

Libyan leader Colonel Muammar Gaddafi refused to extradite the men to the United States (or elsewhere) to stand trial for the bombing. In response to Gaddafi's defiance, the Security Council issued Resolution 748 (1992), which directed Libya to cooperate with foreign authorities investigating the crime, demanded that Libya cease all terrorist activities, and imposed various sanctions on Libya. The sanctions included a ban on international air travel to or from Libya, a ban on the sale of aircraft components to Libya, and a ban on the sale of weapons to Libya.

In 1992, Libya sued the United States, arguing that the requests from the United States were not in accordance with the primary international treaty on civil aviation, the 1971 Convention for the Suppression of Unlawful Acts against the Safety of Civil Aviation (also known as the Montreal Convention). Moreover, Libya asserted that the Security Council was constrained by the scheme created by the Montreal Convention and had impermissibly departed from it by requiring Libya to extradite its nationals. In this case, the ICJ was tasked with determining whether the treaty or the Security Council resolution should take precedence. What did it decide? What provision in the UN Charter supported its decision?

Questions of Interpretation and Application of the 1971 Montreal Convention arising from the Aerial Incident at Lockerbie (Libyan Arab Jamahiriya v. United States of America)

International Court of Justice
1992 I.C.J. 114

Request for the Indication of Provisional Measures

3.   Whereas, in its Application, Libya claims that the Montreal Convention is the only appropriate convention in force between the Parties dealing with such offences, and that the United States is bound by its legal obligations under the Montreal Convention, which require it to act in accordance with the Convention, and only in accordance with the Convention, with respect to the matter involving Pan Am flight 103 and the accused;

5.   Whereas it is stated in the Application that at the time the charge was communicated to Libya, or shortly thereafter, the accused were present in the territory of Libya; that after being apprised of the charge, Libya took such measures as were necessary to establish its jurisdiction over the offences charged, pursuant to Article 5, paragraph 2, of the Montreal Convention; that Libya also took measures to ensure the presence of the accused in Libya in order to enable criminal proceedings to be instituted, that it initiated a preliminary enquiry into

the facts and that it submitted the case to its competent authorities for the purpose of prosecution; that Libya has not extradited the accused, there being no extradition treaty in force between it and the United States, and no basis for the extradition of the accused under Article 8, paragraph 2, of the Montreal Convention, since this provision subjects extradition to the law of the requested State and Libyan law prohibits the extradition of Libyan nationals; and that, pursuant to Article 1 1, paragraph 1, of the Montreal Convention, Libya has sought judicial assistance from the United States in connection with the criminal proceedings instituted by Libya, with the competent Libyan authorities offering to CO-operate with the investigations in the United States or in other countries, but that the United States together with its law enforcement officials have refused to CO-operate in any respect with the Libyan investigations;

38. Whereas in its observations on Security Council resolution 748 (1992) presented in response to the Court's invitation, Libya contends as follows: first, that that resolution does not prejudice the rights of Libya to request the Court to indicate provisional measures, inasmuch as by deciding, in effect, that Libya must surrender its nationals to the United States and the United Kingdom, the Security Council infringes, or threatens to infringe, the enjoyment and the exercise of the rights conferred on Libya by the Montreal Convention and its economic, commercial and diplomatic rights; whereas Libya therefore claims that the United States and the United Kingdom should so act as not to infringe Libya's rights, for example by seeking a suspension of the relevant part of resolution 748 (1992);

39. Whereas Libya in its observations contends, secondly, that the risk of contradiction between the resolution and the provisional measures requested of the Court by Libya does not render the Libyan request inadmissible, since there is in law no competition or hierarchy between the Court and the Security Council, each exercising its own competence; whereas Libya recalls in this connection that it regards the decision of the Security Council as contrary to international law, and considers that the Council has employed its power to characterize the situation for purposes of Chapter VII simply as a pretext to avoid applying the Montreal Convention;

40. Whereas in its observations on Security Council resolution 748 (1992), presented in response to the Court's invitation, the United States observes that that resolution was adopted under Chapter VII rather than Chapter VI of the Charter and was framed as a "decision" and contended that, given that binding decision, no object would be served by provisional measures; that, irrespective of the right claimed by Libya under the Montreal Convention, Libya has a Charter-based duty to accept and carry out the decisions in the resolution, and other States have a Charter-

based duty to seek Libya's compliance; that any indication of provisional measures would run a serious risk of conflicting with the work of the Security Council; that the Council had rejected (inter alia) Libya's contention that the matter should be addressed on the basis of the right claimed by Libya under the Montreal Convention, which Libya asks the Court to protect through provisional measures; and that the Court should therefore decline the request;

41. Whereas the Court, in the context of the present proceedings on a request for provisional measures, has in accordance with Article 41 of the Statute, to consider the circumstances drawn to its attention as requiring the indication of such measures, but cannot make definitive findings either of fact or of law on the issues relating to the merits, and the right of the Parties to contest such issues at the stage of the merits must remain unaffected by the Court's decision;

42. Whereas both Libya and the United States, as Members of the United Nations, are obliged to accept and carry out the decisions of the Security Council in accordance with Article 25 of the Charter; whereas the Court, which is at the stage of proceedings on provisional measures, considers that prima facie this obligation extends to the decision contained in resolution 748 (1992); and whereas, in accordance with Article 103 of the Charter, the obligations of the Parties in that respect prevail over their obligations under any other international agreement, including the Montreal Convention;

43. Whereas the Court, while thus not at this stage called upon to determine definitively the legal effect of Security Council resolution 748 (1992), considers that, whatever the situation previous to the adoption of that resolution, the rights claimed by Libya under the Montreal Convention cannot now be regarded as appropriate for protection by the indication of provisional measures;

44. Whereas, furthermore, an indication of the measures requested by Libya would be likely to impair the rights which appear prima facie to be enjoyed by the United States by virtue of Security Council resolution 748 (1992);

45. Whereas, in order to pronounce on the present request for provisional measures, the Court is not called upon to determine any of the other questions which have been raised before it in the present proceedings, including the question of its jurisdiction to entertain the merits of the case; and whereas the decision given in these proceedings in no way prejudges any such question, and leaves unaffected the rights of the Government of Libya and the Government of the United States to submit arguments in respect of any of these questions;

46. For these reasons. . . by eleven votes to five. . . finds that the circumstances of the case are not such as to require the exercise of its power under Article 41 of the Statute to indicate provisional measures.

AFTERWORD

After Libya lost its case at the ICJ and the UN imposed sanctions on Libya, intensive negotiations continued with Libya over the extradition of the alleged bombers. In 1999, Gaddafi turned over two suspects who were tried before a Scottish court, convened for this case in the Netherlands on the location of a former American airbase. Abdelbaset al-Megrahi was convicted of 270 counts of murder and sentenced to life in prison, while Lamin Khalifah Fhimah was acquitted. The UN lifted sanctions in 2003 after Libya officially renounced terrorism and Libya enjoyed increasingly normalized relations with western democracies.

Scottish authorities released Megrahi from prison in 2009 on medical grounds after he was diagnosed with prostate cancer and his doctors estimated that he had three months to live. He was flown to Libya where he received an enthusiastic welcome from the Gaddafi regime.

Gaddafi was deposed and killed in 2011 in a civil war when NATO air forces intervened on behalf of rebels fighting against the Gaddafi regime. Gaddafi was traveling in a military convoy that was attacked by NATO air forces. Gaddafi survived the air assault but was captured after a subsequent ground assault by a local militia. An angry mob then beat him to death.

Megrahi died in Libya in 2012.

---

4. SECURITY COUNCIL RESOLUTIONS VERSUS HUMAN RIGHTS LAW

In the prior ICJ decisions, the Court reiterated the primacy of the Security Council and its authority to issue binding resolutions that are hierarchically superior to subsidiary forms of law. Does this imply that the Security Council's authority is essentially unbounded? Can the Security Council simply do whatever it believes is necessary to restore international peace and security, or are their limits to this authority? If yes, where would these limits come from?

The following case involves sanctions that were imposed by the Security Council following the 9/11 terrorist attacks. Some members of the Council became concerned about the financial pipelines used to finance terrorist activities. Consequently, the Council used its Chapter VII authority to impose sanctions against specific individuals who were believed to be involved in the financing of terrorism. The sanctions required states to freeze the assets of, among others, Yassin Abdullah Kadi, a national of Saudi Arabia, and a charity named Al Barakaat. Kadi complained that his assets were frozen without any opportunity for him to contest the allegations against him in violation of his human rights as protected by various international treaties.

The case was heard by the European Court of Justice (ECJ), not the ICJ, because Kadi was contesting the European regulations that directed European countries to freeze Kadi's assets. However, the case directly confronts the question of the hierarchy between Security Council resolutions and other obligations under international law. Once again, are Security Council resolutions unbounded by law? What limits apply to the Security Council? How does the ECJ square its decision with article 103 of the UN Charter?

Kadi and Al Barakaat v. Council and Commission
European Court of Justice
September 3, 2008

Background to the disputes

13. On 15 October 1999 the Security Council adopted Resolution 1267 (1999), in which it, inter alia, condemned the fact that Afghan territory continued to be used for the sheltering and training of terrorists and planning of terrorist acts, reaffirmed its conviction that the suppression of international terrorism was essential for the maintenance of international peace and security and deplored the fact that the Taliban continued to provide safe haven to Usama bin Laden and to allow him and others associated with him to operate a network of terrorist training camps from territory held by the Taliban and to use Afghanistan as a base from which to sponsor international terrorist operations.

14. In the second paragraph of the resolution the Security Council demanded that the Taliban should without further delay turn Usama bin Laden over to appropriate authorities in a country where he has been indicted, or to appropriate authorities in a country where he will be arrested and effectively brought to justice. In order to ensure compliance with that demand, paragraph 4(b) of Resolution 1267 (1999) provides that all the States must, in particular, "freeze funds and other financial resources, including funds derived or generated from property owned or controlled directly or indirectly by the Taliban, or by any undertaking owned or controlled by the Taliban, as designated by the Committee established by paragraph 6 below, and ensure that neither they nor any other funds or financial resources so designated are made available, by their nationals or by any persons within their territory, to or for the benefit of the Taliban or any undertaking owned or controlled, directly or indirectly, by the Taliban, except as may be authorised by the Committee on a case-by-case basis on the grounds of humanitarian need."

15. In paragraph 6 of Resolution 1267 (1999), the Security Council decided to establish, in accordance with rule 28 of its provisional rules of procedure, a committee of the Security Council composed of all its members ("the Sanctions Committee"), responsible in particular for ensuring that the States implement the measures imposed by paragraph 4, designating the funds or other financial resources referred to in paragraph 4 and considering requests for exemptions from the measures imposed by paragraph 4.

16. Taking the view that action by the Community was necessary in order to implement Resolution 1267 (1999), on 15 November 1999 the Council adopted Common Position 1999/727/CFSP concerning restrictive measures against the Taliban.

17. Article 2 of that Common Position prescribes the freezing of funds and other financial resources held abroad by the Taliban under the conditions set out in Security Council Resolution 1267 (1999).

18. On 14 February 2000, on the basis of Articles 60 EC and 301 EC, the Council adopted Regulation (EC) No 337/2000 concerning a flight ban and a freeze of funds and other financial resources in respect of the Taliban of Afghanistan.

19. On 19 December 2000 the Security Council adopted Resolution 1333 (2000), demanding, inter alia, that the Taliban should comply with Resolution 1267 (1999), and, in particular, that they should cease to provide sanctuary and training for international terrorists and their organisations and turn Usama bin Laden over to appropriate authorities to be brought to justice. The Security Council decided, in particular, to strengthen the flight ban and freezing of funds imposed under Resolution 1267 (1999).

20. Accordingly, paragraph 8(c) of Resolution 1333 (2000) provides that the States are, inter alia, "[t]o freeze without delay funds and other financial assets of Usama bin Laden and individuals and entities associated with him as designated by the [Sanctions Committee], including those in the Al-Qaeda organisation, and including funds derived or generated from property owned or controlled directly or indirectly by Usama bin Laden and individuals and entities associated with him, and to ensure that neither they nor any other funds or financial resources are made available, by their nationals or by any persons within their territory, directly or indirectly for the benefit of Usama bin Laden, his associates or any entities owned or controlled, directly or indirectly, by Usama bin Laden or individuals and entities associated with him including the Al-Qaeda organization."

21. In the same provision, the Security Council instructed the Sanctions Committee to maintain an updated list, based on information provided by the States and regional organisations, of the individuals and entities designated as associated with Usama bin Laden, including those in the Al-Qaeda organisation.

23. Taking the view that action by the European Community was necessary in order to implement that resolution, on 26 February 2001 the Council adopted Common Position 2001/154/CFSP concerning additional restrictive measures against the Taliban and amending Common Position 96/746/CFSP.

24. Article 4 of that common position provides: "Funds and other financial assets of Usama bin Laden and individuals and entities associated with him, as designated by the Sanctions Committee, will be frozen, and funds or other financial resources will not be made available to Usama bin Laden and individuals or entities associated with him as designated by the Sanctions Committee, under the conditions set out in [Resolution 1333 (2000)]."

25. On 6 March 2001, on the basis of Articles 60 EC and 301 EC, the Council adopted Regulation (EC) No 467/2001 prohibiting the export of certain goods and services to Afghanistan, strengthening the flight ban and extending the freeze of funds and other financial resources in respect of the Taliban of Afghanistan, and repealing Regulation No 337/2000.

26. The third recital in the preamble to that regulation states that the measures provided for by Resolution 1333 (2000) "fall under the scope of the Treaty and, therefore, notably with a view to avoiding distortion of competition, Community legislation is necessary to implement the relevant decisions of the Security Council as far as the territory of the Community is concerned."

The grounds of challenge to the judgments under appeal

116. Mr Kadi puts forward two grounds of appeal, the first alleging lack of any legal basis for the contested regulation and the second concerning breach of several rules of international law by the Court of First Instance and the consequences of that breach as regards the assessment of his arguments relating to the infringement of certain of his fundamental rights which he pleaded before the Court of First Instance.

117. Al Barakaat puts forward three grounds of appeal, the first alleging lack of any legal basis for the contested regulation, the second infringement of Article 249 EC and the third infringement of certain of its fundamental rights.

Findings of the Court

280. The Court will now consider the heads of claim in which the appellants complain that the Court of First Instance, in essence, held that it followed from the principles governing the relationship between the international legal order under the United Nations and the Community legal order that the contested regulation, since it is designed to give effect to a resolution adopted by the Security Council under Chapter VII of the Charter of the United Nations affording no latitude in that respect, could not be subject to judicial review of its internal lawfulness, save with regard to its compatibility with the norms of jus cogens, and therefore to that extent enjoyed immunity from jurisdiction.

281. In this connection it is to be borne in mind that the Community is based on the rule of law, inasmuch as neither its Member States nor its institutions can avoid review of the conformity of their acts with the basic constitutional charter, the EC Treaty, which established a complete system of legal remedies and procedures designed to enable the Court of Justice to review the legality of acts of the institutions.

282. It is also to be recalled that an international agreement cannot affect the allocation of powers fixed by the Treaties or, consequently, the autonomy of the Community legal system, observance of which is ensured by the Court by virtue of the exclusive jurisdiction conferred on it by Article 220 EC, jurisdiction that the Court has, moreover, already held to form part of the very foundations of the Community.

283. In addition, according to settled case-law, fundamental rights form an integral part of the general principles of law whose observance the Court ensures. For that purpose, the Court draws inspiration from the constitutional traditions common to the Member States and from the guidelines supplied by international instruments for the protection of human rights on which the Member States have collaborated or to which they are signatories. In that regard, the ECHR has special significance.

284. It is also clear from the case-law that respect for human rights is a condition of the lawfulness of Community acts and that measures incompatible with respect for human rights are not acceptable in the Community.

285. It follows from all those considerations that the obligations imposed by an international agreement cannot have the effect of prejudicing the constitutional principles of the EC Treaty, which include the principle that all Community acts must respect fundamental rights, that respect constituting a condition of their lawfulness which it is for the Court to review in the framework of the complete system of legal remedies established by the Treaty.

286. In this regard it must be emphasised that, in circumstances such as those of these cases, the review of lawfulness thus to be ensured by the Community judicature applies to the Community act intended to give effect to the international agreement at issue, and not to the latter as such.

287. With more particular regard to a Community act which, like the contested regulation, is intended to give effect to a resolution adopted by the Security Council under Chapter VII of the Charter of the United Nations, it is not, therefore, for the Community judicature, under the exclusive jurisdiction provided for by Article 220 EC, to review the lawfulness of such a resolution adopted by an international body, even if that review were to be limited to examination of the compatibility of that resolution with jus cogens.

288. However, any judgment given by the Community judicature deciding that a Community measure intended to give effect to such a resolution is contrary to a higher rule of law in the Community legal order would not entail any challenge to the primacy of that resolution in international law.

290. It must therefore be considered whether, as the Court of First Instance held, as a result of the principles governing the relationship between the international legal order under the United Nations and the Community legal order, any judicial review of the internal lawfulness of the contested regulation in the light of fundamental freedoms is in principle excluded, notwithstanding the fact that... such review is a constitutional guarantee forming part of the very foundations of the Community.

291. In this respect it is first to be borne in mind that the European Community must respect international law in the exercise of its powers, the Court having in addition stated, in the same paragraph of the first of those judgments, that a measure adopted by virtue of those powers must be interpreted, and its scope limited, in the light of the relevant rules of international law.

292. Moreover, the Court has held that the powers of the Community provided for by Articles 177 EC to 181 EC in the sphere of cooperation and development must be exercised in observance of the undertakings given in the context of the United Nations and other international organisations.

293. Observance of the undertakings given in the context of the United Nations is required just as much in the sphere of the maintenance of international peace and security when the Community gives effect, by means of the adoption of Community measures taken on the basis of Articles 60 EC and 301 EC, to resolutions adopted by the Security Council under Chapter VII of the Charter of the United Nations.

294. In the exercise of that latter power it is necessary for the Community to attach special importance to the fact that, in accordance with Article 24 of the Charter of the United Nations, the adoption by the Security Council of resolutions under Chapter VII of the Charter constitutes the exercise of the primary responsibility with which that international body is invested for the maintenance of peace and security at the global level, a responsibility which, under Chapter VII, includes the power to determine what and who poses a threat to international peace and security and to take the measures necessary to maintain or restore them.

295. Next, it is to be noted that the powers provided for in Articles 60 EC and 301 EC may be exercised only in pursuance of the adoption of

a common position or joint action by virtue of the provisions of the EC Treaty relating to the CFSP which provides for action by the Community.

296. Although, because of the adoption of such an act, the Community is bound to take, under the EC Treaty, the measures necessitated by that act, that obligation means, when the object is to implement a resolution of the Security Council adopted under Chapter VII of the Charter of the United Nations, that in drawing up those measures the Community is to take due account of the terms and objectives of the resolution concerned and of the relevant obligations under the Charter of the United Nations relating to such implementation.

297. Furthermore, the Court has previously held that, for the purposes of the interpretation of the contested regulation, account must also be taken of the wording and purpose of Resolution 1390 (2002) which that regulation, according to the fourth recital in the preamble thereto, is designed to implement.

298. It must however be noted that the Charter of the United Nations does not impose the choice of a particular model for the implementation of resolutions adopted by the Security Council under Chapter VII of the Charter, since they are to be given effect in accordance with the procedure applicable in that respect in the domestic legal order of each Member of the United Nations. The Charter of the United Nations leaves the Members of the United Nations a free choice among the various possible models for transposition of those resolutions into their domestic legal order.

299. It follows from all those considerations that it is not a consequence of the principles governing the international legal order under the United Nations that any judicial review of the internal lawfulness of the contested regulation in the light of fundamental freedoms is excluded by virtue of the fact that that measure is intended to give effect to a resolution of the Security Council adopted under Chapter VII of the Charter of the United Nations.

300. What is more, such immunity from jurisdiction for a Community measure like the contested regulation, as a corollary of the principle of the primacy at the level of international law of obligations under the Charter of the United Nations, especially those relating to the implementation of resolutions of the Security Council adopted under Chapter VII of the Charter, cannot find a basis in the EC Treaty. . .

305. Nor can an immunity from jurisdiction for the contested regulation with regard to the review of its compatibility with fundamental rights, arising from the alleged absolute primacy of the resolutions of the Security Council to which that measure is designed to give effect, find any basis in the place that obligations under the Charter

of the United Nations would occupy in the hierarchy of norms within the Community legal order if those obligations were to be classified in that hierarchy.

310. It has however been maintained before the Court, in particular at the hearing, that the Community judicature ought, like the European Court of Human Rights, which in several recent decisions has declined jurisdiction to review the compatibility of certain measures taken in the implementing of resolutions adopted by the Security Council under Chapter VII of the Charter of the United Nations, to refrain from reviewing the lawfulness of the contested regulation in the light of fundamental freedoms, because that regulation is also intended to give effect to such resolutions.

311. In this respect, it is to be found that, as the European Court of Human Rights itself has noted, there exists a fundamental difference between the nature of the measures concerned by those decisions, with regard to which that court declined jurisdiction to carry out a review of consistency with the ECHR, and the nature of other measures with regard to which its jurisdiction would seem to be unquestionable.

314. In the instant case it must be declared that the contested regulation cannot be considered to be an act directly attributable to the United Nations as an action of one of its subsidiary organs created under Chapter VII of the Charter of the United Nations or an action falling within the exercise of powers lawfully delegated by the Security Council pursuant to that chapter.

316. As noted above in paragraphs 281 to 284, the review by the Court of the validity of any Community measure in the light of fundamental rights must be considered to be the expression, in a community based on the rule of law, of a constitutional guarantee stemming from the EC Treaty as an autonomous legal system which is not to be prejudiced by an international agreement.

317. The question of the Court's jurisdiction arises in the context of the internal and autonomous legal order of the Community, within whose ambit the contested regulation falls and in which the Court has jurisdiction to review the validity of Community measures in the light of fundamental rights.

318. It has in addition been maintained that, having regard to the deference required of the Community institutions vis-à-vis the institutions of the United Nations, the Court must forgo the exercise of any review of the lawfulness of the contested regulation in the light of fundamental rights, even if such review were possible, given that, under the system of sanctions set up by the United Nations, having particular regard to the re-examination procedure which has recently been

significantly improved by various resolutions of the Security Council, fundamental rights are adequately protected.

319. According to the Commission, so long as under that system of sanctions the individuals or entities concerned have an acceptable opportunity to be heard through a mechanism of administrative review forming part of the United Nations legal system, the Court must not intervene in any way whatsoever.

320. In this connection it may be observed, first of all, that if in fact, as a result of the Security Council's adoption of various resolutions, amendments have been made to the system of restrictive measures set up by the United Nations with regard both to entry in the summary list and to removal from it [see, in particular, Resolutions 1730 (2006) of 19 December 2006, and 1735 (2006) of 22 December 2006], those amendments were made after the contested regulation had been adopted so that, in principle, they cannot be taken into consideration in these appeals.

321. In any event, the existence, within that United Nations system, of the re-examination procedure before the Sanctions Committee, even having regard to the amendments recently made to it, cannot give rise to generalised immunity from jurisdiction within the internal legal order of the Community.

322. Indeed, such immunity, constituting a significant derogation from the scheme of judicial protection of fundamental rights laid down by the EC Treaty, appears unjustified, for clearly that re-examination procedure does not offer the guarantees of judicial protection.

323. In that regard, although it is now open to any person or entity to approach the Sanctions Committee directly, submitting a request to be removed from the summary list at what is called the "focal" point, the fact remains that the procedure before that Committee is still in essence diplomatic and intergovernmental, the persons or entities concerned having no real opportunity of asserting their rights and that committee taking its decisions by consensus, each of its members having a right of veto.

324. The Guidelines of the Sanctions Committee, as last amended on 12 February 2007, make it plain that an applicant submitting a request for removal from the list may in no way assert his rights himself during the procedure before the Sanctions Committee or be represented for that purpose, the Government of his State of residence or of citizenship alone having the right to submit observations on that request.

325. Moreover, those Guidelines do not require the Sanctions Committee to communicate to the applicant the reasons and evidence justifying his appearance in the summary list or to give him access, even

restricted, to that information. Last, if that Committee rejects the request for removal from the list, it is under no obligation to give reasons.

326. It follows from the foregoing that the Community judicature must, in accordance with the powers conferred on it by the EC Treaty, ensure the review, in principle the full review, of the lawfulness of all Community acts in the light of the fundamental rights forming an integral part of the general principles of Community law, including review of Community measures which, like the contested regulation, are designed to give effect to the resolutions adopted by the Security Council under Chapter VII of the Charter of the United Nations.

327. The Court of First Instance erred in law, therefore, when it held. . . that it followed from the principles governing the relationship between the international legal order under the United Nations and the Community legal order that the contested regulation, since it is designed to give effect to a resolution adopted by the Security Council under Chapter VII of the Charter of the United Nations affording no latitude in that respect, must enjoy immunity from jurisdiction so far as concerns its internal lawfulness save with regard to its compatibility with the norms of jus cogens.

328. The appellants' grounds of appeal are therefore well founded on that point, with the result that the judgments under appeal must be set aside in this respect.

NOTES & QUESTIONS

1. *A Normative Hierarchy of Legal Norms.* Is the *Kadi* judgment consistent with the ICJ approach in *Lockerbie* or *Legal Consequences for States of the Continued Presence of South Africa in Namibia*? What would the ICJ decide if confronted by the argument advanced by Kadi? Article 103 of the UN Charter specifically states that obligations arising from the UN Charter take precedence over conflicting international obligations. Does this suggest that an obligation to comply with a Security Council resolution should take precedence over an obligation to comply with international human rights law? How did the ECJ interpret article 103? Did you find convincing the ECJ's conclusion that "the contested regulation cannot be considered to be an act directly attributable to the United Nations as an action of one of its subsidiary organs created under Chapter VII of the Charter of the United Nations"? This statement seems to draw a distinction between the Security Council resolution and the European regulation that implemented it. Does this distinction carry the significance that the ECJ assigns it? For a discussion, see Marko Milanovic, *Norm Conflict in International Law: Whither Human Rights?*, 20 Duke J. Comp. & Int'l L. 69, 76–77 (2009) ("Article 103 is not a simple rule of priority—it also precludes or removes any wrongfulness due to the breach of the conflicting norm. In other words, a state cannot be called to account for complying with its

obligations under the Charter, even if in doing so it must violate some other rule—any rule, that is, except a rule of jus cogens."). Were the human rights norms in the *Kadi* case jus cogens norms? Does the concept of jus cogens explain the ECJ's view on the limits of the Security Council's authority?

2. *Monism Versus Dualism.* The Court of First Instance concluded that it had no jurisdiction to consider the lawfulness of the Security Council's resolution. Why did the ECJ disagree? The Court of First Instance had concluded that international law and European law were two separate "legal orders." This conclusion rested on a dualist outlook, and for this reason, the Court of First Instance concluded that it had no basis to oversee the legality of a Security Council resolution. However, the ECJ adopted a monist approach and insisted that European and international law were part of the same "legal order." Although this monist approach suggested that Security Council resolutions trumped conflicting legal norms from domestic law, the ECJ concluded that there was a limit to this normative hierarchy. It applies in all cases *except* in a case involving jus cogens. In that case, the jus cogens norm is even higher than the Security Council resolution. For a discussion, see Katja S. Ziegler, *Strengthening the Rule of Law, but Fragmenting International Law: The Kadi Decision of the ECJ from the Perspective of Human Rights*, 9 Hum. Rts. L. Rev. 288–305 (2009).

3. *The Right to Be Heard.* The ECJ concluded that Kadi's human rights were violated because the European regulations failed to give Kadi an adequate forum to press his legal objections. Do you agree that this constituted a human rights violation?

4. *Collective Versus Individual Sanctions.* Usually, the Security Council issues orders that affect legal rights at the *collective level*. For example, the Security Council might order a naval blockade against an entire country or a military defensive operation against a state whose actions have threatened international peace and security. These military measures are never targeted against single individuals. But in *Kadi*, the sanctions were against specific *individuals*. Did that change in strategy open the Security Council to legal vulnerability flowing from human rights law? Could the Security Council have avoided a human rights problem simply by imposing the same sanctions on a greater number of individuals?

B. THE GENERAL ASSEMBLY

The General Assembly is the legislative organ of the United Nations. However, unlike the United States Congress or a domestic parliament, the General Assembly does not enjoy plenary authority to pass legislation that is automatically binding over all members of the United Nations. (The one exception is the power to grant "membership" in the United Nations, which is squarely within the purview of the General Assembly.) As we saw above, the power to issue binding law resides with the Security Council. In contrast, the General Assembly (upon a majority vote) may pass resolutions that function as recommendations.

1. THE AUTHORITY OF THE GENERAL ASSEMBLY UNDER THE UN CHARTER

In the following provisions, the UN Charter lays out the specific powers of the General Assembly. Pay particular attention to how the UN Charter allocates the division of power between the General Assembly and the Security Council.

Charter of the United Nations
June 26, 1945

Chapter IV: The General Assembly

Article 10

The General Assembly may discuss any questions or any matters within the scope of the present Charter or relating to the powers and functions of any organs provided for in the present Charter, and, except as provided in Article 12, may make recommendations to the Members of the United Nations or to the Security Council or to both on any such questions or matters.

Article 11

1.   The General Assembly may consider the general principles of co-operation in the maintenance of international peace and security, including the principles governing disarmament and the regulation of armaments, and may make recommendations with regard to such principles to the Members or to the Security Council or to both.

2.   The General Assembly may discuss any questions relating to the maintenance of international peace and security brought before it by any Member of the United Nations, or by the Security Council, or by a state which is not a Member of the United Nations in accordance with Article 35, paragraph 2, and, except as provided in Article 12, may make recommendations with regard to any such questions to the state or states concerned or to the Security Council or to both. Any such question on which action is necessary shall be referred to the Security Council by the General Assembly either before or after discussion.

3.   The General Assembly may call the attention of the Security Council to situations which are likely to endanger international peace and security.

4.   The powers of the General Assembly set forth in this Article shall not limit the general scope of Article 10.

Article 12

1.   While the Security Council is exercising in respect of any dispute or situation the functions assigned to it in the present Charter, the General

Assembly shall not make any recommendation with regard to that dispute or situation unless the Security Council so requests.

2.   The Secretary-General, with the consent of the Security Council, shall notify the General Assembly at each session of any matters relative to the maintenance of international peace and security which are being dealt with by the Security Council and shall similarly notify the General Assembly, or the Members of the United Nations if the General Assembly is not in session, immediately the Security Council ceases to deal with such matters.

2.   THE UNITING FOR PEACE RESOLUTION

There is some dispute over the proper role of the General Assembly in matters pertaining to international peace and security. Recall that the Security Council has "primary" authority over that domain. But what does that mean?

The issue came to a head in 1950, just five years after the creation of the United Nations, in the midst of the Cold War. At the end of World War II, Korea was divided into two nations, North Korea and South Korea, roughly corresponding to the territories on the peninsula that Russia and the United States had occupied at the end of World War II. In 1950, communist North Korea, supported by the Soviet Union, invaded South Korea, provoking the Korean War.

The United States pushed the Security Council to condemn the North Korean military incursion into the South. The Soviet Union sought to block the Security Council from issuing resolutions by boycotting Security Council meetings, apparently under the erroneous assumption that its absence would prevent the Security Council from acting. Instead, the rest of the permanent members of the Security Council used the Soviet absence to pass a resolution declaring the North Korean invasion a breach of the peace. Realizing its strategic error, the Soviet Union returned to the Security Council, this time promising to use its veto power to block further Security Council resolutions critical of North Korea.

The United States and its allies were faced with the threat of a deadlocked Security Council unable to act on the pressing matters of the day. Neither the Soviet Union nor China would permit a resolution critical of its interests or its allies, nor would the United States, Britain, or France permit a resolution critical of its policies. In order to break through the deadlock, the United States and France turned to the General Assembly as a possible solution. The result was a "Uniting for Peace" Resolution that articulated a role for General Assembly action in the face of Security Council inaction. As you read the resolution, ask yourself how it squares with the UN Charter. Is it consistent with the authority of the Security Council outlined in the Charter?

Uniting for Peace Resolution
General Assembly Resolution 377
November 3, 1950

The General Assembly,

Recognizing that the first two stated *Purposes of the United Nations* are:

"To maintain international peace and security, and to that end: to take effective collective measures for the prevention and removal of threats to the peace, and for the suppression of acts of aggression or other breaches of the peace, and to bring about by peaceful means, and in conformity with the principles of justice and international law, adjustment or settlement of international disputes or situations which might lead to a breach of the peace", and

"To develop friendly relations among nations based on respect for the principle of equal rights and self-determination of peoples, and to take other appropriate measures to strengthen universal peace",

Reaffirming that it remains the primary duty of all Members of the United Nations, when involved in an international dispute, to seek settlement of such a dispute by peaceful means through the procedures laid down in *Chapter VI of the Charter*, and recalling the successful achievements of the United Nations in this regard on a number of previous occasions,

Finding that international tension exists on a dangerous scale,

Recalling its *resolution 290 (IV)* entitled "Essentials of peace", which states that disregard of the Principles of the Charter of the United Nations is primarily responsible for the continuance of international tension, and desiring to contribute further to the objectives of that resolution,

Reaffirming the importance of the exercise by the Security Council of its primary responsibility for the maintenance of international peace and security, and the duty of the permanent members to seek unanimity and to exercise restraint in the use of the veto,

Reaffirming that the initiative in negotiating the agreements for armed forces provided for in *Article 43 of the Charter* belongs to the Security Council, and desiring to ensure that, pending the conclusion of such agreements, the United Nations has at its disposal means for maintaining international peace and security,

Conscious that failure of the Security Council to discharge its responsibilities on behalf of all the Member States, particularly those responsibilities referred to in the two preceding paragraphs, does not relieve Member States of their obligations or the United Nations of its responsibility under the Charter to maintain international peace and security,

Recognizing in particular that such failure does not deprive the General Assembly of its rights or relieve it of its responsibilities under the Charter in regard to the maintenance of international peace and security,

Recognizing that discharge by the General Assembly of its responsibilities in these respects calls for possibilities of observation which would ascertain the facts and expose aggressors; for the existence of armed forces which could be used collectively; and for the possibility of timely recommendation by the General Assembly to Members of the United Nations for collective action which, to be effective, should be prompt,

1.   Resolves that if the Security Council, because of lack of unanimity of the permanent members, fails to exercise its primary responsibility for the maintenance of international peace and security in any case where there appears to be a threat to the peace, breach of the peace, or act of aggression, the General Assembly shall consider the matter immediately with a view to making appropriate recommendations to Members for collective measures, including in the case of a breach of the peace or act of aggression the use of armed force when necessary, to maintain or restore international peace and security. If not in session at the time, the General Assembly may meet in emergency special session within twenty-four hours of the request therefor. Such emergency special session shall be called if requested by the Security Council on the vote of any seven members, or by a majority of the Members of the United Nations;

2.   Adopts for this purpose the amendments to its rules of procedure set forth in the annex to the present resolution;

3.   Establishes a Peace Observation Commission which, for the calendar years 1951 and 1952, shall be composed of fourteen Members, namely: China, Colombia, Czechoslovakia, France, India, Iraq, Israel, New Zealand, Pakistan, Sweden, the Union of Soviet Socialist Republics, the United Kingdom of Great Britain and Northern Ireland, the United States of America and Uruguay, and which could observe and report on the situation in any area where there exists international tension the continuance of which is likely to endanger the maintenance of international peace and security. Upon the invitation or with the consent of the State into whose territory the Commission would go, the General

Assembly, or the Interim Committee when the Assembly is not in session, may utilize the Commission if the Security Council is not exercising the functions assigned to it by the Charter with respect to the matter in question. Decisions to utilize the Commission shall be made on the affirmative vote of two-thirds of the members present and voting. The Security Council may also utilize the Commission in accordance with its authority under the Charter;

4. Decides that the Commission shall have authority in its discretion to appoint sub-commissions and to utilize the services of observers to assist it in the performance of its functions;

5. Recommends to all governments and authorities that they co-operate with the Commission and assist it in the performance of its functions;

6. Requests the Secretary-General to provide the necessary staff and facilities, utilizing, where directed by the Commission, the United Nations Panel of Field Observers envisaged in General Assembly resolution 297 B (IV);

7. Invites each Member of the United Nations to survey its resources in order to determine the nature and scope of the assistance it may be in a position to render in support of any recommendations of the Security Council or of the General Assembly for the restoration of international peace and security;

8. Recommends to the States Members of the United Nations that each Member maintain within its national armed forces elements so trained, organized and equipped that they could promptly be made available, in accordance with its constitutional processes, for service as a United Nations unit or units, upon recommendation by the Security Council or the General Assembly, without prejudice to the use of such elements in exercise of the right of individual or collective self-defence recognized in *Article 51 of the Charter*;

9. Invites the Members of the United Nations to inform the Collective Measures Committee provided for in paragraph 11 as soon as possible of the measures taken in implementation of the preceding paragraph;

10. Requests the Secretary-General to appoint, with the approval of the Committee provided for in paragraph 11, a panel of military experts who could be made available, on request, to Member States wishing to obtain technical advice regarding the organization, training, and equipment for prompt service as United Nations units or the elements referred to in paragraph 8;

11. Establishes a Collective Measures Committee consisting of fourteen Members, namely: Australia, Belgium, Brazil, Burma, Canada,

Egypt, France, Mexico, Philippines, Turkey, the United Kingdom of Great Britain and Northern Ireland, the United States of America, Venezuela and Yugoslavia, and directs the Committee, in consultation with the Secretary-General and with such Member States as the Committee finds appropriate, to study and make a report to the Security Council and the General Assembly, not later than 1 September 1951, on methods, including those in section C of the present resolution, which might be used to maintain and strengthen international peace and security in accordance with the Purposes and Principles of the Charter, taking account of collective self-defence and regional arrangements (*Articles 51 and 52 of the Charter*);

12. Recommends to all Member States that they co-operate with the Committee and assist it in the performance of its functions;

13. Requests the Secretary-General to furnish the staff and facilities necessary for the effective accomplishment of the purposes set forth in. . . the present resolution;

14. Is fully conscious that, in adopting the proposals set forth above, enduring peace will not be secured solely by collective security arrangements against breaches of international peace and acts of aggression but that a genuine and lasting peace depends also upon the observance of all the *Principles and Purposes* established in the Charter of the United Nations, upon the implementation of the resolutions of the Security Council, the General Assembly and other principal organs of the United Nations intended to achieve the maintenance of international peace and security, and especially upon respect for and observance of human rights and fundamental freedoms for all and on the establishment and maintenance of conditions of economic and social well-being in all countries; and accordingly

15. Urges Member States to respect fully, and to intensify, joint action, in co-operation with the United Nations, to develop and stimulate universal respect for and observance of human rights and fundamental freedoms, and to intensify individual and collective efforts to achieve conditions of economic stability and social progress, particularly through the development of under-developed countries and areas.

NOTES & QUESTIONS

1.   *The Aftermath of "Uniting for Peace."* In the ensuing years, the General Assembly issued a few recommendations pursuant to the Uniting for Peace resolution, but over time the mechanism fell into disuse. Although the United States was originally enthusiastic about using the General Assembly as a workaround for a deadlocked Security Council, the U.S. attitude eventually changed. After all, the General Assembly could be used *against* U.S. interests as well, when the U.S. or its allies blocked an unfriendly resolution in the Security Council. Indeed, this happened during

the Suez Crisis in 1956. This explains why the U.S. and Russia have pulled back from the mechanism because both have an interest in maintaining the Security Council's exclusive role in matters of peace and security, because that is where they have their greatest legal clout. But what explains the failure of smaller states in the General Assembly to use the Uniting for Peace mechanism more aggressively? See Christian Tomuschat, *Uniting for Peace*, United Nations Audiovisual Library of International Law, at 4 ("Notwithstanding their sheer numerical superiority, the many Members of the United Nations are much too weak to attempt to challenge the decisions made at the Security Council.").

2.   *Consistency with the Charter.* Given the role of the Security Council outlined in the UN Charter, one might view the Uniting for Peace Resolution as an illegal attempt to amend the UN Charter without going through the proscribed amendment process. There is nothing in the UN Charter which expressly grants the General Assembly the powers that are normally associated with the Security Council when the latter body is deadlocked due to a veto. Moreover, the Charter seems to *exclude* the General Assembly. (Pay particular attention to article 12 of the UN Charter.) Was the Uniting for Peace Resolution illegal? There are two important details in the resolution that arguably prevent it from being a violation of the Charter structure. The first is that the resolution calls for the General Assembly to make "recommendations"—and nowhere indicates that the General Assembly can make "binding" pronouncements in the same manner as the Security Council. Second, the resolution contemplates that the General Assembly will make recommendations for "collective measures" to be taken by UN members. There is some ambiguity about the meaning of "collective measures." These might be enforcement measures in the sense in which the Security Council can sometimes issue binding enforcement measures in the face of a breach of international peace and security. However, "collective measures" might also refer to acts of collective self-defense. In that sense, the General Assembly might simply recommend that member states exercise their *independent* authority to engage in collective self-defense—a right that is protected in article 51 of the UN Charter and which does not require Security Council authorization. Under that interpretation, the recommendation of "collective measures" contemplated by the Uniting for Peace Resolution would not offend the UN Charter because these are measures that states are free to engage in anyway, so a General Assembly resolution would not add further legal weight to them.

3.   *General Assembly Resolutions.* Are General Assembly resolutions binding expressions of international law? Most international lawyers would say no and would cite Article 10 of the UN Charter, which states that the General Assembly has the power to "discuss" any matter "within the scope" of the Charter and may issue "recommendations." Furthermore, article 38 of the ICJ Statute does not list General Assembly resolutions as a source of international law. That being said, a General Assembly resolution may *indirectly* constitute customary international law insofar as a state's decision

to support a resolution may be evidence of opinio juris. Some scholars have questioned the subsidiary status of General Assembly resolutions, arguing that this subsidiary status embodies international law's failure to adequately involve Third World states in the creation of international law, especially within the United Nations. Why did the framers of the UN Charter not grant the General Assembly greater powers? Did that decision encode a colonial mindset within the UN Charter document? For a discussion of the status of General Assembly resolutions, see Obed Y. Asamoah, *The Legal Significance of the Declarations of the General Assembly of the United Nations* 6 (1966) (noting that "a resolution may contain an assertion that a particular line of conduct is contrary to a principle of customary international law or it may contain a principle agreed upon by the Members of the United Nations to guide their future conduct on an issue" and arguing that "[t]hese statements of principle are not merely recommendations but evidence of what the community of states regards as law").

C. INTERNATIONAL COURT OF JUSTICE

The International Court of Justice is the principal legal organ of the United Nations, created in 1945 at the same time as the General Assembly and the Security Council. The operations of the court are governed by the Statute of the International Court of Justice. As we saw in prior chapters, article 38 of the Statute establishes the sources of law to be applied by the court, including custom, treaties, general principles, and as subsidiary means the decisions of international tribunals and international legal scholarship.

The rules regarding the Court's jurisdiction are complex and will be covered in greater detail in the subsequent chapter on international dispute adjudication. For the moment, it is sufficient to recall that the Court's jurisdiction is based on the principle of consent: either consent to the court's plenary jurisdiction for all cases or limited consent to the court as a dispute resolution mechanism for particular treaties. Also, as a formal matter, the Court's rulings are only binding on the parties to a case; the court has no jurisdiction to impose new legal obligations on non-parties.

One structural consideration is the role of the ICJ in relation to the other UN organs, including the General Assembly and the Security Council. In the United States, the United States Supreme Court has the power of "judicial review," i.e., the power to test legislation and executive action for its compliance with the U.S. Constitution and to declare null and void any action that violates constitutional norms. See *Marbury v. Madison*, 5 U.S. 137, 177 (1803) ("It is emphatically the province and duty of the judicial department to say what the law is."). In contrast, the ICJ has never explicitly invoked a *Marbury*-esque authority to review the legality of Security Council or General Assembly resolution. However, this has not prevented a number of judges and scholars from voicing their opinions on the matter.

In the following excerpts, two ICJ judges present differing views on whether the court enjoys the power of judicial review.

Legal Consequences for States of the Continued Presence of South Africa in Namibia (S. W. Africa) Notwithstanding Security Council Resolution 276

International Court of Justice
1971 I.C.J. 16

Separate Opinion of Judge Onyeama

It would be tedious to reproduce here all the written and oral submissions made to the Court and tending in the direction of confining the Court to an uncritical acceptance of the correctness in law of resolutions and decisions of the General Assembly and the Security Council directly relevant to the question upon which the Court's opinion is requested, and it suffices to say that a number of representatives urged this view upon the Court. The Court had therefore to decide whether it was competent or not to examine resolutions and decisions of the General Assembly and the Security Council relevant to the question before it, with a view to determining their accordance with the Charter of the United Nations, and, therefore, their validity.

In dealing with this matter the Court said:

> Undoubtedly, the Court does not possess powers of judicial review or appeal in respect of the decisions taken by the United Nations organs concerned. The question of the validity or conformity with the Charter of General Assembly resolution 2145 (XXI) or of related Security Council resolutions does not form the subject of the request for advisory opinion. However, in the exercise of its judicial function and since objections have been advanced the Court, in the course of its reasoning, will consider these objections before determining any legal consequences arising from these resolutions.

I do not think that this approach to the question of the Court's competence to examine and pass upon decisions and resolutions of the General Assembly and the Security Council which touch upon issues before it leads to a sufficiently definitive answer.

The Court was established as the principal judicial organ of the United Nations, and, as such, adjudicates upon disputes between States when such disputes are properly brought within its jurisdiction. It is authorized by the Charter and the Statute of the Court to render advisory opinions on legal questions to the General Assembly, the Security Council and other organs of the United Nations and specialized agencies.

In exercising its functions the Court is wholly independent of the other organs of the United Nations and is in no way obliged or concerned to render a judgment or opinion which would be "politically acceptable." Its function is, in the words of Article 38 of the Statute, "to decide in accordance with international law."

The Court's powers are clearly defined by the Statute, and do not include powers to review decisions of other organs of the United Nations; but when, as in the present proceedings, such decisions bear upon a case properly before the Court, and a correct judgment or opinion could not be rendered without determining the validity of such decisions, the Court could not possibly avoid such a determination without abdicating its role of a judicial organ.

The question put to the Court does not, in terms, ask the Court to give an opinion on whether General Assembly resolution 2145 (XXI) is valid, but the "legal consequences" which the Court is requested to define, are postulated upon its validity. Were the Court to accept this postulate without examination, it would run the risk of rendering an opinion based on a false premise. The question itself has not expressly excluded examination of the validity of this and other related resolutions; and, as this Court had in the past modified and interpreted questions put to it, it cannot be assumed that the Security Council intended to fetter the Court in its considerations of the question on which it had itself requested an advisory opinion; it would require the clearest inhibiting words to establish that such a limitation of the scope of the Court's consideration was intended.

I do not conceive it as compatible with the judicial function that the Court will proceed to state the consequences of acts whose validity is assumed, without itself testing the lawfulness of the origin of those acts. I am therefore of the view that, whether an objection had been raised or not, the Court had a duty to examine General Assembly resolution 2145 (XXI) with a view to ascertaining its legal value; it had an equal duty to examine all relevant resolutions of the Security Council for the same purpose.

I can find nothing in the wording of the present request which excludes consideration of the validity of all pertinent resolutions. The words "notwithstanding Security Council resolution 276 (1970)" appear to me to indicate that the Security Council has assumed that resolution 276 (1970) validly created a situation in which South Africa's continued presence in Namibia gives rise to legal consequences for States; but, in my view, those words do not oblige the Court to make the same assumptions or to accept their correctness without examination.

The matter is, in my view, concluded by the principle stated by the Court in the *Certain Expenses of the United Nations* case as follows: ". . .the Court must have full liberty to consider all relevant data available to it in forming an opinion on a question posed to it for an advisory opinion."

Where the question put to the Court is in such terms that the Court could not properly perform its judicial function of a thorough consideration of all relevant data, or where for any other reason the Court is not permitted the full liberty it is entitled to in considering a question posed to it, the Court's discretion to render or withhold an opinion would protect the Court from the danger of rendering an opinion based on, conceivably, false assumptions or incomplete data.

I conclude that in the present request, the Court had a duty to examine all General Assembly and Security Council resolutions which are relevant to the question posed to it, whether objections had been taken to them or not, in order to determine their validity and effect, and so that the Court can arrive at a satisfactory opinion.

Questions of Interpretation and Application of the 1971 Montreal Convention arising from the Aerial Incident at Lockerbie (Libyan Arab Jamahiriya v. United States of America)

International Court of Justice
1998 I.C.J. 115

Dissenting Opinion of Judge Schwebel

. . . .That last spectre raises the question of whether the Court is empowered to exercise judicial review of the decisions of the Security Council, a question as to which I think it right to express my current views. The Court is not generally so empowered, and it is particularly without power to overrule or undercut decisions of the Security Council made by it in pursuance of its authority under Articles 39, 41 and 42 of the Charter to determine the existence of any threat to the peace, breach of the peace, or act of aggression and to decide upon responsive measures to be taken to maintain or restore international peace and security.

The Court more than once has disclaimed possessing a power of judicial review. In its Advisory Opinion in the case concerning *Certain Expenses of the United Nations*, the Court declared:

> In the legal systems of States, there is often some procedure for determining the validity of even a legislative or governmental act, but no analogous procedure is to be found in the structure of the United Nations. Proposals made during the drafting of the Charter to place the ultimate authority to interpret the

Charter in the International Court of Justice were not accepted; the opinion which the Court is in course of rendering is an advisory opinion. As anticipated in 1945, therefore, each organ must, in the first place at least, determine its own jurisdiction. If the Security Council, for example, adopts a resolution purportedly for the maintenance of international peace and security and if, in accordance with a mandate or authorization in such resolution, the Secretary-General incurs financial obligations, these amounts must be presumed to constitute "expenses of the Organization." (1. C.J. Reports 1962, p. 168.)

In its Advisory Opinion on *Legal Consequences for States of the Continued Presence of South Africa in Namibia (South West Africa) notwithstanding Security Council Resolution 276 (1970)*, the Court reiterated that: "Undoubtedly, the Court does not possess powers of judicial review or appeal in respect of the decisions taken by the United Nations organs concerned."

It should be noted that the Court made these holdings in advisory proceedings, in which the Security Council and the General Assembly are entitled to request the Court's opinion "on any legal question." The authority of the Court to respond to such questions, and, in the course of so doing, to pass upon relevant resolutions of the Security Council and General Assembly, is not disputed. Nevertheless, if the Court could hold as it did in advisory proceedings, a fortiori in contentious proceedings the Court can hardly be entitled to invent, assert and apply powers of judicial review.

While the Court so far has not had occasion in contentious proceedings to pass upon an alleged authority to judicially review decisions of the Security Council, it may be recalled that in Military and Paramilitary Activities in and against Nicaragua the Court observed that:

> The Court is not asked to say that the Security Council was wrong in its decision, nor that there was anything inconsistent with law in the way in which the members of the Council employed their right to vote. The Court is asked to pass judgment on certain legal aspects of a situation which has also been considered by the Security Council, a procedure which is entirely consonant with its position as the principal judicial organ of the United Nations. (*Military and Paramilitary Activities in and against Nicaragua (Nicaragua v. United States of America)*, Jurisdiction and Admissibility, Judgment, I.C.J. Reports 1984, p. 436.)

The implication of this statement is that, if the Court had been asked by the Applicant to say that the Security Council had been wrong in its decision, the Court would have reached another conclusion.

The texts of the Charter of the United Nations and of the Statute of the Court furnish no shred of support for a conclusion that the Court possesses a power of judicial review in general, or a power to supervene the decisions of the Security Council in particular. On the contrary, by the absence of any such provision, and by according the Security Council "primary responsibility for the maintenance of international peace and security," the Charter and the Statute import the contrary. So extraordinary a power as that of judicial review is not ordinarily to be implied and never has been on the international plane. If the Court were to generate such a power, the Security Council would no longer be primary in its assigned responsibilities, because if the Court could overrule, negate, modify—or, as in this case, hold as proposed that decisions of the Security Council are not "opposable" to the principal object State of those decisions and to the object of its sanctions—it would be the Court and not the Council that would exercise, or purport to exercise, the dispositive and hence primary authority.

The drafters of the Charter above all resolved to accord the Security Council alone extraordinary powers. They did so in order to further realization of the first Purpose of the United Nations,

> To maintain international peace and security, and to that end: to take effective collective measures for the prevention and removal of threats to the peace, and for the suppression of acts of aggression or other breaches of the peace, and to bring about by peaceful means, and in conformity with the principles of justice and international law, adjustment or settlement of international disputes or situations which might lead to a breach of the peace.

Article 24 thus provides:

> 1. In order to ensure prompt and effective action by the United Nations, its Members confer on the Security Council primary responsibility for the maintenance of international peace and security, and agree that in carrying out its duties under this responsibility the Security Council acts on their behalf.

> 2. In discharging these duties the Security Council shall act in accordance with the Purposes and Principles of the United Nations. . .

Article 25 provides that: "The Members of the United Nations agree to accept and carry out the decisions of the Security Council in accordance with the present Charter."

These provisions—the very heart of the Charter's design for the maintenance of international peace—manifest the plenitude of the powers of the Security Council, which are elaborated by the provisions of Chapters VI, VII, and VIII of the Charter. They also demonstrate that the Security Council is subject to the rule of law; it shall act in accordance with the Purposes and Principles of the United Nations and its decisions must be adopted in accordance with the Charter. At the same time, as Article 103 imports, it may lawfully decide upon measures which may in the interests of the maintenance or restoration of international peace and security derogate from the rights of a State under international law. The first Purpose of the United Nations quoted above also so indicates, for the reference to the principles of justice and international law designedly relates only to adjustment or settlement by peaceful means, and not to the taking of effective collective measures for the prevention and removal of threats to and breaches of the peace. It was deliberately so provided to ensure that the vital duty of preventing and removing threats to and breaches of the peace would not be limited by existing law.

It does not follow from the facts that the decisions of the Security Council must be in accordance with the Charter, and that the International Court of Justice is the principal judicial organ of the United Nations, that the Court is empowered to ensure that the Council's decisions do accord with the Charter. To hold that it does so follow is a monumental non sequitur, which overlooks the truth that, in many legal systems, national and international, the subjection of the acts of an organ to law by no means entails subjection of the legality of its actions to judicial review. In many cases, the system relies not upon judicial review but on self-censorship by the organ concerned or by its members or on review by another political organ.

Judicial review could have been provided for at San Francisco, in full or lesser measure, directly or indirectly, but both directly and indirectly it was not in any measure contemplated or enacted. Not only was the Court not authorized to be the ultimate interpreter of the Charter, as the Court acknowledged in the case concerning Certain Expenses of the United Nations. Proposals which in restricted measure would have accorded the Court a degree of authority, by way of advisory proceedings, to pass upon the legality of proposed resolutions of the Security Council in the sphere of peaceful settlement—what came to be Chapter VI of the Charter—were not accepted. What was never proposed, considered, or, so far as the records reveal, even imagined, was that the International Court of Justice would be entrusted with, or would develop, a power of judicial review at large, or a power to supervene, modify, negate or confine the applicability of resolutions of the Security Council whether directly or in the guise of interpretation.

That this is understandable, indeed obvious, is the clearer in the light of the conjunction of political circumstances at the time that the Charter was conceived, drafted and adopted. The Charter was largely a concept and draft of the United States, and secondarily of the United Kingdom; the other most influential State concerned was the USSR, The United States was cautious about the endowments of the Court. Recalling the rejection by the Senate of the United States a decade earlier of adherence to the Statute of the Permanent Court of International Justice, the Department of State was concerned to assure that nothing in the Charter concerning the Court, and nothing in the Statute which was to be an integral part of the Charter, could prejudice the giving of advice and consent by the Senate to the ratification of the Charter. Thus the Report of the Senate Committee on Foreign Relations on the United Nations Charter of 16 July 1945 to the Senate recommending ratification of the Charter specified:

> The Charter does not permit the Security Council or the General Assembly to force states to bring cases to the Court, nor does it or the Statute permit the Court to interfere with the functions of the Security Council or the General Assembly... Your committee recommends that the Senate accept the International Court of Justice in the form and with the authority set forth in chapter XIV of the Charter and the annexed Statute of the Court.

The British Government which, together with the United States, was the principal proponent of the creation of the Permanent Court of International Justice and which had played a large and constructive part in respect of that Court, was hardly less cautious in its approach to the powers of the International Court of Justice, as is illustrated by a quotation from the proceedings of the San Francisco Conference set out below.

As for the Government of the Union of Soviet Socialist Republics—a Government which had been ideologically hostile to the Court since its creation (as a reading of the *Eastern Carelia* case so vividly illustrates)—can it be thought that Stalin, whose preoccupation in the days of San Francisco was giving the veto power the widest possible reach, could have assented to the establishment of a Court authorized to possess or develop the authority to review and Vary the application of resolutions adopted by the Security Council under Chapter VII of the Charter?

At San Francisco, Belgium proposed the following amendment:

> Any State, party to a dispute brought before the Security Council, shall have the right to ask the Permanent Court of International Justice whether a recommendation or a decision made by the Council or proposed in it infringes on its essential

rights. If the Court considers that such rights have been disregarded or are threatened, it is for the Council either to reconsider the question or to refer the dispute to the Assembly for decision.

The purpose of the amendment, the Belgian delegate explained, was to allow the State concerned to seek an advisory opinion from the Court if that State believed that a Security Council recommendation infringed upon its essential rights. It was not in any sense the purpose of the amendment to limit the legitimate powers of the Security Council.

The Belgian proposal gave rise to a mixed reaction, support from States such as Ecuador and Colombia, and opposition from Great Power Sponsors of the Conference. The delegate of the Soviet Union

considered that the Belgian Amendment would have the effect of weakening the authority of the Council to maintain international peace and security. If it were possible for a state to appeal from the Council to the International Court of Justice. . . the Council would find itself handicapped in carrying out its functions. In such circumstances, the Council might even be placed in a position of being a defendant before the Court.

The delegate of the United States explained the importance of the requirement that the action of the Security Council in dealing with a dispute involving a threat to the peace be taken "in accordance with the purposes and principles of the Organization." One of the purposes is to bring about peaceful settlement of disputes "with due regard for principles of justice and international law." He did not interpret the Proposals as preventing any State from appealing to the International Court of Justice at any time on any matter which might properly go before the Court. On the whole, he did not consider the acceptance of the Belgian Amendment advisable, particularly since he believed that "the Security Council was bound to act in accordance with the principles of justice and international law." (It should be noted that this statement of 17 May 1945 antedated revision of the draft of the Charter's Purposes and Principles in June to provide that "the principles of justice and international law" relate only to the adjustment or settlement of international disputes by peaceful means and not to measures of collective security.)

The delegate of France declared that, while he viewed with great sympathy the ideas in the Belgian Amendment, he was doubtful that "it would be effective in obtaining its desired end, especially since it involved a dispersal of responsibilities in the Organization." The delegate of the United Kingdom stated that the adoption of the Belgian Amendment "would be prejudicial to the success of the Organization." The amendment would result in the decision by the Court. . . of political questions in addition to legal questions. The performance of this function by the Court. . . would seriously impair the success of its role as a judicial body. Further, the procedures proposed by the amendment would cause delay, at a time when prompt action by the Security Council was most desirable. A powerful weapon would thus be placed in the hands of a state contemplating aggression, and the Council would not be able to play the part in maintaining peace which was intended for it. . . he considered it necessary that the Council possess the trust and confidence of all states; its majority would be composed of small states, and it would be obligated to act in a manner consistent with the purposes and principles of the Organization.

After a few other statements in this vein, the delegate of Belgium stated that, since it was now clearly understood that a recommendation under what was to become Chapter VI did not possess obligatory effect, he wished to withdraw his amendment. Subsequently, the Conference rejected a proposal by Belgium to refer disagreements between organs of the United Nations on interpretation of the Charter to the Court. The pertinent report concludes:

Under unitary forms of national government the final determination of such a question may be vested in the highest court or in some other national authority. However, the nature of the Organization and of its operation would not seem to be such as to invite the inclusion in the Charter of any provision of this nature. If two member states are at variance concerning the correct interpretation of the Charter, they are of course free to submit the dispute to the International Court of Justice as in the case of any other treaty. Similarly, it would also be open to the General Assembly or to the Security Council, in appropriate circumstances, to ask the International Court of Justice for an advisory opinion concerning the meaning of a provision of the Charter.

It may finally be recalled that, at San Francisco, it was resolved "to leave to the Council the entire decision, and also the entire responsibility for that decision, as to what constitutes a threat to peace, a breach of the peace, or an act of aggression."

The conclusions to which the *travaux préparatoires* and text of the Charter lead are that the Court was not and was not meant to be invested with a power of judicial review of the legality or effects of decisions of the Security Council. Only the Security Council can determine what is a threat to or breach of the peace or act of aggression under Article 39, and under Article 39 only it can "decide what measures shall be taken. . . to maintain or restore international peace and security." Two States at variance in the interpretation of the Charter may submit a dispute to the Court, but that facility does not empower the Court to set aside or second-guess the determinations of the Security Council under Article 39. Contentious cases may come before the Court that call for its passing upon questions of law raised by Council decisions and for interpreting pertinent Council resolutions. But that power cannot be equated with an authority to review and confute the decisions of the Security Council.

It may of course be maintained that the Charter is a living instrument; that the present-day interpreters of the Charter are not bound by the intentions of its drafters of 50 years ago; that the Court has interpreted the powers of the United Nations constructively in other respects, and could take a constructive view of its own powers in respect of judicial review or some variation of it. The difficulty with this approach is that for the Court to engraft upon the Charter régime a power to review, and revise the reach of, resolutions of the Security Council would not be evolutionary but revolutionary. It would be not a development but a departure, and a great and grave departure. It would not be a development even arguably derived from the terms or structure of the Charter and Statute. It would not be a development arising out of customary international law, which has no principle of or provision for judicial review. It would not be a development drawn from the general principles of law. Judicial review, in varying forms, is found in a number of democratic polities, most famously that of the United States, where it was developed by the Supreme Court itself. But it is by no means a universal or even general principle of government or law. It is hardly found outside the democratic world and is not uniformly found in it. Where it exists internationally, as in the European Union, it is expressly provided for by treaty in specific terms. The United Nations is far from being a government, or an international organization comparable in its integration to the European Union, and it is not democratic.

The conclusion that the Court cannot judicially review or revise the resolutions of the Security Council is buttressed by the fact that only States may be parties in cases before the Court. The Security Council cannot be a party. For the Court to adjudge the legality of the Council's decisions in a proceeding brought by one State against another would be for the Court to adjudicate the Council's rights without giving the Council a hearing, which would run counter to fundamental judicial principles. It would run counter as well to the jurisprudence of the Court. Any such judgment could not bind the Council, because, by the terms of Article 59 of the Statute, the decision of the Court has no binding force except between the parties and in respect of that particular case.

At the same time, a judgment of the Court which held resolutions of the Security Council adopted under Chapter VII of the Charter not to bind or to be "opposable" to a State, despite the terms of Article 25 of the

Charter, would seriously prejudice the effectiveness of the Council's resolutions and subvert the integrity of the Charter. Such a holding would be tantamount to a judgment that the resolutions of the Security Council were ultra vires, at any rate in relation to that State. That could set the stage for an extraordinary confrontation between the Court and the Security Council. It could give rise to the question, is a holding by the Court that the Council has acted ultra vires a holding which of itself is ultra vires?

For some 45 years, the world rightly criticized stalemate in the Security Council. With the end of the Cold War, the Security Council has taken great strides towards performing as it was empowered to perform. That in turn has given rise to the complaint by some Members of the United Nations that they lack influence over the Council's decision-making. However understandable that complaint may be, it cannot furnish the Court with the legal authority to supervene the resolutions of the Security Council. The argument that it does is a purely political argument; the complaints that give rise to it should be addressed to and by the United Nations in its consideration of the reform of the Security Council. It is not an argument that can be heard in a court of law.

NOTES & QUESTIONS

1. *Judicial Review of the Security Council.* Which judge has the better view? Does the ICJ have the power to review and cancel any resolution that violates the UN Charter? Judicial review of the General Assembly is one thing—judicial review of the Security Council quite the other. The UN Charter assigns primary authority to the Security Council to make binding decisions regarding international peace and security. If the ICJ were to review those decisions, it would effectively be placing itself above the Security Council—something not explicitly mentioned in the Charter. For another view, see Dapo Akande, *The International Court of Justice and the Security Council: Is There Room for Judicial Control of Decisions of the Political Organs of the United Nations?*, 46 Int'l & Comp. L.Q. 309, 332 (1997) ("As has been seen, the limitations on the powers of the Council stem from the Charter itself. Where the Court is asked to choose between the application of a provision of the Charter and a Security Council resolution or decision, the Court is bound to choose the 'higher law'—which in this case is the Charter.").

2. *The Judicial Function.* On the other hand, perhaps the power of judicial review is *implicit* in the court's status as the "principal judicial organ of the United Nations," in the words of article 1 of the ICJ Statute. Indeed, the U.S. Constitution does not explicitly refer to judicial review either, but the Supreme Court concluded that this power was implicit in the judicial function. When the UN Charter and the Statute of the International Court of Justice were negotiated and drafted, Belgium proposed a provision that would have explicitly given the ICJ the power of judicial review. The proposal

was rejected by the majority of states participating in the drafting process. Is this historical fact dispositive? Or did the states opt instead to preserve some ambiguity in the final text of the ICJ Statute? For a discussion, see V. Gowlland-Debbas, *Article 7*, in *The Statute of the International Court of Justice* 79, 98 (A. Zimmermann et al eds., 2006) ("the Court has always acted on a presumption of legality of the acts of UN Organs, and it is obvious that only fundamental irregularities would lead the Court to question the validity of an act of an international organization").

D. THE SECRETARY-GENERAL

In a sense, the Secretary-General is the executive branch of the United Nations. Unlike the President of the United States, however, the Secretary-General has few executive powers that he or she can wield independently. The Secretary-General oversees a staff called the "Secretariat" that manages the United Nations bureaucracy. But the Secretary-General has no power to create international law or issue executive orders that bind states.

That being said, the Secretary-General is the public face of the United Nations, and historically his statements carry significant legal and moral impact. During a diplomatic or military crisis, the Secretary-General often speaks publicly, urging one party (or both parties) to respect international law generally, applicable Security Council resolutions specifically, or the laws of war. This process of "naming and shaming" is a significant tool for the Secretary-General to induce compliance. Also, article 99 of the UN Charter allows the Secretary-General to "bring to the attention of the Security Council any matter which in his opinion may threaten the maintenance of international peace and security." The ultimate decision on what actions should be taken rests with the Security Council.

Occasionally, the Secretary General gets directly involved in the negotiated resolution of diplomatic disputes. For example, departing Secretary-General Boutros Boutros-Ghali summarized his role:

> There is a long history of the utilization by the United Nations of distinguished statesmen to facilitate the processes of peace. They can bring a personal prestige that, in addition to their experience, can encourage the parties to enter serious negotiations. There is a wide willingness to serve in this capacity, from which I shall continue to benefit as the need arises. Frequently it is the Secretary-General himself who undertakes the task. While the mediator's effectiveness is enhanced by strong and evident support from the Council, the General Assembly and the relevant Member States acting in their national capacity, the good offices of the Secretary-General may at times be employed most effectively when conducted

independently of the deliberative bodies. Close and continuous consultation between the Secretary-General and the Security Council is, however, essential to ensure full awareness of how the Council's influence can best be applied and to develop a common strategy for the peaceful settlement of specific disputes.

See Boutros Boutros-Ghali, *An Agenda for Peace: Preventive Diplomacy, Peacemaking and Peace-keeping*, Report of the Secretary-General pursuant to the statement adopted by the Summit Meeting of the Security Council on 31 January 1992. SC Doc. S/24111 (June 17, 1992).

For example, Secretary-General Javier Pérez de Cuéllar played a major role in the resolution of the Rainbow Warrior Affair. In 1985, French commandos boarded the Greenpeace vessel *Rainbow Warrior*, located in New Zealand, and destroyed the vessel, killing a Dutch photographer on the boat. The *Rainbow Warrior* was involved in anti-nuclear protests against the French government, which had recently conducted nuclear testing in French Polynesia. The destruction of the vessel and the killing of the photographer by the French commandos prompted a major diplomatic crisis between France and New Zealand—the latter viewing the operation as a major violation of its territorial sovereignty. Instead of relying on the ICJ, the two governments agreed to arbitral resolution by the Secretary-General. A major issue in the crisis was the fate of two French security agents involved in the operation who were arrested in New Zealand. France sought their return but New Zealand refused and insisted on their trial and imprisonment in New Zealand. The two agents pleaded guilty to manslaughter and other charges and received a 10-year prison sentence.

De Cuéllar found that France was responsible for the incursion and ordered France to apologize and pay $7 million in compensation. In return, New Zealand was required to turn over the two French agents, who would be imprisoned by France on "an isolated island outside of Europe for a period of three years." The implementation of the decision proved complicated. France removed one of the agents from the island for medical treatment in Paris. France then evacuated the second agent when she became pregnant and her father became ill with cancer. Neither agent was returned to the island to finish serving the original three-year sentence. The original decision from the Secretary-General included a provision stipulating that disputes arising from the implementation of the agreement could be settled by binding arbitration. Angered by France's failure to return the agents to the island, New Zealand triggered the arbitration provision. An arbitral panel ruled in New Zealand's favor but declined to assess a damage award. For more discussion of this case, see J. Scott Davidson, *The Rainbow Warrior Arbitration Concerning the Treatment of the French Agents Mafart and Prieur*, 40 Int'l & Comp. L.Q. 446 (1991).

It is not common for the Secretary-General to act as an official arbitrator in an international dispute. However, it *is* common for the Secretary-General to act as a behind-the-scenes negotiator, facilitating diplomatic conversations and resolutions in contentious situations. Indeed, it is possible to see the *Rainbow Warrior* affair in that light, as a form of quasi-adjudication bordering on facilitated negotiation. As one commentator noted, "Under art. 33(1) of the Charter, a state may opt to bring in any outside party to aid in peaceful settlement through a variety of measures, including binding authority. The Secretary-General assumed such a role in the North Borneo dispute in 1963, the Bahrain dispute in 1970, and the *Rainbow Warrior* dispute of 1986." Karl J. Irving, *The United Nations and Democratic Intervention: Is "Swords into Ballot Boxes" Enough?*, 25 Denv. J. Int'l L. & Pol'y 41, 66 (1996). Article 33 of the UN Charter states: "The parties to any dispute, the continuance of which is likely to endanger the maintenance of international peace and security, shall, first of all, seek a solution by negotiation, enquiry, mediation, conciliation, arbitration, judicial settlement, resort to regional agencies or arrangements, or other peaceful means of their own choice."

E. INTERNATIONAL ORGANIZATIONS AS LEGAL PERSONS

All states are legal persons under international law. Indeed, their legality personality embodies their ability to operate on the international stage, that is, to be subjects and objects of international law. But what of international organizations such as the United Nations? Is the UN a legal person under international law? The UN enjoys something akin to sovereignty, though it has no independent territory and no subjects to govern. On the other hand, the UN issues its own postage stamps, collects its own taxes, and its offices enjoy diplomatic protection. One might think of it as a "supra-sovereign"—an entity that enjoys some of the trappings of sovereignty because it is an entity created from the "pooled" sovereignty of its members.

Specifically, article 104 of the UN Charter states that the UN "shall enjoy in the territory of each of its Members such legal capacity as may be necessary for the exercise of its functions and the fulfilment of its purposes." Similarly, article 105 grants both the UN and its officials "such privileges and immunities as are necessary for the fulfilment of its purposes." On February 13, 1946, the UN General Assembly passed the Convention on the Privileges and Immunities of the United Nations, which outlines many of the specific rights enjoyed by the organization, including the inviolability of its premises, exemption from taxation and immigration regulations, and diplomatic immunity for its officers. But does "legal capacity" entail full personhood under international law? In a 1949 case, the ICJ answered that question in the affirmative:

In the opinion of the Court, the Organization was intended to exercise and enjoy, and is in fact exercising and enjoying, functions and rights which can only be explained on the basis of the possession of a large measure of international personality and the capacity to operate upon an international plane. It is at present the supreme type of international organization, and it could not carry out the intentions of its founders if it was devoid of international personality. It must be acknowledged that its Members, by entrusting certain functions to it, with the attendant duties and responsibilities, have clothed it with the competence required to enable those functions to be effectively discharged.

Accordingly, the Court has come to the conclusion that the Organization is an international person. That is not the same thing as saying that it is a State, which it certainly is not, or that its legal personality and rights and duties are the same as those of a State. Still less is it the same thing as saying that it is "a super-State," whatever that expression may mean. It does not even imply that all its rights and duties must be upon the international plane, any more than all the rights and duties of a State must be upon that plane. What it does mean is that it is a subject of international law and capable of possessing international rights and duties, and that it has capacity to maintain its rights by bringing international claims.

Reparation for Injuries Suffered in the Service of the United Nations, 1949 I.C.J. 174, 179 (Apr. 11, 1949).

What does it matter that the UN is a legal person? There are two possible consequences. The first is that UN can sign an international agreement, just like any state. The second is that the UN might be subject to the same responsibility for its actions as any state—at least in theory.

As an example of the first, consider the creation of the Special Tribunal for Lebanon (STL) in 2007. The tribunal was initially created by a bilateral agreement between the UN and Lebanon. The agreement was negotiated and signed by the Secretary-General on behalf of the UN, after receiving pre-authorization from the Security Council to negotiate the agreement. The agreement called for the creation of a so-called hybrid tribunal to investigate and prosecute crimes related to the 2005 assassination of former Prime Minister of Lebanon Rafic Hariri in a car bomb attack that killed 22 people. The tribunal was designed as a "hybrid" institution with a mixture of procedural and substantive elements from international law and domestic Lebanese law. Because of opposition from the Speaker of Parliament in Lebanon, the agreement was not submitted for domestic ratification. To resolve this problem, the

Security Council created the tribunal with a binding resolution pursuant to its Chapter VII authority. This is just one example; the UN has signed many agreements which generate binding treaty obligations under international law.

As for responsibility, one question is whether the UN is legally responsible for damage caused by its operations, including peacekeeping operations. These operations frequently involve military officers from one or more state operating under UN Command and often identified by their UN "blue helmets." Is the UN responsible for damage caused by these troops, including criminal violations? There have been reports of widespread sexual abuse by UN troops on some peacekeeping missions. Section 29 of the 1946 Convention referred to above calls for the UN to settle private claims arising from its operations, and in fulfillment of that directive, the UN has a standing claims commission to hear disputes and award compensation. See Daphna Shraga, *UN Peacekeeping Operations: Applicability of International Humanitarian Law and Responsibility for Operations-Related Damage*, 94 Am. J. Int'l L. 406, 409 (2000).

Can the UN be sued in a domestic court? The UN in most cases enjoys the same sovereign immunity as any state, making it difficult to hold it responsible in a domestic court. For example, Haiti suffered a horrendous cholera outbreak in Haiti in 2010 during a UN peacekeeping mission there. Critics claimed that the cholera outbreak was either caused by, or exacerbated by, the negligence of the peacekeepers. Victims of the outbreak and their families filed suit against the UN in a U.S. federal district court. The case was dismissed by the district court. In upholding the dismissal, the Second Circuit noted that the Convention on the Privileges and Immunities of the United Nations guarantees the UN "immunity from every form of legal process except insofar as in any particular case it has expressly waived its immunity." *Georges v. United Nations*, 834 F.3d 88, 90 (2d Cir. 2016). In the same vein, consider also the following Problem Case.

PROBLEM CASE

In July 1995, several thousand Bosnian Muslim civilians sought refuge in Srebrenica from Bosnian Serb forces that were advancing on the area. The United Nations declared Srebrenica a safe area under UN protection—a declaration that encouraged the civilians to seek protection there. Undeterred, the Bosnian Serb Army and allied paramilitary forces advanced on Srebrenica, which was guarded by a few hundred Dutch soldiers under UN command.

Faced with superior firepower from the Bosnian Serb Army, the UN soldiers essentially surrendered and allowed the city to fall to the Bosnian Serb Army, which subsequently committed a massacre of more than 8,000 unarmed civilians trapped there. The International Criminal Tribunal for Yugoslavia convicted General Radislav Krstić for aiding and abetting the genocide. The International Court of Justice also concluded that the massacre constituted genocide.

Critics blamed the United Nations for its role in the crime. Although it was the members of the Bosnian Serb army that committed the genocide, the UN declared the area a safe haven and then refused to defend it; civilians moved into the area in reliance on an implicit promise that the area would be defended by the peacekeepers—by force if necessary. That never happened.

Should the UN be subject to civil responsibility in a domestic court? If not, what other remedies are available for the families of the victims? An organization called Mothers of Srebrenica filed a lawsuit in the Netherlands, alleging that both the Dutch government and the United Nations were jointly responsible for their part in the disaster. A Dutch court concluded that the UN enjoyed immunity from suit:

> With regard to the question whether the immunity from prosecution of the UN is in proportion to the goal aimed for in this case the Court of Appeal postulates the following. Amongst the international organisations the UN has a special position, for under article 42 of the Charter the Security Council may take such actions by air, sea or land forces as may be necessary to maintain or restore international peace and security. No other international organisation has such far-reaching powers. In connection with these extensive powers, which may involve the UN and the troops made available to them in conflict situations more often than not entailing conflicting interests of several parties, there is a real risk that if the UN did not enjoy, or only partially enjoyed immunity from prosecution, the UN would be exposed to claims by parties to the conflict and summoned before national courts of law of the country in which the conflict takes place. In view of the sensitivity of the conflicts in which the UN may be involved this might include situations in which the UN is summoned for the sole reason of obstructing any action undertaken by the Security Council, or even preventing it altogether. . . The immunity from prosecution granted to the UN therefore is closely connected to the public interest pertaining to keeping peace and safety in the world. For this reason it is very important that the UN has the broadest immunity possible allowing for as little discussion as possible. In this light the Court of Appeal believes that only compelling reasons should be allowed to lead to the conclusion that the United Nations' immunity is not in proportion to the objective aimed for.

Mothers of Srebrenica v. Netherlands & United Nations (Neth. App. Ct. 2010), 49 I.L.M. 1021, 1026. Do you believe that responsibility for a case involving genocide is one such "compelling reason"? The court thought not, noting that the Mothers of Srebrenica "blame the UN for failing to have prevented genocide. The Court of Appeal is of the opinion that although this reproach directed at the UN is serious, it is not that pressing that immunity should be waived or that the UN's invocation of immunity is, straightaway, unacceptable." Do you agree?

Conclusion & Summary

The United Nations is the primary international organization and the focal point for international relations. Its various components are divided into legislative, executive, and judicial branches, though their relative authority is far different from their cousin branches in the U.S. government:

1. The Security Council has primary authority and responsibility for the maintenance of international peace and security. Its resolutions are binding on all members of the United Nations and prevail over conflicting legal obligations, such as obligations contained in treaties. However, at least some courts have concluded that Security

Council resolutions cannot trump jus cogens norms, such as human rights.

2. The General Assembly votes on recommendations but does not have the power to issue binding resolutions as the Security Council does. However, as noted in prior chapters, General Assembly resolutions may provide evidence of *opinio juris* and facilitate the formation of customary international law. The Assembly's Uniting for Peace Resolution suggested a framework for acting on matters of international peace and security in the wake of a Security Council deadlock, but a General Assembly resolution passed in this context would not have the same binding effect as a Security Council resolution.

3. The ICJ is the principal judicial organ of the UN and hears cases between parties that have consented to its jurisdiction. The ICJ does not have a general appellate jurisdiction that would allow it to automatically review decisions from other international tribunals. In some cases, it issues advisory opinions as requested by the General Assembly. Its power to engage in judicial review of resolutions from the General Assembly and the Security Council is highly contested, but in any event the court has generally shied away from asserting this power.

4. The Secretary-General's Secretariat is the executive organ of the UN, though the Secretary-General has few formal executive powers other than his or her administration of the organization. However, the Secretary-General can play a major role in the resolution of international disputes through mediation and arbitration. He or she often serves as the public face of the UN, urging members to comply with international law and even calling out states that have flouted its requirements.

5. The UN is a legal person under international law, giving it many of the rights and privileges of statehood without technically being a state. The UN can sign international agreements with other states. In terms of its legal responsibility for potential misdeeds, the organization cannot be sued in domestic courts because it enjoys a corollary to the sovereign immunity enjoyed by states.

CHAPTER 6

PRINCIPLES OF STATE RESPONSIBILITY

Introduction

As explored in previous chapters, states are legal persons under international law and are therefore the subject of both rights and responsibilities. Just as individuals in domestic law are responsible for their wrongdoing, either through civil or criminal liability, so too states are responsible for their wrongdoing under international law. So, the concept of state responsibility is rather uncontroversial; one might even describe it as *axiomatic*. A system of international law would hardly be effective as a legal order if states were not responsible for their own behavior.

The difficulty stems from deciding *which* actions are state actions and therefore subject to international legal responsibility, and why. These principles, which are often abstract but gain content through their application in concrete cases, flow from customary international law. There is no meta-treaty that outlines general principles of state responsibility. However, the International Law Commission codified many of these principles in its Draft Articles on State Responsibility. The document was highly influential among international lawyers and is widely viewed as an accurate statement of the principles that gain their validity from customary law. The Draft Articles start from first principles, such as article 1 which states that "[e]very internationally wrongful act of a State entails the international responsibility of that State." From there, the Draft Articles canvass a range of more specific doctrines, many of which will be explored in this chapter.

For example, states are responsive for actions carried out by the state or actions carried out by others that may be attributed to the state. As to the former, actions carried out by state organs are deemed to be state actions. So, for example, if the State Department or the Interior Department of a country commits an action—international law treats that action as an act performed by the state itself. Similarly, an action carried out by members of the country's Defense Department or military forces would be a state action because it is conducted by an organ of the state.

There are other situations—not just those dealing with the actions of a state organ—where an individual actor's action might be attributable to the state itself. These cases of attribution might involve a state's control over external individuals or groups, a state's acceptance or adoption of the action as its own, or more controversially, a state's harboring of the group on its territory. Each of these situations, which will be outlined in Section A below, may give rise to the state's responsibility for the actions because the law will vicariously "attribute" the actions to the state. Of particular importance is the relevant standard for exercising "control" over external forces, a doctrine that has generated competing standards or tests.

A state can also be connected to another state's wrongdoing by aiding or assisting that state—a complicity doctrine that will be explored in Section B. The basic foundation of state complicity is *derivative*; a state can only be responsible via complicity if there is a primary actor—usually another state—that has violated international law. Finally, Section C will consider the defenses that negate a state's wrongdoing, such as necessity, self-defense, and counter-measures. Although there are other customary principles of state responsibility articulated in the Draft Articles, this chapter focuses on the key doctrines most likely to be at issue in an international controversy or dispute.

A. ATTRIBUTION

The actions of an individual or a group of individuals may be attributed to a state and therefore make the state responsible for any violations of international law flowing from it. There are a variety of circumstances under which this "attribution" might occur. According to article 8 of the Draft Articles of State Responsibility, the "conduct of a person or group of persons shall be considered an act of a State under international law if the person or group of persons is in fact acting on the instructions of, or under the direction or control of, that State in carrying out the conduct." The key word in that provision is "control." What counts as control? Also, what type of control is required? For years, these questions have perplexed international lawyers, who continue to be divided over the appropriate definition of "control" for purposes of establishing attribution to a state.

There are two competing standards for the concept of control. The first is the "effective control" test, which was outlined and applied by the ICJ in the *Nicaragua* case. The second is a broader "overall control" test that was articulated by the International Criminal Tribunal for the Former Yugoslavia (ICTY) in the *Tadić* case. The effective control test is probably best labelled a "majority" view because it is well-entrenched in the practice of the ICJ and many other international tribunals. That being said, the effective control test is not without its critics and the academic literature includes trenchant criticisms of the test. The judges of the ICTY Appeals Chamber eventually formulated a competing test, the overall control test, which is best viewed as an insurgent competitor to the more established effective control test first articulated by the ICJ. The task for the student of international law is to determine whether the ICJ or the ICTY has best articulated the correct criterion for control in this context.

There is a third alternative avenue for establishing attribution—one that has nothing to do with the concept of control. The actions of an individual or group of individuals may be attributed to a state if a state later endorses those actions and adopts them as its own. In other words, even in the absence of control, the state may assume responsibility associated with some actions simply by adopting those actions as its own. Although this may sound odd, there are many situations where a state is unwilling to distance itself or unwilling to disavow the actions of the individuals involved. In those situations, the actions of the individuals are attributed to the state through the state's voluntary endorsement and acceptance of them.

Finally, a fourth test has recently emerged on the scheme: state responsibility for a state that harbors a terrorist organization and fails to take adequate steps to prevent that organization from using its territory as a base of operations from which to launch attacks against third states.

1. THE EFFECTIVE CONTROL TEST

The background of the *Nicaragua* case is important for understanding the genesis of the effective control test. The case takes place against the background of Cold War politics and the geo-political struggle between the United States and the Soviet Union as the world's two super-powers. In its foreign policy, the United States was particularly concerned with the growth of communist governments in foreign states that might tip the balance of geopolitical power toward the Soviet Union and against the United States. The communist government of Nicaragua was politically aligned with the Soviet Union. To counter this perceived threat, the United States supported anti-communist rebels in Nicaragua called the Contras, who were engaged in an insurgency and seeking to overthrow the communist government of Nicaragua.

Nicaragua filed suit against the United States before the ICJ. At issue in the case were two categories of actions. The first were actions that the United States engaged in directly in the region, including the mining of Nicaraguan ports. The second were actions performed by the Contras, who were supported financially, logistically, and militarily by the United States through various overt and covert channels. In the following excerpt, the ICJ considers whether the actions of the Contras may be attributed to the United States and whether the U.S. is responsible for any violations of international law perpetrated by the

Contras. As you read this case, pay particular attention to the factual basis for the court's conclusion.

Case Concerning Military and Paramilitary Activities in and Against Nicaragua (Nicaragua v. United States)

International Court of Justice
1986 I.C.J. 14

95.   The financing by the United States of the aid to the contras was initially undisclosed, but subsequently became the subject of specific legislative provisions and ultimately the stake in a conflict between the legislative and executive organs of the United States. Initial activities in 1981 seem to have been financed out of the funds available to the CIA for "covert" action; according to subsequent press reports quoted by Nicaragua, $19.5 million was allocated to these activities. Subsequently, again according to press sources, a further $19 million was approved in late 1981 for the purpose of the CIA plan for military and paramilitary operations authorized by National Security Decision Directive 17. . .

99.   The Court finds at all events that from 1981 until 30 September 1984 the United States Government was providing funds for military and paramilitary activities by the contras in Nicaragua, and thereafter for "humanitarian assistance." . . .

100.   Evidence of how the funds appropriated were spent, during the period up to autumn 1984, has been provided in the affidavit of the former FDN leader, Mr. Chamorro; in that affidavit he gives considerable detail as to the assistance given to the FDN. . . Mr. Chamorro states that in 1981 former National Guardsmen in exile were offered regular salaries from the CIA, and that from then on arms (FAL and AK-47 assault rifles and mortars), ammunition, equipment and food were supplied by the CIA. When he worked full time for the FDN, he himself received a salary, as did the other FDN directors. There was also a budget from CIA funds for communications, assistance to Nicaraguan refugees or family members of FDN combatants, and a military and logistics budget; however, the latter was not large since all arms, munitions and military equipment, including uniforms, boots and radio equipment, were acquired and delivered by the CIA.

101.   According to Mr. Chamorro, training was at the outset provided by Argentine military officers, paid by the CIA, gradually replaced by CIA personnel. The training given was in "guerrilla warfare, sabotage, demolitions, and in the use of a variety of weapons, including assault rifles, machine guns, mortars, grenade launchers, and explosives, such as Claymore mines. . . also. . . in field communications, and the CIA taught us how to use certain sophisticated codes that the Nicaraguan

Government forces would not be able to decipher." The CIA also supplied the FDN with intelligence, particularly as to Nicaraguan troop movements, derived from radio and telephonic interception, code-breaking, and surveillance by aircraft and satellites...

102. It appears to be recognized by Nicaragua that... operations on Nicaraguan territory were carried out by the contras alone, all United States trainers or advisers remaining on the other side of the frontier, or in international waters. It is however claimed by Nicaragua that the United States Government has devised the strategy and directed the tactics of the contra force, and provided direct combat support for its military operations.

103. In support of the claim that the United States devised the strategy and directed the tactics of the contras, counsel for Nicaragua referred to the successive stages of the United States legislative authorization for funding the contras, and observed that every offensive by the contras was preceded by a new infusion of funds from the United States. From this, it is argued, the conclusion follows that the timing of each of those offensives was determined by the United States. In the sense that an offensive could not be launched until the funds were available, that may well be so; but, in the Court's view, it does not follow that each provision of funds by the United States was made in order to set in motion a particular offensive, and that that offensive was planned by the United States.

104. The evidence in support of the assertion that the United States devised the strategy and directed the tactics of the contras appears to the Court to be as follows. There is considerable material in press reports of statements by FDN officials indicating participation of CIA advisers in planning and the discussion of strategy or tactics, confirmed by the affidavit of Mr. Chamorro. Mr. Chamorro attributes virtually a power of command to the CIA operatives: he refers to them as having "ordered" or "instructed" the FDN to take various action. The specific instances of influence of United States agents on strategy or tactics which he gives are as follows: the CIA, he says, was at the end of 1982 "urging" the FDN to launch an offensive designed to take and hold Nicaraguan territory. After the failure of that offensive, the CIA told the FDN to move its men back into Nicaragua and keep fighting. The CIA in 1983 gave a tactical directive not to destroy farms and crops, and in 1984 gave a directive to the opposite effect. In 1983, the CIA again indicated that they wanted the FDN to launch an offensive to seize and hold Nicaraguan territory. In this respect, attention should also be drawn to the statement of Mr. Chamorro that the CIA supplied the FDN with intelligence, particularly as to Nicaraguan troop movements, and small aircraft suitable for reconnaissance and a certain amount of supply-dropping. Emphasis has been placed, by Mr. Chamorro, by Commander Carrion, and by counsel

for Nicaragua, on the impact on contra tactics of the availability of intelligence assistance and, still more important, supply aircraft.

105. It has been contended by Nicaragua that in 1983 a "new strategy" for contra operations in and against Nicaragua was adopted at the highest level of the United States Government. From the evidence offered in support of this, it appears to the Court however that there was, around this time, a change in contra strategy, and a new policy by the United States administration of more overt support for the contras, culminating in the express legislative authorization in the Department of Defense Appropriations Act, 1984, section 775, and the Intelligence Authorization Act for Fiscal Year 1984, section 108. The new contra strategy was said to be to attack "economic targets like electrical plants and storage facilities" and fighting in the cities.

106. In the light of the evidence and material available to it, the Court is not satisfied that all the operations launched by the contra force, at every stage of the conflict, reflected strategy and tactics wholly devised by the United States. However, it is in the Court's view established that the support of the United States authorities for the activities of the contras took various forms over the years, such as logistic support, the supply of information on the location and movements of the Sandinista troops, the use of sophisticated methods of communication, the deployment of field broadcasting networks, radar coverage, etc. The Court finds it clear that a number of military and paramilitary operations by this force were decided and planned, if not actually by United States advisers, then at least in close collaboration with them, and on the basis of the intelligence and logistic support which the United States was able to offer, particularly the supply aircraft provided to the contras by the United States.

107. To sum up, despite the secrecy which surrounded it, at least initially, the financial support given by the Government of the United States to the military and paramilitary activities of the contras in Nicaragua is a fully established fact. The legislative and executive bodies of the respondent State have moreover, subsequent to the controversy which has been sparked off in the United States, openly admitted the nature, volume and frequency of this support. Indeed, they clearly take responsibility for it, this government aid having now become the major element of United States foreign policy in the region. As to the ways in which such financial support has been translated into practical assistance, the Court has been able to reach a general finding.

108. Despite the large quantity of documentary evidence and testimony which it has examined, the Court has not been able to satisfy itself that the respondent State "created" the contra force in Nicaragua. It seems certain that members of the former Somoza National Guard, together with civilian opponents to the Sandinista regime, withdrew from

Nicaragua soon after that regime was installed in Managua, and sought to continue their struggle against it, even if in a disorganized way and with limited and ineffectual resources, before the Respondent took advantage of the existence of these opponents and incorporated this fact into its policies vis-a-vis the regime of the Applicant. Nor does the evidence warrant a finding that the United States gave "direct and critical combat support," at least if that form of words is taken to mean that this support was tantamount to direct intervention by the United States combat forces, or that all contra operations reflected strategy and tactics wholly devised by the United States. On the other hand, the Court holds it established that the United States authorities largely financed, trained, equipped, armed and organized the FDN.

109. What the Court has to determine at this point is whether or not the relationship of the contras to the United States Government was so much one of dependence on the one side and control on the other that it would be right to equate the contras, for legal purposes, with an organ of the United States Government, or as acting on behalf of that Government. Here it is relevant to note that in May 1983 the assessment of the Intelligence Committee, was that the contras "constitute[d] an independent force" and that the "only element of control that could be exercised by the United States" was "cessation of aid." Paradoxically this assessment serves to underline, *a contrario*, the potential for control inherent in the degree of the contras' dependence on aid. Yet despite the heavy subsides and other support provided to them by the United States, there is no clear evidence of the United States having actually exercised such a degree of control in all fields as to justify treating the contras as acting on its behalf.

110. So far as the potential control constituted by the possibility of cessation of United States military aid is concerned, it may be noted that after 1 October 1984 such aid was no longer authorized, though the sharing of intelligence, and the provision of "humanitarian assistance" as defined in the above-cited legislation may continue. Yet, according to Nicaragua's own case, and according to press reports, contra activity has continued. In sum, the evidence available to the Court indicates that the various forms of assistance provided to the contras by the United States have been crucial to the pursuit of their activities, but is insufficient to demonstrate their complete dependence on United States aid. On the other hand, it indicates that in the initial years of United States assistance the contra force was so dependent. However, whether the United States Government at any stage devised the strategy and directed the tactics of the contras depends on the extent to which the United States made use of the potential for control inherent in that dependence. The Court already indicated that it has insufficient evidence to reach a finding on this point. It is *a fortiori* unable to determine that the contra

force may be equated for legal purposes with the forces of the United States. This conclusion, however, does not of course suffice to resolve the entire question of the responsibility incurred by the United States through its assistance to the contras.

111. In the view of the Court it is established that the contra force has, at least at one period, been so dependent on the United States that it could not conduct its crucial or most significant military and paramilitary activities without the multi-faceted support of the United States. This finding is fundamental in the present case. Nevertheless, adequate direct proof that all or the great majority of contra activities during that period received this support has not been, and indeed probably could not be, advanced in every respect. It will suffice the Court to stress that a degree of control by the United States Government, as described above, is inherent in the position in which the contra force finds itself in relation to that Government.

112. To show the existence of this control, the Applicant argued before the Court that the political leaders of the contra force had been selected, installed and paid by the United States; it also argued that the purpose herein was both to guarantee United States control over this force, and to excite sympathy for the Government's policy within Congress and among the public in the United States. According to the affidavit of Mr. Chamorro, who was directly concerned, when the FDN was formed "the name of the organization, the members of the political junta, and the members of the general staff were all chosen or approved by the CIA"; later the CIA asked that a particular person be made head of the political directorate of the FDN, and this was done. However, the question of the selection, installation and payment of the leaders of the contra force is merely one aspect among others of the degree of dependency of that force. This partial dependency on the United States authorities, the exact extent of which the Court cannot establish, may certainly be inferred inter alia from the fact that the leaders were selected by the United States. But it may also be inferred from other factors, some of which have been examined by the Court, such as the organization, training and equipping of the force, the planning of operations, the choosing of targets and the operational support provided.

113. The question of the degree of control of the contras by the United States Government is relevant to the claim of Nicaragua attributing responsibility to the United States for activities of the contras whereby the United States has, it is alleged, violated an obligation of international law not to kill, wound or kidnap citizens of Nicaragua. The activities in question are said to represent a tactic which includes "the spreading of terror and danger to non-combatants as an end in itself with no attempt to observe humanitarian standards and no reference to the concept of military necessity." In support of this, Nicaragua has

catalogued numerous incidents, attributed to "CIA-trained mercenaries" or "mercenary forces," of kidnapping, assassination, torture, rape, killing of prisoners, and killing of civilians not dictated by military necessity. . .

114. In this respect, the Court notes that according to Nicaragua, the contras are no more than bands of mercenaries which have been recruited, organized, paid and commanded by the Government of the United States. This would mean that they have no real autonomy in relation to that Government. Consequently, any offences which they have committed would be imputable to the Government of the United States, like those of any other forces placed under the latter's command. In the view of Nicaragua, "stricto sensu, the military and paramilitary attacks launched by the United States against Nicaragua do not constitute a case of civil strife. They are essentially the acts of the United States." If such a finding of the imputability of the acts of the contras to the United States were to be made, no question would arise of mere complicity in those acts, or of incitement of the contras to commit them.

115. The Court has taken the view that United States participation, even if preponderant or decisive, in the financing, organizing, training, supplying and equipping of the contras, the selection of its military or paramilitary targets, and the planning of the whole of its operation, is still insufficient in itself, on the basis of the evidence in the possession of the Court, for the purpose of attributing to the United States the acts committed by the contras in the course of their military or paramilitary operations in Nicaragua. All the forms of United States participation mentioned above, and even the general control by the respondent State over a force with a high degree of dependency on it, would not in themselves mean, without further evidence, that the United States directed or enforced the perpetration of the acts contrary to human rights and humanitarian law alleged by the applicant State. Such acts could well be committed by members of the contras without the control of the United States. For this conduct to give rise to legal responsibility of the United States, it would in principle have to be proved that that State had effective control of the military or paramilitary operations in the course of which the alleged violations were committed.

116. The Court does not consider that the assistance given by the United States to the contras warrants the conclusion that these forces are subject to the United States to such an extent that any acts they have committed are imputable to that State. It takes the view that the contras remain responsible for their acts, and that the United States is not responsible for the acts of the contras, but for its own conduct vis-a-vis Nicaragua, including conduct related to the acts of the contras. What the Court has to investigate is not the complaints relating to alleged violations of humanitarian law by the contras, regarded by Nicaragua as imputable to the United States, but rather unlawful acts for which the

United States may be responsible directly in connection with the activities of the contras. . .

NOTES & QUESTIONS

Evidence of Control. Since the ICJ rejected a finding of control in *Nicaragua*, it is unclear exactly what type of evidence would be sufficient to establish effective control. For a discussion of the effective control test, see Oona A. Hathaway, Emily Chertoff, Lara Domínguez, Zachary Manfredi, & Peter Tzeng, *Ensuring Responsibility: Common Article 1 and State Responsibility for Non-State Actors*, 95 Tex. L. Rev. 539, 552 (2017) ("Because the ICJ did not find effective control in either *Nicaragua* or *Bosnian Genocide*, it is unclear exactly what set of facts would satisfy the 'effective control' test. However, it is clear that it sets a high threshold."). Does the high threshold of the effective control test allow states to interfere in foreign states but remain shielded from international responsibility for the actions committed by their surrogates? Here is the argument from one leading commentator, Professor Antonio Cassese, who was a judge on the ICTY Appeals Chamber and one of the leading critics of the effective control test:

> [T]he "effective control" test, to the extent that it is also applied to organized armed groups, is inconsistent with a basic principle underpinning the whole body of rules and principles on state responsibility: states may not evade responsibility towards other states when they, instead of acting through their own officials, *use* groups of individuals to undertake actions that are intended to damage, or in the event do damage, other states; if states so behave, they must answer for the actions of those individuals, even if such individuals have gone beyond their mandate or agreed upon tasks—lest the worst abuses should go unchecked. This is the rationale behind the rule providing that whenever persons lawfully acting on behalf of a state exceed their authority or contravene state instructions, the state is nonetheless answerable for such actions.

See Antonio Cassese, *The Nicaragua and Tadić Tests Revisited in Light of the ICJ Judgment on Genocide in Bosnia*, 18 Eur. J. Int'l L. 649, 654 (2007).

2. THE OVERALL CONTROL TEST

Not content to simply follow and apply the ICJ's effective control test, the ICTY articulated a rival standard in 1999—the overall control test. The Appeals Chamber was focused on the issue of control in order to determine whether the armed conflict on the territory of the former Yugoslavia was an international or non-international armed conflict. If the Bosnian-Serb forces were under the control of the government of Serbia, then the conflict would effectively be internationalized—and the grave breaches regime of the Geneva Conventions would apply. On the other hand, if the Bosnian-Serb forces were not under the control of the government of Serbia, then the conflict was an internal conflict—a civil war—governed by a different set of legal provisions regarding the conduct of hostilities. In other words, before a war crimes tribunal is to adjudicate allegations of war crimes, it must first decide which rules apply to the conflict. That decision requires answering whether the war is an international war or an internal conflict. That decision turns on the question of control.

With that background in mind, read the Appeals Chamber and its criticism of the effective control test. Do you find the criticisms legitimate? Is the overall control test a better rubric for deciding these cases?

Prosecutor v. Tadić

International Criminal Tribunal for the Former Yugoslavia
Appeals Chamber Judgment
July 15, 1999

115. The "effective control" test enunciated by the International Court of Justice was regarded as correct and upheld by Trial Chamber II in the Judgement. The Appeals Chamber, with respect, does not hold the *Nicaragua* test to be persuasive. There are two grounds supporting this conclusion.

116. A first ground on which the *Nicaragua* test as such may be held to be unconvincing is based on the very logic of the entire system of international law on State responsibility.

117. The principles of international law concerning the attribution to States of acts performed by private individuals are not based on rigid and uniform criteria. These principles are reflected in Article 8 of the Draft on State Responsibility adopted on first reading by the United Nations International Law Commission and, even more clearly, in the text of the same provisions as provisionally adopted in 1998 by the ILC Drafting Committee. Under this Article, if it is proved that individuals who are not regarded as organs of a State by its legislation nevertheless do in fact act on behalf of that State, their acts are attributable to the State. The rationale behind this rule is to prevent States from escaping international responsibility by having private individuals carry out tasks that may not or should not be performed by State officials, or by claiming that individuals actually participating in governmental authority are not classified as State organs under national legislation and therefore do not engage State responsibility. In other words, States are not allowed on the one hand to act de facto through individuals and on the other to disassociate themselves from such conduct when these individuals breach international law. The requirement of international law for the attribution to States of acts performed by private individuals is that the State exercises control over the individuals. The degree of control may,

however, vary according to the factual circumstances of each case. The Appeals Chamber fails to see why in each and every circumstance international law should require a high threshold for the test of control. Rather, various situations may be distinguished.

118. One situation is the case of a private individual who is engaged by a State to perform some specific illegal acts in the territory of another State (for instance, kidnapping a State official, murdering a dignitary or a high-ranking State official, blowing up a power station or, especially in times of war, carrying out acts of sabotage). In such a case, it would be necessary to show that the State issued specific instructions concerning the commission of the breach in order to prove—if only by necessary implication—that the individual acted as a de facto State agent. Alternatively it would be necessary to show that the State has publicly given retroactive approval to the action of that individual. A generic authority over the individual would not be sufficient to engage the international responsibility of the State. A similar situation may come about when an unorganised group of individuals commits acts contrary to international law. For these acts to be attributed to the State it would seem necessary to prove not only that the State exercised some measure of authority over those individuals but also that it issued specific instructions to them concerning the performance of the acts at issue, or that it ex post facto publicly endorsed those acts.

119. To these situations another one may be added, which arises when a State entrusts a private individual (or group of individuals) with the specific task of performing lawful actions on its behalf, but then the individuals, in discharging that task, breach an international obligation of the State (for instance, a private detective is requested by State authorities to protect a senior foreign diplomat but he instead seriously mistreats him while performing that task). In this case, by analogy with the rules concerning State responsibility for acts of State officials acting ultra vires, it can be held that the State incurs responsibility on account of its specific request to the private individual or individuals to discharge a task on its behalf.

120. One should distinguish the situation of individuals acting on behalf of a State without specific instructions, from that of individuals making up an organised and hierarchically structured group, such as a military unit or, in case of war or civil strife, armed bands of irregulars or rebels. Plainly, an organised group differs from an individual in that the former normally has a structure, a chain of command and a set of rules as well as the outward symbols of authority. Normally a member of the group does not act on his own but conforms to the standards prevailing in the group and is subject to the authority of the head of the group. Consequently, for the attribution to a State of acts of these groups

it is sufficient to require that the group as a whole be under the overall control of the State.

121. This kind of State control over a military group and the fact that the State is held responsible for acts performed by a group independently of any State instructions, or even contrary to instructions, to some extent equates the group with State organs proper. Under the rules of State responsibility, as restated in Article 10 of the Draft on State Responsibility as provisionally adopted by the International Law Commission, a State is internationally accountable for ultra vires acts or transactions of its organs. In other words it incurs responsibility even for acts committed by its officials outside their remit or contrary to its behest. The rationale behind this provision is that a State must be held accountable for acts of its organs whether or not these organs complied with instructions, if any, from the higher authorities. Generally speaking, it can be maintained that the whole body of international law on State responsibility is based on a realistic concept of accountability, which disregards legal formalities and aims at ensuring that States entrusting some functions to individuals or groups of individuals must answer for their actions, even when they act contrary to their directives.

122. The same logic should apply to the situation under discussion. As noted above, the situation of an organised group is different from that of a single private individual performing a specific act on behalf of a State. In the case of an organised group, the group normally engages in a series of activities. If it is under the overall control of a State, it must perforce engage the responsibility of that State for its activities, whether or not each of them was specifically imposed, requested or directed by the State. To a large extent the wise words used by the United States-Mexico General Claims Commission in the Youmans case with regard to State responsibility for acts of State military officials should hold true for acts of organised groups over which a State exercises overall control.

123. What has just been said should not, of course, blur the necessary distinction between the various legal situations described. In the case envisaged by Article 10 of the Draft on State Responsibility (as well as in the situation envisaged in Article 7 of the same Draft), State responsibility objectively follows from the fact that the individuals who engage in certain internationally wrongful acts possess, under the relevant legislation, the status of State officials or of officials of a State's public entity. In the case under discussion here, that of organised groups, State responsibility is instead the objective corollary of the overall control exercised by the State over the group. Despite these legal differences, the fact nevertheless remains that international law renders any State responsible for acts in breach of international law performed (i) by individuals having the formal status of organs of a State (and this occurs even when these organs act ultra vires or contra legem), or (ii) by

individuals who make up organised groups subject to the State's control. International law does so regardless of whether or not the State has issued specific instructions to those individuals. Clearly, the rationale behind this legal regulation is that otherwise, States might easily shelter behind, or use as a pretext, their internal legal system or the lack of any specific instructions in order to disclaim international responsibility.

124. There is a second ground—of a similarly general nature as the one just expounded—on which the Nicaragua test as such may be held to be unpersuasive. This ground is determinative of the issue. The "effective control" test propounded by the International Court of Justice as an exclusive and all-embracing test is at variance with international judicial and State practice: such practice has envisaged State responsibility in circumstances where a lower degree of control than that demanded by the Nicaragua test was exercised. In short, as shall be seen, this practice has upheld the Nicaragua test with regard to individuals or unorganised groups of individuals acting on behalf of States. By contrast, it has applied a different test with regard to military or paramilitary groups.

125. In cases dealing with members of military or paramilitary groups, courts have clearly departed from the notion of "effective control" set out by the International Court of Justice (i.e., control that extends to the issuance of specific instructions concerning the various activities of the individuals in question). Thus, for instance, in the *Stephens* case, the Mexico-United States General Claims Commission attributed to Mexico acts committed during a civil war by a member of the Mexican "irregular auxiliary" of the army, which among other things lacked both uniforms and insignia. In this case the Commission did not enquire as to whether or not specific instructions had been issued concerning the killing of the United States national by that guard.

126. Similarly, in the Kenneth P. Yeager case, the Iran-United States Claims Tribunal ("Claims Tribunal") held that wrongful acts of the Iranian "revolutionary guards" or "revolutionary Komitehs" vis-à-vis American nationals carried out between 13 and 17 February 1979 were attributable to Iran (the Claims Tribunal referred in particular to the fact that two members of the "Guards" had forced the Americans to leave their house in order to depart from Iran, that the Americans had then been kept inside the Hilton Hotel for three days while the "Guards" manned the exits, and had subsequently been searched at the airport by other "Guards" who had taken their money). . . .

127. . . . Be that as it may, what is notable is that the Iran-United States Claims Tribunal did not enquire as to whether specific instructions had been issued to the "Guards" with regard to the forced expulsion of Americans. The Claims Tribunal took the same stance in other cases.

128. A similar approach was adopted by the European Court of Human Rights in *Loizidou v. Turkey* (although in this case the question revolved around the possible control of a sovereign State over a State entity, rather than control by a State over armed forces operating in the territory of another State). The Court had to determine whether Turkey was responsible for the continuous denial to the applicant of access to her property in northern Cyprus and the ensuing loss of control over the property. The respondent State, Turkey, denied that the Court had jurisdiction, on the grounds that the act complained of was not committed by one of its authorities but, rather, was attributable to the authorities of the Turkish Republic of Northern Cyprus ("TRNC"). The Court dismissed these arguments and found that Turkey was responsible. In reaching the conclusion that the restrictions on the right to property complained of by the applicant were attributable to Turkey, the Court did not find it necessary to ascertain whether the Turkish authorities had exercised "detailed" control over the specific "policies and actions" of the authorities of the "TRNC". The Court was satisfied by the showing that the local authorities were under the "effective overall control" of Turkey.

130. Precisely what measure of State control does international law require for organized military groups? Judging from international case law and State practice, it would seem that for such control to come about, it is not sufficient for the group to be financially or even militarily assisted by a State. This proposition is confirmed by the international practice concerning national liberation movements. Although some States provided movements such as the PLO, SWAPO or the ANC with a territorial base or with economic and military assistance (short of sending their own troops to aid them), other States, including those against which these movements were fighting, did not attribute international responsibility for the acts of the movements to the assisting States. *Nicaragua* also supports this proposition, since the United States, although it aided the contras financially, and otherwise, was not held responsible for their acts (whereas on account of this financial and other assistance to the contras, the United States was held by the Court to be responsible for breaching the principle of non-intervention as well as "its obligation. . . not to use force against another State." This was clearly a case of responsibility for the acts of its own organs).

131. In order to attribute the acts of a military or paramilitary group to a State, it must be proved that the State wields overall control over the group, not only by equipping and financing the group, but also by coordinating or helping in the general planning of its military activity. Only then can the State be held internationally accountable for any misconduct of the group. However, it is not necessary that, in addition, the State should also issue, either to the head or to members of the group,

instructions for the commission of specific acts contrary to international law.

132. It should be added that courts have taken a different approach with regard to individuals or groups not organised into military structures. With regard to such individuals or groups, courts have not considered an overall or general level of control to be sufficient, but have instead insisted upon specific instructions or directives aimed at the commission of specific acts, or have required public approval of those acts following their commission.

133. The Appeals Chamber will mention, first of all, the United States Diplomatic and Consular Staff in Tehran case. There, the International Court of Justice rightly found that the Iranian students (who did not comprise an organised armed group) who had stormed the United States embassy and taken hostage 52 United States nationals, had not initially acted on behalf of Iran, for the Iranian authorities had not specifically instructed them to perform those acts. Nevertheless, Iran was held internationally responsible for failing to prevent the attack on the United States' diplomatic premises and subsequently to put an end to that attack. Later on, the Iranian authorities formally approved and endorsed the occupation of the Embassy and the detention of the United States nationals by the militants and even went so far as to order the students not to put an end to that occupation. At this stage, according to the Court, the militants became de facto agents of the Iranian State and their acts became internationally attributable to that State.

134. The same approach was adopted in 1986 by the International Court itself in *Nicaragua* with regard to the UCLAs (which the Court defined as "persons of the nationality of unidentified Latin American countries"). For specific internationally wrongful acts of these "persons" to be imputable to the United States, it was deemed necessary by the Court that these persons not only be paid by United States organs but also act "on the instructions" of those organs (in addition to their being supervised and receiving logistical support from them).

135. Similar views were propounded in 1987 by the Iran-United States Claims Tribunal in Short. Iran was not held internationally responsible for the allegedly wrongful expulsion of the claimant. The Claims Tribunal found that the Iranian "revolutionaries" (armed but not comprising an organised group) who ordered the claimant's departure from Iran were not State organs, nor did Ayatollah Khomeini's declarations amount to specific incitement to the "revolutionaries" to expel foreigners.

136. It should be added that State practice also seems to clearly support the approach under discussion.

137. In sum, the Appeals Chamber holds the view that international rules do not always require the same degree of control over armed groups or private individuals for the purpose of determining whether an individual not having the status of a State official under internal legislation can be regarded as a de facto organ of the State. The extent of the requisite State control varies. Where the question at issue is whether a single private individual or a group that is not militarily organised has acted as a de facto State organ when performing a specific act, it is necessary to ascertain whether specific instructions concerning the commission of that particular act had been issued by that State to the individual or group in question; alternatively, it must be established whether the unlawful act had been publicly endorsed or approved ex post facto by the State at issue. By contrast, control by a State over subordinate armed forces or militias or paramilitary units may be of an overall character (and must comprise more than the mere provision of financial assistance or military equipment or training). This requirement, however, does not go so far as to include the issuing of specific orders by the State, or its direction of each individual operation. Under international law it is by no means necessary that the controlling authorities should plan all the operations of the units dependent on them, choose their targets, or give specific instructions concerning the conduct of military operations and any alleged violations of international humanitarian law. The control required by international law may be deemed to exist when a State (or, in the context of an armed conflict, the Party to the conflict) has a role in organising, coordinating or planning the military actions of the military group, in addition to financing, training and equipping or providing operational support to that group. Acts performed by the group or members thereof may be regarded as acts of de facto State organs regardless of any specific instruction by the controlling State concerning the commission of each of those acts.

138. Of course, if, as in Nicaragua, the controlling State is not the territorial State where the armed clashes occur or where at any rate the armed units perform their acts, more extensive and compelling evidence is required to show that the State is genuinely in control of the units or groups not merely by financing and equipping them, but also by generally directing or helping plan their actions.

139. The same substantial evidence is required when, although the State in question is the territorial State where armed clashes occur, the general situation is one of turmoil, civil strife and weakened State authority.

140. Where the controlling State in question is an adjacent State with territorial ambitions on the State where the conflict is taking place, and the controlling State is attempting to achieve its territorial

enlargement through the armed forces which it controls, it may be easier to establish the threshold.

In 2007, the ICJ considered whether Serbia was responsible for committing genocide for massacres committed at Srebrenica by ethnic Serb forces in Bosnia, which was engulfed in a civil war at the time. The question for the ICJ was whether those ethnic Serb forces in Bosnia were under the effective control of the Serbian government. The case gave the ICJ the opportunity to revisit its holding in *Nicaragua* and perhaps adopt the competing overall control test articulated by the ICTY. In keeping with its settled jurisprudence, the ICJ applied the effective control test first articulated in *Nicaragua* and explained why it would not adopt the ICTY approach.

This case demonstrates that the effective control test can either establish a link or deny such a link when the control in question falls below the threshold of "effective." As you read the following case, ask yourself whether the effective control test is appropriate or whether it is overly restrictive. In particular, why did the court conclude that Serbia did not have the requisite level of control over the Bosnian Serb forces?

Case Concerning Application of the Convention on the Prevention & Punishment of the Crime of Genocide (Bosnia & Herzegovina v. Serbia & Montenegro)

International Court of Justice
2007 I.C.J. 47

The Question of Attribution of the Srebrenica Genocide to the Respondent on the Basis of Direction or Control

396. As noted above, the Court must now determine whether the massacres at Srebrenica were committed by persons who, though not having the status of organs of the Respondent, nevertheless acted on its instructions or under its direction or control, as the Applicant argues in the alternative; the Respondent denies that such was the case.

397. The Court must emphasize, at this stage in its reasoning, that the question just stated is not the same as those dealt with thus far. It is obvious that it is different from the question whether the persons who committed the acts of genocide had the status of organs of the Respondent under its internal law; nor however, and despite some appearance to the contrary, is it the same as the question whether those persons should be equated with State organs de facto, even though not enjoying that status under internal law. The answer to the latter question depends, as previously explained, on whether those persons were in a relationship of

such complete dependence on the State that they cannot be considered otherwise than as organs of the State, so that all their actions performed in such capacity would be attributable to the State for purposes of international responsibility. Having answered that question in the negative, the Court now addresses a completely separate issue: whether, in the specific circumstances surrounding the events at Srebrenica the perpetrators of genocide were acting on the Respondent's instructions, or under its direction or control. An affirmative answer to this question would in no way imply that the perpetrators should be characterized as organs of the FRY, or equated with such organs. It would merely mean that the FRY's international responsibility would be incurred owing to the conduct of those of its own organs which gave the instructions or exercised the control resulting in the commission of acts in breach of its international obligations. In other words, it is no longer a question of ascertaining whether the persons who directly committed the genocide were acting as organs of the FRY, or could be equated with those organs—this question having already been answered in the negative. What must be determined is whether FRY organs—incontestably having that status under the FRY's internal law—originated the genocide by issuing instructions to the perpetrators or exercising direction or control, and whether, as a result, the conduct of organs of the Respondent, having been the cause of the commission of acts in breach of its international obligations, constituted a violation of those obligations.

398. On this subject the applicable rule, which is one of customary law of international responsibility, is laid down in Article 8 of the ILC Articles on State Responsibility as follows: "Article 8 Conduct directed or controlled by a State. The conduct of a person or group of persons shall be considered an act of a State under international law if the person or group of persons is in fact acting on the instructions of, or under the direction or control of, that State in carrying out the conduct."

399. This provision must be understood in the light of the Court's jurisprudence on the subject, particularly that of the 1986 Judgment in the case concerning Military and Paramilitary Activities in and against Nicaragua *(Nicaragua v. United States of America)*. In that Judgment the Court, as noted above, after having rejected the argument that the contras were to be equated with organs of the United States because they were "completely dependent" on it, added that the responsibility of the Respondent could still arise if it were proved that it had itself "directed or enforced the perpetration of the acts contrary to human rights and humanitarian law alleged by the applicant State"; this led to the following significant conclusion: "For this conduct to give rise to legal responsibility of the United States, it would in principle have to be proved that that State had effective control of the military or paramilitary operations in the course of which the alleged violations were committed."

400. The test thus formulated differs in two respects from the test—described above—to determine whether a person or entity may be equated with a State organ even if not having that status under internal law. First, in this context it is not necessary to show that the persons who performed the acts alleged to have violated international law were in general in a relationship of "complete dependence" on the respondent State; it has to be proved that they acted in accordance with that State's instructions or under its "effective control." It must however be shown that this "effective control" was exercised, or that the State's instructions were given, in respect of each operation in which the alleged violations occurred, not generally in respect of the overall actions taken by the persons or groups of persons having committed the violations.

401. The Applicant has, it is true, contended that the crime of genocide has a particular nature, in that it may be composed of a considerable number of specific acts separate, to a greater or lesser extent, in time and space. According to the Applicant, this particular nature would justify, among other consequences, assessing the "effective control" of the State allegedly responsible, not in relation to each of these specific acts, but in relation to the whole body of operations carried out by the direct perpetrators of the genocide. The Court is however of the view that the particular characteristics of genocide do not justify the Court in departing from the criterion elaborated in the Judgment in *Nicaragua v. United States of America*. The rules for attributing alleged internationally wrongful conduct to a State do not vary with the nature of the wrongful act in question in the absence of a clearly expressed *lex specialis*. Genocide will be considered as attributable to a State if and to the extent that the physical acts constitutive of genocide that have been committed by organs or persons other than the State's own agents were carried out, wholly or in part, on the instructions or directions of the State, or under its effective control. This is the state of customary international law, as reflected in the ILC Articles on State Responsibility.

402. The Court notes however that the Applicant has further questioned the validity of applying, in the present case, the criterion adopted in the Military and Paramilitary Activities Judgment. It has drawn attention to the Judgment of the ICTY Appeals Chamber in the *Tadić* case. In that case the Chamber did not follow the jurisprudence of the Court in the Military and Paramilitary Activities case: it held that the appropriate criterion, applicable in its view both to the characterization of the armed conflict in Bosnia and Herzegovina as international, and to imputing the acts committed by Bosnian Serbs to the FRY under the law of State responsibility, was that of the "overall control" exercised over the Bosnian Serbs by the FRY; and further that that criterion was satisfied in the case. In other words, the Appeals Chamber took the view that acts committed by Bosnian Serbs could give

rise to international responsibility of the FRY on the basis of the overall control exercised by the FRY over the Republika Srpska and the VRS, without there being any need to prove that each operation during which acts were committed in breach of international law was carried out on the FRY's instructions, or under its effective control.

403. The Court has given careful consideration to the Appeals Chamber's reasoning in support of the foregoing conclusion, but finds itself unable to subscribe to the Chamber's view. First, the Court observes that the ICTY was not called upon in the *Tadić* case, nor is it in general called upon, to rule on questions of State responsibility, since its jurisdiction is criminal and extends over persons only. Thus, in that Judgment the Tribunal addressed an issue which was not indispensable for the exercise of its jurisdiction. As stated above, the Court attaches the utmost importance to the factual and legal findings made by the ICTY in ruling on the criminal liability of the accused before it and, in the present case, the Court takes fullest account of the ICTY's trial and appellate judgments dealing with the events underlying the dispute. The situation is not the same for positions adopted by the ICTY on issues of general international law which do not lie within the specific purview of its jurisdiction and, moreover, the resolution of which is not always necessary for deciding the criminal cases before it.

404. This is the case of the doctrine laid down in the *Tadić* Judgment. Insofar as the "overall control" test is employed to determine whether or not an armed conflict is international, which was the sole question which the Appeals Chamber was called upon to decide, it may well be that the test is applicable and suitable; the Court does not however think it appropriate to take a position on the point in the present case, as there is no need to resolve it for purposes of the present Judgment. On the other hand, the ICTY presented the "overall control" test as equally applicable under the law of State responsibility for the purpose of determining—as the Court is required to do in the present case—when a State is responsible for acts committed by paramilitary units, armed forces which are not among its official organs. In this context, the argument in favour of that test is unpersuasive.

405. It should first be observed that logic does not require the same test to be adopted in resolving the two issues, which are very different in nature: the degree and nature of a State's involvement in an armed conflict on another State's territory which is required for the conflict to be characterized as international, can very well, and without logical inconsistency, differ from the degree and nature of involvement required to give rise to that State's responsibility for a specific act committed in the course of the conflict.

406. It must next be noted that the "overall control" test has the major drawback of broadening the scope of State responsibility well

beyond the fundamental principle governing the law of international responsibility: a State is responsible only for its own conduct, that is to say the conduct of persons acting, on whatever basis, on its behalf. That is true of acts carried out by its official organs, and also by persons or entities which are not formally recognized as official organs under internal law but which must nevertheless be equated with State organs because they are in a relationship of complete dependence on the State. Apart from these cases, a State's responsibility can be incurred for acts committed by persons or groups of persons—neither State organs nor to be equated with such organs—only if, assuming those acts to be internationally wrongful, they are attributable to it under the rule of customary international law reflected in Article 8 cited above. This is so where an organ of the State gave the instructions or provided the direction pursuant to which the perpetrators of the wrongful act acted or where it exercised effective control over the action during which the wrong was committed. In this regard the "overall control" test is unsuitable, for it stretches too far, almost to breaking point, the connection which must exist between the conduct of a State's organs and its international responsibility.

407. Thus it is on the basis of its settled jurisprudence that the Court will determine whether the Respondent has incurred responsibility under the rule of customary international law set out in Article 8 of the ILC Articles on State Responsibility.

408. The Respondent has emphasized that in the final judgments of the Chambers of the ICTY relating to genocide in Srebrenica, none of its leaders have been found to have been implicated. The Applicant does not challenge that reading, but makes the point that that issue has not been before the ICTY for decision. The Court observes that the ICTY has indeed not up to the present been directly concerned in final judgments with the question whether those leaders might bear responsibility in that respect. The Court notes the fact that the report of the United Nations Secretary-General does not establish any direct involvement by President Milošević with the massacre. . .

410. The Court was referred to other evidence supporting or denying the Respondent's effective control over, participation in, involvement in, or influence over the events in and around Srebrenica in July 1995. The Respondent quotes two substantial reports prepared seven years after the events, both of which are in the public domain, and readily accessible. The first, Srebrenica—a "Safe" Area, published in 2002 by the Netherlands Institute for War Documentation was prepared over a lengthy period by an expert team. The Respondent has drawn attention to the fact that this report contains no suggestion that the FRY leadership was involved in planning the attack or inciting the killing of non-Serbs; nor any hard evidence of assistance by the Yugoslav army to

the armed forces of the Republika Srpska before the attack; nor any suggestion that the Belgrade Government had advance knowledge of the attack. The Respondent also quotes this passage from point 10 of the Epilogue to the Report relating to the "mass slaughter" and "the executions" following the fall of Srebrenica: "There is no evidence to suggest any political or military liaison with Belgrade, and in the case of this mass murder such a liaison is highly improbable." The Respondent further observes that the Applicant's only response to this submission is to point out that "the report, by its own admission, is not exhaustive," and that this Court has been referred to evidence not used by the authors.

411. The Court observes, in respect of the Respondent's submissions, that the authors of the Report do conclude that Belgrade was aware of the intended attack on Srebrenica. They record that the Dutch Military Intelligence Service and another Western intelligence service concluded that the July 1995 operations were coordinated with Belgrade. More significantly for present purposes, however, the authors state that "there is no evidence to suggest participation in the preparations for executions on the part of Yugoslav military personnel or the security agency (RDB). In fact there is some evidence to support the opposite view. . ." . . .

412. The second report is Balkan Battlegrounds, prepared by the United States Central Intelligence Agency, also published in 2002. The first volume under the heading "The Possibility of Yugoslav involvement" arrives at the following conclusion:

> No basis has been established to implicate Belgrade's military or security forces in the post-Srebrenica atrocities. While there are indications that the VJ or RDB [the Serbian State Security Department] may have contributed elements to the Srebrenica battle, there is no similar evidence that Belgrade-directed forces were involved in any of the subsequent massacres. Eyewitness accounts by survivors may be imperfect recollections of events, and details may have been overlooked. Narrations and other available evidence suggest that only Bosnian Serb troops were employed in the atrocities and executions that followed the military conquest of Srebrenica. . .

Conclusion as to Responsibility for Events at Srebrenica under
Article III, Paragraph (a), of the Genocide Convention

413. In the light of the information available to it, the Court finds, as indicated above, that it has not been established that the massacres at Srebrenica were committed by persons or entities ranking as organs of the Respondent. It finds also that it has not been established that those massacres were committed on the instructions or under the direction of organs of the respondent State, nor that the Respondent exercised

effective control over the operations in the course of which those massacres, which. . . constituted the crime of genocide, were perpetrated.

The Applicant has not proved that instructions were issued by the federal authorities in Belgrade, or by any other organ of the FRY, to commit the massacres, still less that any such instructions were given with the specific intent (dolus specialis) characterizing the crime of genocide, which would have had to be present in order for the Respondent to be held responsible on this basis. All indications are to the contrary: that the decision to kill the adult male population of the Muslim community in Srebrenica was taken by some members of the VRS Main Staff, but without instructions from or effective control by the FRY. . .

414. Finally, the Court observes that none of the situations, other than those referred to in Articles 4 and 8 of the ILC's Articles on State Responsibility, in which specific conduct may be attributed to a State, matches the circumstances of the present case in regard to the possibility of attributing the genocide at Srebrenica to the Respondent. The Court does not see itself required to decide at this stage whether the ILC's Articles dealing with attribution, apart from Articles 4 and 8, express present customary international law, it being clear that none of them apply in this case. The acts constituting genocide were not committed by persons or entities which, while not being organs of the FRY, were empowered by it to exercise elements of the governmental authority (Art. 5), nor by organs placed at the Respondent's disposal by another State (Art. 6), nor by persons in fact exercising elements of the governmental authority in the absence or default of the official authorities of the Respondent (Art. 9); finally, the Respondent has not acknowledged and adopted the conduct of the perpetrators of the acts of genocide as its own (Art. 11).

415. The Court concludes from the foregoing that the acts of those who committed genocide at Srebrenica cannot be attributed to the Respondent under the rules of international law of State responsibility: thus, the international responsibility of the Respondent is not engaged on this basis.

AFTERWORD

The ICJ concluded that there was insufficient factual evidence before the court that Serbia enjoyed effective control over the Bosnian Serb forces that committed the genocide in Srebrenica. But did the Court have access to all of the relevant evidence? The government of Serbia, along with other governments, was ordered by the Security Council to cooperate with the ICTY, which prosecuted Slobodan Milošević, the former president of Serbia. In connection with that case, the Serbian government was asked for access to confidential documents related to the war in Bosnia. The Serbian government complied with that request and provided the documents to the ICTY, but only on the condition that the documents not be provided to the ICJ, where the Serbian government was facing liability for the genocide in the case filed against it by Bosnia. The ICTY Prosecutor agreed to the condition.

In a secret opinion, an ICTY panel upheld that condition and concluded that the documents should be shielded from the ICJ. Although the ICTY concluded that the Prosecutor was wrong to promise that the documents would remain confidential, nonetheless Serbia had only provided the documents in reliance on that promise, which the ICTY concluded should be respected. Although the opinion from the ICTY panel was not publicly released, it was discussed and criticized in a memoir written by Florence Hartmann, a former spokesperson for the tribunal. See Florence Hartmann, *Paix et Châtiment, Les Guerres Secretes De La Politique et de La Justice Internationales* (2007). For disclosing the existence of the opinion, Hartmann was eventually prosecuted and convicted by the tribunal for the crime of contempt.

Consequently, the ICJ was forced to evaluate the issue of "effective control" without all of the relevant evidence. In a dissenting opinion, Vice-President Al-Khasawneh made the following observation:

> It should be observed that Article 49 of the Statute provides that "formal note should be taken of any refusal" and not of the Applicant's suggestion. In addition to this completely unbalanced statement that does not meet the requirement of Article 49, no conclusions whatsoever were drawn from noting the Respondent's refusal to divulge the contents of the unedited documents. It would normally be expected that the consequences of the note taken by the Court would be to shift the onus probandi or to allow a more liberal recourse to inference as the Court's past practice and considerations of common sense and fairness would all demand.

Do you believe that the ICJ should have altered (or lowered) Bosnia's evidentiary burden because Serbia refused to turn over the requested documents?

NOTES & QUESTIONS

1. *Overall Versus Effective Control.* What is the basic difference between overall and effective control? In *Tadić*, the Appeals Chamber suggested that "overall control" requires more than the provision of money, military equipment, or training. On the other hand, it is not necessary for the state to have issued specific orders or to have directed specific military operations. Indeed, that seems to be the very difference between overall control and effective control. The latter requires some level of operational or tactical direction, while the former does not. Overall control presumably can be established if the outside state controls the individuals in question but leaves the details regarding specific operations to their local discretion.

2. *Could Both Tests Be Correct?* One solution for reconciling the two tests would be to apply the overall control test in the case of outside support for rebel forces (as in *Tadić*) but then use the effective control test in all other circumstances. Indeed, the International Committee for the Red Cross (ICRC) has noted that there are particular reasons for employing the overall control test in civil war situations:

> In order to classify a situation under humanitarian law involving a close relationship, if not a relationship of subordination, between a non-State armed group and a third State, the overall control test is appropriate because the notion of overall control better reflects the real relationship between the armed group and the third State, including for the purpose of attribution. It implies that the armed group may be subordinate to the State even if there are no specific

instructions given for every act of belligerency. Additionally, recourse to the overall control test enables the assessment of the level of control over the *de facto* entity or non-State armed group as a whole and thus allows for the attribution of several actions to the third State. Relying on the effective control test, on the other hand, might require reclassifying the conflict with every operation, which would be unworkable.

See ICRC, *Commentary to the Geneva Conventions*, art. 3, para. 409 (2016). Is it possible that each test has its own place in international law, depending on the factual and legal circumstances? For example, the commentary to the ILC Draft Articles on State Responsibility simply states that the ICTY's "mandate is directed to issues of individual criminal responsibility, not State responsibility, and the question in that case concerned not responsibility but the applicable rules of international humanitarian law."

PROBLEM CASE

To get a sense of the practical difference between (and legal significance of) the effective and overall control tests, consider the destruction of Malaysia Airlines Flight 17 over eastern Ukraine in 2014. The Amsterdam to Kuala Lumpur flight was brought down by a missile near the border between Ukraine and Russia, killing all 298 individuals aboard. At the time, pro-Russian rebels in Eastern Ukraine were fighting an insurgency against the Ukrainian government. There were media reports that during the conflict, Russian troops were providing assistance and equipment to the rebel forces and in some cases may even have fought alongside the rebels against the Ukrainian government.

An international investigation suggested that the flight was taken down by a "BUK" anti-aircraft missile system. With the assumption that there was no way that the rebels would have had access to such sophisticated weaponry on their own, some intelligence analysts concluded that the system was probably provided to the rebel forces by the Russian military. (The other possibility is that the rebels captured the missile system from a Ukrainian missile base.) There is some uncertainty over who was operating the missile system when Flight 17 was destroyed, but assume for the sake of argument that the BUK was operated by rebel forces who were trained by Russian military advisors in how to use the system. Assuming that the downing of Flight 17 was an internationally wrongful act, what liability would Russia have for the incident?

Does the answer depend on the test used to evaluate the situation? Under the effective control test, the answer depends on whether the Russian government exercised a form of direct control over the rebel forces in eastern Ukraine that exceeded the level of control that the United States enjoyed over the Contras in Nicaragua. Under the overall control test, the actions of the rebels might be attributed to Russia even if the Russian military did not direct the rebels at the level of specific military operations. Do you think the actions of the rebels should be attributed to Russia? Is Russia responsible for the downing of Flight 17?

Several states, including the United States, drafted a Security Council resolution authorizing the creation of an international tribunal to prosecute individuals responsible for the incident, but the resolution was vetoed by Russia. See S.C. Draft Res. S/2015/562 (2015).

3. ACKNOWLEDGEMENT AND ADOPTION

A state might inherit responsibility for the actions of individuals even if the state did not exercise control over the individuals. According to article 11 of the Draft Articles on State Responsibility, "[c]onduct which is not attributable to a State under the preceding articles shall nevertheless be considered an act of that State under international law if and to the extent that the State acknowledges and adopts the conduct in question as its own." In other words, by voluntarily adopting the action of the individuals as its own, the state has assumed state responsibility for them. According to the commentaries to the Draft Articles, acknowledgement and adoptions should be distinguished from cases of mere endorsement or approval, which fall below the threshold for attributing state responsibility:

> In international controversies, States often take positions which amount to "approval" or "endorsement" of conduct in some general sense but do not involve any assumption of responsibility. The language of "adoption," on the other hand, carries with it the idea that the conduct is acknowledged by the State as, in effect, its own conduct. Indeed, provided the State's intention to accept responsibility for otherwise non-attributable conduct is clearly indicated, article 11 may cover cases where a State has accepted responsibility for conduct of which it did not approve, which it had sought to prevent and which it deeply regretted. However such acceptance may be phrased in the particular case, the term "acknowledges and adopts" in article 11 makes it clear that what is required is something more than a general acknowledgement of a factual situation, but rather that the State identifies the conduct in question and makes it its own.

See ILC, Commentaries to the Draft Articles on State Responsibility, art. 11, para. 6, at 53.

The adoption and acknowledgement principle was applied by the ICJ in *United States v. Iran*, which concerned the takeover of the American Embassy in Tehran by student revolutionaries.

Case Concerning United States Diplomatic & Consular Staff in Tehran (United States of America v. Iran)

International Court of Justice
1980 I.C.J. 3

71. In any event expressions of approval of the take-over of the Embassy, and indeed also of the Consulates at Tabriz and Shiraz, by militants came immediately from numerous Iranian authorities, including religious, judicial, executive, police and broadcasting authorities. Above all, the Ayatollah Khomeini himself made crystal clear the endorsement by the State both of the take-over of the Embassy

and Consulates and of the detention of the Embassy staff as hostages. At a reception in Qom on 5 November, the Ayatollah Khomeini left his audience in no doubt as to his approval of the action of the militants in occupying the Embassy, to which he said they had resorted "because they saw that the shah was allowed in America." Saying that he had been informed that the "centre occupied by our young men. . . has been a lair of espionage and plotting," he asked how the young people could be expected "simply to remain idle and witness all these things." Furthermore he expressly stigmatized as "rotten roots" those in Iran who were "hoping we would mediate and tell the young people to leave this place." The Ayatollah's refusal to order "the young people" to put an end to their occupation of the Embassy, or the militants in Tabriz and Shiraz to evacuate the United States Consulates there, must have appeared the more significant when, on 6 November, he instructed "the young people" who had occupied the Iraqi Consulate in Kermanshah that they should leave it as soon as possible. The true significance of this was only reinforced when, next day, he expressly forbade members of the Revolutionary Council and all responsible officials to meet the special representatives sent by President Carter to try and obtain the release of the hostages and evacuation of the Embassy.

72. At any rate, thus fortified in their action, the militants at the Embassy at once went one step farther. On 6 November they proclaimed that the Embassy, which they too referred to as "the U.S. centre of plots and espionage," would remain under their occupation, and that they were watching "most closely" the members of the diplomatic staff taken hostage whom they called "U.S. mercenaries and spies."

73. The seal of official government approval was finally set on this situation by a decree issued on 17 November 1979 by the Ayatollah Khomeini. His decree began with the assertion that the American Embassy was "a centre of espionage and conspiracy" and that "those people who hatched plots against our Islamic movement in that place do not enjoy international diplomatic respect." He went on expressly to declare that the premises of the Embassy and the hostages would remain as they were until the United States had handed over the former Shah for trial and returned his property to Iran. This statement of policy the Ayatollah qualified only to the extent of requesting the militants holding the hostages to "hand over the blacks and the women, if it is proven that they did not spy, to the Ministry of Foreign Affairs so that they may be immediately expelled from Iran." As to the rest of the hostages, he made the Iranian Government's intentions all too clear: "The noble Iranian nation will not give permission for the release of the rest of them. Therefore, the rest of them will be under arrest until the American Government acts according to the wish of the nation."

74. The policy thus announced by the Ayatollah Khomeini, of maintaining the occupation of the Embassy and the detention of its inmates as hostages for the purpose of exerting pressure on the United States Government was complied with by other Iranian authorities and endorsed by them repeatedly in statements made in various contexts. The result of that policy was fundamentally to transform the legal nature of the situation created by the occupation of the Embassy and the detention of its diplomatic and consular staff as hostages. The approval given to these facts by the Ayatollah Khomeini and other organs of the Iranian State, and the decision to perpetuate them, translated continuing occupation of the Embassy and detention of the hostages into acts of that State. The militants, authors of the invasion and jailers of the hostages, had now become agents of the Iranian State for whose acts the State itself was internationally responsible. On 6 May 1980, the Minister for Foreign Affairs, Mr. Ghotbzadeh, is reported to have said in a television interview that the occupation of the United States Embassy had been "done by our nation." Moreover, in the prevailing circumstances the situation of the hostages was aggravated by the fact that their detention by the militants did not even offer the normal guarantees which might have been afforded by police and security forces subject to the discipline and the control of official superiors.

4. HARBORING

Recently, some international lawyers have suggested that states should be responsible for the actions of the terrorist organizations that they harbor on their territory. One recent example of this phenomenon came shortly after the 9/11 attacks against the United States. The attacks were perpetrated by al-Qaeda, which had set up terrorist training camps in Afghanistan, with the tacit acknowledgement and understanding of the Taliban, the government of Afghanistan at the time. It was unlikely that the Taliban was "controlling" Al-Qaeda in any direct sense—certainly not in the sense required by the effective control test. Nor is it clear that the Taliban "adopted" or "acknowledged" the actions of Al-Qaeda as its own. However, it is possible that the Taliban harbored the terrorist organization by giving it free reign to operate training and operational facilities on its territory. Is that enough to attribute the actions to Afghanistan?

The U.S. government argued that Al-Qaeda's attack was attributable to Afghanistan and therefore the U.S. had a right to engage in self-defense against Afghanistan:

> The attacks on 11 September 2001 and the ongoing threat to the
> United States and its nationals posed by the Al-Qaeda
> organization have been made possible by the decision of the
> Taliban regime to allow the parts of Afghanistan that it controls

to be used by this organization as a base of operation. Despite every effort by the United States and the international community, the Taliban regime has refused to change its policy. From the territory of Afghanistan, the Al-Qaeda organization continues to train and support agents of terror who attack innocent people throughout the world and target United States nationals and interests in the United States and abroad.

Letter from the Permanent Representative of the United States of America to the United Nations Addressed to the President of the Security Council, 40 I.L.M. 1281 (Oct. 7, 2001).

The U.S. government position was met with mixed reactions. Some found the "harboring" theory inadequate or not having a sound basis in existing international legal doctrine. See, e.g., Steven R. Ratner, *Jus Ad Bellum and Jus in Bello After September 11*, 96 Am. J. Int'l L. 905, 908 (2002) ("Whether or not the U.S. position on self-defense is consonant with the Charter scheme on armed attacks or the customary law limits regarding necessity (my own view is that it is), it seems clear, on the issue of state responsibility, that none of the tests cited above—those of the ICJ, the ICTY, or the ILC—supports the harboring theory of the United States. That position, stated by President Bush, effectively imputes responsibility based on the toleration of such acts by the government."); Frédéric Mégret, *"War"? Legal Semantics and the Move to Violence*, 13 Eur. J. Int'l L. 361, 383–84 (2002) ("The mere tolerance of the presence of terrorist groups on a state's territory, however, is otherwise insufficient under the present state of international law to allow a state victim of a terrorist attack to impute that attack to the state which tolerates the presence of the terrorists. Indeed, the Afghan case illustrates in extreme form the dilemmas of contemporary collapsed statehood and efforts to suppress terrorism.")

On the other hand, the other member states of NATO joined the United States in pursuing a collective military action against Afghanistan—suggesting that NATO members agreed that Afghanistan was legally responsible for the actions of al-Qaeda. This suggests a certain degree of state support (and state practice) under customary international law for the notion that harboring a terrorist organization justifies attribution of its acts to the harboring state. Indeed, in the immediate aftermath of 9/11, the UN Security Council passed a resolution calling on "all States to work together urgently to bring to justice the perpetrators, organizers and sponsors of these terrorist attacks and stresses that those responsible for aiding, supporting or harbouring the perpetrators, organizers and sponsors of these acts will be held accountable." UN Security Council Res. 1368 (Sept. 12, 2001).

There is a third, intermediate position. One might argue that harboring is sufficient to establish state responsibility in general but that self-defense (in the sense of military measures) is only permissible when a state either directly launches an attack or is somehow more closely connected to it than the "harboring" doctrine suggests. See, e.g., Jordan J. Paust, *Use of Armed Force Against Terrorists in Afghanistan, Iraq, and Beyond,* 35 Cornell Int'l L.J. 533, 540 (2002) ("Harboring terrorists, providing formal or effective amnesty for terrorists in violation of the customary and treaty-based duty to initiate prosecution of or to extradite terrorists, otherwise tolerating, acquiescing, encouraging, or inciting terrorists within one's borders, or providing certain other forms of assistance to terrorists can implicate state responsibility and justify various political, diplomatic, economic, and juridic sanctions in response, including international claims for reparations and domestic lawsuits. Yet, unless the state is organizing, fomenting, directing, or otherwise directly participating in armed attacks by non-state terrorists, the use of military force against the state, as opposed to only the non-state terrorists, would be impermissible.").

B. COMPLICITY

States can be derivatively responsible for another state's violation of international law. The doctrine of complicity provides the "linking principle" to connect a state to the wrongdoing performed by another state. Similar to the criminal law notion of "aiding and abetting," a state can be complicit in another's wrongdoing when it provides aid or assistance to the wrongdoer. According to article 16 of the ILC Draft Articles, "A State which aids or assists another State in the commission of an internationally wrongful act by the latter is internationally responsible for doing so if: (a) that State does so with knowledge of the circumstances of the internationally wrongful act; and (b) the act would be internationally wrongful if committed by that State."

The doctrine of complicity for internationally wrongful acts should be carefully distinguished from the attribution doctrines outlined in the previous section. At its core, attribution involves drawing a link from the acts of individuals or groups to a particular state, thus making the state the "author" of the acts in question. If those acts transgress a particular prohibition of international law, then the state has violated international law. On the other hand, the complicity doctrine usually involves situations where a state is held responsible for the actions of *another state* that violate international law. In other words, complicity is a form of derivative responsibility. If the principal state has violated international law, other states may inherit legal responsibility if they aided or assisted the principal state.

The following case involves one of the darkest hours of post-9/11 counter-terrorism policy. Under the administration of President George W. Bush, the United States government undertook an official policy of torturing detainees suspected of involvement with al-Qaeda or other terrorist organizations. The detainees were not interrogated in the United States—they were captured oversees and then transferred to secret CIA prisons in third-party states such as Poland. In the following case, Abu Zubaydah argued before the ECHR that the United States violated the international prohibition against torture—and that Poland was complicit for having assisted the United States. As you read the case, pay attention to the legal conclusions that the court reached not just about Poland's complicity, but also the U.S. violations of international law as well.

Case of Husayn (Abu Zubaydah) v. Poland
European Court of Human Rights
Application No. 7511/13
July 24, 2014

425. Several sources of evidence before the Court have suggested the existence of a special bilateral agreement between Poland and the USA on the setting up and running of a secret prison in Poland.

426. The 2007 Marty Report, based on evidence from confidential sources, states that the CIA brokered an "operating agreement" with Poland to hold its High-Value Detainees in a secret detention facility and that Poland agreed to "provide the premises in which [that facility was] established, the highest degrees of physical security and secrecy, and steadfast guarantees of non-interference" (see paragraphs 248–249 above).

In the context of the authorisation of Poland's role in the CIA rendition operations, the 2007 Report mentioned a number of names of the Polish high-ranking officials, stating that they had known and authorised the country's role "in the CIA operation of secret detention facilities for High-Value Detainees on Polish territory" and that they "could therefore be held accountable for these activities."

Senator Marty confirmed those statements before the Court and added that the operation had been organised within the framework of NATO. It had been decided that the CIA would be in sole charge of the operation and, if requested, the member countries would provide cooperation. As regards the specific names of Polish officials that had been given in the 2007 Marty Report, he explained that they had been indicated "because the sources that [had] provided us with these names [had been] of such value, they [had been] so authoritative and there [had been] so much concurring evidence of the involvement of those persons."

427. Mr J.G.S., when heard by the Court, said that whilst in the course of the Marty Inquiry they had not seen the classified documents in question, they had been made aware of the existence of authorising

agreements, which granted extraordinary protections and permissions to the CIA in its execution of the rendition operations.

428. Senator Pinior, both in his affidavit and oral testimony before the Court, stated that he had been informed by an authoritative confidential source of a document—a draft prepared by the Polish intelligence—drawn up under the auspices of Mr Miller's Government for the purpose of regulating the operation of the CIA prison in Poland. According to him, that document, which was currently in the Polish prosecution authority's possession, contained precise regulations concerning the functioning of the prison and, among other things, a proposed protocol for action in the event of a prisoner's death. The word "detainees" was used in the text. The draft had not been signed on behalf of the US.

429. The 2007 EP Resolution "note[d] with concern" that the Polish authorities' official reply of 10 March 2006 to the Secretary General of the Council of Europe, "indicate[d] the existence of secret cooperation agreements initialled by the two countries' secret services' themselves, which exclude[d] the activities of foreign secret services from the jurisdiction of the Polish judicial bodies."

430. The Court does not find it necessary for its examination of the present case to establish whether such agreement or agreements existed and if so, in what format and what was specifically provided therein. It considers that it is inconceivable that the rendition aircraft crossed Polish airspace, landed in and departed from a Polish airport and that the CIA occupied the premises in Stare Kiejkuty without some kind of pre-existing arrangement enabling the CIA operation in Poland to be first prepared and then executed.

437. The Court further notes that Mr Fava also referred to the meeting held in the context of the Fava Inquiry with the former Polish head of the security service who, "although. . . with great diplomacy," had confirmed that the CIA officials often landed in Szymany and that the Polish intelligence and the CIA had had "frequent relations of cooperation. . . consisting in sharing certain practices and objectives."

438. Former President of Poland, Mr Kwaśniewski, in his press interview given on 30 April 2012, also referred to the "intelligence cooperation" with the CIA and stated that "the decision to cooperate with the CIA carried the risk that the Americans would use inadmissible methods."

439. Having regard to the procedure for High-Value Detainees' transfers under which, as established above, a detainee such as the applicant was blindfolded, wore black goggles and was shackled by his hands and feet for the duration of his transfer, the Court considers that those of the Polish authorities who received the CIA personnel on the

Szymany airport runway, put them on the vans and drove them to the black site could not be unaware that the persons brought there with them were the CIA prisoners. In particular, the Court finds it inconceivable they would not have seen or, as described by Mr J.G.S., "witnessed. . . the unloading of bound and shackled detainees from aircraft."

440. There are also other elements that the Court considers relevant for its assessment of Poland's knowledge of the nature and purposes of the CIA activities on its territory at the material time.

As recounted by Senator Pinior in his affidavit and subsequently confirmed in his oral testimony given to the Court, "in the period when the CIA prisoners were detained in Stare Kiejkuty" the authorities of the military base ordered from a Polish company a metal cage of the size fitting a grown man with the option of adding a portable chemical toilet. No explanations have been offered by the respondent Government as to what kind of purposes that cage was to serve.

Furthermore, there were, as pointed out by one of the experts, other aspects of the CIA activity in Poland that were extraordinary from the perspective of the normal operation of an airport like Szymany.

For instance, the landing of the Boeing 737 on September 22, 2003 at Szymany took place despite the fact that the airport did not have the necessary technical conditions for receiving such a large aircraft, in particular the facilities to refuel it, and the fact that the airport fire brigade was not adequately equipped for that purpose. In the view of Ms M.P., the airport manager at the relevant time, "there must have been some very pressing reasons" for allowing that landing.

On another occasion in the winter, notwithstanding the severe weather conditions and the fact that snow had not been cleared at the airport for six weeks, the airport management were not in a position to refuse the CIA aircraft's landing and had to clear the runway because "if the aircraft concerned did not land, 'heads would roll'."

For the airport civilian staff, the landing of the CIA aircraft was a "major event." Despite the fact that they were excluded from the handling of the aircraft and were taken to the airport terminal building during the CIA landings and departures, they perceived those events as "spies" coming or a "changeover of intelligence staff."

441. Lastly, the Court attaches importance to the fact that already between January 2002 and August 2003 ill-treatment and abuse to which captured terrorist suspects were subjected in US custody at different places, including Guantánamo Bay or Bagram base in Afghanistan was largely in the public domain through numerous statements or reports of international organisations. At the material time that topic was also present in the international and Polish media, which paid considerable attention to the situation of Al-Qaeda prisoners in US custody.

442. The Court has taken due note of the fact that knowledge of the CIA rendition and secret detention operations and the scale of abuse to which High-Value Detainees were subjected in CIA custody evolved over time... As already stated above, the Court has relied extensively on those sources of evidence in its retrospective reconstruction and establishment of the facts concerning the applicant's transfers to and from Poland and his secret detention and ill-treatment by the CIA in Poland. However, the Polish State's knowledge of and complicity in the HVD Programme must be established with reference to the elements that it knew or ought to have known at or closely around the relevant time...

443. In that regard, the Court has taken into account the various attendant circumstances referred to above. In the Court's view, those elements taken as a whole demonstrate that at that time the Polish authorities knew that the CIA used its airport in Szymany and the Stare Kiejkuty military base for the purposes of detaining secretly terrorist suspects captured within the "war on terror" operation by the US authorities. It is inconceivable that the rendition aircraft could have crossed Polish airspace, landed in and departed from a Polish airport, or that the CIA occupied the premises in Stare Kiejkuty and transported detainees there, without the Polish State being informed of and involved in the preparation and execution of the HVD Programme on its territory. It is also inconceivable that activities of that character and scale, possibly vital for the country's military and political interests, could have been undertaken on Polish territory without Poland's knowledge and without the necessary authorisation being given at the appropriate level of the State authorities.

The Court would again refer to the testimony given by the experts who, in the course of their inquiries, had the benefit of contact with various, including confidential, sources. They all stated, in unambiguous terms, that at the relevant time Poland had had, or should have had, knowledge of the CIA rendition operations. Poland had ensured the security of the area and had collaborated in concealing the rendition flights. The Polish officials' liaison units must have been aware of the preparation or execution of particular operations and their timing. They had known that the CIA interrogations had contributed intelligence to the United States' war on terror.

This did not mean, in the experts' view, that the Polish authorities had known the details of what went on inside the black site, since the interrogations had been the exclusive responsibility of the CIA, or that they had witnessed treatment to which High-Value Detainees had been subjected in Poland. The Court, being confronted with no evidence to the contrary, accepts the experts' above-mentioned assessment.

Notwithstanding the foregoing proviso as to the lack of direct knowledge of the treatment to which the applicant was subjected in

Poland, as noted above, already between January 2002 and August 2003 numerous public sources were consistently reporting ill-treatment and abuse to which captured terrorist suspects were subjected in US custody in different places. Moreover, in the 2003 PACE Resolution adopted in June 2003—of which Poland, as any other Contracting State was aware—the Parliamentary Assembly of the Council of Europe was "deeply concerned at the conditions of detention" of captured "unlawful combatants" held in the custody of the US authorities. All these sources reported practices resorted to or tolerated by the US authorities that were manifestly contrary to the principles of the Convention. Consequently, there were good reasons to believe that a person in US custody under the HVD Programme could be exposed to a serious risk of treatment contrary to those principles.

444. Taking into consideration all the material in its possession, the Court finds that there is abundant and coherent circumstantial evidence, which leads inevitably to the following conclusions:

(a) that Poland knew of the nature and purposes of the CIA's activities on its territory at the material time and that, by enabling the CIA to use its airspace and the airport, by its complicity in disguising the movements of rendition aircraft and by its provision of logistics and services, including the special security arrangements, the special procedure for landings, the transportation of the CIA teams with detainees on land, and the securing of the Stare Kiejkuty base for the CIA's secret detention, Poland cooperated in the preparation and execution of the CIA rendition, secret detention and interrogation operations on its territory;

(b) that, given that knowledge and the emerging widespread public information about ill-treatment and abuse of detained terrorist suspects in the custody of the US authorities, Poland ought to have known that, by enabling the CIA to detain such persons on its territory, it was exposing them to a serious risk of treatment contrary to the Convention.

445. Consequently, Poland was in a position where its responsibility for securing "to everyone within [its] jurisdiction the rights and freedoms defined. . . . in [the] Convention" set forth in Article 1 was engaged in respect of the applicant at the material time.

447. The applicant submitted that Poland was responsible under Article 1 of the Convention for the violation of his rights because it had knowingly, intentionally and actively collaborated with the CIA in the rendition programme and facilitated his secret detention in Poland and his transfer from Poland to other CIA secret detention facilities

elsewhere. While the full form and extent of Poland's involvement was not known, it was beyond any credible dispute that the Polish authorities had cooperated with the CIA and made possible his secret detention and torture on Polish soil. In the applicant's view, Poland had been aware that those transferred to, detained on and transferred from its territory under the HVD Programme would be subjected to practices manifestly inconsistent with the Convention. Since Poland had actively facilitated the applicant's detention and transfer, it was also responsible for his ill-treatment and unlawful, secret detention during the period following his transfer from Poland.

448. The Court notes that the applicant's complaints relate both to the events that occurred on Poland's territory and to the consequences of his transfer from Poland to other places of his undisclosed detention. In that regard, the Court would wish to reiterate the relevant applicable principles.

449. The Court reiterates that, in accordance with its settled case-law, the respondent State must be regarded as responsible under the Convention for acts performed by foreign officials on its territory with the acquiescence or connivance of its authorities.

450. According to the Court's settled case-law, removal of an applicant from the territory of a respondent State may engage the responsibility of that State under the Convention if this action has as a direct consequence the exposure of an individual to a foreseeable violation of his Convention rights in the country of his destination.

451. In that context, the Court has repeatedly held that the decision of a Contracting State to remove a person—and, *a fortiori*, the actual removal itself—may give rise to an issue under Article 3 where substantial grounds have been shown for believing that the person in question would, if removed, face a real risk of being subjected to treatment contrary to that provision in the destination country. Where it has been established that the sending State knew, or ought to have known at the relevant time that a person removed from its territory was subjected to "extraordinary rendition," that is, "an extra-judicial transfer of persons from one jurisdiction or State to another, for the purposes of detention and interrogation outside the normal legal system, where there was a real risk of torture or cruel, inhuman or degrading treatment," the possibility of a breach of Article 3 is particularly strong and must be considered intrinsic in the transfer.

452. Furthermore, a Contracting State would be in violation of Article 5 of the Convention if it removed, or enabled the removal, of an applicant to a State where he or she was at real risk of a flagrant breach of that Article. Again, that risk is inherent where an applicant has been subjected to "extraordinary rendition," which entails detention...

"outside the normal legal system" and which, "by its deliberate circumvention of due process, is anathema to the rule of law and the values protected by the Convention."

453. Similar principles apply to cases where there are substantial grounds for believing that, if removed from a Contracting State, an applicant would be exposed to a real risk of being subjected to a flagrant denial of justice.

454. While the establishment of the sending State's responsibility inevitably involves an assessment of conditions in the destination country against the standards set out in the Convention, there is no question of adjudicating on or establishing the responsibility of the destination country, whether under general international law, under the Convention or otherwise. In so far as any liability under the Convention is or may be incurred, it is liability incurred by the sending Contracting State by reason of its having taken action which has as a direct consequence the exposure of an individual to proscribed ill-treatment or other violations of the Convention.

455. In determining whether substantial grounds have been shown for believing that a real risk of the Convention violations exists, the Court will assess the issue in the light of all the material placed before it or, if necessary, material it has obtained *proprio motu*. It must examine the foreseeable consequences of sending the applicant to the destination country, bearing in mind the general situation there and his personal circumstances. The existence of the alleged risk must be assessed primarily with reference to those facts which were known or ought to have been known to the Contracting State at the time of the removal. However, where the transfer has already taken place at the date of the Court's examination, the Court is not precluded from having regard to information which comes to light subsequently.

456. The Court will accordingly examine the complaints and the extent to which the events complained of are imputable to the Polish State in the light of the above principles of State responsibility under the Convention, as deriving from its case-law.

AFTERWORD

The United States eventually ended its torture program after a combination of factors: concerns that the program was ineffective, immoral, illegal, and undermining the international and diplomatic standing of the United States. On January 22, 2009, President Obama signed Executive Order 13491, which revoked the CIA's detention authority (and therefore its ability to operate prisons or conduct interrogations at them). The CIA retained the authority to hold individuals "on a short-term, transitory basis." Most importantly, the Executive Order required that all individuals in the custody of a federal officer, employee, or agent could not be subject to "any interrogation technique or approach, or any treatment related to interrogation, that is not authorized by and listed in Army Field Manual. . ." The order required that detainees "shall in all circumstances be treated humanely and shall not be subjected to violence to life and person (including murder of all kinds, mutilation, cruel treatment, and torture), nor to outrages upon personal dignity (including humiliating and degrading treatment). . ."

In 2012, the U.S. Senate Intelligence Committee finalized a report analyzing in exhausting detail the U.S. torture program. In 2014, the Committee released an unclassified "key findings" and "executive summary," because the full report remained classified. Among the report's findings were the following conclusions:

1.   The CIA's use of its enhanced interrogation techniques was not an effective means of acquiring intelligence or gaining cooperation from detainees.

2.   The CIA's justification for the use of its enhanced interrogation techniques rested on inaccurate claims of their effectiveness.

3.   The interrogations of CIA detainees were brutal and far worse than the CIA represented to policymakers and others.

4.   The conditions of confinement for CIA detainees were harsher than the CIA had represented to policymakers and others.

See Senate Select Committee on Intelligence, Committee Study of the CIA's Detention and Interrogation Program, Findings and Conclusions (2012). On June 2, 2017, the Trump Administration returned most of its copies of the full classified version of the report back to the Senate, which was unable to release the document because it was still classified.

NOTES & QUESTIONS

1.   *Knowledge Versus Purpose.* Like criminal law's doctrine of complicity, international law could apply complicity using either a knowledge or a purpose standard. Under a knowledge standard, the state would be responsible if it knows that its actions will assist or aid the principal state in its violation of international law. Under a purpose standard, the state would be responsible if it acts with the purpose to assist the principal state in its violation of international law. Which standard did the ECHR use in the Poland case? Did Poland merely *know* about the CIA torture or did it act with the *purpose* to facilitate the torture? As discussed in the introductory text before the case, article 16 of the ILC Draft Articles refers to the "knowledge" required for international complicity. However, the commentaries to the Draft articles include the following statement:

> The second requirement is that the aid or assistance must be given with a view to facilitating the commission of the wrongful act, and must actually do so. This limits the application of article 16 to those cases where the aid or assistance given is clearly linked to the subsequent wrongful conduct. A State is not responsible for aid or assistance under article 16 unless the relevant State organ intended, by the aid or assistance given, to facilitate the occurrence of the wrongful conduct and the internationally wrongful conduct is actually committed by the aided or assisted State. There is no requirement that the aid or assistance should have been essential to the performance of the internationally wrongful act; it is sufficient if it contributed significantly to that act.

ILC Draft Articles, commentary to art. 16, para 5, at 66. Does this paragraph sound like a knowledge standard or a purpose standard? For more discussion of complicity in international law, see Miles Jackson, *Complicity in International Law* (2015).

2.   *State Complicity for Non-State Actors.* Although the doctrine of complicity is usually used to establish responsibility between two *states* (one principal and the other acting as an accomplice), might it also connect a state with the actions of a non-state actor? The ICJ considered this possibility in the *Bosnia v. Serbia* genocide case reprinted above. Although the ICJ ultimately concluded that Serbia did not provide sufficient "aid or assistance" to the non-state actors who carried out the genocide in Srebrenica, this conclusion suggested that, in theory, the doctrine of complicity as expressed in article 16 of the Draft Articles on State Responsibility might be used to connect a state with the actions of a non-state actor. Of course, article 16 refers to assisting another *state* in its commission of an internationally wrongful act, so strictly speaking the ICJ, in applying the principle to non-state actors, may have been suggesting an extension of the principle by analogy.

C. DEFENSES

Even if a state engages in an action that usually constitutes a violation of international law, it is not necessarily the case that the state has committed an internationally wrongful act. States have at their disposal a number of affirmative defenses under international law. In domestic criminal law, an affirmative defense negates the wrongfulness of the individual's action. Much the same could be said of international defenses. Because of the affirmative defense recognized under international law, the wrongfulness of the state's action is negated. Consequently, under these circumstances, the state is not responsible for the putative violation of international law.

What follows is a brief and introductory exploration of the most common defenses: necessity, self-defense, and counter-measures. The necessity defense will be considered again in the Chapter on Humanitarian Intervention, while self-defense will be the exclusive focus of an entire chapter in this casebook's unit on the use of force under international law. But these introductory materials are necessary to understand the basic structure of state responsibility and its incorporation of affirmative defenses. As you read the following materials, it might be helpful to compare and contrast these international defenses with their correlates in domestic criminal law.

1. NECESSITY

Imagine, as a hypothetical, that a state faces a massive flood that requires the mass evacuation of a large percentage of its population. The safest solution to limit loss of life involves moving the population to higher ground. Unfortunately, that higher ground is located just across the border in a second state. Assuming that officials from the flooded state cross the border and set up a refugee camp on foreign territory, how should we evaluate this course of action? Has the flooded state violated international law?

Clearly the actions of the flooded state involve a border transgression, which normally would violate principles of sovereignty and territorial integrity deeply embedded in international law. The question, though, is whether the defense of necessity might provide an affirmative defense that precludes liability. In order for the doctrine to successfully exonerate the transgressing state, the specific requirements of the doctrine must be satisfied. In reading the following case, identify the requirements for the necessity defense. What constitutes a state of necessity? How urgent or immediate must the danger be? What of future dangers that might manifest themselves on the horizon? What kind of danger rises to the level required for the necessity defense?

The prelude to the following case involves the 1977 "Budapest" treaty signed by Czechoslovakia and Hungary. The treaty called for the joint construction of dams along the Danube river, which runs along the border between the two countries. The dams were designed to control flooding, produce hydroelectricity, and improve navigation along the river. But the Hungarian government pulled out of the project as Hungarians objected vociferously to the project on environmental grounds. The newly independent Slovak Republic continued with the project on its own, though it was forced to downscale the project substantially without Hungarian involvement.

At the ICJ, Hungary sought to justify its abrogation of its treaty responsibilities through the defense of necessity. In other words, its violation of the treaty was "necessary" to protect the state from peril. In the following judgment, the ICJ articulates and applies a standard for asserting this necessity defense. Can an ecological disaster constitute a state of necessity?

Case Concerning the Gabcikovo-Nagymaros Project (Hungary v. Slovakia)

International Court of Justice
1997 I.C.J. 7

40. Throughout the proceedings, Hungary contended that, although it did suspend or abandon certain works, on the contrary, it never suspended the application of the 1977 Treaty itself. To justify its conduct, it relied essentially on a "state of ecological necessity." . . .

44. In the course of the proceedings, Slovakia argued at length that the state of necessity upon which Hungary relied did not constitute a reason for the suspension of a treaty obligation recognized by the law of

treaties. At the same time, it cast doubt upon whether "ecological necessity" or "ecological risk" could, in relation to the law of State responsibility, constitute a circumstance precluding the wrongfulness of an act.

In any event, Slovakia denied that there had been any kind of "ecological state of necessity" in this case either in 1989 or subsequently. It invoked the authority of various scientific studies when it claimed that Hungary had given an exaggeratedly pessimistic description of the situation. Slovakia did not, of course, deny that ecological problems could have arisen. However, it asserted that they could to a large extent have been remedied. . .

49. The Court will now consider the question of whether there was, in 1989, a state of necessity which would have permitted Hungary, without incurring international responsibility, to suspend and abandon works that it was committed to perform in accordance with the 1977 Treaty and related instruments.

50. In the present case, the Parties are in agreement in considering that the existence of a state of necessity must be evaluated in the light of the criteria laid down by the International Law Commission in Article 33 of the Draft Articles on the International Responsibility of States that it adopted on first reading. That provision is worded as follows:

Article 33.   State of Necessity.

1.   A state of necessity may not be invoked by a State as a ground for precluding the wrongfulness of an act of that State not in conformity with an international obligation of the State unless:

(a) the act was the only means of safeguarding an essential interest of the State against a grave and imminent peril; and

(b) the act did not seriously impair an essential interest of the State towards which the obligation existed.

2.   In any case, a state of necessity may not be invoked by a State as a ground for precluding wrongfulness:

(a) if the international obligation with which the act of the State is not in conformity arises out of a peremptory norm of general international law; or

(b) if the international obligation with which the act of the State is not in conformity is laid down by a treaty which, explicitly or implicitly, excludes the possibility of invoking the state of necessity with respect to that obligation; or

(c) if the State in question has contributed to the occurrence of the state of necessity.

In its Commentary, the Commission defined the "state of necessity" as being "the situation of a State whose sole means of safeguarding an essential interest threatened by a grave and imminent peril is to adopt conduct not in conformity with what is required of it by an international obligation to another State." It concluded that "the notion of state of necessity is . . . deeply rooted in general legal thinking."

51. The Court considers, first of all, that the state of necessity is a ground recognized by customary international law for precluding the wrongfulness of an act not in conformity with an international obligation. It observes moreover that such ground for precluding wrongfulness can only be accepted on an exceptional basis. The International Law Commission was of the same opinion when it explained that it had opted for a negative form of words in Article 33 of its Draft: "in order to show, by this formal means also, that the case of invocation of a state of necessity as a justification must be considered as really constituting an exception—and one even more rarely admissible than is the case with the other circumstances precluding wrongfulness. . ."

Thus, according to the Commission, the state of necessity can only be invoked under certain strictly defined conditions which must be cumulatively satisfied; and the State concerned is not the sole judge of whether those conditions have been met.

52. In the present case, the following basic conditions set forth in Draft Article 33 are relevant: it must have been occasioned by an "essential interest" of the State which is the author of the act conflicting with one of its international obligations; that interest must have been threatened by a "grave and imminent peril"; the act being challenged must have been the "only means" of safeguarding that interest; that act must not have "seriously impair[ed] an essential interest" of the State towards which the obligation existed; and the State which is the author of that act must not have "contributed to the occurrence of the state of necessity." Those conditions reflect customary international law.

The Court will now endeavour to ascertain whether those conditions had been met at the time of the suspension and abandonment, by Hungary, of the works that it was to carry out in accordance with the 1977 Treaty.

53. The Court has no difficulty in acknowledging that the concerns expressed by Hungary for its natural environment in the region affected by the Gabcikovo-Nagymaros Project related to an "essential interest" of that State, within the meaning given to that expression in Article 33 of the Draft of the International Law Commission.

The Commission, in its Commentary, indicated that one should not, in that context, reduce an "essential interest" to a matter only of the "existence" of the State, and that the whole question was, ultimately, to be judged in the light of the particular case; at the same time, it included among the situations that could occasion a state of necessity, "a grave danger to . . . the ecological preservation of all or some of [the] territory [of a State]"; and specified, with reference to State practice, that "It is primarily in the last two decades that safeguarding the ecological balance has come to be considered an 'essential interest' of all States."

The Court recalls that it has recently had occasion to stress, in the following terms, the great significance that it attaches to respect for the environment, not only for States but also for the whole of mankind: "the environment is not an abstraction but represents the living space, the quality of life and the very health of human beings, including generations unborn. The existence of the general obligation of States to ensure that activities within their jurisdiction and control respect the environment of other States or of areas beyond national control is now part of the corpus of international law relating to the environment." *Legality of the Threat or Use of Nuclear Weapons,* ICJ Advisory Opinion, para. 29.

54. The verification of the existence, in 1989, of the "peril" invoked by Hungary, of its "grave and imminent" nature, as well as of the absence of any "means" to respond to it, other than the measures taken by Hungary to suspend and abandon the works, are all complex processes.

As the Court has already indicated, Hungary on several occasions expressed, in 1989, its "uncertainties" as to the ecological impact of putting in place the Gabcikovo-Nagymaros barrage system, which is why it asked insistently for new scientific studies to be carried out.

The Court considers, however, that, serious though these uncertainties might have been they could not, alone, establish the objective existence of a "peril" in the sense of a component element of a state of necessity. The word "peril" certainly evokes the idea of "risk"; that is precisely what distinguishes "peril" from material damage. But a state of necessity could not exist without a "peril" duly established at the relevant point in time; the mere apprehension of a possible "peril" could not suffice in that respect. It could moreover hardly be otherwise, when the "peril" constituting the state of necessity has at the same time to be "grave" and "imminent." "Imminence" is synonymous with "immediacy" or "proximity" and goes far beyond the concept of "possibility." As the International Law Commission emphasized in its commentary, the "extremely grave and imminent" peril must "have been a threat to the interest at the actual time." That does not exclude, in the view of the Court, that a "peril" appearing in the long term might be held to be "imminent" as soon as it is established, at the relevant point in time, that the realization of that peril, however far off it might be, is not thereby any less certain and inevitable.

The Hungarian argument on the state of necessity could not convince the Court unless it was at least proven that a real, "grave" and "imminent" "peril" existed in 1989 and that the measures taken by Hungary were the only possible response to it. . .

NOTES & QUESTIONS

1. *The Imminence Requirement.* In the *Hungary* case above, the ICJ clarified that the peril must be both grave and imminent. Is imminence a temporal notion or a requirement of certainty? In this regard, the court's judgment was somewhat ambiguous, since it simply noted that a possible peril in the future could not qualify as a state of necessity. Imagine a situation where a state anticipates that climate change, the melting of ice in Antarctica, and rising ocean levels will someday inundate the state's territory and make it unlivable. Should this qualify as a state of necessity? On the one hand, the "grave peril" will not materialize for several centuries. On the other hand, the result would not be a mere "possibility"—it would be a certainly that scientists can predict based on rising temperatures and the inevitability of rising ocean levels when ice melts. Could such a situation justify an imperiled state's recourse to actions that otherwise violate international law? For more on the imminence requirement, see Jens David Ohlin & Larry May, *Necessity in International Law* 47 (2016).

2. *Justifications Versus Excuses.* Is the necessity defense a justification or an excuse? The difference hinges on how the defense operates. Generally speaking, a justification negates the wrongfulness of the action, while an excuse simply negates the culpability of the actor. In domestic criminal law, the distinction between justifications and excuses is well analyzed. See George P. Fletcher, *Rethinking Criminal Law* 760–62 (2000). In most American jurisdictions, the criminal law defense of necessity is viewed as a justification, because it suggests that the actor acted rightly in order to select the lesser of two evils. However, not all domestic jurisdictions classify the necessity defense in this way. For example, German criminal law includes two necessity defenses—one a justification based on the lesser evils principle, and an excuse based on the idea that some threats are so severe that a person cannot be expected to live up to the demands of the law. Unfortunately, international lawyers have historically ignored the distinction between justification and excuses and have instead simply referred to all of the available doctrines as "defenses." Recent scholarship has suggested that international law should begin to recognize excuses that do not negate the wrongfulness of the action but make clear that the wrongful state is not culpable and should not face international liability for the action. See, e.g., George P. Fletcher & Jens David Ohlin, *Defending Humanity: When Force is Justified and Why* 125–128 (2008); Arthur Kutoroff, *Excuse in International Law*, 44 Cap. U. L. Rev. 189, 200 (2016) ("The neglect of excuses for states is part and parcel of more general conceptual confusion about defenses to violations of international law.").

2. SELF-DEFENSE

Self-defense is a justification in international law just as it is in domestic criminal law. In domestic law, if an individual is attacked by an aggressor, the victim is allowed to fight back with defensive force to repel the assault, assuming certain conditions are met: e.g., the threat was imminent and the response was necessary and proportionate to the peril. Similarly, in international law, states are entitled to respond with military force when faced with an actual or imminent armed attack. Self-defense is so important as a legal doctrine in international law that it will be analyzed in its own chapter.

In many ways, the particularities of the self-defense doctrine are *sui generis* because they form the essential building blocks of the international legal regime governing the recourse to force, or what is often referred to as the *jus ad bellum*. Generally speaking, all states must refrain from the use or threat of military force to settle international disputes. If any state violates that legal prohibition and launches an attack against another state, the victim state may respond in two situations. First, the military response can be authorized by the UN Security Council pursuant to its Chapter VII authority under the UN Charter to maintain international peace and security. Second, the victim state may take unilateral action to repel the assault using military measures. Just as in domestic law, international self-defense is only permissible if it is necessary and proportionate under the circumstances. Disproportionate self-defense is not allowed.

There are many specifics to the doctrine of self-defense, all of which will be explored later. The key point at this juncture is to understand the basic structure of self-defense and how it relates to state responsibility. States are under an international legal obligation not to exercise military force against other states. However, if they *do* resort to military force, their actions may be authorized by international law if they can successfully invoke the principle of self-defense. In that situation, the defense transforms what would otherwise be a wrongful action into a rightful one.

Conclusion & Summary

States are legal persons and therefore suffer legal responsibility for their violations of international law. State responsibility is governed by basic principles, many of which are analogous to principles that govern the responsibility of individuals in domestic law. However, there are also key differences in that regard, since the content of international legal obligations are far different from the legal obligations of domestic law. This chapter has outlined the most fundamental principles of state responsibility, including the following:

1. States are responsible for the actions of individuals if the individuals are functioning as a state organ, e.g., they are members of its government or armed forces. In these situations, individual action simply *is* state action.

2. States can also be held responsible for the actions of outside individuals or groups if these actions can be attributed to the state through a recognized principle of state responsibility. The classic attribution doctrines include control and acceptance/adoption.

3. There are two competing standards for evaluating control over outside forces—effective control and overall control. Effective control requires more direct, operational control over the group's actions through specific orders, while the overall control test is satisfied if the state has diffuse control over the group even if the state does not give it specific orders. The ICJ applies the effective control standard while the ICTY applied the overall control test.

4. States have sometimes argued that the actions of a non-state actor, such as a terrorist organization, can be attributed to a state that "harbors" the non-state actor on its territory. This principle of attribution remains controversial among some international lawyers.

5. A state that assists or aids a second state in violating international law is derivatively responsible for the second state's international wrongdoing. This doctrine of complicity requires at least that the assisting state act with knowledge of the second state's wrongdoing and with the knowledge that their actions will assist that endeavor. There is some debate over whether this complicity doctrine requires that complicit states act with the *purpose* to facilitate the primary state's wrongdoing.

6. States are not responsible for putative violations of international law if they can assert an affirmative defense. Examples of these defenses include necessity, self-defense, and occasionally counter-measures. In order for a state to successfully assert a state of necessity as an affirmative defense, the state must show that it imminently faced a grave peril that threatened an essential state interest. A future harm that is uncertain or hypothetical does not constitute a state of necessity. International lawyers are not accustomed to distinguishing between justifications and excuses, although this is slowly changing.

CHAPTER 7

ADJUDICATING INTERNATIONAL DISPUTES

Introduction

International disputes can be "resolved" in any number of ways, including diplomatic negotiation, legal adjudication, and recourse to military force. This chapter focuses on legal adjudication—the legal institutions that provide for judicial recourse when states suffer seemingly intractable disputes with each other. In some ways, though, military force and diplomatic negotiation are never completely irrelevant. There is always the possibility that states may decide to press their interests outside traditional legal venues through unilateral military force. Just as "bargaining" in domestic legal systems takes place in the "shadow of the trial," so too "bargaining" in international relations takes place against a larger strategic landscape that offers states a variety of avenues, both legal and extra-legal, to pursue their national interests.

Skeptics might ask why so few international disputes reach formal legal adjudication; the number of international legal judgments pales in comparison to the number of cases filed and resolved in any domestic system of law. But the picture looks far different if one selects a more appropriate baseline. The surprising result is not how few cases reach formal adjudication, but how many. Every day, thousands of international lawyers across the globe are making legal arguments on behalf of their clients, presenting claims in international tribunals, preparing legal submissions, and negotiating with opposing lawyers on matters of international dispute. Law structures each of these encounters. Even in situations where international adjudication is very unlikely, the mere possibility of adjudication helps structure a discursive enterprise of justifying behavior with legal norms. In many situations, the "adjudication" of international disputes will take place in the court of world opinion, where the community of states will brand some states as law-compliant and others as rogues, and will structure their relations with them accordingly. The result of these assessments will be increased cooperation and reputational benefits for those states whose behavior complies with international law, and isolation and reputational sanctions for those states that eschew compliance with international norms. One might describe this entire process as a form of radically decentralized international adjudication—where "adjudication" is used in its metaphorical sense.

The present chapter focus on the literal sense of adjudication—the process of one state holding another state responsible for its actions before an international tribunal. Of course, international disputes are sometimes litigated in domestic courts, even though domestic courts are often ill-suited to the task, and there are sometimes doctrinal barriers (including sovereign immunity) that limit the ability of domestic courts to hold foreign states responsible for their behavior. However, the question of international law's application in domestic courts will be the exclusive focus of a later chapter; presently we focus on international mechanisms for adjudication. Section A focuses on the International Court of Justice (ICJ) and the complex mechanisms that can trigger the jurisdiction of that court. The jurisdiction of the ICJ is by no means universal, and most international disputes never end up before the court. Nonetheless, it remains a viable forum for adjudication of important international disputes in limited circumstances, and most states expend considerable effort to ensure that their legal interests and positions are adequately expressed before the court.

Section B focuses on two of the many ad hoc tribunals that exist under international law—specific, subject-matter-related tribunals, often constituted by a particular convention or treaty that regulates some activity under international law. Although there are many of these tribunals, two competing examples will be analyzed: an arbitral tribunal constituted under the UN Convention on the Law of the Sea (UNCLOS), and a case heard by the US-Iran Claims Tribunal. The two examples feature wildly divergent outcomes. In the case of the UNCLOS tribunal, its decision has failed to resolve the international dispute over competing claims of sovereignty over the South China Sea, in part because China refused to recognize the legitimacy of the proceedings. In contrast, the US-Iran Claims Tribunal has issued many decisions in the decades since its creation—decisions that have been respected and largely complied with by the parties involved. This is especially striking given the fraught and tense relationship between Iran and the United States, who are strategic and military enemies in many ways. What accounts for the failure of UNCLOS to settle the South China Sea matter and the success of the US-Iran Claims Tribunal? From these examples, can one infer a general theory of international adjudication?

A. THE INTERNATIONAL COURT OF JUSTICE

The International Court of Justice was created in 1945 as part of the larger United Nations System. Its operations are governed by the Statute of the International Court of Justice, which was adopted at the same time as the U.N. Charter. It is considered a successor court to the Permanent Court of Justice, which was created as the principal legal organ of the League of Nations, which was formed in the aftermath of World War I.

Although the two courts are distinct legal organs, the International Court of Justice is considered its legal successor and both courts are often referred to colloquially as the "World Court."

There are two major avenues that can bring an international dispute before the International Court of Justice, which is located in The Hague with 15 judges, and only hears disputes between states. The first avenue is an advisory opinion requested by another UN body or agency, pursuant to article 96 of the UN Charter. The second is a "contentious case," i.e., a dispute between two states that have agreed to the court's jurisdiction. In that sense, the bedrock principle of consent provides the foundation for the court's jurisdiction in contentious cases.

Consent can be manifested in one of several ways:

1. *Ad Hoc Jurisdiction.* Two or more states may agree to submit a *particular* international dispute to the ICJ for resolution. In that case, the ICJ would be functioning as a de facto arbitral panel with an ad hoc jurisdiction.

2. *Compulsory Jurisdiction.* States might agree to the court's plenary jurisdiction if they "declare that they recognize as compulsory ipso facto and without special agreement, in relation to any other State accepting the same obligation, the jurisdiction of the Court." Art. 36(2) of the ICJ Statute. This is sometimes described as "joining" the World Court, or agreeing to its "compulsory" jurisdiction. The word compulsory here carries a special meaning, because it does not entail that a state may be brought before the ICJ against its will. Rather, the concept suggests that a state can be subject to the court's jurisdiction without consenting to its jurisdiction *in that particular case*, because the state has agreed to the court's *overall* jurisdiction. Consenting to this overall jurisdiction also gives states the right to file a case against another state. In other words, in order to make offensive use of the court's compulsory jurisdiction (to file cases), the state must also accept that jurisdiction and allow other states to file cases against it. According to Article 36(2) of the ICJ Statute, a state has accepted the court's compulsory jurisdiction if it made a declaration of the same to the predecessor Permanent Court of Justice.

3. *Treaty-Based Jurisdiction.* States can agree to the court's jurisdiction by signing treaties that include a provision granting the court jurisdiction to hear disputes arising from the treaty. In some treaties, the provision granting the court jurisdiction is contained in an optional protocol, which states can sign or not, which is separate from the main

treaty. In other examples, though, the jurisdictional provision is integral to the treaty and part of its main text.

As you will see below, the court's jurisdiction is very much based on the principle of reciprocity. This is especially true for the court's compulsory jurisdiction described above in number 2. A state can only use the court's compulsory jurisdiction if it has consented to allow other states to do the same, thus placing themselves on an equal footing before the court. For example, if France accepts the court's compulsory jurisdiction but attaches a reservation to that commitment, that reservation does more than limit France's exposure to the court's jurisdiction—it also limits the exposure of any state that France might sue before the court. In other words, a state cannot exempt themselves from the court's jurisdiction in some way but then get the court to impose that same jurisdiction on another state. It is always a two-way street.

In the following opinion, Nicaragua filed a case against the United States, accusing it of violating international law through a program of covert military and paramilitary activities in the region. Days before the case was filed, the United States deposited a declaration with the United Nations asserting its withdrawal from the ICJ's compulsory jurisdiction in circumstances arising from Central America. What effect did this declaration have?

Nicaragua is a classic case of a complex jurisdictional dispute, demonstrating almost all of the jurisdiction principles described above. Ultimately, what was the basis for the court's acceptance of jurisdiction? Was it the court's compulsory jurisdiction? Or did the ICJ gain jurisdiction through a jurisdictional provision in a particular treaty between Nicaragua and the United States? What was the United States reaction to the court's decision on jurisdiction?

Case Concerning Military and Paramilitary Activities in and Against Nicaragua (Nicaragua v. United States)

International Court of Justice
1984 I.C.J. 392

Jurisdiction of the Court and Admissibility of the Application

11. The present case concerns a dispute between the Government of the Republic of Nicaragua and the Government of the United States of America occasioned, Nicaragua contends, by certain military and paramilitary activities conducted in Nicaragua and in the waters off its coasts, responsibility for which is attributed by Nicaragua to the United States. In the present phase the case concerns the jurisdiction of the Court to entertain and pronounce upon this dispute, and the

admissibility of the Application by which it was brought before the Court. . .

12. To found the jurisdiction of the Court in the present proceedings, Nicaragua in its Application relied on Article 36 of the Statute of the Court and the declarations, described below, made by the Parties accepting compulsory jurisdiction pursuant to that Article. In its Memorial, Nicaragua, relying on a reservation contained in its Application of the right to "supplement or to amend this Application," also contended that the Court has jurisdiction under Article XXIV, paragraph 2, of a Treaty of Friendship, Commerce and Navigation between the Parties signed at Managua on 21 January 1956.

13. Article 36, paragraph 2, of the Statute of the Court provides that:

> The States parties to the present Statute may at any time declare that they recognize as compulsory ipso facto and without special agreement, in relation to any other State accepting the same obligation, the jurisdiction of the Court in all legal disputes concerning:
>
> (a) the interpretation of a treaty;
>
> (b) any question of international law;
>
> (c) the existence of any fact which, if established, would constitute a breach of an international obligation;
>
> (d) the nature or extent of the reparation to be made for the breach of an international obligation.

The United States made a declaration, pursuant to this provision, on 14 August 1946, containing certain reservations, to be examined below, and expressed to "remain in force for a period of five years and thereafter until the expiration of six months after notice may be given to terminate this declaration." On 6 April 1984 the Government of the United States of America deposited with the Secretary-General of the United Nations a notification, signed by the United States Secretary of State. Mr. George Shultz, referring to the Declaration deposited on 26 August 1946, and stating that:

> the aforesaid declaration shall not apply to disputes with any Central American State or arising out of or related to events in Central America, any of which disputes shall be settled in such manner as the parties to them may agree.

> Notwithstanding the terms of the aforesaid declaration, this proviso shall take effect immediately and shall remain in force for two years, so as to foster the continuing regional dispute settlement process which seeks a negotiated solution to the

interrelated political, economic and security problems of Central America.

This notification will be referred to, for convenience, as the "1984 notification."

14. In order to be able to rely upon the United States Declaration of 1946 to found jurisdiction in the present case, Nicaragua has to show that it is a "State accepting the same obligation" within the meaning of Article 36, paragraph 2, of the Statute. For this purpose, Nicaragua relies on a Declaration made by it on 24 September 1929 pursuant to Article 36, paragraph 2, of the Statute of the Permanent Court of International Justice. . .

15. The circumstances of Nicaragua's Declaration of 1929 were as follows. The Members of the League of Nations (and the States mentioned in the Annex to the League of Nations Covenant) were entitled to sign the Protocol of Signature of the Statute of the Permanent Court of International Justice, which was drawn up at Geneva on 16 December 1920. That Protocol provided that it was subject to ratification; and that instruments of ratification were to be sent to the Secretary-General of the League of Nations. On 24 September 1929, Nicaragua, as a Member of the League, signed this Protocol and made a declaration under Article 36, paragraph 2, of the Statute of the Permanent Court which read:

> [Translation from the French] "On behalf of the Republic] of Nicaragua I recognize as compulsory unconditionally the jurisdiction of the Permanent Court of International Justice. Geneva, 24 September 1929. (Signed) T. F. MEDINA.

The files of the League of Nations however contain no record of an instrument of ratification ever having been received. No evidence has been adduced before the Court to show that such an instrument of ratification was ever despatched to Geneva. . .

17. On the basis of these facts, the United States contends, first, that Nicaragua never became a party to the Statute of the Permanent Court of International Justice, and that accordingly it could not and did not make an effective acceptance of the compulsory jurisdiction of the Permanent Court; the 1929 acceptance was therefore not "still in force" within the meaning of the English version of Article 36, paragraph 5, of the Statute of the present Court. . .

18. Nicaragua does not contend that its 1929 Declaration was in itself sufficient to establish a binding acceptance of the compulsory jurisdiction of the Permanent Court of International Justice, for which it would have been necessary that Nicaragua complete the ratification of the Protocol of Signature of the Statute of that Court. It rejects however the interpretation of Article 36, paragraph 5, of the Statute of the present

Court advanced by the United States: Nicaragua argues that the phrase "which are still in force" or "pour une duree qui n'est pas encore expiree" was designed to exclude from the operation of the Article only declarations that had already expired, and has no bearing whatever on a declaration, like Nicaragua's, that had not expired, but which, for some reason or another, had not been perfected. . .

25. So far as the characteristics of Nicaragua's declaration are concerned, the Court notes that, at the time when the question of the applicability of the new Statute arose, that is, on its coming into force, that declaration was certainly valid, for under the system of the Permanent Court of International Justice a declaration was valid on condition that it had been made by a State "either when signing or ratifying" the Protocol of Signature of the Statute "or at a later moment," whereas under the present Statute, declarations under Article 36, paragraph 2, can only be made by "States parties to the present Statute." Since Nicaragua had signed that Protocol, its declaration concerning the compulsory jurisdiction of the Permanent Court, which was not subject to ratification, was undoubtedly valid from the moment it was received by the Secretary-General of the League of Nations. The Statute of the Permanent Court did not lay down any set form or procedure to be followed for the making of such declarations, and in practice a number of different methods were used by States. Nevertheless this declaration, though valid, had not become binding under the Statute of the Permanent Court. It may be granted that the necessary steps had been taken at national level for ratification of the Protocol of Signature of the Statute. But Nicaragua has not been able to prove that it accomplished the indispensable step of sending its instrument of ratification to the Secretary-General of the League of Nations. It did announce that the instrument would be sent: but there is no evidence to show whether it was. Even after having been duly informed, by the Acting Legal Adviser of the League of Nations Secretariat, of the consequences that this might have upon its position vis-a-vis the jurisdiction of the Permanent Court, Nicaragua failed to take the one step that would have easily enabled it to be counted beyond question as one of the States that had recognized the compulsory jurisdiction of the Permanent Court of International Justice. Nicaragua has in effect admitted as much.

26. The Court therefore notes that Nicaragua, having failed to deposit its instrument of ratification of the Protocol of Signature of the Statute of the Permanent Court, was not a party to that treaty. Consequently the Declaration made by Nicaragua in 1929 had not acquired binding force prior to such effect as Article 36, paragraph 5, of the Statute of the International Court of Justice might produce.

27. However, while the declaration had not acquired binding force, it is not disputed that it could have done so, for example at the beginning

of 1945, if Nicaragua had ratified the Protocol of Signature of the Statute of the Permanent Court. The correspondence brought to the Court's attention by the Parties, between the Secretariat of the League of Nations and various Governments including the Government of Nicaragua, leaves no doubt as to the fact that, at any time between the making of Nicaragua's declaration and the day on which the new Court came into existence, if not later, ratification of the Protocol of Signature would have sufficed to transform the content of the 1929 Declaration into a binding commitment; no one would have asked Nicaragua to make a new declaration. It follows that such a declaration as that made by Nicaragua had a certain potential effect which could be maintained indefinitely. This durability of potential effect flowed from a certain characteristic of Nicaragua's declaration; being made "unconditionally," it was valid for an unlimited period. Had it provided, for example, that it would apply for only five years to disputes arising after its signature, its potential effect would admittedly have disappeared as from 24 September 1934. In sum, Nicaragua's 1929 Declaration was valid at the moment when Nicaragua became a party to the Statute of the new Court; it had retained its potential effect because Nicaragua, which could have limited the duration of that effect, had expressly refrained from doing so.

52. The acceptance of jurisdiction by the United States which is relied on by Nicaragua is, as noted above, that dated 14 August 1946. The United States contends however that effect must also be given to the "1984 notification"—the declaration deposited with the Secretary-General of the United Nations on 6 April 1984. It is conceded by Nicaragua that if this declaration is effective as a modification or termination of the Declaration of 14 August 1946, and valid as against Nicaragua at the date of its filing of the Application instituting the present proceedings (9 April 1984), then the Court is without jurisdiction to entertain those proceedings, at least under Article 36, paragraphs 2 and 5, of the Statute. It is however contended by Nicaragua that the 1984 notification is ineffective because international law provides no basis for unilateral modification of declarations made under Article 36 of the Statute of the Court, unless a right to do so has been expressly reserved.

53. The United States insists that the effect of the 1984 notification was a modification and not a termination of its 1946 Declaration. It argues that, notwithstanding the fact that its 1946 Declaration did not expressly reserve a right of modification (as do the declarations made under Article 36 by a number of other States), the 1984 notification effected a valid modification of the 1946 Declaration temporarily suspending the consent of the United States to the adjudication of the claims of Nicaragua. For the United States, declarations under Article 36 are sui generis, are not treaties, and are not governed by the law of treaties, and States have the sovereign right to qualify an acceptance of

the Court's compulsory jurisdiction, which is an inherent feature of the Optional-Clause system as reflected in, and developed by, State practice. It is suggested that the Court has recognized the existence of an inherent, extra-statutory, right to modify declarations in any manner not inconsistent with the Statute at any time until the date of filing of an Application. The United States also draws attention to the fact that its declaration dates from 1946, since when, it asserts, fundamental changes have occurred in State practice under the Optional Clause, and argues that to deny a right of modification to a State which had, in such an older declaration, not expressly reserved such a right would be inequitable and unjustified in the light of those changes in State practice.

60. In fact, the declarations, even though they are unilateral acts, establish a series of bilateral engagements with other States accepting the same obligation of compulsory jurisdiction, in which the conditions, reservations and time-limit clauses are taken into consideration. In the establishment of this network of engagements, which constitutes the Optional-Clause system, the principle of good faith plays an important role. . .

61. The most important question relating to the effect of the 1984 notification is whether the United States was free to disregard the clause of six months' notice which, freely and by its own choice, it had appended to its 1946 Declaration. In so doing the United States entered into an obligation which is binding upon it vis-a-vis other States parties to the Optional-Clause system. Although the United States retained the right to modify the contents of the 1946 Declaration or to terminate it, a power which is inherent in any unilateral act of a State, it has, nevertheless assumed an inescapable obligation towards other States accepting the Optional Clause, by stating formally and solemnly that any such change should take effect only after six months have elapsed as from the date of notice.

63. Moreover, since the United States purported to act on 6 April 1984 in such a way as to modify its 1946 Declaration with sufficiently immediate effect to bar an Application filed on 9 April 1984, it would be necessary, if reciprocity is to be relied on, for the Nicaraguan Declaration to be terminable with immediate effect. But the right of immediate termination of declarations with indefinite duration is far from established. It appears from the requirements of good faith that they should be treated, by analogy, according to the law of treaties, which requires a reasonable time for withdrawal from or termination of treaties that contain no provision regarding the duration of their validity. Since Nicaragua has in fact not manifested any intention to withdraw its own declaration, the question of what reasonable period of notice would legally be required does not need to be further examined: it need only be observed that from 6 to 9 April would not amount to a "reasonable time."

67. The question remains to be resolved whether the United States Declaration of 1946, though not suspended in its effects vis-a-vis Nicaragua by the 1984 notification, constitutes the necessary consent of the United States to the jurisdiction of the Court in the present case, taking into account the reservations which were attached to the declaration. Specifically, the United States has invoked proviso (c) to that declaration, which provides that the United States acceptance of the Court's compulsory jurisdiction shall not extend to

> disputes arising under a multilateral treaty, unless (1) all parties to the treaty affected by the decision are also parties to the case before the Court, or (2) the United States of America specially agrees to jurisdiction.

This reservation will be referred to for convenience as the "multilateral treaty reservation." Of the two remaining provisos to the declaration, it has not been suggested that proviso (a), referring to disputes the solution of which is entrusted to other tribunals, has any relevance to the present case. As for proviso (b), excluding jurisdiction over "disputes with regard to matters which are essentially within the domestic jurisdiction of the United States of America as determined by the United States of America," the United States has informed the Court that it has determined not to invoke this proviso, but "without prejudice to the rights of the United States under that proviso in relation to any subsequent pleadings, proceedings, or cases before this Court."

76. At any rate, this is a question concerning matters of substance relating to the merits of the case: obviously the question of what States may be "affected" by the decision on the merits is not in itself a jurisdictional problem. The present phase of examination of jurisdictional questions was opened by the Court itself by its Order of 10 May 1984, not by a formal preliminary objection submitted by the United States; but it is appropriate to consider the grounds put forward by the United States for alleged lack of jurisdiction in the light of the procedural provisions for such objections. That being so, and since the procedural technique formerly available of joinder of preliminary objections to the merits has been done away with since the 1972 revision of the Rules of Court, the Court has no choice but to avail itself of Article 79, paragraph 7, of the present Rules of Court, and declare that the objection based on the multilateral treaty reservation of the United States Declaration of Acceptance does not possess, in the circumstances of the case, an exclusively preliminary character, and that consequently it does not constitute an obstacle for the Court to entertain the proceedings instituted by Nicaragua under the Application of 9 April 1984.

77. It is in view of this finding on the United States multilateral treaty reservation that the Court has to turn to the other ground of jurisdiction relied on by Nicaragua, even though it is prima facie

narrower in scope than the jurisdiction deriving from the declarations of the two Parties under the Optional Clause. As noted in paragraphs 1 and 12 above, Nicaragua in its Application relies on the declarations of the Parties accepting the compulsory jurisdiction of the Court in order to found jurisdiction, but in its Memorial it invokes also a 1956 Treaty of Friendship, Commerce and Navigation between Nicaragua and the United States as a complementary foundation for the Court's jurisdiction. Since the multilateral treaty reservation obviously does not affect the jurisdiction of the Court under the 1956 Treaty, it is appropriate to ascertain the existence of such jurisdiction, limited as it is.

81. Article XXIV, paragraph 2, of the Treaty of Friendship, Commerce and Navigation between the United States of America and Nicaragua, signed at Managua on 21 January 1956, reads as follows:

> Any dispute between the Parties as to the interpretation or application of the present Treaty, not satisfactorily adjusted by diplomacy, shall be submitted to the International Court of Justice, unless the Parties agree to settlement by some other pacific means.

The treaty entered into force on 24 May 1958 on exchange of ratifications; it was registered with the Secretariat of the United Nations by the United States on 11 July 1960. The provisions of Article XXIV, paragraph 2, are in terms which are very common in bilateral treaties of amity or of establishment, and the intention of the parties in accepting such clauses is clearly to provide for such a right of unilateral recourse to the Court in the absence of agreement to employ some other pacific means of settlement. In the present case, the United States does not deny either that the Treaty is in force, or that Article XXIV is in general capable of conferring jurisdiction on the Court. It contends however that if the basis of jurisdiction is limited to the Treaty, since Nicaragua's Application presents no claims of any violations of it, there are no claims properly before the Court for adjudication. In order to establish the Court's jurisdiction over the present dispute under the Treaty, Nicaragua must establish a reasonable connection between the Treaty and the claims submitted to the Court; but according to the United States, Nicaragua cannot establish such a connection. . .

82. Nicaragua in its Memorial submits that the 1956 Treaty has been and was being violated by the military and paramilitary activities of the United States in and against Nicaragua, as described in the Application; specifically, it is submitted that these activities directly violate the following Articles:

> Article XIX: providing for freedom of commerce and navigation, and for vessels of either party to have liberty "to come with their cargoes to all ports, places and waters of such other party open

to foreign commerce and navigation," and to be accorded national treatment and most-favored nation treatment within those ports, places and waters.

Article XIV: forbidding the imposition of restrictions or prohibitions on the importation of any product of the other party, or on the exportation of any product to the territories of the other party.

Article XVII: forbidding any measure of a discriminatory nature that hinders or prevents the importer or exporter of products of either country from obtaining marine insurance on such products in companies of either party.

Article XX: providing for freedom of transit through the territories of each party.

Article I: providing that each party shall at all times accord equitable treatment to the persons, property, enterprises and other interests of nationals and companies of the other party.

83. Taking into account these Articles of the Treaty of 1956, particularly the provision in, inter alia, Article XIX, for the freedom of commerce and navigation, and the references in the Preamble to peace and friendship, there can be no doubt that, in the circumstances in which Nicaragua brought its Application to the Court, and on the basis of the facts there asserted, there is a dispute between the Parties, inter alia, as to the "interpretation or application" of the Treaty. . . Accordingly, the Court finds that, to the extent that the claims in Nicaragua's Application constitute a dispute as to the interpretation or the application of the Articles of the Treaty of 1956 described in paragraph 82 above, the Court has jurisdiction under that Treaty to entertain such claims.

———————

The ICJ's decision on jurisdiction and admissibility angered the United States, and triggered its gradual estrangement from the court. The U.S. was a member of the court's compulsory jurisdiction from the court's inception in 1946 until 1986, when it formally withdrew its declaration entirely. Although the U.S. continued to accept the court's jurisdiction pursuant to individual treaties, in some situations it withdrew from them as well. For example, in 2005 the U.S. withdrew its consent to ICJ jurisdiction pursuant to the Vienna Convention on Consular Relations, again after adverse rulings by the ICJ against the United States.

The following statement was released by the U.S. State Department after the ICJ issued its decision on jurisdiction in the *Nicaragua* case. Was it smart for the United States to withdraw from participation in the case? The ICJ subsequently heard the case on the merits without the participation of the United States, and held that the actions of the U.S. in Nicaragua violated international law. Should the U.S. have stayed involved in the case?

U.S. Withdrawal from the Proceedings Initiated by Nicaragua in the International Court of Justice

U.S. Department of State
January 18, 1985

The United States has consistently taken the position that the proceedings initiated by Nicaragua in the International Court of Justice are a misuse of the Court for political purposes and that the Court lacks jurisdiction and competence over such a case. The Court's decision of Nov. 26, 1984, finding that it has jurisdiction, is contrary to law and fact. With great reluctance, the United States has decided not to participate in further proceedings in this case.

U.S. Policy in Central America

United States policy in Central America has been to promote democracy, reform and freedom; to support economic development; to help provide a security shield against those—like Nicaragua, Cuba and the U.S.S.R.—who seek to spread tyranny by force, and to support dialogue and negotiation both within and among the countries of the region. In providing a security shield, we have acted in the exercise of the inherent right of collective self-defense, enshrined in the United Nations Charter and the Rio Treaty. We have done so in defense of the vital national security interests of the United States and in support of the peace and security of the hemisphere.

Nicaragua's efforts to portray the conflict in Central America as a bilateral issue between itself and the United States cannot hide the obvious fact that the scope of the problem is far broader. In the security dimension, it involves a wide range of issues: Nicaragua's huge buildup of Soviet arms and Cuban advisers, its cross-border attacks and promotion of insurgency within various nations of the region, and the activities of indigenous opposition groups within Nicaragua. It is also clear that any effort to stop the fighting in the region would be fruitless unless it were part of a comprehensive approach to political settlement, regional security, economic reform and development, and the spread of democracy and human rights.

Role of the International Court of Justice

The conflict in Central America, therefore, is not a narrow legal dispute; it is an inherently political problem that is not appropriate for judicial resolution. The conflict will be solved only by political and diplomatic means—not through a judicial tribunal. The International Court of Justice was never intended to resolve issues of collective security and self-defense and is patently unsuited for such a role. Unlike domestic courts, the World Court has jurisdiction only to the extent that nation-states have consented to it. When the United States accepted the Court's compulsory jurisdiction in 1946, it certainly never conceived of such a role for the Court in such controversies. Nicaragua's suit against the United States—which includes an absurd demand for hundreds of millions of dollars in reparations—is a blatant misuse of the Court for political and propaganda purposes.

As one of the foremost supporters of the International Court of Justice, the United States is one of only 44 of 159 member states of the United Nations that have accepted the Court's compulsory jurisdiction at all. Furthermore, the vast majority of these 44 states have attached to their acceptance reservations that substantially limit its scope. Along with the United Kingdom, the United States is one of only two permanent members of the U.N. Security Council that have accepted that jurisdiction. And of the 16 judges now claiming to sit in judgment on the United States in this case, 11 are from countries that do not accept the Court's compulsory jurisdiction.

Few if any other countries in the world would have appeared at all in a case such as this which they considered to be improperly brought. Nevertheless, out of its traditional respect for the rule of law, the United States has participated fully in the Court's proceedings thus far, to present its view that the Court does not have jurisdiction or competence in this case.

The Decision of November 26

On November 26, 1984, the Court decided—in spite of the overwhelming evidence before it—that it does have jurisdiction over Nicaragua's claims and that it will proceed to a full hearing on the merits of these claims.

This decision is erroneous as a matter of law and is based on a misreading and distortion of the evidence and precedent:

- The Court chose to ignore the irrefutable evidence that Nicaragua itself never accepted the Court's compulsory jurisdiction. Allowing Nicaragua to sue where it could not be sued was a violation of the Court's basic principle of reciprocity, which necessarily underlies our own consent to the Court's compulsory jurisdiction. On this pivotal issue in the Nov. 26 decision—decided by a vote of 11–5—dissenting judges called the Court's judgment "untenable" and "astonishing" and described the U.S. position as "beyond doubt." We agree.

- El Salvador sought to participate in the suit to argue that the Court was not the appropriate forum to address the

Central American conflict. El Salvador declared that it was under armed attack by Nicaragua and, in exercise of its inherent right of self-defense, had requested assistance from the United States. The Court rejected El Salvador's application summarily—without giving reasons and without even granting El Salvador a hearing, in violation of El Salvador's right and in disregard of the Court's own rules.

The Court's decision is a marked departure from its past, cautious approach to jurisdictional questions. The haste with which the Court proceeded to a judgment on these issues—noted in several of the separate and dissenting opinions—only adds to the impression that the Court is determined to find in favor of Nicaragua in this case.

For these reasons, we are forced to conclude that our continued participation in this case could not be justified.

In addition, much of the evidence that would establish Nicaragua's aggression against its neighbors is of a highly sensitive intelligence character. We will not risk U.S. national security by presenting such sensitive material in public or before a Court that includes two judges from Warsaw Pact nations. This problem only confirms the reality that such issues are not suited for the International Court of Justice.

Longer-Term Implications of the Court's Decision

The Court's decision raises a basic issue of sovereignty. The right of a state to defend itself or to participate in collective self-defense against aggression is an inherent sovereign right that cannot be compromised by an inappropriate proceeding before the World Court.

We are profoundly concerned also about the long-term implications for the Court itself. The decision of Nov. 26 represents an overreaching of the Court's limits, a departure from its tradition of judicial restraint and a risky venture into treacherous political waters. We have seen in the United Nations, in the last decade or more, how international organizations have become more and more politicized against the interests of the Western democracies. It would be a tragedy if these trends were to infect the International Court of Justice. We hope this will not happen, because a politicized Court would mean the end of the Court as a serious, respected institution. Such a result would do grievous harm to the goal of the rule of law.

These implications compel us to clarify our 1946 acceptance of the Court's compulsory jurisdiction. Important premises on which our initial acceptance was based now appear to be in doubt in this type of case. We are therefore taking steps to clarify our acceptance of the Court's compulsory jurisdiction in order to make explicit what we have understood from the beginning, namely that cases of this nature are not proper for adjudication by the Court.

We will continue to support the International Court of Justice where it acts within its competence—as, for example, where specific disputes are brought before it by special agreement of the parties. One such example is the recent case between the United States and Canada before a special five-member Chamber of the Court to delimit the maritime boundary in the Gulf of Maine area. Nonetheless, because of our commitment to the rule of law, we must declare our firm conviction that the course on which the Court may now be embarked could do enormous harm to it as an institution and to the cause of international law.

NOTES & QUESTIONS

1.   *The Role of Reciprocity.* Ultimately, the ICJ made a number of findings in the *Nicaragua* case. First, Nicaragua's declaration accepting the jurisdiction of the Permanent Court of Justice, though not formally binding, remained in place when the International Court of Justice was created, thus making Nicaragua a member of the court's jurisdiction. The U.S. attempt to withdraw from the court's jurisdiction at the last minute was not effective, and the court concluded that the validity of the U.S. "multilateral treaty reservation" was not a question of jurisdiction suitable for resolution at this phase of the litigation. The court concluded that it had jurisdiction under the 1956 treaty. Do you agree with these conclusions? In the end, what practical effect did the court's decision have, given that the U.S. subsequently withdrew from the case? Did the U.S. suffer a loss of international standing? For more discussion, see Thomas Franck, *The Power of Legitimacy Among Nations* (1990); Mary Ellen O'Connell, *The Power and Purpose of International Law* 84 (2008).

2.   *American Exceptionalism.* Is the U.S. withdrawal from the ICJ an example of American exceptionalism? Exceptionalism is the idea that the United States should be treated differently from other countries, owing to the special status it occupies on the world stage. In theory, all states have equal sovereignty in the eyes of international law, but the practical reality is that states have different levels of power in international affairs. According to Professor Sean Murphy: "For exceptionalists, an international court may be a good thing for keeping other states in line, but the United States almost always does the right thing and, when it does not, any repercussions should flow from national legal and political institutions, not from abroad." See Sean Murphy, *The United States and the International Court of Justice: Coping with Antinomies,* in *The United States and International Courts and Tribunals* (Cesare Romano ed. 2008). Is exceptionalism a viable strategy for dealing with international institutions such as the ICJ? What risks does the United States run if its conduct is criticized as illegal by these institutions? See also Herbert W. Briggs, *Nicaragua v. United States: Jurisdiction and Admissibility,* 79 Am. J. Int'l L. 373, 378 (1985) ("For the future, if the United

States is prepared—as it always claims—to have its international behavior judged by standards of law and justice, the 1946 Declaration accepting the compulsory jurisdiction of the Court. . . would serve it well.").

3. *Jurisdiction Under the Vienna Convention.* The United States' withdrawal from the compulsory jurisdiction of the ICJ did not, by itself, end litigation against the U.S. at the Court. As noted above, the ICJ also enjoys jurisdiction over disputes arising under individual treaties where that treaty, or an optional protocol to that treaty, explicitly confers that jurisdiction on the Court. So, for example, the United States was sued by Mexico for violations of the Vienna Convention on Consular Relations, resulting in a negative judgment against the U.S. in 2004 (excerpted in Chapter 14 of this casebook). Similarly, on Sept. 28, 2018, Palestine filed a suit at the ICJ claiming that President Trump's decision to move the U.S. Embassy to Jerusalem violated the Vienna Convention because Jerusalem is not a part of Israel, according to Palestine. In response, on Oct. 3, 2018, the U.S. announced its intention to withdraw from the Vienna Convention's Optional Protocol concerning the Compulsory Settlement of Disputes, 596 U.N.T.S. 487 (1963). The ICJ has not yet ruled on whether it has jurisdiction over the dispute between the U.S. and Palestine, nor is it clear that the U.S. withdrawal will prevent future Vienna Convention cases at the ICJ. As one commentator noted: "It is unclear whether the United States has a right under international law to withdraw from the Optional Protocol." See Jean Gailbreath, *Contemporary Practice of the United States Relating to International Law*, 113 Am. J. Int'l L. 131, 135 (2019).

4. *The Standing Requirement.* Typically, a state must assert some particular harm in order to trigger the jurisdiction of ICJ. Lawyers from the United States would refer to this as a "standing" requirement. In some circumstances, though, a state might be able to bring a case to the ICJ even though it has no distinctive interest in the matter and simply has the same interest as the world community in seeking an end to the law-breaking behavior. For example, the Republic of Gambia filed a petition against Myanmar, asserting that Myanmar's mistreatment of the Rohyinga people constituted a genocide in violation of the Genocide Commitment. The Gambia had no specific relationship to the situation, but made a clever legal argument. If the Genocide Convention imposed on its signatures an *ergo omnes* obligation not to commit genocide, then surely any state party could bring a genocide case to the ICJ, regardless of whether the petitioner had been uniquely harmed by that genocide. In short, a petitioner could assert the very same legal violation that any other state could assert, since the legal obligation not to commit genocide was owed to the world community, not to specific bilateral partners. In its decision on The Gambia's request for provisional members, the ICJ concluded that:

> In view of their shared values, all the States parties to the Genocide Convention have a common interest to ensure that acts of genocide are prevented and that, if they occur, their authors do not enjoy impunity. That common interest implies that the obligations in

question are owed by any State party to all the other States parties to the Convention. In its Judgment in the case concerning *Questions relating to the Obligation to Prosecute or Extradite (Belgium v. Senegal)*, the Court observed that the relevant provisions in the Convention against Torture were "similar" to those in the Genocide Convention. The Court held that these provisions generated "obligations [which] may be defined as 'obligations erga omnes partes' in the sense that each State party has an interest in compliance with them in any given case" (Judgment, I.C.J. Reports 2012 (II), p. 449, para. 68). It follows that any State party to the Genocide Convention, and not only a specially affected State, may invoke the responsibility of another State party with a view to ascertaining the alleged failure to comply with its obligations *erga omnes* partes, and to bring that failure to an end. The Court concludes that The Gambia has prima facie standing to submit to it the dispute with Myanmar on the basis of alleged violations of obligations under the Genocide Convention.

The Gambia v. Myanmar, Decision on Request for Provisional Measures (Jan. 23, 2020), paras. 41–42. If The Gambia has standing to sue Myanmar at the ICJ, does this mean that every other state party to the Genocide Convention could join the case as a co-petitioner? Does this cause any procedural problems? Are there other *erga omnes* obligations that might be conducive to similar universal standing arguments, or is genocide unique and distinct?

B. AD HOC TRIBUNALS

Although the ICJ is the court's only true general court and is known as the "World Court," in fact there are many other fora for adjudicating international disputes. Many of these are specialty tribunals that deal with particular subject areas within international law, and as such their subject-matter jurisdiction is carefully limited. For example, the World Trade Organization includes a dispute resolution mechanism of arbitral panels that will be considered in more detail in the chapter on international economic law.

The present section focuses on two examples of ad hoc tribunals with limited subject matter jurisdiction. The first is an arbitral panel constituted under the UN Convention on the Law of the Sea, and the second is the US-Iran Claims Tribunal, which was created by the Algiers Accords signed by the United States and Iran in 1981, to adjudicate economic claims arising from the Iranian revolution and the Iran Hostage Crisis of 1979–1981. In many ways, the two examples paint competing portraits of the significance of international legal adjudication. China, the losing party in the South China Sea arbitration, has ignored the decision. In contrast, both Iran and the United States have followed the decisions of the US-Iran Claims Tribunal, and it has played an integral part in the resolution of some of the most pressing international disputes between the two countries. What accounts for the different legacies of the two cases?

1. UN CONVENTION ON THE LAW OF THE SEA

The South China Sea is a body of water between the coast of China and the coasts of several neighboring countries, including Vietnam, Thailand, Malaysia, Indonesia, Brunei, and the Philippines. China claims a right to an expansive area of the Sea frequently called the "nine-dotted line," because the area is often presented on maps with nine dashes (also referred to as the "cow's tongue" because of the shape of the dashes). The Philippines argues that nine-dotted line violates the provisions of the UN Convention on the Law of the Sea (UNCLOS), which governs maritime boundaries and economic activities related thereto. China's position is that the dispute is not governed by UNCLOS because the dispute is, fundamentally, a dispute about territorial boundaries—an issue that is different and far broader than any dispute about maritime rights.

To buttress its claims to the South China Sea, the Chinese government has expanded existing landmasses in the sea into artificial islands, complete with military installations and aircraft runways, and conducts extensive naval patrols in the region. In response, the United States has occasionally sailed its naval vessels close to the islands to establish that it objects to China's claim of exclusive sovereignty over the South China Sea.

In the Matter of the South China Sea Arbitration (Philippines v. China)

Permanent Court of Arbitration
Case No. 2013–19
July 12, 2016

1. The Parties to this arbitration are the Republic of the Philippines (the "Philippines") and the People's Republic of China ("China") (together, the "Parties").

2. This arbitration concerns disputes between the Parties regarding the legal basis of maritime rights and entitlements in the South China Sea, the status of certain geographic features in the South China Sea, and the lawfulness of certain actions taken by China in the South China Sea.

3. The South China Sea is a semi-enclosed sea in the western Pacific Ocean, spanning an area of almost 3.5 million square kilometres, and is depicted in Map 1 on page 9 below. The South China Sea lies to the south of China; to the west of the Philippines; to the east of Viet Nam;

and to the north of Malaysia, Brunei, Singapore, and Indonesia. The South China Sea is a crucial shipping lane, a rich fishing ground, home to a highly biodiverse coral reef ecosystem, and believed to hold substantial oil and gas resources. The southern portion of the South China Sea is also the location of the Spratly Islands, a constellation of small islands and coral reefs, existing just above or below water, that comprise the peaks of undersea mountains rising from the deep ocean floor. Long known principally as a hazard to navigation and identified on nautical charts as the "dangerous ground", the Spratly Islands are the site of longstanding territorial disputes among some of the littoral States of the South China Sea.

4.   The basis for this arbitration is the 1982 United Nations Convention on the Law of the Sea (the "Convention" or "UNCLOS"). Both the Philippines and China are parties to the Convention, the Philippines having ratified it on 8 May 1984, and China on 7 June 1996. The Convention was adopted as a "constitution for the oceans," in order to "settle all issues relating to the law of the sea," and has been ratified by 168 parties. The Convention addresses a wide range of issues and includes as an integral part a system for the peaceful settlement of disputes. This system is set out in Part XV of the Convention, which provides for a variety of dispute settlement procedures, including compulsory arbitration in accordance with a procedure contained in Annex VII to the Convention. It was pursuant to Part XV of, and Annex VII to, the Convention that the Philippines commenced this arbitration against China on 22 January 2013.

5.   The Convention, however, does not address the sovereignty of States over land territory. Accordingly, this Tribunal has not been asked to, and does not purport to, make any ruling as to which State enjoys sovereignty over any land territory in the South China Sea, in particular with respect to the disputes concerning sovereignty over the Spratly Islands or Scarborough Shoal. None of the Tribunal's decisions in this Award are dependent on a finding of sovereignty, nor should anything in this Award be understood to imply a view with respect to questions of land sovereignty.

6.   Similarly, although the Convention does contain provisions concerning the delimitation of maritime boundaries, China made a declaration in 2006 to exclude maritime boundary delimitation from its acceptance of compulsory dispute settlement, something the Convention expressly permits for maritime boundaries and certain other matters. Accordingly, the Tribunal has not been asked to, and does not purport to, delimit any maritime boundary between the Parties or involving any other State bordering on the South China Sea. To the extent that certain of the Philippines' claims relate to events at particular locations in the South China Sea, the Tribunal will address them only insofar as the two

Parties' respective rights and obligations are not dependent on any maritime boundary or where no delimitation of a boundary would be necessary because the application of the Convention would not lead to any overlap of the two Parties' respective entitlements.

7. The disputes that the Philippines has placed before the Tribunal fall broadly within four categories. First, the Philippines has asked the Tribunal to resolve a dispute between the Parties concerning the source of maritime rights and entitlements in the South China Sea. Specifically, the Philippines seeks a declaration from the Tribunal that China's rights and entitlements in the South China Sea must be based on the Convention and not on any claim to historic rights. In this respect, the Philippines seeks a declaration that China's claim to rights within the 'nine-dash line' marked on Chinese maps are without lawful effect to the extent that they exceed the entitlements that China would be permitted by the Convention.

8. Second, the Philippines has asked the Tribunal to resolve a dispute between the Parties concerning the entitlements to maritime zones that would be generated under the Convention by Scarborough Shoal and certain maritime features in the Spratly Islands that are claimed by both the Philippines and China. The Convention provides that submerged banks and low-tide elevations are incapable on their own of generating any entitlements to maritime areas and that "[r]ocks which cannot sustain human habitation or economic life of their own" do not generate an entitlement to an exclusive economic zone of 200 nautical miles or to a continental shelf. The Philippines seeks a declaration that all of the features claimed by China in the Spratly Islands, as well as Scarborough Shoal, fall within one or the other of these categories and that none of these features generates an entitlement to an exclusive economic zone or to a continental shelf.

9. Third, the Philippines has asked the Tribunal to resolve a series of disputes between the Parties concerning the lawfulness of China's actions in the South China Sea. The Philippines seeks declarations that China has violated the Convention by: (a) interfering with the exercise of the Philippines' rights under the Convention, including with respect to fishing, oil exploration, navigation, and the construction of artificial islands and installations; (b) failing to protect and preserve the marine environment by tolerating and actively supporting Chinese fishermen in the harvesting of endangered species and the use of harmful fishing methods that damage the fragile coral reef ecosystem in the South China Sea; and (c) inflicting severe harm on the marine environment by constructing artificial islands and engaging in extensive land reclamation at seven reefs in the Spratly Islands.

10. Fourth, the Philippines has asked the Tribunal to find that China has aggravated and extended the disputes between the Parties

during the course of this arbitration by restricting access to a detachment of Philippine marines stationed at Second Thomas Shoal and by engaging in the large-scale construction of artificial islands and land reclamation at seven reefs in the Spratly Islands.

11. China has consistently rejected the Philippines' recourse to arbitration and adhered to a position of neither accepting nor participating in these proceedings. It has articulated this position in public statements and in many diplomatic Notes Verbales, both to the Philippines and to the Permanent Court of Arbitration (the "PCA" or the "Registry"), which serves as the Registry in this arbitration. China's Foreign Ministry has also highlighted in its statements, press briefings, and interviews that it considers non-participation in the arbitration to be its lawful right under the Convention.

12. The possibility of a party refraining from participating in dispute resolution proceedings is expressly addressed by the Convention, which provides in Article 9 of its Annex VII that the "[a]bsence of a party or failure of a party to defend its case shall not constitute a bar to the proceedings." The Tribunal has thus held that China's non-participation does not prevent the arbitration from continuing. The Tribunal has also observed that China is still a Party to the arbitration and, pursuant to the terms of Article 296(1) of the Convention and Article 11 of Annex VII, shall be bound by any award the Tribunal issues. The situation of a non-participating Party, however, imposes a special responsibility on the Tribunal. It cannot, in China's absence, simply accept the Philippines' claims or enter a default judgment. Rather, Article 9 requires the Tribunal, before making its award, to satisfy itself "not only that it has jurisdiction over the dispute but also that the claim is well founded in fact and law."

13. Despite its decision not to appear formally at any point in these proceedings, China has taken steps to informally make clear its view that the Tribunal lacks jurisdiction to consider any of the Philippines' claims. On 7 December 2014, China's Foreign Ministry published a "Position Paper of the Government of the People's Republic of China on the Matter of Jurisdiction in the South China Sea Arbitration Initiated by the Republic of the Philippines" ("China's Position Paper"). In its Position Paper, China argued that the Tribunal lacks jurisdiction because (a) "[t]he essence of the subject-matter of the arbitration is the territorial sovereignty over the relevant maritime features in the South China Sea"; (b) "China and the Philippines have agreed, through bilateral instruments and the Declaration on the Conduct of Parties in the South China Sea, to settle their relevant disputes through negotiations"; and (c) the disputes submitted by the Philippines "would constitute an integral part of maritime delimitation between the two countries." The Chinese Ambassador to the Netherlands has also sent several

communications to the individual members of the Tribunal, directly and via the Registry, to draw certain statements of Foreign Ministry officials and others to the attention of the arbitrators, while at the same time making clear that such communications should not be interpreted as China's participation in the arbitral proceedings.

14. The Tribunal decided to treat the Position Paper and communications from China as equivalent to an objection to jurisdiction and to conduct a separate hearing and rule on its jurisdiction as a preliminary question, except insofar as an issue of jurisdiction "does not possess an exclusively preliminary character." The Tribunal issued its Award on Jurisdiction and Admissibility (the "Award on Jurisdiction") on 29 October 2015, addressing the objections to jurisdiction set out in China's Position Paper, as well as other questions concerning the scope of the Tribunal's jurisdiction. In its Award on Jurisdiction, the Tribunal reached conclusions with respect to seven of the Philippines' fifteen Submissions while deferring decisions on seven other Submissions for further consideration in conjunction with the merits of the Philippines' claims. The Tribunal also requested the Philippines to clarify one of its Submissions. Those questions regarding the scope of the Tribunal's jurisdiction that were not decided in the Award on Jurisdiction have all been considered and are addressed in the course of this Award.

15. The Tribunal outlined in its Award on Jurisdiction the steps it took to satisfy itself of its jurisdiction, including treating China's communications as a plea on jurisdiction, bifurcating the dispute to have a separate hearing and exchange of questions and answers on issues of jurisdiction and admissibility, probing the Philippines on jurisdictional questions beyond even those in China's Position Paper, and in relation to the seven matters not decided in the Award on Jurisdiction, deferring for later consideration those jurisdictional issues so intertwined with the merits that they lacked an exclusively preliminary character. In the merits phase of the dispute, as set out in more detail elsewhere in this Award, the Tribunal has been particularly vigilant with respect to establishing whether the Philippines' claims are well founded in fact and law. It has done so, for example, by retaining independent experts on technical matters raised by the Philippines' pleadings; inviting comments from both Parties on materials that were not originally part of the record submitted to the Tribunal by the Philippines; and posing questions to the Philippines' counsel and experts before, during, and after the hearing on the merits that was held in The Hague from 24 to 30 November 2015. While China did not attend the hearing, it was provided with daily transcripts and all documents submitted during the course of the hearing and was given an opportunity to comment thereon. In addition to a large delegation from the Philippines, representatives from Australia, the Republic of Indonesia, Japan, Malaysia, Singapore, the

Kingdom of Thailand, and the Socialist Republic of Viet Nam attended the hearing as observers.

16. In this Award, the Tribunal addresses those matters of jurisdiction and admissibility that remained outstanding after the Award on Jurisdiction, as well as the merits of those of the Philippines' claims for which the Tribunal has jurisdiction. The Award is structured as follows.

17. Chapter II sets out the procedural history of the arbitration, focusing on the events which postdate the issuance of the Award on Jurisdiction. The Chapter demonstrates that, in line with the Tribunal's duty under Article 5 of Annex VII to "assure each party a full opportunity to be heard and to present its case," the Tribunal has communicated to both Parties all developments in this arbitration and provided them with the opportunity to comment on substance and procedure. The Tribunal has consistently reminded China that it remained open to it to participate at any stage, and has taken note of its Position Paper, public statements, and multiple communications from its Ambassador to the Netherlands. The Tribunal has also taken steps, in line with its duty under Article 10 of the Rules of Procedure, to "avoid unnecessary delay and expense and to provide a fair and efficient process for resolving the Parties' dispute." Chapter III sets out the Philippines' requests for relief, including the fifteen final Submissions as amended on 30 November 2015, with leave from the Tribunal communicated on 16 December 2015. This Chapter notes that while China has not participated in the proceedings, the Tribunal has sought to discern from China's official statements its position on each of the Philippines' claims.

21. In Chapter VI, the Tribunal addresses the Philippines' requests concerning the status of, and maritime entitlements generated by, certain maritime features in the South China Sea (the Philippines' Submissions No. 3 to 7), namely Cuarteron Reef, Fiery Cross Reef, the Gaven Reefs, Johnson Reef, Hughes Reef, McKennan Reef, Mischief Reef, Scarborough Shoal, Second Thomas Shoal, and Subi Reef. In arriving at its decisions on Submissions No. 3, 5 and 7, the Tribunal also addresses in Chapter VI whether any feature in the Spratly Islands constitutes a fully entitled island, capable in its natural condition of sustaining human habitation or an economic life of its own within the meaning of Article 121(3) of the Convention, such as to be entitled to potential maritime zones that could overlap with those of the Philippines.

22. In Chapter VII, the Tribunal considers the various allegations by the Philippines that China has violated provisions of the Convention, including with respect to:

(a)   China's interference with the Philippines' sovereign rights over non-living and living resources (the Philippines' Submission No. 8);

(b)   China's failure to prevent exploitation of the Philippines' living resources by Chinese fishing vessels (the Philippines' Submission No. 9);

(c)   China's interference with the traditional fishing activities of Philippine fishermen at Scarborough Shoal (the Philippines' Submission No. 10);

(d)   China's failure to protect and preserve the marine environment through (a) its tolerance and active support of Chinese fishing vessels harvesting endangered species and engaging in harmful fishing methods; and (b) its extensive land reclamation, artificial island-building, and construction activities at seven coral reefs in the Spratly Islands (the Philippines' Submissions No. 11 and 12(b));

(e)   China's construction of artificial islands, installations, and structures at Mischief Reef without the Philippines' authorisation (the Philippines' Submissions No. 12(a) and 12(c)); and

(f)   China's operation of its law enforcement vessels in such a way as to create serious risk of collision and danger to Philippine vessels in the vicinity of Scarborough Shoal during two incidents in April and May 2012 (the Philippines' Submission No. 13).

23.   In Chapter VIII, the Tribunal considers the Philippines' claim that China has, through its activities near Second Thomas Shoal and its artificial island-building activities at seven coral reefs in the Spratly Islands, aggravated and extended the Parties' disputes since the commencement of the arbitration.

24.   Chapter IX examines the Philippines' Submission No. 15 on the future conduct of the Parties and discusses the obligations on both Parties going forward to resolve their disputes peacefully and to comply with the Convention and this Award in good faith. . .

[The Tribunal] FINDS that, during the time in which these dispute resolution proceedings were ongoing, China:

(a)   has built a large artificial island on Mischief Reef, a low-tide elevation located in the exclusive economic zone of the Philippines;

(b)   has caused—through its land reclamation and construction of artificial islands, installations, and structures—severe, irreparable harm to the coral reef ecosystem at Mischief Reef,

Cuarteron Reef, Fiery Cross Reef, Gaven Reef (North), Johnson Reef, Hughes Reef, and Subi Reef; and

(c) has permanently destroyed—through its land reclamation and construction of artificial islands, installations, and structures—evidence of the natural condition of Mischief Reef, Cuarteron Reef, Fiery Cross Reef, Gaven Reef (North), Johnson Reef, Hughes Reef, and Subi Reef; and

FINDS further that China:

(d) has aggravated the Parties' dispute concerning their respective rights and entitlements in the area of Mischief Reef;

(e) has aggravated the Parties' dispute concerning the protection and preservation of the marine environment at Mischief Reef;

(f) has extended the scope of the Parties' dispute concerning the protection and preservation of the marine environment to Cuarteron Reef, Fiery Cross Reef, Gaven Reef (North), Johnson Reef, Hughes Reef, and Subi Reef; and

(g) has aggravated the Parties' dispute concerning the status of maritime features in the Spratly Islands and their capacity to generate entitlements to maritime zones; and

DECLARES that China has breached its obligations pursuant to Articles 279, 296, and 300 of the Convention, as well as pursuant to general international law, to abstain from any measure capable of exercising a prejudicial effect in regard to the execution of the decisions to be given and in general, not to allow any step of any kind to be taken which might aggravate or extend the dispute during such time as dispute resolution proceedings were ongoing.

China rejected the tribunal's decision and has not altered its conduct in the South China Sea. In the following statement, China's Ministry of Foreign Affairs articulates its position that the UNCLOS tribunal had no jurisdiction to issue its award. As you read the statement, ask yourself whether the tribunal's award will alter the situation on the ground given China's refusal to accept its legitimacy.

Statement of the Ministry of Foreign Affairs of the People's Republic of China on the Award of 12 July 2016 of the Arbitral Tribunal in the South China Sea Arbitration Established at the Request of the Republic of the Philippines

With regard to the award rendered on 12 July 2016 by the Arbitral Tribunal in the South China Sea arbitration established at the unilateral request of the Republic of the Philippines (hereinafter referred to as the "Arbitral Tribunal"), the Ministry of Foreign Affairs of the People's Republic of China solemnly declares that the award is null and void and has no binding force. China neither accepts nor recognizes it.

1.   On 22 January 2013, the then government of the Republic of the Philippines unilaterally initiated arbitration on the relevant disputes in the South China Sea between China and the Philippines. On 19 February 2013, the Chinese government solemnly declared that it neither accepts nor participates in that arbitration and has since repeatedly reiterated that position. On 7 December 2014, the Chinese government released the *Position Paper of the Government of the People's Republic of China on the Matter of Jurisdiction in the South China Sea Arbitration Initiated by the Republic of the Philippines*, pointing out that the Philippines' initiation of arbitration breaches the agreement between the two states, violates the United Nations Convention on the Law of the Sea (UNCLOS), and goes against the general practice of international arbitration, and that the Arbitral Tribunal has no jurisdiction. On 29 October 2015, the Arbitral Tribunal rendered an award on jurisdiction and admissibility. The Chinese government immediately stated that the award is null and void and has no binding force. China's positions are clear and consistent.

2.   The unilateral initiation of arbitration by the Philippines is out of bad faith. It aims not to resolve the relevant disputes between China and the Philippines, or to maintain peace and stability in the South China Sea, but to deny China's territorial sovereignty and maritime rights and interests in the South China Sea. The initiation of this arbitration violates international law. First, the subject-matter of the arbitration initiated by the Philippines is in essence an issue of territorial sovereignty over some islands and reefs of Nansha Qundao (the Nansha Islands), and inevitably concerns and cannot be separated from maritime delimitation between China and the Philippines. Fully aware that territorial issues are not subject to UNCLOS, and that maritime delimitation disputes have been excluded from the UNCLOS compulsory dispute settlement procedures by China's 2006 declaration, the Philippines deliberately packaged the relevant disputes as mere issues concerning the interpretation or application of UNCLOS. Second, the Philippines' unilateral initiation of arbitration infringes upon China's right as a state party to UNCLOS to choose on its own will the procedures

and means for dispute settlement. As early as in 2006, pursuant to Article 298 of UNCLOS, China excluded from the compulsory dispute settlement procedures of UNCLOS disputes concerning, among others, maritime delimitation, historic bays or titles, military and law enforcement activities. Third, the Philippines' unilateral initiation of arbitration violates the bilateral agreement reached between China and the Philippines, and repeatedly reaffirmed over the years, to resolve relevant disputes in the South China Sea through negotiations. Fourth, the Philippines' unilateral initiation of arbitration violates the commitment made by China and ASEAN Member States, including the Philippines, in the 2002 Declaration on the Conduct of Parties in the South China Sea (DOC) to resolve the relevant disputes through negotiations by states directly concerned. By unilaterally initiating the arbitration, the Philippines violates UNCLOS and its provisions on the application of dispute settlement procedures, the principle of *pacta sunt servanda* and other rules and principles of international law.

3.   The Arbitral Tribunal disregards the fact that the essence of the subject-matter of the arbitration initiated by the Philippines is issues of territorial sovereignty and maritime delimitation, erroneously interprets the common choice of means of dispute settlement already made jointly by China and the Philippines, erroneously construes the legal effect of the relevant commitment in the DOC, deliberately circumvents the optional exceptions declaration made by China under Article 298 of UNCLOS, selectively takes relevant islands and reefs out of the macro-geographical framework of Nanhai Zhudao (the South China Sea Islands), subjectively and speculatively interprets and applies UNCLOS, and obviously errs in ascertaining facts and applying the law. The conduct of the Arbitral Tribunal and its awards seriously contravene the general practice of international arbitration, completely deviate from the object and purpose of UNCLOS to promote peaceful settlement of disputes, substantially impair the integrity and authority of UNCLOS, gravely infringe upon China's legitimate rights as a sovereign state and state party to UNCLOS, and are unjust and unlawful.

4.   China's territorial sovereignty and maritime rights and interests in the South China Sea shall under no circumstances be affected by those awards. China opposes and will never accept any claim or action based on those awards.

5.   The Chinese government reiterates that, regarding territorial issues and maritime delimitation disputes, China does not accept any means of third party dispute settlement or any solution imposed on China. The Chinese government will continue to abide by international law and basic norms governing international relations as enshrined in the Charter of the United Nations, including the principles of respecting state sovereignty and territorial integrity and peaceful settlement of

disputes, and continue to work with states directly concerned to resolve the relevant disputes in the South China Sea through negotiations and consultations on the basis of respecting historical facts and in accordance with international law, so as to maintain peace and stability in the South China Sea.

NOTES & QUESTIONS

Customary Versus Treaty Law. In adjudicating the dispute between the Philippines and China, the panel applied the provisions of UNCLOS. However, China rejects this approach and believes that the dispute is best governed by customary international law. Is this one reason why China is so insistent on building artificial islands in the sea and why the United States continues to sail its naval assets close to them? Furthermore, while both China and the Philippines are parties to UNCLOS, the United States is not. Is it hypocritical for the United States to insist that China respect the arbitral award when the U.S. is not even a party to the convention? For a discussion, see Ryan Mitchell, *An International Commission of Inquiry for the South China Sea? Defining the Law of Sovereignty to Determine the Chance for Peace*, 49 Vand. J. Transnat'l L. 749, 767 (2016) ("the key challenge of resolving the South China Sea dispute is to balance these states' lawful enjoyment of Westphalian sovereign rights equal to those of any other member of the international community with the separate geopolitical goal of promoting regional peace and integration, as well as the continued socialization of regional powers into international law norms and processes").

2. US-IRAN CLAIMS TRIBUNAL

The US-Iran Claims Tribunal was created by the Algiers Accord in 1981 and continues to hear cases arising from the Iranian revolution. Before the revolution, Iran was controlled by an American-supported Shah, who was deposed by Islamist forces during the revolution. Iranian revolutionaries, many of whom were university students, stormed the American Embassy in Tehran and took its diplomats hostage, provoking an international military and diplomatic dispute. The new Iranian government, hostile to the United States and angered over its past support for the Shah, seized the private assets of U.S. corporations. In response, the U.S. government froze Iranian funds located in U.S. bank accounts. Under the Algiers Accords, private claimants (mostly American) were permitted to file claims with the tribunal, with awards to be paid from an escrow account seeded with the seized Iranian funds. The hostages, who were eventually released, are not permitted to file claims with the tribunal.

An essential ingredient of the Accord was the American promise to terminate all current and future domestic cases against Iran (filed in U.S. courts) and divert them to the newly created US-Iran Claims Tribunal in

The Hague. (The Supreme Court upheld the authority of President Reagan to suspend the claims.) In the following case, Iran accused the United States of failing to live up to this obligation, forcing it to spend money defending suits in federal court.

Iran v. United States

US-Iran Claims Tribunal
Case No. A15 & A24
July 2, 2014

1.   At issue in these consolidated Cases is the United States' obligation under the Algiers Declarations to terminate litigation initiated by United States nationals against the Islamic Republic of Iran ("Iran") in United States courts. These Cases center on General Principle B of the Declaration of the Government of the Democratic and Popular Republic of Algeria of 19 January 1981 ("General Declaration") and Article VII, paragraph 2, of the Declaration of the Government of the Democratic and Popular Republic of Algeria Concerning the Settlement of Claims by the Government of the United States of America and the Government of the Islamic Republic of Iran of 19 January 1981 ("Claims Settlement Declaration").

2.   General Principle B of the General Declaration ("General Principle B") obliges the United States, through the procedures provided in the Claims Settlement Declaration,

> to terminate all legal proceedings in United States courts involving claims of United States persons and institutions against Iran and its state enterprises, to nullify all attachments and judgments obtained therein, to prohibit all further litigation based on such claims, and to bring about the termination of such claims through binding arbitration.

3.   Article VII, paragraph 2, of the Claims Settlement Declaration provides, in relevant part, that "[c]laims referred to the arbitration Tribunal shall, as of the date of filing of such claims with the Tribunal, be considered excluded from the jurisdiction of the courts of Iran, or of the United States, or of any other court."

6.   In Case No. A15 (IV), Iran contended that Executive Order No. 12294, issued by the President of the United States on 24 February 1981 ("Executive Order 12294"), and certain of the Treasury Regulations that the United States issued after 19 January 1981 to implement the United States obligation to terminate litigation, violated the United States' obligations under the Algiers Declarations. . .

7.   Executive Order 12294 provides, in pertinent part:

Section 1. All claims which may be presented to the Iran-United States Claims Tribunal under the terms of Article II of [the Claims Settlement Declaration] and all claims for equitable or other judicial relief in connection with such claims, are hereby suspended, except as they may be presented to the Tribunal. During the period of this suspension, all such claims shall have no legal effect in any action now pending in any court of the United States, including the courts of any state or any locality thereof, the District of Columbia and Puerto Rico, or in any action commenced in any such court after the effective date of this Order. Nothing in this action precludes the commencement of an action after the effective date of this Order for the purpose of tolling the period of limitations for commencement of such action. [. . .]

Section 3. Suspension under this Order of a claim or a portion thereof submitted to the Iran-United States Claims Tribunal for adjudication shall terminate upon a determination by the Tribunal that it does not have jurisdiction over such claim or such portion thereof.

Section 4. A determination by the Iran-United States Claims Tribunal on the merits that a claimant is not entitled to recover on a claim shall operate as a final resolution and discharge of the claim for all purposes. A determination by the Tribunal that a claimant shall have recovery on a claim in a specified amount shall operate as a final resolution and discharge of the claim for all purposes upon payment to the claimant of the full amount of the award, including any interest awarded by the Tribunal.

[. . .]

Section 6. Nothing in this Order shall prohibit the assertion of a counterclaim or set-off by a United States national in any judicial proceeding pending or hereafter commenced by the Government of Iran, any political subdivision of Iran, or any agency, instrumentality, or entity controlled by the Government of Iran or any political subdivision thereof.

8.   In Case No. A24, Iran asserted that the United States allowed a case that had been decided by the Tribunal, Foremost Tehran ("Foremost"), to be revived and to proceed in a United States court as *Foremost-McKesson, Inc. v. Islamic Republic of Iran*, thereby breaching its obligation under the Algiers Declarations to prohibit relitigation of claims already decided by the Tribunal.

10. In Claim A, Iran contended that the United States had breached General Principle B by failing to terminate with prejudice all litigation

in United States courts involving claims of United States nationals against Iran that arose before 19 January 1981. Iran asserted that, rather than terminating those legal proceedings, the United States, through Executive Order 12294, had limited itself to suspending some of them. In addition, Iran maintained that the United States had breached General Principle B by permitting cases dismissed by the Tribunal for want of jurisdiction to be revived in United States courts and by allowing United States nationals to assert counterclaims or set-offs in cases brought by Iran in United States courts.

11. The Tribunal notes that General Principle B, Article VII, paragraph 2, of the Claims Settlement Declaration, and Partial Award No. 590 may be characterized as a cascade developing the nature and content of the United States' obligation from the general to the more detailed to the operational.

12. General Principle B provides:

> It is the purpose of both parties, within the framework of and pursuant to the provisions of the two Declarations of the Government of the Democratic and Popular Republic of Algeria, to terminate all litigation as between the government of each party and the nationals of the other, and to bring about the settlement and termination of all such claims through binding arbitration. Through the procedures provided in the Declaration relating to the Claims Settlement Agreement, the United States agrees to terminate all legal proceedings in United States courts involving claims of United States persons and institutions against Iran and its state enterprises, to nullify all attachments and judgments obtained therein, to prohibit all further litigation based on such claims, and to bring about the termination of such claims through binding arbitration.

13. Article VII, paragraph 2, of the Claims Settlement Declaration specifies that "[c]laims referred to the arbitration Tribunal shall, as of the date of filing of such claims with the Tribunal, be considered excluded from the jurisdiction of the courts of Iran, or of the United States, or of any other court."

33. Iran contends that Article VII, paragraph 2, imposes on the United States an obligation to terminate all litigation in United States courts involving claims that were also filed with the Tribunal. According to Iran, this termination obligation arises as soon as the relevant claim is filed with the Tribunal and ceases once the Tribunal dismisses it for lack of jurisdiction.

34. The United States asserts that Article VII, paragraph 2, requires it only to suspend legal proceedings involving claims filed with the Tribunal until the Tribunal dismisses those claims for want of

jurisdiction. With respect to the scope of this provision, the United States asserts that it obligated the United States merely to suspend those few cases that fell outside the Tribunal's jurisdiction but that were nonetheless filed with the Tribunal and subsequently rejected on jurisdictional grounds.

35. In line with its conclusion in Partial Award No. 590,29 the Tribunal holds that Article VII, paragraph 2, obligates the United States to halt legal proceedings in its courts with respect to all claims filed with the Tribunal from the date they are so filed, irrespective of whether they fall, or arguably fall, within the Tribunal's jurisdiction. The objective of Article VII, paragraph 2, is to avoid parallel litigation before domestic courts and the Tribunal.

Meaning of "Arguably [Falling] within the Tribunal's Jurisdiction"

36. In Partial Award No. 590, in the context of Claim A, the Tribunal held that the Algiers Declarations oblige the United States "to terminate all legal proceedings initiated by United States nationals against Iran in United States courts involving claims that arguably fall within the Tribunal's jurisdiction." In Partial Award No. 590, the Tribunal did not clarify the meaning of the phrase "claims that arguably fall within the Tribunal's jurisdiction," and the Parties have differing views on the matter. It is the Tribunal's task—indeed its duty—to add flesh and specificity to the findings in Partial Award No. 590 where, like here, those findings require clarification. It is in the nature of a partial award that it does not cover the ground of all issues presented to the Tribunal at the time because the arbitrators know that there will be a further award, and they defer consideration and discussion of details to that later point in time. Certainly, it would be counter-intuitive to define language such as "in principle," "generally," "arguably," and the like, in a partial award because it is the very purpose of such wording to be broad and to allow for further reflection before it is actually applied.

37. Iran contends that the following types of claims arguably fall within the Tribunal's jurisdiction: (i) all claims that have been filed with the Tribunal, regardless of whether the Tribunal ultimately dismisses them for want of jurisdiction; (ii) all claims with respect to which the United States took the position, in a statement of interest or otherwise, that they were subject to the Tribunal's jurisdiction; and (iii) any claims that were arguably subject to the Tribunal's jurisdiction, regardless of whether they were filed with the Tribunal. Iran further argues, in essence, that, if there was any doubt at the times here relevant whether a claim was within the Tribunal's jurisdiction, then the United States should have considered it arguably falling within the Tribunal's jurisdiction and therefore terminated the related legal proceedings in its courts.

38. The United States disputes that filing a claim with the Tribunal automatically brings the related claim in United States court arguably within the Tribunal's jurisdiction. It asserts, rather, that what brings a claim arguably within that jurisdiction is what the Tribunal itself thinks of the strength of the jurisdictional claim.

39. According to the United States, Partial Award No. 590 used the word "arguably" to refer to "those few cases that fell outside the Tribunal's jurisdiction but that were nonetheless filed with the Tribunal and rejected on jurisdictional grounds." Therefore, the United States concludes, the term "arguably" is limited to the United States' obligation under Article VII, paragraph 2, to halt legal proceedings in cases that were filed with the Tribunal until such time as the Tribunal dismissed them for lack of jurisdiction.

40. As an initial matter, the filing of a claim with the Tribunal triggers the United States' obligation under Article VII, paragraph 2, to halt parallel proceedings in its courts. Accordingly, it is of no consequence in such cases whether the related United States court claim arguably or actually falls within the Tribunal's jurisdiction.

41. In a holding repeated no less than five times throughout Partial Award No. 590,34 paragraph 214 A (a) (2) of the Partial Award (dispositif) states, in the context of Claim A, that the Algiers Declarations oblige the United States "to terminate all legal proceedings. . . against Iran in United States courts involving claims that arguably fall within the Tribunal's jurisdiction." This evidently crucial holding guides the understanding of, and complements, the Tribunal's further holding in paragraph 214 A (a) (3) of Partial Award No. 590. The Tribunal cannot, and does not, ignore either of these two holdings; rather, it reads them together. The "arguably" language found in Paragraph 214 A (a) (2) of Partial Award No. 590 (dispositif), which a Member of the Tribunal, in his Separate Opinion, feels compelled to dismiss as "unnecessary and unfortunate," represents a binding interpretation of the Algiers Declarations by the Tribunal in Partial Award No. 590 and is res judicata.

42. The term "arguably" is an essential element of the Tribunal's decision of Claim A and reflects the fact that (i) only the Tribunal has the power to determine whether it has jurisdiction over a claim; and (ii) the United States, when implementing its obligation to terminate litigation, could not know in advance the claims over which the Tribunal ultimately would take jurisdiction. In its effort to comply with its treaty obligations, the United States understandably construed the language of General Principle B with the utmost prudence—and the Tribunal's ruling in Partial Award No. 590 confirmed that the United States was correct in so construing the content of its obligations. Thus, to read the word "arguably" out of Partial Award No. 590 would be illogical because the

United States could not determine whether a claim actually fell within the Tribunal's jurisdiction. The United States itself recognized this situation by articulating a similar "arguably" standard in the statements of interest it filed in February 1981 in the cases against Iran in United States courts of which it was then aware: it requested that the courts stay litigation of all claims that were "arguably" within the Tribunal's jurisdiction. The courts acceded to this request by the United States in numerous instances, which demonstrates that the "arguably" standard was capable of practical application—and that it does not represent "an ex post rationale created by the Majority to justify adoption of one of two plausible constructions of Partial Award No. 590," as one Member states in his Separate Opinion.

43. In light of the foregoing, the Tribunal concludes that, under Partial Award No. 590, if Iran was reasonably compelled in the prudent defense of its interests to make appearances or file documents in United States courts subsequent to 19 January 1981 in any litigation involving claims arguably falling within the Tribunal's jurisdiction or involving claims filed with the Tribunal until such time as those claims are dismissed by the Tribunal for lack of jurisdiction, the United States will not have complied with its obligations under the Algiers Declarations.

44. Partial Award No. 590 has held that, by adopting the suspension mechanism provided for in Executive Order 12294, the United States adhered to its obligations under the Algiers Declarations only if, in effect, the mechanism resulted in a termination of litigation as required by those Declarations. Accordingly, under Partial Award No. 590, suspension of claims pursuant to Executive Order 12294 was in compliance with the United States' obligations under the Algiers Declarations so long as Iran was not reasonably compelled in the prudent defense of its interests to make appearances or file documents in United States courts subsequent to 19 January 1981 in any litigation involving claims arguably falling within the Tribunal's jurisdiction or involving claims filed with the Tribunal until such time as those claims are dismissed by the Tribunal for lack of jurisdiction.

45. In deciding whether a claim arguably fell within the Tribunal's jurisdiction, the Tribunal will not rely on hindsight and will therefore not be guided by Tribunal jurisprudence that crystallized after the United States' obligation to terminate litigation arose. With this parameter in mind, the Tribunal holds that, if, at the time that termination obligation arose, there was any possibility that a claim could have fallen within the Tribunal's jurisdiction, as defined in Article II, paragraph 1, of the Claims Settlement Declaration, the United States should have terminated (suspended) the related legal proceedings in United States court. The position the United States took contemporaneously (for example, in a statement of interest) may be a relevant, but not conclusive,

factor in assessing whether a claim arguably fell within the Tribunal's jurisdiction. The Tribunal recognizes that the "any possibility"-test seems to be rather broad. The Tribunal, however, considers it to be a functionally pertinent test, consistent with the intentions of the Parties to the Algiers Declarations, as reflected in the statements of interest of the United States Government, that United States courts exercise utmost prudence in deciding whether jurisdiction was theirs or the Tribunal's.

46. The Tribunal will limit the determination of whether a claim arguably fell within the Tribunal's jurisdiction to claims that were not filed with the Tribunal. This is because, as the Tribunal has found, Article VII, paragraph 2, determines the United States' obligations with respect to litigation involving claims that had been filed with the Tribunal.

47. Based on Iran's evidence, the Tribunal has identified Tribunal counterparts for all but 24 of the United States court cases with respect to which Iran claims litigation expenses. While some of these cases contain claims that fall squarely within, or clearly outside, the description of Article II, paragraph 1, of the Claims Settlement Declaration, others present more complex facts and have been extensively discussed by the Parties in their briefs and at the Hearing. Based on the considerations set forth supra, at paras. 40–46, and the evidence presented, the Tribunal concludes that, of those 24 cases, 11 only contained claims that "arguably" fell within its jurisdiction for the purpose of triggering the United States' termination of litigation obligation under General Principle B. . .

NOTES & QUESTIONS

A Story of Compliance. Both the United States and Iran have complied with decisions from the tribunal. Why? While many of the decisions resulted in payments to U.S. private entities, some of the decisions found the United States responsible and ordered damages, which were subsequently paid, either to satisfy the judgments or as part of settlement negotiations. For example, on January 17, 2016, the State Department announced that it paid Iran $1.7 billion to satisfy claims that the United States blocked military exports to Iran in the 1970s. The settlement included $400 million from an Iranian trust fund for the arms sales and $1.3 billion in partial interest payments. The announcement came on the same day in 2016 that Iran released five Americans who were incarcerated in Iran. Skeptics suggested that the U.S. effectively paid a $1.7 billion ransom to Iran to return the Americans. For others, the U.S. had good reason to settle the case because it might lose if the case went to judgment at the tribunal; if the U.S. secured the release of its nationals in exchange for a settlement it was inclined to pay anyway, so much the better. For a discussion, see John Bellinger, *U.S. Settlement of Iran Claims Tribunal Claim was Prudent but Possible Linkage to Release of Americans Is Regrettable*, Lawfare (January 18, 2016) (concluding that the tribunal, while highly successful in the past, "has outlived its original utility and should be terminated").

Conclusion & Summary

International disputes can be adjudicated in a variety of forums, through a variety of overlapping mechanisms and institutions:

1. The ICJ is the principal judicial organ of the United Nations. Its compulsory jurisdiction allows states to file suits at the court if they agree to be subject to the court's general jurisdiction. This reciprocity explains why many states voluntarily accept the court's jurisdiction. Although states can withdraw their consent to this jurisdiction, there are procedural hurdles and the withdrawal declaration may not be immediately effective, as the *Nicaragua* case demonstrates.

2. Perhaps more important than the ICJ's "compulsory" jurisdiction is the court's specific jurisdiction as a dispute resolution mechanism for particular treaties. Many states that reject the court's compulsory jurisdiction nonetheless accept this more specific jurisdiction. Lawyers for a state might strategically argue that the ICJ has multiple grounds for jurisdiction, as Nicaragua did above, just in case one of the arguments is rejected.

3. Although the ICJ gains much attention as the so-called "World Court," the clear majority of international adjudication takes place at specialized ad hoc tribunals. A state might participate in one ad hoc court but refuse to participate in another, thereby picking and choosing the particular subjects and venues where it considers international adjudication appropriate.

4. States faced with an adverse ruling from either the ICJ or a specialized tribunal sometimes withdraw from the proceedings and refuse to participate, as the U.S. did in the *Nicaragua* case and China did in the *South China Sea Arbitration*. However, this strategic consequence carries dire risks. The withdrawing state may have little or no ability to present its legal case to either the tribunal or the world community and may suffer reputational sanctions— or other negative consequences—if the tribunal ultimately renders a negative decision.

CHAPTER 8

ENFORCING INTERNATIONAL LAW

Introduction

Does international law have a system for enforcing its legal determinations? Consider the following hypothetical scenario. A state feels aggrieved by the actions of a second state. The first state files suit before the ICJ or another tribunal that has jurisdiction over the dispute and the parties. The tribunal concludes, unambiguously, that the second state has violated international law, and the tribunal orders the second state to stop its behavior. Perhaps the tribunal also orders the second state to take some measures—like paying a fine—to remediate the consequences of its prior actions. What then? How does the first state enforce this judgment? Or to take another example, what if there's no court case—because no tribunal has jurisdiction—but it's clear that a state has violated international law. How do other states enforce the normative requirements of international law against the offending state that just refuses to comply?

In a domestic system of law, the remedies are complex but the mechanisms are relatively well known. The winning party of a litigation can ask the court to execute the judgment if the losing party fails to pay the judgment. This process might end with a bailiff seizing property by order of the court, followed by an involuntary sale with the proceeds going to the winning litigant. In criminal cases, the police simply drag the offending party to the court for trial, and upon conviction and sentencing, the defendant might be delivered by the bailiff to the custody of the department of corrections.

But there is no secret police force and no bailiffs in the international legal system. The United Nations does not even have its own army. Although the UN uses peace-keeping forces composed of soldiers on loan from member states, these "blue helmet" forces are usually tasked with protecting civilians in dangerous situations, rather than traditional law enforcement functions. How then is international law enforced?

To understand international legal enforcement, one must first resist the temptation to define "enforcement" based purely on its domestic exemplar. The international legal system uses a variety of unique mechanisms to enforce its legal norms, and these mechanisms are the focus of this chapter. Section A focuses on the Security Council—the organ within the United Nations tasked with imposing truly coercive measures to enforce legal compliance. In extreme circumstances, the Security Council may rely on military measures carried out by member states of the United Nations, pursuant to an authorization contained in a Security Council resolution. More frequently, though, the Security Council will impose economic sanctions—basically trade and investment restrictions—against an offending party.

Since economic sanctions are, in many ways, the pre-eminent form of modern enforcement, Section B offers a comprehensive analysis of this coercive mechanism. Economic sanctions come in two basic flavors. First, "collective" sanctions are organized and enforced by the Security Council, often through a sanctions committee. Second, "multilateral" or "unilateral" sanctions are organized by one or more states outside of the Security Council framework. In both cases, though, the goal is the same: to impose economic hardship to encourage the offending state to alter its behavior.

Section C focuses on the self-help measures that dominate international enforcement, especially counter-measures and retorsions. Counter-measures are quasi-punitive actions taken by one state against another to induce the violating state to comply with its international legal obligations. The counter-measure is an action that would usually constitute a violation of international law, but because the action is taken for enforcement purposes, it is considered lawful. Obviously, the legal concept of counter-measures is powerful because of its ability to transform what would otherwise be unlawful conduct into lawful action simply because of the underlying motive for engaging in the action. However, this powerful concept is limited by the concept of proportionality—counter-measures are only legitimate to the extent that they are proportionate to the situation. Finally, retorsions are a similar form of self-help enforcement except that the coercive measure is inherently lawful and within the state's discretion anyway, such as recalling an ambassador or refusing to engage in diplomatic relations with an offending state.

The riddle of the international enforcement may require new language and concepts. Section D therefore focuses on one recent effort to reconceptualize international enforcement as "outcasting," that is, the process of denying rogue states the benefits of social cooperation on the global stage. Seen through this prism, international law offers distinctive and real methods of enforcement. But unlike the typical methods of domestic enforcement—police and bailiffs—international enforcement often involves non-physical measures imposed by external actors, i.e., the states themselves rather than some non-existent world government. The task of this chapter is to understand the legal requirements and complexity of these methods.

A. THE ROLE OF THE SECURITY COUNCIL

The Security Council is the <u>principal organ for organizing</u> enforcement measures against states that fail to live up to their obligations under international law. For example, judgements of the International Court of Justice may be referred to the Security Council for enforcement measures. According to article 94(2) of the UN Charter, "If any party to a case fails to perform the obligations incumbent upon it under a judgment rendered by the Court, the other party may have recourse to the Security Council, which may, if it deems necessary, make recommendations or decide upon measures to be taken to give effect to the judgment." Similarly, the Security Council might also take enforcement measures in a more general context but not flowing from a case at the ICJ, i.e., situations where a state fails to live up to its general obligations under international law. Such measures, which might include economic sanctions or even military measures, are addressed in Section B of this chapter.

In reality, though, the UN Security Council rarely takes enforcement actions after referrals regarding ICJ judgments, preferring instead to concentrate on larger enforcement issues such as economic sanctions relating to Iran's or North Korea's nuclear programs. For example, in 1986, Nicaragua referred the U.S. to the Security Council for enforcement of the ICJ's *Nicaragua* judgment, which Nicaragua argued that the U.S. ignored by continuing to fund the Contras after the judgment was delivered. Predictably, the United States exercised its authority as a permanent member of the Security Council and vetoed the resolution. However, the action was not without consequences. Some major allies, including Britain and France, abstained from the vote rather than explicitly siding with the United States in voting against the resolution, perhaps sending a soft signal to Washington that its actions in the matter were not beyond reproach.

To take another more recent example, consider South Africa's recent decision to refuse to arrest Sudanese President Omar al-Bashir, despite a valid arrest warrant issued by the International Criminal Court (ICC). After the situation in the Darfur region of Sudan was referred to the ICC by the UN Security Council for investigation, Al-Bashir was charged in 2008 with genocide, crimes against humanity, and war crimes. The charges related to atrocities committed by government and militia troops during a civil war in the Darfur region of Sudan. In 2009, an ICC Pre-Trial Chamber officially authorized an international warrant for his arrest. In the ensuing decade, Bashir has remained free and in office as President of Sudan.

According to article 86 of the Rome Statute of the International Criminal Court, member states are required to "cooperate fully with the

Court in its investigation and prosecution of crimes within the jurisdiction of the Court." Nonetheless, Bashir has not been arrested and in some instances travelled to third party states that failed to detain him and transfer him to ICC custody in The Hague.

In one prominent example, Bashir visited South Africa in June 2015 for a diplomatic conference of the African Union—a group of African states that has been sharply critical of the ICC's prosecutorial focus on crimes committed on the African continent. Rather than execute the ICC's search warrant, South African officials allowed Bashir free movement during the meetings. When word emerged that Bashir was in South Africa, domestic human rights groups filed suit in a South African court, arguing that South Africa was under a legal obligation to arrest Bashir because South Africa was a signatory to the Rome Statute treaty and a member of the court. The local court agreed, but South African officials had hastily arranged for Bashir to leave the country and return to Sudan again. What followed was an internal political struggle within South Africa, with the judicial branch reaffirming the country's obligation to comply with the arrest warrant, and South African executive officials attempting to withdraw from the Rome Statute without first consulting the South African parliament.

In 2017, the ICC Pre-Trial Chamber issued a final decision regarding South Africa's failure to cooperate in the case. In particular, the Chamber was tasked with deciding whether South Africa should be referred to the Security Council for enforcement measures related to its non-compliance. Article 87(7) of the Rome Statute provides that "[w]here a State Party fails to comply with a request to cooperate by the Court contrary to the provisions of this Statute, thereby preventing the Court from exercising its functions and powers under this Statute, the Court may make a finding to that effect and refer the matter to the Assembly of States Parties or, where the Security Council referred the matter to the Court, to the Security Council."

Prosecutor v. Al-Bashir
International Criminal Court
Pre-Trial Chamber II
July 6, 2017

123. The Chamber concludes that, by not arresting Omar Al-Bashir while he was on its territory between 13 and 15 June 2015, South Africa failed to comply with the Court's request for the arrest and surrender of Omar Al-Bashir contrary to the provisions of the Statute, thereby preventing the Court from exercising its functions and powers under the Statute in connection with the criminal proceedings instituted against Omar Al-Bashir.

Whether a referral of the matter to the Assembly of States
Parties and/or the Security Council is warranted

124. The Chamber now turns to the second question before it, namely "whether circumstances are such that a formal finding of non-compliance by South Africa and a referral of the matter to the Assembly of States Parties to the Rome Statute and/or the Security Council of the United Nations within the meaning of article 87(7) of the Statute is warranted." Having found that South Africa failed to comply with a request to cooperate issued by the Court contrary to the provisions of the Statute, thereby preventing the Court from exercising its functions and powers under this Statute, the substantive question to be addressed at this juncture is whether it is appropriate to refer this matter to the Assembly of States Parties and/or the Security Council. This is a separate question from that of whether there has been non-compliance on the part of the requested State. Indeed, as confirmed by the Appeals Chamber, "an automatic referral to external actors is not required as a matter of law."

125. In addition, the Appeals Chamber has held that, when deciding whether to refer a matter of non-cooperation to the Assembly of States Parties and/or the Security Council of the United Nations, a Chamber "has discretion to consider all factors that may be relevant in the circumstances of the case, including whether external actors could indeed provide concrete assistance to obtain cooperation requested taking into account the form and content of the cooperation." The Chamber will be guided by these considerations in its determination and, irrespective of its finding that South Africa failed to comply with a request to cooperate under article 87(7) of the Statute, it will determine, in light of the relevant circumstances of the instant case, whether it is warranted to refer to either the Assembly of States Parties or the Security Council of the United Nations the matter of South Africa's non-compliance with the Court's request for the arrest and surrender of Omar Al-Bashir. In particular, the Chamber will provide below its considerations with respect to the manner in which South Africa has approached its obligation to execute the Court's request for the arrest and surrender of Omar Al-Bashir and interacted with the Court on the matter at issue, as well as on the issue of whether engaging external actors by resorting to measures under article 87(7) of the Statute would be an efficient way to obtain cooperation from South Africa.

126. The Chamber clarifies that the considerations below are relevant exclusively with respect to the Chamber's discretionary determination on whether to engage external actors under article 87(7) of the Statute in the matter of South Africa's noncompliance with its obligations under the Statute. In other words, nothing in the factual considerations expressed in this section of the present decision can be

considered as negating or mitigating the Chamber's conclusion that by not arresting Omar Al-Bashir and surrendering him to the Court South Africa failed to comply with its obligations under the Statute.

127. At first, the Chamber considers that the manner in which South Africa has approached its obligation to cooperate with the Court is a significant consideration in the determination of whether a referral under article 87(7) of the Statute is warranted. In this regard, the Appeals Chamber has indeed held that "[w]ith regard to the conduct of parties in the proceedings, the primary obligation to cooperate lies with the requested State." The Chamber considers that South Africa's request to consult with the Court under article 97 of the Statute—which was made with a view to obtaining a final determination on the legal questions before the Chamber—distinguishes the conduct of South Africa from that of other States that, in the past, have been involved in proceedings under article 87(7) of the Statute.

128. In particular, the Chamber notes that South Africa is the first State Party specifically to invoke article 97 of the Statute following receipt of a request for arrest and surrender. The Chamber recalls that, in accordance with general practice, when the Registry becomes aware that Omar Al-Bashir may be about to travel to a State Party, it routinely reminds that State of its obligations to arrest and surrender Omar Al-Bashir and requests it to consult with the Court under article 97 of the Statute if difficulties regarding the request for cooperation are identified. No State Party involved, however, has thus far triggered article 97 of the Statute. This Chamber has in fact previously held that another State Party "should have consulted or notified the Court in accordance with article 97 of the Statute and rule 195 of the Rules of the existence of a problem related to article 98(1) of the Statute which prevented it from discharging its obligations as a State Party to the Statute prior to or during the visit of Omar Al Bashir and before his departure." It is this previous holding that prompted South Africa's request for consultations under article 97 of the Statute.

129. South Africa triggered article 97 of the Statute in an attempt to resolve what it perceived to be conflicting obligations under international law. South Africa's subsequent conduct is also of relevance in this regard. South Africa presented extensive written and oral legal arguments on the matter at hand and indicated its intention to avail itself of the possible remedy of lodging an appeal in the event that the Chamber found that it had violated its obligations under the Statute.

130. The Chamber considers that the fact that South Africa was the first State Party to seek to consult with the Court under article 97 of the Statute and sought—including in the present proceedings under article 87(7) of the Statute—a final legal determination by the Court of the relevant legal issues is a significant factor in that it sets it apart from

other situations involving failure to comply with the request for arrest and surrender of Omar Al-Bashir.

131. In the view of the Chamber, these considerations are not negated or called into question by the arguments advanced by the Prosecutor to the contrary. In this regard, the Chamber notes that the Prosecutor, in her written observations, submitted that "[t]he fact that South Africa took measures to create a legal impediment to the execution of the pending warrants of arrest for Omar Al-Bashir, and only sought consultations with the Court on the eve of the visit, despite having been in a position to do so earlier, are relevant factors for the Chamber to consider when determining the good faith of the parties involved in the cooperation process." At the hearing, the Prosecutor added that the shifting legal position of South Africa before its domestic courts and/or this Court establishes that South Africa first identified a legal and political problem and then sought a legal impediment to rely upon.

132. At first, the Chamber notes that South Africa explained that any delay in approaching the Court arose as a result of domestic processes. The Chamber considers this to be a reasonable explanation in the circumstances of the case, including the complexity and lack of full clarity on the matters that needed to be addressed by South Africa and a certain level of uncertainty due to the novelty of the issues involving the use of the instrument of consultations with the Court. The Chamber is accordingly of the view that, contrary to the Prosecutor's submission, the fact that South Africa did not approach the Court until 11 June 2015 does not indicate per se absence of good faith on its part.

133. Similarly, the Chamber is not persuaded by the Prosecutor's argument that South Africa "took measures to create a legal impediment to the execution of the pending Arrest Warrants against Omar Al-Bashir." In this regard, the Prosecutor referred to the purported granting of immunity to Omar Al-Bashir by virtue of the Host Agreement for the African Union Summit in June 2015. First, the Chamber recalls, as observed above, that the Host Agreement did not provide immunity and privileges to Heads of State attending the African Union Summit. In any case, the Chamber notes that the Host Agreement is a common instrument in the preparation of an international meeting such as the African Union Summit and that the document in question appears to be framed in the manner usual for such instruments. The Chamber also notes that according to article 31 of the Vienna Convention on the Law of Treaties, the Host State Agreement should be interpreted in good faith. In this regard, the Chamber finds that the Host Agreement did not concern Omar Al-Bashir specifically, but is a general legal document regulating a broad scope of issues. Thus, it cannot be concluded that the signing of the Host Agreement by South Africa reflected an intention on

its part to implement obstacles for the execution of the Court's request for the arrest and surrender of Omar Al-Bashir.

134. The related submission by the Prosecutor to the effect that South Africa would have espoused conflicting legal positions is also immaterial to the matter under consideration. The Chamber notes that the issue before it concerns a multi-faceted legal problem whose resolution is not straightforward in that distinct legal aspects must be considered in their mutual interaction. It is also acknowledged that previous decisions by the Court, while invariably concluding that States Parties to the Statute have a duty to arrest Omar Al-Bashir and surrender him to the Court, have not employed exactly the same legal argumentation on the matter. In these circumstances, the Chamber does not consider that any variation by South Africa in its legal argumentation on the matter in its submissions before the Chamber evidences an intent to impose a legal obstacle to the execution of the request for the arrest and surrender of Omar Al-Bashir.

135. The Chamber also recalls that the Appeals Chamber has found that, since the object and purpose of article 87(7) of the Statute is to foster cooperation, a referral to the Assembly of States Parties and/or the Security Council of the United Nations "was not intended to be the standard response to each instance of non-compliance, but only one that may be sought when the Chamber concludes that it is the most effective way of obtaining cooperation in the concrete circumstances at hand." The Chamber should therefore consider whether engaging external actors would, in the circumstances of the case, be an effective way to obtain cooperation.

136. The Chamber notes that South Africa's domestic courts have found that the Government of South Africa acted in breach of its obligations under its domestic legal framework by not arresting Omar Al-Bashir and surrendering him to the Court. In particular, the Supreme Court of Appeal of South Africa has concluded that the conduct of the Government of South Africa was "inconsistent with South Africa's obligations in terms of the Rome Statute and section 10 of the Implementation of the Rome Statute of the International Criminal Court Act 27 of 2002, and unlawful." Importantly, this ruling has become final as the Government of South Africa has withdrawn its previously lodged appeal against it. It therefore appears that the Government of South Africa has accepted its obligation to cooperate with the Court under its domestic legal framework. In addition, the present decision comprehensively and conclusively disposes of the matter as concerns South Africa's obligations under the Rome Statute.

137. Therefore, should there have existed any doubt in this regard, it has now been unequivocally established, both domestically and by this Court, that South Africa must arrest Omar Al-Bashir and surrender him

to the Court. In these circumstances, as any possible ambiguity as to the law concerning South Africa's obligations has been removed, a referral of South Africa's non-compliance with the Court's request for the arrest and surrender of Omar Al-Bashir would be of no consequence as a mechanism for the Court to obtain cooperation.

138. In addition, the Chamber observes that States Parties have been referred to both the Assembly of States Parties and the United Nations Security Council in six instances in relation to failures to arrest and surrender Omar Al-Bashir. However, the past 24 meetings of the Security Council of the United Nations following the adoption of Resolution 1593 (2005), including meetings held on the occasion of the biannual reports made by the Prosecutor to the Security Council of the United Nations, have not resulted in measures against States Parties that have failed to comply with their obligations to cooperate with the Court, despite proposals from different States to develop a follow-up mechanism concerning the referral of States to the Security Council by the Court. The Chamber considers that these considerations further strengthen its belief that a referral of South Africa is not warranted as a way to obtain cooperation.

139. In sum, the Chamber considers of significance that South Africa is the first State Party to seek from the Court a final legal determination on the extent of its obligations to execute a request for arrest and surrender of Omar Al-Bashir. In addition, the Chamber is not convinced that a referral to the Assembly of States Parties and/or the Security Council of the United Nations would be warranted in order to achieve cooperation from South Africa, in light of the fact that South Africa's domestic courts have already found South Africa to be in breach of its obligations under its domestic legal framework and in light of the resolution of any remaining open matter by virtue of the present decision. In view of the specific circumstances of this case, and bearing in mind its discretion under article 87(7) of the Statute, the Chamber therefore considers that a referral to the Assembly of States Parties or the Security Council of the United Nations of South Africa's non-compliance with the Court's request for arrest and surrender of Omar Al-Bashir is not warranted.

NOTES & QUESTIONS

Security Council Inaction. Why did the Pre-Trial Chamber decline to refer South Africa to the Security Council for enforcement measures? The chamber noted several factors, including the fact that state parties had been referred to the Security Council six times in the past for failing to arrest al-Bashir, and in none of the situations did the Security Council take an enforcement mechanisms. This suggests a kind of fatalism on the part of the ICC. Given the Security Council's inaction in the past, what value would another referral have? Indeed, this portion of the decision reads like an attempt to shame the Security Council into taking a more assertive role in helping the ICC enforce its own decisions. The chamber also noted that South African courts had already pushed back on the government's refusal to arrest Bashir. This might be the relevant answer: the domestic judiciary might be a more potent enforcement mechanism for enforcing international law than a Security Council resolution. For discussion of the Security Council's discretion in enforcement matters, see Karin Iellers-Frahm, *Article 94 UN Charter*, in *The Statute of the International Court of Justice: A Commentary* 159, 170 (2006).

B. ECONOMIC SANCTIONS

What if the Security Council orders a state to comply with its international legal obligations, but the state continues to flout these requirements? At that point, the Security Council is authorized to take more coercive measures to induce compliance. Chief among these are economic sanctions. It is helpful to distinguish between collective sanctions enforced through the Security Council, and economic sanctions imposed by individual states, or groups of states, outside the framework of the Security Council.

1. COLLECTIVE SANCTIONS

Collective sanctions are imposed as a coercive measure by the UN Security Council, in keeping with its authority under article 41 of the UN Charter, which grants the Security Council the authority to "decide what measures not involving the use of armed force are to be employed to give effect to its decisions" and to "call upon the Members of the United Nations to apply such measures." Specifically, article 41 refers to these non-military measures as "complete or partial interruption of economic relations and of rail, sea, air, postal, telegraphic, radio, and other means of communication, and the severance of diplomatic relations." This coercive power is triggered by a Security Council finding under article 39 that there exists a "threat to the peace, breach of the peace, or act of aggression," followed by a decision regarding "what measures shall be taken in accordance with Articles 41 and 42, to maintain or restore international peace and security." If economic measures prove fruitless in the resolution of the breach or threat to international peace or security, military measures under article 42 may be imposed.

The value of imposing sanctions through the Security Council, rather than unilaterally, is that the sanctions become mandatory for all members of the United Nations. States that violate the sanctions and trade with the offending state may be "punished" by the Security Council with their own economic sanctions. Also, the Security Council can take an active role in overseeing the sanctions and updating them as necessary.

Although economic sanctions are a powerful tool for inducing compliance with international legal norms, they are often criticized for being too blunt of a tool. In many recent examples, the people of the sanctioned state suffered terribly, because they might have limited access to goods and services required for daily living. For example, sanctions imposed against Iraq while it was ruled by Saddam Hussein resulted in profound humanitarian costs to the Iraqi people. In that vein, consider the following UN expert report, which concludes with a plea for imposing "smarter" economic sanctions.

Adverse Consequences of Economic Sanctions on the Enjoyment of Human Rights

UN Commission on Human Rights
UN Doc. E/CN.4/Sub.2/2000/33
June 21, 2000

II. SANCTIONS AND THE CHARTER OF THE UNITED NATIONS: LEGITIMATION AND LIMITATION

19. Article 39 of the Charter of the United Nations allows the Security Council to take measures such as sanctions only to "maintain or restore international peace and security" following its determination that there exists a threat to or breach of the peace, or an act of aggression. Thus, sanctions may only be imposed upon a Government, "quasi-Government" or other entity that is capable of being a threat to international peace or security or that is in fact threatening international peace and security. While armed groups within a country may pose a threat to international peace and security, a generally unarmed civilian population is, in all likelihood, unable to pose such a threat. Other States not presenting a threat to, or actually breaching, peace and security must not be affected by sanctions imposed on the violating State.

20. Furthermore, the "threat" may not be determined on the basis of ulterior political motives—there must be genuine "international concern" behind the sanctions, not the foreign or domestic policy considerations of a single State or group of States.

21. Sanctions may not be imposed to secure any of the other Purposes and Principles of the United Nations as set out in Article 1 of the Charter, unless there is a credible determination of a threat to or a breach of the peace or an act of aggression.

22. In addition to these limitations, other provisions that would limit sanctions are found throughout the Charter.

23. Article 24 requires the Security Council to "act in accordance with the Purposes and Principles of the United Nations." Thus, no act of the Security Council is exempt from scrutiny as to whether or not that act is in conformity with the Purposes and Principles of the United Nations.

24. Article 1, paragraph 1, requires that sanctions or other measures undertaken to maintain international peace and security must be "effective" and must be "in conformity with the principles of justice and international law." Sanctions must be evaluated to ensure that they are not unjust or that they do not in any way violate principles of international law stemming from sources "outside" the Charter. Likewise, sanctions must be constantly reviewed to ascertain whether or not they are effective in maintaining peace and security. Ineffective or unjust sanctions or those that violate other norms of international law may not be imposed, or must be lifted if they have been imposed.

25. Article 1, paragraph 2, requires that sanctions or other measures "respect the principle of equal rights and the self-determination of peoples." Sanctions that cause international dissention, that interfere with a State's legal rights, or that unduly affect a people's right to self-determination may not be imposed or must be lifted if imposed.

26. The United Nations purpose of promoting and encouraging respect for human rights set out in article 1, paragraph 3, necessarily limits sanctions. Article 1, paragraph 3, also requires the United Nations to solve issues of a pressing humanitarian nature, not to cause them. Sanctions, therefore, must not result in undue hardships for the people of a country. Sanctions that directly or indirectly cause deaths would be a violation of the right to life. Other human rights could also be violated by sanctions regimes, such as the rights to security of the person, health, education or employment.

27. Article 1, paragraph 4, requires that sanctions or other measures facilitate the harmonization of national or international action. Sanctions imposed on one country but not on another for the same wrongs would violate this requirement of harmonization. Sanctions imposed unequally on two countries for the same wrongs would also violate the harmony provision.

28. Article 55 of the Charter reinforces the limitations of article 1, paragraph 3, in its requirement that the United Nations promote: Higher standards of living and economic and social progress (para. a); Solutions to international economic, social, health and other problems (para. b); and Respect for and observance of human rights (para. c). Sanctions regimes that lower economic standards, create health problems or are detrimental to the observance of human rights would violate Article 55.

29. The General Assembly has passed a number of resolutions that elaborate on Article 1 and that must also be taken into consideration regarding sanctions. They include the following: (i) Declaration on Principles of International Law Concerning Friendly Relations and Cooperation among States in Accordance with the Charter of the United Nations; (ii) Charter of Economic Rights and Duties of States (Economic Charter); (iii) Permanent sovereignty over natural resources; (iv) Universal Declaration on the Eradication of Hunger and Malnutrition.

30. While the whole of the Universal Declaration of Human Rights must be taken into consideration, some provisions are especially important: the right to life (art. 3), the right to freedom from inhuman or degrading treatment (art. 5), the right to an adequate standard of living, including food, clothing, housing and medical care (art. 25) are especially vulnerable to violation under sanctions regimes. Article 25 also establishes the right to social security in the event of lack of livelihood in circumstances beyond a person's control and the entitlement to special care of mothers and children, both of which are vulnerable to violations. The rights of prisoners or others under detention or involuntary committal are especially vulnerable.

31. The two International Covenants on Human Rights reiterate the rights set out in the Universal Declaration of Human Rights. For example, the International Covenant on Economic, Social and Cultural Rights provides for the right to an adequate standard of living (art. 11); the right to health (art. 12) and the right to education (art. 13). The right to life is protected in article 6 of the International Covenant on Civil and Political Rights. Article 4 of the latter Covenant contains the additional concept of the non-derogability of basic rights.

32. Any sanctions regime imposed during a war or as a consequence of a war is governed by humanitarian law. Under humanitarian law the civilian population must be protected from war and its consequences as much as possible. This requires that the civilian population must always be provided with or allowed to secure the essentials for survival: food, potable water, shelter, medicines and medical care.

33. The Hague Convention and Regulations of 1907 contain a number of provisions that could substantially limit sanctions regimes. For example, the Martens Clause (eighth preambular paragraph, re-stated in the Geneva Conventions of 1949 and Additional Protocol I thereto) mandates that all situations arising from war be governed by principles of law of civilized nations, principles of humanity, and the dictates of the public conscience. Article 50 of the Regulations provides: "No general penalty, pecuniary or otherwise, shall be inflicted upon the population on account of the acts of individuals for which they cannot be regarded as jointly and severally responsible."

34. The Geneva Conventions have many provisions relevant to the imposition of sanctions. For example, they mandate the free passage of medical provisions and objects necessary for religious worship (see, for example, Convention IV, art. 23).

35. The Conventions also set out rules relating to medical convoys and evacuation (see, for example, Convention IV, arts. 21–22), which could be violated by a sanctions regime that limited land or air convoys of humanitarian goods. Because the fundamental purpose of the Geneva Conventions is to provide for the medical needs of military personnel wounded in battle as a result of armed conflict, any provision of a sanctions regime that limits the ability of a State to provide for its war wounded must be viewed as illegal. Geneva Convention rights may not be abrogated or waived in any circumstance.

36. The two protocols Additional to the Geneva Conventions of 1949 reinforce some of the provisions. For example, Protocol I, article 54, requires the protection of objects indispensable to the survival of the civilian population. A provision of a sanctions regime that authorizes military action against such objects or that denies the repair and recommissioning of those illegally damaged in the course of armed conflict must be viewed as illegal. Protocol I, article 70, provides for relief actions for the benefit of the civilian population and would be violated by any provision of a sanctions regime that limits or modifies relief action.

37. Protocol II contains parallel provisions to many of the provisions set out in Protocol I. For example, Protocol Additional II, article 14, provides for the protection of objects indispensable to the survival of the civilian population.

38. The General Assembly has passed many resolutions relating to the protection of persons in times of armed conflict. For example, General Assembly Resolution, 3318 (XXIX), of 14 December 1974, on the Declaration on the Protection of Women and Children in Emergency and Armed Conflict provides, in paragraph 6: "Women and children belonging to the civilian population and finding themselves in circumstances of emergency and armed conflict . . . shall not be deprived of shelter, food, medical aid or other inalienable rights, in accordance with the provisions of the Universal Declaration of Human Rights, the International Covenant on Civil and Political Rights, the International Covenant on Economic, Social and Cultural Rights, the Declaration on the Rights of the Child or other instruments of international law."

39. Regional bodies and individual countries also have a role in sanctions regimes and, on their own or in concert with the United Nations, have imposed sanctions on countries in their areas. Europe, Africa and the Americas also have regional human rights forums with regional human rights requirements that could be violated by a

particular sanctions regime. Sanctions have been imposed, for example, by the Council of Europe, the Organization of African Unity and sub-groupings of it, and by the Organization of American States. Individual countries and component parts of individual countries have also imposed sanctions.

40.   The Charter of the United Nations limits the sanctions that may be imposed regionally or by a group of States or by a single Government. Article 52 mandates that regional arrangements and their activities be "consistent with the Purposes and Principles of the United Nations". A sanctions regime imposed unilaterally or by a regional body must meet all the requirements for such sanctions inherent in the Charter, including conformity with the principles of justice and international law.

Evaluating sanctions: the six-prong test

41.   The above-listed limitations to sanctions allow the extrapolation of a six-prong test to evaluate sanctions.

1.   *Are the sanctions imposed for valid reasons?*

42.   Sanctions under the United Nations must be imposed only when there is a threat of or actual breach of international peace and security. Sanctions may not be imposed for invalid political reasons (personal grudges, "East-West" or "North-South" politics, "left-right" politics and the like). Sanctions may not arise from or produce an economic benefit for one State or group of States at the expense of the sanctioned State or other States. Sanctions may not result in undue interference with a State's sovereignty rights under international law.

2.   *Do the sanctions target the proper parties?*

43.   Sanctions may not target civilians who are uninvolved with the threat to peace or international security. Sanctions that would result in an abrogation of Geneva Convention rights are void; there can be no effective, presumed or actual waiver of these rights. Sanctions may not target, or result in collateral damage to, "third party" States or peoples.

3.   *Do the sanctions target the proper goods or objects?*

44.   Sanctions may not interfere with the free flow of humanitarian goods under the Geneva Conventions and other provisions of humanitarian law. Sanctions may not target goods needed to ensure the basic subsistence of the civilian population (food, drinking water, basic medicines and immunizations), regardless of whether there is an armed conflict. Sanctions may not target essential medical provisions or educational materials of any kind. Even if a target is otherwise legal, the target must still have a reasonable relationship to the threat of or actual breach of peace and international security.

4. Are the sanctions reasonably time-limited?

45. Legal sanctions may become illegal when they have been applied for too long without meaningful results. Sanctions that continue for too long can have a negative effect long after the wrong ceases (the so-called "undue future burden" effect). Sanctions that go on too long may also be viewed as ineffective.

5. Are the sanctions effective?

46. Sanctions must be reasonably capable of achieving a desired result in terms of threat or actual breach of international peace and security. Sanctions that are targeted in ways that would not affect the wrongs may be viewed as ineffective.

6. Are the sanctions free from protest arising from violations of the "principles of humanity and the dictates of the public conscience"?

47. The reaction of Governments, intergovernmental bodies, non-governmental organizations, scholars and, of course, the public must be taken into account in evaluating sanctions regimes. This prong, the so-called "Martens Clause test," is important not only in terms of the human rights and humanitarian law from which it derives, but also in terms of the Charter's call for international solidarity and the need to address pressing humanitarian concerns. The public outcry over the sanctions regime in Iraq clearly invokes the Martens Clause test. Individuals and groups are even willing to violate the sanctions and to carry out Gandhi-like passive resistance, including a planned "die-in" for the summer of 2000. Regarding the sanctions imposed on Burundi and Cuba, numerous public officials (United Nations and otherwise) have pointed to their disastrous consequences.

III. DESIGNING "SMARTER" SANCTIONS

A. Theory and efficacy of economic sanctions

48. The "theory" behind economic sanctions is that economic pressure on civilians will translate into pressure on the Government for change. This "theory" is bankrupt both legally and practically, as more and more evidence testifies to the inefficacy of comprehensive economic sanctions as a coercive tool. The traditional calculation of balancing civilian suffering against the desired political effects is giving way to the realization that the efficacy of a sanctions regime is in inverse proportion to its impact on civilians.

49. The case of Iraq by itself points to serious problems in the traditional theory of economic sanctions. In regimes where political decision-making is not democratic, there is simply no pathway through which civilian pressure can bring about change in the Government. In addition, civilian hardship can easily be translated into political

advantage by a ruling regime. The targeted Government, especially if it
has a strong grip on the media, will push its citizens to unite behind it in
defiance of the foreign States. Sanctions can be used by the targeted
Government as a scapegoat for its problems and give leaders fuel for
political extremism.

50. Under sanctions, the middle class is eliminated, the poor get
poorer, and the rich get richer as they take control of smuggling and the
black market. The Government and elite can actually benefit
economically from sanctions, owing to this monopoly on illegal trade. As
many commentators have pointed out, in the long run, as democratic
participation, independent institutions and the middle class are
weakened, and as social disruption leaves the population less able to
resist the Government, the possibility of democracy shrinks. In sum, the
civilian suffering that is believed to be the effective factor in
comprehensive economic sanctions renders those sanctions ineffectual,
even reinforcing the Government and its policies.

51. The Secretary-General recognized this, writing in his
Millennium Report: "When robust and comprehensive economic
sanctions are directed against authoritarian regimes, a different problem
is encountered. Then it is usually the people who suffer, not the political
elites whose behaviour triggered the sanctions in the first place. Indeed,
those in power, perversely, often benefit from such sanctions by their
ability to control and profit from black market activity, and by exploiting
them as a pretext for eliminating domestic sources of political
opposition." The data support this argument. There is a no small debate
around the interpretation of successes and failures of sanctions regimes,
but even the most optimistic point to only about a third of all sanctions
having even "partial" success, while others looking at the data have come
up with a 5 per cent success rate, and a dismal 2 per cent success rate for
sanctions against "authoritarian regimes." In addition, it has been noted
that financial sanctions alone have a greater success than trade
sanctions or combined trade and financial sanctions. Finally, if the
purpose of the sanctions is anything beyond merely the "destabilization
of the regime," an aim that all Security Council sanctions ostensibly
share, researchers have shown that the severity of sanctions is
statistically insignificant in determining their success, and that the
longer a sanctions regime stays in place, the lower its success. The same
researchers demonstrated that when the economic elite are targeted,
there is a significant increase in success.

52. Part of the debate on sanctions focuses on ways to mitigate
civilian suffering to the point where it does not produce unwanted
counter-effects, thus allowing a regime of comprehensive economic
sanctions to put pressure on the government. Under the proviso of
"humanitarian exemptions", certain necessary humanitarian goods can

pass through the sanctions barricade. The primary example of this is the "oil-for-food" programme in Iraq. However, this policy is rife with problems. As was exemplified in Iraq, humanitarian exemptions can in no way fully compensate for the damage done by comprehensive economic sanctions. To quote one analyst: "There was general consensus at the seminar that humanitarian exemptions could not provide an adequate safety net against the social and economic dislocation that prolonged trade embargoes cause. Such embargoes have an impact at macro-level. Humanitarian exemptions only mitigate the situation at micro-level and, even when generous, do not constitute a resource flow that can compensate for dramatic overall economic recession."

53. Comprehensive economic sanctions, even qualified by "humanitarian exemptions", do not make any practical sense for changing a recalcitrant State's policies. The traditional theory behind sanctions is disproved by evidence from recent sanctions regimes, and the doctrine of "humanitarian exemptions" amounts to a futile attempt to mitigate disasters. Instead of trying to patch the sunk ship of comprehensive economic sanctions (likened to "medieval military sieges" by one writer) through "humanitarian exemptions", sanctions should be rethought entirely. This is the "smart sanctions" debate set out below.

B. Smart sanctions

54. In response to the tragic consequences of comprehensive economic sanctions on civilians, an increasingly concerted public discourse has arisen around "targeted" or "smart" sanctions. These targeted sanctions are conceived of as directly affecting the political leaders or those responsible for the breach of peace, while leaving the innocent civilian population alone. Properly targeting sanctions, it is hoped, can eliminate civilian suffering while putting significant pressure on the Government itself, thus bringing sanctions regimes into compliance with human rights and humanitarian law and increasing their chances of success.

55. Targeted economic sanctions, especially targeted financial sanctions, have become an international policy focus lately, giving rise to the Interlaken Process centred around two conferences held in Interlaken, Switzerland, in 1998 and 1999, and to a number of other seminars, conferences and research projects around the world. They have been repeatedly endorsed by the Secretary-General, especially in his Millennium Report.

56. Targeted economic sanctions may target the personal foreign assets and access to foreign financial markets of members of the Government, the ruling elite, or members of the military. The assets of government-owned businesses may also be frozen and investment in those businesses prohibited. Imports of luxury goods and other goods

generally only consumed by the ruling elite can be banned. It is generally advised that lists be drawn up with the names of political and/or military leaders whose assets are to be frozen and who are subject to travel restrictions; such a list for the imposition of targeted financial sanctions has only been drawn up by the United Nations once, during the sanctions against Haiti, but in that case the list was not even legally binding.

57. Carefully targeted sanctions, it is argued, can also reduce the harm done to third-party States, thus removing incentives to defy the sanctions, as has recently happened in Africa, with many countries ignoring the travel ban against the Libyan Arab Jamahiriya. Use of the six-prong test to ensure proper targeting, clearly defined goals, a definitive exit clause, and regional unanimity, sanctions regimes could be effective while not harming the civilian population. It is up to the international community to demand that the Security Council introduce such changes.

NOTES & QUESTIONS

1. *Do Sanctions Work?* The basic problem is that sanctions are designed to alter the behavior of governments, but they often end up hurting the local population the most. Ideally, the population would then put political pressure on the government to change its behavior and get the sanctions lifted. But this process assumes a government with democratic legitimacy. What if the government is a dictatorship or some other illiberal regime? Will the government care if its subjects are suffering? Would so-called "smart" sanctions work better? Instead of targeting an entire economy, targeted sanctions might isolate specific political and economic leaders who are closer to the decision-making power of the state, with the result being far less collateral damage to the population as a whole. For more discussion of sanctions, see Abram Chayes & Antonia Handler Chayes, *The New Sovereignty: Compliance with International Regulatory Agreements* 29–108 (1995).

2. *Enforcing Compliance with Sanctions.* Sanctions imposed by the Security Council have the benefit of being mandatory. Member states are required to comply with them. If a state fails to comply and engages in illegal trade with the sanctioned state, the trading state can be reported to the Security Council for enforcement measures of its own. In other words, the Security Council has the authority to enforce the enforcement mechanism. For more discussion, see Jeremy Matam Farrall, *United Nations Sanctions and the Rule of Law* (2007).

3. *The Role of Sanctions Committees.* The day-to-day administration of UN sanctions often falls to a "sanctions committee" that works under the auspices of the Security Council. In practice, there is little public scrutiny of the work of these international bureaucrats. Is this problematic? Do sanctions committees have too much discretion? Are they transparent enough? See David Cortright & George A. Lopez, *The Sanctions Decade:*

Assessing UN Strategies in the 1990s 234–35 (2000) (discussing need for greater transparency in the work of the sanctions committees). The sanctions committees are particularly important in the context of targeted or smart sanctions against particular individuals or entities. As discussed in Chapter 5, critics of the sanctions committees have complained that the process violates basic human rights of due process—an issue that was litigated successfully in the *Kadi* case before the European Court of Justice. In response, the UN has reformed the process somewhat, allowing individuals identified by sanctions committees an opportunity to present evidence and arguments that they do not fall within the scope of a sanction regime. For example, the Al-Qaeda Sanctions Committee regulations said that "A petitioner (an individual, group, undertaking, and/or entity on the Al-Qaida Sanctions List or their legal representative or estate) seeking to submit a request for delisting can do so either directly to the Office of the Ombudsperson. . . or through his/her State of residence or nationality. . ." See Security Council Committee Pursuant to Resolutions 1267 (1999) and 1989 (2011) Concerning Al-Qaida and Associated Individuals and Entities, Guidelines of the Committee for the Conduct of its Work (April 15, 2013).

2. UNILATERAL AND MULTILATERAL SANCTIONS

Security Council-backed sanctions may be preferable because states that ignore the sanctions and continue doing business with the offending state may be themselves subject to enforcement measures. However, in some situations the Security Council is unavailable as a mechanism for sanctions. For example, if the target of the sanction is a major power with a Security Council veto (or a client state of a major power), there simply is no possibility of using the Security Council to impose sanctions. If the sanctions are to be imposed, they must be imposed unilaterally.

In the following case, the European Court of Justice considered a legal filing questioning the legality of the European Union sanctions imposed on a Russian corporation called Rosneft. The targeted measures were part of a sanctions regime designed to pressure the Kremlin to change its activities in eastern Ukraine, where it has militarily supported pro-Russian rebels fighting a civil war against the Ukraine government. The ECJ considered several arguments from Rosneft, including its complaint that the sanctions violated its fundamental rights. As you read the case, ask yourself whether it is appropriate for the EU to impose such sanctions outside of a judicial process. Is ex post judicial review sufficient to protect the interests of the corporations subject to the sanctions?

Rosneft Sanctions Case

European Court of Justice
Grand Chamber
March 28, 2017

26. On 6 March 2014 the Heads of State or Government of the Member States of the European Union condemned the "unprovoked infringement of Ukrainian sovereignty and territorial integrity by the Russian Federation," decided to suspend bilateral talks with the Russian Federation on visas and on the new comprehensive agreement which was to replace the EU-Russia Partnership Agreement, and declared that any further steps by the Russian Federation to destabilise the situation in Ukraine would lead to additional and far reaching consequences for relations in a broad range of economic areas between the European Union and its Member States, on the one hand, and the Russian Federation, on the other.

27. Thereafter, in the course of 2014, the Council established, within the framework of the Common Foreign and Security Policy (CFSP), a set of restrictive measures in response to the actions of the Russian Federation that were regarded as destabilising the situation in Ukraine. In view of the gravity of the situation in Ukraine notwithstanding the adoption, in March 2014, of travel restrictions and a freeze on the assets of certain natural and legal persons, the Council adopted, on 31 July 2014, Decision 2014/512, which was subsequently amended in September and December of 2014, in order to introduce targeted restrictive measures concerning the areas of access to capital markets, defence, dual-use goods, and sensitive technologies, including in the energy sector.

28. The Council considered that the latter measures fell within the scope of the FEU Treaty and that their implementation required regulatory action at the Union level, and therefore adopted Regulation No 833/2014, which contains more detailed provisions to give effect, both at Union level and in the Member States, to the requirements of Decision 2014/512. Adopted initially on the same day as that decision, that regulation was adjusted in parallel with that decision so as to reflect the amendments subsequently made to that decision.

29. The declared objective of those restrictive measures was to increase the costs of the actions of the Russian Federation designed to undermine Ukraine's territorial integrity, sovereignty and independence and to promote a peaceful settlement of the crisis. To that end, Decision 2014/512 established, in particular, prohibitions on the export of certain sensitive products and technologies to the oil sector in Russia and restrictions on the access of certain operators in that sector to the European capital market.

30. Rosneft is a company incorporated in Russia, specialising in the oil and gas sectors. According to the information provided by the referring court, 69.5% of the capital of that company is owned by OJSC Rosneftegaz, a body owned by the Russian State. A minority shareholding in Rosneft (19.75%) is owned by BP Russian Investments Ltd., a subsidiary of the British oil company BP plc. The remaining 10.75% of Rosneft's issued share capital is publicly traded. According to the order for reference, the activities of Rosneft and its group companies include hydrocarbon exploration and production, upstream offshore projects, hydrocarbon refining and crude oil, gas and product marketing in Russia and abroad. Its exploration activities include operations in waters deeper than 150 metres, in the Arctic, and in shale formations.

31. Since 8 September 2014, Decision 2014/512 and, consequently, Regulation No 833/2014, have made specific reference to Rosneft in their annexes as an entity that is subject to some of the restrictions imposed by those acts.

32. Rosneft brought actions against the restrictive measures both before the Courts of the European Union and before the national courts in the United Kingdom. On 9 October 2014 Rosneft brought an action, currently pending, before the General Court of the European Union, seeking the annulment of the contested acts. Subsequently, on 20 November 2014 Rosneft brought an application for judicial review before the High Court of Justice (England & Wales), Queen's Bench Division (Divisional Court). In the context of the latter proceedings, Rosneft claims that both the restrictive measures adopted by the Council and the national measures to implement them are invalid.

33. According to the referring court, the application for judicial review brought before it concerns, primarily, the national measures adopted by the defendants in the main proceedings in order to implement the European Union acts imposing the restrictive measures at issue. That judicial review concerns, first, the legality of the legislation imposing criminal penalties for breach of the provisions of Regulation No 833/2014 relating to financial services and the oil sector and, second, the accuracy of certain statements of the FCA concerning the concept of 'financial assistance' and the application of that regulation to transferable securities that are issued in the form of Global Depositary Receipts ('GDRs').

34. However, the referring court states that that action also concerns the validity of acts of EU law. In that regard, it considers, by reference to the judgment of 22 October 1987, *Foto-Frost* (314/85, EU:C:1987:452), that it has no jurisdiction to review the validity of those acts. While not wishing to express any view on the jurisdiction of the Court to carry out such a review with respect to, inter alia, acts adopted within the framework of the CFSP, the referring court states, however,

that the measures adopted in that field can have a serious impact on natural and legal persons and that the principle of access to a court to review the legality of acts of the executive is a fundamental right.

35. According to the referring court, Rosneft considers, in essence, that: (i) the contested acts infringe a number of articles of the EU-Russia Partnership Agreement; (ii) they do not comply with the obligation to state reasons, laid down in Article 296 TFEU, and, consequently, the right to a fair hearing and to effective judicial protection; (iii) the provisions in those acts relating to the oil sector are incompatible with the principle of equal treatment and their adoption constitutes a misuse of powers by the Council; (iv) those provisions are disproportionate with respect to the objective pursued by those acts and interfere with Rosneft's freedom to conduct business and right to property; (v) Regulation No 833/2014 fails to give proper effect to Decision 2014/512; (vi) to the extent that the Member States are obliged to impose penalties in order to ensure the implementation of the contested acts, the lack of clarity in their provisions is contrary to the principles of legal certainty and *nulla poena sine lege certa.*

36. In the event that the Court finds that the contested acts are valid, the referring court is doubtful as to their interpretation. The referring court considers that it is important to interpret the terms of the restrictive measures at issue in the main proceedings uniformly throughout the European Union and explains that it has discovered, in the course of the proceedings before it, that the practices of the authorities of other Member States diverge with respect to the interpretation to be adopted of certain provisions of the contested acts.

The principle of proportionality and Rosneft's fundamental rights

143. According to the order for reference, Rosneft has claimed that Article 1(2)(b) to (d) and (3) and Article 7 of, and Annex III to, Decision 2014/512 as well as Articles 3 and 3a, Article 4(3) and (4), Article 5(2)(b) to (d) and (3), and Article 11 of, together with Annexes II and VI to, Regulation No 833/2014 are invalid on the ground that the restrictive measures that are imposed are disproportionate with respect to the declared objective and constitute a disproportionate interference in its freedom to conduct a business and in its right to property, enshrined, respectively, in Articles 16 and 17 of the Charter.

144. Referring to [prior] judgments. . . Rosneft considers that the restrictive measures at issue in the main proceedings are neither necessary nor appropriate since there is no reasonable relationship between the aims pursued by those measures and the means for giving effect to them. Accordingly, those measures amount to a disproportionate interference in Rosneft's freedom to conduct business.

145. Rosneft submits, further, that Article 7(1) of Decision 2014/512 and Article 11(1) of Regulation No 833/2014 permit the confiscation of its assets and interference with its accrued contractual rights, that is to say, with its property rights. Those provisions exceed what is necessary by providing, in essence, that non-Russian parties to contracts can be relieved of any obligations under contracts concluded with the entities that are subject to those provisions, even where the obligation involved is to supply a wide range of equipment of which only a small part relates to technologies referred to in Annex II to that regulation.

146. In so far as Rosneft challenges the proportionality of the general rules on the basis of which it was decided that it should be listed in the annexes to the contested acts, it must be noted, first, that, with regard to judicial review of compliance with the principle of proportionality, the Court has held that the European Union legislature must be allowed a broad discretion in areas which involve political, economic and social choices on its part, and in which it is called upon to undertake complex assessments. The Court has concluded that the legality of a measure adopted in those areas can be affected only if the measure is manifestly inappropriate having regard to the objective which the competent institution is seeking to pursue.

147. Contrary to what is claimed by Rosneft, there is a reasonable relationship between the content of the contested acts and the objective pursued by them. In so far as that objective is, inter alia, to increase the costs to be borne by the Russian Federation for its actions to undermine Ukraine's territorial integrity, sovereignty and independence, the approach of targeting a major player in the oil sector, which is moreover predominantly owned by the Russian State, is consistent with that objective and cannot, in any event, be considered to be manifestly inappropriate with respect to the objective pursued.

148. Second, the fundamental rights relied on by Rosneft, namely the freedom to conduct a business and the right to property, are not absolute, and their exercise may be subject to restrictions justified by objectives of public interest pursued by the European Union, provided that such restrictions in fact correspond to objectives of general interest and do not constitute, in relation to the aim pursued, a disproportionate and intolerable interference, impairing the very essence of the rights guaranteed.

149. In that regard, it is clear, as the Court stated in the context of the implementation of the embargo against the Federal Republic of Yugoslavia (Serbia and Montenegro), that restrictive measures, by definition, have consequences which affect rights to property and the freedom to pursue a trade or business, thereby causing harm to persons who are in no way responsible for the situation which led to the adoption of the sanctions. That is *a fortiori* the case with respect to the

consequences of targeted restrictive measures on the entities subject to those measures.

150. In the main proceedings, it must be observed that the importance of the objectives pursued by the contested acts, namely the protection of Ukraine's territorial integrity, sovereignty and independence and the promotion of a peaceful settlement of the crisis in that country, the achievement of which. . . is part of the wider objective of maintaining peace and international security, in accordance with the objectives of the Union's external action stated in Article 21 TEU, is such as to justify the possibility that, for certain operators, the consequences may be negative, even significantly so. In those circumstances, and having regard, inter alia, to the fact that the restrictive measures adopted by the Council in reaction to the crisis in Ukraine have become progressively more severe, interference with Rosneft's freedom to conduct a business and its right to property cannot be considered to be disproportionate.

NOTES & QUESTIONS

Why Were the Sanctions Unilateral? One might argue that in order for sanctions to be legitimate, they should be imposed by, and coordinated through, the Security Council. But in some situations, Security Council action is impossible. Why didn't the EU go through the Security Council? The simple answer is because Russia was the target, and Russia holds a veto on the Security Council. Consequently, the only way of pursuing sanctions against a major power, or a smaller power that is a client state of a major power, is to impose the sanctions outside of the Security Council process. What legitimacy do these sanctions have? For a discussion, see Barry E. Carter, *International Economic Sanctions: Improving the Haphazard U.S. Legal Regime*, 75 Cal. L. Rev. 1159, 1225 (1987) ("In recent decades, the Security Council has had trouble mandating any action, usually because of a veto by one or more of its five permanent members. In particular, the conflicting interests of the United States and the Soviet Union generally make it difficult for the Council to agree on unified action in any international crises."). Do states have unfettered discretion to impose their own trade restrictions?

C. COUNTER-MEASURES AND RETORSIONS

The enforcement of international law represents a complex puzzle that readers will consider throughout this entire casebook. If a state violates international law, aggrieved states have only a few options for inducing the violator to comply with its legal obligations. The victim state might seek adjudication before the ICJ or other international tribunal, or through the Security Council, but a resolution through these mechanisms may come too slowly, if they are available at all. In some circumstances, the victim state may seek to induce compliance more quickly and unilaterally. These "decentralized" mechanisms of enforcement should not be discounted. In many ways, they are the preeminent form of enforcing international law. Sometimes, the mere threat of these decentralized mechanisms is enough to induce compliance among other states. The following sections consider counter-measures/reprisals, and retorsions. As you read these matters, carefully track the key differences between these fundamental categories. What distinguishes a counter-measure from a retorsion?

1. COUNTER-MEASURES AND BELLIGERENT REPRISALS

Historically, international law was almost always enforced through decentralized mechanisms of enforcement, including imposing reputational costs against the violator or isolating it in other diplomatic or legal arenas. The development of a relatively robust system of international adjudication and centralized enforcement by a Security Council is a relatively new phenomenon—certainly one restricted to the post-World War II era. Before then, enforcement was generally pursued through decentralized mechanisms. One especially coercive mechanism was the imposing of a "counter-measure" against the violator.

The definition of a counter-measure is an action that would otherwise violate international law, taken against another state to induce that state to honor its legal obligations. In that sense, a counter-measure is a defense to international law, because it turns the putative violation of international law into an ersatz punishment. To understand the concept better, consider the notion of punishment under domestic criminal law. In normal circumstances, locking someone up would constitute kidnapping, but when performed by the jailor the action is not a crime—it is lawful punishment. The difference with international counter-measures is that the punishment is inflicted in a decentralized fashion by the victim itself, since there is no world government to do it for them. Also, domestic punishment is often backward looking, imposing punishment for prior culpability. In contrast, counter-measures are designed to be forward-looking: to induce compliance in future cases.

Counter-measures were once common in armed conflict, where they were known as "belligerent reprisals." A common example of a belligerent reprisal might involve an enemy's failure to grant prisoner-of-war status to captured soldiers—perhaps summarily executing them in violation of the law of war. In response, the other side of the armed conflict might engage in a "reprisal" by executing a similar number of captured soldiers with the goal of inducing a more compliant attitude toward the law of war. In essence, the reprisal sends a simple message: If you continue to violate international law, we will punish you for it, so you should reconsider your approach and start complying. In the pre-World War II era, belligerent reprisals were once a recognized—if somewhat disturbing—brick in the basic architecture of the legal regulation of warfare. However, during and after World War II, legal attitudes about belligerent reprisals sharply changed, with the result that reprisals in most situations are no longer tolerated in the law of war. The basic understanding is that parties to an armed conflict are expected to live up to the demands of the law even if their enemy refuses to do so.

Generally speaking, counter-measures are strictly limited by the principle of proportionality. In other words, a state may not take a counter-measure that is grossly disproportionate to the gravity of the conduct that it is seeking to deter. A disproportionate counter-measure is illegal, because the state has engaged in a wrongful act. More specifically, *a portion* of the action might be justified as a counter-measure, but whatever is "left over" after one takes into account the principle of proportionality would no longer be a counter-measure at all— it would simply be a violation of international law. To understand this point, consider the following case from a "belligerent reprisal" that the Nazis carried out in an Italian cave in 1944.

Trial of General von Mackensen
and General Maelzer

British Military Court in Rome
Case No. 43
November 18–30, 1945

The accused were jointly charged with committing a war crime by being concerned in the killing as a reprisal of 335 Italians in the Ardeatine Cave.

The evidence showed that on 23rd March, 1944, a bomb exploded amongst a company of German police marching through Rosella Street in Rome. Twenty-eight German policemen were killed outright and a great number wounded, four of the wounded died during the day, thus raising the death toll to thirty-two. When the news of the bomb attack reached Hitler's Headquarters an order was issued to Field Marshal Kesselring, the Commander of Army Group "C" in Italy, to shoot within 24 hours 10 Italians for every German policeman killed.

The order was silent on the question how the persons who were to be shot as a reprisal were to be selected. This order was passed on to the accused General von Mackensen, who was the Commander of the German 14th Army, in whose sector of operations Rome was situated. He telephoned the accused General Maelzer, who was the Military Commander of the City of Rome, to find out whether there were enough persons under sentence of death to make up the required number. Maelzer passed on this enquiry to Lieut.-Colonel Kappler, who was head of the S.D. (German Security Service) at Rome, and was responsible for the prisons of the city.

These facts were agreed upon by Counsel for the Defence, and Prosecution, but from here onwards the claims of the two were at variance. The Prosecution relied upon the evidence of Kappler and maintained that Kappler told both accused that he did not have enough prisoners to make up the required number, but that he would compile a list of 280 people "worthy of death." This phrase signified persons imprisoned who were either sentenced to death and awaiting execution or serving long sentences of imprisonment or persons detained for partisan activities or acts of sabotage.

The Defence, basing themselves on the testimony of the two accused as well as that of Field Marshal Kesselring and Colonel Baelitz, one of Kesselring's staff officers, claimed that Kappler completely misled the army authorities by telling Kesselring that he had enough prisoners under sentence of death to make up the number, and by promising von Mackensen that if the number of prisoners under sentence of death should be less than 320 he would only execute whatever number there were, but would, nevertheless, publish a communique that 320 had been shot as a reprisal, so that the execution of his order could be reported to the Fuhrer. The Prosecution and the Defence agreed that Kappler told both accused that only four of the selected victims had anything to do with the placing of the bomb in Rosella Street.

The result of the orders given by von Mackensen and Maelzer, whatever these orders were, was neither the formal execution of 320 Italians as ordered by Hitler, nor the execution of all persons in the prisons of Rome who were sentenced to death or long terms of imprisonment as intended by the accused, but an indiscriminate massacre by the S.D. under Kappler.

The rest of the evidence was common ground between the Prosecution and the Defence. After both the Army and the Police authorities had refused to carry out this mass execution, the S.D. under Kappler was ordered to do so. The final number of prisoners executed was 335. Kappler accounted for this number by claiming that another policeman died, making a total death roll of thirty-three, and that he asked the Italian Police to send fifty prisoners to make up the numbers and that they sent fifty-five instead. The victims included a boy of fourteen, a man of seventy, one person who had been acquitted by a Court, and fifty-seven Jews who had nothing to do with any partisan activities and some of whom were not even Italians. The victims' were herded together in the Ardeatine Cave on 24th March, and shot in the back at close range by a section of the S.D. under Kappler. They were divided into groups of five and each group was made to kneel on top of or beside the corpses of the previous group. No priest or doctor was present. After all 335 had been killed the cave was blown up by a battalion of engineers. Kappler reported the execution of the Hitler order to the accused Maelzer and von Mackensen, who passed the report on to Kesselring's headquarters.

Neither von Mackensen or Maelzer pleaded superior orders in the strict sense. They pleaded that they were of the opinion that the reprisal as such was justified as the month preceding the bomb attack had seen a long series of crimes against German troops in Rome to which only drastic action could put a stop. Both accused said that they were anxious to take the sting out of the Hitler order by having only people shot who were sentenced to death or long terms of imprisonment. Both accused disclaimed all knowledge of the manner in which the reprisal was eventually carried out by the S.D. and there was no evidence to show that they knew how the 335 died in the Ardeatine Cave.

Both accused were found guilty and sentenced to death by being shot. The Confirming Officer confirmed the findings on both accused but commuted both sentences to imprisonment for life.

NOTES & QUESTIONS

Disproportionate Counter-Measures. Why were Mackensen or Maelzer convicted? The report above is somewhat vague, but the military court's reasoning seemed to focus on the fact that the actual massacre exceeded the scope of Hitler's order. Hitler ordered the killings of 320 Italians as a reprisal to stop their illegal behavior. However, the massacre killed 335 Italians. Does this suggest that if the reprisal killings were strictly limited to 320, they would have been lawful? Incidentally, the massacre was again the subject of prosecutions in 1996 and 1997, this time by the Italian government against Hass and Priebke, who were also involved. In both cases, Italian courts considered the 10–1 ratio of Hitler's reprisal inherently disproportionate. Part of the complication of the case is whether the victims were subject to lawful execution because they were already criminals in custody. Under today's law, reprisal killings are unquestionably a war crime when the victims are legitimate POWs or innocent civilians. But in the Ardeatine case, the victims were criminal prisoners who were arguably eligible for death sentences under local criminal law. For that reason, the case was decided on grounds of proportionality.

2. RETORSIONS

Counter-measures should be distinguished from retorsions, which are lawful measures taken to induce another state to comply with its legal obligations. A classic example is expelling ambassadors in response to a state's illegal conduct. Since a state has no legal obligation to engage in diplomatic relations with another state, it may expel a foreign ambassador at any time. Counter-measures, by contrast, involve putatively illegal actions taken to induce compliance, which is why they are classified as a defense. A retorsion is not a defense because there is no defense required—the underlying action is lawful. For a discussion, see Oscar Schachter, *International Law in Theory and Practice* 186 (1991).

In recent years, retorsions have taken a prominent place in discussions of cyber-conflict. When an aggressive state engages in cyber-activity against another state that arguably violates international law, what responses might the victim state take? In these situations, military force might be ill-advised as a counter-productive escalation and arguably not consistent with the law of self-defense, which only permits defensive force in response to an armed attack. The better response might be to punish the offending state with a series of retorsions designed to induce compliance in the future. For a discussion of retorsions in the cyber-context, see Mark R. Shulman, *Discrimination in the Laws of Information Warfare*, 37 Colum. J. Transnat'l L. 939, 951 (1999) ("retorsion should be limited to shutting down (either temporarily or permanently) the computer system believed to be generating the original attack"); Manny Halberstam, *Hacking Back: Reevaluating the Legality of Retaliatory Cyberattacks*, 46 Geo. Wash. Int'l L. Rev. 199, 215 (2013) (arguing that "a counter cyber operation that falls short of a use of force is not a valid retorsion if it unlawfully intervenes in the sovereignty of another state").

PROBLEM CASE

In 2016, Russian hackers interfered in the U.S. presidential election by, among other things, hacking the emails of the Democratic National Committee and releasing them to the public. Intelligence officials working for the Obama Administration concluded that these actions constituted a cyber-attack, authorized and ordered by the Russian government, against the United States. Although President Obama said little about the event at the time, he eventually publicly condemned the Russian government for the action and announced a set of responses. For example, the federal government expelled several Russian diplomats and also ordered the shuttering of several diplomatic buildings operated by the Russians in the United States. The U.S. administration may also have taken other responses that were never publicly acknowledged, including limited cyber-attacks against Russia, although this is certainly unclear.

How should one analyze the status of these legal actions? More importantly, why did the U.S. limit its public response to expelling ambassadors and shutting diplomatic outposts? One possibility is that the legal status of the original cyber-attack by Russia was uncertain. While the hacking certainly violated American law, experts were divided over whether the attacks violated international law. See Jens David Ohlin, *Did Russian Cyber Interference in the 2016 Election Violate International Law?*, 95 Texas L. Rev. 1579 (2017). If they did not, then any U.S. "counter-measure" would not have been a real counter-measure at all—it simply would have been a violation of international law.

How do you think the U.S. should have reacted? Are counter-measures a legitimate defense for violating international law? Do they induce compliance or do they spark a continuing spiral of violations?

D. OUTCASTING AND NON-COOPERATION

"Outcasting" is one way to understand international law's distinctive form of enforcement. In the following excerpt, Professors Hathaway and Shapiro coin the term outcasting to describe—and model—international law's model of enforcement whereby offending states are denied "the benefits of social cooperation." For Hathaway and Shapiro, the outcasting concept brings together a variety of enforcement mechanisms that impose different levels of social cost on offending states. This process differs from the type of enforcement that we usually associate with domestic law—the police coming with brute force to enforce a statutory requirement or execute a court's judgment. As you see below, Hathaway and Shapiro identify two relevant characteristics of domestic law enforcement. The first is that the enforcement is often performed by internal actors—agents within the legal system specifically tasked with enforcement, such as the police. The second is that the enforcement is often physical, i.e., backed up by brute force.

But is the physical and internal form of enforcement often found in domestic law the only type of enforcement possible? In theory, one might have enforcement that is completed by external actors—the community itself—and might involve non-physical measures. If Hathaway and Shapiro are correct, outcasting in international law deserves the label "enforcement" because it involves the use of external actors to enforce the law through non-physical means. Although this process "looks" different from much of the enforcement found in domestic law, that does not entail the conclusion that it is not enforcement. It just means that the international system leverages unique mechanisms to accomplish its enforcement goals. Does domestic law sometimes use outcasting too?

Outcasting: Enforcement in Domestic and International Law

Oona Hathaway & Scott J. Shapiro
121 Yale L.J. 252 (2011)

IV. OUTCASTING AND EXTERNAL ENFORCEMENT IN INTERNATIONAL LAW

With the blinders imposed by the Modern State Conception removed—and a fuller vision of law that includes outcasting and external enforcement as really and truly law—international law appears in an entirely new light. We are able to see that allowing the Modern State Conception to set the terms of the debate over international law leads us to ask and answer the wrong questions. Yes, very little of international law meets the Modern State Conception of international law—very little (if any) of it is enforced through brute physical force deployed by an institution enforcing its own rules. But what is interesting is not so much what international law is not, but what it is. And that is law that operates almost entirely through outcasting and external enforcement.

In this Part, we document how international law works in light of the broader understanding of law that we have put forth. What we see is that, time and again, international legal institutions use others (usually states) to enforce their rules, and they typically deploy outcasting—denying individuals the benefits of social cooperation—rather than physical force. The much more complete picture of law offered above thus not only gives the lie to the Modern State Conception, but also provides a new way of understanding international law and how it functions.

Different international legal regimes can be classified depending on the particular modes of enforcement on which they depend. We illustrate this by dividing law enforcement into internal and external enforcement, and into that which resorts to physical force and that which does not. These two different axes can overlap to create four separate categories: (1) internal and physical; (2) external and physical; (3) internal and nonphysical; and (4) external and nonphysical. To illustrate this, consider the following four-square diagram:

Figure 1.

	INTERNAL	EXTERNAL
PHYSICAL	Modern State Conception	External Physical Enforcement
NONPHYSICAL	Internal Outcasting	External Outcasting

As this diagram makes clear, the Modern State Conception of law enforcement is only one part of the larger picture—it encompasses law that is enforced through internal systems using physical force. But there are three other forms of law enforcement: external physical enforcement (enforced by external actors using physical force), internal outcasting (enforced by internal actors using nonphysical means), and external outcasting (enforced by external actors using nonphysical means). As we described the Modern State Conception of law in some depth above, we focus here on completing the picture with more detailed descriptions of the other three forms of law enforcement. This serves as a prelude to a closer examination in the next Part of the type of legal enforcement regime that is most prevalent in international law: external outcasting.

A.   *External Physical Enforcement*

External physical enforcement operates by externalizing enforcement onto other actors that, in turn, resort to physical force. As we noted above, the Modern State Conception demands that enforcement be enforced internally—that is, by the regime itself. All external legal enforcement (whether physical or nonphysical) violates this demand. It instead tasks some party outside the regime with ensuring compliance with the rules. Classical canon law, for example, provided that the ecclesiastical courts could "relax" a person to external actors—the secular authorities—for physical punishment.

Nearly all physical enforcement of international law is external physical enforcement. As noted above, a central principle of international law—codified in Article 2(4) of the United Nations Charter—is the prohibition on the use of aggressive force by a sovereign state against the sovereign territory or political independence of another state. Although the original intention was for the United Nations to have troops at its disposal to carry out enforcement actions, in practice such actions have been carried out by states acting with the approval of the United Nations Security Council.

In the Korean War, for example, the Security Council encouraged member states to "furnish such assistance to the Republic of Korea as may be necessary to repel the armed attack and to restore international peace and security in the area." Similarly, the first U.S. Gulf War was initiated pursuant to Security Council Resolution 678, which authorized "Member States co-operating with the Government of Kuwait. . . to use all necessary means. . . to restore international peace and security in the area." The resolution "[r]equest[ed] all States to provide appropriate support for the actions undertaken" pursuant to that authorization and "[r]equest[ed] the States concerned to keep the Security Council regularly informed on the progress of actions undertaken." In these cases and many others like them, the use of physical force under Chapter VII was carried out by actors outside the institutional bureaucracy of the United Nations, thus making the use of physical force to enforce the law external to the United Nations.

External physical enforcement also occurs through the use of self-defense (authorized by Article 51 of the U.N. Charter) and, as we argued earlier, through mutual defense treaties authorizing states to come to the aid of one another in the event of an attack. States are permitted to use physical force to engage in self-defense and collective self-defense to repel an armed attack. Mutual defense treaties enforce this principle of international law by providing that if one of the parties to the treaty is attacked, the other will come to its aid, thereby enforcing the right of the first state to repel aggression against it. In both cases, the use of physical force is external to the treaty organization.

B. Internal Outcasting

Internal outcasting occurs when the internal bureaucratic structures of a legal system enforce the law without resorting to the threat or use of physical force. Internal outcasting meets the internality condition of the Modern State Conception—it has at least one secondary enforcement link that is addressed to officials of the regime in question. But it does not provide for the use of violence—it does not require or permit officials of the regime to use physical force to enforce the law. For example, minor excommunication in classical canon law entailed separation of a person from the sacraments of the Church. This penalty relied on enforcement by Church officials (internal to the Church) by denying the benefits of membership in the Church (outcasting).

Internal outcasting is used in international law any time a regime sanctions lawbreaking behavior of a state by excluding the state from participation in the treaty bodies. The World Health Organization (WHO) offers an example. The WHO directs and coordinates a vast array of international public health programs aimed at everything from combating infectious diseases (such as HIV/AIDS, swine flu, and SARS) to setting health-related norms and standards to improving access to clean water. State parties have the right to appoint delegations to the World Health Assembly, which is the WHO's decisionmaking body. The Health Assembly elects its President and other officers, elects the Executive Board of the WHO (which serves as the executive arm of the WHO), adopts its rules of procedure, appoints the WHO Director-General, and establishes committees necessary for the work of the Organization, to name just a few of its enumerated functions. The Health Assembly also has the authority to adopt health regulations and standards that are binding on parties that do not expressly opt out within a specified time period.

The WHO is supported by mandatory contributions by state parties, as well as voluntary donor contributions. The mandatory state party contributions are enforced, moreover, by the prospect of internal outcasting. If a Member "fails to meet its financial obligations to the Organization. . . the Health Assembly may, on such conditions as it thinks proper, suspend the voting privileges and services to which a Member is entitled. The Health Assembly shall have the authority to restore such voting privileges and services." Note that the state party is not ejected from the WHO altogether. Instead, the state party loses the ability to participate as a voting member in the Health Assembly—and thus loses control over the activities of the WHO that the Health Assembly oversees and directs. In other words, the sanction for the offense of nonpayment is exclusion from the benefit of participating in the governance of the institution—an enforcement action carried out by the Health Assembly itself. Hence, the enforcement regime is internal outcasting: "internal" because the punishment is carried out by officials internal to the regime, and "outcasting" because the punishment constitutes exclusion from some of the benefits of community membership.

C. External Outcasting

This brings us to the final form of law enforcement—external outcasting. To put external outcasting into context, recall that external physical enforcement violates the requirement of the Modern State Conception that the law be enforced by officials of the regime. Internal outcasting, on the other hand, meets the internality requirement but violates the brute force requirement—it does not require or permit officials to use physical force. External outcasting is distinguished from these two forms of law enforcement in that it violates both the internality and the brute force requirements—it is enforced by officials outside the legal regime without the use of physical force at any point in the enforcement chain. Outlawry under medieval Icelandic law, for example, was enforced not by the Allthing itself but by individual members of society. And the enforcement operated primarily (though not exclusively) by denying the outlaw the benefits of social cooperation and membership, rather than through physical force.

To see how external outcasting applies in international law, we return to the example of the WTO. As we noted in Part I, the WTO falls far short in the estimation of the Modern State Conception: it violates both the internality and the brute force requirements. And yet, the WTO is widely regarded as one of the strongest and most effective international legal regimes in existence. How is that possible?

We can now see that the WTO uses external outcasting to enforce its rules. The trade law principles established in the General Agreement on Tariffs and Trade are not enforced internally—that is, by the officials of the WTO itself. Yes, the WTO has a compulsory dispute resolution system. But the decisions rendered by the WTO's Dispute Settlement Body are enforced through authorized retaliation by the aggrieved state party. It is the states, not the legal regime of the WTO itself, that impose the sanction. Enforcement is thus external to the legal regime. The enforcement regime of the WTO is also devoid of any threat or use of physical force. As we noted earlier, "[t]he WTO has no jailhouse, no bail bondsmen, no blue helmets, no truncheons or tear gas." Nor are member states permitted recourse to violence to enforce the rules. Instead, enforcement is limited to specific, approved, retaliatory trade measures taken by the aggrieved parties after a process of adjudication. Like the Icelandic outlaw, the state party found in violation of the General Agreement on Tariffs and Trade simply loses a measure of protection under the legal regime. And just as in medieval Iceland, the threat of losing the protections of the legal regime provides a powerful inducement to compliance.

The WTO is far from alone. Indeed, once we begin to look at international law through the prism of external outcasting, we see that it is everywhere. It is used to enforce international regulatory regimes such as the Convention on International Civil Aviation and the International Telecommunication Union; it is used to enforce the rules of regional organizations such as the European Convention on Human Rights; it is used by the United Nations Security Council to "give effect to its decisions"; and it is used to enforce environmental legal agreements such as the Montreal Protocol and the Convention on International Trade in Endangered Species. External outcasting is so pervasive that it is fair to say that it is the primary mode of law enforcement utilized by international legal regimes.

Conclusion & Summary

International law has multiple avenues of coercive enforcement, though the methods and processes are somewhat different than domestic law:

1. Within the United Nations, the task of enforcing international law primarily falls to the Security Council. Judgments of the ICJ and other tribunals may be enforced by coercive measures imposed by the Council, including military measures and economic sanctions. In reality, though, few disputes are enforced through the Security Council, which often refuses to act. In some cases, the lack of action may be attributed to the veto power enjoyed by the permanent members of the Security Council, whose interests may compel them to veto, or threaten to veto, an enforcement action. In other situations, Security Council inaction may be harder to explain, such as the Security Council's decision to refer the Sudan situation to the International Criminal Court but then refuse to engage in enforcement actions when states refuse to enforce a valid arrest warrant for the Sudanese President al-Bashir.

2. Economic sanctions may be imposed either through the Security Council or unilateral/multilateral state action. In the former case, the Security Council has the power to enforce compliance with the sanctions, which is often managed by a sanctions committee. In the latter case, states take on the burden of managing the sanctions themselves.

3. In the last two decades, largely in response to criticism that economic sanctions were too harmful for innocent civilians unconnected to government decision-making, "smart" or "targeted" sanctions have been increasingly common. These sanctions target specific individuals or corporations more closely connected to the government of the offending state, or more closely connected to the illegal behavior that

triggered the sanctions. For example, military actions that violate international law might trigger targeted sanctions against companies from that state involved in arms manufacturing, procurement, or trading. As sanctions have become more individualized, corporations and individuals have argued for greater procedural protections to contest their inclusion on the sanctions lists.

4. When all else fails, states engage in counter-measures and retorsions to induce compliance from offending states. In the context of armed conflict, counter-measures are referred to as belligerent reprisals. Although belligerent reprisals were once accepted as a practical means of enforcing the law of war, the modern view is that states engaged in an armed conflict may not commit war crimes and escape liability simply by calling them a "counter-measure."

5. Disproportionate counter-measures are illegal because they are—by definition—unnecessary. The issue of proportionality usually does not arise for retorsions, because retorsions involve lawful conduct already within the sovereign discretion of the state. In that sense, a state is free to engage in retorsions whenever it wants, without the need to justify its behavior.

6. A complete theory of international legal enforcement must recognize that the enforcement is completed by the actors themselves rather than an external police force. States usually use non-physical coercive measures to induce others to comply with international law. However, the difference between international and domestic legal enforcement is probably one of degree rather than kind, since even domestic law makes use of non-physical coercive measures.

CHAPTER 9

SELF-DEFENSE

Introduction

The standard rule in international law is that a state's use of military force against another state is lawful if authorized by the Security Council or if taken in self-defense (or *légitime défense* in French). These are the only two circumstances under which states are relieved from their obligations under Article 2(4) of the UN Charter to "refrain in their international relations from the threat or use of force against the territorial integrity or political independence of any state."

Under article 39 of the UN Charter, the Security Council has the authority and responsibility to determine the "existence of any threat to the peace, breach of the peace, or act of aggression." Once that determination is made, the Security Council may authorize non-military counter-measures pursuant to article 41. If those avenues prove fruitless or are otherwise unavailable, the Security Council may authorize military action pursuant to article 42, up to and including "demonstrations, blockade, and other operations by air, sea, or land forces of Members of the United Nations."

But what if the Security Council refuses to act? Because of the veto power exercised by the permanent five voting members, in many cases the Security Council is gridlocked and will not authorize military force in response to a possible act of aggression. In that situation, states still enjoy a unilateral right of response, provided that the requirements for self-defense are satisfied. Article 51 articulates the basic parameters of the defense:

> Nothing in the present Charter shall impair the inherent right of individual or collective self-defence if an armed attack occurs against a Member of the United Nations, until the Security Council has taken measures necessary to maintain international peace and security. Measures taken by Members in the exercise of this right of self-defence shall be immediately reported to the Security Council and shall not in any way affect the authority and responsibility of the Security Council under the present Charter to take at any time such action as it deems necessary in order to maintain or restore international peace and security.

Unfortunately, nothing else in the UN Charter explicitly articulates the standards for the exercise of national self-defense. However, the basic requirements for national self-defense can generally be divined by consulting the scholarly literature and customary international law. These sources suggest broad agreement over the following criteria for lawful self-defense: (i) the existence of an armed attack against the state; (ii) the attack must be imminent or in progress; (iii) defensive force must be necessary to repel the attack; and (iv) the defensive force must be proportionate to the legitimate interests of the state. Although there is broad agreement on these requirements, the devil is always in the details; defining and applying each of these requirements is controversial and contested. For example, in *United States v. Nicaragua*, the ICJ concluded that the U.S. exceeded the scope of collective self-defense when it mined nearby waters and also armed and supported a paramilitary force, known as the Contras, fighting the Nicaraguan government. In making this conclusion, the ICJ noted that the requirements for lawful self-defense include the existence of an armed attack as well as a necessary and proportionate response.

The following materials explore the formal requirements for a successful claim of national self-defense as well as the controversies surrounding their proper application in concrete cases.

A. THE ARMED ATTACK REQUIREMENT

In order to trigger a right of unilateral force, the state that seeks to deploy the defensive force must have been victimized by an armed attack. Although other infringements against the territorial or political sovereignty of a state may give rise to other counter-measures, a full *military* response is only warranted "if an armed attack occurs" in the language of the UN Charter. Two immediate questions have complicated the proper application of this principle to concrete disputes: what is the temporal dimension for the attack? And how severe must the incursion be to constitute an "armed attack"? The temporal dimension will be explored below in Section C on imminence. We now consider the severity prong.

Generally speaking, a border guard firing his rifle once across the range would not be considered an armed attack—it would be a mere border incident. On the other hand, a full military invasion would certainly constitute an armed attack triggering a right of self-defense. The disagreements start in between these two extremes of the spectrum. For example, if the military of the attacking state flies its air force through the airspace of a non-consenting state, has the attacking state performed an armed attack? Assume for the sake of argument that the attacking state was merely flying *through* the territory of the non-consenting state in order to reach a second state, its ultimate target, which it bombed. If the first non-consenting state was never bombed, was it the victim of an armed attack? Given that the state was not harmed by any bombs or missiles, most international lawyers would probably conclude that the territorial violation did not constitute an armed attack.

Of course, this hypothetical demonstrates the centrality of consent as a key principle behind territorial violations. If the territorial state gives consent for the fly-overs, then it is axiomatic that the flyovers do not constitute a violation of the prohibition against illegal force. Indeed, most scholars agree that the prohibition against the use of military force, codified in article 2(4) of the UN Charter, is only triggered if the military forces are present on the territory of another state *without* the consent of that state.

We now turn to two recent controversies regarding the application of the armed attack requirement that have generated substantial controversy. The first is whether an armed attack from a non-state actor counts as an "armed attack" for purposes of triggering the right of self-defense. The second is whether a *cyber* attack can constitute the "armed attack" that could trigger the target state's right of self-defense. Finally, the section closes with a discussion of collective self-defense.

1. ATTACKS FROM NON-STATE ACTORS

The armed attack requirement is ambiguous and can be interpreted in two different ways. First, one could argue that the *origin* of the armed attack is irrelevant and that all that matters is whether the target state was actually subject to a military incursion. Second, one could argue in the alternative that the origin of the armed attack is absolutely paramount and that it must come from another state. Or, more precisely, the armed attack must be *attributable* to another state using the standard international law rules regarding state responsibility for wrongful acts. In the absence of this attribution, the armed attack does not constitute a violation of the international prohibition against the use of military force (articulated in article 2(4) of the UN Charter), and therefore no right of self-defense flows from the original encounter.

For example, in 1994 the International Court of Justice concluded that the doctrine of self-defense is inapplicable as a justification for acts taken in response to armed attacks from non-state actors. The discussion came in its advisory opinion, *Legal Consequences of the Construction of a Wall in the Occupied Palestinian Territory*, which arose from Israel's erection of a security wall to separate Israel from occupied territories and thereby prevent terrorists from moving easily into Israel to commit attacks. In a breezy passage, the court concluded:

> 138. The Court has thus concluded that the construction of the wall constitutes action not in conformity with various international legal obligations incumbent upon Israel. However, Annex 1 to the report of the Secretary-General states that,

according to Israel: "the construction of the Barrier is consistent with Article 51 of the Charter of the United Nations, its inherent right to self-defence and Security Council resolutions 1368 (2001) and 1373 (2001)". More specifically, Israel's Permanent Representative to the United Nations asserted in the General Assembly on 20 October 2003 that "the fence is a measure wholly consistent with the right of States to self-defence enshrined in Article 51 of the Charter"; the Security Council resolutions referred to, he continued, "have clearly recognized the right of States to use force in self-defence against terrorist attacks", and therefore surely recognize the right to use non-forcible measures to that end.

139. Under the terms of Article 51 of the Charter of the United Nations: "Nothing in the present Charter shall impair the inherent right of individual or collective self-defence if an armed attack occurs against a Member of the United Nations, until the Security Council has taken measures necessary to maintain international peace and security." Article 51 of the Charter thus recognizes the existence of an inherent right of self-defence in the case of armed attack by one State against another State. However, Israel does not claim that the attacks against it are imputable to a foreign State. The Court also notes that Israel exercises control in the Occupied Palestinian Territory and that, as Israel itself states, the threat which it regards as justifying the construction of the wall originates within, and not outside, that territory. The situation is thus different from that contemplated by Security Council resolutions 1368 (2001) and 1373 (2001), and therefore Israel could not in any event invoke those resolutions in support of its claim to be exercising a right of self-defence. Consequently, the Court concludes that Article 51 of the Charter has no relevance in this case.

Unfortunately, the court did not articulate a deeper reason for its conclusion that attacks from non-state actors do not implicate the right of self-defense, nor did it cite a legal authority or precedent for this point of law.

Can you construct the outlines of such an argument?

One possible argument is that the international law of *jus ad bellum* only regulates the use of force between sovereign states. In order to justify the use of force against the target state, the doctrine of self-defense must demonstrate that the target state launched an attack first—thus triggering a right of self-defense. In the absence of an original attack from a sovereign state, there is no self-defense justification for violating the sovereign territory of that state. For example, the ICJ in

United States v. Nicaragua described the right of self-defense in the following way:

> 195. In the case of individual self-defence, the exercise of this right is subject to the State concerned having been the victim of an armed attack. Reliance on collective self-defence of course does not remove the need for this. There appears now to be general agreement on the nature of the acts which can be treated as constituting armed attacks. In particular, it may be considered to be agreed that an armed attack must be understood as including not merely action by regular armed forces across an international border, but also "the sending by or on behalf of a State of armed bands, groups, irregulars or mercenaries, which carry out acts of armed force against another State of such gravity as to amount to" (inter alia) an actual armed attack conducted by regular forces, "or its substantial involvement therein". This description, contained in Article 3, paragraph (g), of the Definition of Aggression annexed to General Assembly resolution 3314 (XXIX), may be taken to reflect customary international law. The Court sees no reason to deny that, in customary law, the prohibition of armed attacks may apply to the sending by a State of armed bands to the territory of another State, if such an operation, because of its scale and effects, would have been classified as an armed attack rather than as a mere frontier incident had it been carried out by regular armed forces. But the Court does not believe that the concept of "armed attack" includes not only acts by armed bands where such acts occur on a significant scale but also assistance to rebels in the form of the provision of weapons or logistical or other support. Such assistance may be regarded as a threat or use of force, or amount to intervention in the internal or external affairs of other States. It is also clear that it is the State which is the victim of an armed attack which must form and declare the view that it has been so attacked. There is no rule in customary international law permitting another State to exercise the right of collective self-defence on the basis of its own assessment of the situation. Where collective self-defence is invoked, it is to be expected that the State for whose benefit this right is used will have declared itself to be the victim of an armed attack.

Note the language from the "Definition of Aggression" resolution that was cited by the ICJ: "the sending by or on behalf of a State. . ." This suggests that the original attack must be at the behest of some state. At least one scholar has argued that although the *Nicaragua* approach governed the pre-9/11 understanding on the matter, at least some states changed their view of the matter after the al-Qaeda attacks:

> One of the most difficult questions arising out of 9/11 is whether the concept of "armed attack" in Article 51 has undergone a revolutionary change so that it now extends to attacks by non-state actors even if there is very little or no state complicity. But even if there could hypothetically be an armed attack in the absence of state complicity in that attack, the question of the permissible response is much more problematic. For many states and commentators the concept of self-defence against non-state actors was unacceptable before 9/11.

Christine Gray, *International Law and the Use of Force* 199 (3d ed. 2008). That being the case, the fact that a few states altered their thinking on the matter is not, by itself, conclusive evidence in a shift in customary international law on the matter. The question is which interpretation of Article 51 is correct.

The other side of the argument is that Article 51 of the UN Charter says nothing about the source of the armed attack. Indeed, the language of Article 51 seems to make a deliberate point of using the passive voice in the phrase "if an armed attack occurs" against a Member State. By its own terms, Article 51 does not impose any restriction on the source of the armed attack. For example, after the September 9/11 attacks against the United States, the UN Security Council explicitly noted that the attacks triggered the right of self-defense, even though it was clear by that time that the attacks were most probably a terrorist attack from a non-state actor. See S.C. Res. 1368 (2001) ("*Recognizing* the inherent right of individual or collective self-defence in accordance with the Charter. . . . *Unequivocally condemns* in the strongest terms the horrifying terrorist attacks which took place on 11 September 2001 in New York, Washington (D.C.) and Pennsylvania and *regards* such acts, like any act of international terrorism, as a threat to international peace and security. . .").

In fact, two judges in the ICJ *Wall* Case vigorously dissented on this point and argued that self-defense applies in response to attacks from non-state actors. One of them, the Dutch jurist Pieter Koojimans, made the following observations:

> 35. *Self-defence*—Israel based the construction of the wall on its inherent right of self-defence as contained in Article 51 of the Charter. In this respect it relied on Security Council resolutions 1368 (2001) and 1373 (2001), adopted after the terrorist attacks of 11 September 2001 against targets located in the United States. The Court starts its response to this argument by stating that Article 51 recognizes the existence of an inherent right of

self-defence in the case of an armed attack by one State against another State. Although this statement is undoubtedly correct, as a reply to Israel's argument it is, with all due respect, beside the point. Resolutions 1368 (2001) and 1373 (2001) recognize the inherent right of individual or collective self-defence without making any reference to an armed attack by a State. The Security Council called acts of international terrorism, without any further qualification, a threat to international peace and security which authorizes it to act under Chapter VII of the Charter. And it actually did so in resolution 1373 (2001) without ascribing these acts of terrorism to a particular State. This is the completely new element in these resolutions. This new element is not excluded by the terms of Article 51 since this conditions the exercise of the inherent right of self-defence on a previous armed attack without saying that this armed attack must come from another State even if this has been the generally accepted interpretation for more than 50 years. The Court has regrettably by-passed this new element, the legal implications of which cannot as yet be assessed but which marks undeniably a new approach to the concept of self-defence.

Separate Opinion of Judge Koojimans, para. 35. For an extensive discussion of this dispute, see also Noam Lubell, *Extraterritorial Use of Force Against Non-State Actors* 30–36 (2010).

Which argument is most convincing?

2.   CYBER-ATTACKS AS 'ARMED ATTACKS'

Imagine that a state uses computer hackers to launch a cyber-attack against the physical or computer infrastructure of another state. Attacks of this nature are becoming increasingly common as some states lean on cyber-superiority as a way of neutralizing another state's superiority in conventional military technology. With great sophistication (and sometimes anonymity), a state could launch a cyber-attack that neutralizes or damages any number of systems in a target state, including: banking systems, environmental systems, water treatment plants, or electrical grids. A cyber-attack might also be designed to steal confidential security information (regarding either personnel or weapons systems) or to steal financial information such as credit card numbers. Any of these attacks can be quite destructive to the security or economy of the target state. Some of these attacks might be described as cyber-espionage or cyber-theft. But might some of them constitute an "armed attack" within the definition of Article 51 of the UN Charter, thus triggering a right of self-defense? If the answer to that question is yes, would the right to defensive force require a cyber-response or might the victim of the original attack respond with traditional military force?

In 2009, an international group of experts were convened in Estonia by NATO to craft a document that articulated the governing principles of cyber-war. The resulting document, the *Tallinn Manual on the International Law Applicable to Cyber Warfare*, articulates a series of rules that ought to govern cyber-attacks. With regard to whether cyber-attacks can trigger self-defense under Article 51 of the UN Charter, here is what the Tallinn Manual says: "A State that is the target of a cyber operation that rises to the level of an armed attack may exercise its inherent right of self-defence. Whether a cyber operation constitutes an armed attack depends on its scale and effects." See *Tallinn Manual*, Rule 13, at 54. Accordingly, the experts concluded that a cyber-attack could constitute an "armed attack" within the meaning of the doctrine of self-defense, though only if the "scale and effects" were sufficient—language that was borrowed from the ICJ's *Nicaragua* case. How should the test be applied? The experts could not predetermine the outcome of this analysis:

> Therefore, the parameters of the scale and effects criteria remain unsettled beyond the indication that they need to be grave. That said, some cases are clear. The International Group of Experts agreed that any use of force that injures or kills persons or damages or destroys property would satisfy the scale and effects requirement. They also agreed that acts of cyber intelligence gathering and cyber theft, as well as cyber operations that involve brief or periodic interruption of non-essential cyber services, do not qualify as armed attacks.

See *Tallinn Manual* at 55. Under this approach, a state may fall victim to a number of cyber-intrusions that are not significant enough to trigger a right of military self-defense (because they do not cross the "scale and effects" threshold). In those cases, the intrusions would be internationally wrongful acts for which non-military responses are permitted (including judicial complaints with relevant international bodies, economic sanctions against the offending state, etc.), but no military response would be permitted. What if the offending state engages in a constant barrage of these "pin pricks," none of which is sufficient by itself to trigger a right of self-defense? As one scholar has noted:

> Low-intensity cyber operations, actions taken short of destructive or violent attacks, present a far more likely picture of future state cyber interactions. In addition to being highly feasible and often inexpensive, low-intensity cyber operations offer attractive prospects for anonymity, appear to frustrate attack correlation by targets, and may also reduce the likelihood of provoking severe retaliation.

Sean Watts, *Low-Intensity Cyber Operations and the Principle of Non-Intervention*, in *Cyberwar: Law and Ethics for Virtual Conflicts* 250 (Jens David Ohlin, Kevin Govern, & Claire Finkelstein eds., 2015).

On this point, the *Tallinn* experts concluded that "there are grounds for treating the incidents as a composite armed attack," but they could not reach agreement on the deeper issue of whether cyber-attacks that do not cause physical damage could constitute an "armed attack" for purposes of self defense. At least some scholars—and states—have concluded that "a large-scale cyber attack that shuts down NCIs such as the financial market for a prolonged time and cripples a state's economy or causes the collapse of the national currency would, if the effects are serious enough, potentially amount to an 'armed attack' for the purposes of self-defense." See Marco Roscini, *Cyber Operations and the Use of Force in International Law* 74 (2014) (concluding also that a military response would only be legitimate if the other requirements for self-defense, including necessity and proportionality, were satisfied); Heather Harrison Dinniss, *Cyber Warfare and the Laws of War* 64 (2012) (concluding that in a "military age typified by remote weaponry and stand-off tactics, the criterion of a violated border is also losing its relevance"). As you consider the following problem case, ask yourself under what circumstances a devastating—but non-violent—cyber-attack should constitute an armed attack and trigger the right of self-defense.

PROBLEM CASE

In June 2015, American officials announced that Chinese hackers had penetrated the computer systems of the Office of Personnel Management (OPM), a division of the Interior Department. From that computer system, the Chinese hackers were able to secretly extract unencrypted personnel files on almost a million federal employees who had applied for security clearances. The data trove included sensitive information regarding finances and health. Federal officials believe that the data was stolen, not for financial gain by criminals, but to further the statecraft of the Chinese government.

The Obama Administration sent a stern warning to Chinese officials that cyber-attacks of this sort would not be tolerated by the United States. At the same time, the federal government debated how to retaliate against China for the intrusion.

Applying the principals described in the above section, did the ongoing Chinese attack on the OPM computer server constitute an armed attack for purposes of the doctrine of self-defense? Would the United States be justified in defending itself either through cyber-countermeasures or a military strike in self-defense? In the end, was this a cyber-attack or a case of cyber-espionage, and are the two concepts mutually exclusive?

Now consider two more complex examples, both of which are hypothetical. First, imagine that China had launched a cyber-attack that had disabled the New York Stock Exchange for 7 days. As a result of the vulnerability of the stock exchange computer system, the attack generated widespread investor panic. When the exchange opened again, spooked investors sold frantically and pushed down the value of the market to the lowest level in 10 years. As a result, the U.S. economy plunged back into a deep recession. Would this cyber-attack constitute an "armed attack" under Article 51 of the UN Charter?

> Consider a second hypothetical example. This time imagine that China used a cyber-attack to disable an aircraft carrier. Imagine that the attack was perpetrated when the propulsion system of the ship was outfitted with a new computer system. Hackers managed to penetrate the computer systems of a vendor preparing the computer system and inserted malicious code into the propulsion system. After it was installed, the code was activated and prevented the aircraft carrier from moving. Applying the principles of the *Tallinn Manual*, did this constitute an armed attack?

3. THE CONCEPT OF COLLECTIVE SELF-DEFENSE

There is one situation when the state that deploys defensive force need not have suffered an unlawful attack. Article 51 of the UN Charter explicitly recognizes the legitimacy of collective self-defense, when a group of like-minded states bind together to vindicate the right of self-defense that is triggered by an attack against *one* of the states. In that situation, some of the states exercising defensive force will not have suffered an armed attack. This situation is roughly analogous to defense of others under domestic criminal law, which involves the deployment of defensive force to protect a third party from an unlawful attack. The key principle that unifies both of these doctrines—defense of others or collective self-defense—is that the third party's right to use defensive force is conceptually linked to the right of the victim state to use self-defense in his or her own capacity. If the victim state has no right of self-defense, third party states have no legal right under international law to come to their aid with military assistance.

In the *Nicaragua* case, the ICJ expounded upon the doctrine of collective self-defense and imposed an additional constraint: the victim state must formally declare that it has been attacked and must formally request assistance from the state that then seeks to justify its military intervention by appealing to collective self-defense. In the absence of a formal request, collective self-defense is not allowed, according to the ICJ. See *Military and Paramilitary Activities in and Against Nicaragua (Nicaragua v. United States)*, 1986 I.C.J. 14 (June 27), para. 165. Why should international law impose this additional hurtle? One argument is that it reduces the danger of pretextual uses of force. One can well imagine a state that uses military force in an aggressive manner and then justifies the behavior by claiming that it is "vindicating" the right of some state that has been attacked. This would give stronger military states the opportunity to opportunistically intervene in any military dispute to their own advantage.

However, the formal request requirement imposes substantial burdens on states whose formal machinery of government may have been compromised by the very attack that triggers their need for assistance. Imagine a state that has been victimized by a swift attack—a Blitzkrieg if you will—that quickly engulfs its territory. If the government is dissolved before a formal request for assistance can be issued, then under the ICJ requirement, there would be no state that could assist the victim state in reclaiming its sovereignty and control over its own territory. This factual situation was not presented in the *Nicaragua* case, so it is unclear whether the ICJ would require formal requests in such a scenario.

Often, mutual assistance is formalized in the form of regional security arrangements such as NATO. Indeed, the negotiating history of Article 51 indicates that the drafters of the UN Charter specifically inserted the language of collective self-defense to clarify that regional security arrangements, such as NATO or the Warsaw Pact, were still legitimate and consistent with the Charter and were not disallowed by the Security Council's primary authority over security matters. See Ruth B. Russell, *A History of the United Nations Charter: The Role of the United States, 1940–1945* (1958).

B. IMMINENCE

Article 51 of the UN Charter uses the phrase "if an armed attack occurs" but it is silent—or at the very least vague—on the temporal requirement. One strict interpretation of the requirement is that the attack must be ongoing, i.e., in progress, before the target of the attack is given a right of military response under international law. See Jordan J. Paust, *Armed Attacks and Imputation: Would a Nuclear Weaponized Iran Trigger Permissible Israeli and U.S. Measures of Self-Defense?*, 45 Georgetown J. Int'l L. 411, 415–17, 419 (2014) ("It is important to note, however, that an imminent threat logically and by definition is not even a present threat and use of such a remarkably expansive criterion as a trigger for permissible use of force in self-defense would be legal nonsense."). In contrast, a more permissive interpretation of Article 51 suggests that the attack must be "imminent"—i.e., on the horizon. Although most publicists support the imminence standard for self-defense, that does not end the matter. The difficulty comes in applying the imminence standard and providing additional content to what remains a rather vague and indeterminate legal standard.

In one sense, though, the concept of an imminent armed attack is no more indeterminate than in the law of self-defense in criminal law, which also requires an imminent threat to an actor's life or bodily integrity before a lethal response will be justified by the criminal law. In that situation, it is up to the jury, as the fact-finder, to determine whether the attack was sufficiently imminent to warrant a lethal response. Public International Law is no different, with the possible exception that avenues for direct litigation in court are comparatively fewer. Nonetheless, there are concrete examples of imminent attacks where self-defense has been supported by the world community, and cases of non-imminent attacks where putative self-defense has been widely condemned. These responses help articulate the outer contours of the imminence standard.

1. BATTERED NATIONS

Recently, some governments have started pushing for a more relaxed understanding of the imminence requirement. This relaxation can take one of two forms: either the state can argue that imminence in practice should be broadly construed, or the state can argue that imminence itself is a quaint relic of the past and ought to be abandoned. This argument is sometimes buttressed by the fact that, as explained above, Article 51 of the UN Charter says nothing specific about the temporality requirement.

To understand and evaluate the legitimacy of these proposals, one must consider other areas of the law where imminence has historically played a central role, but has recently withstood substantial criticism. Consider, for example, the imminence requirement for self-defense as a justification under domestic criminal law. Most state jurisdictions in the United States have required, and continue to require, the existence of an *imminent* threat to a person's life or bodily integrity before that person is entitled to use lethal force in self-defense. Some defense attorneys believed that the imminence requirement was too strict and prevented some defendants from succeeding in their self-defense claims when their actions ought to have been vindicated by the law. These arguments were pressed in cases involving women who were tormented for years by abusive husbands or boyfriends. In at least some of these cases, the women killed their abusers during moments of relative tranquility, such as when the abusers were sleeping or resting. In these cases, the imminence requirement was possibly fatal to the self-defense claim; when the abuser was sleeping, it could not be the case that the woman faced an imminent threat to her life or serious bodily injury. In response, counselors for these women pressed courts to allow them to present psychological evidence of Battered Women's Syndrome—a psychiatric condition whereby the women were so overwhelmed by years of abuse that they believed that force was required even when no threatening attack was imminent upon them. Similarly, the U.S. Model Penal Code, adopted in 1962, abandoned the imminence requirement in favor of a standard of "immediate necessity," which will be discussed below.

Some advocates have suggested, by analogy, that imminence should be dropped as a requirement for self-defense under international law. At least some of these arguments have adapted the language of Battered Women's Syndrome for the international context. The resulting academic theory, Battered Nations Syndrome, suggests that states under a constant threat of military invasion ought to be judged by a different standard. For them, military action might seem reasonable even if an armed attack is not imminent. Should these "battered nations" receive preferential treatment, just like a battered spouse? See, e.g., Kimberly Kessler Ferzan, *Defending Imminence: From Battered Women to Iraq*, 46 Ariz. L. Rev. 213 (2004); Shana Wallace, Comment, *Beyond Imminence: Evolving International Law and Battered Women's Right to Self-Defense*, 71 U. Chi. L. Rev. 1749, 1751 (2004); Jane Campbell Moriarty, *"While Dangers Gather": The Bush Preemption Doctrine, Battered Women, Imminence and Anticipatory Self-Defense*, 30 N.Y.U. Rev. L. & Soc. Change 1 (2005). Although this theory has received extensive treatment in the scholarly literature, no state has explicitly justified its behavior using these terms. However, as described below, several states *have* questioned how imminence should be applied and whether the traditional understanding of the concept should be widened.

2.   PREEMPTIVE VERSUS PREVENTIVE SELF-DEFENSE

Some states have attempted to broaden the insights described above into a broader doctrine called preemptive war. Under this theory, the goal of self-defense is to "preempt" the launching of the very attack that will threaten the innocent nation. The whole point of preemptive self-defense is to preempt the need to use self-defense during an *actual* armed attack. The doctrine of preemptive force is consistent with the imminence requirement in the sense that defensive force is being used to preemptively repel an imminent armed attack. However, in some instances the language of "preemption" is designed to emphasize that the imminence requirement should be broadly construed. For example, in a speech at West Point Military Academy on June 1, 2002, President George W. Bush declared that:

> We must adapt the concept of imminent threat to the capabilities and objectives of today's adversaries. Rogue states and terrorists do not seek to attack us using conventional means. They know such attacks would fail. Instead, they rely on acts of terror and, potentially, the use of weapons of mass destruction—weapons that can be easily concealed, delivered covertly, and used without warning. The targets of these attacks are our military forces and our civilian population, in direct violation of one of the principal norms of the law of warfare. As was demonstrated by the losses on September 11, 2001, mass civilian casualties is the specific objective of terrorists and these losses would be exponentially more severe if terrorists acquired and used weapons of mass destruction. The United States has long maintained the option of preemptive actions to counter a sufficient threat to our national security. The greater the threat, the greater is the risk of inaction—and the more compelling the case for taking anticipatory action to defend ourselves, even if uncertainty remains as to the time and place of the enemy's

attack. To forestall or prevent such hostile acts by our adversaries, the United States will, if necessary, act preemptively.

After 9/11, the United States government, under the leadership of President George W. Bush, occasionally advanced an even broader doctrine—the concept of Preventive Self-Defense. Under this doctrine, sometimes referred to as the Bush Doctrine, an innocent state is entitled to exercise military force in self-defense against a rogue nation in order to prevent that state from acquiring the capacity to use military force against the innocent state. In one speech, President Bush declared:

> The cause of peace requires all free nations to recognize new and undeniable realities. In the 20th century, some chose to appease murderous dictators, whose threats were allowed to grow into genocide and global war. In this century, when evil men plot chemical, biological and nuclear terror, a policy of appeasement could bring destruction of a kind never before seen on this earth. Terrorists and terror states do not reveal these threats with fair notice, in formal declarations—and responding to such enemies only after they have struck first is not self-defense, it is suicide. The security of the world requires disarming Saddam Hussein now.

George W. Bush, Televised Address, Washington, D.C., March 17, 2003. Members of the Bush Administration argued that the Bush Doctrine was a necessary amendment to the rules regarding self-defense for the 21st Century. For example, two administration lawyers wrote that:

> We argue that there are deep and pervasive similarities between, on the one hand, a preventive war undertaken to protect American or allied civilian populations from an emerging threat that weapons of mass destruction might be used against them and, on the other hand, a humanitarian intervention—like that in Kosovo—to protect another population from genocide, forcible deportations, or other grave human rights abuses. In both circumstances, the intervening powers would have a protective purpose in view. In the first case, the objective of the intervening powers would be the protection of their own people; in the second case, the objective would be the protection of another people or at-risk group. In both cases, the intervening powers would also be employing force to counteract a threat of violence-a threat that would be large in scale and gross in illegality in either context. In the first case, the threat would involve intentional mass attacks on non-combatants. In the second case, the threat would involve severe and widespread danger to basic human rights. The targeted states in both cases would have wrongfully subjected others to

unacceptable harm or risk of harm-either internally, by failing to protect their citizens from genocide and other gross human rights violations, or externally, by posing security threats to the citizens of other states, whether by acquiring weapons of mass destruction themselves for aggressive purposes, or by sheltering (or failing to control) terrorists willing to use such weapons. Fundamentally, the aims of both the preventive and humanitarian interventions in question are to uphold the "strong global ethic" against the mass killing of civilians and other equally catastrophic events.

Robert J. Delahunty & John Yoo, *The "Bush Doctrine": Can Preventive War Be Justified?*, 32 Harv. J. L. & Pub. Pol'y 843 (2009).

Is preventive self-defense consistent with the principles articulated in the UN Charter? Do you believe that preventive self-defense is consistent with customary international law?

PROBLEM CASE

After 9/11, the United States was on heightened alert. President George W. Bush argued that the government of Iraq, led by its dictator Saddam Hussein, was planning to launch attacks against the United States and its allies. This was not the first war between the United States and Iraq. Iraq had invaded its neighbor Kuwait in 1990, prompting an international coalition led by the United States to invade Iraqi territory to push its military out of Kuwait. The American-led coalition succeeded in its effort and the Iraqi army was crushed, though Saddam Hussein retained control over his government. After the war was ended, the U.S.-led coalition imposed a no-fly zone over parts of Iraq to keep Hussein in check, and also instituted a system of weapons inspections overseen by the United Nations to ensure that Hussein did not produce more weapons of mass destruction (WMD).

After 9/11, the Bush Administration became convinced that Hussein had successfully eluded the weapons inspections and was stockpiling new weapons that could be used to target the United States. The Bush Administration also suggested that the Iraqi government was cooperating with terrorist organizations such as al-Qaeda to launch future terrorist attacks against the United States.

Based on these concerns, President Bush ordered an invasion of Iraq on March 19, 2003. The legal arguments in support of the intervention were multiple. First, the Bush Administration argued that the U.N. Security Council authorizations for the first war in 1990 were still in effect—and could be used by the United States has a justification for the 2003 invasion. Second, some administration officials suggested that the 2003 invasion was justified by self-defense under a theory of either preemptive or preventive self-defense. In other words, the U.S. could legally strike first even though there was no attack against the U.S. on the horizon.

Was the 2003 invasion consistent with Article 51 of the UN Charter? Was the imminence requirement for self-defense satisfied in this case? After the invasion, the U.S. military dedicated a special team to searching Iraq for Hussein's stockpile of WMD; they were never found. Apparently, Hussein was complying with the relevant Security Council resolutions that he forgo producing WMD. Furthermore, intelligence reports indicating that Iraqi officials were conspiring with al-Qaeda operatives were eventually discredited.

With this information in mind, evaluate the legality of the invasion with particular regard to the requirement of imminence. How should imminence be defined in this context? Did the U.S. stretch the requirements of imminence too far?

Having considered the problem case, now examine an excerpt from the Chilcot Report, the formal outcome of an exhaustive public inquiry in Britain into the legality of the invasion of Iraq by UK and US forces.

Report of the Iraq Inquiry

(The "Chilcot Report")
July 6, 2016

Was Iraq a serious or imminent threat?

On 18 March 2003, the House of Commons was asked:

- to recognise that Iraq's weapons of mass destruction and long-range missiles, and its continuing non-compliance with Security Council resolutions, posed a threat to international peace and security; and

- to support the use of all means necessary to ensure the disarmament of Iraq's weapons of mass destruction, on the basis that the United Kingdom must uphold the authority of the United Nations as set out in resolution 1441 and many resolutions preceding it.

In his statement, Mr. Blair addressed both the threat to international peace and security presented by Iraq's defiance of the UN and its failure to comply with its disarmament obligations as set out in resolution 1441 (2002). Iraq was "the test of whether we treat the threat seriously".

Mr. Blair rehearsed the Government's position on Iraq's past pursuit and use of weapons of mass destruction; its failures to comply with the obligations imposed by the UN Security Council between 1991 and 1998; Iraq's repeated declarations which proved to be false; and the "large quantities of weapons of mass destruction" which were "unaccounted for". He described UNSCOM's final report (in January 1999) as "a withering indictment of Saddam's lies, deception and obstruction". Mr. Blair cited the UNMOVIC "clusters" document issued on 7 March as "a remarkable document", detailing "all the unanswered questions about Iraq's weapons of mass destruction", listing "29 different areas in which the inspectors have been unable to obtain information". He stated that, based on Iraq's false declaration, its failure to co-operate, the unanswered questions in the UNMOVIC "clusters" document, and the unaccounted for material, the Security Council should have convened and condemned Iraq as in material breach of its obligations. If Saddam Hussein continued to fail to co-operate, force should be used.

Addressing the wider message from the issue of Iraq, Mr. Blair asked: ". . . what . . . would any tyrannical regime possessing weapons of mass destruction think when viewing the history of the world's diplomatic dance with Saddam over . . . 12 years? That our capacity to pass firm resolutions has only been matched by our feebleness in implementing them."

Mr. Blair acknowledged that Iraq was "not the only country with weapons of mass destruction", but declared: "back away from this confrontation now, and future conflicts will be infinitely worse and more devastating in their effects". Mr. Blair added: "The real problem is that . . . people dispute Iraq is a threat, dispute the link between terrorism and weapons of mass destruction, and dispute in other words, the whole basis of our assertion that the two together constitute a fundamental assault on our way of life." Mr. Blair also described a "threat of chaos and disorder" arising from "tyrannical regimes with weapons of mass destruction and extreme terrorist groups" prepared to use them. Mr. Blair set out his concerns about:

- proliferators of nuclear equipment or expertise;

- "dictatorships with highly repressive regimes" who were "desperately trying to acquire" chemical, biological or, "particularly, nuclear weapons capability"—some of those were "a short time away from having a serviceable nuclear weapon," and that activity was increasing, not diminishing; and

- the possibility of terrorist groups obtaining and using weapons of mass destruction, including a "radiological bomb."

Those two threats had very different motives and different origins. He accepted "fully" that the association between the two was: ". . . loose— but it is hardening. The possibility of the two coming together—of terrorist groups in possession of weapons of mass destruction or even of a so called dirty radiological bomb—is now in my judgement, a real and present danger to Britain and its national security." Later in his speech, Mr. Blair stated that the threat which Saddam Hussein's arsenal posed: ". . . to British citizens at home and abroad cannot simply be contained. Whether in the hands of his regime or in the hands of the terrorists to whom he would give his weapons, they pose a clear danger to British citizens. . ."

This fusion of long-standing concerns about proliferation with the post-9/11 concerns about mass-casualty terrorism was at the heart of the Government's case for taking action at this time against Iraq. The UK assessment of Iraq's capabilities set out in Section 4 of the Report shows:

- The proliferation of nuclear, chemical and biological weapons and their delivery systems, particularly ballistic missiles, was regarded as a major threat. But Iran, North Korea and Libya were of greater concern than Iraq in terms of the risk of nuclear and missile proliferation.

- JIC Assessments, reflected in the September 2002 dossier, had consistently taken the view that, if sanctions were removed or became ineffective, it would take Iraq at least five years following the end of sanctions to produce enough fissile material for a weapon. On 7 March, the IAEA had reported to the Security Council that there was no indication that Iraq had resumed its nuclear activities.

- The September dossier stated that Iraq could produce a nuclear weapon within one to two years if it obtained fissile material and other essential components from a foreign supplier. There was no evidence that Iraq had tried to acquire fissile material and other components or—were it able to do so—that it had the technical capabilities to turn these materials into a usable weapon.

- JIC Assessments had identified the possible stocks of chemical and biological weapons which would largely have been for short-range, battlefield use by the Iraqi armed forces. The JIC had also judged in the September dossier that Iraq was producing chemical and biological agents and that there were development programmes for longer-range missiles capable of delivering them.

- Iraq's proscribed Al Samoud 2 missiles were being destroyed.

The UK Government did have significant concerns about the potential risks of all types of weapons of mass destruction being obtained by Islamist extremists (in particular Al Qaida) who would be prepared to use such weapons. Saddam Hussein's regime had the potential to proliferate material and know-how, to terrorist groups, but it was not judged likely to do so. On 28 November 2001, the JIC assessed that:

- Saddam Hussein had "refused to permit any Al Qaida presence in Iraq".

- Evidence of contact between Iraq and Usama Bin Laden (UBL) was "fragmentary and uncorroborated"; including that Iraq had been in contact with Al Qaida for exploratory discussions on toxic materials in late 1988.

- "With common enemies ... there was clearly scope for collaboration."

- There was "no evidence that these contacts led to practical co-operation; we judge it unlikely . . . There is no evidence UBL's organisation has ever had a presence in Iraq."

- Practical co-operation between Iraq and Al Qaida was "unlikely because of mutual mistrust".

- There was "no credible evidence of covert transfers of WMD-related technology and expertise to terrorist groups".

On 29 January 2003, the JIC assessed that, despite the presence of terrorists in Iraq "with links to Al Qaida", there was "no intelligence of current co-operation between Iraq and Al Qaida". On 10 February 2003, the JIC judged that Al Qaida would "not carry out attacks under Iraqi direction". Sir Richard Dearlove told the Inquiry: ". . . I don't think the Prime Minister ever accepted the link between Iraq and terrorism. I think it would be fair to say that the Prime Minister was very worried about the possible conjunction of terrorism and WMD, but not specifically in relation to Iraq . . . [I] think, one could say this is one of his primary national security concerns given the nature of Al Qaida."

The JIC assessed that Iraq was likely to mount a terrorist attack only in response to military action and if the existence of the regime was threatened. The JIC Assessment of 10 October 2002 stated that Saddam Hussein's "overriding objective" was to "avoid a US attack that would threaten his regime". The JIC judged that, in the event of US-led military action against Iraq, Saddam would: ". . . aim to use terrorism or the threat of it. Fearing the US response, he is likely to weigh the costs and benefits carefully in deciding the timing and circumstances in which terrorism is used. But intelligence on Iraq's capabilities and intentions in this field is limited." The JIC also judged that:

- Saddam's "capability to conduct effective terrorist attacks" was "very limited."

- Iraq's "terrorism capability" was "inadequate to carry out chemical or biological attacks beyond individual assassination attempts using poisons."

The JIC Assessment of 29 January 2003 sustained its earlier judgements on Iraq's ability and intent to conduct terrorist operations. Sir David Omand, the Security and Intelligence Co-ordinator in the Cabinet Office from 2002 to 2005, told the Inquiry that, in March 2002, the Security Service judged that the "threat from terrorism from Saddam's own intelligence apparatus in the event of an intervention in Iraq . . . was judged to be limited and containable."

Baroness Manningham-Buller, the Director General of the Security Service from 2002 to 2007, confirmed that position, stating that the Security Service felt there was "a pretty good intelligence picture of a threat from Iraq within the UK and to British interests". Baroness Manningham-Buller added that subsequent events showed the judgement that Saddam Hussein did not have the capability to do anything much in the UK, had "turned out to be the right judgement."

While it was reasonable for the Government to be concerned about the fusion of proliferation and terrorism, there was no basis in the JIC Assessments to suggest that Iraq itself represented such a threat. The UK Government assessed that Iraq had failed to comply with a series of UN resolutions. Instead of disarming as these resolutions had demanded, Iraq was assessed to have concealed materials from past inspections and to have taken the opportunity of the absence of inspections to revive its WMD programmes.

In Section 4, the Inquiry has identified the importance of the ingrained belief of the Government and the intelligence community that Saddam Hussein's regime retained chemical and biological warfare capabilities, was determined to preserve and if possible enhance its capabilities, including at some point in the future a nuclear capability, and was pursuing an active and successful policy of deception and concealment.

This construct remained influential despite the lack of significant finds by inspectors in the period leading up to military action in March 2003, and even after the Occupation of Iraq. Challenging Saddam Hussein's "claim" that he had no weapons of mass destruction, Mr. Blair said in his speech on 18 March:

- "...we are asked to believe that after seven years of obstruction and non-compliance... he [Saddam Hussein] voluntarily decided to do what he had consistently refused to do under coercion."

- "We are asked now seriously to accept that in the last few years—contrary to all history, contrary to all intelligence— Saddam decided unilaterally to destroy those weapons. I say that such a claim is palpably absurd."

- "...Iraq continues to deny that it has any weapons of mass destruction, although no serious intelligence service anywhere in the world believes it."

- "What is perfectly clear is that Saddam is playing the same old games in the same old way. Yes, there are minor concessions, but there has been no fundamental change of heart or mind."

At no stage was the proposition that Iraq might no longer have chemical, biological or nuclear weapons or programmes identified and examined by either the JIC or the policy community.

Intelligence and assessments were used to prepare material to be used to support Government statements in a way which conveyed certainty without acknowledging the limitations of the intelligence. Mr. Blair's statement to the House of Commons on 18 March was the culmination of a series of public statements and interviews setting out the urgent need for the international community to act to bring about Iraq's disarmament in accordance with those resolutions, dating back to February 2002, before his meeting with President Bush at Crawford on 5 and 6 April.

As Mr. Cook's resignation statement on 17 March made clear, it was possible for a Minister to draw different conclusions from the same information. Mr. Cook set out his doubts about Saddam Hussein's ability to deliver a strategic attack and the degree to which Iraq posed a "clear and present danger" to the UK. The points Mr. Cook made included:

- "...neither the international community nor the British public is persuaded that there is an urgent and compelling reason for this military action in Iraq."

- "Over the past decade that strategy [of containment] had destroyed more weapons than in the Gulf War, dismantled Iraq's nuclear weapons programme and halted Saddam's medium and long range missile programmes."

- "Iraq probably has no weapons of mass destruction in the commonly understood sense of the term—namely a credible device capable of being delivered against a strategic city target. It probably . . . has biological toxins and battlefield chemical munitions, but it has had them since the 1980s when US companies sold Saddam anthrax agents and the then British Government approved chemical and munitions factories. Why is it now so urgent that we should take military action to disarm a military capacity that has been there for twenty years, and which we helped to create? Why is it necessary to resort to war this week, while Saddam's ambition to complete his weapons programme is blocked by the presence of UN inspectors?"

On 12 October 2004, announcing the withdrawal of two lines of intelligence reporting which had contributed to the pre-conflict judgements on mobile biological production facilities and the regime's intentions, Mr. Straw stated that he did: ". . . not accept, even with hindsight, that we were wrong to act as we did in the circumstances that we faced at the time. Even after reading all the evidence detailed by the Iraq Survey Group, it is still hard to believe that any regime could behave in so self-destructive a manner as to pretend that it had forbidden weaponry, when in fact it had not."

Iraq had acted suspiciously over many years, which led to the inferences drawn by the Government and the intelligence community that it had been seeking to protect concealed WMD assets. When Iraq denied that it had retained any WMD capabilities, the UK Government accused it of lying. This led the Government to emphasise the ability of Iraq successfully to deceive the inspectors, and cast doubt on the investigative capacity of the inspectors. The role of the inspectors, however, as was often pointed out, was not to seek out assets that had been hidden, but rather to validate Iraqi claims. By March 2003, however:

- The Al Samoud 2 missiles which exceeded the range permitted by the UN, were being destroyed.

- The IAEA had concluded that there was no Iraqi nuclear programme of any significance.

- The inspectors believed that they were making progress and expected to achieve more co-operation from Iraq.

- The inspectors were preparing to step up their activities with U2 flights and interviews outside Iraq.

When the UK sought a further Security Council resolution in March 2003, the majority of the Council's members were not persuaded that the inspections process, and the diplomatic efforts surrounding it, had reached the end of the road. They did not agree that the time had come to terminate inspections and resort to force. The UK went to war without the explicit authorisation which it had sought from the Security Council. At the time of the Parliamentary vote of 18 March, diplomatic options had not been exhausted. The point had not been reached where military action was the last resort.

3. IMMINENCE IN TARGETED KILLINGS

During the Obama Administration, the United States began an aggressive campaign of targeted killings against suspected members of al-Qaeda and other terrorist organizations who were involved in planning or perpetrating future attacks against the United States and its allies. In most cases these killings were carried out using Remotely Piloted Vehicles—drones—although in some instances manned aircraft or special operations ground forces were used. The official U.S. position is that these killings were performed pursuant to an armed conflict against Al-Qaeda and other terrorist organizations and that U.S. actions were justified by national self-defense and consistent with the principles embodied in Article 51 of the UN Charter.

It is a little unclear whether the U.S. government believes that international law requires that *each* killing must satisfy the imminence requirement, or whether international law simply requires that the entire campaign in general meet the imminence standard. In any event, U.S. officials have made clear that, at the very least as a policy matter, targeted killings are only authorized if the target in question is involved in an imminent attack. But what definition of "imminence" do they use? Consider the following quote from Attorney General Eric Holder regarding drone strikes:

> Let me be clear: an operation using lethal force in a foreign country, targeted against a U.S. citizen who is a senior operational leader of al Qaeda or associated forces, and who is actively engaged in planning to kill Americans, would be lawful at least in the following circumstances: First, the U.S. government has determined, after a thorough and careful review, that the individual poses an imminent threat of violent attack against the United States; second, capture is not feasible; and third, the operation would be conducted in a manner consistent with applicable law of war principles.
>
> The evaluation of whether an individual presents an "imminent threat" incorporates considerations of the relevant window of opportunity to act, the possible harm that missing the window would cause to civilians, and the likelihood of heading off future disastrous attacks against the United States. As we learned on 9/11, al Qaeda has demonstrated the ability to strike with little or no notice—and to cause devastating casualties. Its leaders are continually planning attacks against the United States, and they do not behave like a traditional military—wearing uniforms, carrying arms openly, or massing forces in preparation for an attack. Given these facts, the Constitution does not require the President to delay action until some theoretical end-stage of planning—when the precise time, place, and manner of an attack become clear. Such a requirement would create an unacceptably high risk that our efforts would fail, and that Americans would be killed.

Eric Holder, Attorney General of the United States, Speech at Northwestern University School of Law, Chicago, Illinois, March 5, 2012.

How would you evaluate Holder's definition of imminence? Is it consistent with basic principles of international law? In particular, Holder referred to the "relevant window of opportunity to act. . ." This has little to do with the time gap between the defensive force and the future threat. Rather, it relates to the time gap between the defensive force and the necessity for acting. Is this consistent with a basic definition of imminence? Indeed, Holder went out of his way to suggest that the President of the United States need not wait until the final "end-stage" of planning (i.e., when the terrorist attack is imminent) in order to defend itself. One could interpret Holder's argument as an expression of "elongated imminence." See Pardiss Kebriaei, *Distance between Principle and Practice in the Obama Administration's Targeted Killing Program: A Response to Jeh Johnson*, 31 Yale L. & Pol'y Rev 151, 160 (2012). Or one might interpret it as a form of the "immediate necessity" standard that is embodied in the Model Penal Code.

Do you think that Holder's definition bears any resemblance to the doctrine of preemptive self-defense? Although Holder never invoked that label explicitly, he seemed to suggest that the U.S. would kill a suspected terrorist if he or she was planning a terrorist attack far in the future, but the *only* opportunity for the U.S. to act was the moment when they deployed defensive force. Does this suggest a type of *preemptive* force? With that question in mind, consider the following report issued by the British parliament regarding the legal justification for drone strikes carried out by the British forces:

The Government's Policy on the Use of Drones for Targeted Killing

House of Lords & House of Commons Joint Committee on Human Rights
April 27, 2016

The Right of Self-Defence in International Law

As the Government rightly observes, any use of lethal force abroad outside of armed conflict must, first, be lawful under the international law on the use of force which governs whether a State is entitled to resort to force at all. The Government invokes the inherent right to self-defence against a threat of imminent armed attack.

Whether the right of self-defence can be exercised where the threat of armed attack emanates from non-state actors such as ISIL/Da'esh who are not acting under the control or direction of another state is an issue which is not clearly settled in international law. Some international lawyers appear to take the view that the right of self-defence can only be invoked against another State. Others, including the Government, take the view that a State's inherent right of self-defence extends to attacks originating from non-state actors such as ISIL/Da'esh. State practice since 9/11 certainly supports the view that a State's right of self-defence includes the right to respond with force to an actual or imminent armed attack by a non-State actor, and the most recent UN Security Council Resolution 2249 (2015) lends support to this view. To be entitled to rely on self-defence against non-state actors, the State from whose territory the armed attack is being launched or prepared for must be unable or unwilling to prevent the attack.

The Government's position is that the right of self-defence can be invoked against nonstate actors such as ISIL/Da'esh operating in another state which is unwilling or unable to prevent the attack by the non-state actors. The Prime Minister told the Commons in the run up to the debate on extending authorisation for use of military force to Syria that "there is a solid basis of evidence on which to conclude, first, that there is a direct link between the presence and activities of ISIL in Syria and its ongoing attack on Iraq, and secondly, that the Assad regime is unwilling and/or unable to take action necessary to prevent ISIL's continuing attack on Iraq, or indeed attacks on us."

We accept the Government's argument that there is a right of self-defence against armed attack by non-State actors such as ISIL/Da'esh, and that anticipatory self-defence is also permitted. We have examined carefully two particular aspects of the Government's individual self-defence argument: first, the assertion that the scale and effects of ISIL's campaign reach the level of an "armed attack" and, second, the assertion that the armed attack the UK faces is "imminent" in the sense required by the right of self-defence.

The meaning of "armed attack"

For a State to invoke the right of self-defence there must be an "armed attack" or the threat of an imminent armed attack. To constitute an "armed attack" for the purposes of the right of self-defence the attack must cross a certain threshold of seriousness or intensity. A series of minor attacks is not necessarily enough to constitute an armed attack. The scale and effect of the attack must reach a certain threshold of gravity.

The Prime Minister told the House of Commons that "It is [. . .] clear that ISIL's campaign against the UK and our allies has reached the level of an 'armed attack', such that force may lawfully be used in self-defence to prevent further atrocities being committed by ISIL." The Government's Memorandum similarly states that the scale and effects of ISIL's campaign reach the level of an armed attack against the UK which justifies the use of force to counter it.

It is clear that terrorist attacks by non-State actors such as ISIL/Da'esh can amount to an armed attack on a State. It is not clear, however, what level the Government considers they have to reach in order to constitute an armed attack. The Prime Minister, in his statement on 7 September, referred to six terrorist plots having been foiled in the UK in the preceding 12 months. A number of written submissions that we received pointed out that this raises a question as to the level and scale of violence that the UK considers to be sufficient to cross the threshold between criminal offences and armed attack such that the State is entitled to go beyond counterterrorism law enforcement and use military force on the territory of another state to defend itself.

We note that the UN Security Council, in its Resolution 2249 (2015), refers to "the horrifying terrorist attacks perpetrated by ISIL also known as Da'esh which took place on 26 June 2015 in Sousse, on 10 October 2015 in Ankara, on 31 October 2015 over Sinaï, on 12 November 2015 in Beirut and on 13 November 2015 in Paris, and all other attacks perpetrated by ISIL also known as Da'esh, including hostage-taking and killing", and determines that the threat from ISIL/Da'esh "affects all regions and Member States, even those far from conflict zones."

We accept, as does the UN Security Council, that the attacks on the UK already mounted by ISIL/Da'esh satisfy the requirement that there must be an armed attack on the UK which entitles it to invoke the right to self-defence. However, to provide certainty for the future, we recommend that in its response to our Report the Government provide clarification of its view about the threshold that needs to be met in order for a terrorist attack or threatened attack to constitute an "armed attack" which entitles the Government to invoke its right of self-defence in international law.

The meaning of "imminence"

Although it is not expressly provided for in the UN charter, it is well-established that a State's right of self-defence can be invoked preventively, in anticipation of an armed attack. The UK Government's view has always been that such preventive action in self-defence may only be taken to avert an imminent armed attack.

However the precise meaning of imminence is disputed in international law. Under the long established "Caroline test" for imminence (so called after a 19th century case on the use of force), the need to use force in self-defence must be "instant, overwhelming, leaving no choice of means and no moment for deliberation." However, others argue that the Caroline test is too narrow in the light of modern conditions. In 2004, the then Attorney-General Lord Goldsmith said in the House of Lords: "The concept of what constitutes an 'imminent' armed attack will develop to meet new circumstances and new threats [. . .] It must be right that States are able to act in self-defence in circumstances where there is evidence of further imminent attacks by terrorist groups, even if there is no specific evidence of where such an attack will take place or of the precise nature of the attack."

However, the then Attorney-General distinguished the UK Government's position from the much more expansive US doctrine of pre-emptive self-defence set out in the US's 2002 National Security Strategy: "It is [. . .] the Government's view that international law permits the use of force in self-defence against an imminent attack but does not authorise the use of force to mount a pre-emptive attack against a threat that is more remote."

The Government has made clear, in the course of our inquiry, that it favours a more flexible approach to the meaning of "imminence", to include an ongoing threat of a terrorist attack from an identified individual who has both the intent and the capability to carry out such an attack without notice.

The Attorney General, for example, indicated that he considers that the traditional "Caroline" test for imminence (that the threat must be "instant, overwhelming, leaving no choice of means and no moment for deliberation") needs to be reassessed in the light of modern conditions: "The Caroline case, as you will appreciate, goes back to the 19th century, and we are talking about very different circumstances now. [. . .] One of the things we probably need to think about as a society in any event is what imminence means in the context of a terrorist threat, compared with back in the 1890s when you were probably able to judge imminence by a measure of how many troops you could see on the horizon. That is something that everyone—including the academic world, no doubt—will want to consider, but the basic tenets of acting in self-defence have not changed."

The Secretary of State for Defence also preferred a much more flexible approach to the meaning of imminence:

> Jeremy Lefroy: Secretary of State, to return to the understanding of the word "imminence", because it is clearly very important, in the past an armed attack was considered imminent only if it was so proximate in time that it left no moment for deliberation. Clearly, we live in an era of instant communication and the fact that we are dealing with people who have made it quite clear that they want to kill us at any time and in any way possible means that that definition of "imminent" may have changed a bit. Is your understanding that "imminence" means what it used to mean—that is, so proximate that it leaves no time for deliberation—or have circumstances changed so that an ongoing threat from a specific terrorist is considered imminent all the time?

> Michael Fallon MP: Circumstances have certainly changed from the definition that you have quoted. I would not want to rest on that. You look at these things on a case-by-case basis in the light of the assessment that you make in each particular case. I do not think it is possible to have a hard and fast rule about how you would define "imminent". [. . .]

> The Chair: Basically, to summarise your response to Jeremy's question, an imminent threat can be ongoing: somebody by their very nature, by their ongoing commitment to a particular course of action, can be an ongoing imminent threat by virtue of what they have done in the past and their general way of going about things?

Michael Fallon MP: I am not, as you have probably realised, a lawyer. But yes, an imminent threat can presumably grow in immediacy. It may grow in seriousness. It may grow in likelihood. It may exist for some period of time, absolutely."

We accept that the meaning of "imminence" in the international law of self-defence must be interpreted with a degree of flexibility, in light of modern conditions and in particular the fact that we live in an era of instantaneous communication. A terrorist on the other side of the world may well have the capability to launch a terrorist attack in the UK literally at the touch of a button. While opinion is divided amongst international law experts as to the legally correct interpretation of "imminence" in the international law of self-defence, we note that the broader interpretation of "imminence" preferred by the Government appears to have the implicit support of the UN Security Council in its most recent resolution concerning ISIL/Da'esh in Syria and Iraq.

We welcome the implicit indication in the Government's Memorandum that for the test of imminence to be satisfied the threat must be "genuine" in the sense that there was both an intention to attack and the capability to do so; and that the attack could happen at any moment and without warning. We also note the Government's recent answer to a written question asking the Secretary of State for Defence "what working definition of imminence his Department uses in the application of Article 51 of the UN Charter?" "It has long been the position of successive UK Governments that "the inherent right of self-defence", as recognised in Article 51 of the UN Charter, does not require a State to wait until an armed attack is actually under way before it can lawfully use force to alleviate the threat. A State may use force in anticipation of an armed attack where such an attack is imminent, provided that such force is both necessary and proportionate to averting the threat. The assessments would depend on the facts of each case, with consideration likely to include issues such as the nature and immediacy of the threat, the probability of an attack, its scale and effects and whether it can be prevented without force."

We welcome the Government's indication in this written answer that, while the assessment of imminence will be fact-dependent, it will include consideration of relevant issues which clearly go to the question of imminence, such as the nature and immediacy of the threat and the probability of an attack.

We nevertheless have some concerns about the implications of too expansive a definition of "imminence" for the width of the right of self-defence in international law. Introducing flexibility into the meaning of imminence raises important questions about the degree of proximity that is required between preparatory acts and threatened attacks. Is it enough to trigger the right of self-defence, for example, if there is evidence that an individual is planning terrorist attacks in the UK, or does the preparation need to have gone beyond mere planning? Once a specific individual has been identified as being involved in planning or directing attacks in the UK, does the wider meaning of imminence mean that an ongoing threat from that individual is, in effect, permanently imminent? These questions arise directly in relation to the UK drone strike in Syria on 21 August, as it appears that the authorisation of the use of force may have been given by the National Security Council in May 2015, up to three months before the actual use of lethal force. Whether the test of imminence was in fact satisfied on that occasion will, of course, turn on the intelligence and should therefore be a question for the ISC to consider, not us.

We do not feel that all of these questions about the Government's understanding of the meaning of "imminence" in the international law of self-defence have been fully answered by the end of our inquiry. The Government's interpretation of the concept of "imminence" is crucial because it determines the scope of its policy of using lethal force outside areas of armed conflict. Too flexible an interpretation of imminence risks leading to an overbroad policy, which could be used to justify any member of ISIL/Da'esh anywhere being considered a legitimate target, which in our view would begin to resemble a targeted killing policy.

We therefore recommend that the Government provides, in its response to our Report, clarification of its understanding of the meaning of "imminence" in the international law of self-defence. In particular, we ask the Government to clarify whether it agrees with our understanding of the legal position, that while international law permits the use of force in self-defence against an imminent attack, it does not authorise the use of force pre-emptively against a threat which is too remote, such as attacks which have been discussed or planned but which remain at a very preparatory stage.

Subject to the two questions we have raised above about the Government's understanding of the meaning of "armed attack" and "imminence", we accept the Government's understanding of the international law of self-defence which forms the first part of the legal basis for its policy of using lethal force abroad outside of armed conflict.

C. NECESSITY

In order to qualify as self-defense, a state's deployment of military force must be necessary under the circumstances. In other words, military force in self-defense is only permitted if non-military means of vindicating the state's protective interests are unavailable or have already been exhausted. To take an obvious example, a superficial injury that could be cured with a simple diplomatic overture cannot provide the foundation for military self-defense.

The necessity requirement for self-defense has an ancient lineage. The word "necessity" or "necessary" were mainstays of the 19th Century publicists who wrote about the principle of national self-defense. Also, the concept of necessity took center stage in the famous Caroline incident, which is still cited to this day by international lawyers applying the principles of national self-defense.

1. THE CAROLINE INCIDENT

The first most noteworthy example of the necessity principle is the Caroline incident. In 1837, a group of Canadian rebels were fighting the British and had carved out a self-declared independent Canadian republic near the Niagara River. Their attempt to foment a larger rebellion in Canada had failed. Nonetheless, the Canadian rebels had some sympathizers, including some Americans, who provided them with support. A Canadian militia, which was loyal to the British Government, received intelligence that Americans were supplying arms to the Canadian rebels using a ship called the SS Caroline. The Canadian militia crossed into American waters to capture the Caroline and destroy it.

The destruction of the Caroline, in American waters, by a Canadian militia, sparked a diplomatic row between the United States and Britain, which at that point still ruled Canada. In a letter to the British Government complaining about the incident and demanding a justification for it, U.S. Secretary of State Daniel Webster made the following observations:

> Under these circumstances, and under those immediately connected with the transaction itself, it will be for Her Majesty's Government to show, upon what state of facts, and what rules of national law, the destruction of the "Caroline" is to be defended. It will be for that Government to show a necessity of self-defence, instant, overwhelming, leaving no choice of means, and no moment for deliberation. It will be for it to show, also, that the local authorities of Canada,—even supposing the necessity of the moment authorized them to enter the territories of the United States at all,—did nothing unreasonable or excessive; since the act justified by the necessity of self-defence, must be limited by that necessity, and kept clearly within it. It must be shown that admonition or remonstrance to the persons on board the "Caroline" was impracticable, or would have been unavailing; it must be shown that daylight could not be waited for; that there could be no attempt at discrimination, between the innocent and the guilty; that it would not have been enough to seize and detain the vessel; but that there was a necessity, present and inevitable, for attacking her, in the darkness of the

night, while moored to the shore, and while unarmed men were asleep on board, killing some, and wounding others, and then drawing her into the current, above the cataract, setting her on fire, and, careless to know whether there might not be in her the innocent with the guilty, or the living with the dead, committing her to a fate, which fills the imagination with horror. A necessity for all this, the Government of the United States cannot believe to have existed.

See Letter from Daniel Webster, U.S. Secretary of State, to Lord Ashburton, August 6, 1842, reprinted in 2 *A Digest of International Law* 412 (John Bassett Moore ed., 1906).

The key phrase here is that Webster described the temporal requirement as highly acute: "instant, overwhelming, leaving no choice of means, and no moment for deliberation." This phrase is often cited as evidence for the imminence requirement under customary international law. Although the Webster letter regarding the sinking of the Caroline is merely an expression of one government's views, it is widely regarded as classic example of *opinio juris*: a statement regarding the belief in the legality or illegality of some state practice, backed up in this case by diplomatic objection to the actions of the Canadian militia operating from British territory (Canada). Although the British maintained that the actions of the Canadian loyalists were appropriate under international law—in essence disagreeing with Webster's conclusion—they nonetheless failed to disagree with the Webster's *articulation* of the relevant standard.

Webster's letter in the Caroline affair is often cited as evidence that self-defense is only justified in response to an actual or imminent attack. The Canadian loyalists were only justified in sinking the SS Caroline if it was indeed preparing to imminently participate in another attack by the Canadian rebels. This conclusion might be a misreading of the Webster letter. On closer inspection, the Webster formulation referred somewhat obliquely to questions about imminence, but its central focus was not the temporal nature of the coming attack. Rather, the core of Webster's letter is the temporal nature of the *response*—how important is it for the responding state to attack *now*. That temporal notion is part of Webster's larger complaint about the lack of necessity for the defensive force on the part of the Canadian loyalists. Did they have to act when they did? Could they have not waited until the Caroline crossed into Canadian waters? Did they have to destroy the ship? Were other alternatives available? These constraints apply in any case when a state exercises self-defense. To be necessary, military force must be a last resort.

2. THE UNWILLING OR UNABLE DOCTRINE

The United States has asserted the right to use defensive force against non-state actors, even when the group is located on the territory of a host state that does not consent to the territorial incursion caused by the defensive force. In these situations, there are two legal questions raised by the use of defensive force. First, is self-defense against the non-state actor legitimate? Second, what justification under international law permits the infringement of the host nation's territorial integrity, a potential violation of Article 2(3) of the UN Charter?

Scholars and government lawyers have developed several legal arguments to justify these territorial incursions. The first possibility is that the host state is responsible for, or complicit with, the behavior of the terrorist organization, but that argument depends on an organizational connection between the host state and the non-state actor, which in many cases will be absent. The second possibility is that the territorial incursion is not a use of force against the host state and for that reason does not trigger the prohibition on the use of force articulated in Article 2(3). The far more popular theory is to assert that intervention on the territory of the host nation is permitted when the host state is either "unwilling or unable" to address the threat posed by the non-state actor. Under this theory, the "unwilling or unable" doctrine is an *application* of the criterion of necessity in the doctrine of self-defense. In other words, military force by the intervening state is only necessary in such cases when the host state is unwilling or unable to remediate the threat. For example, the government of Canada wrote in a letter to the Security Council in 2015 that "States must be able to act in self-defence when the Government of the State where a threat is located is unwilling or unable to prevent attacks emanating from its territory." At the time, Canadian military forces were engaged in a coalition fighting the Islamic State on the territory of Syria. Other states have invoked the unwilling or unable test to justify this and similar military incursions against extraterritorial terrorist threats, though other states have spoken out against the legal theory.

Proponents of the unwilling or unable test consider it a relatively straightforward application of the Caroline test. In the Caroline, the Canadian rebels were being assisted by non-state actors on the American side, thus making it "necessary" for the British to cross the border to destroy the ship because the U.S. government was either unwilling or unable to stop the non-state actors operating on its territory. For proponents, just as the historical British were justified in crossing into U.S. territory, so too in the modern age the U.S. is permitted to surge into foreign territory to engage a terrorist threat that a foreign state is unwilling or unable to resolve.

However, the "unwilling or unable" doctrine is controversial among legal scholars and many state governments. Some consider the Caroline an irrelevant historical example because it occurred prior to the adoption of the U.N. Charter and its rules regarding self-defense expressed in article 51. Under this view, article 51 only permits defensive force if the triggering attack can be attributed to the state against which the defensive force is used. For these scholars, the attribution requirement is central to the basic architecture of *jus ad bellum*. It should be noted, though, that the text of article 51 uses open-ended language and simply refers to defensive force "if an armed attack occurs" and does not explicitly specify the required author of the armed attack.

For a discussion of this controversy, compare Ashley S. Deeks, *"Unwilling or Unable": Toward A Normative Framework For Extraterritorial Self-Defense*, 52 Va. J. Int'l L. 483 (2011) ("In today's world, the 'unwilling or unable' test is a key piece in the puzzle of how to regulate force on the international plane."), with Dawood I. Ahmed, *Defending Weak States Against the "Unwilling or Unable" Doctrine of Self-Defense*, 9 J. Int'l L. & Int'l Rel. 1, 14 (2013) ("A lack of any substantive clarity robs the 'unwilling or unable' doctrine of much of its efficacy in guiding state behavior... Alleging that another state is unwilling or unable/ineffective can be a very subjective claim that is open to significant manipulation, particularly because a state's effectiveness to deal with non-state actors may often not be easily observable to other states and thus provides greater room for conflicting and self-serving interpretations.").

The following materials contain a UN report regarding the unwilling or unable doctrine, as well as a Security Council resolution passed in the wake of the 9/11 attacks. Ask yourself what obligations a state has to prevent its territory from being used as a base for terrorist attacks and what consequences—if any—flow from a state's failure to fulfill this obligation of due diligence.

Excerpt from the Report of the Special Rapporteur (Ben Emmerson) on the Promotion and Protection of Human Rights and Fundamental Freedoms While Countering Terrorism

September 18, 2013
UN Doc. A/68/389

Self-defence is the central justification advanced by the Government of the United States for the extraterritorial use of deadly force in counter-terrorism operations. The International Court of Justice has held that in the absence of consent the use of force in self-defence by one State against a non-State armed group located on the territory of another State can be justified only where the actions of the group concerned are imputable to the host State. This may extend to situations in which a non-State armed group is being harboured by the host State. In this analysis, however, absent such a connection, extraterritorial use of force against a non-State armed group in another State is an unlawful violation of sovereignty, and thus potentially an act of aggression, unless it takes place with the host State's consent or the prior authorization of the Security Council.

On the other hand, the United States and some other countries take the view that, subject to particular conditions, the law of self-defence entitles States to engage in non-consensual military operations on the territory of another State against armed groups that pose a direct and immediate threat of attack, even where those groups have no operational connection with their host State. They derive support for this approach from Security Council resolutions 1368 (2001) and 1373 (2001), which were adopted in the wake of the attacks of 11 September 2001. Borrowing from the law of neutrality applicable to international armed conflicts, the United States considers that if, after a reasonable opportunity, the host State has failed effectively to neutralize the threat that emanates from armed groups located within its borders, either because it is unwilling or unable to do so, then the State that is threatened with attack is entitled under the law of self-defence to cross the host State's borders and deploy armed force on its territory for the purpose of taking effective military action in self-defence against the armed group that presents the threat.

Security Council Resolution 1368
September 28, 2001

The Security Council,

Reaffirming the principles and purposes of the Charter of the United Nations,

Determined to combat by all means threats to international peace and security caused by terrorist acts,

Recognizing the inherent right of individual or collective self-defence in accordance with the Charter,

1.   *Unequivocally* condemns in the strongest terms the horrifying terrorist attacks which took place on 11 September 2001 in New York, Washington, D.C. and Pennsylvania and regards such acts, like any act of international terrorism, as a threat to international peace and security;

2.   *Expresses* its deepest sympathy and condolences to the victims and their families and to the people and Government of the United States of America;

3.   *Calls* on all States to work together urgently to bring to justice the perpetrators, organizers and sponsors of these terrorist attacks and

stresses that those responsible for aiding, supporting or harbouring the perpetrators, organizers and sponsors of these acts will be held accountable;

4. *Calls* also on the international community to redouble their efforts to prevent and suppress terrorist acts including by increased cooperation and full implementation of the relevant international anti-terrorist conventions and Security Council resolutions, in particular resolution 1269 (1999) of 19 October 1999;

5. *Expresses* its readiness to take all necessary steps to respond to the terrorist attacks of 11 September 2001, and to combat all forms of terrorism, in accordance with its responsibilities under the Charter of the United Nations;

6. *Decides* to remain seized of the matter.

D. PROPORTIONALITY

Just because a state has a right to exercise self-defense under international law does not necessarily entail that the state can engage in *any* military action it wants once the right of self-defense is triggered. Commentators and scholars agree that the right of national self-defense is limited by the principle of proportionality. See *Military and Paramilitary Activities in and Against Nicaragua (Nicaragua v. United States)*, 1986 I.C.J. 14 (June 27), para. 194 ("The Parties also agree in holding that whether the response to the attack is lawful depends on observance of the criteria of the necessity and the proportionality of the measures taken in self-defence."). Specifically, the nation's exercise of military self-defense must be proportional to the interest that it seeks to vindicate.

Discussions of proportionality in wartime are often confused because the concept of proportionality shows up in at least two different bodies of law. In this chapter we analyze the principle of proportionality with regard to national self-defense. This requires consideration of the threat against the innocent state and asking whether its military actions taken in self-defense are proportional to the nature of the threat it faces. However, the principle of proportionality shows up in a different manner in International Humanitarian Law (IHL), which regulates the *conduct* of warfare during an armed conflict. One basic principle of IHL is that soldiers must limit their attacks to military personnel and military objects. However, attacks against those legitimate targets are still permissible if they also cause collateral damage to innocent civilians—as long as the damage to the civilians is not disproportionate to the military advantage that will be secured by the attack. This principle of proportionality—the prohibition against causing disproportionate civilian casualties—is separate from the proportionality requirement for self-defense under general public international law.

How should the principle of proportionality be applied in cases of national self-defense? Launching a full-scale invasion in response to a metaphorical pinprick is hardly proportional and would exceed the bounds of national self-defense. In real-life situations, though, the self-defense proportionality constraint is much more difficult to evaluate.

Consider one well-known example. On April 2, 1982, the naval forces of Argentina invaded the Falkland Islands. Sovereignty over the islands was disputed, with the Argentinian government claiming a lawful interest in the territory. At the time, however, the islands were controlled by the British government. Their outpost there was guarded by less than 100 members of the British armed forces. The Argentinian naval forces landed with a marine force that quickly overran the British defenses and took control over the islands. In response, the British government sent a much larger naval force to the Falkland Islands to retake the territory, which they succeeded in doing with a combination of air, naval, and marine engagements. The conflict ended on June 14, 1982, after hundreds of casualties.

Putting aside the question of the competing claims to sovereignty over the Islands, analyze the British government's justification for its military action as a case of international self-defense. In response to what they considered to be an unlawful attack against their territory, British forces launched a military response to vindicate their right to the territory. This created an armed conflict between Britain and Argentina. The principle of proportionality restricts the aim that Britain could seek to advance by using military force. In this case, Britain limited its military objective to reclaiming the territory that had been seized, allegedly without legal justification, by Argentina. What if Britain had launched a series of military strikes—by air for example—against strategic targets located on the Argentinian homeland? Or more controversially, what if Britain had launched a ground invasion of Argentina with the goal of occupying Buenos Aires and removing from power the military junta that had ruled Argentina since a coup d'état in 1976? Would such a military campaign be considered proportional under the right of self-defense?

In light of these considerations, consider the following problem case.

PROBLEM CASE

On August 2, 1990, the military forces of Iraq launched a military invasion of Kuwait. Under the leadership of Saddam Hussein, the Iraqi military quickly overran the Kuwaiti armed forces and succeeded in annexing the country of Kuwait. International condemnation of the invasion was quick and near universal. The U.N. Security Council declared the annexation null and void under international law. See S.C. Res. 661, August 6, 1990 ("Decides that annexation of Kuwait by Iraq under any form and whatever pretext has no legal validity, and is considered null and void. . .").

In response to the invasion, American and allied military forces launched a military campaign to push Hussein's forces from Kuwait and restore its previous government to power. The resulting Gulf War was successful in this regard, and Iraqi forces soon retreated back into Iraqi territory. However, coalition forces did not cease military action once Kuwait's territory was secured. Military forces continued to engage the Iraqi army in an attempt, which was largely successful, to degrade the military capability of the Iraqi forces. However, President George H.W. Bush halted military action well before coalition forces could enter Baghdad, the capital of Iraq. Instead, a surrender agreement was negotiated with the government of Saddam Hussein that permitted him to remain in power in Iraq, albeit with substantial constraints. A "no-fly zone" was instituted in the southern and northern areas of Iraq, which prevented Iraqi air forces from flying in those areas, although helicopters were permitted. Also, Hussein was required to give up weapons of mass destruction.

Apply the principle of proportionality to the coalition engagement against Hussein's military forces. Was it proportional for the military forces to continue engaging with Iraqi forces after Kuwait's sovereignty was restored? Or did the proportionality principle require coalition forces to disengage at that point? Would the principle of proportionality have justified a military campaign to take over Iraq, remove Saddam Hussein from power, and institute a regime change? President Bush, in announcing the decision to halt force, simply said: "Kuwait is liberated. Iraq's army is defeated. Our military objectives are met." He did not say that international law, or some deeper principle of proportionality, obligated the coalition to offensive halt military operations. Did it?

Conclusion & Summary

International law permits a state to exercise self-defense to protect itself. This doctrine justifies the use of military force that would otherwise constitute an illegal use of force in violation of the prohibition against the use of military force that is codified in Article 2(4) of the UN Charter. The requirements for the exercise of lawful self-defense include: (1) the existence of an unlawful attack; (2) that is either in progress or imminent; (3) prompting a military response that is necessary (because non-military options are either unavailable or have been exhausted); and (4) the military response is not disproportionate.

In summary, the following observations regarding self-defense are important to remember when applying the materials discussed in this chapter:

1. The ICJ has not applied the doctrine of self-defense in cases involving attacks from non-state actors, though after 9/11 this issue remains deeply contested. The Security Council

indicated that the 9/11 attacks triggered the right of self-defense, suggesting a different view from the ICJ.

2.   The scope and frequency of cyber-attacks will add greater urgency to the question of whether a cyber-attack can constitute an armed attack under Article 51 of the UN Charter, and if so under what conditions. The *Tallinn Manual* concludes that some cyber-attacks could trigger the right of self-defense if the cyber-attack has sufficient "scale and effects."

3.   Applying the temporal scope of the imminence requirement requires a prior determination regarding how much preemptive force is permitted by Article 51 of the UN Charter. The United States, under both the Bush and Obama Administrations, has at times argued for a wide interpretation of imminence.

4.   The principle of proportionality limits what objectives a state may lawfully seek when it responds militarily in self-defense against an imminent or actual attack. The right to respond in self-defense does not automatically entail the right to invade the enemy's territory and overthrow its government.

CHAPTER 10

HUMANITARIAN INTERVENTION

Introduction

The rules on the use of force under international law would appear to be clear. A state may only make recourse to armed force if authorized by the Security Council under Chapter VII of the UN Charter or if justified by the doctrine of self-defense under Article 51. In some situations, however, the Security Council will decline to authorize military force, either because it does not agree that the situation constitutes a threat to international peace and security, or because one of its permanent members uses its veto to block the passage of a binding resolution.

The UN Charter provision on self-defense clearly contemplates that defensive force can be taken in the absence of a Security Council authorization. Indeed, failure to reserve this power to individual states would surely have doomed the UN Charter when it was being negotiated and drafted. However, absent the conditions giving rise to self-defense, many international lawyers believe that the UN Charter grants exclusive authority to the Security Council to determine when and where military intervention is appropriate.

This creates a dilemma. In situations where a state wishes to intervene for purely altruistic reasons—say to stop an on-going massacre or crime against humanity, or relieve a humanitarian catastrophe—the doctrine of self-defense does not apply. The *self* in self-defense is missing in these cases. Is intervention permissible in this context? These cases of humanitarian intervention have plagued international lawyers in recent years. The number of options is limited. Either one concludes that the interventions are illegal and should not be undertaken or one constructs an argument that they are lawful notwithstanding the clear language of the UN Charter. The final possibility is to concede that humanitarian interventions are illegal but that they should be pursued anyway.

The following materials examine the various doctrines that might be used to justify a unilateral humanitarian intervention—a proposition that is highly contested. Section A outlines the genesis of the problem: the decision of NATO to intervene militarily against Serbia over its conduct in the Kosovo region, despite the absence of a Security Council authorization. Section B focuses on the Responsibility to Protect doctrine, which was specifically formulated in the years following the Kosovo intervention as a potential solution to the "problem" of humanitarian intervention. Finally, Section C looks at the doctrine of necessity as an alternative doctrine that some practitioners and scholars have advanced as a possible foundation for unilateral intervention.

A. THE KOSOVO DILEMMA

The Kosovo crisis began in 1998. The former Yugoslavia had broken apart into several independent republics, one of which was Serbia and Montenegro, during the course of several wars that featured widespread violations of the laws and customs of warfare. One region of the newly formed Serbia and Montenegro was called Kosovo, which was composed of mostly ethnic Albanians. Kosovo, while located within Serbia, is geographically close to Albania. Rebels within Kosovo, a fighting unit called the Kosovo Liberation Army (KLA), fought for independence from Serbia in an all-out civil war. The government forces were composed of regular military troops from Serbia and there were reports of paramilitary groups fighting alongside the regular Serbian government troops. Although there were reports of human rights violations on both sides of the conflict, the majority of international observers concluded that the Serbian forces were responsible for the worst of the abuses, which included deportations, murders, sexual assaults, and persecution of ethnic Albanians in an attempt to change the ethnic character of the Kosovo region. (Several Serbian officials were eventually prosecuted at an international tribunal for the offenses).

When diplomatic initiatives failed to stop the civil war, the international community decided to act. On September 23, 1998, the UN Security Council issued Resolution 1199, which made, inter alia, the following demands pursuant to its Chapter VII authority to restore international peace and security:

(a) cease all action by the security forces affecting the civilian population and order the withdrawal of security units used for civilian repression;

(b) enable effective and continuous international monitoring in Kosovo by the European Community Monitoring Mission and diplomatic missions accredited to the Federal Republic of Yugoslavia, including access and complete freedom of movement of such monitors to, from and within Kosovo unimpeded by government authorities, and expeditious issuance of appropriate travel documents to international personnel contributing to the monitoring;

(c) facilitate, in agreement with the UNHCR and the International Committee of the Red Cross (ICRC), the safe return of refugees and displaced persons to their homes and allow free and unimpeded access for humanitarian organizations and supplies to Kosovo;

(d) make rapid progress to a clear timetable, in the dialogue referred to in paragraph 3 with the Kosovo Albanian community called for in resolution 1160 (1998), with the aim of agreeing confidence-building measures and finding a political solution to the problems of Kosovo. . .

Notably absent from the resolution, however, was any authorization for the use of force by member states of the United Nations. On March 24, 1999, military forces under the command of the North Atlantic Treaty Organization (NATO) launched a military campaign against Serbian forces with the stated goal of getting the Serbs to withdraw from Kosovo. Ultimately, the pressure worked, and Serbian leader Slobodan Milosevic agreed to a peace deal that resulted in a Serbian withdrawal from Kosovo, which allowed the Kosovo people to initiate a political process that would eventually result in de facto independence under the protection of UN peacekeepers. The NATO bombing stopped in June of 1999.

The aftermath of the NATO bombing prompted no shortage of hand-wringing among international lawyers and diplomats. Most observers outside of Serbia (and Russia) considered the end-result extremely positive: the Serbs withdrew from Kosovo, the ethnic cleansing was stopped, many refugees returned home, and the Kosovo right to self-determination was protected. However, the *method* by which these results were achieved had troubling implications for the international rule of law. The NATO intervention was neither an example of self-defense nor authorized by the Security Council. Was it therefore illegal? Some international lawyers asked whether the result was indeed a Pyrrhic victory. If the cost of pushing Serbia out of Kosovo was destroying the rule of law and weakening the UN Charter, the downstream results might be disastrous.

In 1999, the Secretary General of the UN, Kofi Annan, gave a speech in which he noted in stark terms the legal conundrum of Kosovo: "It has cast in stark relief the dilemma of what has been called humanitarian intervention: on one side, the question of the legitimacy of an action taken by a regional organization without a United Nations mandate; on the other, the universally recognized imperative of effectively halting gross and systematic violations of human rights with grave humanitarian consequences." The government of Sweden responded by creating an international commission of jurists to study and resolve this question.

As you read the following excerpts from the report, ask yourself whether the NATO intervention against Serbia violated international law. Should the UN Charter provisions on the use of force be interpreted strictly or was Kofi Annan correct when he referred to the UN Charter as a "living document"?

The Kosovo Report
Independent International Commission on Kosovo (2000)*

Military Intervention and International Law

. . . International law as embodied textually in the UN Charter is on the surface clear with respect to the permissible scope for the use of force in international life. The threat or use of force by states is categorically prohibited by Article 2(4). The sole exception set forth in Article 51 is a right of self-defense, but only if exercised in response to a prior armed attack across an international frontier, and then only provisionally. A claim to act in self-defense must be promptly communicated to the UNSC, which is empowered to pass final judgment. The UNSC, in discharging its responsibility for international peace and security under Chapter VII is empowered to authorize the use of force. This narrow interpretation of the legal framework governing the use of force was strongly endorsed by a commanding majority within the International Court of Justice in the *Nicaragua* Case decided in 1986. The only other relevant directive as to the use of force is contained in Article 53, which allows regional organizations to engage in enforcement actions provided that they do so on the basis of UNSC authorization. Although there is a subsidiary argument about implied authorization to use force once a conflict has been formally treated by the UNSC as a threat to international peace and security under Chapter vii of the Charter, it remains difficult to reconcile NATO's recourse to armed intervention on behalf of Kosovo with the general framework of legal rights and duties which determines the legality of the use of force.

It is, however, possible to argue that, running parallel to the Charter's limitations on the use of force, is Charter support for the international promotion and protection of human rights. In this vein it has been asserted that, given the unfolding humanitarian catastrophe precipitated by the Serb pattern of oppressive criminality toward the civilian Albanian population in Kosovo, the use of force by NATO was legitimate, as it was the only practical means available to protect the Albanian Kosovars from further violent abuse. The main difficulty with such a line of argument is that Charter restrictions on the use of force represented a core commitment when the United Nations was established in 1945—a commitment which has reshaped general international law. In contrast, the Charter provisions relating to human rights were left deliberately vague, and were clearly not intended when written to provide a legal rationale for any kind of enforcement, much less a free-standing mandate for military intervention without UNSC approval. Human rights were given a subordinate and marginal role in

---

the UN system in 1945, a role that was understood to be, at most, aspirational.

Any interventionary claim based on human rights would face the additional legal obstacle posed by Article 2(7) which forbids intervention, even by the United Nations, in matters that fall essentially within the "domestic jurisdiction" of states. Even serious infractions of human rights were considered to be matters of domestic jurisdiction when the Charter was drafted, and were not thought to provide any grounds for an external use of force. The more sovereignty-oriented members of the United Nations, including notably China and Russia, continue to support such a view of human rights. Additionally, there has been as yet no clarification by the ICJ or other authoritative body as to the extent to which the evolution of law in relation to international human rights erodes the prohibition on non-defensive uses of force.

However, the Commission recognizes that, in the more than fifty years of UN existence, the status of human rights has changed dramatically. International legal standards have been agreed upon. Numerous NGOs have devoted great energy to their implementation. During the anti-apartheid campaigns of the 1980s, the UN committed itself to the implementation of human rights with respect to South Africa, and even went so far as to reject claims of sovereign rights. European states have shown a willingness to accept external accountability for upholding human rights, including giving their citizens the right to petition for relief to the European Commission on Human Rights. . .

Such developments have led Secretary General Kofi Annan and his two predecessors, Javier Perez de Cuellar and Boutros Boutros Ghali, to insist that the evolution of international human rights standards and support for their implementation has now reached the stage where norms of non-intervention, and the related deference to sovereign rights, no longer apply to the same extent in the face of severe human rights or humanitarian abuses. The organized international community, according to this view, now enjoys a permissible option of humanitarian intervention as one way to protect vulnerable people against severe abuses of human rights, crimes against humanity, and genocide. Nevertheless, prudential considerations still inhibit humanitarian intervention, especially when the effort is likely to require a serious military commitment or involves the risk of provoking a major war. Still, this process of evolution could suggest that interventionary force to uphold human rights in extreme situations of abuse is less inconsistent with the spirit of the UN Charter and general international law than has been suggested by some. . .

International law on these matters is not yet settled, and the fluidity caused by competing doctrines generates controversy and uncertainty. In these settings "coalitions of the willing" provide a subsidiary source of protection for a beleaguered people that cannot summon a response from the UN System, but this in turn creates a concern about the loosening of legal restraints on war and intervention. The Rwanda genocide in 1994 reinforced a perception that effective action to prevent such a tragedy should not be inhibited by deference to the UN or to outmoded or overly rigid restrictions governing use of force. But much of the non-Western world remains unconvinced, and is suspicious of validating use of force that endow the powerful countries of the North with such a discretionary option in this regard. This suspicion is associated not only with NATO action in Bosnia and Kosovo, but with the sort of open-ended mandate provided by the UNSC regarding the use force against Iraq to recover the sovereignty of Kuwait in 1990–91, and the indefinite prolongation of this use of force without a subsequent renewal of the mandate.

It is also suggested by advocates of intervention that UN practice has created greater flexibility and permissiveness with respect to the use of force than can be derived from the most relevant international law texts, including the Charter. On this reading of international law, the Charter is overly restrictive. This conclusion is arguably reinforced by the failure of UN membership, even after the end of the cold war, to implement the collective security provisions of Chapter VII (including the designation of standby forces and the active operation of the Military Staff Committee). As a result, all claims to use force must be considered in each context, and evaluated as reasonable or not, based on their specific merit. Such a view is usually coupled with the argument that states have often acted in apparent opposition to these Charter restrictions, and have not encountered legal censure. In part, this more flexible approach to the interpretation of international law governing the use of force acknowledges the reasonableness of taking transnational action to respond to either international terrorism or genocidal behavior. It also accepts the necessity of acting in some circumstances without a UN authorization, when such authorization might be unavailable due to a veto being cast or anticipated by a Permanent Member of the UNSC. . .

One way to analyze the international law status of the NATO campaign is to consider legality a matter of degree. This approach acknowledges the current fluidity of international law on humanitarian intervention, caught between strict Charter prohibitions of non-defensive uses of force and more permissive patterns of state practice with respect to humanitarian interventions and counter-terrorist use of force. The Chapter vii resolutions prior to March 1999 usefully support this analysis, as does the one-sided rejection of the Russian-sponsored resolution of censure after the intervention. Even more indicative of a quasi-ratification of the NATO action was the willingness of the UNSC in Resolution 1244 to accept a central role for restoring normality to Kosovo on the basis of the NATO negotiating position at Rambouillet and elsewhere, including the imposition of an UNMIK regime that amounts to de facto independence for the former province. These factors supportive of "legality" are offset in part, though, by the negotiating ambiguities outlined in the previous chapter, the exclusive reliance on air warfare, and the ambivalent relationship to the KLA.

Another fundamental legal concern relates to the kind of precedent being established by forceful intervention in Kosovo and Serbia. To endow the NATO campaign with an aura of legality on the basis of "implicit" authorization to use force by the UNSC seems an undesirable precedent. This is likely to encourage an even greater reliance on the veto by those Permanent Members who fear expansive subsequent interpretations. Such states may well be concerned that their concurring vote on what seems like a preliminary resolution on a threat to peace might later be relied upon by some states to justify force and what they would regard as unwarranted intrusions on sovereign rights. There is little doubt that any move toward an implicit authorization for force tends to undermine "the bright red line" that the Charter has attempted to draw around permissible force, although this dilution, it must be admitted, may already be occurring in practice.

Several non-legal or quasi-legal justifications for the intervention have been put forward after the fact by supporters of the NATO undertaking. These include assertions that the Charter framework is obsolete in the current era of intrastate conflict, and that the moral priority of preventing genocide and severe crimes against humanity justifies action even when the UNSC cannot find a political consensus. This geopolitically grounded argument suggests that a coalition of like-minded or "enlightened" states excluding the blocking Permanent Members can still wield sufficient moral authority for the international community to justify bypassing a paralyzed UNSC when the circumstances demand it. At the very least, such an argument demands that it be demonstrable that what is at stake is indeed as morally extreme as genocide or severe criminality, and that no course of action within the capacity of the UNSC could reasonably be expected to stop it. Despite this high threshold and the ambiguities surrounding whether Kosovo met such conditions, the recognition of such a vaguely defined right to "coalition" action has disturbing implications for future world stability. If the Kosovo war is employed as a precedent for allowing states, whether singly or in coalition, to ignore or contradict the UNSC based on their own interpretation of international morality, the stabilizing function of the UNSC will be seriously imperiled, as will the effort to circumscribe the conditions under which recourse to force by states is permissible. . .

NATO and its supporters have wisely avoided staking out any doctrinal claims for its action either prior to or after the war. Rather than defining the Kosovo intervention as a precedent, most NATO supporters among international jurists presented the intervention as an unfortunate but necessary and reasonable exception. Nevertheless, NATO cannot hope to preclude states, and especially other regional organizations, from referring to its claims of intervention in Kosovo as a precedent. NATO could in theory formally commit itself not to repeat such an unauthorized intervention in the event of similar circumstances arising in the future, but such a step would be seen as amounting to the repudiation of its campaign on behalf of Kosovo, and is extremely unlikely. . .

On the Doctrine of Humanitarian Intervention

With the ending of the Cold War, new conditions of world order have complicated earlier priorities with respect to the use of force in international relations. The post-1945 preoccupation was with the prevention of international wars between two or more states, and especially between major states. Nuclear weaponry and missile guidance systems lent a geopolitical urgency to this undertaking. Nevertheless, even before the Soviet collapse, many of the most serious challenges to international peace and security were arising in the course of intra-national crises of a wide variety. The UN Charter discouraged responses to such crises with its assurance that matters "essentially within the domestic jurisdiction" of states were beyond its purview unless defined by the UNSC as threats to international peace and security. Although the UNSC has increasingly identified domestic crises as threats to international peace and security, the feeling persists that the Charter as originally written is not satisfactory for a world order that is increasingly called upon to respond to humanitarian challenges. This concern had already been clearly articulated before the Kosovo challenge, but it was accentuated by the NATO response.

The Commission's initial discussion above of the legality of the NATO campaign ended inconclusively with an appreciation of the difficulty of reconciling what was done to protect the people of Kosovo with the core prohibition on recourse to non-defensive force that has not been authorized by the United Nations. At the same time, the Commission takes the view that the pattern of Serb oppression in Kosovo, the experience of ethnic cleansing a few years earlier in Bosnia, and the lack of international response to genocide in Rwanda in 1994 combine to create a strong moral and political duty on the part of the international community to act effectively, and to express solidarity with civilian societies victimized by governments guilty of grave breaches of human rights. This duty pertains both to the protection of the Kosovar Albanians and to the reestablishment of autonomy for the province. Arguably, it extends to the realization of the right of self-determination for the people of Kosovo. As the previous has argued, diplomacy failed to produce these results in a reliable manner, leaving the options of doing nothing or mounting a military intervention under NATO auspices. This situation supports the general conclusion that the NATO campaign was illegal, yet legitimate. Such a conclusion is related to the controversial idea that a "right" of humanitarian intervention is not consistent with the UN Charter if conceived as a legal text, but that it may, depending on context, nevertheless, reflect the spirit of the Charter as it relates to the overall protection of people against gross abuse. Humanitarian intervention may also thus be legitimately authorized by the UN, but will often be challenged legally from the perspective of Charter obligations to respect the sovereignty of states.

Allowing this gap between legality and legitimacy to persist is not healthy, for several reasons. Acknowledging the tension with most interpretations of international law either inhibits solidarity with civilian victims of severe abuse by territorial governments, or seriously erodes the prohibition on the use of force that the World Court and other authorities have deemed valid. Closely related to this effect, recourse to force without proper UN authorization tends to weaken the authority of, and respect for, the United Nations, especially the UNSC, in the domain of international peace and security. It needs to be observed, at the same time, that a failure to act on behalf of the Kosovars, or a repetition of the Bosnian or Rwandan experience of an insufficient UN mandate and capabilities, would have also weakened the United Nations, probably to a greater degree. Therefore, although the Commission's finding is that the use of force by NATO in intervening in Kosovo is validated from the perspective of the legitimacy of the undertaking and its overall societal effects, the Commission feels that it would be most beneficial to work diligently to close the gap between legality and legitimacy in a convincing manner for the future.

The Commission is of the opinion that the best way to do this is to conceive of an emergent doctrine of humanitarian intervention that consists of a process of three phases:

- a recommended framework of principles useful in a setting where humanitarian intervention is proposed as an international response and where it actually occurs;

- the formal adoption of such a framework by the General Assembly of the United Nations in the form of a Declaration on the Right and Responsibility of Humanitarian Intervention, accompanied by UNSC interpretations of the UN Charter that reconciles such practice with the balance between respect for sovereign rights, implementation of human rights, and prevention of humanitarian catastrophe;

- the amendment of the Charter to incorporate these changes in the role and responsibility of the United Nations and other collective actors in international society to implement the Declaration on the Right and Responsibility of Humanitarian Intervention.

The main problems relating to the protection of human rights and the prevention of humanitarian catastrophes are political rather than legal. In the face of serious abuses of human rights, even genocide, or the need to prevent or mitigate a humanitarian catastrophe, armed or unarmed intervention will not occur in an effective form unless such action conforms to the interests of potential intervening states; the action does not fly in the face of prudential concerns about sustaining the stability of world order; and, above all, the action does not risk the outbreak of a major war among states with nuclear capacity. For these reasons, it is unrealistic to expect humanitarian intervention to evolve according to the rule of law such that equal cases are treated equally. The only viable option is to prohibit such interventionary claims altogether, or to accept their selective implementation, ensuring only that in appropriate instances such intervention proceeds on a principled basis that is as consistent as possible with the humanitarian rationale. . .

The Commission believes that the end of the Cold War has brought about some dramatic changes in circumstances, which make the case for a doctrine of humanitarian intervention much more compelling than in the past. There has been an impressive evolution of international standards governing human rights, and some expectation of implementation both by the organized international community (such as the anti-apartheid campaign) and through the initiative of civil society organizations and concerned governments. Further, there is a growing trend toward an insistence on accountability of leaders for crimes of states, demonstrated by the controversy over the extradition case against General Augusto Pinochet, and epitomized by the ICTY and by the Rome Treaty of 1998, which sets the framework for the establishment of an International Criminal Court. . .

We acknowledge that a framework for intervention is thus a controversial step. One opposing position argues that it is not necessary, because of the possibility of loosening the interpretation of the prohibition on force to an extent that "international law" encompasses what is here called "legitimacy." The second position insists that positing such a principles regime would contribute further to a revival of geopolitical discretion with respect to force, weakening both international law and the United Nations in the process. This position was particularly firmly emphasized to the Commission by participants at its Johannesburg seminar.

However, the importance of agreeing upon a principled regime for humanitarian intervention or human rights enforcement has assumed prominence throughout the 1990s. Somalia, Bosnia, Haiti, Rwanda, and East Timor are only the most salient cases in which great moral pressure was exerted on the international community and the UN system to take forcible action to end a humanitarian catastrophe in the making-pressure exerted as a result of domestic circumstances. Kosovo underscored the challenge, and the NATO response is being treated by many commentators as the defining moment in the debate on humanitarian intervention.

A Framework for Principled Humanitarian Intervention

The Commission's recommended framework of principles is divided into two parts. The first suggests threshold principles that must be satisfied in order for any claim of humanitarian intervention to be legitimate. The second puts forward principles that enhance or diminish the degree of legitimacy possessed by forceful intervention. These "contextual principles" can be applied either before an intervention in order to determine whether force should be used, or to assess whether an intervention was justifiable. Unless it is apparent from the text that a principle is relevant only to instances of intervention without a UN mandate, these principles should be understood to be capable of application to coercive humanitarian intervention either by the UN, or by a coalition of the willing acting with or without the approval of the UN. It should further be kept in mind that the term "intervention" is not applicable to a situation where a government in power gives its consent to an international presence, given that, in such a situation, no legal problem arises regarding the legitimacy of the humanitarian participation.

Threshold Principles

1. There are two valid triggers of humanitarian intervention. The first is severe violations of international human rights or humanitarian law on a sustained basis. The second is the subjection of a civilian society to great suffering and risk due to the "failure" of their state, which entails the breakdown of governance at the level of the territorial sovereign state.

2. The overriding aim of all phases of the intervention involving the threat and the use of force must be the direct protection of the victimized population.

3. The method of intervention must be reasonably calculated to end the humanitarian catastrophe as rapidly as possible, and must specifically take measures to protect all civilians, to avoid collateral damage to civilian society, and to

preclude any secondary punitive or retaliatory action against the target government.

Contextual Principles

4. There must be a serious attempt to find a peaceful solution to the conflict. This solution must ensure that the pattern of abuse is terminated in a reliable and sustainable fashion, or that a process of restoring adequate governance is undertaken.

5. Recourse to the United Nations UNSC, or the lack thereof, is not conclusive. This is so if approaching the Council fails because of the exercise of a veto by one or more of the permanent members; or if the failure to have recourse to the UNSC is due to the reasonable anticipation of such a veto, where subsequent further appeal to the General Assembly is not practical. Effectively, the latter case suggests that the veto right is superseded by a 2/3 or better majority determination by "a coalition of the willing" that a humanitarian catastrophe is present or imminent.

6. Before military action is taken, lesser measures of mediating and coercive action, including sanctions, embargoes and non-violent methods of peace observation, must have been attempted without success. Further delay must be reasonably deemed to significantly increase the prospect of a humanitarian catastrophe;

7. Any recourse to the threat or use of force should not be unilateral, but enjoy some established collective support that is expressed both by a multilateral process of authorization and the participation of countries in the undertaking;

8. There should not be any formal act of censure or condemnation of the intervention by a principle organ of the United Nations, especially by the International Court of Justice or the UNSC.

9. There must be even stricter adherence to the laws of war and international humanitarian law than in standard military operations. This applies to all aspects of the military operation, including any post cease-fire occupation.

10. Territorial or economic goals are illegitimate as justification for intervention, and there should be a credible willingness on their part of intervening states to withdraw military forces and to end economic coercive measures at

the earliest point in time consistent with the humanitarian objectives.

11. After the use of armed force has achieved its objectives, there should be energetic implementation of the humanitarian mission by a sufficient commitment of resources to sustain the population in the target society and to ensure speedy and humane reconstruction of that society in order for the whole population to return to normality. This implies a rejection of prolonged comprehensive or punitive sanctions.

Suggested Revisions to the UN Charter

The distribution of powers between the different organs of the UN is part of a complex political and legal construction with the collective security system at its center. Under the collective security system, the role of the UNSC is, or has been until now, to ensure international peace and international order. The issue of human rights protection has been of only secondary importance to the UNSC within this framework. Ideally, the Charter must be amended to enhance the role of human rights in their own right within the system for collective security.

Such amendment would both put pressure on and make it possible for the UNSC to invoke violations of human rights and humanitarian law directly as a reason for taking a variety of types of measures. The Council would consequently no longer have to stretch reality to invoke the notion of "threat to the peace" in every case, and would also have greater difficulty standing by and doing nothing.

References to human rights could be inserted into a number of existing articles in the UN Charter. For example, in Article 1 of the Charter concerning the purposes of the UN a reference to human rights could be inserted in sub-paragraph 1 after "international peace and security" in the very first sentence. The first sentence of sub-paragraph 1 would then read "To maintain international peace and security and respect for human rights (. . .)"

In Article 24 sub-paragraph 1 on the functions and powers of the UNSC, the passage "and respect for fundamental human rights" could be inserted after "maintenance of international peace and security," so that Article 24(1) would read: "In order to ensure prompt and effective action by the United Nations, its Members confer on the UNSC primary responsibility for the maintenance of international peace and security and respect for fundamental human rights, and agree that in carrying out its duties under this responsibility the UNSC acts on their behalf."
. . .

At the end of Article 39, a reference to "respect for human rights" could also be inserted. This article would then read: "The UNSC shall determine the existence of any threat to the peace, breach of the peace, act of aggression or serious violation of human rights and shall make recommendations, or decide what measures shall be taken in accordance with Articles 41 and 42, to maintain or restore international peace and security and respect for human rights." . . .

NOTES & QUESTIONS

1.   *Illegal but Legitimate.* The International Commission concluded that the NATO intervention was illegal but legitimate. What is the difference between legality and legitimacy? What relevance does legitimacy have if the underlying action is illegal? Does legitimacy in this context refer to a *moral* evaluation, as in the intervention was illegal but morally necessary? Or does legitimacy refer to a statement about the law itself, as in the action violated the law but the law is unjust and should be changed? Furthermore, should world leaders and states strive to ensure that they act lawfully or act legitimately? The argument of the International Commission appeared to boil down to the idea that the intervention, though technically a violation of the UN Charter, was necessary under the circumstances and the product of multilateral consensus. For more discussion, see also Bruno Simma, *NATO, the UN and the Use of Force: Legal Aspects*, 10 Eur. J. Int'l L. 1 (1999) ("The lesson which can be drawn from this is that unfortunately there do occur 'hard cases' in which terrible dilemmas must be faced and imperative political and moral considerations may appear to leave no choice but to act outside the law. The more insolated these instances remain, the smaller will be their potential to erode the precepts of international law, in our case the UN Charter.").

2.   *Conditions for the Exercise of Legitimate Intervention.* The International Commission was clearly concerned about opening a Pandora's Box of unrestrained interventions. Consequently, the commission identified a variety of requirements that must be met before the intervention should be considered "legitimate." Other groups have proposed alternative, but largely overlapping, requirements. For example, the international jurist Antonio Cassese proposed the following requirements: (1) "egregious" breaches of human rights consisting in the slaughter of hundreds or thousands of innocent individuals; (2) proof of the territorial state's complete inability to stop the violence when the violence occurs during a period of anarchy; (3) inaction by the Security Council due to disagreement or veto; (4) exhaustion of peaceful and diplomatic solutions; (5) multilateral support for intervention; and (6) military force is used exclusively for the purpose of stopping the atrocities. See Antonio Cassese, *Ex iniuria ius oritur: Are We Moving towards International Legitimation of Forcible Humanitarian Countermeasures in the World Community?*, 10 Eur. J. Int'l L. 23, 27 (1999). Would you impose any *additional* conditions on the legitimate use of humanitarian intervention?

B. THE RESPONSIBILITY TO PROTECT

In response to Kofi Annan's continued discussion at the United Nations of the problem of humanitarian intervention, the Canadian government formed an independent commission to study the problem, called the International Commission on Intervention and State Sovereignty. Their report created a new principle—the Responsibility to Protect (RTP)—that envisions a legal obligation on the part of the world community to protect civilians from violence, human rights abuses, and other catastrophes. However, the new RTP doctrine raises as many questions as it answered, in particular whether RTP can provide a justification for unilateral humanitarian intervention.

The following report was filed by the Secretary General of the United Nations, and clarified how RTP might be translated from doctrine to practice. As you read the following excerpt, ask yourself how the Responsibility to Protect can help prevent, or stop, a major humanitarian crisis.

Implementing the Responsibility to Protect
Report of the Secretary-General
January 12, 1999

The twentieth century was marred by the Holocaust, the killing fields of Cambodia, the genocide in Rwanda and the mass killings in Srebrenica, the latter two under the watch of the Security Council and United Nations peacekeepers. Genocide, war crimes, ethnic cleansing and crimes against humanity: the brutal legacy of the twentieth century speaks bitterly and graphically of the profound failure of individual States to live up to their most basic and compelling responsibilities, as well as the collective inadequacies of international institutions. Those tragic events led my distinguished predecessor, Kofi Annan, and other world leaders to ask whether the United Nations and other international institutions should be exclusively focused on the security of States without regard to the safety of the people within them. Could sovereignty, the essential building block of the nation-State era and of the United Nations itself, they queried, be misused as a shield behind which mass violence could be inflicted on populations with impunity? How deeply and irreparably had the legitimacy and credibility of the United Nations and its partners been damaged by such revelations? Could we not find the will and the capacity in the new century to do better?

Before responding, we should note that the worst human tragedies of the past century were not confined to any particular part of the world. They occurred in the North and in the South, in poor, medium-income and relatively affluent countries. Sometimes they were linked to ongoing conflicts but quite often—including in some of the worst cases—they were not. In retrospect, three factors stand out. First, in each case there were warning signs. Violence of this magnitude takes planning and preparation, as well as a contributing political, social and economic context. Second, the signals of trouble ahead were, time and again, ignored, set aside or minimized by high-level national and international decision makers with competing political agendas. Third, at times the United Nations—its intergovernmental organs and its Secretariat— failed to do its part. Citing a "lack of resources and political commitment," the Independent Inquiry into the actions of the United Nations during the 1994 genocide in Rwanda, commissioned by then Secretary-General Annan, concluded in its report that "the United Nations failed the people of Rwanda during the genocide in 1994." The report of the Secretary-General on the fall of Srebrenica, while also underscoring "the gulf between mandate and means", went on to question "the pervasive ambivalence within the United Nations regarding the role of force in the pursuit of peace" and "an institutional ideology of impartiality even when confronted with attempted genocide." A prime lesson of Srebrenica, the Secretary-General noted, was that "the United Nations global commitment to ending conflict does not preclude moral judgments, but makes them necessary." Nine years after those sobering reports, many of their institutional recommendations, including on early warning, analysis and training, have not been fully implemented, despite efforts to improve the prevention capacities of the Organization. The United Nations and its Member States remain underprepared to meet their most fundamental prevention and protection responsibilities. We can, and must, do better. Humanity expects it and history demands it.

Part of the problem has been conceptual and doctrinal: how we understand the issue and the policy alternatives. Two distinct approaches emerged during the final years of the twentieth century. Humanitarian intervention posed a false choice between two extremes: either standing by in the face of mounting civilian deaths or deploying coercive military force to protect the vulnerable and threatened populations. Member States have been understandably reluctant to choose between those unpalatable alternatives. Meanwhile, Francis Deng, at that time the Representative of the Secretary-General on internally displaced persons, and his colleagues had been refining a conceptually distinct approach centred on the notion of "sovereignty as responsibility." They underscored that sovereignty entailed enduring obligations towards one's people, as well as certain international privileges. The State, by fulfilling fundamental protection obligations and respecting core human rights, would have far less reason to be concerned about unwelcome intervention from abroad.

Neither concerns about sovereignty nor the understanding that sovereignty implies responsibility are confined to one part of the world. The evolution of thinking and practice in Africa in that regard has been especially impressive. While the Organization of African Unity emphasized non-intervention, its successor, the African Union, has stressed non-indifference. In 2000, five years before the 2005 World Summit endorsed the responsibility to protect, the Constitutive Act of the African Union provided, in article 4(h), for "the right of the Union to intervene in a Member State pursuant to a decision of the Assembly in respect to grave circumstances, namely: war crimes, genocide, and crimes against humanity." It made a clear distinction between Member States, which were not to interfere "in the internal affairs of another" (article 4(g)), and the Union, which could do so in response to the three "grave circumstances" noted above. As concluded by the Independent Inquiry into the actions of the United Nations during the 1994 Rwanda genocide, the Convention on the Prevention and Punishment of the Crime of Genocide had long since imposed "the responsibility to act."

Concerns about how to respond to such conscience-shocking events, and better yet to prevent them in the first place, were not confined to Africa or the global South. In 2000, Canada convened an independent International Commission on Intervention and State Sovereignty, co-chaired by Gareth Evans of Australia and Mohamed Sahnoun of Algeria. According to the Commission, "external military intervention for humanitarian protection purposes has been controversial both when it has happened—as in Somalia, Bosnia and Herzegovina and Kosovo—and when it has failed to happen, as in Rwanda." The geographically diverse Commission, however, came to understand that protection was neither primarily a military matter nor essentially a contest between State and individual sovereignty. Coining the phrase "responsibility to protect," the Commission identified a responsibility to prevent, a responsibility to react and a responsibility to rebuild, posing a continuum of graduated policy instruments across that spectrum. Although it addressed the proper authority and rules for the use of force, the report of the Commission highlighted the advantages of prevention through encouraging States to meet their core protection responsibilities. A number of the Commission's key recommendations were included in the conclusions of the High-level Panel on Threats, Challenges and Change convened in 2004 by then Secretary-General Kofi Annan and in his subsequent report entitled "In larger freedom: towards development, security and human rights for all." These reports, in turn, provided material for consideration at the 2005 World Summit.

While the approach to the responsibility to protect described in the present report draws from the above-mentioned history in important ways, it has been defined by the provisions of paragraphs 138 and 139 of the Summit Outcome as follows:

(a) As the assembled Heads of State and Government made absolutely clear, the responsibility to protect is an ally of sovereignty, not an adversary. It grows from the positive and affirmative notion of sovereignty as responsibility, rather than from the narrower idea of humanitarian intervention. By helping States to meet their core protection responsibilities, the responsibility to protect seeks to strengthen sovereignty, not weaken it. It seeks to help States to succeed, not just to react when they fail;

(b) The responsibility to protect applies, until Member States decide otherwise, only to the four specified crimes and violations: genocide, war crimes, ethnic cleansing and crimes against humanity. To try to extend it to cover other calamities, such as HIV/AIDS, climate change or the response to natural disasters, would undermine the 2005 consensus and stretch the concept beyond recognition or operational utility;

(c) While the scope should be kept narrow, the response ought to be deep, employing the wide array of prevention and protection instruments available to Member States, the United Nations system, regional and subregional organizations and their civil society partners. To that end, in paragraph 138 of the Summit Outcome, States were called on to use "appropriate and necessary means" to prevent such crimes and their incitement, and the international community was called on to "encourage and help" States to exercise their responsibility and to "support the United Nations in establishing an early warning capability". In paragraph 139 of the Summit Outcome, reference is made both to "appropriate diplomatic, humanitarian and peaceful means" under Chapters VI and VIII of the Charter and to "collective action" under Chapter VII. Our approach to the responsibility to protect should therefore be both narrow and deep;

(d) The Summit recognized that early warning and assessment was a necessary, though hardly sufficient, ingredient for successful preventive and protective action by Member States, through the United Nations. As asserted in paragraph 138 of the Summit Outcome, the international community should "support the United Nations in establishing an early warning capability." This would require: (i) the timely flow to United Nations decision makers of accurate, authoritative, reliable and relevant information about the incitement, preparation or perpetration of the four specified crimes and violations; (ii) the capacity for the United Nations Secretariat to assess that information and to understand the patterns of events properly within the context of local conditions; and (iii) ready access to the office of the Secretary-General. Too often, the alarm bells were not sounded at all or they failed to command attention or spur effective action at senior political ranks, whether in the Secretariat or in intergovernmental bodies. But a pattern of false alarms or, worse, selective reporting could also damage the credibility of the Organization. It is therefore important that early warning and assessment be effected fairly, prudently and professionally, without political interference or double standards. . .

Pillar Three

Timely and Decisive Response

As the first two sentences of paragraph 139 of the Summit Outcome make unambiguously clear, pillar three is integral to the strategy for fulfilling the responsibility to protect that was agreed upon by the assembled Heads of State and Government. According to the opening sentence, "the international community, through the United Nations, also has the responsibility to use appropriate diplomatic, humanitarian and other peaceful means, in accordance with Chapters VI and VIII of the Charter, to help protect populations from genocide, war crimes, ethnic cleansing and crimes against humanity." The wording suggests that the intent is for this to be an ongoing, generic responsibility that employs the kind of peaceful, pacific measures specified in Chapter VI and in Article 52, Chapter VIII. The second sentence of paragraph 139 underscores that a wider range of collective actions, either peaceful or non-peaceful, could be invoked by the international community if two conditions are met: (a) "should peaceful means be inadequate," and (b) "national authorities are manifestly failing to protect their populations" from the four specified crimes and violations. In those two cases, paragraph 139 affirms that "we are prepared to take collective action, in a timely and decisive manner, through the Security Council, in accordance with the Charter, including Chapter VII, on a case-by-case basis and in cooperation with relevant regional organizations as appropriate." As I noted in a speech delivered in Berlin, Germany, on 15 July 2008, the wording of this sentence suggests the need for an early and flexible response in such cases, one both tailored to the circumstances of the situation and fully in accord with the provisions of the Charter.

In dealing with the diverse circumstances in which crimes and violations relating to the responsibility to protect are planned, incited and/or committed, there is no room for a rigidly sequenced strategy or for tightly defined "triggers" for action. The threshold for prevention, capacity-building or rebuilding efforts under pillar two would certainly be lower than the threshold for a response under pillar three, namely that "national authorities are manifestly failing to protect their populations." Similarly, under pillar three, the threshold for Chapter VI measures would be lower than the threshold for enforcement action under Chapter VII, which can only be authorized at the intergovernmental level. The more robust the response, the higher the standard for authorization. In a rapidly unfolding emergency situation, the United Nations, regional, subregional and national decision makers must remain focused on saving lives through "timely and decisive" action, not on following arbitrary, sequential or graduated policy ladders that prize procedure over substance and process over results.

The United Nations has a strong preference for dialogue and peaceful persuasion. Therefore, pillar three encompasses, in addition to more robust steps, a wide range of non-coercive and non-violent response measures under Chapters VI and VIII of the Charter. Under the Charter, many of these can be undertaken by the Secretary-General or by regional or subregional arrangements, without the explicit authorization of the Security Council. This was the case in Kenya in early 2008, when for the first time both regional actors and the United Nations viewed the crisis in part from the perspective of the responsibility to protect.

Intergovernmental bodies can play pivotal roles in conducting on-site investigations and fact-finding missions. Under Article 34 of the Charter, the Security Council "may investigate any dispute, or any situation which might lead to international friction or give rise to a dispute, in order to determine whether the continuation of the dispute or situation is likely to endanger the maintenance of international peace and security". Subject to the provisions of Article 12 of the Charter, the General Assembly can avail itself of similar opportunities in some cases, under the provisions of Articles 11, 13, and 14. Either the Assembly or the Council, for instance, may appoint a fact-finding mission to investigate and report on alleged violations of international law, as the latter did in the case of Darfur. The Human Rights Council may deploy a fact-finding mission, appoint a special rapporteur to advise on the situation or refer the situation to existing special procedures. Parallel instruments and possibilities may exist in a number of regions and subregions.

Investigation, of course, is not a substitute for "timely and decisive" protective action but rather should be seen as an initial step towards it. If undertaken early in a crisis, at the first sign that a State is failing to meet its obligations relating to the responsibility to protect, such on-site missions can also provide opportunities for delivering messages directly to key decision makers on behalf of the larger international community, for example, by trying to dissuade them from destructive courses of action that could make them subject to prosecution by the International Criminal Court or ad hoc tribunals. Such candid messages have been voiced effectively by the United Nations High Commissioner for Human Rights, the United Nations High Commissioner for Refugees and the Special Adviser on the Prevention of Genocide, among others, as well as by the office of the Secretary-General. In recent years, the international criminal justice system has made important strides towards ensuring accountability and ending impunity, but more could be done to address perceptions of selectivity and to ensure its global reach.

It is now well established in international law and practice that sovereignty does not bestow impunity on those who organize, incite or commit crimes relating to the responsibility to protect. In paragraph 138 of the Summit Outcome, States affirmed their responsibility to prevent the incitement of the four specified crimes and violations. When a State manifestly fails to prevent such incitement, the international community should remind the authorities of this obligation and that such acts could be referred to the International Criminal Court, under the Rome Statute. As noted above, in cases of imminent or unfolding violence of this magnitude against populations, this message may be more effectively and persuasively delivered in person than from afar. Until recently, however, the practice at the United Nations and in many capitals had too often been to ignore or minimize the signs of looming mass murder. The world body failed to take notice when the Khmer Rouge called for a socially and ethnically homogenous Cambodia with a "clean social system" and its radio urged listeners to "purify" the "masses of the people" of Cambodia. Nor did it respond vigorously to ethnically inflammatory broadcasts and rhetoric in the Balkans in the early 1990s or in Rwanda in 1993 and 1994 in the months preceding the genocide. Despite several reports during those critical months by the United Nations Assistance Mission in Rwanda and the Special Rapporteur on extrajudicial, arbitrary or summary executions on the incendiary programming of Radio Mille Collines, there was no attempt by the international community to jam those hateful and fateful broadcasts.

There is some reason to believe, however, that the United Nations and its Member States have learned some painful, but enduring, lessons from these calamities. It is true that we have yet to develop the tools or display the will to respond consistently and effectively to all emergencies relating to the responsibility to protect, as the tragic events in Darfur, the Democratic Republic of the Congo and Somalia remind us. Nonetheless, when confronted with crimes or violations relating to the responsibility to protect or their incitement, today the world is less likely to look the other way than in the last century. For example, in November 2004, then Special Adviser on the Prevention of Genocide Juan Méndez reminded the authorities in Côte d'Ivoire, where xenophobic hate speech had exacerbated domestic tensions and spurred further violence, that they could be held criminally responsible for the consequences. The offensive messages soon ceased. Similarly, during the early 2008 post-election violence in Kenya, I urged leaders on all sides, as did my Special Adviser on the Prevention of Genocide, Francis Deng, to call publicly for an end to the violence and to statements inciting violence, noting that political and community leaders could be held accountable for violations of international law committed at their instigation. Live broadcasts were banned during the heat of the crisis, when tensions were running high, and former Secretary General Kofi Annan, who was mediating the dispute, cautioned Kenyan lawmakers that those engaged in acts of violence could not be allowed to act with impunity. Leaders everywhere should be reminded that incitement to racial hatred is condemned by the International Convention on the Elimination of All Forms of Racial Discrimination. Because of the typically public and explicit character of such incitement, it should be relatively easy to identify it and to rally international support for efforts to discourage it. Moreover, where the United Nations has a peacekeeping presence or a means of accomplishing this from offshore or from a neighbouring country, it can counter such messages with its own broadcasts and information services.

Talk is not an end in itself, and there should be no hesitation to seek authorization for more robust measures if quiet diplomacy is being used as a delaying tactic when an earlier and more direct response could save lives and restore order. Paragraph 139 of the Summit Outcome reflects the hard truth that no strategy for fulfilling the responsibility to protect would be complete without the possibility of collective enforcement measures, including through sanctions or coercive military action in extreme cases. When a State refuses to accept international prevention and protection assistance, commits egregious crimes and violations relating to the responsibility to protect and fails to respond to less coercive measures, it is, in effect, challenging the international community to live up to its own responsibilities under paragraph 139 of the Summit Outcome. Such collective measures could be authorized by the Security Council under Articles 41 or 42 of the Charter, by the General Assembly under the "Uniting for peace" procedure or by regional or subregional arrangements under Article 53, with the prior authorization of the Security Council.

Diplomatic sanctions, if fully and consistently implemented by Member States, provide another way for the international community to underscore the message that committing crimes and violations relating to the responsibility to protect is unacceptable behaviour for a United Nations Member State in the twenty-first century. Leaders responsible for such atrocities, at the very least, should not be welcome among their peers. Nor should they or their countries be eligible for election to leadership posts in subregional, regional or global bodies. Targeted sanctions, such as on travel, financial transfers, luxury goods and arms, should also be considered by the Security Council, on a case-by-case basis and in cooperation with relevant regional organizations, as appropriate, under Articles 41 and 53 of the Charter and in accordance with paragraph 139 of the Summit Outcome (and in the case of sexual violence, in accordance with the terms contained in Council resolution 1820 (2008)). The General Assembly could also consider such measures under its resolution 377 (V), entitled "Uniting for peace," although they would then not be legally binding. While sanctions may be inadequate to stop abuses by a determined authoritarian regime, if applied sufficiently early they can demonstrate the international community's commitment to meeting its collective responsibilities under paragraph 139 of the Summit Outcome and serve as a warning of possibly tougher measures if the violence against a population persists.

Particular attention should be paid to restricting the flow of arms or police equipment, which could be misused by repressive regimes that are manifestly failing to meet their core responsibilities under paragraph 138 of the Summit Outcome, or in situations where an ongoing conflict threatens to escalate into the perpetration by one side or another of large-scale crimes and violations relating to the responsibility to protect. While the General Assembly has at times called for arms embargoes, only the Security Council has the authority to make them binding. Under Article 53 of the Charter, regional arrangements may take such enforcement steps with the authorization of the Council. In practice, however, it has not been uncommon for regional or subregional bodies or ad hoc groups of Member States to undertake such measures without formal prior authorization from the Council.

States and intergovernmental organizations, of course, are hardly the only influential actors in situations relating to the responsibility to protect, as underscored in the discussion of pillars one and two in sections II and III above. The multiple roles of domestic or transnational civil society in advocacy, early warning, monitoring, research, training and education are well known and are readily and repeatedly acknowledged in the present report. Less well known is the role of individuals, advocacy groups, women's groups and the private sector in shaping the international response to crimes and violations relating to the responsibility to protect. Like the United Nations itself, international civil society learned lessons from the relatively muted, slow and scattered public response to the genocides in Cambodia and Rwanda. The mass, well organized and highly visible transnational campaigns against the violence in Darfur have demonstrated both the power and the limitations of such movements. They have shown the depth and breadth of public concern over ending the violence against the beleaguered population of Darfur, even as they have highlighted how inadequate our policy tools are and how fleeting is the political will to use them. Over the longer term, however, as noted above, those who would commit crimes and violations relating to the responsibility to protect should consider the enduring and wide-ranging damage such atrocities have both on society and on its capacity to recover. Foreign direct investment, cultural exchanges and tourism may be negatively affected for decades to come since the costs to a country's reputation of such unacceptable behaviour are high and growing. Even if the Security Council does not impose an embargo, individual public and private investors, spurred by non-governmental organizations advocacy networks, are likely to do so instead. Individual financial and trade embargoes may prove far harder to lift without visible and sustainable change within the country concerned.

As repeatedly underscored above, there are substantial gaps in capacity, imagination and will across the whole spectrum of prevention and protection measures relating to the responsibility to protect. Nowhere is that gap more pronounced or more damaging than in the realm of forceful and timely response to the most flagrant crimes and violations relating to the responsibility to protect. Here, weaknesses of capacity and the paucity of will, including in many capitals that speak in favour of advancing goals relating to the responsibility to protect, feed off each other in a particularly vicious cycle of hesitation and finger-pointing in the face of unfolding atrocities. Most visibly and tragically, the international community's failure to stem the mass violence and displacements in Darfur, as well as in the Democratic Republic of the Congo and Somalia, has undermined public confidence in the United Nations and our collective espousal of the principles relating to the responsibility to protect. I am firmly convinced that we can and will do better in the future, acting fully within the framework of the Charter and the provisions of paragraphs 138 and 139 of the Summit Outcome.

While the first and enduring responsibility resides with each State to meet its obligations relating to the responsibility to protect, when it manifestly fails to do so the Secretary-General bears particular responsibility for ensuring that the international community responds in a "timely and decisive" manner, as called for in paragraph 139 of the Summit Outcome. For my part, I recognize that, as noted in the report of the Panel on United Nations Peace Operations in a similar context, the Secretary-General has an obligation to tell the Security Council—and in this case the General Assembly as well—what it needs to know, not what it wants to hear. The Secretary-General must be the spokesperson for the vulnerable and the threatened when their Governments become their persecutors instead of their protectors or can no longer shield them from marauding armed groups. Within the Security Council, the five permanent members bear particular responsibility because of the privileges of tenure and the veto power they have been granted under the Charter. I would urge them to refrain from employing or threatening to employ the veto in situations of manifest failure to meet obligations relating to the responsibility to protect, as defined in paragraph 139 of the Summit Outcome, and to reach a mutual understanding to that effect. Across the globe, attitudes have changed in important ways since Cambodia, Rwanda and Srebrenica, raising the political costs, domestically and internationally, for anyone seen to be blocking an effective international response to an unfolding genocide or other high-visibility crime relating to the responsibility to protect. All Member States, not just the 15 members of the Security Council, should be acutely aware of both public expectations and shared responsibilities. If the General Assembly is to play a leading role in shaping a United Nations response, then all 192 Member States should share the responsibility to make it an effective instrument for advancing the principles relating to the responsibility to protect expressed so clearly in paragraphs 138 and 139 of the Summit Outcome.

As noted above, the credibility, authority and hence effectiveness of the United Nations in advancing the principles relating to the responsibility to protect depend, in large part, on the consistency with which they are applied. This is particularly true when military force is used to enforce them. In that regard, Member States may want to consider the principles, rules and doctrine that should guide the application of coercive force in extreme situations relating to the responsibility to protect. This issue was addressed in the 2001 report of the International Commission on Intervention and State Sovereignty and by my predecessor, Kofi Annan, in his 2005 report entitled "In larger freedom: towards development, security and human rights for all."

The General Assembly has an important role to play, even under pillar three. Its peace and security functions are addressed in Articles 11, 12, 14, and 15 of the Charter. Article 24 of the Charter confers on the Security Council "primary," not total, responsibility for the maintenance of peace and security, and in some cases the perpetration of crimes relating to the responsibility to protect may not be deemed to pose a threat to international peace and security. Moreover, under the "Uniting for peace" procedure, the Assembly can address such issues when the Council fails to exercise its responsibility with regard to international peace and security because of the lack of unanimity among its five permanent members. Even in such cases, however, Assembly decisions are not legally binding on the parties.

Despite years of study and public discussion, the United Nations is still far from developing the kind of rapid-response military capacity most needed to handle the sort of rapidly unfolding atrocity crimes referred to in paragraph 139 of the Summit Outcome. I appreciate the efforts by a number of Member States to consider the components of such a capacity, including doctrine, training and command-and-control issues. Much more needs to be done, however, to internationalize such efforts and put them in the larger context of finding better ways to protect civilians. The continuing consideration of the latter issue by the Security Council and General Assembly is most timely in that regard.

Better modes of collaboration between the United Nations and regional and subregional arrangements are also needed. Such arrangements need to consider capacity-sharing and not just capacity-building, as is now the case in mediation support. The African Union-United Nations 10-year capacity building programme is particularly crucial in that regard. We must redouble our efforts to ensure that it succeeds and that the African Standby Force realizes its full potential. Global-regional collaboration is a key plank of our strategy for operationalizing the responsibility to protect, including for establishing the early warning capability mandated in paragraph 138 of the Summit Outcome, and it deserves our full and unambiguous support.

In sum, as the United Nations community comes to articulate and implement a response strategy consistent with both the call in paragraph 139 of the Summit Outcome for "timely and decisive" action and the provisions of the Charter, including its purposes and principles, this will make it more difficult for States or groups of States to claim that they need to act unilaterally or outside of United Nations channels, rules and procedures to respond to emergencies relating to the responsibility to protect. The more consistently, fairly and reliably such a United Nations-based response system operates, the more confidence there will be in the capacity of the United Nations to provide a credible multilateral alternative. This would also help to deter or dissuade potential perpetrators of such crimes and violations. . .

NOTES & QUESTIONS

1.   *RTP and Unilateral Intervention.* Does the Responsibility to Protect provide a legal justification for unilateral humanitarian intervention? If so, how does it do so? Recall that the UN Charter provisions on the use of force and self-defense are crystal clear. Furthermore, the UN Charter includes a provision for amending the Charter (article 108), which has not been utilized in this case. Some scholars have suggested that the Responsibility to Protect doctrine is an example of an emerging norm of customary international law. If that is the case, can a new norm of customary international law supplant the clear law of the Charter? Recall that article 103 of the Charter states that "[i]n the event of a conflict between the obligations of the Members of the United Nations under the present Charter and their obligations under any other international agreement, their obligations under the present Charter shall prevail." This suggests, perhaps, that the Charter regime should take precedence over any conflicting rule of customary international law.

2.   *The Many Faces of RTP.* When states express their support for RTP, it can sometimes be unclear which aspect of the doctrine they are

supporting. As is clear from the above materials, the notion of RTP covers a lot of ground and can include, among other things, unilateral intervention, Security Council authorized missions, support for refugees and civilians suffering from exposure to armed conflict, and many other humanitarian situations. In other words, the RTP doctrine is far wider than just the notion of humanitarian intervention, and it is possible for a state to express support for RTP without necessarily endorsing the possibility of intervention in the absence of Security Council authorization. For more discussion of the many faces of RTP, see Carsten Stahn, *Responsibility to Protect: Political Rhetoric or Emerging Legal Norm?*, 191 Am. J. Int'l L. 99, 102 (2007) ("the concept currently encompasses a spectrum of different normative propositions that vary considerably in their status and degree or legal support").

PROBLEM CASE

In the spring of 2011, peaceful protests erupted in Damascus, Syria, as protestors took to the streets to express their dissatisfaction with the regime of President Bashar al-Assad. The protestors viewed Assad as increasingly authoritarian, and were no doubt encouraged by the so-called Arab Spring of 2011, in which anti-government protests erupted across the Arab world.

But instead of negotiating with the protestors or giving up power, Assad dug in his heels and sought to repress the insurrection. The dispute was soon militarized, with the protestors forming an armed opposition group, which included members of the Syrian army that had defected, and eventually erupted into a full-blown civil war between the rebels and the government.

The civil war was, and as of 2017 continues to be, brutal. Published reports indicate that both sides of the conflict have engaged in numerous abuses and violations of the laws of war. The most severe condemnation has been lodged against Assad's government forces, which are accused of having engaged in torture and execution of captured rebel soldiers and suspected traitors. Perhaps the most scandalous accusations surround the type of weaponry used by the government. Reports indicate that government forces have repeatedly shelled civilians locations in rebel held territory, especially around the city of Aleppo, and have used so-called barrel bombs in civilian neighborhoods. (Barrel bombs are, quite literally, barrels filled with shrapnel and explosive compound that are dropped from helicopters).

For the international community, the triggering event came when Assad reportedly used chemical weapons against rebel forces. If true, the deployment of chemical weapons violated the Chemical Weapons Convention, and established norms for the conduct of warfare. Many observers called on the US and NATO to intervene militarily in Syria. However, the Security Council was unwilling to authorize a military strike against Syria, because both Russia and China had promised to veto such a resolution. Consequently, several foreign governments provided financial support and arms to the Syrian rebels, but no government was willing to send ground troops of their own without Security Council authorization.

Should NATO have intervened militarily in this case? If you were a legal advisor for a foreign government that wished to intervene, what advice would you provide to your client? Is this a situation where the "Responsibility to Protect" doctrine would justify military intervention? Most importantly, is there any way to reconcile unilateral intervention with the text of the UN Charter, which prohibits the use of force in the absence of self-defense or Security Council authorization?

C. NECESSITY

Another possibility for justifying humanitarian intervention is the doctrine of necessity. The doctrine is a defense that precludes a finding of state responsibility under international law. In other words, the doctrine of necessity transforms what would otherwise constitute an internationally wrongful act into a rightful act, assuming that the doctrinal elements of the defense are satisfied.

After the NATO intervention, the Serbian government sued Belgium and other NATO member states, claiming that the bombing campaign was illegal. Although the case was eventually dismissed on jurisdictional grounds, the court heard oral arguments on the merits. During the discussion, lawyers for Belgium argued that the intervention was justified by necessity.

Read the following excerpt of the oral argument, and immediately following Article 25 of the Draft Articles on State Responsibility, and ask yourself whether the requirements for the defense of necessity were satisfied in this case.

Legality of Use of Force
(Serbia and Montenegro v. Belgium)

International Court of Justice
Oral Proceedings
May 10, 1999

As regards the intervention, the Kingdom of Belgium takes the view that the Security Council's resolutions which I have just cited provide an unchallengeable basis for the armed intervention. They are clear, and they are based on Chapter VII of the Charter, under which the Security Council may determine the existence of any threat to international peace and security. But we need to go further and develop the idea of armed humanitarian intervention. NATO, and the Kingdom of Belgium in particular, felt obliged to intervene to forestall an ongoing humanitarian catastrophe, acknowledged in Security Council resolutions. To safeguard what? To safeguard, Mr. President, essential values which also rank as jus cogens. Are the right to life, physical integrity, the prohibition of torture, are these not norms with the status of jus cogens? They undeniably have this status, so much so that international instruments on human rights (the European Human Rights Convention, the agreements mentioned above) protect them in a waiver clause (the power of suspension in case of war of all human rights except right to life and integrity of the individual): thus they are absolute rights, from which we may conclude that they belong to the jus cogens. Thus, NATO intervened to protect fundamental values enshrined in the jus cogens and to prevent an impending catastrophe recognized as such by the Security Council.

There is another important feature of NATO's action: NATO has never questioned the political independence and the territorial integrity of the Federal Republic of Yugoslavia—the Security Council's resolutions, the NATO decisions, and the press releases have, moreover, consistently stressed this. Thus this is not an intervention against the territorial integrity or independence of the former Republic of Yugoslavia. The purpose of NATO's intervention is to rescue a people in peril, in deep distress. For this reason the Kingdom of Belgium takes the view that this is an armed humanitarian intervention, compatible with Article 2, paragraph 4, of the Charter, which covers only intervention against the territorial integrity or political independence of a State.

There is no shortage of precedents. India's intervention in Eastern Pakistan; Tanzania's intervention in Uganda; Vietnam in Cambodia, the West African countries' interventions first in Liberia and then in Sierra Leone. While there may have been certain doubts expressed in the doctrine, and among some members of the international community, these interventions have not been expressly condemned by the relevant United Nations bodies. These precedents, combined with Security Council resolutions and the rejection of the draft Russian resolution on 26 March, which I have already referred to, undoubtedly support and substantiate our contention that the NATO intervention is entirely legal. Allow me to remind the Court of the three features of the intervention which have been noted by the international authorities, in this case the Security Council; there was a humanitarian catastrophe, recognised by the Security Council, imminent danger, i.e., a situation constituting a threat to peace as noted by the Security Council resolution; and the power responsible for this—as is made clear in the three Security Council resolutions—is the Federal Republic of Yugoslavia.

The intervention is of a quite exceptional character, prompted by entirely objective criteria. In the circumstances do we need to add another consideration, the tendency in contemporary international law towards a steadily greater protection of minorities? We are accused of encroaching on sovereignty, but the Government of the Kingdom of Belgium would like to quote a passage from a speech given by Mr. Kofi Annan, United Nations Secretary-General, on 30 April last, at the University of Michigan. Mr. Annan said "no Government has the right to hide behind national sovereignty in order to violate the human rights or fundamental freedoms of its peoples," and he added a very important point, "Emerging slowly, but I believe surely is an international norm against the violent repression of minorities that will and must take precedence over concerns of State sovereignty."

NATO's action has had and still has a further dimension. The aim is to protect a distressed population in the throes of a humanitarian catastrophe, but there is also a need to safeguard the stability of an entire region, for the Security Council resolutions have also noted that the behavior of the Federal Republic of Yugoslavia in Kosovo was generating a threat to international peace and security by impairing the stability of the whole area. This is a case of a lawful armed humanitarian intervention for which there is a compelling necessity. And, Mr. President, Members of the Court, if we have failed to convince you that what has been taking place is armed humanitarian intervention justified by international law, the Government of the Kingdom of Belgium will also plead, in the alternative, that there is a state of necessity.

The notion of a state of necessity, which is enshrined in all branches of the law, is unquestionably acknowledged in international law; and the draft Article 33 proposed by the International Law Commission reflects this.

Allow me to suggest a definition to the Court: what is a state of necessity? A state of necessity is the cause which justifies the violation of a binding rule in order to safeguard, in face of grave and imminent peril, values which are higher than those protected by the rule which has been breached. Let me review the elements of this definition one at a time and set them against the case we are dealing with today.

First, what rule has been breached? We do not accept that any rule has been breached. However, for the sake of argument, let us say that it is the rule prohibiting the use of force. Where is the imminent peril, the grave and imminent peril? There it was—no doubt about it—at the time of the armed intervention; there it is still, the humanitarian catastrophe recorded in the resolutions of the Security Council—an impending peril. What are the higher values which this intervention attempts to safeguard? They are rights of jus cogens. It is the collective security of an entire region. And the final element of a state of necessity, I almost forgot, is that the acts must be proportionate; the intervention must be proportional to the threat. The intervention is wholly in proportion to the gravity of the peril; it is limited to aerial bombardments directed solely and exclusively against the war machine of the aggressor and against its military-industrial complex.

The Court will see that this is a use of force which is utterly unlike the parallel drawn this morning by one of my esteemed opponents; a parallel with what was the diktats of the Nazi régime to its peaceful neighbours. The Kingdom of Belgium regrets to have to say that it finds such a parallel totally unacceptable, and apt to shock the civilized legal conscience. The situation is the total reverse. It is we, the member countries of NATO, democratic countries with freely elected governments, who find ourselves confronted by a régime which rejects the most fundamental values of humanity. . .

Draft Articles on State Responsibility

Article 25 Necessity

1.   Necessity may not be invoked by a State as a ground for precluding the wrongfulness of an act not in conformity with an international obligation of that State unless the act:

(a)   is the only way for the State to safeguard an essential interest against a grave and imminent peril; and

(b)   does not seriously impair an essential interest of the State or States towards which the obligation exists, or of the international community as a whole.

2.   In any case, necessity may not be invoked by a State as a ground for precluding wrongfulness if:

(a)   the international obligation in question excludes the possibility of invoking necessity; or

(b)   the State has contributed to the situation of necessity.

NOTES & QUESTIONS

1.   *The Limits of Necessity.* Ultimately, did the representative from Belgium have a convincing argument? If not, what was missing in the argument? The doctrine of necessity, at least according to the ILC Draft Articles, requires that the state face "an essential interest against a grave and imminent peril." In this case, what was Belgium's essential interest? The problem, of course, is that Belgium intervened against Serbia in order to protect an essential interest of the Kosovo people, not to safeguard an interest of the Belgium nation. Is there an answer to this problem? One possibility is to suggest that the "essential value" of humanitarian protection and respect for the right to life is itself an "essential interest" of Belgium. Is this argument convincing? For a discussion, see O. Spiermann, *Humanitarian Intervention as a Necessity and the Threat or Use of Jus Cogens,* 71 Nordic J. Int'l L. 523 (2002) (concluding that necessity might justify unilateral intervention in "extraordinary circumstances"); Nicholas Tsagourias, *Necessity and the Use of Force: A Special Regime*, 41 Netherlands Yearbook Int'l L. 11, 42 (2010) (necessity might excuse but not justify unilateral humanitarian intervention). Some scholars have argued that article 25 of the ILC Draft Articles was never intended to apply to the use of force at all. See Robert Sloane, *On the Use and Abuse of Necessity in the Law of State Responsibility*, 106 Am. J. Int'l L. 447, 494 (2012).

2.   *Legitimate Defense.* There may be other avenues to justify unilateral humanitarian intervention without resorting to new doctrines such as RTP or necessity. One possibility is to delve deeper into the language of article 51 and its codification of the right of self-defense. Article 51 refers to the "inherent right of individual or collective self-defence." What exactly does this phrase mean? Most scholars have assumed that the phrase's

meaning is relatively obvious. But in looking at the equally authoritative French version of the Charter (and other translations), the phrase is rendered as *droit naturel de légitime défense*. In foreign criminal law systems, the notion of *légitime défense* is a broad notion that includes not just self-defense but also defense of others. One way of understanding humanitarian intervention is as an example of defense of others, which would be one component of this broader notion of legitimate defense. Moreover, the invocation of *droit naturel*—i.e., natural rights—suggests that the true meaning of article 51 was to preserve the pre-Charter rights of intervention that existed by virtue of natural law, which were more permissive, as long as the intervention was motivated by either self-defense or defense of others. The virtue of this argument is that it justifies humanitarian intervention through an *interpretation* of article 51 instead of by positing the existence of a norm (such as RTP) that is *external* to the UN Charter, which runs into the problem that the Charter is always superior to contradictory legal norms. For more on the doctrine of legitimate defense, see George P. Fletcher & Jens David Ohlin, *Defending Humanity: When Force is Justified and Why* (2008); Jens David Ohlin, *The Doctrine of Legitimate Defense*, 91 Int'l L. Stud. 119 (2015).

3.   *The Pretext Problem.* Is there a danger that recognizing a unilateral right of humanitarian intervention might allow some states to intervene militarily while using the doctrine as a pretext for their behavior? See Ryan Goodman, *Humanitarian Intervention and Pretexts for War*, 100 Am. J. Int'l L. 107 (2006) (concluding that "the pretext objection should not remain an obstacle" to recognizing the doctrine of humanitarian intervention). Goodman argues that as an empirical matter, the benefits of unilateral intervention would far outweigh any potential abuses caused by pretextual invocations of the doctrine. Do you agree?

4.   *The Fiduciary Theory.* A third possibility for justifying humanitarian intervention is a fiduciary theory of obligation. Under this argument, states that use military force are acting as fiduciaries of the local population they are seeking to save from humanitarian crisis. See Evan J. Criddle, *Three Grotian Theories of Humanitarian Intervention*, 16 Theoretical Inquiries in Law 473, 476 (2015) ("states that engage in humanitarian intervention hold discretionary power over the legal and practical interests of their designated beneficiaries (foreign nationals), and they bear a concomitant fiduciary obligation to exercise this power exclusively for their beneficiaries' benefit"). However, Criddle concedes that the Security Council is the legal institution tasked with authorizing intervention. Could the fiduciary theory be extended to justify *unilateral* intervention? Is it possible to argue that authoritarian states have a fiduciary obligation to their citizens and that if they violate it (by killing their citizens) their sovereign right to rule evaporates? This argument implies that the concept of sovereignty is a conditional entitlement granted to each state from the international community.

Conclusion & Summary

The status of humanitarian intervention under international law is highly contested. However, despite the uncertainty, a number of clear conclusions can be drawn:

1. Although the UN Charter rules on authorizing military force are clear, the Kosovo intervention was retroactively supported by many actors, leading many of them to envision an emerging norm of humanitarian intervention under highly restrictive circumstances. Many legal scholars suggested that the intervention was illegal but legitimate in some deeper sense.

2. A number of doctrines have emerged as potential justifications for humanitarian intervention. The Responsibility to Protect (RTP) is the most prominent example, although the doctrine is sufficiently broad that many statements of support for the doctrine may not be endorsements of a right to unilateral intervention. Furthermore, the doctrine may not be consistent with the text of article 51 of the UN Charter.

3. There are other doctrinal possibilities for justifying intervention, including the defense of necessity, the doctrine of legitimate defense, and the fiduciary theory, though none of these theories have attracted widespread support among states.

4. The UN and other NGO groups have emphasized prevention of atrocities in the absence of broad support for a new norm of unilateral intervention.

CHAPTER 11

HUMAN RIGHTS

Introduction

The end of War World II brought, along with the creation of the United Nations, a renewed focus on individual human rights. The centerpiece of that process was the Universal Declaration of Human Rights, which was passed in the form of a United Nations General Assembly resolution in 1948. The Declaration was one piece of a larger legal architecture that included the creation of the United Nations and its subsidiary organs, including the Security Council, the General Assembly, and the International Court of Justice. In just 30 terse articles, the Declaration articulates a series of individual rights that all nation states must accept. These include, to name just a few: right to life, liberty and security (art. 3); prohibition on slavery (art. 4); prohibition on torture (art. 5); recognition before the law (art. 6); and anti-discrimination (art. 7). Perhaps more important than the specific rights articulated in the document is the underlying assumption guiding the entire effort: How a state treats its own citizens is no longer a matter of sovereign prerogative but rather is a matter of international concern and an appropriate subject for international legal regulation. That change, more than any other, represents the heart of the human rights revolution.

However, it is possible to overstate the significance of the Universal Declaration as a source of law. Because it was passed as a General Assembly resolution, rather than as a treaty, its provisions are not legally binding on member states as a matter of positive law. Rather, the Declaration is considered aspirational only—a broad policy statement of what rights all human beings ought to have, without necessarily creating a formal legal obligation to bring those rights to fruition.

That formalized process came later, when work began on translating the aspirational rights of the Declaration into a formal bilateral human rights convention. Unfortunately, the devil was in the details, and the process of deciding which human rights would be formalized in a binding treaty became embroiled in Cold War geopolitics.

According to the United States and its closest allies, the new human rights treaty should protect individual rights *against* government misconduct, mistreatment, or interference—rights that an American lawyer might refer to as "civil rights." Among these would be freedom of expression and religion, the right to participate in the political process, rights to due process, etc. In contrast, the Soviet Union and its allies were skeptical of these rights, which were sharply limited under Communist rule, and they worried that a document focused on these civil rights would be used as a rhetorical tool for Western states to criticize communist rule. The Soviet Union believed that a human rights treaty should focus on economic and social rights, i.e., the right to food, housing, employment, and healthcare—entitlements that communist or socialist governments seek to provide to their citizens.

The dividing line between these two categories of rights is often referred to with the somewhat imprecise language of "negative" and "positive" rights. Negative rights involve freedom *from* governmental misconduct. So, for example, the right to free speech means that the government cannot prosecute someone for what they say, and freedom of religion means the government cannot discriminate on the basis of religion. On the other hand, positive rights are "freedom to" something, and require positive action—possibly even redistribution of wealth—on the part of the government to ensure that the right is fulfilled. With this distinction between positive and negative rights in mind, one can see why the United States and the Soviet Union had polar opposite views regarding the nature of human rights. For the Soviet Union, negative rights had the potential to place its country's political practices under far too much international scrutiny. For the United States, positive rights—taken to their logical extreme—might actually require the implementation of economic socialism.

This tension proved too difficult to navigate in a single document. The result was a bifurcation of the proposed human rights treaty into two distinct documents focusing on separate spheres of justice. The negative rights document ripened into the International Covenant on Civil and Political Rights (ICCPR), while the positive rights document ripened into the International Covenant on Economic, Social, and Cultural Rights (ICESCR). Both were signed in 1966 and entered into force in 1976. In subsequent years, regional bodies have emerged with their own foundational documents to protect human rights in a particular geographical region, such as the European Convention on Human Rights and the African Charter on Human and Peoples' Rights. These regional conventions overlap *partially* with their international cousins in that they exclude some rights recognized at the international level and include some rights not codified in the international conventions. Consequently, human rights law is composed of an overlapping matrix of international, regional, and domestic legal obligations.

The following materials lay out the basic building blocks of this new international legal regime that protects individuals, rather than states (the original objects of international legal obligations). Section A briefly explains the courts and tribunals where individual rights might be vindicated. Section B focuses on civil and political rights, with special emphasis on the right to religion. Section C focuses on one economic right—the right to food—and what obligations states might have to ensure that all human beings are adequately fed. Section D considers the fate of human rights in times of emergency and whether states may suspend or otherwise "bend" these individual protections when the safety of the state is at stake. Finally, Section E considers whether international human rights treaties apply extraterritorially, that is, whether a state is constrained by this body of law when it is acting outside of its own territories (in its dealing with foreign nationals), for example during a military operation abroad.

In reading these materials, it is essential to recall how quickly international law has transformed itself from a legal regime that focused exclusively on what states may or may not do to each other, into a body of law that also directly protects the interests of individual human beings.

A. COURTS AND TRIBUNALS

International human rights can be vindicated in a number of fora. Although international tribunals receive the greatest attention in popular discourse, in the human rights field a greater role is played by non-adjudicatory bodies at the international level, regional courts, and even national courts. In some situations, the vindication is performed through formal litigation, in the same way that constitutional rights are vindicated in a domestic legal system, but in other cases less formal avenues allow petitioners to file complaints or allow bodies to review and assess whether states are complying with their human rights obligations.

1. INTERNATIONAL BODIES

The ICCPR includes its own enforcement mechanism, though it is not an adversarial "court" or "tribunal." The Human Rights Committee was created under the ICCPR and has two major functions. First, state parties to the ICCPR are required to submit regular reports, every five years, regarding their compliance with international obligations under the Convention. The Committee then reviews the report and has the opportunity to comment on these self-assessments. Given that the assessments are drafted by the state parties, they are inevitably non-critical. The second mechanism is an individual complaint process whereby nationals from state parties can file petitions against their *own* state for violations of the ICCPR. This individual complaint process is only available if the state has signed and ratified the First Optional Protocol to the ICCPR. The complaint process provides an opportunity for individuals to file a complaint, at which point the Committee will consider both the complaint's admissibility and, if the first is positive, the merits of the complaint. States are entitled to withdraw from the First

Optional Protocol, but doing so would not deprive the Committee of jurisdiction over a complaint first filed when the state was still a state party. If the Committee issues a decision finding that a violation has occurred, the state is supposed to report back indicating the measures taken to remedy the violation. However, the Committee does not have the power to order coercive legal remedies in the same manner as a domestic court hearing an allegation of a constitutional violation. That coercive power would reside with the UN Security Council.

There are international bodies associated with many of the major human rights conventions. For example, compliance with the ICESCR is monitored by the UN Committee on Economic, Social and Cultural Rights. The Convention on the Elimination of all Forms of Discrimination Against Women (CEDAW) created the Committee on the Elimination of Discrimination Against Women. The Committee against Torture was created by the Convention against Torture and Other Cruel, Inhuman or Degrading Treatment or Punishment. Like the Human Rights Council tasked with monitoring compliance with the ICCPR, many of these treaty bodies are empowered to hear complaints from individuals.

The United Nations also included a Commission on Human Rights, which provides an opportunity for states to discuss concerns related to human rights protections and violations. Created by the UN Charter, the Commission and its discussions had a reputation for being highly politicized. Some western states, including the United States, complained that human rights violators on the Commission were using their membership on the Commission to simultaneously shield themselves from scrutiny and strategically criticize their geopolitical adversaries. Amid fears that the Commission was irreparably broken, it was replaced in 2006 with a new Human Rights Council, which includes 47 states selected by election. While opinions differ, several human rights activists consider the Human Rights Council an improvement over its predecessor commission. Nonetheless, some have complained that disputes between Israel and Arab states—in particular over Israel's conduct towards Palestinians—continue to occupy a disproportionate amount of the council's efforts.

2. REGIONAL COURTS

One of the most active tribunals is the European Court on Human Rights, which considers complaints of misconduct under the European Convention on Human Rights. Based in Strasbourg, France, the court's members include all 47 states of the Council of Europe. Its decisions are binding on its members, and refusal to abide by the court's decisions would run the risk that a state might be excluded from the European Union, a highly desirable political, economic, and legal union of European states. For this reason, the ECHR has a strong track record of inducing compliance among European states. The decisions of the ECHR have produced a rich jurisprudence of European human rights law. Although this law is best described as "regional human rights law," because the European Convention is only binding on signatory states in Europe, most of its provisions overlap significantly with provisions in international legal instruments.

There are corollary courts on other continents, although none has had the same practical effect as the European Court. For example, the Inter-American Court of Human Rights was created in 1979 pursuant to the American Convention on Human Rights, though it does not create a provision for the filing of complaints by individuals. Its judges are elected by a regional entity called the Organization of American States (OAS). Similarly, the African Court on Human and Peoples' Rights was created by a protocol to the African Charter on Human and Peoples' Rights. The African Charter is somewhat unique in that it codifies, in addition to individual human rights, select "duties" that individuals have towards their family, community, and society.

3. NATIONAL COURTS

International human rights can also be vindicated in domestic courts. This can happen either directly or indirectly. For example, a state may codify a human right in its domestic constitution. If that right was codified domestically in response to an international legal obligation—for example a right expressed in an international convention—then in some sense the enforcement of the domestic constitutional right is an indirect enforcement of the more foundational international human right. However, there are also many examples of direct enforcement of international legal norms in domestic courts. Signatories of the European Court of Human Rights allow citizens to file individual complaints before domestic courts as a first step; only once they have exhausted all domestic remedies are they permitted to appeal to the European Court in Strasbourg. In some states, domestic courts use international human rights as the foundation for a "constitutional" review of governmental practice. In that vein, a court in say, the Netherlands, will review domestic legislation for its consistency with international law, including human rights law, and will strike down the legislation if it conflicts with the state's legal obligations. Although this process is most robust in states, like the Netherlands, with a monist approach to international law, it is present in any state that allows litigants to express arguments in the language of international human rights. Although the forum for these arguments may be provided by an individual state (i.e., its domestic courts), the content of these legal arguments flows from international human rights law. In that sense, international human rights law is often enforced domestically by domestic actors.

B. CIVIL AND POLITICAL RIGHTS

The category of "civil" and "political" rights represents a vast conceptual territory of rights as diverse as rights to equal treatment before the law; freedom from discrimination; the right not to be deprived of life arbitrarily; freedom from torture, slavery, and servitude; due process and fair trial rights; freedom of movement and the right to leave their country; freedom of thought, conscience, expression, and religion; participation and voting in the political process; and many other rights. Although these rights are codified in the ICCPR and other international and regional human rights instruments, their content usually requires judicial elaboration. The following materials explore two recent examples: domestic prohibitions on face coverings and domestic prohibitions on female genital mutilation. Each example implicates multiple and perhaps conflicting rights. As you read the materials, try to determine the borderline between the public and the private, between an individual's right to religious expression and the state's authority to enact protective legislation, and the proper scope of state secularity.

1. PROHIBITIONS ON FACE VEILS

In 2010, the French legislature passed a law banning face coverings in public. France was not the only state to regulate the wearing of face coverings. Spain, Belgium, and Turkey have passed similar legislation, though in each case the details of the prohibition are different. Advocates for the legislation have pointed to a variety of arguments in support of the ban, including that the veil is a symbol of female subordination within Islam or that the veil's anonymity poses a security threat in public spaces. However, the ban in France was also justified by a particularly French notion—the idea that public space should be "secular." In the following case, a French national contested the ban before the ECHR. How did the Court evaluate the French legislation? Which human rights were possibly implicated by the ban? If the ban implicates a particular human right, does that automatically entail that the legislation is illegal?

S.A.S. v. France
European Court of Human Rights
Application No. 43835/11 (2014)

10. The applicant is a French national who was born in 1990 and lives in France.

11. In the applicant's submission, she is a devout Muslim and she wears the burqa and niqab in accordance with her religious faith, culture and personal convictions. According to her explanation, the burqa is a full-body covering including a mesh over the face, and the niqab is a full-face veil leaving an opening only for the eyes. The applicant emphasised

that neither her husband nor any other member of her family put pressure on her to dress in this manner.

12. The applicant added that she wore the niqab in public and in private, but not systematically: she might not wear it, for example, when she visited the doctor, when meeting friends in a public place, or when she wanted to socialise in public. She was thus content not to wear the niqab in public places at all times but wished to be able to wear it when she chose to do so, depending in particular on her spiritual feelings. There were certain times (for example, during religious events such as Ramadan) when she believed that she ought to wear it in public in order to express her religious, personal and cultural faith. Her aim was not to annoy others but to feel at inner peace with herself.

13. The applicant did not claim that she should be able to keep the niqab on when undergoing a security check, at the bank or in airports, and she agreed to show her face when requested to do so for necessary identity checks.

14. Since 11 April 2011, the date of entry into force of Law No. 2010–1192 of 11 October 2010 throughout France, it has been prohibited for anyone to conceal their face in public places.

15. The conference of Presidents of the National Assembly, on 23 June 2009, established a parliamentary commission comprising members from various parties with the task of drafting a report on "the wearing of the full-face veil on national territory."

16. The report of some 200 pages, deposited on 26 January 2010, described and analysed the existing situation. It showed, in particular, that the wearing of the full-face veil was a recent phenomenon in France (almost no women wore it before 2000) and that about 1,900 women were concerned by the end of 2009 (of whom about 270 were living in French overseas administrative areas); nine out of ten were under 40, two-thirds were French nationals and one in four were converts to Islam. According to the report, the wearing of this clothing existed before the advent of Islam and did not have the nature of a religious precept, but stemmed from a radical affirmation of individuals in search of identity in society and from the action of extremist fundamentalist movements. The report further indicated that the phenomenon was non-existent in countries of central and eastern Europe, specifically mentioning the Czech Republic, Bulgaria, Romania, Hungary, Latvia and Germany. It was not therefore a matter of debate in those countries, unlike the situation in Sweden and Denmark, where the wearing of such veils nevertheless remained marginal. Moreover, the question of a general ban had been discussed in the Netherlands and in Belgium. The report was also critical of the situation in the United Kingdom, where it pointed to a sectarian trend driven by radical and fundamental Muslim groups, who were taking

advantage of a legal system that was very protective of individual fundamental rights and freedoms in order to obtain recognition of rights that were specifically applicable to residents of Muslim faith or origin.

17. The report went on to criticise "a practice at odds with the values of the Republic," as expressed in the maxim "liberty, equality, fraternity." It emphasised that, going beyond mere incompatibility with secularism, the full-face veil was an infringement of the principle of liberty, because it was a symbol of a form of subservience and, by its very existence, negated both the principle of gender equality and that of the equal dignity of human beings. The report further found that the full-face veil represented a denial of fraternity, constituting the negation of contact with others and a flagrant infringement of the French principle of living together.

The report, thus finding it necessary to "release women from the subservience of the full-face veil," advocated a three-pronged course of action: to convince, protect women and envisage a ban. It made the following four proposals: first, to adopt a resolution reasserting Republican values and condemning as contrary to such values the wearing of the full-face veil; secondly, to initiate a general survey of the phenomena of amalgamation, discrimination and rejection of others on account of their origins or faith, and of the conditions of fair representation of spiritual diversity; thirdly, to reinforce actions of awareness and education in mutual respect and diversity and the generalising of mediation mechanisms; and fourthly, to enact legislation guaranteeing the protection of women who were victims of duress, which would strengthen the position of public officials confronted with this phenomenon and curb such practices. The report emphasised that among both the parliamentary commission's members and those of the political formations represented in Parliament, there was no unanimous support for the enactment of a law introducing a general and absolute ban on the wearing of the full-face veil in public places.

18. In the meantime, on 21 January 2010, the National Advisory Commission on Human Rights (CNCDH) had issued an "opinion on the wearing of the full-face veil," stating that it was not in favour of a law introducing a general and absolute ban. It took the view, in particular, that the principle of secularism alone could not serve as a basis for such a general measure, since it was not for the State to determine whether or not a given matter fell within the realm of religion, and that public order could justify a prohibition only if it were limited in space and time. The opinion also emphasised the risk of stigmatising Muslims and pointed out that a general prohibition could be detrimental to women, in particular because those who were made to wear the full-face veil would additionally become deprived of access to public areas.

19. That being said, the CNCDH observed that support for women who were subjected to any kind of violence had to be a political priority; it advocated, in order to combat any form of obscurantism, encouraging the promotion of a culture of dialogue, openness and moderation, with a view to fostering better knowledge of religions and the principles of the Republic; it called for the strengthening of civic education courses— including education and training in human rights—at all levels, for both men and women; it sought the strict application of the principles of secularism and neutrality in public services, and the application of existing legislation; and it expressed the wish that, in parallel, sociological and statistical studies should be carried out in order to monitor the evolution of the wearing of the full-face veil.

28. Sections 1 to 3 of Law No. 2010–1192... "prohibiting the concealment of one's face in public places" read as follows:

Section 1: No one may, in public places, wear clothing that is designed to conceal the face.

Section 2: (I) For the purposes of section 1 hereof, 'public places' comprise the public highway and any places open to the public or assigned to a public service. (II) The prohibition provided for in section 1 hereof shall not apply if the clothing is prescribed or authorised by primary or secondary legislation, if it is justified for health or occupational reasons, or if it is worn in the context of sports, festivities or artistic or traditional events."

Section 3: Any breach of the prohibition laid down in section 1 hereof shall be punishable by a fine, at the rate applying to second-class petty offences (*contraventions*) [150 euros maximum]. An obligation to follow a citizenship course, as provided at paragraph 80 of Article 131–16 of the Criminal Code, may be imposed in addition to or instead of the payment of a fine.

The provisions for the obligation to follow a citizenship course can be found in Articles R. 131–35 to R. 131–44 of the Criminal Code. The purpose of the course is to remind the convicted persons of the Republican values of tolerance and respect for the dignity of the human being and to make them aware of their criminal and civil liability, together with the duties that stem from life in society. It also seeks to further the person's social integration.

29. Law no. 2010–1192 also inserted the following... into the Criminal Code:

Any person who forces one or more other persons to conceal their face, by threat, duress, coercion, abuse of authority or of office, on account of their gender, shall be liable to imprisonment for one year and a fine of 30,000 euros. Where the offence is committed against a minor, such punishment shall be increased to two years' imprisonment and a fine of 60,000 euros.

40. To date, only Belgium has passed a law that is comparable to the French Law of 11 October 2010, and the Belgian Constitutional Court has found it compatible with the right to freedom of thought, conscience and religion. However, the question of a ban on concealing one's face in public has been or is being discussed in a number of other European States. A blanket ban remains a possibility in some of them. In particular, a bill has been tabled to that end in Italy: although it has not yet passed into law, it appears that the discussion is still open. In Switzerland the Federal Assembly rejected, in September 2012, an initiative of the Canton of Aargau seeking to ban the wearing in public of clothing covering all or a large part of the face, but in Ticino there was a vote on 23 September 2013 for a ban of that kind (the text still has to be validated, however, by the Federal Assembly). Such an option is also being discussed in the Netherlands, notwithstanding unfavourable opinions by the Council of State. It should also be noted that the Spanish Supreme Court has ruled on the legality of a ban of that kind.

74. The applicant complained for the same reasons of a violation of her right to respect for her private life, her right to freedom to manifest her religion or beliefs and her right to freedom of expression, together with discrimination in the exercise of these rights. She relied on Articles 8, 9 and 10 of the Convention, taken separately and in conjunction with Article 14. Those first three Articles read as follows.

Article 8

1. Everyone has the right to respect for his private and family life, his home and his correspondence.

2. There shall be no interference by a public authority with the exercise of this right except such as is in accordance with the law and is necessary in a democratic society in the interests of national security, public safety or the economic well-being of the country, for the prevention of disorder or crime, for the protection of health or morals, or for the protection of the rights and freedoms of others.

Article 9

1. Everyone has the right to freedom of thought, conscience and religion; this right includes freedom to change his religion or belief and freedom, either alone or in community with others and in public or private, to manifest his religion or belief, in worship, teaching, practice and observance. 2. Freedom to manifest one's religion or beliefs shall be subject only to such limitations as are prescribed by law and are necessary in a democratic society in the interests of public safety, for the

protection of public order, health or morals, or for the protection of the rights and freedoms of others.

Article 10

1. Everyone has the right to freedom of expression. This right shall include freedom to hold opinions and to receive and impart information and ideas without interference by public authority and regardless of frontiers. This Article shall not prevent States from requiring the licensing of broadcasting, television or cinema enterprises.

2. The exercise of these freedoms, since it carries with it duties and responsibilities, may be subject to such formalities, conditions, restrictions or penalties as are prescribed by law and are necessary in a democratic society, in the interests of national security, territorial integrity or public safety, for the prevention of disorder or crime, for the protection of health or morals, for the protection of the reputation or rights of others, for preventing the disclosure of information received in confidence, or for maintaining the authority and impartiality of the judiciary.

106. The ban on wearing, in public places, clothing designed to conceal the face raises questions in terms of the right to respect for private life of women who wish to wear the full-face veil for reasons related to their beliefs, and in terms of their freedom to manifest those beliefs.

107. The Court is thus of the view that personal choices as to an individual's desired appearance, whether in public or in private places, relate to the expression of his or her personality and thus fall within the notion of private life. It has found to this effect previously as regards a haircut. It considers, like the Commission, that this is also true for a choice of clothing. A measure emanating from a public authority which restricts a choice of this kind will therefore, in principle, constitute an interference with the exercise of the right to respect for private life within the meaning of Article 8 of the Convention. Consequently, the ban on wearing clothing designed to conceal the face in public places, pursuant to the Law of 11 October 2010, falls under Article 8 of the Convention.

108. That being said, in so far as that ban is criticised by individuals who, like the applicant, complain that they are consequently prevented from wearing in public places clothing that the practice of their religion requires them to wear, it mainly raises an issue with regard to the freedom to manifest one's religion or beliefs. The fact that this is a minority practice and appears to be contested is of no relevance in this connection.

109. The Court will thus examine this part of the application under both Article 8 and Article 9, but with emphasis on the second of those provisions.

Whether there has been a "limitation" or an "interference"

110. As the Court has already pointed out, the Law of 11 October 2010 confronts the applicant with a dilemma comparable to that which it identified in the *Dudgeon* and *Norris* judgments: either she complies with the ban and thus refrains from dressing in accordance with her approach to religion; or she refuses to comply and faces criminal sanctions. She thus finds herself, in the light of both Article 9 and Article 8 of the Convention, in a similar situation to that of the applicants in *Dudgeon* and *Norris*, where the Court found a "continuing interference" with the exercise of the rights guaranteed by the second of those provisions. There has therefore been, in the present case, an "interference" with or a "limitation" of the exercise of the rights protected by Articles 8 and 9 of the Convention.

111. Such a limitation or interference will not be compatible with the second paragraphs of those Articles unless it is "prescribed by law," pursues one or more of the legitimate aims set out in those paragraphs and is "necessary in a democratic society" to achieve the aim or aims concerned.

Whether the measure is "prescribed by law"

112. The Court finds that the limitation in question is prescribed by sections 1, 2 and 3 of the Law of 11 October 2010. It further notes that the applicant has not disputed that these provisions satisfy the criteria laid down in the Court's case-law concerning Article 8 § 2 and Article 9 § 2 of the Convention.

Whether there is a legitimate aim

113. The Court reiterates that the enumeration of the exceptions to the individual's freedom to manifest his or her religion or beliefs, as listed in Article 9 § 2, is exhaustive and that their definition is restrictive. For it to be compatible with the Convention, a limitation of this freedom must, in particular, pursue an aim that can be linked to one of those listed in this provision. The same approach applies in respect of Article 8 of the Convention.

114. The Court's practice is to be quite succinct when it verifies the existence of a legitimate aim within the meaning of the second paragraphs of Articles 8 to 11 of the Convention. However, in the present case, the substance of the objectives invoked in this connection by the Government, and strongly disputed by the applicant, call for an in-depth examination. The applicant took the view that the interference with the exercise of her freedom to manifest her religion and of her right to respect

for her private life, as a result of the ban introduced by the Law of 11 October 2010, did not correspond to any of the aims listed in the second paragraphs of Articles 8 and 9. The Government argued, for their part, that the Law pursued two legitimate aims: public safety and "respect for the minimum set of values of an open and democratic society." The Court observes that the second paragraphs of Articles 8 and 9 do not refer expressly to the second of those aims or to the three values mentioned by the Government in that connection.

115. As regards the first of the aims invoked by the Government, the Court first observes that "public safety" is one of the aims enumerated in the second paragraph of Article 9 of the Convention and also in the second paragraph of Article 8. It further notes the Government's observation in this connection that the impugned ban on wearing, in public places, clothing designed to conceal the face satisfied the need to identify individuals in order to prevent danger for the safety of persons and property and to combat identity fraud. Having regard to the case file, it may admittedly be wondered whether the Law's drafters attached much weight to such concerns. It must nevertheless be observed that the explanatory memorandum which accompanied the bill indicated—albeit secondarily—that the practice of concealing the face "could also represent a danger for public safety in certain situations," and that the Constitutional Council noted that the legislature had been of the view that this practice might be dangerous for public safety. Similarly, in its study report of 25 March 2010, the *Conseil d'État* indicated that public safety might constitute a basis for prohibiting concealment of the face, but pointed out that this could be the case only in specific circumstances. Consequently, the Court accepts that, in adopting the impugned ban, the legislature sought to address questions of "public safety" within the meaning of the second paragraphs of Articles 8 and 9 of the Convention.

116. As regards the second of the aims invoked—to ensure "respect for the minimum set of values of an open and democratic society"—the Government referred to three values: respect for equality between men and women, respect for human dignity and respect for the minimum requirements of life in society. They submitted that this aim could be linked to the "protection of the rights and freedoms of others," within the meaning of the second paragraphs of Articles 8 and 9 of the Convention.

117. As the Court has previously noted, these three values do not expressly correspond to any of the legitimate aims enumerated in the second paragraphs of Articles 8 and 9 of the Convention. Among those aims, the only ones that may be relevant in the present case, in relation to the values in question, are "public order" and the "protection of the rights and freedoms of others." The former is not, however, mentioned in Article 8 § 2. Moreover, the Government did not refer to it either in their written observations or in their answer to the question put to them in

that connection during the public hearing, preferring to refer solely to the "protection of the rights and freedoms of others." The Court will thus focus its examination on the latter "legitimate aim". . .

118. Firstly, the Court is not convinced by the Government's submission in so far as it concerns respect for equality between men and women.

119. It does not doubt that gender equality might rightly justify an interference with the exercise of certain rights and freedoms enshrined in the Convention. It reiterates in this connection that advancement of gender equality is today a major goal in the member States of the Council of Europe. Thus a State Party which, in the name of gender equality, prohibits anyone from forcing women to conceal their face pursues an aim which corresponds to the "protection of the rights and freedoms of others" within the meaning of the second paragraphs of Articles 8 and 9 of the Convention. The Court takes the view, however, that a State Party cannot invoke gender equality in order to ban a practice that is defended by women—such as the applicant—in the context of the exercise of the rights enshrined in those provisions, unless it were to be understood that individuals could be protected on that basis from the exercise of their own fundamental rights and freedoms. It further observes that the *Conseil d'État* reached a similar conclusion in its study report of 25 March 2010.

Moreover, in so far as the Government thus sought to show that the wearing of the full-face veil by certain women shocked the majority of the French population because it infringed the principle of gender equality as generally accepted in France, the Court would refer to its reasoning as to the other two values that they have invoked.

120. Secondly, the Court takes the view that, however essential it may be, respect for human dignity cannot legitimately justify a blanket ban on the wearing of the full-face veil in public places. The Court is aware that the clothing in question is perceived as strange by many of those who observe it. It would point out, however, that it is the expression of a cultural identity which contributes to the pluralism that is inherent in democracy. It notes in this connection the variability of the notions of virtuousness and decency that are applied to the uncovering of the human body. Moreover, it does not have any evidence capable of leading it to consider that women who wear the full-face veil seek to express a form of contempt against those they encounter or otherwise to offend against the dignity of others.

121. Thirdly, the Court finds, by contrast, that under certain conditions the "respect for the minimum requirements of life in society" referred to by the Government—or of "living together," as stated in the explanatory memorandum accompanying the bill—can be linked to the legitimate aim of the "protection of the rights and freedoms of others."

122. The Court takes into account the respondent State's point that the face plays an important role in social interaction. It can understand the view that individuals who are present in places open to all may not wish to see practices or attitudes developing there which would fundamentally call into question the possibility of open interpersonal relationships, which, by virtue of an established consensus, forms an indispensable element of community life within the society in question. The Court is therefore able to accept that the barrier raised against others by a veil concealing the face is perceived by the respondent State as breaching the right of others to live in a space of socialisation which makes living together easier. That being said, in view of the flexibility of the notion of "living together" and the resulting risk of abuse, the Court must engage in a careful examination of the necessity of the impugned limitation.

Whether the measure is necessary in a democratic society

123. As the Court has decided to focus on Article 9 of the Convention in examining this part of the application, it finds it appropriate to reiterate the general principles concerning that provision.

124. As enshrined in Article 9, freedom of thought, conscience and religion is one of the foundations of a "democratic society" within the meaning of the Convention. This freedom is, in its religious dimension, one of the most vital elements that go to make up the identity of believers and their conception of life, but it is also a precious asset for atheists, agnostics, sceptics and the unconcerned. The pluralism indissociable from a democratic society, which has been dearly won over the centuries, depends on it. That freedom entails, *inter alia*, freedom to hold or not to hold religious beliefs and to practise or not to practise a religion.

125. While religious freedom is primarily a matter of individual conscience, it also implies freedom to manifest one's religion, alone and in private, or in community with others, in public and within the circle of those whose faith one shares. Article 9 lists the various forms which the manifestation of one's religion or beliefs may take, namely worship, teaching, practice and observance. Article 9 does not, however, protect every act motivated or inspired by a religion or belief and does not always guarantee the right to behave in the public sphere in a manner which is dictated by one's religion or beliefs.

126. In democratic societies, in which several religions coexist within one and the same population, it may be necessary to place limitations on freedom to manifest one's religion or beliefs in order to reconcile the interests of the various groups and ensure that everyone's beliefs are respected. This follows both from paragraph 2 of Article 9 and from the State's positive obligations under Article 1 of the Convention to

secure to everyone within its jurisdiction the rights and freedoms defined therein.

127. The Court has frequently emphasised the State's role as the neutral and impartial organiser of the exercise of various religions, faiths and beliefs, and has stated that this role is conducive to public order, religious harmony and tolerance in a democratic society. As indicated previously, it also considers that the State's duty of neutrality and impartiality is incompatible with any power on the State's part to assess the legitimacy of religious beliefs or the ways in which those beliefs are expressed, and that this duty requires the State to ensure mutual tolerance between opposing groups. Accordingly, the role of the authorities in such circumstances is not to remove the cause of tension by eliminating pluralism, but to ensure that the competing groups tolerate each other.

128. Pluralism, tolerance and broadmindedness are hallmarks of a "democratic society." Although individual interests must on occasion be subordinated to those of a group, democracy does not simply mean that the views of a majority must always prevail: a balance must be achieved which ensures the fair treatment of people from minorities and avoids any abuse of a dominant position. Pluralism and democracy must also be based on dialogue and a spirit of compromise necessarily entailing various concessions on the part of individuals or groups of individuals which are justified in order to maintain and promote the ideals and values of a democratic society. Where these "rights and freedoms of others" are themselves among those guaranteed by the Convention or the Protocols thereto, it must be accepted that the need to protect them may lead States to restrict other rights or freedoms likewise set forth in the Convention. It is precisely this constant search for a balance between the fundamental rights of each individual which constitutes the foundation of a "democratic society."

129. It is also important to emphasise the fundamentally subsidiary role of the Convention mechanism. The national authorities have direct democratic legitimation and are, as the Court has held on many occasions, in principle better placed than an international court to evaluate local needs and conditions. In matters of general policy, on which opinions within a democratic society may reasonably differ widely, the role of the domestic policy-maker should be given special weight. This is the case, in particular, where questions concerning the relationship between State and religions are at stake. As regards Article 9 of the Convention, the State should thus, in principle, be afforded a wide margin of appreciation in deciding whether and to what extent a limitation of the right to manifest one's religion or beliefs is "necessary." That being said, in delimiting the extent of the margin of appreciation in a given case, the Court must also have regard to what is at stake therein.

It may also, if appropriate, have regard to any consensus and common values emerging from the practices of the States Parties to the Convention.

130. In the judgment in *Leyla Şahin,* the Court pointed out that this would notably be the case when it came to regulating the wearing of religious symbols in educational institutions, especially in view of the diversity of the approaches taken by national authorities on the issue. Referring to the judgment in *Otto-Preminger-Institut v. Austria* and the decision in *Dahlab v. Switzerland,* it added that it was thus not possible to discern throughout Europe a uniform conception of the significance of religion in society and that the meaning or impact of the public expression of a religious belief would differ according to time and context. It observed that the rules in this sphere would consequently vary from one country to another according to national traditions and the requirements imposed by the need to protect the rights and freedoms of others and to maintain public order. It concluded from this that the choice of the extent and form of such rules must inevitably be left up to a point to the State concerned, as it would depend on the specific domestic context.

131. This margin of appreciation, however, goes hand in hand with a European supervision embracing both the law and the decisions applying it. The Court's task is to determine whether the measures taken at national level were justified in principle and proportionate.

137. The Court would first emphasise that the argument put forward by the applicant and some of the third-party interveners, to the effect that the ban introduced by sections 1 to 3 of the Law of 11 October 2010 was based on the erroneous supposition that the women concerned wore the full-face veil under duress, is not pertinent. It can clearly be seen from the explanatory memorandum accompanying the bill that it was not the principal aim of the ban to protect women against a practice which was imposed on them or would be detrimental to them.

138. That being clarified, the Court must verify whether the impugned interference is "necessary in a democratic society" for public safety or for the "protection of the rights and freedoms of others."

139. As regards the question of necessity in relation to public safety, within the meaning of Articles 8 and 9, the Court understands that a State may find it essential to be able to identify individuals in order to prevent danger for the safety of persons and property and to combat identity fraud. It has thus found no violation of Article 9 of the Convention in cases concerning the obligation to remove clothing with a religious connotation in the context of security checks and the obligation to appear bareheaded on identity photos for use on official documents. However, in view of its impact on the rights of women who wish to wear

the full-face veil for religious reasons, a blanket ban on the wearing in public places of clothing designed to conceal the face can be regarded as proportionate only in a context where there is a general threat to public safety. The Government have not shown that the ban introduced by the Law of 11 October 2010 falls into such a context. As to the women concerned, they are thus obliged to give up completely an element of their identity that they consider important, together with their chosen manner of manifesting their religion or beliefs, whereas the objective alluded to by the Government could be attained by a mere obligation to show their face and to identify themselves where a risk for the safety of persons and property has been established, or where particular circumstances entail a suspicion of identity fraud. It cannot therefore be found that the blanket ban imposed by the Law of 11 October 2010 is necessary, in a democratic society, for public safety, within the meaning of Articles 8 and 9 of the Convention.

140. The Court will now examine the questions raised by the other aim that it has found legitimate: to ensure the observance of the minimum requirements of life in society as part of the "protection of the rights and freedoms of others."

141. The Court observes that this is an aim to which the authorities have given much weight. This can be seen, in particular, from the explanatory memorandum accompanying the bill, which indicates that "[t]he voluntary and systematic concealment of the face is problematic because it is quite simply incompatible with the fundamental requirements of 'living together' in French society" and that "[t]he systematic concealment of the face in public places, contrary to the ideal of fraternity, . . . falls short of the minimum requirement of civility that is necessary for social interaction." It indeed falls within the powers of the State to secure the conditions whereby individuals can live together in their diversity. Moreover, the Court is able to accept that a State may find it essential to give particular weight in this connection to the interaction between individuals and may consider this to be adversely affected by the fact that some conceal their faces in public places.

142. Consequently, the Court finds that the impugned ban can be regarded as justified in its principle solely in so far as it seeks to guarantee the conditions of "living together."

143. It remains to be ascertained whether the ban is proportionate to that aim.

144. Some of the arguments put forward by the applicant and the intervening non-governmental organisations warrant particular attention.

145. Firstly, it is true that only a small number of women are affected. It can be seen, among other things, from the report "on the

wearing of the full-face veil on national territory", prepared by a commission of the National Assembly and deposited on 26 January 2010, that about 1,900 women wore the Islamic full-face veil in France at the end of 2009, of whom about 270 were living in French overseas administrative areas. This is a small proportion in relation to the French population of about sixty-five million and to the number of Muslims living in France. It may thus seem excessive to respond to such a situation by imposing a blanket ban.

146. In addition, there is no doubt that the ban has a significant negative impact on the situation of women who, like the applicant, have chosen to wear the full-face veil for reasons related to their beliefs. As stated previously, they are thus confronted with a complex dilemma, and the ban may have the effect of isolating them and restricting their autonomy, as well as impairing the exercise of their freedom to manifest their beliefs and their right to respect for their private life. It is also understandable that the women concerned may perceive the ban as a threat to their identity.

147. It should furthermore be observed that a large number of actors, both international and national, in the field of fundamental rights protection have found a blanket ban to be disproportionate. This is the case, for example, of the French National Advisory Commission on Human Rights, non-governmental organisations such as the third-party interveners, the Parliamentary Assembly of the Council of Europe and the Commissioner for Human Rights of the Council of Europe.

148. The Court is also aware that the Law of 11 October 2010, together with certain debates surrounding its drafting, may have upset part of the Muslim community, including some members who are not in favour of the full-face veil being worn.

149. In this connection, the Court is very concerned by the indications of some of the third-party interveners to the effect that certain Islamophobic remarks marked the debate which preceded the adoption of the Law of 11 October 2010. It is admittedly not for the Court to rule on whether legislation is desirable in such matters. It would, however, emphasise that a State which enters into a legislative process of this kind takes the risk of contributing to the consolidation of the stereotypes which affect certain categories of the population and of encouraging the expression of intolerance, when it has a duty, on the contrary, to promote tolerance. The Court reiterates that remarks which constitute a general, vehement attack on a religious or ethnic group are incompatible with the values of tolerance, social peace and non-discrimination which underlie the Convention and do not fall within the right to freedom of expression that it protects.

150. The other arguments put forward in support of the application must, however, be qualified.

151. Thus, while it is true that the scope of the ban is broad, since it concerns all places accessible to the public (except for places of worship), the Law of 11 October 2010 does not affect the freedom to wear in public any garment or item of clothing—with or without a religious connotation—which does not have the effect of concealing the face. The Court is aware of the fact that the impugned ban mainly affects Muslim women who wish to wear the full-face veil. It nevertheless finds it to be of some significance that the ban is not expressly based on the religious connotation of the clothing in question but solely on the fact that it conceals the face. . .

152. As to the fact that criminal sanctions are attached to the ban, this no doubt increases the impact of the measure on those concerned. It is certainly understandable that the idea of being prosecuted for concealing one's face in a public place is traumatising for women who have chosen to wear the full-face veil for reasons related to their beliefs. It should nevertheless be taken into account that the sanctions provided for by the Law's drafters are among the lightest that could be envisaged, since they consist of a fine at the rate applying to second-class petty offences (currently EUR 150 maximum), with the possibility for the court to impose, in addition to or instead of the fine, an obligation to follow a citizenship course.

153. Furthermore, admittedly, as the applicant pointed out, by prohibiting everyone from wearing clothing designed to conceal the face in public places, the respondent State has to a certain extent restricted the reach of pluralism, since the ban prevents certain women from expressing their personality and their beliefs by wearing the full-face veil in public. However, for their part, the Government indicated that it was a question of responding to a practice that the State deemed incompatible, in French society, with the ground rules of social communication and more broadly the requirements of "living together." From that perspective, the respondent State is seeking to protect a principle of interaction between individuals, which in its view is essential for the expression not only of pluralism, but also of tolerance and broadmindedness without which there is no democratic society. It can thus be said that the question whether or not it should be permitted to wear the full-face veil in public places constitutes a choice of society.

154. In such circumstances, the Court has a duty to exercise a degree of restraint in its review of Convention compliance, since such review will lead it to assess a balance that has been struck by means of a democratic process within the society in question. The Court has, moreover, already had occasion to observe that in matters of general policy, on which opinions within a democratic society may reasonably

differ widely, the role of the domestic policy-maker should be given special weight.

155. In other words, France had a wide margin of appreciation in the present case.

157. Consequently, having regard in particular to the breadth of the margin of appreciation afforded to the respondent State in the present case, the Court finds that the ban imposed by the Law of 11 October 2010 can be regarded as proportionate to the aim pursued, namely the preservation of the conditions of "living together" as an element of the "protection of the rights and freedoms of others."

158. The impugned limitation can thus be regarded as "necessary in a democratic society." This conclusion holds true with respect both to Article 8 of the Convention and to Article 9.

159. Accordingly, there has been no violation either of Article 8 or of Article 9 of the Convention.

NOTES & QUESTIONS

1. *Living Together.* Ultimately, why did the ECHR conclude that France had not violated the human rights of the applicant? What role did the notion of "living together" play in the court's analysis? Why is the ban a legitimate response to the need to create a public space where socialization may occur? Recall that the court ultimately rejected the notion that the ban was a proportional response to the security threat posed by the veil. Why then was the ban upheld as proportional to the legitimate government aim of protecting the "minimum requirements of life in society"? What role did the "margin of appreciation" play? For a discussion of the ECHR's margin of appreciation that it affords states, see Raffaella Nigro, *The Margin of Appreciation Doctrine and the Case-Law of the European Court of Human Rights on the Islamic Veil*, 11 Hum. Rts. Rev. 531 (2010); Natan Lerner, *How Wide the Margin of Appreciation? The Turkish Headscarf Case, the Strasbourg Court, and Secularist Tolerance*, 13 Willamette J. Int'l L. & Disp. Resol. 65, 85 (2005) ("From a purely human rights angle, one is tempted to say that the European Court of Human Rights reasserted its respect for the margin of appreciation of states, but ignored the individual right to manifest bona fide religious convictions and did not attempt to show how a total prohibition of such manifestations, at all levels in the educational sphere including universities, was necessary to protect a democratic society.").

2. *Methodology: Proportionality Review.* The Court's determination that the French legislation infringed a particular right was the beginning—not the end—of its analysis. After that threshold determination, the Court went on to ask whether the state had an essential interest and then whether the state's infringement of the individual right was proportional to the state interest. This analytical process is often described as proportionality review, and it is now a common metric for evaluating human rights claims in

domestic and international tribunals. Of course, some prohibitions are immune from balancing, such as the prohibition on torture or other forms of mistreatment. In contrast, other rights, such as expression and religion, are subject to regulation under the European Convention if restrictions "are necessary in a democratic society in the interests of public safety, for the protection of public order, health or morals, or for the protection of the rights and freedoms of others" (art. 9). Whether a restriction is "necessary" depends on whether it is proportional to the government interest. National courts are now using a similar methodology for evaluating rights' claims. Professor Alec Stone Sweet argues that "Under the Court's supervision, [proportionality review] is now in the process of diffusing to every national legal order in Europe, where it will typically be absorbed as a constitutional principle." See Alec Stone Sweet & Jud Mathews, *Proportionality Balancing and Global Constitutionalism*, 47 Colum. J. Transnat'l L. 72, 150 (2008). Do you think that proportionality review yielded the correct outcome in *S.A.S. v. France*?

2. FEDERAL BAN ON FEMALE GENITAL MUTILATION

Many states have bans on female genital mutilation, a practice of cutting all or parts of a young girl's genitalia. In some cases, the procedure is performed shortly after birth as a form of female "circumcision." In other cases, it happens at an older age as the child reaches puberty, in an attempt to limit or control the woman's capacity for sexual enjoyment. The procedure is particularly prevalent in some countries in Africa and Asia, where it is considered a religious practice. Although there are multiple reasons for the practice, the United Nations has concluded that "[i]n every society in which it is practised, female genital mutilation is a manifestation of gender inequality that is deeply entrenched in social, economic and political structures." See World Health Organization, Eliminating Female Genital Mutilation: An Interagency Statement 5 (2008). Many states have criminalized the practice. For example, in 2017 federal prosecutors in the U.S. charged several individuals in the Detroit area with female genital mutilation, including two doctors. Lawyers for the charged individuals asserted that the procedures they performed did not constitute female genital mutilation. The case was the first prosecution under the federal criminal provision, but the case was thrown out by a district judge because there was "no rational relationship between the FGM statute" and the ICCPR, which includes a provision prohibiting sex discrimination but no specific reference to genital mutilation. *United States v. Nagarwala*, 350 F. Supp. 3d 613, 618 (E.D. Mich. 2018). The Trump Administration's Department of Justice declined to defend the statute before the Sixth Circuit Court of Appeals and moved to dismiss the prosecution.

Reprinted below is the relevant provision from the U.S. Criminal Code, as well as General Recommendation No. 14 from the Committee on the Elimination of Discrimination against Women, the human rights body associated with CEDAW, the international convention on women's rights. Given that female genital mutilation is often practiced as a religious or cultural observance, these prohibitions implicate both the right to religious practice and the government's need to undertake proactive measures to protect women and girls from discriminatory practices. How should these two international human rights be balanced with each other? If the state has the right to prohibit female genital mutilation, does it have the right to prohibit other religious practices that are inherently discriminatory?

18 U.S.C. § 116

(a) Except as provided in subsection (b), whoever knowingly circumcises, excises, or infibulates the whole or any part of the labia majora or labia minora or clitoris of another person who has not attained the age of 18 years shall be fined under this title or imprisoned not more than 5 years, or both.

(b) A surgical operation is not a violation of this section if the operation is—

(1) necessary to the health of the person on whom it is performed, and is performed by a person licensed in the place of its performance as a medical practitioner; or

(2) performed on a person in labor or who has just given birth and is performed for medical purposes connected with that labor or birth by a person licensed in the place it is performed as a medical practitioner, midwife, or person in training to become such a practitioner or midwife.

(c) In applying subsection (b)(1), no account shall be taken of the effect on the person on whom the operation is to be performed of any belief on the part of that person, or any other person, that the operation is required as a matter of custom or ritual.

(d) Whoever knowingly transports from the United States and its territories a person in foreign commerce for the purpose of conduct with regard to that person that would be a violation of subsection (a) if the conduct occurred within the United States, or attempts to do so, shall be fined under this title or imprisoned not more than 5 years, or both.

General Recommendation No. 14
Committee on the Elimination of
Discrimination against Women
Ninth Session (1990)

The Committee on the Elimination of Discrimination against Women,

Concerned about the continuation of the practice of female circumcision and other traditional practices harmful to the health of women,

Noting with satisfaction that Governments, where such practices exist, national women's organizations, non-governmental organizations, and bodies of the United Nations system, such as the World Health Organization and the United Nations Children's Fund, as well as the Commission on Human Rights and its Sub-Commission on Prevention of Discrimination and Protection of Minorities, remain seized of the issue having particularly recognized that such traditional practices as female circumcision have serious health and other consequences for women and children,

Taking note with interest the study of the Special Rapporteur on Traditional Practices Affecting the Health of Women and Children, and of the study of the Special Working Group on Traditional Practices,

Recognizing that women are taking important action themselves to identify and to combat practices that are prejudicial to the health and well-being of women and children,

Convinced that the important action that is being taken by women and by all interested groups needs to be supported and encourage by Governments,

Noting with grave concern that there are continuing cultural, traditional and economic pressures which help to perpetuate harmful practices, such as female circumcision,

Recommends that States parties:

(a) Take appropriate and effective measures with a view to eradicating the practice of female circumcision. Such measures could include:

    i.   The collection and dissemination by universities, medical or nursing associations, national women's organizations or other bodies of basic data about such traditional practices;

    ii.   The support of women's organizations at the national and local levels working for the elimination of female circumcision and other practices harmful to women;

    iii. The encouragement of politicians, professionals, religious and community leaders at all levels, including the media and the arts, to co-operate in influencing attitudes towards the eradication of female circumcision;

    iv. The introduction of appropriate educational and training programmes and seminars based on research findings about the problems arising from female circumcision;

(b) Include in their national health policies appropriate strategies aimed at eradicating female circumcision in public health care. Such strategies could include the special responsibility of health personnel, including traditional birth attendants, to explain the harmful effects of female circumcision;

(c) Invite assistance, information and advice from the appropriate organizations of the United Nations system to support and assist efforts being deployed to eliminate harmful traditional practices;

(d) Include in their reports to the Committee under articles 10 and 12 of the Convention on the Elimination of All Forms of Discrimination against Women information about measures taken to eliminate female circumcision.

C. ECONOMIC AND SOCIAL RIGHTS

As noted above, the ICESCR codifies positive rights, including the right to work (art. 6); the right to appropriate working conditions (art. 7); the right to unionization and collective bargaining, including the right to strike (art. 8); the right to an adequate standard of living, including food, clothing and housing (art. 11); the right to education (art. 13); and other social and cultural rights. Of these, one of the most unfulfilled rights is the right to food. Each year, millions of individuals across the globe suffer from malnutrition and do not have access to adequate nutritional resources. This raises two related questions. First, what obligation does a state have to its own citizens to ensure that they are adequately fed? Second, what obligation does one state have to another state to assist the second state in feeding its citizens? Does the international human right to food entail a system of wealth redistribution? If not, what other mechanisms might fulfill the right to food? In 1999, the Committee on Economic, Social and Cultural Rights considered these and other issues and released the following General Comment.

General Comment No. 12
The Right to Adequate Food

Committee on Economic, Social and Cultural Rights
UN Doc. E/C.12/1999/5 (1999)

1.   The human right to adequate food is recognized in several instruments under international law. The International Covenant on Economic, Social and Cultural Rights deals more comprehensively than any other instrument with this right. Pursuant to article 11.1 of the Covenant, States parties recognize "the right of everyone to an adequate standard of living for himself and his family, including adequate food, clothing and housing, and to the continuous improvement of living conditions," while pursuant to article 11.2 they recognize that more immediate and urgent steps may be needed to ensure "the fundamental right to freedom from hunger and malnutrition." The human right to adequate food is of crucial importance for the enjoyment of all rights. It applies to everyone; thus the reference in Article 11.1 to "himself and his family" does not imply any limitation upon the applicability of this right to individuals or to female-headed households.

4.   The Committee affirms that the right to adequate food is indivisibly linked to the inherent dignity of the human person and is indispensable for the fulfilment of other human rights enshrined in the International Bill of Human Rights. It is also inseparable from social justice, requiring the adoption of appropriate economic, environmental and social policies, at both the national and international levels, oriented to the eradication of poverty and the fulfilment of all human rights for all.

5.   Despite the fact that the international community has frequently reaffirmed the importance of full respect for the right to adequate food, a disturbing gap still exists between the standards set in article 11 of the Covenant and the situation prevailing in many parts of the world. More than 840 million people throughout the world, most of them in developing countries, are chronically hungry; millions of people are suffering from famine as the result of natural disasters, the increasing incidence of civil strife and wars in some regions and the use of food as a political weapon. The Committee observes that while the problems of hunger and malnutrition are often particularly acute in developing countries, malnutrition, under-nutrition and other problems which relate to the right to adequate food and the right to freedom from hunger, also exist in some of the most economically developed countries. Fundamentally, the roots of the problem of hunger and malnutrition are not lack of food but lack of access to available food, inter alia because of poverty, by large segments of the world's population.

6.   The right to adequate food is realized when every man, woman and child, alone or in community with others, have physical and economic

access at all times to adequate food or means for its procurement. The right to adequate food shall therefore not be interpreted in a narrow or restrictive sense which equates it with a minimum package of calories, proteins and other specific nutrients. The right to adequate food will have to be realized progressively. However, States have a core obligation to take the necessary action to mitigate and alleviate hunger as provided for in paragraph 2 of article 11, even in times of natural or other disasters.

7.   The concept of adequacy is particularly significant in relation to the right to food since it serves to underline a number of factors which must be taken into account in determining whether particular foods or diets that are accessible can be considered the most appropriate under given circumstances for the purposes of article 11 of the Covenant. The notion of sustainability is intrinsically linked to the notion of adequate food or food security, implying food being accessible for both present and future generations. The precise meaning of "adequacy" is to a large extent determined by prevailing social, economic, cultural, climatic, ecological and other conditions, while "sustainability" incorporates the notion of long-term availability and accessibility.

8.   The Committee considers that the core content of the right to adequate food implies: (i) The availability of food in a quantity and quality sufficient to satisfy the dietary needs of individuals, free from adverse substances, and acceptable within a given culture; (ii) The accessibility of such food in ways that are sustainable and that do not interfere with the enjoyment of other human rights.

9.   Dietary needs implies that the diet as a whole contains a mix of nutrients for physical and mental growth, development and maintenance, and physical activity that are in compliance with human physiological needs at all stages throughout the life cycle and according to gender and occupation. Measures may therefore need to be taken to maintain, adapt or strengthen dietary diversity and appropriate consumption and feeding patterns, including breast-feeding, while ensuring that changes in availability and access to food supply as a minimum do not negatively affect dietary composition and intake.

10.   Free from adverse substances sets requirements for food safety and for a range of protective measures by both public and private means to prevent contamination of foodstuffs through adulteration and/or through bad environmental hygiene or inappropriate handling at different stages throughout the food chain; care must also be taken to identify and avoid or destroy naturally occurring toxins.

11.   Cultural or consumer acceptability implies the need also to take into account, as far as possible, perceived non nutrient-based values

attached to food and food consumption and informed consumer concerns regarding the nature of accessible food supplies.

12. Availability refers to the possibilities either for feeding oneself directly from productive land or other natural resources, or for well functioning distribution, processing and market systems that can move food from the site of production to where it is needed in accordance with demand.

13. Accessibility encompasses both economic and physical accessibility:

Economic accessibility implies that personal or household financial costs associated with the acquisition of food for an adequate diet should be at a level such that the attainment and satisfaction of other basic needs are not threatened or compromised. Economic accessibility applies to any acquisition pattern or entitlement through which people procure their food and is a measure of the extent to which it is satisfactory for the enjoyment of the right to adequate food. Socially vulnerable groups such as landless persons and other particularly impoverished segments of the population may need attention through special programmes.

Physical accessibility implies that adequate food must be accessible to everyone, including physically vulnerable individuals, such as infants and young children, elderly people, the physically disabled, the terminally ill and persons with persistent medical problems, including the mentally ill. Victims of natural disasters, people living in disaster-prone areas and other specially disadvantaged groups may need special attention and sometimes priority consideration with respect to accessibility of food. A particular vulnerability is that of many indigenous population groups whose access to their ancestral lands may be threatened.

14. The nature of the legal obligations of States parties are set out in article 2 of the Covenant and has been dealt with in the Committee's General Comment No. 3 (1990). The principal obligation is to take steps to achieve progressively the full realization of the right to adequate food. This imposes an obligation to move as expeditiously as possible towards that goal. Every State is obliged to ensure for everyone under its jurisdiction access to the minimum essential food which is sufficient, nutritionally adequate and safe, to ensure their freedom from hunger.

15. The right to adequate food, like any other human right, imposes three types or levels of obligations on States parties: the obligations to respect, to protect and to fulfil. In turn, the obligation to fulfil incorporates both an obligation to facilitate and an obligation to provide. The obligation to respect existing access to adequate food requires States parties not to take any measures that result in preventing such access. The obligation to protect requires measures by the State to ensure that

enterprises or individuals do not deprive individuals of their access to adequate food. The obligation to fulfil (facilitate) means the State must proactively engage in activities intended to strengthen people's access to and utilization of resources and means to ensure their livelihood, including food security. Finally, whenever an individual or group is unable, for reasons beyond their control, to enjoy the right to adequate food by the means at their disposal, States have the obligation to fulfil (provide) that right directly. This obligation also applies for persons who are victims of natural or other disasters.

16. Some measures at these different levels of obligations of States parties are of a more immediate nature, while other measures are more of a longterm character, to achieve progressively the full realization of the right to food.

17. Violations of the Covenant occur when a State fails to ensure the satisfaction of, at the very least, the minimum essential level required to be free from hunger. In determining which actions or omissions amount to a violation of the right to food, it is important to distinguish the inability from the unwillingness of a State party to comply. Should a State party argue that resource constraints make it impossible to provide access to food for those who are unable by themselves to secure such access, the State has to demonstrate that every effort has been made to use all the resources at its disposal in an effort to satisfy, as a matter of priority, those minimum obligations. This follows from Article 2.1 of the Covenant, which obliges a State party to take the necessary steps to the maximum of its available resources, as previously pointed out by the Committee in its General Comment No. 3, paragraph 10. A State claiming that it is unable to carry out its obligation for reasons beyond its control therefore has the burden of proving that this is the case and that it has unsuccessfully sought to obtain international support to ensure the availability and accessibility of the necessary food.

21. The most appropriate ways and means of implementing the right to adequate food will inevitably vary significantly from one State party to another. Every State will have a margin of discretion in choosing its own approaches, but the Covenant clearly requires that each State party take whatever steps are necessary to ensure that everyone is free from hunger and as soon as possible can enjoy the right to adequate food. This will require the adoption of a national strategy to ensure food and nutrition security for all, based on human rights principles that define the objectives, and the formulation of policies and corresponding benchmarks. It should also identify the resources available to meet the objectives and the most cost effective way of using them.

28. Even where a State faces severe resource constraints, whether caused by a process of economic adjustment, economic recession, climatic

conditions or other factors, measures should be undertaken to ensure that the right to adequate food is especially fulfilled for vulnerable population groups and individuals.

32. Any person or group who is a victim of a violation of the right to adequate food should have access to effective judicial or other appropriate remedies at both national and international levels. All victims of such violations are entitled to adequate reparation, which may take the form of restitution, compensation, satisfaction or guarantees of nonrepetition. National Ombudsmen and human rights commissions should address violations of the right to food.

33. The incorporation in the domestic legal order of international instruments recognizing the right to food, or recognition of their applicability, can significantly enhance the scope and effectiveness of remedial measures and should be encouraged in all cases. Courts would then be empowered to adjudicate violations of the core content of the right to food by direct reference to obligations under the Covenant.

36. In the spirit of article 56 of the Charter of the United Nations, the specific provisions contained in articles 11, 2.1, and 23 of the Covenant and the Rome Declaration of the World Food Summit, States parties should recognize the essential role of international cooperation and comply with their commitment to take joint and separate action to achieve the full realization of the right to adequate food. In implementing this commitment, States parties should take steps to respect the enjoyment of the right to food in other countries, to protect that right, to facilitate access to food and to provide the necessary aid when required. States parties should, in international agreements whenever relevant, ensure that the right to adequate food is given due attention and consider the development of further international legal instruments to that end.

38. States have a joint and individual responsibility, in accordance with the Charter of the United Nations, to cooperate in providing disaster relief and humanitarian assistance in times of emergency, including assistance to refugees and internally displaced persons. Each State should contribute to this task in accordance with its ability. The role of the World Food Programme (WFP) and the Office of the United Nations High Commissioner for Refugees (UNHCR), and increasingly that of UNICEF and FAO is of particular importance in this respect and should be strengthened. Priority in food aid should be given to the most vulnerable populations.

Notes & Questions

1. *Fulfilling the Right to Food.* What specifically should states do to comply with the right to food? The committee concluded that the right "will have to be realized progressively" and that each state will have "a margin of

discretion in choosing its own approaches." Most importantly, the committee concluded that a state is only obligated to take "necessary steps to the maximum of its available resources," a reference to article 2(1) of the Convention which requires states to act "to the maximum of its available resources." This arguably entails a relative scale, with richer states under a greater obligation to fulfill the right to food than poorer nations.

2.   *A Global Resources Dividend?* One way for richer nations to fulfill their obligations to poorer nations would be to redistribute a small percentage of their national wealth for the sole purpose of alleviating global hunger and poverty. How might this be achieved? Political philosopher Thomas Pogge once suggested the creation of a Global Resources Dividend (GRD), which would require states to pay a small "tax" on all natural resources they use, which would then be redistributed to developing states and their populations. One possible argument for the GRD is that states have access to natural resource through sheer luck—the materials located on their sovereign territory—and that all human beings have a right to share in the bounty created from the earth's natural resources. A second possible argument is that states have a duty to mitigate the negative consequences associated with their participation in the global economic order. Would the GRD proposal work? For more discussion, see Tim Hayward, *Thomas Pogge's Global Resources Dividend: A Critique and an Alternative*, 2 J. Moral Phil. 317 (2005) ("If a tax on natural resources is to have progressive redistributive effects, there is a case for suggesting it should be levied on those who ultimately derive more economic benefit from the exploitation of raw resources rather than on those who, engaged in primary extraction, will generally yield the least added value from the resource."); Smita Narula, *The Right to Food: Holding Global Actors Accountable Under International Law*, 44 Colum. J. Transnat'l L. 691, 797 (2006) ("While the right to food is both hard law and a strong moral imperative, the inability to reconcile states' obligations with global processes has allowed the world's most powerful actors (transnational corporations, international financial institutions, and influential states) to opt out of legal obligation.").

3.   *Economic Inequality.* Did the increasing focus on civil and political rights in the 20th Century lead the human rights movement, at least in the west, to ignore or downplay economic equality as a fundamental human right? It is certainly true that while civil and political rights have flourished in the last 50 years, economic rights have largely withered, if by economic rights one means an equal distribution of wealth and income across the globe. To some critics, the primacy of civil and political rights within the human rights system has largely masked the darker reality that economic inequality has grown steadily over the last few decades, resulting in entrenched poverty and misery. Why has international law focused so much on civil and political rights and so little on economic inequality? For one such critique of the human rights movement, see Samuel Moyn, *Not Enough: Human Rights in an Unequal World* (2018). But for an argument that civil and political rights are a necessary and laudatory precursor before any

genuine socialist economic order can be achieved, see Heiner Bielefeldt, *Human Rights as a 'Substitute Utopia'? Questionable Assumptions in Samuel Moyn's Work*, 38 Nordic J. Hum. Rts. (2020) (arguing that "human rights provide support against policies of intimidation, typically employed by those defending old privileges against new social and political utopias").

D. HUMAN RIGHTS DURING PUBLIC EMERGENCIES

Should states have any wiggle room in their international legal obligations when faced with a national emergency? For example, what if a state is in the midst of a major environmental disaster, or a critical medical situation like a pandemic? There are two doctrinal possibilities for answering this question. The first is an official "derogation" wherein a state explicitly states that it has entered into a state of emergency requiring it to derogate from its human rights obligations. However, as will be outlined below, not all rights are derogable. The second doctrinal possibility is the concept of necessity, i.e., the notion that the infringement of the protected interest is "necessary" for the protection of society. As will be explored in the second sub-section below, some domestic and international courts have placed limits on a state's ability to argue that fundamental rights can be balanced away in order to secure protections for a greater number of individuals in the community at large.

1. DEROGATIONS

The "derogation" mechanism is explicitly codified in major human rights instruments. For example, article 4 of the ICCPR proclaims that "[i]n time of public emergency which threatens the life of the nation and the existence of which is officially proclaimed, the States Parties to the present Covenant may take measures derogating from their obligations under the present Covenant to the extent strictly required by the exigencies of the situation, provided that such measures are not inconsistent with their other obligations under international law and do not involve discrimination solely on the ground of race, colour, sex, language, religion or social origin." Article 4 goes on to require that state parties relying on the derogation provision inform all other state parties to the ICCPR, thus establishing that a state cannot covertly rely on derogations as a way of exempting itself from international legal responsibility. Rather, the state must stand up and declare its intention to derogate, thus opening itself up to criticism and scrutiny if other states believe that its situation does not rise to the level of a public emergency. Also, some rights are explicitly listed as "non-derogable," meaning that they must be respected even in times of public emergency. This includes the right not to be deprived of life arbitrarily, the prohibition on torture and slavery, the prohibition on ex post facto criminal punishment, and freedom of thought, conscience, and religion.

The European Convention has parallel provisions for derogations in times of public emergency. Under article 15, parties to the European Convention are entitled to derogate from their obligations "in time of war or other public emergency," though derogations do not apply to the provisions regarding torture, slavery, punishment without law, or the right to life (except lawful acts of war). One reason for issuing a derogation is to limit the number of cases filed against the state during an armed conflict. So, for example, the British Government announced in 2016 a new policy of derogating during any armed conflict so as to limit litigation against the state and its armed forces. In making this announcement, the British Government noted that the European Court's jurisprudence on extraterritorial jurisdiction was subjecting British military forces to constant legal scrutiny which the government sought to avoid through the derogation mechanism.

In the following General Comment, the Human Rights Committee considered the issue of derogations and what limits, if any, should be placed on the power.

General Comment Number 29
Human Rights Committee
CCPR/C/21/Rev.1/Add.11 (2001)

1.   Article 4 of the Covenant is of paramount importance for the system of protection for human rights under the Covenant. On the one hand, it allows for a State party unilaterally to derogate temporarily from a part of its obligations under the Covenant. On the other hand, article 4 subjects both this very measure of derogation, as well as its material consequences, to a specific regime of safeguards. The restoration of a state of normalcy where full respect for the Covenant can again be secured must be the predominant objective of a State party derogating from the Covenant. In this general comment. . . the Committee seeks to assist States parties to meet the requirements of article 4.

2.   Measures derogating from the provisions of the Covenant must be of an exceptional and temporary nature. Before a State moves to invoke article 4, two fundamental conditions must be met: the situation must amount to a public emergency which threatens the life of the nation, and the State party must have officially proclaimed a state of emergency. The latter requirement is essential for the maintenance of the principles of legality and rule of law at times when they are most needed. When proclaiming a state of emergency with consequences that could entail derogation from any provision of the Covenant, States must act within their constitutional and other provisions of law that govern

such proclamation and the exercise of emergency powers; it is the task of the Committee to monitor the laws in question with respect to whether they enable and secure compliance with article 4. In order that the Committee can perform its task, States parties to the Covenant should include in their reports submitted under article 40 sufficient and precise information about their law and practice in the field of emergency powers.

3. Not every disturbance or catastrophe qualifies as a public emergency which threatens the life of the nation, as required by article 4, paragraph 1. During armed conflict, whether international or non-international, rules of international humanitarian law become applicable and help, in addition to the provisions in article 4 and article 5, paragraph 1, of the Covenant, to prevent the abuse of a State's emergency powers. The Covenant requires that even during an armed conflict measures derogating from the Covenant are allowed only if and to the extent that the situation constitutes a threat to the life of the nation. If States parties consider invoking article 4 in other situations than an armed conflict, they should carefully consider the justification and why such a measure is necessary and legitimate in the circumstances. On a number of occasions the Committee has expressed its concern over States parties that appear to have derogated from rights protected by the Covenant, or whose domestic law appears to allow such derogation in situations not covered by article 4.

4. A fundamental requirement for any measures derogating from the Covenant, as set forth in article 4, paragraph 1, is that such measures are limited to the extent strictly required by the exigencies of the situation. This requirement relates to the duration, geographical coverage and material scope of the state of emergency and any measures of derogation resorted to because of the emergency. Derogation from some Covenant obligations in emergency situations is clearly distinct from restrictions or limitations allowed even in normal times under several provisions of the Covenant. Nevertheless, the obligation to limit any derogations to those strictly required by the exigencies of the situation reflects the principle of proportionality which is common to derogation and limitation powers. Moreover, the mere fact that a permissible derogation from a specific provision may, of itself, be justified by the exigencies of the situation does not obviate the requirement that specific measures taken pursuant to the derogation must also be shown to be required by the exigencies of the situation. In practice, this will ensure that no provision of the Covenant, however validly derogated from will be entirely inapplicable to the behaviour of a State party. When considering States parties' reports the Committee has expressed its concern over insufficient attention being paid to the principle of proportionality.

5. The issues of when rights can be derogated from, and to what extent, cannot be separated from the provision in article 4, paragraph 1, of the Covenant according to which any measures derogating from a State party's obligations under the Covenant must be limited "to the extent strictly required by the exigencies of the situation." This condition requires that States parties provide careful justification not only for their decision to proclaim a state of emergency but also for any specific measures based on such a proclamation. If States purport to invoke the right to derogate from the Covenant during, for instance, a natural catastrophe, a mass demonstration including instances of violence, or a major industrial accident, they must be able to justify not only that such a situation constitutes a threat to the life of the nation, but also that all their measures derogating from the Covenant are strictly required by the exigencies of the situation. In the opinion of the Committee, the possibility of restricting certain Covenant rights under the terms of, for instance, freedom of movement (article 12) or freedom of assembly (article 21) is generally sufficient during such situations and no derogation from the provisions in question would be justified by the exigencies of the situation.

6. The fact that some of the provisions of the Covenant have been listed in article 4 (paragraph 2), as not being subject to derogation does not mean that other articles in the Covenant may be subjected to derogations at will, even where a threat to the life of the nation exists. The legal obligation to narrow down all derogations to those strictly required by the exigencies of the situation establishes both for States parties and for the Committee a duty to conduct a careful analysis under each article of the Covenant based on an objective assessment of the actual situation.

7. Article 4, paragraph 2, of the Covenant explicitly prescribes that no derogation from the following articles may be made: article 6 (right to life), article 7 (prohibition of torture or cruel, inhuman or degrading punishment, or of medical or scientific experimentation without consent), article 8, paragraphs 1 and 2 (prohibition of slavery, slave-trade and servitude), article 11 (prohibition of imprisonment because of inability to fulfil a contractual obligation), article 15 (the principle of legality in the field of criminal law, i.e., the requirement of both criminal liability and punishment being limited to clear and precise provisions in the law that was in place and applicable at the time the act or omission took place, except in cases where a later law imposes a lighter penalty), article 16 (the recognition of everyone as a person before the law), and article 18 (freedom of thought, conscience and religion). The rights enshrined in these provisions are non-derogable by the very fact that they are listed in article 4, paragraph 2. The same applies, in relation to States that are parties to the Second Optional Protocol to the Covenant, aiming at the

abolition of the death penalty, as prescribed in article 6 of that Protocol. Conceptually, the qualification of a Covenant provision as a non-derogable one does not mean that no limitations or restrictions would ever be justified. The reference in article 4, paragraph 2, to article 18, a provision that includes a specific clause on restrictions in its paragraph 3, demonstrates that the permissibility of restrictions is independent of the issue of derogability. Even in times of most serious public emergencies, States that interfere with the freedom to manifest one's religion or belief must justify their actions by referring to the requirements specified in article 18, paragraph 3. On several occasions the Committee has expressed its concern about rights that are non-derogable according to article 4, paragraph 2, being either derogated from or under a risk of derogation owing to inadequacies in the legal regime of the State party.

8.   According to article 4, paragraph 1, one of the conditions for the justifiability of any derogation from the Covenant is that the measures taken do not involve discrimination solely on the ground of race, colour, sex, language, religion or social origin. Even though article 26 or the other Covenant provisions related to non-discrimination have not been listed among the non-derogable provisions in article 4, paragraph 2, there are elements or dimensions of the right to non-discrimination that cannot be derogated from in any circumstances. In particular, this provision of article 4, paragraph 1, must be complied with if any distinctions between persons are made when resorting to measures that derogate from the Covenant.

9.   Furthermore, article 4, paragraph 1, requires that no measure derogating from the provisions of the Covenant may be inconsistent with the State party's other obligations under international law, particularly the rules of international humanitarian law. Article 4 of the Covenant cannot be read as justification for derogation from the Covenant if such derogation would entail a breach of the State's other international obligations, whether based on treaty or general international law. This is reflected also in article 5, paragraph 2, of the Covenant according to which there shall be no restriction upon or derogation from any fundamental rights recognized in other instruments on the pretext that the Covenant does not recognize such rights or that it recognizes them to a lesser extent.

10.   Although it is not the function of the Human Rights Committee to review the conduct of a State party under other treaties, in exercising its functions under the Covenant the Committee has the competence to take a State party's other international obligations into account when it considers whether the Covenant allows the State party to derogate from specific provisions of the Covenant. Therefore, when invoking article 4, paragraph 1, or when reporting under article 40 on the legal framework

related to emergencies, States parties should present information on their other international obligations relevant for the protection of the rights in question, in particular those obligations that are applicable in times of emergency. In this respect, States parties should duly take into account the developments within international law as to human rights standards applicable in emergency situations.

11. The enumeration of non-derogable provisions in article 4 is related to, but not identical with, the question whether certain human rights obligations bear the nature of peremptory norms of international law. The proclamation of certain provisions of the Covenant as being of a non-derogable nature, in article 4, paragraph 2, is to be seen partly as recognition of the peremptory nature of some fundamental rights ensured in treaty form in the Covenant (e.g., articles 6 and 7). However, it is apparent that some other provisions of the Covenant were included in the list of non-derogable provisions because it can never become necessary to derogate from these rights during a state of emergency (e.g., articles 11 and 18). Furthermore, the category of peremptory norms extends beyond the list of non-derogable provisions as given in article 4, paragraph 2. States parties may in no circumstances invoke article 4 of the Covenant as justification for acting in violation of humanitarian law or peremptory norms of international law, for instance by taking hostages, by imposing collective punishments, through arbitrary deprivations of liberty or by deviating from fundamental principles of fair trial, including the presumption of innocence.

12. In assessing the scope of legitimate derogation from the Covenant, one criterion can be found in the definition of certain human rights violations as crimes against humanity. If action conducted under the authority of a State constitutes a basis for individual criminal responsibility for a crime against humanity by the persons involved in that action, article 4 of the Covenant cannot be used as justification that a state of emergency exempted the State in question from its responsibility in relation to the same conduct. Therefore, the recent codification of crimes against humanity, for jurisdictional purposes, in the Rome Statute of the International Criminal Court is of relevance in the interpretation of article 4 of the Covenant.

13. In those provisions of the Covenant that are not listed in article 4, paragraph 2, there are elements that in the Committee's opinion cannot be made subject to lawful derogation under article 4. Some illustrative examples are presented below.

(a) All persons deprived of their liberty shall be treated with humanity and with respect for the inherent dignity of the human person. Although this right, prescribed in article 10 of the Covenant, is not separately mentioned in the list of non-derogable rights in article 4, paragraph 2, the Committee believes that here the Covenant expresses a norm of general international law not subject to derogation. This is supported by the reference to the inherent dignity of the human person in the preamble to the Covenant and by the close connection between articles 7 and 10.

(b)   The prohibitions against taking of hostages, abductions or unacknowledged detention are not subject to derogation. The absolute nature of these prohibitions, even in times of emergency, is justified by their status as norms of general international law.

(c)   The Committee is of the opinion that the international protection of the rights of persons belonging to minorities includes elements that must be respected in all circumstances. This is reflected in the prohibition against genocide in international law, in the inclusion of a non-discrimination clause in article 4 itself, as well as in the non-derogable nature of article 18.

(d)   As confirmed by the Rome Statute of the International Criminal Court, deportation or forcible transfer of population without grounds permitted under international law, in the form of forced displacement by expulsion or other coercive means from the area in which the persons concerned are lawfully present, constitutes a crime against humanity. The legitimate right to derogate from article 12 of the Covenant during a state of emergency can never be accepted as justifying such measures.

(e)   No declaration of a state of emergency made pursuant to article 4, paragraph 1, may be invoked as justification for a State party to engage itself, contrary to article 20, in propaganda for war, or in advocacy of national, racial or religious hatred that would constitute incitement to discrimination, hostility or violence.

14.   Article 2, paragraph 3, of the Covenant requires a State party to the Covenant to provide remedies for any violation of the provisions of the Covenant. This clause is not mentioned in the list of non-derogable provisions in article 4, paragraph 2, but it constitutes a treaty obligation inherent in the Covenant as a whole. Even if a State party, during a state of emergency, and to the extent that such measures are strictly required by the exigencies of the situation, may introduce adjustments to the practical functioning of its procedures governing judicial or other remedies, the State party must comply with the fundamental obligation, under article 2, paragraph 3, of the Covenant to provide a remedy that is effective.

15.   It is inherent in the protection of rights explicitly recognized as non-derogable in article 4, paragraph 2, that they must be secured by procedural guarantees, including, often, judicial guarantees. The provisions of the Covenant relating to procedural safeguards may never be made subject to measures that would circumvent the protection of non-derogable rights. Article 4 may not be resorted to in a way that would

result in derogation from non-derogable rights. Thus, for example, as article 6 of the Covenant is non-derogable in its entirety, any trial leading to the imposition of the death penalty during a state of emergency must conform to the provisions of the Covenant, including all the requirements of articles 14 and 15.

16. Safeguards related to derogation, as embodied in article 4 of the Covenant, are based on the principles of legality and the rule of law inherent in the Covenant as a whole. As certain elements of the right to a fair trial are explicitly guaranteed under international humanitarian law during armed conflict, the Committee finds no justification for derogation from these guarantees during other emergency situations. The Committee is of the opinion that the principles of legality and the rule of law require that fundamental requirements of fair trial must be respected during a state of emergency. Only a court of law may try and convict a person for a criminal offence. The presumption of innocence must be respected. In order to protect non-derogable rights, the right to take proceedings before a court to enable the court to decide without delay on the lawfulness of detention, must not be diminished by a State party's decision to derogate from the Covenant.

17. In paragraph 3 of article 4, States parties, when they resort to their power of derogation under article 4, commit themselves to a regime of international notification. A State party availing itself of the right of derogation must immediately inform the other States parties, through the United Nations Secretary-General, of the provisions it has derogated from and of the reasons for such measures. Such notification is essential not only for the discharge of the Committee's functions, in particular in assessing whether the measures taken by the State party were strictly required by the exigencies of the situation, but also to permit other States parties to monitor compliance with the provisions of the Covenant. In view of the summary character of many of the notifications received in the past, the Committee emphasizes that the notification by States parties should include full information about the measures taken and a clear explanation of the reasons for them, with full documentation attached regarding their law. Additional notifications are required if the State party subsequently takes further measures under article 4, for instance by extending the duration of a state of emergency. The requirement of immediate notification applies equally in relation to the termination of derogation. These obligations have not always been respected: States parties have failed to notify other States parties, through the Secretary-General, of a proclamation of a state of emergency and of the resulting measures of derogation from one or more provisions of the Covenant, and States parties have sometimes neglected to submit a notification of territorial or other changes in the exercise of their emergency powers. Sometimes, the existence of a state of emergency and

the question of whether a State party has derogated from provisions of the Covenant have come to the attention of the Committee only incidentally, in the course of the consideration of a State party's report. The Committee emphasizes the obligation of immediate international notification whenever a State party takes measures derogating from its obligations under the Covenant. The duty of the Committee to monitor the law and practice of a State party for compliance with article 4 does not depend on whether that State party has submitted a notification.

2. THE LIMITS OF UTILITARIAN BALANCING

The basic conceptual structure of derogations is a notion of utilitarian balancing, or the idea that the interests of an individual can be outweighed by the needs of the many. Utilitarianism is the view that it is good to promote outcomes that maximize overall utility in society. Under this view, harming one individual may be morally justified if it results in substantial gains to others that outweigh the costs imposed on the harmed individual. This "balancing" approach underlies the basic idea of derogations discussed above; the infringement on an individual's human right may be justified if that infringement is outweighed by the positive benefits that flow to the community at large during times of public emergency.

As we saw above, however, there are limits to this balancing process. Both the ICCPR and the European Convention define some rights as non-derogable. The question is *why*. Why are some rights immune from utilitarian balancing in the name of the common good? In the following two cases, two domestic courts—one in Israel and one in Germany—answer that question. In the first, human rights activists objected to Israel's policy of using torture against detainees suspected of involvement in terrorism. In the second, the German Constitutional Court considered whether the government could shoot down a hijacked passenger airplane in order to prevent it from being used in a 9/11 terrorist attack against a skyscraper. In both cases, the judges referred to the concept of "human dignity" as a basis for their decision that some rights are immune from utilitarian balancing.

Public Committee Against Torture v. Israel
Supreme Court of Israel
September 6, 1999

1. Ever since it was established, the State of Israel has been engaged in an unceasing struggle for its security—indeed, its very existence. Terrorist organizations have set Israel's annihilation as their goal. Terrorist acts and the general disruption of order are their means of choice. In employing such methods, these groups do not distinguish between civilian and military targets. They carry out terrorist attacks in

which scores are murdered in public areas—in areas of public transportation, city squares and centers, theaters and coffee shops. They do not distinguish between men, women and children. They act out of cruelty and without mercy.

The facts before this Court reveal that 121 people died in terrorist attacks between January 1, 1996 and May 14, 1998. Seven hundred and seven people were injured. A large number of those killed and injured were victims of harrowing suicide bombings in the heart of Israel's cities. Many attacks—including suicide bombings, attempts to detonate car bombs, kidnappings of citizens and soldiers, attempts to highjack buses, murders, and the placing of explosives—were prevented due to daily measures taken by authorities responsible for fighting terrorist activities. The GSS is the main body responsible for fighting terrorism.

In order to fulfill this function, the GSS also investigates those suspected of hostile terrorist activities. The purpose of these interrogations includes the gathering of information regarding terrorists in order to prevent them from carrying out terrorist attacks. In the context of these interrogations, GSS investigators also make use of physical means. . .

The decision to utilize physical means in a particular instance is based on internal regulations, which requires obtaining permission from the higher ranks of the GSS. The regulations themselves were approved by a special Ministerial Committee on GSS interrogations. Among other guidelines, the committee set forth directives regarding the rank required of an officer who was to authorize such interrogation practices. These directives were not examined by this Court. Different interrogation methods are employed in each situation, depending what is necessary in that situation and the likelihood of obtaining authorization. The GSS does not resort to every interrogation method at its disposal in each case. . .

Indeed, the authority to conduct interrogations, like any administrative power, is designed for a specific purpose, and must be exercised in conformity with the basic principles of the democratic regime. In setting out the rules of interrogation, two values clash. On the one hand, lies the desire to uncover the truth, in accord with the public interest in exposing crime and preventing it. On the other hand is the need to protect the dignity and liberty of the individual being interrogated. This having been said, these values are not absolute. A democratic, freedom-loving society does not accept that investigators may use any means for the purpose of uncovering the truth. "The interrogation practices of the police in a given regime," noted Justice Landau, "are indicative of a regime's very character." At times, the price of truth is so high that a democratic society is not prepared to pay. To the same extent, however, a democratic society, desirous of liberty, seeks to fight crime and, to that end, is prepared to accept that an interrogation may infringe the human dignity and liberty of a suspect—provided that it is done for a proper purpose and that the harm does not exceed that which is necessary. . .

23. It is not necessary for us to engage in an in-depth inquiry into the "law of interrogation" for the purposes of the petitions before us. These laws vary, depending on the context. For instance, the law of interrogation is different in the context of an investigator's potential criminal liability, and in the context of admitting evidence obtained by questionable means. Here we deal with the "law of interrogation" as a power of an administrative authority. The "law of interrogation" by its very nature, is intrinsically linked to the circumstances of each case. This having been said, a number of general principles are nonetheless worth noting. . .

First, a reasonable investigation is necessarily one free of torture, free of cruel, inhuman treatment, and free of any degrading conduct whatsoever. There is a prohibition on the use of "brutal or inhuman means" in the course of an investigation. Human dignity also includes the dignity of the suspect being interrogated. This conclusion is in accord with international treaties, to which Israel is a signatory, which prohibit the use of torture, "cruel, inhuman treatment" and "degrading treatment." These prohibitions are "absolute." There are no exceptions to them and there is no room for balancing. Indeed, violence directed at a suspect's body or spirit does not constitute a reasonable investigation practice. The use of violence during investigations can lead to the investigator being held criminally liable. . .

Second, a reasonable investigation is likely to cause discomfort. It may result in insufficient sleep. The conditions under which it is conducted risk being unpleasant. Of course, it is possible to conduct an effective investigation without resorting to violence. Within the confines of the law, it is permitted to resort to various sophisticated techniques. Such techniques—accepted in the most progressive of societies—can be effective in achieving their goals. In the end result, the legality of an investigation is deduced from the propriety of its purpose and from its methods. Thus, for instance, sleep deprivation for a prolonged period, or sleep deprivation at night when this is not necessary to the investigation time-wise, may be deemed disproportionate.

24. We shall now turn from the general to the particular. Clearly, shaking is a prohibited investigation method. It harms the suspect's body. It violates his dignity. It is a violent method which can not form part of a legal investigation. It surpasses that which is necessary. Even the state did not argue that shaking is an "ordinary" investigatory method which every investigator, whether in the GSS or the police, is permitted to employ. The argument before us was that the justification

for shaking is found in the "necessity defense." That argument shall be dealt with below. In any event, there is no doubt that shaking is not to be resorted to in cases outside the bounds of "necessity" or as part of an "ordinary" investigation.

25. It was argued before the Court that one of the employed investigation methods consists of compelling the suspect to crouch on the tips of his toes for periods of five minutes. The state did not deny this practice. This is a prohibited investigation method. It does not serve any purpose inherent to an investigation. It is degrading and infringes an individual's human dignity.

26. The "Shabach" method is composed of several components: the cuffing of the suspect, seating him on a low chair, covering his head with a sack, and playing loud music in the area. Does the general power to investigate authorize any of the above acts? Our point of departure is that there are actions which are inherent to the investigatory power. Therefore, we accept that the suspect's cuffing, for the purpose of preserving the investigators' safety, is included in the general power to investigate. Provided the suspect is cuffed for this purpose, it is within the investigator's authority to cuff him. The state's position is that the suspects are indeed cuffed with the intention of ensuring the investigators' safety or to prevent the suspect from fleeing from legal custody. Even petitioners agree that it is permissible to cuff a suspect in such circumstances and that cuffing constitutes an integral part of an interrogation. The cuffing associated with the "Shabach" position, however, is unlike routine cuffing. The suspect is cuffed with his hands tied behind his back. One hand is placed inside the gap between the chair's seat and back support, while the other is tied behind him, against the chair's back support. This is a distorted and unnatural position. The investigators' safety does not require it. Similarly, there is no justification for handcuffing the suspect's hands with especially small handcuffs, if this is in fact the practice. The use of these methods is prohibited. As has been noted, "cuffing that causes pain is prohibited." Moreover, there are other ways of preventing the suspect from fleeing which do not involve causing pain and suffering.

27. The same applies to seating the suspect in question in the "Shabach" position. We accept that seating a man is inherent to the investigation. This is not the case, however, when the chair upon which he is seated is a very low one, tilted forward facing the ground, and when he is seated in this position for long hours. This sort of seating is not authorized by the general power to interrogate. Even if we suppose that the seating of the suspect on a chair lower than that of his investigator can potentially serve a legitimate investigation objective—for instance, to establish the "rules of the game" in the contest of wills between the parties, or to emphasize the investigator's superiority over the suspect—

there is no inherent investigative need to seat the suspect on a chair so low and tilted forward towards the ground, in a manner that causes him real pain and suffering. Clearly, the general power to conduct interrogations does not authorize seating a suspect on a tilted chair, in a manner that applies pressure and causes pain to his back, all the more so when his hands are tied behind the chair, in the manner described. All these methods do not fall within the sphere of a "fair" interrogation. They are not reasonable. They infringe the suspect's dignity, his bodily integrity and his basic rights in an excessive manner. They are not to be deemed as included within the general power to conduct interrogations.

30. To the above, we must add that the "Shabach" position employs all the above methods simultaneously. This combination gives rise to pain and suffering. This is a harmful method, particularly when it is employed for a prolonged period of time. For these reasons, this method is not authorized by the powers of interrogation. It is an unacceptable method. "The duty to safeguard the detainee's dignity includes his right not to be degraded and not to be submitted to sub-human conditions in the course of his detention, of the sort likely to harm his health and potentially his dignity."

A similar—though not identical—combination of interrogation methods were discussed in the case of *Ireland v. United Kingdom*, 23 Eur. Ct. H.R. (ser. B) at 3 (1976). In that case, the Court examined five interrogation methods used by England to investigate detainees suspected of terrorist activities in Northern Ireland. The methods included protracted standing against a wall on the tip of one's toes, covering of the suspect's head throughout the detention (except during the actual interrogation), exposing the suspect to very loud noise for a prolonged period of time, and deprivation of sleep, food and drink. The Court held that these methods did not constitute "torture." However, since they subjected the suspect to "inhuman and degrading" treatment, they were nonetheless prohibited.

31. The interrogation of a person is likely to be lengthy, due to the suspect's failure to cooperate, the complexity of the information sought, or in light of the need to obtain information urgently and immediately. Indeed, a person undergoing interrogation cannot sleep like one who is not being interrogated. The suspect, subject to the investigators' questions for a prolonged period of time, is at times exhausted. This is often the inevitable result of an interrogation. This is part of the "discomfort" inherent to an interrogation. This being the case, depriving the suspect of sleep is, in our opinion, included in the general authority of the investigator. . . The above described situation is different from one in which sleep deprivation shifts from being a "side effect" of the interrogation to an end in itself. If the suspect is intentionally deprived of sleep for a prolonged period of time, for the purpose of tiring him out

or "breaking" him, it is not part of the scope of a fair and reasonable investigation. Such means harm the rights and dignity of the suspect in a manner beyond what is necessary.

32. All these limitations on an interrogation, which flow from the requirement that an interrogation be fair and reasonable, is the law with respect to a regular police interrogation. The power to interrogate granted to the GSS investigator is the same power the law bestows upon the ordinary police investigator. The restrictions upon the police investigations are equally applicable to GSS investigations. There is no statute that grants GSS investigators special interrogating powers that are different or more significant than those granted the police investigator. From this we conclude that a GSS investigator, whose duty it is to conduct the interrogation according to the law, is subject to the same restrictions applicable to police interrogators.

33. We have arrived at the conclusion that GSS personnel who have received permission to conduct interrogations, as per the Criminal Procedure Statute [Testimony], are authorized to do so. This authority—like that of the police investigator—does not include most of the physical means of interrogation in the petition before us. Can the authority to employ these methods be anchored in a legal source beyond the authority to conduct an interrogation? This question was answered by the state in the affirmative. As noted, our law does not contain an explicit authorization permitting the GSS to employ physical means. An authorization of this nature can, however, in the state's opinion, be obtained in specific cases by virtue of the criminal law defense of "necessity," as provided in section 34(1) of the Penal Law. The statute provides:

> A person will not bear criminal liability for committing any act immediately necessary for the purpose of saving the life, liberty, body or property, of either himself or his fellow person, from substantial danger of serious harm, in response to particular circumstances during a specific time, and absent alternative means for avoiding the harm.

The state's position is that by virtue of this defense against criminal liability, GSS investigators are authorized to apply physical means—such as shaking—in the appropriate circumstances and in the absence of other alternatives, in order to prevent serious harm to human life or limb. The state maintains that an act committed under conditions of "necessity" does not constitute a crime. Instead, the state sees such acts as worth committing in order to prevent serious harm to human life or limb. These are actions that society has an interest in encouraging, which should be seen as proper under the circumstances. In this, society is choosing the lesser evil. Not only is it legitimately permitted to engage in fighting terrorism, it is our moral duty to employ the means necessary for this purpose. This duty is particularly incumbent on the state authorities—and, for our purposes, on the GSS investigators—who carry the burden of safeguarding the public peace. As this is the case, there is no obstacle preventing the investigators' superiors from instructing and guiding them as to when the conditions of the "necessity" defense are fulfilled. This, the state contends, implies the legality of the use of physical means in GSS interrogations.

In the course of their argument, the state presented the "ticking bomb" argument. A given suspect is arrested by the GSS. He holds information regarding the location of a bomb that was set and will imminently explode. There is no way to diffuse the bomb without this information. If the information is obtained, the bomb may be neutralized. If the bomb is not neutralized, scores will be killed and injured. Is a GSS investigator authorized to employ physical means in order to obtain this information? The state answers in the affirmative. The use of physical means should not constitute a criminal offence, and their use should be sanctioned, according to the state, by the "necessity" defense.

34. We are prepared to assume, although this matter is open to debate, that the "necessity defense" is available to all, including an investigator, during an interrogation, acting in the capacity of the state. Likewise, we are prepared to accept—although this matter is equally contentious—that the "necessity defense" can arise in instances of "ticking bombs," and that the phrase "immediate need" in the statute refers to the imminent nature of the act rather than that of the danger. Hence, the imminence criteria is satisfied even if the bomb is set to explode in a few days, or even in a few weeks, provided the danger is certain to materialize and there is no alternative means of preventing it. In other words, there exists a concrete level of imminent danger of the explosion's occurrence.

Consequently we are prepared to presume, as was held by the Report of the Commission of Inquiry, that if a GSS investigator—who applied physical interrogation methods for the purpose of saving human life—is criminally indicted, the "necessity defense" is likely to be open to him in the appropriate circumstances. A long list of arguments, from the fields of ethics and political science, may be raised in support of and against the use of the "necessity defense." This matter, however, has already been decided under Israeli law. Israeli penal law recognizes the "necessity defense."

35. Indeed, we are prepared to accept that, in the appropriate circumstances, GSS investigators may avail themselves of the "necessity defense" if criminally indicted. This, however, is not the issue before this Court. We are not dealing with the criminal liability of a GSS investigator who employed physical interrogation methods under circumstances of "necessity." Nor are we addressing the issue of the

admissibility or probative value of evidence obtained as a result of a GSS investigator's application of physical means against a suspect. We are dealing with a different question. The question before us is whether it is possible, *ex ante*, to establish permanent directives setting out the physical interrogation means that may be used under conditions of "necessity." Moreover, we must decide whether the "necessity defense" can constitute a basis for the authority of a GSS investigator to investigate, in the performance of his duty. According to the state, it is possible to imply from the "necessity defense"—available *post factum* to an investigator indicted of a criminal offence—the *ex ante* legal authorization to allow the investigator to use physical interrogation methods. Is this position correct?

36. In the Court's opinion, the authority to establish directives respecting the use of physical means during the course of a GSS interrogation cannot be implied from the "necessity defense." The "necessity defense" does not constitute a source of authority, which would allow GSS investigators to make use physical means during the course of interrogations. The reasoning underlying our position is anchored in the nature of the "necessity defense." The defense deals with cases involving an individual reacting to a given set of facts. It is an improvised reaction to an unpredictable event. Thus, the very nature of the defense does not allow it to serve as the source of authorization. . .

37. In other words, general directives governing the use of physical means during interrogations must be rooted in an authorization prescribed by law and not in defenses to criminal liability. The principle of "necessity" cannot serve as a basis of authority. If the state wishes to enable GSS investigators to utilize physical means in interrogations, it must enact legislation for this purpose....

38. We conclude, therefore, that, according to the existing state of the law, neither the government nor the heads of the security services have the authority to establish directives regarding the use of physical means during the interrogation of suspects suspected of hostile terrorist activities, beyond the general rules which can be inferred from the very concept of an interrogation itself. Similarly, the individual GSS investigator—like any police officer—does not possess the authority to employ physical means that infringe a suspect's liberty during the interrogation, unless these means are inherent to the very essence of an interrogation and are both fair and reasonable. An investigator who employs these methods exceeds his authority. His responsibility shall be fixed according to law. His potential criminal liability shall be examined in the context of the "necessity defense." Provided the conditions of the defense are met by the circumstances of the case, the investigator may find refuge under its wings. Just as the existence of the "necessity defense" does not bestow authority, the lack of authority does not negate

the applicability of the necessity defense or of other defenses from criminal liability. The Attorney-General can establish guidelines regarding circumstances in which investigators shall not stand trial, if they claim to have acted from "necessity." . . .

NOTES & QUESTIONS

1.   *The Criminal Law Defense.* The Israeli Supreme Court conceded that domestic criminal law may offer a defense, in some circumstances, to the crime of torture. But the judges concluded that one could not infer, on the basis of that defense, an ex ante policy justification for the practice of torture. Why not? For a discussion, see Alon Harel and Assaf Sharon, *What is Really Wrong with Torture?*, 6 J. Int'l Crim. Just. 241, 251 (2008) ("When torture is called for, we want torture to be performed *as an exception* grounded in practical necessity rather than as a rule-governed principle or norm.").

2.   *The Concept of Human Dignity.* What is the concept of human dignity? In both the German and Israeli legal systems, the constitution protects the right of human dignity. Indeed, in both countries the protection of human dignity is the first provision in the constitution. For example, the German Constitution states in article 1 that "Human dignity shall be inviolable. To respect and protect it shall be the duty of all state authority. . . The German people therefore acknowledge inviolable and inalienable human rights as the basis of every community, of peace and of justice in the world." Is this notion of human dignity also implicit in the ICCPR and European Convention provisions that identify some rights as non-derogable? The concept of human dignity is often associated with the work of Immanuel Kant, who developed a non-utilitarian framework that could ground the inherent moral worth of each individual. According to Kant, morality requires that each individual be treated as an end onto himself (or herself), rather than a means to an end. How might this notion apply to a detainee subject to torture during an interrogation? In what way is the tortured detainee being used as a mere means to an end? For a discussion of torture and human dignity, see David Luban, *Torture, Power, and Law* 146 (2014) (arguing that "the paradigm case of violating human dignity consists in humiliating someone").

3.   *Failure to Prosecute.* In the opinion, the Supreme Court says that the necessity defense cannot act as a forward-looking legal authorization for torture. But in paragraph 38, the Supreme Court states that the Attorney General may establish ex ante "guidelines" to announce when interrogators acting under necessity will stand trial and when they will not. Is it possible that these guidelines, though technically related to prosecutorial discretion, will act as a kind of de facto legal authorization, since they are announced in advance and known to investigators? Recall that the proposed guidelines would not simply dictate who will be convicted and who will acquitted, but rather who will even stand trial. If an investigator knows in advance that

their behavior will not generate a criminal charge, how different is this from the ex ante authorization that the Israeli Supreme Court rejected?

In the following case, the concept of human dignity once again takes center stage to prevent the German government from invoking the requirement of public emergency—an imminent terrorist attack—to justify the killing of innocent passengers on a hijacked airplane. Would killing the innocent passengers on a hijacked airplane (by downing the airplane to prevent it from hitting a building) constitute an impermissible instrumentalization of the passengers?

Aviation Security Act Case
German Constitutional Court
1 BvR 357/05 (2006)

The constitutional complaint challenges the armed forces' authorisation by the Aviation Security Act to shoot down, by the direct use of armed force, aircraft that are intended to be used as weapons in crimes against human lives.

On 11 September 2001, four passenger planes of US American airlines were hijacked in the United States of America by an international terrorist organisation and caused to crash. Two of the planes hit the World Trade Center in New York, one crashed into the Pentagon, the Ministry of Defence of the United States of America. The crash of the fourth plane occurred southeast of Pittsburgh in the state of Pennsylvania, after, possibly, the intervention of passengers on board had resulted in a change of the plane's course. More than 3,000 persons in the planes, in the area of the World Trade Center, and in the Pentagon died in the attacks.

On 5 January 2003, an armed man captured a sports plane, circled above the banking district of Frankfurt/Main and threatened to crash the plane into the highrise of the European Central Bank if he was not granted the possibility of making a phone call to the United States of America. A police helicopter and two jet fighters of the German Air Force took off and circled the powered glider. The police ordered major alert, the city centre of Frankfurt was cleared, highrises were evacuated. Slightly more than half an hour after the capture, it was evident that the hijacker was a mentally confused person acting on his own. After his demand had been complied with, he landed on Rhein-Main Airport and did not resist his arrest.

Both incidents caused a large number of measures aimed at preventing unlawful interference with civil aviation, at improving the security of civil aviation as a whole and at protecting it, in doing so, also from dangers that are imminent where aircraft are taken command of by people who want to abuse them for objectives that are unrelated to air traffic. . .

In the Federal Republic of Germany, factual as well as legal measures have been taken whose intended objectives are to increase the security of air traffic and to protect it from attacks. . .

The operations that are permissible in accordance with the Aviation Security Act and the principles that apply as regards their choice are specified in §§ 14 and 15 of the Aviation Security Act. Pursuant to § 15.1 of the Aviation Security Act, operations intended to prevent the occurrence of an especially grave accident within the meaning of § 14.1 and 14.3 of the Aviation Security Act may be taken only if the aircraft from which the danger of such accident emanates has previously been checked by the armed forces in the air space and if it has then been unsuccessfully tried to warn and to divert it. If this prerequisite has been met, the armed forces may, pursuant to § 14.1 of the Aviation Security Act, force the aircraft off its course in the air space, force it to land, threaten to use armed force, or fire warning shots. The principle of proportionality applies to the choice among these measures. Pursuant to § 14.3 of the Aviation Security Act, the direct use of armed force against the aircraft is permissible only if the occurrence of an especially grave accident cannot be prevented even by such measures. This, however, only applies where it must be assumed under the circumstances that the aircraft is intended to be used as a weapon against human lives, and where the direct use of armed force is the only means to avert this imminent danger. Pursuant to § 14.4 sentence 1 of the Aviation Security Act, the exclusive competence for ordering this measure rests with the Federal Minister of Defence, or in the event of the Minister of Defence having to be represented, with the member of the Federal Government who is authorised to represent the Minister. . .

The fundamental right to life guaranteed by Article 2.2 sentence 1 of the Basic Law is subject to the requirement of the specific enactment of a statute pursuant to Article 2.2 sentence 3 of the Basic Law. The Act, however, that restricts the fundamental right must in its turn be regarded in the light of the fundamental right and of the guarantee of human dignity under Article 1.1 of the Basic Law, which is closely linked with it. Human life is the vital basis of human dignity as the essential constitutive principle, and as the supreme value, of the constitution. All human beings possess this dignity as persons, irrespective of their qualities, their physical or mental state, their achievements and their social status. It cannot be taken away from any human being. What can be violated, however, is the claim to respect which results from it. This applies irrespective, inter alia, of the probable duration of the individual human life on the human being's claim to respect of his or her dignity even after death.

In view of this relation between the right to life and human dignity, the state is prohibited, on the one hand, from encroaching upon the fundamental right to life by measures of its own, thereby violating the ban on the disregard of human dignity. On the other hand, the state is also obliged to protect every human life. This duty of protection demands of the state and its bodies to shield and to promote the life of every individual, which means above all to also protect it from unlawful attacks, and interference, by third parties. Also this duty of protection has its foundations in Article 1.1 sentence 2 of the Basic Law, which explicitly obliges the state to respect and protect human dignity.

What this obligation means in concrete terms for state action cannot be definitely determined once and for all. Article 1.1 of the Basic Law protects the individual human being not only against humiliation, branding, persecution, outlawing and similar actions by third parties or by the state itself. Taking as a starting point the idea of the constitution-creating legislature that it is part of the nature of human beings to exercise self-determination in freedom and to freely develop themselves, and that the individual can claim, in principle, to be recognised in society as a member with equal rights and with a value of his or her own, the obligation to respect and protect human dignity generally precludes making a human being a mere object of the state. What is thus absolutely prohibited is any treatment of a human being by public authority which fundamentally calls into question his or her quality of a subject, his or her status as a legal entity by its lack of the respect of the value which is due to every human being for his or her own sake, by virtue of his or her being a person. When it is that such a treatment occurs must be stated in concrete terms in the individual case in view of the specific situation in which a conflict can arise.

According to these standards, § 14.3 of the Aviation Security Act is also incompatible with Article 2.2 sentence 1 in conjunction with Article 1.1 of the Basic Law to the extent that the shooting down of an aircraft affects people who, as its crew and passengers, have not exerted any influence on the occurrence of the non-warlike aerial incident assumed under § 14.3 of the Aviation Security Act.

In the situation in which these persons are at the moment in which the order to use direct armed force against the aircraft involved in the aerial incident pursuant to § 14.4 sentence 1 of the Aviation Security Act is made, it must be possible, pursuant to § 14.3 of the Aviation Security Act, to assume with certainty that the aircraft is intended to be used against human lives. As has been stated in the reasoning for the Act, the aircraft must have been converted into an assault weapon by those who have brought it under their command; the aircraft itself must be used by the perpetrators in a targeted manner as a weapon for the crime, not merely as an auxiliary means for committing the crime, against the lives of people who stay in the area in which the aircraft is intended to crash. In such an extreme situation, which is, moreover, characterised by the cramped conditions of an aircraft in flight, the passengers and the crew are typically in a desperate situation. They can no longer influence the circumstances of their lives independently from others in a self-determined manner.

This makes them objects not only of the perpetrators of the crime. Also the state which in such a situation resorts to the measure provided by § 14.3 of the Aviation Security Act treats them as mere objects of its rescue operation for the protection of others. The desperateness and inescapability which characterise the situation of the people on board the aircraft who are affected as victims also exist vis-à-vis those who order and execute the shooting down of the aircraft. Due to the circumstances, which cannot be controlled by them in any way, the crew and the passengers of the plane cannot escape this state action but are helpless and defenceless in the face of it with the consequence that they are shot down in a targeted manner together with the aircraft and as result of this will be killed with near certainty. Such a treatment ignores the status of the persons affected as subjects endowed with dignity and inalienable rights. By their killing being used as a means to save others, they are treated as objects and at the same time deprived of their rights; with their lives being disposed of unilaterally by the state, the persons on board the aircraft, who, as victims, are themselves in need of protection, are denied the value which is due to a human being for his or her own sake. . .

Even if in the area of police power, insecurities concerning forecasts often cannot be completely avoided, it is absolutely inconceivable under the applicability of Article 1.1 of the Basic Law to intentionally kill persons such as the crew and the passengers of a hijacked plane, who are in a situation that is hopeless for them, on the basis of a statutory authorisation which even accepts such imponderabilities if necessary. It need not be decided here how a shooting down that is performed all the same, and an order relating to it, would have to be assessed under criminal law. What is solely decisive for the constitutional appraisal is that the legislature may not, by establishing a statutory authorisation for intervention, give authority to perform operations of the nature regulated in § 14.3 of the Aviation Security Act vis-à-vis people who are not participants in the crime and may not in this manner qualify such operations as legal and thus permit them. As missions of the armed forces of a non-warlike nature, they are incompatible with the right to life and the obligation of the state to respect and protect human dignity.

Therefore it cannot be assumed—differently from arguments that are advanced sometimes—that someone boarding an aircraft as a crew member or as a passenger will presumably consent to its being shot down, and thus to his or her own killing, in the case of the aircraft becoming involved in an aerial incident within the meaning of § 13.1 of the Aviation Security Act which results in a measure averting the danger pursuant to § 14.3 of the Aviation Security Act. Such an assumption lacks any realistic grounds and is no more than an unrealistic fiction.

Also the assessment that the persons who are on board a plane that is intended to be used against other people's lives within the meaning of § 14.3 of the Aviation Security Act are doomed anyway cannot remove its nature of an infringement of their right to dignity from the killing of innocent people in a situation that is desperate for them which an operation performed pursuant to this provisions as a general rule involves. Human life and human dignity enjoy the same constitutional protection regardless of the duration of the physical existence of the individual human being. Whoever denies this or calls this into question denies those who, such as the victims of a hijacking, are in a desperate situation that offers no alternative to them, precisely the respect which is due to them for the sake of their human dignity.

In addition, uncertainties as regards the factual situation exist here as well. These uncertainties, which characterise the assessment of the situation in the area of application of §§ 13 to 15 of the Aviation Security Act in general, necessarily also influence a prediction of how long people who are on board a plane which has been converted into an assault weapon will live and whether there is still a chance of rescuing them. As a general rule, it will therefore not be possible to make a reliable statement about these people's lives being "lost anyway already."

The assumption that anyone who is held on board an aircraft under the command of persons who intend to use the aircraft as a weapon of a crime against other people's lives within the meaning of § 14.3 of the Aviation Security Act has become part of a weapon and must bear being treated as such also does not justify a different assessment. This opinion expresses in a virtually undisguised manner that the victims of such an incident are no longer perceived as human beings but as part of an object, a view by which they themselves become objects. This cannot be reconciled with the Basic Law's concept of the human being and with the idea of the human being as a creature whose nature it is to exercise self-determination in freedom, and who therefore may not be made a mere object of state action. . .

NOTES & QUESTIONS

The View from the ECHR. The German Constitutional Court took a particularly extreme view of the right to life and its non-derogable nature.

Would the ECHR have taken the same position if it had heard this case? Although this question is highly speculative, the ECHR has considered the right to life in other cases and given states a wider margin of appreciation. For example, in *Finogenov and Others v. Russia*, the ECHR considered an application from victims of a terrorist attack in the Dubrovka theater in Moscow on October 23–26, 2002. The attack by Chechen separatists resulted in a hostage situation that was ended by Russian security forces, resulting in the deaths of approximately 130 hostages and 40 terrorists. The applicants alleged a violation of article 2 of the European Convention, which states:

> 1. Everyone's right to life shall be protected by law... 2. Deprivation of life shall not be regarded as inflicted in contravention of this article when it results from the use of force which is no more than absolutely necessary: (a) in defence of any person from unlawful violence; (b) in order to effect a lawful arrest or to prevent the escape of a person lawfully detained; (c) in action lawfully taken for the purpose of quelling a riot or insurrection.

Specifically, the applicants argued that many deaths were caused by the security service's use of gas during the storming of the theater. The ECHR concluded that:

> In sum, the situation appeared very alarming. Heavily armed separatists dedicated to their cause had taken hostages and put forward unrealistic demands. The first days of negotiations did not bring any visible success; in addition, the humanitarian situation (the hostages' physical and psychological condition) had been worsening and made the hostages even more vulnerable. The Court concludes that there existed a real, serious and immediate risk of mass human losses and that the authorities had every reason to believe that a forced intervention was the "lesser evil" in the circumstances. Therefore, the authorities' decision to end the negotiations and storm the building did not in the circumstances run counter to Article 2 of the Convention (para. 226).

Is there a factual difference between using lethal force to stop a hostage crisis, knowing that it will inevitably result in the death of some usages, versus using physical force to bring down a hijacked airliner?

E. EXTRATERRITORIAL APPLICATION OF HUMAN RIGHTS

Although human rights are, in a sense, universal, there is lingering controversy over the exact geographical scope of international human rights protections. It is uncontroversial that these obligations apply when state officials act on their own territory. But when these officials act extraterritorially—on another state's territory—do the same protections apply? One common way of asking the question is whether human rights law *follows the flag* and applies wherever the state acts or whether, in contrast, human rights law is territorially bounded.

Article 2(1) of the ICCPR states that "[e]ach State Party to the present Covenant undertakes to respect and to ensure to all individuals within its territory and subject to its jurisdiction the rights recognized in the present Covenant. . ." Although this sounds relatively straightforward, the following excerpt from a U.S. State Department memorandum demonstrates how complex article 2 really is. Does the ICCPR apply extraterritorially?

Memorandum Opinion on the Geographic Scope of the International Covenant on Civil and Political Rights

Office of Legal Advisor Harold Koh
October 19, 2010

The geographic scope of States Parties' obligations under the International Covenant on Civil and Political Rights ("ICCPR") is governed by Article 2(1), which provides that "[e]ach State Party to the present Covenant undertakes to respect and to ensure to all individuals within its territory and subject to its jurisdiction the rights recognized in the present Covenant, without distinction of any kind" . . . . (emphasis added). In 1995, in a brief oral response to a question regarding the geographic scope of the Covenant during the United States' Initial Report to the Human Rights Committee ("Committee" or "HRC"), then-Legal Adviser Conrad Harper stated that "[t]he Covenant was not regarded as having extraterritorial application." Since that time, the U.S. Government has maintained, under the 1995 Interpretation, that Article 2(1) obligates States Parties to recognize Covenant rights only for "individuals who are both within the territory of a State Party and subject to that State Party's sovereign authority, so that "the terms of the Covenant apply exclusively within the territory" of the United States. Under this "strict territoriality" reading, the Covenant would not impose any obligations on a State Party either to respect or to ensure the rights in the Covenant for any individual who is located outside the territory of a State Party—even for persons who are subject to complete U.S. authority abroad, and even with respect to such fundamental Covenant rights as the right to be free of torture or cruel, inhuman or degrading treatment. One obvious implication of the 1995 Interpretation is that the States Parties would not have intended the Covenant to pose a legal barrier to a State Party torturing a person outside its territorial borders, even if that person were subject to that state's total and effective control.

As I noted during my confirmation hearing as Legal Adviser, I approach prior legal opinions of the Legal Adviser's Office as enjoying a presumption of stare decisis, while at the same time recognizing that, under certain circumstances, that presumption can and should be overcome. Since 1995, the 1995 Interpretation has been brought into question by the International Court of Justice ("ICI") (writing in two important opinions), the Human Rights Committee (writing in its General Comment 31, in its responses to individual petitions and in its observations and recommendations regarding State reports), and a number of our closest allies in their written comments to the Human Rights Committee. All have taken the considered position—contrary to the 1995 Interpretation—that the protections afforded by the Covenant do not in all cases stop at the water's edge. The 1995 Interpretation has been questioned repeatedly by numerous academics, human rights experts and NGO commentators. It also stands in tension with the recognition by regional human rights bodies of extraterritorial obligations under other human rights instruments.

Given these challenges, we conducted an initial investigation which established that, with respect to this Issue, the 1995 Interpretation overstated the clarity of the text and negotiating history (*travaux preparatoires*) of the Covenant. Upon fuller analysis, we found that neither the text nor the travaux of the Covenant requires the extraordinarily strict territorial interpretation that the United States has asserted regarding the geographic scope of the Covenant— particularly when taking into account the treaty's broader context and object and purpose, as standard rules of treaty interpretation require. Nor, despite frequent citation to Eleanor Roosevelt's contemporaneous views as claimed support for the strict territorial view, do the travaux establish that this was in fact the U.S. understanding at the time when Eleanor Roosevelt presided over the Covenant's drafting. Nor, finally, was the 1995 Interpretation clearly embraced by the President at either the time of signature or of ratification, nor was it anywhere reflected in the understanding of the ratifying Senate.

All of this contradictory evidence raises the question whether the United States should continue to urge a rigidly territorial reading of the ICCPR. We cannot continue to adhere to the then-Legal Adviser's 1995 Interpretation to the Human Rights Committee without taking into account and explaining the competing evidence from the text, context, object and purpose, travaux, and ratification history of the Covenant, as well as the growing body of jurisprudential, governmental and scholarly interpretation articulating a broader interpretation of the treaty's territorial scope.

To resolve this disagreement, this Office has now conducted an exhaustive review of: (1) the language of the Covenant in its context; (2) the treaty's object and purpose; (3) the negotiating history; (4) all prior U.S. positions of which we are aware regarding the Covenant, including positions taken during the negotiation, signature and ratification of the treaty, as well as later interpretations; (5) the interpretations of other States Parties; (6) the interpretations of the U.N. Human Rights Committee, and (7) Advisory Opinions and judgments of the International Court of Justice ("ICJ").

Based upon this comprehensive review, I have now reached the considered legal judgment, as Legal Adviser:

First, that the 1995 Interpretation is not compelled by either the language or the negotiating history of the Covenant;

Second, that the 1995 Interpretation is in fact in significant tension with the treaty's language, context, and object and purpose, as well as with interpretations of important U.S. allies, the Human Rights Committee and the ICJ, and developments in related bodies of law;

Third, that an interpretation of Article 2(1) that is truer to the Covenant's language, context, object and purpose, negotiating history, and subsequent understandings of other States Parties, as well as the interpretations of other international bodies, would provide that in fact, the Covenant does impose certain obligations on a State Party's extraterritorial conduct under certain circumstances:

- In particular, as detailed below, it is my considered opinion that a better legal reading would distinguish between the territorial scope of the Covenant's obligation to "respect" and to "ensure" Covenant rights.

- A state incurs obligations to *respect* Covenant rights—i.e., is itself obligated not to violate those rights through its own actions or the actions of its agents—in those circumstances where a state exercises authority or effective control over the person or context at issue.

- A state incurs obligations to *ensure* Covenant rights— either by legislating or otherwise affirmatively acting to protect individuals abroad from harm by other states or entities—only where such individuals are both within its territory and subject to its jurisdiction, since in such cases the exercise of such affirmative authority would not conflict with the jurisdiction of any other sovereign.

In my view, the 1995 Interpretation is no longer tenable and the USG legal position should be reviewed and revised accordingly. A presumption in favor of stare decisis in executive interpretation does not compel rote repetition of incorrect legal positions in reports to international bodies, particularly when those positions can be reexamined in a way that enables this Administration to turn the page on the past by disengaging from an increasingly implausible legal interpretation.

Our prior position has been a source of ongoing international tension, with significant deleterious effects on our international human rights reputation and our ability to promote international human rights internationally. The prior administration was severely criticized in U.N. fora, by important U.S. allies, by members of Congress, by domestic and international human rights groups, and in the domestic and international media. The 1995 Interpretation is seen as allowing alleged incidents of abusive extraterritorial practices such as torture and "extraordinary rendition," and as immunizing such practices from legal review by preserving the policy option for U.S. personnel to act in a "legal black hole" once they step outside the territorial United States. By contrast, revising our legal position to recognize some application of the ICCPR to U.S. conduct abroad would have a salutary effect on our international reputation. It would significantly advance our international standing and reputation for respect for the international rule of law, which are primary commitments of this Administration.

In addition, reviewing and modifying the rigidly territorial reading of the ICCPR would offer a stronger legal foundation for current policy practices. To adhere to the 1995 Interpretation, in the face of extensive contrary evidence and authority, would place our attorneys in the position of providing legal advice to the U.S. government that does not reflect the best reading of the law. Nor is a "strict territorial" interpretation an accurate predictor of how authoritative interpreters, our allies, and other important interlocutors will likely evaluate the United States' legal obligations.

Adopting the sounder legal interpretation need not require a dramatic change in our actual practices abroad. For example, President Obama has already ordered compliance with U.S. treaty obligations mandating humane treatment in armed conflict with respect to all persons "in the custody or under the effective control of" U.S. authorities "or detained within a facility owned, operated, or controlled by. . . the United States." Many of the obligations recognized by the ICCPR that would apply to U.S. conduct overseas already apply in that context through the operation of other international legal obligations (such as the Geneva, Genocide and Torture Conventions, as well as customary international law). Indeed, some of those legal obligations already form part of the body of specialized international humanitarian law rules (lex specialis) that governs armed conflict. . .

Treaty Language, Context, Object and Purpose

. . . .Significantly, the 1995 Interpretation of the territorial scope of the ICCPR has turned primarily on treating the Article 2(1) text as clear, with some limited consideration of the negotiating history. To our knowledge, the 1995 Interpretation did not conduct a deeper analysis of the text to consider how that reading comported with the context, object and purpose of the treaty, subsequent state practice, and other primary interpretive sources set forth in [the Vienna Convention on the Law of Treaties]. To the contrary, the 1995 Interpretation avoided extensive examination of these interpretive sources other than the text of Article 2(1) itself, by viewing that language as unambiguous on its face. In 2005, the U.S. ICCPR Report repeated that " 'the plain and ordinary meaning" of the Article "establishes that States Parties are required to ensure the rights in the Covenant only to individuals who are both within the territory of a State Party and subject to that State Party's sovereign authority." The 2005 USG analysis—repeated virtually without change in 2007—asserted that this conclusion was "inescapable."

Yet in fact, far from being "unambiguous," even on its face, the obligation of a state "to respect and to ensure to all individuals within its territory and subject to its jurisdiction the rights recognized in the. . . Covenant" has proven susceptible to not one, but several, possible interpretations: the first concerns whether the term "and" should be read as conjunctive or disjunctive; the second concerns whether the territorial limit equally modifies both the obligation to "respect" and the obligation to "ensure."

The first ambiguity involves the function of the word "and" in the treaty phrase at issue. On one hand, the word "and" in Article 2(1) could be read in the conjunctive, to apply to all persons who are "within [a state's] territory and [who are also] subject to its jurisdiction," as the United States has advocated. "Territory" and "jurisdiction" are not coterminous concepts, although they often overlap significantly in practice. Thus, individuals may be present within a state's territory but not be subject to its jurisdiction for all purposes, such as foreign diplomats and consuls (and foreign embassies and missions), who generally remain within the jurisdiction of their home state. Conversely, persons outside of a state's territory may nevertheless remain under its jurisdiction—either because they are present in territory under the state's de facto or de jure jurisdiction (potentially including embassies, military bases, and state-flagged ships and aircraft), because they are agents acting on the state's behalf or because they are nationals of the state, among other grounds. By reading "and" in the conjunctive, this reading would apply all of the Covenant's protections only to the limited set of individuals who fell within both its "territory" and its "jurisdiction." The 1995 Interpretation took the position that "and" must be read in this context as connective, which would mean that no person who is located outside a State Party's territory would ever be covered by the Covenant, even if the state used its jurisdiction over a person located outside its territory to harm that individual's interests from within the state's own territory. But as we elaborate below, such a stringent reading of the Covenant does not appear to be consistent with the United States' original interpretation or its modem application of the Covenant in practice.

On the other hand, depending upon the context, "and" could also be used disjunctively, for example, when used to connect alternatives. The Human Rights Committee, the ICJ, and others have read "and" in this manner, as applying the Covenant to all persons "within [a state's] territory and [also to all persons] subject to its jurisdiction." The 1995 Interpretation argues that, on the face of Article 2(1), "and" must be read as conjunctive. But even accepting that reading, this would not by itself establish that the entire phrase is unambiguous. To the contrary, at least two possible interpretations still remain available:

i.   *Territorially Limiting Both the Obligation to Respect and the Obligation to Ensure*: Under this reading, the phrase "within its territory and subject to its jurisdiction" would modify both the obligation "to respect" and the obligation "to ensure," so that both of these obligations would apply only to persons who are both within a state's sovereign territory and also subject to its jurisdiction. Put another way, Article 2 would place an obligation on a State Party "to respect Covenant rights only for all individuals within its territory and subject to its jurisdiction and to ensure Covenant rights only to all individuals within its territory and subject to its jurisdiction." As noted above, this "strict territoriality" approach has been the U.S. reading since 1995.

ii. *Territorially Limiting Only the Obligation to Ensure ("Effective Control")*: Under this reading, the geographic limitation of "[w]ithin its territory and subject to its jurisdiction" modifies only the obligation to which it is textually appended: "to ensure" Covenant rights, not the obligation "to respect" those rights. A State Party would undertake "to respect" Covenant obligations by refraining from infringing protected rights, but undertake "to ensure" Covenant rights only to persons who are both "within its territory and subject to its jurisdiction." Put another way, this reading of Article 2 would place a general obligation on a State to respect Covenant rights whenever it exercises authority or effective control, without regard to geographic location, but to ensure Covenant rights only to those individuals who are "within its territory and subject to its jurisdiction." This has been the reading of certain commentators and Special Rapporteurs, and is informed by the development of the concept of "effective control" in U.S. and other national courts and regional tribunals.

In choosing between the "strictly territorial" 1995 Interpretation (reading (i), above), and the alternative "effective control" interpretation (reading (ii), above), which permits some extraterritorial application of the ICCPR, in light of the treaty text, context, object and purpose, we note at least five difficulties that arise with the 1995 Interpretation:

First, the 1995 Interpretation could be understood to render redundant or meaningless the Article 2(1) obligation "to respect" rights. It is canonical in treaty interpretation that all the words of a treaty are to be given meaning and that a treaty should not be construed so as to render some words redundant. If the words "to respect and to ensure" are both modified by the limiting clause "to all individuals within its territory and subject to its jurisdiction," as under reading (i) above, the obligation to "respect" could be understood to be subsumed by the obligation "to ensure" and thus to have no independent effect.

Although the Covenant on its face does not elaborate on how these two terms differ, today the concepts "to respect" and "to ensure" are widely understood to bear separate and specific meanings under the ICCPR. The obligation "to respect" means that a state commits to negative obligations, i.e., to refrain itself from violating these rights through its own actions. By contrast, the obligation "to ensure" encompasses broader positive obligations to guarantee rights to individuals by protecting them from violation of their rights and facilitating the affirmative enjoyment of rights, including through the adoption of legislation. It would make little sense to say that a State Party was obligated to ensure rights of the kind recognized by the ICCPR (i.e., to promote them positively and protect against violations), but not also to respect them (i.e., refrain from violating those rights itself).

Significantly, as the travaux reflect, the text of the treaty that was originally proposed by the United States only included the word "ensure;" the obligation to "respect" was later added. In defending the original U.S. text, Eleanor Roosevelt "thought it was unnecessary to insert the words 'respect and' . . . She felt that if a State ensured all the rights and obligations of the covenant, it must necessarily respect those rights and obligations." The French delegate Mr. Rene Cassin, by contrast, considered it "essential that a State should not only guarantee the enjoyment of [i.e., ensure] human rights to individuals but also respect those rights itself."

On the other hand, reading (ii) above would read the territorial and jurisdictional limitation clause to modify only the obligation to "ensure," giving both words clear distinct import. These two obligations would function independently, with differing geographic scopes. Under this interpretation, the treaty language creates not one, but two obligations: a geographically unconstrained obligation to respect—or avoid violating—the ICCPR rights of persons wherever the state may act with authority or effective control, coupled with a geographically constrained obligation to ensure—or affirmatively guarantee—rights for the more circumscribed category of persons who are both within the State's territory and subject to its jurisdiction.

Second, the 1995 Interpretation is grammatically problematic in both English and other official Covenant languages. Under the English version of the treaty, the literal meaning of the phrase "to respect and to ensure to all individuals within its territory and subject to its jurisdiction the rights recognized in the present Covenant" does not apply the italicized territorial restriction to both the obligation "to respect" and the obligation "to ensure." Rather, under normal English grammar, the territorially-limited prepositional phrase modifies only the verb "to ensure." While it is appropriate to speak of ensuring rights "to" rights holders, it is not idiomatic English to speak of respecting rights "to" right holders. Yet, a reading that assumes that the territorial restriction modifies not just "to ensure," but also "to respect," would yield the ungrammatical reading that States Parties are obligated "to respect. . . to all individuals within its territory and subject to its jurisdiction the rights" in the Covenant. The more grammatically correct reading of the passage would obligate States Parties "to respect. . . the rights recognized in the present Covenant," and also to ensure those rights to all persons within its territory and subject to its jurisdiction. Consistent with reading (ii), which also offers a solution to the redundancy concern above, this grammatically correct reading would place a territorial constraint on the positive obligation to ensure rights in the Covenant, but would apply the obligation to respect those rights wherever a state acts. . .

Third, an interpretation that limits all Covenant obligations to a State Party's territory renders the territorial restriction in Article 12(1) superfluous. Article 12(1) provides that "Everyone lawfully within the territory of a state shall, within that territory, have the right to liberty of movement and freedom to choose his residence." (Emphasis added). But if through the operation of Article 2(1), the entire Covenant already applied only within a state's territory, it would be entirely redundant to add the second, italicized reference in this particular clause, which limits the right of persons lawfully within a state's territory to freedom of movement "within that territory." On the other hand, if the Covenant has the potential to apply extraterritorially in certain contexts, then the second territorial restriction in Article 12(1) would become meaningful to limit the operation of that particular Article to the territory of a State Party.

Fourth, a strict territorial reading places the Covenant in tension with its own Optional Protocol. The First Optional Protocol to the ICCPR, a related instrument which was adopted simultaneously with the Covenant in 1966 (and which the United States has not signed or ratified), provides for review by the HRC of individual petitions brought by "individuals subject to [the State Party's] jurisdiction who claim to be victims of a violation by that State Party of any of the rights set forth in the Covenant." Note that the Optional Protocol does not limit the Committee's authority over individual claims that also arise within the territory of the State Party. Reading Article 2(1) as strictly territorial, therefore, appears to create an anomalous authority for the HRC to review individual petitions under the Optional Protocol that would extend more broadly than the scope of a State Party's substantive obligations under the ICCPR.

Fifth and finally, contrary to VCLT articles 31 and 32, a reading that the Covenant applies solely and exclusively within a State Party's territory (a) does not comport with the treaty's object and purpose, and (b) produces unreasonable or absurd results.

a. *Object and purpose:* The purpose of the Covenant, as set forth in the Preamble and acknowledged by the U.S. transmittal documents for ratification, is to advance the U.N. Charter and Universal Declaration of Human Rights goals of promoting "the inherent dignity and . . . the equal and inalienable rights of all members of the human family," and "universal respect for, and observance of, human rights and freedoms." Logically, the treaty drafters may have assumed that the goal of universal protection for human rights could be achieved primarily by securing universal state adherence to the Covenant, together with uniform compliance within each state's territory. It also seems logical that the drafters would not have sought to impose obligations on States Parties to ensure rights extraterritorially in regions subject to another State's legal authority, since such obligations could "impose excessive extraterritorial burdens on States Parties and provoke conflicts of jurisdiction. The drafters also appear to have understood that in certain situations, the ICCPR would complement other bodies of international law (such as international humanitarian law) which would primarily regulate state behavior in armed conflict. But none of these purposes or potential understandings of the Covenant would be served by a rigidly territorial construction that reads the treaty as mandating comprehensive protection of human rights within a State Party's borders, while imposing absolutely no obligation on the State not to violate rights when it acts affirmatively beyond those borders—whether on the high seas or in the territory of another sovereign. Such a construction would underserve the Covenant's broad and protective object and purpose. Indeed, such an interpretation would have flouted the animating purpose of post-World War II human rights regime, which was to develop legal tools to respond effectively to Nazi and other atrocities. Moreover, as the Human Rights Committee and other commentators have noted, a strictly territorial reading of Article 2(1) would create tension with other aspects of the treaty, such as Article 5(1) of the Covenant, which provides that

> Nothing in the present Covenant may be interpreted as implying for any State, group or person any right to engage in any activity or perform any act aimed at the destruction of any of the rights and freedoms recognized herein or at their limitation to a greater extent than is provided for in the present Covenant.

In 1981, the HRC construed this article as establishing a strong negative inference against a rigid territorial restriction. The Committee concluded that in light of this article, "it would be unconscionable" to interpret Article 2(1) "to permit a State party to perpetrate violations of the Covenant on the territory of another State, which violations it could not perpetrate on its own territory."

b.   *Unreasonable or absurd results:* The interpretation that "the terms of the Covenant apply exclusively within the territory" of a State Party also yields unreasonable or absurd results. A rigidly territorial restriction on State obligations under the Covenant, for example, would yield the bizarre result that a state that was obligated to protect citizens within its borders could act against those same citizens with impunity under the Covenant, the moment they stepped outside the state's borders. Absent other complementary treaty regimes regulating such conduct, such a construction would permit a state to torture, commit extrajudicial killing, or violate other human rights just outside its borders. As HRC Member Professor Christian Tomuschat noted: "To construe the words 'within its territory'. . . as excluding any responsibility for conduct occurring beyond the national boundaries would. . . lead to utterly absurd results. . . . [by] grant[ing] States parties unfettered discretionary power to carry out wilful and deliberate attacks against the freedom and personal integrity of their citizens living abroad. . ."

Moreover, it is unclear precisely what it means for a state's obligations under the ICCPR to apply only to persons within its borders. Governments may act in a variety of ways to affect the rights of persons inside or outside of their territory. For example, a government may (a) act externally and affect a person externally; (b) act internally but affect a person externally; or (c) act externally but affect a person internally. Under a rigidly territorial restriction, a State Party could act internally but affect a person externally (situation (b) above), for example, by conducting a flagrantly unfair trial within its territory to adjudicate rights of a citizen who lived abroad, including applying a presumption of guilt rather than innocence or subjecting the person to double jeopardy, contrary to Article 14 of the Covenant. A State could likewise act within its territory to interfere with the privacy or family of a national residing abroad, contrary to Article 17, or deny a passport to a citizen living abroad, thereby denying the individual the right to enter his own country guaranteed under Article 12(4). *Indeed, it is unclear what the Covenant's explicit right to enter a country could mean if it does not bestow protection on persons who are outside the territory.* The 1995 Interpretation of the territorial scope of the Covenant fails to take account of these various means by which reading strict territorial limits into Covenant provisions may lead states to affect the rights of individuals in a way that yields unreasonable or absurd results. In short, for all of these reasons—the multiple plausible readings of the text of Article 2(1) itself, the textual redundancies and grammatical difficulties created by the 1995 Interpretation, the tensions with other treaty provisions such as Article 12(1) and the Optional Protocol, the conflict with the Covenant's object and purpose, and the potential for unreasonable or absurd results—the text of Article 2(1), standing alone, does not plainly and unambiguously dictate a rigidly territorial delimitation of all Covenant obligations. To the contrary, an interpretation more consistent with the treaty's language, context, and object and purpose would acknowledge some extraterritorial application of the Covenant in some limited circumstances, for example, when a state itself acts abroad with authority or effective control to directly violate Covenant rights (such as reading (ii), supra). At a minimum, these concerns should call into question the repeated assertions that the 1995 Interpretation is "unambiguous" or "inescapable." . . .

In the following case, the ECHR considers the analogous question: Does the European Convention apply when European governmental officials act outside of Europe? For example, does the ECHR have jurisdiction over complaints alleging human rights violations by British soldiers deployed in Iraq?

Al-Skeini and Others v. United Kingdom

European Court of Human Rights
Application No. 55721/07 (2011)

9.   On 8 November 2002 the United Nations Security Council, acting under Chapter VII of the Charter of the United Nations, adopted Resolution 1441. The Resolution decided, *inter alia*, that Iraq had been and remained in material breach of its obligations under previous United Nations Security Council resolutions to disarm and to cooperate with United Nations and International Atomic Energy Agency weapons inspectors. Resolution 1441 decided to afford Iraq a final opportunity to comply with its disarmament obligations and set up an enhanced inspection regime. It requested the Secretary-General of the United

Nations immediately to notify Iraq of the Resolution and demanded that Iraq cooperate immediately, unconditionally, and actively with the inspectors. Resolution 1441 concluded by recalling that the Security Council had "repeatedly warned Iraq that it w[ould] face serious consequences as a result of its continued violations of its obligations." The Security Council decided to remain seised of the matter.

Major combat operations: 20 March to 1 May 2003

10. On 20 March 2003 a Coalition of armed forces under unified command, led by the United States of America with a large force from the United Kingdom and small contingents from Australia, Denmark and Poland, commenced the invasion of Iraq. By 5 April 2003 the British had captured Basra and by 9 April 2003 United States troops had gained control of Baghdad. Major combat operations in Iraq were declared complete on 1 May 2003. Thereafter, other States sent personnel to help with the reconstruction effort.

12. As mentioned in the above letter, the occupying States, acting through the Commander of Coalition Forces, created the Coalition Provisional Authority (CPA) to act as a "caretaker administration" until an Iraqi government could be established. It had power, *inter alia*, to issue legislation. On 13 May 2003 the US Secretary of Defence, Donald Rumsfeld, issued a memorandum formally appointing Ambassador Paul Bremer as Administrator of the CPA with responsibility for the temporary governance of Iraq. . . .

13. The CPA administration was divided into regional areas. CPA South was placed under United Kingdom responsibility and control, with a United Kingdom Regional Coordinator. It covered the southernmost four of Iraq's eighteen provinces, each having a governorate coordinator. United Kingdom troops were deployed in the same area. The United Kingdom was represented at CPA headquarters through the Office of the United Kingdom Special Representative. According to the Government, although the United Kingdom Special Representative and his Office sought to influence CPA policy and decisions, United Kingdom personnel had no formal decision-making power within the Authority. All the CPA's administrative and legislative decisions were taken by Ambassador Bremer.

15. In July 2003 the Governing Council of Iraq was established. The CPA was required to consult with it on all matters concerning the temporary governance of Iraq. . .

17. On 8 March 2004 the Governing Council of Iraq promulgated the Law of Administration for the State of Iraq for the Transitional Period (known as the "Transitional Administrative Law"). This provided a temporary legal framework for the administration of Iraq for the transitional period which was due to commence by 30 June 2004 with the

establishment of an interim Iraqi government and the dissolution of the CPA.

19. On 28 June 2004 full authority was transferred from the CPA to the Iraqi interim government and the CPA ceased to exist. Subsequently, the Multinational Force, including the British forces forming part of it, remained in Iraq pursuant to requests by the Iraqi government and authorisations from the United Nations Security Council.

20. During this period, the Coalition Forces consisted of six divisions that were under the overall command of US generals. Four were US divisions and two were multinational. Each division was given responsibility for a particular geographical area of Iraq. The United Kingdom was given command of the Multinational Division (South-East), which comprised the provinces of Basra, Maysan, Thi Qar and Al-Muthanna, an area of 96,000 square kilometres with a population of 4.6 million. There were 14,500 Coalition troops, including 8,150 United Kingdom troops, stationed in the Multinational Division (South-East). The main theatre for operations by United Kingdom forces in the Multinational Division (South-East) were the Basra and Maysan provinces, with a total population of about 2.75 million people. Just over 8,000 British troops were deployed there, of whom just over 5,000 had operational responsibilities.

21. From 1 May 2003 onwards British forces in Iraq carried out two main functions. The first was to maintain security in the Multinational Division (South-East) area, in particular in the Basra and Maysan provinces. The principal security task was the effort to re-establish the Iraqi security forces, including the Iraqi police. Other tasks included patrols, arrests, anti-terrorist operations, policing of civil demonstrations, protection of essential utilities and infrastructure and protecting police stations. The second main function of the British troops was the support of the civil administration in Iraq in a variety of ways, from liaison with the CPA and Governing Council of Iraq and local government, to assisting with the rebuilding of the infrastructure.

23. United Kingdom military records show that, as at 30 June 2004, there had been approximately 178 demonstrations and 1,050 violent attacks against Coalition Forces in the Multinational Division (South-East) since 1 May 2003. The violent attacks consisted of 5 anti-aircraft attacks, 12 grenade attacks, 101 attacks using improvised explosive devices, 52 attempted attacks using improvised explosive devices, 145 mortar attacks, 147 rocket-propelled grenade attacks, 535 shootings and 53 others. The same records show that, between May 2003 and March 2004, 49 Iraqis were known to have been killed in incidents in which British troops used force.

33. The following accounts are based on the witness statements of the applicants and the British soldiers involved in each incident. These statements were also submitted to the domestic courts and, as regards all but the fifth applicant, summarised in their judgments (particularly the judgment of the Divisional Court).

34. The first applicant is the brother of Hazim Jum'aa Gatteh Al-Skeini ("Hazim Al-Skeini"), who was 23 years old at the time of his death. Hazim Al-Skeini was one of two Iraqis from the Beini Skein tribe who were shot dead in the Al-Majidiyah area of Basra just before midnight on 4 August 2003 by Sergeant A., the Commander of a British patrol.

35. In his witness statement, the first applicant explained that, during the evening in question, various members of his family had been gathering at a house in Al-Majidiyah for a funeral ceremony. In Iraq it is customary for guns to be discharged at a funeral. The first applicant stated that he was engaged in receiving guests at the house, as they arrived for the ceremony, and saw his brother fired upon by British soldiers as he was walking along the street towards the house. According to the first applicant, his brother was unarmed and only about ten metres away from the soldiers when he was shot and killed. Another man with him was also killed. He had no idea why the soldiers opened fire.

36. According to the British account of the incident, the patrol, approaching on foot and on a very dark night, heard heavy gunfire from a number of different points in Al-Majidiyah. As the patrol got deeper into the village they came upon two Iraqi men in the street. One was about five metres from Sergeant A., who was leading the patrol. Sergeant A. saw that he was armed and pointing the gun in his direction. In the dark, it was impossible to tell the position of the second man. Believing that his life and those of the other soldiers in the patrol were at immediate risk, Sergeant A. opened fire on the two men without giving any verbal warning.

37. The following day, Sergeant A. produced a written statement describing the incident. This was passed to the Commanding Officer of his battalion, Colonel G., who took the view that the incident fell within the rules of engagement and duly wrote a report to that effect. Colonel G. sent the report to the Brigade, where it was considered by Brigadier Moore. Brigadier Moore queried whether the other man had been pointing his gun at the patrol. Colonel G. wrote a further report that dealt with this query to Brigadier Moore's satisfaction. The original report was not retained in the Brigade records. Having considered Colonel G.'s further report, as did his Deputy Chief of Staff and his legal adviser, Brigadier Moore was satisfied that the actions of Sergeant A. fell within the rules of engagement and so he did not order any further investigation.

38. On 11, 13 and 16 August 2003 Colonel G. met with members of the dead men's tribe. He explained why Sergeant A. had opened fire and gave the tribe a charitable donation of 2,500 United States dollars (USD) from the British Army Goodwill Payment Committee, together with a letter explaining the circumstances of the deaths and acknowledging that the deceased had not intended to attack anyone.

95. The applicants contended that their relatives were within the jurisdiction of the United Kingdom under Article 1 of the Convention at the moment of death and that, except in relation to the sixth applicant, the United Kingdom had not complied with its investigative duty under Article 2.

96. The Government accepted that the sixth applicant's son had been within United Kingdom jurisdiction but denied that the United Kingdom had jurisdiction over any of the other deceased. They contended that, since the second and third applicants' relatives had been killed after the adoption of United Nations Security Council Resolution 1511, the acts which led to their deaths were attributable to the United Nations and not to the United Kingdom. In addition, the Government contended that the fifth applicant's case should be declared inadmissible for non-exhaustion of domestic remedies and that the fifth and sixth applicants no longer had victim status.

130. Article 1 of the Convention reads as follows: "The High Contracting Parties shall secure to everyone within their jurisdiction the rights and freedoms defined in Section I of [the] Convention." As provided by this Article, the engagement undertaken by a Contracting State is confined to "securing" the listed rights and freedoms to persons within its own "jurisdiction". "Jurisdiction" under Article 1 is a threshold criterion. The exercise of jurisdiction is a necessary condition for a Contracting State to be able to be held responsible for acts or omissions imputable to it which give rise to an allegation of the infringement of rights and freedoms set forth in the Convention.

The territorial principle

131. A State's jurisdictional competence under Article 1 is primarily territorial. Jurisdiction is presumed to be exercised normally throughout the State's territory. Conversely, acts of the Contracting States performed, or producing effects, outside their territories can constitute an exercise of jurisdiction within the meaning of Article 1 only in exceptional cases.

132. To date, the Court in its case-law has recognised a number of exceptional circumstances capable of giving rise to the exercise of jurisdiction by a Contracting State outside its own territorial boundaries. In each case, the question whether exceptional circumstances exist which require and justify a finding by the Court that the State was exercising

jurisdiction extraterritorially must be determined with reference to the particular facts.

State agent authority and control

133. The Court has recognised in its case-law that, as an exception to the principle of territoriality, a Contracting State's jurisdiction under Article 1 may extend to acts of its authorities which produce effects outside its own territory. The statement of principle, as it appears in *Drozd and Janousek* and the other cases just cited, is very broad: the Court states merely that the Contracting Party's responsibility "can be involved" in these circumstances. It is necessary to examine the Court's case-law to identify the defining principles.

134. Firstly, it is clear that the acts of diplomatic and consular agents, who are present on foreign territory in accordance with provisions of international law, may amount to an exercise of jurisdiction when these agents exert authority and control over others.

135. Secondly, the Court has recognised the exercise of extraterritorial jurisdiction by a Contracting State when, through the consent, invitation or acquiescence of the Government of that territory, it exercises all or some of the public powers normally to be exercised by that Government. Thus, where, in accordance with custom, treaty or other agreement, authorities of the Contracting State carry out executive or judicial functions on the territory of another State, the Contracting State may be responsible for breaches of the Convention thereby incurred, as long as the acts in question are attributable to it rather than to the territorial State.

136. In addition, the Court's case-law demonstrates that, in certain circumstances, the use of force by a State's agents operating outside its territory may bring the individual thereby brought under the control of the State's authorities into the State's Article 1 jurisdiction. This principle has been applied where an individual is taken into the custody of State agents abroad. For example, in *Öcalan*, the Court held that "directly after being handed over to the Turkish officials by the Kenyan officials, the applicant was effectively under Turkish authority and therefore within the 'jurisdiction' of that State for the purposes of Article 1 of the Convention, even though in this instance Turkey exercised its authority outside its territory". In *Issa and Others,* the Court indicated that, had it been established that Turkish soldiers had taken the applicants' relatives into custody in northern Iraq, taken them to a nearby cave and executed them, the deceased would have been within Turkish jurisdiction by virtue of the soldiers' authority and control over them. In *Al-Saadoon and Mufdhi v. the United Kingdom,* the Court held that two Iraqi nationals detained in British-controlled military prisons in Iraq fell within the jurisdiction of the United Kingdom, since the

United Kingdom exercised total and exclusive control over the prisons and the individuals detained in them. Finally, in *Medvedyev and Others v. France,* the Court held that the applicants were within French jurisdiction for the purposes of Article 1 of the Convention by virtue of the exercise by French agents of full and exclusive control over a ship and its crew from the time of its interception in international waters. The Court does not consider that jurisdiction in the above cases arose solely from the control exercised by the Contracting State over the buildings, aircraft or ship in which the individuals were held. What is decisive in such cases is the exercise of physical power and control over the person in question.

137. It is clear that, whenever the State, through its agents, exercises control and authority over an individual, and thus jurisdiction, the State is under an obligation under Article 1 to secure to that individual the rights and freedoms under Section I of the Convention that are relevant to the situation of that individual. . .

Effective control over an area

138. Another exception to the principle that jurisdiction under Article 1 is limited to a State's own territory occurs when, as a consequence of lawful or unlawful military action, a Contracting State exercises effective control of an area outside that national territory. The obligation to secure, in such an area, the rights and freedoms set out in the Convention, derives from the fact of such control, whether it be exercised directly, through the Contracting State's own armed forces, or through a subordinate local administration. Where the fact of such domination over the territory is established, it is not necessary to determine whether the Contracting State exercises detailed control over the policies and actions of the subordinate local administration. The fact that the local administration survives as a result of the Contracting State's military and other support entails that State's responsibility for its policies and actions. The controlling State has the responsibility under Article 1 to secure, within the area under its control, the entire range of substantive rights set out in the Convention and those additional Protocols which it has ratified. It will be liable for any violations of those rights.

139. It is a question of fact whether a Contracting State exercises effective control over an area outside its own territory. In determining whether effective control exists, the Court will primarily have reference to the strength of the State's military presence in the area. Other indicators may also be relevant, such as the extent to which its military, economic and political support for the local subordinate administration provides it with influence and control over the region.

Application of these principles to the facts of the case

143. In determining whether the United Kingdom had jurisdiction over any of the applicants' relatives when they died, the Court takes as its starting-point that, on 20 March 2003, the United Kingdom together with the United States of America and their Coalition partners, through their armed forces, entered Iraq with the aim of displacing the Ba'ath regime then in power. This aim was achieved by 1 May 2003, when major combat operations were declared to be complete and the United States of America and the United Kingdom became Occupying Powers within the meaning of Article 42 of the Hague Regulations.

144. As explained in the letter dated 8 May 2003 sent jointly by the Permanent Representatives of the United Kingdom and the United States of America to the President of the United Nations Security Council, the United States of America and the United Kingdom, having displaced the previous regime, created the CPA "to exercise powers of government temporarily." One of the powers of government specifically referred to in the letter of 8 May 2003 to be exercised by the United States of America and the United Kingdom through the CPA was the provision of security in Iraq, including the maintenance of civil law and order. The letter further stated that "[t]he United States, the United Kingdom and Coalition partners, working through the Coalition Provisional Authority, shall, *inter alia*, provide for security in and for the provisional administration of Iraq, including by. . . assuming immediate control of Iraqi institutions responsible for military and security matters."

145. In its first legislative act, CPA Regulation No. 1 of 16 May 2003, the CPA declared that it would "exercise powers of government temporarily in order to provide for the effective administration of Iraq during the period of transitional administration, to restore conditions of security and stability."

146. The contents of the letter of 8 May 2003 were noted by the Security Council in Resolution 1483, adopted on 22 May 2003. This Resolution gave further recognition to the security role which had been assumed by the United States of America and the United Kingdom when, in paragraph 4, it called upon the Occupying Powers "to promote the welfare of the Iraqi people through the effective administration of the territory, including in particular working towards the restoration of conditions of security and stability."

147. During this period, the United Kingdom had command of the military division Multinational Division (South-East), which included the province of Al-Basra, where the applicants' relatives died. From 1 May 2003 onwards the British forces in Al-Basra took responsibility for maintaining security and supporting the civil administration. Among the United Kingdom's security tasks were patrols, arrests, anti-terrorist

operations, policing of civil demonstrations, protection of essential utilities and infrastructure and protecting police stations.

Conclusion as regards jurisdiction

149. It can be seen, therefore, that following the removal from power of the Ba'ath regime and until the accession of the interim Iraqi government, the United Kingdom (together with the United States of America) assumed in Iraq the exercise of some of the public powers normally to be exercised by a sovereign government. In particular, the United Kingdom assumed authority and responsibility for the maintenance of security in south-east Iraq. In these exceptional circumstances, the Court considers that the United Kingdom, through its soldiers engaged in security operations in Basra during the period in question, exercised authority and control over individuals killed in the course of such security operations, so as to establish a jurisdictional link between the deceased and the United Kingdom for the purposes of Article 1 of the Convention.

161. The Court is conscious that the deaths in the present case occurred in Basra City in south-east Iraq in the aftermath of the invasion, during a period when crime and violence were endemic. Although major combat operations had ceased on 1 May 2003, the Coalition Forces in south-east Iraq, including British soldiers and military police, were the target of over a thousand violent attacks in the subsequent thirteen months. In tandem with the security problems, there were serious breakdowns in the civilian infrastructure, including the law enforcement and criminal justice systems.

162. While remaining fully aware of this context, the Court's approach must be guided by the knowledge that the object and purpose of the Convention as an instrument for the protection of individual human beings requires that its provisions be interpreted and applied so as to make its safeguards practical and effective. Article 2, which protects the right to life and sets out the circumstances when deprivation of life may be justified, ranks as one of the most fundamental provisions of the Convention. No derogation from it is permitted under Article 15, "except in respect of deaths resulting from lawful acts of war." Article 2 covers both intentional killing and also the situations in which it is permitted to use force which may result, as an unintended outcome, in the deprivation of life. Any use of force must be no more than "absolutely necessary" for the achievement of one or more of the purposes set out in sub-paragraphs (a) to (c).

168. The Court takes as its starting-point the practical problems caused to the investigating authorities by the fact that the United Kingdom was an Occupying Power in a foreign and hostile region in the immediate aftermath of invasion and war. These practical problems

included the breakdown in the civil infrastructure, leading, *inter alia*, to shortages of local pathologists and facilities for autopsies; the scope for linguistic and cultural misunderstandings between the occupiers and the local population; and the danger inherent in any activity in Iraq at that time. As stated above, the Court considers that in circumstances such as these the procedural duty under Article 2 must be applied realistically, to take account of specific problems faced by investigators.

169. Nonetheless, the fact that the United Kingdom was in occupation also entailed that, if any investigation into acts allegedly committed by British soldiers was to be effective, it was particularly important that the investigating authority was, and was seen to be, operationally independent of the military chain of command.

170. It was not in issue in the first, second and fourth applicants' cases that their relatives were shot by British soldiers, whose identities were known. The question for investigation was whether in each case the soldier fired in conformity with the rules of engagement. In respect of the third applicant, Article 2 required an investigation to determine the circumstances of the shooting, including whether appropriate steps were taken to safeguard civilians in the vicinity. As regards the fifth applicant's son, although the Court has not been provided with the documents relating to the court martial, it appears to have been accepted that he died of drowning. It needed to be determined whether British soldiers had, as alleged, beaten the boy and forced him into the water. In each case, eyewitness testimony was crucial. It was therefore essential that, as quickly after the event as possible, the military witnesses, and in particular the alleged perpetrators, should have been questioned by an expert and fully independent investigator. Similarly, every effort should have been taken to identify Iraqi eyewitnesses and to persuade them that they would not place themselves at risk by coming forward and giving information and that their evidence would be treated seriously and acted upon without delay.

171. It is clear that the investigations into the shooting of the first, second and third applicants' relatives fell short of the requirements of Article 2, since the investigation process remained entirely within the military chain of command and was limited to taking statements from the soldiers involved. . .

Notes & Questions

Personal Control Versus Spatial Control. Why did the ECHR conclude that the United Kingdom had jurisdiction over the applicants in Iraq? Was the court's conclusion affected by the fact that Iraq was officially governed by the Coalition Provisional Authority, with the United Kingdom taking responsibility for control of one zone? It is not wholly surprising that the ECHR would conclude that the Convention applies when a signatory is engaged in a belligerent occupation of foreign territory. But could the principle be extended even further? What if European troops have "control" over a city street or a building? Is this enough to trigger the application of human rights law? In 2010, the ECHR concluded in *Al-Saadoon and Mufdhi v. United Kingdom*, Application No. 61498/08, that UK forces had jurisdiction over detainees in an Iraqi prison. What if the troops have "control" over a particular individual? One possibility is that convention rights apply whenever a state has "personal" control over an individual. But would that make every battlefield killing of an individual subject to the jurisdiction of the ECHR? For more discussion, see Marko Milanovic, *Extraterritorial Application of Human Rights Treaties* 173 (2011) ("[E]ven if the personal model presented a legitimate option in principle, what would actually count as state control over an individual? . . . [I]t is hard to say whether it is possible to give any meaningful answer to that question."). Indeed, in 2021 the ECHR rejected the possibility that a state can have effective control during active hostilities because "the very reality of armed confrontation and fighting between enemy military forces seeking to establish control over an area in a context of chaos not only means that there is no 'effective control' over an area . . . but also excludes any form of 'State agent authority and control' over individuals." *Georgia v. Russia (II)*, Application No. 38263/08, para. 137 (Jan. 21, 2021).

Conclusion & Summary

Since World War II, human rights law has radically reoriented the relationship between the state and the individual. No longer can a state claim that its treatment of its own citizens, on its own territory, is a private matter immune from international scrutiny. Human rights law, by treaty and custom, grants basic rights to individuals that can be vindicated in both international and domestic arenas:

1.   Though aspirational, the Universal Declaration of Human Rights articulates a vision for the universal respect of human rights that was subsequently codified in two major treaties, the ICCPR and the ICESCR. The former deals mostly with negative rights to be free from governmental interference, while the latter grants positive rights to basic economic and social necessities.

2.   Many of the protections in international legal instruments are mirrored in regional human rights instruments that are enforceable in regional courts such as the ECHR.

3.   For example, the right to religion is recognized by both the ICCPR and the ECHR. However, the ECHR grants states a wide "margin of appreciation" and has upheld regulations that infringe on the practice of religion, such as the ban on face coverings in France.

4.   Social and economic rights, such as the right to food, are relative to the resources of the state in question. States with lesser resources are not required to bring their citizens up to the same standard of living as governments in fully developed states. According to some international lawyers, developed states that are parties to the ICESCR are under an affirmative obligation to help fulfill these rights in developing nations. As of yet there is no formal mechanism to ensure this fulfillment, other than voluntary contributions and foreign aid.

5.   The protections in the ICCPR and the ECHR are subject to derogation in times of public emergency, though such situations must be publicly announced. However, some rights are non-derogable, including the right to be free from torture and servitude. Some national courts have argued that the right to be free from torture (Israel) and the right to life (Germany) are universal and cannot be suspended, even in moments of extreme emergency. The rationale for this conclusion is that "human dignity" of the individual is inviolable and cannot be "balanced away" by the competing interest of society at large.

6.   Human rights treaties usually apply when the state has jurisdiction or control over a particular individual—but applying that standard is deeply contested. In the past, the U.S. has argued that the ICCPR has no extraterritorial application, though the U.S. State Department in 2010 recommended that the U.S. revise its position (it has not). The ECHR has concluded that the European Convention has extraterritorial application in certain situations, such as the occupation of Iraqi territory by British soldiers under the auspices of the Coalition Provisional Authority.

CHAPTER 12

INTERNATIONAL HUMANITARIAN LAW

Introduction

The legal regulation of the conduct of hostilities has ancient roots. For many centuries, the conduct of battle was regulated by norms of conduct that sounded in codes of morality and professionalism. For example, the practice of knights was guided by notions of chivalry and honor that guided when, and how, killing was appropriate. Over time, these abstract norms of behavior ripened into legal constraints—at first customary in nature and later codified by treaty.

The first major codification of the law of war was drafted by Francis Lieber, a German-American lawyer and lecturer at Columbia University, who was selected by President Lincoln to draft a pamphlet that Union soldiers could carry with them into battle. The resulting document, titled General Orders Number 100 but more commonly referred to as the Lieber Code, had an enormous impact. Although it is no longer binding law, long since replaced by more recent enactments, lawyers and historians continue to cite its provisions when interpreting today's law of war.

International diplomatic conferences in The Hague, Netherlands, led to the signing of the Hague Conventions in 1899 and 1907, which were a package of major treaties that banned the use of poisonous gas and regulated the conduct of naval and land battle. Like most treaties codifying the laws of war, the agreements were signed by a large number of states, though a few major powers, like the United States, signed some but not all of them. A major treaty on the treatment of prisoners of war (POWs) was signed in 1929 and is officially referred to as the Convention Relative to the Treatment of Prisoners of War, Geneva, July 27, 1929.

World War II included a breakdown of customs of warfare, including the widespread intentional bombing of civilian populations by air, resulting in hundreds of thousands of casualties. Historians debate whether the strategic bombing of civilians in World War II was an aberration or in keeping with the limited respect for civilians in that era. Either way, the end of World War II ushered in a collective desire for more robust legal constraints on the conduct of warfare.

The major result of that effort was the Geneva Conventions signed in 1949. This package of four treaties regulated the following conduct: treatment of wounded and sick soldiers during land warfare, treatment of wounded and sick sailors during naval warfare, treatment of POWs, and the protection of civilians during armed conflict and occupation. The Conventions lay out a series of obligations during international armed conflict. However, each Convention also includes the following provision that applies during all "non-international" armed conflicts, such as civil wars. Known as "Common Article 3" because it is common to all four of the Geneva Conventions, the provision states:

> In the case of armed conflict not of an international character occurring in the territory of one of the High Contracting Parties, each Party to the conflict shall be bound to apply, as a minimum, the following provisions:
>
> (1) Persons taking no active part in the hostilities, including members of armed forces who have laid down their arms and those placed 'hors de combat' by sickness, wounds, detention, or any other cause, shall in all circumstances be treated humanely, without any adverse distinction founded on race, colour, religion or faith, sex, birth or wealth, or any other similar criteria. To this end, the following acts are and shall remain prohibited at any time and in any place whatsoever with respect to the above-mentioned persons:
>
> (a) violence to life and person, in particular murder of all kinds, mutilation, cruel treatment and torture;
>
> (b) taking of hostages;
>
> (c) outrages upon personal dignity, in particular humiliating and degrading treatment;
>
> (d) the passing of sentences and the carrying out of executions without previous judgment pronounced by a regularly constituted court, affording all the judicial guarantees which are recognized as indispensable by civilized peoples.
>
> (2) The wounded and sick shall be collected and cared for.
>
> An impartial humanitarian body, such as the International Committee of the Red Cross, may offer its services to the Parties to the conflict.
>
> The Parties to the conflict should further endeavour to bring into force, by means of special agreements, all or part of the other provisions of the present Convention. The application of the preceding provisions shall not affect the legal status of the Parties to the conflict.

Common Article 3 therefore explicitly declares that a state's behavior during an internal armed conflict is a matter of international concern and is regulated by International Humanitarian Law. No longer could states argue that their conduct during a civil war was a matter of sovereign discretion.

In the mid-1970s, diplomats began a process to update the Geneva Conventions for the next generation. This process resulted in the signing of two new treaties in 1979, called Additional Protocol I (API) and Additional Protocol II (APII). Officially the protocols are considered additions to the Geneva Conventions of 1949 because they are meant to clarify and extend the protections in them. API governs the conduct of hostilities in international armed conflicts between states, while APII governs non-international conflicts, such as civil wars. Although API has garnered 174 ratifications, a number of major powers, including the U.S., are not parties to the Protocol. APII has 168 state parties.

Even if a state is not a party to API or APII, the content of its provisions are, in some cases, operative as a matter of customary international law and therefore bind non-signatories unless they are persistent objectors. Consequently, despite the great wave of codification of IHL over the last century, customary international law continues to play a major role in its development and application in specific armed conflicts. The International Committee of the Red Cross (ICRC) has digested state practice and opinio juris, resulting in a lengthy written study of the customary laws of war. In the practice of IHL, citing a customary rule recognized by the ICRC carries great weight.

The following materials analyze the major elements of today's IHL. Section A focuses on the definition of armed conflict, which triggers the application of the law of war. This includes separate definitions for international conflicts and non-international conflicts. Sections B and C focus on the major pillars of IHL, the principles of distinction and proportionality. The former principle requires forces to refrain from attacking civilians. The latter principle allows forces to cause collateral damage to civilians as long as that damage is not disproportionate. Section D explains the detention regime of IHL, which confers POW status on privileged belligerents who meet certain criteria and who must be returned to their home country following the end of hostilities. Section E details the prohibition on certain tactics and weapons, either outlawed by a convention or illegal because of their inherently indiscriminate nature. Section F explores one of today's most pressing, unresolved controversy: the application of human rights law during armed conflict and the relationship between that body of law and IHL. Finally, Section G provides an overview of the law of occupation.

A. ARMED CONFLICT

If IHL governs the conduct of hostilities during armed conflict, this raises the most preliminary of questions: What counts as an armed conflict? Although the concept of war is, in some basic sense, self-explanatory, its exact legal definition is not codified in one single treaty. However, by mining customary international law and what types of conflicts states have treated as "armed conflicts," as well as considering the specific treaties that regulate armed conflict, one may certainly infer a legal definition.

The criteria for what counts as an armed conflict depends on what type of armed conflict it is. International armed conflicts (IACs) are "traditional" wars fought between two or more nation-states. In contrast, non-international armed conflicts (NIACs) are conflicts between a state and a non-state actor, or a conflict between two non-state actors. The typical example of a NIAC is a civil war, that is, an armed conflict between a state and a rebel force seeking to overthrow its government and take control over the state. However, other examples of NIACs may exist.

In the following case, the ICTY Appeals Chamber offered its own definition for both IACs and NIACs, based on its analysis of the relevant legal precedents. Although the criteria were announced in the context of a criminal case that sought to determine whether the defendant could be convicted for war crimes, the so-called "*Tadić* criteria" have been immensely influential among military and humanitarian lawyers. Indeed, the International Committee on the Red Cross considers these criteria to be a persuasive articulation of existing customary law.

Prosecutor v. Dusko Tadić

International Criminal Tribunal for the Former Yugoslavia
Decision on the Defense Motion for Interlocutory Appeal on Jurisdiction
October 2, 1995

65. Appellant's third ground of appeal is the claim that the International Tribunal lacks subject-matter jurisdiction over the crimes alleged. The basis for this allegation is Appellant's claim that the subject-matter jurisdiction under Articles 2, 3 and 5 of the Statute of the International Tribunal is limited to crimes committed in the context of an international armed conflict. Before the Trial Chamber, Appellant claimed that the alleged crimes, even if proven, were committed in the context of an internal armed conflict. On appeal an additional alternative claim is asserted to the effect that there was no armed conflict at all in the region where the crimes were allegedly committed. . . .

Preliminary Issue: The Existence of an Armed Conflict

66. Appellant now asserts the new position that there did not exist a legally cognizable armed conflict—either internal or international—at the time and place that the alleged offences were committed. Appellant's argument is based on a concept of armed conflict covering only the precise time and place of actual hostilities. Appellant claims that the conflict in

the Prijedor region (where the alleged crimes are said to have taken place) was limited to a political assumption of power by the Bosnian Serbs and did not involve armed combat (though movements of tanks are admitted). This argument presents a preliminary issue to which we turn first.

67. International humanitarian law governs the conduct of both internal and international armed conflicts. Appellant correctly points out that for there to be a violation of this body of law, there must be an armed conflict. The definition of "armed conflict" varies depending on whether the hostilities are international or internal but, contrary to Appellant's contention, the temporal and geographical scope of both internal and international armed conflicts extends beyond the exact time and place of hostilities. With respect to the temporal frame of reference of international armed conflicts, each of the four Geneva Conventions contains language intimating that their application may extend beyond the cessation of fighting. For example, both Conventions I and III apply until protected persons who have fallen into the power of the enemy have been released and repatriated.

68. Although the Geneva Conventions are silent as to the geographical scope of international "armed conflicts," the provisions suggest that at least some of the provisions of the Conventions apply to the entire territory of the Parties to the conflict, not just to the vicinity of actual hostilities. Certainly, some of the provisions are clearly bound up with the hostilities and the geographical scope of those provisions should be so limited. Others, particularly those relating to the protection of prisoners of war and civilians, are not so limited. With respect to prisoners of war, the Convention applies to combatants in the power of the enemy; it makes no difference whether they are kept in the vicinity of hostilities. In the same vein, Geneva Convention IV protects civilians anywhere in the territory of the Parties. This construction is implicit in Article 6, paragraph 2, of the Convention, which stipulates that: "[i]n the territory of Parties to the conflict, the application of the present Convention shall cease on the general close of military operations." Article 3(b) of Protocol I to the Geneva Conventions contains similar language. In addition to these textual references, the very nature of the Conventions—particularly Conventions III and IV—dictates their application throughout the territories of the parties to the conflict; any other construction would substantially defeat their purpose.

69. The geographical and temporal frame of reference for internal armed conflicts is similarly broad. This conception is reflected in the fact that beneficiaries of common Article 3 of the Geneva Conventions are those taking no active part (or no longer taking active part) in the hostilities. This indicates that the rules contained in Article 3 also apply outside the narrow geographical context of the actual theatre of combat

operations. Similarly, certain language in Protocol II to the Geneva Conventions (a treaty which, as we shall see in paragraphs 88 and 114 below, may be regarded as applicable to some aspects of the conflicts in the former Yugoslavia) also suggests a broad scope. First, like common Article 3, it explicitly protects "[a]ll persons who do not take a direct part or who have ceased to take part in hostilities." Article 2, paragraph 1, provides: "[t]his Protocol shall be applied. . . to all persons *affected* by an armed conflict as defined in Article 1." The same provision specifies in paragraph 2 that:

> [A]t the end of the conflict, all the persons who have been deprived of their liberty or whose liberty has been restricted for reasons related to such conflict, as well as those deprived of their liberty or whose liberty is restricted after the conflict for the same reasons, shall enjoy the protection of Articles 5 and 6 until the end of such deprivation or restriction of liberty.

Under this last provision, the temporal scope of the applicable rules clearly reaches beyond the actual hostilities. Moreover, the relatively loose nature of the language "for reasons related to such conflict," suggests a broad geographical scope as well. The nexus required is only a relationship between the conflict and the deprivation of liberty, not that the deprivation occurred in the midst of battle.

70. On the basis of the foregoing, we find that an armed conflict exists whenever there is a resort to armed force between States or protracted armed violence between governmental authorities and organized armed groups or between such groups within a State. International humanitarian law applies from the initiation of such armed conflicts and extends beyond the cessation of hostilities until a general conclusion of peace is reached; or, in the case of internal conflicts, a peaceful settlement is achieved. Until that moment, international humanitarian law continues to apply in the whole territory of the warring States or, in the case of internal conflicts, the whole territory under the control of a party, whether or not actual combat takes place there.

Applying the foregoing concept of armed conflicts to this case, we hold that the alleged crimes were committed in the context of an armed conflict. Fighting among the various entities within the former Yugoslavia began in 1991, continued through the summer of 1992 when the alleged crimes are said to have been committed, and persists to this day. Notwithstanding various temporary cease-fire agreements, no general conclusion of peace has brought military operations in the region to a close. These hostilities exceed the intensity requirements applicable to both international and internal armed conflicts. There has been protracted, large-scale violence between the armed forces of different States and between governmental forces and organized insurgent groups.

Even if substantial clashes were not occurring in the Prijedor region at the time and place the crimes allegedly were committed—a factual issue on which the Appeals Chamber does not pronounce—international humanitarian law applies. It is sufficient that the alleged crimes were closely related to the hostilities occurring in other parts of the territories controlled by the parties to the conflict. There is no doubt that the allegations at issue here bear the required relationship. The indictment states that in 1992 Bosnian Serbs took control of the Opstina of Prijedor and established a prison camp in Omarska. It further alleges that crimes were committed against civilians inside and outside the Omarska prison camp as part of the Bosnian Serb take-over and consolidation of power in the Prijedor region, which was, in turn, part of the larger Bosnian Serb military campaign to obtain control over Bosnian territory. Appellant offers no contrary evidence but has admitted in oral argument that in the Prijedor region there were detention camps run not by the central authorities of Bosnia-Herzegovina but by Bosnian Serbs. In light of the foregoing, we conclude that, for the purposes of applying international humanitarian law, the crimes alleged were committed in the context of an armed conflict.

NOTES & QUESTIONS

1. *Armed Conflicts with Terrorists.* A civil war is clearly a NIAC, because the state battles a group of rebels fighting to take control of the state's territory. But what if a non-state actor is located *outside* the territory of the state that it attacks? These "extraterritorial" conflicts are more commonly associated with contemporary terrorist organizations that do not aspire to control a state's territory. For example, is the armed conflict between the United States and al-Qaeda a NIAC? Some lawyers have argued that NIACs are, by definition, internal conflicts confined to the territory of a single state. But certainly, the armed conflict against al-Qaeda cannot be an IAC, because one party to the conflict is a non-state actor. This argument led the administration of President George W. Bush to argue, early in his first term, that the conflict with al-Qaeda was no armed conflict at all, and therefore the constraints imposed by the law of war were inapplicable. In *Hamdan*, the U.S. Supreme Court rejected this view, and concluded that the conflict was indeed a NIAC, and therefore subject to prohibitions that the laws of war impose on the conduct of hostilities in a NIAC. Writing for the majority, Justice Stevens concluded that

> [T]he Government asserts. . . that Common Article 3 does not apply to Hamdan because the conflict with al Qaeda, being "international in scope," does not qualify as a "conflict not of an international character." That reasoning is erroneous. The term "conflict not of an international character" is used here in contradistinction to a conflict between nations. . . In context, then, the phrase "not of an international character" bears its literal meaning.

Hamdan v. Rumsfeld, 548 U.S. 557, 630–31 (2006). Some international lawyers have suggested that we should refer to the armed conflict with al-Qaeda as an "extraterritorial NIAC" or "transnational NIAC" to distinguish it from a civil war. For a discussion, see Geoffrey S. Corn, *Hamdan, Lebanon, and the Regulation of Armed Conflict: The Need to Recognize a Hybrid Category of Armed Conflict*, 40 Vanderbilt J Transnat'l L. 295 (2007); Naz K. Modirzadeh, *Folk International Law: 9/11 Lawyering and the Transformation of the Law of Armed Conflict to Human Rights Policy and Human Rights Law to War Governance*, 5 Harv. Nat'l Sec. J. 225, 281 (2014).

2.   *Overlapping Armed Conflicts.* Just because hostilities are one "war" in common parlance does not necessarily entail that the situation is a single armed conflict in the legal sense of that expression. An armed conflict involves a state of hostilities between two or more belligerent parties, and may overlap with another armed conflict with a different set of belligerent parties. Similarly, a NIAC might start between a state and a non-state group but then spill over the border and become internationalized. Take, for example, the situation in Syria and Iraq in 2017. In that year, the government of Syria was involved in a NIAC against anti-government rebel forces seeking to depose President Assad of Syria. At the same time, Syria was involved in a NIAC against the "Islamic State" or "ISIS" (which, despite its name, is a non-state actor). At the same time, Russia intervened to help Syria against both the anti-Assad rebels and ISIS, while the United States for a time supported the rebels. Despite being on opposite sides of the armed conflict between the Syrian government and the rebels, both Russia and the United States were on the same side in fighting ISIS. Furthermore, the government of Iraq was also fighting an armed conflict on its territory against ISIS. This complex web of overlapping armed conflicts throws in sharp relief the need to describe armed conflicts with particularity.

3.   *The Geography of Armed Conflict.* Some international lawyers argue that armed conflict has a particular geography. In other words, armed conflicts do not exist in some ambiguous space, but rather exist in a defined area. For example, Professor O'Connell argues that:

> In addition to exchange, intensity, and duration, armed conflicts have a spatial dimension. It is not the case that if there is an armed conflict in one state—for example, Afghanistan—that all the world is at war, or even that Afghanis and Americans are at war with each other all over the planet. Armed conflicts inevitably have a limited and identifiable territorial or spatial dimension because human beings who participate in armed conflict require territory in which to carry out intense, protracted, armed exchanges.

See Mary Ellen O'Connell, *Combatants and the Combat Zone*, 43 U. Rich. L. Rev. 845, 858 (2009). According to this view, then, the syntactical grammar of armed conflict requires a description of: 1) the parties to the armed conflict; 2) the status of the conflict (IAC or NIAC); and 3) the territory where the armed conflict is being fought. The legal geography of armed conflict is important because it determines *where* the legal regime of IHL applies. For example, a state engulfed in a NIAC might have one region of the country engulfed in sustained violence, while other regions of the state are left untouched by violence. Does IHL apply in the whole country or just the "hot" battlefield? In contrast to the highly localized interpretation of the geography of IHL, some scholars argue that IHL applies broadly across the territory of a state engulfed in armed conflict, a position that was articulated by the ICTY in *Tadić* when it stated that the "geographical and temporal frame of reference for internal armed conflicts is. . . broad." For a discussion, see Michael N. Schmitt, *Charting the Legal Geography of Non-International Armed Conflict*, 90 Int'l L. Stud. 1, 9 (2014) (concluding that "it is clear that [IHL] extends throughout the territory of the State involved" in a NIAC); Jennifer C. Daskal, *The Geography of the Battlefield: A Framework for Detention and Targeting Outside the "Hot" Conflict Zone*, 161 U. Pa. L. Rev. 1165, 1176 (2013).

B. DISTINCTION

According to the ICRC, the principle of distinction is "Rule Number 1" of IHL, owing to its centrality in the basic architecture of the law of war. The ICRC defines the principle of distinction in the following way: "The parties to the conflict must at all times distinguish between civilians and combatants. Attacks may only be directed against combatants. Attacks must not be directed against civilians." In a sense, the principle of distinction is really a bilateral obligation. Attacking forces have an obligation to direct their attacks against enemy combatants, not civilians. In return, the military forces being attacked have an obligation to distinguish themselves from the civilian population by, for example, wearing a uniform or a fixed emblem recognizable at a distance, and carrying their arms openly. These broad legal obligations form the cornerstone of the law of war: Soldiers are entitled to attack each other but civilians, as much as possible, should be spared from direct attack. The following two subsections focus on the prohibition against intentionally attacking civilians and the exception that allows attacking forces to target civilians who are "directly participating in hostilities" as de facto combatants.

1. PROHIBITION ON ATTACKING CIVILIANS

The wars in the former Yugoslavia featured widespread violations of the principle of distinction. In the following case, an ICTY Trial Chamber discusses the legal requirements for the war crime of intentionally attacking civilians. As you read the case, pay particular attention to how the Trial Chamber defines the concepts of "intentionally" and an "attack."

Prosecutor v. Galić

International Criminal Tribunal for the Former Yugoslavia
Trial Chamber Judgment
December 5, 2003

14. The paragraph introducing Count 4 alleges that the Accused, General Galić, as commander of the SRK, "conducted a coordinated and protracted campaign of sniper attacks upon the civilian population of Sarajevo, killing and wounding a large number of civilians of all ages and both sexes, such attacks by their nature involving the deliberate targeting of civilians with direct fire weapons."

15. Count 7 of the Indictment is in terms identical to Count 4, except that the paragraph preceding Count 7 alleges that the Accused "conducted a coordinated and protracted campaign of artillery and mortar shelling onto civilian areas of Sarajevo and upon its civilian population. The campaign of shelling resulted in thousands of civilians being killed or injured."

16. Counts 4 and 7 of the Indictment are clearly based on rules of international humanitarian law, namely Article 51(2) of Additional Protocol I and Article 13(2) of Additional Protocol II. Both provide, in relevant part, that: "The civilian population as such, as well as individual civilians, shall not be made the object of attack." . . .

41. Although the Indictment refers in general terms to Article 51 of Additional Protocol I, the Trial Chamber understands the first sentence of the second paragraph of that article to be the legal basis of the charges of attack on civilians in Counts 4 and 7. This sentence will hereinafter be referred to as "the first part" of the second paragraph of Article 51 of Additional Protocol I, or simply as the "first part of Article 51(2)."

42. The constitutive elements of the offence of attack on civilians have not yet been the subject of a definitive statement by the Appeals Chamber. In only two cases before the Tribunal have persons been charged and tried of attack on civilians under Article 3 of the Statute pursuant to Article 51(2) of Additional Protocol I. In each case a brief exposition was given of the offence, together with the offence of attacks on civilian property. In the *Blaskić* case the Trial Chamber observed in relation to the actus reus that "the attack must have caused deaths and/or serious bodily injury within the civilian population or damage to civilian property. [. . .] Targeting civilians or civilian property is an offence when not justified by military necessity." On the mens rea it found that "such an attack must have been conducted intentionally in the knowledge, or when it was impossible not to know, that civilians or civilian property were being targeted not through military necessity." The Trial Chamber in the *Kordić and Cerkez* case held that "prohibited attacks are those launched deliberately against civilians or civilian

objects in the course of an armed conflict and are not justified by military necessity. They must have caused deaths and/or serious bodily injuries within the civilian population or extensive damage to civilian objects."

43. The Trial Chamber follows the above-mentioned jurisprudence to the extent that it states that an attack which causes death or serious bodily injury within the civilian population constitutes an offence. As noted above, such an attack when committed wilfully is punishable as a grave breach of Additional Protocol I. The question remains whether attacks resulting in non-serious civilian casualties, or in no casualties at all, may also entail the individual criminal responsibility of the perpetrator under the type of charge considered here, and thus fall within the jurisdiction of the Tribunal, even though they do not amount to grave breaches of Additional Protocol I. The present Indictment refers only to killing and wounding of civilians; therefore the Trial Chamber does not deem it necessary to express its opinion on that question.

44. The Trial Chamber does not however subscribe to the view that the prohibited conduct set out in the first part of Article 51(2) of Additional Protocol I is adequately described as "targeting civilians when not justified by military necessity." This provision states in clear language that civilians and the civilian population as such should not be the object of attack. It does not mention any exceptions. In particular, it does not contemplate derogating from this rule by invoking military necessity.

45. The Trial Chamber recalls that the provision in question explicitly confirms the customary rule that civilians must enjoy general protection against the danger arising from hostilities. The prohibition against attacking civilians stems from a fundamental principle of international humanitarian law, the principle of distinction, which obliges warring parties to distinguish at all times between the civilian population and combatants and between civilian objects and military objectives and accordingly to direct their operations only against military objectives. In its *Advisory Opinion on the Legality of Nuclear Weapons*, the International Court of Justice described the principle of distinction, along with the principle of protection of the civilian population, as "the cardinal principles contained in the texts constituting the fabric of humanitarian law" and stated that "States must never make civilians the object of attack. . ."

46. Part IV of Additional Protocol I, entitled "Civilian Population" (articles 48 to 58), develops and augments earlier legal protections afforded to civilians through specific rules aimed at guiding belligerents to respect and protect the civilian population and individual civilians during the conduct of hostilities. The general prohibition mentioned above forms integral part of and is complemented and reinforced by this set of rules. In order to properly define the conduct outlawed in the first

part of Article 51(2) of Additional Protocol I, this rule must be interpreted in light of the ordinary meaning of the terms of Additional Protocol I, as well as of its spirit and purpose.

47. As already stated, the first part of Article 51(2) of Additional Protocol I proscribes making the civilian population as such, or individual civilians, the object of attack. According to Article 50 of Additional Protocol I, "a civilian is any person who does not belong to one of the categories of persons referred to in Article 4(A)(1), (2), (3) and (6) of the Third Geneva Convention and in Article 43 of Additional Protocol I." For the purpose of the protection of victims of armed conflict, the term "civilian" is defined negatively as anyone who is not a member of the armed forces or of an organized military group belonging to a party to the conflict. It is a matter of evidence in each particular case to determine whether an individual has the status of civilian.

48. The protection from attack afforded to individual civilians by Article 51 of Additional Protocol I is suspended when and for such time as they directly participate in hostilities. To take a "direct" part in the hostilities means acts of war which by their nature or purpose are likely to cause actual harm to the personnel or matériel of the enemy armed forces. As the *Kupreškić* Trial Chamber explained: the protection of civilian and civilian objects provided by modern international law may cease entirely or be reduced or suspended. . . if a group of civilians takes up arms. . . and engages in fighting against the enemy belligerent, they may be legitimately attacked by the enemy belligerent whether or not they meet the requirements laid down in Article 4(A)(2) of the Third Geneva Convention of 1949. Combatants and other individuals directly engaged in hostilities are considered to be legitimate military targets.

49. The civilian population comprises all persons who are civilians, as defined above. The use of the expression "civilian population as such" in Article 51(2) of Additional Protocol I indicates that "the population must never be used as a target or as a tactical objective."

50. The presence of individual combatants within the population does not change its civilian character. In order to promote the protection of civilians, combatants are under the obligation to distinguish themselves at all times from the civilian population; the generally accepted practice is that they do so by wearing uniforms, or at least a distinctive sign, and by carrying their weapons openly. In certain situations it may be difficult to ascertain the status of particular persons in the population. The clothing, activity, age, or sex of a person are among the factors which may be considered in deciding whether he or she is a civilian. A person shall be considered to be a civilian for as long as there is a doubt as to his or her real status. The Commentary to Additional Protocol I explains that the presumption of civilian status concerns "persons who have not committed hostile acts, but whose status seems

doubtful because of the circumstances. They should be considered to be civilians until further information is available, and should therefore not be attacked." The Trial Chamber understands that a person shall not be made the object of attack when it is not reasonable to believe, in the circumstances of the person contemplating the attack, including the information available to the latter, that the potential target is a combatant.

51. As mentioned above, in accordance with the principles of distinction and protection of the civilian population, only military objectives may be lawfully attacked. A widely accepted definition of military objectives is given by Article 52 of Additional Protocol I as "those objects which by their nature, location, purpose or use make an effective contribution to military action and whose total or partial destruction, capture or neutralization, in the circumstances ruling at the time, offers a definite military advantage." In case of doubt as to whether an object which is normally dedicated to civilian purposes is being used to make an effective contribution to military action, it shall be presumed not to be so used. The Trial Chamber understands that such an object shall not be attacked when it is not reasonable to believe, in the circumstances of the person contemplating the attack, including the information available to the latter, that the object is being used to make an effective contribution to military action.

52. "Attack" is defined in Article 49 of Additional Protocol I as "acts of violence against the adversary, whether in offence or in defence." The Commentary makes the point that "attack" is a technical term relating to a specific military operation limited in time and place, and covers attacks carried out both in offence and in defence. The jurisprudence of the Tribunal has defined "attack" as a course of conduct involving the commission of acts of violence. In order to be punishable under Article 3 of the Statute, these acts have to be carried out during the course of an armed conflict.

53. In light of the discussion above, the Trial Chamber holds that the prohibited conduct set out in the first part of Article 51(2) is to direct an attack (as defined in Article 49 of Additional Protocol I) against the civilian population and against individual civilians not taking part in hostilities.

54. The Trial Chamber will now consider the mental element of the offence of attack on civilians, when it results in death or serious injury to body or health. Article 85 of Additional Protocol I explains the intent required for the application of the first part of Article 51(2). It expressly qualifies as a grave breach the act of wilfully "making the civilian population or individual civilians the object of attack." The Commentary to Article 85 of Additional Protocol I explains the term as follows:

wilfully: the accused must have acted consciously and with intent, i.e., with his mind on the act and its consequences, and willing them ("criminal intent" or "malice aforethought"); this encompasses the concepts of "wrongful intent" or "recklessness," viz., the attitude of an agent who, without being certain of a particular result, accepts the possibility of it happening; on the other hand, ordinary negligence or lack of foresight is not covered, i.e., when a man acts without having his mind on the act or its consequences.

The Trial Chamber accepts this explanation, according to which the notion of "wilfully" incorporates the concept of recklessness, whilst excluding mere negligence. The perpetrator who recklessly attacks civilians acts "willfully."

55. For the mens rea recognized by Additional Protocol I to be proven, the Prosecution must show that the perpetrator was aware or should have been aware of the civilian status of the persons attacked. In case of doubt as to the status of a person, that person shall be considered to be a civilian. However, in such cases, the Prosecution must show that in the given circumstances a reasonable person could not have believed that the individual he or she attacked was a combatant.

56. In sum, the Trial Chamber finds that the crime of attack on civilians is constituted of the elements common to offences falling under Article 3 of the Statute, as well as of the following specific elements: 1. Acts of violence directed against the civilian population or individual civilians not taking direct part in hostilities causing death or serious injury to body or health within the civilian population. 2. The offender wilfully made the civilian population or individual civilians not taking direct part in hostilities the object of those acts of violence.

PROBLEM CASE

On October 3, 2015, a U.S. Air Force gunship opened fire on a Médecins Sans Frontières (MSF) hospital in Kunduz, Afghanistan. At the time of the attack, the U.S. military believed that they were attacking a group of Taliban insurgents in the area who were launching attacks against allied Afghanistan military forces. The Afghanistan forces called for tactical assistance from the U.S. military, which launched the gunship. However, instead of engaging the Taliban insurgents, the gunship killed dozens of people in the MSF hospital. The attack allegedly continued even after MSF officials called U.S. commanders pleading for the attack to be discontinued.

A U.S. military investigation into the attack documented a series of fatal errors by U.S. commanders, pilots, and airmen involved in the attack. In particular, the report into the errant strike faulted the Americans for their lack of "situational awareness." Specifically, the Americans confused the MSF hospital with a government building nearby where the Taliban forces were located. Furthermore, the Americans involved in the strike failed to consult their "no-strike" list, which included the coordinates of the hospital. Had they double-checked the coordinates of their target with the coordinates listed on the "no-strike" list, they would have realized that they were about to engage the wrong building.

Did the Kunduz hospital attack constitute a war crime? The answer is not so simple. The Rome Statute includes "willful killing" as a war crime, though the question is how to define willfulness in this context. Also, article 8(2)(b)(i) of the Rome Statute refers to the war crime of "intentionally directing attacks against the civilian population as such or against individual civilians not taking direct part in hostilities." However, some decisions from the ICTY have suggested that under customary international law, " 'wilfully' incorporates the concept of recklessness, whilst excluding mere negligence. The perpetrator who recklessly attacks civilians acts 'wilfully'." See *Prosecutor v. Galić*, above, para. 54.

Did the attack on the Kunduz hospital constitute a war crime? How should international criminal law treat crimes of recklessness?

2.   CIVILIANS DIRECTLY PARTICIPATING IN HOSTILITIES

There is one major exception to the prohibition on intentionally attacking civilians. Civilians who directly participate in hostilities are subject to direct attack. To understand the rationale for this rule, consider what combat would look like if the prohibition against attacking civilians applied to civilians who directly participate in hostilities. These civilians would have the best of both worlds: they would participate in hostilities yet be immune from targeting. Professional armies would do better to fight in battle as civilians.

So IHL permits the targeting of civilians participating in hostilities. For example, article 51 of Additional Protocol I to the Geneva Conventions articulates the rule this way:

1.   The civilian population and individual civilians shall enjoy general protection against dangers arising from military operations. To give effect to this protection, the following rules, which are additional to other applicable rules of international law, shall be observed in all circumstances.

2.   The civilian population as such, as well as individual civilians, shall not be the object of attack. Acts or threats of violence the primary purpose of which is to spread terror among the civilian population are prohibited.

3.   Civilians shall enjoy the protection afforded by this Section, unless and for such time as they take a direct part in hostilities.

Another way of understanding this rule is that it allows for "conduct-based" targeting. Usually, individuals are targeted based on "status," i.e., their membership in an enemy army. In contrast, civilians who directly participate in hostilities are targetable based on their conduct, because "directly participating in hostilities" is a type of conduct.

The question is how to apply the standard of "direct participation in hostilities" to concrete situations. What does this mean in practice?

The standard raises two central questions. The first is which types of participation are "direct" and which are "indirect." In theory, civilians who indirectly participate in hostilities retain their protection from direct attack. Consequently, the task of the international lawyer is to construct compelling arguments about which types of participation are direct and which are indirect.

The second is the scope of the temporal condition. Paragraph (3) of article 51 notes that the exception applies "for such time" as the civilian directly participates in hostilities. How long does this last? When does this status end? The question is crucial to answer because once the temporal condition evaporates, the civilian regains his or her protection from attack.

In 2009, the ICRC published its *Interpretive Guidance on the Notion of Direct Participation in Hostilities*. The document, prepared after a lengthy study involving consultation with state governments and legal experts, offered concrete guidance for unpacking the notion of direct participation in hostilities. In particular, the *Interpretive Guidance* argued that civilians who belong to a non-state organized armed group are always targetable by virtue of their status within that organization as individuals dedicated to a continuous combat function:

> Continuous combat function requires lasting integration into an organized armed group acting as the armed forces of a non-state party to an armed conflict. Thus, individuals whose continuous function involves the preparation, execution, or command of acts or operations amounting to direct participation in hostilities are assuming a continuous combat function. An individual recruited, trained and equipped by such a group to continuously and directly participate in hostilities on its behalf can be considered to assume a continuous combat function even before he or she first carries out a hostile act.

What implication does this have for the targeting of terrorists who belong to organized armed groups such as al-Qaeda? Does this mean that a member of al-Qaeda with a continuous combat function within the group may be targeted based on status instead of conduct? If yes, how does an individual shed this status? Again, according to the ICRC, withdrawal can be accomplished by "conclusive behaviour, such as a lasting physical distancing from the group and reintegration into civilian life or the permanent resumption of an exclusively non-combat function." For more discussion of the "continuous combat function" standard, see Bill Boothby, *"And for Such Time As": The Time Dimension to Direct Participation in Hostilities*, 42 N.Y.U. J. Int'l L. & Pol. 741, 745 (2010).

PROBLEM CASE

On September 30, 2011, the United States fired a drone missile in Yemen that killed 40-year-old Anwar al-Awlaki, an American-born religious cleric who was well known in extremist circles for a series of fiery online speeches urging his followers to wage violent Jihad against the

United States and the west. Over time, al-Awlaki had risen from a minor online presence in extremist circles to what U.S. intelligence agencies described as the chief propagandist for Al-Qaeda in the Arabian Peninsula (AQAP), al-Qaeda's affiliate branch headquartered in Yemen.

Was Al-Awlaki directly participating in hostilities when he was killed? Were his speeches alone enough to qualify for "continuous combat function" status within AWAP? In justifying the strike, U.S. officials indicated that the Awlaki's role had been "operationalized" and that his role was no longer confined to mere dissemination of propaganda, and that he had supervised and approved a plan to attempt to bomb an airliner traveling between Amsterdam and Detroit. The Justice Department's Office of Legal Counsel drafted a memorandum justifying the strike, concluding that "Al-Aulaqi, an active, high-level leader of an enemy force who is continually involved in planning and recruiting for terrorist attacks, can on that basis fairly be said to be taking 'an active part in hostilities'. . . and targeting him in the circumstances posited to us would not [be illegal]. . ." See U.S. Dept. of Justice, Office of Legal Counsel, Memorandum for the Attorney General, Re: Applicability of Federal Criminal Laws and the Constitution to Contemplated Lethal Operations Against Shaykh Anwar al-Aulaqi (July 16, 2010).

Did Awlaki qualify as a civilian directly participating in hostilities? Was he a legitimate target? For a discussion of this case, see Robert Chesney, *Who May Be Killed? Anwar al-Awlaki as a Case Study in the International Legal Regulation of Lethal Force*, 13 Yearbook of Int'l Humanitarian L. 3, 45 (2010) ("If. . . the facts show that he. . . engaged solely in propaganda and generalized recruiting, the case for targeting is stronger yet still relatively weak in the sense that such conduct would fail the [continuous combat function] test. . ." but if al-Awlaki had taken on a recurring "operational planning function. . ." [then] this would satisfy the continuous combat function standard.).

3. THE PROHIBITION ON INDISCRIMINATE ATTACKS

International Humanitarian Law also includes a related yet distinct prohibition on indiscriminate attacks. The use of the word "indiscriminate" in this context literally means that the attack failed to discriminate between combatants and civilians. For example, article 51 of Additional Protocol I describes indiscriminate acts as:

(a) those which are not directed at a specific military objective;

(b) those which employ a method or means of combat which cannot be directed at a specific military objective; or

(c) those which employ a method or means of combat the effects of which cannot be limited as required by this Protocol; and consequently, in each such case, are of a nature to strike military objectives and civilians or civilian objects without distinction.

Typically, an indiscriminate attack is one that rains down munitions around a wide area, without any concern for whether combatants or civilians will be harmed. Similarly, an indiscriminate attack might involve the use of a weapon that is not sufficiently precise to be aimed at a particular target. In that situation, the attacker does not launch the weapon with the explicit desire to harm a civilian, but rather launches the weapon without any expectation of whether it will hit a combatant or a civilian. Article 51(5) of API also includes the following further examples of indiscriminate attacks:

(a)   an attack by bombardment by any methods or means which treats as a single military objective a number of clearly separated and distinct military objectives located in a city, town, village or other area containing a similar concentration of civilians or civilian objects; and

(b)   an attack which may be expected to cause incidental loss of civilian life, injury to civilians, damage to civilian objects, or a combination thereof, which would be excessive in relation to the concrete and direct military advantage anticipated.

The second of these examples is a reference to the principle of proportionality, which is the subject of the next section.

C. PROPORTIONALITY

Notwithstanding the principle of distinction, attacking forces are permitted to kill civilians—just not intentionally or directly. IHL recognizes that civilians may be killed as collateral damage. This means that if an attacking force launches an attack against military personnel or military objects, the attack is still lawful even if it kills nearby civilians. The one enduring constraint on this possibility is that the civilian casualties cannot be disproportionate to the anticipated value of the military target. Or, in the words of article 51(5)(b) of the 1977 Additional Protocol I, military forces are prohibited from launching "an attack which may be expected to cause incidental loss of civilian life, injury to civilians, damage to civilian objects, or a combination thereof, which would be excessive in relation to the concrete and direct military advantage anticipated."

There are few court cases involving the prohibition on causing disproportionate collateral damage. However, in the following case, the ICTY considered whether the destruction of a civilian bridge was disproportionate under the circumstances.

Prosecutor v. Prlić et al.

International Criminal Tribunal for the Former Yugoslavia
Trial Chamber Judgment
May 29, 2013

121. The offence of extensive destruction of property not justified by military necessity and carried out unlawfully and wantonly towards which Count 19 of the Indictment is directed is punishable under Article 2(d) of the Statute, and constitutes a grave breach under the Geneva Conventions.

122. The Chamber recalls that two categories of property are protected pursuant to Article 2(d) of the Statute, which forbids both the destruction of property falling under the general protection of the Geneva Conventions as well as the destruction of property in occupied territory.

123. Military necessity may be defined in reference to the military objectives defined in Article 52(2) of Additional Protocol I,240 which provides that "military objectives are limited to those objects which by their nature, location, purpose or use make an effective contribution to military action and whose total or partial destruction, capture or neutralization, in the circumstances ruling at the time, offers a definite military advantage." Where there is uncertainty, Article 52(3) of Additional Protocol I provides that "an object which is normally dedicated to civilian purposes, such as a place of worship, a house or other dwelling or a school, is being used to make an effective contribution to military action, it shall be presumed not to be so used." Objects of property which, by their very nature, afford a definite military advantage include property used directly by the armed forces, such as equipment, structures that provide shelter for the armed forces, depots or communications centres. The criterion dealing with the location of property is aimed at objects of particular significance to military operations, such as bridges or other structures. The purpose of an object relates to its future use whereas its use relates to its present function. The military advantage for each object of property must be definite and cannot offer merely an indeterminate or potential advantage. Knowing whether a definite military advantage may be achieved must be decided from the perspective of the person contemplating the attack, taking into account the information available to the latter at the moment of the attack.

124. The Appeals Chamber has, moreover, recalled that although attacks may be conducted against military objectives, "collateral civilian damage" is not by nature unlawful, provided that the customary rules of proportionality in the conduct of hostilities are observed. This proportionality principle is defined by Article 51.5(b) of Additional Protocol I, which prohibits attacks "which may be expected to cause incidental loss of civilian life, injury to civilians, damage to civilian objects, or a combination thereof, which would be excessive in relation to the concrete and direct military advantage anticipated."

125. Objects of property that receive broad protection, such as fixed medical establishments and mobile medical units, hospital ships and civilian hospitals may "in no circumstances" be attacked, and must at all times be respected and protected by the Parties to the conflict. The Chamber notes, however, that this protection may expire if these are used to commit "acts harmful to the enemy," once due warning setting a reasonable time limit has gone unheeded.

126. To violate the prohibition set out in Article 2(d) of the Statute, the destruction of property must be extensive in scope. The Chamber considers, however, that the criterion that the destruction be extensive in scope must be evaluated in light of the facts of the case, and that a single incident, such as the destruction of a hospital, may suffice to constitute an offence under this count.

127. The deliberate nature of the offence of the destruction of property is established when the perpetrator acts knowingly with the intent to destroy the property in question or when the property has been destroyed "in reckless disregard of the likelihood of its destruction."

1581. The Chamber also established that on 8 November 1993, as part of the offensive on Mostar ordered by Milivoj Petković and carried out by Miljenko Lasić, an HVO tank positioned on Stotina Hill fired on the Old Bridge of Mostar all day long. It noted that on the evening of 8 November 1993, the Old Bridge could be considered destroyed since it was on the point of collapse.

1582. The Chamber established that the Old Bridge, real property normally used by civilians, was used by both the ABiH and the inhabitants of the right and left banks of the Neretva between May and November 1993 as a means of communication and supply. In this respect, it considers that the Old Bridge was essential to the ABiH for combat activities of its units on the front line, for evacuations, for the sending of troops, food and material, and that it was indeed utilised to this end. Furthermore, the ABiH was holding positions in the immediate vicinity of the Old Bridge. For this reason, the armed forces of the HVO had a military interest in destroying this structure since its destruction cut off practically all possibilities for the ABiH to continue its supply operations. Consequently, at the time of the attack, the Old Bridge was a military target.

1583. The Chamber, however, also noted that the destruction of the Old Bridge put the residents of Donja Mahala, the Muslim enclave on the right bank of the Neretva, in virtually total isolation, making it impossible for them to get food and medical supplies resulting in a serious deterioration of the humanitarian situation for the population living there. The Chamber determined that there were very few supply routes available to the inhabitants, other than the Old Bridge; that between May and November 1993, in addition to the Old Bridge, they could only use the Kamenica bridge, a makeshift bridge constructed by the ABiH in March 1993 and used until November 1993, or a path over the mountain from the neighbourhood of Donja Mahala to Jablanica, which was considered very dangerous; and that, as such, the destruction of the Kamenica bridge by the armed forces of the HVO on 10, 11 or 17 November 1993, that is, only a few days after the destruction of the Old Bridge, cut off all access across the Neretva River in Mostar definitively.

The Chamber also determined that the destruction of the Old Bridge had a very significant psychological impact on the Muslim population of Mostar.

1584. The Chamber therefore holds that although the destruction of the Old Bridge by the HVO may have been justified by military necessity, the damage to the civilian population was indisputable and substantial. It therefore holds by a majority, with Judge Antonetti dissenting, that the impact on the Muslim civilian population of Mostar was disproportionate to the concrete and direct military advantage expected by the destruction of the Old Bridge.

Dissenting Opinion of Judge Antonetti

. . .In 1969, the Institute for International Law also provided a fairly similar definition of the notion of "military objective." Thus, the Institute of International Law "included [in its definition of] military objectives only those which by their very nature or purpose or use, make an effective contribution to military action, or exhibit a generally recognized military significance, such that their total or partial destruction in the actual circumstances gives a substantial, specific and immediate military advantage to those who are in a position to destroy them."

The ICRC also proposed a mixed definition for the draft Protocol in 1970–1971. According to this draft,

> [a]ttacks shall be strictly limited to military objectives, namely, to those objectives which are, by their nature, purpose or use, recognized to be of military interest and whose total or partial destruction, in the circumstances ruling at the time, offers a distinct and substantial military advantage. Consequently, objects designed for civilian use, such as houses, dwellings, installations and means of transport, and all objects which are not military objectives, shall not be made the object of attack, except if they are used mainly in support of the military effort.

The diplomatic conference that established the notion of "military objectives" declared that immunity was conferred on civilian property, which it then defined in contrast with "military objectives." This was the first time that an international treaty provided a definition of the notion of "military objective." The definition adopted at the conference was to a large extent inspired by the previous documents. Thus, according to the definition that appears in the Second Protocol to the Hague Convention, a "military objective" consists of two elements. The target is considered a military objective as soon as both these elements are present.

According to the first condition, such objects must be "objects which by their nature, location, purpose or use make an effective contribution to military action." This element refers to objects that by their "nature" make an effective contribution to military action. All property directly used by the armed forces—weapons, equipment, means of transport, fortifications, depots, edifices sheltering the armed forces, staffs, communication centres, etc.—is included in this category.

The requirement for fulfilling the second condition is that "total or partial destruction, capture or neutralisation, in the circumstances ruling at the time, offers a definite military advantage." The second criterion concerns "the location" of objects. It is obvious that there are objects which, although not military by nature, make an effective contribution to military action as a result of their location. For example, such an object could be a bridge or some other construction; it could also be, as noted above, an area of particular importance for military operations on account of its location whether because the objective is to take it, to prevent the enemy from occupying it, or to force the enemy to abandon it. It should be noted that the Working Group of Commission III introduced the criterion of location without providing any reasons.

The criterion of "purpose" relates to the future and current "use" of property. Most property that is civilian by nature can be transformed into property useful to the armed forces. For example, a school or a hotel are civilian property but become military objectives if used to accommodate troops or staffs. We will see, in relation to paragraph 3, that in case of doubt, they are presumed to be civilian property.

Other establishments or edifices dedicated to the production of civilian property can also be used to the advantage of the military; in such cases this refers to mixed property which has value both to the civilian population and to the soldiers. In such situations, the time and place of the attack must be considered together with the expected military advantage on the one hand, and the expected loss of human life among the civilian population and the damage that will be caused to civilian property on the other hand.

Last, the destruction, capture or neutralisation must offer a "definite military advantage" under the prevailing spatial and temporal circumstances. In other words, it is not lawful to launch an attack that offers only indefinite or potential advantages. Those ordering or carrying out the attack must have sufficient intelligence to allow them to take this requirement into account; in the case of doubt, safeguarding the population—which is the Protocol's objective—is what must be considered.

In respect of the two elements constituting a military objective according to the commonly accepted definition, the conclusion that can be drawn from the testimony is that because of the Stari Most's location and use, it made an effective contribution to ABiH military action during the period preceding its destruction. The fact that the Stari Most was one of the two remaining bridges still intact in Mostar must be taken into account.

The Old Bridge in Mostar allowed the ABiH to transport supplies and personnel and was the only route through which one part of East Mostar was resupplied with military materiel. By destroying the Old Bridge, the HVO cut off the supply route for food and ammunition, which gave it a military advantage. The Old Bridge in Mostar was therefore a military objective for the HVO. . .

I fail to see how the principle of proportionality could be applicable in this case. If the Old Bridge was a military objective, it quite simply had to be destroyed. In any event, there is no such thing as proportionate destruction.

During the NATO bombing of Serbia in 1999, many civilians were killed or injured by the NATO strikes. The ICTY's Office of the Prosecutor received complaints that the killings violated the laws of war—specifically, the principle of proportionality. The Prosecutor investigated the allegations and issued the following report. As you read the following report, ask yourself whether a large number of civilian deaths in armed conflict is evidence, by itself, that the principle of proportionality was violated.

Final Report to the Prosecutor by the Committee Established to Review the NATO Bombing Campaign Against the Federal Republic of Yugoslavia
June 13, 2000

The Principle of Proportionality

48. The main problem with the principle of proportionality is not whether or not it exists but what it means and how it is to be applied. It is relatively simple to state that there must be an acceptable relation between the legitimate destructive effect and undesirable collateral effects. For example, bombing a refugee camp is obviously prohibited if its only military significance is that people in the camp are knitting socks for soldiers. Conversely, an air strike on an ammunition dump should not be prohibited merely because a farmer is plowing a field in the area. Unfortunately, most applications of the principle of proportionality are not quite so clear cut. It is much easier to formulate the principle of proportionality in general terms than it is to apply it to a particular set of circumstances because the comparison is often between unlike quantities and values. One cannot easily assess the value of innocent human lives as opposed to capturing a particular military objective.

49. The questions which remain unresolved once one decides to apply the principle of proportionality include the following:

a)   What are the relative values to be assigned to the military advantage gained and the injury to non-combatants and or the damage to civilian objects?

b)   What do you include or exclude in totaling your sums?

c)   What is the standard of measurement in time or space? and

d)   To what extent is a military commander obligated to expose his own forces to danger in order to limit civilian casualties or damage to civilian objects?

50. The answers to these questions are not simple. It may be necessary to resolve them on a case by case basis, and the answers may differ depending on the background and values of the decision maker. It is unlikely that a human rights lawyer and an experienced combat commander would assign the same relative values to military advantage and to injury to noncombatants. Further, it is unlikely that military commanders with different doctrinal backgrounds and differing degrees of combat experience or national military histories would always agree in close cases. It is suggested that the determination of relative values must be that of the "reasonable military commander." Although there will be room for argument in close cases, there will be many cases where reasonable military commanders will agree that the injury to noncombatants or the damage to civilian objects was clearly disproportionate to the military advantage gained.

51. Much of the material submitted to the OTP consisted of reports that civilians had been killed, often inviting the conclusion to be drawn that crimes had therefore been committed. Collateral casualties to civilians and collateral damage to civilian objects can occur for a variety of reasons. Despite an obligation to avoid locating military objectives within or near densely populated areas, to remove civilians from the vicinity of military objectives, and to protect their civilians from the dangers of military operations, very little prevention may be feasible in many cases. Today's technological society has given rise to many dual use facilities and resources. City planners rarely pay heed to the possibility of future warfare. Military objectives are often located in densely populated areas and fighting occasionally occurs in such areas. Civilians present within or near military objectives must, however, be taken into account in the proportionality equation even if a party to the conflict has failed to exercise its obligation to remove them.

52. In the *Kupreskic* Judgment (Case No: IT–95–16–T 14 Jan 2000) the Trial Chamber addressed the issue of proportionality as follows:

526. As an example of the way in which the Martens clause may be utilised, regard might be had to considerations such as the cumulative effect of attacks on military objectives causing incidental damage to civilians. In other words, it may happen that single attacks on military objectives causing incidental damage to civilians, although they may raise doubts as to their lawfulness, nevertheless do not appear on their face to fall foul *per se* of the loose prescriptions of Articles 57 and 58 (or of the corresponding customary rules). However, in case of repeated attacks, all or most of them falling within the grey area between indisputable legality and unlawfulness, it might be warranted to conclude that the cumulative effect of such acts entails that they may not be in keeping with international law. Indeed, this pattern of military conduct may turn out to jeopardise excessively the lives and assets of civilians, contrary to the demands of humanity.

This formulation in *Kupreskic* can be regarded as a progressive statement of the applicable law with regard to the obligation to protect civilians. Its practical import, however, is somewhat ambiguous and its application far from clear. It is the committee's view that where individual (and legitimate) attacks on military objectives are concerned, the mere *cumulation* of such instances, all of which are deemed to have been lawful, cannot *ipso facto* be said to amount to a crime. The committee understands the above formulation, instead, to refer to an *overall* assessment of the totality of civilian victims as against the goals of the military campaign.

Casualty Figures

53. In its report, *Civilian Deaths in the NATO Air Campaign*, Human Rights Watch documented some 500 civilian deaths in 90 separate incidents. It concluded: "on the basis available on these ninety incidents that as few as 488 and as many as 527 Yugoslav civilians were killed as a result of NATO bombing. Between 62 and 66 percent of the total registered civilian deaths occurred in just twelve incidents. These twelve incidents accounted for 303 to 352 civilian deaths. These were the only incidents among the ninety documented in which ten or more civilian deaths were confirmed." Ten of these twelve incidents were included among the incidents which were reviewed with considerable care by the committee and our estimate was that between 273 and 317 civilians were killed in these ten incidents. Human Rights Watch also found the FRY Ministry of Foreign Affairs publication NATO Crimes in Yugoslavia to be largely credible on the basis of its own filed research and correlation with other sources. A review of this publication indicates it provides an estimated total of approximately 495 civilians killed and 820 civilians wounded in specific documented instances. For the purposes of

this report, the committee operates on the basis of the number of persons allegedly killed as found in both publications. It appears that a figure similar to both publications would be in the range of 500 civilians killed.

General Assessment of the Bombing Campaign

54. During the bombing campaign, NATO aircraft flew 38,400 sorties, including 10,484 strike sorties. During these sorties, 23, 614 air munitions were released (figures from NATO). As indicated in the preceding paragraph, it appears that approximately 500 civilians were killed during the campaign. These figures do not indicate that NATO may have conducted a campaign aimed at causing substantial civilian casualties either directly or incidentally.

55. The choice of targets by NATO includes some loosely defined categories such as military-industrial infrastructure and government ministries and some potential problem categories such as media and refineries. All targets must meet the criteria for military objectives. If they do not do so, they are unlawful. A general label is insufficient. The targeted components of the military-industrial infrastructure and of government ministries must make an effective contribution to military action and their total or partial destruction must offer a definite military advantage in the circumstances ruling at the time. Refineries are certainly traditional military objectives but tradition is not enough and due regard must be paid to environmental damage if they are attacked. The media as such is not a traditional target category. To the extent particular media components are part of the C3 (command, control and communications) network they are military objectives. If media components are not part of the C3 network then they may become military objectives depending upon their use. As a bottom line, civilians, civilian objects and civilian morale as such are not legitimate military objectives. The media does have an effect on civilian morale. If that effect is merely to foster support for the war effort, the media is not a legitimate military objective. If the media is used to incite crimes, as in Rwanda, it can become a legitimate military objective. If the media is the nerve system that keeps a war-monger in power and thus perpetuates the war effort, it may fall within the definition of a legitimate military objective. As a general statement, in the particular incidents reviewed by the committee, it is the view of the committee that NATO was attempting to attack objects it perceived to be legitimate military objectives.

56. The committee agrees there is nothing inherently unlawful about flying above the height which can be reached by enemy air defences. However, NATO air commanders have a duty to take practicable measures to distinguish military objectives from civilians or civilian objectives. The 15,000 feet minimum altitude adopted for part of the campaign may have meant the target could not be verified with the naked eye. However, it appears that with the use of modern technology,

the obligation to distinguish was effectively carried out in the vast majority of cases during the bombing campaign.

NOTES & QUESTIONS

1. *The Reasonable Military Commander.* Should the proportionality calculation be evaluated based on the information available at the time or should it be evaluated using the benefit of hindsight? The NATO Final Report refers to the "reasonable military commander." This suggests a hybrid subjective-objective standard, i.e., evaluating the information available to the commander at the time and asking whether a reasonable military commander under the circumstances would have initiated the attack. For more discussion, see Lieutenant Commander Luke A. Whittemore, *Proportionality Decision Making in Targeting: Heuristics, Cognitive Biases, and the Law,* 7 Harv. Nat'l Sec. J. 577, 578 (2016) ("More has been written about proportionality than perhaps any other IHL principle, but few writers have sought to explain and predict how those commanders actually make decisions as human beings limited by their cognitive capacities in a suboptimal decision making environment, thus a descriptive decision theory analysis of the proportionality principle."); Robert D. Sloane, *Puzzles of Proportion and the "Reasonable Military Commander": Reflections on the Law, Ethics, and Geopolitics of Proportionality,* 6 Harv. Nat'l Sec. J. 299, 302 (2015) (proportionality's "implementation in the field is guided by the nebulous standard of the good-faith and optimally informed 'reasonable military commander.' ").

2. *All Feasible Precautions.* In addition to the customary prohibition against causing disproportionate collateral damage, signatories to Additional Protocol I to the Geneva Conventions are subject to a more exacting standard. Article 57 requires that attacking forces "take all feasible precautions in the choice of means and methods of attack with a view to avoiding, and in any event to minimizing, incidental loss of civilian life, injury to civilians and damage to civilian objects. . ." This goes well beyond the demands of proportionality because it requires reducing collateral damage *as far as possible.* However, only "feasible" precautions are required. What does this mean? The answer is presumably context dependent. In its 1987 *Commentary to Additional Protocol I,* the ICRC remarked that:

> Finally, mention may be made of the precautionary measures taken by the Allied forces during bombardments carried out during the Second World War against factories located in territories occupied by German forces; in order to avoid hitting the people working in these factories, the attacks took place on days or at times when the factories were empty; the desired effect was to destroy the factories without killing the workers.

The United States is not a signatory to Additional Protocol I. Is the requirement to take "all feasible precautions" now a part of customary international law? Finally, is an attacking force required to take measures that will *reduce* the risk to civilians but will *increase* the risk to the attacking soldiers? Is that a "feasible" precaution?

3.   *Human Shields.* IHL also includes a prohibition on using human shields, which is the practice of moving civilians into close proximity of military forces in order to dissuade an attacking force from launching a military strike. The attacking force is thereby forced into a difficult situation: Either launch the attack and cause massive collateral damage to the human shields, or forego the attack and suffer the military consequences of allowing the enemy to continue holding its position. Neither is a particularly attractive position. Although it is clear that customary international law prohibits the use of human shields, the question is what attacking forces are permitted to do about it. The answer depends on the distinction between voluntary and involuntary human shields. Involuntary human shields are civilians who, against their will, are brought in close proximity to the battle for the purpose of dissuading the attacking force from launching a strike. In that situation, the attacking force is required to take into account the human shields when calculating collateral damage. If the civilian deaths will be disproportionate, then the attack cannot go forward. On the other hand, if the human shields are voluntary—i.e., they willingly place themselves near the battle to dissuade an attack—they might be considered directly participating in hostilities and therefore subject to *direct* attack. For example, the ICRC in its Interpretive Guidance argued that when civilians "voluntarily and deliberately position themselves to create a physical obstacle to military operations of a party to the conflict, they could directly cause the threshold of harm required for a qualification as direct participation in hostilities." The U.S. Department of Defense Law of War Manual includes the following statement:

> Harm to Human Shields. Use of human shields violates the rule that civilians may not be used to shield, favor, or impede military operations. The party that employs human shields in an attempt to shield military objectives from attack assumes responsibility for their injury, provided that the attacker takes feasible precautions in conducting its attack.

> If the proportionality rule were interpreted to permit the use of human shields to prohibit attacks, such an interpretation would perversely encourage the use of human shields and allow violations by the defending force to increase the legal obligations on the attacking force.

Law of War Manual § 5.12.3.3. Some lawyers have criticized this articulation, suggesting that it conflicts with the well-established rule that involuntary shields must be considered in the proportionality calculation. For a discussion, see Adil Ahmad Haque, *Off Target: Selection, Precaution, and Proportionality in the DoD Manual*, 92 Int'l L. Stud. 31, 65 (2016) ("The Manual cites no State practice or opinio juris directly supporting its claim that harm to human shields cannot render an attack disproportionate.").

D. DETENTION

If a soldier effectively communicates his or her surrender, the soldier is immune from attack and cannot be killed. If the soldier is then captured, what happens next? The answer is governed by the combatant's privilege, also known as combatant immunity. This principle, universally recognized by nation-states with modern armies, entails that soldiers are immune from prosecution under domestic criminal law for their belligerent actions that complied with IHL. In other words, a soldier cannot be prosecuted in an enemy court for killing other soldiers on the battlefield. (Of course, a soldier can be prosecuted for war crimes.) Instead, the soldier should be granted Prisoner of War (POW) status and detained in humane conditions until the conclusion of hostilities and then released to his or her home country. The point of POW detention is not to punish soldiers but rather to incapacitate and prevent their return to the battlefield.

1. PRISONER OF WAR STATUS

Not all soldiers qualify for POW status. The qualifications for POW status are laid out in article 4 of the Convention (III) relative to the Treatment of Prisoners of War, Geneva, 12 August 1949, colloquially referred to as the Third Geneva Convention:

A. Prisoners of war, in the sense of the present Convention, are persons belonging to one of the following categories, who have fallen into the power of the enemy:

(1) Members of the armed forces of a Party to the conflict, as well as members of militias or volunteer corps forming part of such armed forces.

(2) Members of other militias and members of other volunteer corps, including those of organized resistance movements, belonging to a Party to the conflict and operating in or outside their own territory, even if this territory is occupied, provided that such militias or volunteer corps, including such organized resistance movements, fulfil the following conditions:

(a) that of being commanded by a person responsible for his subordinates;

(b) that of having a fixed distinctive sign recognizable at a distance;

(c) that of carrying arms openly;

(d) that of conducting their operations in accordance with the laws and customs of war.

This means that all members of the regular armed forces are eligible for POW status. Members of militia are also eligible for POW status if they meet the four "functional" criteria referenced above: a responsible command, a fixed emblem, open arms, and general compliance with the laws of war. There is some controversy about whether members of the regular armed forces—as opposed to a militia—would be eligible for POW status if they did not meet the functional criteria. One view is that subcategory one above does not list the four functional criteria, which only appear under subsection two, thus suggesting that the criteria only apply to militia. However, another possibility is that the four criteria represent a definition of what it means to be part of armed force, so that the criteria are implicit in the first sub-section.

Article 4 also includes a few other categories of individuals entitled to POW status:

(3) Members of regular armed forces who profess allegiance to a government or an authority not recognized by the Detaining Power.

(4) Persons who accompany the armed forces without actually being members thereof, such as civilian members of military aircraft crews, war correspondents, supply contractors, members of labour units or of services responsible for the welfare of the armed forces, provided that they have received authorization, from the armed forces which they accompany, who shall provide them for that purpose with an identity card similar to the annexed model.

(5) Members of crews, including masters, pilots and apprentices, of the merchant marine and the crews of civil aircraft of the Parties to the conflict, who do not benefit by more favourable treatment under any other provisions of international law.

(6) Inhabitants of a non-occupied territory, who on the approach of the enemy spontaneously take up arms to resist the invading forces, without having had time to form themselves into regular armed units, provided they carry arms openly and respect the laws and customs of war.

Subsection 6 is particularly noteworthy and refers to a *levee en masse*, a situation where citizen-soldiers band together to fight off an armed invasion. Though not formally an army or even a militia, these residents would be entitled to POW status provided they carry their arms openly and respect the laws of war.

2. DETENTION OF UNPRIVILEGED BELLIGERENTS

What if a combatant is not entitled to Prisoner of War status? In many ways, this conundrum has plagued international law since the 9/11 attacks. Since 9/11, the United States has transferred combatants captured overseas to the military prison at Guantanamo Bay. The U.S. has denied these combatants POW status because they are unprivileged, meaning they do not meet the functional criteria for the privilege. Although al-Qaeda has a responsible command structure, its members do not wear a fixed sign, carry arms openly, or follow the laws and customs of war. Since al-Qaeda targets civilians and launches attacks perfidiously, its members are unprivileged combatants. The status of the Taliban in Afghanistan is somewhat more complicated. The Taliban was the official government of Afghanistan between 1996 and 2001, although they were subsequently ousted from power in an American-led invasion in 2001. At that point, the Taliban transformed itself into a rebel insurgency, fighting against the new U.S.-supported government of Afghanistan.

Where does the authorization come to detain unprivileged combatants? Some international lawyers argue that the authorization is implicit in article 4 of the Geneva Conventions, reprinted above. Others argue that the Geneva Conventions merely regulate detention (in the sense that they impose restrictions), so that the authorization must come from elsewhere, such as domestic law. In the context of the armed conflict against al-Qaeda, what would constitute authorization. In the immediate aftermath of 9/11, Congress passed the Authorization for the Use of Military Force (AUMF), which included the following language:

> That the President is authorized to use all necessary and appropriate force against those nations, organizations, or persons he determines planned, authorized, committed, or aided the terrorist attacks that occurred on September 11, 2001, or harbored such organizations or persons, in order to prevent any future acts of international terrorism against the United States by such nations, organizations or persons.

Does this language implicitly authorize detention of suspected members of al-Qaeda? Does it extend to members of co-sympathetic terrorist organizations other than al-Qaeda?

President George W. Bush initially declared, by executive fiat, that all members of al-Qaeda and the Taliban were unprivileged combatants and not eligible for POW status. One alleged Taliban detainee, the American citizen Yaser Hamdi, contested his detention in federal court. On appeal, the U.S. Supreme Court concluded that the President had a right to subject enemy combatants to detention, consistent with the

AUMF, but that Hamdi had a right to contest his detention before a neutral decisionmaker.

Hamdi v. Rumsfeld

Supreme Court of the United States
542 U.S. 507 (2004)

The AUMF authorizes the President to use "all necessary and appropriate force" against "nations, organizations, or persons" associated with the September 11, 2001, terrorist attacks. There can be no doubt that individuals who fought against the United States in Afghanistan as part of the Taliban, an organization known to have supported the al Qaeda terrorist network responsible for those attacks, are individuals Congress sought to target in passing the AUMF. We conclude that detention of individuals falling into the limited category we are considering, for the duration of the particular conflict in which they were captured, is so fundamental and accepted an incident to war as to be an exercise of the "necessary and appropriate force" Congress has authorized the President to use.

The capture and detention of lawful combatants and the capture, detention, and trial of unlawful combatants, by "universal agreement and practice," are "important incident[s] of war." The purpose of detention is to prevent captured individuals from returning to the field of battle and taking up arms once again.

There is no bar to this Nation's holding one of its own citizens as an enemy combatant. In *Quirin,* one of the detainees, Haupt, alleged that he was a naturalized United States citizen. We held that "[c]itizens who associate themselves with the military arm of the enemy government, and with its aid, guidance and direction enter this country bent on hostile acts, are enemy belligerents within the meaning of. . . the law of war." While Haupt was tried for violations of the law of war, nothing in *Quirin* suggests that his citizenship would have precluded his mere detention for the duration of the relevant hostilities. Nor can we see any reason for drawing such a line here. A citizen, no less than an alien, can be "part of or supporting forces hostile to the United States or coalition partners" and "engaged in an armed conflict against the United States"; such a citizen, if released, would pose the same threat of returning to the front during the ongoing conflict.

In light of these principles, it is of no moment that the AUMF does not use specific language of detention. Because detention to prevent a combatant's return to the battlefield is a fundamental incident of waging war, in permitting the use of "necessary and appropriate force," Congress has clearly and unmistakably authorized detention in the narrow circumstances considered here.

Hamdi objects, nevertheless, that Congress has not authorized the *indefinite* detention to which he is now subject. The Government responds that "the detention of enemy combatants during World War II was just as 'indefinite' while that war was being fought." We take Hamdi's objection to be not to the lack of certainty regarding the date on which the conflict will end, but to the substantial prospect of perpetual detention. We recognize that the national security underpinnings of the "war on terror," although crucially important, are broad and malleable. As the Government concedes, "given its unconventional nature, the current conflict is unlikely to end with a formal cease-fire agreement." The prospect Hamdi raises is therefore not farfetched. If the Government does not consider this unconventional war won for two generations, and if it maintains during that time that Hamdi might, if released, rejoin forces fighting against the United States, then the position it has taken throughout the litigation of this case suggests that Hamdi's detention could last for the rest of his life.

It is a clearly established principle of the law of war that detention may last no longer than active hostilities.

Hamdi contends that the AUMF does not authorize indefinite or perpetual detention. Certainly, we agree that indefinite detention for the purpose of interrogation is not authorized. Further, we understand Congress' grant of authority for the use of "necessary and appropriate force" to include the authority to detain for the duration of the relevant conflict, and our understanding is based on longstanding law-of-war principles. If the practical circumstances of a given conflict are entirely unlike those of the conflicts that informed the development of the law of war, that understanding may unravel. But that is not the situation we face as of this date. Active combat operations against Taliban fighters apparently are ongoing in Afghanistan. The United States may detain, for the duration of these hostilities, individuals legitimately determined to be Taliban combatants who "engaged in an armed conflict against the United States." If the record establishes that United States troops are still involved in active combat in Afghanistan, those detentions are part of the exercise of "necessary and appropriate force," and therefore are authorized by the AUMF. . .

With due recognition of these competing concerns, we believe that neither the process proposed by the Government nor the process apparently envisioned by the District Court below strikes the proper constitutional balance when a United States citizen is detained in the United States as an enemy combatant. That is, "the risk of an erroneous deprivation" of a detainee's liberty interest is unacceptably high under the Government's proposed rule, while some of the "additional or substitute procedural safeguards" suggested by the District Court are unwarranted in light of their limited "probable value" and the burdens they may impose on the military in such cases.

We therefore hold that a citizen-detainee seeking to challenge his classification as an enemy combatant must receive notice of the factual basis for his classification, and a fair opportunity to rebut the Government's factual assertions before a neutral decisionmaker. These essential constitutional promises may not be eroded.

At the same time, the exigencies of the circumstances may demand that, aside from these core elements, enemy-combatant proceedings may be tailored to alleviate their uncommon potential to burden the Executive at a time of ongoing military conflict. Hearsay, for example, may need to be accepted as the most reliable available evidence from the Government in such a proceeding. Likewise, the Constitution would not be offended by a presumption in favor of the Government's evidence, so long as that presumption remained a rebuttable one and fair opportunity for rebuttal were provided. Thus, once the Government puts forth credible evidence that the habeas petitioner meets the enemy-combatant criteria, the onus could shift to the petitioner to rebut that evidence with more persuasive evidence that he falls outside the criteria. A burden-shifting scheme of this sort would meet the goal of ensuring that the errant tourist, embedded journalist, or local aid worker has a chance to prove military error while giving due regard to the Executive once it has put forth meaningful support for its conclusion that the detainee is in fact an enemy combatant. . .

We think it unlikely that this basic process will have the dire impact on the central functions of warmaking that the Government forecasts. The parties agree that initial captures on the battlefield need not receive the process we have discussed here; that process is due only when the determination is made to *continue* to hold those who have been seized. The Government has made clear in its briefing that documentation regarding battlefield detainees already is kept in the ordinary course of military affairs. Any factfinding imposition created by requiring a knowledgeable affiant to summarize these records to an independent tribunal is a minimal one. Likewise, arguments that military officers ought not have to wage war under the threat of litigation lose much of their steam when factual disputes at enemy-combatant hearings are limited to the alleged combatant's acts. This focus meddles little, if at all, in the strategy or conduct of war, inquiring only into the appropriateness of continuing to detain an individual claimed to have taken up arms against the United States. While we accord the greatest respect and consideration to the judgments of military authorities in matters relating to the actual prosecution of a war, and recognize that the scope of that discretion necessarily is wide, it does not infringe on the core role of the military for the courts to exercise their own time-honored and constitutionally mandated roles of reviewing and resolving claims like those presented here.

In sum, while the full protections that accompany challenges to detentions in other settings may prove unworkable and inappropriate in the enemy-combatant setting, the threats to military operations posed by a basic system of independent review are not so weighty as to trump a citizen's core rights to challenge meaningfully the Government's case and to be heard by an impartial adjudicator.

AFTERMATH

Although Hamdi was a U.S. citizen and the *Hamdi* case adjudicated his due process rights under the Constitution, the content of those rights was largely provided by the procedural rights that international law guarantees to all detainees, whether citizens or aliens, captured during armed conflict. In particular, article 5 of the Geneva Conventions states: "Should any doubt arise as to whether persons, having committed a belligerent act and having fallen into the hands of the enemy, belong to any of the categories enumerated in Article 4, such persons shall enjoy the protection of the present Convention until such time as their status has been determined by a competent tribunal." In *Hamdi*, the Supreme Court concluded that a competent tribunal requires, at the very least, that a detainee has the right to contest his detention before a neutral decisionmaker.

In response to the *Hamdi* ruling, the Bush Administration created a system of military tribunals to review detention decisions. The new review tribunals, called Combatant Status Review Tribunals (CSRTs), were designed to satisfy the requirements of Article 5. They were not civilian tribunals, but rather rough-and-ready hearings, presided over by military officers, that simply gave the detainee a chance to contest detention. Somewhat predictably, the vast majority of the CSRTs concluded that continued detention was justified.

In subsequent litigation before the Supreme Court, Guantanamo detainees earned the right to file habeas corpus petitions in federal court to contest their detention. See *Rasul v. Bush*, 542 U.S. 466 (2004) (concluding that federal courts have habeas jurisdiction over detainees at Guantanamo). Following *Rasul*, Congress passed the Detainee Treatment Act, which stripped federal courts of their jurisdiction to hear the petitions. See 28 U.S.C. § 2241 ("no court, justice, or judge shall have jurisdiction to hear or consider. . . an application for a writ of habeas corpus filed by or on behalf of an alien detained by the Department of Defense at Guantanamo Bay, Cuba."). The Supreme Court again upheld the constitutional right of the detainees to file habeas petitions, despite the congressional statutes. See *Boumediene v. Bush*, 553 U.S. 723, 739 (2008) (rejecting government argument that "noncitizens designated as enemy combatants and detained in territory located outside our Nation's borders have no constitutional rights and no privilege of habeas corpus").

However, the *Boumediene* holding was based in part on the fact that the United States has exclusive control over Guantanamo. See *Boumediene*, 553 U.S. at 755 ("As we did in *Rasul*, however, we take notice of the obvious and uncontested fact that the United States, by virtue of its complete jurisdiction and control over the base, maintains *de facto* sovereignty over this territory."). No federal court has reached a similar conclusion regarding detainees housed by the United States or its allies in oversees locations, such as Afghanistan.

E. PROHIBITED WEAPONS

Parties to an armed conflict do not have unlimited means to pursue their military objectives. IHL imposes substantial restrictions on the type of weapons and their manner of use. The following broad categories of prohibitions are relevant:

1. Specific weapons explicitly prohibited by treaty, such as biological or chemical weapons. For example, the Chemical Weapons Convention has roughly 192 state parties, thus establishing nearly universal agreement that chemical weapons are illegal under international law.

2. Weapons that cause unnecessary suffering (*maux superflus*). See Article 35 of Additional Protocol I ("It is prohibited to employ weapons, projectiles and material and methods of warfare of a nature to cause superfluous injury or unnecessary suffering."). For example, if a commander has at his disposal two weapons that are equally effective, but one causes less suffering to enemy soldiers, the unit must use the less painful weapon. To do otherwise would accomplish no legitimate military aim and would presumably be motivated only by sadism or revenge.

3. Weapons that are inherently indiscriminate. Some human rights lawyers argue that cluster munitions are indiscriminate because they cover too wide an area. For this reason, more than 100 states have signed a Convention on Cluster Munitions to ban the bombs. Similarly, a total of 38 states have ratified the Treaty on the Prohibition of Nuclear Weapons and 81 more have signed it. Under the treaty, parties promise never to "develop, test, produce, manufacture, otherwise acquire, possess or stockpile nuclear weapons or other nuclear explosive devices." The treaty extends the norms first outlined in the Non-Proliferation Treaty of 1970. However, the world's major nuclear powers have not consented to the new treaty.

In the following case, the ICJ was asked by the General Assembly to issue an advisory opinion on whether the use or threat of nuclear weapons violated International Humanitarian Law. As you read the opinion, ask yourself whether nuclear weapons are necessarily indiscriminate in all circumstances.

Legality of Threat or Use of Nuclear Weapons
International Court of Justice
1996 I.C.J. 226

74. The Court not having found a conventional rule of general scope, nor a customary rule specifically proscribing the threat or use of nuclear weapons *per se,* it will now deal with the question whether recourse to nuclear weapons must be considered as illegal in the light of the

principles and rules of international humanitarian law applicable in armed conflict and of the law of neutrality.

75. A large number of customary rules have been developed by the practice of States and are an integral part of the international law relevant to the question posed. The "laws and customs of war"—as they were traditionally called—were the subject of efforts at codification undertaken in The Hague (including the Conventions of 1899 and 1907), and were based partly upon the St. Petersburg Declaration of 1868 as well as the results of the Brussels Conference of 1874. This "Hague Law" and, more particularly, the Regulations Respecting the Laws and Customs of War on Land, fixed the rights and duties of belligerents in their conduct of operations and limited the choice of methods and means of injuring the enemy in an international armed conflict. One should add to this the "Geneva Law" (the Conventions of 1864, 1906, 1929 and 1949), which protects the victims of war and aims to provide safeguards for disabled armed forces personnel and persons not taking part in the hostilities. These two branches of the law applicable in armed conflict have become so closely interrelated that they are considered to have gradually formed one single complex system, known today as international humanitarian law. The provisions of the Additional Protocols of 1977 give expression and attest to the unity and complexity of that law.

76. Since the turn of the century, the appearance of new means of combat has—without calling into question the longstanding principles and rules of international law—rendered necessary some specific prohibitions of the use of certain weapons, such as explosive projectiles under 400 grammes, dum-dum bullets and asphyxiating gases. Chemical and bacteriological weapons were then prohibited by the 1925 Geneva Protocol. More recently, the use of weapons producing "non-detectable fragments," of other types of "mines, booby traps and other devices," and of "incendiary weapons," was either prohibited or limited, depending on the case, by the Convention of 10 October 1980 on Prohibitions or Restrictions on the Use of Certain Conventional Weapons Which May Be Deemed to Be Excessively Injurious or to Have Indiscriminate Effects. The provisions of the Convention on "mines, booby traps and other devices" have just been amended, on 3 May 1996, and now regulate in greater detail, for example, the use of anti-personnel land mines.

77. All this shows that the conduct of military operations is governed by a body of legal prescriptions. This is so because "the right of belligerents to adopt means of injuring the enemy is not unlimited" as stated in Article 22 of the 1907 Hague Regulations relating to the laws and customs of war on land. The St. Petersburg Declaration had already condemned the use of weapons "which uselessly aggravate the suffering of disabled men or make their death inevitable." The aforementioned

Regulations relating to the laws and customs of war on land, annexed to the Hague Convention IV of 1907, prohibit the use of "arms, projectiles, or material calculated to cause unnecessary suffering" (Art. 23).

78. The cardinal principles contained in the texts constituting the fabric of humanitarian law are the following. The first is aimed at the protection of the civilian population and civilian objects and establishes the distinction between combatants and non-combatants; States must never make civilians the object of attack and must consequently never use weapons that are incapable of distinguishing between civilian and military targets. According to the second principle, it is prohibited to cause unnecessary suffering to combatants: it is accordingly prohibited to use weapons causing them such harm or uselessly aggravating their suffering. In application of that second principle, States do not have unlimited freedom of choice of means in the weapons they use.

The Court would likewise refer, in relation to these principles, to the Martens Clause, which was first included in the Hague Convention II with Respect to the Laws and Customs of War on Land of 1899 and which has proved to be an effective means of addressing the rapid evolution of military technology. A modern version of that clause is to be found in Article 1, paragraph 2, of Additional Protocol I of 1977, which reads as follows:

> In cases not covered by this Protocol or by other international agreements, civilians and combatants remain under the protection and authority of the principles of international law derived from established custom, from the principles of humanity and from the dictates of public conscience.

In conformity with the aforementioned principles, humanitarian law, at a very early stage, prohibited certain types of weapons either because of their indiscriminate effect on combatants and civilians or because of the unnecessary suffering caused to combatants, that is to say, a harm greater than that unavoidable to achieve legitimate military objectives. If an envisaged use of weapons would not meet the requirements of humanitarian law, a threat to engage in such use would also be contrary to that law.

79. It is undoubtedly because a great many rules of humanitarian law applicable in armed conflict are so fundamental to the respect of the human person and "elementary considerations of humanity" as the Court put it in its Judgment of 9 April 1949 in the *Corfu Channel* case, that the Hague and Geneva Conventions have enjoyed a broad accession. Further these fundamental rules are to be observed by all States whether or not they have ratified the conventions that contain them, because they constitute intransgressible principles of international customary law.

80. The Nuremberg International Military Tribunal had already found in 1945 that the humanitarian rules included in the Regulations annexed to the Hague Convention IV of 1907 "were recognized by all civilized nations and were regarded as being declaratory of the laws and customs of war."

81. The Report of the Secretary-General pursuant to paragraph 2 of Security Council resolution 808 (1993), with which he introduced the Statute of the International Tribunal for the Prosecution of Persons Responsible for Serious Violations of International Humanitarian Law Committed in the Territory of the Former Yugoslavia since 1991, and which was unanimously approved by the Security Council (resolution 827 (1993)), stated:

> In the view of the Secretary-General, the application of the principle *nullum crimen sine lege* requires that the international tribunal should apply rules of international humanitarian law which are beyond any doubt part of customary law... The part of conventional international humanitarian law which has beyond doubt become part of international customary law is the law applicable in armed conflict as embodied in: the Geneva Conventions of 12 August 1949 for the Protection of War Victims; the Hague Convention (IV) Respecting the Laws and Customs of War on Land and the Regulations annexed thereto of 18 October 1907; the Convention on the Prevention and Punishment of the Crime of Genocide of 9 December 1948; and the Charter of the International Military Tribunal of 8 August 1945.

82. The extensive codification of humanitarian law and the extent of the accession to the resultant treaties, as well as the fact that the denunciation clauses that existed in the codification instruments have never been used, have provided the international community with a corpus of treaty rules the great majority of which had already become customary and which reflected the most universally recognized humanitarian principles. These rules indicate the normal conduct and behaviour expected of States.

84. Nor is there any need for the Court to elaborate on the question of the applicability of Additional Protocol I of 1977 to nuclear weapons. It need only observe that while, at the Diplomatic Conference of 1974–1977, there was no substantive debate on the nuclear issue and no specific solution concerning this question was put forward, Additional Protocol I in no way replaced the general customary rules applicable to all means and methods of combat including nuclear weapons. In particular, the Court recalls that all States are bound by those rules in Additional Protocol I which, when adopted, were merely the expression of the pre-existing customary law, such as the Martens Clause,

reaffirmed in the first article of Additional Protocol I. The fact that certain types of weapons were not specifically dealt with by the 1974–1977 Conference does not permit the drawing of any legal conclusions relating to the substantive issues which the use of such weapons would raise.

85. Turning now to the applicability of the principles and rules of humanitarian law to a possible threat or use of nuclear weapons, the Court notes that doubts in this respect have sometimes been voiced on the ground that these principles and rules had evolved prior to the invention of nuclear weapons and that the Conferences of Geneva of 1949 and 1974–1977 which respectively adopted the four Geneva Conventions of 1949 and the two Additional Protocols thereto did not deal with nuclear weapons specifically. Such views, however, are only held by a small minority. In the view of the vast majority of States as well as writers there can be no doubt as to the applicability of humanitarian law to nuclear weapons.

86. The Court shares that view. Indeed, nuclear weapons were invented after most of the principles and rules of humanitarian law applicable in armed conflict had already come into existence; the Conferences of 1949 and 1974–1977 left these weapons aside, and there is a qualitative as well as quantitative difference between nuclear weapons and all conventional arms. However, it cannot be concluded from this that the established principles and rules of humanitarian law applicable in armed conflict did not apply to nuclear weapons. Such a conclusion would be incompatible with the intrinsically humanitarian character of the legal principles in question which permeates the entire law of armed conflict and applies to all forms of warfare and to all kinds of weapons, those of the past, those of the present and those of the future. In this respect it seems significant that the thesis that the rules of humanitarian law do not apply to the new weaponry, because of the newness of the latter, has not been advocated in the present proceedings. On the contrary, the newness of nuclear weapons has been expressly rejected as an argument against the application to them of international humanitarian law. . .

87. Finally, the Court points to the Martens Clause, whose continuing existence and applicability is not to be doubted, as an affirmation that the principles and rules of humanitarian law apply to nuclear weapons.

90. Although the applicability of the principles and rules of humanitarian law and of the principle of neutrality to nuclear weapons is hardly disputed, the conclusions to be drawn from this applicability are, on the other hand, controversial.

91. According to one point of view, the fact that recourse to nuclear weapons is subject to and regulated by the law of armed conflict does not necessarily mean that such recourse is as such prohibited. As one State put it to the Court:

> Assuming that a State's use of nuclear weapons meets the requirements of self-defence, it must then be considered whether it conforms to the fundamental principles of the law of armed conflict regulating the conduct of hostilities. . . the legality of the use of nuclear weapons must therefore be assessed in the light of the applicable principles of international law regarding the use of force and the conduct of hostilities, as is the case with other methods and means of warfare. . . The reality. . . is that nuclear weapons might be used in a wide variety of circumstances with very different results in terms of likely civilian casualties. In some cases, such as the use of a low yield nuclear weapon against warships on the High Seas or troops in sparsely populated areas, it is possible to envisage a nuclear attack which caused comparatively few civilian casualties. It is by no means the case that every use of nuclear weapons against a military objective would inevitably cause very great collateral civilian casualties (United Kingdom).

92. Another view holds that recourse to nuclear weapons could never be compatible with the principles and rules of humanitarian law and is therefore prohibited. In the event of their use, nuclear weapons would in all circumstances be unable to draw any distinction between the civilian population and combatants, or between civilian objects and military objectives, and their effects, largely uncontrollable, could not be restricted, either in time or in space, to lawful military targets. Such weapons would kill and destroy in a necessarily indiscriminate manner, on account of the blast, heat and radiation occasioned by the nuclear explosion and the effects induced; and the number of casualties which would ensue would be enormous. The use of nuclear weapons would therefore be prohibited in any circumstance, notwithstanding the absence of any explicit conventional prohibition. That view lay at the basis of the assertions by certain States before the Court that nuclear weapons are by their nature illegal under customary international law, by virtue of the fundamental principle of humanity.

93. A similar view has been expressed with respect to the effects of the principle of neutrality. Like the principles and rules of humanitarian law, that principle has therefore been considered by some to rule out the use of a weapon the effects of which simply cannot be contained within the territories of the contending States.

94. The Court would observe that none of the States advocating the legality of the use of nuclear weapons under certain circumstances,

including the "clean" use of smaller, low yield, tactical nuclear weapons, has indicated what, supposing such limited use were feasible, would be the precise circumstances justifying such use; nor whether such limited use would not tend to escalate into the all-out use of high yield nuclear weapons. This being so, the Court does not consider that it has a sufficient basis for a determination on the validity of this view.

95. Nor can the Court make a determination on the validity of the view that the recourse to nuclear weapons would be illegal in any circumstance owing to their inherent and total incompatibility with the law applicable in armed conflict. Certainly, as the Court has already indicated, the principles and rules of law applicable in armed conflict—at the heart of which is the overriding consideration of humanity—make the conduct of armed hostilities subject to a number of strict requirements. Thus, methods and means of warfare, which would preclude any distinction between civilian and military targets, or which would result in unnecessary suffering to combatants, are prohibited. In view of the unique characteristics of nuclear weapons, to which the Court has referred above, the use of such weapons in fact seems scarcely reconcilable with respect for such requirements. Nevertheless, the Court considers that it does not have sufficient elements to enable it to conclude with certainty that the use of nuclear weapons would necessarily be at variance with the principles and rules of law applicable in armed conflict in any circumstance.

96. Furthermore, the Court cannot lose sight of the fundamental right of every State to survival, and thus its right to resort to self-defence, in accordance with Article 51 of the Charter, when its survival is at stake.

Nor can it ignore the practice referred to as "policy of deterrence," to which an appreciable section of the international community adhered for many years. The Court also notes the reservations which certain nuclear-weapon States have appended to the undertakings they have given, notably under the Protocols to the Treaties of Tlatelolco and Rarotonga, and also under the declarations made by them in connection with the extension of the Treaty on the Non-Proliferation of Nuclear Weapons, not to resort to such weapons.

97. Accordingly, in view of the present state of international law viewed as a whole, as examined above by the Court, and of the elements of fact at its disposal, the Court is led to observe that it cannot reach a definitive conclusion as to the legality or illegality of the use of nuclear weapons by a State in an extreme circumstance of self-defence, in which its very survival would be at stake.

105. For these reasons, THE COURT, replies in the following manner to the question put by the General Assembly: E. By seven votes to seven, by the President's casting vote, it follows from the above-mentioned

requirements that the threat or use of nuclear weapons would generally be contrary to the rules of international law applicable in armed conflict, and in particular the principles and rules of humanitarian law; however, in view of the current state of international law, and of the elements of fact at its disposal, the Court cannot conclude definitively whether the threat or use of nuclear weapons would be lawful or unlawful in an extreme circumstance of self-defence, in which the very survival of a State would be at stake;

Dissenting Opinion of Vice-President Schwebel

While it is not difficult to conclude that the principles of international humanitarian law—above all, proportionality in the application of force, and discrimination between military and civilian targets—govern the use of nuclear weapons, it does not follow that the application of those principles to the threat or use of nuclear weapons "in any circumstance" is easy. Cases at the extremes are relatively clear; cases closer to the centre of the spectrum of possible uses are less so.

At one extreme is the use of strategic nuclear weapons in quantities against enemy cities and industries. This so-called "countervalue" use (as contrasted with "counterforce" uses directed only against enemy nuclear forces and installations) could cause an enormous number of deaths and injuries, running in some cases into the millions; and, in addition to those immediately affected by the heat and blast of those weapons, vast numbers could be affected, many fatally, by spreading radiation. Large-scale "exchanges" of such nuclear weaponry could destroy not only cities but countries, and render continents, perhaps the whole of the earth, uninhabitable, if not at once then through longer-range effects of nuclear fallout. It cannot be accepted that the use of nuclear weapons on a scale which would—or could—result in the deaths of many millions in indiscriminate inferno and by far-reaching fallout, have profoundly pernicious effects in space and time, and render uninhabitable much or all of the earth, could be lawful.

At the other extreme is the use of tactical nuclear weapons against discrete military or naval targets so situated that substantial civilian casualties would not ensue. For example, the use of a nuclear depth-charge to destroy a nuclear submarine that is about to fire nuclear missiles, or has fired one or more of a number of its nuclear missiles, might well be lawful. By the circumstance of its use, the nuclear depth-charge would not give rise to immediate civilian casualties. It would easily meet the test of proportionality; the damage that the submarine's missiles could inflict on the population and territory of the target State would infinitely outweigh that entailed in the destruction of the submarine and its crew. The submarine's destruction by a nuclear weapon would produce radiation in the sea, but far less than the radiation that firing of its missiles would produce on and over land. Nor is it as certain that the use of a conventional depth-charge would discharge the mission successfully; the far greater force of a nuclear weapon could ensure destruction of the submarine whereas a conventional depth-charge might not.

An intermediate case would be the use of nuclear weapons to destroy an enemy army situated in a desert. In certain circumstances, such a use of nuclear weapons might meet the tests of discrimination and proportionality; in others not. The argument that the use of nuclear weapons is inevitably disproportionate raises troubling questions, which the British Attorney-General addressed in the Court's oral proceedings in these terms:

> If one is to speak of "disproportionality," the question arises: disproportionate to what? The answer must be "to the threat posed to the victim State." It is by reference to that threat that proportionality must be measured. So one has to look at all the circumstances, in particular the scale, kind and location of the threat. To assume that any defensive use of nuclear weapons must be disproportionate, no matter how serious the threat to the safety and the very survival of the State resorting to such use, is wholly unfounded. Moreover, it suggests an overbearing assumption by the critics of nuclear weapons that they can determine in advance that no threat, including a nuclear, chemical or biological threat, is ever worth the use of any nuclear weapon. It cannot be right to say that if an aggressor hits hard enough, his victim loses the right to take the only measure by which he can defend himself and reverse the aggression. That would not be the rule of law. It would be an aggressor's charter.

For its part, the body of the Court's Opinion is cautious in treating problems of the application of the principles of international humanitarian law to concrete cases. It evidences a measure of uncertainty in a case in which the tension between State practice and legal principle is unparalleled. It concludes, in paragraph 2 E of the *dispositif,* that, "It follows from the above-mentioned requirements that the threat or use of nuclear weapons would generally be contrary to the rules of international law applicable in armed conflict, and in particular the principles and rules of international humanitarian law."

That conclusion, while imprecise, is not unreasonable. The use of nuclear weapons is, for the reasons examined above, exceptionally difficult to reconcile with the rules of international law applicable in armed conflict, particularly the principles and rules of international humanitarian law. But that is by no means to say that the use of nuclear weapons, in any and all circumstances, would necessarily and invariably conflict with those rules of international law. On the contrary, as the *dispositif* in effect acknowledges, while they might "generally" do so, in specific cases they might not. It all depends upon the facts of the case. . .

Desert Storm

The most recent and effective threat of the use of nuclear weapons took place on the eve of "Desert Storm." The circumstances merit exposition, for they constitute a striking illustration of a circumstance in which the perceived threat of the use of nuclear weapons was not only eminently lawful but intensely desirable.

Iraq, condemned by the Security Council for its invasion and annexation of Kuwait and for its attendant grave breaches of international humanitarian law, had demonstrated that it was prepared to use weapons of mass destruction. It had recently and repeatedly used gas in large quantities against the military formations of Iran, with substantial and perhaps decisive effect. It had even used gas against its own Kurdish citizens. There was no ground for believing that legal or humanitarian scruple would prevent it from using weapons of mass destruction—notably chemical, perhaps bacteriological or nuclear weapons—against the coalition forces arrayed against it. Moreover, it was engaged in extraordinary efforts to construct nuclear weapons in violation of its obligations as a party to the Non-Proliferation Treaty.

General Norman Schwarzkopf stated on 10 January 1996 over national public television in the United States on *Frontline*:

> My nightmare scenario was that our forces would attack into Iraq and find themselves in such a great concentration that they became targeted by chemical weapons or some sort of rudimentary nuclear device that would cause mass casualties. That's exactly what the Iraqis did in the Iran-Iraq war. They would take the attacking masses of the Iranians, let them run up against their barrier system, and when there were thousands of people massed against the barrier system, they would drop chemical weapons on them and kill thousands of people.

To exorcise that nightmare, the United States took action as described by then Secretary of State James A. Baker in the following terms, in which he recounts his climactic meeting of 9 January 1990 in Geneva with the then Foreign Minister of Iraq, Tariq Aziz:

> I then made a point "on the dark side of the issue" that Colin Powell had specifically asked me to deliver in the plainest possible terms. "If the conflict involves your use of chemical or biological weapons against our forces," I warned, "the American people will demand vengeance. We have the means to exact it. With regard to this part of my presentation, that is not a threat, it is a promise. If there is any use of weapons like that, our objective won't just be the liberation of Kuwait, but the

elimination of the current Iraqi regime, and anyone responsible for using those weapons would be held accountable.

The President had decided, at Camp David in December, that the best deterrent of the use of weapons of mass destruction by Iraq would be a threat to go after the Ba'ath regime itself. He had also decided that U.S. forces would not retaliate with chemical or nuclear response if the Iraqis attacked with chemical munitions. There was obviously no reason to inform the Iraqis of this. In hope of persuading them to consider more soberly the folly of war, I purposely left the impression that the use of chemical or biological agents by Iraq could invite tactical nuclear retaliation. (We do not really know whether this was the reason there appears to have been no confirmed use by Iraq of chemical weapons during the war. My own view is that the calculated ambiguity how we might respond has to be part of the reason.)

. . . Thus there is on record remarkable evidence indicating that an aggressor was or may have been deterred from using outlawed weapons of mass destruction against forces and countries arrayed against its aggression at the call of the United Nations by what the aggressor perceived to be a threat to use nuclear weapons against it should it first use weapons of mass destruction against the forces of the coalition. Can it seriously be maintained that Mr. Baker's calculated—and apparently successful—threat was unlawful? Surely the principles of the United Nations Charter were sustained rather than transgressed by the threat. "Desert Storm" and the resolutions of the Security Council that preceded and followed it may represent the greatest achievement of the principles of collective security since the founding of the League of Nations. The defeat of this supreme effort of the United Nations to overcome an act of aggression by the use of weapons of mass destruction against coalition forces and countries would have been catastrophic, not only for coalition forces and populations, but for those principles and for the United Nations. But the United Nations did triumph, and to that triumph what Iraq perceived as a threat to use nuclear weapons against it may have made a critical contribution. Nor is this a case of the end justifying the means. It rather demonstrates that, in some circumstances, the threat of the use of nuclear weapons—as long as they remain weapons unproscribed by international law—may be both lawful and rational. . .

F. HUMAN RIGHTS IN ARMED CONFLICT

During armed conflict, the belligerent parties are clearly constrained by International Armed Conflict. But what of Human Rights Law? Does it still apply during armed conflict? Or is human rights law effectively "displaced" by IHL during times of armed conflict? At times, the United

States government has invoked this displacement model, suggesting that the only relevant body of law during armed conflict is IHL. However, more human rights-oriented scholars have criticized this view. For one, they ask, why do human rights treaties contain derogation clauses that although state parties to "derogate" from some of their human rights obligations during time of armed conflict? If IHL automatically "displaces" human rights law, such clauses would be unnecessary. See Marko Milanovic, *The Lost Origins of Lex Specialis: Rethinking the Relationship Between Human Rights and International Humanitarian Law*, in *Theoretical Boundaries of Armed Conflict and Human Rights* 104 (Jens David Ohlin ed., 2016).

Some human rights lawyers argue that since human rights law is universal, it must apply at all times, including during armed conflict. But is human rights law consistent with the largescale killing of enemy combatants that is permitted by IHL. Recall that while IHL prohibits the intentional killing of civilians, it allows the intentional killing of enemy combatants, and even the foreseeable killing of enemy civilians in the form of collateral damage. Furthermore, article 6 of the International Covenant on Civil and Political Rights (ICCPR) states that "Every human being has the inherent right to life. This right shall be protected by law. No one shall be arbitrarily deprived of his life." Is this consistent with the rules of IHL? How can human rights law apply during armed conflict?

In an earlier section of its Advisory Opinion on the *Legality of Nuclear Weapons*, the ICJ concluded that human rights law applies during armed conflict:

24. Some of the proponents of the illegality of the use of nuclear weapons have argued that such use would violate the right to life as guaranteed in Article 6 of the International Covenant on Civil and Political Rights, as well as in certain regional instruments for the protection of human rights. Article 6, paragraph 1, of the International Covenant provides as follows: "Every human being has the inherent right to life. This right shall be protected by law. No one shall be arbitrarily deprived of his life."

In reply, others contended that the International Covenant on Civil and Political Rights made no mention of war or weapons, and it had never been envisaged that the legality of nuclear weapons was regulated by that instrument. It was suggested that the Covenant was directed to the protection of human rights in peacetime, but that questions relating to unlawful loss of life in hostilities were governed by the law applicable in armed conflict.

25. The Court observes that the protection of the International Covenant of Civil and Political Rights does not cease in times of war, except by operation of Article 4 of the Covenant whereby certain provisions may be derogated from in a time of national emergency. Respect for the right to life is not, however, such a provision. In principle, the right not arbitrarily to be deprived of one's life applies also in hostilities. The test of what is an arbitrary deprivation of life, however, then falls to be determined by the applicable *lex specialis,* namely, the law applicable in armed conflict which is designed to regulate the conduct of hostilities. Thus whether a particular loss of life, through the use of a certain weapon in warfare, is to be considered an arbitrary deprivation of life contrary to Article 6 of the Covenant, can only be decided by reference to the law applicable in armed conflict and not deduced from the terms of the Covenant itself.

What does the court's reference to *lex specialis* mean? The phrase *lex specialis* refers to the Latin maxim *lex specialis derogat legi generali*—the specific law prevails over the more general law. To understand the principle better, consider the concept of legislative intent in domestic law. Imagine that a legislature has passed two conflicting statutes: a very general statute and a very specific one. All other things being equal, one should assume that the legislature desired that the more specific law should prevail over the general one.

In this context, the invocation of *lex specialis* would mean that IHL is the more specific law and prevails in times of armed conflict. According to the ICJ, this does not mean that human rights law disappears, but rather that the *content* of human rights law is provided by the more specific law, that is, IHL. For example, in order to determine whether someone has been arbitrarily denied their right to life under human rights law, one should look to the rules articulated in IHL. If the killing complied with the more specific legal requirements of IHL, then the killing was not "arbitrary" as a matter of human rights law.

Others argue that the *lex specialis* principle requires a comparison between two norms of IHL and human rights law, with the result that the more specific *rule* between them will govern in any situation. For an expression of this view, see Oona A. Hathaway, Rebecca Crootof, Philip Levitz, Haley Nix, William Perdue, Chelsea Purvis, & Julia Spiegel, *Which Law Governs During Armed Conflict? The Relationship Between International Humanitarian Law and Human Rights Law*, 96 Minn. L. Rev. 1883, 1887 (2012) ("The specificity rule of conflict resolution that we detail derives from the broader *lex specialis* maxim, which states that 'whenever two or more norms deal with the same subject matter, priority should be given to the norm that is more specific.' However, the specificity rule applies at the level of the operation, situation, or encounter, so that whichever body of law is eclipsed in that operation, situation, or encounter still remains relevant in the broader armed conflict.").

However, not everyone is convinced that the concept of *lex specialis* is a helpful one. For a dissenting view, see Milanovic, *supra*, at 114 ("The appeal of *lex specialis* lies in the veneer of antiquity of its Latin formula, in its apparent formality, simplicity and objectivity. But all it really does is disguise a series of policy judgments about what outcomes are the most sensible, realistic and practicable in any given situation."). For more discussion of *lex specialis*, see Ashika Singh, *The United States, the Torture Convention, and Lex Specialis: The Quest for A Coherent Approach to the CAT in Armed Conflict*, 47 Colum. Hum. Rts. L. Rev. 134, 177 (2016).

One practical consequence of this debate is the question of whether a human rights court has jurisdiction over alleged human rights abuses that occur armed conflict or whether those violations are exclusively regulated by the norms of IHL. The most active human rights court in the world is the European Court of Human Rights and several of its judgments have grappled with the question of whether the court can apply the provisions of the European Convention of Human Rights during active military hostilities. Doctrinally, the question comes down to whether the state that is sued had "effective control" over the alleged victims, which is the jurisdictional condition for the Convention to apply. For example, consider a military strike that kills a group of individuals. Does the killing suggest that, by definition, the state had "control" over the individuals because it had the power to kill them? Or does "control" suggest something more than control over an individual person, such as exclusive control over the territory on which the individual is located?

In 2021, a Grand Chamber of the European Court of Human Rights ruled that it did *not* have jurisdiction to review military targeting decisions that occurred during the phase of active hostilities between Russia and Georgia because "the very reality of armed confrontation and fighting between enemy military forces seeking to establish control over an area in a context of chaos not only means that there is no 'effective control' over an area ... but also excludes any form of 'State agent authority and control' over individuals." *Russia v. Georgia (II)*, Application No. 38263/08, para. 137. However, the Chamber concluded that it *did* have jurisdiction over abuses that occurred after the active hostilities ceased, because during that occupation phase Russian and South Ossetian forces had secured effective control over the relevant areas. Although future Grand Chambers may decide to go in a different direction, the decision highlighted the court's reluctance to stray too far into the conceptual terrain of IHL.

However, many human rights lawyers continue to press the idea that human rights law has an important role to play in the regulation of armed conflict. In addition to the arguments discussed above that human rights governs the conduct of hostilities alongside IHL, some lawyers have suggested that human rights law also governs the *resort* to armed conflict as embodied by *jus ad bellum* and Article 51 of the UN Charter. Specifically, these lawyers argue that any killing that occurs during a military campaign that violates *jus ad bellum* is a human rights violation of the right to life. In that vein, consider the following Draft Comment from the Human Rights Committee on the right to life. What legal standards does it set for determining whether a killing in armed conflict constitutes an "arbitrary" deprivation of life? From which bodies of law do these standards arise?

Draft General Comment No. 36
Human Rights Committee

16. Although it inheres in every human being the right to life is not absolute. By requiring that deprivations of life must not be arbitrary, Article 6, paragraph 1 implicitly recognizes that some deprivations of life may be non-arbitrary. For example, the use of lethal force in self-defence, under the conditions specified in paragraph 18 below would not constitute an arbitrary deprivation of life. Even those exceptional measures leading to deprivations of life which are not arbitrary per se must be applied in a manner which is not arbitrary in fact. Such exceptional measures should be established by law and accompanied by effective institutional safeguards designed to prevent arbitrary deprivations of life. . .

17. The second sentence of paragraph 1 requires that the right to life be protected by law, while the third sentence requires that no one should be arbitrarily deprived of life. The two requirements overlap in that a deprivation of life that lacks a legal basis or is otherwise inconsistent with life-protecting laws and procedures is, as a rule, arbitrary in nature. . .

18. A deprivation of life may be authorized by domestic law and still be arbitrary. The notion of "arbitrariness" is not to be equated with "against the law," but must be interpreted more broadly to include elements of inappropriateness, injustice, lack of predictability, and due process of law as well as elements of reasonableness, necessity, and proportionality. For example, in order not to be qualified as arbitrary under article 6, the application of lethal force by a person acting in self-defense, or by another person coming to his or her defence, must be reasonable and necessary in view of the threat posed by the attacker; it must represent a method of last resort after non-lethal alternatives, including warnings, have been exhausted or deemed inadequate; the

amount of force applied cannot exceed the amount strictly needed for responding to the threat; the force applied must be carefully directed, as far as possible, only against the attacker; and the threat responded to must be extreme, involving imminent death or serious injury. The deliberate use of potentially lethal force for law enforcement purposes which is intended to address threats, not of extreme gravity, such as protecting private property or preventing the escape from custody of a suspected criminal or a convict who does not pose a serious and imminent threat to the lives or bodily integrity of others, cannot be regarded as a proportionate use of force.

67. Like the rest of the Covenant, article 6 continues to apply also. . . in situations of armed conflict to which the rules of international humanitarian law are applicable. While rules of international humanitarian law may be relevant for the interpretation and application of article 6, both spheres of law are complementary, not mutually exclusive. Uses of lethal force authorized and regulated by and complying with international humanitarian law are, in principle, not arbitrary. By contrast, practices inconsistent with international humanitarian law, entailing a risk to the lives of civilians and persons hors de combat, including the targeting of civilians and civilian objects, indiscriminate attacks, failure to apply adequate measures of precaution to prevent collateral death of civilians, and the use of human shields, violate article 6 of the Covenant. States parties should. . . disclose the criteria for attacking with lethal force individuals or objects whose targeting is expected to result in deprivation of life, including the legal basis for specific attacks, the process of identification of military targets and combatants or persons taking a direct part in hostilities, the circumstances in which relevant means and methods of warfare have been used, and whether non-lethal alternatives for attaining the same military objective were considered. They must also investigate allegations of violations of article 6 in situations of armed conflict in accordance with the relevant international standards.

71. States parties engaged in acts of aggression contrary to the United Nations Charter violate ipso facto article 6 of the Covenant. Moreover, States parties that fail to take all reasonable measures to settle their international disputes by peaceful means so as to avoid resort to the use of force do not comply in full with their positive obligation to ensure the right to life. At the same time, all States are reminded of their responsibility as members of the international community to protect lives and to oppose widespread or systematic attacks on the right to life, including acts of aggression, international terrorism and crimes against humanity, while respecting all of their obligations under the United Nations Charter.

NOTES & QUESTIONS

Arbitrary Killings. Which legal norms provide content to the human rights notion of an "arbitrary" killing? According to the Draft Comment, killings "authorized and regulated by and complying with international humanitarian law are, in principle, not arbitrary." Also, the Draft Comment asserts that acts of aggression automatically involve arbitrary killings. If this is true, then every killing of an enemy soldier during a military campaign in contravention of article 2(4) of the UN Charter would constitute a human rights violation. If 100,000 combatants are killed, each one is a human rights violation. This seems to suggest that during armed conflict, the content of human rights law—at least with regard to the right to life—is provided *both* by IHL (jus in bello) *and* the Charter regime (jus ad bellum). Is this the same concept of *lex specialis* discussed above?

G. THE LAW OF OCCUPATION

After the conclusion of hostilities, international law does not fall silent regarding a belligerent power's treatment of the civilian population. The triggering condition for this body of law—the law of occupation—is the belligerent's control over the territory of its enemy. At that point in time, the military transitions from being a belligerent in an armed conflict to being a belligerent occupying power.

It is important to note that international law's recognition of a belligerent occupation does not entail anything about the sovereignty of the territory in question. A state's occupation of a particular territory does not allow that state to legally annex that territory, nor does it allow the occupying power to unilaterally alter the boundary of its state or of its enemy. The question of sovereignty and statehood is controlled by the criteria of statehood that was outlined in Chapter 4. Indeed, the animating impulse behind the law of occupation is to insist that an occupying power has obligations to "govern" a territory in a responsible manner if that territory falls within its control. At the same time, though, international law insists that occupational control does not equate with sovereign control.

The requirements of the law of occupation are outlined, in treaty form, in both the 1907 Hague Regulations and the 1949 Geneva Conventions. The provisions of the Hague Regulations articulate the triggering conditions for the law of occupation and also outline the basic set of obligations that an occupying force must respect:

> Art. 42. Territory is considered occupied when it is actually placed under the authority of the hostile army. The occupation extends only to the territory where such authority has been established and can be exercised.

Art. 43. The authority of the legitimate power having in fact passed into the hands of the occupant, the latter shall take all the measures in his power to restore, and ensure, as far as possible, public order and safety, while respecting, unless absolutely prevented, the laws in force in the country.

Convention (IV) respecting the Laws and Customs of War on Land and its annex: Regulations concerning the Laws and Customs of War on Land, The Hague, October 18, 1907. In broad strokes, articles 42–43 of the Regulations obligate the occupying power to provide for the civilian population in several core domains—food, health, education, security— because the occupying power has displaced the original government that would normally provide these services.

The provisions in the 1949 Geneva Convention (IV) Relative to the Protection of Civilian Persons in Time of War are far more detailed and add specificity to the broad provisions that were codified in 1907. So, for example, the Fourth Geneva Convention includes provisions that prohibit transferring the local population out of occupied territory and also prohibit transferring its own civilians into occupied territory (art. 49). This latter prohibition is particularly important because the transfer of settlers into an occupied territory could slowly help the occupying power annex the territory by changing the national makeup of the local population. The occupying power is required to "facilitate the proper working of all institutions devoted to the care and education of children" (art. 50). Military conscription of the local population is prohibited (art. 51), as is destruction of private property (art. 53). The occupying power is responsible for providing adequate food, medicine, and hospital services for the local population (art. 55–56). Penal and other laws of the occupying territory remain in force and shall not be suspended by the occupying power unless "they constitute a threat to its security or an obstacle to the application of the present Convention" (art. 64). These are just a few of the rules codified in the Fourth Geneva Convention; the rest of the document is a complete roadmap for the legal requirements of a belligerent occupation, outlined in great detail over the course of 159 articles and three annexes.

Some of the provisions in the Fourth Geneva Convention are limited by qualifying clauses that exempt the occupying power from its responsibilities when doing so would not be consistent with "military necessity" or similar notions of feasibility. So, for example, the Fourth Geneva Convention allows an occupying power to requisition civilian hospitals for the care of military wounded in cases of "urgent necessity" (art. 57) or to evacuate the civilian population of an area for "imperative military reasons" (art. 49). These exceptions, while not completely open ended, nevertheless concede much ground to the exigencies of military operations.

Most major military powers are parties to the Fourth Geneva Convention, although a few states, such as Israel, have refused to join the Convention. In relation to those non-parties, the legal analysis often revolves around the status of the above provisions under customary international law. Although the analysis must be conducted on a provision-by-provision basis, there is widespread agreement that most occupation provisions of the Hague Regulations and the Geneva Conventions are now a part of customary international law.

Conceptually, the law of occupation stands at the intersection of IHL and International Human Rights Law. It owes much to its progenitor, IHL, because occupation occurs after the cessation of hostilities, once one belligerent is successful enough to enjoy control over enemy territory. Furthermore, the inspiration behind the Fourth Geneva Convention is the same as the inspiration behind IHL, which is to protect civilians, to the extent feasible, from the horrors of war. Of course, the protection of civilians, embodied in what IHL lawyers often call the principle of humanity, must be balanced by the needs of the military to conduct operations, or what IHL lawyers call military necessity. This dynamic interaction also is embodied in the law of occupation, which grants substantial protections to the civilian population while at the same time recognizing that occupation forces have military needs.

On the other hand, the law of occupation is structurally similar to human rights law because the occupying power has control over the local population—similar to the control or jurisdiction that must exist for human rights law to apply. Indeed, this has caused some, including the ICJ, to conclude that human rights treaties can also apply during a state of occupation. See *Legal Consequences of Construction of a Wall in the Occupied Palestinian Territory,* 2004 I.C.J. 136 (July 9, 2004). Although the occupying power does not enjoy any form of de jure legitimacy as a government, the occupying power does exercise a form of de facto quasi-governmental authority that triggers the application of legal restraints regarding the treatment of the civilian population. Indeed, article 6 of the Fourth Geneva Convention clarifies that "[i]n the case of occupied territory, the application of the present Convention shall cease one year after the general close of military operations; however, the Occupying Power shall be bound, for the duration of the occupation, to the extent that such Power exercises the functions of government in such territory. . . ."

Conclusion & Summary

International Humanitarian Law represents one of international law's greatest successes. Although many armed conflicts feature violations and war crimes, IHL has succeeded in constraining belligerents and protecting civilians from war's worst excesses. Here are the key features of the system of regulation:

1. IHL applies during an armed conflict, whether international (IAC) or non-international (NIAC). An IAC is triggered when there is recourse to force between states, and a NIAC is triggered when there is a sustained violence that rises to a sufficient level of scope and intensity between a state and a non-state actor, or between two non-state actors. If the non-state actor is located outside of the state, many lawyers refer to this as an extraterritorial NIAC. Lawyers disagree about the temporal and geographic scope of IHL and whether it applies only on a narrowly defined "hot" battlefield or whether its targeting rules apply across a broader geographical space.

2. The principle of distinction requires combatants to distinguish themselves from civilians and also requires attacking forces to direct their attacks against combatants. The major exception to that requirement is the case of civilians directly participating in hostilities, who may be targeted "for such time" as they are directly participating. The exact contours of "direct participation" are hotly debated among IHL experts, though one proposal, by the ICRC, concludes that members of an organized armed group who exercise a "continuous combat function" should qualify as directly participating in hostilities and therefore targetable. Under this view, terrorists whose permanent role in a terrorist group is to launch attacks would be targetable during an armed conflict.

3. Civilian collateral damage is tolerated in IHL, as long as the damage is not disproportionate to the anticipated value of the military target. Such calculations are notoriously hard to make and there are almost no cases of prosecutions before international tribunals for causing disproportionate collateral damage. When lawyers do scrutinize these decisions, the relevant framework is not an ex post evaluation but rather an ex ante determination from the perspective of the "reasonable military commander" in that situation.

4. Privileged combatants are entitled to Prisoner of War status and may be detained in humane conditions until the end of hostilities. To qualify as a privileged combatant, the soldier must be a member of the regular armed forces of a state, or militia, and satisfy the functional criteria: a responsible command, wear a fixed sign, carry arms openly,

and respects the laws and customs of war. POWs are entitled to combatant immunity, which means the detaining power is not permitted to prosecute or punish them for lawful acts of belligerency. Unprivileged combatants (who fail to satisfy the functional criteria) are always subject to detention, though unlike privileged combatants, they may be prosecuted under domestic law for their illegal acts of belligerency. However, both international and domestic law confers procedural protections on these detainees, including the right to contest the lawfulness of their detention before a competent tribunal.

5.   International Humanitarian Law is not the only body of law relevant during armed conflict. Almost all lawyers agree that there is some role for human rights law to play. The center of the dispute is the manner and scope of human rights law's application in armed conflict. According to the ICJ, IHL is *lex specialis* and therefore one must look to the more specific rules of IHL to the determine the content of the human right not to be deprived of life arbitrarily. Under this view, a killing during armed conflict which is IHL compliant would not be "arbitrary."

6.   After hostilities have ended, a belligerent power in control of enemy territory will be regulated by the law of occupation.

CHAPTER 13

INTERNATIONAL CRIMINAL LAW

Introduction

International criminal law focuses on the criminal responsibility of individuals for certain violations of international law. Not all violations of international law generate individual criminal responsibility. In fact, most do not. The more typical scheme is for *states* to be responsible for violations of international law. But there is a limited subset of international norms that are considered so pressing that their violation justifies the imposition of punishment against individual perpetrators.

However, this concentration on the "individual" does not take place in an utter vacuum, but rather is the ultimate extension of a process outlined in the prior two chapters on Human Rights and International Humanitarian Law. Both of these domains invariably sprung from state obligations, in the sense that states signed major treaties protecting human rights and states are bound by the laws of war that came into force through treaty or customary law. In both cases, though, it is *individuals* who are the primary beneficiaries of the law because the law protects them from state excess or the horrors of war.

The individual takes center stage in international criminal law, though in a different manner. In this case, individuals bear *responsibility* for the illegal conduct. In many ways, this is the central move of international criminal justice, highlighted by the Nuremberg "moment" in 1945. When Nazi leaders were prosecuted at the end of World War II, it signified, if it was not already apparent, that individuals could be personally punished for violating international law. Indeed, it was already well established that there were legal restrictions on the conduct of warfare (although perhaps there was disagreement on the exact scope of these restrictions). Nuremberg solidified the idea that criminal responsibility could, and should, attach to individuals for violating some of those restrictions.

Of course, not all violations of international law are *criminalized*, just as not all illegal behavior in a domestic system of justice falls under the penal law. The classic core crimes include war crimes, crimes against humanity, genocide, and aggression. Also, there is no central court where the crimes might be prosecuted, though the International Criminal Court comes close. In reality, international crimes are prosecuted at an array of international and domestic courts with different grants of jurisdiction.

Some criminals escape scrutiny because no international tribunal has jurisdiction over the case. At least in theory, though, international criminal justice abhors impunity, and the development over the last half century has been to create more tribunals, with greater jurisdiction, to limit or even eliminate the number of criminals who may successfully evade justice. In this chapter, we focus on the major international venues, though it should not be forgotten that in many cases national courts prosecute their citizens for international crimes in accordance with domestic statutes that criminalize war crimes, crimes against humanity, and genocide. There is a difference between international crimes and international courts and the two do not always coincide; domestic courts may prosecute international offenses too.

The following chapter starts in Section A by explaining the key differences between the so-called "ad hoc" tribunals and the International Criminal Court. Then, Section B analyzes the major international crimes, focusing on the doctrinal requirements for each that has prompted the most litigation or controversy in prosecutions at international tribunals. Section C focuses on the modes of liability that courts use to "link" defendants with the physical perpetration of the crimes. International tribunals with scarce resources prefer to focus their attention on higher-echelon defendants, rather than the soldiers "on the ground" who did the actual killing. The modes of liability, such as Joint Criminal Enterprise, the Control Theory, and command responsibility, all function to establish a link between behind-the-scenes individuals who played a role in the criminality. Section D focuses on the defenses available to international defendants, with special emphasis on the controversy surrounding necessity and duress.

A. COURTS

Despite popular belief, there is no single world court for the prosecution of international war criminals, but rather an array of tribunals with different temporal and geographic jurisdictions. However, one can certainly categorize the tribunals into two categories: ad hoc tribunals versus the permanent International Criminal Court (ICC). Ad hoc tribunals are specialty courts, created by either the United Nations or by national jurisdictions to investigate and prosecute allegations of atrocities committed during specific conflicts. These tribunals usually operate for a specific duration and eventually shut down. In contrast, the ICC is a treaty-based, permanent court with a more general jurisdiction. However, as will be demonstrated below, the jurisdiction of the ICC is still limited by multiple principles and legal doctrines; the ICC certainly does not have universal jurisdiction.

1. AD HOC TRIBUNALS

After World War II, the victorious military powers negotiated a treaty to create the International Military Tribunal at Nuremberg, an ad hoc tribunal to prosecute Nazis for atrocities as well as for starting the war in the first place. A separate tribunal was convened to prosecute offenses related to the conflict against Japan. Although Nuremberg was a watershed moment in the history of international criminal law, the project of individual accountability and punishment for war crimes dimmed in the ensuing decades. However, in the 1990s, two conflicts— and reports of widespread abuses committed during them—shocked the world community. The first was the breakup of Yugoslavia and the military conflicts that arose from them. These conflicts included reports of killings of civilians, rapes, and ethnic cleansing. The second conflict was a civil war in Rwanda that quickly turned genocidal, with reports that thousands of Hutu perpetrators killed roughly 800,000 ethnic Tutsi in the span of a few weeks.

In response to these humanitarian catastrophes, the UN Security Council created two ad hoc international criminal tribunals in 1993 and 1994 respectively, with jurisdiction to prosecute international offenses related to conflicts. Known as the International Criminal Tribunal for the Former Yugoslavia (ICTY) and the International Criminal Tribunal for Rwanda (ICTR), the tribunals were granted *primary* jurisdiction over their defendants, meaning that as a matter of international law, the jurisdiction of the tribunals takes priority over competing claims of criminal jurisdiction from domestic legal systems. The tribunals were located in The Hague and applied the crimes (war crimes, crimes against humanity, and genocide) defined in a statute drafted by the UN Security Council.

In creating the ICTY and ICTR, the Security Council broke new legal ground. Never before had the Council created an ad hoc tribunal to prosecute international crimes. In this instance, the Council invoked its Chapter VII authority under the UN Charter to take measures to restore international peace and security. The first defendants brought before the ICTY questioned the legitimacy of the tribunal and argued that the Council had acted *ultra vires* when it created the tribunals. Did the UN Charter give the Security Council the authority to create a criminal court from whole cloth? In the following case, the first to go to trial, the ICTY Appeals Chamber gave its answer.

Prosecutor v. Dusko Tadić

International Criminal Tribunal for the Former Yugoslavia
Decision on the Defense Motion for Interlocutory Appeal on Jurisdiction
October 2, 1995

The Power of The Security Council to Invoke Chapter VII

28. Article 39 opens Chapter VII of the Charter of the United Nations and determines the conditions of application of this Chapter. It provides:

> The Security Council shall determine the existence of any threat to the peace, breach of the peace, or act of aggression and shall make recommendations, or decide what measures shall be taken in accordance with Articles 41 and 42, to maintain or restore international peace and security.

It is clear from this text that the Security Council plays a pivotal role and exercises a very wide discretion under this Article. But this does not mean that its powers are unlimited. The Security Council is an organ of an international organization, established by a treaty which serves as a constitutional framework for that organization. The Security Council is thus subjected to certain constitutional limitations, however broad its powers under the constitution may be. Those powers cannot, in any case, go beyond the limits of the jurisdiction of the Organization at large, not to mention other specific limitations or those which may derive from the internal division of power within the Organization. In any case, neither the text nor the spirit of the Charter conceives of the Security Council as *legibus solutus* (unbound by law). In particular, Article 24, after declaring, in paragraph 1, that the Members of the United Nations "confer on the Security Council primary responsibility for the maintenance of international peace and security," imposes on it, in paragraph 3, the obligation to report annually (or more frequently) to the General Assembly, and provides, more importantly, in paragraph 2, that: "In discharging these duties the Security Council shall act in accordance with the Purposes and Principles of the United Nations. The specific powers granted to the Security Council for the discharge of these duties are laid down in Chapters VI, VII, VIII, and XII." The Charter thus speaks the language of specific powers, not of absolute fiat.

29. What is the extent of the powers of the Security Council under Article 39 and the limits thereon, if any? The Security Council plays the central role in the application of both parts of the Article. It is the Security Council that makes the determination that there exists one of the situations justifying the use of the "exceptional powers" of Chapter VII. And it is also the Security Council that chooses the reaction to such a situation: it either makes recommendations (i.e., opts not to use the exceptional powers but to continue to operate under Chapter VI) or

decides to use the exceptional powers by ordering measures to be taken in accordance with Articles 41 and 42 with a view to maintaining or restoring international peace and security. The situations justifying resort to the powers provided for in Chapter VII are a "threat to the peace," a "breach of the peace" or an "act of aggression." While the "act of aggression" is more amenable to a legal determination, the "threat to the peace" is more of a political concept. But the determination that there exists such a threat is not a totally unfettered discretion, as it has to remain, at the very least, within the limits of the Purposes and Principles of the Charter.

30. It is not necessary for the purposes of the present decision to examine any further the question of the limits of the discretion of the Security Council in determining the existence of a "threat to the peace". . . . [A]n armed conflict (or a series of armed conflicts) has been taking place in the territory of the former Yugoslavia since long before the decision of the Security Council to establish this International Tribunal. If it is considered an international armed conflict, there is no doubt that it falls within the literal sense of the words "breach of the peace" (between the parties or, at the very least, would be a as a "threat to the peace" of others). But even if it were considered merely as an "internal armed conflict," it would still constitute a "threat to the peace" according to the settled practice of the Security Council and the common understanding of the United Nations membership in general. Indeed, the practice of the Security Council is rich with cases of civil war or internal strife which it classified as a "threat to the peace" and dealt with under Chapter VII. . .

The Range of Measures Envisaged Under Chapter VII

31. Once the Security Council determines that a particular situation poses a threat to the peace or that there exists a breach of the peace or an act of aggression, it enjoys a wide margin of discretion in choosing the course of action: as noted above it can either continue, in spite of its determination, to act via recommendations, i.e., as if it were still within Chapter VI ("Pacific Settlement of Disputes") or it can exercise its exceptional powers under Chapter VII. In the words of Article 39, it would then "decide what measures shall be taken in accordance with Articles 41 and 42, to maintain or restore international peace and security."

A question arises in this respect as to whether the choice of the Security Council is limited to the measures provided for in Articles 41 and 42 of the Charter (as the language of Article 39 suggests), or whether it has even larger discretion in the form of general powers to maintain and restore international peace and security under Chapter VII at large. In the latter case, one of course does not have to locate every measure decided by the Security Council under Chapter VII within the confines of

Articles 41 and 42, or possibly Article 40. In any case, under both interpretations, the Security Council has a broad discretion in deciding on the course of action and evaluating the appropriateness of the measures to be taken. The language of Article 39 is quite clear as to the channeling of the very broad and exceptional powers of the Security Council under Chapter VII through Articles 41 and 42. These two Articles leave to the Security Council such a wide choice as not to warrant searching, on functional or other grounds, for even wider and more general powers than those already expressly provided for in the Charter. These powers are coercive *vis-à-vis* the culprit State or entity. But they are also mandatory *vis-à-vis* the other Member States, who are under an obligation to cooperate with the Organization (Article 2, paragraph 5, Articles 25, 48) and with one another (Articles 49), in the implementation of the action or measures decided by the Security Council.

The Establishment of The International Tribunal as a Measure Under Chapter VII

32. As with the determination of the existence of a threat to the peace, a breach of the peace or an act of aggression, the Security Council has a very wide margin of discretion under Article 39 to choose the appropriate course of action and to evaluate the suitability of the measures chosen, as well as their potential contribution to the restoration or maintenance of peace. But here again, this discretion is not unfettered; moreover, it is limited to the measures provided for in Articles 41 and 42. Indeed, in the case at hand, this last point serves as a basis for the Appellant's contention of invalidity of the establishment of the International Tribunal. In its resolution 827, the Security Council considers that "in the particular circumstances of the former Yugoslavia," the establishment of the International Tribunal "would contribute to the restoration and maintenance of peace" and indicates that, in establishing it, the Security Council was acting under Chapter VII. However, it did not specify a particular Article as a basis for this action.

Appellant has attacked the legality of this decision at different stages before the Trial Chamber as well as before this Chamber on at least three grounds:

    a.   that the establishment of such a tribunal was never contemplated by the framers of the Charter as one of the measures to be taken under Chapter VII; as witnessed by the fact that it figures nowhere in the provisions of that Chapter, and more particularly in Articles 41 and 42 which detail these measures;

    b.   that the Security Council is constitutionally or inherently incapable of creating a judicial organ, as it is conceived in the Charter as an executive organ, hence not possessed of judicial powers which can be exercised through a subsidiary organ;

c. that the establishment of the International Tribunal has neither promoted, nor was capable of promoting, international peace, as demonstrated by the current situation in the former Yugoslavia.

33. The establishment of an international criminal tribunal is not expressly mentioned among the enforcement measures provided for in Chapter VII, and more particularly in Articles 41 and 42. Obviously, the establishment of the International Tribunal is not a measure under Article 42, as these are measures of a military nature, implying the use of armed force. Nor can it be considered a "provisional measure" under Article 40. These measures, as their denomination indicates, are intended to act as a "holding operation," producing a "stand-still" or a "cooling-off" effect, "without prejudice to the rights, claims or position of the parties concerned." They are akin to emergency police action rather than to the activity of a judicial organ dispensing justice according to law. Moreover, not being enforcement action, according to the language of Article 40 itself ("before making the recommendations or deciding upon the measures provided for in Article 39"), such provisional measures are subject to the Charter limitation of Article 2, paragraph 7, and the question of their mandatory or recommendatory character is subject to great controversy; all of which renders inappropriate the classification of the International Tribunal under these measures.

34. *Prima facie*, the International Tribunal matches perfectly the description in Article 41 of "measures not involving the use of force." Appellant, however, has argued before both the Trial Chamber and this Appeals Chamber, that: ". . .[I]t is clear that the establishment of a war crimes tribunal was not intended. The examples mentioned in this article focus upon economic and political measures and do not in any way suggest judicial measures." It has also been argued that the measures contemplated under Article 41 are all measures to be undertaken by Member States, which is not the case with the establishment of the International Tribunal.

35. The first argument does not stand by its own language. Article 41 reads as follows:

The Security Council may decide what measures not involving the use of armed force are to be employed to give effect to its decisions, and it may call upon the Members of the United Nations to apply such measures. These may include complete or partial interruption of economic relations and of rail, sea, air, postal, telegraphic, radio, and other means of communication, and the severance of diplomatic relations.

It is evident that the measures set out in Article 41 are merely illustrative examples which obviously do not exclude other measures. All the Article requires is that they do not involve "the use of force." It is a negative definition.

That the examples do not suggest judicial measures goes some way towards the other argument that the Article does not contemplate institutional measures implemented directly by the United Nations through one of its organs but, as the given examples suggest, only action by Member States, such as economic sanctions (though possibly coordinated through an organ of the Organization). However, as mentioned above, nothing in the Article suggests the limitation of the measures to those implemented by States. The Article only prescribes what these measures cannot be. Beyond that it does not say or suggest what they have to be.

Moreover, even a simple literal analysis of the Article shows that the first phrase of the first sentence carries a very general prescription which can accommodate both institutional and Member State action. The second phrase can be read as referring particularly to one species of this very large category of measures referred to in the first phrase, but not necessarily the only one, namely, measures undertaken directly by States. It is also clear that the second sentence, starting with "These [measures]" not "Those [measures]," refers to the species mentioned in the second phrase rather than to the "genus" referred to in the first phrase of this sentence.

36. Logically, if the Organization can undertake measures which have to be implemented through the intermediary of its Members, it can a fortiori undertake measures which it can implement directly via its organs, if it happens to have the resources to do so. It is only for want of such resources that the United Nations has to act through its Members. But it is of the essence of "collective measures" that they are collectively undertaken. Action by Member States on behalf of the Organization is but a poor substitute *faute de mieux,* or a "second best" for want of the first. This is also the pattern of Article 42 on measures involving the use of armed force. In sum, the establishment of the International Tribunal falls squarely within the powers of the Security Council under Article 41.

Can the Security Council Establish A Subsidiary Organ With Judicial Powers?

37. The argument that the Security Council, not being endowed with judicial powers, cannot establish a subsidiary organ possessed of such powers is untenable: it results from a fundamental misunderstanding of the constitutional set-up of the Charter. Plainly, the Security Council is not a judicial organ and is not provided with judicial powers (though it may incidentally perform certain quasi-judicial

activities such as effecting determinations or findings). The principal function of the Security Council is the maintenance of international peace and security, in the discharge of which the Security Council exercises both decision-making and executive powers.

38. The establishment of the International Tribunal by the Security Council does not signify, however, that the Security Council has delegated to it some of its own functions or the exercise of some of its own powers. Nor does it mean, in reverse, that the Security Council was usurping for itself part of a judicial function which does not belong to it but to other organs of the United Nations according to the Charter. The Security Council has resorted to the establishment of a judicial organ in the form of an international criminal tribunal as an instrument for the exercise of its own principal function of maintenance of peace and security, i.e., as a measure contributing to the restoration and maintenance of peace in the former Yugoslavia. . .

Was the Establishment of the International Tribunal an Appropriate Measure?

39. The third argument is directed against the discretionary power of the Security Council in evaluating the appropriateness of the chosen measure and its effectiveness in achieving its objective, the restoration of peace. Article 39 leaves the choice of means and their evaluation to the Security Council, which enjoys wide discretionary powers in this regard; and it could not have been otherwise, as such a choice involves political evaluation of highly complex and dynamic situations. It would be a total misconception of what are the criteria of legality and validity in law to test the legality of such measures *ex post facto* by their success or failure to achieve their ends (in the present case, the restoration of peace in the former Yugoslavia, in quest of which the establishment of the International Tribunal is but one of many measures adopted by the Security Council).

40. For the aforementioned reasons, the Appeals Chamber considers that the International Tribunal has been lawfully established as a measure under Chapter VII of the Charter.

Was the Establishment of the International Tribunal Contrary to The General Principle Whereby Courts Must be "Established by Law"?

41. Appellant challenges the establishment of the International Tribunal by contending that it has not been established by law. The entitlement of an individual to have a criminal charge against him determined by a tribunal which has been established by law is provided in Article 14, paragraph 1, of the International Covenant on Civil and Political Rights. It provides: "In the determination of any criminal charge against him, or of his rights and obligations in a suit at law, everyone

shall be entitled to a fair and public hearing by a competent, independent and impartial tribunal established by law." Similar provisions can be found in Article 6(1) of the European Convention on Human Rights, which states: "In the determination of his civil rights and obligations or of any criminal charge against him, everyone is entitled to a fair and public hearing within a reasonable time by an independent and impartial tribunal established by law" . . . and in Article 8(1) of the American Convention on Human Rights, which provides: "Every person has the right to a hearing, with due guarantees and within a reasonable time, by a competent, independent and impartial tribunal, previously established by law."

Appellant argues that the right to have a criminal charge determined by a tribunal established by law is one which forms part of international law as a "general principle of law recognized by civilized nations," one of the sources of international law in Article 38 of the Statute of the International Court of Justice. In support of this assertion, Appellant emphasises the fundamental nature of the "fair trial" or "due process" guarantees afforded in the International Covenant on Civil and Political Rights, the European Convention on Human Rights and the American Convention on Human Rights. Appellant asserts that they are minimum requirements in international law for the administration of criminal justice.

42. For the reasons outlined below, Appellant has not satisfied this Chamber that the requirements laid down in these three conventions must apply not only in the context of national legal systems but also with respect to proceedings conducted before an international court. This Chamber is, however, satisfied that the principle that a tribunal must be established by law, as explained below, is a general principle of law imposing an international obligation which only applies to the administration of criminal justice in a municipal setting. It follows from this principle that it is incumbent on all States to organize their system of criminal justice in such a way as to ensure that all individuals are guaranteed the right to have a criminal charge determined by a tribunal established by law. This does not mean, however, that, by contrast, an international criminal court could be set up at the mere whim of a group of governments. Such a court ought to be rooted in the rule of law and offer all guarantees embodied in the relevant international instruments. Then the court may be said to be "established by law."

43. Indeed, there are three possible interpretations of the term "established by law." First, as Appellant argues, "established by law" could mean established by a legislature. Appellant claims that the International Tribunal is the product of a "mere executive order" and not of a "decision making process under democratic control, necessary to create a judicial organisation in a democratic society." Therefore

Appellant maintains that the International Tribunal not been "established by law." The case law applying the words "established by law" in the European Convention on Human Rights has favoured this interpretation of the expression. This case law bears out the view that the relevant provision is intended to ensure that tribunals in a democratic society must not depend on the discretion of the executive; rather they should be regulated by law emanating from Parliament. Or, put another way, the guarantee is intended to ensure that the administration of justice is not a matter of executive discretion, but is regulated by laws made by the legislature.

It is clear that the legislative, executive and judicial division of powers which is largely followed in most municipal systems does not apply to the international setting nor, more specifically, to the setting of an international organization such as the United Nations. Among the principal organs of the United Nations the divisions between judicial, executive and legislative functions are not clear cut. Regarding the judicial function, the International Court of Justice is clearly the "principal judicial organ." There is, however, no legislature, in the technical sense of the term, in the United Nations system and, more generally, no Parliament in the world community. That is to say, there exists no corporate organ formally empowered to enact laws directly binding on international legal subjects.

It is clearly impossible to classify the organs of the United Nations into the above-discussed divisions which exist in the national law of States. Indeed, Appellant has agreed that the constitutional structure of the United Nations does not follow the division of powers often found in national constitutions. Consequently the separation of powers element of the requirement that a tribunal be "established by law" finds no application in an international law setting. The aforementioned principle can only impose an obligation on States concerning the functioning of their own national systems.

44. A second possible interpretation is that the words "established by law" refer to establishment of international courts by a body which, though not a Parliament, has a limited power to take binding decisions. In our view, one such body is the Security Council when, acting under Chapter VII of the United Nations Charter, it makes decisions binding by virtue of Article 25 of the Charter. . .

NOTES & QUESTIONS

1. *Judicial Review of the Security Council?* Ultimately, the Appeals Chamber decided that the Security Council acted lawfully when it created the ICTY. In a sense, the Appeals Chamber was engaging in de facto judicial review of the Security Council, because it was evaluating the legality of the Council's actions. What authority did the Appeals Chamber have to engage

in this review? Certainly nothing in the UN Charter grants the ICTY—or any other body—the explicit authority to review Security Council resolutions for legality. In another section of its Decision, the *Tadić* Appeals Chamber concluded that it had the inherent authority to determine the lawfulness of its own creation, based on the principle of the "*la compétence de la compétence*," or jurisdiction to decide jurisdiction, which it considered to be "a necessary component in the exercise of the judicial function."

2.   *Other Ad Hoc Tribunals.* Although the ICTY and ICTR were the first ad hoc tribunals created by the Security Council, they were not the last. The Security Council created the Special Tribunal for Lebanon in 2007 when it invoked its Chapter VII authority in Resolution 1757. Initially the tribunal's design was negotiated in an agreement between Lebanon and the United Nations, but when the agreement was not submitted for ratification in Lebanon, the Security Council simply used its Chapter VII authority to create the tribunal unilaterally. Other ad hoc tribunals are sometimes called "hybrid" tribunals because their composition includes a mixture of international and domestic elements. For example, the Special Court for Sierra Leone was created by special agreement between that country and the United Nations; the Court convicted former President of Liberia Charles Taylor for crimes committed during the war. Finally, the Extraordinary Chambers of the Courts of Cambodia (ECCC) was created by special agreement with the Government of Cambodia to investigate and prosecute crimes, including genocide, committed during the rule of the Khmer Rouge regime. The ECCC includes a unique structure, with the prosecutor's office run by co-prosecutors—one domestic prosecutor selected by the Cambodian government and an international prosecutor selected by the United Nations.

2.   THE INTERNATIONAL CRIMINAL COURT

In contrast to the ICTY and ICTR, which were created by the Security Council as official organs of the UN, the ICC is a treaty-based court created by the Rome Statute, which was signed in 1998 and entered into force in 2002. The ICC currently has 123 states as members, giving it wide representation across the globe, although several major military powers are not members: China, Russia, the United States, Israel, India, and Pakistan.

The ICC's jurisdiction is far from universal. In order for it to exercise jurisdiction in a case, one of the following circumstances, outlined in article 13 of the Rome Statute, must apply:

a)   A referral from a state party, provided that the crime either occurred on the territory of a state party or the accused is a national of a state party.

b)   The ICC prosecutor initiates an investigation on his or her own authority, provided that the crime either occurred on the territory of a state party or the accused is a national of a state party.

c) The situation is referred to the ICC Prosecutor by the UN Security Council acting under its Chapter VII authority under the UN Charter.

Taken together, these jurisdictional "pathways" substantially limit the ability of the ICC to exercise its jurisdiction when crimes occur on the territory of states that refuse to accept the court's jurisdiction. The notable exception is the case of a Security Council referral—which harnesses the Security Council's power to coercively impose jurisdiction on non-consenting states when required by the demands of international peace and security. However, Security Council referrals are relatively rare, with the only examples being the situation in Darfur, Sudan (2005), and the situation in Libya (2011). In those situations, the ICC referral follows a similar pathway as the creation of the ICTY and the ICTR—a determination by the Security Council that criminal investigation and prosecution is necessary for international peace and security.

There are other constraints on the ICC's exercise of jurisdiction—most notably the principle of complementarity. This principle, which is codified in article 17 of the Rome Statute, entails that the ICC's jurisdiction is designed to "complement" the jurisdiction of national criminal courts. In plainer terms, the ICC is designed to be a jurisdictional gap-filler. If a domestic court is willing and able to investigate and prosecute (if warranted) the offences in question, the domestic court retains primary jurisdiction.

After the Libyan revolution (and civil war) in 2011, the Security Council referred the situation to the ICC Prosecutor, who applied for arrest warrants against several individuals, including Saif Gaddafi (the son of deposed dictator Colonel Gaddafi). Libya objected to the ICC's jurisdiction on complementarity grounds, arguing that the case should be handled in Libyan criminal court. Ironically, Saif Gaddafi's lawyers argued in favor of the ICC exercising jurisdiction, presumably because ICC does not use capital punishment, whereas their client faced execution if he went on trial in Libya.

In the following case, an ICC Pre-Trial Chamber evaluated the evidence and decided whether the Libyan government was willing and able to prosecute the case, or whether it should proceed in The Hague at the ICC.

Prosecutor v. Gaddafi

International Criminal Court
Pre-Trial Chamber I
May 31, 2013

1.   On 26 February 2011, the United Nations Security Council ("Security Council") adopted Resolution 1970, whereby it referred to the Prosecutor of the Court the situation in Libya since 15 February 2011.

2.   On 27 June 2011, the Chamber issued the Warrant of Arrest for Saif Al-Islam Gaddafi (the "Warrant of Arrest"), having found reasonable grounds to believe that he is criminally responsible under article 25(3)(a) of the Statute for the commission of crimes against humanity of murder and persecution in various locations of the Libyan territory, in particular in Benghazi, Misrata, Tripoli and other neighbouring cities, from 15 February 2011 until at least 28 February 2011 in violation of articles 7(1)(a) and (h) of the Statute.

3.   On 1 May 2012, Libya filed a challenge to the admissibility of the case against Mr Gaddafi (the "Admissibility Challenge") and requested that the Chamber postpone the execution of the surrender request pursuant to article 95 of the Statute. Libya subsequently filed perfected translations of the annexes to its Admissibility Challenge and a compilation of the relevant provisions of Libyan law referred to in the Admissibility Challenge.

25.   Libya challenges the admissibility of the case on the basis that its national judicial system is actively investigating Mr Gaddafi for his alleged criminal responsibility for multiple acts of murder and persecution, committed pursuant to or in furtherance of a state policy, amounting to crimes against humanity.

26.   Libya submits that investigations into Mr Gaddafi's alleged criminal conduct began on the date of his capture, 23 November 2011, in particular with respect to financial crimes and corruption. A decision was taken on 17 December 2011 to extend this investigation to include crimes against the person under Libyan law. On 8 January 2012, the Prosecutor-General commenced an investigation against Mr Gaddafi for serious crimes (including murder and rape) allegedly committed by Mr Gaddafi during the revolution (including in the period between 15 February to 28 February 2011).

27.   Libya contends that very substantial resources were deployed to interview witnesses and gather other evidence and sets out the further investigative steps that it intends to take in the future. Once the final step of interviewing Mr Gaddafi to confirm his identity and confront him with the allegations against him has been completed, the case could move onto the accusation stage of proceedings and later to trial.

28. At the time of the filing of the Admissibility Challenge, Libya envisaged that the likely charges against Mr Gaddafi would be: intentional murder; torture; incitement to civil war; indiscriminate killings; misuse of authority against individuals; arresting people without just cause; and the unjustified deprivation of personal liberty pursuant to articles 368, 435, 293, 296, 431, 433, 434 of the Libyan Criminal Code. It affirmed that the National Transitional Council was considering the adoption of a draft law incorporating international crimes, modes of responsibility and penalties under the Statute.

58. The Chamber notes that the Appeals Chamber has stated that article 17(1)(a) of the Statute contemplates a two-step test, according to which the Chamber, in considering an admissibility challenge, shall address in turn two questions: (i) whether, at the time of the proceedings in respect of an admissibility challenge, there is an ongoing investigation or prosecution of the case at the national level; and, in case the answer to the first question is in the affirmative, (ii) whether the State is unwilling or unable genuinely to carry out such investigation or prosecution.

73. As recalled above, the first analysis that the Chamber is required to undertake is to determine whether the Libyan and the ICC investigations cover the same case. Accordingly, the evidence presented in support of the Admissibility Challenge must demonstrate that the Libyan authorities are taking concrete and progressive investigative steps in relation to such "case."

74. In the *Lubanga* case, Pre-Trial Chamber I found for the first time that for a case to be inadmissible before the Court, national proceedings must "encompass both the person and the conduct which is the subject of the case before the Court." This test later became the settled jurisprudence of the Pre-Trial Chambers.

75. Pre-Trial Chambers have also indicated that a case encompasses "specific incidents during which one or more crimes within the jurisdiction of the Court seem to have been committed by one or more identified suspects," without clarifying, however, what would be encompassed by the notion of "incident."

76. The Appeals Chamber endorsed the Pre-Trial Chambers' approach with respect to the specific nature of the admissibility test when it found that "article 19 of the Statute relates to the admissibility of concrete cases" and that "the defining elements of a concrete case before the Court are the individual and the alleged conduct." Thus, the validity of the "same person/same conduct" test has been confirmed by the Appeals Chamber. However, rather than referring to "incidents," the Appeals Chamber referred to the conduct "as alleged in the proceedings before the Court." In addition, the Appeals Chamber has stated that the

investigation or prosecution must cover "substantially" the same conduct: "[T]he defining elements of a concrete case before the Court are the individual and the alleged conduct. It follows that for such a case to be inadmissible under article 17(1)(a) of the Statute, the national investigation must cover the same individual and substantially the same conduct as alleged in the proceedings before the Court."

77. The Chamber considers that the determination of what is "substantially the same conduct as alleged in the proceedings before the Court" will vary according to the concrete facts and circumstances of the case and, therefore, requires a case-by-case analysis.

78. In the case at hand, the conduct allegedly under investigation by Libya must be compared to the conduct attributed to Mr Gaddafi in the Warrant of Arrest issued against him by the Chamber, as well as in the Chamber's decision on the Prosecutor's application for the warrant of arrest.

79. In the Warrant of Arrest, the Chamber found reasonable grounds to believe that: Saif Al-Islam Gaddafi is criminally responsible as an indirect co-perpetrator, under article 25(3)(a) of the Statute, for the following crimes committed by Security Forces under his control in various localities of the Libyan territory, in particular in Benghazi, Misrata, Tripoli and other neighboring cities, from 15 February 2011 until at least 28 February 2011: i) murder as a crime against humanity, within the meaning of article 7(1)(a) of the Statute; and ii) persecution as a crime against humanity, within the meaning of article 7(1)(h) of the Statute.

80. The Warrant of Arrest does not refer to specific instances of killings and acts of persecution, but rather refers to acts of such a nature resulting from Mr Gaddafi's use of the Libyan Security Forces to target the civilian population which was demonstrating against Gaddafi's regime or those perceived to be dissidents to the regime.

81. Conversely, the Article 58 Decision includes a long, non-exhaustive list of alleged acts of murder and persecution committed against an identified category of people within certain temporal and geographical parameters, on the basis of which the Chamber was satisfied that throughout Libya—in particular in Tripoli, Misrata, Benghazi, Al-Bayda, Dema, Tobruk and Ajdabiya—killings and inhuman acts amounting to persecution on political grounds were committed by the Security Forces from 15 February 2011 until at least 28 February 2011 as part of an attack against the civilian demonstrators and/or perceived dissidents to Gaddafi's regime.

82. The Chamber notes that the events expressly mentioned in the Article 58 Decision do not represent unique manifestations of the form of criminality alleged against Mr Gaddafi in the proceedings before the

Court. They constitute rather samples of a course of conduct of the Security Forces, under Mr Gaddafi's control, that allegedly carried out an attack committed across Libya from 15 February 2011 onwards against the civilians who were dissidents or perceived dissidents to Gaddafi's regime, which resulted in an unspecified number of killings and acts of persecution.

83. Therefore, in the circumstances of the case at hand and bearing in mind the purpose of the complementarity principle, the Chamber considers that it would not be appropriate to expect Libya's investigation to cover exactly the same acts of murder and persecution mentioned in the Article 58 Decision as constituting instances of Mr Gaddafi's alleged course of conduct. Instead, the Chamber will assess, on the basis of the evidence provided by Libya, whether the alleged domestic investigation addresses the same conduct underlying the Warrant of Arrest and Article 58 Decision, namely that: Mr Gaddafi used his control over relevant parts of the Libyan State apparatus and Security Forces to deter and quell, by any means, including by the use of lethal force, the demonstrations of civilians, which started in February 2011 against Muammar Gaddafi's regime; in particular, that Mr Gaddafi activated the Security Forces under his control to kill and persecute hundreds of civilian demonstrators or alleged dissidents to Muammar Gaddafi's regime, across Libya, in particular in Benghazi, Misrata, Tripoli and other neighbouring cities, from 15 February 2011 to at least 28 February 2011.

84. The Chamber notes that a draft bill incorporating international crimes at the time of the current admissibility decision has not yet been adopted by Libya.

85. The Chamber is of the view that the assessment of domestic proceedings should focus on the alleged conduct and not its legal characterisation. The question of whether domestic investigations are carried out with a view to prosecuting "international crimes" is not determinative of an admissibility challenge.

86. The Chamber notes that the Statute does not make a distinction between ordinary and international crimes. Article 20(3) of the Statute allows for a successful ne bis in idem challenge whenever a person "has been tried by another court for conduct also proscribed by article 6, 7, 8 or 8 bis." In contrast to similar provisions in the Statutes of the International Criminal Tribunal for the Former Yugoslavia (the "ICTY") and the International Criminal Tribunal for Rwanda (the "ICTR"), article 20(3) of the Statute does not require the same legal characterisation of the crime in order to satisfy the ne bis in idem principle.

87. The *travaux préparatoires* demonstrate that the decision to depart from the language of the ICTY and ICTR Statutes and to exclude reference to the ordinary crimes exception was a deliberate decision that

followed extensive discussions during the negotiating process. The reference to ordinary crimes met a considerable amount of resistance and the concept was finally excluded from the Draft Statute in 1998.

88. It follows that a domestic investigation or prosecution for "ordinary crimes," to the extent that the case covers the same conduct, shall be considered sufficient. It is the Chamber's view that Libya's current lack of legislation criminalising crimes against humanity does not per se render the case admissible before the Court.

134. On the basis of the materials placed before it, the Chamber is not persuaded that the evidence presented sufficiently demonstrates that Libya is investigating the same case as that before the Court. As found above, the Chamber is satisfied that some items of evidence show that a number of investigative steps have been taken by Libya with respect to certain discrete aspects that arguably relate to the conduct of Mr Gaddafi as alleged in the proceedings before the Court. These aspects include instances of mobilisation of militias and equipment by air, the assembly and the mobilization of military forces at the Abraq Airport, certain events in Benghazi on 17 February 2011, and the arrest of journalists and activists against the Gaddafi regime.

135. Nevertheless, the evidence, taken as a whole, does not allow the Chamber to discern the actual contours of the national case against Mr Gaddafi such that the scope of the domestic investigation could be said to cover the same case as that set out in the Warrant of Arrest issued by the Court. Libya has fallen short of substantiating, by means of evidence of a sufficient degree of specificity and probative value, the submission that the domestic investigation covers the same case that is before the Court.

Willingness or Ability Genuinely to Investigate and Prosecute

138. The Chamber received submissions related to the second limb of the admissibility analysis. In relation to the issue of "inability," in light of the initial submissions and evidence received, the Chamber raised a number of additional specific questions in order to ascertain the ability of Libya genuinely to investigate and prosecute the case at hand. Given that, as explained below, Libya is found to be unable genuinely to carry out the investigation or prosecution against Mr Gaddafi the Chamber will not address the alternative requirement of "willingness."

204. Having considered the responses and evidence received, the Chamber takes note of the efforts deployed by Libya under extremely difficult circumstances to improve security conditions, rebuild institutions and restore the rule of law. In this regard, it takes note, in particular, of the Libyan submissions on specific measures of assistance received from national governments and regional and international organizations to enhance capacity, inter alia, with respect to transitional

justice. The Chamber emphasises the relevance of specific submissions related to progress made, as well as those regarding the proposed strategy to improve the effectiveness and accountability of the police service, the security for the courts and participants in the proceedings, to reform the detention centres and to bring practices of torture to an end.

205. Without prejudice to these achievements, it is apparent from the submissions that multiple challenges remain and that Libya continues to face substantial difficulties in exercising its judicial powers fully across the entire territory. Due to these difficulties, which are further explained below, the Chamber is of the view that its national system cannot yet be applied in full in areas or aspects relevant to the case, being thus "unavailable" within the terms of article 17(3) of the Statute. As a consequence, Libya is "unable to obtain the accused" and the necessary testimony and is also "otherwise unable to carry out [the] proceedings" in the case against Mr Gaddafi in compliance with its national laws, in accordance with the same provision.

206. The Chamber notes that Libya has not yet been able to secure the transfer of Mr Gaddafi from his place of detention under the custody of the Zintan militia into State authority. In response to a specific request for clarification from the Chamber, the Libyan representatives indicated that "[e]fforts to arrange Mr. Gaddafi's transfer to a detention facility in Tripoli where other Gaddafi-era officials are presently held are still ongoing." Libya subsequently reiterated that efforts to arrange Mr Gaddafi's transfer to detention in Tripoli are ongoing and that it will shortly begin implementation of its recently devised proposal to train members of the Zintan brigade so that they may form part of the judicial police who will be responsible for guarding Mr Gaddafi upon his transfer to Tripoli. It estimated that the transfer will take place "before the earliest possible estimated commencement date of the trial in May 2013" and that the national security proceedings in Zintan will also be transferred to the Tripoli court at this point if they proceed to trial.

207. The Chamber has no doubt that the central Government is deploying all efforts to obtain Mr Gaddafi's transfer but, in spite of Libya's recent assurances, no concrete progress to this effect has been shown since the date of his apprehension on 19 November 2011. The Chamber is not persuaded that this problem may be resolved in the near future and no evidence has been produced in support of that contention.

208. The Chamber notes the submissions of Libya that in absentia trials are not permitted under Libyan law when the accused is present on Libyan territory and his location is known to the authorities. As a result, without the transfer of Mr Gaddafi into the control of the central authorities, the trial cannot take place.

NOTES & QUESTIONS

Positive Complementarity. Recently, international lawyers have started talking of "positive complementarity." This seemingly paradoxical notion suggests that the ICC has an important role to play even in cases when complementarity bars it from exercising jurisdiction. Consider the following train of thought: A state is faced with a situation where international crimes occurred on its territory. However, the state is hostile to the idea of an outside institution (the ICC) taking over the case because it would involve an infringement of the state's sovereignty. Consequently, the state pours more effort and resources into its judicial process, ensuring that it can conduct a credible criminal investigation that will satisfy the ICC Prosecutor and an ICC Pre-Trial Chamber. In that case, if the ICC never succeeds in gaining jurisdiction because the domestic system engages in an independent and impartial effort, should that be counted as a defeat for the ICC or a victory? In the end, this seems like a victory for justice, even though the ICC does not prosecute the crimes. For more discussion of positive complementarity, see Sarah M. H. Nouwen, *Complementarity in the Line of Fire* 97 (2013).

B. CRIMES

What crimes may an international tribunal prosecute? Although plenty of crimes have an international or transnational dimension (including drug smuggling and money laundering), international tribunals invariably prosecute a limited menu of international offenses. A few tribunals have jurisdiction over domestic offenses as well. For example, the Special Tribunal for Lebanon has jurisdiction not only over international offenses but also violations of Lebanese criminal law. However, with regard to the most active international tribunals such as the ICC, ICTY, and ICTR, their dockets are dominated by accusations of war crimes, crimes against humanity, and genocide. The ICC recently acquired jurisdiction over a fourth crime—aggression—which will be explored last in this section.

When scholars refer to the "core" international crimes, they are usually referring to war crimes, crimes against humanity, and genocide. (Aggression is a distinctive crime because it resides at the interplay of individual action and a state's violation of the international rules regarding the use of force.) These crimes all share a distinct conceptual structure. First, in order for the crime to apply, the defendant must have committed any one of a long list of predicate criminal acts, such as a killing, rape or torture. The exact list of relevant predicate acts changes depending on the crime. Then, the defendant's conduct must also satisfy larger "chapeau" elements. To take just one example, the crime of genocide includes a chapeau element that the defendant acted with "genocidal intent," which will be explained below. In order to satisfy its burden, then, the prosecution must prove that the defendant committed one or more of the predicate acts and did so with genocidal intent, and any other chapeau-level requirements.

The sub-sections that follow will focus on the distinct chapeau elements that apply to each of the core international crimes, and difficulties in interpretation and application that arise from them. But one should never forget that in addition to satisfying the chapeau elements, the prosecution must demonstrate that the defendant committed at least one predicate act, including the legal elements associated with that predicate. In order to determine which acts qualify as predicate acts, one should consult the ICTY and ICTR statutes, the Rome Statute of the ICC, as well as an ICC document called the "Elements of Crimes."

1. WAR CRIMES

The first chapeau element for war crimes is the existence of an armed conflict. Put simply, there are no war crimes without there first being a war. The legal standards for the existence of an armed conflict were first analyzed in the prior chapter on International Humanitarian Law (IHL). According to one widely accepted articulation of the relevant criteria, the ICTY's decision in the *Tadić* case, an armed conflict exists when there is: (i) any recourse to military force between two states; or ii) sustained hostilities between a state and a non-state actor, or between two non-state actors, that rises to a sufficient level of scope and intensity. Traditionally, these armed conflicts have been distinguished as International Armed Conflicts (IACs) and Non-International Armed Conflicts (NIACs). In the absence of this chapeau requirement, the killings would simply be violations of domestic criminal law, rather than a war crime. (However, crimes against humanity and genocide do not require a nexus to an armed conflict, so the killings might constitute an international crime if they meet the legal standard for these offenses.)

In terms of specific war crimes, they are all violations of IHL that are sufficiently grave that they generate individual criminal responsibility, i.e., soldiers or commanders can go to prison for violating them, rather than responsibility simply attaching to the state. Examples of IHL that constitute war crimes include executing prisoners of war, intentionally targeting civilians, or causing disproportionate collateral damage to civilians.

There is a long history of war crimes committed and prosecuted during international armed conflicts. But in another section of the *Tadić* decision, the ICTY was forced to inquire whether war crimes can be committed in non-international conflicts, e.g. the civil wars in the former Yugoslavia, and whether the ICTY's statute granted it jurisdiction to prosecute offenses committed during *internal* conflicts. As you read the following opinion, identify the methodology that the tribunal used to answer this question.

Prosecutor v. Dusko Tadić

International Criminal Tribunal for the Former Yugoslavia
Decision on the Defense Motion for Interlocutory Appeal on Jurisdiction
October 2, 1995

B.   Does the Statute Refer only to
International Armed Conflicts?

1.   Literal Interpretation of the Statute

71. On the face of it, some provisions of the Statute are unclear as to whether they apply to offences occurring in international armed conflicts only, or to those perpetrated in internal armed conflicts as well. Article 2 refers to "grave breaches" of the Geneva Conventions of 1949, which are widely understood to be committed only in international armed conflicts, so the reference in Article 2 would seem to suggest that the Article is limited to international armed conflicts. Article 3 also lacks any express reference to the nature of the underlying conflict required. A literal reading of this provision standing alone may lead one to believe that it applies to both kinds of conflict. By contrast, Article 5 explicitly confers jurisdiction over crimes committed in either internal or international armed conflicts. An argument *a contrario* based on the absence of a similar provision in Article 3 might suggest that Article 3 applies only to one class of conflict rather than to both of them. In order better to ascertain the meaning and scope of these provisions, the Appeals Chamber will therefore consider the object and purpose behind the enactment of the Statute.

2.   Teleological Interpretation of the Statute

72. In adopting resolution 827, the Security Council established the International Tribunal with the stated purpose of bringing to justice persons responsible for serious violations of international humanitarian law in the former Yugoslavia, thereby deterring future violations and contributing to the re-establishment of peace and security in the region. The context in which the Security Council acted indicates that it intended to achieve this purpose without reference to whether the conflicts in the former Yugoslavia were internal or international.

As the members of the Security Council well knew, in 1993, when the Statute was drafted, the conflicts in the former Yugoslavia could have been characterized as both internal and international, or alternatively, as an internal conflict alongside an international one, or as an internal conflict that had become internationalized because of external support, or as an international conflict that had subsequently been replaced by one or more internal conflicts, or some combination thereof. The conflict in the former Yugoslavia had been rendered international by the involvement of the Croatian Army in Bosnia-Herzegovina and by the involvement of the Yugoslav National Army ("JNA") in hostilities in Croatia, as well as in Bosnia-Herzegovina at least until its formal withdrawal on 19 May 1992. To the extent that the conflicts had been limited to clashes between Bosnian Government forces and Bosnian Serb rebel forces in Bosnia-Herzegovina, as well as between the Croatian Government and Croatian Serb rebel forces in Krajina (Croatia), they had been internal (unless direct involvement of the Federal Republic of Yugoslavia (Serbia-Montenegro) could be proven). It is notable that the parties to this case also agree that the conflicts in the former Yugoslavia since 1991 have had both internal and international aspects.

73. The varying nature of the conflicts is evidenced by the agreements reached by various parties to abide by certain rules of humanitarian law. Reflecting the international aspects of the conflicts, on 27 November 1991 representatives of the Federal Republic of Yugoslavia, the Yugoslavia Peoples' Army, the Republic of Croatia, and the Republic of Serbia entered into an agreement on the implementation of the Geneva Conventions of 1949 and the 1977 Additional Protocol I to those Conventions. Significantly, the parties refrained from making any mention of common Article 3 of the Geneva Conventions, concerning non-international armed conflicts.

By contrast, an agreement reached on 22 May 1992 between the various factions of the conflict within the Republic of Bosnia and Herzegovina reflects the internal aspects of the conflicts. The agreement was based on common Article 3 of the Geneva Conventions which, in addition to setting forth rules governing internal conflicts, provides in paragraph 3 that the parties to such conflicts may agree to bring into force provisions of the Geneva Conventions that are generally applicable only in international armed conflicts. In the Agreement, the representatives of Mr. Alija Izetbegovic (President of the Republic of Bosnia and Herzegovina and the Party of Democratic Action), Mr. Radovan Karadzic (President of the Serbian Democratic Party), and Mr. Miljenko Brkic (President of the Croatian Democratic Community) committed the parties to abide by the substantive rules of internal armed conflict contained in common Article 3 and in addition agreed, on the strength of common Article 3, paragraph 3, to apply certain provisions of the Geneva Conventions concerning international conflicts. Clearly, this Agreement shows that the parties concerned regarded the armed conflicts in which they were involved as internal but, in view of their magnitude, they agreed to extend to them the application of some provisions of the Geneva Conventions that are normally applicable in international armed conflicts only. The same position was implicitly taken by the International Committee of the Red Cross ("ICRC"), at whose invitation and under whose auspices the agreement was reached. In this connection it should be noted that, had the ICRC not believed that the conflicts governed by the agreement at issue were internal, it would have acted blatantly contrary to a common provision of the four Geneva Conventions (Article 6/6/6/7). This is a provision formally banning any agreement designed to restrict the application of the Geneva Conventions in case of international armed conflicts. If the conflicts were, in fact, viewed as international, for the ICRC to accept that they would be governed only by common Article 3, plus the provisions contained in Article 2, paragraphs 1 to 6, of Agreement No. 1, would have constituted clear disregard of the aforementioned Geneva provisions. On account of the unanimously recognized authority, competence and impartiality of the ICRC, as well as its statutory mission to promote and supervise respect for international humanitarian law, it is inconceivable that, even if there were some doubt as to the nature of the conflict, the ICRC would promote and endorse an agreement contrary to a basic provision of the Geneva Conventions. The conclusion is therefore warranted that the ICRC regarded the conflicts governed by the agreement in question as internal.

Taken together, the agreements reached between the various parties to the conflict(s) in the former Yugoslavia bear out the proposition that, when the Security Council adopted the Statute of the International Tribunal in 1993, it did so with reference to situations that the parties themselves considered at different times and places as either internal or international armed conflicts, or as a mixed internal-international conflict.

74. The Security Council's many statements leading up to the establishment of the International Tribunal reflect an awareness of the mixed character of the conflicts. On the one hand, prior to creating the International Tribunal, the Security Council adopted several resolutions condemning the presence of JNA forces in Bosnia-Herzegovina and Croatia as a violation of the sovereignty of these latter States. On the other hand, in none of these many resolutions did the Security Council explicitly state that the conflicts were international.

In each of its successive resolutions, the Security Council focused on the practices with which it was concerned, without reference to the nature of the conflict. For example, in resolution 771 of 13 August 1992, the Security Council expressed "grave alarm" at the

> [c]ontinuing reports of widespread violations of international humanitarian law occurring within the territory of the former Yugoslavia and especially in Bosnia and Herzegovina including reports of mass forcible expulsion and deportation of civilians, imprisonment and abuse of civilians in detention centres, deliberate attacks on non-combatants, hospitals and

ambulances, impeding the delivery of food and medical supplies to the civilian population, and wanton devastation and destruction of property.

As with every other Security Council statement on the subject, this resolution makes no mention of the nature of the armed conflict at issue. The Security Council was clearly preoccupied with bringing to justice those responsible for these specifically condemned acts, regardless of context. The Prosecutor makes much of the Security Council's repeated reference to the grave breaches provisions of the Geneva Conventions, which are generally deemed applicable only to international armed conflicts. This argument ignores, however, that, as often as the Security Council has invoked the grave breaches provisions, it has also referred generally to "other violations of international humanitarian law," an expression which covers the law applicable in internal armed conflicts as well.

75. The intent of the Security Council to promote a peaceful solution of the conflict without pronouncing upon the question of its international or internal nature is reflected by the Report of the Secretary-General of 3 May 1993 and by statements of Security Council members regarding their interpretation of the Statute. The Report of the Secretary-General explicitly states that the clause of the Statute concerning the temporal jurisdiction of the International Tribunal was "clearly intended to convey the notion that no judgement as to the international or internal character of the conflict was being exercised."

In a similar vein, at the meeting at which the Security Council adopted the Statute, three members indicated their understanding that the jurisdiction of the International Tribunal under Article 3, with respect to laws or customs of war, included any humanitarian law agreement in force in the former Yugoslavia. As an example of such supplementary agreements, the United States cited the rules on internal armed conflict contained in Article 3 of the Geneva Conventions as well as "the 1977 Additional Protocols to these [Geneva] Conventions [of 1949]." This reference clearly embraces Additional Protocol II of 1977, relating to internal armed conflict. No other State contradicted this interpretation, which clearly reflects an understanding of the conflict as both internal and international (it should be emphasized that the United States representative, before setting out the American views on the interpretation of the Statute of the International Tribunal, pointed out: "[W]e understand that other members of the [Security] Council share our view regarding the following clarifications related to the Statute."

76. That the Security Council purposely refrained from classifying the armed conflicts in the former Yugoslavia as either international or internal and, in particular, did not intend to bind the International Tribunal by a classification of the conflicts as international, is borne out

by a *reductio ad absurdum* argument. If the Security Council had categorized the conflict as exclusively international and, in addition, had decided to bind the International Tribunal thereby, it would follow that the International Tribunal would have to consider the conflict between Bosnian Serbs and the central authorities of Bosnia-Herzegovina as international. Since it cannot be contended that the Bosnian Serbs constitute a State, arguably the classification just referred to would be based on the implicit assumption that the Bosnian Serbs are acting not as a rebellious entity but as organs or agents of another State, the Federal Republic of Yugoslavia (Serbia-Montenegro). As a consequence, serious infringements of international humanitarian law committed by the government army of Bosnia-Herzegovina against Bosnian Serbian civilians in their power would not be regarded as "grave breaches," because such civilians, having the nationality of Bosnia-Herzegovina, would not be regarded as "protected persons" under Article 4, paragraph 1 of Geneva Convention IV. By contrast, atrocities committed by Bosnian Serbs against Bosnian civilians in their hands would be regarded as "grave breaches," because such civilians would be "protected persons" under the Convention, in that the Bosnian Serbs would be acting as organs or agents of another State, the Federal Republic of Yugoslavia (Serbia-Montenegro) of which the Bosnians would not possess the nationality. This would be, of course, an absurd outcome, in that it would place the Bosnian Serbs at a substantial legal disadvantage *vis-à-vis* the central authorities of Bosnia-Herzegovina. This absurdity bears out the fallacy of the argument advanced by the Prosecutor before the Appeals Chamber.

77. On the basis of the foregoing, we conclude that the conflicts in the former Yugoslavia have both internal and international aspects, that the members of the Security Council clearly had both aspects of the conflicts in mind when they adopted the Statute of the International Tribunal, and that they intended to empower the International Tribunal to adjudicate violations of humanitarian law that occurred in either context. To the extent possible under existing international law, the Statute should therefore be construed to give effect to that purpose.

78. With the exception of Article 5 dealing with crimes against humanity, none of the statutory provisions makes explicit reference to the type of conflict as an element of the crime; and, as will be shown below, the reference in Article 5 is made to distinguish the nexus required by the Statute from the nexus required by Article 6 of the London Agreement of 8 August 1945 establishing the International Military Tribunal at Nuremberg. Since customary international law no longer requires any nexus between crimes against humanity and armed conflict, Article 5 was intended to reintroduce this nexus for the purposes of this Tribunal. As previously noted, although Article 2 does not explicitly refer

to the nature of the conflicts, its reference to the grave breaches provisions suggest that it is limited to international armed conflicts. It would however defeat the Security Council's purpose to read a similar international armed conflict requirement into the remaining jurisdictional provisions of the Statute. Contrary to the drafters' apparent indifference to the nature of the underlying conflicts, such an interpretation would authorize the International Tribunal to prosecute and punish certain conduct in an international armed conflict, while turning a blind eye to the very same conduct in an internal armed conflict. To illustrate, the Security Council has repeatedly condemned the wanton devastation and destruction of property, which is explicitly punishable only under Articles 2 and 3 of the Statute. Appellant maintains that these Articles apply only to international armed conflicts. However, it would have been illogical for the drafters of the Statute to confer on the International Tribunal the competence to adjudicate the very conduct about which they were concerned, only in the event that the context was an international conflict, when they knew that the conflicts at issue in the former Yugoslavia could have been classified, at varying times and places, as internal, international, or both.

Thus, the Security Council's object in enacting the Statute—to prosecute and punish persons responsible for certain condemned acts being committed in a conflict understood to contain both internal and international aspects—suggests that the Security Council intended that, to the extent possible, the subject-matter jurisdiction of the International Tribunal should extend to both internal and international armed conflicts.

In light of this understanding of the Security Council's purpose in creating the International Tribunal, we turn below to discussion of Appellant's specific arguments regarding the scope of the jurisdiction of the International Tribunal under Articles 2, 3 and 5 of the Statute.

91. Article 3 thus confers on the International Tribunal jurisdiction over any serious offence against international humanitarian law not covered by Article 2, 4 or 5. Article 3 is a fundamental provision laying down that any "serious violation of international humanitarian law" must be prosecuted by the International Tribunal. In other words, Article 3 functions as a residual clause designed to ensure that no serious violation of international humanitarian law is taken away from the jurisdiction of the International Tribunal. Article 3 aims to make such jurisdiction watertight and inescapable.

92. This construction of Article 3 is also corroborated by the object and purpose of the provision. When it decided to establish the International Tribunal, the Security Council did so to put a stop to all serious violations of international humanitarian law occurring in the former Yugoslavia and not only special classes of them, namely "grave

breaches" of the Geneva Conventions or violations of the "Hague law." Thus, if correctly interpreted, Article 3 fully realizes the primary purpose of the establishment of the International Tribunal, that is, not to leave unpunished any person guilty of any such serious violation, whatever the context within which it may have been committed.

2. CRIMES AGAINST HUMANITY

According to article 7 of the Rome Statute, crimes against humanity involve the commission of a predicate act "committed as part of a widespread or systematic attack directed against any civilian population, with knowledge of the attack." The relevant predicate acts include murder, extermination, enslavement, deportation, torture, rape and sexual violence, persecution, enforced disappearances, apartheid, and other "inhumane acts of a similar character intentionally causing great suffering."

The key chapeau elements are the requirement that the crime be directed against civilians (as opposed to combatants), pursuant to a state or organizational plan or policy, and be widespread or systematic. In the following case, an ICC Pre-Trial Chamber must decide whether election-related violence in Kenya was widespread or systematic, and also whether it was committed pursuant to an organizational plan or policy. As you read this decision, look for the types of evidence that the chamber scrutinized to evaluate the plan or policy requirement.

Situation in the Republic of Kenya
International Criminal Court Pre-Trial Chamber II
March 31, 2010

77. Article 7(1) of the Statute describes the contextual elements of crimes against humanity as follows: " 'crimes against humanity' means any of the following acts when committed as part of a widespread or systematic attack directed against any civilian population, with knowledge of the attack."

78. Article 7(2)(a) of the Statute further indicates that: " '[a]ttack directed against any civilian population' means a course of conduct involving the multiple commission of acts referred to in paragraph 1 against any civilian population, pursuant to or in furtherance of a State or organizational policy to commit such attack."

79. The Chamber observes that the following requirements can be distinguished: (i) an attack directed against any civilian population, (ii) a State or organizational policy, (iii) the widespread or systematic nature of the attack, (iv) a nexus between the individual act and the attack, and (v) knowledge of the attack. In light of the nature of the current stage of the proceedings, bearing in mind that there is presently no suspect before

the Court, the Chamber considers that the last requirement cannot be adequately addressed at this stage, as knowledge is an aspect of the mental element under article 30(3) of the Statute. Therefore, the Chamber's analysis will be limited to the first four enumerated requirements.

An attack directed against any civilian population

80. The meaning of the term "attack," although not addressed in the Statute, is clarified by the Elements of Crimes, which state that, for the purposes of article 7(1) of the Statute, an attack is not restricted to a "military attack." Instead, the term refers to "a campaign or operation carried out against the civilian population." As provided for in article 7(2)(a) of the Statute, an attack consists of a course of conduct involving the multiple commission of acts referred to in article 7(1).

81. Moreover, the chapeau of article 7(1) of the Statute defines crimes against humanity as any of the acts specified therein, when committed as part of an attack "directed against any civilian population." The Chamber considers that the potential civilian victims of a crime under article 7 of the Statute are groups distinguished by nationality, ethnicity or other distinguishing features. The Prosecutor will need to demonstrate, to the standard of proof applicable, that the attack was directed against the civilian population as a whole and not merely against randomly selected individuals.

82. The Chamber need not be satisfied that the entire civilian population of the geographical area in question was being targeted. However, the civilian population must be the primary object of the attack in question and cannot merely be an incidental victim. The term "civilian population" refers to persons who are civilians, as opposed to members of armed forces and other legitimate combatants.

State or organizational policy

83. Further, article 7(2)(a) of the Statute imposes the additional requirement that the attack against any civilian population be committed "pursuant to or in furtherance of a State or organizational policy to commit such attack." The Elements of Crimes offer further clarification in paragraph 3, in fine, of the Introduction to Crimes against humanity, where it is stated that:

> [i]t is understood that "policy to commit such an attack" requires that the State or organization actively promote or encourage such an attack against a civilian population;

and in footnote 6 of the same Introduction to Crimes against Humanity, where it is stated that:

> [a] policy which has a civilian population as the object of the attack would be implemented by State or organizational action.

Such a policy may, in exceptional circumstances, be implemented by a deliberate failure to take action, which is consciously aimed at encouraging such attack. The existence of such a policy cannot be inferred solely from the absence of governmental or organizational action.

84.   The Chamber notes that the Statute does not provide definitions of the terms "policy" or "State or organizational." However, both this Chamber and Pre-Trial Chamber I have addressed the policy requirement in previous decisions. In the case against *Katanga and Ngudjolo Chui*, Pre-Trial Chamber I found that this requirement:

> . . .ensures that the attack, even if carried out over a large geographical area or directed against a large number of victims, must still be thoroughly organised and follow a regular pattern. It must also be conducted in furtherance of a common policy involving public or private resources. Such a policy may be made either by groups of persons who govern a specific territory or by any organisation with the capability to commit a widespread or systematic attack against a civilian population. The policy need not be explicitly defined by the organisational group. Indeed, an attack which is planned, directed or organized—as opposed to spontaneous or isolated acts of violence—will satisfy this criterion.

85.   In the "Decision Pursuant to Article 61(7)(a) and (b) of the Rome Statute on the Charges of the Prosecutor Against Jean-Pierre Bemba Gombo," this Chamber also addressed the issue, stating that:

> [t]he requirement of "a State or organizational policy" implies that the attack follows a regular pattern. Such a policy may be made by groups of person who govern a specific territory or by any organization with the capability to commit a widespread or systematic attack against a civilian population. The policy need not be formalised. Indeed, an attack which is planned, directed or organized—as opposed to spontaneous or isolated acts of violence—will satisfy this criterion.

86.   Regarding the meaning of the term "policy," the Chamber will apply, in accordance with article 21(2) of the Statute, the definitions given in the abovementioned precedents. The Chamber also takes note of the jurisprudence of the ad hoc tribunals, and the work of the International Law Commission (the "ILC"). While the Chamber is mindful of the jurisprudential evolution and the eventual abandonment of the policy requirement before the ad hoc tribunals, it nevertheless deems it useful and thus appropriate to consider their definition of the concept in earlier cases.

87. In particular, the Chamber takes note of the judgment in the case against Tihomir Blaskic, in which the ICTY Trial Chamber held that the plan to commit an attack:

> ...need not necessarily be declared expressly or even stated clearly and precisely. It may be surmised from the occurrence of a series of events, inter alia:
>
> - the general historical circumstances and the overall political background against which the criminal acts are set;
>
> - the establishment and implementation of autonomous political structures at any level of authority in a given territory;
>
> - the general content of a political programme, as it appears in the writings and speeches of its authors; media propaganda;
>
> - the establishment and implementation of autonomous military structures;
>
> - the mobilisation of armed forces;
>
> - temporally and geographically repeated and co-ordinated military offensives;
>
> - links between the military hierarchy and the political structure and its political programme;
>
> - alterations to the "ethnic" composition of populations;
>
> - discriminatory measures, whether administrative or other (banking restrictions, laissez-passer,. . .);
>
> - the scale of the acts of violence perpetrated—in particular, murders and other physical acts of violence, rape, arbitrary imprisonment, deportations and expulsions or the destruction of non-military property, in particular, sacral sites.

88. The Chamber may refer to these factors, inter alia, when determining whether there was a policy to commit an attack against the Kenyan civilian population.

89. With regard to the definition of the terms "State or organizational," the Chamber firstly notes that while, in the present case, the term "State" is self-explanatory, it is worth mentioning that in the case of a State policy to commit an attack, this policy "does not necessarily need to have been conceived 'at the highest level of the State machinery'." Hence, a policy adopted by regional or even local organs of the State could satisfy the requirement of a State policy.

90. With regard to the term "organizational," the Chamber notes that the Statute is unclear as to the criteria pursuant to which a group may qualify as an "organization" for the purposes of article 7(2) (a) of the Statute. Whereas some have argued that only State-like organizations may qualify, the Chamber opines that the formal nature of a group and the level of its organization should not be the defining criterion. Instead, as others have convincingly put forward, a distinction should be drawn on whether a group has the capability to perform acts which infringe on basic human values:

> the associative element, and its inherently aggravating effect, could eventually be satisfied by "purely" private criminal organizations, thus not finding sufficient reasons for distinguishing the gravity of patterns of conduct directed by "territorial" entities or by private groups, given the latter's acquired capacity to infringe basic human values.

91. The Chamber deems it useful to turn to the work of the ILC which determined in the Commentary to the Draft Code adopted during its 43rd session, that one shall not:

> confine possible perpetrators of the crimes to public officials or representatives alone. Admittedly, they would, in view of their official position, have far-reaching factual opportunity to commit the crimes covered by the draft article; yet the article does not rule out the possibility that private individuals with de facto power or organized in criminal gangs or groups might also commit the kind of systematic or mass violations of human rights covered by the article; in that case, their acts would come under the draft Code.

92. The Chamber finds that had the drafters of the Statute intended to exclude non-State actors from the term "organization," they would not have included this term in article 7(2)(a) of the Statute. The Chamber thus determines that organizations not linked to a State may, for the purposes of the Statute, elaborate and carry out a policy to commit an attack against a civilian population.

93. In the view of the Chamber, the determination of whether a given group qualifies as an organization under the Statute must be made on a case-by-case basis. In making this determination, the Chamber may take into account a number of considerations, inter alia: (i) whether the group is under a responsible command, or has an established hierarchy; (ii) whether the group possesses, in fact, the means to carry out a widespread or systematic attack against a civilian population; (iii) whether the group exercises control over part of the territory of a State; (iv) whether the group has criminal activities against the civilian population as a primary purpose; (v) whether the group articulates,

explicitly or implicitly, an intention to attack a civilian population; (vi) whether the group is part of a larger group, which fulfils some or all of the abovementioned criteria. It is important to clarify that, while these considerations may assist the Chamber in its determination, they do not constitute a rigid legal definition, and do not need to be exhaustively fulfilled.

Widespread or systematic nature of the attack

94. Under article 7(1) of the Statute, an act listed therein constitutes a crime against humanity when committed as part of a widespread or systematic attack directed against any civilian population. The Chamber considers that this contextual element applies disjunctively, such that the alleged acts must be either widespread or systematic to warrant classification as crimes against humanity. The rationale behind this contextual element is to "exclude isolated or random acts from the notion of crimes against humanity." Importantly, only the attack, and not the alleged individual acts are required to be "widespread" or "systematic."

95. Insofar as the "widespread" element is concerned, this has long been defined as encompassing "the large scale nature of the attack, which should be massive, frequent, carried out collectively with considerable seriousness and directed against a multiplicity of victims." As such, the element refers to both the large-scale nature of the attack and the number of resultant victims. The assessment is neither exclusively quantitative nor geographical, but must be carried out on the basis of the individual facts. Accordingly, a widespread attack may be the "cumulative effect of a series of inhumane acts or the singular effect of an inhumane act of extraordinary magnitude."

96. In contrast to the large-scale character of "widespread," the term "systematic" refers to the "organised nature of the acts of violence and the improbability of their random occurrence." An attack's systematic nature can "often be expressed through patterns of crimes, in the sense of non-accidental repetition of similar criminal conduct on a regular basis." The Chamber notes that the "systematic" element has been defined by the ICTR as (i) being thoroughly organised, (ii) following a regular pattern, (iii) on the basis of a common policy, and (iv) involving substantial public or private resources, whilst the ICTY has determined that the element requires (i) a political objective or plan, (ii) large-scale or continuous commission of crimes which are linked, (iii) use of significant public or private resources, and (iv) the implication of high-level political and/or military authorities.

Nexus between the individual acts and the attack

97. As previously noted, the chapeau of article 7(1) of the Statute defines crimes against humanity as any of the acts specified therein

insofar as they are committed "as part of a widespread or systematic attack directed against any civilian population." Thus, the nexus between such acts and the attack against a civilian population is one of the requirements that must be satisfied in order for the commission of crimes against humanity to be established.

98. In determining whether an act falling within the scope of article 7(1) of the Statute forms part of an attack, the Chamber must consider the nature, aims and consequences of such act. Isolated acts which clearly differ, in their nature, aims and consequences, from other acts forming part of an attack, would fall outside the scope of article 7(1) of the Statute.

Dissenting Opinion of Judge Hans-Peter Kaul

45. A legal dictionary offers the meaning of an "organization" to be "a body of persons (such as a union or corporation)." Clearly, the "organization" is an entity different from a "State" if the legislator was to avoid redundancy. Thus, it is permissive to conclude that an "organization" may be a private entity (a nonstate actor) which is not an organ of a State or acting on behalf of a State. But how can this non-state "organization" be further delineated? A look at previous rulings of this Court reveals that jurisprudence of both Pre-Trial Chambers exists in which some findings addressing this aspect have been made, namely in the cases of *Prosecutor v. Germain Katanga and Mathieu Ngudjolo Chui* and *Prosecutor v. Jean-Pierre Bemba Gombo*.

48. But I read this jurisprudence against the backdrop that the Pre-Trial Chambers at that time assessed, to the standard of proof applicable, the acts of military-like organized armed groups in the context of an armed conflict not of an international character who over a prolonged period of time allegedly committed crimes according to a policy.

49. The jurisprudence of other international and national tribunals, to the extent that it may be applied in accordance with article 21 of the Statute, offers only little guidance as the tribunals have not further clarified the constitutive characteristics and contours of non-state "organizations," in case they alluded to this possibility.

50. A look at the academic literature, for reasons of completeness, reveals a more dissonant dialogue. One prominent academic argues that the wording "organizational policy" refers only to a policy of an organ of the State. Other commentators have argued to interpret that notion quite broadly, inter alia, in light of the need to protect basic human values. Others have advanced a more restricted reading of the term "organization," linking it to state-like entities.

51. I read the provision such that the juxtaposition of the notions "State" and "organization" in article 7(2)(a) of the Statute are an indication that even though the constitutive elements of statehood need

not be established those "organizations" should partake of some
characteristics of a State. Those characteristics eventually turn the
private "organization" into an entity which may act like a State or has
quasi-State abilities. These characteristics could involve the following:
(a) a collectivity of persons; (b) which was established and acts for a
common purpose; (c) over a prolonged period of time; (d) which is under
responsible command or adopted a certain degree of hierarchical
structure, including, as a minimum, some kind of policy level; (e) with
the capacity to impose the policy on its members and to sanction them;
and (f) which has the capacity and means available to attack any civilian
population on a large scale.

52. In contrast, I believe that non-state actors which do not reach
the level described above are not able to carry out a policy of this nature,
such as groups of organized crime, a mob, groups of (armed) civilians or
criminal gangs. They would generally fall outside the scope of article
7(2)(a) of the Statute. To give a concrete example, violence-prone groups
of persons formed on an ad hoc basis, randomly, spontaneously, for a
passing occasion, with fluctuating membership and without a structure
and level to set up a policy are not within the ambit of the Statute, even
if they engage in numerous serious and organized crimes. Further
elements are needed for a private entity to reach the level of an
"organization" within the meaning of article 7 of the Statute. For it is not
the cruelty or mass victimization that turns a crime into a delictum iuris
gentium but the constitutive contextual elements in which the act is
embedded.

53. In this respect, the general argument that any kind of non-state
actors may be qualified as an "organization" within the meaning of article
7(2)(a) of the Statute on the grounds that it "has the capability to perform
acts which infringe on basic human values" without any further
specification seems unconvincing to me. In fact this approach may
expand the concept of crimes against humanity to any infringement of
human rights. I am convinced that a distinction must be upheld between
human rights violations on the one side and international crimes on the
other side, the latter forming the nucleus of the most heinous violations
of human rights representing the most serious crimes of concern to the
international community as a whole.

NOTES & QUESTIONS

1. *The "Organization" in Organizational Policy.* What is the point of
the plan or policy requirement? Presumably, the plan or policy requirement
is closely connected with the widespread or systematic requirement. In other
words, crimes against humanity are not isolated crimes, or even a large
number of isolated acts that all take place in close spatial or temporal
proximity. The individual predicate acts must be related to each other in the

right way, i.e., elements of a larger plan or policy. But does the plan or policy require *state* action? At Nuremberg, the relevant organizations connected with the Holocaust were sub-state organizations like the Gestapo, or elements of the Nazi leadership operating at the highest echelons of government. This historical precedent has led some, such as Judge Kaul, to suggest that the "organization" in the plan or policy requirement must be a sub-component of the state, or at the very least bear some state-like qualities. Under this view, the plan or policy can be located at the state level, in one bureaucratic agency of the government, or in an organization that bears some similarities to a state. In contrast, others have suggested that a wholly non-state organization, completely divorced from government, may constitute an "organization" capable of forming a plan or policy that forms the foundation for a crime against humanity. Which view has the ICC adopted? For more discussion, see William A. Schabas, *State Policy as an Element of International Crimes*, 98 J. Crim. L. & Criminology 953, 972 (2008) ("Dictionary definitions consider an organization to comprise any organized group of people, such as a club, society, trade union, or business. Surely the drafters of the Rome Statute did not intend for Article 7 to have such a broad scope, given that all previous case law concerning crimes against humanity, and all evidence of national prosecutions for crimes against humanity, had concerned State-supported atrocities."); Leila Nadya Sadat, *Crimes Against Humanity in the Modern Age*, 107 Am. J. Int'l L. 334, 336 (2013) ("Kaul's position would sharply limit the scope of prosecution of crimes against humanity at the ICC, which could affect the Court's utility as a tool for punishing and preventing atrocity crimes.").

2.   *The Concept of Humanity.* Why are "crimes against humanity" crimes against *humanity*? What exactly does this mean? Is it just a *façon de parler* that roughly corresponds to any large atrocity, or does the language of "humanity" confer some special meaning? Certainly, not all atrocities qualify as crimes against humanity, due to the technical chapeau requirements analyzed above. Several scholars have tried to articulate a deeper rationale for the crime. For example, Professor Luban argues that some crimes are sufficiently grave that they implicate the interests of humanity at large, not just individual victims, because the crimes "assault one particular aspect of human being, namely our character as political animals." In this sense, Luban's theory owes much to Aristotle, who first described human beings as *zoon politikon* (political animals). Luban argues that as human beings we "are creatures whose nature compels us to live socially, but who cannot do so without artificial political organization that inevitably poses threats to our well-being, and, at the limit, to our very survival." Crimes against humanity "represent the worst of those threats" because "they are the limiting case of politics gone cancerous." See David Luban, *A Theory of Crimes Against Humanity*, 29 Yale J. Int'l L. 85, 90 (2004). Is this a good description of the political violence in Kenya?

3. GENOCIDE

The crime of genocide requires that the defendant committed a predicate act with genocidal intent. Article 6 of the Rome Statute defines genocidal intent as the "intent to destroy, in whole or in part, a national, ethnical, racial or religious group, as such. . ." In other words, what matters is why the defendant committed the particular predicate crime. If the crime was committed to destroy the group, then it could qualify as genocide. Note that it is not necessary to intend to destroy the entire group. If, for example, someone intends to destroy *part* of the group (such as the members of that group located in a particular geographic region), based on an overwhelming animosity towards that group, this more modest project would still be genocide.

According to article 6, the predicate acts must fit into one of a defined list of relevant acts: "(a) killing members of the group; (b) causing serious bodily or mental harm to members of the group; (c) deliberately inflicting on the group conditions of life calculated to bring about its physical destruction in whole or in part; (d) imposing measures intended to prevent births within the group; (e) forcibly transferring children of the group to another group." Although the most common examples of genocide involve group destruction through killing, the list above makes clear that other methods of group destruction (e.g. preventing births or transferring children from the group) qualify as genocide.

The intended victims must be members of a protected group. Consequently, one of the first tasks for a prosecutor and court is to determine whether the crime targeted a group that qualifies as national, ethnical, racial, or religious. In some cases, this is rather obvious, but in others, what counts as "national" or "ethnical" may be open to dispute, and require some reference to sociological or anthropological evidence to adjudicate. Other groups, for example "political groups," are not protected by the law of genocide, though an attack against the group's members may qualify as a crime against humanity. For example, if a political leader targets and destroys members of a political group that opposes him, this atrocity may not meet the current doctrinal definition of genocide.

Unlike crimes against humanity, which unquestionably include a plan or policy requirement, there is some uncertainty over whether genocide necessarily includes this chapeau element. All prior examples of genocide adjudicated by international tribunals have taken place in the larger context of a state or organizational plan or policy, yet some tribunals have held that, strictly speaking, the plan or policy prong is not a doctrinal requirement for a genocide conviction. According to this view, genocide could be a purely individual crime (rather than a collective crime), as strange as that sounds.

In the following case, the ICTR focused on the sexual violence that occurred in Rwanda in order to determine whether it qualified as a crime of genocide.

Prosecutor v. Akayesu
International Criminal Tribunal for Rwanda
Trial Chamber Judgment
September 2, 1998

492. Article 2 of the Statute stipulates that the Tribunal shall have the power to prosecute persons responsible for genocide, complicity to commit genocide, direct and public incitement to commit genocide, attempt to commit genocide and complicity in genocide.

493. In accordance with the said provisions of the Statute, the Prosecutor has charged Akayesu with the crimes legally defined as genocide (count 1), complicity in genocide (count 2) and incitement to commit genocide (count 4).

494. The definition of genocide, as given in Article 2 of the Tribunal's Statute, is taken verbatim from Articles 2 and 3 of the Convention on the Prevention and Punishment of the Crime of Genocide (the "Genocide Convention"). It states: "Genocide means any of the following acts committed with intent to destroy, in whole or in part, a national, ethnical, racial or religious group, as such: (a) Killing members of the group; (b) Causing serious bodily or mental harm to members of the group; (c) Deliberately inflicting on the group conditions of life calculated to bring about its physical destruction in whole or in part; (d) Imposing measures intended to prevent births within the group; (e) Forcibly transferring children of the group to another group."

495. The Genocide Convention is undeniably considered part of customary international law, as can be seen in the opinion of the International Court of Justice on the provisions of the Genocide Convention, and as was recalled by the United Nations' Secretary-General in his Report on the establishment of the International Criminal Tribunal for the former Yugoslavia.

496. The Chamber notes that Rwanda acceded, by legislative decree, to the Convention on Genocide on 12 February 197593. Thus, punishment of the crime of genocide did exist in Rwanda in 1994, at the time of the acts alleged in the Indictment, and the perpetrator was liable to be brought before the competent courts of Rwanda to answer for this crime.

497. Contrary to popular belief, the crime of genocide does not imply the actual extermination of group in its entirety, but is understood as such once any one of the acts mentioned in Article 2(2)(a) through 2(2)(e)

is committed with the specific intent to destroy "in whole or in part" a national, ethnical, racial or religious group.

498. Genocide is distinct from other crimes inasmuch as it embodies a special intent or *dolus specialis*. Special intent of a crime is the specific intention, required as a constitutive element of the crime, which demands that the perpetrator clearly seeks to produce the act charged. Thus, the special intent in the crime of genocide lies in "the intent to destroy, in whole or in part, a national, ethnical, racial or religious group, as such."

499. Thus, for a crime of genocide to have been committed, it is necessary that one of the acts listed under Article 2(2) of the Statute be committed, that the particular act be committed against a specifically targeted group, it being a national, ethnical, racial or religious group. Consequently, in order to clarify the constitutive elements of the crime of genocide, the Chamber will first state its findings on the acts provided for under Article 2(2)(a) through Article 2(2)(e) of the Statute, the groups protected by the Genocide Convention, and the special intent or *dolus specialis* necessary for genocide to take place.

Killing members of the group

500. With regard to Article 2(2)(a) of the Statute, like in the Genocide Convention, the Chamber notes that the said paragraph states "meurtre" in the French version while the English version states "killing." The Trial Chamber is of the opinion that the term "killing" used in the English version is too general, since it could very well include both intentional and unintentional homicides, whereas the term "meurtre," used in the French version, is more precise. It is accepted that there is murder when death has been caused with the intention to do so, as provided for, incidentally, in the Penal Code of Rwanda which stipulates in its Article 311 that "Homicide committed with intent to cause death shall be treated as murder". 501. Given the presumption of innocence of the accused, and pursuant to the general principles of criminal law, the Chamber holds that the version more favourable to the accused should be upheld and finds that Article 2(2)(a) of the Statute must be interpreted in accordance with the definition of murder given in the Penal Code of Rwanda, according to which "meurtre" (killing) is homicide committed with the intent to cause death. The Chamber notes in this regard that the travaux préparatoires of the Genocide Convention 94, show that the proposal by certain delegations that premeditation be made a necessary condition for there to be genocide, was rejected, because some delegates deemed it unnecessary for premeditation to be made a requirement; in their opinion, by its constitutive physical elements, the very crime of genocide, necessarily entails premeditation.

Causing serious bodily or mental harm to members of the group

502. Causing serious bodily or mental harm to members of the group does not necessarily mean that the harm is permanent and irremediable.

503. In the Adolf Eichmann case, who was convicted of crimes against the Jewish people, genocide under another legal definition, the District Court of Jerusalem stated in its judgment of 12 December 1961, that serious bodily or mental harm of members of the group can be caused "by the enslavement, starvation, deportation and persecution [. . .] and by their detention in ghettos, transit camps and concentration camps in conditions which were designed to cause their degradation, deprivation of their rights as human beings, and to suppress them and cause them inhumane suffering and torture."

504. For purposes of interpreting Article 2 (2)(b) of the Statute, the Chamber takes serious bodily or mental harm, without limiting itself thereto, to mean acts of torture, be they bodily or mental, inhumane or degrading treatment, persecution.

Deliberately inflicting on the group conditions of life calculated to bring about its physical destruction in whole or in part

505. The Chamber holds that the expression deliberately inflicting on the group conditions of life calculated to bring about its physical destruction in whole or in part, should be construed as the methods of destruction by which the perpetrator does not immediately kill the members of the group, but which, ultimately, seek their physical destruction.

506. For purposes of interpreting Article 2(2)(c) of the Statute, the Chamber is of the opinion that the means of deliberate inflicting on the group conditions of life calculated to bring about its physical destruction, in whole or part, include, inter alia, subjecting a group of people to a subsistence diet, systematic expulsion from homes and the reduction of essential medical services below minimum requirement.

Imposing measures intended to prevent births within the group

507. For purposes of interpreting Article 2(2)(d) of the Statute, the Chamber holds that the measures intended to prevent births within the group, should be construed as sexual mutilation, the practice of sterilization, forced birth control, separation of the sexes and prohibition of marriages. In patriarchal societies, where membership of a group is determined by the identity of the father, an example of a measure intended to prevent births within a group is the case where, during rape, a woman of the said group is deliberately impregnated by a man of another group, with the intent to have her give birth to a child who will consequently not belong to its mother's group.

508. Furthermore, the Chamber notes that measures intended to prevent births within the group may be physical, but can also be mental. For instance, rape can be a measure intended to prevent births when the person raped refuses subsequently to procreate, in the same way that members of a group can be led, through threats or trauma, not to procreate.

Forcibly transferring children of the group to another group

509. With respect to forcibly transferring children of the group to another group, the Chamber is of the opinion that, as in the case of measures intended to prevent births, the objective is not only to sanction a direct act of forcible physical transfer, but also to sanction acts of threats or trauma which would lead to the forcible transfer of children from one group to another.

510. Since the special intent to commit genocide lies in the intent to "destroy, in whole or in part, a national, ethnical, racial or religious group, as such," it is necessary to consider a definition of the group as such. Article 2 of the Statute, just like the Genocide Convention, stipulates four types of victim groups, namely national, ethnical, racial or religious groups.

511. On reading through the travaux préparatoires of the Genocide Convention 96, it appears that the crime of genocide was allegedly perceived as targeting only "stable" groups, constituted in a permanent fashion and membership of which is determined by birth, with the exclusion of the more "mobile" groups which one joins through individual voluntary commitment, such as political and economic groups. Therefore, a common criterion in the four types of groups protected by the Genocide Convention is that membership in such groups would seem to be normally not challengeable by its members, who belong to it automatically, by birth, in a continuous and often irremediable manner.

512. Based on the Nottebohm decision rendered by the International Court of Justice, the Chamber holds that a national group is defined as a collection of people who are perceived to share a legal bond based on common citizenship, coupled with reciprocity of rights and duties.

513. An ethnic group is generally defined as a group whose members share a common language or culture.

514. The conventional definition of racial group is based on the hereditary physical traits often identified with a geographical region, irrespective of linguistic, cultural, national or religious factors.

515. The religious group is one whose members share the same religion, denomination or mode of worship.

516. Moreover, the Chamber considered whether the groups protected by the Genocide Convention, echoed in Article 2 of the Statute, should be limited to only the four groups expressly mentioned and whether they should not also include any group which is stable and permanent like the said four groups. In other words, the question that arises is whether it would be impossible to punish the physical destruction of a group as such under the Genocide Convention, if the said group, although stable and membership is by birth, does not meet the definition of any one of the four groups expressly protected by the Genocide Convention. In the opinion of the Chamber, it is particularly important to respect the intention of the drafters of the Genocide Convention, which according to the travaux préparatoires, was patently to ensure the protection of any stable and permanent group.

517. As stated above, the crime of genocide is characterized by its *dolus specialis*, or special intent, which lies in the fact that the acts charged, listed in Article 2(2) of the Statute, must have been "committed with intent to destroy, in whole or in part, a national, ethnical, racial or religious group, as such."

518. Special intent is a well-known criminal law concept in the Roman-continental legal systems. It is required as a constituent element of certain offences and demands that the perpetrator have the clear intent to cause the offence charged. According to this meaning, special intent is the key element of an intentional offence, which offence is characterized by a psychological relationship between the physical result and the mental state of the perpetrator.

519. As observed by the representative of Brazil during the travaux préparatoires of the Genocide Convention, "genocide [is] characterised by the factor of particular intent to destroy a group. In the absence of that factor, whatever the degree of atrocity of an act and however similar it might be to the acts described in the convention, that act could still not be called genocide."

520. With regard to the crime of genocide, the offender is culpable only when he has committed one of the offences charged under Article 2(2) of the Statute with the clear intent to destroy, in whole or in part, a particular group. The offender is culpable because he knew or should have known that the act committed would destroy, in whole or in part, a group.

521. In concrete terms, for any of the acts charged under Article 2(2) of the Statute to be a constitutive element of genocide, the act must have been committed against one or several individuals, because such individual or individuals were members of a specific group, and specifically because they belonged to this group. Thus, the victim is chosen not because of his individual identity, but rather on account of his

membership of a national, ethnical, racial or religious group. The victim of the act is therefore a member of a group, chosen as such, which, hence, means that the victim of the crime of genocide is the group itself and not only the individual.

522. The perpetration of the act charged therefore extends beyond its actual commission, for example, the murder of a particular individual, for the realisation of an ulterior motive, which is to destroy, in whole or part, the group of which the individual is just one element.

523. On the issue of determining the offender's specific intent, the Chamber considers that intent is a mental factor which is difficult, even impossible, to determine. This is the reason why, in the absence of a confession from the accused, his intent can be inferred from a certain number of presumptions of fact. The Chamber considers that it is possible to deduce the genocidal intent inherent in a particular act charged from the general context of the perpetration of other culpable acts systematically directed against that same group, whether these acts were committed by the same offender or by others. Other factors, such as the scale of atrocities committed, their general nature, in a region or a country, or furthermore, the fact of deliberately and systematically targeting victims on account of their membership of a particular group, while excluding the members of other groups, can enable the Chamber to infer the genocidal intent of a particular act.

524. Trial Chamber I of the International Criminal Tribunal for the former Yugoslavia also stated that the specific intent of the crime of genocide

> may be inferred from a number of facts such as the general political doctrine which gave rise to the acts possibly covered by the definition in Article 4, or the repetition of destructive and discriminatory acts. The intent may also be inferred from the perpetration of acts which violate, or which the perpetrators themselves consider to violate the very foundation of the group—acts which are not in themselves covered by the list in Article 4(2) but which are committed as part of the same pattern of conduct.

Thus, in the matter brought before the International Criminal Tribunal for the former Yugoslavia, the Trial Chamber, in its findings, found that

> this intent derives from the combined effect of speeches or projects laying the groundwork for and justifying the acts, from the massive scale of their destructive effect and from their specific nature, which aims at undermining what is considered to be the foundation of the group.

702. In the light of the facts brought to its attention during the trial, the Chamber is of the opinion that, in Rwanda in 1994, the Tutsi

constituted a group referred to as "ethnic" in official classifications. Thus, the identity cards at the time included a reference to "ubwoko" in Kinyarwanda or "ethnie" (ethnic group) in French which, depending on the case, referred to the designation Hutu or Tutsi, for example. The Chamber further noted that all the Rwandan witnesses who appeared before it invariably answered spontaneously and without hesitation the questions of the Prosecutor regarding their ethnic identity. Accordingly, the Chamber finds that, in any case, at the time of the alleged events, the Tutsi did indeed constitute a stable and permanent group and were identified as such by all.

706. With regard to the acts alleged in paragraphs 12(A) and 12(B) of the Indictment, the Prosecutor has shown beyond a reasonable doubt that between 7 April and the end of June 1994, numerous Tutsi who sought refuge at the Taba Bureau communal were frequently beaten by members of the Interahamwe on or near the premises of the Bureau communal. Some of them were killed. Numerous Tutsi women were forced to endure acts of sexual violence, mutilations and rape, often repeatedly, often publicly and often by more than one assailant. Tutsi women were systematically raped, as one female victim testified to by saying that "each time that you met assailants, they raped you." Numerous incidents of such rape and sexual violence against Tutsi women occurred inside or near the Bureau communal. It has been proven that some communal policemen armed with guns and the accused himself were present while some of these rapes and sexual violence were being committed. Furthermore, it is proven that on several occasions, by his presence, his attitude and his utterances, Akayesu encouraged such acts, one particular witness testifying that Akayesu, addressed the Interahamwe who were committing the rapes and said that "never ask me again what a Tutsi woman tastes like." In the opinion of the Chamber, this constitutes tacit encouragement to the rapes that were being committed.

731. With regard, particularly, to the acts described in paragraphs 12(A) and 12(B) of the Indictment, that is, rape and sexual violence, the Chamber wishes to underscore the fact that in its opinion, they constitute genocide in the same way as any other act as long as they were committed with the specific intent to destroy, in whole or in part, a particular group, targeted as such. Indeed, rape and sexual violence certainly constitute infliction of serious bodily and mental harm on the victims and are even, according to the Chamber, one of the worst ways of inflict harm on the victim as he or she suffers both bodily and mental harm. In light of all the evidence before it, the Chamber is satisfied that the acts of rape and sexual violence described above, were committed solely against Tutsi women, many of whom were subjected to the worst public humiliation, mutilated, and raped several times, often in public, in the Bureau

Communal premises or in other public places, and often by more than one assailant. These rapes resulted in physical and psychological destruction of Tutsi women, their families and their communities. Sexual violence was an integral part of the process of destruction, specifically targeting Tutsi women and specifically contributing to their destruction and to the destruction of the Tutsi group as a whole.

732. The rape of Tutsi women was systematic and was perpetrated against all Tutsi women and solely against them. A Tutsi woman, married to a Hutu, testified before the Chamber that she was not raped because her ethnic background was unknown. As part of the propaganda campaign geared to mobilizing the Hutu against the Tutsi, the Tutsi women were presented as sexual objects. Indeed, the Chamber was told, for an example, that before being raped and killed, Alexia, who was the wife of the Professor, Ntereye, and her two nieces, were forced by the Interahamwe to undress and ordered to run and do exercises "in order to display the thighs of Tutsi women." The Interahamwe who raped Alexia said, as he threw her on the ground and got on top of her, "let us now see what the vagina of a Tutsi woman tastes like." As stated above, Akayesu himself, speaking to the Interahamwe who were committing the rapes, said to them: "don't ever ask again what a Tutsi woman tastes like." This sexualized representation of ethnic identity graphically illustrates that Tutsi women were subjected to sexual violence because they were Tutsi. Sexual violence was a step in the process of destruction of the Tutsi group—destruction of the spirit, of the will to live, and of life itself.

733. On the basis of the substantial testimonies brought before it, the Chamber finds that in most cases, the rapes of Tutsi women in Taba, were accompanied with the intent to kill those women. Many rapes were perpetrated near mass graves where the women were taken to be killed. A victim testified that Tutsi women caught could be taken away by peasants and men with the promise that they would be collected later to be executed. Following an act of gang rape, a witness heard Akayesu say "tomorrow they will be killed" and they were actually killed. In this respect, it appears clearly to the Chamber that the acts of rape and sexual violence, as other acts of serious bodily and mental harm committed against the Tutsi, reflected the determination to make Tutsi women suffer and to mutilate them even before killing them, the intent being to destroy the Tutsi group while inflicting acute suffering on its members in the process.

734. In light of the foregoing, the Chamber finds firstly that the acts described supra are indeed acts as enumerated in Article 2(2) of the Statute, which constitute the factual elements of the crime of genocide, namely the killings of Tutsi or the serious bodily and mental harm inflicted on the Tutsi. The Chamber is further satisfied beyond

reasonable doubt that these various acts were committed by Akayesu with the specific intent to destroy the Tutsi group, as such. . .

NOTES & QUESTIONS

1.   *Ethnical Groups.* How does one determine whether a particular group qualifies as an "ethnical" or "national" group? In *Akayesu*, the Trial Chamber concluded that the Tutsi were an ethnical group, though that conclusion was not preordained. The Chamber seemed particularly influenced by the fact that many witnesses spontaneously and unambiguously identified themselves as Tutsi, which the chamber concluded was a "stable and permanent group." Another possibility is that protected groups are *negatively* defined by others, perhaps even by the perpetrators of the genocide. In other words, even if members of a group do not self-identify as a national, ethnical, racial, or religious group, it is enough that the perpetrators viewed the victims as belonging to a group of this type, thus leading to the genocide. The ICTR supported this "negative attribution" theory in the *Rutaganda* case. For a discussion of these issues, see Alexander Zahar and Goran Sluiter, *International Criminal Law: A Critical Introduction* 161–162 (2008).

2.   *Political Groups.* Why are political groups excluded from the definition of genocide? One possible answer is that genocide involves crimes against groups that are relatively immutable. Or, more precisely, one can place group membership on a spectrum that ranges from more or less immutable. One can, for example, change one's nationality, but one cannot change the nation of one's birth. One can change one's religion though one cannot change the religion you were assigned at birth. Ethnicity is mostly immutable, i.e., not something that an individual voluntarily selects. In contrast, membership in a political group is *chosen* by the member, who decides to join the group. Is this relevant? Should the law be changed to include political groups within the protective umbrella of genocide? For an argument, see David L. Neressian, *Genocide and Political Groups* 205 (2010) ("There are good reasons to treat genocide against political groups as a separate international crime. The concept is supported by strong theoretical and public policy grounds, and the need is great.").

4. AGGRESSION

In some ways, aggression is the criminal offence that never was. It has a distinguished pedigree and formed the backdrop to the allied prosecution of Nazi war criminals at Nuremberg after World War II. Although the Holocaust is synonymous with atrocities and the concept of genocide, the Nuremberg case focused primarily on a massive Nazi conspiracy to commit "crimes against peace," which in today's language would be called "aggression." However, in the intervening years, no major prosecution for aggression has occurred at an international tribunal. Aggression was not included in the ICTY or ICTR statutes. And although aggression was included as a crime in the Rome Statute, the crime had no definition and provisions for its prosecution at the ICC were only added after a diplomatic conference took place in Kampala, Uganda, in 2010. The conference agreed on the following definition:

1. For the purpose of this Statute, "crime of aggression" means the planning, preparation, initiation or execution, by a person in a position effectively to exercise control over or to direct the political or military action of a State, of an act of aggression which, by its character, gravity and scale, constitutes a manifest violation of the Charter of the United Nations.

2. For the purpose of paragraph 1, "act of aggression" means the use of armed force by a State against the sovereignty, territorial integrity or political independence of another State, or in any other manner inconsistent with the Charter of the United Nations. . .

One reason the crime of aggression might be disfavored as a prosecutorial tool is that it necessarily involves questions of *jus ad bellum* under public international law. An individual is only guilty of aggression if they participated in a war of aggression. This means that the crime requires an underlying chapeau requirement of a state that commences a war without justification under international law. The rules regarding the use of force are governed primarily by the UN Charter; force is lawful when authorized by the Security Council pursuant to its Chapter VII authority, or when taken in self-defense. But the scope of the right of self-defense is among the most contested areas of public international law. Any prosecutor charging the crime of aggression would need to demonstrate not only the defendant's culpability but also the state's responsibility for the overall war.

At Nuremberg, the prosecution did just that. It established that Germany engaged in a war of aggression against its European neighbors, Russia, and the United States, and from that criminal war came the specific atrocities that produced the Holocaust.

International Military Tribunal at Nuremberg
Final Judgment
September 30–October 1, 1946

The Common Plan or Conspiracy and Aggressive War

The Tribunal now turns to the consideration of the Crimes against peace charged in the Indictment. Count One of the Indictment charges the defendants with conspiring or having a common plan to commit crimes against peace.

Count Two of the Indictment charges the defendants with committing specific crimes against peace by planning, preparing, initiating, and waging wars of aggression against a number of other States. It will be convenient to consider the question of the existence of a common plan and the question of aggressive war together, and to deal later in this Judgment with the question of the individual responsibility of the defendants.

The charges in the Indictment that the defendants planned and waged aggressive wars are charges of the utmost gravity. War is essentially an evil thing. Its consequences are not confined to the belligerent states alone, but affect the whole world.

To initiate a war of aggression, therefore, is not only an international crime; it is the supreme international crime differing only from other war crimes in that it contains within itself the accumulated evil of the whole.

The first acts of aggression referred to in the Indictment are the seizure of Austria and Czechoslovakia and the first war of aggression charged in the Indictment is the war against Poland begun on the 1st September, 1939.

Before examining that charge it is necessary to look more closely at some of the events which preceded these acts of aggression. The war against Poland did not come suddenly out of an otherwise clear sky; the evidence has made it plain that this war of aggression, as well as the seizure of Austria and Czechoslovakia, was pre-meditated and carefully prepared, and was not undertaken until the moment was thought opportune for it to be carried through as a definite part of the pre-ordained scheme and plan.

For the aggressive designs of the Nazi Government were not accidents arising out of the immediate political situation in Europe and the world; they were a deliberate and essential part of Nazi foreign policy.

From the beginning, the National Socialist movement claimed that its object was to unite the German people in the consciousness of their mission and destiny, based on inherent qualities of race, and under the guidance of the Fuehrer.

For its achievement, two things were deemed to be essential: the disruption of the European order as it had existed since the Treaty of Versailles, and the creation of a Greater Germany beyond the frontiers of 1914. This necessarily involved the seizure of foreign territories.

War was seen to be inevitable, or at the very least, highly probable, if these purposes were to be accomplished. The German people, therefore, with all their resources were to be organised as a great political-military army. schooled to obey without question any policy decreed by the State.

Preparation for Aggression

In *Mein Kampf* Hitler had made this view quite plain. It must be remembered that *Mein Kampf* was no mere private diary in which the secret thoughts of Hitler were set down. Its contents were rather proclaimed from the house-tops. It was used in the schools and Universities and among the Hitler Youth, in the SS and the SA, and among the German people generally, even down to the presentation of an official copy to all newly married people. By the year 1945 over 61 million copies had been circulated. The general contents are well known. Over and over again Hitler asserted his belief in the necessity of force as the means of solving international problems, as in the following quotation:

> The soil on which we now live was not a gift bestowed by Heaven on our forefathers. They had to conquer it by risking their lives. So also in the future, our people will not obtain territory, and therewith the means of existence, as a favour from any other people, but will have to win it by the power of a triumphant sword.

Mein Kampf contains many such passages, and the extolling of force as an instrument of foreign policy is openly proclaimed.

The precise objectives of this policy of force are also set forth in detail. The very first page of the book asserts that "German-Austria must be restored to the great German Motherland," not on economic grounds, but because "people of the same blood should be in the same Reich."

The restoration of the German frontiers of 1914 is declared to be wholly insufficient, and if Germany is to exist at all, it must be as a world power with the necessary territorial magnitude.

Mein Kampf is quite explicit in stating where the increased territory is to be found:

> Therefore we National Socialists have purposely drawn a line through the line of conduct followed by pre-war Germany in foreign policy. We put an end to the perpetual Germanic march towards the South and West of Europe, and turn our eyes towards the lands of the East. We finally put a stop to the colonial and trade policy of the pre-war times, and pass over to the territorial policy of the future.

> But when we speak of new territory in Europe to-day, we must think principally of Russia and the border states subject to her.

Mein Kampf is not to be regarded as a mere literary exercise, nor as an inflexible policy or plan incapable of modification. Its importance lies in the unmistakable attitude of aggression revealed throughout its pages.

The Planning of Aggression

Evidence from captured documents has revealed that Hitler held four secret meetings to which the Tribunal proposes to make special reference because of the light they shed upon the question of the common plan and aggressive war.

These meetings took place on the 5th of November, 1937, the 23rd of May, 1939, the 22nd of August, 1939, and the 23rd of November, 1939.

At these meetings important declarations were made by Hitler as to his purposes, which are quite unmistakable in their terms.

The documents which record what took place at these meetings have been subject to some criticism at the hands of defending Counsel.

Their essential authenticity is not denied, but it is said, for example that they do not purpose to be verbatim transcripts of the speeches they record, that the document dealing with the meeting on the 5th November, 1937, was dated five days after the meeting had taken place, and that the two documents dealing with the meeting of August 22nd, 1939, differ from one another, and are unsigned.

Making the fullest allowance for criticism of this kind, the Tribunal is of the opinion that the documents are documents of the highest value, and that their authenticity and substantial truth are established.

They are obviously careful records of the events they describe, and they have been preserved as such in the archives of the German Government, from whose custody they were captured. Such documents could never be dismissed as inventions, nor even as inaccurate or distorted, they plainly record events which actually took place.

Conferences of the 23rd November, 1939
and 5th November, 1937

It will perhaps be useful to deal first of all with the meeting of the 23rd November, 1939, when Hitler called his Supreme Commanders together. A record was made of what was said, by one of those present. At the date of the meeting, Austria and Czechoslovakia had been incorporated into the German Reich, Poland had been conquered by the German armies, and the war with Great Britain and France was still in its static phase. The moment was opportune for a review of past events. Hitler informed the Commanders that the purpose of the Conference was to give them an idea of the world of his thoughts, and to tell them his decision. He thereupon reviewed his political task since 1919, and referred to the secession of Germany from the League of Nations, the denunciation of the Disarmament Conference, the order for re-armament, the introduction of compulsory armed service, the occupation of the Rhineland, the seizure of Austria, and the action against Czechoslovakia. He stated:

One year later, Austria came; this step also was considered doubtful. It brought about a considerable reinforcement of the Reich. The next step was Bohemia, Moravia and Poland. This step also was not possible to accomplish in one campaign. First of all, the western fortification had to be finished. It was not possible to reach the goal in one effort. It was clear to me from the first moment that I could not be satisfied with the Sudeten German territory. That was only a partial solution. The decision to march into Bohemia was made. Then followed the erection of the Protectorate and with that the basis for the action against Poland was laid, but I wasn't quite clear at that time whether I should start first against the East and then in the West or vice versa. . . Basically I did not organise the armed forces in order not to strike. The decision to strike was always in me. Earlier or later I wanted to solve the problem. Under pressure it was decided that the East was to be attacked first.

This address, reviewing past events and re-affirming the aggressive intentions present from the beginning, puts beyond any question of doubt the character of the actions against Austria and Czechoslovakia, and the war against Poland.

For they had all been accomplished according to plan, and the nature of that plan must now be examined in a little more detail.

At the meeting of the 23rd November, 1939, Hitler was looking back to things accomplished, at the earlier meetings now to be considered, he was looking forward, and revealing his plans to his confederates. The comparison is instructive.

The meeting held at the Reich Chancellery in Berlin on the 5th November 1937, was attended by Lieut.-Colonel Hoszbach, Hitler's personal adjutant, who compiled a long note of the proceedings, which he dated the 10th November, 1937, and signed.

The persons present were Hitler, and the defendants Goering, von Neurath and Raeder, in their capacities as Commander-in-Chief of the Luftwaffe, Reich Foreign Minister and Commander-in-Chief of the Navy respectively, General von Blomberg, Minister of War, and General von Fritsch, the Commander-in-Chief of the Army.

Hitler began by saying that the subject of the conference was of such high importance that in other States it would have taken place before the Cabinet. He went on to say that the subject matter of his speech was the result of his detailed deliberations, and of his experience during his four and a half years of Government. He requested that the statements he was about to make should be looked upon in the case of his death as his last will and testament. Hitler's main theme was the problem of living space, and he discussed various possible solutions, only to set them aside.

He then said that the seizure of living space on the continent of Europe was therefore necessary, expressing himself in these words:

> It is not a case of conquering people, but of conquering agriculturally useful space. It would also be more to the purpose to seek raw material producing territory in Europe directly adjoining the Reich and not overseas, and this solution would have to be brought into effect for one or two generations. . . . The history of all times Roman Empire, British Empire has proved that every space expansion can only be effected by breaking resistance and taking risks. Even setbacks are unavoidable: neither formerly nor to-day has space been found without an owner; the attacker always comes up against the proprietor.

He concluded with this observation: "The question for Germany is where the greatest possible conquest could be made at the lowest cost."

Nothing could indicate more plainly the aggressive intentions of Hitler, and the events which soon followed showed the reality of his purpose. It is impossible to accept the contention that Hitler did not actually mean war; for after pointing out that Germany might expect the opposition of England and France, and analysing the strength and the weakness of those powers in particular situations, he continued:

> The German question can be solved only by way of force, and this is never without risk. . . . If we place the decision to apply force with risk at the head of the following expositions, then we are left to reply to the questions "when" and "how." In this regard we have to decide upon three different cases.

The first of these three cases set forth a hypothetical international situation, in which he would take action not later than 1943 to 1945, saying: "If the Fuehrer is still living then it will be his irrevocable decision to solve the German space problem not later than 1943 to 1945. The necessity for action before 1943 to 1945 will come under consideration in Cases 2 and 3."

The second and third cases to which Hitler referred show the plain intention to seize Austria and Czechoslovakia, and in this connection Hitler said: "For the improvement of our military-political position, it must be our first aim in every case of entanglement by war to conquer Czechoslovakia and Austria simultaneously in order to remove any threat from the flanks in case of a possible advance westwards."

He further added: "The annexation of the two states to Germany militarily and politically would constitute a considerable relief, owing to shorter and better frontiers, the freeing of fighting personnel for other purposes, and the possibility of reconstituting new armies up to a strength of about twelve divisions."

This decision to seize Austria and Czechoslovakia was discussed in some detail, the action was to be taken as soon as a favourable opportunity presented itself.

The military strength which Germany had been building up since 1933 was now to be directed at the two specific countries, Austria and Czechoslovakia.

The defendant Goering testified that he did not believe at that time that Hitler actually meant to attack Austria and Czechoslovakia, and that the purpose of the conference was only to put pressure on von Fritsch to speed up the re-armament of the Army.

The defendant Raeder testified that neither he, nor von Fritsch, nor von Blomberg, believed that Hitler actually meant war, a conviction which the defendant Raeder claims that he held up to the 22nd August, 1939. The basis of this conviction was his hope that Hitler would obtain a "political solution" of Germany's problems. But all that this means, when examined, is the belief that Germany's position would be so good, and Germany's armed might so overwhelming, that the territory desired could be obtained without fighting for it. It must be remembered too that Hitler's declared intention with regard to Austria was actually carried out within a little over four months from the date of the meeting, and within less than a year the first portion of Czechoslovakia was absorbed, and Bohemia and Moravia a few months later. If any doubts had existed in the minds of any of his hearers in November, 1937, after March of 1939 there could no longer be any question that Hitler was in deadly earnest in his decision to resort to war. The Tribunal is satisfied that Lt.-Col. Hoszbach's account of the meeting is substantially correct, and that those present knew that Austria and Czechoslovakia would be annexed by Germany at the first possible opportunity.

NOTES & QUESTIONS

1.   *The Supreme International Crime.* Why did the Nuremberg tribunal refer to crimes against peace as the "supreme" international crime? Is it true that aggression contains "within itself the accumulated evil of the whole"? Recall that under modern jurisprudence, crimes against humanity and genocide do not require a nexus with armed conflict and may occur in peacetime. Similarly, while war crimes require an armed conflict, most war crimes today take place during civil wars, or so-called non-international armed conflicts, which are internal to a state. In those situations, there is no possibility for aggression because only one state is involved. Is it still accurate to call aggression the "supreme" international crime?

2.   *The Kampala Compromise.* The ICC finally gained jurisdiction over aggression after the 2010 Kampala review conference, which brought together state parties to the Rome Statute to adopt amendments to the treaty. Originally, both Germany and the United States wanted to limit the

ICC's jurisdiction over aggression to situations where the UN Security Council has declared that aggression occurred. However, Germany eventually changed its mind, and the negotiations proceeded with a more complicated jurisdictional triggering mechanism. First, the ICC cannot exercise jurisdiction over non-state parties, and even state parties to the ICC may exempt themselves from the court's jurisdiction in aggression cases by filing a declaration with the Registrar. Second, the ICC Prosecutor needs a declaration from the Security Council that an act of aggression was committed, *or* the prosecutor needs authorization to proceed from an ICC Pre-Trial Chamber.

C. MODES OF LIABILITY

Most defendants at international tribunals are not accused of physically perpetrating crimes by their own hand. More typically, the defendants are higher-level officials who were physically removed from the commission of the crimes, but nonetheless participated in important ways. Modes of liability are "linking principles" that connect the defendant with the actor who physically perpetrated the crime at the street level. In domestic criminal law, the relevant modes of liability are conspiracy, solicitation, and aiding and abetting. Conspiracy is generally disfavored as a mode of liability in international criminal law, having been the subject of an intense dispute between jurists at the Nuremberg tribunal. Although U.S. lawyers working at the tribunal felt that conspiracy best described the larger context of Nazi criminality, European lawyers at the tribunal were skeptical of the concept and found it too American and insufficiently international for inclusion in the tribunal's jurisprudence. Ultimately, a compromise was reached and conspiracy formed the basis for the convictions of crimes against peace (reprinted directly above), but was rejected for war crimes and crimes against humanity. It was felt that crimes against the peace were already collective in nature—because they included a state action requirement—so conspiracy was not adding another layer of collective criminality. However, conspiracy remains a viable mode of liability in genocide cases, in part because the Genocide Convention explicitly includes a reference to conspiracy to commit genocide.

Consequently, international criminal law has developed its own, sui generis modes of liability, that are uniquely suited to the collective context. Although the more common modes of liability still exist—such as aiding and abetting—the bulk of the jurisprudence of the tribunals has been focused on three: Joint Criminal Enterprise, the Control Theory, and command responsibility (also known as superior responsibility).

1. JOINT CRIMINAL ENTERPRISE

In the first prosecution before the ICTY, the Appeals Chamber took the opportunity to lay the groundwork for a distinctively international mode of liability called Joint Criminal Enterprise, known more colloquially as JCE. The doctrine applies when an individual participates, with others, in a common plan or purpose to perpetrate an international crime. Like conspiracy, the physical perpetration of the crime need not be performed by the defendant. More typically, the plan involves a division of labor where physical tasks are assigned to foot soldiers, and upper echelon participants remain behind the scenes. Nonetheless, all participants are criminally responsible for the crimes carried out by the JCE.

The *Tadić* decision was the ICTY's first articulation of the doctrine, which has been refined in subsequent decisions. The doctrine comes in three flavors, JCE I, JCE II, and JCE III. As you read the decision, focus on the difference between the three variants and the doctrinal requirements for each.

Prosecutor v. Tadić

International Criminal Tribunal for the Former Yugoslavia
Appeals Chamber Judgment
July 15, 1999

Article 7(1) of the Statute and the Notion of Common Purpose

185. The question therefore arises whether under international criminal law the Appellant can be held criminally responsible for the killing of the five men from Jaskići even though there is no evidence that he personally killed any of them. The two central issues are: (i) whether the acts of one person can give rise to the criminal culpability of another where both participate in the execution of a common criminal plan; and (ii) what degree of mens rea is required in such a case.

186. The basic assumption must be that in international law as much as in national systems, the foundation of criminal responsibility is the principle of personal culpability: nobody may be held criminally responsible for acts or transactions in which he has not personally engaged or in some other way participated (*nulla poena sine culpa*). In national legal systems this principle is laid down in Constitutions, in laws, or in judicial decisions. In international criminal law the principle is laid down, inter alia, in Article 7(1) of the Statute of the International Tribunal which states that: "A person who planned, instigated, ordered, committed or otherwise aided and abetted in the planning, preparation or execution of a crime referred to in Articles 2 to 5 of the present Statute, shall be individually responsible for the crime." This provision is aptly

explained by the Report of the Secretary-General on the establishment of the International Tribunal, which states the following:

> An important element in relation to the competence ratione personae (personal jurisdiction) of the International Tribunal is the principle of individual criminal responsibility. As noted above, the Security Council has reaffirmed in a number of resolutions that persons committing serious violations of international humanitarian law in the former Yugoslavia are individually responsible for such violations.

Article 7(1) also sets out the parameters of personal criminal responsibility under the Statute. Any act falling under one of the five categories contained in the provision may entail the criminal responsibility of the perpetrator or whoever has participated in the crime in one of the ways specified in the same provision of the Statute.

187. Bearing in mind the preceding general propositions, it must be ascertained whether criminal responsibility for participating in a common criminal purpose falls within the ambit of Article 7(1) of the Statute.

188. This provision covers first and foremost the physical perpetration of a crime by the offender himself, or the culpable omission of an act that was mandated by a rule of criminal law. However, the commission of one of the crimes envisaged in Articles 2, 3, 4 or 5 of the Statute might also occur through participation in the realisation of a common design or purpose.

189. An interpretation of the Statute based on its object and purpose leads to the conclusion that the Statute intends to extend the jurisdiction of the International Tribunal to all those "responsible for serious violations of international humanitarian law" committed in the former Yugoslavia (Article 1). As is apparent from the wording of both Article 7(1) and the provisions setting forth the crimes over which the International Tribunal has jurisdiction (Articles 2 to 5), such responsibility for serious violations of international humanitarian law is not limited merely to those who actually carry out the actus reus of the enumerated crimes but appears to extend also to other offenders (see in particular Article 2, which refers to committing or ordering to be committed grave breaches of the Geneva Conventions and Article 4 which sets forth various types of offences in relation to genocide, including conspiracy, incitement, attempt and complicity).

190. It should be noted that this notion is spelled out in the Secretary General's Report, according to which: "The Secretary-General believes that all persons who participate in the planning, preparation or execution of serious violations of international humanitarian law in the former Yugoslavia are individually responsible for such violations." Thus,

all those who have engaged in serious violations of international humanitarian law, whatever the manner in which they may have perpetrated, or participated in the perpetration of those violations, must be brought to justice. If this is so, it is fair to conclude that the Statute does not confine itself to providing for jurisdiction over those persons who plan, instigate, order, physically perpetrate a crime or otherwise aid and abet in its planning, preparation or execution. The Statute does not stop there. It does not exclude those modes of participating in the commission of crimes which occur where several persons having a common purpose embark on criminal activity that is then carried out either jointly or by some members of this plurality of persons. Whoever contributes to the commission of crimes by the group of persons or some members of the group, in execution of a common criminal purpose, may be held to be criminally liable, subject to certain conditions, which are specified below.

191. The above interpretation is not only dictated by the object and purpose of the Statute but is also warranted by the very nature of many international crimes which are committed most commonly in wartime situations. Most of the time these crimes do not result from the criminal propensity of single individuals but constitute manifestations of collective criminality: the crimes are often carried out by groups of individuals acting in pursuance of a common criminal design. Although only some members of the group may physically perpetrate the criminal act (murder, extermination, wanton destruction of cities, towns or villages, etc.), the participation and contribution of the other members of the group is often vital in facilitating the commission of the offence in question. It follows that the moral gravity of such participation is often no less—or indeed no different—from that of those actually carrying out the acts in question.

192. Under these circumstances, to hold criminally liable as a perpetrator only the person who materially performs the criminal act would disregard the role as co-perpetrators of all those who in some way made it possible for the perpetrator physically to carry out that criminal act. At the same time, depending upon the circumstances, to hold the latter liable only as aiders and abettors might understate the degree of their criminal responsibility.

193. This interpretation, based on the Statute and the inherent characteristics of many crimes perpetrated in wartime, warrants the conclusion that international criminal responsibility embraces actions perpetrated by a collectivity of persons in furtherance of a common criminal design. It may also be noted that—as will be mentioned below—international criminal rules on common purpose are substantially rooted in, and to a large extent reflect, the position taken by many States of the world in their national legal systems.

194. However, the Tribunal's Statute does not specify (either expressly or by implication) the objective and subjective elements (actus reus and mens rea) of this category of collective criminality. To identify these elements one must turn to customary international law. Customary rules on this matter are discernible on the basis of various elements: chiefly case law and a few instances of international legislation.

195. Many post-World War II cases concerning war crimes proceed upon the principle that when two or more persons act together to further a common criminal purpose, offences perpetrated by any of them may entail the criminal liability of all the members of the group. Close scrutiny of the relevant case law shows that broadly speaking, the notion of common purpose encompasses three distinct categories of collective criminality.

196. The first such category is represented by cases where all co-defendants, acting pursuant to a common design, possess the same criminal intention; for instance, the formulation of a plan among the co-perpetrators to kill, where, in effecting this common design (and even if each co-perpetrator carries out a different role within it), they nevertheless all possess the intent to kill. The objective and subjective prerequisites for imputing criminal responsibility to a participant who did not, or cannot be proven to have, effected the killing are as follows: (i) the accused must voluntarily participate in one aspect of the common design (for instance, by inflicting non-fatal violence upon the victim, or by providing material assistance to or facilitating the activities of his co-perpetrators); and (ii) the accused, even if not personally effecting the killing, must nevertheless intend this result.

202. The second distinct category of cases is in many respects similar to that set forth above, and embraces the so-called "concentration camp" cases. The notion of common purpose was applied to instances where the offences charged were alleged to have been committed by members of military or administrative units such as those running concentration camps; i.e., by groups of persons acting pursuant to a concerted plan. Cases illustrative of this category are *Dachau Concentration Camp*, decided by a United States court sitting in Germany and *Belsen*, decided by a British military court sitting in Germany. In these cases the accused held some position of authority within the hierarchy of the concentration camps. Generally speaking, the charges against them were that they had acted in pursuance of a common design to kill or mistreat prisoners and hence to commit war crimes. In his summing up in the *Belsen* case, the Judge Advocate adopted the three requirements identified by the Prosecution as necessary to establish guilt in each case: (i) the existence of an organised system to ill-treat the detainees and commit the various crimes alleged; (ii) the accused's awareness of the nature of the system; and (iii) the fact that the accused

in some way actively participated in enforcing the system, i.e., encouraged, aided and abetted or in any case participated in the realisation of the common criminal design. The convictions of several of the accused appear to have been explicitly based upon these criteria.

203. This category of cases (which obviously is not applicable to the facts of the present case) is really a variant of the first category, considered above. The accused, when they were found guilty, were regarded as co-perpetrators of the crimes of ill-treatment, because of their objective "position of authority" within the concentration camp system and because they had "the power to look after the inmates and make their life satisfactory" but failed to do so. It would seem that in these cases the required actus reus was the active participation in the enforcement of a system of repression, as it could be inferred from the position of authority and the specific functions held by each accused. The mens rea element comprised: (i) knowledge of the nature of the system and (ii) the intent to further the common concerted design to ill-treat inmates. It is important to note that, in these cases, the requisite intent could also be inferred from the position of authority held by the camp personnel. Indeed, it was scarcely necessary to prove intent where the individual's high rank or authority would have, in and of itself, indicated an awareness of the common design and an intent to participate therein. All those convicted were found guilty of the war crime of ill-treatment, although of course the penalty varied according to the degree of participation of each accused in the commission of the war crime.

204. The third category concerns cases involving a common design to pursue one course of conduct where one of the perpetrators commits an act which, while outside the common design, was nevertheless a natural and foreseeable consequence of the effecting of that common purpose. An example of this would be a common, shared intention on the part of a group to forcibly remove members of one ethnicity from their town, village or region (to effect "ethnic cleansing") with the consequence that, in the course of doing so, one or more of the victims is shot and killed. While murder may not have been explicitly acknowledged to be part of the common design, it was nevertheless foreseeable that the forcible removal of civilians at gunpoint might well result in the deaths of one or more of those civilians. Criminal responsibility may be imputed to all participants within the common enterprise where the risk of death occurring was both a predictable consequence of the execution of the common design and the accused was either reckless or indifferent to that risk. Another example is that of a common plan to forcibly evict civilians belonging to a particular ethnic group by burning their houses; if some of the participants in the plan, in carrying out this plan, kill civilians by setting their houses on fire, all the other participants in the plan are criminally responsible for the killing if these deaths were predictable.

220. In sum, the Appeals Chamber holds the view that the notion of common design as a form of accomplice liability is firmly established in customary international law and in addition is upheld, albeit implicitly, in the Statute of the International Tribunal. As for the objective and subjective elements of the crime, the case law shows that the notion has been applied to three distinct categories of cases. First, in cases of co-perpetration, where all participants in the common design possess the same criminal intent to commit a crime (and one or more of them actually perpetrate the crime, with intent). Secondly, in the so-called "concentration camp" cases, where the requisite mens rea comprises knowledge of the nature of the system of ill-treatment and intent to further the common design of ill-treatment. Such intent may be proved either directly or as a matter of inference from the nature of the accused's authority within the camp or organisational hierarchy. With regard to the third category of cases, it is appropriate to apply the notion of "common purpose" only where the following requirements concerning mens rea are fulfilled: (i) the intention to take part in a joint criminal enterprise and to further—individually and jointly—the criminal purposes of that enterprise; and (ii) the foreseeability of the possible commission by other members of the group of offences that do not constitute the object of the common criminal purpose. Hence, the participants must have had in mind the intent, for instance, to ill-treat prisoners of war (even if such a plan arose extemporaneously) and one or some members of the group must have actually killed them. In order for responsibility for the deaths to be imputable to the others, however, everyone in the group must have been able to predict this result. It should be noted that more than negligence is required. What is required is a state of mind in which a person, although he did not intend to bring about a certain result, was aware that the actions of the group were most likely to lead to that result but nevertheless willingly took that risk. In other words, the so-called *dolus eventualis* is required (also called "advertent recklessness" in some national legal systems).

NOTES & QUESTIONS

Just Convict Everyone. Is JCE III too expansive as a mode of liability? According to the ICTY in *Tadić*, a defendant can be held responsible for actions that fall *outside* the scope of the common plan if the crime was reasonably foreseeable. In some ways, the standard for JCE III is similar to the requirements for the American *Pinkerton* doctrine, which allows a defendant to be convicted for crimes that fall outside the scope of a criminal conspiracy as long as the crime was a reasonably foreseeable consequence of the conspiracy. What mens rea does a defendant in that situation have? Is recklessness an appropriate mens rea for an international crime? Some scholars (and defense attorneys) have criticized JCE III for failing to make distinctions in the relative culpability of participants in a JCE, some of whom may have had different attitudes about the resulting crime. For a discussion, see Mohamed Elewa Badar, *Just Convict Everyone! Joint Perpetration: From Tadić to Stakić and Back Again*, 6 Int'l Crim. L. Rev. 293 (2006); Jens David Ohlin, *Three Conceptual Problems with the Doctrine of JCE*, 5 J. Int'l Crim. Jus. 69 (2007).

2. THE CONTROL THEORY

When the ICC began its operations after the Rome Statute came into force, the judges established early precedents regarding modes of liability. Instead of adopting the ICTY's version of Joint Criminal Enterprise, the ICC Pre-Trial Chamber charted a different course. Article 25(3)(a) of the Rome Statute states that an individual is criminally responsible if he or she commits a crime, "whether as an individual, jointly with another or through another person, regardless of whether that other person is criminally responsible. . ." The judges of the Pre-Trial Chamber interpreted this provision as reference to co-perpetration and indirect perpetration. The question is how these concepts should be defined.

The first judicial application of the Control Theory happened in German domestic penal courts. When Germany was split into two states, East Germany and West Germany, residents of East Germany were not permitted to leave and were shot by border guards if they attempted to flee the country. After reunification, German government officials were held responsible as indirect perpetrators for these killings, because they crafted the policy that was then implemented by the border guards.

In the following case, the Pre-Trial Chamber adopted the Control Theory, which stipulates that the person who "controls" the crime—i.e., decides whether it will occur or not—should be defined as the principal perpetrator, rather than as a mere accomplice. If two or more individuals "control" the crime, they are labeled co-perpetrators. If an individual controls the crime by "using" another individual to carry out the crime for him, he is an indirect perpetrator.

Prosecutor v. Lubanga
International Criminal Court Pre-Trial Chamber I
Decision on the Confirmation of Charges

317. Pursuant to regulation 52(c) of the Regulations of the Court, the Document Containing the Charges must include "a legal characterisation of the facts to accord both with the crimes under articles 6, 7 or 8 and the precise form of participation under articles 25 and 28."

318. Accordingly, in the Document Containing the Charges, the Prosecution charges Thomas Lubanga Dyilo with criminal responsibility under article 25(3)(a) of the Statute, which covers the notions of direct

perpetration (commission of a crime in person), co-perpetration (commission of a crime jointly with another person) and indirect perpetration (commission of a crime through another person, regardless of whether that other person is criminally responsible).

319. Furthermore, the Chamber observes that in the part of the document containing the charges dealing with individual criminal responsibility, the Prosecution charges Thomas Lubanga Dyilo only with individual criminal responsibility as a co-perpetrator within the meaning of article 25(3)(a) of the Statute. Likewise, in its closing brief, the Prosecution asserts that "[f]rom the beginning and continuing throughout the proceedings, the Prosecution has pleaded one form of individual criminal responsibility, namely co-perpetration pursuant to article 25(3)(a) of the Statute" because it "best represents the criminal responsibility for crimes with which Thomas Lubanga Dyilo is charged."

320. The Chamber recalls that in the decision concerning the issuance of a warrant of arrest, it distinguished between (i) the commission strictu senso of a crime by a person as an individual, jointly with another or through another person within the meaning of article 25(3)(a) of the Statute, and (ii) the responsibility of superiors under article 28 of the Statute and "any other forms of accessory, as opposed to principal, liability provided for in article 25(3)(b) to (d) of the Statute."

321. Hence, if the Chamber finds that there is sufficient evidence to establish substantial grounds to believe that Thomas Lubanga Dyilo is criminally responsible as a co-perpetrator for the crimes listed in the Document Containing the Charges, for the purpose of the confirmation of the charges, the question as to whether it may also consider the other forms of accessory liability provided for in articles 25(3)(b) to (d) of the Statute or the alleged superior responsibility of Thomas Lubanga Dyilo under article 28 of the Statute becomes moot, even though these modes of liability have not been expressly pleaded in the Document Containing the Charges.

The concept of co-perpetration as embodied in the Statute

322. The concept of co-perpetration embodied in article 25(3)(a) of the Statute requires analysis. The Prosecution is of the opinion that article 25(3)(a) of the Statute adopts a concept of co-perpetration based on the notion of control of the crime in the sense that a person can become a co-perpetrator of a crime only if he or she has "joint control" over the crime as a result of the "essential contribution" ascribed to him or her.

323. The Prosecution acknowledges that the concept of co-perpetration pursuant to article 25(3)(a) of the Statute differs from that of co-perpetration based on the existence of a joint criminal enterprise or common purpose as reflected, in particular, in the jurisprudence of the ICTY. In this regard, the Prosecution submits that it is important to take

into consideration the fundamental differences between the ad hoc tribunals and the Court, because the latter operates under a Statute which not only sets out modes of criminal liability in great detail, but also deliberately avoids the broader definitions found in, for example, article 7(1) of the ICTY Statute.

324. The Defence does not suggest any interpretation of the concept of co-perpetration, but it challenges the Prosecution's approach saying that it "goes beyond the clear terms of co-perpetration and indirect perpetration set out in the Statute, and is not supported by either customary international law, or general principles of law derived from legal systems of the world."

326. The Chamber is of the view that the concept of co-perpetration is originally rooted in the idea that when the sum of the co-ordinated individual contributions of a plurality of persons results in the realisation of all the objective elements of a crime, any person making a contribution can be held vicariously responsible for the contributions of all the others and, as a result, can be considered as a principal to the whole crime.

327. In this regard, the definitional criterion of the concept of co-perpetration is linked to the distinguishing criterion between principals and accessories to a crime where a criminal offence is committed by a plurality of persons.

328. The objective approach to such a distinction focuses on the realisation of one or more of the objective elements of the crime. From this perspective, only those who physically carry out one or more of the objective elements of the offence can be considered principals to the crime.

329. The subjective approach—which is the approach adopted by the jurisprudence of the ICTY through the concept of joint criminal enterprise or the common purpose doctrine—moves the focus from the level of contribution to the commission of the offence as the distinguishing criterion between principals and accessories, and places it instead on the state of mind in which the contribution to the crime was made. As a result, only those who make their contribution with the shared intent to commit the offence can be considered principals to the crime, regardless of the level of their contribution to its commission.

330. The concept of control over the crime constitutes a third approach for distinguishing between principals and accessories which, contrary to the Defence claim, is applied in numerous legal systems. The notion underpinning this third approach is that principals to a crime are not limited to those who physically carry out the objective elements of the offence, but also include those who, in spite of being removed from the scene of the crime, control or mastermind its commission because they decide whether and how the offence will be committed.

331. This approach involves an objective element, consisting of the appropriate factual circumstances for exercising control over the crime, and a subjective element, consisting of the awareness of such circumstances.

332. According to this approach, only those who have control over the commission of the offence—and are aware of having such control—may be principals because:

i.   they physically carry out the objective elements of the offence (commission of the crime in person, or direct perpetration);

ii. they control the will of those who carry out the objective elements of the offence (commission of the crime through another person, or indirect perpetration); or

iii. they have, along with others, control over the offence by reason of the essential tasks assigned to them (commission of the crime jointly with others, or co-perpetration).

333. Article 25(3)(a) of the Statute does not take into account the objective criterion for distinguishing between principals and accessories because the notion of committing an offence through another person—particularly when the latter is not criminally responsible—cannot be reconciled with the idea of limiting the class of principals to those who physically carry out one or more of the objective elements of the offence.

334. Article 25(3)(a) of the Statute, read in conjunction with article 25(3)(d), also does not take into account the subjective criteria for distinguishing between principals and accessories. In this regard, the Chamber notes that, by moving away from the concept of co-perpetration embodied in article 25(3)(a), article 25(3)(d) defines the concept of (i) contribution to the commission or attempted commission of a crime by a group of persons acting with a common purpose, (ii) with the aim of furthering the criminal activity of the group or in the knowledge of the criminal purpose.

335. The Chamber considers that this latter concept—which is closely akin to the concept of joint criminal enterprise or the common purpose doctrine adopted by the jurisprudence of the ICTY—would have been the basis of the concept of co-perpetration within the meaning of article 25(3)(a), had the drafters of the Statute opted for a subjective approach for distinguishing between principals and accessories.

336. Moreover, the Chamber observes that the wording of article 25(3)(d) of the Statute begins with the words "[i]n any other way contributes to the commission or attempted commission of such a crime."

337. Hence, in the view of the Chamber, article 25(3)(d) of the Statute provides for a residual form of accessory liability which makes it

possible to criminalise those contributions to a crime which cannot be characterised as ordering, soliciting, inducing, aiding, abetting or assisting within the meaning of article 25(3)(b) or article 25(3)(c) of the Statute, by reason of the state of mind in which the contributions were made.

338. Not having accepted the objective and subjective approaches for distinguishing between principals and accessories to a crime, the Chamber considers, as does the Prosecution and, unlike the jurisprudence of the ad hoc tribunals, that the Statute embraces the third approach, which is based on the concept of control over the crime.

339. In this regard, the Chamber notes that the most typical manifestation of the concept of control over the crime, which is the commission of a crime through another person, is expressly provided for in article 25(3)(a) of the Statute. In addition, the use of the phrase "regardless of whether that other person is criminally responsible" in article 25(3)(a) of the Statute militates in favour of the conclusion that this provision extends to the commission of a crime not only through an innocent agent (that is, through another person who is not criminally responsible), but also through another person who is fully criminally responsible.

340. The Chamber considers that the concept of co-perpetration embodied in article 25(3)(a) of the Statute by the reference to the commission of a crime "jointly with. . . another person" must cohere with the choice of the concept of control over the crime as a criterion for distinguishing between principals and accessories.

341. Hence, as stated in its Decision to Issue a Warrant of Arrest,420 the Chamber considers that the concept of co-perpetration embodied in article 25(3)(a) of the Statute coincides with that of joint control over the crime by reason of the essential nature of the various contributions to the commission of the crime.

Elements of co-perpetration based on joint control over the crime

342. The concept of co-perpetration based on joint control over the crime is rooted in the principle of the division of essential tasks for the purpose of committing a crime between two or more persons acting in a concerted manner. Hence, although none of the participants has overall control over the offence because they all depend on one another for its commission, they all share control because each of them could frustrate the commission of the crime by not carrying out his or her task.

*Existence of an agreement or common plan
between two or more persons*

343. In the view of the Chamber, the first objective requirement of co-perpetration based on joint control over the crime is the existence of an agreement or common plan between two or more persons. Accordingly, participation in the commission of a crime without co-ordination with one's co-perpetrators falls outside the scope of co-perpetration within the meaning of article 25(3)(a) of the Statute.

344. The common plan must include an element of criminality, although it does not need to be specifically directed at the commission of a crime. It suffices:

   i.   that the co-perpetrators have agreed (a) to start the implementation of the common plan to achieve a non-criminal goal, and (b) to only commit the crime if certain conditions are met; or

   ii. that the co-perpetrators (a) are aware of the risk that implementing the common plan (which is specifically directed at the achievement of a non-criminal goal) will result in the commission of the crime, and (b) accept such an outcome.

345. Furthermore, the Chamber considers that the agreement need not be explicit and that its existence can be inferred from the subsequent concerted action of the co-perpetrators.

*Co-ordinated essential contribution by each co-perpetrator
resulting in the realisation of the objective
elements of the crime*

346. The Chamber considers that the second objective requirement of co-perpetration based on joint control over the crime is the co-ordinated essential contribution made by each co-perpetrator resulting in the realisation of the objective elements of the crime.

347. In the view of the Chamber, when the objective elements of an offence are carried out by a plurality of persons acting within the framework of a common plan, only those to whom essential tasks have been assigned—and who, consequently, have the power to frustrate the commission of the crime by not performing their tasks—can be said to have joint control over the crime.

348. The Chamber observes that, although some authors have linked the essential character of a task—and hence the ability to exercise joint control over the crime—to its performance at the execution stage of the crime,[425] the Statute does not contain any such restriction.

*The suspect must fulfil the subjective
elements of the crime in question*

349. The Chamber considers that co-perpetration based on joint control over the crime requires above all that the suspect fulfil the subjective elements of the crime with which he or she is charged, including any requisite *dolus specialis* or ulterior intent for the type of crime involved.

350. Article 30 of the Statute sets out the general subjective element for all crimes within the jurisdiction of the Court by specifying that "[u]nless otherwise provided, a person shall be criminally responsible and liable for punishment for a crime within the jurisdiction of the Court only if the material elements are committed with intent and knowledge," that is:

i.   if the person is "[aware] that a circumstance exists or a consequence will occur in the ordinary course of events"; and

ii.   if the person means to engage in the relevant conduct and means to cause the relevant consequence or is aware that it will occur in the ordinary course of events.

351. The cumulative reference to "intent" and "knowledge" requires the existence of a volitional element on the part of the suspect. This volitional element encompasses, first and foremost, those situations in which the suspect (i) knows that his or her actions or omissions will bring about the objective elements of the crime, and (ii) undertakes such actions or omissions with the concrete intent to bring about the objective elements of the crime (also known as *dolus directus* of the first degree).

352. The above-mentioned volitional element also encompasses other forms of the concept of dolus which have already been resorted to by the jurisprudence of the ad hoc tribunals, that is:

i.   situations in which the suspect, without having the concrete intent to bring about the objective elements of the crime, is aware that such elements will be the necessary outcome of his or her actions or omissions (also known as *dolus directus* of the second degree); and

ii.   situations in which the suspect (a) is aware of the risk that the objective elements of the crime may result from his or her actions or omissions, and (b) accepts such an outcome by reconciling himself or herself with it or consenting to it (also known as *dolus eventualis*).

353. The Chamber considers that in the latter type of situation, two kinds of scenarios are distinguishable. Firstly, if the risk of bringing about the objective elements of the crime is substantial (that is, there is a likelihood that it "will occur in the ordinary course of events"), the fact

that the suspect accepts the idea of bringing about the objective elements of the crime can be inferred from:

> i.   the awareness by the suspect of the substantial likelihood that his or her actions or omissions would result in the realisation of the objective elements of the crime; and

> ii.   the decision by the suspect to carry out his or her actions or omissions despite such awareness.

354. Secondly, if the risk of bringing about the objective elements of the crime is low, the suspect must have clearly or expressly accepted the idea that such objective elements may result from his or her actions or omissions.

355. Where the state of mind of the suspect falls short of accepting that the objective elements of the crime may result from his or her actions or omissions, such a state of mind cannot qualify as a truly intentional realisation of the objective elements, and hence would not meet the "intent and knowledge" requirement embodied in article 30 of the Statute.

356. As provided for in article 30(1) of the Statute, the general subjective element ("intent and knowledge") therein contemplated applies to any crime within the jurisdiction of the Court "[u]nless otherwise provided," that is, as long as the definition of the relevant crime does not expressly contain a different subjective element.

NOTES & QUESTIONS

1.   *Indirect Perpetration Through an Organization.* In subsequent cases, the ICC articulated a sub-variant of the Control Theory called indirect perpetration through an organization. The doctrine is also referred to by its German name, *Organisationsherrschaft*, which literally refers to perpetration through an organized apparatus of power. The doctrine applies to individuals who use another to commit a crime. But instead of simply using another human being to commit the crime, the indirect perpetrator uses an entire organization—say a bureaucratic agency or a militia—to carry out the crime. Does this doctrine better capture the collective reality of international atrocities than JCE?

2.   *Indirect Co-Perpetration.* Another variant of the Control Theory is called indirect co-perpetration. Under that scenario, a defendant is twice removed from the physical perpetrators—one step vertically removed and one step horizontally removed. At the leadership level, the defendant cooperates with other co-perpetrators in designing the crime. However, the indirect control is exercised by the defendant's co-perpetrator, rather than the defendant personally. This doctrine was applied in *Prosecutor v. Germain Katanga and Mathieu Ngudjolo Chui,* Decision on Confirmation of Charges, ICC Pre-Trial Chamber (September 30, 2008). For a critical discussion, see

Jens David Ohlin, *Second-Order Linking Principles: Combining Vertical and Horizontal Modes of Liability*, 25 Leiden J. Int'l L. 771 (2012).

3. SUPERIOR OR COMMAND RESPONSIBILITY

The doctrine of command responsibility was first articulated in the case of General Tomoyuki Yamashita, who was prosecuted before an American military tribunal at the end of World War II for atrocities committed by troops under his command. The U.S. Supreme Court upheld his conviction, noting that:

> These provisions plainly imposed on petitioner, who at the time specified was military governor of the Philippines, as well as commander of the Japanese forces, an affirmative duty to take such measures as were within his power and appropriate in the circumstances to protect prisoners of war and the civilian population. This duty of a commanding officer has heretofore been recognized, and its breach penalized by our own military tribunals

Application of Yamashita, 327 U.S. 1, 16 (1946). The doctrine is now applied by all international tribunals and is sometimes referred to as "superior responsibility," since the defendant need not be a member of the military forces to exercise authority over military forces.

The Rome Statute articulates the requirements for the doctrine in article 28:

> A military commander or person effectively acting as a military commander shall be criminally responsible for crimes within the jurisdiction of the Court committed by forces under his or her effective command and control, or effective authority and control as the case may be, as a result of his or her failure to exercise control properly over such forces, where:
>
> (i)   That military commander or person either knew or, owing to the circumstances at the time, should have known that the forces were committing or about to commit such crimes; and
>
> (ii) That military commander or person failed to take all necessary and reasonable measures within his or her power to prevent or repress their commission or to submit the matter to the competent authorities for investigation and prosecution.

There is some controversy in the case law over whether the defendant's actions must make a causal contribution to the crimes committed by his subordinates. Consider the following scenario. The military commander takes command of his unit on June 1. On May 1, the unit committed several atrocities. In June, the military commander fails to adequately investigate the allegations or prosecute the offenders, thus triggering the command responsibility doctrine. But did the failure to punish causally contribute to the crimes? Certainly not, since the crimes occurred *before* the failure to punish. This has led some judges to conclude that a causal contribution to the crime is not required under the doctrine. See, e.g., *Prosecutor v. Orić*, ICTY Trial Chamber II (June 30, 2006), paras. 280–288. Several legal scholars have suggested that the causal contribution requirement be reinstated. See Darryl Robinson, *How Command Responsibility Got So Complicated: A Culpability Contradiction, Its Obfuscation, and A Simple Solution*, 13 Melb. J. Int'l L. 1, 57 (2012) ("Tribunal jurisprudence took an early misstep in rejecting causal contribution for inadequate reasons. This put the jurisprudence and discourse onto a particular path."). For more discussion on command responsibility generally, see Mirjan Damaska, *The Shadow Side of Command Responsibility*, 49 Am. J. Comp. L. 455, 468 (2001) ("When this severe treatment of the commander is observed from the perspective of just desserts, the only plausible ground on which it can be justified is that his failure to punish implies a superior's approval, or subsequent ratification, of his subordinates' transgression. Used as a vehicle for vicarious liability, however, approval of a transgression is alien to the tenets of modern criminal law.").

D. DEFENSES

International defendants are entitled to assert affirmative defenses, just like defendants in domestic criminal law. Self-defense, defense of others, intoxication, duress and necessity, mistake of fact and law, are all possible defenses, though their doctrinal requirements are often stringent. Moreover, the factual predicates for these defenses rarely apply in armed conflict situations, so in practice, defenses have not played the same role when compared to domestic criminal law. Nonetheless, there are situations at the margins where the defenses might apply. Also, some critics suggest that defenses should be more widely recognized in international criminal law, taking into account the often untenable situation that soldiers often find themselves in. The overarching question raised by these doctrines is how sympathetic the law should be when individual perpetrators fail to live up to the demands of the law?

1. DURESS AND NECESSITY

The case of Dražen Erdemović certainly ranks as one of the most disturbing crimes to come out of the war in Bosnia. The Trial Chamber described the event in the following terms:

> On the morning of 16 July 1995, Dražen Erdemović and seven members of the 10th Sabotage Unit of the Bosnian Serb army were ordered to leave their base at Vlasenica and go to the Pilica

farm north-west of Zvornik. When they arrived there, they were informed by their superiors that buses from Srebrenica carrying Bosnian Muslim civilians between 17 and 60 years of age who had surrendered to the members of the Bosnian Serb police or army would be arriving throughout the day. Starting at 10 o'clock in the morning, members of the military police made the civilians in the first buses, all men, get off in groups of ten.

The men were escorted to a field adjacent to the farm buildings where they were lined up with their backs to the firing squad. The members of the 10th Sabotage Unit, including Dražen Erdemović, who composed the firing squad then killed them. Dražen Erdemović carried out the work with an automatic weapon. The executions continued until about 3 o'clock in the afternoon. The accused estimated that there were about 20 buses in all, each carrying approximately 60 men and boys. He believes that he personally killed about seventy people.

Dražen Erdemović claims that he received the order from Brano Gojković, commander of the operations at the Branjevo farm at Pilica, to prepare himself along with seven members of his unit for a mission the purpose of which they had absolutely no knowledge. He claimed it was only when they arrived on-site that the members of the unit were informed that they were to massacre hundreds of Muslims. He asserted his immediate refusal to do this but was threatened with instant death and told "If you don't wish to do it, stand in the line with the rest of them and give others your rifle so that they can shoot you." He declared that had he not carried out the order, he is sure he would have been killed or that his wife or child would have been directly threatened. Regarding this, he claimed to have seen Milorad Pelemis ordering someone to be killed because he had refused to obey. He reported that despite this, he attempted to spare a man between 50 and 60 years of age who said that he had saved Serbs from Srebrenica. Brano Gojković then told him that he did not want any surviving witness to the crime. Dražen Erdemović asserted that he then opposed the order of a lieutenant colonel to participate in the execution of five hundred Muslim men being detained in the Pilica public building. He was able not to commit this further crime because three of his comrades supported him when he refused to obey.

Should Erdemović be excused for his crime? As the following excerpt makes clear, the answer depends in part on whether international criminal law should adopt the common law or civil law approach to necessity and duress. In American criminal law, defendants are not entitled to assert the duress and necessity defenses in cases of murder.

This is the common-law rule ever since *Dudley and Stephens*, 14 Q.B.D. 273 (1884) (the case of the shipwrecked sailors who resorted to cannibalism and were convicted of murder).

As you read the following case, ask yourself whether the law should expect that Erdemović, and those like him, live up to the demands of the law. Is the majority correct that the purpose of IHL will be undermined if the excuse is entertained by international tribunals?

Prosecutor v. Erdemović

International Criminal Tribunal for the Former Yugoslavia
Appeals Chamber Judgment
October 7, 1997

Separate Opinion of Judge McDonald and Judge Vohrah

49. . . . To the extent that the domestic decisions and national laws of States relating to the issue of duress as a defence to murder may be regarded as state practice, it is quite plain that this practice is not at all consistent. The defence in its Notice of Appeal surveys the criminal codes and legislation of 14 civil law jurisdictions in which necessity or duress is prescribed as a general exculpatory principle applying to all crimes. The surveyed jurisdictions comprise those of Austria, Belgium, Brazil, Greece, Italy, Finland, the Netherlands, France, Germany, Peru, Spain, Switzerland, Sweden and the former Yugoslavia. Indeed, the war crimes decisions cited in the Separate Opinion of Judge Cassese are based upon the acceptance of duress as a general defence to all crimes in the criminal codes of France, Italy, Germany, the Netherlands and Belgium. In stark contrast to this acceptance of duress as a defence to the killing of innocents is the clear position of the various countries throughout the world applying the common law. These common law systems categorically reject duress as a defence to murder. The sole exception is the United States where a few states have accepted Section 2.09 of the United States Penal Code which currently provides that duress is a general defence to all crimes. . .

50. Not only is State practice on the question as to whether duress is a defence to murder far from consistent, this practice of States is not, in our view, underpinned by opinio juris. Again to the extent that state practice on the question of duress as a defence to murder may be evidenced by the opinions on this question in decisions of national military tribunals and national laws, we find quite unacceptable any proposition that States adopt this practice because they "feel that they are conforming to what amounts to a legal obligation" at an international level.

59. The penal codes of civil law systems, with some exceptions, consistently recognise duress as a complete defence to all crimes. The

criminal codes of civil law nations provide that an accused acting under duress "commits no crime" or "is not criminally responsible" or "shall not be punished." We would note that some civil law systems distinguish between the notion of necessity and that of duress. Necessity is taken to refer to situations of emergency arising from natural forces. Duress, however, is taken to refer to compulsion by threats of another human being. Where a civil law system makes this distinction, only the provision relating to duress will be referred to.

60. In England, duress is a complete defence to all crimes except murder, attempted murder and, it would appear, treason. Although there is no direct authority on whether duress is available in respect of attempted murder, the prevailing view is that there is no reason in logic, morality or law in granting the defence to a charge of attempted murder whilst withholding it in respect of a charge of murder. United States and Australia The English position that duress operates as a complete defence in respect of crimes generally is followed in the United States and Australia with variations in the federal state jurisdictions as to the precise definition of the defence and the range of offences for which the defence is not available.

66. Having regard to the above survey relating to the treatment of duress in the various legal systems, it is, in our view, a general principle of law recognised by civilised nations that an accused person is less blameworthy and less deserving of the full punishment when he performs a certain prohibited act under duress. We would use the term "duress" in this context to mean "imminent threats to the life of an accused if he refuses to commit a crime" and do not refer to the legal terms of art which have the equivalent meaning of the English word "duress" in the languages of most civil law systems. This alleviation of blameworthiness is manifest in the different rules with differing content in the principal legal systems of the world as the above survey reveals. On the one hand, a large number of jurisdictions recognise duress as a complete defence absolving the accused from all criminal responsibility. On the other hand, in other jurisdictions, duress does not afford a complete defence to offences generally but serves merely as a factor which would mitigate the punishment to be imposed on a convicted person. Mitigation is also relevant in two other respects. Firstly, punishment may be mitigated in respect of offences which have been specifically excepted from the operation of the defence of duress by the legislatures of some jurisdictions. Secondly, courts have the power to mitigate sentences where the strict elements of a defence of duress are not made out on the facts. It is only when national legislatures have prescribed a mandatory life sentence or death penalty for particular offences that no consideration is given in national legal systems to the general principle

that a person who commits a crime under duress is less blameworthy and less deserving of the full punishment in respect of that particular offence.

72. It is clear from the differing positions of the principal legal systems of the world that there is no consistent concrete rule which answers the question whether or not duress is a defence to the killing of innocent persons. It is not possible to reconcile the opposing positions and, indeed, we do not believe that the issue should be reduced to a contest between common law and civil law. We would therefore approach this problem bearing in mind the specific context in which the International Tribunal was established, the types of crimes over which it has jurisdiction, and the fact that the International Tribunals mandate is expressed in the Statute as being in relation to "serious violations of international humanitarian law."

75. . . .[T]he law should not be the product or slave of logic or intellectual hair-splitting, but must serve broader normative purposes in light of its social, political and economic role. It is noteworthy that the authorities. . . issued their cautionary words in respect of domestic society and in respect of a range of ordinary crimes including kidnapping, assault, robbery and murder. Whilst reserving our comments on the appropriate rule for domestic national contexts, we cannot but stress that we are not, in the International Tribunal, concerned with ordinary domestic crimes. The purview of the International Tribunal relates to war crimes and crimes against humanity committed in armed conflicts of extreme violence with egregious dimensions. We are not concerned with the actions of domestic terrorists, gang-leaders and kidnappers. We are concerned that, in relation to the most heinous crimes known to humankind, the principles of law to which we give credence have the appropriate normative effect upon soldiers bearing weapons of destruction and upon the commanders who control them in armed conflict situations. The facts of this particular case, for example, involved the cold-blooded slaughter of 1200 men and boys by soldiers using automatic weapons. We must bear in mind that we are operating in the realm of international humanitarian law which has, as one of its prime objectives, the protection of the weak and vulnerable in such a situation where their lives and security are endangered. Concerns about the harm which could arise from admitting duress as a defence to murder were sufficient to persuade a majority of the House of Lords and the Privy Council to categorically deny the defence in the national context to prevent the growth of domestic crime and the impunity of miscreants. Are they now insufficient to persuade us to similarly reject duress as a complete defence in our application of laws designed to take account of humanitarian concerns in the arena of brutal war, to punish perpetrators of crimes against humanity and war crimes, and to deter the commission of such crimes in the future? If national law denies recognition of duress

as a defence in respect of the killing of innocent persons, international criminal law can do no less than match that policy since it deals with murders often of far greater magnitude. If national law denies duress as a defence even in a case in which a single innocent life is extinguished due to action under duress, international law, in our view, cannot admit duress in cases which involve the slaughter of innocent human beings on a large scale. It must be our concern to facilitate the development and effectiveness of international humanitarian law and to promote its aims and application by recognising the normative effect which criminal law should have upon those subject to them. Indeed, Security Council resolution 827 (1993) establishes the International Tribunal expressly as a measure to "halt and effectively redress" the widespread and flagrant violations of international humanitarian law occurring in the territory of the former Yugoslavia and to contribute thereby to the restoration and maintenance of peace.

76. It might be urged that although the civil law jurisdictions allow duress as a defence to murder, there is no evidence that crimes such as murder and terrorism are any more prevalent in these societies than in common law jurisdictions. We are not persuaded by this argument. We are concerned primarily with armed conflict in which civilian lives, the lives of the most vulnerable, are at great risk. Historical records, past and recent, concerned with armed conflict give countless examples of threats being brought to bear upon combatants by their superiors when confronted with any show of reluctance or refusal on the part of the combatants to carry out orders to perform acts which are in clear breach of international humanitarian law. It cannot be denied that in an armed conflict, the frequency of situations in which persons are forced under duress to commit crimes and the magnitude of the crimes they are forced to commit are far greater than in any peacetime domestic environment.

79. It was suggested during the hearing of 26 May 1997 that neither the English national cases nor the post-World War Two military tribunal decisions specifically addressed the situation in which the accused faced the choice between his own death for not obeying an order to kill or participating in a killing which was inevitably going to occur regardless of whether he participated in it or not. It has been argued that in such a situation where the fate of the victim was already sealed, duress should constitute a complete defence. This is because the accused is then not choosing that one innocent human being should die rather than another. In a situation where the victim or victims would have died in any event, such as in the present case where the victims were to be executed by firing squad, there would be no reason for the accused to have sacrificed his life. The accused could not have saved the victims life by giving his own and thus, according to this argument, it is unjust and illogical for the law to expect an accused to sacrifice his life in the knowledge that the

victim's will die anyway. . . For the reasons given below we would reject [this] approach. . .

80. [This] approach proceeds from the starting point of strict utilitarian logic based on the fact that if the victim will die anyway, the accused is not at all morally blameworthy for taking part in the execution; there is absolutely no reason why the accused should die as it would be unjust for the law to expect the accused to die for nothing. It should be immediately apparent that the assertion that the accused is not morally blameworthy where the victim would have died in any case depends entirely again upon a view of morality based on utilitarian logic. This does not, in our opinion, address the true rationale for our rejection of duress as a defence to the killing of innocent human beings. The approach we take does not involve a balancing of harms for and against killing but rests upon an application in the context of international humanitarian law of the rule that duress does not justify or excuse the killing of an innocent person. Our view is based upon a recognition that international humanitarian law should guide the conduct of combatants and their commanders. There must be legal limits as to the conduct of combatants and their commanders in armed conflict. In accordance with the spirit of international humanitarian law, we deny the availability of duress as a complete defence to combatants who have killed innocent persons. In so doing, we give notice in no uncertain terms that those who kill innocent persons will not be able to take advantage of duress as a defence and thus get away with impunity for their criminal acts in the taking of innocent lives.

84. . . . [W]e are of the view that soldiers or combatants are expected to exercise fortitude and a greater degree of resistance to a threat than civilians, at least when it is their own lives which are being threatened. Soldiers, by the very nature of their occupation, must have envisaged the possibility of violent death in pursuance of the cause for which they fight. The relevant question must therefore be framed in terms of what may be expected from the ordinary soldier in the situation of the Appellant. What is to be expected of such an ordinary soldier is not, by our approach, analysed in terms of a utilitarian approach involving the weighing up of harms. Rather, it is based on the proposition that it is unacceptable to allow a trained fighter, whose job necessarily entails the occupational hazard of dying, to avail himself of a complete defence to a crime in which he killed one or more innocent persons.

85. Finally, we think, with respect, that it is inaccurate to say that by rejecting duress as a defence to the killing of innocent persons, the law "expects" a person who knows that the victims will die anyway to throw his life away in vain. If there were a mandatory life sentence which we would be bound to impose upon a person convicted of killing with only an executive pardon available to do justice to the accused, it may well be

said that the law "expects" heroism from its subjects. Indeed, such a mandatory life-term was prescribed for murder in England at the time the relevant English cases were decided and featured prominently in the considerations of the judges. We are not bound to impose any such mandatory term. One cannot superficially gauge what the law "expects" by the existence of only two alternatives: conviction or acquittal. In reality, the law employs mitigation of punishment as a far more sophisticated and flexible tool for the purpose of doing justice in an individual case. The law, in our view, does not "expect" a person whose life is threatened to be hero and to sacrifice his life by refusing to commit the criminal act demanded of him. The law does not "expect" that person to be a hero because in recognition of human frailty and the threat under which he acted, it will mitigate his punishment. In appropriate cases, the offender may receive no punishment at all. . .

Separate Opinion of Judge Cassese

47. I contend that the international legal regulation of duress in case of murder, as I have endeavoured to infer it from case-law and practice, is both realistic and flexible. It also takes account of social expectations more than the rule suggested by the Prosecution and that propounded by the majority.

Law is based on what society can reasonably expect of its members. It should not set intractable standards of behaviour which require mankind to perform acts of martyrdom, and brand as criminal any behaviour falling below those standards.

Consider the following example. A driver of a van unwittingly transporting victims to a place of execution, upon arrival is told by the executioners he must shoot one of the victims or he himself will be shot. This, of course, is done in order to assure his silence since he will then be implicated in the unlawful killing. The victims who are at the execution site will certainly die in any event. Can society reasonably expect the driver in these circumstances to sacrifice his life? In such situations it may be too demanding to require of the person under duress that they do not perpetrate the offence. I should add that the war in the former Yugoslavia furnishes us with so many examples of such atrocities that this International Tribunal ought not to dismiss any possible scenario as fanciful or farfetched.

Let us consider another case, a variation of an example drawn from proceedings which have taken place before this very International Tribunal. An inmate of a concentration camp, starved and beaten for months, is then told, after a savage beating, that if he does not kill another inmate, who has already been beaten with metal bars and will certainly be beaten to death before long, then his eyes will, then and there, be gouged out. He kills the other inmate as a result. Perhaps a hero could accept a swift bullet in his skull to avoid having to kill, but it would require an extraordinary—and perhaps impossible—act of courage to accept one's eyes being plucked out. Can one truly say that the man in this example should have allowed his eyes to be gouged out and that he is a criminal for not having done so? This example, and one can imagine still worse, is one of those rare cases, in my opinion, where duress should be entertained as a complete defence. Any answer to the question of duress has to be able to cope with such examples which the war in Yugoslavia—and wars throughout the world—have generated and, regretfully, will continue to generate.

48. Another remark seems apposite. I do not see any point in contending that, since duress can be urged in mitigation, a court of law could take account of the situations just discussed by sentencing the person who acted under duress to a minimum or token penalty. Any such contention would neglect a critical, inescapable point, namely that the purpose of criminal law, including international criminal law, is to punish behaviour which is criminal, i.e., morally reprehensible or injurious to society, not to condemn behaviour which is "the product of coercion that is truly irresistible" or the choice of the lesser of two evils. No matter how much mitigation a court allows an accused, the fundamental fact remains that if it convicts him, it regards his behaviour as criminal, and considers that he should have behaved differently. I have tried to demonstrate that this may be unjust and unreasonable where the accused can do nothing to save the victims by laying down his own life. . .

49. What I have argued so far leads me to the conclusion that international criminal law on duress is not ambiguous or uncertain. Here lies the main point of my disagreement with the Appeals Chamber's majority. Admittedly, when duress is urged as a defence for a war crime or a crime against humanity where the underlying offence is the killing of innocent persons, it proves particularly difficult for the international judge to establish whether the relevant facts are present and the necessary high requirements laid down in law are satisfied. But this is a matter for the trial judge to look into. However difficult and tricky his judicial investigation, he is not left emptyhanded by law: on the contrary, he can draw from international law fairly accurate guidelines, spelled out in a number of national cases dealing with war crimes and crimes against humanity.

It should therefore be no surprise that I do not share the views of the majority of the Appeals Chamber, according to which, since international criminal law is ambiguous or uncertain on this matter, it is warranted to make a policy-directed choice and thus rely on "considerations of social and economic policy." I disagree not only because, as I have already repeatedly stated, in my view international law is not ambiguous or uncertain, but also because to uphold in this area of criminal law the concept of recourse to a policy-directed choice is tantamount to running foul of the customary principle *nullum crimen sine lege.* An international court must apply *lex lata,* that is to say, the existing rules of international law as they are created through the sources of the international legal system. If it has instead recourse to policy considerations or moral principles, it acts *ultra vires.*

In any event, even assuming that no clear legal regulation of the matter were available in international law, arguably the Appeals Chamber majority should have drawn upon the law applicable in the former Yugoslavia. In the former Yugoslavia and in the present States of the area the relevant criminal law provides that duress (called "extreme necessity") may amount to a total defence for any crime, whether or not implying the killing of persons. A national of one of the States of that region fighting in an armed conflict was required to know those national criminal provisions and base his expectations on their contents. Were *ex hypothesi* international criminal law really ambiguous on duress or were it even to contain a gap, it would therefore be appropriate and judicious to have recourse—as a last resort—to the national legislation of the accused, rather than to moral considerations or policy-oriented principles. . .

NOTES & QUESTIONS

The View from the ICC. Although the ICTY sided with the common law view and concluded that duress and necessity should be unavailable as defenses, the Rome Statute seems to side with the civil law position. Article 31(1)(d) confers a defense if "[t]he conduct which is alleged to constitute a crime within the jurisdiction of the Court has been caused by duress resulting from a threat of imminent death or of continuing or imminent serious bodily harm against that person or another person, and the person acts necessarily and reasonably to avoid this threat, provided that the person does not intend to cause a greater harm than the one sought to be avoided." Would this provision have benefited Erdemović? Did he act "reasonably"? Did he cause greater or lesser harm that the one he avoided?

2. MISTAKES OF FACT OR LAW

Under some circumstances, defendants may assert a mistake defense. This is rare, because just like domestic criminal law, ignorance of the law is no excuse. However, legal systems are more tolerant of mistake of fact. The general rule is that mistakes of fact constitute a defense only when the mistake "negates" a required element of the crime.

Article 32 of the Rome Statute stipulates that "a mistake of law as to whether a particular type of conduct is a crime within the jurisdiction of the Court shall not be a ground for excluding criminal responsibility."

However, the provision continues with this qualification: "A mistake of law may, however, be a ground for excluding criminal responsibility if it negates the mental element required by such a crime or as provided for in article 33." The reference to article 33 is the Rome Statute's provision on superior orders, which provides that a defense of "just following orders" is applicable if the following conditions are met:

(a)   The person was under a legal obligation to obey orders of the Government or the superior in question;

(b)   The person did not know that the order was unlawful; and

(c)   The order was not manifestly unlawful.

This sounds as if a defendant could argue the defense of superior orders in many situations. However, the next sub-section of article 33 stipulates that crimes against humanity and genocide are always "manifestly unlawful." In reality, then, the defense of superior orders is only possible for war crimes, if at all.

3.   LEGAL INCAPACITY

International criminal law criminalizes the use or conscription of child soldiers. Indeed, the first conviction at the ICC—against Thomas Lubanga—was for the war crime of conscripting child soldiers. But what if the child soldiers commit crimes themselves? Can the children be prosecuted at an international tribunal?

The simple answer is that the ICC does not have jurisdiction over defendants who were less than 18 years old when the crimes were committed. This provision (article 26) is considered a jurisdictional provision rather than an excuse. In theory, then, child soldiers may be responsible for their behavior and subject to criminal liability elsewhere. Generally speaking, though, the field of international criminal justice often views child soldiers as victims rather than perpetrators.

The more complex answer is that the phenomenon of child soldiers demonstrates that the categories of "victim" and "perpetrator" are not mutually exclusive. It is possible to be both at the same time. This is especially problematic when one realizes that adult perpetrators may be *former* child soldiers. They may have been conscripted, or even kidnapped, years or decades earlier and forced to fight with a militia. Then, if they commit crimes years later as adults, how should courts treat the coercive conditions that led them to become combatants? These are, in many ways, unresolved questions in the field of international criminal justice. For more discussion, see Mark Drumbl, *Reimagining Child Soldiers in International Law and Policy* 40 (2012) ("particularized evidence from disparate sources warns that discourses of innocence, non-responsibility, and excuse are of limited utility in the reintegration of minoritorian—albeit key—at-risk subgroups of child soldiers").

Conclusion & Summary

International criminal law has a rich tradition going back to Nuremberg, but since the mid-1990s has experienced an explosion of activity that has quickly produced a rich jurisprudence from various tribunals:

1. The ICTY, ICTR, and other ad hoc tribunals have tightly defined jurisdictions, while the ICC has a more general jurisdiction. That being the case, a variety of mechanisms limit the capacity of the ICC to exercise jurisdiction, including the principle of complementarity. Also, the ICC generally cannot exercise jurisdiction over crimes committed on the territory of a non-state party, unless the Security Council exercises its Chapter VII authority to refer a case to the ICC.

2. The core crimes applicable at most international tribunals include war crimes, crimes against humanity, and genocide. War crimes are violations of IHL that occur during an armed conflict, either international or non-international. Neither crimes against humanity nor genocide require a nexus with armed conflict and can be perpetrated in peacetime. Crimes against humanity require a widespread and systematic attack against a civilian population as part of a state or organizational plan or policy, though the definition of "organizational" is highly contested. Although some courts have ruled that genocide does not include a plan or policy requirement, it does require the special mental element of genocidal intent. The only protected groups are national, ethnical, racial, or religious groups, and political groups do not, per se, qualify.

3. In addition to proving the chapeau elements for the international crime, a prosecutor must establish the elements for the underlying predicate crime.

4. International criminal law uses distinctive modes of liability, in part because conspiracy was so controversial at Nuremberg. The ICTY and ICTR have focused on JCE, while the ICC applies the Control Theory, a version of co-perpetration. Although both doctrines involve collective action, their doctrinal elements are different. JCE requires that the defendant participate with others in a criminal plan or purpose to carry out an international crime. JCE III is particularly controversial because it is based on the mens rea of recklessness; the defendant takes the risk that their participation in a collective crime might yield unintended

consequences. In contrast, the Control Theory declares that whoever controls the crime is the principal perpetrator, even if others under their direction carried out the physical perpetration of the crime. Command responsibility allows a court to prosecute a commander for failing to adequately prevent or punish atrocities committed by subordinates.

5.   In a narrow 3–2 decision, the ICTY rejected the necessity and duress defenses for a defendant charged with the killing of innocent civilians. However, the ultimate fate of these defenses is somewhat unresolved, since the ICC Statute allows for duress and necessity defenses if the defendant acts reasonably and also meets a "lesser evils" standard. One central worry with the defenses is that they will unwind the protections that innocent civilians are owed under the law of war. At issue is whether soldiers are under a legal (and underlying moral) obligation to sacrifice themselves rather than take the life of innocent civilians.

CHAPTER 14

APPLYING INTERNATIONAL LAW IN DOMESTIC COURTS

Introduction

One might assume that the central location for the enforcement of international law is international courts and tribunals. In reality, though, international legal norms are applied, interpreted, and enforced in domestic courts all the time. However, legal systems have different ways of incorporating international law into their domestic legal systems.

For example, some countries are strongly monist in their legal culture. Monism is the view that there is one legal system in the world—international law—and domestic legal systems are essentially sub-units of that larger system. This monist worldview means that all domestic legal systems are subordinate to international law, which represents a universal framework that is hierarchically superior to the various "municipal" legal systems in each country.

On the other hand, some countries adopt a more dualist approach to their relationship with international law. Dualism is the view that there are many legal systems in the world, none of which are hierarchically superior to any other. Under this view, international law is just one legal system among many in the world, and therefore not necessarily entitled to privileged treatment. In a sense, dualism treats international law as a "foreign" legal system, just as much as the law of Germany or France or Japan.

One practical consequence of the distinction between monism and dualism is that monist legal systems, such as the Netherlands, are more likely to apply and enforce international legal norms in their domestic legal systems, in part because their lawyers view this process as natural and expected since Dutch law and international law are both part of the same legal system. In contrast, courts and judges with a dualist worldview are more likely to require a specific *incorporation* of international law into their domestic legal system before these norms can be applied or enforced in the domestic sphere. Under this view, domestic courts apply domestic law; international law needs to be brought home *into* domestic law before a court might apply it.

Although such generalizations can be hazardous, it is probably safe to conclude that the United States is more dualist than monist in its attitude toward international law. International law is not regarded as *automatically* enforceable in a federal court, but rather must be incorporated through some mechanism. For treaty-based legal norms, that incorporation happens when the Senate gives advice and consent to the treaty's ratification, combined with the fact that the U.S. Constitution explicitly includes treaties within the federal Supremacy Clause. But what about customary international law?

This chapter focuses on the fate of international law in U.S. courts and the mechanisms by which international law might be enforced and applied domestically. The first section examines the mechanism by which customary international law is incorporated into the U.S. legal system— an incorporation with a rich history that dates back at least as far as the War of Independence and the birth of the American nation. As *Paquete Habana* demonstrates, customary international law is incorporated into domestic law through the common law, which the U.S. inherited from England at the time of independence. The second section focuses on the Alien Tort Statute, a federal statute that grants federal courts the jurisdiction to adjudicate allegations of torts committed in violation of the "law of nations," or what today would be called customary international law. In the last 30 years, human rights lawyers have used the Alien Tort Statute to file dozens of cases against alleged violators for atrocities and other human rights violations committed overseas. However, the exact meaning of the Statute, and the jurisdiction it gives federal courts, has remained controversial despite more than one intervention by the U.S. Supreme Court to clarify the Statute's meaning. Finally, the third section of the chapter analyzes the degree to which international judgments— particularly those from the International Court of Justice—are automatically enforceable in U.S. courts. Taken together, these materials present a portrait of a dualistic legal system struggling to navigate the complex, evolving—and at time contentious—relationship between domestic and international law and their respective institutions.

A. INTERNATIONAL LAW AS FEDERAL LAW

In the following case, the Supreme Court was tasked with adjudicating the fate of two fishing vessels seized off the coast of Cuba. Under normal rules of international law governing armed conflict, vessels interdicted on the high seas were subject to capture as prizes of war—though fishing vessels were exempted from this rule of customary international law. Much of *Paquete Habana* is devoted to a lengthy and sophisticated analysis of international custom. But also pay attention to the deeper point articulated by Justice Gray, i.e., why the court has the authority to find and apply customary international law in the first place. How and when was customary international law incorporated into U.S. law?

The Paquete Habana
Supreme Court of the United States
175 U.S. 677 (1900)

■ MR. JUSTICE GRAY delivered the opinion of the court:

These are two appeals from decrees of the district court of the United States for the southern district of Florida condemning two fishing vessels and their cargoes as prize of war.

Each vessel was a fishing smack, running in and out of Havana, and regularly engaged in fishing on the coast of Cuba; sailed under the Spanish flag; was owned by a Spanish subject of Cuban birth, living in the city of Havana; was commanded by a subject of Spain, also residing in Havana; and her master and crew had no interest in the vessel, but were entitled to shares, amounting in all to two thirds, of her catch, the other third belonging to her owner. Her cargo consisted of fresh fish, caught by her crew from the sea, put on board as they were caught, and kept and sold alive. Until stopped by the blockading squadron she had no knowledge of the existence of the war or of any blockade. She had no arms or ammunition on board, and made no attempt to run the blockade after she knew of its existence, nor any resistance at the time of the capture.

The Paquete Habana was a sloop, 43 feet long on the keel, and of 25 tons burden, and had a crew of three Cubans, including the master, who had a fishing license from the Spanish government, and no other commission or license. She left Havana March 25, 1898; sailed along the coast of Cuba to Cape San Antonio, at the western end of the island, and there fished for twenty-five days, lying between the reefs off the cape, within the territorial waters of Spain; and then started back for Havana, with a cargo of about 40 quintals of live fish. On April 25, 1898, about 2 miles off Mariel, and 11 miles from Havana, she was captured by the United States gunboat Castine.

The Lola was a schooner, 51 feet long on the keel, and of 35 tons burden, and had a crew of six Cubans, including the master, and no commission or license. She left Havana April 11, 1898, and proceeded to Campeachy sound, off Yucatan, fished there eight days, and started back for Havana with a cargo of about 10,000 pounds of live fish. On April 26, 1898, near Havana, she was stopped by the United States steamship Cincinnati, and was warned not to go into Havana, but was told that she would be allowed to land at Bahia Honda. She then changed her course, and put for Bahia Honda, but on the next morning, when near that port, was captured by the United States steamship Dolphin.

Both the fishing vessels were brought by their captors into Key West. A libel for the condemnation of each vessel and her cargo as prize of war was there filed on April 27, 1898; a claim was interposed by her master on behalf of himself and the other members of the crew, and of her owner;

evidence was taken, showing the facts above stated; and on May 30, 1898, a final decree of condemnation and sale was entered, "the court not being satisfied that as a matter of law, without any ordinance, treaty, or proclamation, fishing vessels of this class are exempt from seizure." . . .

We are then brought to the consideration of the question whether, upon the facts appearing in these records, the fishing smacks were subject to capture by the armed vessels of the United States during the recent war with Spain.

By an ancient usage among civilized nations, beginning centuries ago, and gradually ripening into a rule of international law, coast fishing vessels, pursuing their vocation of catching and bringing in fresh fish, have been recognized as exempt, with their cargoes and crews, from capture as prize of war.

This doctrine, however, has been earnestly contested at the bar; and no complete collection of the instances illustrating it is to be found, so far as we are aware, in a single published work although many are referred to and discussed by the writers on international law. . . It is therefore worth the while to trace the history of the rule, from the earliest accessible sources, through the increasing recognition of it, with occasional setbacks, to what we may now justly consider as its final establishment in our own country and generally throughout the civilized world.

The earliest acts of any government on the subject, mentioned in the books, either emanated from, or were approved by, a King of England.

In 1403 and 1406 Henry IV. issued orders to his admirals and other officers, entitled "Concerning Safety for Fishermen—*De Securitate pro Piscatoribus.*" By an order of October 26, 1403, reciting that it was made pursuant to a treaty between himself and the King of France; and for the greater safety of the fishermen of either country, and so that they could be, and carry on their industry, the more safely on the sea, and deal with each other in peace; and that the French King had consented that English fishermen should be treated likewise,—it was ordained that French fishermen might, during the then pending season for the herring fishery, safely fish for herrings and all other fish, from the harbor of Gravelines and the island of Thanet to the mouth of the Seine and the harbor of Hautoune. . .

The treaty made October 2, 1521, between the Emperor Charles V. and Francis I. of France, through their ambassadors, recited that a great and fierce war had arisen between them, because of which there had been, both by land and by sea, frequent depredations and incursions on either side, to the grave detriment and intolerable injury of the innocent subjects of each; and that a suitable time for the herring fishery was at hand, and, by reason of the sea being beset by the enemy, the fishermen did not dare to go out, whereby the subject of their industry, bestowed by heaven to allay the hunger of the poor, whould wholly fail for the year, unless it were otherwise provided. . . And it was therefore agreed that the subjects of each sovereign, fishing in the sea, or exercising the calling of fishermen, could and might, until the end of the next January, without incurring any attack, depredation, molestation, trouble, or hindrance soever, safely and freely, everywhere in the sea, take herrings and every other kind of fish, the existing war by land and sea notwithstanding; and, further, that during the time aforesaid no subject of either sovereign should commit, or attempt or presume to commit, any depredation, force, violence, molestation, or vexation to or upon such fishermen or their vessels, supplies, equipments, nets, and fish, or other goods soever truly appeartaining to fishing. . .

The herring fishery was permitted, in time of war, by French and Dutch edicts in 1536.

France, from remote times, set the example of alleviating the evils of war in favor of all coast fishermen. . . The same custom would seem to have prevailed in France until towards the end of the seventeenth century. For example, in 1675, Louis XIV. and the States General of Holland by mutual agreement granted to Dutch and French fishermen the liberty, undisturbed by their vessels of war, of fishing along the coats of France, Holland, and England. But by the ordinances of 1681 and 1692 the practice was discontinued, because, Valin says, of the faithless conduct of the enemies of France, who, abusing the good faith with which she had always observed the treaties, habitually carried off her fishermen, while their own fished in safety.

The doctrine which exempts coast fishermen, with their vessels and cargoes, from capture as prize of war, has been familiar to the United States from the time of the War of Independence. . .

Since the United States became a nation, the only serious interruptions, so far as we are informed, of the general recognition of the exemption of coast fishing vessels from hostile capture, arose out of the mutual suspicions and recriminations of England and France during the wars of the French Revolution. . .

International law is part of our law, and must be ascertained and administered by the courts of justice of appropriate jurisdiction as often as questions of right depending upon it are duly presented for their determination. For this purpose, where there is no treaty and no controlling executive or legislative act or judicial decision, resort must be had to the customs and usages of civilized nations, and, as evidence of these, to the works of jurists and commentators who by years of labor, research, and experience have made themselves peculiarly well acquainted with the subjects of which they treat. Such works are resorted to by judicial tribunals, not for the speculations of their authors concerning what the law ought to be, but for trustworthy evidence of what the law really is.

Wheaton places among the principal sources international law "text-writers of authority, showing what is the approved usage of nations, or the general opinion respecting their mutual conduct, with the definitions and modifications introduced by general consent." As to these he forcibly observes: "Without wishing to exaggerate the importance of these writers, or to substitute, in any case, their authority for the principles of reason, it may be affirmed that they are generally impartial in their judgment. They are witnesses of the sentiments and usages of civilized nations, and the weight of their testimony increases every time that their authority is invoked by statesmen, and every year that passes without the rules laid down in their works being impugned by the avowal of contrary principles."

Chancellor Kent says: "In the absence of higher and more authoritative sanctions, the ordinances of foreign states, the opinions of eminent statesmen, and the writings of distinguished jurists, are regarded as of great consideration on questions not settled by conventional law. In cases where the principal jurists agree, the presumption will be very great in favor of the solidity of their maxims; and no civilized nation that does not arrogantly set all ordinary law and justice at defiance will venture to disregard the uniform sense of the established writers on international law."

It will be convenient, in the first place, to refer to some leading French treatises on international law, which deal with the question now before us, not as one of the law of France only, but as one determined by the general consent of civilized nations. . .

This review of the precedents and authorities on the subject appears to us abundantly to demonstrate that at the present day, by the general consent of the civilized nations of the world, and independently of any express treaty or other public act, it is an established rule of international law, founded on considerations of humanity to a poor and industrious order of men, and of the mutual convenience of belligerent states, that coast fishing vessels, with their implements and supplies, cargoes and crews, unarmed and honestly pursuing their peaceful calling of catching and bringing in fresh fish, are exempt from capture as prize of war.

The exemption, of course, does not apply to coast fishermen or their vessels if employed for a warlike purpose, or in such a way as to give aid or information to the enemy; nor when military or naval operations create a necessity to which all private interests must give way.

Nor has the exemption been extended to ships or vessels employed on the high sea in taking whales or seals or cod or other fish which are not brought fresh to market, but are salted or otherwise cured and made a regular article of commerce.

This rule of international law is one which prize courts administering the law of nations are bound to take judicial notice of, and to give effect to, in the absence of any treaty or other public act of their own government in relation to the matter. . .

To this subject in more than one aspect are singularly applicable the words uttered by Mr. Justice Strong, speaking for this court: "Undoubtedly no single nation can change the law of the sea. The law is of universal obligation and no statute of one or two nations can create obligations for the world. Like all the laws of nations, it rests upon the common consent of civilized communities. It is of force, not because it was prescribed by any superior power, but because it has been generally accepted as a rule of conduct. Whatever may have been its origin, whether in the usages of navigation, or in the ordinances of maritime states, or in both, it has become the law of the sea only by the concurrent sanction of those nations who may be said to constitute the commercial world. Many of the usages which prevail, and which have the force of law, doubtless originated in the positive prescriptions of some single state, which were at first of limited effect, but which, when generally accepted, became of universal obligation." "This is not giving to the statutes of any nation extraterritorial effect. It is not treating them as general maritime laws; but it is recognition of the historical fact that by common consent of mankind these rules have been acquiesced in as of general obligation. Of that fact, we think, we may take judicial notice. Foreign municipal laws must indeed be proved as facts, but it is not so with the law of nations." *The Scotia,* 14 Wall. 170, 187, 188.

The position taken by the United States during the recent war with Spain was quite in accord with the rule of international law, now generally recognized by civilized nations, in regard to coast fishing vessels. . .

[I]t is the duty of this court, sitting as the highest prize court of the United States, and administering the law of nations, to declare and adjudge that the capture was unlawful and without probable cause. . .

NOTES & QUESTIONS

1. *Did Paquete Survive Erie? Paquete Habana* stands for the proposition that "international law is part of our law"—incorporated into the common law at the founding of the nation because international law was part of the common law of England. In an influential article, Professors Curtis Bradley and Jack Goldsmith questioned this legacy, arguing that the holding of *Paquete Habana* was fundamentally undermined by the Supreme Court's holding in *Erie R.R. Co. v. Tompkins,* 304 U.S. 64 (1938). In *Erie,* the Court ruled that district court judges in diversity cases should apply the common

law of the state in which they sit (articulated by state courts), rather than consulting a "general common law" articulated by federal judges. This ended the era of a federal common law and ushered in a post-*Erie* era of common law as state law. If *Paquete Habana* means that international law is incorporated into federal common law, where did international law go when *Erie* effectively eliminated the federal common law in 1938? According to Bradley and Goldsmith, the authority to apply international law devolved to state courts. See Curtis Bradley & Jack L. Goldsmith, *Customary International Law as Federal Common Law: A Critique of the Modern Position*, 110 Harv. L. Rev. 815, 816–17 (1997). Do you agree?

2.   *Understanding the Modern Position.* In a brief article written shortly after *Erie* was decided, Professor Jessup, an American jurist who would later serve as a judge on the ICJ, conceded that "[i]f the dictum of Mr. Justice Brandeis in the *Tompkins* case is to be applied broadly, it would follow that hereafter a state court's determination of a rule of international law would be a finding regarding the law of the state and would not be reviewed by the Supreme Court of the United States." Jessup argued that this result would lead to untenable pluralism, each state deciding for itself how to apply and interpret international law: "Any question of applying international law in our courts involves the foreign relations of the United States and can thus be brought within a federal power." See Philip C. Jessup, *The Doctrine of Erie Railroad v. Tompkins Applied to International Law*, 33 Am. J. Int'l L. 740 (1939). In other words, international law should not be subject to the *Erie* rule.

In *Banco Nacional de Cuba v. Sabbatino*, 376 U.S. 398, 425 (1964), the Supreme Court sided with Jessup and reached this conclusion:

> [W]e are constrained to make it clear that an issue concerned with a basic choice regarding the competence and function of the Judiciary and the National Executive in ordering our relationships with other members of the international community must be treated exclusively as an aspect of federal law. It seems fair to assume that the Court did not have rules like the act of state doctrine in mind when it decided *Erie R. Co. v. Tompkins*. Soon thereafter, Professor Philip C. Jessup, now a judge of the International Court of Justice, recognized the potential dangers were *Erie* extended to legal problems affecting international relations. He cautioned that rules of international law should not be left to divergent and perhaps parochial state interpretations.

Most international law scholars viewed the *Sabbatino* decision as reinforcing the continuing validity of *Paquete Habana*'s conclusion that international law remains "part of our law." See Harold Hongju Koh, *Is International Law Really State Law?*, 111 Harv. L. Rev. 1824, 1835 (1998) ("The proper reading of this doctrine, in my view, is that even after *Erie* and *Sabbatino*, federal courts retain legitimate authority to incorporate bona fide rules of customary international law into federal common law.")

B. THE ALIEN TORT STATUTE

As you will read below, Judge Friendly described the Alien Tort Statute as a "legal Lohengrin," a character from Germanic literature and later a Wagner opera, because "no one seems to know whence it came." *IIT v. Vencap, Ltd.*, 519 F.2d 1001, 1015 (2d Cir. 1975). In the opera, the character Elsa asks God to send her a champion; Lohengrin the knight appears from nowhere on a boat pulled by a giant swan. Friendly's reference to Lohengrin the knight suggested that the ATS was a powerful force, but that asking about its origin and meaning would raise difficult and uncomfortable questions—about the role of federal courts, about the relationship between domestic and international law, and indeed about the nature of law itself.

The Alien Tort Statute laid essentially dormant for centuries until revived by cases like *Filartiga v. Pena-Irala*. As you read *Filartiga*, ask yourself which cases regarding international law violations the judiciary is committing itself to adjudicating. Are the doors of the federal judiciary open to the entire world? Does the Alien Tort Statute represent a kind of universal jurisdiction for civil claims arising from violations of international law? If the ATS is a legal Lohengrin, who sent it and why?

Filartiga v. Pena-Irala
U.S. Court of Appeals for the Second Circuit
630 F.2d 876 (1980)

■ IRVING R. KAUFMAN, CIRCUIT JUDGE:

Upon ratification of the Constitution, the thirteen former colonies were fused into a single nation, one which, in its relations with foreign states, is bound both to observe and construe the accepted norms of international law, formerly known as the law of nations. Under the Articles of Confederation, the several states had interpreted and applied this body of doctrine as a part of their common law, but with the founding of the "more perfect Union" of 1789, the law of nations became preeminently a federal concern.

Implementing the constitutional mandate for national control over foreign relations, the First Congress established original district court jurisdiction over "all causes where an alien sues for a tort only (committed) in violation of the law of nations." Judiciary Act of 1789, ch. 20, § 9(b), 1 Stat. 73, 77 (1789), codified at 28 U.S.C. § 1350. Construing this rarely-invoked provision, we hold that deliberate torture perpetrated under color of official authority violates universally accepted norms of the international law of human rights, regardless of the nationality of the parties. Thus, whenever an alleged torturer is found and served with process by an alien within our borders, § 1350 provides federal jurisdiction. Accordingly, we reverse the judgment of the district court dismissing the complaint for want of federal jurisdiction.

I

The appellants, plaintiffs below, are citizens of the Republic of Paraguay. Dr. Joel Filartiga, a physician, describes himself as a longstanding opponent of the government of President Alfredo Stroessner, which has held power in Paraguay since 1954. His daughter, Dolly Filartiga, arrived in the United States in 1978 under a visitor's visa, and has since applied for permanent political asylum. The Filartigas brought this action in the Eastern District of New York against Americo Norberto Pena-Irala (Pena), also a citizen of Paraguay, for wrongfully causing the death of Dr. Filartiga's seventeen-year old son, Joelito. Because the district court dismissed the action for want of subject matter jurisdiction, we must accept as true the allegations contained in the Filartigas' complaint and affidavits for purposes of this appeal.

The appellants contend that on March 29, 1976, Joelito Filartiga was kidnapped and tortured to death by Pena, who was then Inspector General of Police in Asuncion, Paraguay. Later that day, the police brought Dolly Filartiga to Pena's home where she was confronted with the body of her brother, which evidenced marks of severe torture. As she fled, horrified, from the house, Pena followed after her shouting, "Here you have what you have been looking for for so long and what you deserve. Now shut up." The Filartigas claim that Joelito was tortured and killed in retaliation for his father's political activities and beliefs.

Shortly thereafter, Dr. Filartiga commenced a criminal action in the Paraguayan courts against Pena and the police for the murder of his son. As a result, Dr. Filartiga's attorney was arrested and brought to police headquarters where, shackled to a wall, Pena threatened him with death. This attorney, it is alleged, has since been disbarred without just cause. . .

In July of 1978, Pena sold his house in Paraguay and entered the United States under a visitor's visa. He was accompanied by Juana Bautista Fernandez Villalba, who had lived with him in Paraguay. The couple remained in the United States beyond the term of their visas, and were living in Brooklyn, New York, when Dolly Filartiga, who was then living in Washington, D. C., learned of their presence. Acting on information provided by Dolly the Immigration and Naturalization Service arrested Pena and his companion, both of whom were subsequently ordered deported on April 5, 1979 following a hearing. They had then resided in the United States for more than nine months. . .

II

Appellants rest their principal argument in support of federal jurisdiction upon the Alien Tort Statute, 28 U.S.C. § 1350, which provides: "The district courts shall have original jurisdiction of any civil action by an alien for a tort only, committed in violation of the law of nations or a treaty of the United States." Since appellants do not contend that their action arises directly under a treaty of the United States, a threshold question on the jurisdictional issue is whether the conduct alleged violates the law of nations. In light of the universal condemnation of torture in numerous international agreements, and the renunciation of torture as an instrument of official policy by virtually all of the nations of the world (in principle if not in practice), we find that an act of torture committed by a state official against one held in detention violates established norms of the international law of human rights, and hence the law of nations.

The Supreme Court has enumerated the appropriate sources of international law. The law of nations "may be ascertained by consulting the works of jurists, writing professedly on public law; or by the general usage and practice of nations; or by judicial decisions recognizing and enforcing that law." In *Smith*, a statute proscribing "the crime of piracy (on the high seas) as defined by the law of nations," 3 Stat. 510(a) (1819), was held sufficiently determinate in meaning to afford the basis for a death sentence. The *Smith* Court discovered among the works of Lord Bacon, Grotius, Bochard and other commentators a genuine consensus that rendered the crime "sufficiently and constitutionally defined." *United States v. Smith*, 18 U.S. (5 Wheat.) 153, 162 (1820).

The Paquete Habana, 175 U.S. 677 (1900), reaffirmed that

> where there is no treaty, and no controlling executive or legislative act or judicial decision, resort must be had to the customs and usages of civilized nations; and, as evidence of these, to the works of jurists and commentators, who by years of labor, research and experience, have made themselves peculiarly well acquainted with the subjects of which they treat. Such works are resorted to by judicial tribunals, not for the speculations of their authors concerning what the law ought to be, but for trustworthy evidence of what the law really is.

Modern international sources confirm the propriety of this approach.

Habana is particularly instructive for present purposes, for it held that the traditional prohibition against seizure of an enemy's coastal fishing vessels during wartime, a standard that began as one of comity only, had ripened over the preceding century into "a settled rule of international law" by "the general assent of civilized nations." Thus it is clear that courts must interpret international law not as it was in 1789, but as it has evolved and exists among the nations of the world today.

The requirement that a rule command the "general assent of civilized nations" to become binding upon them all is a stringent one.

Were this not so, the courts of one nation might feel free to impose idiosyncratic legal rules upon others, in the name of applying international law. Thus, in *Banco Nacional de Cuba v. Sabbatino*, 376 U.S. 398 (1964), the Court declined to pass on the validity of the Cuban government's expropriation of a foreign-owned corporation's assets, noting the sharply conflicting views on the issue propounded by the capital-exporting, capital-importing, socialist and capitalist nations.

The case at bar presents us with a situation diametrically opposed to the conflicted state of law that confronted the *Sabbatino* Court. Indeed, to paraphrase that Court's statement, there are few, if any, issues in international law today on which opinion seems to be so united as the limitations on a state's power to torture persons held in its custody.

The United Nations Charter (a treaty of the United States, see 59 Stat. 1033 (1945)) makes it clear that in this modern age a state's treatment of its own citizens is a matter of international concern. It provides: "With a view to the creation of conditions of stability and well-being which are necessary for peaceful and friendly relations among nations. . . the United Nations shall promote. . . universal respect for, and observance of, human rights and fundamental freedoms for all without distinctions as to race, sex, language or religion." Art. 55. And further: "All members pledge themselves to take joint and separate action in cooperation with the Organization for the achievement of the purposes set forth in Article 55." Art. 56.

While this broad mandate has been held not to be wholly self-executing, this observation alone does not end our inquiry. For although there is no universal agreement as to the precise extent of the "human rights and fundamental freedoms" guaranteed to all by the Charter, there is at present no dissent from the view that the guaranties include, at a bare minimum, the right to be free from torture. This prohibition has become part of customary international law, as evidenced and defined by the Universal Declaration of Human Rights, which states, in the plainest of terms, "no one shall be subjected to torture." The General Assembly has declared that the Charter precepts embodied in this Universal Declaration "constitute basic principles of international law."

Particularly relevant is the Declaration on the Protection of All Persons from Being Subjected to Torture, General Assembly Resolution 3452 (1975). The Declaration expressly prohibits any state from permitting the dastardly and totally inhuman act of torture. Torture, in turn, is defined as "any act by which severe pain and suffering, whether physical or mental, is intentionally inflicted by or at the instigation of a public official on a person for such purposes as. . . intimidating him or other persons." The Declaration goes on to provide that "(w)here it is proved that an act of torture or other cruel, inhuman or degrading treatment or punishment has been committed by or at the instigation of a public official, the victim shall be afforded redress and compensation, in accordance with national law." This Declaration, like the Declaration of Human Rights before it, was adopted without dissent by the General Assembly. . .

Turning to the act of torture, we have little difficulty discerning its universal renunciation in the modern usage and practice of nations. The international consensus surrounding torture has found expression in numerous international treaties and accords. The substance of these international agreements is reflected in modern municipal i.e., national law as well. Although torture was once a routine concomitant of criminal interrogations in many nations, during the modern and hopefully more enlightened era it has been universally renounced. According to one survey, torture is prohibited, expressly or implicitly, by the constitutions of over fifty-five nations, including both the United States and Paraguay. Our State Department reports a general recognition of this principle: "There now exists an international consensus that recognizes basic human rights and obligations owed by all governments to their citizens. . . . There is no doubt that these rights are often violated; but virtually all governments acknowledge their validity." We have been directed to no assertion by any contemporary state of a right to torture its own or another nation's citizens. . .

Having examined the sources from which customary international law is derived the usage of nations, judicial opinions and the works of jurists we conclude that official torture is now prohibited by the law of nations. The prohibition is clear and unambiguous, and admits of no distinction between treatment of aliens and citizens. . . The treaties and accords cited above, as well as the express foreign policy of our own government, all make it clear that international law confers fundamental rights upon all people vis-a-vis their own governments. . .

III

Appellee submits that even if the tort alleged is a violation of modern international law, federal jurisdiction may not be exercised consistent with the dictates of Article III of the Constitution. The claim is without merit. Common law courts of general jurisdiction regularly adjudicate transitory tort claims between individuals over whom they exercise personal jurisdiction, wherever the tort occurred. Moreover, as part of an articulated scheme of federal control over external affairs, Congress provided, in the first Judiciary Act, for federal jurisdiction over suits by aliens where principles of international law are in issue. The constitutional basis for the Alien Tort Statute is the law of nations, which has always been part of the federal common law.

It is not extraordinary for a court to adjudicate a tort claim arising outside of its territorial jurisdiction. A state or nation has a legitimate

ATS— gives JX in fed common law

interest in the orderly resolution of disputes among those within its borders, and where the lex loci delicti commissi is applied, it is an expression of comity to give effect to the laws of the state where the wrong occurred...

As ratified, the judiciary article contained no express reference to cases arising under the law of nations. Indeed, the only express reference to that body of law is contained in Article I, sec. 8, cl. 10, which grants to the Congress the power to "define and punish... offenses against the law of nations." Appellees seize upon this circumstance and advance the proposition that the law of nations forms a part of the laws of the United States only to the extent that Congress has acted to define it. This extravagant claim is amply refuted by the numerous decisions applying rules of international law uncodified in any act of Congress. A similar argument was offered to and rejected by the Supreme Court in *United States v. Smith*, 18 U.S. (5 Wheat.) 153, 158–60, and we reject it today. As John Jay wrote in The Federalist No. 3, "Under the national government, treaties and articles of treaties, as well as the laws of nations, will always be expounded in one sense and executed in the same manner, whereas adjudications on the same points and questions in the thirteen states will not always accord or be consistent." Federal jurisdiction over cases involving international law is clear.

Thus, it was hardly a radical initiative for Chief Justice Marshall to state in *The Nereide*, 13 U.S. (9 Cranch) 388, 422 (1815), that in the absence of a congressional enactment, United States courts are "bound by the law of nations, which is a part of the law of the land." These words were echoed in *The Paquete Habana*, *supra*, "(i)nternational law is part of our law, and must be ascertained and administered by the courts of justice of appropriate jurisdiction, as often as questions of right depending upon it are duly presented for their determination." ...

Although the Alien Tort Statute has rarely been the basis for jurisdiction during its long history, in light of the foregoing discussion, there can be little doubt that this action is properly brought in federal court. This is undeniably an action by an alien, for a tort only, committed in violation of the law of nations. The paucity of suits successfully maintained under the section is readily attributable to the statute's requirement of alleging a "violation of the law of nations" (emphasis supplied) at the jurisdictional threshold. Courts have, accordingly, engaged in a more searching preliminary review of the merits than is required, for example, under the more flexible "arising under" formulation. Thus, the narrowing construction that the Alien Tort Statute has previously received reflects the fact that earlier cases did not involve such well-established, universally recognized norms of international law that are here at issue...

IV

In the twentieth century the international community has come to recognize the common danger posed by the flagrant disregard of basic human rights and particularly the right to be free of torture. Spurred first by the Great War, and then the Second, civilized nations have banded together to prescribe acceptable norms of international behavior. From the ashes of the Second World War arose the United Nations Organization, amid hopes that an era of peace and cooperation had at last begun. Though many of these aspirations have remained elusive goals, that circumstance cannot diminish the true progress that has been made. In the modern age, humanitarian and practical considerations have combined to lead the nations of the world to recognize that respect for fundamental human rights is in their individual and collective interest. Among the rights universally proclaimed by all nations, as we have noted, is the right to be free of physical torture. Indeed, for purposes of civil liability, the torturer has become like the pirate and slave trader before him *hostis humani generis*, an enemy of all mankind. Our holding today, giving effect to a jurisdictional provision enacted by our First Congress, is a small but important step in the fulfillment of the ageless dream to free all people from brutal violence.

1. THE STANDARD FOR ATS LIABILITY

After the *Filartiga* decision, federal courts began to hear many ATS cases, resulting in a new brand of human rights litigation. The Supreme Court steadfastly refused to hear appeals arising from those cases, until 2004 when the Supreme Court opined on whether the Alien Tort Statute conferred a "cause of action" that could be heard in federal courts or whether the cause of action emanated from international law. Along the way, the Supreme Court provided guidance to lower federal courts regarding which norms of international law could be the basis for a successful ATS case. What if the relevant rule of international law is contested, unclear, or has an uncertain application to the facts of the case? As you read the case, look for how the Supreme Court evokes Blackstone to answer this question.

Sosa v. Alvarez-Machain
Supreme Court of the United States
542 U.S. 692 (2004)

■ JUSTICE SOUTER delivered the opinion of the Court.

The two issues are whether respondent Alvarez-Machain's allegation that the Drug Enforcement Administration instigated his abduction from Mexico for criminal trial in the United States supports a claim against the Government under the Federal Tort Claims Act (FTCA or Act), and whether he may recover under the Alien Tort Statute (ATS). We hold that he is not entitled to a remedy under either statute.

I

We have considered the underlying facts before, *United States v. Alvarez-Machain*, 504 U.S. 655 (1992). In 1985, an agent of the Drug Enforcement Administration (DEA), Enrique Camarena-Salazar, was captured on assignment in Mexico and taken to a house in Guadalajara, where he was tortured over the course of a 2-day interrogation, then murdered. Based in part on eyewitness testimony, DEA officials in the United States came to believe that respondent Humberto Alvarez-Machain (Alvarez), a Mexican physician, was present at the house and acted to prolong the agent's life in order to extend the interrogation and torture.

In 1990, a federal grand jury indicted Alvarez for the torture and murder of Camarena-Salazar, and the United States District Court for the Central District of California issued a warrant for his arrest. The DEA asked the Mexican Government for help in getting Alvarez into the United States, but when the requests and negotiations proved fruitless, the DEA approved a plan to hire Mexican nationals to seize Alvarez and bring him to the United States for trial. As so planned, a group of Mexicans, including petitioner Jose Francisco Sosa, abducted Alvarez from his house, held him overnight in a motel, and brought him by private plane to El Paso, Texas, where he was arrested by federal officers.

Once in American custody, Alvarez moved to dismiss the indictment on the ground that his seizure was "outrageous governmental conduct," and violated the extradition treaty between the United States and Mexico. The District Court agreed, the Ninth Circuit affirmed, and we reversed, holding that the fact of Alvarez's forcible seizure did not affect the jurisdiction of a federal court. The case was tried in 1992, and ended at the close of the Government's case, when the District Court granted Alvarez's motion for a judgment of acquittal.

In 1993, after returning to Mexico, Alvarez began the civil action before us here. He sued Sosa, Mexican citizen and DEA operative Antonio Garate-Bustamante, five unnamed Mexican civilians, the United States, and four DEA agents. So far as it matters here, Alvarez sought damages from the United States under the FTCA, alleging false arrest, and from Sosa under the ATS, for a violation of the law of nations. The former statute authorizes suit "for. . . personal injury. . . caused by the negligent or wrongful act or omission of any employee of the Government while acting within the scope of his office or employment." The latter provides in its entirety that "[t]he district courts shall have original jurisdiction of any civil action by an alien for a tort only, committed in violation of the law of nations or a treaty of the United States." . . .

III

Alvarez has also brought an action under the ATS against petitioner Sosa, who argues (as does the United States supporting him) that there is no relief under the ATS because the statute does no more than vest federal courts with jurisdiction, neither creating nor authorizing the courts to recognize any particular right of action without further congressional action. Although we agree the statute is in terms only jurisdictional, we think that at the time of enactment the jurisdiction enabled federal courts to hear claims in a very limited category defined by the law of nations and recognized at common law. We do not believe, however, that the limited, implicit sanction to entertain the handful of international law cum common law claims understood in 1789 should be taken as authority to recognize the right of action asserted by Alvarez here.

Judge Friendly called the ATS a "legal Lohengrin. . . no one seems to know whence it came," and for over 170 years after its enactment it provided jurisdiction in only one case. The first Congress passed it as part of the Judiciary Act of 1789, in providing that the new federal district courts "shall also have cognizance, concurrent with the courts of the several States, or the circuit courts, as the case may be, of all causes where an alien sues for a tort only in violation of the law of nations or a treaty of the United States."

The parties and amici here advance radically different historical interpretations of this terse provision. Alvarez says that the ATS was intended not simply as a jurisdictional grant, but as authority for the creation of a new cause of action for torts in violation of international law. We think that reading is implausible. As enacted in 1789, the ATS gave the district courts "cognizance" of certain causes of action, and the term bespoke a grant of jurisdiction, not power to mold substantive law. The fact that the ATS was placed in § 9 of the Judiciary Act, a statute otherwise exclusively concerned with federal-court jurisdiction, is itself support for its strictly jurisdictional nature. Nor would the distinction between jurisdiction and cause of action have been elided by the drafters of the Act or those who voted on it. . . It is unsurprising, then, that an authority on the historical origins of the ATS has written that "section 1350 clearly does not create a statutory cause of action," and that the contrary suggestion is "simply frivolous." In sum, we think the statute was intended as jurisdictional in the sense of addressing the power of the courts to entertain cases concerned with a certain subject.

But holding the ATS jurisdictional raises a new question, this one about the interaction between the ATS at the time of its enactment and the ambient law of the era. Sosa would have it that the ATS was stillborn because there could be no claim for relief without a further statute expressly authorizing adoption of causes of action. Amici professors of federal jurisdiction and legal history take a different tack, that federal courts could entertain claims once the jurisdictional grant was on the books, because torts in violation of the law of nations would have been recognized within the common law of the time. We think history and practice give the edge to this latter position.

"When the United States declared their independence, they were bound to receive the law of nations, in its modern state of purity and refinement." In the years of the early Republic, this law of nations comprised two principal elements, the first covering the general norms governing the behavior of national states with each other: "the science which teaches the rights subsisting between nations or states, and the obligations correspondent to those rights," E. de Vattel, Law of Nations, or "that code of public instruction which defines the rights and prescribes the duties of nations, in their intercourse with each other," 1 J. Kent, Commentaries on American Law. This aspect of the law of nations thus occupied the executive and legislative domains, not the judicial. See 4 W. Blackstone, Commentaries on the Laws of England 68 (1769) (hereinafter Commentaries) ("[O]ffences against" the law of nations are "principally incident to whole states or nations").

The law of nations included a second, more pedestrian element, however, that did fall within the judicial sphere, as a body of judge-made law regulating the conduct of individuals situated outside domestic boundaries and consequently carrying an international savor. To Blackstone, the law of nations in this sense was implicated "in mercantile questions, such as bills of exchange and the like; in all marine causes, relating to freight, average, demurrage, insurances, bottomry . . .; [and] in all disputes relating to prizes, to shipwrecks, to hostages, and ransom bills." The law merchant emerged from the customary practices of international traders and admiralty required its own transnational regulation. And it was the law of nations in this sense that our precursors spoke about when the Court explained the status of coast fishing vessels in wartime grew from "ancient usage among civilized nations, beginning centuries ago, and gradually ripening into a rule of international law . . . ." *The Paquete Habana*, 175 U.S. 677, 686 (1900).

There was, finally, a sphere in which these rules binding individuals for the benefit of other individuals overlapped with the norms of state relationships. Blackstone referred to it when he mentioned three specific offenses against the law of nations addressed by the criminal law of England: violation of safe conducts, infringement of the rights of ambassadors, and piracy. An assault against an ambassador, for example, impinged upon the sovereignty of the foreign nation and if not adequately redressed could rise to an issue of war. It was this narrow set of violations of the law of nations, admitting of a judicial remedy and at the same time threatening serious consequences in international affairs, that was probably on minds of the men who drafted the ATS with its reference to tort.

Before there was any ATS, a distinctly American preoccupation with these hybrid international norms had taken shape owing to the distribution of political power from independence through the period of confederation. The Continental Congress was hamstrung by its inability to "cause infractions of treaties, or of the law of nations to be punished," and in 1781 the Congress implored the States to vindicate rights under the law of nations. In words that echo Blackstone, the congressional resolution called upon state legislatures to "provide expeditious, exemplary and adequate punishment" for "the violation of safe conducts or passports,. . . of hostility against such as are in amity. . . with the United States,. . . infractions of the immunities of ambassadors and other public ministers. . . [and] infractions of treaties and conventions to which the United States are a party." The resolution recommended that the States "authorise suits. . . for damages by the party injured, and for compensation to the United States for damage sustained by them from an injury done to a foreign power by a citizen." Apparently only one State acted upon the recommendation, but Congress had done what it could to signal a commitment to enforce the law of nations.

Appreciation of the Continental Congress's incapacity to deal with this class of cases was intensified by the so-called Marbois incident of May 1784, in which a French adventurer, De Longchamps, verbally and physically assaulted the Secretary of the French Legion in Philadelphia. Congress called again for state legislation addressing such matters, and concern over the inadequate vindication of the law of nations persisted through the time of the Constitutional Convention. During the Convention itself, in fact, a New York City constable produced a reprise of the Marbois affair and Secretary Jay reported to Congress on the Dutch Ambassador's protest, with the explanation that "the federal government does not appear. . . to be vested with any judicial Powers competent to the Cognizance and Judgment of such Cases."

The Framers responded by vesting the Supreme Court with original jurisdiction over "all Cases affecting Ambassadors, other public ministers and Consuls." The Judiciary Act reinforced this Court's original jurisdiction over suits brought by diplomats, created alienage jurisdiction, and, of course, included the ATS.

Although Congress modified the draft of what became the Judiciary Act, it made hardly any changes to the provisions on aliens, including what became the ATS. There is no record of congressional discussion about private actions that might be subject to the jurisdictional provision, or about any need for further legislation to create private remedies; there is no record even of debate on the section. Given the poverty of drafting history, modern commentators have necessarily concentrated on the text, remarking on the innovative use of the word "tort," and the statute's mixture of terms expansive ("all suits"), and restrictive ("for a tort only"). The historical scholarship has also placed the ATS within the competition between federalist and antifederalist forces over the national role in foreign relations. But despite considerable scholarly attention, it is fair to say that a consensus understanding of what Congress intended has proven elusive.

Still, the history does tend to support two propositions. First, there is every reason to suppose that the First Congress did not pass the ATS as a jurisdictional convenience to be placed on the shelf for use by a future Congress or state legislature that might, someday, authorize the creation of causes of action or itself decide to make some element of the law of nations actionable for the benefit of foreigners. The anxieties of the preconstitutional period cannot be ignored easily enough to think that the statute was not meant to have a practical effect. Consider that the principal draftsman of the ATS was apparently Oliver Ellsworth, previously a member of the Continental Congress that had passed the 1781 resolution and a member of the Connecticut Legislature that made good on that congressional request. Consider, too, that the First Congress was attentive enough to the law of nations to recognize certain offenses expressly as criminal, including the three mentioned by Blackstone. It would have been passing strange for Ellsworth and this very Congress to vest federal courts expressly with jurisdiction to entertain civil causes brought by aliens alleging violations of the law of nations, but to no effect whatever until the Congress should take further action. There is too much in the historical record to believe that Congress would have enacted the ATS only to leave it lying fallow indefinitely.

The second inference to be drawn from the history is that Congress intended the ATS to furnish jurisdiction for a relatively modest set of actions alleging violations of the law of nations. Uppermost in the legislative mind appears to have been offenses against ambassadors; violations of safe conduct were probably understood to be actionable, and individual actions arising out of prize captures and piracy may well have also been contemplated. But the common law appears to have understood only those three of the hybrid variety as definite and actionable, or at any rate, to have assumed only a very limited set of claims. As Blackstone had put it, "offences against this law [of nations] are principally incident to whole states or nations," and not individuals seeking relief in court.

The sparse contemporaneous cases and legal materials referring to the ATS tend to confirm both inferences, that some, but few, torts in violation of the law of nations were understood to be within the common law. In *Bolchos v. Darrel* (S.C. 1795), the District Court's doubt about admiralty jurisdiction over a suit for damages brought by a French privateer against the mortgagee of a British slave ship was assuaged by assuming that the ATS was a jurisdictional basis for the court's action. . .

Then there was the 1795 opinion of Attorney General William Bradford, who was asked whether criminal prosecution was available against Americans who had taken part in the French plunder of a British slave colony in Sierra Leone. Bradford was uncertain, but he made it clear that a federal court was open for the prosecution of a tort action growing out of the episode. . . Although it is conceivable that Bradford (who had prosecuted in the Marbois incident) assumed that there had been a violation of a treaty, that is certainly not obvious, and it appears likely that Bradford understood the ATS to provide jurisdiction over what must have amounted to common law causes of action. . .

In sum, although the ATS is a jurisdictional statute creating no new causes of action, the reasonable inference from the historical materials is that the statute was intended to have practical effect the moment it became law. The jurisdictional grant is best read as having been enacted on the understanding that the common law would provide a cause of action for the modest number of international law violations with a potential for personal liability at the time.

IV

We think it is correct, then, to assume that the First Congress understood that the district courts would recognize private causes of action for certain torts in violation of the law of nations, though we have found no basis to suspect Congress had any examples in mind beyond those torts corresponding to Blackstone's three primary offenses: violation of safe conducts, infringement of the rights of ambassadors, and piracy. We assume, too, that no development in the two centuries from the enactment of § 1350 to the birth of the modern line of cases beginning with *Filartiga v. Pena-Irala* (1980), has categorically precluded federal courts from recognizing a claim under the law of nations as an element of common law; Congress has not in any relevant way amended § 1350 or limited civil common law power by another statute. Still, there are good reasons for a restrained conception of the discretion a federal court should exercise in considering a new cause of action of this kind. Accordingly, we think courts should require any claim based on the present-day law of nations to rest on a norm of international character accepted by the civilized world and defined with a specificity comparable to the features of the 18th-century paradigms we have recognized. This requirement is fatal to Alvarez's claim.

A series of reasons argue for judicial caution when considering the kinds of individual claims that might implement the jurisdiction conferred by the early statute. First, the prevailing conception of the common law has changed since 1789 in a way that counsels restraint in judicially applying internationally generated norms. When § 1350 was enacted, the accepted conception was of the common law as "a transcendental body of law outside of any particular State but obligatory within it unless and until changed by statute." Now, however, in most cases where a court is asked to state or formulate a common law principle in a new context, there is a general understanding that the law is not so much found or discovered as it is either made or created. . . One need not accept the Holmesian view as far as its ultimate implications to acknowledge that a judge deciding in reliance on an international norm will find a substantial element of discretionary judgment in the decision.

Second, along with, and in part driven by, that conceptual development in understanding common law has come an equally significant rethinking of the role of the federal courts in making it. *Erie R. Co. v. Tompkins*, 304 U.S. 64 (1938), was the watershed in which we denied the existence of any federal "general" common law, which largely withdrew to havens of specialty, some of them defined by express congressional authorization to devise a body of law directly. Elsewhere, this Court has thought it was in order to create federal common law rules in interstitial areas of particular federal interest. And although we have even assumed competence to make judicial rules of decision of particular importance to foreign relations, such as the act of state doctrine, the general practice has been to look for legislative guidance before exercising innovative authority over substantive law. It would be remarkable to take a more aggressive role in exercising a jurisdiction that remained largely in shadow for much of the prior two centuries.

Third, this Court has recently and repeatedly said that a decision to create a private right of action is one better left to legislative judgment in the great majority of cases. The creation of a private right of action raises issues beyond the mere consideration whether underlying primary conduct should be allowed or not, entailing, for example, a decision to permit enforcement without the check imposed by prosecutorial discretion. Accordingly, even when Congress has made it clear by statute that a rule applies to purely domestic conduct, we are reluctant to infer intent to provide a private cause of action where the statute does not supply one expressly. While the absence of congressional action addressing private rights of action under an international norm is more equivocal than its failure to provide such a right when it creates a statute, the possible collateral consequences of making international rules privately actionable argue for judicial caution.

Fourth, the subject of those collateral consequences is itself a reason for a high bar to new private causes of action for violating international law, for the potential implications for the foreign relations of the United States of recognizing such causes should make courts particularly wary of impinging on the discretion of the Legislative and Executive Branches in managing foreign affairs. It is one thing for American courts to enforce constitutional limits on our own State and Federal Governments' power, but quite another to consider suits under rules that would go so far as to claim a limit on the power of foreign governments over their own citizens, and to hold that a foreign government or its agent has transgressed those limits. Yet modern international law is very much concerned with just such questions, and apt to stimulate calls for vindicating private interests in § 1350 cases. Since many attempts by federal courts to craft remedies for the violation of new norms of international law would raise risks of adverse foreign policy consequences, they should be undertaken, if at all, with great caution.

The fifth reason is particularly important in light of the first four. We have no congressional mandate to seek out and define new and debatable violations of the law of nations, and modern indications of congressional understanding of the judicial role in the field have not affirmatively encouraged greater judicial creativity. . . Several times, indeed, the Senate has expressly declined to give the federal courts the task of interpreting and applying international human rights law, as when its ratification of the International Covenant on Civil and Political Rights declared that the substantive provisions of the document were not self-executing.

These reasons argue for great caution in adapting the law of nations to private rights. Justice Scalia concludes that caution is too hospitable, and a word is in order to summarize where we have come so far and to focus our difference with him on whether some norms of today's law of nations may ever be recognized legitimately by federal courts in the absence of congressional action beyond § 1350. All Members of the Court agree that § 1350 is only jurisdictional. We also agree, or at least Justice Scala does not dispute, that the jurisdiction was originally understood to be available to enforce a small number of international norms that a federal court could properly recognize as within the common law enforceable without further statutory authority. Justice Scalia concludes, however, that two subsequent developments should be understood to preclude federal courts from recognizing any further international norms as judicially enforceable today, absent further congressional action. As described before, we now tend to understand common law not as a discoverable reflection of universal reason but, in a positivistic way, as a product of human choice. And we now adhere to a conception of limited judicial power first expressed in reorienting federal diversity jurisdiction, see *Erie R. Co. v. Tompkins*, that federal courts have no authority to derive "general" common law.

Whereas Justice Scalia sees these developments as sufficient to close the door to further independent judicial recognition of actionable international norms, other considerations persuade us that the judicial power should be exercised on the understanding that the door is still ajar subject to vigilant doorkeeping, and thus open to a narrow class of international norms today. *Erie* did not in terms bar any judicial recognition of new substantive rules, no matter what the circumstances, and post-*Erie* understanding has identified limited enclaves in which federal courts may derive some substantive law in a common law way. For two centuries we have affirmed that the domestic law of the United States recognizes the law of nations. It would take some explaining to say now that federal courts must avert their gaze entirely from any international norm intended to protect individuals.

We think an attempt to justify such a position would be particularly unconvincing in light of what we know about congressional understanding bearing on this issue lying at the intersection of the judicial and legislative powers. The First Congress, which reflected the understanding of the framing generation and included some of the Framers, assumed that federal courts could properly identify some international norms as enforceable in the exercise of § 1350 jurisdiction. We think it would be unreasonable to assume that the First Congress would have expected federal courts to lose all capacity to recognize enforceable international norms simply because the common law might lose some metaphysical cachet on the road to modern realism. Later Congresses seem to have shared our view. The position we take today has been assumed by some federal courts for 24 years, ever since the Second Circuit decided *Filartiga v. Pena-Irala.* . .

We must still, however, derive a standard or set of standards for assessing the particular claim Alvarez raises, and for this action it suffices to look to the historical antecedents. Whatever the ultimate criteria for accepting a cause of action subject to jurisdiction under § 1350, we are persuaded that federal courts should not recognize private claims under federal common law for violations of any international law norm with less definite content and acceptance among civilized nations than the historical paradigms familiar when § 1350 was enacted. This limit upon judicial recognition is generally consistent with the reasoning of many of the courts and judges who faced the issue before it reached this Court. And the determination whether a norm is sufficiently definite to support a cause of action should (and, indeed, inevitably must) involve an element of judgment about the practical consequences of making that cause available to litigants in the federal courts.

Thus, Alvarez's detention claim must be gauged against the current state of international law, looking to those sources we have long, albeit cautiously, recognized. . . To begin with, Alvarez cites two well-known international agreements that, despite their moral authority, have little utility under the standard set out in this opinion. He says that his abduction by Sosa was an "arbitrary arrest" within the meaning of the

Universal Declaration of Human Rights. And he traces the rule against arbitrary arrest not only to the Declaration, but also to article nine of the International Covenant on Civil and Political Rights, to which the United States is a party, and to various other conventions to which it is not. But the Declaration does not of its own force impose obligations as a matter of international law. And, although the Covenant does bind the United States as a matter of international law, the United States ratified the Covenant on the express understanding that it was not self-executing and so did not itself create obligations enforceable in the federal courts. Accordingly, Alvarez cannot say that the Declaration and Covenant themselves establish the relevant and applicable rule of international law. He instead attempts to show that prohibition of arbitrary arrest has attained the status of binding customary international law. . .

Alvarez's failure to marshal support for his proposed rule is underscored by the Restatement (Third) of Foreign Relations Law of the United States (1986), which says in its discussion of customary international human rights law that a "state violates international law if, as a matter of state policy, it practices, encourages, or condones . . . prolonged arbitrary detention." Although the Restatement does not explain its requirements of a "state policy" and of "prolonged" detention, the implication is clear. Any credible invocation of a principle against arbitrary detention that the civilized world accepts as binding customary international law requires a factual basis beyond relatively brief detention in excess of positive authority. Even the Restatement's limits are only the beginning of the enquiry, because although it is easy to say that some policies of prolonged arbitrary detentions are so bad that those who enforce them become enemies of the human race, it may be harder to say which policies cross that line with the certainty afforded by Blackstone's three common law offenses. In any event, the label would never fit the reckless policeman who botches his warrant, even though that same officer might pay damages under municipal law.

Whatever may be said for the broad principle Alvarez advances, in the present, imperfect world, it expresses an aspiration that exceeds any binding customary rule having the specificity we require. Creating a private cause of action to further that aspiration would go beyond any residual common law discretion we think it appropriate to exercise. It is enough to hold that a single illegal detention of less than a day, followed by the transfer of custody to lawful authorities and a prompt arraignment, violates no norm of customary international law so well defined as to support the creation of a federal remedy.

NOTES & QUESTIONS

1. *Closing the Door.* Did *Sosa* close the door of federal courts to ATS claims? Not exactly, because the Court concluded that the ATS provided

jurisdiction to federal courts and that the "cause of action" came from international law. In this way, the court reaffirmed the basic premise articulated in *Filartiga*. However, the court imposed strict standards for which cases could proceed under the ATS. International norms would be excluded from the scope of the ATS if they had "less definite content and acceptance among civilized nations than the historical paradigms familiar when § 1350 was enacted." As a benchmark, the court looked to the examples cited by Blackstone, including violations of safe conduct, rights of ambassadors, and piracy. What unites this diverse and eclectic list of international obligations? Does this list of examples provide lower federal courts with sufficient guidance for which international legal norms can be enforced via the ATS? How should courts understand the requirement that the norms be "accepted by the civilized world and defined with a specificity comparable to" Blackstone's examples. Which international legal norms have the same acceptance and specificity as piracy?

2. *Which Victims? Which Perpetrators?* Was the ATS designed to protect aliens from violations committed by other aliens or violations committed by Americans? A recent article suggests that the ATS was designed to provide redress for wrongdoing performed by U.S. citizens. See Anthony J. Bellia Jr & Bradford R. Clark, *The Alien Tort Statute and the Law of Nations*, 78 U. Chi. L. Rev. 445, 448 (2011) ("Neither the broader approach initially endorsed by lower federal courts nor the more restrictive approach subsequently adopted by *Sosa* fully captures the original meaning and purpose of the ATS."). Bellia and Clark conclude, on the basis of historical research, that the ATS was designed to cover torts committed by U.S. citizens against aliens, because these actions violate the state's international obligation to ensure that its citizens not harm foreigners. If that standard was adopted, should courts have heard the allegations of torture in *Filartiga*?

3. *The Erie Argument.* The Supreme Court in *Sosa* explicitly rejected Bradley and Goldsmith's argument that *Paquete Habana* did not survive *Erie*'s destruction of federal common law. Justice Souter concluded that "it would be unreasonable to assume that the First Congress would have expected federal courts to lose all capacity to recognize enforceable international norms simply because the common law might lose some metaphysical cachet on the road to modern realism." However, in response, Bradley and Goldsmith insisted that their *Erie*-critique was still valid. See Curtis A. Bradley, Jack L. Goldsmith, & David H. Moore, *Sosa, Customary International Law, and the Continuing Relevance of Erie*, 120 Harv. L. Rev. 869, 902 (2007) ("In particular, the Court's insistence in *Sosa* that any federal common law relating to [customary international law] be grounded in, conform to, and not exceed the contours of what the political branches have authorized; its recognition that the ATS authorizes courts to enforce only a very small subset of [customary international law]; and its limited view of judicial power vis-à-vis the federal political branches and even the states in cases involving [customary international law] simply cannot be

reconciled with the modern position that all of [customary international law] is automatically part of judge-made federal common law even in the absence of political branch authorization.").

2. EXTRATERRITORIAL APPLICATION

In the aftermath of *Sosa*, federal courts continued to hear ATS cases, usually involving allegations of human rights abuses in foreign countries. Many of these cases were against multinational corporations accused of aiding and abetting human rights abuses perpetrated by foreign governments that the corporations were in business with. On appeal, several corporations argued that corporate liability was not provided for by either the ATS or international law generally. A vigorous circuit split on this question developed. Compare *Kiobel v. Royal Dutch Petroleum Co.*, 621 F.3d 111, 119 (2d Cir. 2010), with *Sarei v. Rio Tinto, PLC*, 671 F.3d 736, 748 (9th Cir. 2011) ("The ATS contains no such language and has no such legislative history to suggest that corporate liability was excluded and that only liability of natural persons was intended.").

The Supreme Court accepted certiorari in the case of *Kiobel v. Royal Dutch Petroleum Co.* to determine the scope of corporate liability under the ATS. The parties to the case briefed this issue, but during oral argument a number of justices questioned whether the ATS should apply to cases that are foreign "cubed," i.e., foreign plaintiffs suing foreign defendants for foreign conduct. Subsequently, the court asked the parties to brief this issue and the court scheduled a second oral argument with a new question presented: the presumption against extraterritoriality. The following opinion provided the court's answer to whether the ATS applied to these entirely foreign cases.

Kiobel v. Royal Dutch Petroleum Co.
Supreme Court of the United States
569 U.S. 108 (2013)

■ CHIEF JUSTICE ROBERTS delivered the opinion of the Court.

Petitioners, a group of Nigerian nationals residing in the United States, filed suit in federal court against certain Dutch, British, and Nigerian corporations. Petitioners sued under the Alien Tort Statute, 28 U.S.C. § 1350, alleging that the corporations aided and abetted the Nigerian Government in committing violations of the law of nations in Nigeria. The question presented is whether and under what circumstances courts may recognize a cause of action under the Alien Tort Statute, for violations of the law of nations occurring within the territory of a sovereign other than the United States.

I

Petitioners were residents of Ogoniland, an area of 250 square miles located in the Niger delta area of Nigeria and populated by roughly half a million people. When the complaint was filed, respondents Royal Dutch Petroleum Company and Shell Transport and Trading Company, were holding companies incorporated in the Netherlands and England, respectively. Their joint subsidiary, respondent Shell Petroleum Development Company of Nigeria, Ltd. (SPDC), was incorporated in Nigeria, and engaged in oil exploration and production in Ogoniland. According to the complaint, after concerned residents of Ogoniland began protesting the environmental effects of SPDC's practices, respondents enlisted the Nigerian Government to violently suppress the burgeoning demonstrations. Throughout the early 1990's, the complaint alleges, Nigerian military and police forces attacked Ogoni villages, beating, raping, killing, and arresting residents and destroying or looting property. Petitioners further allege that respondents aided and abetted these atrocities by, among other things, providing the Nigerian forces with food, transportation, and compensation, as well as by allowing the Nigerian military to use respondents' property as a staging ground for attacks.

Following the alleged atrocities, petitioners moved to the United States where they have been granted political asylum and now reside as legal residents. They filed suit in the United States District Court for the Southern District of New York, alleging jurisdiction under the Alien Tort Statute and requesting relief under customary international law. The ATS provides, in full, that "[t]he district courts shall have original jurisdiction of any civil action by an alien for a tort only, committed in violation of the law of nations or a treaty of the United States." According to petitioners, respondents violated the law of nations by aiding and abetting the Nigerian Government in committing (1) extrajudicial killings; (2) crimes against humanity; (3) torture and cruel treatment; (4) arbitrary arrest and detention; (5) violations of the rights to life, liberty, security, and association; (6) forced exile; and (7) property destruction. . .

II

Passed as part of the Judiciary Act of 1789, the ATS was invoked twice in the late 18th century, but then only once more over the next 167 years. The statute provides district courts with jurisdiction to hear certain claims, but does not expressly provide any causes of action. We held in *Sosa v. Alvarez-Machain* (2004), however, that the First Congress did not intend the provision to be "stillborn." The grant of jurisdiction is instead "best read as having been enacted on the understanding that the common law would provide a cause of action for [a] modest number of international law violations." . . .

The question here is not whether petitioners have stated a proper claim under the ATS, but whether a claim may reach conduct occurring in the territory of a foreign sovereign. Respondents contend that claims under the ATS do not, relying primarily on a canon of statutory interpretation known as the presumption against extraterritorial application. That canon provides that "[w]hen a statute gives no clear indication of an extraterritorial application, it has none," *Morrison v. National Australia Bank*, 561 U.S. 247 (2010), and reflects the "presumption that United States law governs domestically but does not rule the world." . . .

The presumption against extraterritorial application helps ensure that the Judiciary does not erroneously adopt an interpretation of U.S. law that carries foreign policy consequences not clearly intended by the political branches.

We typically apply the presumption to discern whether an Act of Congress regulating conduct applies abroad. The ATS, on the other hand, is "strictly jurisdictional." It does not directly regulate conduct or afford relief. It instead allows federal courts to recognize certain causes of action based on sufficiently definite norms of international law. But we think the principles underlying the canon of interpretation similarly constrain courts considering causes of action that may be brought under the ATS.

Indeed, the danger of unwarranted judicial interference in the conduct of foreign policy is magnified in the context of the ATS, because the question is not what Congress has done but instead what courts may do. This Court in *Sosa* repeatedly stressed the need for judicial caution in considering which claims could be brought under the ATS, in light of foreign policy concerns. As the Court explained, "the potential [foreign policy] implications. . . of recognizing. . . . causes [under the ATS] should make courts particularly wary of impinging on the discretion of the Legislative and Executive Branches in managing foreign affairs." These concerns, which are implicated in any case arising under the ATS, are all the more pressing when the question is whether a cause of action under the ATS reaches conduct within the territory of another sovereign.

These concerns are not diminished by the fact that *Sosa* limited federal courts to recognizing causes of action only for alleged violations of international law norms that are "specific, universal, and obligatory." As demonstrated by Congress's enactment of the Torture Victim Protection Act of 1991, identifying such a norm is only the beginning of defining a cause of action. Each of these decisions carries with it significant foreign policy implications.

The principles underlying the presumption against extraterritoriality thus constrain courts exercising their power under the ATS.

III

Petitioners contend that even if the presumption applies, the text, history, and purposes of the ATS rebut it for causes of action brought under that statute. It is true that Congress, even in a jurisdictional provision, can indicate that it intends federal law to apply to conduct occurring abroad. But to rebut the presumption, the ATS would need to evince a "clear indication of extraterritoriality." It does not.

To begin, nothing in the text of the statute suggests that Congress intended causes of action recognized under it to have extraterritorial reach. The ATS covers actions by aliens for violations of the law of nations, but that does not imply extraterritorial reach—such violations affecting aliens can occur either within or outside the United States. Nor does the fact that the text reaches "any civil action" suggest application to torts committed abroad; it is well established that generic terms like "any" or "every" do not rebut the presumption against extraterritoriality.

Petitioners make much of the fact that the ATS provides jurisdiction over civil actions for "torts" in violation of the law of nations. They claim that in using that word, the First Congress "necessarily meant to provide for jurisdiction over extraterritorial transitory torts that could arise on foreign soil." For support, they cite the common-law doctrine that allowed courts to assume jurisdiction over such "transitory torts," including actions for personal injury, arising abroad.

Under the transitory torts doctrine, however, "the only justification for allowing a party to recover when the cause of action arose in another civilized jurisdiction is a well founded belief that it was a cause of action in that place." The question under Sosa is not whether a federal court has jurisdiction to entertain a cause of action provided by foreign or even international law. The question is instead whether the court has authority to recognize a cause of action under U.S. law to enforce a norm of international law. The reference to "tort" does not demonstrate that the First Congress "necessarily meant" for those causes of action to reach conduct in the territory of a foreign sovereign. In the end, nothing in the text of the ATS evinces the requisite clear indication of extraterritoriality.

Nor does the historical background against which the ATS was enacted overcome the presumption against application to conduct in the territory of another sovereign. We explained in Sosa that when Congress passed the ATS, "three principal offenses against the law of nations" had been identified by Blackstone: violation of safe conducts, infringement of the rights of ambassadors, and piracy. The first two offenses have no necessary extraterritorial application. Indeed, Blackstone—in describing them—did so in terms of conduct occurring within the forum nation.

Two notorious episodes involving violations of the law of nations occurred in the United States shortly before passage of the ATS. Each concerned the rights of ambassadors, and each involved conduct within the Union. In 1784, a French adventurer verbally and physically assaulted Francis Barbe Marbois—the Secretary of the French Legion—in Philadelphia. The assault led the French Minister Plenipotentiary to lodge a formal protest with the Continental Congress and threaten to leave the country unless an adequate remedy were provided. *Respublica v. De Longchamps*. And in 1787, a New York constable entered the Dutch Ambassador's house and arrested one of his domestic servants. At the request of Secretary of Foreign Affairs John Jay, the Mayor of New York City arrested the constable in turn, but cautioned that because "neither Congress nor our [State] Legislature have yet passed any act respecting a breach of the privileges of Ambassadors," the extent of any available relief would depend on the common law. The two cases in which the ATS was invoked shortly after its passage also concerned conduct within the territory of the United States.

These prominent contemporary examples—immediately before and after passage of the ATS—provide no support for the proposition that Congress expected causes of action to be brought under the statute for violations of the law of nations occurring abroad.

The third example of a violation of the law of nations familiar to the Congress that enacted the ATS was piracy. Piracy typically occurs on the high seas, beyond the territorial jurisdiction of the United States or any other country. This Court has generally treated the high seas the same as foreign soil for purposes of the presumption against extraterritorial application. Petitioners contend that because Congress surely intended the ATS to provide jurisdiction for actions against pirates, it necessarily anticipated the statute would apply to conduct occurring abroad.

Applying U.S. law to pirates, however, does not typically impose the sovereign will of the United States onto conduct occurring within the territorial jurisdiction of another sovereign, and therefore carries less direct foreign policy consequences. Pirates were fair game wherever found, by any nation, because they generally did not operate within any jurisdiction. We do not think that the existence of a cause of action against them is a sufficient basis for concluding that other causes of action under the ATS reach conduct that does occur within the territory of another sovereign; pirates may well be a category unto themselves.

Petitioners also point to a 1795 opinion authored by Attorney General William Bradford. In 1794, in the midst of war between France and Great Britain, and notwithstanding the American official policy of neutrality, several U.S. citizens joined a French privateer fleet and attacked and plundered the British colony of Sierra Leone. In response to a protest from the British Ambassador, Attorney General Bradford responded as follows:

> So far . . . as the transactions complained of originated or took place in a foreign country, they are not within the cognizance of our courts; nor can the actors be legally prosecuted or punished for them by the United States. But crimes committed on the high seas are within the jurisdiction of the . . . courts of the United States; and, so far as the offence was committed thereon, I am inclined to think that it may be legally prosecuted in . . . those courts. . . . But some doubt rests on this point, in consequence of the terms in which the [applicable criminal law] is expressed. But there can be no doubt that the company or individuals who have been injured by these acts of hostility have a remedy by a civil suit in the courts of the United States; jurisdiction being expressly given to these courts in all cases where an alien sues for a tort only, in violation of the laws of nations, or a treaty of the United States. . . .

Petitioners read the last sentence as confirming that "the Founding generation understood the ATS to apply to law of nations violations committed on the territory of a foreign sovereign." Respondents counter that when Attorney General Bradford referred to "these acts of hostility," he meant the acts only insofar as they took place on the high seas, and even if his conclusion were broader, it was only because the applicable treaty had extraterritorial reach. The Solicitor General, having once read the opinion to stand for the proposition that an "ATS suit could be brought against American citizens for breaching neutrality with Britain only if acts did not take place in a foreign country," now suggests the opinion "could have been meant to encompass . . . conduct [occurring within the foreign territory]."

Attorney General Bradford's opinion defies a definitive reading and we need not adopt one here. Whatever its precise meaning, it deals with U.S. citizens who, by participating in an attack taking place both on the high seas and on a foreign shore, violated a treaty between the United States and Great Britain. The opinion hardly suffices to counter the weighty concerns underlying the presumption against extraterritoriality.

Finally, there is no indication that the ATS was passed to make the United States a uniquely hospitable forum for the enforcement of international norms. As Justice Story put it, "No nation has ever yet pretended to be the custos morum of the whole world. . . ." *United States v. The La Jeune Eugenie* (1822). It is implausible to suppose that the First Congress wanted their fledgling Republic—struggling to receive international recognition—to be the first. Indeed, the parties offer no evidence that any nation, meek or mighty, presumed to do such a thing.

The United States was, however, embarrassed by its potential inability to provide judicial relief to foreign officials injured in the United States. Such offenses against ambassadors violated the law of nations, "and if not adequately redressed could rise to an issue of war." The ATS ensured that the United States could provide a forum for adjudicating such incidents. Nothing about this historical context suggests that Congress also intended federal common law under the ATS to provide a cause of action for conduct occurring in the territory of another sovereign.

Indeed, far from avoiding diplomatic strife, providing such a cause of action could have generated it. Recent experience bears this out. Moreover, accepting petitioners' view would imply that other nations, also applying the law of nations, could hale our citizens into their courts for alleged violations of the law of nations occurring in the United States, or anywhere else in the world. The presumption against extraterritoriality guards against our courts triggering such serious foreign policy consequences, and instead defers such decisions, quite appropriately, to the political branches.

We therefore conclude that the presumption against extraterritoriality applies to claims under the ATS, and that nothing in the statute rebuts that presumption. . .

IV

On these facts, all the relevant conduct took place outside the United States. And even where the claims touch and concern the territory of the United States, they must do so with sufficient force to displace the presumption against extraterritorial application. Corporations are often present in many countries, and it would reach too far to say that mere corporate presence suffices. If Congress were to determine otherwise, a statute more specific than the ATS would be required.

NOTES & QUESTIONS

1. *The Morrison Presumption.* When the Supreme Court finally decided *Kiobel* after the second oral argument, it held that absent express indication from Congress, courts should assume that statutes have no extraterritorial effect. Does this so-called *Morrison* presumption apply equally to statutes that craft domestic legal norms *and* to statutes that apply international legal norms? If a statute pertains to *international law*, perhaps the presumption ought to be reversed, and courts should assume that the regulation applies extraterritorially unless Congress declares otherwise. Recall that the ATS is purely jurisdictional, i.e., it does not create any new cause of action. The cause of action flows from international law, which clearly has extraterritorial effect. So why should one assume that the grant of jurisdiction is limited to cases arising from the territory of the United States, when the underlying norm clearly applies universally? For a discussion of this issue, see Anthony J. Colangelo, *A Unified Approach to*

Extraterritoriality, 97 Va. L. Rev. 1019, 1023 (2011) (suggesting that "when Congress implements international law, courts should presume Congress intended to implement all of international law—including international jurisdictional law, which may permit, encourage, or even obligate extraterritoriality").

2.   *Other Statues.* The twin decisions of *Sosa* and *Kiobel* severely limited the extraterritorial reach of the Alien Tort Statute. However, some subject-specific human rights statutes explicitly permit litigation over foreign conduct. These statutes are clear enough in their congressional intent to overcome the *Morrison* presumption against extraterritoriality. For example, the Torture Victims Protection Act (TVPA) confers jurisdiction on federal courts to hear allegations of "torture and extrajudicial killing carried out by an individual with 'actual or apparent authority, or color of law, of any foreign nation.'" *Chowdhury v. Worldtel Bangladesh Holding, Ltd.*, 746 F.3d 42, 51 (2d Cir. 2014) (concluding that "the TVPA, unlike the ATS, has extraterritorial application"). If the Supreme Court continues to narrow the scope of the ATS, might these more limited statutes be the future of human rights litigation in federal courts?

3.   *Aiding and Abetting.* As noted above, many of the *Kiobel*-style cases rely on an "aiding and abetting" theory of liability. Under this theory, the plaintiffs seek to hold a corporation responsible for business arrangements that facilitated the commission of human rights violations by foreign governments. Courts have struggled over the proper standard to apply in these cases, with plaintiffs arguing for a knowledge standard and defendants pushing for a purpose standard. Under a knowledge standard, the corporation would be responsible if it merely had knowledge that its actions would contribute to the government's violation of international law. Under the purpose standard, though, the corporation is only responsible if it provided assistance to the government with the purpose to facilitate the legal violations. If the corporation acted merely with the purpose to make money, and was genuinely indifferent to the commission of the abuses, the corporation might escape liability. Courts are split on this issue, although the purpose standard has gained the most traction in recent decisions. See, e.g., *Presbyterian Church of Sudan v. Talisman Energy*, 582 F.3d 244, 259 (2d Cir. 2009) (applying purpose standard).

4.   *The "Touch and Concern" Test.* *Kiobel* announced that district courts do not have jurisdiction to try foreign cases that do not sufficiently "touch and concern" the territory of the United States to rebut the presumption against extraterritoriality. Under what conditions might a foreign case have sufficient contacts with the United States to rebut the presumption? In *Jane W. v. Thomas*, 354 F. Supp. 3d 630 (E.D. Pa. 2018), a district court concluded that it had jurisdiction over a case alleging torture in Liberia by a foreign national because: 1) the defendant was residing in the United States at the time the case was filed; 2) the torture occurred during a raid at a compound leased by a U.S. agency in Liberia; and 3) the defendant fraudulently received a visa from a U.S. immigration program designed to

assist the victims of atrocities in Liberia. Do you agree that these factors sufficiently distinguish the case from the facts in *Kiobel* and other "foreign-cubed" cases?

3. CORPORATE LIABILITY

After *Kiobel*, ATS cases against corporations continued, as long as those cases touched and concerned the territory of the United States sufficiently to displace the *Morrison* presumption against extraterritoriality. Corporate defendants pressed the Supreme Court to finally answer the question it had originally intended to answer in *Kiobel*, i.e., whether the ATS allows for corporate liability. The following case involved a foreign bank accused by plaintiffs of being connected with foreign terrorism in violation of international law. The bank was headquartered in Jordan but like many foreign banks had a branch in New York.

Jesner v. Arab Bank, PLC
Supreme Court of the United States
138 S.Ct. 1386 (2018)

■ JUSTICE KENNEDY announced the judgment of the Court and delivered the opinion of the Court with respect to Parts I, II-B-1, and II-C, and an opinion with respect to Parts II-A, II-B-2, II-B-3, and III, in which THE CHIEF JUSTICE and JUSTICE THOMAS join.

II

B

Petitioners and Arab Bank disagree as to whether corporate liability is a question of international law or only a question of judicial authority and discretion under domestic law. The dispute centers on a footnote in *Sosa*. In the course of holding that international norms must be "sufficiently definite to support a cause of action," the Court in *Sosa* noted that a "related consideration is whether international law extends the scope of liability for a violation of a given norm to the perpetrator being sued, if the defendant is a private actor such as a corporation or individual."

In the Court of Appeals' decision in *Kiobel*, the majority opinion by Judge Cabranes interpreted footnote 20 to mean that corporate defendants may be held liable under the ATS only if there is a specific, universal, and obligatory norm that corporations are liable for violations of international law. In Judge Cabranes' view, "[i]nternational law is not silent on the question of the subjects of international law—that is, those that, to varying extents, have legal status, personality, rights, and duties under international law," "[n]or does international law leave to individual States the responsibility of defining those subjects." There is considerable force and weight to the position articulated by Judge Cabranes. And, assuming the Court of Appeals was correct that under *Sosa* corporate liability is a question of international law, there is an equally strong argument that petitioners cannot satisfy the high bar of demonstrating a specific, universal, and obligatory norm of liability for corporations. Indeed, Judge Leval agreed with the conclusion that international law does "not provide for any form of liability of corporations."

1

In modern times, there is no doubt, of course, that "the international community has come to recognize the common danger posed by the flagrant disregard of basic human rights," leading "the nations of the world to recognize that respect for fundamental human rights is in their individual and collective interest." That principle and commitment support the conclusion that human-rights norms must bind the individual men and women responsible for committing humanity's most terrible crimes, not just nation-states in their interactions with one another. "The singular achievement of international law since the Second World War has come in the area of human rights," where international law now imposes duties on individuals as well as nation-states.

It does not follow, however, that current principles of international law extend liability—civil or criminal—for human-rights violations to corporations or other artificial entities. This is confirmed by the fact that the charters of respective international criminal tribunals often exclude corporations from their jurisdictional reach.

The Charter for the Nuremberg Tribunal, created by the Allies after World War II, provided that the Tribunal had jurisdiction over natural persons only. Later, a United States Military Tribunal prosecuted 24 executives of the German corporation IG Farben. Among other crimes, Farben's employees had operated a slave-labor camp at Auschwitz and "knowingly and intentionally manufactured and provided" the poison gas used in the Nazi death chambers. Although the Military Tribunal "used the term 'Farben' as descriptive of the instrumentality of cohesion in the name of which" the crimes were committed, the Tribunal noted that "corporations act through individuals." Farben itself was not held liable.

The jurisdictional reach of more recent international tribunals also has been limited to "natural persons." The Rome Statute of the International Criminal Court, for example, limits that tribunal's jurisdiction to "natural persons." The drafters of the Rome Statute considered, but rejected, a proposal to give the International Criminal Court jurisdiction over corporations.

The international community's conscious decision to limit the authority of these international tribunals to natural persons counsels against a broad holding that there is a specific, universal, and obligatory norm of corporate liability under currently prevailing international law.

2

In light of the sources just discussed, the sources petitioners rely on to support their contention that liability for corporations is well established as a matter of international law lend weak support to their position.

Petitioners first point to the International Convention for the Suppression of the Financing of Terrorism. This Convention imposes an obligation on "Each State Party" "to enable a legal entity located in its territory or organized under its laws to be held liable when a person responsible for the management or control of that legal entity has, in that capacity," violated the Convention. But by its terms the Convention imposes its obligations only on nation-states "to enable" corporations to be held liable in certain circumstances under domestic law. The United States and other nations, including Jordan, may fulfill their obligations under the Convention by adopting detailed regulatory regimes governing financial institutions. The Convention neither requires nor authorizes courts, without congressional authorization, to displace those detailed regulatory regimes by allowing common-law actions under the ATS. And nothing in the Convention's text requires signatories to hold corporations liable in common-law tort actions raising claims under international law.

In addition, petitioners and their amici cite a few cases from other nations and the Special Tribunal for Lebanon that, according to petitioners, are examples of corporations being held liable for violations of international law. Yet even assuming that these cases are relevant examples, at most they demonstrate that corporate liability might be permissible under international law in some circumstances. That falls far short of establishing a specific, universal, and obligatory norm of corporate liability.

It must be remembered that international law is distinct from domestic law in its domain as well as its objectives. International human-rights norms prohibit acts repugnant to all civilized peoples—crimes like genocide, torture, and slavery, that make their perpetrators "enem[ies] of all mankind." In the American legal system, of course, corporations are often subject to liability for the conduct of their human employees, and so it may seem necessary and natural that corporate entities are liable for violations of international law under the ATS. It is true, furthermore, that the enormity of the offenses that can be committed against persons in violation of international human-rights protections can be cited to show that corporations should be subject to liability for the crimes of their human agents. But the international community has not yet taken that step, at least in the specific, universal, and obligatory manner required by Sosa. Indeed, there is precedent to the contrary in the statement during the Nuremberg proceedings that "[c]rimes against international law are committed by men, not by abstract entities, and only by punishing individuals who commit such crimes can the provisions of international law be enforced." . . .

C

The ATS was intended to promote harmony in international relations by ensuring foreign plaintiffs a remedy for international-law violations in circumstances where the absence of such a remedy might provoke foreign nations to hold the United States accountable. But here, and in similar cases, the opposite is occurring.

Petitioners are foreign nationals seeking hundreds of millions of dollars in damages from a major Jordanian financial institution for injuries suffered in attacks by foreign terrorists in the Middle East. The only alleged connections to the United States are the CHIPS transactions in Arab Bank's New York branch and a brief allegation regarding a charity in Texas. The Court of Appeals did not address, and the Court need not now decide, whether these allegations are sufficient to "touch and concern" the United States under *Kiobel*.

At a minimum, the relatively minor connection between the terrorist attacks at issue in this case and the alleged conduct in the United States well illustrates the perils of extending the scope of ATS liability to foreign multinational corporations like Arab Bank. For 13 years, this litigation has "caused significant diplomatic tensions" with Jordan, a critical ally in one of the world's most sensitive regions. "Jordan is a key counterterrorism partner, especially in the global campaign to defeat the Islamic State in Iraq and Syria. The United States explains that Arab Bank itself is "a constructive partner with the United States in working to prevent terrorist financing." Jordan considers the instant litigation to be a "grave affront" to its sovereignty.

This is not the first time, furthermore, that a foreign sovereign has appeared in this Court to note its objections to ATS litigation. These are the very foreign-relations tensions the First Congress sought to avoid.

Petitioners insist that whatever the faults of this litigation—for example, its tenuous connections to the United States and the prolonged diplomatic disruptions it has caused—the fact that Arab Bank is a foreign corporate entity, as distinct from a natural person, is not one of them. That misses the point. As demonstrated by this litigation, foreign corporate defendants create unique problems. And courts are not well suited to make the required policy judgments that are implicated by corporate liability in cases like this one.

Like the presumption against extraterritoriality, judicial caution under *Sosa* "guards against our courts triggering . . . serious foreign policy consequences, and instead defers such decisions, quite appropriately, to the political branches." If, in light of all the concerns that must be weighed before imposing liability on foreign corporations via ATS suits, the Court were to hold that it has the discretion to make that determination, then the cautionary language of *Sosa* would be little more than empty rhetoric. Accordingly, the Court holds that foreign corporations may not be defendants in suits brought under the ATS. . . .

NOTES & QUESTIONS

1. *Domestic Corporate Liability.* The *Jesner* case did not fully resolve the question of corporate liability under the ATS. The case produced a fractured set of opinions, with some members of the five-member majority, such as Kennedy, rejecting corporate liability entirely and others, such as Alito, focusing more on the fate of foreign corporations under the *Kiobel* "touch and concern" test. This left open the question of whether a U.S. corporation could be sued under the ATS. That question is now working its way before the circuit courts of appeal and may be addressed by the Supreme Court in the future.

2. *Historical Research Regarding Domestic Defendants.* Recent historical research suggests that Secretary of State Thomas Jefferson and Attorney General William Randolph were concerned about diplomatic controversies triggered by international law violations by U.S. citizens abroad and more importantly viewed the ATS as an important remedy for this problem. For example, historian David Golove has brought to light two diplomatic controversies of importance during the presidency of George Washington. In the first, a dispute arose between the U.S. and Spain regarding U.S. citizens from Georgia, who crossed into East Florida, which at the time was Spanish territory, and kidnapped five enslaved persons and forcibly transported them back to Georgia. In the second, a dispute broke out between the U.S. and France regarding a U.S. vessel in St. Domingo, which was involved in the illegal transportation of enslaved persons to the United States. According to documents unearthed by Golove, Jefferson and Randolph both viewed the ATS as applicable to these controversies, as long as an individual foreigner suffered the injury (as opposed to a foreign state). Does this historical evidence suggest that modern ATS cases should proceed against U.S. corporations that engage in violations of international law abroad? See David Golove, *The Alien Tort Statute and the Law of Nations: New Historical Evidence of Founding-Era Understandings*, Just Security, Nov. 17, 2020.

3. *Jurisdiction.* What significance should we draw from the fact that most international criminal law tribunals do not enjoy jurisdiction over corporations? With the exception of the Special Tribunal for Lebanon, the major tribunals such as the ICC, the ICTY, and the ICTR, only enjoy jurisdiction over "natural persons." But does this argument prove too much? Many of these international tribunals do not have jurisdiction over states

either, but it would be fallacious to conclude that states are not responsible agents under international law. Indeed, states are the paradigmatic agents of Westphalian international law. Should we separate the question of jurisdiction at tribunals with the deeper question of whether a type of defendant is capable of violating international law?

4. *Corporate Liability at the STL.* The Special Tribunal for Lebanon (STL) is a hybrid tribunal created by the UN Security Council to investigate the assassination of former Lebanese Prime Minister Rafik Hariri in 2005. The tribunal is based in The Hague and has jurisdiction to try individuals for violations of both Lebanese domestic penal law and international criminal law. The Office of the Prosecutor initiated an investigation of television station Al Jadeed for broadcasting confidential information about tribunal witnesses. The tribunal ordered the station to stop disseminating the confidential information but it refused. The resulting contempt proceeding forced the tribunal to determine two related questions. First, did the tribunal have the inherent power to punish contempt of court? Second, did that power extend to corporations? In answering the second question in the affirmative, the tribunal concluded in 2014 that corporations could be held criminally responsible under international law. Does this case undermine the holding in *Jesner*? Or does it merely reinforce, as Justice Kennedy suggested, that corporate liability may be emerging in international law in isolated contexts but not yet as a general rule? See *Prosecutor v. Al Khayat*, Case No. STL–14–05/PT/AP/ARI26.1, Decision on Interlocutory Appeal Concerning Personal Jurisdiction in Contempt Proceedings (Special Trib. For Lebanon, Oct. 2, 2014).

5. *The Canadian Approach.* In 2020, the Canadian Supreme Court concluded that corporate liability was recognized by international law. Canadian law allows individuals to file suit in Canadian courts for violations of human rights law through a mechanism that bears some similarity to the ATS, though in the Canadian case it is judicially created. (Canada recognizes the doctrine of "adoption" which holds that customary international law is incorporated into the common law and can be applied by Canadian courts, in the absence of conflicting legislation, without any legislative action.) In reaching its decision, the Canadian Supreme Court was aware of *Kiobel* but concluded that corporate liability was consistent with international law because the international legal system has long since moved away from the assumption that only states are responsible agents under international law. The Canadian Supreme Court noted that individuals can be punished under international criminal law and then concluded that the idea that corporations cannot be responsible for international law violations was a pure "myth," a phrase it attributed to Harold Koh. *Nevsun Resources Ltd. v. Araya*, 2020 S.C.C. 5.

PROBLEM CASE

During the Vietnam War, U.S. infantry forces and their allies were facing fierce resistance from Viet Cong troops. The Viet Cong were trained in guerilla tactics and were able to use the jungle environment as a strategic advantage for general concealment of movement and launching ambushes. In order to counter-act this strategic imbalance, the U.S. military used airplanes to drop a chemical called "Agent Orange" to act as a defoliant. After the war, U.S. service members blamed a host of medical conditions on the toxicity of the Agent Orange they were exposed to.

Decades later, residents in Vietnam exposed to Agent Orange filed suit in a U.S. district court, arguing that the deployment of the chemical violated international law. The Alien Tort Statute case listed as defendants the U.S. companies that manufactured the chemical and alleged that the companies were complicit in the international law violation perpetrated by the U.S. government.

Dueling experts on both sides of the case debated whether the laws of war prohibited the use of chemicals as a deforestation agent. While it is clear that the use of poisonous gases, i.e., chemical weapons, violate both the Chemical Weapons Convention, contemporary customary international law, and older prohibitions under the law of war, Agent Orange was deployed to kill forests, not people. Ultimately, the Second Circuit ruled that Agent Orange did not violate international law because "[p]laintiffs have, at best, alleged a customary international norm proscribing the purposeful use of poison as a weapon against human beings that is inapplicable in this case. *Vietnam Ass'n for Victims of Agent Orange v. Dow Chem. Co.*, 517 F.3d 104, 123 (2d Cir. 2008).

Setting aside for the moment the dispute over the content of the laws of war, are U.S. courts the best place to adjudicate disputes that occurred overseas? What if the conduct involved a foreign military but the defendants were still U.S. companies? What if the military and the companies were both foreign?

C. ENFORCING INTERNATIONAL JUDGMENTS

The Alien Tort Statute deals exclusively with private litigants pursuing legal claims directly in U.S. courts. But what of disputes between nation-states that are adjudicated in an international forum? What effect does the decision of an international tribunal have in a domestic court? Is the international judgment automatically enforceable in domestic court? The following three cases represent a tense and fraught back and forth between the ICJ and the U.S. Supreme Court. The background setting involves the Vienna Convention on Consular Relations, which requires state parties to allow foreign detainees access to consular visitation, and more importantly obligates state parties to notify foreign detainees of this right. Unfortunately, police departments in the U.S. were not in the habit of issuing these notifications as part of the standard *Miranda* warnings.

In the first case, the ICJ issues preliminary measures against the United States with regards to the Mexican nationals on death row in the U.S. In the second case, the U.S. Supreme Court concludes that ICJ judgments are not automatically enforceable in U.S. courts, despite the fact that the U.S. was, at the time, a signatory to the U.N. Charter, the Charter of the International Court of Justice, and the Vienna Convention on Consular Relations and its optional protocol giving the ICJ jurisdiction to hear disputes arising under the Convention. As you read the case, ask yourself why the Supreme Court did not give the ICJ judgment automatic effect in federal court. Does the answer have something to do with the distinction between monism and dualism?

Finally, as you read the third case, the ICJ's final judgment after learning of the Supreme Court's decision, ask yourself whether the failure of the U.S. court system to implement the ICJ decision is itself a violation of international law. Can the U.S. use its own federal structure (including horizontal and vertical separation of powers) as an excuse for failing to live up to its international obligations? Is it possible that U.S. law and international law might yield different answers to this question?

Avena and Other Mexican Nationals
(Mexico v. United States)

International Court of Justice
2004 I.C.J. 12

19. The underlying facts alleged by Mexico may be briefly described as follows: some are conceded by the United States, and some disputed. Mexico states that all the individuals the subject of its claims were Mexican nationals at the time of their arrest. It further contends that the United States authorities that arrested and interrogated these individuals had sufficient information at their disposal to be aware of the foreign nationality of those individuals. According to Mexico's account, in 50 of the specified cases, Mexican nationals were never informed by the competent United States authorities of their rights under Article 36, paragraph 1 (b), of the Vienna Convention and, in the two remaining cases, such information was not provided "without delay," as required by that provision. Mexico has indicated that in 29 or the 52 cases its consular authorities learned of the detention of the Mexican nationals only after death sentences had been handed down. In the 23 remaining cases, Mexico contends that it learned of the cases through means other than notification to the consular post by the competent United States authorities under Article 36, paragraph 1(b). It explains that in five cases this was too late to affect the trials, that in 15 cases the defendants had already made incriminating statements, and that it became aware of the other three cases only after considerable delay.

20. Of the 52 cases referred to in Mexico's final submissions, 49 are currently at different stages of the proceedings before United States judicial authorities at state or federal level, and in three cases. . . judicial remedies within the United States have already been exhausted. The Court has been informed of the variety of types of proceedings and forms of relief available in the criminal justice systems of the United States, which can differ from state to state. In very general terms, and according to the description offered by both Parties in their pleadings, it appears that the 52 cases may be classified into three categories: 24 cases which are currently in direct appeal; 25 cases in which means of direct appeal

have been exhausted, but post-conviction relief (habeas corpus), either at slate or at federal level, is still available; and three cases in which no judicial remedies remain. The Court also notes that, in at least 33 cases, the alleged breach of the Vienna Convention was raised by the defendant either during pre-trial, at trial, on appeal or in habeas corpus proceedings, and that some of these claims were dismissed on procedural or substantive grounds and others are still pending. To date, in none of the 52 cases have the defendants had recourse to the clemency process.

21. On 9 January 2003, the day on which Mexico filed its Application and a request for the indication of provisional measures, all 52 individuals the subject of the claims were on death row. However, two days later the Governor of the State of Illinois, exercising his power of clemency review, commuted the sentences of all convicted individuals awaiting execution in that State, including those of three individuals named in Mexico's Application. By a letter dated 20 January 2003, Mexico informed the Court that, further to that decision, it withdrew its request for the indication of provisional measures on behalf of these three individuals, but that its Application remained unchanged. In the Order of 5 February 2003, mentioned in paragraph 3 above, on the request by Mexico for the indication of provisional measures, the Court considered that it was apparent from the information before it that the three Mexican nationals named in the Application who had exhausted all judicial remedies in the United States (see paragraph 20 above) were at risk of execution in the following months, or even weeks. Consequently, it ordered by way of provisional measure that the United States take all measures necessary to ensure that these individuals would not be executed pending final judgment in these proceedings. The Court notes that, at the date of the present Judgment, these three individuals have not been executed, but further notes with great concern that, by an Order dated 1 March 2004, the Oklahoma Court of Criminal Appeals has set an execution date of 18 May 2004 for Mr. Torres.

The third objection by the United States to the jurisdiction of the Court refers to the first of the submissions in the Mexican Memorial concerning remedies. By that submission, which was confirmed in substance in the final submissions. Mexico claimed that "Mexico is entitled to restitutio in integrum, and the United States therefore is under an obligation to restore the status quo ante, that is, re-establish the situation that existed at the time of the detention and prior to the interrogation of, proceedings against, and convictions and sentences of, Mexico's nationals in violation of the United States' international legal obligations. . ." On that basis, Mexico went on in its first submission to invite the Court to declare that the United States was bound to vacate the convictions and sentences of the Mexican nationals concerned, to exclude from any subsequent proceedings any statements and confessions obtained from them, to prevent the application of any procedural penalty for failure to raise a timely defence on the basis of the Convention, and to prevent the application of any municipal law rule preventing courts in the United States from providing a remedy for the violation of Article 36 rights.

32. The United States objects that so to require specific acts by the United States in its municipal criminal justice systems would intrude deeply into the independence of its courts; and that for the Court to declare that the United States is under a specific obligation to vacate convictions and sentences would be beyond its jurisdiction. The Court, the United States claims, has no jurisdiction to review appropriateness of sentences in criminal cases, and even less to determine guilt or innocence, matters which only a court of criminal appeal could go into.

33. For its part, Mexico points out that the United States accepts that the Court has jurisdiction to interpret the Vienna Convention and to determine the appropriate form of reparation under international law. In Mexico's view, these two considerations are sufficient to defeat the third objection to jurisdiction of the United States.

34. For the same reason as in respect of the second jurisdictional objection, the Court is unable to uphold the contention of the United States that, even if the Court were to find that breaches of the Vienna Convention have been committed by the United States of the kind alleged by Mexico, it would still be without jurisdiction to order restitution in integrum as requested by Mexico. The Court would recall in this regard, as it did in the *LaGrand* case, that, where jurisdiction exists over a dispute on a particular matter, no separate basis for jurisdiction is required by the Court in order to consider the remedies a party has requested for the breach of the obligation. Whether or how far the Court may order the remedy requested by Mexico are matters to be determined as part of the merits of the dispute. The third objection of the United States to jurisdiction cannot therefore be upheld.

111. The "procedural default" rule in United States law has already been brought to the attention of the Court in the *LaGrand* case. The following brief definition of the rule was provided by Mexico in its Memorial in this case and has not been challenged by the United States: "a defendant who could have raised, but fails to raise, a legal issue at trial will generally not be permitted to raise it in future proceedings, on appeal or in a petition for a writ of habeas corpus." The rule requires exhaustion of remedies, inter alia, at the state level and before a habeas corpus motion call be filed with federal courts. In the *LaGrand* case, the rule in question was applied by United Stales federal courts; in the present case, Mexico also complains of the application of the rule in certain state courts of criminal appeal.

112. The Court has already considered the application of the "procedural default" rule, alleged by Mexico to be a hindrance to the full implementation of the international obligations of the United States under Article 36, in the *LaGrand* case, when the Court addressed the issue of its implications for the application of Article 36, paragraph 2, of the Vienna Convention. The Court emphasized that "a distinction must be drawn between that rule as such and its specific application in the present case". The Court stated: "In itself, the rule does not violate Article 36 of the Vienna Convention. The problem arises when the procedural default rule does not allow the detained individual to challenge a conviction and sentence by claiming, in reliance on Article 36, paragraph 1, of the Convention, that the competent national authorities failed to comply with their obligation to provide the requisite consular information 'without delay', thus preventing the person from seeking and obtaining consular assistance from the sending State."

On this basis, the Court concluded that "the procedural default rule prevented counsel for the LaGrands to effectively challenge their convictions and sentences other than on United States constitutional grounds." This statement of the Court seems equally valid in relation to the present case, where a number of Mexican nationals have been placed exactly in such a situation.

113. The Court will return to this aspect below, in the context of Mexico's claims as to remedies. For the moment, the Court simply notes that the procedural default rule has not been revised, nor has any provision been made to prevent its application in cases where it has been the failure of the United States itself to inform that may have precluded counsel from being in a position to have raised the question of a violation of the Vienna Convention in the initial trial. It thus remains the case that the procedural default rule may continue to prevent courts from attaching legal significance to the fact, inter alia, that the violation of the rights set forth in Article 36, paragraph 1, prevented Mexico, in a timely fashion, from retaining private counsel for certain nationals and otherwise assisting in their defence. In such cases, application of the procedural default rule would have the effect of preventing "full effect [from being] given to the purposes for which the rights accorded under this article are intended," and thus violate paragraph 2 of Article 36. The Court notes moreover that in several of the cases cited in Mexico's final submissions the procedural default rule has already been applied, and that in others it could be applied at subsequent stages in the proceedings. However, in none of the cases, save for the three mentioned in paragraph 114 below, have the criminal proceedings against the Mexican nationals concerned already reached a stage at which there is no further possibility of judicial reexamination of those cases; that is to say, all possibility is not yet excluded of "review and reconsideration" of conviction and

sentence, as called for in the *LaGrand* case... It would therefore be premature For the Court to conclude at this stage that, in those cases, there is already a violation of the obligations under Article 36, paragraph 2, of the Vienna Convention.

121. Similarly, in the present case, the Court's task is to determine what would be adequate reparation for the violations of Article 36. It should be clear from what has been observed above that the internationally wrongful acts committed by the United States were the failure of its competent authorities to inform the Mexican nationals concerned, to notify Mexican consular posts and to enable Mexico to provide consular assistance. It follows that the remedy to make good these violations should consist in an obligation on the United States to permit review and reconsideration of these nationals' cases by the United States courts... with a view to ascertaining whether in each case the violation of Article 36 committed by the competent authorities caused actual prejudice to the defendant in the process of administration of criminal justice.

122. The Court reaffirms that the case before it concerns Article 36 of the Vienna Convention and not the correctness as such of any conviction or sentencing. The question of whether the violations of Article 36, paragraph 1, are to be regarded as having, in the causal sequence of events, ultimately led to convictions and severe penalties is an integral part of criminal proceedings before the courts of the United States and is for them to determine in the process of review and reconsideration. In so doing, it is for the courts of the United States to examine the facts, and in particular the prejudice and its causes, taking account of the violation of the rights set forth in the Convention.

After the ICJ decision was handed down, the defendants who were denied their rights under the Vienna Convention sought to have their death sentences overturned in the United States. But there turned out to be many doctrinal and conceptual roadblocks to implementing the ICJ's decision in a U.S. court. In order to implement the United States' obligations under the Vienna Convention and the ICJ judgment, President Bush sent a Memorandum ordering Texas to review the death sentences of the relevant defendants. In the following case, the Supreme Court was asked to determine whether an ICJ judgment is directly enforceable in a U.S. court by criminal defendants and whether President Bush had the constitutional authority to intervene in state criminal law cases in order to implement an international decision from the ICJ. These twin questions implicate important issues regarding the relationship between domestic and international law, between the federal government and the states, and between the executive and judicial branches. Underlying these issues is one fundamental question: How is international law in general—and an ICJ judgment in particular—incorporated into the U.S. legal system?

Medellín v. Texas

United States Supreme Court
552 U.S. 491 (2008)

■ CHIEF JUSTICE ROBERTS delivered the opinion of the Court.

The International Court of Justice (ICJ), located in the Hague, is a tribunal established pursuant to the United Nations Charter to adjudicate disputes between member states. In the *Case Concerning Avena and Other Mexican Nationals (Mex. v. U.S.)*, that tribunal considered a claim brought by Mexico against the United States. The ICJ held that, based on violations of the Vienna Convention, 51 named Mexican nationals were entitled to review and reconsideration of their state-court convictions and sentences in the United States. This was so regardless of any forfeiture of the right to raise Vienna Convention claims because of a failure to comply with generally applicable state rules governing challenges to criminal convictions.

In *Sanchez-Llamas v. Oregon*, 548 U.S. 331 (2006)—issued after *Avena* but involving individuals who were not named in the *Avena* judgment—we held that, contrary to the ICJ's determination, the Vienna Convention did not preclude the application of state default rules. After the *Avena* decision, President George W. Bush determined, through a Memorandum for the Attorney General, that the United States would "discharge its international obligations" under *Avena* "by having State courts give effect to the decision."

Petitioner José Ernesto Medellín, who had been convicted and sentenced in Texas state court for murder, is one of the 51 Mexican nationals named in the *Avena* decision. Relying on the ICJ's decision and the President's Memorandum, Medellín filed an application for a writ of habeas corpus in state court. The Texas Court of Criminal Appeals dismissed Medellín's application as an abuse of the writ under state law, given Medellín's failure to raise his Vienna Convention claim in a timely manner under state law. We granted certiorari to decide two questions. *First,* is the ICJ's judgment in *Avena* directly enforceable as domestic law in a state court in the United States? *Second,* does the President's Memorandum independently require the States to provide review and reconsideration of the claims of the 51 Mexican nationals named in *Avena* without regard to state procedural default rules? We conclude that neither *Avena* nor the President's Memorandum constitutes directly enforceable federal law that pre-empts state limitations on the filing of successive habeas petitions. We therefore affirm the decision below.

I

In 1969, the United States, upon the advice and consent of the Senate, ratified the Vienna Convention on Consular Relations, and the Optional Protocol Concerning the Compulsory Settlement of Disputes to the Vienna Convention. The preamble to the Convention provides that its purpose is to "contribute to the development of friendly relations among nations." Toward that end, Article 36 of the Convention was drafted to "facilitat[e] the exercise of consular functions." It provides that if a person detained by a foreign country "so requests, the competent authorities of the receiving State shall, without delay, inform the consular post of the sending State" of such detention, and "inform the [detainee] of his righ[t]" to request assistance from the consul of his own state.

The Optional Protocol provides a venue for the resolution of disputes arising out of the interpretation or application of the Vienna Convention. Under the Protocol, such disputes "shall lie within the compulsory jurisdiction of the International Court of Justice" and "may accordingly be brought before the [ICJ]. . . by any party to the dispute being a Party to the present Protocol."

The ICJ is "the principal judicial organ of the United Nations." It was established in 1945 pursuant to the United Nations Charter. The ICJ Statute—annexed to the U.N. Charter—provides the organizational framework and governing procedures for cases brought before the ICJ.

Under Article 94(1) of the U.N. Charter, "[e]ach Member of the United Nations undertakes to comply with the decision of the [ICJ] in any case to which it is a party." The ICJ's jurisdiction in any particular case, however, is dependent upon the consent of the parties. The ICJ Statute delineates two ways in which a nation may consent to ICJ jurisdiction: It may consent generally to jurisdiction on any question arising under a treaty or general international law, or it may consent specifically to jurisdiction over a particular category of cases or disputes pursuant to a separate treaty. The United States originally consented to the general jurisdiction of the ICJ when it filed a declaration recognizing compulsory jurisdiction under Art. 36(2) in 1946. The United States withdrew from general ICJ jurisdiction in 1985. By ratifying the Optional Protocol to the Vienna Convention, the United States consented to the specific jurisdiction of the ICJ with respect to claims arising out of the Vienna Convention. On March 7, 2005, subsequent to the ICJ's judgment in *Avena,* the United States gave notice of withdrawal from the Optional Protocol to the Vienna Convention.

Petitioner José Ernesto Medellín, a Mexican national, has lived in the United States since preschool. A member of the "Black and Whites" gang, Medellín was convicted of capital murder and sentenced to death in Texas for the gang rape and brutal murders of two Houston teenagers.

On June 24, 1993, 14-year-old Jennifer Ertman and 16-year-old Elizabeth Pena were walking home when they encountered Medellín and several fellow gang members. Medellín attempted to engage Elizabeth in conversation. When she tried to run, petitioner threw her to the ground. Jennifer was grabbed by other gang members when she, in response to her friend's cries, ran back to help. The gang members raped both girls for over an hour. Then, to prevent their victims from identifying them, Medellín and his fellow gang members murdered the girls and discarded their bodies in a wooded area. Medellín was personally responsible for strangling at least one of the girls with her own shoelace.

Medellín was arrested at approximately 4 a.m. on June 29, 1993. A few hours later, between 5:54 and 7:23 a.m., Medellín was given *Miranda* warnings; he then signed a written waiver and gave a detailed written confession. Local law enforcement officers did not, however, inform Medellín of his Vienna Convention right to notify the Mexican consulate of his detention. Medellín was convicted of capital murder and sentenced to death; his conviction and sentence were affirmed on appeal.

Medellín first raised his Vienna Convention claim in his first application for state post-conviction relief. The state trial court held that the claim was procedurally defaulted because Medellín had failed to raise it at trial or on direct review. The trial court also rejected the Vienna Convention claim on the merits, finding that Medellín had "fail[ed] to show that any non-notification of the Mexican authorities impacted on the validity of his conviction or punishment." The Texas Court of Criminal Appeals affirmed.

Medellín then filed a habeas petition in Federal District Court. The District Court denied relief, holding that Medellín's Vienna Convention claim was procedurally defaulted and that Medellín had failed to show prejudice arising from the Vienna Convention violation.

While Medellín's application for a certificate of appealability was pending in the Fifth Circuit, the ICJ issued its decision in *Avena*. The ICJ held that the United States had violated Article 36(1)(b) of the Vienna Convention by failing to inform the 51 named Mexican nationals, including Medellín, of their Vienna Convention rights. In the ICJ's determination, the United States was obligated "to provide, by means of its own choosing, review and reconsideration of the convictions and sentences of the [affected] Mexican nationals." The ICJ indicated that such review was required without regard to state procedural default rules.

The Fifth Circuit denied a certificate of appealability. The court concluded that the Vienna Convention did not confer individually enforceable rights. The court further ruled that it was in any event bound by this Court's decision in *Breard v. Greene,* 523 U.S. 371, 375 (1998), which held that Vienna Convention claims are subject to procedural default rules, rather than by the ICJ's contrary decision in *Avena.*

This Court granted certiorari. Before we heard oral argument, however, President George W. Bush issued his Memorandum for the United States Attorney General, providing:

> I have determined, pursuant to the authority vested in me as President by the Constitution and the laws of the United States of America, that the United States will discharge its international obligations under the decision of the International Court of Justice in [*Avena*], by having State courts give effect to the decision in accordance with general principles of comity in cases filed by the 51 Mexican nationals addressed in that decision.

Medellín, relying on the President's Memorandum and the ICJ's decision in *Avena,* filed a second application for habeas relief in state court. Because the state-court proceedings might have provided Medellín with the review and reconsideration he requested, and because his claim for federal relief might otherwise have been barred, we dismissed his petition for certiorari as improvidently granted.

The Texas Court of Criminal Appeals subsequently dismissed Medellín's second state habeas application as an abuse of the writ. In the court's view, neither the *Avena* decision nor the President's Memorandum was "binding federal law" that could displace the State's limitations on the filing of successive habeas applications. We again granted certiorari.

II

Medellín first contends that the ICJ's judgment in *Avena* constitutes a "binding" obligation on the state and federal courts of the United States. He argues that "by virtue of the Supremacy Clause, the treaties requiring compliance with the *Avena* judgment are *already* the 'Law of the Land' by which all state and federal courts in this country are 'bound.'" Accordingly, Medellín argues, *Avena* is a binding federal rule of decision that pre-empts contrary state limitations on successive habeas petitions.

No one disputes that the *Avena* decision—a decision that flows from the treaties through which the United States submitted to ICJ jurisdiction with respect to Vienna Convention disputes—constitutes an *international* law obligation on the part of the United States. But not all international law obligations automatically constitute binding federal law enforceable in United States courts. The question we confront here is whether the *Avena* judgment has automatic *domestic* legal effect such that the judgment of its own force applies in state and federal courts.

This Court has long recognized the distinction between treaties that automatically have effect as domestic law, and those that—while they constitute international law commitments—do not by themselves function as binding federal law. The distinction was well explained by Chief Justice Marshall's opinion in *Foster v. Neilson* (1829), which held that a treaty is "equivalent to an act of the legislature," and hence self-executing, when it "operates of itself without the aid of any legislative provision." When, in contrast, "[treaty] stipulations are not self-executing they can only be enforced pursuant to legislation to carry them into effect." In sum, while treaties "may comprise international commitments. . . they are not domestic law unless Congress has either enacted implementing statutes or the treaty itself conveys an intention that it be 'self-executing' and is ratified on these terms."

A treaty is, of course, "primarily a compact between independent nations." It ordinarily "depends for the enforcement of its provisions on the interest and the honor of the governments which are parties to it." "If these [interests] fail, its infraction becomes the subject of international negotiations and reclamations . . . . It is obvious that with all this the judicial courts have nothing to do and can give no redress." Only "[i]f the treaty contains stipulations which are self-executing, that is, require no legislation to make them operative, [will] they have the force and effect of a legislative enactment."

Medellín and his *amici* nonetheless contend that the Optional Protocol, United Nations Charter, and ICJ Statute supply the "relevant obligation" to give the *Avena* judgment binding effect in the domestic courts of the United States. Because none of these treaty sources creates binding federal law in the absence of implementing legislation, and because it is uncontested that no such legislation exists, we conclude that the *Avena* judgment is not automatically binding domestic law. . .

As a signatory to the Optional Protocol, the United States agreed to submit disputes arising out of the Vienna Convention to the ICJ. The Protocol provides: "Disputes arising out of the interpretation or application of the [Vienna] Convention shall lie within the compulsory jurisdiction of the International Court of Justice." Of course, submitting to jurisdiction and agreeing to be bound are two different things. A party could, for example, agree to compulsory nonbinding arbitration. Such an agreement would require the party to appear before the arbitral tribunal without obligating the party to treat the tribunal's decision as binding.

The most natural reading of the Optional Protocol is as a bare grant of jurisdiction. It provides only that "[d]isputes arising out of the interpretation or application of the [Vienna] Convention shall lie within the compulsory jurisdiction of the International Court of Justice" and "may accordingly be brought before the [ICJ]. . . by any party to the dispute being a Party to the present Protocol." The Protocol says nothing about the effect of an ICJ decision and does not itself commit signatories to comply with an ICJ judgment. The Protocol is similarly silent as to any enforcement mechanism.

The obligation on the part of signatory nations to comply with ICJ judgments derives not from the Optional Protocol, but rather from Article 94 of the United Nations Charter—the provision that specifically addresses the effect of ICJ decisions. Article 94(1) provides that "[e]ach Member of the United Nations *undertakes to comply* with the decision of the [ICJ] in any case to which it is a party." The Executive Branch contends that the phrase "undertakes to comply" is not "an acknowledgement that an ICJ decision will have immediate legal effect in the courts of U.N. members," but rather "a *commitment* on the part of U.N. members to take *future* action through their political branches to comply with an ICJ decision."

We agree with this construction of Article 94. The Article is not a directive to domestic courts. It does not provide that the United States "shall" or "must" comply with an ICJ decision, nor indicate that the Senate that ratified the U.N. Charter intended to vest ICJ decisions with immediate legal effect in domestic courts. Instead, "[t]he words of Article 94. . . call upon governments to take certain action." In other words, the U.N. Charter reads like "a compact between independent nations" that "depends for the enforcement of its provisions on the interest and the honor of the governments which are parties to it."

The remainder of Article 94 confirms that the U.N. Charter does not contemplate the automatic enforceability of ICJ decisions in domestic courts. Article 94(2)—the enforcement provision—provides the sole remedy for noncompliance: referral to the United Nations Security Council by an aggrieved state.

The U.N. Charter's provision of an express diplomatic—that is, nonjudicial—remedy is itself evidence that ICJ judgments were not meant to be enforceable in domestic courts. And even this "quintessentially *international* remed[y]" is not absolute. First, the Security Council must "dee[m] necessary" the issuance of a recommendation or measure to effectuate the judgment. Second, as the President and Senate were undoubtedly aware in subscribing to the U.N. Charter and Optional Protocol, the United States retained the unqualified right to exercise its veto of any Security Council resolution.

This was the understanding of the Executive Branch when the President agreed to the U.N. Charter and the declaration accepting general compulsory ICJ jurisdiction. . . If ICJ judgments were instead regarded as automatically enforceable domestic law, they would be immediately and directly binding on state and federal courts pursuant to the Supremacy Clause. Mexico or the ICJ would have no need to proceed to the Security Council to enforce the judgment in this case. Noncompliance with an ICJ judgment through exercise of the Security Council veto—always regarded as an option by the Executive and ratifying Senate during and after consideration of the U.N. Charter, Optional Protocol, and ICJ Statute—would no longer be a viable alternative. There would be nothing to veto. In light of the U.N. Charter's remedial scheme, there is no reason to believe that the President and Senate signed up for such a result.

In sum, Medellín's view that ICJ decisions are automatically enforceable as domestic law is fatally undermined by the enforcement structure established by Article 94. His construction would eliminate the option of noncompliance contemplated by Article 94(2), undermining the ability of the political branches to determine whether and how to comply with an ICJ judgment. Those sensitive foreign policy decisions would instead be transferred to state and federal courts charged with applying an ICJ judgment directly as domestic law. And those courts would not be empowered to decide whether to comply with the judgment—again, always regarded as an option by the political branches—any more than courts may consider whether to comply with any other species of domestic law. . .

The ICJ Statute, incorporated into the U.N. Charter, provides further evidence that the ICJ's judgment in *Avena* does not automatically constitute federal law judicially enforceable in United States courts. To begin with, the ICJ's "principal purpose" is said to be to "arbitrate particular disputes between national governments." Accordingly, the ICJ can hear disputes only between nations, not individuals. More important, Article 59 of the statute provides that "[t]he decision of the [ICJ] has *no binding force* except between the parties and in respect of that particular case." The dissent does not explain how Medellín, an individual, can be a party to the ICJ proceeding.

Medellín argues that because the *Avena* case involves him, it is clear that he—and the 50 other Mexican nationals named in the *Avena* decision—should be regarded as parties to the *Avena* judgment. But cases before the ICJ are often precipitated by disputes involving particular persons or entities, disputes that a nation elects to take up as its own. That has never been understood to alter the express and established rules that only nation-states may be parties before the ICJ and—contrary to the position of the dissent—that ICJ judgments are binding only between those parties. . .

Our conclusion that *Avena* does not by itself constitute binding federal law is confirmed by the "post-ratification understanding" of signatory nations. There are currently 47 nations that are parties to the Optional Protocol and 171 nations that are parties to the Vienna Convention. Yet neither Medellín nor his *amici* have identified a single nation that treats ICJ judgments as binding in domestic courts. In determining that the Vienna Convention did not require certain relief in United States courts in *Sanchez-Llamas,* we found it pertinent that the requested relief would not be available under the treaty in any other signatory country. So too here the lack of any basis for supposing that any other country would treat ICJ judgments as directly enforceable as a matter of their domestic law strongly suggests that the treaty should not be so viewed in our courts. . .

Moreover, the consequences of Medellín's argument give pause. An ICJ judgment, the argument goes, is not only binding domestic law but is also unassailable. As a result, neither Texas nor this Court may look behind a judgment and quarrel with its reasoning or result. (We already know, from *Sanchez-Llamas,* that this Court disagrees with both the reasoning and result in *Avena.*) Medellín's interpretation would allow ICJ judgments to override otherwise binding state law; there is nothing in his logic that would exempt contrary federal law from the same fate. And there is nothing to prevent the ICJ from ordering state courts to annul criminal convictions and sentences, for any reason deemed sufficient by the ICJ. Indeed, that is precisely the relief Mexico requested. . .

In short, and as we observed in *Sanchez-Llamas,* "[n]othing in the structure or purpose of the ICJ suggests that its interpretations were intended to be conclusive on our courts." Given that holding, it is difficult to see how that same structure and purpose can establish, as Medellín argues, that *judgments* of the ICJ nonetheless were intended to be conclusive on our courts. A judgment is binding only if there is a rule of law that makes it so. And the question whether ICJ judgments can bind domestic courts depends upon the same analysis undertaken in *Sanchez-Llamas* and set forth above. . .

In sum, while the ICJ's judgment in *Avena* creates an international law obligation on the part of the United States, it does not of its own force constitute binding federal law that pre-empts state restrictions on the filing of successive habeas petitions. As we noted in *Sanchez-Llamas,* a contrary conclusion would be extraordinary, given that basic rights guaranteed by our own Constitution do not have the effect of displacing state procedural rules. Nothing in the text, background, negotiating and drafting history, or practice among signatory nations suggests that the President or Senate intended the improbable result of giving the judgments of an international tribunal a higher status than that enjoyed by "many of our most fundamental constitutional protections."

III

Medellín next argues that the ICJ's judgment in *Avena* is binding on state courts by virtue of the President's February 28, 2005 Memorandum. The United States contends that while the *Avena* judgment does not of its own force require domestic courts to set aside ordinary rules of procedural default, that judgment became the law of the land with precisely that effect pursuant to the President's Memorandum and his power "to establish binding rules of decision that preempt contrary state law." Accordingly, we must decide whether the President's declaration alters our conclusion that the *Avena* judgment is not a rule of domestic law binding in state and federal courts.

The United States maintains that the President's constitutional role "uniquely qualifies" him to resolve the sensitive foreign policy decisions that bear on compliance with an ICJ decision and "to do so expeditiously." We do not question these propositions. In this case, the President seeks to vindicate United States interests in ensuring the reciprocal observance of the Vienna Convention, protecting relations with foreign governments, and demonstrating commitment to the role of international law. These interests are plainly compelling.

Such considerations, however, do not allow us to set aside first principles. The President's authority to act, as with the exercise of any governmental power, "must stem either from an act of Congress or from the Constitution itself." *Youngstown* at 585. Justice Jackson's familiar tripartite scheme provides the accepted framework for evaluating executive action in this area. First, "[w]hen the President acts pursuant to an express or implied authorization of Congress, his authority is at its maximum, for it includes all that he possesses in his own right plus all that Congress can delegate." Second, "[w]hen the President acts in absence of either a congressional grant or denial of authority, he can only rely upon his own independent powers, but there is a zone of twilight in which he and Congress may have concurrent authority, or in which its distribution is uncertain." In this circumstance, Presidential authority can derive support from "congressional inertia, indifference or quiescence." Finally, "[w]hen the President takes measures incompatible with the expressed or implied will of Congress, his power is at its lowest ebb," and the Court can sustain his actions "only by disabling the Congress from acting upon the subject."

The United States marshals two principal arguments in favor of the President's authority "to establish binding rules of decision that preempt contrary state law." The Solicitor General first argues that the relevant treaties give the President the authority to implement the *Avena* judgment and that Congress has acquiesced in the exercise of such authority. The United States also relies upon an "independent" international dispute-resolution power wholly apart from the asserted authority based on the pertinent treaties. Medellín adds the additional argument that the President's Memorandum is a valid exercise of his power to take care that the laws be faithfully executed.

The United States maintains that the President's Memorandum is authorized by the Optional Protocol and the U.N. Charter. That is, because the relevant treaties "create an obligation to comply with *Avena*," they "*implicitly* give the President authority to implement that treaty-based obligation." As a result, the President's Memorandum is well grounded in the first category of the *Youngstown* framework.

We disagree. The President has an array of political and diplomatic means available to enforce international obligations, but unilaterally converting a non-self-executing treaty into a self-executing one is not among them. The responsibility for transforming an international obligation arising from a non-self-executing treaty into domestic law falls to Congress. As this Court has explained, when treaty stipulations are "not self-executing they can only be enforced pursuant to legislation to carry them into effect." Moreover, "[u]ntil such act shall be passed, the Court is not at liberty to disregard the existing laws on the subject."

The requirement that Congress, rather than the President, implement a non-self-executing treaty derives from the text of the Constitution, which divides the treaty-making power between the President and the Senate. The Constitution vests the President with the authority to "make" a treaty. If the Executive determines that a treaty should have domestic effect of its own force, that determination may be implemented in "mak[ing]" the treaty, by ensuring that it contains language plainly providing for domestic enforceability. If the treaty is to be self-executing in this respect, the Senate must consent to the treaty by the requisite two-thirds vote, consistent with all other constitutional restraints. . .

We thus turn to the United States' claim that—independent of the United States' treaty obligations—the Memorandum is a valid exercise of the President's foreign affairs authority to resolve claims disputes with foreign nations. The United States relies on a series of cases in which this Court has upheld the authority of the President to settle foreign claims pursuant to an executive agreement. In these cases this Court has explained that, if pervasive enough, a history of congressional acquiescence can be treated as a "gloss on 'Executive Power' vested in the President by § 1 of Art. II." . . .

The claims-settlement cases involve a narrow set of circumstances: the making of executive agreements to settle civil claims between American citizens and foreign governments or foreign nationals. They are based on the view that "a systematic, unbroken, executive practice, long pursued to the knowledge of the Congress and never before questioned," can "raise a presumption that the [action] had been [taken] in pursuance of its consent." . . .

The President's Memorandum is not supported by a "particularly longstanding practice" of congressional acquiescence, but rather is what the United States itself has described as "unprecedented action." Indeed, the Government has not identified a single instance in which the President has attempted (or Congress has acquiesced in) a Presidential directive issued to state courts, much less one that reaches deep into the heart of the State's police powers and compels state courts to reopen final criminal judgments and set aside neutrally applicable state laws. . .

After the *Medellín* judgment, Governor Rick Perry refused to commute the death sentences involved. Despite a last minute appeal to the Supreme Court, the State of Texas executed José E. Medellín in 2008, essentially ignoring the ICJ judgment and also ignoring the views of the Bush Administration. In denying the petition from Medellín, the Supreme Court stated in a per curiam opinion that "Petitioner seeks a stay of execution on the theory that either Congress or the Legislature of the State of Texas might determine that actions of the International Court of Justice (ICJ) should be given controlling weight in determining that a violation of the Vienna Convention on Consular Relations is grounds for vacating the sentence imposed in this suit. Under settled principles, these possibilities are too remote to justify an order from this Court staying the sentence imposed by the Texas courts." *Medellín v. Texas*, 554 U.S. 759, 759 (2008). A bill to implement the ICJ decision was introduced in the U.S. House of Representatives but never passed into law. See Avena Case Implementation Act of 2008, H.R. 6481, 110th Cong., 2d Sess. (2008). In dissent, Justice Breyer noted that Medellín's execution "will place this Nation in violation of international law." 554 U.S. 759, at 766. After the execution, the case between the United States and Mexico continued, resulting in the following judgment from the ICJ. As you read this final judgment, consider the costs and benefits of the U.S. approach for incorporating international law into the domestic legal system.

Request for Interpretation of the Judgment of 31 March 2004 in the Case Concerning Avena and Other Mexican Nationals (Mexico v. United States of America)

International Court of Justice
2009 I.C.J. 3

47. Before proceeding to the additional requests of Mexico, the Court observes that considerations of domestic law which have so far

hindered the implementation of the obligation incumbent upon the United States, cannot relieve it of its obligation. A choice of means was allowed to the United States in the implementation of its obligation and, failing success within a reasonable period of time through the means chosen, it must rapidly turn to alternative and effective means of attaining that result.

52. Mr. Medellín was executed in the State of Texas on 5 August 2008 after having unsuccessfully filed an application for a writ of habeas corpus and applications for stay of execution and after having been refused a stay of execution through the clemency process. Mr. Medellín was executed without being afforded the review and reconsideration provided for by paragraphs 138 to 141 of the Avena Judgment, contrary to what was directed by the Court in its Order indicating provisional measures of 16 July 2008.

53. The Court thus finds that the United States did not discharge its obligation under the Court's Order of 16 July 2008, in the case of Mr. José Ernesto Medellín Rojas.

54. The Court further notes that the Order of 16 July 2008 stipulated that five named persons were to be protected from execution until they received review and reconsideration or until the Court had rendered its Judgment upon Mexico's Request for interpretation. The Court recalls that the obligation upon the United States not to execute Messrs. César Roberto Fierro Reyna, Rubén Ramírez Cárdenas, Humberto Leal García, and Roberto Moreno Ramos pending review and reconsideration being afforded to them is fully intact... The Court further notes that the other persons named in the Avena Judgment are also to be afforded review and reconsideration in the terms there specified.

55. The Court finally recalls that, as the United States has itself acknowledged, until all of the Mexican nationals referred to in subparagraphs (4), (5), (6) and (7) of paragraph 153 of the Avena Judgment have had their convictions and sentences reviewed and reconsidered, by taking account of Article 36 of the Vienna Convention on Consular Relations and paragraphs 138 to 141 of the Avena Judgment, the United States has not complied with the obligation incumbent upon it...

58. Lastly, Mexico requests the Court to order the United States to provide guarantees of non-repetition (point (2) (c) of Mexico's submissions) so that none of the Mexican nationals mentioned in the Avena Judgment is executed without having benefited from the review and reconsideration provided for by the operative part of that Judgment.

59. The United States disputes the jurisdiction of the Court to order it to furnish guarantees of non-repetition, principally inasmuch as the

Court lacks jurisdiction under Article 60 of the Statute to entertain Mexico's Request for interpretation or, in the alternative, since the Court cannot, in any event, order the provision of such guarantees within the context of interpretation proceedings.

60. The Court finds it sufficient to reiterate that its Avena Judgment remains binding and that the United States continues to be under an obligation fully to implement it. . .

NOTES & QUESTIONS

1. *Non-Self-Executing Treaties*. One reason for the Supreme Court's refusal to give automatic effect to the ICJ judgment was the Court's conclusion that both the UN Charter and the Charter of the International Court of Justice were non-self-executing treaties. Recall the prior discussion of the distinction between self-executing and non-self-executing treaties in Chapter 3 of this casebook. Do you agree with the Court's conclusion about these specific treaties? More generally, is it appropriate for a country to use the distinction between the two types of treaties as a reason for failing to comply with the preliminary measures ordered by the ICJ in *Avena*? Is the United States responsible under international law for signing what it considered a non-self-executing treaty and then not following up with appropriate domestic legislation to fulfill its international obligations? For an argument that the American distinction between self-executing and non-self-executing treaties is a judicial distortion of the Constitution, see Jordan J. Paust, *Self-Executing Treaties*, 82 Am. J. Int'l L. 760 (1988).

2. *Presidential Power*. The Bush Administration intervened in the dispute and effectively ordered state governments to comply with the ICJ's *Avena* judgment. Why did this argument not persuade the Supreme Court? The Court conceded that the President has at least *some* independent foreign affairs power under Article II of the Constitution. More importantly, the Supreme Court in the past has upheld the President's authority to engage in international claims settlement. See, e.g., *Dames and Moore v. Reagan*, 453 U.S. 654 (1981) (upholding President's authority to suspend pending claims in federal court pursuant to the Algiers Accords signed with the government of Iran). Why couldn't the President use his claims settlement authority to direct the state court to comply with an ICJ decision? In *Medellín*, the court focused on the fact that the President had no delegated authority from Congress to directly implement the ICJ's decisions. If Congress had wanted to give the President that authority, it could have ratified a self-executing treaty or passed implementing legislation giving the President that authority (which it never did).

3. *Monism Versus Dualism*. What role, if any, does dualism play in the dispute between the ICJ and the U.S. courts? Recall that the distinction between self-executing and non-self-executive treaties is a doctrine of U.S. law, and not all countries utilize the distinction to the same extent as American jurists. In some jurisdictions, international agreements are

automatically enforceable in domestic court without any further implementing legislation. What explains the different treatment that international obligations receive in domestic law? Are monist legal systems more likely to grant blanket enforceability of international obligations in domestic court? For more reading on this subject, see Curtis A. Bradley, *Breard, Our Dualist Constitution, and the Internationalist Conception*, 51 Stan. L. Rev. 529, 531 (1999) ("the U.S. approach to international law has been and continues to be fundamentally dualist"). In contrast, the Netherlands Constitution specifically provides that treaties are directly enforceable in their domestic courts and that they supplant conflicting domestic law. See John H. Jackson, *Status of Treaties in Domestic Legal Systems: A Policy Analysis*, 86 Am. J. Int'l L. 310, 320 (1992). How would the Netherlands have responded from an order of the ICJ in a case arising out of the Vienna Convention?

Conclusion & Summary

International law can be applied and enforced in domestic U.S. courts, though numerous obstacles and doctrinal limitations sometimes limit the ability of litigants to get courts to directly apply international law in their cases. In this chapter, the following elements of international law application were articulated:

1. Historically, international law was considered part of U.S. federal law because it was incorporated by the common law, which the U.S. inherited from England at the time of independence. For that reason, federal courts may consider customary international law (the "law of nations") in addition to applying treaties which are already considered federal law by virtue of the Supremacy Clause in the U.S. Constitution. Although some scholars have suggested that the elimination of federal common law in *Erie* poses problem for this incorporation of international law through the common law, the Supreme Court in *Sosa* reiterated that international law is still part of federal law and can be applied in federal court.

2. The Alien Tort Statute grants federal courts jurisdiction to hear claims by aliens for violations of the law of nations. Although the ATS laid dormant for many years, human rights lawyers have used the ATS to file many cases for atrocities committed abroad. In *Sosa*, the Supreme Court, drawing on the offenses originally described Blackstone, clarified that the alleged violations must be specific, universal, and obligatory. Then, in *Kiobel*, the Supreme Court applied the presumption against extraterritoriality and barred ATS cases that do not touch and concern the

territory of the United States, though extraterritorial
jurisdiction still exists under more specific statutes such as
the Torture Victims Protection Act. *Jesner* foreclosed ATS
cases against foreign corporations.

3.   Although decisions by the International Court of Justice are
binding on the parties as a matter of international law, they
may not be automatically enforceable in federal court.
Litigants cannot simply walk into federal court, cite an ICJ
decision, and expect federal judges to enforce it. In
Medellín, the Supreme Court concluded that the UN
Charter and the Charter of the ICJ were both non-self-
executing treaties, and therefore not directly enforceable in
federal court absent some further domestic legislation by
Congress. Moreover, the Court concluded that the
President could not transform a non-self-executing treaty
into a self-executing treaty by executive fiat. Some nations,
such as the Netherlands, take a more monist approach to
their international obligations and allow litigants to enforce
any international treaty in their domestic courts.

CHAPTER 15

PRINCIPLES OF JURISDICTION

Introduction

A state's exercise of jurisdiction over particular conduct is not simply a matter of domestic concern. In a world increasingly dominated by transnational business activities, global tourism, and cross-border information technology, multiple states often have competing interests in regulating that human conduct. Consequently, international law has developed a series of principles that guide the exercise of a state's jurisdiction. In order to regulate conduct, a state should point to at least one principle to justify its assertion of jurisdiction.

There are three domains of jurisdiction:

A. *Jurisdiction to prescribe* involves the state's capacity to issue regulations, such as when its legislature passes a statute.

B. *Jurisdiction to adjudicate* involves a court's capacity to entertain a legal dispute or resolve a particular legal controversy.

C. *Jurisdiction to enforce* involves the state's capacity to enforce the law by, say, sending its police or other officials to arrest an individual or to enforce a monetary judgment.

Although international lawyers are accustomed to discussing these domains separately, in practice they are usually intertwined. When a court adjudicates a dispute it usually does so pursuant to some statutory authorization. Similarly, when a state official arrests an individual (jurisdiction to enforce) they usually bring that individual to court to decide the charges (jurisdiction to adjudicate). Consequently, "regulation" of conduct usually involves the combination of these government functions: prescribing rules by a legislature or other law-making governmental body, a court's adjudication of alleged violations of those rules, and an executive official's enforcement of those rules and decisions.

A. JURISDICTION TO PRESCRIBE

In this section, we consider five major principles of jurisdiction: (i) territoriality, (ii) active personality, (iii) passive personality, (iv) protective, and (v) universal.

The territorial principle allows a state to regulate conduct occurring on its territory and, in some circumstances, extraterritorial conduct that has "effects" on its domestic territory. In many ways, the primary task of the international law of jurisdiction is to articulate which domestic effects of foreign conduct are significant and closely connected enough to ground a claim of jurisdiction. The active personality principle allows a state to regulate the foreign conduct of its own nationals, while the passive personality principle allows a state to regulate foreign conduct that victimizes its citizens. (These principles are sometimes referred to as active *nationality* and passive *nationality* respectively.) For example, think of an American who commits a crime in France; if the United States enforces its laws against that individual, it would be exercising jurisdiction based on the active personality principle. Similarly, imagine that a foreigner commits a terrorist attack abroad that kills one or more American citizens; if the United States indicts the terrorist, it would be exercising jurisdiction based on the passive personality principle. Under the protective principle, states may exercise jurisdiction to protect essential government functions; so, for example, a foreign conspiracy to counterfeit a state's currency would be a valid subject of sovereign concern. Finally, universal jurisdiction allows any state to prosecute an individual who commits an international crime or other serious atrocity. However, as will be discussed below, the exact scope of universal jurisdiction is hotly contested and states have recently responded to these criticisms by restricting their assertion of universal jurisdiction to situations with *some* connection to their sovereign territory or sovereign interest, which in some sense is not really "universal" jurisdiction at all. The doctrine of universal jurisdiction—and the exact scope of each jurisdictional principle below—continues to evolve.

1. TERRITORIAL JURISDICTION

There is nothing controversial about a state exerting jurisdiction over acts committed on its territory. Indeed, that forms the baseline paradigm for territorial jurisdiction. However, states have gradually expanded their notion of territorial jurisdiction from acts committed on its territory to extraterritorial acts that have *effects* on its territory. In the United States, the watershed case discussing this development was *United States v. Aluminum Co. of America (Alcoa),* 148 F.2d 416 (2d Cir. 1945). In *Alcoa,* Judge Learned Hand wrote that "it is settled law... that any state may impose liabilities, even upon persons not within its allegiance, for conduct outside its borders that has consequences within its borders which the state reprehends; and these liabilities other states will ordinarily recognize." Consequently, the Second Circuit concluded that the United States could apply its antitrust laws to foreign price-fixing conspiracies that have effects in the United States.

However, in today's globalized economy, a lot of foreign commercial activity will have some downstream "effect" in the United States.

Without any future limitation, a broad effects test runs the risk of granting de facto universal jurisdiction over worldwide commercial activity—all under the pretense of adhering to the principle of territoriality. This runs the risk that a state's exercise of jurisdiction may interfere with the sovereignty of another state that has a greater interest in regulating the behavior. As the Ninth Circuit said in *Timberlane*, "The effects test by itself is incomplete because it fails to consider other nations' interests." *Timberlane Lumber Co. v. Bank of America*, 549 F.2d 597, 611–12 (9th Cir. 1976). Furthermore, the Ninth Circuit noted that "[d]espite its description as 'settled law,' *Alcoa*'s assertion has been roundly disputed by many foreign commentators as being in conflict with international law, comity, and good judgment."

Consequently, the Ninth Circuit in *Timberlane* developed an influential test for guiding U.S. courts in exercising their jurisdiction in a manner consistent with international law. The three-prong standard included the following factors: (1) there be some effect actual or intended on American foreign commerce (the *Alcoa* framework); (2) the effect is sufficiently large to present a cognizable injury to the plaintiffs; and (3) whether the interests of, and links to, the United States are sufficiently strong, relative to other nations, to justify extraterritorial jurisdiction. The third prong required a consideration of seven factors:

i.   The degree of conflict with foreign law or policy;

ii.   The nationality or allegiance of the parties and the locations or principal places of businesses or corporations;

iii.   The extent to which enforcement by either state can be expected to achieve compliance;

iv.   The relative significance of effects on the United States as compared with those elsewhere;

v.   The extent to which there is explicit purpose to harm or affect American commerce;

vi.   The foreseeability of such effect; and

vii.   The relative importance to the violations charged of conduct within the United States as compared with conduct abroad.

The goal of these seven *Timberlane* factors was to limit the potential conflict with international law and international comity posed by the aggressive use of United States jurisdiction over extraterritorial conduct with effects on U.S. territory. Although the criteria were influential and designed to limit these conflicts, some of the criteria were easy to satisfy. For example, in *Hartford Fire Ins. Co. v. California*, 509 U.S. 764, 769 (1993), the Supreme Court considered the first *Timberlane* factor, the degree of conflict with foreign law or policy, and concluded that a "conflict" does not exist if a person "subject to regulation by two states can comply with the laws of both." In most cases, this is possible by simply complying with the more restrictive of the two regulations. It is rarely the case where two nations issue contrary regulations that are literally *impossible* to comply with because one state requires that a person do *x* while a second requires that a person not do *x*.

The basic idea behind the *Timberlane* factors—the need to set some limits on U.S. antitrust enforcement and bring it in line with international principles of jurisdiction—also inspired Congress to enter the fray with an explicit statutory scheme. The result was the Foreign Trade Antitrust Improvements Act of 1982 (FTAIA). The FTAIA provided, in part:

> Sections 1 to 7 of this title shall not apply to conduct involving trade or commerce (other than import trade or import commerce) with foreign nations unless—
>
> (1) such conduct has a direct, substantial, and reasonably foreseeable effect—
>
> (A) on trade or commerce which is not trade or commerce with foreign nations, or on import trade or import commerce with foreign nations; or
>
> (B) on export trade or export commerce with foreign nations, of a person engaged in such trade or commerce in the United States; and
>
> (2) such effect gives rise to a claim under the provisions of sections 1 to 7 of this title, other than this section.
>
> If sections 1 to 7 of this title apply to such conduct only because of the operation of paragraph (1)(B), then sections 1 to 7 of this title shall apply to such conduct only for injury to export business in the United States.

The key limitation here is the requirement that the *Alcoa*-type effect must be "direct, substantial, and reasonably foreseeable." That language, incidentally, also appears in the *Restatement (Third) of Foreign Relations Law*, which argues that one factor in determining the reasonableness of a state's exercise of jurisdiction over a "person or activity having connections with another state" is "the link of the activity to the territory of the regulating state, i.e., the extent to which the activity takes place within the territory, or has substantial, direct, and foreseeable effect upon or in the territory. . ." Although not every state may use the same language in articulating these factors, the basic idea is that an unlimited effects test might place a state in conflict with another's sovereign right to regulate conduct occurring on its territory, and therefore violate international law. Consequently, effects-based jurisdiction must be substantially curtailed and only be asserted in situations where the effects in the state asserting jurisdiction are substantial, direct, and foreseeable.

Nonetheless, many questions about these constraints remained. They are not self-applying. Consider the following fact pattern which is common in antitrust price-fixing conspiracies. Foreign parties outside of the United States engage in a price-fixing conspiracy, which results in harm to foreign purchasers in the form of inappropriately high prices and also higher prices for United States customers. Can the *foreign* purchasers bring suit in the United States based on the argument that the conspiracy had a foreign effect *and* a "direct, substantial, and reasonably foreseeable" effect on prices in the United States? Or would the assertion of jurisdiction in such a case trample on the rights of the sovereign rights of the foreign nation, which should have exclusive rights to regulate the conduct in question? In the following case, the U.S. Supreme Court answers that question. Although the case is very much based on statutory interpretation of the FTAIA, the statute was intertwined with, and motived by, a respect for international legal restraints on the exercise of extraterritorial jurisdiction.

F. Hoffmann-La Roche Ltd. v. Empagran
Supreme Court of the United States
542 U.S. 155 (2004)

■ JUSTICE BREYER delivered the opinion of the Court.

The Foreign Trade Antitrust Improvements Act of 1982 (FTAIA) excludes from the Sherman Act's reach much anticompetitive conduct that causes only foreign injury. It does so by setting forth a general rule stating that the Sherman Act "shall not apply to conduct involving trade or commerce... with foreign nations." It then creates exceptions to the general rule, applicable where (roughly speaking) that conduct significantly harms imports, domestic commerce, or American exporters.

We here focus upon anticompetitive price-fixing activity that is in significant part foreign, that causes some domestic antitrust injury, and that independently causes separate foreign injury. We ask two questions about the price-fixing conduct and the foreign injury that it causes. First, does that conduct fall within the FTAIA's general rule excluding the Sherman Act's application? That is to say, does the price-fixing activity constitute "conduct involving trade or commerce... with foreign nations"? We conclude that it does.

Second, we ask whether the conduct nonetheless falls within a domestic-injury exception to the general rule, an exception that applies (and makes the Sherman Act nonetheless applicable) where the conduct (1) has a "direct, substantial, and reasonably foreseeable effect" on domestic commerce, and (2) "such effect gives rise to a [Sherman Act] claim." §§ 6a(1)(A), (2). We conclude that the exception does not apply where the plaintiff's claim rests solely on the independent foreign harm.

To clarify: The issue before us concerns (1) significant foreign anticompetitive conduct with (2) an adverse domestic effect and (3) an independent foreign effect giving rise to the claim. In more concrete terms, this case involves vitamin sellers around the world that agreed to fix prices, leading to higher vitamin prices in the United States and independently leading to higher vitamin prices in other countries such as Ecuador. We conclude that, in this scenario, a purchaser in the United States could bring a Sherman Act claim under the FTAIA based on domestic injury, but a purchaser in Ecuador could not bring a Sherman Act claim based on foreign harm.

I

The plaintiffs in this case originally filed a class-action suit on behalf of foreign and domestic purchasers of vitamins under, inter alia, § 1 of the Sherman Act, and §§ 4 and 16 of the Clayton Act. Their complaint alleged that petitioners, foreign and domestic vitamin manufacturers and distributors, had engaged in a price-fixing conspiracy, raising the price of vitamin products to customers in the United States and to customers in foreign countries.

As relevant here, petitioners moved to dismiss the suit as to the foreign purchasers (the respondents here), five foreign vitamin distributors located in Ukraine, Australia, Ecuador, and Panama, each of which bought vitamins from petitioners for delivery outside the United States. Respondents have never asserted that they purchased any vitamins in the United States or in transactions in United States commerce, and the question presented assumes that the relevant "transactions occurr[ed] entirely outside U.S. commerce."

II

The FTAIA seeks to make clear to American exporters (and to firms doing business abroad) that the Sherman Act does not prevent them from entering into business arrangements (say, joint-selling arrangements), however anticompetitive, as long as those arrangements adversely affect only foreign markets. It does so by removing from the Sherman Act's reach, (1) export activities and (2) other commercial activities taking place abroad, unless those activities adversely affect domestic commerce, imports to the United States, or exporting activities of one engaged in such activities within the United States.

The FTAIA says:

Sections 1 to 7 of this title [the Sherman Act] shall not apply to conduct involving trade or commerce (other than import trade or import commerce) with foreign nations unless—

(1) such conduct has a direct, substantial, and reasonably foreseeable effect—

(A) on trade or commerce which is not trade or commerce with foreign nations [i.e., domestic trade or commerce], or on import trade or import commerce with foreign nations; or

(B) on export trade or export commerce with foreign nations, of a person engaged in such trade or commerce in the United States [i.e., on an American export competitor]; and

(2) such effect gives rise to a claim under the provisions of sections 1 to 7 of this title, other than this section.

If sections 1 to 7 of this title apply to such conduct only because of the operation of paragraph (1)(B), then sections 1 to 7 of this title shall apply to such conduct only for injury to export business in the United States.

This technical language initially lays down a general rule placing all (non-import) activity involving foreign commerce outside the Sherman Act's reach. It then brings such conduct back within the Sherman Act's reach provided that the conduct both (1) sufficiently affects American commerce, i.e., it has a "direct, substantial, and reasonably foreseeable effect" on American domestic, import, or (certain) export commerce, and (2) has an effect of a kind that antitrust law considers harmful, i.e., the "effect" must "giv[e] rise to a [Sherman Act] claim."

We ask here how this language applies to price-fixing activity that is in significant part foreign, that has the requisite domestic effect, and that also has independent foreign effects giving rise to the plaintiff's claim.

IV

We turn now to the basic question presented, that of the exception's application. Because the underlying antitrust action is complex, potentially raising questions not directly at issue here, we reemphasize that we base our decision upon the following: The price-fixing conduct significantly and adversely affects both customers outside the United States and customers within the United States, but the adverse foreign effect is independent of any adverse domestic effect. In these circumstances, we find that the FTAIA exception does not apply (and thus the Sherman Act does not apply) for two main reasons.

First, this Court ordinarily construes ambiguous statutes to avoid unreasonable interference with the sovereign authority of other nations. This rule of construction reflects principles of customary international law—law that (we must assume) Congress ordinarily seeks to follow. See *Restatement (Third) of Foreign Relations Law of the United States* §§ 403(1), 403(2) (1986) (hereinafter Restatement) (limiting the unreasonable exercise of prescriptive jurisdiction with respect to a person or activity having connections with another State); *Murray v. Schooner Charming Betsy*, 2 Cranch 64, 118 (1804) ("[A]n act of Congress ought never to be construed to violate the law of nations if any other possible construction remains"); *Hartford Fire Insurance Co. v. California*, 509 U.S. 764, 817 (1993) (Scalia, J., dissenting) (identifying rule of construction as derived from the principle of "prescriptive comity").

This rule of statutory construction cautions courts to assume that legislators take account of the legitimate sovereign interests of other nations when they write American laws. It thereby helps the potentially conflicting laws of different nations work together in harmony—a harmony particularly needed in today's highly interdependent commercial world.

No one denies that America's antitrust laws, when applied to foreign conduct, can interfere with a foreign nation's ability independently to regulate its own commercial affairs. But our courts have long held that application of our antitrust laws to foreign anticompetitive conduct is nonetheless reasonable, and hence consistent with principles of prescriptive comity, insofar as they reflect a legislative effort to redress domestic antitrust injury that foreign anticompetitive conduct has caused. See *United States v. Aluminum Co. of America*, 148 F.2d 416, 443–444 (2d Cir. 1945).

But why is it reasonable to apply those laws to foreign conduct insofar as that conduct causes independent foreign harm and that foreign harm alone gives rise to the plaintiff's claim? Like the former case, application of those laws creates a serious risk of interference with a foreign nation's ability independently to regulate its own commercial affairs. But, unlike the former case, the justification for that interference seems insubstantial. See Restatement § 403(2) (determining reasonableness on basis of such factors as connections with regulating nation, harm to that nation's interests, extent to which other nations regulate, and the potential for conflict). Why should American law supplant, for example, Canada's or Great Britain's or Japan's own determination about how best to protect Canadian or British or Japanese customers from anticompetitive conduct engaged in significant part by Canadian or British or Japanese or other foreign companies?

We recognize that principles of comity provide Congress greater leeway when it seeks to control through legislation the actions of American companies, see Restatement § 402; and some of the anticompetitive price-fixing conduct alleged here took place in America. But the higher foreign prices of which the foreign plaintiffs here complain are not the consequence of any domestic anticompetitive conduct that Congress sought to forbid, for Congress did not seek to forbid any such conduct insofar as it is here relevant, i.e., insofar as it is intertwined with foreign conduct that causes independent foreign harm. Rather Congress sought to release domestic (and foreign) anticompetitive conduct from Sherman Act constraints when that conduct causes foreign harm. Congress, of course, did make an exception where that conduct also causes domestic harm. See House Report 13 (concerns about American firms' participation in international cartels addressed through "domestic injury" exception). But any independent domestic harm the foreign conduct causes here has, by definition, little or nothing to do with the matter.

We thus repeat the basic question: Why is it reasonable to apply this law to conduct that is significantly foreign insofar as that conduct causes independent foreign harm and that foreign harm alone gives rise to the plaintiff's claim? We can find no good answer to the question.

The Areeda and Hovenkamp treatise notes that under the Court of Appeals' interpretation of the statute

> a Malaysian customer could. . . maintain an action under United States law in a United States court against its own Malaysian supplier, another cartel member, simply by noting that unnamed third parties injured [in the United States] by the American [cartel member's] conduct would also have a cause of action. Effectively, the United States courts would provide worldwide subject matter jurisdiction to any foreign suitor wishing to sue its own local supplier, but unhappy with its own sovereign's provisions for private antitrust enforcement, provided that a different plaintiff had a cause of action against a different firm for injuries that were within U.S. [other-than-import] commerce. It does not seem excessively rigid to infer that Congress would not have intended that result.

P. Areeda & H. Hovenkamp, Antitrust Law ¶ 273, pp. 51–52 (Supp. 2003). We agree with the comment. We can find no convincing justification for the extension of the Sherman Act's scope that it describes.

Respondents reply that many nations have adopted antitrust laws similar to our own, to the point where the practical likelihood of interference with the relevant interests of other nations is minimal. Leaving price fixing to the side, however, this Court has found to the contrary. See, e.g., *Hartford Fire*, 509 U.S. at 797–799 (noting that the alleged conduct in the London reinsurance market, while illegal under United States antitrust laws, was assumed to be perfectly consistent with British law and policy).

Regardless, even where nations agree about primary conduct, say price fixing, they disagree dramatically about appropriate remedies. The application, for example, of American private treble-damages remedies to anticompetitive conduct taking place abroad has generated considerable controversy. And several foreign nations have filed briefs here arguing that to apply our remedies would unjustifiably permit their citizens to bypass their own less generous remedial schemes, thereby upsetting a balance of competing considerations that their own domestic antitrust laws embody.

These briefs add that a decision permitting independently injured foreign plaintiffs to pursue private treble-damages remedies would undermine foreign nations' own antitrust enforcement policies by diminishing foreign firms' incentive to cooperate with antitrust authorities in return for prosecutorial amnesty.

Respondents alternatively argue that comity does not demand an interpretation of the FTAIA that would exclude independent foreign injury cases across the board. Rather, courts can take (and sometimes have taken) account of comity considerations case by case, abstaining where comity considerations so dictate.

In our view, however, this approach is too complex to prove workable. The Sherman Act covers many different kinds of anticompetitive agreements. Courts would have to examine how foreign law, compared with American law, treats not only price fixing but also, say, information-sharing agreements, patent-licensing price conditions, territorial product resale limitations, and various forms of joint venture, in respect to both primary conduct and remedy. The legally and economically technical nature of that enterprise means lengthier proceedings, appeals, and more proceedings—to the point where procedural costs and delays could themselves threaten interference with a foreign nation's ability to maintain the integrity of its own antitrust enforcement system. Even in this relatively simple price-fixing case, for example, competing briefs tell us (1) that potential treble-damage liability would help enforce widespread anti-price-fixing norms (through added deterrence) and (2) the opposite, namely that such liability would hinder antitrust enforcement (by reducing incentives to enter amnesty programs). How could a court seriously interested in resolving so empirical a matter—a matter potentially related to impact on foreign interests—do so simply and expeditiously?

We conclude that principles of prescriptive comity counsel against the Court of Appeals' interpretation of the FTAIA. Where foreign anticompetitive conduct plays a significant role and where foreign injury is independent of domestic effects, Congress might have hoped that America's antitrust laws, so fundamental a component of our own economic system, would commend themselves to other nations as well. But, if America's antitrust policies could not win their own way in the international marketplace for such ideas, Congress, we must assume, would not have tried to impose them, in an act of legal imperialism, through legislative fiat.

Second, the FTAIA's language and history suggest that Congress designed the FTAIA to clarify, perhaps to limit, but not to expand in any significant way, the Sherman Act's scope as applied to foreign commerce. And we have found no significant indication that at the time Congress wrote this statute courts would have thought the Sherman Act applicable in these circumstances.

The Solicitor General and petitioners tell us that they have found no case in which any court applied the Sherman Act to redress foreign injury in such circumstances. And respondents themselves apparently conceded as much at a May 23, 2001, hearing before the District Court below. Nevertheless, respondents now have called to our attention six cases, three decided by this Court and three decided by lower courts. In the first three cases the defendants included both American companies and foreign companies jointly engaged in anticompetitive behavior having both foreign and domestic effects. In all three cases the plaintiff sought relief, including relief that might have helped to protect those injured abroad. . .

In all three cases, however, the plaintiff was the Government of the United States. A Government plaintiff, unlike a private plaintiff, must seek to obtain the relief necessary to protect the public from further anticompetitive conduct and to redress anticompetitive harm. And a Government plaintiff has legal authority broad enough to allow it to carry out this mission. Private plaintiffs, by way of contrast, are far less likely to be able to secure broad relief. This difference means that the Government's ability, in these three cases, to obtain relief helpful to those injured abroad tells us little or nothing about whether this Court would have awarded similar relief at the request of private plaintiffs.

Neither did the Court focus explicitly in its opinions on a claim that the remedies sought to cure only independently caused foreign harm. Thus the three cases tell us even less about whether this Court then thought that foreign private plaintiffs could have obtained foreign relief based solely upon such independently caused foreign injury. . .

Taken together, these two sets of considerations, the one derived from comity and the other reflecting history, convince us that Congress would not have intended the FTAIA's exception to bring independently caused foreign injury within the Sherman Act's reach. . .

NOTES & QUESTIONS

1. *The Presumption Against Extraterritoriality.* Generally speaking, U.S. courts will assume, all other things being equal, that Congress did not intend for its statutes to have extraterritorial effect. What is the basis for

this canon of interpretation? Does it flow from the intersection of the *Charming Betsy* canon and international principles of jurisdiction? In other words, courts assume—again all other things being equal—that Congress acts consistent with, rather than against, its international legal obligations. And if aggressive extraterritorial jurisdiction runs the risk that the United States might be acting contrary to international legal principles of jurisdiction, then courts have strong reasons to avoid reading congressional statutes in this way—unless Congress is explicit about the matter. In *Morrison v. Nat'l Australia Bank Ltd.*, 561 U.S. 247, 255 (2010), the Supreme Court noted that the rule "rests on the perception that Congress ordinarily legislates with respect to domestic, not foreign matters" but that it "applies regardless of whether there is a risk of conflict between the American statute and a foreign law." In *Kiobel*, reprinted and discussed in Chapter 14 of this casebook, the Supreme Court applied the *Morrison* presumption to claims under the Alien Tort Statute, ultimately concluding that the ATS did not give U.S. federal courts jurisdiction over most torts committed overseas.

2.   *Civil Versus Criminal Territorial Jurisdiction.* Should territorial jurisdiction play out differently in criminal and civil cases? In the United States, federal and state courts have understood territorial jurisdiction in broader terms in criminal cases and in narrower terms in civil cases. For a discussion, see Zachary C. Clopton, *Bowman Lives: The Extraterritorial Application of U.S. Criminal Law After Morrison v. National Australia Bank,* 67 N.Y.U. Ann. Surv. Am. L. 137 (2011) (concluding that U.S. courts are more willing to apply criminal statutes extraterritorially compared with private-law counterparts). Why would courts treat criminal laws differently from civil statutes? One possibility involves the concern that extraterritorial jurisdiction will negatively impact relations with foreign states. Civil cases are triggered by private plaintiffs filing claims with a court; the judiciary must then decide if the exercise of jurisdiction will negatively impact the state's conduct of foreign relations. In contrast, criminal cases, at least at the federal level, are triggered by the executive branch, which presumably has already determined that the potential risks to foreign relations are outweighed by the benefits of enforcing the criminal statute. In that situation, a court may have fewer qualms about judicial involvement.

2. ACTIVE NATIONALITY PRINCIPLE

Under the active nationality principle, a state may regulate the conduct of its nationals, even when they are overseas. The basic idea is that an important relationship between the state and its nationals endures even when that national is located on the sovereign territory of another state. This means, for example, that a U.S. national living abroad who commits a crime may be subject to prosecution in an American court. Of course, not all penal statutes in the United States have this extraterritorial effect. For example, 18 U.S.C. § 1119 prohibits "A person who, being a national of the United States, kills or attempts to kill a national of the United States while such national is outside the

United States but within the jurisdiction of another country. . ." However, this statute limits jurisdiction to cases where the victim also is a U.S. national, thus establishing a deeper connection between the United States and the act in question.

In what circumstances would it be permissible under international law for a state to exercise jurisdiction over its nationals for extraterritorial conduct that victimizes foreign nationals? The following case answers that question. At the very least, the exercise of jurisdiction based on the active nationality principle is uncontroversial when the state is under a pre-existing obligation under international law to prosecute the offense, as is true for genocide and, in the case of Chuckie Taylor, torture. Taylor was prosecuted for violating the federal Torture Act, which includes extraterritorial jurisdiction under specific circumstances.

United States v. Belfast (Chuckie Taylor)
United States Court of Appeals for the Eleventh Circuit
611 F.3d 783 (2010)

■ MARCUS, CIRCUIT JUDGE:

Roy M. Belfast, Jr., a/k/a Charles McArthur Emmanuel, a/k/a Charles Taylor, Jr., a/k/a Chuckie Taylor, II ("Emmanuel"), appeals his convictions and 97-year sentence for committing numerous acts of torture and other atrocities in Liberia between 1999 and 2003, during the presidency of his father, Charles Taylor. Emmanuel, who is the first individual to be prosecuted under the Torture Act, 18 U.S.C. § 2340–2340A ("the Torture Act"), seeks reversal of his convictions on the ground that the Torture Act is unconstitutional. Primarily, Emmanuel contends that congressional authority to pass the Torture Act derives solely from the United States's obligations as a signatory to the Convention Against Torture and Other Cruel, Inhuman or Degrading Treatment or Punishment (the "CAT"); he says the Torture Act impermissibly exceeds the bounds of that authority, both in its definition of torture and its proscription against conspiracies to commit torture. Emmanuel also challenges his convictions under 18 U.S.C. § 924(c), which criminalizes the use or possession of a firearm in connection with a crime of violence. He says, among other things, that this provision cannot apply extraterritorially to his actions in Liberia. Finally, he claims that an accumulation of procedural errors made his trial fundamentally unfair, and that the district court erred in sentencing him.

After thorough review, we conclude that all of Emmanuel's convictions are constitutional. The United States validly adopted the CAT pursuant to the President's Article II treaty-making authority, and it was well within Congress's power under the Necessary and Proper

Clause to criminalize both torture, as defined by the Torture Act, and conspiracy to commit torture. Furthermore, we hold that both the Torture Act and the firearm statute apply to extraterritorial conduct, and that their application in this case was proper. . . Accordingly, we affirm Emmanuel's convictions and sentence in all respects.

I.

The facts of this case are riddled with extraordinary cruelty and evil. The defendant, Charles McArthur Emmanuel, was born in Massachusetts in 1977, the son of Bernice Yolanda Emmanuel and Charles Taylor. Taylor returned to his native Liberia sometime thereafter. Emmanuel's mother married Roy Belfast in 1983. Apparently out of fear that Taylor would try to take her son, Bernice Emmanuel moved with him and Belfast to Orlando, FL. There, the couple also changed Emmanuel's name to Roy Belfast, Jr.

In 1992, Emmanuel visited Liberia, where a bloody civil war had been raging for three years. At the time of Emmanuel's visit, his father, Taylor, led the National Patriotic Front of Liberia ("NPFL"), an armed insurgent group. The NPFL was one faction in the struggle for national power following the assassination of Liberian President Samuel Doe in 1990. After some months, Emmanuel returned to the United States. Two years later, however, Emmanuel again visited Liberia; this time, he did not return. In 1997, Taylor was elected to the presidency. President Taylor soon charged the twenty-year-old Emmanuel with overseeing the state's creation of an Anti-Terrorism Unit ("ATU")—also known in Liberia as the "Demon Forces"—which was responsible for protecting Taylor and his family.

Under Emmanuel's direction, the ATU began recruiting men to fill its ranks, and installed them at a former training camp known as Gbatala Base. The base was situated in a swampy area. As described by one recruit, Wesley Sieh, Emmanuel directed the ATU soldiers to dig around twenty grave-size prison pits, which were eventually covered with metal bars or barbed wire. A periodically overflowing river in the vicinity caused some of the pits to fill with water, which then stagnated. Aside from the prison pits, the base included a shooting range, a building containing a holding cell for disobedient ATU soldiers, and an "educational" training facility known as the College of Knowledge. The base was under the command of David Compari; he took orders from Emmanuel, who appeared several times a week wearing the ATU's green tiger-striped uniform and red emblem bearing a cobra and scorpion.

The ATU was Emmanuel's self-described "pet project." At Gbatala and elsewhere, ATU affiliates referred to Emmanuel as "Chief," and his license plate read "Demon." Between 1999 and 2002, the defendant wielded his power in a terrifying and violent manner, torturing numerous individuals in his custody who were never charged with any crime or given any legal process. . .

III

Next, Emmanuel argues that his convictions are invalid because the Torture Act allows federal courts to take jurisdiction over an act of torture based solely on the presence of the alleged torturer in the United States, something he claims is not authorized by the CAT or any other provision of law. Notably, there was no need to invoke this so-called "present-in" jurisdiction in this case because Emmanuel is a United States citizen. See 18 U.S.C. § 2340A(b)(1) (conferring jurisdiction over acts of torture where "the alleged offender is a national of the United States"). Thus, we address Emmanuel's objection to "present-in" jurisdiction only in the context of his facial challenge to the Torture Act.

Article 5(2) of the CAT obligates a signatory nation to assert jurisdiction over an "alleged offender" who is "present in any territory under its jurisdiction" and whom it does not extradite. It is difficult to see what clearer authorization of "present-in" jurisdiction the CAT might have contained. Consistent with the plain language of the CAT, Congress placed the following jurisdictional provision in the Torture Act:

(b) Jurisdiction—There is jurisdiction over the activity prohibited in subsection (a) if—

(1) the alleged offender is a national of the United States; or

(2) the alleged offender is present in the United States, irrespective of the nationality of the victim or alleged offender.

18 U.S.C. § 2340A(b). Plainly, even if subsection (b)(2) had provided the exclusive basis for jurisdiction in this case—and it did not—that fact would not have rendered Emmanuel's convictions infirm in any way.

Emmanuel also challenges his Torture Act convictions on the ground that the Torture Act does not apply to the extraterritorial conduct of a United States citizen. He is, once again, incorrect, because Congress has the power to regulate extraterritorial conduct, and the requisite expression of congressional intent to do so is found in the Torture Act.

It has long been established that Congress has the power to regulate the extraterritorial acts of U.S. citizens. *United States v. Plummer,* 221 F.3d 1298, 1304 (11th Cir. 2000); see also *United States v. Baker,* 609 F.2d 134, 136 (5th Cir. 1980) (noting that "[s]ince an early date, it has been recognized that Congress may attach extraterritorial effect to its penal enactments," and that "a nation's power to secure itself from injury may certainly be exercised beyond the limits of its territory."). As we have explained, however,

[w]hether Congress has chosen to exercise that authority. . . is an issue of statutory construction. It is a longstanding principle of American law that legislation of Congress, unless a contrary intent appears, is meant to apply only within the territorial jurisdiction of the United States.

Nieman v. Dryclean U.S.A. Franchise Co., 178 F.3d 1126, 1129 (11th Cir. 1999). "The presumption against extraterritoriality can be overcome only by clear expression of Congress' intention to extend the reach of the relevant Act beyond those places where the United States has sovereignty or has some measure of legislative control." See also *Morrison v. Nat'l Austl. Bank Ltd* (2010) ("When a statute gives no clear indication of an extraterritorial application, it has none."). Such an intention of course may appear on the face of the statute, but it may also be "inferred from. . . the nature of the harm the statute is designed to prevent," from the self-evident "international focus of the statute," and from the fact that "limit[ing] [the statute's] prohibitions to acts occurring within the United States would undermine the statute's effectiveness."

The language of the Torture Act itself evinces an unmistakable congressional intent to apply the statute extraterritorially. It punishes "[w]hoever *outside the United States* commits. . . torture." Further, even if the language of the Torture Act were not so remarkably clear, the intent to apply the statute to acts occurring outside United States territory could be inferred along the lines set forth in *Plummer,* 221 F.3d at 1310. First, the nature of the harm to which the CAT and the Torture Act are directed—"torture and other cruel, inhuman or degrading treatment or punishment throughout the world"—is quintessentially international in scope. Second, and relatedly, the international focus of the statute is "self-evident": Congress's concern was not to prevent official torture within the borders of the United States, but in nations where the rule of law has broken down and the ruling government has become the enemy, rather than the protector, of its citizens. Finally, limiting the prohibitions of the Torture Act to conduct occurring in the United States would dramatically, if not entirely, reduce their efficacy.

In short, all of Emmanuel's substantive convictions under the Torture Act are fully consonant with the United States Constitution. . .

NOTES & QUESTIONS

A Citizen's Duty of Loyalty. Why is a United States citizen bound to follow the laws of the United States when residing abroad? And what right does the United States have to enforce those laws? In *Blackmer v. United States,* 284 U.S. 421, 436 (1932), the Supreme Court upheld contempt proceedings against an American living in France who ignored a subpoena issued by an American court. In reaching this conclusion, the court stated that though Blackmer moved to France, he continued to owe "allegiance to the United States. By virtue of the obligations of citizenship, the United States retained its authority over him, and he was bound by its laws made applicable to him in a foreign country." Similarly, in *United States v. King*, 552 F.2d 833, 851 (1976), the Ninth Circuit upheld narcotics charges against Americans engaged in international narcotics smuggling because "American authority over them could be based upon the allegiance they owe this country and its laws if the statute. . . evinces a legislative intent to control actions within and without the United States." Does this statement suggest that the active nationality principle supports the prosecution of citizens for their extraterritorial conduct even in the case of minor crimes?

3. PASSIVE PERSONALITY PRINCIPLE

What if a foreigner engages in actions contrary to U.S. law, outside the territory of the United States, but the individual harmed by the action is an American citizen? In that case, the United States (or any state in a similar position) has a national interest in regulating the conduct and enforcing its laws. Jurisdiction under these circumstances is possible under the "passive personality principle," a label that captures that it is the individual affected by the action that provides the foundation for the state's exercise of jurisdiction over the situation. As you read the following case, ask yourself whether the passive personality principle can be asserted to regulate any conduct or whether only conduct of a sufficient gravity should be subject to jurisdiction under this principle.

United States v. Neil
U.S. Court of Appeals for the Ninth Circuit
312 F.3d 419 (2002)

■ WILLIAM A. FLETCHER, CIRCUIT JUDGE.

Emmanuel Ormand Neil appeals his conviction for sexual contact with a minor in violation of 18 U.S.C. § 2244(a)(3). Neil is a citizen of St. Vincent and the Grenadines who was employed on a cruise ship departing from and returning to an American port. The victim, a 12-year-old girl, was a United States citizen, and the crime took place in Mexican territorial waters. Neil contends that the United States did not have extraterritorial jurisdiction over the crime. We disagree and affirm the judgment of the district court.

I

During the week of October 1–7, 2000, Neil worked as a cabin steward on the Carnival Cruise Lines ship Elation on a round-trip vacation cruise from San Pedro Harbor in California to various ports in Mexico. The Elation has Panamanian registry, and is wholly owned by

Carnival Cruise Lines. The majority of passengers on the Elation's weekly round-trip cruise to Mexico are American.

During the cruise, Neil was responsible for cleaning the cabin of a 12-year-old girl. On October 5, 6, and 7, Neil felt the girl's breasts and buttocks through her clothing. At the end of the voyage, the girl's parents lodged a complaint and referral to the Federal Bureau of Investigation. Neil eventually admitted the sexual molestation and signed a written confession. After she returned to the United States, the girl missed several days of school for psychological counseling, which cost her family approximately $2000.

In February 2001, a grand jury charged Neil with three counts of sexual contact with a minor in violation of 18 U.S.C. § 2244(a)(3). Neil filed a motion to dismiss the indictment for lack of jurisdiction, which the district court denied. Neil then filed a motion for reconsideration, which the district court also denied. Neil conditionally pled guilty to two counts of sexual contact, reserving the right to appeal the district court's jurisdictional holding. The district court sentenced him to six months in custody. . .

II

We hold that the United States properly exercised jurisdiction. The Constitution does not bar extraterritorial application of United States penal laws. *See United States v. Felix-Gutierrez,* 940 F.2d 1200, 1204 (9th Cir. 1991); *Chua Han Mow v. United States,* 730 F.2d 1308, 1311 (9th Cir. 1984). However, acts of Congress generally do not have extraterritorial application unless Congress clearly so intends.

We undertake a two-part inquiry to determine whether extraterritorial jurisdiction is proper. First, we look to the text of the statute for an indication that Congress intended it to apply extraterritorially. Second, we look to the operation of the statute to determine whether the exercise of extraterritorial jurisdiction comports with principles of international law. Because the statute in question here explicitly applies outside the United States and because exercising jurisdiction does not offend any principle of international law, we hold that extraterritorial jurisdiction is proper.

We look first to the text of the statute to determine whether Congress intended it to apply extraterritorially in this case. *See United States v. Bowman,* 260 U.S. 94, 97–98 (1922); *United States v. Vasquez-Velasco,* 15 F.3d 833, 839 (9th Cir. 1994). The text of § 2244(a)(3), the statute under which Neil was convicted, specifically invokes the "special maritime and territorial jurisdiction of the United States." It provides, in relevant part:

(a) *Sexual conduct in circumstances where sexual acts are punished by this chapter.*—Whoever, in the special maritime and territorial jurisdiction of the United States or in a Federal prison, knowingly engages in or causes sexual contact with or by another person, if so to do would violate. . . .

(3) subsection (a) of section 2243 of this title had the sexual contact been a sexual act, shall be fined under this title, imprisoned not more than two years, or both.

18 U.S.C. § 2244(a)(3). Section 2243(a)(1), in turn, prohibits "knowingly engag[ing] in a sexual act with another person who has attained the age of 12 years but has not attained the age of 16 years." Like § 2244, § 2243 applies in the "special maritime and territorial jurisdiction of the United States."

Congress has defined the "special maritime and territorial jurisdiction of the United States" as including, "[t]o the extent permitted by international law, any foreign vessel during a voyage having a scheduled departure from or arrival in the United States with respect to an offense committed by or against a national of the United States." 18 U.S.C. § 7(8). The criminal sexual contact between Neil and the victim occurred on a foreign vessel that departed from and arrived in the United States, and the victim was a United States national. This conduct thus falls squarely into the definition of special maritime and territorial jurisdiction set out in § 7(8).

It remains to examine whether the exercise of jurisdiction by the United States in this case would violate international law. In general, we consult international law as part of our analysis of statutes that do not make explicit their intent to exercise extraterritorial jurisdiction. In this particular case, we consult international law because the text of the statute qualifies the grant of extraterritorial jurisdiction by providing that such jurisdiction is available only "[t]o the extent permitted by international law."

International law supports extraterritorial jurisdiction in this case. Two principles of international law permitting extraterritorial jurisdiction are potentially relevant: the territorial principle and the passive personality principle. Under the territorial principle, the United States may assert jurisdiction when acts performed outside of its borders have detrimental effects within the United States. The sexual contact occurred during a cruise that originated and terminated in California. Neil's conduct prompted an investigation by the FBI, and an agent arrested Neil in the United States. The victim was an American citizen who lives and goes to school in the United States, and who sought counseling in this country after the attack. These facts are enough to support jurisdiction under the territorial principle. See *Hill,* 279 F.3d at 739–40 (applying the territorial principle to find extraterritorial jurisdiction in a case involving a failure to make child support payments);

see also *United States v. Roberts,* 1 F. Supp. 2d 601, 608 (E.D. La. 1998) (applying the territorial principle to find extraterritorial jurisdiction over a sexual assault on an American aboard a Carnival Cruise Lines ship); *United States v. Pizdrint,* 983 F. Supp. 1110, 1112–13 (M.D. Fla. 1997) (applying the territorial principle to find extraterritorial jurisdiction over an assault on two people, one of whom was an American citizen, aboard a Carnival Cruise Lines ship).

Extraterritorial jurisdiction is also appropriate under the passive personality principle. Under this principle, a state may, under certain circumstances, assert jurisdiction over crimes committed against its nationals. We have previously sustained jurisdiction based on the passive personality principle. See, e.g., *Hill,* 279 F.3d at 740 (applying the passive personality principle to find extraterritorial jurisdiction when the victims of the defendant's failure to make child support payments were American citizens); *Felix-Gutierrez,* 940 F.2d at 1206 (applying territorial, protective, and passive personality principles "cumulatively" to find extraterritorial jurisdiction over a prosecution of a Mexican national for assisting in the kidnapping and murder of an American Drug Enforcement Agency agent in Mexico).

Neil contends that the passive personality principle is inappropriate in this case based on our discussion in *United States v. Vasquez-Velasco,* 15 F.3d 833 (9th Cir. 1994). In that case, two American tourists had been murdered in Mexico by members of a drug cartel. We held that the passive personality principle applied because the defendants believed that the two Americans were agents of the federal Drug Enforcement Agency, but we wrote that "[i]f the evidence at trial only suggested that two tourists were randomly murdered, extraterritorial application of § 1959 would be inappropriate." Citing the [*Restatement (Third) of Foreign Relations Law of the United States* § 402 cmt. G], we noted that, in general, the passive personality principle has not been accepted as a sufficient basis for extraterritorial jurisdiction over ordinary torts and crimes.

Neil overreads our statements in *Vasquez-Velasco.* The defendants in that case were charged with committing violent crimes in aid of a racketeering enterprise under 18 U.S.C. § 1959. Unlike § 2244, that statute does not explicitly state that it applies extraterritorially, and we were obliged to infer an intent to exercise extraterritorial jurisdiction. We therefore construed the statute somewhat narrowly, stating that we did not believe that Congress intended to invoke the passive personality principle in § 1959, and thereby to criminalize extraterritorial crimes against all Americans under that statute. By contrast, § 2244(a)(3) relies on § 7(8), which invokes the passive personality principle by explicitly stating its intent to authorize extraterritorial jurisdiction, to the extent permitted by international law, when a foreign vessel departs from or arrives in an American port and an American national is a victim. We conclude that the passive personality principle is appropriately invoked to justify the exercise of extraterritorial jurisdiction in the circumstances specified in the statute.

NOTES & QUESTIONS

The View from the Restatement. Consider the following statement from the *Restatement (Third) of Foreign Relations Law*: "The passive personality principle asserts that a state may apply law—particularly criminal law—to an act committed outside its territory by a person not its national where the victim of the act was its national. The principle has not been generally accepted for ordinary torts or crimes, but it is increasingly accepted as applied to terrorist and other organized attacks on a state's nationals by reason of their nationality, or to assassination of a state's diplomatic representatives or other officials." Does this contradict *Neil*? In *Neil*, the defendant was charged with sexual assault, not terrorism or assassination. Is the passive personality principle as controversial as the *Restatement* suggests? Prior Restatements were even more categorical, concluding that the passive personality principle was not recognized by international law. However, since the 1970s, the United States has started to exercise jurisdiction on the basis of the passive personality principle more often. See Geoffrey R. Watson, *The Passive Personality Principle*, 28 Tex. Int'l L.J. 1, 9 (1993) ("Despite these statements, passive personality jurisdiction began to creep into United States law in the early 1970s when the United States entered into a series of multilateral terrorism conventions, sometimes founded on passive personality jurisdiction, that obliged states to extradite or prosecute offenders for various terrorist offenses."). However, Professor Watson goes on to conclude: "Outside of terrorism, however, the United States still seems reluctant to embrace passive personality jurisdiction. Although Congress has recognized passive personality jurisdiction for some terrorist offenses, it has not extended such jurisdiction to common crimes of violence against Americans on foreign soil." Can you think of some particular reason why the United States was willing to invoke the passive personality principle in the case of Emmanuel Ormand Neil?

4.   THE PROTECTIVE PRINCIPLE

In addition to the passive personality principle, states have also occasionally invoked the "protective principle" as grounds for jurisdiction. The idea behind the principle is that international law permits states to take actions necessary for their sovereign defense and protection, and this right sometimes requires the exercise of jurisdiction over extraterritorial acts. The classic examples are terrorism and other national security threats that might threaten either the homeland or foreign assets of the state in a way that might interfere with a state's governmental functions. In a sense, the protective principle is conceptually close to the passive personality principle, which focuses on the victims of the act to be regulated. Similarly, the protective principle focuses on who or what might be negatively impacted by the action. However, the protective principle operates with a wider focus than the passive personality principle in the sense that it is not necessary to identify specific victims. Instead, the protective principle looks to the legitimate national interests of a state—usually its governmental functions—and asks whether jurisdiction is a necessarily element of protecting those endeavors. At the same time, though, the protective principle is arguably narrower than the passive personality principle because it only applies to a limited category of offenses that implicate particular state interests. The following case presents an interesting example of the protective principle in action.

United States v. Yousef
U.S. Court of Appeals for the Second Circuit
327 F.3d 56 (2003)

. . . The conspiracy to bomb the World Trade Center began in the Spring of 1992, when Yousef met Ahmad Mohammad Ajaj at a terrorist training camp on the border of Afghanistan and Pakistan. After formulating their terrorist plot, Yousef and Ajaj traveled to New York together in September 1992. In Ajaj's luggage, he carried a "terrorist kit" that included, among other things, bomb-making manuals. After Yousef and Ajaj arrived at John F. Kennedy International Airport, inspectors of the Immigration and Naturalization Service ("INS") discovered the "terrorist kit" in Ajaj's luggage and arrested him. Although Yousef was also stopped, he and Ajaj did not disclose their connection to one another, and INS officials allowed Yousef to enter the United States.

Once in New York, Yousef began to put together the manpower and the supplies that he would need to carry out his plan to bomb the World Trade Center. Yousef assembled a group of co-conspirators to execute his plan, including defendants Mohammad Salameh, Nidal Ayyad, Mahmud Abouhalima, and Abdul Rahman Yasin. Next, Yousef began accumulating the necessary ingredients for the bomb. He ordered the required chemicals, and his associates rented a shed in which to store them. Yousef and Salameh established their headquarters at an apartment they rented in Jersey City, New Jersey, an urban center located across the Hudson River from Manhattan. The apartment also functioned as their bomb-making factory.

In December 1992, Yousef contacted Ismoil, who was then living in Dallas, Texas. On February 22, 1993, Ismoil joined Yousef and the others in New York to help complete the bomb preparations.

On February 26, 1993, Yousef and Ismoil drove a bomb-laden van onto the B-2 level of the parking garage below the World Trade Center. They then set the bomb's timer to detonate minutes later. At approximately 12:18 p.m. that day, the bomb exploded, killing six people, injuring more than a thousand others, and causing widespread fear and more than $500 million in property damage.

Soon after the bombing, Yousef and Ismoil fled from the United States. Yousef and Ismoil were indicted for their participation in the bombing on March 31, 1993 and August 8, 1994, respectively. Yousef was captured in Pakistan nearly two years after the bombing, and Ismoil was arrested in Jordan a little over two years after the attack. Both were returned to the United States to answer the charges in the indictment.

Airline Bombing

A year and a half after the World Trade Center bombing, Yousef entered Manila, the capital of the Philippines, under an assumed name. By September 1994, Yousef had devised a plan to attack United States airliners. According to the plan, five individuals would place bombs aboard twelve United States-flag aircraft that served routes in Southeast Asia. The conspirators would board an airliner in Southeast Asia, assemble a bomb on the plane, and then exit the plane during its first layover. As the planes continued on toward their next destinations, the time-bombs would detonate. Eleven of the twelve flights targeted were ultimately destined for cities in the United States.

Yousef and his co-conspirators performed several tests in preparation for the airline bombings. In December 1994, Yousef and Wali Khan Amin Shah placed one of the bombs they had constructed in a Manila movie theater. The bomb exploded, injuring several patrons of the theater. Ten days later, Yousef planted another test bomb under a passenger's seat during the first leg of a Philippine Airlines flight from Manila to Japan. Yousef disembarked from the plane during the stopover and then made his way back to Manila. During the second leg of the flight, the bomb exploded, killing one passenger, a Japanese national, and injuring others.

The plot to bomb the United States-flag airliners was uncovered in January 1995, only two weeks before the conspirators intended to carry it out. Yousef and Murad were burning chemicals in their Manila apartment and accidentally caused a fire. An apartment security guard saw the smoke coming from the apartment and called the fire department. After the firemen left, the Philippine police arrived at the apartment, where they discovered chemicals and bomb components, a laptop computer on which Yousef had set forth the aircraft bombing plans, and other incriminating evidence. Philippine authorities arrested Murad and Shah, though Shah escaped and was not recaptured until nearly a year later. Yousef fled the country, but was captured in Pakistan the next month.

On February 21, 1996, a grand jury in the Southern District of New York filed a twenty-count superseding indictment against the defendants and others. Counts One through Eleven charged Yousef and Ismoil with various offenses arising from their participation in the February 26, 1993 bombing of the World Trade Center. Counts Twelve through Nineteen charged Yousef, Murad, and Shah with various crimes relating to their conspiracy to bomb United States airliners in Southeast Asia in 1994 and 1995.

The trial of Yousef, Murad, and Shah on the airline bombing charges began on May 29, 1996 and ended on September 5, 1996, when the jury found all three defendants guilty on all counts. Yousef and Ismoil's trial on charges relating to the World Trade Center bombing began on July 15, 1997 and concluded on November 12, 1997, when the jury found both defendants guilty on all counts.

Yousef was sentenced for both convictions on January 8, 1998. For the World Trade Center convictions he was sentenced principally to a total of 240 years of imprisonment: 180 years on Counts One through Eight, plus two 30-year terms on Counts Nine and Ten for violations of 18 U.S.C. § 924(c) to be served consecutively to the 180-year sentence and to each other. For the airline bombing convictions, Yousef was sentenced principally to a term of life imprisonment, to be served consecutively to his 240-year sentence for the World Trade Center bombing.

Jurisdiction to Prosecute Defendants' Extraterritorial Conduct Under Federal Law

It is beyond doubt that, as a general proposition, Congress has the authority to "enforce its laws beyond the territorial boundaries of the United States." Although there is a presumption that Congress does not intend a statute to apply to conduct outside the territorial jurisdiction of the United States, that presumption can be overcome when Congress clearly expresses its intent to do so. As long as Congress has indicated its intent to reach such conduct, a United States court is "bound to follow the Congressional direction unless this would violate the due process clause of the Fifth Amendment." Moreover, the presumption against extraterritorial application does not apply to those "criminal statutes which are, as a class, not logically dependent on their locality for the Government's jurisdiction."

In determining whether Congress intended a federal statute to apply to overseas conduct, "an act of Congress ought never to be construed to violate the law of nations if any other possible construction remains." Nonetheless, in fashioning the reach of our criminal law, "Congress is not bound by international law." "If it chooses to do so, it may legislate with

respect to conduct outside the United States, in excess of the limits posed
by international law."

Exercise of United States Extraterritorial Jurisdiction
and Customary International Law

On appeal, Yousef challenges the District Court's jurisdiction over
Counts Twelve through Nineteen of the indictment by arguing that
customary international law does not provide a basis for jurisdiction over
these counts and that United States law is subordinate to customary
international law and therefore cannot provide a basis for jurisdiction.
He particularly contests the District Court's conclusion that customary
international law permits the United States to prosecute him under the
so-called universality principle for the bombing of Philippine Airline
Flight 434 charged in Count Nineteen. Yousef claims that, absent a
universally agreed-upon definition of "terrorism" and an international
consensus that terrorism is a subject matter over which universal
jurisdiction may be exercised, the United States cannot rest jurisdiction
over him for this "terrorist" act *either* on the universality principle or on
any United States positive law, which, he claims, necessarily is
subordinate to customary international law.

Yousef's arguments fail. First, irrespective of whether customary
international law provides a basis for jurisdiction over Yousef for Counts
Twelve through Nineteen, United States law provides a separate and
complete basis for jurisdiction over each of these counts and, contrary to
Yousef's assertions, United States law is not subordinate to customary
international law or necessarily subordinate to treaty-based
international law and, in fact, may conflict with both. Further contrary
to Yousef's claims, customary international law *does* provide a
substantial basis for jurisdiction by the United States over each of these
counts, although not (as the District Court held) under the universality
principle.

While the District Court correctly held that jurisdiction was proper
over each count, and we affirm the substance of its rulings in full, we hold
that the District Court erred in partially grounding its exercise of
jurisdiction over Count Nineteen—the bombing of Philippine Airlines
Flight 434 while en route from Manila, the Philippines, via Cebu, to
Japan—on the universality principle.

We conclude, instead, that jurisdiction over Count Nineteen was
proper, first, under domestic law, 18 U.S.C. § 32; second, under the *aut
dedere aut punire* ("extradite or prosecute") jurisdiction created by the
Montreal Convention, as implemented in 18 U.S.C. § 32 (destruction of
aircraft) and 49 U.S.C. § 46502 (aircraft piracy); and third, under the
protective principle of the customary international law of criminal
jurisdiction.

Jurisdiction over Counts Twelve through Eighteen is straight-forward, and we affirm both the District Court's finding of jurisdiction and its reasoning. United States domestic law provides a complete basis for jurisdiction over the conduct charged in these counts, independent of customary international law. Nevertheless, contrary to Yousef's claims, jurisdiction is consistent with three of the five principles of customary international law criminal jurisdiction—the objective, protective, and passive personality principles.

First, jurisdiction over Counts Twelve through Eighteen is consistent with the "passive personality principle" of customary international jurisdiction because each of these counts involved a plot to bomb United States-flag aircraft that would have been carrying United States citizens and crews and that were destined for cities in the United States. Moreover, assertion of jurisdiction is appropriate under the "objective territorial principle" because the purpose of the attack was to influence United States foreign policy and the defendants intended their actions to have an effect—in this case, a devastating effect—on and within the United States. Finally, there is no doubt that jurisdiction is proper under the "protective principle" because the planned attacks were intended to affect the United States and to alter its foreign policy.

Although the government is not required to prove that its prosecution of Yousef comported with any of the customary international law bases of criminal jurisdiction, we note that, in fact, Yousef's prosecution by the United States *is* consistent with the "protective principle" of international law. The protective (or "security") principle permits a State to assume jurisdiction over non-nationals for acts done abroad that affect the security of the State. The protective principle generally is invoked to obtain jurisdiction over politically motivated acts but is not limited to acts with a political purpose. *In re Marc Rich & Co.,* 707 F.2d 663, 666 (2d Cir. 1983) (stating that the protective principle provides jurisdiction over acts committed outside of a State's territory that are directed at interfering with the State's "governmental functions," provided that the act also is contrary to the laws of the host State, if such State has a "reasonably developed" legal system).

The stated purpose of Yousef's plot to destroy United States commercial aircraft was to influence United States foreign policy, the making of which clearly constitutes a "governmental function." The bombing of the Philippine Airlines flight at issue in Count Nineteen, which killed one Japanese national and maimed another, was merely a test-run that Yousef executed to ensure that the tactics and devices the conspirators planned to use on United States aircraft operated properly.

Documentation stored on Yousef's laptop computer and adduced at trial, demonstrates that the Philippine Airlines bombing constituted part of the co-conspirators' plan to detonate numerous bombs on United

States-flag aircraft. A letter, with a file date of November 19, 1994, found in Yousef's laptop states, in pertinent part:

> We, the Fifth Division of the Liberation Army... declare our responsibility for striking at some American targets in the near future in retaliation for the financial, political, and military support extended by the American government to the Jewish State.... [T]he Jewish State continues its massacres... with American money, weapons, and ammunition, in addition to the support and blessing given... by the U.S. Congress. The American people are quite aware of all this. [Therefore] [we] *will consider all American nationals as part of our legitimate targets because they are responsible for the behavior of their government and its foreign policies,* for the policy of the government represents the will of the people.

Letter from Fifth Division of the Liberation Army (Nov. 19, 1994) (emphasis added).

Extensive additional documentation was found on Yousef's laptop and presented at trial. These documents, which set forth, *inter alia,* the flight schedules and paths of United States-flag aircraft and detailed plans for planting bombs on these flights, confirmed that the co-conspirators intended to bomb United States-flag aircraft using a *modus operandi* identical to that which permitted them to place the bomb on Philippine Airlines flight 434. All of these flights were scheduled to depart from cities in Southeast Asia where the bomber would board the plane, make a stopover in that region where the bomber would disembark, and then continue on to a United States destination, at which point the previously-planted explosive device would detonate. This is more than enough to permit the United States to claim jurisdiction over Yousef under the protective principle.

To summarize, we hold that the District Court erred in holding that jurisdiction over the acts charged in Count Nineteen is proper under the customary international law principle of universal jurisdiction, but conclude that the District Court properly asserted jurisdiction over Counts Twelve through Nineteen under United States law, the treaty obligations of the United States, and various principles of customary international law other than the universality principle. We reject Yousef's claim that the absence of jurisdiction under the universality principle over so-called "terrorist" acts precludes his prosecution under United States law.

NOTES & QUESTIONS

Which State Interests? What is the basis for the protective principle? The *Restatement (Third) of Foreign Relations Law* states that that a state may regulate "certain conduct outside its territory by persons not its nationals that is directed against the security of the state or against a limited class of other state interests." See § 402(3). What actions might this apply to? Clearly a terrorism plot, but are there other examples? The *Restatement* goes on to note that

> International law recognizes the right of a state to punish a limited class of offenses committed outside its territory by persons who are not its nationals—offenses directed against the security of the state or other offenses threatening the integrity of governmental functions that are generally recognized as crimes by developed legal systems, e.g., espionage, counterfeiting of the state's seal or currency, falsification of official documents, as well as perjury before consular officials, and conspiracy to violate the immigration or customs laws.

Is this really a separate principle of jurisdiction or is it a sub-category of the principle of territorial effects described in Section A? In each of these cases, the extraterritorial crimes have a substantial, direct, and foreseeable effect on the territory of the United States. In any event, international lawyers have grown accustomed to describing the protective principle as a distinct principle of jurisdiction. For more discussion, see Richard G. Alexander, *Iran and Libya Sanctions Act of 1996: Congress Exceeds Its Jurisdiction to Prescribe Law*, 54 Wash. & Lee L. Rev. 1601, 1616 (1997) (concluding that a state may "prescribe laws governing conduct outside its territory directed against the security of the state or against a limited class of other state interests," but that the principle only applies to "acts generally recognized as crimes by developed legal systems" such as "espionage, counterfeiting of the state's seal or currency, falsification of official documents, perjury before consular officials, and conspiracy to violate immigration or customs laws").

5. UNIVERSAL JURISDICTION

On May 11, 1960, Ricardo Klement rode the bus from his job at a Mercedes Benz factory in Buenos Aires, Argentina. He got off the bus and walked down to his house on Garibaldi Street. But before he could reach the house, he was waylaid by Israeli Mossad agents who shoved him into a car and took him to a Mossad safe house. There he was interrogated and admitted that he was real name was Adolf Eichmann, the Nazi officer responsible for the bureaucratic implementation of the Final Solution—the destruction of the Jewish People in Nazi-constructed gas chambers.

The Mossad exfiltrated Eichmann out of Argentina by smuggling him aboard a diplomatic flight that was returning to Israel. Upon Eichmann's arrival in Israel, Mossad director Issar Harel reportedly walked into the office of Prime Minister David Ben-Gurion and said: "I brought you a present. Eichmann is here." Eichmann was then placed on trial for his role in the Holocaust.

Putting aside for the moment whether the Israeli snatch-and-grab operation was a violation of Argentina's sovereignty, what principle of jurisdiction justified Israel's prosecution of Eichmann? Eichmann's crimes occurred in Germany (and other European states), not on the territory of Israel, which in any event did not even exist during World War II. Are some crimes so horrific that every state has jurisdiction to prosecute them?

Attorney General of the Government of Israel v. Eichmann

Supreme Court of Israel
Criminal Appeal 336/61 (1962)

1.   The Appellant, Adolf Eichmann, was found guilty by the District Court of Jerusalem of offences of the most extreme gravity against the Nazis and Nazi Collaborators (Punishment) Law 5710–1950 (hereinafter "the Law") and was sentenced to death. These offences may be divided into four groups: Group One: Crimes against the Jewish People, contrary to Section I(a) (1) of the Law; Group Two: Crimes against Humanity, contrary to Section 1(a) (2); Group Three: War Crimes, contrary to Section 1(a) (3); Group Four: Membership of Hostile Organizations, contrary to Section 3.

2.   The acts constituting these offences, which the Court attributed to the Appellant, have been specified in paragraph 244 of the Judgment. The acts belonging to Group One are:

1)   That during the period from August 1941 to May 1945, in Germany, in the territories of the Axis States, and in the areas which were subject to the authority of Germany and the Axis States, he, together with others, caused the deaths of millions of Jews, with the purpose of implementing the plan which was known as "the Final Solution of the Jewish Question," with intent to exterminate the Jewish People;

2)   that during that period and in the same places he, together with others, subjected millions of Jews to living conditions which were likely to bring about their physical destruction, in order to implement the said plan, with intent to exterminate the Jewish People;

3)   that during that period and in the same places he, together with others, caused grave bodily and mental harm to millions of Jews, with intent to exterminate the Jewish People;

4)   that during the years 1943 and 1944 he, together with others, "took measures to prevent births among Jews, by directing that births be banned and pregnancies

terminated among Jewish women in the Therezin Ghetto, with intent to exterminate the Jewish People."

The acts constituting the crimes in Group Two are as follows:

5) That during the period from August 1941 to May 1945 "he, together with others, caused in the places mentioned in Clause (1), the murder, extermination, enslavement, starvation and deportation of the Jewish civilian population;"

6) that during the period from December 1939 to March 1941 "he, together with others, caused the deportation of Jews to Nisko, and the deportation of Jews from the areas in the East annexed to the Reich, and from the Reich area proper, into the German-occupied area in the East, and to France;"

7) that in carrying out the above-mentioned activities he persecuted Jews on national, racial, religious and political grounds;

8) that during the period from March 1938 to May 1945 in the places mentioned above "he, together with others, caused the plunder of the property of millions of Jews through mass terror, linked with the murder, destruction, starvation and deportation of those Jews;"

9) that "during the years 1940–1942 he, together with others, caused the expulsion of hundreds of thousands of Poles from their homes;"

10) that in 1941, he, together with others, caused "the expulsion of more than fourteen thousand Slovenes from their homes;"

11) that during World War II he, together with others, caused the expulsion of "tens of thousands of Gypsies from Germany and German-occupied areas and their transportation to the German-occupied areas in the East;"

12) that in 1942 "he, together with others, caused the expulsion of 93 children of the Czech village Lidice."

The acts comprised in Group Three of the crimes are:

13) That "he committed the acts of persecution, expulsion and murder mentioned in Counts 1–7, so far as these were done during World War II, against Jews from among the populations of the countries occupied by the Germans and by the other Axis States."

The acts comprised in Group Four are:

14) That as from May 1940 he was "a member of three Nazi police organizations which were declared criminal organizations by the International Military Tribunal which tried the major war criminals, and as a member of such organizations he took part in acts declared criminal in Article 6 of the London Charter of 8 August 1945."

3.   The Appellant has appealed to this Court against both the conviction and the sentence.

6.   Most of the legal contentions of Counsel for the Appellant concentrate on the argument that the District Court, in assuming jurisdiction to try the Appellant, acted contrary to the principles of international law. These contentions are as follows:

(2)   The offences for which the Appellant was tried are in the nature of "extra-territorial offences," that is to say, offences that were committed outside the territory of Israel by a citizen of a foreign state; and even though the above-mentioned Law confers jurisdiction in respect of such offences, it conflicts, in so doing, with the principle of territorial sovereignty, which postulates that only the country within whose territory the offence was committed, or to which the offender belongs—in this case, Germany—has jurisdiction to punish therefor.

9.   The same applies to the second contention as well. It will be recalled that according to that contention the enactment of a criminal law applicable to an act committed in a foreign country by a foreign national conflicts with the principle of territorial sovereignty. But here, too, we must hold that there is no such rule in customary international law, and that to this day it has not won universal international recognition. This is established by the judgment of the Permanent Court of International Justice in the *Lotus* case (P.C.I.J. Series No. 10, 1927). In that case, the judges of the majority recognized the competence of the State of Turkey to enact a criminal statute extending to the negligent conduct of a French citizen while on duty as Officer-of-the-Watch of a French ship, at the time of her collision on the high seas—and therefore outside Turkey's territorial waters—with a ship flying the Turkish flag. The collision caused the sinking of the Turkish ship and also the death of eight of her passengers who were of Turkish nationality. It was held in that case that the principle of territorial sovereignty merely requires that a state exercise its power to punish within its own borders, not outside them; that subject to this restriction every state may exercise a wide discretion as to the application of its laws and the jurisdiction of its courts in respect of acts committed outside the state; and that only insofar as it is possible to point to a specific rule prohibiting the exercise

of this discretion—a rule agreed upon by international treaty—is a state prevented from exercising it. That view was based on the following two grounds: (1) It is precisely the conception of state sovereignty which demands the preclusion of any presumption that there is a restriction on its independence; (2) even if it is true that the principle of the territorial character of criminal law is firmly established in various states, it is no less true that in almost all such states criminal jurisdiction has been extended, in ways that vary from state to state, so as to embrace offences committed outside its territory.

As to the first ground, it was stated in the Judgment: "Restrictions upon the independence of states cannot. . . be presumed." As to the second ground, it was stated:

> Though it is true that in all systems of law the principle of the territorial character of criminal law is fundamental, it is equally true that all or nearly all these systems of law extend their action to offences committed outside the territory of the state which adopts them, and they do so in ways which vary from state to state. The territoriality of criminal law, therefore, is not an absolute principle of international law and by no means coincides with territorial sovereignty.

The view based on these two grounds was expressed in the following terms:

> Now the first and foremost restriction imposed by international law upon a state is that—failing the existence of a permissive rule to the contrary—it may not exercise its power in any form in the territory state. In this sense jurisdiction is certainly territorial; it cannot be exercised by a state outside its territory except by virtue of a permissive rule derived from international custom or from a convention.

> It does not, however, follow that international law prohibits a state from exercising jurisdiction in its own territory, in respect of any case which relates to acts which have taken place abroad, and in which it cannot rely on some permissive rule of international law. Such a view would only be tenable if international law contained a general prohibition to states to extend the application of their laws and the jurisdiction of their courts to persons, property and acts outside its territory, and if, as an exception to their general prohibition of another, it allowed states to do so in certain specific cases. But this is certainly not the case under international law as it stands at present. Far from laying down a general prohibition to the effect that states may not extend the application of their laws and the jurisdiction of their courts to persons, property and acts outside

their territory, it leaves them in this respect a wide measure of discretion which is only limited in certain cases by prohibitive rules; as regards other cases, every state remains free to adopt the principles which it regards as best and most suitable. . .

In these circumstances, all that can be required of a state is that it should not overstep the limits which international law places upon its jurisdiction; within these limits, its title to exercise jurisdiction rests in its sovereignty.

We have no intention of dealing extensively with the above-mentioned divided opinion, or of associating ourselves with any one of them. Our only object in setting forth these views, including the majority view in the *Lotus* case, is to point to the fact that on the question of the jurisdiction of a state to punish persons who are not its nationals for acts committed beyond its borders, there is as yet no international accord. . .

We should add that even if Counsel for the Appellant were right in his view that international law prohibits a state from trying a foreign national for an act committed outside its borders, this would not avail his client in any way. The reason for this is that, according to the theory of international law, in the absence of an international treaty which vests rights in an individual, that law only recognizes the rights of a state; in other words, assuming that there is such a prohibition in international law, the violation of it is deemed to be a violation of the rights of the state to which the accused belongs, and not a violation of his own rights. . .

10.   We have thus far stated our reasons for dismissing the first two contentions of Counsel for the Appellant on the strength of the rules that determine the relationship between Israel municipal law and international law. Our principal object was to make it clear—and this is a negative approach that there was no prohibition whatever by international law of the enactment of the Law of 1950, either because it created ex post facto offences or because such offences are of an extra-territorial character. However, we too, like the District Court, do not content ourselves with this solution, but have undertaken the task of showing that these contentions are unjustifiable also from a positive approach, namely that, when enacting the Law in question, the Knesset only sought to apply the principles of international law and to realize its objectives. The two propositions on which we propose to base ourselves will therefore be as follows: (1) The crimes created by the Law and of which the Appellant was convicted must be deemed today to have always borne the stamp of international crimes, banned by international law and entailing individual criminal liability; (2) It is the particular universal character of these crimes that vests in each state the power to try and punish anyone who assisted in their commission. But before we substantiate these propositions, and in order to lighten our task on this

point, we must make a few observations on the four categories of the offences in question, and especially on the inter-relation between them.

The definitions in the Law of these offences have been clearly explained by the District Court in paragraph 16 of its Judgment. It was there explained in the light of a detailed comparative analysis that the sources of these definitions are to be found in international documents that define the corresponding crimes. We do not intend to repeat the explanatory and comparative observations made there, but only to make it clear that the local category of a "Crime against Humanity"—which includes the murder, extermination, starving and deportation of a civilian population, on the one hand, and the persecution on national, racial, religious or political grounds on the other—may be seen as extending also to the three other categories, as these were proved in the proceedings in this case.

12. It will be recalled that, according to this proposition, it is the universal character of the crimes in question which vests in every state the power to try those who participated in the perpetration of such crimes and to punish them therefor. This proposition is closely linked with the one adduced in the preceding paragraph from which, indeed, it follows as a logical outcome. The reasoning behind it is as follows:

(a) One of the principles whereby states assume, in one degree or another, the power to try and punish a person for an offence he has committed, is the principle of universality. Its meaning is, in essence, that that power is vested in every state regardless of the fact that the offence was committed outside its territory by a person who did not belong to it, provided he is in its custody at the time he is brought to trial. This principle has wide support and is universally acknowledged with respect to the offence of piracy jure gentium. But while there exists general agreement as to its application to this offence, there is a difference of opinion as to the scope of its application. Thus one school of thought holds that it cannot be applied to any offence other than the one mentioned above, lest this entail excessive interference with the competence of the state in which the offence was committed. This view is reflected in the following extract from the judgment of Judge Moor in the *Lotus* case: "It is important to bear in mind the foregoing opinions of eminent authorities as to the essential nature of piracy by law of nations, especially for the reason that nations have shown the strongest repugnance to extending the scope of the offence, because it carried with it. . .the principle of universal jurisdiction. . ." and "Piracy by law of nations, in its jurisdictional aspects, is sui generis."

A second school of thought. . . though agreeing to the extension of the principle to all manner of extra-territorial offences committed by foreign nationals, considers it to be no more than an auxiliary principle, to be applied in circumstances in which no resort can be had to the principle of territorial sovereignty or to the nationality principle, both of which are universally agreed to. The authors of this draft, therefore, impose various restrictions on the application of the principle of universal jurisdiction, which are designed to obviate opposition by those states that find themselves competent to punish the offender according to either of the other two principles mentioned. One of these reservations—to which we shall yet revert—is that the state contemplating the exercise of the power in question must first offer the extradition of the offender to the state within whose territory the offence was committed (forum delicti commissi). The justification seen by that school of thought—as distinct from the first-mentioned school—for the adoption of this principle, albeit as a purely auxiliary principle, is the consideration that it is calculated to prove useful in circumstances in which the offender is likely to evade punishment, if it is not applied.

A third school of thought holds that the rule of universal jurisdiction, which is valid in cases of piracy, logically applies also to all such criminal acts of commission or omission which constitute offences under the law of nations (delicta juris gentium) without any reservation whatever or, at most, subject to a reservation of the kind mentioned above. This view has been opposed in the past because of the difficulty in securing general agreement as to the offences to be included in the above-mentioned class.

A fourth view is that expressed de lege ferenda by Lauterpacht in the Cambridge Law Journal of 1947: "It would be in accordance with an enlightened principle of justice—a principle which has not yet become part of the law of nations—if in the absence of effective extradition, the courts of a state were to assume jurisdiction over common crimes, by whomsoever and wherever committed, of a heinous character. . ."

(b) This brief survey of views set out above shows that, notwithstanding the differences between them, there is full justification for applying here the principle of universal jurisdiction, since the international character of the "crimes against humanity" (in the wide meaning of the term) is, in this case, not in doubt, and the unprecedented extent of their injurious and murderous effects is not open to dispute at the present day. In other words, the basic reason for which international law recognizes the right of each state to exercise such jurisdiction in piracy offences—notwithstanding the fact that its own jurisdiction does not extend to the scene of the commission of the offence (the high seas) and the offender is a national of another state or is stateless—applies with all the greater force to the above-mentioned crimes. That reason is, it will be recalled, that the interest to prevent bodily and material harm to those who sail the seas, and to persons engaged in free trade between nations, is a vital interest, common to all civilized states and of universal scope, as was emphasized by the authors of the Harvard Research:

> . . .The competence to prosecute and punish for piracy was commonly explained by saying that the pirate. . .was the enemy of all alike. . . The competence is better justified at the present time upon the ground that the punishable acts are committed upon the seas where all have an interest in the safety of commerce and where no state has territorial jurisdiction. Notwithstanding the more effective policing of the seas in modern times, the common interest and mutual convenience which gave rise to the principle have conserved its vitality as a means of preventing the recurrence of maritime depredations of a piratical character.

That is to say that it was not the recognition of the universal jurisdiction to try and punish the person who committed "piracy" that justified the viewing of such an act as an international crime sui generis, but it was the agreed vital interest of the international community that justified the exercise of the jurisdiction in question: "As a result of this attitude of mankind towards these two great public crimes. . .piracy and the slave trade, wherever practised, are subject to punishment by any political authority apprehending the persons engaged therein irrespective of their nationality or allegiance."

It follows that the state which prosecutes and punishes a person for that offence acts solely as the organ and agent of the international community, and metes out punishment to the offender for his breach of the prohibition imposed by the law of nations. . .

The above explanation of the substantive basis underlying the exercise of universal jurisdiction in respect of the crime of piracy also justifies its exercise in regard to the crimes with which we are dealing in this case.

(c) The truth is—and this further supports our conclusion—that the application of that principle has been advancing for quite some time beyond the international crime of piracy. We have in mind its application to conventional war crimes as well. As stated [earlier], whenever the "belligerent" countries tried and punished a member of the armed forces of the enemy for any act contrary to "the laws and customs of war," it did so because an international crime was involved which the countries of the world as a whole were anxious to prevent. Thus, in his article mentioned in the same paragraph, Cowles reviewed a series of cases that occurred prior to World War II, in which American military tribunals tried the offenders for war crimes committed within territory which was not, at the time, under the control of the armed forces of the United States, but was reached by them only subsequently. On the strength of that review he summarized the position by saying:

Actual practice shows that the jurisdiction assumed by military courts, trying offences against the law of war, has been personal, or universal, not territorial. The jurisdiction, exercised over war crimes, has been of the same nature as that exercised in the case of the pirate, and this broad jurisdiction has been assumed for the same fundamental reason.

He therefore reached the conclusion: "under international law, every independent state has jurisdiction to punish war criminals in its custody regardless of the nationality of the victim, the time it entered the war, or the place where the offence was committed."

In his article "Legal Basis of Jurisdiction over War Crimes," Baxter stated that at the end of World War II cases of war crimes were tried by the British military tribunals in Germany, in which victims were not British subjects but nationals of allied countries: "In the Zyklon B case...those killed by poison gas supplied by the accused included Belgian, Dutch, French, Czech and Polish nationals, and it was not alleged that any British subjects were among the victims."

In this connection, mention should also be made of a case which was tried by a British military court in Singapore. In that case, the court, composed of British officers, sentenced to death a member of the Japanese army for unlawfully killing American prisoners of war in Saigon (then French Indo-China); that is to say, the court so composed exercised jurisdiction, notwithstanding the fact that the scene of the crime was in French territory, and the victims were not British nationals.

True, the fact that the victims of the crimes in these cases were nationals of countries in alliance with the state prosecuting the offender derogates somewhat from the universal character of the jurisdiction exercised, but, on the other hand, they indicate that substantial strides were made towards extending the use of that principle.

Indeed, Baxter concluded, on the basis of these cases and also of those that were tried by the American tribunals in Germany under Control Law No. 10, that: "International law also surmounts the jurisdictional barrier, as municipal law cannot, by recognizing the universality of jurisdiction enjoyed by war crimes tribunals."

Moreover, according to this expert's opinion, even a neutral country has the right to try a person for a war crime. This is also the view of Greenspan: "Since each sovereign power stands in the position of a guardian of international law, and is equally interested in upholding it, any state has the legal right to try war crimes, even though the crimes have been committed against the nationals of another power and in a conflict to which that state is not a party."

(d) This is the place to discuss the limitation imposed by most of those who support this principle upon the exercise of universal jurisdiction, namely, that the state which has apprehended the offender must first offer his extradition to the state in which the offence was committed. This means that only if the second state does not respond to the offer of extradition may the first state arrogate to itself the jurisdiction to try and punish. The above limitation is based upon the approach implicit in the maxim aut dedere aut punire. Counsel for the Appellant also took this approach, and accordingly submitted that, so long as the State of Israel had not offered to extradite his client to Germany—the forum delicti commissi of many of the crimes attributed to him—it has no right to place him on trial. He further contended that the fact of the Appellant's German nationality also obliged Israel to follow the course of extraditing him to that state. As to the last fact, let it be said at once that it cannot avail him, as the requirement of making an offer to extradite the offender to the state of his national origin is supported neither by international law nor by the practice of states.

As to the limitation itself in the sense explained above, we are of the opinion that it has no place in the circumstances of this case. First, as already stated, Counsel for the Appellant has himself admitted that his application to the Government of Western Germany to demand the extradition of his client was refused, and therefore an offer in this sense by the Government of Israel could be of no practical use. Secondly—and this is the principal reason for the rejection of his submission—the idea behind the above-mentioned limitation is not that the requirement to offer the offender to the state in which the offence was committed was designed to prevent the violation of its territorial sovereignty. Its reason is rather a purely practical one: The great majority of the witnesses and the greater part of the evidence are concentrated in that state, and it becomes, therefore, the most convenient place (forum convenicus) for the conduct of the trial. This point was taken by Lauterpacht... "Territoriality of jurisdiction is a rule of convenience in the sphere of the law of evidence. It is not a requirement of justice or even a necessary postulate of the sovereignty of the state." Baxter, too, had this meaning of the limitation in mind when he stated: "If a neutral state should, by reason of the availability of the accused witnesses, and evidence, be the most convenient locus in which to try a war crime, there is no reason why that state should not perform that function."

If, therefore, we should consider the above-mentioned contention of Counsel for the Appellant in the light of this practical test, it must be said that the great majority of the witnesses who gave evidence here on the grave crimes attributed to the Appellant, especially those against the Jews, were residents of Israel, and, moreover, the bulk of the vast mass of documents produced was previously gathered and preserved (through Yad Vashem) in the State of Israel. It should be noted that the Appellant himself has relied for his defence on a number of the documents which are in this country and have been made available to him. It is clear, therefore, that it is the State of Israel—not the State of Germany—that must be regarded as the forum convenicus for the trial.

We have also taken into consideration the possible desire of other countries to try the Appellant, insofar as the crimes included in the indictment were committed in those countries or their evil effects were felt there. But what has been said of the practical object that has justified the holding of the trial here is equally applicable to them. It is to be observed that we have not heard of a single protest by any of these countries against conducting the trial in Israel, and it is reasonable to believe that, as Israel has exercised its jurisdiction in this matter, no other state has demanded the right to do so. What is more, it is precisely the fact that the crimes in question and their effects have extended to numerous countries that empties the territorial principle of its content in the present case and justifies Israel in assuming criminal jurisdiction by virtue of the "universal" principle. This is so because Israel could not possibly have decided to which particular country the Appellant ought to have been extradited without the selection being arbitrary. . .

(e) Counsel for the Appellant has further submitted that, under Article 6 of the Genocide Convention, a person accused of this crime shall be tried by a court of competent jurisdiction of the state in which it was committed. According to his submission, that Article has confirmed the application of the "territorial" principle, and the "universal" principle, therefore, is implicitly negated. The reply to this contention was given by the District Court in its judgment: That Article 6 imposes upon the parties contractual obligations with future effect, that is to say, obligations which bind them to prosecute for crimes of "genocide" which will be committed within their territories in the future. This obligation, however, has nothing to do with the universal power vested in every state to prosecute for crimes of this type committed in the past—a power which is based on customary international law.

(f) We sum up our views on this subject as follows: Not only are all the crimes attributed to the Appellant of an international character, but they are crimes whose evil and murderous effects were so widespread as to shake the stability of the international community to its very foundations. The State of Israel, therefore, was entitled, pursuant to the principle of universal jurisdiction, and acting in the capacity of guardian of international law and agents for its enforcement, to try the Appellant. This being the case, it is immaterial that the State of Israel did not exist at the time the offences were committed. Here, therefore, is an additional reason—one based on a positive approach—for rejecting the second "jurisdictional" contention of Counsel for the Appellant.

We wish to add one further observation. In regard to the crimes directed against the Jews, the District Court found additional support for its jurisdiction in the connecting link between the State of Israel and the Jewish People, including that between the State of Israel and the Jewish victims of the Catastrophe, and the National Home in Palestine, as explained in its judgment. It therefore upheld its criminal jurisdiction also by virtue of the protective principle and the principle of passive personality. It should be clear that we fully agree with every word said by the Court on this subject. . . If we, in our judgment, have concentrated on the international and universal character of the crimes for which the Appellant has been convicted, one of the reasons for our doing so is that some of them were directed against non-Jewish groups (Poles, Slovenes, Czechs and Gypsies). . .

NOTES & QUESTIONS

1.   *The Rise and Fall of Universal Jurisdiction.* The *Eichmann* precedent inspired other states to exercise universal jurisdiction over international crimes that have little or no connection to their territory. In 1985, Spain gave its courts jurisdiction over a host of offenses, including genocide, terrorism, piracy, hijacking, counterfeiting, prostitution-related crimes, narcotics trafficking, and any other offenses criminalized pursuant to an international treaty. Spain subsequently launched investigations into atrocities committed during the military junta in Argentina, Chinese repression in Tibet, the conduct of Guatemala's military dictatorship, Israeli military operations in Gaza, and many others. In 1993, Belgium's parliament passed a statute giving its courts universal jurisdiction over war crimes, crimes against humanity, and genocide committed outside of Belgian territory. However, many of these investigations caused complications for foreign relations—other states resented that Belgian and Spanish courts were investigating crimes that had connections to their territory or citizens. Consequently, both Spain and Belgium rolled back the most expansive elements of their universal jurisdiction statutes. In 2003, Belgium revised the law so that courts only have jurisdiction if the accused is located or domiciled in Belgium, the victim is Belgian or lives in Belgium, or if jurisdiction is required by an international treaty. Similarly, Spain revised its law in 2009 so that the exercise of jurisdiction is limited to cases where the perpetrators are in Spain, the victims are Spanish, or there is some other link to Spain, and no other state is currently investigating or prosecuting the crimes. These limitations substantially limit the "universal" aspect of this universal jurisdiction statute.

2.   *The Princeton Principles.* In 2001, a group of legal scholars gathered to draft a set of "best practices" for the exercise of universal jurisdiction. Known as the *Princeton Principles on Universal Jurisdiction*, the document includes the following limitations:

i.   Courts exercising universal jurisdiction must respect due process rights including "the rights of the accused and victims, the fairness of the proceedings, and the independence and impartiality of the judiciary."

ii.   Where multiple states might assert overlapping claims of jurisdiction, courts should only exercise jurisdiction after considering the following factors: (a) treaty obligations; (b) the location of the crime; (c) the connections between the alleged perpetrator and the prosecuting state; (d) the connections between the victims and the prosecuting state; (e) effectiveness of the prosecution; (f) fairness and impartiality of the proceedings; (g) convenience to the parties and witnesses; and (h) the interests of justice.

Do these principles adequately respond to the risk of international strife caused by competing claims of jurisdiction?

3.   *Universal Civil Jurisdiction.* Although *Eichmann* highlights the importance of universal criminal jurisdiction, states can also exercise universal jurisdiction over civil claims as well. In a sense, the United States Alien Tort Statute is an example of universal jurisdiction, insofar as it granted federal courts jurisdiction over suits by foreign nationals for torts committed outside the territory of the United States. As discussed in Chapter 14, the Supreme Court substantially limited the extraterritorial reach of the ATS in *Kiobel v. Royal Dutch Petroleum Co.*, 569 U.S. 108 (2013). That result can be seen as consistent with the global movement to limit or restrict the exercise of universal jurisdiction discussed in Note 1 above. Although some version of universal jurisdiction remains a viable theory under international law, its application is sharply constrained and monitored by domestic actors.

4.   *Is Universal Jurisdiction Subordinate to Other Principles?* Assuming that universal jurisdiction is legitimate in certain circumstances, the question arises whether *any* state might exercise it or whether an assertion of universal jurisdiction is *subordinate* to more traditional principles of jurisdiction that might be asserted by another state. Specifically, if a state with a territorial or personality connection to the crime seeks jurisdiction in a particular case, must the state invoking universal jurisdiction forgo prosecution and transfer the suspect to the other state? For example, the Belgium government explained the concept of universal jurisdiction in the following manner: "Universal jurisdiction is in a sense subsidiary to the jurisdiction of the State in the territory of which a crime was committed. It is a component of cooperation among States, which is an essential element in combating impunity for the most serious crimes." Does this entail that universal jurisdiction is a "lesser" principle of jurisdiction?

B. JURISDICTION TO ADJUDICATE

Jurisdiction to adjudicate often coincides with jurisdiction to prescribe, because courts are usually in the business of adjudicating claims arising from statutes passed by their local legislature. Consequently, the state's exercise of jurisdiction in such a case, in order to comply with international law, requires that the legislature was permitted to regulate the conduct (jurisdiction to prescribe) and the court was permitted to adjudicate an allegation of wrongful conduct under the statute (jurisdiction to adjudicate). In that case, the latter type of jurisdiction is parasitic upon the former type of jurisdiction. However, it is important to remember that jurisdiction to adjudicate is logically distinct from jurisdiction to prescribe, and the international limitations on the two forms of jurisdiction are not the same. In order to understand the difference, consider a domestic court that hears a case where it is called upon to apply the law of a different forum, i.e., the law of a foreign state. In that situation, one state is exercising jurisdiction to adjudicate while a different state is exercising jurisdiction to prescribe.

According to the Third Restatement, jurisdiction to adjudicate is based on the concept of reasonableness, which is often cashed out in terms of the territorial presence of the person or thing within the forum state. Consider the following excerpt from the Restatement:

Restatement (Third) of Foreign Relations Law § 421 (1987)

(1) A state may exercise jurisdiction through its courts to adjudicate with respect to a person or thing if the relationship of the state to the person or thing is such as to make the exercise of jurisdiction reasonable.

(2) In general, a state's exercise of jurisdiction to adjudicate with respect to a person or thing is reasonable if, at the time jurisdiction is asserted:

- (a) the person or thing is present in the territory of the state, other than transitorily;

- (b) the person, if a natural person, is domiciled in the state;

- (c) the person, if a natural person, is resident in the state;

- (d) the person, if a natural person, is a national of the state;

- (e) the person, if a corporation or comparable juridical person, is organized pursuant to the law of the state;

- (f) a ship, aircraft or other vehicle to which the adjudication relates is registered under the laws of the state;

- (g) the person, whether natural or juridical, has consented to the exercise of jurisdiction;

- (h) the person, whether natural or juridical, regularly carries on business in the state;

- (i) the person, whether natural or juridical, had carried on activity in the state, but only in respect of such activity;

- (j) the person, whether natural or juridical, had carried on outside the state an activity having a substantial, direct, and foreseeable effect within the state, but only in respect of such activity; or

(k) the thing that is the subject of adjudication is owned, possessed, or used in the state, but only in respect of a claim reasonably connected with that thing.

(3) A defense of lack of jurisdiction is generally waived by any appearance by or on behalf of a person or thing (whether as plaintiff, defendant, or third party), if the appearance is for a purpose that does not include a challenge to the exercise of jurisdiction.

Notice the reference to extraterritorial activities having a "substantial, direct, and foreseeable effect within the state." Does this standard sound familiar? The phrase also appears as the standard regarding extraterritorial jurisdiction for the jurisdiction to prescribe. The phrase's reappearance as a standard for jurisdiction to adjudicate shows the conceptual overlap between the two forms of jurisdiction.

C. JURISDICTION TO ENFORCE

Jurisdiction to enforce overlaps with the jurisdiction to adjudicate because usually a state's exercise of enforcement will follow from the fact that the state's judiciary has adjudicated the case. But not always. Sometimes a case is litigated in one state but then the prevailing party seeks to have a judgment enforced in another state, for example where the losing party controls assets that might be seized to satisfy a judgment. In that situation, one state is exercising jurisdiction to adjudicate while another state is exercising jurisdiction to enforce. As the following Restatement excerpt notes, in situations where the enforcement is *judicial* in nature, the state also must satisfy the requirements of jurisdiction to adjudicate.

Restatement (Third) of Foreign Relations Law § 431 (1987)

(1) A state may employ judicial or nonjudicial measures to induce or compel compliance or punish noncompliance with its laws or regulations, provided it has jurisdiction to prescribe in accordance with §§ 402 and 403.

(2) Enforcement measures must be reasonably related to the laws or regulations to which they are directed; punishment for noncompliance must be preceded by an appropriate determination of violation and must be proportional to the gravity of the violation.

(3) A state may employ enforcement measures against a person located outside its territory

(a) if the person is given notice of the claims or charges against him that is reasonable in the circumstances;

(b) if the person is given an opportunity to be heard, ordinarily in advance of enforcement, whether in person or by counsel or other representative; and

(c) when enforcement is through the courts, if the state has jurisdiction to adjudicate.

Conclusion & Summary

International law regulates jurisdiction to prevent states from exercising their jurisdiction in a way that unjustly interferes with the sovereignty of other states. Even when these principles are observed, however, it is still possible that more than one state will have some foundation to exercise jurisdiction over the same individual or the same act. Nonetheless, adherence to the international principles of jurisdiction will reduce the likelihood and intensity of conflict over competing claims of jurisdiction. The materials in this chapter yielded the following insights:

1. Jurisdiction includes the jurisdiction to prescribe, adjudicate, and enforce, though in practice all three forms of jurisdiction are implicated when a state legislates, litigates, and enforces a legal rule.

2. The territoriality principle certainly allows a state to regulate actions occurring on its territory. The principle also allows a state to regulate extraterritorial actions that have effects on its domestic territory. However, an "effects-based" territoriality principle runs the risk of allowing states to exercise unduly expansive jurisdiction, because most foreign transactions have *some* minimal effect on domestic territory. Consequently, customary international law severely restricts effects-based territorial jurisdiction, though these restrictions are often expressed in different formulations. One popular formulation limits jurisdiction to foreign conduct that has a domestic effect that is direct, substantial, and foreseeable.

3. The active personality principle allows a state to exercise jurisdiction over its nationals even when they act abroad. In contrast, the passive personality principle allows a state to exercise jurisdiction over foreigners who commit crimes against a state's nationals. However, passive personality jurisdiction is controversial outside of major crimes like terrorism. In practice, most states are reluctant to exercise jurisdiction when their nationals are harmed abroad for

garden-variety criminal offenses, and often defer to the territorial state where the crime occurred and where the perpetrator and evidence are located. There is some uncertainty over whether this deference is motivated by pragmatic considerations or the *opinio juris* necessary to establish a rule of customary international law.

4. The protective principle allows a state to exercise jurisdiction to protect essential governmental functions. In practice, the protective principle is most often invoked in terrorism situations that involve foreign plots designed to disrupt the functioning of the state or influence its political direction. The protective principle might also be invoked to protect governmental functions such as the state's currency or other economic devices.

5. The concept of universal jurisdiction suggests that any state has jurisdiction over certain egregious crimes. Historically, piracy was treated in this way because pirates were stateless, acting on the high seas and outside the territorial jurisdiction of any state, and their crimes threatened the safety of navigation for all, thus making them "enemies of all mankind." In modern times, a few states have sought to extend this reasoning to crimes of torture, genocide, crimes against humanity, war crimes, and similar atrocities. The reasoning here is that some crimes are so universally condemned that extraordinary measures should be taken to ensure that no one enjoys impunity for these atrocities. This suggests that even states with no direct territorial or personality connection with the crime might nonetheless assert jurisdiction. These efforts have met with mixed results. The criticism of universal jurisdiction is that it threatens to embroil a state in diplomatic controversy as it asserts jurisdiction over crimes that occurred on the territory of other states and by nationals of other states. In response, states such as Belgium and Spain have amended their universal jurisdiction statutes to sharply limit the type of situations in which their courts might assert this jurisdiction, often requiring a finding that no other state is exerting jurisdiction or that the state exercising jurisdiction has some connection to the crime, such as the location of the alleged perpetrators on its territory. In the United States, federal courts exercised a form of universal jurisdiction in civil cases, through the Alien Tort Statute, until the

Supreme   Court   sharply   limited   the   statute's extraterritorial scope in the *Kiobel* case.

CHAPTER 16

IMMUNITIES

Introduction

Sovereignty means many things under international law. Perhaps no other concept has been at once foundational and controversial in contemporary legal practice. The concept of sovereignty captures a core notion of non-interference in a foreign state's affairs, yet at the same time sovereignty is a porous concept. It is porous because some matters are *not* simply a matter of a state's sovereign concern, but rather are legitimate targets of international regulation. The task of international law is to distinguish between these two spheres—the personal and the public, as it were. Personal matters are protected by sovereignty and should not be interfered with, while public matters are not shielded in this way because they are regulated by the "body politic" of the international community and its legal norms.

Certainly, subjecting a state or its officials to judicial scrutiny constitutes a substantial interference. For this reason, international law has developed a range of doctrines to articulate when a state or its officials may be subject to civil or criminal litigation in a foreign court, and when they are immune from judicial process. However, as the following materials demonstrate, these cases are regulated not by a single doctrine but rather a group of related doctrines—arguably flowing from the concept of sovereignty and its *limited* or conditional promise of non-interference.

Section A will focus on diplomatic immunity, the protection afforded to embassy and consular workers. However, as these materials demonstrate, this protection is not absolute and does not cover all activities. More importantly, though individual employees are beneficiaries of this immunity, the immunity itself belongs to the sovereign state and as such can be waived when the state no longer wishes to shield the individual from judicial scrutiny.

Section B focuses on the immunity afforded to heads of state and other high governmental officers, such as ministers. This immunity has a different conceptual structure from diplomatic immunity, which is based on a conditional promise on the part of the receiving state to afford the diplomats of the sending state with certain protections, namely immunity from judicial process. In contrast, head of state immunity seems designed to prevent an untoward judicialization of international disputes best resolved through the practice of negotiation and diplomacy. Head of state immunity runs right into the growing—or perhaps declining, depending on your view—exercise of universal jurisdiction. Human rights litigators have relished the opportunity to use universal jurisdiction statutes to bring foreign heads of state to account for their alleged abuses. These attempts have forced heads of state to assert immunity claims—a legal dispute that effectively places the protection of international diplomacy in some tension with the anti-impunity norm, or the idea that violators of international law must be brought to account, even if the costs of doing so are high. In many ways, the materials on universal jurisdiction in the prior chapter raise important questions that are best answered by the materials on immunity in this chapter.

Section C focuses on sovereign immunity, the promise that each state makes to foreign states to exempt them from civil and criminal suit in a domestic court. Of course, there are exceptions to sovereign immunity—sovereign activity is immune but commercial activity undertaken by the state is not—and the task of this section is to explore and apply these criteria. Finally, Section D focuses on the act of state doctrine, a doctrine that precludes U.S. courts from passing judgment on the acts of a foreign sovereign, even if the foreign state is not a party to the litigation. As the readings make clear, there are two ways of understanding the act of state doctrine. The first is to view it as a codification of the United States' international obligations to non-interference with foreign sovereigns. The second is to view it as a doctrine that structures the relative allocation of power between the branches of the federal government. Should the judiciary entertain such questions or should it defer out of consideration for the work of the Executive Branch in the area of foreign affairs?

A. DIPLOMATIC IMMUNITY

Diplomatic immunity holds a special place in the popular imagination. The idea, so often the plot of television shows and films, involves a diplomat who perpetrates a crime and escapes justice. These depictions are often caricatures that obfuscate the underlying conceptual structure of diplomatic immunity. The most elementary confusion is that diplomatic immunity is often falsely portrayed as an *individual* immunity. In reality, diplomatic immunity flows from a bilateral relationship between two states, the "sending" state and the "receiving" state. The sending state is the country that the diplomat represents. The receiving state is the country where the embassy, consulate, or other diplomatic mission is located. At its heart, diplomatic immunity involves a set of bilateral obligations between two sovereigns over how their respective diplomats will be treated.

The core elements of this legal relationship were codified in the Vienna Convention on Diplomatic Relations, signed in 1961 and entered into force in 1964, though many of its norms were already well entrenched in customary international law by that time. The Convention is detailed. It does not obligate a receiving state to receive any particular foreign diplomat and indeed some states have no diplomatic relations with each other and therefore do not exchange diplomats. Once received, a foreign diplomat may also be expelled. On this point, consider article 9 of the Convention:

> 1.   The receiving State may at any time and without having to explain its decision, notify the sending State that the head of the mission or any member of the diplomatic staff of the mission is persona non grata or that any other member of the staff of the mission is not acceptable. In any such case, the sending State shall, as appropriate, either recall the person concerned or terminate his functions with the mission. A person may be declared non grata or not acceptable before arriving in the territory of the receiving State.

However, once a receiving state accepts a foreign diplomat on its territory, the Convention constrains how the receiving state treats officers of the sending state.

Of those obligations, immunity from prosecution is the most famous. Because diplomatic immunity is an obligation that the receiving state owes to the sending state, the sending state may *waive* the immunity of its diplomat—notwithstanding any obligations voiced by the diplomat facing legal jeopardy. In practice, serious crimes committed by a diplomat and not performed in the service of statecraft would trigger negotiations by the two states, with the receiving state asking the sending state to waive the immunity and allow a prosecution to continue in the receiving state's court system. Also, diplomatic immunity is not absolute; commercial and professional activities are excluded, in part because diplomats are admitted to the receiving state for the sole purpose of carrying out state functions and are not supposed to be engaged in private business matters, according to article 42 of the Convention.

The following excerpt from the Vienna Convention outlines the details of diplomatic immunity. Following that, the case of *Sabbithi v. Al Saleh* provides a working example of diplomatic immunity on the ground, including the application of the commercial activity exception and an official request for a waiver diplomatic immunity. As you read the case, ask yourself why Kuwait denied the waiver request and what consequences that decision might have had for Kuwait.

Vienna Convention on Diplomatic Relations (1961)
500 U.N.T.S. 95

Article 31

1. A diplomatic agent shall enjoy immunity from the criminal jurisdiction of the receiving State. He shall also enjoy immunity from its civil and administrative jurisdiction, except in the case of:

(*a*) A real action relating to private immovable property situated in the territory of the receiving State, unless he holds it on behalf of the sending State for the purposes of the mission;

(*b*) An action relating to succession in which the diplomatic agent is involved as executor, administrator, heir or legatee as a private person and not on behalf of the sending State;

(*c*) An action relating to any professional or commercial activity exercised by the diplomatic agent in the receiving State outside his official functions.

2. A diplomatic agent is not obliged to give evidence as a witness.

3. No measures of execution may be taken in respect of a diplomatic agent except in the cases coming under subparagraphs (*a*), (*b*) and (*c*) of paragraph 1 of this article, and provided that the measures concerned can be taken without infringing the inviolability of his person or of his residence.

4. The immunity of a diplomatic agent from the jurisdiction of the receiving State does not exempt him from the jurisdiction of the sending State.

Article 32

1. The immunity from jurisdiction of diplomatic agents and of persons enjoying immunity under article 37 may be waived by the sending State.

2. Waiver must always be express.

3. The initiation of proceedings by a diplomatic agent or by a person enjoying immunity from jurisdiction under article 37 shall preclude him from invoking immunity from jurisdiction in respect of any counterclaim directly connected with the principal claim.

4. Waiver of immunity from jurisdiction in respect of civil or administrative proceedings shall not be held to imply waiver of immunity in respect of the execution of the judgement, for which a separate waiver shall be necessary.

Sabbithi v. Al Saleh

U.S. District Court for the District of Columbia
605 F. Supp. 2d 122 (2009)

■ EMMET G. SULLIVAN, DISTRICT JUDGE.

Plaintiffs Mani Kumari Sabbithi, Joaquina Quadros, and Gila Sixtina Fernandes, domestic workers from India, bring this action against their former employers Major Waleed KH N.S. Al Saleh, his wife, Maysaa KH A.O.A. Al Omar, (together "defendants"), and the State of Kuwait. Plaintiffs bring suit under the Trafficking Victims Protection Act of 2000 ("TVPA"), 18 U.S.C. § 1581, the Fair Labor Standards Act, 29 U.S.C. §§ 201, and assert various contract and tort claims. Before this Court is the defendants' motion to dismiss the complaint and quash service of process based on diplomatic immunity. Upon consideration of the motion, the responses and replies thereto, the *amici curiae* brief and response thereto, the Statement of the United States and responses thereto, and the applicable law, the Court grants defendants Al Saleh and Al Omar's motion to dismiss and quashes service of process as to those defendants.

Background

Defendant Major Waleed KH N.S. Al Saleh is a Kuwaiti diplomat. Al Saleh and his wife, defendant Maysaa KH A.O.A. Al Omar, lived in the United States from 2005 to 2007, while Al Saleh served as Attaché to the Embassy of Kuwait. Prior to moving to the United States, the defendants employed plaintiffs as domestic workers in the defendants' home in Kuwait. The individual plaintiffs worked for the defendants in Kuwait for a period ranging from five and a half years to eight and a half months. In Kuwait, plaintiffs allegedly worked seven days a week, for long hours each day, and were paid between 35 Kuwaiti Dinar (KD) (approximately $121 U.S. dollars) and 40 KD (approximately $138 U.S. dollars) per month. According to plaintiffs, however, before coming to the United States the defendants signed an employment contract promising to pay plaintiffs $1,314 U.S. dollars per month and agreeing to comply with United States labor laws in exchange for plaintiffs' domestic work in the defendants' home in the United States. Plaintiffs assert that these employment contracts were presented to the United States Embassy in Kuwait for the purpose of obtaining plaintiffs' A-3 visas, which authorized plaintiffs to work as live-in domestic servants in defendants' home in McLean, Virginia.

Plaintiffs claim that once in the United States, the defendants did not comply with the terms of the employment contracts. Allegedly, plaintiffs worked sixteen to nineteen hours per day, seven days a week, and were not paid directly, but instead defendants sent wages of 70 KD (approximately $242 U.S. dollars) to 100 KD (approximately $346 U.S.

dollars) per month to plaintiffs" families overseas. Plaintiffs allege that the defendants deprived them of their passports, threatened plaintiffs with physical harm, and physically abused Sabbithi.

Plaintiffs eventually escaped the defendants' home, and, on January 18, 2007, plaintiffs filed this complaint against defendants and the State of Kuwait. In addition to this civil action, plaintiffs pursued criminal charges against the defendants through the U.S. Department of Justice ("DOJ"). Pursuant to the DOJ's request, the U.S. Department of State ("State Department") asked the State of Kuwait to waive the defendants' diplomatic immunity. According to the State Department, Kuwait declined to waive the defendants' immunity. As a result, the DOJ closed its investigation into defendants' alleged illegal conduct. . .

Discussion

. . . Defendants argue that they have diplomatic immunity, and that their immunity deprives this Court of jurisdiction in this case, pursuant to the Vienna Convention on Diplomatic Relations ("the Vienna Convention," "Convention" or "VCDR"), to which both Kuwait and the United States are parties. The Vienna Convention provides that a "diplomatic agent shall . . . enjoy immunity from [the receiving state's] civil and administrative jurisdiction. . . ." The Convention further provides that the "members of the family of a diplomatic agent forming part of his household shall, if they are not nationals of the receiving State, enjoy the privileges and immunities specified in Articles 29 to 36." The Vienna Convention also provides that a diplomatic agent "shall not in the receiving State practice for personal profit any professional or commercial activity." Diplomatic immunity can be forfeited "in the case of. . . an action relating to any professional or commercial activity exercised by the diplomatic agent in the receiving State outside his official functions."

In accordance with the Vienna Convention, Congress enacted 22 U.S.C. § 254d, which provides that "[a]ny action or proceeding brought against an individual who is entitled to immunity with respect to such action or proceeding under the Vienna Convention on Diplomatic Relations. . . shall be dismissed." Therefore, if the Court concludes that defendants are immune, it must dismiss the action. . .

A defendant's diplomatic immunity "may be established upon motion or suggestion by or on behalf of the individual. . . ." Defendants filed as an exhibit to their motion to dismiss a letter from the State Department dated March 15, 2007. In that letter, the State Department confirmed that in August 2004, the Embassy of Kuwait had notified the State Department that Al Saleh was a diplomatic agent at the Embassy of Kuwait and, as of March 2007, Al Saleh continued to serve in that capacity. The State Department also certified that the Embassy of

Kuwait had confirmed that Al Omar was a national of Kuwait and Al Saleh's spouse residing in his household. In addition, defendants filed the State Department's Diplomatic List from the summer of 2006, in which the defendants' names appear as diplomats of Kuwait.

In view of the State Department's determination that the defendants are diplomats and its certification that as diplomats they are immune from suit pursuant to the Vienna Convention, the Court concludes that these defendants are entitled to diplomatic immunity.

Despite defendants' status as diplomats, plaintiffs contend that diplomatic immunity should not shield the defendants from liability in this case. In support of this position, plaintiffs argue that: (1) defendants' alleged trafficking of plaintiffs falls within the commercial activities exception to immunity under the Vienna Convention; (2) diplomatic immunity cannot bar plaintiffs' claims challenging defendants' conduct in violation of the Thirteenth Amendment; (3) diplomatic immunity cannot bar plaintiffs' claims because defendants' actions were so egregious they violate jus cogens norms prohibiting slavery and slavery-like practices; and (4) plaintiffs' claims under the TVPA prevail over defendants' conflicting claims of diplomatic immunity according to the "subsequent-in-time" rule.

The purpose of diplomatic immunity is "to contribute to the development of friendly relations among nations and to ensure the efficient performance of the functions of diplomatic missions." Consistent with that purpose, the Vienna Convention provides that a diplomatic agent "shall not in the receiving State practice for personal profit any professional or commercial activity." Because diplomats are not to engage in professional or commercial activity outside of their duties as diplomats, the Vienna Convention includes an exception to diplomatic immunity "in the case of. . . an action relating to any professional or commercial activity exercised by the diplomatic agent in the receiving State outside his official functions."

Plaintiffs allege that defendants' conduct in bringing plaintiffs from Kuwait to the United States to work as domestic servants constituted human trafficking, and was therefore a "commercial activity exercised by the diplomatic agent. . . outside his official functions" within the meaning of the Vienna Convention. Plaintiffs. . . argue at length that human trafficking is a profitable commercial activity that results in severe human rights violations. "But such a literal manner of interpretation is superficial and incomplete, and, [this Court] believe[s], yields an incorrect rendering of the meaning of 'commercial activity' as used in the Vienna Convention." *Tabion v. Mufti,* 73 F.3d 535, 537 (4th Cir. 1996).

Hiring household help is incidental to the daily life of a diplomat and therefore not commercial for purposes of the exception to the Vienna Convention. This Court agrees with the Fourth Circuit in *Tabion:*

> When examined in context, the term "commercial activity" does not have so broad a meaning as to include occasional service contracts as Tabion contends, but rather relates only to trade or business activity engaged in for personal profit. Accepting the broader meaning fails to take into account the treaty's background and negotiating history, as well as its subsequent interpretation. It also ignores the relevance of the remainder of the phrase "outside his official functions."

According to the Statement of Interest filed by the United States, "[t]he 'commercial activity' exception focuses on the pursuit of trade or business activity that is unrelated to the diplomatic assignment; it does not encompass contractual relationships for goods and services that are incidental to the daily life of the diplomat and his family in the receiving State." The United States also stated that "[w]hen diplomats enter into contractual relationships for personal goods or services incidental to residing in the host country, including the employment of domestic workers, they are not engaging in 'commercial activity' as that term is used in the Diplomatic Relations Convention." "Although not conclusive, the meaning attributed to treaty provisions by the Government agencies charged with their negotiation and enforcement is entitled to great weight." Furthermore, the facts in this case support a conclusion that the defendants' conduct in bringing plaintiffs from Kuwait to the United States and employing plaintiffs as domestic servants, albeit for marginal wages, was not commercial activity outside of the defendants' official functions.

This Court finds the reasoning in *Gonzalez Paredes,* a case with very similar facts, persuasive. In *Gonzalez Paredes,* the plaintiff, a citizen of Paraguay, was hired by defendants in Argentina to work as a domestic servant for defendants while they served on a diplomatic mission to the United States. *Gonzalez Paredes,* 479 F. Supp. 2d at 189. Plaintiff alleged that the defendant signed an employment contract agreeing to pay plaintiff $6.72 per hour, plus overtime, and that the contract was presented to the United States Embassy in Argentina for the purposes of obtaining an A-3 visa. Plaintiff claimed that, contrary to the promises made in the contract, she worked seventy-seven hours per week, and was paid only $500 per month. Plaintiff filed suit for violations of federal and local wage laws, breach of contract, and unjust enrichment. The defendants moved to dismiss the complaint and quash service of process based on diplomatic immunity.

In determining whether the hiring of domestic help was a commercial activity outside a diplomat's official functions, the *Gonzalez*

Paredes court considered Statements of Interest filed by the State Department. Those statements mirror the statements the United States provided to the Court in this case. Finding no reason to disagree with the conclusion of the State Department, the *Gonzalez Paredes* court found that a contract for domestic services was not itself "commercial activity" within the meaning of the Vienna Convention.

Similarly, this Court concludes that hiring domestic employees is an activity incidental to the daily life of a diplomat and his or her family, and does not constitute commercial activity outside a diplomat's official function.

Plaintiffs argue that the defendants' actions in this case violated the Thirteenth Amendment of the United States Constitution prohibiting slavery, and that diplomatic immunity does not apply against a constitutional challenge. Plaintiffs do not cite a single case, however, in which diplomatic immunity was withheld in order to provide redress for a constitutional violation. Instead, case law suggests that diplomatic immunity can shield a diplomat from liability for alleged constitutional violations. Plaintiffs constitutional claims must also give way to defendants' diplomatic immunity.

Jus cogen norms are peremptory norms of international law which enjoy the highest status in international law and prevail over both customary international law and treaties. Plaintiffs argue that the defendants' human trafficking conduct violated jus cogen norms, and as such defendants diplomatic immunity pursuant to the Vienna Convention should be denied.

The Court is not persuaded that defendants' conduct constituted human trafficking, and thus no jus cogen norm was at issue. Furthermore, "[i]n the view of the United States, there is no jus cogens exception to diplomatic immunity" and "there is not evidence that the international community has come to recognize a jus cogens exception to diplomatic immunity."

Finally, plaintiffs' argument that the TVPA overrides the Vienna Convention pursuant to the subsequent-in-time rule is wholly unavailing. The subsequent-in-time rule applies "[w]here a treaty and a statute relate to the same subject," and the two cannot be harmonized. The TVPA concerns peonage, slavery, and trafficking in persons, whereas the Vienna Convention provides immunity from criminal prosecution and civil actions to foreign diplomats. Because the treaty and statute do not relate to the same subject, the subsequent in time rule is inapplicable. "A treaty will not be deemed to have been abrogated or modified by a later statute, unless such purpose on the part of Congress has been clearly expressed." There has been no such action on the part of Congress, and inaction is not sufficient to abrogate a treaty. Moreover, "[i]n the view of the United States, the TVPA does not override diplomatic immunity. First, the TVPA is silent as to whether it limits the immunity of diplomats, and courts should not read a statute to modify the United States' treaty obligations in the absence of a clear statement from Congress."

In light of defendants leaving their diplomatic post in 2007 and returning to Kuwait, plaintiffs ask the Court to find that defendants no longer have diplomatic immunity. Although Article 39 of the Vienna Convention states that an official's privileges and immunities end when his diplomatic functions cease, Article 39 provides that a residual immunity subsists with respect to "acts performed by such a person in the exercise of his functions as a member of the mission." Therefore, defendant's immunity remains intact for acts performed in the exercise of his duties as a diplomatic officer of the State of Kuwait. As the Court previously concluded, defendants' conduct in employing plaintiffs was not performed outside the exercise of defendants' diplomatic functions. For this reason, defendants' current status does not affect their immunity from civil jurisdiction.

The Court recognizes that foreclosing plaintiffs' access to the courts may have harsh implications, including even the denial of legal or monetary relief. The application of the doctrine of diplomatic immunity inevitably "deprives others of remedies for harm they have suffered." Congress, however, is the appropriate body for plaintiffs to present their concerns that the effectiveness of enforcing fair labor practices in the United States is compromised by diplomatic immunity. This court will not create new exceptions to the longstanding policy of diplomatic immunity. . .

NOTES & QUESTIONS

1.   *Diplomatic Versus Consular Immunity.* Under international law, it matters whether an official is classified as "diplomatic" or "consular." In practical terms, an embassy is usually located in the receiving state's capital city, while consulates are usually located in subsidiary cities and provide, among other things, services to nationals residing in the receiving state. Receiving states are required to grant consular officials preferred treatment under the 1963 Vienna Convention on Consular Relations. However, the immunity provisions under the 1963 Convention are narrower than the 1961 Convention that applies to embassy diplomats. Article 41 of the 1963 Convention states that "[c]onsular officers shall not be liable to arrest or detention pending trial, except in the case of a grave crime and pursuant to a decision by the competent judicial authority." Why did the state parties to the 1963 Convention limit consular immunity in this way?

2.   *Immunity from Process.* Diplomatic and consular immunity is designed to protect officials from the judicial process of the receiving state.

But it would be wrong to conclude that officials covered by diplomatic or consular immunity are immune from all legal process. Indeed, courts from the sending state could still exercise jurisdiction over the official. See Vienna Convention, art. 31(4) ("The immunity of a diplomatic agent from the jurisdiction of the receiving State does not exempt him from the jurisdiction of the sending State."). See also Restatement (Third) of Foreign Relations Law § 464 (1987) ("That provision was apparently added to encourage sending states to assure a competent forum for hearing cases against members of their diplomatic missions abroad.").

In the context of a criminal case, this "sending-state jurisdiction" would usually involve a determination by a government prosecutor from the sending state that a criminal case should be pursued. In practical terms, this rarely occurs, because the sending state is usually reluctant to punish its own official for conduct that occurred abroad. But see *United States v. Corey,* 232 F.3d 1166, 1182 (9th Cir. 2000). Nonetheless, the possibility of criminal jurisdiction exercised by the sending state is an important element in the conceptual justification for diplomatic immunity. By signing the Vienna Convention, states have agreed that each should be responsible for prosecuting and punishing their own diplomats rather than subjecting them to the criminal jurisdiction of receiving states and the possibility of politicized prosecutions.

Civil jurisdiction presents its own set of issues. For example, in 2019, the wife of an American diplomat was driving in England when she got into a car accident that killed a 19-year-old British individual named Harry Dunn. The accident prompted outrage in Britain when the public learned that the wife, Anne Sacoolas, was immune from prosecution in the United Kingdom even though she allegedly was driving on the wrong side of the road. The United States refused to waive diplomatic immunity and she quickly returned to the United States. Sacoolas' claim to diplomatic immunity was valid but a bit convoluted. Her husband worked as a CIA employee at RAF Croughton, a British Air Force base being used by the Americans as a signals collection outpost. The two countries had reached a special arrangement that categorized CIA employees working there as part of the embassy but specified that they did not enjoy diplomatic immunity. However, that arrangement failed to explicitly mention their family members, so the United States took the position that the default rule applied from the Vienna Convention, which extends diplomatic immunity to spouses and children. (In 2020, the two countries agreed that going forward, family members attached to RAF Croughton would be covered by the special arrangement and would not receive diplomatic immunity.)

When the diplomatic controversy failed to dissipate, a reconciliation between Sacoolas and Dunn's family was arranged at the White House with President Trump presiding, but the meeting never took place because the Dunn family was brought to the White House not knowing that they were scheduled to meet with Sacoolas, which they refused to do. In 2020, Dunn's family filed a wrongful death lawsuit in a federal district court against

Sacoolas, availing themselves of the legal process of the U.S. justice system in accordance with article 31(4) of the Vienna Convention. See *Charles et al. v. Sacoolas et al.,* Case No. 1:20–cv–01052 (Sept. 9, 2020).

PROBLEM CASE

On January 27, 2011, American Raymond Allen Davis killed two men in broad daylight on the streets of Lahore, Pakistan. Davis, who worked for the U.S. State Department, was reportedly in his car and the two men were on motorcycles when the killing occurred. In the immediate aftermath of the shooting, a car with American security officers rushed to pick up Davis, and in the process collided with, and killed, a Pakistani civilian. Davis was unable to escape and was apprehended by Pakistani police officials and was brought in for questioning.

Davis told the Pakistani authorities that he killed the two men in self-defense. According to his statement, Davis was riding in his car when two men on motorcycles approached the car and pointed a gun at him; Davis responded by shooting both men through the windshield and killing them.

Pakistani officials were suspicious of Davis' self-defense story. Although neither the U.S. nor the Pakistanis released a definitive account of what happened on the street, this much is certain. Davis was no ordinary State Department officer, but was rather a covert CIA operative—reportedly acting station chief of the CIA in Pakistan—with diplomatic cover. It is typical for covert intelligence officers, not just in the U.S. but in any country, to have an official state department position that serves as cover for their intelligence activities. Newspaper reports suggested (without offering definitive evidence) that the Pakistani men on motorcycles were working with the ISI, the Pakistani intelligence service.

Pakistani and U.S. officials disagreed about Davis' entitlement to diplomatic immunity. According to the U.S. State Department, Davis was part of the embassy's "administrative and technical staff." Article 37 of the 1961 Vienna Convention grants diplomatic immunity to the administrative and technical staff of the state's mission. However, Pakistan refused to recognize Davis' status and concluded, at least initially, that he was not immune. A factual dispute arose over whether Davis was best classified as working at the U.S. embassy or at the local consulate. If indeed Davis was staffed to the local consulate, his immunity might not extend to grave crimes (the exception codified in the 1963 Vienna Convention governing the treatment of consular officials).

After a series of confidential meetings, Davis was released. The United States payed substantial monetary compensation to the families of the deceased and the charges against Davis were dropped. Davis was flown out of Pakistan to Afghanistan and eventually back to the United States, his career as a covert operative finished.

Did the basic structure of diplomatic immunity work properly in this case? Should Davis have stood trial in Pakistan in connection with the incident? In practice, diplomatic immunity protects not just the daily functioning of diplomatic services but also the tradecraft of intelligence agencies. Is this what the Vienna Convention was designed to accomplish?

B. IMMUNITY FOR STATE OFFICIALS

Diplomatic and consular officials are not the only ones entitled to immunity. Heads of state and other governmental officers—such as a minister of foreign affairs—are entitled to immunity as well. The scope of this immunity is, in some sense, far wider than the immunities conferred by the Vienna Conventions described above. In the case of diplomatic and consular officials, the immunity is attached to the process of the territorial state "receiving" the official on its territory. In contrast, the immunity conferred on high government officers might be an issue even if the official never leaves his or her home state, and moreover flows from customary international law. What happens if the government official never leaves home but is nonetheless the subject of an arrest warrant issued by another state? Is this permissible under international law? In the following case, the ICJ seeks an answer to this question. Does the answer change if the arrest warrant involves an international crime such as crimes against humanity or genocide?

Arrest Warrant Case
(Democratic Republic of Congo v. Belgium)
International Court of Justice
2002 I.C.J. 3

45. [I]n its Application instituting these proceedings, the Congo originally challenged the legality of the arrest warrant of 11 April 2000 on two separate grounds: on the one hand, Belgium's claim to exercise a universal jurisdiction and, on the other, the alleged violation of the immunities of the Minister for Foreign Affairs of the Congo then in office. However, in its submissions in its Memorial, and in its final submissions at the close of the oral proceedings, the Congo invokes only the latter ground.

46. As a matter of logic, the second ground should be addressed only once there has been a determination in respect of the first, since it is only where a State has jurisdiction under international law in relation to a particular matter that there can be any question of immunities in regard to the exercise of that jurisdiction. However, in the present case, and in view of the final form of the Congo's submissions, the Court will address first the question whether, assuming that it had jurisdiction under international law to issue and circulate the arrest warrant of 11 April 2000, Belgium in so doing violated the immunities of the then Minister for Foreign Affairs of the Congo.

47. The Congo maintains that, during his or her term of office, a Minister for Foreign Affairs of a sovereign State is entitled to inviolability and to immunity from criminal process being "absolute or complete," that is to say, they are subject to no exception. Accordingly, the Congo contends that no criminal prosecution may be brought against a Minister for Foreign Affairs in a foreign court as long as he or she remains in office, and that any finding of criminal responsibility by a domestic court in a foreign country, or any act of investigation undertaken with a view to bringing him or her to court, would contravene the principle of immunity from jurisdiction. According to the Congo, the basis of such criminal immunity is purely functional, and immunity is accorded under customary international law simply in order to enable the foreign State

representative enjoying such immunity to perform his or her functions freely and without let or hindrance. The Congo adds that the immunity thus accorded to Ministers for Foreign Affairs when in office covers *all* their acts, including any committed before they took office, and that it is irrelevant whether the acts done whilst in office may be characterized or not as "official acts."

48.   The Congo states further that it does not deny the existence of a principle of international criminal law, deriving from the decisions of the Nuremberg and Tokyo international military tribunals, that the accused's official capacity at the time of the acts cannot, before any court, whether domestic or international, constitute a "ground of exemption from his criminal responsibility or a ground for mitigation of sentence." The Congo then stresses that the fact that an immunity might bar prosecution before a specific court or over a specific period does not mean that the same prosecution cannot be brought, if appropriate, before another court which is not bound by that immunity, or at another time when the immunity need no longer be taken into account. It concludes that immunity does not mean impunity.

49.   Belgium maintains for its part that, while Ministers for Foreign Affairs in office generally enjoy an immunity from jurisdiction before the courts of a foreign State, such immunity applies only to acts carried out in the course of their official functions, and cannot protect such persons in respect of private acts or when they are acting otherwise than in the performance of their official functions.

50.   Belgium further states that, in the circumstances of the present case, Mr. Yerodia enjoyed no immunity at the time when he is alleged to have committed the acts of which he is accused, and that there is no evidence that he was then acting in any official capacity. It observes that the arrest warrant was issued against Mr. Yerodia personally.

51.   The Court would observe at the outset that in international law it is firmly established that, as also diplomatic and consular agents, certain holders of high-ranking office in a State, such as the Head of State, Head of Government and Minister for Foreign Affairs, enjoy immunities from jurisdiction in other States, both civil and criminal. For the purposes of the present case, it is only the immunity from criminal jurisdiction and the inviolability of an incumbent Minister for Foreign Affairs that fall for the Court to consider.

52.   A certain number of treaty instruments were cited by the Parties in this regard. These included, first, the Vienna Convention on Diplomatic Relations of 18 April 1961, which states in its preamble that the purpose of diplomatic privileges and immunities is "to ensure the efficient performance of the functions of diplomatic missions as representing States." It provides in Article 32 that only the sending State

may waive such immunity. On these points, the Vienna Convention on Diplomatic Relations, to which both the Congo and Belgium are parties, reflects customary international law. The same applies to the corresponding provisions of the Vienna Convention on Consular Relations of 24 April 1963, to which the Congo and Belgium are also parties. The Congo and Belgium further cite the New York Convention on Special Missions of 8 December 1969, to which they are not, however, parties. They recall that under Article 21, paragraph 2, of that Convention:

> The Head of the Government, the Minister for Foreign Affairs and other persons of high rank, when they take part in a special mission of the sending State, shall enjoy in the receiving State or in a third State, in addition to what is granted by the present Convention, the facilities, privileges and immunities accorded by international law.

These conventions provide useful guidance on certain aspects of the question of immunities. They do not, however, contain any provision specifically defining the immunities enjoyed by Ministers for Foreign Affairs. It is consequently on the basis of customary international law that the Court must decide the questions relating to the immunities of such Ministers raised in the present case.

53. In customary international law, the immunities accorded to Ministers for Foreign Affairs are not granted for their personal benefit, but to ensure the effective performance of their functions on behalf of their respective States. In order to determine the extent of these immunities, the Court must therefore first consider the nature of the functions exercised by a Minister for Foreign Affairs. He or she is in charge of his or her Government's diplomatic activities and generally acts as its representative in international negotiations and intergovernmental meetings. Ambassadors and other diplomatic agents carry out their duties under his or her authority. His or her acts may bind the State represented, and there is a presumption that a Minister for Foreign Affairs, simply by virtue of that office, has full powers to act on behalf of the State. In the performance of these functions, he or she is frequently required to travel internationally, and thus must be in a position freely to do so whenever the need should arise. He or she must also be in constant communication with the Government, and with its diplomatic missions around the world, and be capable at any time of communicating with representatives of other States. The Court further observes that a Minister for Foreign Affairs, responsible for the conduct of his or her State's relations with all other States, occupies a position such that, like the Head of State or the Head of Government, he or she is recognized under international law as representative of the State solely by virtue of his or her office. He or she does not have to present letters of

credence: to the contrary, it is generally the Minister who determines the authority to be conferred upon diplomatic agents and countersigns their letters of credence. Finally, it is to the Minister for Foreign Affairs that *chargés d'affaires* are accredited.

54. The Court accordingly concludes that the functions of a Minister for Foreign Affairs are such that, throughout the duration of his or her office, he or she when abroad enjoys full immunity from criminal jurisdiction and inviolability. That immunity and that inviolability protect the individual concerned against any act of authority of another State which would hinder him or her in the performance of his or her duties.

55. In this respect, no distinction can be drawn between acts performed by a Minister for Foreign Affairs in an "official" capacity, and those claimed to have been performed in a "private capacity," or, for that matter, between acts performed before the person concerned assumed office as Minister for Foreign Affairs and acts committed during the period of office. Thus, if a Minister for Foreign Affairs is arrested in another State on a criminal charge, he or she is clearly thereby prevented from exercising the functions of his or her office. The consequences of such impediment to the exercise of those official functions are equally serious, regardless of whether the Minister for Foreign Affairs was, at the time of arrest, present in the territory of the arresting State on an "official" visit or a "private" visit, regardless of whether the arrest relates to acts allegedly performed before the person became the Minister for Foreign Affairs or to acts performed while in office, and regardless of whether the arrest relates to alleged acts performed in an "official" capacity or a "private" capacity. Furthermore, even the mere risk that, by travelling to or transiting another State a Minister for Foreign Affairs might be exposing himself or herself to legal proceedings could deter the Minister from travelling internationally when required to do so for the purposes of the performance of his or her official functions.

56. The Court will now address Belgium's argument that immunities accorded to incumbent Ministers for Foreign Affairs can in no case protect them where they are suspected of having committed war crimes or crimes against humanity. In support of this position, Belgium refers in its Counter-Memorial to various legal instruments creating international criminal tribunals, to examples from national legislation, and to the jurisprudence of national and international courts. Belgium begins by pointing out that certain provisions of the instruments creating international criminal tribunals state expressly that the official capacity of a person shall not be a bar to the exercise by such tribunals of their jurisdiction.

Belgium also places emphasis on certain decisions of national courts, and in particular on the judgments rendered on 24 March 1999 by the

House of Lords in the United Kingdom and on 13 March 2001 by the Court of Cassation in France in the *Pinochet* and *Qaddafi* cases respectively, in which it contends that an exception to the immunity rule was accepted in the case of serious crimes under international law. Thus, according to Belgium, the *Pinochet* decision recognizes an exception to the immunity rule when Lord Millett stated that "[i]nternational law cannot be supposed to have established a crime having the character of a jus cogens and at the same time to have provided an immunity which is coextensive with the obligation it seeks to impose," or when Lord Phillips of Worth Matravers said that "no established rule of international law requires state immunity *ratione materiae* to be accorded in respect of prosecution for an international crime." As to the French Court of Cassation, Belgium contends that, in holding that, "under international law as it currently stands, the crime alleged [acts of terrorism], irrespective of its gravity, does not come within the exceptions to the principle of immunity from jurisdiction for incumbent foreign Heads of State," the Court explicitly recognized the existence of such exceptions.

57. The Congo, for its part, states that, under international law as it currently stands, there is no basis for asserting that there is any exception to the principle of absolute immunity from criminal process of an incumbent Minister for Foreign Affairs where he or she is accused of having committed crimes under international law. In support of this contention, the Congo refers to State practice, giving particular consideration in this regard to the *Pinochet* and *Qaddafi* cases, and concluding that such practice does not correspond to that which Belgium claims but, on the contrary, confirms the absolute nature of the immunity from criminal process of Heads of State and Ministers for Foreign Affairs. Thus, in the *Pinochet* case, the Congo cites Lord Browne-Wilkinson's statement that "[t]his immunity enjoyed by a head of state in power and an ambassador in post is a complete immunity attached to the person of the head of state or ambassador and rendering him immune from all actions or prosecutions . . .". According to the Congo, the French Court of Cassation adopted the same position in its *Qaddafi* judgment, in affirming that "international custom bars the prosecution of incumbent Heads of State, in the absence of any contrary international provision binding on the parties concerned, before the criminal courts of a foreign State." As regards the instruments creating international criminal tribunals and the latter's jurisprudence, these, in the Congo's view, concern only those tribunals, and no inference can be drawn from them in regard to criminal proceedings before national courts against persons enjoying immunity under international law.

58. The Court has carefully examined State practice, including national legislation and those few decisions of national higher courts, such as the House of Lords or the French Court of Cassation. It has been

unable to deduce from this practice that there exists under customary international law any form of exception to the rule according immunity from criminal jurisdiction and inviolability to incumbent Ministers for Foreign Affairs, where they are suspected of having committed war crimes or crimes against humanity. The Court has also examined the rules concerning the immunity or criminal responsibility of persons having an official capacity contained in the legal instruments creating international criminal tribunals, and which are specifically applicable to the latter. It finds that these rules likewise do not enable it to conclude that any such an exception exists in customary international law in regard to national courts. Finally, none of the decisions of the Nuremberg and Tokyo international military tribunals, or of the International Criminal Tribunal for the former Yugoslavia, cited by Belgium deal with the question of the immunities of incumbent Ministers for Foreign Affairs before national courts where they are accused of having committed war crimes or crimes against humanity. The Court accordingly notes that those decisions are in no way at variance with the findings it has reached above. In view of the foregoing, the Court accordingly cannot accept Belgium's argument in this regard.

59. It should further be noted that the rules governing the jurisdiction of national courts must be carefully distinguished from those governing jurisdictional immunities: jurisdiction does not imply absence of immunity, while absence of immunity does not imply jurisdiction. Thus, although various international conventions on the prevention and punishment of certain serious crimes impose on States obligations of prosecution or extradition, thereby requiring them to extend their criminal jurisdiction, such extension of jurisdiction in no way affects immunities under customary international law, including those of Ministers for Foreign Affairs. These remain opposable before the courts of a foreign State, even where those courts exercise such a jurisdiction under these conventions.

60. The Court emphasizes, however, that the *immunity* from jurisdiction enjoyed by incumbent Ministers for Foreign Affairs does not mean that they enjoy *impunity* in respect of any crimes they might have committed, irrespective of their gravity. Immunity from criminal jurisdiction and individual criminal responsibility are quite separate concepts. While jurisdictional immunity is procedural in nature, criminal responsibility is a question of substantive law. Jurisdictional immunity may well bar prosecution for a certain period or for certain offences; it cannot exonerate the person to whom it applies from all criminal responsibility.

61. Accordingly, the immunities enjoyed under international law by an incumbent or former Minister for Foreign Affairs do not represent a bar to criminal prosecution in certain circumstances. First, such persons

enjoy no criminal immunity under international law in their own countries, and may thus be tried by those countries' courts in accordance with the relevant rules of domestic law. Secondly, they will cease to enjoy immunity from foreign jurisdiction if the State which they represent or have represented decides to waive that immunity. Thirdly, after a person ceases to hold the office of Minister for Foreign Affairs, he or she will no longer enjoy all of the immunities accorded by international law in other States. Provided that it has jurisdiction under international law, a court of one State may try a former Minister for Foreign Affairs of another State in respect of acts committed prior or subsequent to his or her period of office, as well as in respect of acts committed during that period of office in a private capacity. Fourthly, an incumbent or former Minister for Foreign Affairs may be subject to criminal proceedings before certain international criminal courts, where they have jurisdiction. Examples include the International Criminal Tribunal for the former Yugoslavia, and the International Criminal Tribunal for Rwanda, established pursuant to Security Council resolutions under Chapter VII of the United Nations Charter, and the future International Criminal Court created by the 1998 Rome Convention. The latter's Statute expressly provides, in Article 27, paragraph 2, that "[i]mmunities or special procedural rules which may attach to the official capacity of a person, whether under national or international law, shall not bar the Court from exercising its jurisdiction over such a person."

62. Given the conclusions it has reached above concerning the nature and scope of the rules governing the immunity from criminal jurisdiction enjoyed by incumbent Ministers for Foreign Affairs, the Court must now consider whether in the present case the issue of the arrest warrant of 11 April 2000 and its international circulation violated those rules. The Court recalls in this regard that the Congo requests it, in its first final submission, to adjudge and declare that:

> [B]y issuing and internationally circulating the arrest warrant of 11 April 2000 against Mr. Abdulaye Yerodia Ndombasi, Belgium committed a violation in regard to the Democratic Republic of the Congo of the rule of customary international law concerning the absolute inviolability and immunity from criminal process of incumbent foreign ministers; in so doing, it violated the principle of sovereign equality among States.

63. In support of this submission, the Congo maintains that the arrest warrant of 11 April 2000 as such represents a "coercive legal act" which violates the Congo's immunity and sovereign rights, inasmuch as it seeks to "subject to an organ of domestic criminal jurisdiction a member of a foreign government who is in principle beyond its reach" and is fully enforceable without special formality in Belgium. The Congo considers that the mere issuance of the warrant thus constituted a coercive

measure taken against the person of Mr. Yerodia, even if it was not executed.

64. As regards the international circulation of the said arrest warrant, this, in the Congo's view, not only involved further violations of the rules referred to above, but also aggravated the moral injury which it suffered as a result of the opprobrium "thus cast upon one of the most prominent members of its Government." The Congo further argues that such circulation was a fundamental infringement of its sovereign rights in that it significantly restricted the full and free exercise, by its Minister for Foreign Affairs, of the international negotiation and representation functions entrusted to him by the Congo's former President. In the Congo's view, Belgium "[thus] manifests an intention to have the individual concerned arrested at the place where he is to be found, with a view to procuring his extradition." The Congo emphasizes moreover that it is necessary to avoid any confusion between the arguments concerning the legal effect of the arrest warrant abroad and the question of any responsibility of the foreign authorities giving effect to it. It points out in this regard that no State has acted on the arrest warrant, and that accordingly "no further consideration need be given to the specific responsibility which a State executing it might incur, or to the way in which that responsibility should be related" to that of the Belgian State. The Congo observes that, in such circumstances, "there [would be] a direct causal relationship between the arrest warrant issued in Belgium and any act of enforcement carried out elsewhere."

65. Belgium rejects the Congo's argument on the ground that "the character of the arrest warrant of 11 April 2000 is such that it has neither infringed the sovereignty of, nor created any obligation for, the [Congo]." With regard to the legal effects under Belgian law of the arrest warrant of 11 April 2000, Belgium contends that the clear purpose of the warrant was to procure that, if found in Belgium, Mr. Yerodia would be detained by the relevant Belgian authorities with a view to his prosecution for war crimes and crimes against humanity. According to Belgium, the Belgian investigating judge did, however, draw an explicit distinction in the warrant between, on the one hand, immunity from jurisdiction and, on the other hand, immunity from enforcement as regards representatives of foreign States who visit Belgium on the basis of an official invitation, making it clear that such persons would be immune from enforcement of an arrest warrant in Belgium. Belgium further contends that, in its effect, the disputed arrest warrant is national in character, since it requires the arrest of Mr. Yerodia if he is found in Belgium but it does not have this effect outside Belgium.

66. In respect of the legal effects of the arrest warrant outside Belgium, Belgium maintains that the warrant does not create any obligation for the authorities of any other State to arrest Mr. Yerodia in

the absence of some further step by Belgium completing or validating the arrest warrant (such as a request for the provisional detention of Mr. Yerodia), or the issuing of an arrest warrant by the appropriate authorities in the State concerned following a request to do so, or the issuing of an Interpol Red Notice. Accordingly, outside Belgium, while the purpose of the warrant was admittedly "to establish a legal basis for the arrest of Mr. Yerodia. . . and his subsequent extradition to Belgium," the warrant had no legal effect unless it was validated or completed by some prior act "requiring the arrest of Mr. Yerodia by the relevant authorities in a third State." Belgium further argues that "[i]f a State had executed the arrest warrant, it might infringe Mr. [Yerodia's] criminal immunity," but that "the Party directly responsible for that infringement would have been that State and not Belgium."

70. The Court notes that the *issuance*, as such, of the disputed arrest warrant represents an act by the Belgian judicial authorities intended to enable the arrest on Belgian territory of an incumbent Minister for Foreign Affairs on charges of war crimes and crimes against humanity. The fact that the warrant is enforceable is clearly apparent from the order given to "all bailiffs and agents of public authority. . . to execute this arrest warrant" and from the assertion in the warrant that "the position of Minister for Foreign Affairs currently held by the accused does not entail immunity from jurisdiction and enforcement." The Court notes that the warrant did admittedly make an exception for the case of an official visit by Mr. Yerodia to Belgium, and that Mr. Yerodia never suffered arrest in Belgium. The Court is bound, however, to find that, given the nature and purpose of the warrant, its mere issue violated the immunity which Mr. Yerodia enjoyed as the Congo's incumbent Minister for Foreign Affairs. The Court accordingly concludes that the issue of the warrant constituted a violation of an obligation of Belgium towards the Congo, in that it failed to respect the immunity of that Minister and, more particularly, infringed the immunity from criminal jurisdiction and the inviolability then enjoyed by him under international law. . .

NOTES & QUESTIONS

1. *Domestic Versus International Courts.* The case between Belgium and the Congo involved a domestic court exercising universal jurisdiction. It is not surprising that an international court would uphold immunity in those circumstances. If one country were able to indict a head of state or minister of foreign affairs, the criminal justice system might be hijacked for geopolitical purposes—to decapitate the government of a rival state. However, the case for immunity before an international tribunal is far different, since international tribunals should, in theory, operate with a higher degree of impartiality. Furthermore, article 27 of the Rome Statute of the International Criminal Court states that it "shall apply equally to all persons without any distinction based on official capacity" and that

immunities "shall not bar the Court from exercising its jurisdiction" over government officials. In the *Al-Bashir* case, reprinted in Chapter 8 above, an ICC Pre-Trial Chamber reiterated that Sudanese President Al-Bashir did not have head of state immunity from prosecution. Was the ICC decision in some tension with the ICJ decision in the *Arrest Warrant* case? How should the law resolve a conflict between customary international law and the Rome Statute on this issue?

2.   *Exception for International or Jus Cogens Crimes.* In *Arrest Warrant*, the ICJ considered and rejected the idea that immunity does not apply to allegations of international crimes. The argument in favor of recognizing the exception is that international crimes—by definition—cannot be official government acts, because they are ultra vires and beyond the scope of a state's sovereign prerogative. Under this view, head of state immunity would apply unless a foreign court alleges that the official committed war crimes, crimes against humanity, or genocide. This would also help explain why international tribunals do not respect immunity, since international tribunals like the ICC confine themselves to prosecuting international offenses. For example, in 1999, the British House of Lords concluded that Augusto Pinochet, the former dictator of Chile, was not entitled to head of state immunity for alleged jus cogens violations perpetrated while he was in power. See *Regina v. Bartle, Ex Parte Pinochet*, 38 I.L.M. 581, 593 (House of Lords, 1999) (concluding that there is "strong ground for saying that the implementation of torture as defined by the Torture Convention cannot be a state function"). Do you agree with this argument? Professors Akande and Shah have argued that "this argument is not persuasive and is riddled with problems." See Dapo Akande & Sangeeta Shah, *Immunities of State Officials, International Crimes, and Foreign Domestic Courts*, 21 Eur. J. Int'l L. 815, 830 (2010) ("whether or not an act is *jure imperii* or sovereign for the purposes of state immunity does not depend on the international legality or otherwise of the conduct, but on whether the act in question is intrinsically governmental").

C. SOVEREIGN IMMUNITY

Generally speaking, customary international law does not permit a state's domestic courts to entertain legal claims against another sovereign state. To do so would subject a state to litigation in hundreds of courts worldwide and would risk embroiling a state's judiciary in disputes that are fundamentally diplomatic in nature. For this and other reasons, customary international law confers immunity on sovereign states before domestic courts.

To implement and formalize it, Congress enacted the Foreign Sovereign Immunities Act (FSIA) in 1976, further amended on multiple occasions. The act provides for general immunity but also includes several exceptions, including one for commercial activity:

A foreign state shall not be immune from the jurisdiction of courts of the United States or of the States in any case. . . in which the action is based upon a commercial activity carried on in the United States by the foreign state; or upon an act performed in the United States in connection with a commercial activity of the foreign state elsewhere; or upon an act outside the territory of the United States in connection with a commercial activity of the foreign state elsewhere and that act causes a direct effect in the United States. . .

28 U.S.C. § 1605. So, when a state acts pursuant to a sovereign function, it retains its sovereign immunity, but when a state engages in commercial activity (for example a business transaction), sovereign immunity does not apply. In the following case, the Supreme Court applied the commercial activity exception to determine whether a suit against Argentina could proceed in U.S. courts. Did Argentina's unilateral refinancing of its bonds constitute a commercial activity? Is an American court an appropriate forum for adjudicating a claim that Argentina breached its contract?

Argentina v. Weltover
Supreme Court of the United States
504 U.S. 609 (1992)

■ JUSTICE SCALIA delivered the opinion of the Court.

This case requires us to decide whether the Republic of Argentina's default on certain bonds issued as part of a plan to stabilize its currency was an act taken "in connection with a commercial activity" that had a "direct effect in the United States" so as to subject Argentina to suit in an American court under the Foreign Sovereign Immunities Act of 1976, 28 U.S.C. § 1602.

I

Since Argentina's currency is not one of the mediums of exchange accepted on the international market, Argentine businesses engaging in foreign transactions must pay in United States dollars or some other internationally accepted currency. In the recent past, it was difficult for Argentine borrowers to obtain such funds, principally because of the instability of the Argentine currency. To address these problems, petitioners, the Republic of Argentina and its central bank, Banco Central (collectively Argentina), in 1981 instituted a foreign exchange insurance contract program (FEIC), under which Argentina effectively agreed to assume the risk of currency depreciation in cross-border transactions involving Argentine borrowers. This was accomplished by Argentina's agreeing to sell to domestic borrowers, in exchange for a contractually predetermined amount of local currency, the necessary

United States dollars to repay their foreign debts when they matured, irrespective of intervening devaluations.

Unfortunately, Argentina did not possess sufficient reserves of United States dollars to cover the FEIC contracts as they became due in 1982. The Argentine Government thereupon adopted certain emergency measures, including refinancing of the FEIC-backed debts by issuing to the creditors government bonds. These bonds, called "Bonods," provide for payment of interest and principal in United States dollars; payment may be made through transfer on the London, Frankfurt, Zurich, or New York market, at the election of the creditor. Under this refinancing program, the foreign creditor had the option of either accepting the Bonods in satisfaction of the initial debt, thereby substituting the Argentine Government for the private debtor, or maintaining the debtor/creditor relationship with the private borrower and accepting the Argentine Government as guarantor.

When the Bonods began to mature in May 1986, Argentina concluded that it lacked sufficient foreign exchange to retire them. Pursuant to a Presidential Decree, Argentina unilaterally extended the time for payment and offered bondholders substitute instruments as a means of rescheduling the debts. Respondents, two Panamanian corporations and a Swiss bank who hold, collectively, $1.3 million of Bonods, refused to accept the rescheduling and insisted on full payment, specifying New York as the place where payment should be made. Argentina did not pay, and respondents then brought this breach-of-contract action in the United States District Court for the Southern District of New York, relying on the Foreign Sovereign Immunities Act of 1976 as the basis for jurisdiction. . .

II

The Foreign Sovereign Immunities Act of 1976 (FSIA) establishes a comprehensive framework for determining whether a court in this country, state or federal, may exercise jurisdiction over a foreign state. Under the Act, a "foreign state *shall* be immune from the jurisdiction of the courts of the United States and of the States" unless one of several statutorily defined exceptions applies. The FSIA thus provides the "sole basis" for obtaining jurisdiction over a foreign sovereign in the United States. The most significant of the FSIA's exceptions—and the one at issue in this case—is the "commercial" exception of § 1605(a)(2), which provides that a foreign state is not immune from suit in any case

> in which the action is based upon a commercial activity carried on in the United States by the foreign state; or upon an act performed in the United States in connection with a commercial activity of the foreign state elsewhere; or upon an act outside the territory of the United States in connection with a

commercial activity of the foreign state elsewhere and that act causes a direct effect in the United States.

In the proceedings below, respondents relied only on the third clause of § 1605(a)(2) to establish jurisdiction, and our analysis is therefore limited to considering whether this lawsuit is (1) "based. . . upon an act outside the territory of the United States"; (2) that was taken "in connection with a commercial activity" of Argentina outside this country; and (3) that "cause[d] a direct effect in the United States." The complaint in this case alleges only one cause of action on behalf of each of the respondents, viz., a breach-of-contract claim based on Argentina's attempt to refinance the Bonods rather than to pay them according to their terms. The fact that the cause of action is in compliance with the first of the three requirements—that it is "based upon an act outside the territory of the United States" (presumably Argentina's unilateral extension)—is uncontested. The dispute pertains to whether the unilateral refinancing of the Bonods was taken "in connection with a commercial activity" of Argentina, and whether it had a "direct effect in the United States." We address these issues in turn.

A

Respondents and their *amicus,* the United States, contend that Argentina's issuance of, and continued liability under, the Bonods constitute a "commercial activity" and that the extension of the payment schedules was taken "in connection with" that activity. The latter point is obvious enough, and Argentina does not contest it; the key question is whether the activity is "commercial" under the FSIA.

The FSIA defines "commercial activity" to mean:

> [E]ither a regular course of commercial conduct or a particular commercial transaction or act. The commercial character of an activity shall be determined by reference to the nature of the course of conduct or particular transaction or act, rather than by reference to its purpose.

This definition, however, leaves the critical term "commercial" largely undefined: The first sentence simply establishes that the commercial nature of an activity does *not* depend upon whether it is a single act or a regular course of conduct; and the second sentence merely specifies what element of the conduct determines commerciality (i.e., nature rather than purpose), but still without saying what "commercial" means. Fortunately, however, the FSIA was not written on a clean slate. As we have noted, the Act (and the commercial exception in particular) largely codifies the so-called "restrictive" theory of foreign sovereign immunity first endorsed by the State Department in 1952. The meaning of "commercial" is the meaning generally attached to that term under the restrictive theory at the time the statute was enacted.

This Court did not have occasion to discuss the scope or validity of the restrictive theory of sovereign immunity until our 1976 decision in *Alfred Dunhill of London, Inc. v. Republic of Cuba,* 425 U.S. 682. Although the Court there was evenly divided on the question whether the "commercial" exception that applied in the foreign-sovereign-immunity context also limited the availability of an act-of-state defense, there was little disagreement over the general scope of the exception. The plurality noted that, after the State Department endorsed the restrictive theory of foreign sovereign immunity in 1952, the lower courts consistently held that foreign sovereigns were not immune from the jurisdiction of American courts in cases "arising out of purely commercial transactions." The plurality further recognized that the distinction between state sovereign acts, on the one hand, and state commercial and private acts, on the other, was not entirely novel to American law. The plurality stated that the restrictive theory of foreign sovereign immunity would not bar a suit based upon a foreign state's participation in the marketplace in the manner of a private citizen or corporation. A foreign state engaging in "commercial" activities "do[es] not exercise powers peculiar to sovereigns"; rather, it "exercise[s] only those powers that can also be exercised by private citizens." The dissenters did not disagree with this general description. Given that the FSIA was enacted less than six months after our decision in *Alfred Dunhill* was announced, we think the plurality's contemporaneous description of the then-prevailing restrictive theory of sovereign immunity is of significant assistance in construing the scope of the Act.

In accord with that description, we conclude that when a foreign government acts, not as regulator of a market, but in the manner of a private player within it, the foreign sovereign's actions are "commercial" within the meaning of the FSIA. Moreover, because the Act provides that the commercial character of an act is to be determined by reference to its "nature" rather than its "purpose," the question is not whether the foreign government is acting with a profit motive or instead with the aim of fulfilling uniquely sovereign objectives. Rather, the issue is whether the particular actions that the foreign state performs (whatever the motive behind them) are the *type* of actions by which a private party engages in "trade and traffic or commerce," Black's Law Dictionary 270 (6th ed. 1990). Thus, a foreign government's issuance of regulations limiting foreign currency exchange is a sovereign activity, because such authoritative control of commerce cannot be exercised by a private party; whereas a contract to buy army boots or even bullets is a "commercial" activity, because private companies can similarly use sales contracts to acquire goods.

The commercial character of the Bonods is confirmed by the fact that they are in almost all respects garden-variety debt instruments: They may be held by private parties; they are negotiable and may be traded on the international market (except in Argentina); and they promise a future stream of cash income. We recognize that, prior to the enactment of the FSIA, there was authority suggesting that the issuance of public debt instruments did not constitute a commercial activity. There is, however, nothing distinctive about the state's assumption of debt (other than perhaps its purpose) that would cause it always to be classified as *jure imperii,* and in this regard it is significant that *Victory Transport* expressed confusion as to whether the "nature" or the "purpose" of a transaction was controlling in determining commerciality. Because the FSIA has now clearly established that the "nature" governs, we perceive no basis for concluding that the issuance of debt should be treated as categorically different from other activities of foreign states.

Argentina contends that, although the FSIA bars consideration of "purpose," a court must nonetheless fully consider the *context* of a transaction in order to determine whether it is "commercial." Accordingly, Argentina claims that the Court of Appeals erred by defining the relevant conduct in what Argentina considers an overly generalized, acontextual manner and by essentially adopting a *per se* rule that all "issuance of debt instruments" is "commercial." We have no occasion to consider such a per se rule, because it seems to us that even in full context, there is nothing about the issuance of these Bonods (except perhaps its purpose) that is not analogous to a private commercial transaction.

Argentina points to the fact that the transactions in which the Bonods were issued did not have the ordinary commercial consequence of raising capital or financing acquisitions. Assuming for the sake of argument that this is not an example of judging the commerciality of a transaction by its purpose, the ready answer is that private parties regularly issue bonds, not just to raise capital or to finance purchases, but also to refinance debt. That is what Argentina did here: By virtue of the earlier FEIC contracts, Argentina was *already* obligated to supply the United States dollars needed to retire the FEIC-insured debts; the Bonods simply allowed Argentina to restructure its existing obligations. Argentina further asserts (without proof or even elaboration) that it "received consideration [for the Bonods] in no way commensurate with [their] value." Assuming that to be true, it makes no difference. Engaging in a commercial act does not require the receipt of fair value, or even compliance with the common-law requirements of consideration.

Argentina argues that the Bonods differ from ordinary debt instruments in that they "were created by the Argentine Government to fulfill its obligations under a foreign exchange program designed to address a domestic credit crisis, and as a component of a program designed to control that nation's critical shortage of foreign exchange." In this regard, Argentina relies heavily on *De Sanchez v. Banco Central de Nicaragua,* 770 F.2d 1385 (1985), in which the Fifth Circuit took the view that "[o]ften, the essence of an act is defined by its purpose"; that unless "we can inquire into the purposes of such acts, we cannot determine their nature"; and that, in light of its purpose to control its reserves of foreign currency, Nicaragua's refusal to honor a check it had issued to cover a private bank debt was a sovereign act entitled to immunity. Indeed, Argentina asserts that the line between "nature" and "purpose" rests upon a "formalistic distinction [that] simply is neither useful nor warranted." We think this line of argument is squarely foreclosed by the language of the FSIA. However difficult it may be in some cases to separate "purpose" (i.e., the *reason* why the foreign state engages in the activity) from "nature" (i.e., the outward form of the conduct that the foreign state performs or agrees to perform), the statute unmistakably commands that to be done. We agree with the Court of Appeals that it is irrelevant *why* Argentina participated in the bond market in the manner of a private actor; it matters only that it did so. We conclude that Argentina's issuance of the Bonods was a "commercial activity" under the FSIA.

B

The remaining question is whether Argentina's unilateral rescheduling of the Bonods had a "direct effect" in the United States. In addressing this issue, the Court of Appeals rejected the suggestion in the legislative history of the FSIA that an effect is not "direct" unless it is both "substantial" and "foreseeable." That suggestion is found in the House Report, which states that conduct covered by the third clause of § 1605(a)(2) would be subject to the jurisdiction of American courts "consistent with principles set forth in section 18, Restatement of the Law, Second, Foreign Relations Law of the United States (1965)." Section 18 states that American laws are not given extraterritorial application except with respect to conduct that has, as a "direct and foreseeable result," a "substantial" effect within the United States. Since this obviously deals with jurisdiction to *legislate* rather than jurisdiction to *adjudicate,* this passage of the House Report has been charitably described as "a bit of a *non sequitur.*" Of course the generally applicable principle *de minimis non curat lex* ensures that jurisdiction may not be predicated on purely trivial effects in the United States. But we reject the suggestion that § 1605(a)(2) contains any unexpressed requirement of "substantiality" or "foreseeability." As the Court of Appeals recognized, an effect is "direct" if it follows "as an immediate consequence of the defendant's . . . activity."

The Court of Appeals concluded that the rescheduling of the maturity dates obviously had a "direct effect" on respondents. It further concluded that that effect was sufficiently "in the United States" for purposes of the FSIA, in part because "Congress would have wanted an American court to entertain this action" in order to preserve New York City's status as "a preeminent commercial center." The question, however, is not what Congress "would have wanted" but what Congress enacted in the FSIA. Although we are happy to endorse the Second Circuit's recognition of "New York's status as a world financial leader," the effect of Argentina's rescheduling in diminishing that status (assuming it is not too speculative to be considered an effect at all) is too remote and attenuated to satisfy the "direct effect" requirement of the FSIA.

We nonetheless have little difficulty concluding that Argentina's unilateral rescheduling of the maturity dates on the Bonods had a "direct effect" in the United States. Respondents had designated their accounts in New York as the place of payment, and Argentina made some interest payments into those accounts before announcing that it was rescheduling the payments. Because New York was thus the place of performance for Argentina's ultimate contractual obligations, the rescheduling of those obligations necessarily had a "direct effect" in the United States: Money that was supposed to have been delivered to a New York bank for deposit was not forthcoming. We reject Argentina's suggestion that the "direct effect" requirement cannot be satisfied where the plaintiffs are all foreign corporations with no other connections to the United States. We expressly stated in *Verlinden* that the FSIA permits "a foreign plaintiff to sue a foreign sovereign in the courts of the United States, provided the substantive requirements of the Act are satisfied," 461 U.S., at 489. . .

We conclude that Argentina's issuance of the Bonods was a "commercial activity" under the FSIA; that its rescheduling of the maturity dates on those instruments was taken in connection with that commercial activity and had a "direct effect" in the United States; and that the District Court therefore properly asserted jurisdiction, under the FSIA, over the breach-of-contract claim based on that rescheduling. . .

NOTES & QUESTIONS

1. *Suing Crown Corporations.* Unlike the United States, some countries dominate industries through a government-owned corporation, occasionally with a government-backed monopoly. Examples include airlines, railways, and oil or other energy outfits. In these cases, the foreign state may be subject to litigation if the state corporation is engaged in "commercial activities" in the United States. For example, in *Sachs v. Republic of Austria*, 737 F.3d 584 (9th Cir. 2013), the Ninth Circuit concluded that Austria was not entitled to sovereign immunity. The plaintiff, Sachs, purchased a "Eurail Pass" ticket in the United States for transportation across Europe. While traveling in Austria on board the Austrian national rail carrier, OBB, Sachs was injured, resulting in the amputation of both legs.

The Ninth Circuit concluded that although the accident occurred in Austria, "buying the Eurail pass from [the travel agent in the United States] was the start of Sachs's tragic misadventure." On appeal, the U.S. Supreme Court agreed that the activity was commercial in nature, but disagreed with the Ninth Circuit's conclusion that the sale of the pass in the U.S. was sufficient to establish that Sachs' claim was "based upon" the commercial activity that Austria conducted in the United States. Consequently, the commercial activity exception did not apply. See *OBB Personenverkehr AG v. Sachs*, 577 U.S. 27, 36 (2015).

2.   *Does the FSIA Protect Individuals?* By its terms, the Foreign Sovereign Immunity Act grants sovereign immunity to foreign states. Does the Act, by extension, protect foreign government officials as well? In 2010, the U.S. Supreme Court considered the immunity claim of a former government official from Somalia who was sued by Somali nationals under the Torture Victim Protection Act (TVPA). The Supreme Court concluded that the government official was not entitled to protection under FSIA because the act, by its terms, applies only to "foreign states," not officials of those states. See *Samantar v. Yousuf*, 560 U.S. 305, 314 (2010). However, the Court's holding did not preclude a common-law immunity claim. Put another way, Congress used the FSIA to codify sovereign immunity but head of state and foreign officer immunity remained governed by customary international law as incorporated into federal law. On remand, a federal district court concluded that the defendant was not entitled to head of state immunity, even though Samantar was a former Prime Minister of Somalia. The U.S. State Department did not support Samantar's immunity claim. On appeal, the Fourth Circuit concluded that "under international and domestic law, officials from other countries are not entitled to foreign official immunity for jus cogens violations, even if the acts were performed in the defendant's official capacity." *Yousuf v. Samantar*, 699 F.3d 763, 777 (4th Cir. 2012). Is this consistent with the ICJ's conclusion in the *Arrest Warrant* case?

3.   *The Expropriation Exception.* The FSIA codifies other exceptions to sovereign immunity, including expropriation. That exception applies whenever a foreign state expropriates private property in violation of international law (for example by not providing sufficient compensation to the property holder). However, the statutory exception only applies when there is some commercial connection to the United States, e.g., the "property or any property exchanged for such property is present in the United States in connection with a commercial activity carried on in the United States by the foreign state." 28 U.S.C. § 1605. The doctrine raises a number of important questions, including whether foreign citizens can sue their own governments in a U.S. court alleging an illegal expropriation that occurred in the foreign state. In *Germany v. Philipp*, 894 F.3d 406 (D.C. Cir. 2018), the heirs of Jewish art dealers sued Germany alleging that the Nazis effectively stole their property in the 1930s by forcing the dealers to sell at below-market value. The U.S. Supreme Court granted certiorari in 2020 to

decide if the expropriation exception applies when a sovereign violates international law by taking private property from its own citizens. In *Philipp*, the German plaintiffs argued that an amendment to FSIA created an exception for private takings "in violation of international law." Plaintiffs argued that Germany violated international law by taking their property as part of a genocide, an international crime. The Supreme Court, though, disagreed, ruling unanimously in 2021 that Congress' enactment of the expropriation exception, and the language of "in violation of international law," was designed to refer only to takings by a state against foreigners. 2021 WL 357254, at *10 (U.S. Feb. 3, 2021).

PROBLEM CASE

In 2016, Congress passed the Justice Against Sponsors of Terrorism Act (JASTA), overriding a veto from President Obama, who opposed the measure. JASTA amended the FSIA, 28 U.S.C. § 1605B, to limit sovereign immunity in terrorism cases:

A foreign state shall not be immune from the jurisdiction of the courts of the United States in any case in which money damages are sought against a foreign state for physical injury to person or property or death occurring in the United States and caused by—

(1)   an act of international terrorism in the United States; and

(2)   a tortious act or acts of the foreign state, or of any official, employee, or agent of that foreign state while acting within the scope of his or her office, employment, or agency, regardless where the tortious act or acts of the foreign state occurred.

The legislation was passed after intense lobbying efforts by victims of the 9/11 attacks who wanted to sue Saudi Arabia in federal court in connection with the terrorist attack. Victim families and their supporters argued that Saudi Arabia's alleged involvement in financing the attack was never fully investigated. The alleged links were discussed in a classified section of an early U.S. government report on the attacks, though the official federal 9/11 Commission Report concluded that "Saudi Arabia has long been considered the primary source of al Qaeda funding, but we have found no evidence that the Saudi government as an institution or Saudi officials individually funded the organization. (This conclusion does not exclude the likelihood that charities with significant government sponsorship diverted funds to al Qaeda.)" See 9/11 Commission Report 171 (2004).

Critics of the legislation, including the White House, argued that allowing a lawsuit against Saudi Arabia in federal court would harm relations with an important American ally in the Middle East. Supporters of the legislation argued that any interference in diplomatic relations was a small price to pay for getting an independent judicial inquiry into Saudi Arabia's alleged involvement—or lack thereof—in the 9/11 attacks. As a result of these concerns, the JASTA legislation included a special provision allowing a federal court to "stay a proceeding against a foreign state if the Secretary of State certifies that the United States is engaged in good faith discussions with the foreign state defendant concerning the resolution of the claims against the foreign state, or any other parties as to whom a stay of claims is sought." The maximum length of the stay is 180 days, but the Attorney General may petition for additional 180-day stays after the first one.

Was Congress right to abrogate sovereign immunity for terrorism cases? Will relations with Saudi Arabia be irreparably harmed if a federal district court starts delving into the Kingdom's finances? Is the stay mechanism described above sufficient to resolve these concerns?

D. ACT OF STATE DOCTRINE

Unlike sovereign immunity, which prevents a state from being named as a litigant in a criminal or civil matter, the act of state doctrine is broader: it limits the ability of a court to pass judgment on the actions of a sovereign state. Usually, the former entails the latter, in the sense that suing a foreign state usually involves passing a judgment on its actions. However, there circumstances when a case against non-sovereign litigants might hinge on the actions of a sovereign state. In those situations, sovereign immunity per se is inapplicable, but the act of state doctrine counsels caution when a court must evaluate the actions of the foreign sovereign. These legal assessments can be just as disruptive to foreign relations as the act of suing a sovereign state in a domestic court.

Where does the act of state doctrine come from? At first glance, it would appear to be an extension of the international doctrine of sovereign immunity. However, in the following case, the Supreme Court rejected that interpretation and concluded that the act of state doctrine is a quasi-constitutional principle rooted in the separation of powers. The judiciary should avoid passing judgment on the sovereign actions of a foreign state and should instead defer to the Executive Branch's conduct of foreign affairs through diplomatic channels. As you read the following case, ask yourself why the Supreme Court was so deferential to the Executive Branch on issues of foreign affairs. Do you agree with its conclusion that excessive judicial involvement in such cases could be damaging to national interests?

Banco Nacional de Cuba v. Sabbatino

Supreme Court of the United States
376 U.S. 398 (1964)

■ MR. JUSTICE HARLAN delivered the opinion of the Court.

The question which brought this case here, and is now found to be the dispositive issue, is whether the so-called act of state doctrine serves to sustain petitioner's claims in this litigation. Such claims are ultimately founded on a decree of the Government of Cuba expropriating certain property, the right to the proceeds of which is here in controversy. The act of state doctrine in its traditional formulation precludes the courts of this country from inquiring into the validity of the public acts a recognized foreign sovereign power committed within its own territory.

I.

In February and July of 1960, respondent Farr, Whitlock & Co., an American commodity broker, contracted to purchase Cuban sugar, free alongside the steamer, from a wholly owned subsidiary of Compania

Azucarera Vertientes-Camaguey de Cuba (C.A.V.), a corporation organized under Cuban law whose capital stock was owned principally by United States residents. Farr, Whitlock agreed to pay for the sugar in New York upon presentation of the shipping documents and a sight draft.

On July 6, 1960, the Congress of the United States amended the Sugar Act of 1948 to permit a presidentially directed reduction of the sugar quota for Cuba. On the same day President Eisenhower exercised the granted power. The day of the congressional enactment, the Cuban Council of Ministers adopted Law No. 851, which characterized this reduction in the Cuban sugar quota as an act of "aggression, for political purposes" on the part of the United States, justifying the taking of countermeasures by Cuba. The law gave the Cuban President and Prime Minister discretionary power to nationalize by forced expropriation property or enterprises in which American nationals had an interest. Although a system of compensation was formally provided, the possibility of payment under it may well be deemed illusory. Our State Department has described the Cuban law as "manifestly in violation of those principles of international law which have long been accepted by the free countries of the West. It is in its essence discriminatory, arbitrary and confiscatory."

Between August 6 and August 9, 1960, the sugar covered by the contract between Farr, Whitlock and C.A.V. was loaded, destined for Morocco, onto the S.S. Hornfels, which was standing offshore at the Cuban port of Jucaro (Santa Maria). On the day loading commenced, the Cuban President and Prime Minister, acting pursuant to Law No. 851, issued Executive Power Resolution No. 1. It provided for the compulsory expropriation of all property and enterprises, and of rights and interests arising therefrom, of certain listed companies, including C.A.V., wholly or principally owned by American nationals. The preamble reiterated the alleged injustice of the American reduction of the Cuban sugar quota and emphasized the importance of Cuba's serving as an example for other countries to follow "in their struggle to free themselves from the brutal claws of Imperialism." . . .

IV

The classic American statement of the act of state doctrine, which appears to have taken root in England as early as 1674, and began to emerge in the jurisprudence of this country in the late eighteenth and early nineteenth centuries, is found in *Underhill v. Hernandez*, 168 U.S. 250, 252, where Chief Justice Fuller said for a unanimous Court:

> Every sovereign state is bound to respect the independence of every other sovereign state, and the courts of one country will not sit in judgment on the acts of the government of another, done within its own territory. Redress of grievances by reason

of such acts must be obtained through the means open to be availed of by sovereign powers as between themselves.

Following this precept the Court in that case refused to inquire into acts of Hernandez, a revolutionary Venezuelan military commander whose government had been later recognized by the United States, which were made the basis of a damage action in this country by Underhill, an American citizen, who claimed that he had had unlawfully assaulted, coerced, and detained in Venezuela by Hernandez.

None of this Court's subsequent cases in which the act of state doctrine was directly or peripherally involved manifest any retreat from *Underhill*. . .

In deciding the present case the Court of Appeals relied in part upon an exception to the unqualified teachings of *Underhill*. . . In *Bernstein v. Van Heyghen Freres Societe Anonyme*, 163 F.2d 246 (2d Cir. 1947), suit was brought to recover from an assignee property allegedly taken, in effect, by the Nazi Government because plaintiff was Jewish. Recognizing the odious nature of this act of state, the court, through Judge Learned Hand, nonetheless refused to consider it invalid on that ground. Rather, it looked to see if the Executive had acted in any manner that would indicate that United States Courts should refuse to give effect to such a foreign decree. Finding no such evidence, the court sustained dismissal of the complaint. In a later case involving similar facts the same court again assumed examination of the German acts improper, but, quite evidently following the implications of Judge Hand's opinion in the earlier case, amended its mandate to permit evidence of alleged invalidity, subsequent to receipt by plaintiff's attorney of a letter from the Acting Legal Adviser to the State Department written for the purpose of relieving the court from any constraint upon the exercise of its jurisdiction to pass on that question.

This Court has never had occasion to pass upon the so-called *Bernstein* exception, nor need it do so now. For whatever ambiguity may be thought to exist in the two letters from State Department officials on which the Court of Appeals relied, is now removed by the position which the Executive has taken in this Court on the act of state claim; respondents do not indeed contest the view that these letters were intended to reflect no more than the Department's then wish not to make any statement bearing on this litigation.

The outcome of this case, therefore, turns upon whether any of the contentions urged by respondents against the application of the act of state doctrine in the premises is acceptable: (1) that the doctrine does not apply to acts of state which violate international law, as is claimed to be the case here; (2) that the doctrine is inapplicable unless the Executive specifically interposes it in a particular case; and (3) that, in any event, the doctrine may not be invoked by a foreign government plaintiff in our courts.

V

Preliminarily, we discuss the foundations on which we deem the act of state doctrine to rest, and more particularly the question of whether state or federal law governs its application in a federal diversity case.

We do not believe that this doctrine is compelled either by the inherent nature of sovereign authority, as some of the earlier decision seem to imply, or by some principle of international law. If a transaction takes place in one jurisdiction and the forum is in another, the forum does not by dismissing an action or by applying its own law purport to divest the first jurisdiction of its territorial sovereignty; it merely declines to adjudicate or makes applicable its own law to parties or property before it. The refusal of one country to enforce the penal laws of another is a typical example of an instance when a court will not entertain a cause of action arising in another jurisdiction. While historic notions of sovereign authority do bear upon the wisdom or employing the act of state doctrine, they do not dictate its existence.

That international law does not require application of the doctrine is evidenced by the practice of nations. Most of the countries rendering decisions on the subject to follow the rule rigidly. No international arbitral or judicial decision discovered suggests that international law prescribes recognition of sovereign acts of foreign governments, and apparently no claim has ever been raised before an international tribunal that failure to apply the act of state doctrine constitutes a breach of international obligation. If international law does not prescribe use of the doctrine, neither does it forbid application of the rule even if it is claimed that the act of state in question violated international law. The traditional view of international law is that it establishes substantive principles for determining whether one country has wronged another. Because of its peculiar nation-to-nation character the usual method for an individual to seek relief is to exhaust local remedies and then repair to the executive authorities of his own state to persuade them to champion his claim in diplomacy or before an international tribunal. Although it is, of course, true that United States courts apply international law as a part of our own in appropriate circumstances, the public law of nations can hardly dictate to a country which is in theory wronged how to treat that wrong within its domestic borders.

Despite the broad statement. . . that "The conduct of the foreign relations of our government is committed by the Constitution to the executive and legislative. . . departments," it cannot of course be thought that "every case or controversy which touches foreign relations lies beyond judicial cognizance." The text of the Constitution does not require the act of state doctrine; it does not irrevocably remove from the judiciary the capacity to review the validity of foreign acts of state.

The act of state doctrine does, however, have "constitutional" underpinnings. It arises out of the basic relationships between branches of government in a system of separation of powers. It concerns the competency of dissimilar institutions to make and implement particular kinds of decisions in the area of international relations. The doctrine as formulated in past decisions expresses the strong sense of the Judicial Branch that its engagement in the task of passing on the validity of foreign acts of state may hinder rather than further this country's pursuit of goals both for itself and for the community of nations as a whole in the international sphere. Many commentators disagree with this view; they have striven by means of distinguishing and limiting past decisions and by advancing various considerations of policy to stimulate a narrowing of the apparent scope of the rule. Whatever considerations are thought to predominate, it is plain that the problems involved are uniquely federal in nature. If federal authority, in this instance this Court, orders the field of judicial competence in this area for the federal courts, and the state courts are left free to formulate their own rules, the purposes behind the doctrine could be as effectively undermined as if there had been no federal pronouncement on the subject. . .

VI

If the act of state doctrine is a principle of decision binding on federal and state courts alike but compelled by neither international law nor the Constitution, its continuing vitality depends on its capacity to reflect the proper distribution of functions between the judicial and political branches of the Government on matters bearing upon foreign affairs. It should be apparent that the greater the degree of codification or consensus concerning a particular area of international law, the more appropriate it is for the judiciary to render decisions regarding it, since the courts can then focus on the application of an agreed principle to circumstances of fact rather than on the sensitive task of establishing a principle not inconsistent with the national interest or with international justice. It is also evident that some aspects of international law touch much more sharply on national nerves than do others; the less important the implications of an issue are for our foreign relations, the weaker the justification for exclusivity in the political branches. The balance of relevant considerations may also be shifted if the government which perpetrated the challenged act of state is no longer in existence, as in the *Bernstein* case, for the political interest of this country may, as a result, be measurably altered. Therefore, rather than laying down or reaffirming an inflexible and all-encompassing rule in this case, we decide only that the (Judicial Branch) will not examine the validity of a taking of property within its own territory by a foreign sovereign government, extant and recognized by this country at the time of suit, in the absence of a treaty or other unambiguous agreement regarding controlling legal principles, even if the complaint alleges that the taking violates customary international law. . .

The dangers of such adjudication are present regardless of whether the State Department has, as it did in this case, asserted that the relevant act violated international law. If the Executive Branch has undertaken negotiations with an expropriating country, but has refrained from claims of violation of the law of nations, a determination to that effect by a court might be regarded as a serious insult, while a finding of compliance with international law would greatly strengthen the bargaining hand of the other state with consequent detriment to American interests.

Even if the State Department has proclaimed the impropriety of the expropriation, the stamp of approval of its view by a judicial tribunal, however, impartial, might increase any affront and the judicial decision might occur at a time, almost always well after the taking, when such an impact would be contrary to our national interest. Considerably more serious and far-reaching consequences would flow from a judicial finding that international law standards had been met if that determination flew in the face of a State Department proclamation to the contrary. When articulating principles of international law in its relations with other states, the Executive Branch speaks not only as an interpreter of generally accepted and traditional rules, as would the courts, but also as an advocate of standards it believes desirable for the community of nations and protective of national concerns. In short, whatever way the matter is cut, the possibility of conflict between the Judicial and Executive Branches could hardly be avoided.

Respondents contend that, even if there is not agreement regarding general standards for determining the validity of expropriations, the alleged combination of retaliation, discrimination, and inadequate compensation makes it patently clear that this particular expropriation was in violation of international law. If this view is accurate, it would still be unwise for the courts so to determine. Such a decision now would require the drawing of more difficult lines in subsequent cases and these would involve the possibility of conflict with the Executive view. Even if the courts avoided this course, either by presuming the validity of an act of state whenever the international law standard was thought unclear or by following the State Department declaration in such a situation, the very expression of judicial uncertainty might provide embarrassment to the Executive Branch. . .

It is suggested that if the act of state doctrine is applicable to violations of international law, it should only be so when the Executive Branch expressly stipulates that it does not wish the courts to pass on the question of validity. We should be slow to reject the representations of the Government that such a reversal of the *Bernstein* principle would work serious inroads on the maximum effectiveness of United States diplomacy. Often the State Department will wish to refrain from taking an official position, particularly at a moment that would be dictated by the development of private litigation but might be inopportune diplomatically. Adverse domestic consequences might flow from an official stand which could be assuaged, if at all, only by revealing matters best kept secret. Of course, a relevant consideration for the State Department would be the position contemplated in the court to hear the case. It is highly questionable whether the examination of validity by the judiciary should depend on an educated guess by the Executive as to probable result and, at any rate, should a prediction be wrong, the Executive might be embarrassed in its dealings with other countries. We do not now pass on the *Bernstein* exception, but even if it were deemed valid, its suggested extension is unwarranted.

However offensive to the public policy of this country and its constituent States an expropriation of this kind may be, we conclude that both the national interest and progress toward the goal of establishing the rule of law among nations are best served by maintaining intact the act of state doctrine in this realm of its application. . .

NOTES & QUESTIONS

The Bernstein Exception. The Supreme Court repeatedly refers to the *Bernstein* exception, which was articulated in *Bernstein v. N.V. Nederlandsche-Amerikaansche, Stoomvart-Maatschappij*, 210 F.2d 375 (2d Cir. 1954). The *Bernstein* exception allows the State Department to "waive" the act of state doctrine by issuing a letter declaring that it has no objection to a court's consideration of the actions of the foreign sovereign. In the Bernstein case, the federal government stated in a letter that "The policy of the Executive, with respect to claims asserted in the United States for the restitution of identifiable property (or compensation in lieu thereof) lost through force, coercion, or duress as a result of Nazi persecution in German, is to relieve American courts from any restraint upon the exercise of their jurisdiction to pass upon the validity of the acts of Nazi officials." In keeping with the letter, the Second Circuit considered the act of state doctrine inapplicable. However, not everyone is happy with the *Bernstein* exception. As one legal commentator put it, "[t]he *Bernstein* exception should be abolished because significant foreign policy considerations should not be evaluated by the judiciary on a case-by-case basis; it is simply too risky for the judicial branch to declare foreign acts of state unlawful." See Breana Frankel, *Oy Vey! The* Bernstein *Exception: Rethinking the Doctrine in the Wake of Constitutional Abuses, Corporate Malfeasance, and the 'War on Terror'*, 41 Geo. Wash. Int'l L. Rev. 67 (2009). Does the *Bernstein* exception ensure that diplomatic relations will be protected or does it promote ad hockery?

E. IMMUNITY FOR INTERNATIONAL ORGANIZATIONS

Although international organizations are not states per se, they do nonetheless possess international legal personality, giving them many of the legal entitlements that states enjoy. It is therefore of little surprise that international organizations and their officers are entitled to many of the same immunities as sovereign states. For example, UN offices are inviolable, just like embassies, and state representatives at the UN are entitled to the same diplomatic immunity as embassy workers. This basic structure is repeated for many international organizations, not just the United Nations. Typically, these immunities will be explicitly codified in a bilateral treaty, often called a "Headquarters Agreement," between the international organization and the host state. Will the international organization be subject to taxation from the host state? Will its representatives have diplomatic immunity? Will the criminal law of the host state continue to apply at the headquarters? All of these questions are usually answered in the bilateral agreement.

Reprinted below are excerpts from the United Nations Headquarters Agreement with the United States, outlining the immunities that will apply. After digesting these provisions, consider the case of Radovan Karadžić, who was served with a complaint while in New York City en route to the United Nations. As an invitee to the UN, did this service violate either the letter or spirit of the Headquarters Agreement? How essential is immunity to the functioning of the UN as a center for the diplomatic resolution of global disputes?

Agreement Between the United Nations and the United States Regarding the Headquarters of the United Nations

June 26, 1947
Approved by the General Assembly October 31, 1947

Section 9

(a) The headquarters district shall be inviolable. Federal, state or local officers or officials of the United States, whether administrative, judicial, military or police, shall not enter the headquarters district to perform any official duties therein except with the consent of and under conditions agreed to by the Secretary-General. The service of legal process, including the seizure of private property, may take place within the headquarters district only with the consent of and under conditions approved by the Secretary-General.

(b) Without prejudice to the provisions of the General Convention or Article IV of this agreement, the United Nations shall prevent the headquarters district from becoming a refuge either for persons who are avoiding arrest under the federal, state, or local law of the United States or are required by the Government of the United States for extradition to another country, or for persons who are endeavouring to avoid service of legal process.

Section 11

The federal, state or local authorities of the United States shall not impose any impediments to transit to or from the headquarters district of (1) representatives of Members or officials of the United Nations, or of specialized agencies as defined in Article 57, paragraph 2, of the Charter, or the families of such representatives or officials; (2) experts performing missions for the United Nations or for such specialized agencies; (3) representatives of the press, or of radio, film or other information agencies, who have been accredited by the United Nations (or by such a specialized agency) in its discretion after consultation with the United States; (4) representatives of nongovernmental organizations recognized by the United Nations for the purpose of consultation under Article 71 of the Charter; or (5) other persons invited to the headquarters district by the United Nations or by such specialized agency on official business. The appropriate American authorities shall afford any necessary protection to such persons while in transit to or from the headquarters district. This section does not apply to general interruptions of transportation which are to be dealt with as provided in Section 17, and does not impair the effectiveness of generally applicable laws and regulations as to the operation of means of transportation.

Section 15

(1) Every person designated by a Member as the principal resident representative to the United Nations of such Member or as a resident representative with the rank of ambassador or minister plenipotentiary,

(2) Such resident members of their staffs as may be agreed upon between the Secretary-General, the Government of the United States and the Government of the Member concerned,

(3) Every person designated by a Member of a specialized agency, as defined in Article 57, paragraph 2, of the Charter, as its principal resident representative, with the rank of ambassador or minister plenipotentiary at the headquarters of such agency in the United States, and

(4) Such other principal resident representatives of members of a specialized agency and such resident members of the staffs of representatives of a specialized agency as may be agreed upon between the principal executive officer of the specialized agency, the Government

of the United States and the Government of the Member concerned, shall whether residing inside or outside the headquarters district, be entitled in the territory of the United States to the same privileges and immunities, subject to corresponding conditions and obligations, as it accords to diplomatic envoys accredited to it. In the case of Members whose governments are not recognized by the United States, such privileges and immunities need be extended to such representatives, or persons on the staffs of such representatives, only within the headquarters district, at their residences and offices outside the district, in transit between the district and such residences and offices, and in transit on official business to or from foreign countries.

Kadic v. Karadžić
U.S. Court of Appeals for the Second Circuit
70 F.3d 232 (1995)

■ JON O. NEWMAN, CHIEF JUDGE:

Most Americans would probably be surprised to learn that victims of atrocities committed in Bosnia are suing the leader of the insurgent Bosnian-Serb forces in a United States District Court in Manhattan. Their claims seek to build upon the foundation of this Court's decision in *Filártiga v. Peña-Irala*, 630 F.2d 876 (2d Cir. 1980), which recognized the important principle that the venerable Alien Tort Act, 28 U.S.C. § 1350 (1988), enacted in 1789 but rarely invoked since then, validly creates federal court jurisdiction for suits alleging torts committed anywhere in the world against aliens in violation of the law of nations. The pending appeals pose additional significant issues as to the scope of the Alien Tort Act: whether some violations of the law of nations may be remedied when committed by those not acting under the authority of a state; if so, whether genocide, war crimes, and crimes against humanity are among the violations that do not require state action; and whether a person, otherwise liable for a violation of the law of nations, is immune from service of process because he is present in the United States as an invitee of the United Nations.

These issues arise on appeals by two groups of plaintiffs-appellants from the November 19, 1994, judgment of the United States District Court for the Southern District of New York, dismissing, for lack of subject-matter jurisdiction, their suits against defendant-appellee Radovan Karadžić, President of the self-proclaimed Bosnian-Serb republic of "Srpska." For the reasons set forth below, we hold that subject-matter jurisdiction exists, that Karadžić may be found liable for genocide, war crimes, and crimes against humanity in his private capacity and for other violations in his capacity as a state actor, and that he is not immune from service of process. We therefore reverse and remand.

Background

The plaintiffs-appellants are Croat and Muslim citizens of the internationally recognized nation of Bosnia-Herzegovina, formerly a republic of Yugoslavia. Their complaints, which we accept as true for purposes of this appeal, allege that they are victims, and representatives of victims, of various atrocities, including brutal acts of rape, forced prostitution, forced impregnation, torture, and summary execution, carried out by Bosnian-Serb military forces as part of a genocidal campaign conducted in the course of the Bosnian civil war. Karadžić, formerly a citizen of Yugoslavia and now a citizen of Bosnia-Herzegovina, is the President of a three-man presidency of the self-proclaimed Bosnian-Serb republic within Bosnia-Herzegovina, sometimes referred to as "Srpska," which claims to exercise lawful authority, and does in fact exercise actual control, over large parts of the territory of Bosnia-Herzegovina. In his capacity as President, Karadžić possesses ultimate command authority over the Bosnian-Serb military forces, and the injuries perpetrated upon plaintiffs were committed as part of a pattern of systematic human rights violations that was directed by Karadžić and carried out by the military forces under his command. The complaints allege that Karadžić acted in an official capacity either as the titular head of Srpska or in collaboration with the government of the recognized nation of the former Yugoslavia and its dominant constituent republic, Serbia.

The two groups of plaintiffs asserted causes of action for genocide, rape, forced prostitution and impregnation, torture and other cruel, inhuman, and degrading treatment, assault and battery, sex and ethnic inequality, summary execution, and wrongful death. They sought compensatory and punitive damages, attorney's fees, and, in one of the cases, injunctive relief. . .

In early 1993, Karadžić was admitted to the United States on three separate occasions as an invitee of the United Nations. According to affidavits submitted by the plaintiffs, Karadžić was personally served with the summons and complaint in each action during two of these visits while he was physically present in Manhattan. Karadžić admits that he received the summons and complaint in the *Kadic* action, but disputes whether the attempt to serve him personally in the *Doe* action was effective. . .

Service of Process and Personal Jurisdiction

Appellants aver that Karadžić was personally served with process while he was physically present in the Southern District of New York. In the *Doe* action, the affidavits detail that on February 11, 1993, process servers approached Karadžić in the lobby of the Hotel Intercontinental at 111 East 48th St. in Manhattan, called his name and identified their purpose, and attempted to hand him the complaint from a distance of two feet, that security guards seized the complaint papers, and that the papers fell to the floor. Karadžić submitted an affidavit of a State Department security officer, who generally confirmed the episode, but stated that the process server did not come closer than six feet of the defendant. In the *Kadic* action, the plaintiffs obtained from Judge Owen an order for alternate means of service, directing service by delivering the complaint to a member of defendant's State Department security detail, who was ordered to hand the complaint to the defendant. The security officer's affidavit states that he received the complaint and handed it to Karadžić outside the Russian Embassy in Manhattan. Karadžić's statement confirms that this occurred during his second visit to the United States, sometime between February 27 and March 8, 1993. Appellants also allege that during his visits to New York City, Karadžić stayed at hotels outside the "headquarters district" of the United Nations and engaged in non-United Nations-related activities such as fund-raising.

Fed. R. Civ. P. 4(e)(2) specifically authorizes personal service of a summons and complaint upon an individual physically present within a judicial district of the United States, and such personal service comports with the requirements of due process for the assertion of personal jurisdiction.

Nevertheless, Karadžić maintains that his status as an invitee of the United Nations during his visits to the United States rendered him immune from service of process. He relies on both the Agreement Between the United Nations and the United States of America Regarding the Headquarters of the United Nations, reprinted at 22 U.S.C. § 287 note (1988) ("Headquarters Agreement"), and a claimed federal common law immunity. We reject both bases for immunity from service.

The Headquarters Agreement provides for immunity from suit only in narrowly defined circumstances. First, "service of legal process. . . may take place within the headquarters district only with the consent of and under conditions approved by the Secretary-General." This provision is of no benefit to Karadžić, because he was not served within the well-defined confines of the "headquarters district," which is bounded by Franklin D. Roosevelt Drive, 1st Avenue, 42nd Street, and 48th Street. Second, certain representatives of members of the United Nations, whether residing inside or outside of the "headquarters district," shall be entitled to the same privileges and immunities as the United States extends to accredited diplomatic envoys. This provision is also of no benefit to Karadžić, since he is not a designated representative of any member of the United Nations.

A third provision of the Headquarters Agreement prohibits federal, state, and local authorities of the United States from "impos[ing] any impediments to transit to or from the headquarters district of. . . persons invited to the headquarters district by the United Nations. . . on official business." Karadžić maintains that allowing service of process upon a United Nations invitee who is on official business would violate this section, presumably because it would impose a potential burden— exposure to suit—on the invitee's transit to and from the headquarters district. However, this Court has previously refused "to extend the immunities provided by the Headquarters Agreement beyond those explicitly stated." *See Klinghoffer v. S.N.C. Achille Lauro,* 937 F.2d 44, 48 (2d Cir. 1991). We therefore reject Karadžić's proposed construction of section 11, because it would effectively create an immunity from suit for United Nations invitees where none is provided by the express terms of the Headquarters Agreement.

The parties to the Headquarters Agreement agree with our construction of it. In response to a letter from plaintiffs' attorneys opposing any grant of immunity to Karadžić, a responsible State Department official wrote: "Mr. Karadžić's status during his recent visits to the United States has been solely as an 'invitee' of the United Nations, and as such he enjoys no immunity from the jurisdiction of the courts of the United States." Counsel for the United Nations has also issued an opinion stating that although the United States must allow United Nations invitees access to the Headquarters District, invitees are not immune from legal process while in the United States at locations outside of the Headquarters District.

Karadžić nonetheless invites us to fashion a federal common law immunity for those within a judicial district as a United Nations invitee. He contends that such a rule is necessary to prevent private litigants from inhibiting the United Nations in its ability to consult with invited visitors. Karadžić analogizes his proposed rule to the "government contacts exception" to the District of Columbia's long-arm statute, which has been broadly characterized to mean that "mere entry [into the District of Columbia] by non-residents for the purpose of contacting federal government agencies cannot serve as a basis for in personam jurisdiction." He also points to a similar restriction upon assertion of personal jurisdiction on the basis of the presence of an individual who has entered a jurisdiction in order to attend court or otherwise engage in litigation.

Karadžić also endeavors to find support for a common law immunity in our decision in *Klinghoffer.* Though, as noted above, *Klinghoffer* declined to extend the immunities of the Headquarters Agreement beyond those provided by its express provisions, the decision applied immunity considerations to its construction of New York's long-arm statute, N.Y. Civ. Prac. L. & R. 301 (McKinney 1990), in deciding whether the Palestine Liberation Organization (PLO) was doing business in the state. *Klinghoffer* construed the concept of "doing business" to cover only those activities of the PLO that were not United Nations-related.

Despite the considerations that guided *Klinghoffer* in its narrowing construction of the general terminology of New York's long-arm statute as applied to United Nations activities, we decline the invitation to create a federal common law immunity as an extension of the precise terms of a carefully crafted treaty that struck the balance between the interests of the United Nations and those of the United States.

Finally, we note that the mere possibility that Karadžić might at some future date be recognized by the United States as the head of state of a friendly nation and might thereby acquire head-of-state immunity does not transform the appellants' claims into a nonjusticiable request for an advisory opinion, as the District Court intimated. Even if such future recognition, determined by the Executive Branch, would create head-of-state immunity, it would be entirely inappropriate for a court to create the functional equivalent of such an immunity based on speculation about what the Executive Branch *might* do in the future.

In sum, if appellants personally served Karadžić with the summons and complaint while he was in New York but outside of the U.N. headquarters district, as they are prepared to prove, he is subject to the personal jurisdiction of the District Court. . .

Conclusion & Summary

The immunities discussed in this chapter flow from a cluster of related ideas: a domestic court is not an appropriate forum for seeking redress from a foreign sovereign or even passing judgment on the official actions of that sovereign or its officials. In the materials presented, this chapter explored the following doctrines and principles:

1.   Diplomats are subject to immunity under the 1961 Vienna Convention, though the immunity resides with the sending state, not the individual diplomat, and accordingly can be waived by the sending state. Consular officials are also eligible for immunity under the 1963 Vienna Convention, though it is less absolute because it does not apply to grave crimes. Commercial and professional activities are not eligible for immunity since foreign diplomats and consular officials are not permitted to engage in outside commercial or professional activities while serving in their positions.

2.   Under customary international law, heads of state are immune from judicial process in domestic courts, whether a civil action or a criminal proceeding. This immunity also extends to high governmental officials, such as a minister of foreign affairs, though it is unclear which government

officials are eligible for the immunity. According to the ICJ in the *Arrest Warrant* case, the issuance of the warrant— even if it is never executed—is itself a violation of customary international law because it interferes with the work of the foreign sovereign.

3. Some courts have recognized limitations on head of state and government official immunity. First, the immunity does not apply at international tribunals, such as the International Criminal Court, which has repeatedly confirmed that heads of state should be arrested if they are charged with international crimes that fall within the jurisdiction of the court. However, not every state agrees with this position and some, including South Africa, have cited head of state immunity as one reason for ignoring arrest warrants issued by the ICC.

4. Second, some courts have suggested that heads of state do not have immunity for crimes that constitute jus cogens violations of international law, such as torture or genocide. For example, the United Kingdom concluded that Augusto Pinochet did not have head of state immunity for this very reason, and a few U.S. courts have adopted this reasoning. However, a court needs to reject immunity long before it reaches the merits of the underlying legal claim, thus suggesting that if this exception were universally recognized, heads of state might be subject to judicial scrutiny in factually questionable cases, just because the allegations are presented as violations of jus cogens. For this and other reasons, the ICJ in the *Arrest Warrant* case rejected the idea that there exists an exception to head of state immunity for jus cogens violations. The issue continues to be hotly debated by academic commentators.

5. Sovereign states cannot be sued in domestic courts. This forms the basic contours of a reciprocal agreement between states not to subject each other to burdensome litigation in domestic courts. However, just like diplomatic immunity, there is an exception for commercial activities. When a state functions as a market or commercial actor, rather than as a sovereign state, its actions are no longer shielded from judicial scrutiny. This exception is frequently invoked when the foreign state owns and operates a national corporation.

6. The United States has abrogated sovereign immunity in cases dealing with terrorism, though the Attorney General may request a stay of the proceedings. Critics worry that

these cases risk disrupting carefully constructed diplomatic alliances.

7. Federal courts in the United States recognize an act of state doctrine that prevents courts from passing judgment on the official acts of sovereign states, even if they are not parties to a proceeding. Although the doctrine has some affinity to sovereign immunity, the Supreme Court has grounded the doctrine in separation-of-powers concerns that caution against excessive judicial interference in the Executive Branch's conduct of foreign affairs.

8. U.S. courts have often recognized an exception to sovereign immunity and the act of state doctrine when the State Department certifies that it favors judicial resolution and that litigation will not harm the national interests of the United States. This so-called *Bernstein* exception entails that similar cases might yield different results depending on the attitude of the State Department.

9. Representatives at the UN and other international organizations are entitled to diplomatic immunity. The exact contours of that immunity are usually outlined in a headquarters agreement. In some situations that immunity might extend to invitees and others with business before the international organization, though as the *Karadžić* case demonstrates, that immunity is far from absolute and is often narrowly construed.

CHAPTER 17

INTERNATIONAL ECONOMIC LAW

Introduction

As part of the global economy, goods and capital cross borders. Investors in one state inject capital (money) into business projects in another state, in return for a promise to repay the money (a loan) or in exchange for a portion of the business project (equity). Goods that are produced in one state are exported and sold in other states. Governments that need money issue bonds to foreign investors, raising capital for government spending in exchange for making loan payments back to the bondholders.

In each of these circumstances, transactions can sour quickly. Investors might pour money into a foreign project but then lose money when the government changes its fiscal policy. Producers in one state might have trouble exporting their goods when another state engages in protectionist behavior, that is, protecting their domestic producers at the expense of foreign producers trying to access the market. Or maybe the producers cannot export their product because the target state issues a regulation that defines the product as unsafe. Bondholders might provide capital to a sovereign state that has trouble paying back the debt. Each of these situations involve economic transactions that did not go exactly as planned. In the first two situations (foreign investment and trade), there are well-regarded avenues for legal enforcement in the form of arbitration. In the last situation, sovereign debt, there are proposals for institutional mechanisms but none have been created. For all of them, however, international law regulates the behavior through norms that guide these disputes toward resolution.

Section A focuses on trade disputes, section B focuses on investor-state arbitration, and section C explores sovereign debt restructuring. The disputes in the former two categories are highly structured through arbitral proceedings, while sovereign debt restructuring usually involves negotiation (and possibly litigation in domestic courts). In each case, the materials focus on both substance and process. The substance necessarily involves examples rather than a comprehensive treatment of every rule or legal principle that might be asserted in these disputes. Every treaty and every legal instrument contains dozens or hundreds of legal rules whose violation might trigger some form of redress under international law. Rather, the focus here is on broad principles—such as the principle of non-discrimination in international trade or the defense of necessity in investor-state arbitration—which help illuminate the basic structure of these disputes, why they matter, and how international law structures their resolution. Two of the three sections (investor-state disputes and sovereign debt restructuring) deal with Argentina, a compelling but disturbing case study of the legal consequences of one country's economic collapse and repeated attempts by domestic and international actors to rehabilitate Argentina's economy while at the same time treating investors fairly.

As for the process, international economic law uses arbitration more than other areas explored in prior chapters. As we saw before, international criminal law uses ad hoc or standing tribunals while human rights law is often enforced either in regional courts or human rights commissions or councils. In contrast, trade disputes and investor-state disputes are often resolved through panels composed of professional arbitrators who consider both factual evidence and legal arguments before issuing written decisions. Perhaps arbitration proceedings are more common in economic disputes because corporate actors prefer the certainty, predictability, and lower costs associated with dispute resolution through arbitration. But, in a sense, it is best to view these arbitration possibilities along a spectrum with other international dispute resolution mechanisms, with negotiation on one end of the spectrum and international courts at the other. But as discussed in the chapter on international adjudication, even the International Court of Justice is, in a sense, a kind of arbitration proceeding that resolves disputes between states that have consented to the court's jurisdiction through some treaty or ad hoc declaration. There simply is no international tribunal with the kind of coercive authority akin to a domestic criminal court that has mandatory jurisdiction over all individuals on the state's territory.

As you read the following materials, focus on mastering the institutional structures that have been created to resolve these disputes and the differences between them.

A. WORLD TRADE ORGANIZATION

The foundations of the legal system for regulating international trade were laid after World War II, when the General Agreement on Tariffs and Trade (GATT) was negotiated and signed in 1947. This multilateral treaty created a series of basic principles and rules to be applied in the trading system. The underlying rationale behind the agreement was to reduce barriers to trade, including tariffs and other forms of protectionism (a government's favoring of local economic goods over imported goods), and to promote equity, fairness, and transparency among trading partners. However, the GATT did not produce—nor did it aim to produce—a universal system of global free trade. Tariffs, duties, and taxes were still possible under GATT, though they were subject to its constraints in the hopes that these could be reduced as far as possible. Under the auspices of GATT, international negotiations took place at irregular intervals, resulting in tariff reductions and amendments to the original GATT treaty.

In 1986, a round of negotiations in Uruguay resulted in the creation of the World Trade Organization—an extension of the GATT framework with an improved system for dispute resolution. The original GATT treaty and its amendments remained in effect, but a more robust bureaucratic structure was created for overseeing negotiations and resolution of disputes through arbitral panels.

Under the WTO framework, a member state may file a complaint against another member alleging unfair treatment in violation of a state's legal obligations under the GATT. The rules for these arbitral proceedings are governed by a separate agreement called the Dispute Settlement Understanding (DSU), a document that emerged from the Uruguay round negotiations. If a dispute cannot be resolved through negotiation, a WTO panel is convened to resolve the dispute. The panel decision is automatically adopted unless the full WTO membership unanimously votes to reject the decision. However, the panel decision can be appealed to the WTO Appellate Body, though appeals are limited to points of law rather than factual findings. This WTO process resolved a major defect of the pre-WTO dispute resolution system. Under that older system, panel decisions were only adopted if all state parties to the GATT agreed to the adoption, which rarely occurred, since the very existence of the dispute entailed a lack of consensus. Under the newer WTO system, the default is the reverse: WTO panel decisions are implemented unless there is agreement to block them, which rarely occurs. Consequently, the WTO panel framework has been remarkably effective in resolving trade disputes or lessening their intensity.

Unfortunately, in 2019, the WTO adjudicative system broke down. For several years, the U.S. government had complained about decisions issued by the WTO Appellate Body (AB). For example, the U.S. complained that the Appellate Body's jurisdiction was limited to matters of law but that the AB was issuing decisions that implicitly reviewed questions of fact as well. Also, the U.S. complained that the AB often made "new law" rather than simply applying existing law—an aggressive approach that the U.S. believed was at odds with the Appellate Body's limited judicial role in reviewing arbitral penal decisions. As one commentator put it: "The AB views itself as having a duty to make law. This is problematic because, in doing so, the AB is substituting its judgment for rules that otherwise would be a product of sensitive political negotiations." Richard H. Steinberg, *The Impending Dejudicialization of the WTO Dispute Settlement System?*, 112 Am. Soc'y Int'l L. Proc. 316,

317 (2018). Indeed, article 3.2 of the Dispute Settlement Understanding contains an internal tension: It tasks the Appellate Body with "clarify[ing] the existing provisions" while at the same time insisting that appellate rulings "cannot add to or diminish the rights and obligations" in the WTO agreements. Steinberg, *supra*, at 318–19. European states were generally comfortable with the Appellate Body's use of customary international law or general principles to engage in "gap filling" where WTO law was unclear or ambiguous, while the United States and other powerful countries were generally hostile to this approach.

Although several states shared these and other concerns, they mostly believed that the benefits of the Appellate Body system outweighed its drawbacks. The United States, on the other hand, considered the Appellate Body deeply flawed and sought to grind its work to a halt until the issues could be addressed with structural reforms. To halt the work of the Appellate Body, the U.S. used its veto power to block the appointment of any new members to the Appellate Body. The strategy was effective. Without replacement members, the Appellate Body's membership slowly dwindled as each member retired at the end of their term but could not be replaced. Eventually, the membership of the Appellate Body dipped below the minimum level required for it to hear cases. The Appellate Body was effectively placed in limbo and remains there with an uncertain future.

The substantive law applied by a WTO panel flows from legal obligations first articulated in GATT. Chief among them is a principle of non-discrimination, that is, not discriminating against goods from other countries. The first manifestation of this broad principle is Most-Favored-Nation (MFN) treatment, which is articulated in article 1 of the GATT; its position as the first article in the treaty signals its centrality to the framework. Under the MFN rule, "any advantage, favour, privilege or immunity granted by any contracting party to any product originating in or destined for any other country shall be accorded immediately and unconditionally to the like product originating in or destined for the territories of all other contracting parties." It is, on other words, a rule requiring like treatment among trading partners.

The second manifestation of the non-discrimination principle is found in article 3, which prohibits a government from discriminating against imported goods and favoring locally produced goods, such as imposing burdensome regulations or "internal" taxes on the imported goods that the local goods are exempt from. However, it is important to understand that this obligation only applies once the imported goods have landed in the local marketplace. States are still allowed to impose tariffs and duties on imported goods, but once these import requirements are fulfilled, the goods must receive like treatment with domestically produced goods. The rule is designed to prevent the use of internal taxes and regulation as a form of backdoor protectionism.

Of course, a central goal of the WTO process is to reduce tariffs and duties. As a result, the WTO-sponsored negotiations frequently result in new agreements that lower or eliminate tariffs for particular goods and industries. The overall trend within the WTO is toward *freer* trade, though strictly speaking it is incorrect to call the WTO a free trade zone simpliciter. When the trade agreements are violated, the WTO provides the dispute resolution system to enforce them. Generally speaking, member states comply with the WTO panel decisions because participation in the WTO system yields access to foreign markets on the best possible terms; economic self-interest demands that states work within the WTO framework rather than outside of it.

In the following case, European regulators prohibited the importation of beef with artificial growth hormones. The hormones were commonly used in American beef farming, thus causing a problem for American producers of beef trying to export their product to European markets. However, European regulators argued that the hormones were unsafe and banned the hormones on health and safety grounds. Under the WTO framework, health and safety regulations imposed on imported goods, such as the American beef, must be grounded in a scientific justification. The United States brought the following case to the WTO. Why did the WTO hold that the European regulations were invalid?

EC Measures Concerning Meat and Meat Products (Hormones)
World Trade Organization Appellate Body
January 16, 1998

1.   The European Communities, the United States and Canada appeal from certain issues of law and legal interpretations in the Panel Reports, *EC Measures Concerning Meat and Meat Products (Hormones)*. These two Panel Reports, circulated to Members of the World Trade Organization ("WTO") on 18 August 1997, were rendered by two Panels composed of the same three persons. These Panel Reports are similar, but they are not identical in every respect. The Panel in the complaint brought by the United States was established by the Dispute Settlement Body (the "DSB") on 20 May 1996. On 16 October 1996, the DSB established the Panel in the complaint brought by Canada. The European Communities and Canada agreed, on 4 November 1996, that the composition of the latter Panel would be identical to the composition of the Panel established at the request of the United States.

2.   The Panel dealt with a complaint against the European Communities relating to an EC prohibition of imports of meat and meat

products derived from cattle to which either the natural hormones: oestradiol-17, progesterone or testosterone, or the synthetic hormones: trenbolone acetate, zeranol or melengestrol acetate ("MGA"), had been administered for growth promotion purposes. This import prohibition was set forth in a series of Directives of the Council of Ministers that were enacted before 1 January 1995. . .

3.   Directive 81/602 prohibited the administration to farm animals of substances having a hormonal action and of substances having a thyrostatic action. It also prohibited the placing on the European market of both domestically produced and imported meat and meat products derived from farm animals to which such substances had been administered. Two exceptions to this prohibition were provided for. One exception covered substances with an oestrogenic, androgenic or gestagenic action when used for therapeutic or zootechnical purposes and administered by a veterinarian or under a veterinarian's responsibility. The other exception related to three natural hormones (oestradiol-17, progesterone and testosterone) and two synthetic hormones (trenbolone acetate and zeranol) used for growth promotion purposes if allowed under the regulations of the Member States of the European Economic Community ("EEC"), until a detailed examination of the effects of these substances could be carried out and until the EEC could take a decision on the use of these substances for growth promotion. The sixth hormone involved in this appeal, MGA, was not included in the second exception; it was covered by the general prohibition concerning substances having a hormonal or thyrostatic action.

4.   Seven years later, Directive 88/146 was promulgated prohibiting the administration to farm animals of the synthetic hormones: trenbolone acetate and zeranol, for any purposes, as well as the administration of the natural hormones: oestradiol-17, progesterone and testosterone, for growth promotion or fattening purposes. This Directive permitted Member States of the EEC to authorize, under specified conditions, the use of the three natural hormones for therapeutic and zootechnical purposes. Directive 88/146 explicitly prohibited both the intra-EEC trade and the importation from third countries of meat and meat products obtained from animals to which substances having oestrogenic, androgenic, gestagenic or thyrostatic action had been administered. Trade in meat and meat products derived from animals treated with such substances for therapeutic or zootechnical purposes was allowed only under certain conditions. Those conditions were set out in Directive 88/299.

5.   Effective as of 1 July 1997, Directives 81/602, 88/146 and 88/299 were repealed and replaced with Council Directive 96/22/EC of 29 April 1996 ("Directive 96/22"). This Directive maintains the prohibition of the administration to farm animals of substances having a hormonal or

thyrostatic action. As under the previously applicable Directives, it is prohibited to place on the market, or to import from third countries, meat and meat products from animals to which such substances, including the six hormones at issue in this dispute, were administered. This Directive also continues to allow Member States to authorize the administration, for therapeutic and zootechnical purposes, of certain substances having a hormonal or thyrostatic action. Under certain conditions, Directive 96/22 allows the placing on the market, and the importation from third countries, of meat and meat products from animals to which these substances have been administered for therapeutic and zootechnical purposes.

13. The European Communities claims that the Panel erred in law by not according deference to the following aspects of the EC measures: first, the decision of the European Communities to set and apply a level of sanitary protection higher than that recommended by the Codex Alimentarius (the "Codex") for the risks arising from the use for growth promotion of the hormones in dispute; second, the EC's scientific assessment and management of the risk from the hormones at issue, and third, the EC's adherence to the precautionary principle and its aversion to accepting any increased carcinogenic risk.

14. It is submitted by the European Communities that WTO panels should adopt a deferential "reasonableness" standard when reviewing a Member's decision to adopt a particular science policy or a Member's determination that a particular inference from the available data is scientifically plausible. To the European Communities, the Panel in this case imposed its own assessment of the scientific evidence.

15. The European Communities asserts that GATT 1947 panel reports rejected a de novo standard of review in relation to fact-finding, and that this approach has been maintained by panels established under the DSU. It is contended that the "reasonable deference standard of review" has been given expression in the Marrakesh Agreement Establishing the World Trade Organization (the "WTO Agreement") in Article 17.6 of the Agreement on Implementation of Article VI of the General Agreement on Tariffs and Trade 1994 (the "Anti-Dumping Agreement"). The European Communities considers that the principle of reasonable deference is applicable in all highly complex factual situations, including the assessment of the risks to human health arising from toxins and contaminants, and that therefore, the Panel applied an inappropriate standard of review in the present case.

16. The European Communities submits that the Panel erred in law in considering that the precautionary principle was only relevant for "provisional measures" under Article 5.7 of the SPS Agreement. The precautionary principle is already, in the view of the European Communities, a general customary rule of international law or at least a

general principle of law, the essence of which is that it applies not only in the management of a risk, but also in the assessment thereof. It is claimed that the Panel therefore erred in stating that the application of the precautionary principle "would not override the explicit wording in Articles 5.1 and 5.2 [of the SPS Agreement]," and in suggesting that that principle might be in conflict with those Articles. The European Communities asserts that Articles 5.1 and 5.2 and Annex A.4 of the SPS Agreement do not prescribe a particular type of risk assessment, but rather simply identify factors that need to be taken into account. Thus, these provisions do not prevent Members from being cautious when setting health standards in the face of conflicting scientific information and uncertainty.

17. The European Communities argues that the Panel failed to make an objective assessment of the facts and therefore did not comply with its obligations under Article 11 of the DSU. The Panel, it is alleged, disregarded or distorted the evidence with regard to both the MGA and the other five hormones at issue supplied by the Panel's experts, as well as the scientific evidence presented by the European Communities. In support of this contention, the European Communities submits that the Panel has manifestly distorted the views of both Dr. Lucier and Dr. Andre. According to the European Communities, contrary to what the Panel found, the evidence provided to the Panel by the majority of its own scientific experts indicated that there was a real risk of adverse effects arising from the use of the hormones at issue. It is also claimed that the Panel manifestly distorted the scientific evidence by considering that the 1995 European Communities Scientific Conference on Growth Promotion in Meat Production amounted to a risk assessment in the sense of Articles 5.1 and 5.2. The distinction made by the Panel between general studies on the health risks associated with hormones and specific studies addressing the health risks of residues in food of hormones used for growth promotion purposes was, in the view of the European Communities, devised by the Panel for the sole purpose of enabling it to conclude that the Monographs of the International Agency for Research on Cancer ("IARC") are not relevant as a risk assessment in this case. This, the European Communities asserts, amounts to a distortion of relevant scientific evidence. The European Communities also alleges that the Panel violated Article 11 of the DSU by discarding several articles and opinions of individual scientists invoked by the European Communities.

18. With regard to the problems relating to the control of the correct use of the hormones, the European Communities contends that it submitted convincing specific evidence to the Panel, but that the Panel either failed to take this evidence into account or failed to summarize it properly in the Panel Report. Finally, the Panel allegedly ignored the

arguments made by the European Communities as to why the situations compared by the Panel under Article 5.5 were not comparable. In rejecting the six reasons advanced by the European Communities as to why the distinction in the levels of sanitary protection between carbadox and olaquindox, on the one hand, and the hormones at issue in this dispute, on the other, is not arbitrary or unjustifiable, the European Communities argues that the Panel failed to take into account the evidence before it.

43. In the view of the United States, the claim of the European Communities that there is a generally accepted principle of international law which may be referred to as the "precautionary principle" is erroneous as a matter of international law. The United States does not consider that the "precautionary principle" represents a principle of customary international law; rather, it may be characterized as an "approach"—the content of which may vary from context to context. The SPS Agreement does recognize a precautionary approach; indeed, Article 5.7 permits the provisional adoption of SPS measures even where the relevant scientific evidence is insufficient. Thus, the United States believes that there is no need to invoke a "precautionary principle" in order to be risk-averse since the SPS Agreement, by its terms, recognizes the discretion of Members to determine their own level of sanitary protection. The European Communities does not explain how "the precautionary principle" affects the requirements in the SPS Agreement that a measure be "based on" scientific principles and a risk assessment, and not maintained without sufficient scientific evidence. The EC's invocation of a "precautionary principle" cannot create a risk assessment where there is none, nor can a "principle" create "sufficient scientific evidence" where there is none.

60. The Panel did not take a position on whether the "precautionary principle" constituted part of the body of international law. Rather, in Canada's view, the Panel acknowledged that the "precautionary principle" was reflected in Article 5.7 of the SPS Agreement, and correctly held that the "precautionary principle" could not override Articles 5.1 and 5.2, or any other provision of the SPS Agreement. Canada also regards the issue of whether the "precautionary principle" is "built into" other provisions of the SPS Agreement as irrelevant in this appeal. Moreover, the European Communities has not explained what is meant by the "precautionary principle" having been "built into" other provisions of the SPS Agreement, and how this could in any way affect the conclusions of the Panel. The "precautionary principle" should be characterized as the "precautionary approach" because it has not yet become part of public international law. Canada considers the precautionary approach or concept as an emerging principle of international law, which may in the future crystallize into one of the

"general principles of law recognized by civilized nations", within the meaning of Article 38(1)(c) of the Statute of the International Court of Justice.

120. We are asked by the European Communities to reverse the finding of the Panel relating to the precautionary principle. The Panel's finding and its supporting statements are set out in the Panel Reports in the following terms:

> The European Communities also invokes the precautionary principle in support of its claim that its measures in dispute are based on a risk assessment. To the extent that this principle could be considered as part of customary international law and be used to interpret Articles 5.1 and 5.2 on the assessment of risks as a customary rule of interpretation of public international law (as that phrase is used in Article 3.2 of the DSU), we consider that this principle would not override the explicit wording of Articles 5.1 and 5.2 outlined above, in particular since the precautionary principle has been incorporated and given a specific meaning in Article 5.7 of the SPS Agreement. We note, however, that the European Communities has explicitly stated in this case that it is not invoking Article 5.7.

> We thus find that the precautionary principle cannot override our findings made above, namely that the EC import ban of meat and meat products from animals treated with any of the five hormones at issue for growth promotion purposes, in so far as it also applies to meat and meat products from animals treated with any of these hormones in accordance with good practice, is, from a substantive point of view, not based on a risk assessment. (underlining added)

121. The basic submission of the European Communities is that the precautionary principle is, or has become, "a general customary rule of international law" or at least "a general principle of law." Referring more specifically to Articles 5.1 and 5.2 of the SPS Agreement, applying the precautionary principle means, in the view of the European Communities, that it is not necessary for all scientists around the world to agree on the "possibility and magnitude" of the risk, nor for all or most of the WTO Members to perceive and evaluate the risk in the same way. It is also stressed that Articles 5.1 and 5.2 do not prescribe a particular type of risk assessment and do not prevent Members from being cautious in their risk assessment exercise. The European Communities goes on to state that its measures here at stake were precautionary in nature and satisfied the requirements of Articles 2.2 and 2.3, as well as of Articles 5.1, 5.2, 5.4, 5.5 and 5.6 of the SPS Agreement.

122. The United States does not consider that the "precautionary principle" represents customary international law and suggests it is more an "approach" than a "principle." Canada, too, takes the view that the precautionary principle has not yet been incorporated into the corpus of public international law; however, it concedes that the "precautionary approach" or "concept" is "an emerging principle of law" which may in the future crystallize into one of the "general principles of law recognized by civilized nations" within the meaning of Article 38(1)(c) of the Statute of the International Court of Justice.

123. The status of the precautionary principle in international law continues to be the subject of debate among academics, law practitioners, regulators and judges. The precautionary principle is regarded by some as having crystallized into a general principle of customary international environmental law. Whether it has been widely accepted by Members as a principle of general or customary international law appears less than clear. We consider, however, that it is unnecessary, and probably imprudent, for the Appellate Body in this appeal to take a position on this important, but abstract, question. We note that the Panel itself did not make any definitive finding with regard to the status of the precautionary principle in international law and that the precautionary principle, at least outside the field of international environmental law, still awaits authoritative formulation.

124. It appears to us important, nevertheless, to note some aspects of the relationship of the precautionary principle to the SPS Agreement. First, the principle has not been written into the SPS Agreement as a ground for justifying SPS measures that are otherwise inconsistent with the obligations of Members set out in particular provisions of that Agreement. Secondly, the precautionary principle indeed finds reflection in Article 5.7 of the SPS Agreement. We agree, at the same time, with the European Communities, that there is no need to assume that Article 5.7 exhausts the relevance of a precautionary principle. It is reflected also in the sixth paragraph of the preamble and in Article 3.3. These explicitly recognize the right of Members to establish their own appropriate level of sanitary protection, which level may be higher (i.e., more cautious) than that implied in existing international standards, guidelines and recommendations. Thirdly, a panel charged with determining, for instance, whether "sufficient scientific evidence" exists to warrant the maintenance by a Member of a particular SPS measure may, of course, and should, bear in mind that responsible, representative governments commonly act from perspectives of prudence and precaution where risks of irreversible, e.g. life-terminating, damage to human health are concerned. Lastly, however, the precautionary principle does not, by itself, and without a clear textual directive to that effect, relieve a panel from the duty of applying the normal (i.e., customary international law)

principles of treaty interpretation in reading the provisions of the SPS Agreement.

125. We accordingly agree with the finding of the Panel that the precautionary principle does not override the provisions of Articles 5.1 and 5.2 of the SPS Agreement.

NOTES & QUESTIONS

1.   *The Precautionary Principle.* What role did the Precautionary Principle play in the panel's decision? In broad brushstrokes, the precautionary principle suggests that regulations should be crafted to reduce the *risk* of health or environmental harm. Thus stated, the principle suggests that even in the absence of definitive scientific evidence that a particular practice is harmful, the practice should still be regulated based on an actuarial assessment that the practice might be harmful. The European Community cited the precautionary principle in support of its decision to ban the hormones, while the United States and Canada argued that the precautionary principle was not a principle of international law, that is, not yet incorporated into customary international law and therefore not a valid source of law for the WTO to apply in evaluating the legitimacy of the European regulation. Did the WTO resolve this important methodological question or did they punt it? Ultimately, the appellate body concluded that the principle was already embodied in provisions of the SPS agreement and therefore could not override them. For a discussion, see Jan Bohanes, *Risk Regulation in WTO Law: A Procedure-Based Approach to the Precautionary Principle*, 40 Colum. J. Transnat'l L. 323, 336–37 (2002) ("While [the appellate body] declined to adopt a clear position on the precise meaning and legal status of the precautionary principle under international law, it held that the precautionary principle could not in any case override the explicit wording of articles 5.1 and 5.2 of the SPS Agreement, and that the EC had violated the SPS Agreement by failing to base its hormone ban on a risk assessment.").

2.   *Reviving the Appellate Body.* As noted at the beginning of this section, the WTO Appellate Body was put on ice in 2019 by the United States. Many observers have described this as an existential crisis for the WTO Appellate Body, which had a reputation as an amazing success story for international law. How might other states restart the process? One possibility is for other states to just wait out the United States and see if it will start approving Appellate Body members again. Another approach is for the other state parties of the WTO to accede to the wishes of the United States and open negotiations for major reforms of the WTO panel process. What reforms would respond to the U.S. concerns? Is there any way of preventing or limiting "activist judges" on the Appellate Body? One possibility would be to amend the Dispute Settlement Understanding to clarify that the Appellate Body should not engage in gap filling, should not invoke customary international law in its decision, and should not issue advisory opinions. If you were advising the United States government, would

you recommend, based on these concessions, that it release its hold on appointing new Appellate Body members? See Bruce Hirsh, *Resolving the WTO Appellate Body Crisis*, National Foreign Trade Council (Dec. 2019).

B. INVESTOR-STATE ARBITRATION

Investor-state arbitration shares some similarity with the WTO panel arbitration described in Section A. WTO disputes are formally between two states, though usually one state, such as the United States in the beef hormones dispute, is acting on behalf of its producers who are harmed by the other state's conduct. Similarly, investor-state arbitration involves a combination of private and public actors, though in this case the private corporation aggrieved by the foreign state is a formal party to the arbitration. Consequently, although investor-state arbitration is a creature of public international law, since it applies norms agreed to between states, one side of the arbitration is always a private entity.

In order to encourage foreign investment—which is essential for the free flow of capital across international borders—states have signed agreements that afford certain protections to foreign investors. These agreements, often called Bilateral Investment Treaties (BITs), obligate the state to treat the foreign investors fairly, in exchange for a reciprocal obligation from the other state to treat foreign investors from the other country in like fashion. Since the 1980s, a couple *thousand* BITs have been signed, coinciding with a global expansion of foreign direct investment. In addition to the BITs, investment protections are also contained in some subject-specific multilateral investment treaties. Finally, some trade treaties such as NAFTA include some investment protection provisions.

To take just one obvious example where foreign investment can be dangerous, imagine a foreigner who invests a substantial amount of money in a business interest in a state, only to see the industry nationalized and turned into a crown corporation, or otherwise expropriated in some other fashion by the government. Foreign investors are uniquely vulnerable to such discriminatory deprivations; this risk stops foreign investors from providing much needed capital for expanding a state's economy. Bilateral investment treaties are designed to afford legal protections that lower that risk.

Occasionally, though, foreign investors are mistreated or otherwise allege that a state has violated its obligations under a BIT. Pursuant to these BITs, disputes can be resolved by arbitration, often through the auspices of the International Center for the Settlement of Investment Disputes (ICSID), which currently includes 161 member states, and formally is a subdivision of the World Bank. The working of the Center is governed by the ICSID Convention, which was first signed in 1966. However, arbitration may also occur outside of ICSID under the auspices of another international arbitration organization, such as the United Nations Commission on International Trade Law (UNCITRAL). Or, if the relevant investment protection is contained in a trade agreement such as NAFTA, the aggrieved investor may seek arbitration under that treaty framework. Either way, the hearing panels are true arbitration panels, that is, ad hoc tribunals with arbitrators appointed to hear individual cases, not standing courts with full-time professional judges. If the investor wins, the state will be ordered to pay damages. If the state "wins" because the panel finds that it acted appropriately, the investor will not be liable for damages.

The U.S.-Argentina BIT was signed in 1991 and entered into force in 1994. In the following case, an American energy company named LG&E invested in Argentina's newly formed gas entity, which was in the process of being privatized. The American company made the investment after the Argentinian government made representations regarding the gas rates that it would charge its customers and an Argentinian policy of tying its currency to the U.S. Dollar, thus reducing the risk that local currency fluctuation might devalue the investment. But when Argentina's economy was struck with severe deflation, the government had to radically lower the gas rates it charged its customers, otherwise gas would have remained unaffordable to the local population. Argentina also stopped pegging its currency to the American Dollar. These and other economic changes substantially reduced the value of the American investment. LG&E filed for arbitration under ICSID.

Of particular issue in the arbitration was the interpretation and application of article XI of the U.S.-Argentina BIT, which provides that the "treaty shall not preclude the application by either Party of measures necessary for the maintenance of public order, the fulfillment of its obligations with respect to the maintenance or restoration of international peace or security, or the Protection of its own essential security interests." As you read the following case, ask yourself whether an economic crisis can trigger a state's "essential security interests." What recourse does an investor have if a state takes remedial measures during an emergency that destroys the value of the investment?

LG&E Energy Corp. v. The Argentine Republic

ICSID Case No. ARB/02/1 (Oct. 3, 2006)
46 I.L.M. 40 (2007)

1.   Claimants, LG&E Energy Corp. and LG&E Capital Corp. are corporations created and existing under the laws of the Commonwealth of Kentucky, in the United States of America, with domestic and foreign operations. LG&E International Inc. is a corporation organized and existing under the laws of the State of Delaware, United States of

America. Claimants hereinafter will be referred to collectively as "LG&E" or "Claimants."

2. LG&E has a shareholding interest in three local, gas distributing companies in Argentina created and existing under the laws of Argentina by commandment of the Argentine Government: Distribuidora de Gas del Centro ("Centro"), Distribuidora de Gas Cuyana S.A. ("Cuyana") and Gas Natural BAN S.A. ("GasBan"), hereinafter collectively referred to as "the licensees." LG&E owns a controlling equity interest in Centro and minority equity interests in GasBan and Cuyana.

3. Respondent is the Argentine Republic, which along with the United States of America, is a party to the Convention on the Settlement of Investment Disputes between States and Nationals of other States ("ICSID Convention" or "Convention"), ratified by the Argentine Republic in 1994 and by the United States of America in 1966. The Bilateral Investment Treaty between the United States of America and the Argentine Republic Concerning the Reciprocal Encouragement and Protection of Investments was signed on 14 November 1991 ("BIT", "the Bilateral Treaty" or the "Treaty") (and entered into force on 20 October 1994).

4. On 31 January 2002 the Centre's Secretary-General registered Claimants' Request for Arbitration in accordance with Article 36(3) of the ICSID Convention. In accordance with Rule 7 of the Rules of Procedure for the Institution of Conciliation and Arbitration Proceedings ("the Institution Rules"), the Secretary-General gave notice to the parties of the registration of Claimants' Request and invited them to constitute an Arbitral Tribunal as soon as possible.

5. Forthwith, the parties agreed that the Arbitral Tribunal should be formed by three arbitrators, one appointed by the Claimants, another by the Argentine Republic and the third one, called to preside over the Tribunal, would be appointed by the Centre's Secretary-General in accordance with the method agreed upon by the parties.

Factual Background

33. Before considering the merits of the dispute, the Tribunal deems it necessary to set forth the facts that it considered relevant for its decision.

34. The present claims are to be viewed against the historic background and especially the economic upheaval in Argentina and the Government's reaction to the several economic crises suffered by the country in the late 1980s and 1990s.

35. In the late 1980s, Argentina underwent an economic crisis characterized by deep recession and hyperinflation. As part of its economic recovery plan, the Government began an ambitious

privatization program with the enactment of the State Reform Law in August 1989. Within this framework, large Government-owned businesses and entities were privatized or granted on concession.

36. One March 27, 1991, Argentina enacted Law No. 23,928, referred to as the *Convertibility Law*, which ordered the implementation of a fixed exchange rate, pegging the *austral* (the then-Argentine currency) to the United States dollar. The Convertibility Law also banned price or value indexation.

37. One of the primary goals of the Government's plan was the privatization of *Gas del Estado S.E.*, the national natural-gas transport and distribution monopoly. Pursuant to the Government's privatization plan, investors could purchase shares in newly-formed, licensed private corporations that would offer gas transport and distribution services. Such shares were available to domestic and foreign investors.

38. To implement its plan, the Government enacted in June 1992, the *Ley del Gas* ("Gas Law"), which established a comprehensive regulatory structure for the provision of natural-gas transport and distribution services, and created a public agency, called *Ente Nacional Regulador del Gas* (ENARGAS) to oversee the industry.

39. The Gas Law adopted a tariff structure under which ENARGAS would collect tariffs on the price of gas paid by consumers. Under the provisions of the Gas Law, ENARGAS was required to set the transport and distribution tariffs at fair and reasonable levels that would allow licensed utility providers to recoup a "reasonable rate of return," after accounting for costs, defined as a rate similar to that applied to activities of similar risk and adequately related to the level of efficiency and satisfactory performance of the transport or distribution service. Profitability was to be measured against other activities of comparable risk.

44. By Decree No. 1189/92, published on 17 July 1992, Argentina approved the procedure for the privatization of *Gas del Estado S.E.* It was restructured into two distinct transport business units and eight separate distribution business units, each responsible for a geographic region of the country. Each of the ten business units were transferred to the newly-created companies, which were to operate with a license under the legal framework in force.

45. An international bidding process was set in place by Resolution No. 874/92 issued by the Ministry of Public Works and Services and conducted pursuant to the *Pliego de Bases y Condiciones para la Licitación* ("Bidding Rules"). Under these Bidding Rules, both foreign and domestic investors were free to bid on the shares. The purpose of the Bidding Process was the purchase and sale of the majority interest in each of the licensed companies created by Decree No. 1189/92. Three of

those majority interests were sold during that bidding process: 60% of Cuyana's shares, 70% of GasBan's shares, and 90% of Centro's shares. . .

49. The privatization scheme created by Respondent targeted foreign investors because foreign capital was deemed essential for the successful operation of the Government's economic recovery plan. Foreign investors were encouraged to purchase shares with guarantees, such as tariffs calculated in U.S. dollars, automatic and periodic adjustments to the tariffs based on the PPI, a clear legal framework that could not be unilaterally modified, and the granting of "licenses" instead of "concessions" with a view to offering the highest degree of protection to prospective investors. . . .

51. During this period, Argentina undertook to provide enhanced legal protection to investors so as to attract foreign investment in support of its privatization scheme. The Respondent ratified several treaties relating to international investment obligations, such as the ICSID Convention and a great number of bilateral investment treaties, including the Argentina-U.S. Bilateral Investment Treaty at issue in this dispute. As mentioned above, the Convertibility Law, which pegged the peso to the U.S. dollar, was also enacted at this time.

52. In reliance on the legal guarantees offered by the Argentine Government for the privatized energy industry, and based on its positive prior experience investing in the privatized Argentine gas market in 1992, Claimants chose to purchase shares of three licensed companies in the gas-distribution market. . .

Economic Crisis and the Emergence of the Dispute (1999–2001)

54. A new economic crisis developed in Argentina in the late 1990s. In the third quarter of 1998, the Argentine economy plunged into a period of recession that was to last four years and triggered, in Respondent's opinion, the worst economic crisis since Argentina's inception in 1810.

55. In 1999, Argentina's Gross Domestic Product ("GDP") decreased causing a dramatic fall in domestic prices. Private consumption and investments began falling in August 1998 and Argentina entered a deflationary period. The period was marked by widespread decline in the value of assets located in Argentina. By the end of the 1990s, many economists considered the peso as overvalued, and predicted that the currency board would have to be abandoned, which would inevitably devalue the peso. Argentina's country risk premium increased, gradually excluding the country from the international credit market. These economic indicators were accompanied by social problems— unemployment, poverty and indigence levels began to increase. On 10 December 1999, Mr. Fernando de la Rúa took office as the President of Argentina. His administration tried to maintain the peg of the Argentine peso to the U.S. dollar as mandated by the Convertibility Law.

56. Against this background, public services rates, as specified in the contracts, were due to be adjusted in January 2000 based on the PPI. At the time, the United States was experiencing a high inflationary period, while Argentina was experiencing a significant deflationary period. As established in the Gas Law, the tariffs were to be adjusted to reflect changes in the cost structure of utility providers. Argentina considered that the pending tariff adjustments based on the U.S. rate were unreasonable because they would result in a significant increase in utility rates within a recessionary and deflationary context. . .

62. ENARGAS declared in November 2001 that no further adjustments to the tariffs would be approved. . . No further adjustments to the tariffs have occurred to date.

The Emergency Law (January 6, 2002)

63. Argentina's crisis deepened at the end of 2001. The Government experienced increased difficulties in repaying its foreign debt. As poverty and unemployment soared, Argentines feared that the Government would default on its debt and immobilize bank deposits. Therefore, savings were massively withdrawn from the banks. . . Amid widespread discontent and public demonstrations, including violence that claimed tens of lives, President De la Rúa and his Cabinet resigned on 20 December 2001. A succession of presidents took office and quickly resigned.

64. Finally, President Eduardo Duhalde took office and implemented a new economic plan, which contained measures that form the additional claim submitted by Claimants. On 6 January 2002, Congress enacted Law No. 25,561, the Public Emergency and Foreign Exchange System Reform Law (known as "the Emergency Law"). The Emergency Law abrogated the Convertibility Law so that the one-to-one peg of the Argentine peso to the United States dollar no longer existed. The Emergency Law provided for the switch into Argentine pesos of debts owed to the banking system, debts arising from management contracts governed by public law, and debts under private agreements. The law further provided for the renegotiation of private and public agreements to adapt them to the new exchange system.

65. The Emergency Law adopted measures modifying public-service contracts, such as establishing that tariffs and prices for public services were to be calculated in pesos, instead of U.S. dollars; abolishing all clauses calling for tariff adjustments in U.S. dollars or other foreign currencies; eliminating all indexing mechanisms; and directing the Executive Branch to renegotiate all public-service contracts.

66. By Presidential Decree No. 214 of 3 February 2002, the Government adopted a currency conversion scheme under which all obligations payable in dollars existing on the date of enactment of the

Emergency Law would be converted into pesos at the fixed one-to-one exchange rate.

67. The switch into Argentine pesos, also called "pesification," which affected the entire Argentine economy, was characterized by Respondent as a necessary process to return the country to the path of economic stability...

Request for Relief

132. In light of the foregoing, the Tribunal concludes that Argentina violated the fair and equitable treatment provision in the Bilateral Treaty for the following reasons.

133. Emerging from the economic crisis of the late 1980s, Argentina created an economic recovery plan mainly dependent upon foreign capital. Argentina prepared with the investment banks an attractive framework of laws and regulations that addressed the specific concerns of foreign investors with respect to the country risks involved in Argentina. In light of these risks, Claimants relied upon certain key guarantees in the Gas Law and implementing regulations, such as calculation of the tariffs in U.S. dollars before their conversion into pesos, the semi-annual PPI adjustments, tariffs set to provide sufficient revenues to cover all the costs and a reasonable rate of return, and compensation in the event that the Government altered the tariff scheme. Having created specific expectations among investors, Argentina was bound by its obligations concerning the investment guarantees vis-à-vis public utility licensees, and in particular, the gas-distribution licensees. The abrogation of these specific guarantees violates the stability and predictability underlying the standard of fair and equitable treatment.

134. Specifically, it was unfair and inequitable to pass a law discarding the guarantee... that the tariffs would be calculated in U.S. dollars and then converted into pesos. As pointed out by Claimants, this was not merely an economic and monetary policy of the Argentine Government which materialized through the Convertibility Law. Rather, it was a guarantee laid down in the tariff system. This guarantee was very important to investors to protect their investment, which was made in dollars, from a subsequent devaluation of the peso...

139. The Tribunal nevertheless recognizes the economic hardships that occurred during this period, and certain political and social realities that at the time may have influenced the Government's response to the growing economic difficulties. Certainly, LG&E was aware of the risks inherent in investing in a foreign State. But here, the Tribunal is of the opinion that Argentina went too far by completely dismantling the very legal framework constructed to attract investors.

General Comments on Article XI

204. Article XI of the Bilateral Treaty provides: "This Treaty shall not preclude the application by either Party of measures necessary for the maintenance of public order, the fulfillment of its obligations with respect to the maintenance or restoration of international peace or security, or the protection of its own essential security interests."

205. The Tribunal's analysis to determine the applicability of Article XI of the Bilateral Treaty is twofold. First, the Tribunal must decide whether the conditions that existed in Argentina during the relevant period were such that the State was entitled to invoke the protections included in Article XI of the Treaty. Second, the Tribunal must determine whether the measures implemented by Argentina were necessary to maintain public order or to protect its essential security interests, albeit in violation of the Treaty.

206. The Tribunal reiterates that to carry out the two-fold analysis already mentioned, it shall apply first, the Treaty, second, the general international law to the extent that is necessary and third, the Argentine domestic law. The Tribunal underscores that the claims and defenses mentioned derive from the Treaty and that, to the extent required for the interpretation and application of its provisions, the general international law shall be applied.

Necessary Nature of the Measures Adopted

215. Argentina defends the measures it implemented as necessary to maintain public order and protect its essential security interests. It contends that under any interpretation, the financial crisis, riots and chaos of the years 2000 through 2002 in Argentina constitute a national emergency sufficient to invoke the protections of Article XI.

216. Concerning "public order," Respondent reinforces its arguments on the necessary nature of the measures it had implemented by pointing to numerous reports of waves of sudden economic catastrophe, massive strikes involving millions of workers, fatal shootings, the shut down of schools, businesses, transportation, energy, banking and health services, demonstrations across the country, and a plummeting stock market, culminating in a "final massive social explosion" in which five presidential administrations resigned within a month. Under these circumstances, Argentina argues that price controls by the Argentine Government would have been fully justifiable under the public order provisions of Article XI. Additionally, Respondent argues that actions to freeze price increases in the gas-distribution sector were justifiable to maintain the country's basic infrastructure, which was dependent on natural gas energy.

217. Argentina also defends its measures as necessary to protect its essential security interests. Argentina asserts that Article XI's "essential

security interests" element encompasses economic and political interests, as well as national military defense interests. Respondent cites several United States' officials who have propounded a broad interpretation of "essential security interests."

218. Respondent attacks Claimants' basis for asserting that the clause is narrow, reserved only for military actions. Furthermore, in all of the cases cited by Claimants, the point was whether the use of military force was justifiable under international law—a narrow reading of essential security clauses in these cases would be expected.

219. Because economic stability, in Respondent's view, falls within a State's essential security interests, Respondent defends the measures it took as necessary to protect its economic interests. Respondent argues that during the crisis period, the health, safety and security of the Argentine State and its people were threatened, and that the economic melt-down had the potential to cause catastrophic state failure. Thus, the public emergency that Argentina declared and the Emergency Law the Government passed altering its financial arrangements were necessary to protect the State's essential security interests.

220. Claimants identify the four measures at issue here— suspension and abolishment of the PPI adjustment, freezing the gas-distribution tariffs, and abandonment of the calculation of the tariffs in dollars, all taken unilaterally—and contend that Respondent must prove that each measure was necessary in order to maintain public order and protect Argentina's essential security interests. By the term "necessary," Claimants contend that these measures must have been the only option available to Argentina in order to invoke protection under Article XI.

221. Claimants define public order measures as "actions taken pursuant to a state's police powers, particularly in respect of public health and safety." Based on this definition, Claimants state that the measures in dispute in this case were not aimed at bringing calmness to the collapse that was threatening the country. Consequently, such measures cannot be deemed necessary to maintain public order.

222. With respect to "essential security interests," Claimants reiterate that such interests do not include economic interests—only defense or military concerns. They compare a State's interest in essential security to a national security threat, while a "national emergency," the alleged circumstance in which Respondent invokes the protection, has an entirely different meaning. In Claimants' view, economic crises should not be elevated to an essential security interest, and that doing so would disregard the object and purpose of the Treaty. They argue that an economic crisis is precisely when investors need the protections offered by a BIT.

223. Claimants argue that in any event, Article XI does not relieve Argentina of its obligations to compensate Claimants for damages suffered as a result of breaches of the Treaty.

224. Claimants also reject the possibility of applying the rule provided by Article IV(3) of the Treaty. They are of the opinion that this provision does not apply to economic crises, and it does not authorize the host State to revoke or suspend the protections given to foreign investors

225. Claimants invoke Article 27 of the International Law Commission's Draft Articles on State Responsibility. Claimants contend that even if the state of necessity defense is available to Argentina under the circumstances of this case, Article 27 of the Draft Articles makes clear that Argentina's obligations to Claimants are not extinguished and Argentina must compensate Claimants for losses incurred as a result of the Government's actions. Article 27 provides that "invocation of a circumstance precluding wrongfulness in accordance with this chapter is without prejudice to (a) compliance with the obligation in question... (b) the question of compensation for any material loss caused by the act in question."

The Tribunal's Analysis

226. In the judgment of the Tribunal, from 1 December 2001 until 26 April 2003, Argentina was in a period of crisis during which it was necessary to enact measures to maintain public order and protect its essential security interests.

227. The Tribunal does not consider that the initial date for the state of necessity is the effective date of the Emergency Law, January 6, 2002, because, in the first place, the emergency had already started when the law was enacted. Second, should the Tribunal take as the initial date the day when the Emergency Law became effective, it might be reasonable to take as its closing date the day when the state of emergency is lifted by the Argentine State, a fact that has not yet taken place since the law has been extended several times.

228. It is to be pointed out that there is a factual emergency that began on 1 December 1, 2001 and ended on April 26, 2003, on account of the reasons detailed below, as well as a legislative emergency, that begins and ends with the enactment and abrogation of the Emergency Law, respectively. It should be borne in mind that Argentina declared its state of necessity and has extended such state until the present. Indeed, the country has issued a record number of decrees since 1901, accounting for the fact that the emergency periods in Argentina have been longer than the non-emergency periods. Emergency periods should be only strictly exceptional and should be applied exclusively when faced with extraordinary circumstances. Hence, in order to allege state of necessity as a State defense, it will be necessary to prove the existence of serious

public disorders. Based on the evidence available, the Tribunal has determined that the situation ended at the time President Kirchner was elected.

229. Thus, Argentina is excused under Article XI from liability for any breaches of the Treaty between December 1, 2001 and April 26, 2003. The reasons are the following:

230. These dates coincide, on the one hand, with the Government's announcement of the measure freezing funds, which prohibited bank account owners from withdrawing more than one thousand pesos monthly and, on the other hand, with the election of President Kirchner. The Tribunal marks these dates as the beginning and end of the period of extreme crisis in view of the notorious events that occurred during this period.

231. Evidence has been put before the Tribunal that the conditions as of December 2001 constituted the highest degree of public disorder and threatened Argentina's essential security interests. This was not merely a period of "economic problems" or "business cycle fluctuation" as Claimants described. Extremely severe crises in the economic, political and social sectors reached their apex and converged in December 2001, threatening total collapse of the Government and the Argentine State.

232. All of the major economic indicators reached catastrophic proportions in December 2001. An accelerated deterioration of Argentina's Gross Domestic Product (GDP) began in December 2001, falling 10 to 15 percent faster than the previous year. Private consumption dramatically dropped in the fourth quarter of 2001, accompanied by a severe drop in domestic prices. Argentina experienced at this time widespread decline in the prices and in the value of assets located in Argentina. The Merval Index, which measures the share value of the main companies of Argentina listed on the Buenos Aires Stock Exchange, experienced a dramatic decline of 60% by the end of December 2001. By mid-2001, Argentina's country risk premium was the highest premium worldwide, rendering Argentina unable to borrow on the international markets, and reflecting the severity of the economic crisis.

233. At this time, capital outflow was a critical problem for the Government. In the fourth quarter of 2001, the Central Bank of Argentina lost US$ 11 billion in liquid reserves, amounting to 40%. The banking system lost 25% of its total deposits.

234. While unemployment, poverty and indigency rates gradually increased from the beginning of 1998, they reached intolerable levels by December 2001. Unemployment reached almost 25%, and almost half of the Argentine population was living below poverty. The entire healthcare system teetered on the brink of collapse. Prices of pharmaceuticals soared as the country plunged deeper into the deflationary period,

becoming unavailable for low-income people. Hospitals suffered a severe shortage of basic supplies. Investments in infrastructure and equipment for public hospitals declined as never before. These conditions prompted the Government to declare the nationwide health emergency to ensure the population's access to basic health care goods and services. At the time, one quarter of the population could not afford the minimum amount of food required to ensure their subsistence. Given the level of poverty and lack of access to healthcare and proper nutrition, disease followed. Facing increased pressure to provide social services and security to the masses of indigent and poor people, the Government was forced to decrease its per capita spending on social services by 74%.

235. By December 2001, there was widespread fear among the population that the Government would default on its debt and seize bank deposits to prevent the bankruptcy of the banking system. Faced with a possible run on banks, the Government issued on 1 December 2001 Decree of Necessity and Emergency No. 1570/01. The law triggered widespread social discontent. Widespread violent demonstrations and protests brought the economy to a halt, including effectively shutting down transportation systems. Looting and rioting followed in which tens of people were killed as the conditions in the country approached anarchy. A curfew was imposed to curb lootings.

236. By 20 December 2001, President De la Rúa resigned. His presidency was followed by a succession of presidents over the next days, until Mr. Eduardo Duhalde took office on 1 January 2002, charged with the mandate to bring the country back to normal conditions.

237. All of these devastating conditions—economic, political, social—in the aggregate triggered the protections afforded under Article XI of the Treaty to maintain order and control the civil unrest.

238. The Tribunal rejects the notion that Article XI is only applicable in circumstances amounting to military action and war. Certainly, the conditions in Argentina in December 2001 called for immediate, decisive action to restore civil order and stop the economic decline. To conclude that such a severe economic crisis could not constitute an essential security interest is to diminish the havoc that the economy can wreak on the lives of an entire population and the ability of the Government to lead. When a State's economic foundation is under siege, the severity of the problem can equal that of any military invasion.

239. Claimants contend that the necessity defense should not be applied here because the measures implemented by Argentina were not the only means available to respond to the crisis. The Tribunal rejects this assertion. Article XI refers to situations in which a State has no choice but to act. A State may have several responses at its disposal to maintain public order or protect its essential security interests. In this

sense, it is recognized that Argentina's suspension of the calculation of tariffs in U.S. dollars and the PPI adjustment of tariffs was a legitimate way of protecting its social and economic system.

240. The Tribunal has determined that Argentina's enactment of the Emergency Law was a necessary and legitimate measure on the part of the Argentine Government. Under the conditions the Government faced in December 2001, time was of the essence in crafting a response. Drafted in just six days, the Emergency Law took the swift, unilateral action against the economic crisis that was necessary at the time.

241. In drafting the Emergency Law, the Government considered the interests of the foreign investors, and concluded that it "could not leave sectors of the economy operating with the brutally dollarized economy—[the] system was in crisis, so we had to cut off that process, and we had to establish a new set of rules for everybody." Argentina's strategy to deal with the thousands of public utility contracts that could not be individually assessed during the period of crisis was to implement "across-the-board solutions" and then renegotiate the contracts. The Tribunal accepts the necessity of approaching enactment of a stop-gap measure in this manner and therefore rejects Claimants' objection that Argentina's unilateral response was not necessary.

242. The Tribunal accepts that the provisions of the Emergency Law that abrogated calculation of the tariffs in U.S. dollars and PPI adjustments, as well as freezing tariffs were necessary measures to deal with the extremely serious economic crisis. Indeed, it would be unreasonable to conclude that during this period the Government should have implemented a tariff increase pursuant to an index pegged to an economy experiencing a high inflationary period (the United States). The severe devaluation of the peso against the dollar renders the Government's decision to abandon the calculation of tariffs in dollars reasonable. Similarly, the Government deemed that freezing gas tariffs altogether during the crisis period was necessary, and Claimants have not provided any reason as to why such measure would not provide immediate relief from the crisis.

243. The Tribunal will now turn to Article IV(3) of the Treaty, which provides:

> Nationals or companies of either Party whose investments suffer losses in the territory of the other Party owing to war or other armed conflict, revolution, *state of national emergency*, insurrection, civil disturbance or other similar events shall be accorded treatment by such other Party no less favorable than that accorded to its own nationals or companies or to nationals or companies of any third country, whichever is the more

favorable treatment, as regards any measures it adopts in relation to such losses. (Emphasis added)

244. Article IV(3) of the Treaty confirms that the States Party to the Bilateral Treaty contemplated the state of national emergency as a separate category of exceptional circumstances. That is in line with the Tribunal's interpretation of Article XI of the Treaty. Furthermore, the Tribunal has determined, as a factual matter that the grave crisis in Argentina lasted from December 1, 2001 until April 26, 2003. It has not been shown convincingly to the Tribunal that during that period the provisions of Article IV(3) of the Treaty have been violated by Argentina. On the contrary, during that period, the measures taken by Argentina were "across the board."

245. In the previous analysis, the Tribunal has determined that the conditions in Argentina from December 1, 2001 until April 26, 2003 were such that Argentina is excused from liability for the alleged violation of its Treaty obligations due to the responsive measures it enacted. The concept of excusing a State for the responsibility for violation of its international obligations during what is called a "state of necessity" or "state of emergency" also exists in international law. While the Tribunal considers that the protections afforded by Article XI have been triggered in this case, and are sufficient to excuse Argentina's liability, the Tribunal recognizes that satisfaction of the state of necessity standard as it exists in international law (reflected in Article 25 of the ILC's Draft Articles on State Responsibility) supports the Tribunal's conclusion. . .

257. The essential interests of the Argentine State were threatened in December 2001. It faced an extremely serious threat to its existence, its political and economic survival, to the possibility of maintaining its essential services in operation, and to the preservation of its internal peace. There is no serious evidence in the record that Argentina contributed to the crisis resulting in the state of necessity. In this circumstance, an economic recovery package was the only means to respond to the crisis. Although there may have been a number of ways to draft the economic recovery plan, the evidence before the Tribunal demonstrates that an across-the-board response was necessary, and the tariffs on public utilities had to be addressed. It cannot be said that any other State's rights were seriously impaired by the measures taken by Argentina during the crisis. Finally, as addressed above, Article XI of the Treaty exempts Argentina of responsibility for measures enacted during the state of necessity. . .

Conclusions of the Tribunal

266. Based on the analysis of the state of necessity, the Tribunal concludes that, first, said state started on December 1, 2001 and ended on April 26, 2003; second, during that period Argentina is exempt of

responsibility, and accordingly, the Claimants should bear the consequences of the measures taken by the host State; and finally, the Respondent should have restored the tariff regime on April 27, 2003, or should have compensated the Claimants, which did not occur. As a result, Argentina is liable as from that date to Claimants for damages.

NOTES & QUESTIONS

1. *Argentina's Necessity Defense.* What is the relationship between the necessity principle articulated in article XI of the BIT and the general necessity defense flowing from customary international law? Is the treaty provision simply a codification of custom or does it represent a unique legal doctrine separate from the customary defense of necessity? Some legal scholars have argued that "[w]here the treaty or the particular treaty provision in question is silent as to its relationship with customary law. . . then both the customary and treaty rule should be treated as applicable separately and independently." See William W. Burke-White & Andreas von Staden, *Investment Protection in Extraordinary Times: The Interpretation and Application of Non-Precluded Measures Provisions in Bilateral Investment Treaties*, 48 Va. J. Int'l L. 307, 324 (2008). Do you agree? The panel in the LG&E case analyzed both provisions and found that Argentina was justified in invoking necessity. However, other arbitration panels have concluded that Argentina could not invoke the necessity defense and have awarded larger damages against Argentina. For more discussion, see also Alec Stone Sweet, *Investor-State Arbitration: Proportionality's New Frontier*, 4 Law & Ethics Hum. Rts. 47, 70 (2010) ("As a matter of comparative law, the notion of 'public order' is a broad one, normally encompassing any policy concern rising to some asserted threshold of importance. It would seem impossible to argue that the Argentine crisis would not qualify as touching upon 'public order', even under the narrowest of criteria.").

2. *Regulatory Chill.* Some critics of the investor-state arbitration process worry that the system has a built-in deficiency: it may discourage states from adopting regulations, even legitimate ones. Investors aggrieved by a particular regulatory change—even one that protects the local population, its environment, or its economy—can make life difficult for the host state by filing a complaint. Since the state runs the risk of losing millions of dollars from an adverse arbitration panel decision, the host state may think twice before adopting public-interest regulations. Is the danger of "regulatory chill" a real possibility? For more discussion, see James D. Fry & Odysseas G. Repousis, *Towards A New World for Investor-State Arbitration Through Transparency*, 48 N.Y.U. J. Int'l L. & Pol. 795, 808 (2016) ("there hardly is any evidence that supports the notion that investment treaties can restrain legitimate government regulation"); David P. Riesenberg, *Fee Shifting in Investor-State Arbitration: Doctrine and Policy Justifying Application of the English Rule*, 60 Duke L.J. 977, 989 (2011) ("though little empirical evidence exists to confirm the regulatory chill theory, it is nonetheless a favorite of the system's critics"). In a similar vein, other critics

worry that the investor-state arbitration system is fundamentally pro-investor and biased against the public-oriented perspective of the state. Since only investors can win monetary damages at these tribunals, and investors facing legitimate regulation generally won't file complaints, how can researches prove this bias?

C. SOVEREIGN DEBT

Individuals and corporations are not the only entities that get into debt. Sovereign states frequently raise capital by borrowing money—often through the sale of government bonds to foreign investors. The sovereign state will owe interest payments to the foreign bond-holders and will eventually need to repay the debt. Sometimes, if a state borrows too heavily or experiences economic contraction, these debt payments may become crushing. The state might then seek to renegotiate the debt on more favorable terms. The bond-holders have an incentive to renegotiate because refusal might trigger the state's default on its sovereign debt—leaving the bond-holders in a more precarious position.

Another avenue for a state teetering on the edge of default is a rescue loan from the International Monetary Fund (IMF). The IMF was conceived during the 1944 Bretton Woods Conference, which established the basic building blocks of the post-World War II global economic system. The IMF has 189 member states and oversees a massive fund of capital that can be loaned to countries in economic distress, with the goal of providing stability and predictability to the international financial system. The IMF will sometimes attach conditions to these emergency loans, insisting on changes to a state's fiscal policy in exchange for the capital it provides.

The United Nations has long discussed the possibility of creating a multilateral framework for sovereign debt renegotiation—a way of lessening burdensome payments to debt-ridden states. Proposals for such a framework are often referred to as a sovereign debt restructuring mechanism, or SDRM, and the IMF itself has proposed one iteration of the mechanism. Although there are different proposals, one possibility is the creation of an international tribunal—either with permanent judges or with ad hoc arbitrators for individual cases—with the power to redraw creditor-debtor relations—the international equivalent of a bankruptcy court with the power to discharge debt and revise loan terms. Economist Joseph Stiglitz has argued that "restructurings are necessary for the market economy to work. But unfortunately, while we have a system to deal with private bankruptcy, we have no system for sovereign debt restructuring." See Joseph E. Stiglitz, *A Global System Is Needed for Debt Restructuring*, New York Times (Oct. 27, 2014). Not surprisingly, such a robust mechanism has not come to fruition, in part due to the impact on state sovereignty that a such a tribunal would entail. The United States has not supported the creation of a formal SDRM.

In the absence of an SDRM, sovereign debt restructuring already exists—but it is not undertaken through any formal or centralized process. Instead, states in financial stress simply negotiate with bond-holders for new terms, hoping that the bondholders will accept a "haircut," say 70 cents or 60 cents on the dollar of the value of the original loan, in exchange for a greater likelihood that they will actually be paid. Ideally, the distressed state hopes to reach universal agreement with all foreign bondholders. But what happens if one "hold-out" bondholder rejects the deal and insists that the state can pay more? The following case presents this exact scenario in the context of Argentina's sovereign debt crisis.

NML Capital, Ltd. v. Republic of Argentina
U.S. Court of Appeals for the Second Circuit
727 F.3d 230 (2013)

■ BARRINGTON D. PARKER, CIRCUIT JUDGE:

This is a contract case in which the Republic of Argentina refuses to pay certain holders of sovereign bonds issued under a 1994 Fiscal Agency Agreement (hereinafter, the "FAA" and the "FAA Bonds"). In order to enhance the marketability of the bonds, Argentina made a series of promises to the purchasers. Argentina promised periodic interest payments. Argentina promised that the bonds would be governed by New York law. Argentina promised that, in the event of default, unpaid interest and principal would become due in full. Argentina promised that any disputes concerning the bonds could be adjudicated in the courts of New York. Argentina promised that each bond would be transferable and payable to the transferee, regardless of whether it was a university endowment, a so-called "vulture fund," or a widow or an orphan. Finally, Argentina promised to treat the FAA Bonds at least equally with its other external indebtedness. As we have held, by defaulting on the Bonds, enacting legislation specifically forbidding future payment on them, and continuing to pay interest on subsequently issued debt, Argentina breached its promise of equal treatment.

Specifically, in October 2012, we affirmed injunctions issued by the district court intended to remedy Argentina's breach of the equal treatment obligation in the FAA. Our opinion chronicled pertinent aspects of Argentina's fiscal history and the factual background of this case, familiarity with which is assumed. Those injunctions, fashioned by the Hon. Thomas P. Griesa, directed that whenever Argentina pays on the bonds or other obligations that it issued in 2005 or 2010 exchange offers (the "Exchange Bonds"), the Republic must also make a "ratable payment" to plaintiffs who hold defaulted FAA Bonds. We remanded, however, for the district court to clarify the injunctions' payment formula and effects on third parties and intermediary banks. . .

On November 21, 2012, the district court issued amended injunctions with the clarifications we requested, as well as an opinion explaining them, which are challenged on this appeal by Argentina as well as by non-party appellants and intervenors. Recognizing the unusual nature of this litigation and the importance to Argentina of the issues presented, following oral argument, we invited Argentina to propose to the appellees an alternative payment formula and schedule for the outstanding bonds to which it was prepared to commit. Instead, the proposal submitted by Argentina ignored the outstanding bonds and proposed an entirely new set of substitute bonds. In sum, no productive proposals have been forthcoming. To the contrary, notwithstanding its commitment to resolving disputes involving the FAA in New York courts under New York law, at the February 27, 2013 oral argument, counsel for Argentina told the panel that it "would not voluntarily obey" the district court's injunctions, even if those injunctions were upheld by this Court. Moreover, Argentina's officials have publicly and repeatedly announced their intention to defy any rulings of this Court and the district court with which they disagree. . .

In its opinion, the district court first explained that its "ratable payment" requirement meant that whenever Argentina pays a percentage of what is due on the Exchange Bonds, it must pay plaintiffs the same percentage of what is then due on the FAA Bonds. Under the express terms of the FAA, as negotiated and agreed to by Argentina, the amount currently due on the FAA Bonds, as a consequence of its default, is the outstanding principal and accrued interest. Thus, as the district court explained, if Argentina pays Exchange Bondholders 100% of what has come due on their bonds at a given time, it must also pay plaintiffs 100% of the roughly $1.33 billion of principal and accrued interest that they are currently due. . .

Argentina advances a litany of reasons as to why the amended injunctions unjustly injure itself, the Exchange Bondholders, participants in the Exchange Bond payment system, and the public. None of the alleged injuries leads us to find an abuse of the district court's discretion.

Alleged Injuries to Argentina

Argentina argues that the amended injunctions unjustly injure it in two ways. First, Argentina argues that the amended injunctions violate the Foreign Sovereign Immunities Act ("FSIA") by forcing Argentina to use resources that the statute protects. As discussed in our October opinion, the original injunctions—and now the amended injunctions—do not violate the FSIA because "[t]hey do not attach, arrest, or execute upon any property" as proscribed by the statute. Rather, the injunctions allow Argentina to pay its FAA debts with whatever resources it likes. Absent further guidance from the Supreme Court, we remain convinced that the amended injunctions are consistent with the FSIA.

Second, Argentina argues that the injunctions' ratable payment remedy is inequitable because it calls for plaintiffs to receive their full principal and all accrued interest when Exchange Bondholders receive even a single installment of interest on their bonds. However, the undisputed reason that plaintiffs are entitled immediately to 100% of the principal and interest on their debt is that the FAA guarantees acceleration of principal and interest in the event of default. As the district court concluded, the amount currently owed to plaintiffs by Argentina as a result of its persistent defaults is the accelerated principal plus interest. We believe that it is equitable for one creditor to receive what it bargained for, and is therefore entitled to, even if other creditors, when receiving what they bargained for, do not receive the same thing. The reason is obvious: the first creditor is differently situated from other creditors in terms of what is currently due to it under its contract. Because the district court's decision does no more than hold Argentina to its contractual obligation of equal treatment, we see no abuse of discretion.

Argentina adds that the amended injunctions are invalid because a district court may not issue an injunctive "remedy [that] was historically unavailable from a court of equity." However, English chancery courts traditionally had power to issue injunctions and order specific performance when no effective remedy was available at law. As we explained in our October 2012 opinion, the plaintiffs have no adequate remedy at law because the Republic has made clear its intention to defy any money judgment issued by this Court. Moreover, Argentina has gone considerably farther by passing legislation, the Lock Law, specifically barring payments to FAA bondholders. And it is unremarkable that a court empowered to afford equitable relief may also direct the timing of that relief. Here, that timing requires that it occur before or when Argentina next pays the Exchange Bondholders.

Alleged Injuries to Exchange Bondholders

Invoking the proposition that equitable relief is inappropriate where it would cause unreasonable hardship or loss to third persons, Argentina, EBG, and Fintech argue that the amended injunctions are inequitable to Exchange Bondholders. But this case presents no conflict with that proposition. EBG argues, notwithstanding our affirmance of the district court's finding that Argentina has the financial wherewithal to pay all of its obligations, that the amended injunctions will harm Exchange Bondholders because Argentina "has declared publicly that it has no intention of ever paying holdout bondholders like NML" and, as a result, neither plaintiffs nor Exchange Bondholders will be paid if the amended injunctions stand.

This type of harm—harm threatened to third parties by a party subject to an injunction who avows not to obey it—does not make an otherwise lawful injunction "inequitable." We are unwilling to permit Argentina's threats to punish third parties to dictate the availability or terms of relief under Rule 65. Argentina's contention that the amended injunctions are unfair to Exchange Bondholders is all the less persuasive because, before accepting the exchange offers, they were expressly warned by Argentina in the accompanying prospectus that there could be "no assurance" that litigation over the FAA Bonds would not "interfere with payments" under the Exchange Bonds. Under these circumstances, we conclude that the amended injunctions have no inequitable effect on Exchange Bondholders and find no abuse of discretion. . .

Alleged Injuries to the Public Interest

In our October opinion, we considered the dire predictions from Argentina that enforcing the commitments it made in the FAA would have cataclysmic repercussions in the capital markets and the global economy, and we explained why we disagreed. On this appeal, Argentina essentially recycles those arguments. We are mindful of the fact that courts of equity should pay particular regard to the public consequences of any injunction. However, what the consequences predicted by Argentina have in common is that they are speculative, hyperbolic, and almost entirely of the Republic's own making. None of the arguments demonstrates an abuse of the district court's discretion.

The district court found that Argentina now "has the financial wherewithal to meet its commitment of providing equal treatment to [plaintiffs] and [Exchange Bondholders]." However, Argentina and the Euro Bondholders warn that Argentina may not be able to pay or that paying will cause problems in the Argentine economy, which could affect the global economy. But as we observed in our last opinion, other than this speculation, "Argentina makes no real argument that, to avoid defaulting on its other debt, it cannot afford to service the defaulted debt, and it certainly fails to demonstrate that the district court's finding to the contrary was clearly erroneous." Moreover, and perhaps more critically, Argentina failed to present the district court with any record evidence to support its assertions. . .

Next, Argentina and various *amici* assert that the amended injunctions will imperil future sovereign debt restructurings. They argue essentially that success by holdout creditors in this case will encourage other bondholders to refuse future exchange offers from other sovereigns. They warn that rather than submitting to restructuring, bondholders will hold out for the possibility of full recovery on their bonds at a later time, in turn causing second- and third-order effects detrimental to the global economy and especially to developing countries.

But this case is an exceptional one with little apparent bearing on transactions that can be expected in the future. Our decision here does not control the interpretation of all *pari passu* clauses or the obligations of other sovereign debtors under *pari passu* clauses in other debt instruments. As we explicitly stated in our last opinion, we have not held that a sovereign debtor breaches its *pari passu* clause every time it pays one creditor and not another, or even every time it enacts a law disparately affecting a creditor's rights. We simply affirm the district court's conclusion that Argentina's extraordinary behavior was a violation of the particular *pari passu* clause found in the FAA.

We further observed that cases like this one are unlikely to occur in the future because Argentina has been a uniquely recalcitrant debtor and because newer bonds almost universally include collective action clauses ("CACs") which permit a super-majority of bondholders to impose a restructuring on potential holdouts. Argentina and *amici* respond that, even with CACs, enough bondholders may nonetheless be motivated to refuse restructurings and hold out for full payment—or that holdouts could buy up enough bonds of a single series to defeat restructuring of that series. But a restructuring failure on one series would still allow restructuring of the remainder of a sovereign's debt. And, as one *amicus* notes, "if transaction costs and other procedural inefficiencies are sufficient to block a super-majority of creditors from voting in favor of a proposed restructuring, the proposed restructuring is likely to fail under any circumstances."

Ultimately, though, our role is not to craft a resolution that will solve all the problems that might arise in hypothetical future litigation involving other bonds and other nations. The particular language of the FAA's *pari passu* clause dictated a certain result in this case, but going forward, sovereigns and lenders are free to devise various mechanisms to avoid holdout litigation if that is what they wish to do. They may also draft different *pari passu* clauses that support the goal of avoiding holdout creditors. If, in the future, parties intend to bar preferential payment, they may adopt language like that included in the FAA. If they mean only that subsequently issued securities may not explicitly declare subordination of the earlier bonds, they are free to say so. But none of this establishes why the plaintiffs should be barred from vindicating their rights under the FAA.

For the same reason, we do not believe the outcome of this case threatens to steer bond issuers away from the New York marketplace. On the contrary, our decision affirms a proposition essential to the integrity of the capital markets: borrowers and lenders may, under New

York law, negotiate mutually agreeable terms for their transactions, but they will be held to those terms. We believe that the interest—one widely shared in the financial community—in maintaining New York's status as one of the foremost commercial centers is advanced by requiring debtors, including foreign debtors, to pay their debts. . .

AFTERWORD

NML Capital did not buy the bonds directly from Argentina. Rather, the bonds were purchased by other investors who eventually sold to NML when it became clear that Argentina was in distress and unable to repay the debts. NML then purchased the bonds at a cheap price, hoping to make money by negotiating a repayment price higher than what they originally paid for the bonds. In the alternative, NML has engaged in litigation designed to force Argentina to repay the bonds or risk having their assets confiscated by domestic courts enforcing Argentina's repayment obligations. Critics have called these hedge funds "vulture funds" because they prey on weakened states facing the threat of default. The result of the district court's injunction and the Second Circuit's ruling in the *NML* case was that Argentina was brought to the negotiating table and settled the claim for $2.26 billion. NML Capital reportedly paid about $177 million for the bonds—earning it a return of over 1,000 percent on its original investment.

In addition to the case in the Southern District of New York, NML filed cases in other jurisdictions to secure repayment of Argentina's bond obligations. In particular, NML filed petitions in jurisdictions where sovereign assets of Argentina were located. In one well-known case, NML filed a petition in Ghana, asking its courts to seize an Argentinian military vessel, the ARA Libertad, as partial satisfaction of the judgment. (At the time, the Libertad was berthed at the Port of Tema in Ghana.) The length that NML went to enforce its judgment shocked some observers and only added to the reputation of NML as a "vulture" fund. Moreover, the incident disrupted Argentina's relationship with Ghana. Indeed, Argentina filed a claim against Ghana before the International Tribunal for the Law of the Sea, which ruled in 2012 that the Libertad should be released back to Argentina, essentially accepting Argentina's argument that its military vessels were immune from legal process under principles of sovereign immunity.

NML is not the only so-called "vulture" fund. Plenty of other hedge funds pursue a similar strategy of buying cheap bonds and then seeking to enforce them in court. Is this a legalized form of "ransom," as some critics have suggested, or is it simply an attempt to get sovereign states to live up to their financial and legal obligations? After all, Argentina borrowed the money on the condition that it would repay it to the lenders (or their assignees). Should the UN set up a centralized mechanism for sovereign debt restructuring or is ad hoc negotiation sufficient to resolve these cases?

NOTES & QUESTIONS

1. *The Doctrine of Odious Debt.* In economic terms, the most important continuing legal obligations are debt payments owed in conjunction with prior lending agreements. Lenders are notoriously insistent on being repaid—in any context. The general default assumption is that a change in government—even a change in political structure—does not alleviate a state's obligation to repay its prior debts. This might produce results that are arguably unfair. Consider, for example, a state run by a dictator who borrows large sums of money that is used mostly for the personal enrichment of the dictator. If the dictator is overthrown in favor of democratic self-rule, why should the local population suffer the burden of

crushing repayment terms? The argument in favor of repayment is simple: a change in government does not affect the legal personality of the state, and the debt is owed by the state itself, which endured throughout the political transformation. In recent years, a nascent legal doctrine has emerged to counsel flexibility in such situations, resulting in renegotiation or partial forgiveness of such debts in circumstances when the original debt is "odious," i.e., morally questionable. For more discussion of this theory, see Odette Lieneau, *Rethinking Sovereign Debt* 9 (2004). If sovereignty is viewed purely in statist terms, the debt is owed by the state and must be repaid. However, if sovereignty is viewed in non-statist terms, based on the notion of a people, then perhaps the debt should be forgiven because the loan was never secured with the popular consent of the people. The problem for proponents of the doctrine of odious debt is that contemporary international lawyers almost always view sovereignty through the lens of the state, and very rarely understand sovereignty in deeper terms.

2.   *Reforming the World Economic Order.* The basic building blocks of the global economic order have remained relatively unchanged. The roots of the system date back to Dumbarton Oaks, a diplomatic conference held in 1944 at a mansion in Washington, D.C., where representatives from the U.S., the U.K., China, and the Soviet Union, laid the groundwork for the post-World War II international order. The same wave of international institution building that gave birth to the United Nations also ushered in the World Bank, the International Monetary Fund, and paved the way for the WTO years later. But some economists and legal scholars, especially those writing with a sensitivity to the Third World perspective, would argue that the world economic order has deeper roots going back to colonialism. Has the basic structure of the economic order escaped its colonial past? Today, economic arrangements between nations are largely determined less by the formal equality of states under international law and more by the unequal power distribution between states with the greatest financial resources and those with the least. In the main, that power differential still tracks the First World and Third World axes, with Global North countries dictating financial terms and Global South countries largely forced to accept them. Is there any legal structure that can alter this basic reality? Could a new economic order be negotiated? Why have prior negotiations failed to produce meaningful reform? Given the interdependence of the global economic order, do prosperous states have an incentive to accept reforms in order to reduce the risk of systemic collapse that can spread across borders? For a discussion, see Göran Ohlin, *Can World Order Be Negotiated?*, in *The Spirit of Uppsala* 84, 85 (1984) (noting that "[t]he interdependence of the world economy, which reveals not only the dependence of the poor countries on the rich ones but also the opposite, is used to support the claim that the call for a new world economic order is a proposal that the rich cannot refuse, as it is in fact in their own vital interest").

Conclusion & Summary

This chapter has focused on the following examples of legal disputes arising from the international economic system. This was not a comprehensive treatment of the international economic system, but rather a survey of the major areas where international law regulates or otherwise influences economic disputes on the international stage:

1. Trade dispute are governed by the GATT and other agreements that make promises regarding tariff reductions. Some of these agreements are regional, such as NAFTA, while others are global. The goal of these agreements is to reduce barriers to trade although not necessarily to produce a system of pure free trade. GATT and other agreements codify requirements of non-discrimination—treating imports from multiple countries in similar fashion and treating imports on an equal footing with domestic goods.

2. If a country feels victimized by illegal trade practices, it can file a complaint with the WTO and request an arbitration before a WTO panel. Once the panel issues its decision, there is a provision for appeals to the WTO appellate body on matters of law. WTO panel decisions are usually respected, in part because participation in the WTO is important for modern economies because it gives states access to foreign markets on favorable terms.

3. Foreign producers sometimes complain when they are unfairly treated by government regulations that either prevent them from selling their goods in that market or make it difficult to do so. In that case, a WTO panel can order the state to repeal the regulation if it lacks a valid scientific basis or if the regulation unfairly discriminates against the imported goods and favors domestic producers.

4. When foreign investors provide capital for business projects in another state, the rights of the investors are protected by Bilateral Investment Treaties and other legal instruments, such as multilateral treaties or investor protection provisions in trade compacts. If the government then enacts legislation or takes other actions that impermissibly affect the investment (by lowering its value), the investor can file for investor-state arbitration. These arbitration panels are often, but not always, convened under the auspices of ICSID.

5. Investor-state arbitration, by design, favors investors over states. The investors can recover money that they've lost,

but states do not get anything (except possibly legal costs) if they win the arbitration. Even the mere possibility of a costly investor claim might make a state think twice before enacting a new regulation or an economic reform that might harm foreign investors. So why do states agree to investor arbitration? First, they do so in exchange for reciprocal promises from other states who are similarly constrained. Second, refusing arbitration will make investment in the country seem risky to foreign investors, who might deploy their capital elsewhere, thus harming local industry in need of capital infusion.

6.   In several cases, states such as Argentina have asserted the necessity defense to justify emergency economic reform that damaged the interest of foreign investors. The necessity defense comes from two different sources: general customary international law as well as specific necessity clauses in the relevant BIT or other treaty. At least some arbitration panels have accepted the necessity defense, concluding that avoiding an imminent economic collapse constituted an essential security interest that the state was justified in taking measures to avoid, even if doing so harmed the foreign investors. However, the necessity defense only applies for such time as the state of necessity endures; after the exigency evaporates, the state is required to honor its commitments or pay damages.

7.   Foreign investors can also loan money directly to a sovereign state, usually in the form of a bond. If a state becomes heavily indebted and may not be able to repay the loans, the risk of default lowers the value of the bond. In some cases, the original bondholders cut their losses by selling the bonds—perhaps to financial firms betting that they can make money by buying the bonds at a fire-sale price.

8.   If the state is in danger of defaulting on its loan obligations, it has to negotiate with the bondholders for better terms. However, this can be difficult, especially if there are holdouts among the bondholders. In the best-case scenario, the bondholders agree to revised terms that prevent the state from falling into default. Also, the IMF may provide temporary loan relief in exchange for changes to the state's fiscal policy or other macroeconomic changes. In the worst-case scenario, negotiations fail to restructure the debt, with the result that the state falls into default and has difficulty

acquiring future loan capital on the international bond markets.

9.   The IMF, the United Nations, and other organizations have called for a Sovereign Debt Restructuring Mechanism (SDRM), which would centralize the process of revising sovereign debt obligations through the creation of a tribunal or arbitration process. The United States is not in favor of creating an SDRM.

10. States ruled by dictators or other illiberal regimes sometimes rack up billions of dollars of sovereign debt. This capital is often used to enrich the dictator or other government insiders, to the detriment of the local population. If the dictatorship is overturned and a more democratic regime is installed, the state may argue that it should not be forced to repay the "odious debt." There is no widely accepted rule of customary international law that entails that states are free to ignore their loan obligations in this situation. The standard rule is that a change in government does not obviate a state's prior legal obligations, so it still needs to pay back the prior debt. However, the process of sovereign debt restructuring—by negotiating with bondholders or requesting a loan from the IMF—does not take place in a political vacuum. Arguments about the lack of legitimacy of the prior debt may be a relevant factor for the state's reputation on the international stage.

CHAPTER 18

INTERNATIONAL ENVIRONMENTAL LAW

Introduction

International law regulates environmental concerns through the same mechanisms as any other area, including but not limited to: treaties, custom, litigation before domestic courts and international tribunals. There are a plethora of international treaties and covenants on biological diversity, biosafety, climate change, whaling, water pollution, and organic pollutants. Similarly, unwritten rules of customary international law apply to the protection of the natural environment. The goal of this chapter is not to provide an exhaustive accounting of these legal norms, but rather to canvass the key principles that form the basis architecture of international environmental law. What ideas or principles are truly distinctive in the field of international environmental regulation?

The first is the most obvious: the notion of transboundary harm. In many ways, this is an obvious point, but it is one that required judicial elaboration at some point in time. States are responsible for the pollution they create because it constitutes a transboundary harm. The second principle is the emerging precautionary principle, which counsels in favor of regulatory action even in the face of scientific uncertainty. Although the exact status of the precautionary principle remains murky, it plays an increasingly important role in environmental decisions at both the domestic and international levels. The third area is the challenge posed by climate change. The earth is warming, ice is melting, and sea levels will rise over the coming decades and centuries. This crisis represents a massive collective action problem among states. According to scientists, greenhouse gas emissions from human activity are hastening global warming and making the problem far worse. But if a state lowers its emissions unilaterally while the rest of the world maintains them, the state will bear the economic burdens while receiving none of the environmental benefits. The only solution is to create an international compact of mutually constrained states, each one willing to lower its emissions in exchange for a reciprocal promise from other states to act similarly. The idea is simple in its inspiration but not so easy to implement in practice, especially with international law's unique systems of enforcement.

Section A will focus on transboundary harm, Section B on the precautionary principle, and Section C on legal approaches to redressing climate change.

A. TRANSBOUNDARY HARM

A core pillar of environmental law is the prohibition on using one's territory for hazardous activities to the detriment of others. Does this "no harm" principle exist in international law? Given the relative paucity of environmental litigation before international tribunals, it might be hard to find this norm reflected in a tribunal judgment. It seems more likely that an articulation of this norm would be found in customary international law, i.e., a situation where states complain of the polluting conduct of a neighboring state. However, the "no harm" principle is, in fact, firmly entrenched in international jurisprudence. Back in the late 1930s and early 1940s, a sharp diplomatic dispute arose between the United States and Canada over a factory in British Columbia. Residents of nearby Washington State complained that the Canadian factory was polluting their air and water. The U.S. government pressed Canada to resolve the issue but received what the Americans considered to be marked indifference to the suffering of the Washington residents. A Canadian-American arbitral panel was convened to resolve the environmental dispute.

As you read the following award decision, identify the substantive "no harm" principle articulated by the panel. What areas of law or past jurisprudence did the panel analyze to find this norm?

Trail Smelter Case
Arbitral Award
1941

. . . In 1896, a smelter was started under American auspices near the locality known as Trail, B.C. In 1906, the Consolidated Mining and Smelting Company of Canada, Limited, obtained a charter of incorporation from the Canadian authorities, and that company acquired the smelter plant at Trail as it then existed. Since that time, the Canadian company, without interruption, has operated the Smelter, and from time to time has greatly added to the plant until it has become one of the best and largest equipped smelting plants on the American continent. In 1925 and 1927, two stacks of the plant were erected to 409 feet in height and the Smelter greatly increased its daily smelting of zinc and lead ores. This increased production resulted in more sulphur dioxide fumes and higher concentrations being emitted into the air. In 1916, about 5,000 tons of sulphur per month were emitted; in 1924, about 4,700 tons; in 1926, about 9,000 tons—an amount which rose near to 10,000 tons per month in 1930. In other words, about 300–350 tons of sulphur were being emitted daily in 1930. (It is to be noted that one ton of sulphur is substantially the equivalent of two tons of sulphur dioxide or SO2.)

From 1925, at least, to 1937, damage occurred in the State of Washington, resulting from the sulphur dioxide emitted from the Trail Smelter as stated in the previous decision.

The subject of fumigations and damage claimed to result from them was referred by the two Governments on August 7, 1928, to the International Joint Commission, United States and Canada, under Article IX of the Convention of January 11, 1909, between the United States and Great Britain, providing that the high contracting parties might agree that "any other question or matters of difference arising between them involving the rights, obligations or interests of either in relation to the other, or to the inhabitants of the other, along the common frontier between the United States and the Dominion of Canada shall be referred from time to time to the International Joint Commission for examination and report. Such reports shall not be regarded as decisions of the question or matters so submitted either on the facts or on the law, and shall not, in any way, have the character of an arbitral award."

The questions referred to the International Joint Commission were five in number, the first two of which may be noted: first, the extent to which property in the State of Washington has been damaged by fumes from the Smelter at Trail B.C.; second, the amount of indemnity which would compensate United States' interests in the State of Washington for past damages.

The International Joint Commission sat at Northport, at Nelson, B.C., and in Washington, D.C., in 1928, 1929 and 1930, and on February 28, 1931, rendered a unanimous report which need not be considered in detail. After outlining the plans of the Trail Smelter for extracting sulphur from the fumes, the report recommended (Part I, Paragraphs (a) and (c)) that "the company be required to proceed as expeditiously as may be reasonably possible with the works above referred to and also to erect with due dispatch such further sulphuric acid units and take such further or other action as may be necessary, if any, to reduce the amount and concentration of SO2 fumes drifting from its said plant into the United States until it has reduced the amount by some means to a point where it will do no damage in the United States." . . .

III

The second question under Article III of the Convention is as follows:

In the event of the answer to the first part of the preceding question being in the affirmative, whether the Trail Smelter should be required to refrain from causing damage in the State of Washington in the future and, if so, to what extent?

Damage has occurred since January 1, 1932, as fully set forth in the previous decision. To that extent, the first part of the preceding question has thus been answered in the affirmative.

As has been said above, the report of the International Joint Commission (1 (g)) contained a definition of the word "damage" excluding "occasional damage that may be caused by SO2 fumes being carried across the international boundary in air pockets or by reason of unusual atmospheric conditions," as far, at least, as the duty of the Smelter to reduce the presence of that gas in the air was concerned.

The correspondence between the two Governments during the interval between that report and the conclusion of the Convention shows that the problem thus raised was what parties had primarily in mind in drafting Question No. 2. Whilst Canada wished for the adoption of the report, the United States stated that it could not acquiesce in the proposal to limit consideration of damage to damage as defined in the report (letter of the Minister of the United States of America at Ottawa to the Secretary of State for External Affairs of the Dominion of Canada, January 30, 1934). The view was expressed that "so long as fumigations occur in the State of Washington with such frequency, duration and intensity as to cause injury," the conditions afforded "grounds of complaint on the part of the United States, regardless of the remedial works. . . . and regardless of the effect of those works" (same letter).

The first problem which arises is whether the question should be answered on the basis of the law followed in the United States or on the basis of international law. The Tribunal, however, finds that this problem need not be solved here as the law followed in the United States in dealing with the quasi-sovereign rights of the States of the Union, in the matter of air pollution, whilst more definite, is in conformity with the general rules of international law.

Particularly in reaching its conclusions as regards this question as well as the next, the Tribunal has given consideration to the desire of the high contracting parties "to reach a solution just to all parties concerned."

As Professor Eagleton puts in (Responsibility of States in International Law, 1928, p. 80): "A State owes at all times a duty to protect other States against injurious acts by individuals from within its jurisdiction." A great number of such general pronouncements by leading authorities concerning the duty of a State to respect other States and their territory have been presented to the Tribunal. These and many others have been carefully examined. International decisions, in various matters, from the Alabama case onward, and also earlier ones, are based on the same general principle, and, indeed, this principle, as such, has not been questioned by Canada. But the real difficulty often arises rather when it comes to determine what, pro subjecta materie, is deemed to constitute an injurious act.

A case concerning, as the present one does, territorial relations, decided by the Federal Court of Switzerland between the Cantons of Soleure and Argovia, may serve to illustrate the relativity of the rule. Soleure brought a suit against her sister State to enjoin use of a shooting establishment which endangered her territory. The court, in granting the injunction, said: "This right (sovereignty) excludes. . . . not only the usurpation and exercise of sovereign rights (of another State). . . . but also an actual encroachment which might prejudice the natural use of the territory and the free movement of its inhabitants." As a result of the decision, Argovia made plans for the improvement of the existing installations. These, however, were considered as insufficient protection by Soleure. The Canton of Argovia then moved the Federal Court to decree that the shooting be again permitted after completion of the projected improvements. This motion was granted. "The demand of the Government of Soleure, said the court, "that all endangerment be absolutely abolished apparently goes too far." The court found that all risk whatever had not been eliminated, as the region was flat and absolutely safe shooting ranges were only found in mountain valleys; that there was a federal duty for the communes to provide facilities for military target practice and that "no more precautions may be demanded for shooting ranges near the boundaries of two Cantons than are required for shooting ranges in the interior of a Canton."

No case of air pollution dealt with by an international tribunal has been brought to the attention of the Tribunal nor does the Tribunal know of any such case. The nearest analogy is that of water pollution. But, here also, no decision of an international tribunal has been cited or has been found.

There are, however, as regards both air pollution and water pollution, certain decisions of the Supreme Court of the United States which may legitimately be taken as a guide in this field of international law. For it is reasonable to follow by analogy, in international cases, precedents established by that court in dealing with controversies between States of the Union or with other controversies concerning the quasi-sovereign rights of such States, where no contrary rule prevails in international law and no reason for rejecting such precedents can be adduced from the limitations of sovereignty inherent in the Constitution of the United States.

In the suit of the *State of Missouri v. the State of Illinois* (200 U.S. 496, 521) concerning the pollution, within the boundaries of Illinois, of the Illinois River, an affluent of the Mississippi flowing into the latter where it forms the boundary between that State and Missouri, an injunction was refused. "Before this court ought to intervene," said the court, "the case should be of serious magnitude, clearly and fully proved, and the principle to be applied should be one which the court is prepared deliberately to maintain against all considerations on the other side. (See Kansas v. Colorado, 185 U.S. 125.)" The court found that the practice complained of was general along the shores of the Mississippi River at that time, that it was followed by Missouri itself and that thus a standard was set up by the defendant which the claimant was entitled to invoke.

As the claims of public health became more exacting and methods for removing impurities from the water were perfected, complaints ceased. It is significant that Missouri sided with Illinois when the other riparians of the Great Lakes' system sought to enjoin it to desist from diverting the waters of that system into that of the Illinois and Mississippi for the very purpose of disposing of the Chicago sewage.

In the more recent suit of the *State of New York against the State of New Jersey* (256 U.S. 296, 309), concerning the pollution of New York Bay, the injunction was also refused for lack of proof, some experts believing that the plans which were in dispute would result in the presence of "offensive odors and unsightly deposits," other equally reliable experts testifying that they were confidently of the opinion that the waters would be sufficiently purified. The court, referring to *Missouri v. Illinois*, said: ". . . .the burden upon the State of New York of sustaining the allegations of its bill is much greater than that imposed upon a complainant in an ordinary suit between private parties. Before this court can be moved to exercise its extraordinary power under the Constitution to control the conduct of one State at the suit of another, the threatened invasion of rights must be of serious magnitude and it must be established by clear and convincing evidence."

What the Supreme Court says there of its power under the Constitution equally applies to the extraordinary power granted this Tribunal under the Convention. What is true between States of the Union is, at least, equally true concerning the relations between the United States and the Dominion of Canada.

In another recent case concerning water pollution (283 U.S. 473), the complainant was successful. The City of New York was enjoined, at the request of the State of New Jersey, to desist, within a reasonable time limit, from the practice of disposing of sewage by dumping it into the sea, a practice which was injurious to the coastal waters of New Jersey in the vicinity of her bathing resorts.

In the matter of air pollution itself, the leading decisions are those of the Supreme Court in the *State of Georgia v. Tennessee Copper Co & Ducktown Sulphur, Copper and Iron Co Ltd*. Although dealing with a suit against private companies, the decisions were on questions cognate to those here at issue. Georgia stated that it had in vain sought relief from the State of Tennessee, on whose territory the smelters were located, and the court defined the nature of the suit by saying: "This is a suit by a State for an injury to it in its capacity of quasi-sovereign. In that capacity, the State has an interest independent of and behind the titles of its citizens, in all the earth and air within its domain."

On the question whether an injunction should be granted or not, the court said (206 U.S. 230):

> It (the State) has the last word as to whether its mountains shall be stripped of their forests and its inhabitants shall breathe pure air. . . . It is not lightly to be presumed to give up quasi-sovereign rights for pay and. . . . if that be its choice, it may insist that an infraction of them shall be stopped. This court has not quite the same freedom to balance the harm that will be done by an injunction against that of which the plaintiff complains, that it would have in deciding between two subjects of a single political power. Without excluding the considerations that equity always takes into account. . . . it is a fair and reasonable demand on the part of a sovereign that the air over its territory should not be polluted on a great scale by sulphurous acid gas, that the forests on its mountains, be they better or worse, and whatever domestic destruction they may have suffered, should not be further destroyed or threatened by the act of persons beyond its control, that the crops and orchards on its hills should not be endangered from the same source. . . . Whether Georgia, by insisting upon this claim, is doing more harm than good to her own citizens, is for her to determine. The possible disaster to those outside the State must be accepted as a consequence of her standing upon her extreme rights.

Later on, however, when the court actually framed an injunction, in the case of the Ducktown Company (237 U.S. 474, 477) (an agreement on the basis of an annual compensation was reached with the most important of the two smelters, the Tennessee Copper Company), they did not go beyond a decree "adequate to diminish materially the present probability of damage to its (Georgia's) citizens."

Great progress in the control of fumes has been made by science in the last few years and this progress should be taken into account.

The Tribunal, therefore, finds that the above decisions, taken as a whole, constitute an adequate basis for its conclusions, namely, that, under the principles of international law, as well as of the law of the United States, no State has the right to use or permit the use of its territory in such a manner as to cause injury by fumes in or to the territory of another or the properties or persons therein, when the case is of serious consequence and the injury is established by clear and convincing evidence.

The decisions of the Supreme Court of the United States which are the basis of these conclusions are decisions in equity and a solution inspired by them, together with the régime hereinafter prescribed, will, in the opinion of the Tribunal, be "just to all parties concerned," as long, at least, as the present conditions in the Columbia River Valley continue to prevail.

Considering the circumstances of the case, the Tribunal holds that the Dominion of Canada is responsible in international law for the conduct of the Trail Smelter. Apart from the undertakings in the Convention, it is, therefore, the duty of the Government of the Dominion of Canada to see to it that this conduct should be in conformity with the obligation of the Dominion under international law as herein determined.

The Tribunal, therefore, answers Question No. 2 as follows: (2) So long as the present conditions in the Columbia River Valley prevail, the Trail Smelter shall be required to refrain from causing any damage through fumes in the State of Washington; the damage herein referred to and its extent being such as would be recoverable under the decisions of the courts of the United States in suits between private individuals. The indemnity for such damage should be fixed in such manner as the Governments, acting under Article XI of the Convention, should agree upon. . .

NOTES & QUESTIONS

1.   *The State Analogy.* The *Trail Smelter* panel was plagued by a lack of case-law on transboundary international harm. In the absence of this case law, the panel looked to transboundary environmental harm between states within the American constitutional framework, ultimately looking to the U.S. Supreme Court for an articulation of the rule that "no State has the right to use or permit the use of its territory in such a manner as to cause injury by fumes in or to the territory of another or the properties or persons therein. . ." This is now the definitive statement of the rule in international law as well. Was it legitimate for the panel to reason by analogy from the domestic context to the international system? The panel also concluded that Canada was required to compensate the United States for the harm caused by its factory based on the principle that "the polluter pays." Again, does this principle make sense when applied at the international level?

2.   *The Forward-Looking Obligation.* The *Trail Smelter* arbitration also helped to develop the law of state responsibility. For example, the panel concluded that Canada was under a continuing obligation to prevent the transboundary pollution in the future, specifically: "the Trail Smelter shall be required to refrain from causing any damage through fumes in the State

of Washington." This forward-looking obligation is a critical aspect of the holding. It eventually was incorporated into the ILC Draft Articles on State Responsibility, which state in article 14(3) that "[t]he breach of an international obligation requiring a State to prevent a given event occurs when the event occurs and extends over the entire period during which the event continues and remains not in conformity with that obligation." In other words, this principle is not just a requirement of international environmental law, but also of general international law as well. For more discussion, see Mark A. Drumbl, Trail Smelter *and the International Law Commission's Work on State Responsibility for Internationally Wrongful Acts and State Liability*, in *Transboundary Harm in International Law* 85, 91 (Rebecca M. Bratspies & Russell A. Miller, 2006).

Decades after *Trail Smelter*, the International Law Commission endeavored to codify the principles of transboundary harm first articulated in the path-breaking case. As you read the following excerpt from the draft articles, ask yourself how many of these principles are implicit in *Trail Smelter* and how many are principles that have emerged in the interim.

Draft Articles on Prevention of Transboundary Harm From Hazardous Activities

International Law Commission
2001

Article 1. Scope

The present articles apply to activities not prohibited by international law which involve a risk of causing significant transboundary harm through their physical consequences.

Article 2. Use of terms

For the purposes of the present articles:

(a) "Risk of causing significant transboundary harm" includes risks taking the form of a high probability of causing significant transboundary harm and a low probability of causing disastrous transboundary harm;

(b) "Harm" means harm caused to persons, property or the environment;

(c) "Transboundary harm" means harm caused in the territory of or in other places under the jurisdiction or control of a State other than the State of origin, whether or not the States concerned share a common border;

(d) "State of origin" means the State in the territory or otherwise under the jurisdiction or control of which the activities referred to in article 1 are planned or are carried out;

(e) "State likely to be affected" means the State or States in the territory of which there is the risk of significant transboundary harm or which have jurisdiction or control over any other place where there is such a risk;

(f) "States concerned" means the State of origin and the State likely to be affected.

Article 3. Prevention

The State of origin shall take all appropriate measures to prevent significant transboundary harm or at any event to minimize the risk thereof.

Article 4. Cooperation

States concerned shall cooperate in good faith and, as necessary, seek the assistance of one or more competent international organizations in preventing significant transboundary harm or at any event in minimizing the risk thereof.

Article 5. Implementation

States concerned shall take the necessary legislative, administrative or other action including the establishment of suitable monitoring mechanisms to implement the provisions of the present articles.

Article 6. Authorization

1.   The State of origin shall require its prior authorization for:

(a) any activity within the scope of the present articles carried out in its territory or otherwise under its jurisdiction or control;

(b) any major change in an activity referred to in subparagraph (a);

(c) any plan to change an activity which may transform it into one falling within the scope of the present articles.

2.   The requirement of authorization established by a State shall be made applicable in respect of all preexisting activities within the scope of the present articles. Authorizations already issued by the State for preexisting activities shall be reviewed in order to comply with the present articles.

3.   In case of a failure to conform to the terms of the authorization, the State of origin shall take such actions as appropriate, including where necessary terminating the authorization.

Article 7.   Assessment of risk

Any decision in respect of the authorization of an activity within the scope of the present articles shall, in particular, be based on an assessment of the possible transboundary harm caused by that activity, including any environmental impact assessment.

Article 8.   Notification and information

1.   If the assessment referred to in article 7 indicates a risk of causing significant transboundary harm, the State of origin shall provide the State likely to be affected with timely notification of the risk and the assessment and shall transmit to it the available technical and all other relevant information on which the assessment is based.

2.   The State of origin shall not take any decision on authorization of the activity pending the receipt, within a period not exceeding six months, of the response from the State likely to be affected.

Article 9.   Consultations on preventive measures

1.   The States concerned shall enter into consultations, at the request of any of them, with a view to achieving acceptable solutions regarding measures to be adopted in order to prevent significant transboundary harm or at any event to minimize the risk thereof. The States concerned shall agree, at the commencement of such consultations, on a reasonable time frame for the consultations.

2.   The States concerned shall seek solutions based on an equitable balance of interests in the light of article 10.

3.   If the consultations referred to in paragraph 1 fail to produce an agreed solution, the State of origin shall nevertheless take into account the interests of the State likely to be affected in case it decides to authorize the activity to be pursued, without prejudice to the rights of any State likely to be affected.

Article 10.   Factors involved in an
equitable balance of interests

In order to achieve an equitable balance of interests as referred to in paragraph 2 of article 9, the States concerned shall take into account all relevant factors and circumstances, including:

(a) the degree of risk of significant transboundary harm and of the availability of means of preventing such harm, or minimizing the risk thereof or repairing the harm;

(b) the importance of the activity, taking into account its overall advantages of a social, economic and technical character for the State of origin in relation to the potential harm for the State likely to be affected;

(c) the risk of significant harm to the environment and the availability of means of preventing such harm, or minimizing the risk thereof or restoring the environment;

(d) the degree to which the State of origin and, as appropriate, the State likely to be affected are prepared to contribute to the costs of prevention;

(e) the economic viability of the activity in relation to the costs of prevention and to the possibility of carrying out the activity elsewhere or by other means or replacing it with an alternative activity;

(f) the standards of prevention which the State likely to be affected applies to the same or comparable activities and the standards applied in comparable regional or international practice.

PROBLEM CASE

In 2019, an outbreak of the coronavirus occurred in Wuhan, China and quickly engulfed that region in a major health crisis. Health officials in China struggled to contain the spread of the virus and its associated disease, Covid-19. China eventually stopped the outbreak with a combination of draconian measures, including a quarantine of Wuhan, but not before the virus spread to other nations. Within a few months, the disease spread and became a global pandemic. As of June 2020, the virus had caused almost 10 million infections and nearly 500,000 fatalities globally. It also precipitated a major economic downturn.

Almost immediately, some asked whether China could be responsible under international law for the spread of the coronavirus. While China did not deliberately spread the virus, the question is whether China might be held responsible for failing to adequately respond to the threat posed by the virus. But before assessing whether that response was negligent in some fashion—i.e., whether China could or should have done something differently—one must first determine whether China violated some pre-existing duty under international law.

Could the transboundary harm principle provide one source for the duty? Under this doctrine, a state is required to make sure that nothing on its territory—including, perhaps, a virus or other communicable disease—harms another state or its territory. If it violates this obligation, the state is responsible for any damage caused (the "polluter pays" principle.) Is China responsible for failing to address a global harm that emanated from its territory? Does this represent a simple application of the principle of transboundary harm or does it stretch the principle beyond recognition?

For more discussion, see Written Statement of Prof. Russell A. Miller, Hearing on the Foreign Sovereign Immunities Act, Coronavirus, and Addressing China's Culpability, U.S. Senate Committee on the Judiciary (June 23, 2020) ("The rule announced in the Trail Smelter Arbitration gives states around the world a basis for alleging the Chinese government's international law responsibility for using or allowing the use of its territory—in relation to the coronavirus outbreak—in such a manner as to cause injury of serious consequence to the territory of other states or the properties or persons therein.").

B. PRECAUTIONARY PRINCIPLE

What methodology should international law use to evaluate environmental risk? In the *Beef Hormones* case in the prior chapter, we already saw a WTO panel refer to the precautionary principle in support of Europe's decision to impose strict import controls on American and

Canadian beef raised with hormones. Nonetheless, the panel considered the precautionary principle as an emerging "principle" of international law rather than an existing legal rule carrying the burden of legal obligation. In keeping with this conclusion, the panel ruled that Europe's ban on the American beef was not justified by the scientific evidence—Europe's invocation of the precautionary principle notwithstanding.

In the intervening years, the precautionary principle has taken on renewed energy in discussions relating to the protection of the natural environment. When the scientific evidence on a given question is uncertain, should states err on the side of protecting the environment? In June 1992, the United Nations Conference on Environment and Development convened in Rio de Janeiro and issued a multilateral Declaration on Environment and Development. Principle 15 of the Declaration included the following support for the Precautionary Principle: "In order to protect the environment, the precautionary approach shall be widely applied by States according to their capabilities. Where there are threats of serious or irreversible damage, lack of full scientific certainty shall not be used as a reason for postponing cost-effective measures to prevent environmental degradation." The Rio Declaration was signed by 170 states.

Is there enough state support for the Precautionary Principle to consider it an established part of customary international law? To answer that question, one must consult state practice and *opinio juris* of several states. As a start, consider the following communication from the European Community that both defines the precautionary principle and explains how bureaucracies within the European Community should apply the principle to concrete policy questions. Article 174(2) of the EC Treaty states that European "policy on the environment shall aim at a high level of protection taking into account the diversity of situations in the various regions of the Community. It shall be based on the precautionary principle and on the principles that preventive action should be taken, that environmental damage should as a priority be rectified at source and that the polluter should pay." Is the precautionary principle sufficiently recognized by domestic jurisdictions to be considered a part of international environmental law? If yes, what source of law generates this legal obligation? Is a general principle of international law?

Communication from the Commission on the Precautionary Principle

European Community (2000)

Introduction

A number of recent events has shown that public opinion is becoming increasingly aware of the potential risks to which the population or their environment are potentially exposed.

Enormous advances in communications technology have fostered this growing sensitivity to the emergence of new risks, before scientific research has been able to fully illuminate the problems. Decision-makers have to take account of the fears generated by these perceptions and to put in place preventive measures to eliminate the risk or at least reduce it to the minimum acceptable level. On April 13, 1999 the Council adopted a resolution urging the Commission inter alia "to be in the future even more determined to be guided by the precautionary principle in preparing proposals for legislation and in its other consumer-related activities and develop as priority clear and effective guidelines for the application of this principle." This Communication is part of the Commission's response.

The dimension of the precautionary principle goes beyond the problems associated with a short or medium-term approach to risks. It also concerns the longer run and the well-being of future generations.

A decision to take measures without waiting until all the necessary scientific knowledge is available is clearly a precaution-based approach.

Decision-makers are constantly faced with the dilemma of balancing the freedoms and rights of individuals, industry and organisations with the need to reduce or eliminate the risk of adverse effects to the environment or to health.

Finding the correct balance so that proportionate, non-discriminatory, transparent and coherent decisions can be arrived at, which at the same time provide the chosen level of protection, requires a structured decision making process with detailed scientific and other objective information. This structure is provided by the three elements of risk analysis: the assessment of risk, the choice of risk management strategy and the communication of the risk.

Any assessment of risk that is made should be based on the existing body of scientific and statistical data. Most decisions are taken where there is sufficient information available for appropriate preventive measures to be taken but in other circumstances, these data may be wanting in some respects.

Whether or not to invoke the Precautionary Principle is a decision exercised where scientific information is insufficient, inconclusive, or uncertain and where there are indications that the possible effects on the environment, or human, animal or plant health may be potentially dangerous and inconsistent with the chosen level of protection. . .

3.   *The Precautionary Principle in the European Union*

The Community has consistently endeavoured to achieve a high level of protection, among others in environment and human, animal or plant health. In most cases, measures making it possible to achieve this high level of protection can be determined on a satisfactory scientific basis. However, when there are reasonable grounds for concern that potential hazards may affect the environment or human, animal or plant health, and when at the same time the available data preclude a detailed risk evaluation, the precautionary principle has been politically accepted as a risk management strategy in several fields.

To understand fully the use of the precautionary principle in the European Union, it is necessary to examine the legislative texts, the case law of the Court of Justice and the Court of First Instance, and the policy approaches that have emerged.

The analysis starts with the legal texts which explicitly or implicitly refer to the precautionary principle.

At Community level the only explicit reference to the precautionary principle is to be found in the environment title of the EC Treaty, and more specifically Article 174. However, one cannot conclude from this that the principle applies only to the environment. Although the principle is adumbrated in the Treaty, it is not defined there.

Like other general notions contained in the legislation, such as subsidiarity or proportionality, it is for the decision-makers and ultimately the courts to flesh out the principle. In other words, the scope of the precautionary principle also depends on trends in case law, which to some degree are influenced by prevailing social and political values.

However, it would be wrong to conclude that the absence of a definition has to lead to legal uncertainty. The Community authorities' practical experience with the precautionary principle and its judicial review make it possible to get an ever-better handle on the precautionary principle.

The Court of Justice of the European Communities and the Court of First Instance have already had occasion to review the application of the precautionary principle in cases they have adjudicated and hence to develop case law in this area. . .

Hence the Commission considers that the precautionary principle is a general one which should in particular be taken into consideration in the fields of environmental protection and human, animal and plant health.

Although the precautionary principle is not explicitly mentioned in the Treaty except in the environmental field, its scope is far wider and covers those specific circumstances where scientific evidence is insufficient, inconclusive or uncertain and there are indications through preliminary objective scientific evaluation that there are reasonable grounds for concern that the potentially dangerous effects on the environment, human, animal or plant health may be inconsistent with the chosen level of protection.

4.   The Precautionary Principle in International Law

At international level, the precautionary principle was first recognised in the World Charter for Nature, adopted by the UN General Assembly in 1982. It was subsequently incorporated into various international conventions on the protection of the environment.

This principle was enshrined at the 1992 Rio Conference on the Environment and Development, during which the Rio Declaration was adopted, whose principle 15 states that: "in order to protect the environment, the precautionary approach shall be widely applied by States according to their capability. Where there are threats of serious or irreversible damage, lack of full scientific certainty shall not be used as a reason for postponing cost-effective measures to prevent environmental degradation." Besides, the United Nations' Framework Convention on Climate Change and the Convention of Biological Diversity both refer to the precautionary principle. Recently, on 28 January 2000, at the Conference of the Parties to the Convention on Biological Diversity, the Protocol on Biosafety concerning the safe transfer, handling and use of living modified organisms resulting from modern biotechnology confirmed the key function of the Precautionary Principle.

Hence this principle has been progressively consolidated in international environmental law, and so it has since become a full-fledged and general principle of international law.

The WTO agreements confirm this observation. The preamble to the WTO Agreement highlights the ever-closer links between international trade and environmental protection. A consistent approach means that the precautionary principle must be taken into account in these agreements, notably in the Agreement on Sanitary and Phytosanitary Measures (SPS) and in the Agreement on Technical Barriers to Trade (TBT), to ensure that this general principle is duly enforced in this legal order.

Hence, each Member of the WTO has the independent right to determine the level of environmental or health protection they consider appropriate. Consequently a member may apply measures, including measures based on the precautionary principle, which lead to a higher level of protection than that provided for in the relevant international standards or recommendations.

The Agreement on the Application of Sanitary and Phytosanitary Measures (SPS Agreement) clearly sanctions the use of the precautionary principle, although the term itself is not explicitly used. Although the general rule is that all sanitary and phytosanitary measures must be based on scientific principles and that they should not be maintained without adequate scientific evidence, a derogation from these principles is provided for in Article 5(7) which stipulates that: "in cases where relevant scientific evidence is insufficient, a Member may provisionally adopt sanitary or phytosanitary measures on the basis of available pertinent information, including that from the relevant international organizations as well as from sanitary or phytosanitary measures applied by other Members. In such circumstances, Members shall seek to obtain the additional information necessary for a more objective assessment of risk and review the sanitary or phytosanitary measure accordingly within a reasonable period of time."

Hence, according to the SPS Agreement, measures adopted in application of a precautionary principle when the scientific data are inadequate, are provisional and imply that efforts be undertaken to elicit or generate the necessary scientific data. It is important to stress that the provisional nature is not bound up with a time limit but with the development of scientific knowledge.

The use of the term "more objective assessment of risk" in Article 5.7 infers that a precautionary measure may be based on a less objective appraisal but must nevertheless includes an evaluation of risk.

The concept of risk assessment in the SPS leaves leeway for interpretation of what could be used as a basis for a precautionary approach. The risk assessment on which a measure is based may include non-quantifiable data of a factual or qualitative nature and is not uniquely confined to purely quantitative scientific data. This interpretation has been confirmed by the WTO's Appellate body in the case of growth hormones, which rejected the panel's initial interpretation that the risk assessment had to be quantitative and had to establish a minimum degree of risk.

The principles enshrined in Article 5.7 of the SPS must be respected in the field of sanitary and phytosanitary measures; however, because of the specific nature of other areas, such as the environment, it may be that somewhat different principles will have to be applied.

International guidelines are being considered in relation to the application of the Precautionary Principle in Codex Alimentarius. Such guidance in this, and other sectors, could pave the way to a harmonised approach by the WTO Members, to drawing up health or environment protection measures, while avoiding the misuse of the precautionary principle which could otherwise lead to unjustifiable barriers to trade.

In the light of these observations, the Commission considers that, following the example set by other Members of the WTO, the Community is entitled to prescribe the level of protection, notably as regards the environment and human, animal and plant health, which it considers appropriate. In this context, the Community must respect Articles 6, 95, 152 and 174 of the Treaty. To this end, reliance on the precautionary principle constitutes an essential plank of its policy. It is clear that the choices made will affect its positions at international and notably multilateral level, as regards recourse to the precautionary principle.

Bearing in mind the very origins of the precautionary principle and its growing role in international law, and notably in the agreements of the World Trade Organisation, this principle must be duly addressed at international level in the various areas in which it is likely to be of relevance.

Following the example set by the other members of the WTO, the Commission considers that the Community is entitled to prescribe the level of protection, notably as regards environmental protection and human, animal and plant health, that it considers appropriate. Recourse to the precautionary principle is a central plank of Community policy. The choices made to this end will continue to influence its positions at international level, and notably at multinational level, as regards the precautionary principle.

5.   *The Constituent Parts of the Precautionary Principle*

An analysis of the precautionary principle reveals two quite distinct aspects: (i) the political decision to act or not to act as such, which is linked to the factors triggering recourse to the precautionary principle; (ii) in the affirmative, how to act, i.e., the measures resulting from application of the precautionary principle.

There is a controversy as to the role of scientific uncertainty in risk analysis, and notably as to whether it belongs under risk assessment or risk management. This controversy springs from a confusion between a prudential approach and application of the precautionary principle. These two aspects are complementary but should not be confounded.

The prudential approach is part of risk assessment policy which is determined before any risk assessment takes place and which is based on the elements described [below]; it is therefore an integral part of the scientific opinion delivered by the risk evaluators.

On the other hand, application of the precautionary principle is part of risk management, when scientific uncertainty precludes a full assessment of the risk and when decision-makers consider that the chosen level of environmental protection or of human, animal and plant health may be in jeopardy.

The Commission considers that measures applying the precautionary principle belong in the general framework of risk analysis, and in particular risk management.

5.1. Factors Triggering Recourse to the Precautionary Principle

The precautionary principle is relevant only in the event of a potential risk, even if this risk cannot be fully demonstrated or quantified or its effects determined because of the insufficiency or inclusive nature of the scientific data.

It should however be noted that the precautionary principle can under no circumstances be used to justify the adoption of arbitrary decisions.

Before the precautionary principle is invoked, the scientific data relevant to the risks must first be evaluated. However, one factor logically and chronologically precedes the decision to act, namely identification of the potentially negative effects of a phenomenon. To understand these effects more thoroughly it is necessary to conduct a scientific examination. The decision to conduct this examination without awaiting additional information is bound up with a less theoretical and more concrete perception of the risk.

A scientific evaluation of the potential adverse effects should be undertaken based on the available data when considering whether measures are necessary to protect the environment, the human, animal or plant health. An assessment of risk should be considered where feasible when deciding whether or not to invoke the precautionary principle. This requires reliable scientific data and logical reasoning, leading to a conclusion which expresses the possibility of occurrence and the severity of a hazard's impact on the environment, or health of a given population including the extent of possible damage, persistency, reversibility and delayed effect. However it is not possible in all cases to complete a comprehensive assessment of risk, but all effort should be made to evaluate the available scientific information.

Where possible, a report should be made which indicates the assessment of the existing knowledge and the available information, providing the views of the scientists on the reliability of the assessment as well as on the remaining uncertainties. If necessary, it should also contain the identification of topics for further scientific research.

Risk assessment consists of four components—namely hazard identification, hazard characterisation, appraisal of exposure and risk characterization. The limits of scientific knowledge may affect each of these components, influencing the overall level of attendant uncertainty and ultimately affecting the foundation for protective or preventive action. An attempt to complete these four steps should be performed before decision to act is taken.

Scientific uncertainty results usually from five characteristics of the scientific method: the variable chosen, the measurements made, the samples drawn, the models used and the causal relationship employed. Scientific uncertainty may also arise from a controversy on existing data or lack of some relevant data. Uncertainty may relate to qualitative or quantitative elements of the analysis.

A more abstract and generalised approach preferred by some scientists is to separate all uncertainties into three categories of: Bias, Randomness and True Variability. Some other experts categorise uncertainty in terms of estimation of confidence interval of the probability of occurrence and of the severity of the hazard's impact. . .

Risk evaluators accommodate these uncertainty factors by incorporating prudential aspects such as:

- relying on animal models to establish potential effects in man;

- using body weight ranges to make inter-species comparisons;

- adopting a safety factor in evaluating an acceptable daily intake to account for intra- and inter-species variability; the magnitude of this factor depends on the degree of uncertainty of the available data;

- not adopting an acceptable daily intake for substances recognised as genotoxic or carcinogenic;

- adopting the "ALARA" (as low as reasonably achievable) level as a basis for certain toxic contaminants.

Risk managers should be fully aware of these uncertainty factors when they adopt measures based on the scientific opinion delivered by the evaluators.

However, in some situations the scientific data are not sufficient to allow one to apply these prudential aspects in practice, i.e. in cases in which extrapolations cannot be made because of the absence of parameter modelling and where cause-effect relationships are suspected but have not been demonstrated. It is in situations like these that decision-makers face the dilemma of having to act or not to act.

Recourse to the precautionary principle presupposes:

- identification of potentially negative effects resulting from a phenomenon, product or procedure;

- a scientific evaluation of the risk which because of the insufficiency of the data, their inconclusive or imprecise nature, makes it impossible to determine with sufficient certainty the risk in question.

5.2.   Measures Resulting from Reliance on the Precautionary Principle

In the kind of situation described above—sometimes under varying degrees of pressure from public opinion—decision-makers have to respond. However, responding does not necessarily mean that measures always have to be adopted. The decision to do nothing may be a response in its own right.

The appropriate response in a given situation is thus the result of an eminently political decision, a function of the risk level that is "acceptable" to the society on which the risk is imposed.

The nature of the decision influences the type of control that can be carried out. Recourse to the precautionary principle does not necessarily mean adopting final instruments designed to produce legal effects that are open to judicial review. There is a whole range of actions available to decision-makers under the head of the precautionary principle. The decision to fund a research programme or even the decision to inform the public about the possible adverse effects of a product or procedure may themselves be inspired by the precautionary principle.

It is for the Court of Justice to pronounce on the legality of any measures taken by the Community institutions. The Court has consistently held that when the Commission or any other Community institution has broad discretionary powers, notably as regards the nature and scope of the measures it adopts, review by the Court must be limited to examining whether the institution committed a manifest error or misuse of power or manifestly exceed the limits of its powers of appraisal.

Hence the measures may not be of an arbitrary nature.

Recourse to the precautionary principle does not necessarily mean adopting final instruments designed to produce legal effects, which are subject to judicial review.

6.   Guidelines for Applying the Precautionary Principle

6.1.   Implementation

When decision-makers become aware of a risk to the environment or human, animal or plant health that in the event of non-action may have serious consequences, the question of appropriate protective measures arise. Decision-makers have to obtain, through a structured approach, a scientific evaluation, as complete as possible, of the risk to the environment, or health, in order to select the most appropriate course of action

The determination of appropriate action including measures based on the precautionary principle should start with a scientific evaluation and, if necessary, the decision to commission scientists to perform an as objective and complete as possible scientific evaluation. It will cast light on the existing objective evidence, the gaps in knowledge and the scientific uncertainties.

The implementation of an approach based on the precautionary principle should start with a scientific evaluation, as complete as possible, and where possible, identifying at each stage the degree of scientific uncertainty.

6.2.   The Triggering Factor

Once the scientific evaluation has been performed as best as possible, it may provide a basis for triggering a decision to invoke the precautionary principle. The conclusions of this evaluation should show that the desired level of protection for the environment or a population group could be jeopardised. The conclusions should also include an assessment of the scientific uncertainties and a description of the hypotheses used to compensate for the lack of the scientific or statistical data. An assessment of the potential consequences of inaction should be considered and may be used as a trigger by the decision-makers. The decision to wait or not to wait for new scientific data before considering possible measures should be taken by the decision-makers with a maximum of transparency. The absence of scientific proof of the existence of a cause-effect relationship, a quantifiable dose/response relationship or a quantitative evaluation of the probability of the emergence of adverse effects following exposure should not be used to justify inaction. Even if scientific advice is supported only by a minority fraction of the scientific community, due account should be taken of their views, provided the credibility and reputation of this fraction are recognised.

The Commission has confirmed its wish to rely on procedures as transparent as possible and to involve all interested parties at the earliest possible stage. This will assist decision makers in taking legitimate measures which are likely to achieve the society's chosen level of health or environmental protection. An assessment of the potential consequences of inaction and of the uncertainties of the scientific evaluation should be considered by decision-makers when determining whether to trigger action based on the precautionary principle.

All interested parties should be involved to the fullest extent possible in the study of various risk management options that may be envisaged once the results of the scientific evaluation and/or risk assessment are available and the procedure be as transparent as possible.

6.3.   The General Principles of Application

The general principles are not limited to application of the precautionary principle. They apply to all risk management measures. An approach inspired by the precautionary principle does not exempt one from applying wherever possible these criteria, which are generally used when a complete risk assessment is at hand.

Thus reliance on the precautionary principle is no excuse for derogating from the general principles of risk management.

These general principles include:

- proportionality,

- non-discrimination,

- consistency,

- examination of the benefits and costs of action or lack of action,

- examination of scientific developments.

The measures envisaged must make it possible to achieve the appropriate level of protection. Measures based on the precautionary principle must not be disproportionate to the desired level of protection and must not aim at zero risk, something which rarely exists. However, in certain cases, an incomplete assessment of the risk may considerably limit the number of options available to the risk managers.

In some cases a total ban may not be a proportional response to a potential risk. In other cases, it may be the sole possible response to a potential risk.

Risk reduction measures should include less restrictive alternatives which make it possible to achieve an equivalent level of protection, such as appropriate treatment, reduction of exposure, tightening of controls, adoption of provisional limits, recommendations for populations at risk, etc. One should also consider replacing the products or procedures concerned by safer products or procedures.

The risk reduction measure should not be limited to immediate risks where the proportionality of the action is easier to assess. It is in situations in which the adverse effects do not emerge until long after exposure that the cause-effect relationships are more difficult to prove scientifically and that—for this reason—the precautionary principle often has to be invoked. In this case the potential long-term effects must be taken into account in evaluating the proportionality of measures in the form of rapid action to limit or eliminate a risk whose effects will not surface until ten or twenty years later or will affect future generations. This applies in particular to effects on the eco-system. Risks that are carried forward into the future cannot be eliminated or reduced except at the time of exposure, that is to say immediately.

Measures should be proportional to the desired level of protection.

The principle of non-discrimination means that comparable situations should not be treated differently and that different situations should not be treated in the same way, unless there are objective grounds for doing so.

Measures taken under the precautionary principle should be designed to achieve an equivalent level of protection without invoking the geographical origin or the nature of the production process to apply different treatments in an arbitrary manner.

Measures should not be discriminatory in their application.

Measures should be consistent with the measures already adopted in similar circumstances or using similar approaches. Risk evaluations include a series of factors to be taken into account to ensure that they are as thorough as possible. The goal here is to identify and characterise the hazards, notably by establishing a relationship between the dose and the effect and assessing the exposure of the target population or the environment. If the absence of certain scientific data makes it impossible to characterise the risk, taking into account the uncertainties inherent to the evaluation, the measures taken under the precautionary principle should be comparable in nature and scope with measures already taken in equivalent areas in which all the scientific data are available.

Measures should be consistent with the measures already adopted in similar circumstances or using similar approaches.

A comparison must be made between the most likely positive or negative consequences of the envisaged action and those of inaction in terms of the overall cost to the Community, both in the long- and short-term. The measures envisaged must produce an overall advantage as regards reducing risks to an acceptable level.

Examination of the pros and cons cannot be reduced to an economic cost-benefit analysis. It is wider in scope and includes non-economic considerations.

However, examination of the pros and cons should include an economic cost-benefit analysis where this is appropriate and possible.

Besides, other analysis methods, such as those concerning the efficacy of possible options and their acceptability to the public may also have to be taken into account. A society may be willing to pay a higher cost to protect an interest, such as the environment or health, to which it attaches priority.

The Commission affirms, in accordance with the case law of the Court that requirements linked to the protection of public health should undoubtedly be given greater weight that economic considerations.

The measures adopted presuppose examination of the benefits and costs of action and lack of action. This examination should include an economic cost/benefit analysis when this is appropriate and feasible. However, other analysis methods, such as those concerning efficacy and the socio-economic impact of the various options, may also be relevant. Besides the decision-maker may, in certain circumstances, by guided by non-economic considerations such as the protection of health.

The measures should be maintained as long as the scientific data are inadequate, imprecise or inconclusive and as long as the risk is considered too high to be imposed on society. The measures may have to be modified or abolished by a particular deadline, in the light of new scientific findings. However, this is not always linked to the time factor, but to the development of scientific knowledge.

Besides, scientific research should be carried out with a view to obtaining a more advanced or more complete scientific assessment. In this context, the measures should be subjected to regular scientific monitoring, so that they can be reevaluated in the light of new scientific information. . .

Research could also be conducted for the improvement of the methodologies and instruments for assessing risk, including greater integration of all pertinent factors (e.g. socio-economic information, technological perspectives).

The measures, although provisional, shall be maintained as long as the scientific data remain incomplete, imprecise or inconclusive and as long as the risk is considered too high to be imposed on society.

Maintenance of the measures depends on the development of scientific knowledge, in the light of which they should be reevaluated. This means that scientific research shall be continued with a view to obtaining more complete data.

Measures based on the precautionary principle shall be reexamined and if necessary modified depending on the results of the scientific research and the follow up of their impact.

6.4. The Burden of Proof

Community rules and those of many third countries enshrine the principle of prior approval (positive list) before the placing on the market of certain products, such as drugs, pesticides or food additives. This is one way of applying the precautionary principle, by shifting responsibility for producing scientific evidence. This applies in particular to substances deemed "a priori" hazardous or which are potentially hazardous at a certain level of absorption. In this case the legislator, by way of precaution, has clearly reversed the burden of proof by requiring that the substances be deemed hazardous until proven otherwise. Hence it is up to the business community to carry out the scientific work needed to evaluate the risk. As long as the human health risk cannot be evaluated with sufficient certainty, the legislator is not legally entitled to authorise use of the substance, unless exceptionally for test purposes.

In other cases, where such a prior approval procedure does not exist, it may be for the user, a private individual, a consumer association, citizens or the public authorities to demonstrate the nature of a danger and the level of risk posed by a product or process. Action taken under the head of the precautionary principle must in certain cases include a clause reversing the burden of proof and placing it on the producer, manufacturer or importer, but such an obligation cannot be systematically entertained as a general principle. This possibility should be examined on a case-by-case basis when a measure is adopted under the precautionary principle, pending supplementary scientific data, so as to give professionals who have an economic interest in the production and/or marketing of the procedure or product in question the opportunity to finance the necessary research on a voluntary basis.

Measures based on the precautionary principle may assign responsibility for producing the scientific evidence necessary for a comprehensive risk evaluation.

Conclusion

This Communication of a general scope sets out the Commission's position as regards recourse to the precautionary principle. The Communication reflects the Commission's desire for transparency and dialogue with all stakeholders. At the same it is provides concrete guidance for applying the precautionary principle. . .

This Communication should also contribute to reaffirming the Community's position at [the] international level, where the precautionary principle is receiving increasing attention. However the Commission wishes to stress that this Communication is not meant to be the last word; rather, it should be seen as the point of departure for a broader study of the conditions in which risks should be assessed, appraised, managed and communicated.

NOTES & QUESTIONS

1. *Operationalizing the Precautionary Principle.* How should we understand the precautionary principle? In an influential article, Professor

Cass Sunstein argued that the precautionary principle, strictly understood, was "literally paralyzing" because "every step, including inaction, creates a risk to health, the environment, or both." Sunstein argues that the precautionary principle cannot be universally operationalized because the only way to escape the paralysis is to apply the precautionary principle for some risks but ignore it for others. Sunstein offers an example: "People seem quite concerned about the risks associated with dioxin, a real candidate for use of the precautionary principle, but far less concerned about the statistically equivalent risks associated with aflatoxin, a carcinogen found in peanut butter. When aflatoxin does not trigger public concern, a large part of the reason is that the burdens of banning aflatoxin seem high and indeed intolerable; too many people would object to heavy regulation of peanut butter, for generations a staple of school lunches and many diets." Sunstein is so down on the principle that he concludes that the "precautionary principle leads in the wrong directions, but that if it is taken for all that it is worth, it leads in no direction at all." See Cass R. Sunstein, *Beyond the Precautionary Principle*, 151 U. Pa. L. Rev. 1003, 1054 (2003). Do you agree? If not for the precautionary principle, how should regulators determine an *acceptable* level of risk to the environment?

2. *The Precautionary Principle and Jus Cogens.* Is the precautionary principle a mandatory part of the methodological architecture of international law? Some states and regions, such as Europe, have adopted the principle, while others have rejected it or qualified it, especially with regard to the dangers of climate change. If the latter are understood as persistent objectors, this raises the question of whether the precautionary principle is jus cogens or whether states may derogate from its obligations. For discussions on the exact status of the precautionary principle under international law, see James E. Hickey, Jr. & Vern R. Walker, *Refining the Precautionary Principle in International Environmental Law*, 14 Va. Envt'l L.J. 423, 425–26 (1995) ("If the present precautionary principle is to provide more than platitudinal support for pollution prevention, it must evolve into a refined rule that would adjust to new and evolving factual situations, to more sophisticated norms of international law, and to advances in scientific knowledge."); A.W. Harris, *Derogating the Precautionary Principle*, 19 Vill. Envt'l L.J. 1, 59 (2008) ("Given the potential adverse consequences of future climate change, a stronger and more robust principle is needed."). See also Daniel Bodansky, *Scientific Uncertainty and the Precautionary Principle*, 33 Environment 4, 5 (1991).

C. CLIMATE CHANGE

Climate change represents the most urgent and possibly devastating problem facing humanity. If not abated, climate change runs the risk of raising the entire temperature of the globe, resulting in, among other things, a radical increase in ice-melting and a rise in ocean levels. Some countries may face coastal flooding while others, close to or at sea level, may simply disappear under water. This flooding will trigger the greatest migration in the history of human civilization.

The history of climate change remediation efforts begins with the 1997 Protocol on Climate Change, which was negotiated in Kyoto, Japan. The so-called Kyoto Protocol called for most industrialized nations to reduce greenhouse gas emissions with an initial target of 6 to 8 percent reduction compared with 1990 levels. President Bill Clinton signed the treaty but the agreement was never ratified by the U.S. Senate.

The Kyoto Protocol was followed in 2015 by the Paris Agreement, which called for more ambitious cuts in greenhouse gas emissions. The agreement was signed by 195 states with 160 ratifications. The explicit aim of the Paris Agreement is to hold the increase in global temperature to less than 2 degrees Celsius and, if possible, within 1.5 degrees Celsius. To reach that goal, individual states are required to limit greenhouse gas emissions in differing amounts. Although ambitious in its targets, the Paris Agreement is light on enforcement mechanisms. It creates no tribunal or other framework for adjudication or coercive enforcement, preferring instead to rely on the traditional avenues of enforcement already available in international law. Moreover, the exact amount of emission reductions is set by each state, which individually determines its Nationally Determined Contribution (NDC) towards the overall goal.

Both the Kyoto and the Paris agreements—and the interim agreements signed in the intervening years—were negotiated pursuant to the United Nations Framework Convention on Climate Change (UNFCCC), a 1992 multilateral agreement creating a structure for climate change negotiations. Consider the following excerpts from the UNFCCC. As you read these provisions, identify the conceptual foundations that it lays down regarding the international legal obligations associated with climate change.

United Nations Framework Convention on Climate Change

31 I.L.M. 849 (1992)

Article 2 Objective

The ultimate objective of this Convention and any related legal instruments that the Conference of the Parties may adopt is to achieve, in accordance with the relevant provisions of the Convention, stabilization of greenhouse gas concentrations in the atmosphere at a level that would prevent dangerous anthropogenic interference with the climate system. Such a level should be achieved within a time-frame sufficient to allow ecosystems to adapt naturally to climate change, to ensure that food production is not threatened and to enable economic development to proceed in a sustainable manner.

Article 3 Principles

In their actions to achieve the objective of the Convention and to implement its provisions, the Parties shall be guided, inter alia, by the following:

1.   The Parties should protect the climate system for the benefit of present and future generations of humankind, on the basis of equity and in accordance with their common but differentiated responsibilities and respective capabilities. Accordingly, the developed country Parties should take the lead in combating climate change and the adverse effects thereof.

2.   The specific needs and special circumstances of developing country Parties, especially those that are particularly vulnerable to the adverse effects of climate change, and of those Parties, especially developing country Parties, that would have to bear a disproportionate or abnormal burden under the Convention, should be given full consideration.

3.   The Parties should take precautionary measures to anticipate, prevent or minimize the causes of climate change and mitigate its adverse effects. Where there are threats of serious or irreversible damage, lack of full scientific certainty should not be used as a reason for postponing such measures, taking into account that policies and measures to deal with climate change should be cost-effective so as to ensure global benefits at the lowest possible cost. To achieve this, such policies and measures should take into account different socio-economic contexts, be comprehensive, cover all relevant sources, sinks and reservoirs of greenhouse gases and adaptation, and comprise all economic sectors. Efforts to address climate change may be carried out cooperatively by interested Parties.

4.   The Parties have a right to, and should, promote sustainable development. Policies and measures to protect the climate system against human-induced change should be appropriate for the specific conditions of each Party and should be integrated with national development programmes, taking into account that economic development is essential for adopting measures to address climate change.

5.   The Parties should cooperate to promote a supportive and open international economic system that would lead to sustainable economic growth and development in all Parties, particularly developing country Parties, thus enabling them better to address the problems of climate change. Measures taken to combat climate change, including unilateral ones, should not constitute a means of arbitrary or unjustifiable discrimination or a disguised restriction on international trade.

Article 4 Commitments

1.   All Parties, taking into account their common but differentiated responsibilities and their specific national and regional development priorities, objectives and circumstances, shall:

(a) Develop, periodically update, publish and make available to the Conference of the Parties, in accordance with Article 12, national inventories of anthropogenic emissions by sources and removals by sinks of all greenhouse gases not controlled by the Montreal Protocol, using comparable methodologies to be agreed upon by the Conference of the Parties;

(b) Formulate, implement, publish and regularly update national and, where appropriate, regional programmes containing measures to mitigate climate change by addressing anthropogenic emissions by sources and removals by sinks of all greenhouse gases not controlled by the Montreal Protocol, and measures to facilitate adequate adaptation to climate change;

(c) Promote and cooperate in the development, application and diffusion, including transfer, of technologies, practices and processes that control, reduce or prevent anthropogenic emissions of greenhouse gases not controlled by the Montreal Protocol in all relevant sectors, including the energy, transport, industry, agriculture, forestry and waste management sectors;

(d) Promote sustainable management, and promote and cooperate in the conservation and enhancement, as appropriate, of sinks and reservoirs of all greenhouse gases not controlled by the Montreal Protocol, including biomass, forests and oceans as well as other terrestrial, coastal and marine ecosystems;

(e) Cooperate in preparing for adaptation to the impacts of climate change; develop and elaborate appropriate and integrated plans for coastal zone management, water resources and agriculture, and for the protection and rehabilitation of areas, particularly in Africa, affected by drought and desertification, as well as floods;

(f) Take climate change considerations into account, to the extent feasible, in their relevant social, economic and environmental policies and actions, and employ appropriate methods, for example impact assessments, formulated and determined nationally, with a view to minimizing adverse effects on the economy, on public health and on the quality of the environment, of projects or measures undertaken by them to mitigate or adapt to climate change;

(g) Promote and cooperate in scientific, technological, technical, socio-economic and other research, systematic observation and development of data archives related to the climate system and intended to further the understanding and to reduce or eliminate the remaining uncertainties regarding the causes, effects, magnitude and timing of climate change and the economic and social consequences of various response strategies;

(h) Promote and cooperate in the full, open and prompt exchange of relevant scientific, technological, technical, socio-economic and legal information related to the climate system and climate change, and to the economic and social consequences of various response strategies;

(i) Promote and cooperate in education, training and public awareness related to climate change and encourage the widest participation in this process, including that of non-governmental organizations; and

(j) Communicate to the Conference of the Parties information related to implementation, in accordance with Article 12.

2. The developed country Parties and other Parties included in annex I commit themselves specifically as provided for in the following:

(a) Each of these Parties shall adopt national policies and take corresponding measures on the mitigation of climate change, by limiting its anthropogenic emissions of greenhouse gases and protecting and enhancing its greenhouse gas sinks and reservoirs. These policies and measures will demonstrate that developed countries are taking the lead in modifying longer-term trends in anthropogenic emissions consistent with the objective of the Convention, recognizing that the return by the end of the present decade to earlier levels of anthropogenic emissions of carbon dioxide and other greenhouse gases not controlled by the Montreal Protocol would contribute to such modification, and taking into account the differences in these Parties' starting points and approaches, economic structures and resource bases, the need to maintain strong and sustainable economic growth, available technologies and other individual circumstances, as well as the need for equitable and appropriate contributions by each of these Parties to the global effort regarding that objective. These Parties may implement such policies and measures jointly with other Parties and may assist other Parties in contributing to the achievement of the objective of the Convention and, in particular, that of this subparagraph;

(b) In order to promote progress to this end, each of these Parties shall communicate, within six months of the entry into force of the Convention for it and periodically thereafter, and in accordance with Article 12, detailed information on its policies and measures referred to in subparagraph (a) above, as well as on its resulting projected anthropogenic emissions by sources and removals by sinks of greenhouse gases not controlled by the Montreal Protocol for the period referred to in subparagraph (a), with the aim of returning individually or jointly to their 1990 levels these anthropogenic emissions of carbon dioxide and other greenhouse gases not controlled by the Montreal Protocol. This information will be reviewed by the Conference of the Parties, at its first session and periodically thereafter, in accordance with Article 7;

(c)   Calculations of emissions by sources and removals by sinks of greenhouse gases for the purposes of subparagraph (b) above should take into account the best available scientific knowledge, including of the effective capacity of sinks and the respective contributions of such gases to climate change. The Conference of the Parties shall consider and agree on methodologies for these calculations at its first session and review them regularly thereafter;

(d)   The Conference of the Parties shall, at its first session, review the adequacy of subparagraphs (a) and (b) above. Such review shall be carried out in the light of the best available scientific information and assessment on climate change and its impacts, as well as relevant technical, social and economic information. Based on this review, the Conference of the Parties shall take appropriate action, which may include the adoption of amendments to the commitments in subparagraphs (a) and (b) above. The Conference of the Parties, at its first session, shall also take decisions regarding criteria for joint implementation as indicated in subparagraph (a) above. A second review of subparagraphs (a) and (b) shall take place not later than 31 December 1998, and thereafter at regular intervals determined by the Conference of the Parties, until the objective of the Convention is met;

(e)   Each of these Parties shall:

(i)   coordinate as appropriate with other such Parties, relevant economic and administrative instruments developed to achieve the objective of the Convention; and

(ii) identify and periodically review its own policies and practices which encourage activities that lead to greater levels of anthropogenic emissions of greenhouse gases not controlled by the Montreal Protocol than would otherwise occur;

(f)   The Conference of the Parties shall review, not later than 31 December 1998, available information with a view to taking decisions regarding such amendments to the lists in annexes I and II as may be appropriate, with the approval of the Party concerned;

(g)   Any Party not included in annex I may, in its instrument of ratification, acceptance, approval or accession, or at any time thereafter, notify the Depositary that it intends to be bound by subparagraphs (a) and (b) above. The Depositary shall inform the other signatories and Parties of any such notification.

3.   The developed country Parties and other developed Parties included in annex II shall provide new and additional financial resources to meet the agreed full costs incurred by developing country Parties in complying

with their obligations under Article 12, paragraph 1. They shall also provide such financial resources, including for the transfer of technology, needed by the developing country Parties to meet the agreed full incremental costs of implementing measures that are covered by paragraph 1 of this Article and that are agreed between a developing country Party and the international entity or entities referred to in Article 11, in accordance with that Article. The implementation of these commitments shall take into account the need for adequacy and predictability in the flow of funds and the importance of appropriate burden sharing among the developed country Parties.

4. The developed country Parties and other developed Parties included in annex II shall also assist the developing country Parties that are particularly vulnerable to the adverse effects of climate change in meeting costs of adaptation to those adverse effects.

5. The developed country Parties and other developed Parties included in annex II shall take all practicable steps to promote, facilitate and finance, as appropriate, the transfer of, or access to, environmentally sound technologies and know-how to other Parties, particularly developing country Parties, to enable them to implement the provisions of the Convention. In this process, the developed country Parties shall support the development and enhancement of endogenous capacities and technologies of developing country Parties. Other Parties and organizations in a position to do so may also assist in facilitating the transfer of such technologies.

6. In the implementation of their commitments under paragraph 2 above, a certain degree of flexibility shall be allowed by the Conference of the Parties to the Parties included in annex I undergoing the process of transition to a market economy, in order to enhance the ability of these Parties to address climate change, including with regard to the historical level of anthropogenic emissions of greenhouse gases not controlled by the Montreal Protocol chosen as a reference.

7. The extent to which developing country Parties will effectively implement their commitments under the Convention will depend on the effective implementation by developed country Parties of their commitments under the Convention related to financial resources and transfer of technology and will take fully into account that economic and social development and poverty eradication are the first and overriding priorities of the developing country Parties.

8. In the implementation of the commitments in this Article, the Parties shall give full consideration to what actions are necessary under the Convention, including actions related to funding, insurance and the transfer of technology, to meet the specific needs and concerns of developing country Parties arising from the adverse effects of climate

change and/or the impact of the implementation of response measures, especially on:

(a) Small island countries;

(b) Countries with low-lying coastal areas;

(c) Countries with arid and semi-arid areas, forested areas and areas liable to forest decay;

(d) Countries with areas prone to natural disasters;

(e) Countries with areas liable to drought and desertification;

(f) Countries with areas of high urban atmospheric pollution;

(g) Countries with areas with fragile ecosystems, including mountainous ecosystems;

(h) Countries whose economies are highly dependent on income generated from the production, processing and export, and/or on consumption of fossil fuels and associated energy-intensive products; and

(i) Land-locked and transit countries.

Further, the Conference of the Parties may take actions, as appropriate, with respect to this paragraph.

9.   The Parties shall take full account of the specific needs and special situations of the least developed countries in their actions with regard to funding and transfer of technology.

10. The Parties shall, in accordance with Article 10, take into consideration in the implementation of the commitments of the Convention the situation of Parties, particularly developing country Parties, with economies that are vulnerable to the adverse effects of the implementation of measures to respond to climate change. This applies notably to Parties with economies that are highly dependent on income generated from the production, processing and export, and/or consumption of fossil fuels and associated energy-intensive products and/or the use of fossil fuels for which such Parties have serious difficulties in switching to alternatives.

———————

The agreements produced by the UNFCCC, including the Paris Agreement, are bold in their ambitions but short on coercive mechanisms. What methods are still available to hold states to their commitments under the Paris Agreement? In some sense, the Paris Agreement, like all treaties, is simply a long-term self-binding legal obligation—one that can be reversed if the state decides to withdraw from the treaty accord. Unless a treaty and its norms have ripened into jus cogens or the treaty explicitly prohibits withdrawal, a reversal of legal obligation is permitted under international law. So, what value do these treaties have? One way of thinking of the Paris Agreement is that it provides additional legal support for internal actors to hold their government's feet to the fire—to get them to live up to their legal and moral commitments.

In the following case, a Dutch environmental group called Urgenda filed a lawsuit against the government of Netherlands, claiming that it was not acting aggressively enough to combat global warming. What role did the Paris Agreement and other international instruments play in the court's decision? The court was confronted with two major questions: First, does the Netherlands owe to other states more aggressive action to combat global climate change? Second, does Netherlands owe its own citizens the same thing? In other words, did the Paris Agreement create a private right of action for Urgenda or did the group need to rely on other legal instruments to gain a judicial remedy? As you read the case, ask yourself how the right to life protected by human rights law interfaces with environmental conventions negotiated under international law.

Urgenda Foundation v. Netherlands
Supreme Court of the Netherlands
Dec. 20, 2019

Do Articles 2 and 8 ECHR oblige the State to take measures?

According to the State, Articles 2 and 8 ECHR do not oblige it to offer protection from the genuine threat of dangerous climate change. The State asserts that this danger is not specific enough to fall within the scope of protection afforded by Articles 1, 2 and 8 ECHR. To that end, the State asserts that the threat is global in nature; in other words, that it is global in both cause and scope, and that it relates to the environment, which the State argues is not protected as such by the ECHR.

Article 1 ECHR provides that the contracting parties must secure to everyone within their jurisdiction the rights and freedoms defined in Section I of the ECHR. In other words, ECHR protection is afforded to the persons who fall within the states' jurisdiction. In the Netherlands this regards, primarily and to the extent relevant in this case, the residents of the Netherlands.

Article 2 ECHR protects the right to life. According to established ECtHR case law, this provision also encompasses a contracting state's positive obligation to take appropriate steps to safeguard the lives of those within its jurisdiction. According to that case law, this obligation applies, inter alia, if the situation in question entails hazardous industrial activities regardless of whether these are conducted by the government itself or by others, and also in situations involving natural disasters. The ECtHR has on multiple occasions found that Article 2 ECHR was violated with regard to a state's acts or omissions in relation to a natural or environmental disaster. It is obliged to take appropriate steps if there is a real and immediate risk to persons and the state in question is aware of that risk. In this context, the term "real and immediate risk" must be understood to refer to a risk that is both genuine and imminent. The term "immediate" does not refer to imminence in the sense that the risk must materialise within a short period of time, but rather that the risk in question is directly threatening the persons involved. The protection of Article 2 ECHR also regards risks that may only materialise in the longer term.

Article 8 ECHR protects the right to respect for private and family life. This provision also relates to environmental issues. The ECHR may not entail a right to protection of the living environment, but according to established ECtHR case law, protection may be derived from Article 8 ECHR in cases in which the materialisation of environmental hazards may have direct consequences for a person's private lives and are sufficiently serious, even if that person's health is not in jeopardy. According to that case law, when it comes to environmental issues, Article 8 ECHR encompasses the positive obligation to take reasonable and appropriate measures to protect individuals against possible serious damage to their environment. The ECtHR has found that Article 8 ECHR was violated in various cases involving environmental harm. The obligation to take measures exists if there is a risk that serious environmental contamination may affect individuals' well-being and prevent them from enjoying their homes in such a way as to affect their private and family life adversely. That risk need not exist in the short term.

According to the ECtHR, when it comes to activities that are hazardous to the environment, the positive obligation implied by Article 8 ECHR largely overlaps with the obligation implied by Article 2 ECHR. The case law regarding the former obligation therefore applies to the latter obligation. In the case of environmentally hazardous activities, the state is expected to take the same measures pursuant to Article 8 ECHR that it would have to take pursuant to Article 2 ECHR. Therefore, the obligations pursuant to Articles 2 and 8 ECHR will be referred to collectively below.

The protection afforded by Articles 2 and 8 ECHR is not limited to specific persons, but to society or the population as a whole. The latter is for instance the case with environmental hazards. In the case of environmental hazards that endanger an entire region, Articles 2 and 8 ECHR offer protection to the residents of that region.

The obligation to take appropriate steps pursuant to Articles 2 and 8 ECHR also encompasses the duty of the state to take preventive measures to counter the danger, even if the materialisation of that danger is uncertain. This is consistent with the precautionary principle.

If it is clear that the real and immediate risk referred to above ... exists, states are obliged to take appropriates steps without having a margin of appreciation. The states do have discretion in choosing the steps to be taken, although these must actually be reasonable and suitable.

The obligation pursuant to Articles 2 and 8 ECHR to take appropriate steps to counter an imminent threat may encompass both mitigation measures (measures to prevent the threat from materialising) or adaptation measures (measures to lessen or soften the impact of that materialisation). According to ECtHR case law, which measures are suitable in a given case depends on the circumstances of that case.

The court may determine whether the measures taken by a state are reasonable and suitable. The policy a state implements when taking measures must be consistent and the state must take measures in good time. A state must take due diligence into account in its policy. The court can determine whether the policy implemented satisfies these requirements. In many instances found in ECtHR case law, a state's policy has been found to be inadequate, or a state has failed to provide sufficient substantiation that its policy is not inadequate. . . .

Articles 2 and 8 ECHR must not result in an impossible or under the given circumstances disproportionate burden being imposed on a state. If a state has taken reasonable and suitable measures, the mere fact that those measures were unable to deter the hazard does not mean that the state failed to meet the obligation that had been imposed on it. The obligations ensuing from Articles 2 and 8 ECHR regard measures to be taken by a state, not the achievement, or guarantee of the achievement, of the envisaged result.

According to established ECtHR case law, the provisions of the ECHR must be interpreted and applied so as to make its safeguards practical and effective. According to the ECtHR, this "effectiveness principle" ensues from "the object and purpose of the Convention as an instrument for the protection of individual human beings." This also regards the application of Article 31(1) of the Vienna Convention on the Law of Treaties, which stipulates that a treaty must be interpreted in good faith in accordance with the ordinary meaning to be given to the terms of the treaty in the light of its object and purpose. . . .

Article 13 ECHR is also relevant to the interpretation of Articles 2 and 8 ECHR; Article 13 provides that if the rights and freedoms under the ECHR are violated, there exists the right to an effective remedy before a national authority. According to ECtHR case law, this provision guarantees the existence of a remedy at national level to compel the observance of these rights and freedoms. In cases involving an arguable complaint regarding the violation of those rights and freedoms, national law must therefore offer a remedy that leads to obtaining appropriate relief. The scope of this obligation depends on the nature of the violation. The remedy must be both practically and legally effective.

A remedy is considered effective as meant in Article 13 ECHR if it will prevent or end the violation or if the remedy offers adequate redress for a violation that has already occurred. In the case of more serious violations, the available remedies must provide for both: the prevention or end of the violation as well as redress. National states are thus required to provide remedies that can effectively prevent more serious violations. The remedy must ensure that a national court determines whether the rights and freedoms ensuing from the ECHR have been violated and that this court does so in accordance with the rules of the ECHR and the interpretation of those rules by the ECtHR. In short: the remedy must offer effective legal protection from possible violations of the rights and freedoms ensuing from the ECHR. . . .

Pursuant to the findings above . . . no other conclusion can be drawn but that the State is required pursuant to Articles 2 and 8 ECHR to take measures to counter the genuine threat of dangerous climate change if this were merely a national problem. Given the findings above . . . after all, this constitutes a "real and immediate risk" as referred to above . . . and it entails the risk that the lives and welfare of Dutch residents could be seriously jeopardised. The same applies to, inter alia, the possible sharp rise in the sea level, which could render part of the Netherlands uninhabitable. The fact that this risk will only be able to materialise a few decades from now and that it will not impact specific persons or a specific group of persons but large parts of the population does not mean—contrary to the State's assertions—that Articles 2 and 8 ECHR offer no protection from this threat. This is consistent with the precautionary principle. The mere existence of a sufficiently genuine possibility that this risk will materialise means that suitable measures must be taken. . . .

. . . [U]nder Articles 2 and 8 ECHR, the Netherlands is obliged to do "its part" in order to prevent dangerous climate change, even if it is a global problem. This is based on the following grounds.

The UNFCCC is based on the idea that climate change is a global problem that needs to be solved globally. Where emissions of greenhouse gases take place from the territories of all countries and all countries are affected, measures will have to be taken by all countries. Therefore, all countries will have to do the necessary. The preamble to this convention states, among other things, the following in this context: "Acknowledging that the global nature of climate change calls for the widest possible cooperation by all countries and their participation in an effective and appropriate international response, in accordance with their common but differentiated responsibilities and respective capabilities and their social and economic conditions, (. . .). Recalling also that States have (...) the responsibility to ensure that activities within their jurisdiction or control do not cause damage to the environment of other States or of areas beyond the limits of national jurisdiction."

The objective of the UNFCCC is to stabilise greenhouse gas concentrations in the atmosphere at a level that would prevent dangerous human induced interference with the climate system (Article 2). Article 3 contains various principles to achieve this objective. For instance, Article 3(1) provides that the parties "should protect the climate system for the benefit of present and future generations of humankind, on the basis of equity and in accordance with their common but differentiated responsibilities and respective capabilities." Article 3(3) provides that the parties "should take precautionary measures to anticipate, prevent or minimize the causes of climate change and mitigate its adverse effects." And Article 4 provides, put succinctly, that all parties will take measures and develop policy in this area. It follows from these provisions that each state has an obligation to take the necessary measures in accordance with its specific responsibilities and possibilities. . . .

This understanding corresponds to what is commonly referred to as the "no harm principle," a generally accepted principle of international law which entails that countries must not cause each other harm. This is also referred to in the preamble to the UNFCCC. Countries can be called to account for the duty arising from this principle. Applied to greenhouse gas emissions, this means that they can be called upon to make their contribution to reducing greenhouse gas emissions. This approach justifies partial responsibility: each country is responsible for its part and can therefore be called to account in that respect.

This partial responsibility is in line with what is adopted in national and international practice in the event of unlawful acts that give rise to only part of the cause of the damage. Partial responsibility is in line with, inter alia, the Draft Articles on Responsibility of States for Internationally Wrongful Acts, as proposed by the UN International Law Commission and adopted by the UN General Assembly. . .

Partly in view of the serious consequences of dangerous climate change . . . the defence that a state does not have to take responsibility because other countries do not comply with their partial responsibility, cannot be accepted. Nor can the assertion that a country's own share in global greenhouse gas emissions is very small and that reducing emissions from one's own territory makes little difference on a global scale, be accepted as a defence. Indeed, acceptance of these defences would mean that a country could easily evade its partial responsibility by pointing out other countries or its own small share. If, on the other hand, this defence is ruled out, each country can be effectively called to account for its share of emissions and the chance of all countries actually making their contribution will be greatest, in accordance with the principles laid down in the preamble to the UNFCCC. . . .

Also important in this context is that . . . each reduction of greenhouse gas emissions has a positive effect on combating dangerous climate change, as every reduction means that more room remains in the carbon budget. The defence that a duty to reduce greenhouse gas emissions on the part of the individual states does not help because other countries will continue their emissions cannot be accepted for this reason either: no reduction is negligible. Climate change threatens human rights.... This is also recognised internationally outside the context of the Council of Europe. In order to ensure adequate protection from the threat to those rights resulting from climate change, it should be possible to invoke those rights against individual states, also with regard to the aforementioned partial responsibility. This is in line with the principle of effective interpretation ... that the ECtHR applies when interpreting the ECHR and also with the right to effective legal protection guaranteed by Article 13 ECHR. . . . [T]he Supreme Court finds that Articles 2 and 8 ECHR relating to the risk of climate change should be interpreted in such a way that these provisions oblige the contracting states to do "their part" to counter that danger. . . .

NOTES & QUESTIONS

1.   *Implementation.* On the basis of the above reasoning, the Supreme Court upheld a lower court's order forcing the Dutch government to set a far more ambitious target for lowering greenhouse gasses. The new limit required a reduction of 25 percent at the end of 2020 when compared to the greenhouse emission levels of 1990. Is this new limit ambitious enough? Is there an argument that the human rights articulated in the European Convention require an even greater reduction?

2.   *Doing Their Part.* The Dutch Government argued that it was not required to take more drastic measures because other states were not complying with their obligations to help solve the climate crisis. Their argument boiled down to the idea that a Dutch reduction in greenhouse gases would not be effective in solving a classic coordination problem. In other words, unilateral action by the Netherlands, alone, will not solve the environmental crisis. Why did the Supreme Court reject this argument? How is the notion of "partial responsibility" relevant to this question?

3.   *An Immediate Threat.* Does the risk of climate change, including sea level rise, constitute an "immediate" or "imminent" risk that requires the Dutch government to take action? The Supreme Court concluded that a harm need not fully materialize in the near term for it to constitute an immediate risk, as long as "the risk in question is directly threatening the persons involved." What does it mean for a risk to "directly" threaten a person? Furthermore, does this notion of imminence comport with how that term is

understood in other areas of public international law, such as the use of force?

4. *Right to Life Versus Duty of Care.* Unlike the Supreme Court, the lower court declined to resolve the case on the basis of the right to life under European human rights law. Instead, the lower court concluded that Netherlands had a "duty of care" to its own citizens. Formally speaking, this duty comes from Dutch constitutional law. As two legal commentators noted regarding the lower court decision: "One of the main reasons for a critical reception of the *Urgenda* judgment is that, while the court ruled that no State obligations vis-à-vis Urgenda can be derived from the contents of international agreements and other documents, the court still made use of these international agreements and other documents to establish the scope of the State's duty towards Urgenda." See K. J. de Graaf & J. H. Jans, *The* Urgenda *Decision: Netherlands Liable for Role in Causing Dangerous Global Climate Change*, 27 J. of Envt'l L. 517 (2015). See also Josephine van Zeben, *Establishing a Governmental Duty of Care for Climate Change Mitigation: Will* Urgenda *Turn the Tide?*, 4 Transnat'l Envt'l L. 339 (2015) ("The non-statutory basis for the Court's order to act distinguishes *Urgenda* from previous climate change litigation in which mandatory orders have been based on statutory obligations. This raises the question as to whether suitable equivalents... can be found for similar actions in other jurisdictions. Several elements of the judgment could prove particularly pertinent to the further development of climate change litigation, provided that their application can be extended beyond the Netherlands.")

PROBLEM CASE

Tuvalu is small island in the Pacific Ocean with a population of roughly 10,000. Part of the British Commonwealth, Tuvala gained foreign independence as a sovereign state in 1978. Tuvalu is only two metres above sea level. Consequently, Tuvalu's government is concerned that sea level rise caused by global warming might severely harm Tuvalu's territory. The country risks not just flooding but outright disappearance if it is swallowed into a higher Pacific Ocean. Other nations are in a similar plight. The Netherlands, for example, has an elaborate system of flood control using dams, dikes, and pumps, because the country's low elevation makes it highly vulnerable to sea rise. However, even the best anti-flood technology may prove inadequate in the face of protracted sea-level rise over the coming centuries.

What legal recourse do these states have? Although the Paris Agreement and the UNFCCC create legal obligations to reduce greenhouse gas emissions, these norms are arguably *ergo omnes*— obligations owed to all mankind. But do polluting states have a special responsibility towards states that are uniquely vulnerable to sea rise?

For some time, the government of Tuvalu was making noises of filing a legal complaint against several states before the International Court of Justice, though so far Tuvalu has avoided this approach. Would the ICJ's involvement have some strategic benefits? What remedy might the ICJ order if it found a violation of international law?

Could Tuvalu and similarly situated states make use of the doctrine of necessity to justify unilateral military action against polluting states? The question is largely hypothetical, since the states with the largest militaries also happen to be polluting states, while the states with the most to lose from global climate change are militarily weak.

Conclusion & Summary

Although international environmental law has a reputation for being a new subject, the field is, in fact, an example of applying well developed legal principles to new phenomenon. Here are the key legal principles and the challenges to which they are applied:

1. States are under an obligation not to use their territory to cause environmental harm to neighboring states. This "no harm" principle was articulated in the *Trail Smelter* arbitration and found its way into international law through a consideration of the legal principles that govern the relationship between municipal states under U.S. law. Just as New York State cannot use its territory to harm Pennsylvania's environment, so too Canada cannot use its territory to harm the environment of the United States. If damage does occur, the polluting state is required to compensate the victim state under the "polluter pays" principle.

2. When faced with uncertainty in the scientific evidence, states should not take that scientific uncertainty as a reason not to take precautionary measures, such as regulating risky conduct. This regulatory principle is already well entrenched in many domestic systems. In the context of environmental law, the principle suggests that states should take action now even in the face of scientific uncertainty; it may be too late to act once the scientific controversy is fully resolved. The precautionary principle was articulated in the Rio Declaration and therefore is frequently referred to as an emerging principle of international environmental law. It is already well entrenched as a legal requirement of European law.

3. Climate change represents the greatest single environmental challenge facing humanity. Efforts at emissions reduction take place pursuant to the UNFCCC. Although it may be hard for states to hold other states to their UNFCCC commitments, such as the Paris Agreements, domestic actors can pressure their own states to live up to their international obligations to stop global warming. In the Netherlands, a Dutch court concluded that its government had failed to live up to its duty of care to its own citizens by taking insufficiently aggressive actions to fight climate change. Although the case relied on a particularly Dutch understanding of the notion of the state's "duty of care" to its own citizens, similar

environmental litigation may be possible in other states. Also, international agreements may give domestic environmental groups the rhetorical leverage to pressure, through the political process, their governments into more aggressive action.

INDEX

References are to Pages